EDUCATIONAL PSYCHOLOGY

EIGHTH EDITION

Anita Woolfolk

The Ohio State University

ALLYN AND BACON

Boston ■ London ■ Toronto ■ Sydney ■ Tokyo ■ Singapore

Senior Vice President and Publisher: Nancy Forsyth
Editor-in-Chief: Paul A. Smith
Developmental Editor: Alicia Reilly
Editorial Assistant: Shannon Morrow
Editorial Production Supervisor: Susan McIntyre
Editorial Production Services: Kathy Smith
Photo Research: Laurie Frankenthaler
Cover Administrator: Linda Knowles
Composition Buyer: Linda Cox
Design and Composition: Shelley Davidson
Manufacturing Buyer: Megan Cochran
Marketing Manager: Brad Parkins

Library of Congress Cataloging-in-Publication Data

Woolfolk, Anita.
    Educational psychology / Anita E. Woolfolk. — 8th ed.
      p.   cm.
    Includes bibliographical references and indexes.
    ISBN 0-205-28995-9
    1. Educational psychology. I. Title.
  LB1051.W74 2001
  370.15—dc20   00-036357
                                      CIP

Printed in the United States of America
10 9 8 7 6 5 4 3 2 1 VHP 05 04 03 02 01 00

To Liz, Wayne K., and Kelly,
Teachers, Learners, Innovators:
The future

And to Wayne
For all that is,
And the best that's yet to be.

Brief Contents

Contents

4 Learner Differences   104

5 Culture and Community 154

Part Two *Learning*

6 Behavioral Views of Learning 198

7 Cognitive Views of Learning 238

9 Social Cognitive and Constructivist Views of Learning   320

Part Four   *Teaching*

12   Creating Learning Environments   432

13   Teaching for Learning   472

Part Five   *Assessing*

14   Standardized Testing   520

15 Classroom Assessment and Grading 554

Preface

Many of you reading this book will be enrolled in an educational psychology course as part of your professional preparation for teaching, counseling, speech therapy, or psychology. The material in this text should be of interest to everyone who is concerned about education and learning, from the nursery school volunteer to the instructor in a community program for adults with disabilities. No background in psychology or education is necessary to understand this material. It is as free of jargon and technical language as possible and many people have worked to make this edition clear, relevant, and interesting.

Since the first edition of *Educational Psychology* appeared, there have been many exciting developments in the field. This edition incorporates new insights and current trends while retaining the best features of the previous work. The eighth edition continues to emphasize the educational implications and applications of research on child development, cognitive science, learning, and teaching. Theory and practice are not separated but are considered together; the text shows how information and ideas drawn from research in educational psychology can be applied to solve the everyday problems of teaching. To explore the connections between knowledge and practice, there are many examples, lesson segments, case studies, guidelines, and practical tips from experienced teachers. Throughout the text you will be challenged to think about the value and use of the ideas in each chapter and you will see principles of educational psychology in action. Professors and students who used the first seven editions found these features very helpful. But what about the new developments?

The study of teaching continues to focus on the person being taught—the student doing the learning and how that person makes meaning in a social context. In this revision, there is a new chapter on *social cognitive and constructivist views of learning* that examines the role of social processes in learning. This is an exciting and sometimes controversial area in educational psychology, but one that merits consideration by anyone who wants to understand learning.

Over 250 new citations have been added to this edition to bring prospective teachers the most current information. Topics include the following:

the brain and learning	culturally relevant pedagogy
Vygotsky and sociocultural theories of development	learning strategies
	social cognitive theory and self-efficacy
the role of adults and peers in cognitive development	problem-based learning
	cooperative learning
personal and collective self-esteem	interest and emotions in learning
bullies and victims	self-schemas and motivation
navigating transitions in school	conceptual change teaching in science
person-first language	creating learning communities
emotional intelligence and tacit knowledge	dealing with conflict and violence
	revised taxonomies for learning
ADHD	grading rubrics
stereotype threat	authentic assessment
dialects and teaching	portfolios

The Plan of the Book. The introductory chapter begins with you, the prospective teacher, and the questions you may be asking yourself about a teaching career. What is good teaching and what does it take to become an excellent teacher? How can educational psychology help you to become such a teacher? Part One, "Students," focuses on the learners. How do they develop mentally, physically, emotionally, and socially, and how do all these aspects fit together? Where do individual differences come from, and what do they mean for teachers? What does it mean to create a culturally compatible classroom, one that makes learning accessible to all students? Part Two, "Learning," looks at learning from three major perspectives—behavioral, cognitive, and constructivist—with an emphasis on the last two. Learning theories have important implications for instruction at every level. Cognitive research is particularly vital right now and promises to be a wellspring of ideas for teaching in the immediate future. The new chapter, "Social Cognitive and Constructivist Views of Learning," explores the role of social and cultural processes in learning. Part Three, "Motivating," discusses the ever-present, linked issues of motivating and teaching today's students. Part Four, "Teaching," looks at instruction from two perspectives: a teacher-focused view that emphasizes the teacher's role in planning, providing, and monitoring instruction, and a student-centered view that emphasizes the students' active construction of understanding. This section also examines how teachers can adapt instruction for students with special needs. The material in these chapters is based on the most recent research in real classrooms. Part Five, "Assessing," examines many types of testing and grading, providing a sound basis for determining how well students have learned.

Aids to Understanding. At the beginning of each chapter you will find an *Outline* of the key topics with page numbers for quick reference. An *Overview* begins with a question about a subject related to the chapter. Before you read each chapter, take a moment to reflect on the questions raised. Your answers to the questions and the Overview, along with a list of Learning Objectives (also useful for later review), provide an orientation to the chapter topics.

When you turn the page, you confront another question, "What would you do?" about a real-life classroom situation related to the information in the chapter. By the time you reach the end of the chapter, you should have even more ideas about how to solve the problem raised, so be alert as you read.

Within the chapter, headings point out themes, questions, and problems as they arise, so you can look up information easily. These can also serve as a quick review of important points. When a new term or concept is introduced, it appears in boldface type along with a brief margin definition. These *Key Terms* are also defined in a *Glossary* at the back of the text. After every major section of the chapter, *Checkpoints* ask you to review and apply your knowledge. Can you answer these questions? If not, you might want to reexamine the material. Throughout the book, graphs, tables, photos, and cartoons have been chosen to clarify and extend the text material—and to add to your enjoyment.

Each chapter ends with a *Summary* of the main ideas keyed to the *Checkpoint* questions in each main heading and an alphabetical list of the *Key Terms* from the chapter, along with the page number on which each is discussed.

Other Text Features. As in previous editions, chapters in the eighth edition include *Guidelines*, the *Teachers' Casebook*, and *Point/Counterpoints* on issues such as inclusion, tracking, "paying" kids to learn, and alternatives to direct teaching.

Guidelines. An important reason for studying educational psychology is to gain skills in solving classroom problems. Often, texts give pages of theory and research findings but little assistance in translating theory into practice. This text is different. Included in every chapter after the first one are several sets of *Guidelines*. These are teaching tips and practical suggestions based on the theory and research discussed in the chapter. Each suggestion is clarified by two or three specific examples. Although the *Guidelines* cannot cover every possible situation, they do provide a needed bridge between knowledge and practice and should help you transfer the text's information to new situations. In addition, every chapter after the first has one set of Guidelines that gives ideas for *working with families and the community*—an area of growing importance today.

Connect and Extend. Connect and Extend features appear in the margins several times throughout each chapter, linking content to teaching, students' thinking, research, and the news. They are valuable components for promoting deep level processing and transferring theory to authentic classroom settings.

Teachers' Casebook. This highly acclaimed and popular feature from the first seven editions is back. At the end of each chapter, master teachers from across the country, including many Teacher of the Year award winners, as well as teachers from Australia, Papua New Guinea, and Mexico, offer their own solutions to the *What Would You Do?* sitiuation presented at the beginning of the chapter. *Teachers' Casebook: What Would They Do?* gives you insights into the thinking of expert teachers—compare their solutions to the ones you devised. Their ideas truly show educational psychology at work in a range of everyday situations. The *Teachers' Casebook* brings to life the topics and principles discussed in each chapter.

Point/Counterpoint. Every chapter includes a *Point/Counterpoint* debate that examines two contrasting perspectives on an important question or controversy related to research or practice in educational psychology. Many of the topics considered in these *Point/Counterpoints* have "made the news" recently and are central to the discussions of educational reformers.

Becoming a Professional. At the end of every chapter, beginning with Chapter 2, is a section called "Becoming a Professional" that gives you guidance for developing a personal study guide for professional *Certification Tests* you may be required to take, organizing a professional *Teaching Portfolio*, and developing a *Resource File* for your future classrooms.

Student Supplements. A *Study Guide* designed to help you master the material in the text is also available. The *Study Guide* includes concept maps, case study applications, lists of key points, exercises with key terms and concepts, practice tests, and explanations of why answers are correct. Finally, with this book you got an *Interactive Companion,* a CD-ROM that has audio and video clips, Websites and interactivities, self-tests and study aids, and the voices of teachers and children to connect and extend your learning through multiple modes and media. The *Interactive Companion* provides many opportunities to learn about teaching. Check it out right away so you can use it with all your education classes.

Student Responses. You are invited to respond to any aspect of this text. We welcome your feedback. You may wish to criticize the solutions in the *Teachers' Casebook,* for example, or suggest topics or materials you think should be added to future editions. We would also like to know what you think of the text features and student supplements. Please send letters to:

Woolfolk
EDUCATIONAL PSYCHOLOGY, 8/e
Allyn & Bacon
160 Gould Street
Needham Heights, MA 02494

$\mathcal{A}$cknowledgments

During the years I have worked on this book, from initial draft to this most recent revision, many people have supported the project. Without their help, this text simply could not have been written.

Many educators contributed to this project. Carol Weinstein wrote the section in Chapter 12 on spaces for learning. Kathryn Linden of Purdue University is responsible for the *Test Bank* and the answer feedback material that accompanies each item. The *Instructor's Resource Manual* was created by Angela O'Donnell (Rutgers University) and the *Study Guide* by Beth Mowrer-Popiel (University of Idaho).

My writing was guided by extensive and thoughtful reviews from the following individuals:

Teresa Garcia
University of Texas, Austin

Rosalyn King
Northern Virginia Community College

Nancy Knapp
University of Georgia

Hermine Marshall
San Francisco State University

Elizabeth Mowrer-Popiel
University of Idaho

P. Karen Murphy
The Ohio State University

Angela O'Donnell
Rutgers University

Nancy Perry
University of British Columbia

Philip H. Winne
Simon Fraser University

As I made decisions about how to revise this edition, I benefited from the ideas of professors around the country who took the time to complete surveys and answer my questions. Thanks to:

Arthur Bangs
La Salle University

Janice R. Boone
New Jersey City University

Lucille J. Cantin
Notre Dame College

Edward E. Coates
Abilene University

William Foster
Australian Catholic University

M. Arthur Garmon
Western Michigan University

Larry Harrington
Missouri Baptist College

Gina Hurley
Cape Cod Community College

William Jenlicka
Harper College

Irwin Kahn
Ferris State University

Patricia Kalata
Burlington Community College

William Locke
Hastings College

Elizabeth Mowrer-Popiel
University of Idaho

Eldon Peters
University of Northern Iowa

Regina Peters
Hawkeye Community College

Cynthia Popowicz
University of Pittsburg

Thomas G. Reio
University of Maryland

Lawrence R. Rogien
Boise State University

James G. Stark
Christian Heritage College

Renee Wood Stewart
Weber State University

Many classroom teachers across the country contributed their experience, creativity, and expertise to the *Teachers' Casebook*. Special thanks must go to Professor William Foster, of Australian Catholic University, Brisbane, and Madya Ayala, of Monterrey, Mexico, who helped put me in contact with some wonderful teachers in their countries. I have thoroughly enjoyed my association with these master teachers, whose names are listed below, and I am grateful for the perspective they bring to the book.

Jan Andrews
Dulacca State School
Dulacca QLD 4255 - Australia

Madya Ayala
Campus Garza Sada.
Monterrey, N.L. Mexico

Diane Batty
Orono High School
Orono, Maine

Suzy L. Boswell
Pickens County Middle School
Jasper, Georgia

Constance Carter
Orono High School
Orono, Maine

Valerie A. Chilcoat
Glenmount School
Baltimore, Maryland

Elizabeth Chouinard
MacGregor Elementary School
Houston, Texas

Katie Churchill
Oriole Parke Elementary School
Chicago, Illinois

Maria Cirmia
Hillside School
Needham, Massachusetts

Nicole DePalma Cobb
Sterling Middle School
Quincy, Massachusetts

Kathleen Conroy
Rancho Canada Elementary School
Lake Forest, California

Ashley Dodge
Los Angeles Unified School District
Los Angeles, California

Mary Frances Donohoe
Lawton Chiles Elementary School
Gainesville, Florida

Margaret Doolan
St. Michael's School
Gordonvale QLD 4865 Australia

Michael J. Ellis
Quincy High School
Quincy, Massachusetts

Aimee Fredette
Fisher Elementary School
Walpole, Massachusetts

Frances D. Garland
Winship School
Boston, Massachusetts

Pam Gaskill
Riverside Elementary School
Dublin, Ohio

Sandra Gill
Hudson Middle School
Hudson, New York

Stewart Gill
Hudson Middle School
Hudson, New York

Linda Glisson
St. James Episcopal Day School
Baton Rouge, Louisiana

Carol Grosberg
Bates School
Wellesley, Massachusetts

Jeff D. Horton
Colton School
Colton, Washington

Jeff Hovermill
Colton School
Colton, Washington

Kelly L. Hoy
Faber Elementary School
Dunellen, New Jersey

Mitchell D. Klett
A.C. New Middle School
Springs, Texas

Regina M. LaRose
Hillside School
Needham, Massachusetts

Peggy McDonnell
West Park School
Moscow, Idaho

Kate McMenemy
St. Ignatius Primary School
Grove Crescent, Toowong, Australia

Sandra T. McNeice
Sterling Middle School
Quincy, Massachusetts

Rev. Edward Meli, MSC
Sacred Heart High School - Hagita, Alotou
Milne Bay Province, Papua New Guinea

Wendy Merefield-Ward
Payne Road State School
The Gap QLD 4061- Australia

Sue Middleton
St. James Episcopal Day School
Baton Rouge, Louisiana

Brenda Miller
Yucca Elementary School
Alamogordo, New Mexico

Julie Mohok
Ponam Primary School,
Manus Island, Papua New Guinea

Amy Neal
Katy High School
Katy, Texas

Thomas W. Newkirk
Hamilton Heights Middle School
Arcadia, Indiana

Thomas O'Donnell
Malden High School
Malden, Massachusetts

Allan Osborne
Snug Harbor Community School
Quincy, Massachusetts

Carolyn Ely Parham
Conway Elementary School
Ladue (St. Louis), Missouri

Carey Perkson
Brown School
Natick, Massachusetts

Mary Phillips
Orono High School
Orono, Maine

Katie Piel
West Park School
Moscow, Idaho

María Elena Ramos
Instituto San Roberto
Monterrey, N.L. Mexico

Denise Ready
Snug Harbor Community School
Quincy, Massachusetts

Steven P. Rude
John C. Fremont High School
Los Angeles, California

Ann Sande
Henry Viscardi School
Albertson, New York

Dr. Nancy Sheehan-Melzack
Snug Harbor Community School
Quincy, Massachusetts

Mark Smith
Medford High School
Medford, Massachusetts

Richard T. Smith
Harrison Middle School
Yarmouth, Maine

Susan B. Strauss
Lincoln High School
Lincoln, Rhode Island

Jennifer Hudson Thomas
Armidale High School
Armidale, Australia

Anne Worth
Clardy School
Kansas City, Missouri

In a project of this size so many people make essential contributions. Roberta Broyer, Permissions Coordinator, worked diligently to obtain permissions for the material reproduced in this text and the supplements. Laurie Frankenthaler guided the collection of photographs. The text designer, Shelley Davidson, and cover coordinator, Linda Knowles, made the look of this book the best yet. They make it seem easy to produce a beautiful book—it isn't. Kathy Smith, outside project manager, Susan McIntyre, Production Supervisor, and Elaine Ober, Production Manager, coordinated all aspects of the project, with amazing skill and grace. Somehow they brought order to what could have been chaos and fun to what might have been drudgery. Now the book is in the able hands of Sandi Kirshner, Executive Publisher, Brad Parkins, Marketing Manager, Kate Conway, Director of Advertising, and their staff. I can't wait to see what they are planning for me now! What a talented and creative group—I am honored to work with them all.

On this edition, I was privileged to work with an outstanding editorial group. Bill Barke, President of Allyn and Bacon, brought his distinctive style and leadership to the project, making the effort a pleasure. I was once again privileged to work with Nancy Forsyth, Senior Vice President and Publisher, and Paul A. Smith, Vice President and Editor-in-Chief. Their intelligence, creativity, sound judgment, style, and enduring commitment to quality can be seen on every page of this text. They will always have my deepest respect and enduring friendship. Shannon Morrow, Editorial Assistant, kept everything running smoothly and kept my fax machine and e-mail humming. On this edition I was fortunate again to have the help of Alicia Reilly, an outstanding developmental editor with the perfect combination of knowledge and organizational ability. Once again she guided this revision in all its many aspects, always staying just ahead of whatever had to happen next, communicating with people around the world—remarkable! The supplements package and the excellent pedagogical supports would not exist without her tireless efforts.

Finally, I want to thank my family and friends for their kindness and support during the long days and nights that I worked on this book. Again, to my daughter, Liz, thanks for your insights about teachers and students, shared over the years. You have been my greatest teacher—the source of my greatest joy. Your intelligence and courage continue to amaze me. To my family—Anita Wieckert; Marion, Bob, Lucas, Geoffrey, Eric, and Suzie Pratt; Claudia Casser; and Wayne C., Elsie, Wayne K., Kelly, Tom, and Mike Hoy—you are the greatest.

And finally, to Wayne Hoy, my friend, colleague, inspiration, passion, husband—there will never be enough time to be with you.

Anita Woolfolk Hoy

EDUCATIONAL PSYCHOLOGY

1

Teachers, Teaching, and Educational Psychology

ake a minute to remember the names of the best teachers you ever had, inside or outside a classroom. What was it about these teachers that made you remember them over the years? What effects did they have on you?

If you are like many students, you begin this course with a mixture of anticipation and wariness. Perhaps you are required to take educational psychology as part of a program in teacher education, speech therapy, nursing, or counseling. You may have chosen this class as an elective because you are interested in education or psychology. Whatever your reason for enrolling, you probably have questions about teaching, schools, students—or even about yourself—that you hope this course may answer. I have written the 8th edition of *Educational Psychology* with questions such as these in mind.

In this first chapter, we begin not with educational psychology but with education—more specifically, with the state of teaching today. Only when you are aware of the challenges teachers face can you appreciate the contributions of educational psychology. After a brief introduction to the world of the teacher, we turn to a discussion of educational psychology itself. We will consider what educational psychology is and why you should study it. How can principles identified by educational psychologists benefit teachers, therapists, parents, and others who are interested in teaching and learning? What exactly is the content of educational psychology, and where does this information come from? By the time you have finished this chapter, you will be in a much better position to answer these questions and many others such as:

▶ What is good teaching?
▶ Would teaching be a good career for me?
▶ What do expert teachers know?
▶ What are the greatest concerns of beginning teachers?
▶ Why should I study educational psychology?
▶ What roles do theory and research play in this field?
▶ What kinds of problems will the study of educational psychology help me to solve?

What Would You Do?

It is your second year as a teacher at the Riverside Combined Campus (Kindergarten–8th grade). The district has just received money from the state and a private foundation to give three awards in your school for "excellence in teaching." The principal wants the teachers' recommendations about how to choose the recipients of these awards, so a committee is formed, composed of experienced teachers and one beginner—you. When the principal asked you to serve on the committee, you felt you had to say yes. All week the Teachers' Lounge has been buzzing with discussion about the awards. Some teachers are suspicious—they fear the decisions will be purely political. Others are glad to see teaching honored. Names are mentioned as "sure winners" and a few teachers who seldom speak to you have become very friendly ever since the committee membership was announced. It's clear that the job of determining how to choose winners will not be as easy as you had hoped. The first meeting is next week. How will you prepare for it?

▶ What do you need to know about teaching to complete this task?

▶ What are some indicators of excellent teaching? Do different philosophies of teaching provide different answers to this question?

▶ What are your recommendations, and how would you back them up?

Describing teachers who made a difference in his life, Harvard professor Robert Coles (1990) said:

> I mention these teachers in my life because, in fact, they continue to be a great big part of it still. Their voices are in my head and are part of my voice, I am sure. Their thoughts and values inform what I consider and call my own thoughts and values. Their example—the things they did, the style of their teaching, the strategies they employed—continue to inform the way I work. . . .
>   In a sense, then, all good teachers rescue us from the death of boredom, apathy, self-preoccupation, and self-satisfaction: the teacher as an intellectual and moral life saver who fortunately has come our way and, of course, the teacher as one who is rescued by rescuing others. (p. 59)

What Is Good Teaching?

Connect and Extend
To your own philosophy
What are the goals of education, real and ideal? What does it mean to be an educated person? What makes a teacher effective? Describe the most effective teacher you ever had. How do you learn best? What do you hope to gain from this course? Your answers will provide the basis for developing a philosophy of teaching.

There are hundreds of answers to this question, including ideas based on your own experience. This question has been examined by educators, psychologists, philosophers, novelists, journalists, mathematicians, scientists, historians, policymakers, and parents, to name only a few groups. And good teaching is not confined to classrooms—it occurs in homes and hospitals, museums and sales meetings, therapists' offices and summer camps. In this book, we are primarily concerned with teaching in classrooms, but much of what you will learn applies to other settings as well.

Inside Four Classrooms

To begin our examination of good teaching, let's step inside the classrooms of several outstanding teachers. All the situations that follow are real. The first two teachers worked with my student teachers in local elementary schools. I have chosen them because one of my former colleagues at Rutgers, Carol Weinstein, has written about them in her book on classroom management (Weinstein & Mignano, 1997). The next two are secondary school teachers who have been studied by other educational psychologists.

A Bilingual 1st Grade. There are 25 students in Viviana's class. Most have recently emigrated from the Dominican Republic; the rest come from Nicaragua, Mexico, Puerto Rico, and Honduras. Even though the children speak little or no English when they begin school, by the time they leave in June, Viviana has helped them master the normal 1st-grade curriculum for their district. She accomplishes this by teaching in Spanish early in the year to aid understanding, then gradually introducing English as the students are ready. Viviana does not want her students segregated or labeled as disadvantaged. She encourages them to take pride in their Spanish-speaking heritage while using every available opportunity to support their developing English proficiency.

Viviana's expectations for her students are high, and she makes sure the students have the resources they need. She provides materials—pencils, scissors, crayons— so no child lacks the means to learn. And she supplies constant encouragement. "Viviana's commitment to her students is evident in her 1st-grade bilingual classroom. With an energy level that is rare, she motivates, prods, instructs, models, praises, and captivates her students. . . . The pace is brisk and Viviana clearly has a flair for the dramatic; she uses music, props, gestures, facial expressions, and shifts in voice tone to communicate the material" (Weinstein & Mignano, 1997, p. 13).

Viviana's expectations for herself are high as well. She continually expands her knowledge of teaching through graduate work and participation in special training programs. To know more about her students each year, she spends hours in their homes. For Viviana, teaching is a not just a job; it is a way of life.

A Suburban 6th Grade. Ken teaches 6th grade in a suburban elementary school in central New Jersey. Ken emphasizes "process writing." His students complete first drafts, discuss them with others in the class, revise, edit, and "publish" their work. The students also keep daily journals and often use these to share personal concerns with Ken. They tell him of problems at home, fights, and fears; he always takes the time to respond in writing. The study of science is also placed in the context of the real world. The students use a National Geographic Society computer network to link with other schools in order to identify acid rain patterns around the world. For social studies, the class played two simulation games that focused on the first half of the 1800s. They "lived" as trappers collecting animal skins, and as pioneers heading west to search for gold.

Throughout the year Ken is very interested in the social and emotional development of his students—he wants them to learn about responsibility and fairness as well as science and social studies. This concern is evident in the way he develops his class rules at the beginning of the year. Rather than specifying dos and don'ts, Ken and his students devise a "Bill of Rights" for the class, describing the rights of the students and of the teacher. These rights cover most of the situations that might need a "rule."

Two Advanced Math Classes. Hilda Borko and Carol Livingston (1989) describe two expert secondary school mathematics teachers. In one lesson for her advanced mathematics class, Ellen had her students identify any three problems about ellipses from their text. She asked if there were any questions or uncertainties

Connect and Extend
To the news
An article in the *New York Times* (May 26, 1988, p. B1) described how Cornell University was bringing together some of the high school teachers of its top undergraduates in order to honor both the students and their former teachers. One of these undergraduates said of his high school math teacher, "She had so much enthusiasm in class, she made learning so interesting; we had fun learning calculus." According to the article, the teacher's techniques included such innovations as "classroom coupons" for excellent work, which gave students the privilege of leaving class early or being late to class without penalty. At the same time, the student spoke of his teacher's "absolute dedication and discipline in teaching mathematics. There was no doubt that you were in her class to learn."

Connect and Extend
To other chapters
Ken's process writing, student publishing, and journal writing are examples of a "whole language" approach, discussed in Chapter 13. Ken's "Bill of Rights" is an example of an innovative approach to setting class rules, discussed in Chapter 12.

Connect and Extend
To the research
Borko, H., & Livingston, O. B. (1989). Cognition and improvisation: Differences in mathematics instruction by expert and novice teachers. *American Educational Research Journal, 26,* 473–498.

about these problems. Ellen answered student questions, worked two of the problems, and then used the three problems to derive all the concepts and equations the students needed to understand the material. Ellen's knowledge of the subject and of her students was so thorough that she could create the explanations and derive the formulas on the spot, no matter which problems the students chose.

Another teacher, Randy, worked with his students' confusion to construct a review lesson about strategies for doing integrals. When one student said that a particular section in the book seemed "haphazard," Randy led the class through a process of organizing the material. He asked the class for general statements about useful strategies for doing integrals. He clarified their suggestions, elaborated on some, and helped students improve others. He asked the students to tie their ideas to passages in the text. Even though he accepted all reasonable suggestions, he listed only the key strategies on the board. By the end of the period, the students had transformed the disorganized material from the book into an ordered and useful outline to guide their learning. They also had a better idea about how to read and understand difficult material.

What do you see in these classrooms? The teachers are committed to their students. They must deal with a wide range of student abilities and challenges: different languages, different home lives, different needs. These teachers must understand their subjects and their students' thinking so well that they can spontaneously create new examples and explanations when students are confused. They must make the most abstract concepts, such as integrals, real and understandable for their particular students. And then there is the challenge of new technologies and techniques. The teachers must use them appropriately to accomplish important goals, not just to entertain the students. The whole time that these experts are navigating through the academic material, they also are taking care of the emotional needs of their students, propping up sagging self-esteem and encouraging responsibility. If we followed these individuals from the first day of class, we would see that they carefully plan and teach the basic procedures for living and learning in their classes. They can efficiently correct and collect homework, regroup students, give directions, distribute materials, collect lunch money, and deal with disruptions—and do all of this while also making a mental note to check why one of their students is so tired.

Viviana, Ken, Ellen, and Randy are examples of **expert teachers**, the focus of much recent research in education and psychology. For another perspective on the question "What is good teaching?" let's examine this research on what expert teachers know.

Expert Knowledge

Expert teachers have elaborate *systems of knowledge* for understanding problems in teaching. For example, when a beginning teacher is faced with students' wrong answers on math or history tests, all the wrong answers may seem about the same—wrong. The inexperienced teacher may have trouble connecting other facts or ideas with the students' wrong answers. But for an expert teacher, wrong answers are part of a rich system of knowledge that could include how to recognize several types of wrong answers, the misunderstanding or lack of information behind each kind of mistake, the best way to reteach and correct the misunderstanding, materials and activities that have worked in the past, and several ways to test whether the reteaching was successful (Floden & Klinzing, 1990; Leinhardt, 1988). Peterson and Comeaux (1989) argue that it is the quality of teachers' professional knowledge and their ability to be aware of their own thinking that make them expert.

Connect and Extend
To other classrooms
Another excellent teacher is described in the *Harvard Education Letter*.

Robert Moses, founder of the Algebra Project at the Martin Luther King School in Cambridge, Massachusetts, teaches students the concept of number and sign through a physical event: they go for a ride on a subway. Choosing one subway stop as a starting point, students relate inbound and outbound to positive and negative numbers. They translate their subway ride into mathematical language by considering both the number of stops and their direction. By giving students such experiences before introducing the formal language of algebra, Moses . . . has made math more enjoyable and accessible. (Ruopp & Driscoll, 1990, p. 5)

Connect and Extend
To the research
Carter, K., Sabers, D., Cushing, K., Pinnegar, S., & Berliner, D. (1987). Processing and using information about students: A study of expert, novice, and postulant teachers. *Teaching and Teacher Education, 3*, 147–157.

Connect and Extend
To other chapters
Teachers' knowledge of their own thinking is an example of metacognitive knowledge, discussed in Chapter 7.

Expert Teachers: Experienced, effective teachers who have developed solutions for common classroom problems. Their knowledge of teaching process and content is extensive and well organized.

What do expert teachers know that allows them to be so successful? Lee Shulman (1987) has studied this question, and he has identified seven areas of professional knowledge. Expert teachers know:

1. The academic subjects they teach.

2. General teaching strategies that apply in all subjects (such as the principles of classroom management, effective teaching, and evaluation that you will discover in this book).

3. The curriculum materials and programs appropriate for their subject and grade level.

4. Subject-specific knowledge for teaching: special ways of teaching certain students and particular concepts, such as the best ways to explain negative numbers to lower-ability students.

5. The characteristics and cultural backgrounds of learners.

6. The settings in which students learn—pairs, small groups, teams, classes, schools, and the community.

7. The goals and purposes of teaching.

This is quite a list. Obviously, one course cannot give you all the information you need to teach. In fact, a whole program of courses won't make you an expert. That takes time and experience. But studying educational psychology can add to your professional knowledge. At the heart of educational psychology is a concern with learning wherever it occurs—in classrooms and corporations, in the military, and in medical internships, wherever people strive to become more knowledgeable and competent.

No person can learn for another; students create their own knowledge and skills. The teacher's role is to orchestrate materials, tasks, environments, conversations, and explorations that encourage and support learning and the increasing independence of their students. To become such a teacher, you will need to know about your *students* (Part 1 of this book), *learning* (Part 2), *motivating* (Part 3), *teaching* (Part 4), and *assessing* (Part 5).

How do you grow from beginning teacher to expert? Can you learn to be an expert teacher, or are really great teachers just born? Is good teaching an art or a science? Answers to this last question provide another perspective on good teaching.

Teaching: Artistry, Technique, and a Lot of Work

Because researchers have identified a number of effective teaching techniques, some educators argue that all teachers should learn these practices and be tested on them in order to earn or keep their teaching certificates. Other educators believe that the mark of an excellent teacher is not the ability to apply techniques but the artistry of being **reflective**—thoughtful and inventive—about teaching (Schon, 1983). Educators who adopt this view tend to be more concerned with how teachers plan, solve problems, create instruction, and make decisions than they are with the specific techniques teachers apply. They believe teaching is a complicated, demanding activity that requires creative thinking and a commitment to lifelong learning (Borko, 1989; Peterson & Comeaux, 1989).

Most people agree that teachers must be both technically competent and inventive. They must be able to use a range of strategies, and they must also be able to

▲ *Expert teachers not only know the content of the subjects they teach, they also know how to relate this content to the world outside the classroom and how to keep students involved in learning.*

Connect and Extend
To the research
Jean Piaget (1973) had this to say about teaching: "The art of education is like the art of medicine: it is an art that cannot be practiced without special 'gifts,' but one that assumes exact and experimental knowledge relating to the human beings on which it is exercised" (*To Understand Is to Invent: The Future of Education*. New York: Grossman, p. 94).

Reflective: Thoughtful and inventive. Reflective teachers think back over situations to analyze what they did and why and to consider how they might improve learning for their students.

Connect and Extend
To the research

- Read and discuss the article by Sparks-Langer, G. M., & Colton, A. S. B. (1991). Synthesis of research on teachers' reflective thinking. *Educational Leadership, 48*(6), 37–44. *Focus Questions:* What does it mean to be a reflective teacher? Why is reflection important in teaching?

- For a slightly longer discussion of the value of technique versus reflective thinking in teacher preparation, see pages 109–111 of Hoy, W. K., and Woolfolk, A. E. (1989). Supervising student teachers. In A. Woolfolk (Ed.), *Research perspectives on the graduate preparation of teachers* (pp. 108–131). Boston: Allyn & Bacon.

- See the article by Murphy, J., Evertson, C. M., & Radnofsky, M. L. (1991). Restructuring schools: Fourteen elementary and secondary teachers' perspectives on reform. *Elementary School Journal, 92,* 135–148. *Focus Question:* Are teachers becoming more involved in school decisions?

invent new strategies. They must have some simple routines for managing classes, but they must also be willing and able to break from the routine when the situation calls for change. New problems arise all the time, and when the old solutions do not work, something else is needed.

With the growing understanding that teaching is a complex problem-solving activity has come a call to give teachers more freedom and responsibility. A number of educational reform movements seek to involve teachers in designing the curriculum and making the decisions for their own students, as you can see in the Point/Counterpoint section.

You may be thinking that all this talk about expert teachers and expert knowledge, artistry, and technique is a bit idealistic and abstract. Right now, you may have other, more down-to-earth, concerns about becoming a teacher. You are not alone!

Concerns of Beginning Teachers

Beginning teachers everywhere share many concerns. A review of studies conducted around the world found that beginning teachers regard maintaining classroom discipline, motivating students, accommodating differences among students, evaluating student work, and dealing with parents as the most serious challenges they face. Many teachers also experience what has been called "reality shock" when they take their first job and confront the "harsh and rude reality of everyday classroom life" (Veenman, 1984, p. 143). One source of shock may be that teachers really cannot ease into their responsibilities. On the first day of their first job, beginning teachers face the same tasks as teachers with years of experience. Student teaching, while a critical element, does not really prepare prospective teachers for starting off a school year with a new class. And schools usually offer little chance

Teaching is one of the few professions in which a new teacher must assume all of the responsibilities of an experienced "pro" during the first week on the job. Veteran teachers can be an excellent source of information and support during these early weeks. ▼

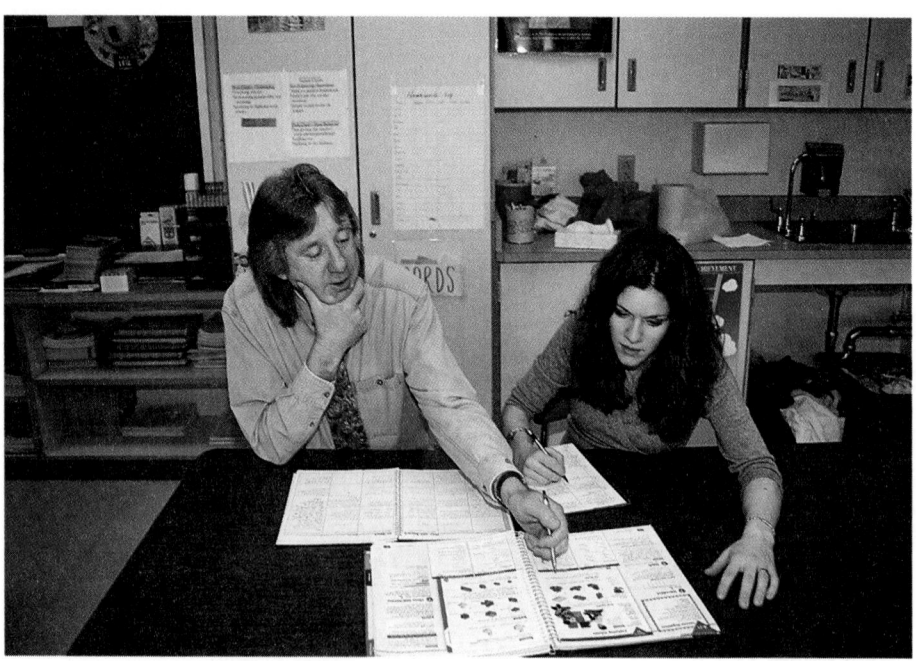

Whose Classroom Is It Anyway?

The Carnegie Forum on Education and the Economy report, *A Nation Prepared: Teachers for the 21st Century* (1986), introduced a new word to the vocabulary of educational reform—*restructuring*. The report argued that we must "restructure schools to provide a professional environment for teachers, freeing [teachers] to decide how to best meet the state and local goals for children" (p. 57). Is this recommendation becoming a reality? Is the structure of schools changing so teachers can use their expertise in deciding how to teach their students?

▶ **POINT** *Teachers have a bigger say.*

The National Governors' Association, the National Education Association, and the National Association of Secondary School Principals have issued reports supporting teacher participation in school decisions. The National Governors' Association (1989) states that restructuring should involve (1) modifying curriculum to support higher-order thinking and problem solving, creativity, and cooperation; (2) bringing together teachers, administrators, and parents at each school to make instructional decisions; (3) creating new staff roles to make better use of the teachers' expertise; and (4) holding schools accountable for students' achievement.

The April 1990 issue of *Educational Leadership* describes many elementary and secondary schools that have radically altered curriculum, decision-making, roles, and accountability systems. For example,

the staff of Central Park East Secondary School decided to limit the number of class periods for its students to allow more in-depth study:

A typical week for students in grades 7–10, for example, includes several two-hour blocks of humanities and math-science, daily one-hour classes in Spanish, two to three hours of community service, and several advisory periods. During an extended lunch period and after school, students may participate in clubs, music, physical education, sports, and other activities. (O'Neil, 1990b, p. 7)

In 119 Dade County, Florida, schools, administrator/teacher/parent councils have been created to redesign the schools. Three of the innovations established by these councils are Saturday classes providing extra help, enrichment, and even ballet instruction; satellite schools in local businesses; and lead teachers who receive extra pay to support and guide their colleagues.

◀ **COUNTERPOINT** *Restructuring is not working.*

In 1987 the Carnegie Foundation for the Advancement of Teaching surveyed teachers across the United States to see if they felt involved in decisions at their schools. Most teachers—about 79%—participated in choosing textbooks, and a good number (63%) felt they were involved in shaping the curriculum. But only 47% helped to set standards for students' behavior, only 43% participated in designing staff

development programs, and a mere 20% had a say in school budgets.

Some researchers suggest that teachers must be so focused on their classrooms and students that they have little time or energy for participating in schoolwide decisions (Lortie, 1977). Other researchers suggest that teachers and administrators have a kind of agreement not to interfere in each other's "territory." In return for leaving school-level decisions to the administrators, teachers get to be autonomous in their classrooms (Corwin, 1981). Some critics fear that restructuring will require teachers to take on more responsibilities without giving them more time or resources to meet these new obligations (Conley, 1991).

Evidently, the problems persist. David Clark and Terry Astuto (1994) ask these questions about restructuring schools so that teachers are more involved in making decisions about their individual students:

Why do we focus on implementing site-based management systems for high schools while we retain the daily schedule of six to eight 50-minute class periods, which ensures that most high school teachers will never get to know about the lives of the 150 to 200 students whom they see each day? Does anyone believe that such an organizational structure provides the time for English teachers to tutor their students in writing? . . .Or that it provides an opportunity for individualized instruction and counseling? (p. 514)

for helpful contact between novice and experienced teachers, making mutual support and assistance difficult. If you have had any of these concerns, you shouldn't be troubled. They come with the job of being a beginning teacher (Borko & Putnam, 1996; Cooke & Pang, 1991; Veenman, 1984).

Review

▶ What do expert teachers know?

▶ What are the artistic and scientific aspects of teaching?

▶ What are the concerns of beginning teachers?

Apply

▶ Analyze one of your current teachers in terms of Shulman's seven kinds of knowledge.

▶ How are your concerns about teaching similar to or different from those reported in studies of beginning teachers?

Connect and Extend

To the research

Evidence for the importance of technique and reflection in teaching can be found in a study of a teacher education program in the Netherlands that strongly emphasizes the development of reflective thinking: Korthagen, F. A. J. (1985). Reflective teaching and preservice teacher education in the Netherlands. *Journal of Teacher Education, 36*(5), 11–15. Over 50% of the program's graduates who responded to a survey said they had been insufficiently prepared for handling problems of motivation and management. Many of these graduates found that they had to abandon their attempts at analysis and inquiry in their early teaching years to develop ways to handle the day-to-day teaching problems. Beginning teachers need to master some basic teaching techniques and procedures in order to protect the capacity for reflection. Otherwise, they may spend all their time in the first years of teaching just learning to survive.

Self-Regulated Learners: Learners who have a combination of academic learning skills and self-control that makes learning easier; they have the *skill* and the *will* to learn.

With experience, however, most teachers meet the challenges that seem difficult for beginners. They have more time to experiment with new methods or materials. Finally, as confidence grows, seasoned teachers can focus on the students' needs. Are my students learning? Are they developing positive attitudes? Is this the best way to teach the slower learners to write a persuasive essay? At this advanced stage, teachers judge their success by the successes of their students (Feiman-Nemser, 1983; Fuller 1969; Putnam & Borko, 1997).

I have talked about good teachers because that is what many of you are planning to become. But all good teaching begins with an understanding of *students* and *learning*. As you will see throughout this text, today there is great interest in studying how people understand and apply knowledge. Just as educational psychologists have investigated how expertise develops in teaching, they have also explored how students come to be experts in particular subjects. Many of the chapters in this book are concerned with these issues.

The Ultimate Goal of Teaching: Lifelong Expert Learning

Today, people change jobs an average of seven times before they retire. Many of these career changes require new knowledge and skills (Weinstein, 1994). Thus, one goal of teaching should be to free students from the need for teachers so the students can continue to learn independently throughout their lives.

To continue learning independently throughout life, you must be a self-regulated learner. **Self-regulated learners** have a combination of academic learning skills and self-control that makes learning easier, so they are more motivated; in other words, they have the *skill* and the *will* to learn (McCombs & Marzano, 1990; Murphy & Alexander, 2000). The concept of self-regulated learning integrates much of what is known about effective learning and motivation. Three factors influence skill and will: knowledge, motivation, and self-discipline or volition.

Knowledge

To be self-regulated learners, students need *knowledge* about themselves, the subject, the task, strategies for learning, and the contexts in which they will apply their learning. "Expert" students know about *themselves* and how they learn best. For example, they know their preferred learning styles, what is easy and what is hard for them, how to cope with the hard parts, what their interests and talents are, and how to use their strengths (see Chapter 4 of this book). These experts also know quite a bit about the *subject* being studied—and the more they know, the easier it is to learn more (Alexander, 1997). They probably understand that different *learning tasks* require different approaches on their part. A simple memory task, for example, might require a mnemonic strategy (see Chapter 7) while a complex comprehension task might be approached by means of concept maps of the key ideas (see Chapter 8). Also, these self-regulated learners know that learning often is difficult and knowledge is seldom absolute—there usually are different ways of looking at problems as well as different solutions (Pressley, 1995; Winne, 1995).

These expert students not only know what each task requires, they can also apply the *strategy* needed. They can skim or read carefully. They can use memory strategies or reorganize the material. As they become more knowledgeable in a field, they apply many of these strategies automatically. In short, they have mastered a large, flexible repertoire of learning strategies and tactics (see Chapter 8).

Finally, expert learners think about the *contexts* in which they will apply their knowledge—when and where they will use their learning—so they can set motivating goals and connect present work to future accomplishments (Wang & Palincsar, 1989; Weinstein, 1994; Winne, 1995).

▲ *Lyn Corno has written extensively about self-regulated learning.*

Motivation

Self-regulated learners are *motivated* to learn (see Chapters 10 and 11). They find many tasks in school interesting because they value learning, not just performing well in the eyes of others. But even if they are not intrinsically motivated by a particular task, they are serious about getting the intended benefit from it. They know *why* they are studying, so their actions and choices are self-determined and not controlled by others. However, knowledge and motivation are not always enough. Self-regulated learners need volition or self-discipline. "Where motivation denotes commitment, volition denotes follow-through" (Corno, 1992, p. 72).

Volition

It is Friday night. I have been writing almost all day and my cold is getting worse. I want to keep writing because the deadline for this chapter is very near. I have knowledge and motivation, but to keep going I need a good dose of volition. **Volition** is an old-fashioned word for will power. Self-regulated learners know how to protect themselves from distractions—where to study, for example, so they are not interrupted. They know how to cope when they feel anxious, drowsy, or lazy (Corno, 1992, 1995; Snow, Corno, & Jackson, 1996). And they know what to do when tempted to stop working and take a nap—the temptation I'm facing now—that, and a large bowl of (low-fat) chips and salsa.

Obviously, not all of your students will be self-regulated learners. In fact, some psychologists suggest that you think of this capacity as an individual difference characteristic (Snow, Corno, & Jackson, 1996). Some students are much better at it than others. How can you help more students

CHECKPOINT

The Ultimate Goal of Teaching: Lifelong Expert Learning

Review

▶ Describe self-regulated learning.

Apply

▶ What aspects of teachers' professional knowledge can you hope to develop by studying educational psychology?

Volition: Will power; self-discipline.

become self-regulated learners? That is where educational psychology and this book can help.

The Role of Educational Psychology

Connect and Extend
To the research
The Spring 1992 issue of *Educational Psychologist, 27*(2), has a special section on "The Nature and Mission of Educational Psychology" with articles by Merle Wittrock, David Berliner, Robert Calfee, and Carol Goodenow.

We begin our consideration of the role of educational psychology in teaching and learning by defining the term. For as long as educational psychology has existed—about 90 years—there have been debates about what it really is. Some people believe educational psychology is simply knowledge gained from psychology and applied to the activities of the classroom. Others believe it involves applying the methods of psychology to study classroom and school life (Clifford, 1984a; Grinder, 1981).

The view generally accepted today is that **educational psychology** is a distinct discipline with its own theories, research methods, problems, and techniques. "Educational psychology is distinct from other branches of psychology because it has the understanding and improvement of education as its primary goal" (Wittrock, 1992, p. 138). Educational psychologists "study what people think and do [I would add *feel*] as they teach and learn a particular curriculum in a particular environment where education and training are intended to take place" (Berliner, 1992, p. 145). But are the findings of educational psychologists really that helpful for teachers? After all, most teaching is just common sense, isn't it? Let's take a few minutes to examine these questions.

Is It Just Common Sense?

In many cases, the principles set forth by educational psychologists—after spending much thought, research, and money—sound pathetically obvious. People are tempted to say, and usually do say, "Everyone knows that!" Consider these examples:

Taking Turns. What method should a teacher use in selecting students to participate in a primary grade reading class?

Common Sense Answer. Teachers should call on students randomly so that everyone will have to follow the lesson carefully. If a teacher were to use the same order every time, the students would know when their turn was coming up.

Answer Based on Research. Years ago, research by Ogden, Brophy, and Evertson (1977) found that the answer to this question is not so simple. In 1st-grade reading classes, for example, going around the circle in order and giving each child a chance to read led to better overall achievement than calling on students randomly. The critical factor in going around the circle may be that each child gets a chance to participate. Without some system for calling on everyone, many students can be overlooked or skipped. Research suggests there are better alternatives for teaching reading than going around the circle, but teachers should make sure that everyone has the chance for practice and feedback whatever approach is used (Tierney, Readence, & Dishner, 1990).

Classroom Management. Students are engaged in an appropriate and educationally meaningful task, but still, some students are repeatedly out of their seats without permission, wandering around the room. What should the teacher do?

These young students are participating in a reading circle. Will their reading skills improve using this approach? Are there better ways to learn to read? Educational research attempts to shed light on such questions. ▼

Common Sense Answer. Each time they get up, the teacher should remind students to remain in their seats. These repeated reminders will help overactive students remember the rule. If the teacher does not remind them and lets them get away with breaking the rules, both the out-of-seat students and the rest of the class may decide the teacher is not really serious about the rule.

Answer Based on Research. In a now-classic study, Madsen, Becker, Thomas, Koser, and Plager (1968) found that the more a teacher told students to sit down when they were out of their seats, the more often the students got out of their seats without permission. When the teacher ignored students who were out of their seats and praised students who were sitting down, the rate of out-of-seat behavior dropped greatly. When the teacher returned to the previous system of telling students to sit down, the rate of out-of-seat behavior increased once again. It seems that—at least under some conditions—the more a teacher says "Sit down!" the more the students stand up!

Skipping Grades. Should a school encourage exceptionally bright students to skip grades or to enter college early?

Common Sense Answer. No! Very intelligent students who are a year or two younger than their classmates are likely to be social misfits. They are neither physically nor emotionally ready for dealing with older students and would be miserable in the social situations that are so important in school, especially in the later grades.

Answer Based on Research. Maybe. According to Samuel Kirk and his colleagues (1993), "From early admissions to school to early admissions to college, research studies invariably report that children who have been accelerated have adjusted as well as or better than have children of similar ability who have not been accelerated" (p. 105). Whether acceleration is the best solution for a student depends on many specific individual characteristics, including the intelligence and maturity of the student, and on the other available options. For some students, moving quickly through the material and working in advanced courses with older students is a very good idea.

Lily Wong (1987) demonstrated that just seeing research results in writing can make them seem obvious. She selected 12 findings from research on teaching; one of them was the "taking turns" result noted above. She presented six of the findings in their correct form and six in *exactly the opposite form* to college students and to experienced teachers. Both the college students and teachers rated about half of the *wrong* findings as "obviously" correct. In a follow-up study, another group of subjects was shown the 12 findings and their opposites and was asked to pick which ones were correct. For 8 of the 12 findings, the subjects chose the wrong result more often than the right one.

You may have thought that educational psychologists spend their time discovering the obvious. The examples above point out the danger of this kind of thinking. When a principle is stated in simple terms, it can sound simplistic. A similar phenomenon takes place when we see a gifted dancer or athlete perform; the well-trained performer makes it look easy. But we see only the results of the training, not all the work that went into mastering the individual movements. And bear in mind that any research finding—or its opposite—may sound like common sense. The issue is not what *sounds* sensible, but what is demonstrated when the principle is put to the test (Gage, 1991).

Connect and Extend
To the research
Read and discuss the article by Gage, N. L. (1991). The obviousness of social and educational research results. *Educational Researcher, 20*(1), 10–16. *Focus Questions:* What makes findings in educational research seem "obvious"? What is the danger in this kind of thinking?

Educational Psychology: The discipline concerned with teaching and learning processes; applies the methods and theories of psychology and has its own as well.

Descriptive Studies: Studies that collect detailed information about specific situations, often using observation, surveys, interviews, recordings, or a combination of these methods.

Ethnography: A descriptive approach to research that focuses on life within a group and tries to understand the meaning of events to the people involved.

Participant Observation: A method for conducting descriptive research in which the researcher becomes a participant in the situation in order to better understand life in that group.

Case Study: Intensive study of one person or one situation.

Correlations: Statistical descriptions of how closely two variables are related.

Positive Correlation: A relationship between two variables in which the two increase or decrease together. Example: calorie intake and weight gain.

Negative Correlation: A relationship between two variables in which a high value on one is associated with a low value on the other. Example: height and distance from top of head to the ceiling.

Connect and Extend
To real life

Perfect positive (1.0) correlation: the radius of a circle and its circumference. Perfect negative (−1.0) correlation: the number of minutes of daylight and the number of minutes of dark each day. Less than perfect positive correlation: the cost of a car and the cost of insuring it; child's IQ score and school grades: .39 (Sattler, 1992). Less than perfect negative correlation: cost of a theater ticket and distance from the stage. Zero correlation: population of India and the winning percentage of the New York Yankees.

Using Research to Understand and Improve Teaching

Conducting research to test possible answers is one of two major tasks of educational psychology. The other is combining the results of various studies into theories that attempt to present a unified view of such things as teaching, learning, and development.

Descriptive Studies. Educational psychologists design and conduct many different kinds of research studies in their attempts to understand teaching and learning. Some of these studies are "descriptive," that is, their purpose is simply to describe events in a particular class or several classes. Reports of **descriptive studies** often include survey results, interview responses, samples of actual classroom dialogue, or records of the class activities.

One descriptive approach, classroom **ethnography**, is borrowed from anthropology. Ethnographic methods involve studying the naturally occurring events in the life of a group and trying to understand the meaning of these events to the people involved. For example, the descriptions of expert high school mathematics teachers in the opening pages of this chapter were taken from an ethnographic study by Hilda Borko and Carol Livingston (1989). The researchers made detailed observations in the teachers' classes and analyzed these observations, along with audio recordings and information from interviews with the teachers, in order to describe differences between novice and expert teachers.

In some descriptive studies, researchers carefully analyze videotapes of classes to identify recurring patterns of teacher and student behaviors. In other studies, the researcher uses **participant observation** and works within the class or school to understand the actions from the perspectives of the teacher and the students. Researchers also may employ case studies. A **case study** investigates in depth how a teacher plans courses, for example, or how a student tries to learn specific material.

Correlational Studies. Often the results of descriptive studies include reports of correlations. We will take a minute to examine this concept, because you will encounter many correlations in the coming chapters. A **correlation** is a number that indicates both the strength and the direction of a relationship between two events or measurements. Correlations range from 1.00 to −1.00. The closer the correlation is to either 1.00 or −1.00, the stronger the relationship. For example, the correlation between height and weight is about .70 (a strong relationship); the correlation between height and number of languages spoken is about .00 (no relationship at all).

The sign of the correlation tells the direction of the relationship. A **positive correlation** indicates that the two factors increase or decrease together. As one gets larger, so does the other. Height and weight are positively correlated because greater height tends to be associated with greater weight. A **negative correlation** means that increases in one factor are related to decreases in the other. For example, the correlation between outside temperature and the weight of clothing worn is negative, because people tend to wear clothing of increasing weight as the temperature decreases.

It is important to note that correlations do not prove cause and effect (see Figure 1.1). Height and weight are correlated—taller people tend to weigh more than shorter people. But gaining weight obviously does not cause you to grow taller. Knowing a person's weight simply allows you to make a general prediction about that person's height. Educational psychologists identify correlations so they can make predictions about important events in the classroom.

Experimental Studies. A second type of research—**experimentation**—allows educational psychologists to go beyond predictions and actually study cause and

FIGURE 1.1

Correlations Do Not Show Causation

When research shows that broken homes and crime are correlated, it does not show causation. Poverty, a third variable, may be the cause of both crime and broken homes.

Faulty Assumption

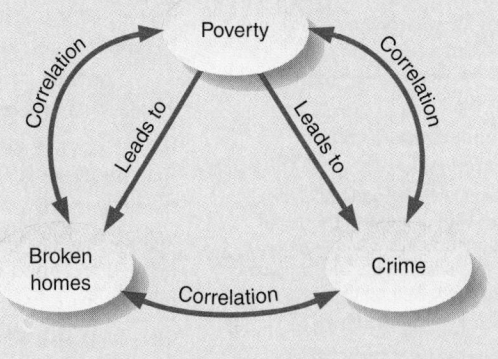

More Likely Assumption

effect. Instead of just observing and describing an existing situation, the investigators introduce changes and note the results. First, a number of comparable groups of subjects are created. In psychological research, the term **subjects** generally refers to the people being studied—such as teachers or 8th graders—not to subjects like math or science. One common way to make sure that groups of subjects are essentially the same is to assign each subject to a group using a random procedure. **Random** means each subject has an equal chance to be in any group.

In one or more of these groups, the experimenters change some aspect of the situation to see if this change or "treatment" has an expected effect. The results in each group are then compared. Usually statistical tests are conducted to see if the differences between the groups are significant. When differences are described as **statistically significant**, it means that they probably did not happen simply by chance. A number of the studies we will examine attempt to identify cause-and-effect relationships by asking questions such as this: If teachers ignore students who are out of their seats without permission and praise students who are working hard at their desks (cause), will students spend more time working at their desks (effect)?

In many cases, both descriptive and experimental research occur together. The study by Ogden, Brophy, and Evertson (1977) described at the beginning of this section is a good example. In order to answer questions about the relationship between how students are selected to read in a primary-grade class and their achievement in reading, these investigators first observed students and teachers in a number of classrooms and then measured the reading achievement of the students. They found that having students read in a predictable order was associated, or correlated, with gains in reading scores. With a simple correlation such as this, however, the researchers could not be sure that the strategy was actually causing the effect. In the second part of the study, Ogden and her colleagues asked several teachers to call on each student in turn. They then compared reading achievement in these groups with achievement in groups where teachers used other strategies. This second part of the research was thus an experimental study.

Theories for Teaching. The major goal of educational psychology is understanding teaching and learning, and research is a primary tool. Reaching this goal is a slow process; there are very few landmark studies that answer a question once and

Connect and Extend
To what you know
Are the following studies descriptive (D) or experimental (E)? (D) 1. Researchers observe teachers of classes that have high achievement in order to determine how these teachers are alike. (E) 2. Teachers give three groups of impulsive children different types of training to determine which type of training is most effective in reducing impulsivity. (D) 3. Researchers administer IQ tests to a group of boys and girls to determine if there is a relationship between sex and verbal ability. (E) 4. Teachers instruct two similar groups of math students by two different methods to determine which method leads to higher scores on a math achievement test.

Experimentation: Research method in which variables are manipulated and the effects recorded.

Subjects: People or animals studied.

Random: Without any definite pattern; following no rule.

Statistically Significant: Not likely to be a chance occurrence.

Principle: Established relationship between factors.

Theory: Integrated statement of principles that attempts to explain a phenomenon and make predictions.

Connect and Extend
To the research
Killion, J. P., & Todnem, G. R. (1991). A process for personal theory building. *Educational Leadership, 48*(6), 14–16. *Focus Question:* Why do teachers need a personal theory for teaching?

for all. Human beings are too complicated. Instead, research in educational psychology examines limited aspects of a situation—perhaps a few variables at a time or life in one or two classrooms. If enough studies are completed in a certain area and findings repeatedly point to the same conclusions, we eventually arrive at a **principle**. This is the term for an established relationship between two or more factors—between a certain teaching strategy, for example, and student achievement.

Another tool for building a better understanding of the teaching and learning processes is **theory**. The common sense notion of theory (as in "Oh well, it was only a theory") is "a guess or hunch." But the scientific meaning of theory is quite different. "A theory in science is an interrelated set of concepts that is used to explain a body of data and to make predictions about the results of future experiments" (Stanovich, 1992, p. 21). Given a number of established principles, educational psychologists have developed explanations for the relationships among many variables and even whole systems of relationships. There are theories to explain how language develops, how differences in intelligence occur, and, as noted earlier, how people learn.

Few theories explain and predict perfectly. In this book, you will see many examples of educational psychologists taking different theoretical positions and disagreeing on the overall explanations of such issues as learning and motivation. Because no one theory offers all the answers, it makes sense to consider what each has to offer.

So why, you may ask, is it necessary to deal with theories? Why not just stick to principles? The answer is that both are useful. Principles of classroom management, for example, will give you help with specific problems. A good theory of classroom management, on the other hand, will give you a new way of thinking about discipline problems; it will give you tools for creating solutions to many different problems and for predicting what might work in new situations. A major goal of this book is to provide you with the best and the most useful theories for teaching—those that have solid evidence behind them. Although you may prefer some theories over others, consider them all as ways of understanding the challenges teachers face.

The study of educational psychology involves both content and process. The content of facts, principles, and theories adds to the store of your professional knowledge for teaching. The process aspect of educational psychology helps you think critically about teaching so you can become a researcher on your own effectiveness.

CHECKPOINT

The Role of Educational Psychology

Review

▶ What is educational psychology?

▶ What are descriptive studies?

▶ What are correlations?

▶ What are experimental studies?

▶ Distinguish between principles and theories.

Apply

▶ What would you say to someone who asserts that "teaching is just common sense"?

How This Book Can Help *You* Learn

Years ago a wonderful principal told me that teachers are the *professional learners* and students are the *amateurs*. She encouraged the teachers in her school to be good guides and learning coaches so that their students would become expert learners too. I tell my class the first day of the semester that I hope they will "take educational psychology personally." By this I mean I want them to apply the ideas to their own lives as students. If you can become a more expert learner by applying the knowledge from this text about study strategies, motivation, active learning, and understanding, then you will be a better teacher as well. So I encourage you to use this book to learn more about learning, motivation, goal setting, studying, test-taking, and self-regulation so you can apply the knowledge to your life now.

The structure, as well as the content of this book, supports learning. Here is how you might use the different elements of the book to help you develop a base of knowledge for use as a student now and always and as a teacher later.

Getting Ready to Learn

Each chapter begins with several features to help you get ready for learning. You are asked several questions to start you thinking about a topic related to the chapter. Your answers may bring to mind information you already know about the topics in the chapter. You will soon see that all learning begins with what students already know and believe. The chapter *Outline* and the *Overview* give you a snapshot of the organization of the material to come. Next you encounter a *"What would you do?"* scenario, asking you to project yourself into a classroom and decide how you would handle a problem situation. As you consider possible actions, you will be confronting issues from the upcoming chapter. So, as you read the chapter, you can check out and perhaps expand your ideas for handling the situation. Reading with a purpose in mind aids comprehension. I hope the "What would you do?" problem gives you good reasons and purposes for reading that tie knowledge in educational psychology to classroom practice.

Aids to Understanding

Throughout the chapters, you will find other aids to understanding and application. Use them fully to get the most from this book. Notice the headings and sub-headings as you read. These headings show the structure of the chapter, the main ideas and the related ideas under each main idea. Key terms are highlighted in bold and defined in the margin the first time they are used. There is a list of key terms at the end of each chapter. When you finish reading, test yourself to see if you can briefly explain these terms in your own words. Also, after each main section of the chapter are *Checkpoint* boxes, asking you to check your understanding by reviewing key ideas and applying concepts. At the end of the chapter is a *Summary* that is organized around the *Checkpoints*.

Applying Knowledge

If the ideas in this book are to be valuable, they need to be used to think about and act on problems of teaching and learning—both your own and those of your students. That emphasis is clear at the beginning of each chapter when I ask you to consider, *"What would you do?"* Throughout every chapter after this one are *Guidelines*, principles that can be applied in teaching. Each principle includes a few examples. These examples are intended to encourage your thinking about applications. One set of Guidelines focuses on families as partners in teaching—a very important consideration today. Every chapter also contains a *Point/Counterpoint* debate about a critical issue in educational psychology. You will see that educators

Connect and Extend
To real life
The August 30, 1988, issue of *USA Today* had several stories about the attitudes of teachers based on a sample of 1,174 teachers randomly selected from the 10,000 delegates to the 1988 national conventions of the American Federation of Teachers and the National Education Association ("What Teachers Think," *USA Today*, August 30, 1988, Section D, p. 1). Some of the results: The teachers averaged 44 years old and 19 years' teaching experience, and worked an average of 8 hours per day. Of the teachers, 69% would go into teaching again; 29% would give their school a grade of A; 50% would give their school a grade of B. About 5% would give their school D or F. Most (71%) gave themselves a grade of A, 28% a grade of B, and 1% a C. When asked what they dreaded most about their jobs, 15% said their bosses, 10% said their too-large classes, 5–6% named the paperwork, and 4% said discipline problems. The biggest problems in teaching: low pay and large classes. The greatest rewards: "Watching those mental lightbulbs go on." Discuss the validity of these results with the rest of the class. Are they representative of all teachers? Why or why not? Who are delegates to these professional meetings? Are they likely to be as satisfied with their careers as teachers in general? More or less satisfied? You might want to continue the discussion by noting the need to be "critical consumers" of the research results often reported in the press.

Certification Tests: In many states, teachers are required to take standardized tests, such as the Praxis series designed by the Educational Testing Service, in order to be certified or licensed as a teacher.

Teaching Portfolio: A depiction of you as a teacher, usually including a curriculum vitae, statement of teaching philosophy, examples of your teaching plans and activities, example assignments and tests, students' work, and even videos or CD excerpts of teaching.

do not always agree about the meaning of research findings or how those findings should be applied. At the end of every chapter after this one is a section called *Becoming a Professional* that gives you guidance for:

▶ Developing a personal study guide for professional **Certification Tests** you may be required to take.

▶ Organizing a professional **Teaching Portfolio.**

▶ Developing a resource file.

Finally, we return to the *"What would you do?"* situation to see what several experienced teachers around the country would do. Compare your ideas with theirs and with the information in the chapter. Do you agree? What would you add?

Becoming a Good Beginning Teacher

Becoming an expert teacher takes time and experience, but you can start now by becoming a good beginner. You can develop a repertoire of effective principles and practices for your first years of teaching so that some activities quickly become automatic. You can also develop the habit of questioning and analyzing these accepted practices and your own teaching so you can solve new problems when they arise. You can learn to look behind the effective techniques identified in research to ask: Why did this approach work with these students? What else might be as good or better? The answers to these questions and your ability to analyze the situations are much more important than the specific techniques themselves. As you ask and answer questions, you will be refining your personal theories of teaching.

My goal in writing this book is to help you become an excellent beginning teacher, one who can both apply and improve many techniques. Even more important, I hope this book will cause you to think about students and teaching in new ways, so you will have the foundation for becoming an expert as you gain experience.

CHECKPOINT

How This Book Can Help *You* Learn

Review

 What methods will you use to learn educational psychology?

Summary

What Is Good Teaching?

What do expert teachers know?

It takes time and experience to become an expert teacher. These teachers have a rich store of well-organized knowledge about the many specific situations of teaching. This includes knowledge about the subjects they teach, their students, general teaching strategies, subject-specific ways of teaching, settings for learning, curriculum materials, and the goals of education.

What are the artistic and scientific aspects of teaching?

Teaching is both an art and a science. Effective teaching requires an understanding of research findings on learning and instruction, and knowledge of effective techniques and routines. Teaching also calls for the creativity, talent, and judgment of an artist.

What are the concerns of beginning teachers?

Learning to teach is a gradual process. The concerns and problems of teachers change as they progress. During the beginning years, attention tends to be focused on survival. Maintaining discipline, motivating students, evaluating students' work, and dealing with parents are universal concerns for beginning teachers. The more experienced teacher can move on to concerns about professional growth and effectiveness with a wide range of students.

The Ultimate Goal of Teaching: Lifelong Expert Learning

Describe self-regulated learning.

One important goal of teaching is to prepare students for lifelong learning. To reach this goal, students must be self-regulated learners; that is, they must have a combination of the knowledge, motivation to learn, and volition that provides the skill and will to learn independently and effectively. Knowledge includes an understanding of self, subject, task, learning strategy, and contexts for application. Motivation to learn provides the commitment, and volition is the follow-through that combats distraction and protects persistence.

The Role of Educational Psychology

What is educational psychology?

The goals of educational psychology are to understand and to improve the teaching and learning processes. Educational psychologists develop knowledge and methods; they also use the knowledge and methods of psychology and other related disciplines to study learning and teaching in everyday situations.

Describe descriptive studies.

Reports of descriptive studies often include survey results, interview responses, samples of actual classroom dialogue, or records of the class activities. One descriptive approach, classroom ethnography, is borrowed from anthropology. Ethnographic methods involve studying the naturally occurring events in the life of a group and trying to understand the meaning of these events to the people involved. Researchers also may employ case studies. A case study investigates in depth how a teacher plans courses, for example, or how a student tries to learn specific material. Both descriptive studies and experimental research can provide valuable information for teachers.

What are correlations?

Correlations allow you to predict events that are likely to occur in the classroom. A correlation is a number that indicates both the strength and the direction of a relationship between two events or measurements. Correlations range from 1.00 to –1.00. The closer the correlation is to either 1.00 or –1.00, the stronger the relationship.

What are experimental studies?

Experimental studies can indicate cause-and-effect relationships and should help teachers implement useful changes. Instead of just observing and describing an existing situation, the investigators introduce changes and note the results.

Distinguish between principles and theories.

Educational psychology involves content and process. A principle is an established relationship between two or more factors—between a certain teaching strategy, for example, and student achievement. A theory is an interrelated set of concepts that is used to explain a body of data and to make predictions about the results of future experiments. There are theories to explain how language develops, how differences in intelligence occur, and, as noted earlier, how people learn. The principles from research offer a number of possible answers to specific problems, and the theories offer perspectives for analyzing almost any situation that may arise. The process of analyzing research and theory will encourage you to think critically about teaching.

How This Book Can Help You Learn

Becoming a good teacher means being a good learner. Much of the information in this text will help you become a more expert learner if you take the ideas personally and apply them to your own life. Take advantage of the book's features—the overviews, outlines, "What would you do?" questions, chapter Checkpoints and Summaries, organizational headings, Guidelines, and Teachers' Casebook—to become an expert learner.

ᴷey Terms

case study, p. 14
certification tests, p. 18
correlations, p. 14
descriptive studies, p. 14
educational psychology, p. 12
ethnography, p. 14
experimentation, p. 14

expert teachers, p. 6
negative correlation, p. 14
participant observation, p. 14
positive correlation, p. 14
principle, p. 16
random, p. 15
reflective, p. 7

self-regulated learners, p. 10
statistically significant, p. 15
subjects, p. 15
teaching portfolio, p. 18
theory, p. 16
volition, p. 11

What Would They Do?

Here is how some practicing teachers responded to the teaching situation presented at the beginning of this chapter about establishing a "Teaching Excellence Award."

MADYA AYALA

High School Teacher of Preperatoria Eugenio Garza Lagüera
Campus Garza Sada, Monterrey, N.L. Mexico

The first thing that I would propose is to establish a set of selection criteria. We know that all teachers have strengths and weaknesses and what works the best for each of us. The set of evaluation criteria could change from time to time depending on international, national, and local needs and values. These factors would influence the interpretation of a teacher's psychological, pedagogical, and epistemological strengths as well. Thus, the committee should recognize the educational needs in society at the current time.

The set of criteria related to the level of competence in teaching should be supported officially with bibliographic references, including what UNESCO would say. Input from colleagues, students, and directors should be considered as well. I would propose to the committee that the colleagues' opinions are very important and should have particular importance in the final decision. Candidates' evaluations of themselves might also be included.

Length of experience should not be a factor, only excellence in performance as a teacher. The main objective should be to make teachers aware of what is expected of them and to set the best examples.

KATIE CHURCHILL

Third Grade Teacher
Oriole Parke Elementary School, Chicago, Illinois

I would prepare for the meeting by researching how other schools have chosen recipients for similar awards in the past. I would recommend that we select different categories of "excellence" to decide who will be nominated for the awards. I would suggest that we choose recipients fairly, based on their teaching abilities. Finally, I would recommend that we have student input regarding which teachers should receive these awards.

CAREY PERKSON

Second Grade Teacher
Brown School, Natick, Massachusetts

I would have a discussion with the experienced teachers before our committee meeting to pinpoint what qualifications we are looking for in our candidates. Establishing a definition of "excellence in teaching" and constructing a list of recommendations should be a priority of the committee to ensure that all committee members are looking for the same qualifications.

It would be extremely important to keep an open mind and an attentive ear during all committee meetings. By constructing a list of key qualities and accomplishments for each nominee, we would be able to assess who would be the most qualified for the award.

DENISE READY

Second Grade Teacher
Snug Harbor Community School, Quincy, Massachusetts

My preparation for this meeting would be to come up with the following list of what I believe are indicators of excellent teaching. An excellent teacher:

▶ Loves children.

▶ Respects all children and parents under all circumstances.

▶ Creates a classroom atmosphere that makes children feel safe and secure—an atmosphere in which they feel the importance of classroom ownership.

▶ Sees potential in all children.

▶ Motivates students to reach their highest potential.

▶ Has a wealth of knowledge on child growth and development, along with the ability to use that knowledge to meet individual children's needs.

- Has an in-depth knowledge of classroom management as well as behavior management.
- Is a spontaneous and creative educator who is able to see a teachable moment and seize the opportunity to go with it.
- Is a good role model and mentor for less experienced teachers.
- Has a sense of belonging to a team and a willingness to share responsibilities.
- Uses new educational ideas and insights and has the ability and desire to change so that the field of education can continue to grow.
- Has a sense of humor.
- Is willing to take the "extra time" and go the "extra mile"—has the desire to be the best teacher that he or she can be.

AIMEE FREDETTE

Second Grade Teacher
Fisher Elementary School, Walpole, Massachusetts

There are many facets to being an effective teacher, the foremost being that the teacher will reach all children no matter what it takes. Effective teachers will modify curriculum and instruction to allow all ability levels to feel success and to foster a learning environment that builds the self-esteem of their students. This environment and confidence will encourage children to succeed at their own attempts to learn.

Another indicator of an effective teacher would be the ability to relate to and work with other staff members. Strong communication skills among the administration, peers, parents, and students is essential. When a teacher is able to positively and clearly inspire a class, those students will become curious investigators of the world. If this happens, the parents of these children will become a strong asset to the teacher. Now the child has a foundation on which to grow in both the school and the home environment.

In today's world, a teacher is a critical professional, and, in order to fulfill this role, a continuous effort of self-improvement and professional development must be undertaken. There are many effective means to improve oneself, from attending workshops and conferences, to enrolling in classes, reading trade journals and articles, and conducting peer focus groups and curriculum reviews. A professional who realizes that growth and learning are lifelong and who works to attain new ideas and skills is a valuable asset to any classroom.

There are a variety of teaching philosophies, and each teacher may have a different interpretation of each teaching approach. The teaching philosophies should always arrive at the same outcomes: the growth of student knowledge and the desire of teachers to learn more on their own. Each philosophy that has these goals in mind will use a different way to obtain success.

Effective teachers, regardless of philosophy, will excite and spark the children's interest. This will help the children to develop their own motivation for learning. I also feel that teachers should fully support the placement of all children into their classroom, regardless of abilities. To be effective, teachers will appropriately modify and implement assignments to meet those levels. A positive learning experience is created with a cooperative relationship among teachers, students, and home.

To reinforce recommendations for the indicators of an effective teacher, researching in professional books and journals would be beneficial. Another suggestion would be to brainstorm a list of things that you feel indicate an effective educator.

2

Cognitive Development and Language

hink for a moment about how you would explain the concept of "symbol" to a 6-year-old and to a 14-year-old. Would you use words? Pictures? Specific examples? What kind? What do you know about how younger and older children differ in their thinking?

The material in this chapter will help you answer these questions and many others about how young people think and how their thinking changes over time. These changes in thinking and understanding are called *cognitive development.*

In this chapter, we begin with a discussion of the general principles of human development and a brief look at the human brain. Then we will examine the ideas of two of the most influential cognitive developmental theorists, Jean Piaget and Lev Vygotsky. Piaget's ideas have implications for teachers about what their students can learn and when the students are ready to learn it. We will examine important criticisms of his ideas as well.

The work of Lev Vygotsky, a Russian psychologist, is becoming more and more influential. His theory highlights the important role teachers and parents play in the cognitive development of the child. Finally, we will explore language development and discuss the role of the school in developing and enriching language skills.

By the time you have completed this chapter, you should be able to:

▶ State three general principles of human development, and give examples of each.
▶ Explain how children's thinking differs at each of Piaget's four stages of development.
▶ Summarize the implications of Piaget's theory for teaching students of different ages.
▶ Contrast Piaget's and Vygotsky's ideas about cognitive development.
▶ Give implications of Vygotsky's theory for teaching students of any age.
▶ Describe briefly the stages of language development.
▶ Suggest ways a teacher can help children expand their language use and comprehension.

What Would You Do?

The district curriculum guide calls for a unit on poetry, including lessons on *symbolism* in poems. You are concerned that many of your 5th-grade students may not be ready to understand this abstract concept. To test the waters, you ask a few students what a symbol is.

"It's sorta like a big metal thing that you bang together." Tracy waves her hands like a drum major.

"Yeah," Sean adds, "My sister plays one in the high school band."

You realize they are on the wrong track here, so you try again. "I was thinking of a different kind of symbol, like a ring as a symbol of marriage or a heart as a symbol of love, or . . . ."

You are met with blank stares.

Trevor ventures, "You mean like the Olympic torch?"

"And what does that symbolize, Trevor?" you ask.

"I said, the torch." Trevor wonders how you could be so dense.

▶ What do these students' reactions tell you about children's thinking?

▶ How would you approach this unit?

▶ What more would you do to "listen" to your students' thinking so you could match your teaching to their level of thinking?

▶ How would you give your students concrete experience with symbolism?

▶ How will you decide if the students are not developmentally ready for this material?

A Definition of Development

Development: Orderly, adaptive changes we go through from conception to death.

Physical Development: Changes in body structure and function over time.

Personal Development: Changes in personality that take place as one grows.

Social Development: Changes over time in the ways we relate to others.

Cognitive Development: Gradual orderly changes by which mental processes become more complex and sophisticated.

Maturation: Genetically programmed, naturally occurring changes over time.

The term **development** in its most general psychological sense refers to certain changes that occur in human beings (or animals) between conception and death. The term is not applied to all changes, but rather to those that appear in orderly ways and remain for a reasonably long period of time. A temporary change caused by a brief illness, for example, is not considered a part of development. Psychologists also make a value judgment in determining which changes qualify as development. The changes, at least those that occur early in life, are generally assumed to be for the better and to result in behavior that is more adaptive, more organized, more effective, and more complex (Mussen, Conger, & Kagan, 1984).

Human development can be divided into a number of different aspects. **Physical development,** as you might guess, deals with changes in the body. **Personal development** is the term generally used for changes in an individual's personality. **Social development** refers to changes in the way an individual relates to others. And **cognitive development** refers to changes in thinking.

Many changes during development are simply matters of growth and maturation. **Maturation** refers to changes that occur naturally and spontaneously and that are, to a large extent, genetically programmed. Such changes emerge over time and are relatively unaffected by environment, except in cases of malnutrition or severe illness. Much of a person's physical development falls into this category. Other changes are brought about through learning, as individuals interact with their environment. Such changes make up a large part of a person's social development. But what about the development of thinking and personality? Most psychologists agree that in these areas, both maturation and interaction with the environment (or nature and nurture, as they are sometimes called) are important, but they disagree about the amount of emphasis to place on each.

General Principles of Development

Although there is disagreement about what is involved in development and about the way it takes place, there are a few general principles almost all theorists would support.

1. *People develop at different rates.* In your own classroom, you will have a whole range of examples of different developmental rates. Some students will be larger, better coordinated, or more mature in their thinking and social relationships. Others will be much slower to mature in these areas. Except in rare cases of very rapid or very slow development, such differences are normal and to be expected in any large group of students.

2. *Development is relatively orderly.* People develop certain abilities before others. In infancy they sit before they walk, babble before they talk, and see the world through their own eyes before they can begin to imagine how others see it. In school, they will master addition before algebra, Bambi before Shakespeare, and so on. Theorists may disagree on exactly what comes before what, but they all seem to find a relatively logical progression.

3. *Development takes place gradually.* Very rarely do changes appear overnight. A student who cannot manipulate a pencil or answer a hypothetical question may well develop this ability, but the change is likely to take time.

The Brain and Cognitive Development

If you have taken an introductory psychology class, you have read about the brain and nervous system. You probably remember, for example, that there are several different areas of the brain and that certain areas are involved in particular functions. For example, the feathery looking cerebellum coordinates and orchestrates smooth, skilled movements—from the graceful gestures of the dancer to the everyday action of eating without stabbing yourself in the nose with a fork. The cerebellum may also play a role in higher cognitive functions such as learning. The thalamus is involved in our ability to learn new information, particularly if it is verbal. The reticular formation plays a role in attention and arousal, blocking some messages and sending others on to higher brain centers for processing (Wood & Wood, 1999).

The outer 1/8-inch-thick covering of the cerebrum is the wrinkled-looking cerebral cortex—the largest area of the brain. The cerebral cortex accounts for about 85% of the brain's weight and contains the greatest number of neurons—the tiny structures that store and transmit information; this part of the brain allows the greatest human accomplishments. This crumpled sheet of neurons serves three major functions: receiving signals from sense organs (such as visual or auditory signals), controlling voluntary movement, and forming associations. In humans, this area of the brain is much larger than in lower animals. The cortex is the last part of the brain to develop, so it is believed to be more susceptible to environmental influences than other areas

Connect & Extend
To the news
See the February, 19, 1996 issue of *Newsweek* for the cover story "Your Child's Brain," a provocative mixture of data and opinion.

FIGURE 2.1

A View of the Cerebral Cortex

This is a simple representation of the left side of the human brain, showing the cerebral cortex. The cortex is divided into different areas or lobes, each having a variety of regions with different functions. A few of the major functions are indicated here.

Body movement and coordination

Body sensation

Frontal lobe

Auditory cortex

Visual cortex

Lateralization: The specialization of the two hemispheres (sides) of the brain cortex.

of the brain. In addition, all parts of the cortex do not mature at the same rate. The part of the cortex that controls physical motor movement develops or matures first, then the areas that control complex senses such as vision and hearing, and last, the frontal lobe that controls higher-order thinking processes (Berk, 2000; Meece, 1997).

Specialization and Integration. Different areas of the cortex seem to have different functions, as shown in Figure 2.1. Even though different functions are found in different areas of the brain, these specialized functions are quite specific and elementary. To accomplish more complex functions such as speaking or reading, the various areas of the cortex must work together (Byrnes & Fox, 1998). For example, many areas of the cortex are necessary in processing language. To answer a question, you must first hear it. This involves the primary auditory cortex. Movements controlled by the motor cortex are required to speak your response. Broca's area (near the area that controls the lips, jaw, and tongue) has a role in setting up a grammatically correct way of expressing an idea, and Wernicke's area (near the auditory cortex) is necessary for connecting meaning with particular words. A person with a functioning Broca's area but a damaged Wernicke's area will say meaningless things in a grammatically correct structure. Damage limited to Broca's area, on the other hand, is associated with short, ungrammatical sentences, but the words are appropriate (Anderson, 1995a).

Another aspect of brain functioning that has implications for cognitive development is **lateralization**, or the specialization of the two hemispheres of the brain. We know that each half of the brain controls the opposite side of the body. Damage to the right side of the brain will affect movement of the left side of the body and vice versa. In addition, certain areas of the brain affect particular behaviors. For most of us, the left hemisphere of the brain is a major factor in language processing, and the right hemisphere handles much of the spatial-visual information and emotions (nonverbal information). For some left-handed people, the relationship may be reversed, but for most left-handers there is less hemispheric specialization altogether (Berk, 2000). In addition, females on average seem to show less hemispheric specialization than males (O'Boyle & Gill, 1998).

These differences in performance by the brain's hemispheres are more relative than absolute, however; one hemisphere is just more efficient than the other in performing certain functions. Nearly any task, particularly the complex skills and abilities that concern teachers, requires participation of many different areas of the brain. For example, the right side of the brain is better at figuring out the meaning of a story, but the left side is where grammar and syntax are understood, so both sides of the brain have to work together in reading. "The primary implication of these findings is that the practice of teaching to 'different sides of the brain' is not supported by the neuroscientific research" (Byrnes & Fox, 1998, p. 310). Thus, beware of educational approaches based on simplistic views of brain functioning—what Keith Stanovich (1998) has called "the left-brain–right-brain nonsense that has inundated education through workshops, inservices, and the trade publications" (p. 420).

Storing and Transferring Information. Neurons (nerve cells that store and transfer information) send messages by releasing chemicals that jump across the synapses (the tiny spaces between the neuron fibers) from one neuron fiber to another. By the time we are born, we have all the neurons we will ever have, about 100 to 200 billion (Baron, 1998). However, the fibers that reach out from the neurons and the synapses between the fiber ends do increase during the first years of life, perhaps into adolescence.

Neurons that are stimulated and used continue to add new synapses, making new connections, but unstimulated neurons lose connections and die off. In fact, animal studies have shown that rats raised in stimulating environments (with toys, tasks for learning, and human handling) develop 25% more synapses than rats who are raised with little stimulation (Greenough, Black, & Wallace, 1987). Early stimulation is important for humans as well. It is clear that extreme deprivation of stimulation can have negative effects on brain development, but this does not mean that extra stimulation will improve development for young children who are getting adequate or typical amounts of stimulation (Byrnes & Fox, 1998; Kolb & Whishaw, 1998). Of course, many factors besides stimulus deprivation, such as the mother's intake of drugs (including alcohol and caffeine) during pregnancy, toxins in the infant's environment, or poor nutrition, can have negative effects on brain development.

Another factor that influences thinking and learning is **myelination**, or the coating of neuron fibers with an insulating fatty covering. This process is something like coating bare electrical wires with rubber or plastic. The myelin coating makes message transmission faster and more efficient. Myelination happens quickly in the early years, but continues gradually into adolescence and is the reason the child's brain grows rapidly in the first few years of life.

In the next decade we should see increasing research on the brain, development, learning, and teaching. For example, in 1998, there was a special issue of *Educational Psychology Review* on cognitive neuroscience and education. The authors of this volume emphasized that the brain is a complex collection of systems working together to construct understanding, detect patterns, create rules, and make sense of experience. These systems change over the lifetime as the individual matures and develops. We turn next to examine this process of change.

The first theory of cognitive development we will consider was developed by a biologist turned psychologist, Jean Piaget.

Myelination: The process by which neural fibers are coated with a fatty sheath called *myelin* that makes message transfer more efficient.

CHECKPOINT

A Definition of Development

Review

▶ Summarize three principles describing how development takes place.

▶ What part of the brain is associated with higher mental functions?

▶ What is lateralization, and why is it important?

Apply

▶ What aspect of development is involved in Trevor's understanding of "symbolism" at the opening of this chapter?

*P*iaget's Theory of Cognitive Development

During the past half-century, Swiss psychologist Jean Piaget devised a model describing how humans go about making sense of their world by gathering and organizing information (Piaget, 1954, 1963, 1970a, b). We will examine Piaget's ideas closely, because they provide an explanation of the development of thinking from infancy to adulthood.

Connect & Extend
To your students' thinking
To experience some of the ways children differ from adults in their thinking, ask children of various ages the following questions:

What does it mean to be alive?

Can you name some things that are alive?

Is the moon alive?

Where do dreams come from?

Where do they go?

Which is farther, to go from the bottom of the hill all the way to the top or go from the top of the hill all the way to the bottom?

Can a person live in Chicago and in Illinois at the same time?

Will you be just as old as your big brother some day?

When is yesterday?

Where does the sun go at night?

Jean Piaget was a Swiss psychologist whose insightful descriptions of children's thinking changed the way we understand cognitive development. ▼

Organization: Ongoing process of arranging information and experience into mental systems or categories.

Adaptation: Adjustment to the environment.

According to Piaget (1954), certain ways of thinking that are quite simple for an adult are not so simple for a child. Sometimes all you need to do to teach a new concept is to give a student a few basic facts as background. At other times, however, all the background facts in the world are useless. The student simply is not ready to learn the concept. With some students, you can discuss the general causes of civil wars and then ask why they think the American Civil War broke out in 1861. But suppose the students respond with "When is 1861?" Obviously their concepts of time are different from your own. They may think, for example, that they will some day catch up to a sibling in age, or they may confuse the past and the future.

Influences on Development

As you can see, cognitive development is much more than the addition of new facts and ideas to an existing store of information. According to Piaget, our thinking processes change radically, though slowly, from birth to maturity because we constantly strive to make sense of the world. How do we do this? Piaget identified four factors—biological maturation, activity, social experiences, and equilibration—that interact to influence changes in thinking (Piaget, 1970a). Let's briefly examine the first three factors. We'll return to a discussion of equilibration in the next section.

One of the most important influences on the way we make sense of the world is *maturation*, the unfolding of the biological changes that are genetically programmed in each human being at conception. Parents and teachers have little impact on this aspect of cognitive development, except to be sure that children get the nourishment and care they need to be healthy.

Activity is another influence. With physical maturation comes the increasing ability to act on the environment and learn from it. When a young child's coordination is reasonably developed, for example, the child may discover principles about balance by experimenting with a seesaw. Thus, as we act on the environment—as we explore, test, observe, and eventually organize information—we are likely to alter our thinking processes at the same time.

As we develop, we are also interacting with the people around us. According to Piaget, our cognitive development is influenced by *social transmission*, or learning from others. Without social transmission, we would need to reinvent all the knowledge already offered by our culture. The amount people can learn from social transmission varies according to their stage of cognitive development.

Maturation, activity, and social transmission all work together to influence cognitive development. How do we respond to these influences?

Basic Tendencies in Thinking

As a result of his early research in biology, Piaget concluded that all species inherit two basic tendencies, or "invariant functions." The first of these tendencies is toward **organization**—the combining, arranging, recombining, and rearranging of behaviors and thoughts into coherent systems. The second tendency is toward **adaptation,** or adjusting to the environment.

Organization. People are born with a tendency to organize their thinking processes into psychological structures. These psychological structures are our systems for understanding and interacting with the world. Simple structures are continually combined and coordinated to become more sophisticated and thus more effective. Very young infants, for example, can either look at an object or grasp it when it comes in contact with their hands. They cannot coordinate looking and grasping at the same time. As they develop, however, infants organize these two separate behavioral structures into a coordinated higher-level structure of looking at, reaching for, and grasping the object. They can, of course, still use each structure separately (Ginsburg & Opper, 1988; Miller, 1993).

Piaget gave a special name to these structures: schemes. In his theory, **schemes** are the basic building blocks of thinking. They are organized systems of actions or thought that allow us to mentally represent or "think about" the objects and events in our world. Schemes may be very small and specific, for example, the sucking-through-a-straw scheme or the recognizing-a-rose scheme. Or they may be larger and more general—the drinking scheme or the categorizing-plants scheme. As a person's thinking processes become more organized and new schemes develop, behavior also becomes more sophisticated and better suited to the environment.

Adaptation. In addition to the tendency to organize their psychological structures, people also inherit the tendency to adapt to their environment. Two basic processes are involved in adaptation: assimilation and accommodation.

Assimilation takes place when people use their existing schemes to make sense of events in their world. Assimilation involves trying to understand something new by fitting it into what we already know. At times, we may have to distort the new information to make it fit. For example, the first time many children see a skunk, they call it a "kitty." They try to match the new experience with an existing scheme for identifying animals.

Accommodation occurs when a person must change existing schemes to respond to a new situation. If data cannot be made to fit any existing schemes, then more appropriate structures must be developed. We adjust our thinking to fit the new information, instead of adjusting the information to fit our thinking. Children demonstrate accommodation when they add the scheme for recognizing skunks to their other systems for identifying animals.

People adapt to their increasingly complex environments by using existing schemes whenever these schemes work (assimilation) and by modifying and adding to their schemes when something new is needed (accommodation). In fact, both processes are required most of the time. Even using an established pattern such as sucking through a straw may require some accommodation if the straw is of a different size or length than the type you are used to. If you have tried drinking juice from box packages, you know that you have to add a new skill to your sucking scheme—don't squeeze the box or you will shoot juice through the straw, straight up into the air and into your lap. Whenever new experiences are assimilated into an existing scheme, the scheme is enlarged and changed somewhat, so assimilation involves some accommodation.

There are also times when neither assimilation nor accommodation is used. If people encounter something that is too unfamiliar, they may ignore it. Experience is filtered to fit the kind of thinking a person is doing at a given time. For example, if you overhear a conversation in a foreign language, you probably will not try to make sense of the exchange unless you have some knowledge of the language.

Equilibration. According to Piaget, organizing, assimilating, and accommodating can be seen as a kind of complex balancing act. In his theory, the actual changes in thinking take place through the process of **equilibration**—the act of

Schemes: Mental systems or categories of perception and experience.

Assimilation: Fitting new information into existing schemes.

Accommodation: Altering existing schemes or creating new ones in response to new information.

Equilibration: Search for mental balance between cognitive schemes and information from the environment.

searching for a balance. Piaget assumed that people continually test the adequacy of their thinking processes in order to achieve that balance.

Briefly, the process of equilibration works like this: If we apply a particular scheme to an event or situation and the scheme works, then equilibrium exists. If the scheme does not produce a satisfying result, then **disequilibrium** exists, and we become uncomfortable. This motivates us to keep searching for a solution through assimilation and accommodation, and thus our thinking changes and moves ahead. In order to maintain a balance between our schemes for understanding the world and the data the world provides, we continually assimilate new information using existing schemes, and we accommodate our thinking whenever unsuccessful attempts to assimilate produce disequilibrium.

Four Stages of Cognitive Development

Now we turn to the actual differences that Piaget hypothesized for children as they grow. Piaget's four stages of cognitive development are called sensorimotor, preoperational, concrete operational, and formal operational. Piaget believed that all people pass through the same four stages in exactly the same order. These stages are generally associated with specific ages, as shown in Table 2.1. When you see ages linked to stages, remember that these are only general guidelines, not labels for all children of a certain age. Piaget was interested in the kinds of thinking abilities people are able to use, not in labeling. Often, people can use one level of thinking to solve one kind of problem and a different level to solve another. Piaget noted that individuals may go through long periods of transition between stages and that a person may show characteristics of one stage in one situation but characteristics of a higher or lower stage in other situations. Therefore, knowing a student's age is never a guarantee that you know how the child will think (Ginsburg & Opper, 1988; Orlando & Machado, 1996).

Infancy: The Sensorimotor Stage. The earliest period is called the **sensorimotor** stage, because the child's thinking involves seeing, hearing, moving, touching, tasting, and so on. During this period, the infant develops **object permanence,** the understanding that objects exist in the environment whether the baby perceives them or not. As most parents discover, before infants develop object permanence, it is relatively easy to take something away from them. The trick is to distract them and remove the object while they are not looking—"out of sight, out of mind." The older infant who searches for the ball that has rolled out of sight is indicating an understanding that objects still exist even when they are not in view. Recent research, however, suggests that infants as young as 3 to 4 months may know that the object still exists, but they do not have the memory skills to "hold on" to the location of the object or the motor skills to coordinate a search (Baillargeon & DeVos, 1991; Meece, 1997).

A second major accomplishment in the sensorimotor period is the beginning of logical, **goal-directed actions.** Think of the familiar container toy for babies. It is usually plastic, has a lid, and contains several colorful items that can be dumped out and replaced. A 6-month-old baby is likely to become frustrated trying to get to the toys inside. An older child who has mastered the basics of the sensorimotor stage will probably be able to deal with the toy in an orderly fashion. Through trial and error the child will slowly build a "container toy" scheme: (1) get the lid off, (2) turn the container upside down, (3) shake if the items jam, (4) watch the items fall. Separate lower-level schemes have been organized into a higher-level scheme to achieve a goal.

Disequilibrium: In Piaget's theory, the "out-of-balance" state that occurs when a person realizes that his or her current ways of thinking are not working to solve a problem or understand a situation.

Sensorimotor: Involving the senses and motor activity.

Object Permanence: The understanding that objects have a separate, permanent existence.

Goal-Directed Actions: Deliberate actions toward a goal.

TABLE 2.1 *Piaget's Stages of Cognitive Development*

Stage	Approximate Age	Characteristics
Sensorimotor	0–2 years	Begins to make use of imitation, memory, and thought.
		Begins to recognize that objects do not cease to exist when they are hidden.
		Moves from reflex actions to goal-directed activity.
Preoperational	2–7 years	Gradually develops use of language and ability to think in symbolic form.
		Able to think operations through logically in one direction.
		Has difficulties seeing another person's point of view.
Concrete operational	7–11 years	Able to solve concrete (hands-on) problems in logical fashion.
		Understands laws of conservation and is able to classify and seriate.
		Understands reversibility.
Formal operational	11–adult	Able to solve abstract problems in logical fashion.
		Becomes more scientific in thinking.
		Develops concerns about social issues, identity.

Source: From *Piaget's Theory of Cognitive and Affective Development* (5th ed.), by B. J. Wadsworth, 1996, Reading, MA: Addison-Wesley. Copyright © 1971, 1979, 1984, 1989, 1996 by Addison-Wesley. Adapted with permission.

The child is soon able to reverse this action by refilling the container. Learning to reverse actions is a basic accomplishment of the sensorimotor stage. As we will soon see, however, learning to reverse thinking—that is, learning to imagine the reverse of a sequence of actions—takes much longer.

Early Childhood to the Early Elementary Years: The Preoperational Stage. By the end of the sensorimotor stage, the child can use many action schemes. As long as these schemes remain tied to physical actions, however, they are of no use in recalling the past, keeping track of information, or planning. For this, children need what Piaget called **operations,** or actions that are carried out and reversed mentally rather than physically. The stage after sensorimotor is called **preoperational,** because the child has not yet mastered these mental operations but is moving toward mastery.

According to Piaget, the first step from action to thinking is the internalization of action, performing an action mentally rather than physically. The first type of thinking that is separate from action involves making action schemes symbolic. The

Operations: Actions a person carries out by thinking them through instead of literally performing the actions.

Preoperational: The stage before a child masters logical mental operations.

Semiotic Function: The ability to use symbols—language, pictures, signs, or gestures—to represent actions or objects mentally.

Reversible Thinking: Thinking backward, from the end to the beginning.

Conservation: Principle that some characteristics of an object remain the same despite changes in appearance.

Decentering: Focusing on more than one aspect at a time.

Egocentric: Assuming that others experience the world the way you do.

Collective Monologue: Form of speech in which children in a group talk but do not really interact or communicate.

The ability to manipulate concrete objects helps children understand abstract relationships such as the connection between symbols and quantity. ▼

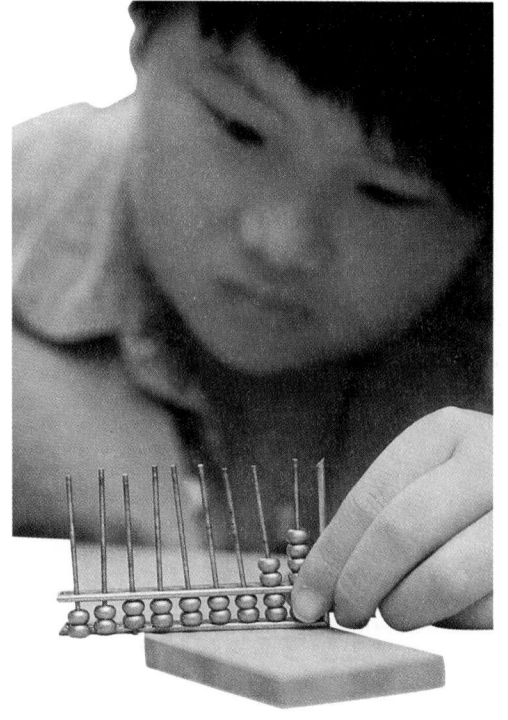

ability to form and use symbols—words, gestures, signs, images, and so on—is thus a major accomplishment of the preoperational period and moves children closer to mastering the mental operations of the next stage. This ability to work with symbols, such as using the word "bicycle" or a picture of a bicycle to represent a real bicycle that is not actually present, is called the **semiotic function.**

The child's earliest use of symbols is in pretending or miming. Children who are not yet able to talk will often use action symbols—pretending to drink from an empty cup or touching a comb to their hair, showing that they know what each object is for. This behavior also shows that their schemes are becoming more general and less tied to specific actions. The eating scheme, for example, may be used in playing house. During the preoperational stage, we also see the rapid development of that very important symbol system, language. Between the ages of 2 and 4, most children enlarge their vocabulary from about 200 to 2,000 words.

As the child moves through the preoperational stage, the developing ability to think about objects in symbolic form remains somewhat limited to thinking in one direction only, or using *one-way logic*. It is very difficult for the child to "think back-wards," or imagine how to reverse the steps in a task.

Reversible thinking is involved in many tasks that are difficult for the preoperational child, such as the conservation of matter. **Conservation** is the principle that the amount or number of something remains the same even if the arrangement or appearance is changed, as long as nothing is added and nothing is taken away. You know that if you tear a piece of paper into several pieces, you will still have the same amount of paper. To prove this, you know that you can reverse the process by taping the pieces back together.

A classic example of difficulty with conservation is found in the preoperational child's response to the following Piagetian task. Leah, a 5-year-old, is shown two identical glasses, both short and wide in shape. Both have exactly the same amount of colored water in them. The experimenter asks Leah if each glass has the same amount of water, and she answers, "Yes." The experimenter then pours the water from one of the glasses into a tall, narrow glass and asks Leah again if each glass has the same amount of water. Now she is likely to insist that there is more water in the tall, narrow glass, because the water level is higher. Notice, by the way, that Leah shows a basic understanding of identity (it's the same water) but not an understanding that the amounts are identical (Ginsburg & Opper, 1988).

Piaget's explanation for Leah's answer is that she is focusing, or centering, attention on the dimension of height. She has difficulty considering more than one aspect of the situation at a time, or **decentering.** The preoperational child cannot understand that increased diameter compensates for decreased height, since this would require taking into account two dimensions at once. Thus, children at the preoperational stage have trouble freeing themselves from their own perceptions of how the world appears.

This brings us to another important characteristic of the preoperational stage. Preoperational children, according to Piaget, are very **egocentric;** they tend to see the world and the experiences of others from their own viewpoint. Egocentric, as Piaget intended it, does not mean selfish; it simply means children often assume that everyone else shares their feelings, reactions, and perspectives. For example, if a little boy at this stage is afraid of dogs, he may assume that all children share this fear. Very young children center on their own perceptions and on the way the situation appears to them. This is one reason it is difficult for these children to understand that your right hand is not on the same side as theirs when you are facing them.

Egocentrism is also evident in the child's language. You may have seen young children happily talking about what they are doing even though no one is listening. This can happen when the child is alone or, even more often, in a group of children—each child talks enthusiastically, without any real interaction or conversation. Piaget called this the **collective monologue.**

Research has shown that young children are not totally egocentric in every situation, however. Children as young as age 4 change the way they talk to 2-year-olds by speaking in simpler sentences, and even before age 2 children show toys to adults by turning the front of the toy to face the other person. So young children do seem quite able to take the needs and different perspectives of others into account, at least in certain situations (Gelman, 1979; Gelman & Ebeling, 1989). The Guidelines below give ideas for working with preoperational thinkers.

Connect & Extend
To your students' thinking
As an example of young children's difficulties with reversibility and egocentric thinking, ask a child with only one sibling, "Do you have a brother (sister)?" The child should say, "Yes." Now ask, "Does your brother (sister) have a brother (sister)?" Young children have difficulty reversing the situation and putting themselves in their sibling's position, so they usually reply, "No." Now face the child and ask the child to point to your right hand. Most young children assume your right hand is on the same side as theirs, even when they are facing you.

Guidelines

Teaching the Preoperational Child

Use concrete props and visual aids whenever possible.
Examples
1. When you discuss concepts such as "part," "whole," or "one-half," use shapes on a felt board or cardboard "pizzas" to demonstrate.
2. Let children add and subtract with sticks, rocks, or colored chips.

Make instructions relatively short, using actions as well as words.
Examples
1. When giving instructions about how to enter the room after recess and prepare for social studies, ask a student to demonstrate the procedure for the rest of the class by walking in quietly, going straight to his or her seat, and placing the text, paper, and a pencil on his or her desk.
2. Explain a game by acting out one of the parts.
3. Show students what their finished papers should look like. Use an overhead projector or display examples where students can see them easily.

Don't expect the students to be consistent in their ability to see the world from someone else's point of view.
Examples
1. Avoid social studies lessons about worlds too far removed from the child's experience.
2. Avoid long lectures on sharing. Be clear about rules for sharing or use of materials, but avoid long explanations of the rationales for the rules.

Be sensitive to the possibility that students may have different meanings for the same word or different words for the same meaning. Students may also expect everyone to understand words they have invented.
Examples
1. If a student protests, "I won't take a nap. I'll just rest!" be aware that a nap may mean something such as "changing into pajamas and being in my bed at home."
2. Ask children to explain the meanings of their invented words.

Give children a great deal of hands-on practice with the skills that serve as building blocks for more complex skills such as reading comprehension.
Examples
1. Provide cut-out letters to build words.
2. Supplement paper-and-pencil tasks in arithmetic with activities that require measuring and simple calculations—cooking, building a display area for class work, dividing a batch of popcorn equally.

Provide a wide range of experiences in order to build a foundation for concept learning and language.
Examples
1. Take field trips to zoos, gardens, theaters, and concerts; invite storytellers to the class.
2. Give students words to describe what they are doing, hearing, seeing, touching, tasting, and smelling.

Connect & Extend
To your teaching
By the time children reach the concrete-operational stage of cognitive development, they have some operations and strategies that they are able to employ. Considering these new skills, how might you go about teaching a child in this stage (a) a history lesson about the American Revolution, and (b) the importance of the five food groups of nutrition.

Later Elementary to the Middle School Years: The Concrete-Operational Stage. Piaget coined the term **concrete operations** to describe this stage of "hands-on" thinking. The basic characteristics of the stage are the recognition of the logical stability of the physical world, the realization that elements can be changed or transformed and still conserve many of their original characteristics, and the understanding that these changes can be reversed.

Figure 2.2 shows examples of the different tasks given to children to assess conservation and the approximate age ranges when most children can solve these problems. According to Piaget, a student's ability to solve conservation problems depends on an understanding of three basic aspects of reasoning: identity, compensation, and reversibility. With a complete mastery of **identity,** the student knows that if nothing is added or taken away, the material remains the same. With an understanding of **compensation,** the student knows that an apparent change in one direction can be compensated for by a change in another direction. That is, if the liquid rises higher in the glass, the glass must be narrower. And with an understanding of **reversibility,** the student can mentally cancel out the change that has been made.

Another important operation mastered at this stage is **classification.** Classification depends on a student's abilities to focus on a single characteristic of objects in a set and group the objects according to that characteristic. Given 12 objects of assorted colors and shapes, the concrete-operational student can invariably pick out the ones that are round.

More advanced classification at this stage involves recognizing that one class fits into another. A city can be in a particular state or province and also in a particular country. As children apply this advanced classification to locations, they often become fascinated with "complete" addresses such as Lee Jary, 5116 Forest Hill Drive, Richmond Hill, Ontario, Canada, North America, Northern Hemisphere, Earth, Solar System, Milky Way, Universe.

Classification is also related to reversibility. The ability to reverse a process mentally now allows the concrete-operational student to see that there is more than one way to classify a group of objects. The student understands, for example, that buttons can be classified by color, then reclassified by size or by the number of holes.

Seriation is the process of making an orderly arrangement from large to small or vice versa. This understanding of sequential relationships permits a student to construct a logical series in which A < B < C (A is less than B is less than C) and so on. Unlike the preoperational child, the concrete-operational child can grasp the notion that B can be larger than A but smaller than C.

With the abilities to handle operations such as conservation, classification, and seriation, the student at the concrete-operational stage has finally developed a complete and very logical system of thinking. This system of thinking, however, is still tied to physical reality. The logic is based on concrete situations that can be organized, classified, or manipulated. Thus, children at this stage can imagine several different arrangements for the furniture in their rooms before they act. They do not have to solve the problem strictly through trial and error by actually making the arrangements. However, the concrete-operational child is not yet able to reason about hypothetical, abstract problems that involve the coordination of many factors at once. This kind of coordination is part of Piaget's next and final stage of cognitive development.

In any grade you teach, a knowledge of concrete-operational thinking will be helpful. In the early grades, the students are moving toward this logical system of thought. In the middle grades, it is in full flower, ready to be applied and extended

▲ *An important operation mastered during the concrete stage is classification, the ability to focus on a single characteristic of objects in a set and group the objects according to that characteristic.*

Concrete Operations: Mental tasks tied to concrete objects and situations.

Identity: Principle that a person or object remains the same over time.

Compensation: The principle that changes in one dimension can be offset by changes in another.

FIGURE 2.2

Some Piagetian Conservation Tasks

In addition to the tasks shown here, other tasks involve the conservation of number, length, weight, and volume. These tasks are all achieved over the concrete-operational period.

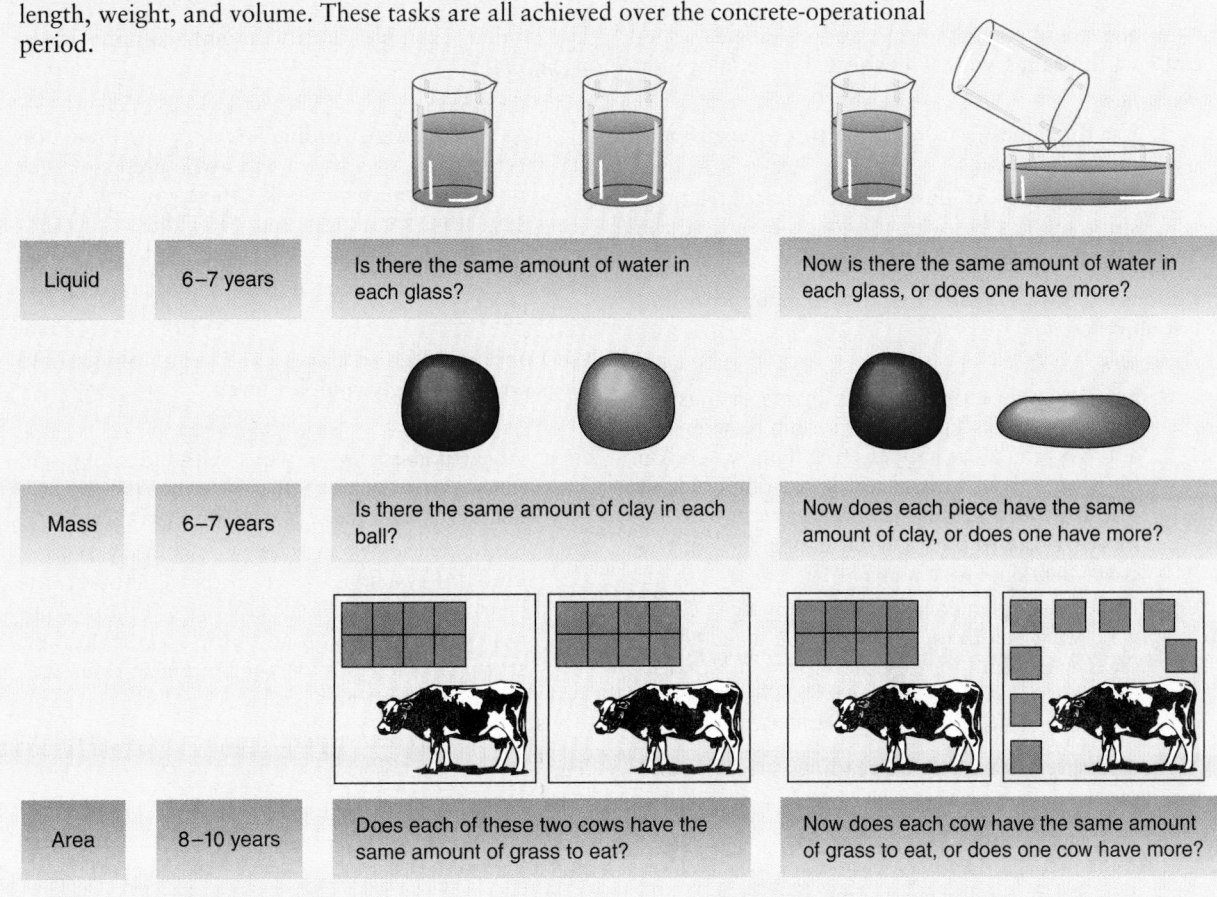

Liquid	6–7 years	Is there the same amount of water in each glass?	Now is there the same amount of water in each glass, or does one have more?
Mass	6–7 years	Is there the same amount of clay in each ball?	Now does each piece have the same amount of clay, or does one have more?
Area	8–10 years	Does each of these two cows have the same amount of grass to eat?	Now does each cow have the same amount of grass to eat, or does one cow have more?

Source: From *Child Development* (4th ed.), by L. E. Berk, 1997, Boston: Allyn & Bacon. Copyright © 1997 by Allyn & Bacon. Adapted with permission.

by your teaching. In the high school years, it is often used by students whose thinking may not have fully developed to the next stage—the stage of formal operations. The Guidelines on page 36 should give you ideas for teaching children who can apply concrete operations.

Junior and Senior High: Formal Operations. Some students remain at the concrete-operational stage throughout their school years, even throughout life. However, new experiences, usually those that take place in school, eventually present most students with problems that they cannot solve using concrete operations. What happens when a number of variables interact, as in a labora-

Reversibility: A characteristic of Piagetian logical operations—the ability to think through a series of steps, then mentally reverse the steps and return to the starting point; also called *reversible thinking.*

Classification: Grouping objects into categories.

Seriation: Arranging objects in sequential order according to one aspect, such as size, weight, or volume.

GUIDELINES

Teaching the Concrete-Operational Child

Continue to use concrete props and visual aids, especially when dealing with sophisticated material.

Examples

1. Use time lines in history and three-dimensional models in science.
2. Use diagrams to illustrate hierarchical relationships such as branches of government and the agencies under each branch.

Continue to give students a chance to manipulate and test objects.

Examples

1. Set up simple scientific experiments such as the following involving the relationship between fire and oxygen. What happens to a flame when you blow on it from a distance? (If you don't blow it out, the flame gets larger briefly, because it has more oxygen to burn.) What happens when you cover the flame with a jar?
2. Have students make candles by dipping wicks in wax, weave cloth on a simple loom, bake bread, set type by hand, or do other craft work that illustrates the daily occupations of people in the colonial period.

Make sure presentations and readings are brief and well organized.

Examples

1. Assign stories or books with short, logical chapters, moving to longer reading assignments only when students are ready.
2. Break up a presentation with a chance to practice the first steps before introducing the next.

Use familiar examples to explain more complex ideas.

Examples

1. Compare students' lives with those of characters in a story. After reading *Island of the Blue Dolphins* (the true story of a girl who grew up alone on a deserted island), ask "Have you ever had to stay alone for a long time? How did you feel?"
2. Teach the concept of area by having students measure two rooms in the school that are different sizes.

Give opportunities to classify and group objects and ideas on increasingly complex levels.

Examples

1. Give students slips of paper with individual sentences written on each paper and ask the students to group the sentences into paragraphs.
2. Compare the systems of the human body to other kinds of systems: the brain to a computer, the heart to a pump. Break down stories into components, from the broad to the specific: author; story; characters, plot, theme; place, time; dialogue, description, actions.

Present problems that require logical, analytical thinking.

Examples

1. Use mind twisters, brain teasers, Master Mind, and riddles.
2. Discuss open-ended questions that stimulate thinking: "Are the brain and the mind the same thing?" "How should the city deal with stray animals?" "What is the largest number?"

Formal Operations: Mental tasks involving abstract thinking and coordination of a number of variables.

Hypothetico-Deductive Reasoning: A formal-operations problem-solving strategy in which an individual begins by identifying all the factors that might affect a problem and then deduces and systematically evaluates specific solutions.

tory experiment? Then a mental system for controlling sets of variables and working through a set of possibilities is needed. These are the abilities Piaget called **formal operations.**

At the level of formal operations, all the earlier operations and abilities continue in force; that is, formal thinking is reversible, internal, and organized in a system of interdependent elements. The focus of thinking shifts, however, from what *is* to what *might be.* Situations do not have to be experienced to be imagined. Ask a young child how life would be different if people did not sleep, and the child might say, "People have to sleep!" In contrast, the adolescent who has mastered formal operations can consider contrary-to-fact questions. In answering, the adolescent demonstrates the hallmark of formal operations—**hypothetico-deductive reasoning.** The formal thinker can consider a hypothetical situation (people do not sleep) and reason deductively (from the general assumption to specific implications, such as longer workdays, more money spent on lighting, or new entertainment industries). Formal operations also include inductive reasoning, or using specific observations to identify general principles. For example, the economist observes many specific changes in the stock market and attempts to identify general principles about economic cycles. Formal-operational thinkers can form hypotheses, set up mental experiments to test them, and isolate or control variables in order to complete a valid test of the hypotheses.

The ability to consider abstract possibilities is critical for much of mathematics and science. After elementary school, most math is concerned with hypothetical situations, assumptions, and givens: "Let $x = 10$," or "Assume $x^2 + y^2 = z^2$," or "Given two sides and an adjacent angle. . . ." Young children cannot reason based on symbols and abstractions, but this kind of reasoning is expected in the later grades (Bjorklund, 1989). Work in social studies and literature requires abstract thinking, too: "What did Wilson mean when he called World War I the 'war to end all wars'?" "What are some metaphors for hope and despair in Shakespeare's sonnets?" "What symbols of old age does T. S. Eliot use in *The Waste Land*?" "How do animals symbolize human character traits in Aesop's fables?"

The organized, scientific thinking of formal operations requires that students systematically generate different possibilities for a given situation. For example, if a child capable of formal operations is asked, "How many different meat/vegetable/salad meals can you make using three meats, three vegetables, and three salads?" the child can systematically identify the 27 possible combinations. A concrete thinker might name just a few meals, focusing on favorite foods or using each food only once. The underlying system of combinations is not yet available.

The ability to think hypothetically, consider alternatives, identify all possible combinations, and analyze one's own thinking has some interesting consequences for adolescents. Since they can think about worlds that do not exist, they often become interested in science fiction. Because they can reason from general principles to specific actions, they often are critical of people whose actions seem to contradict their principles. Adolescents can deduce the set of "best" possibilities and imagine ideal worlds (or ideal parents and teachers, for that matter). This explains why many students at this age develop interests in utopias, political causes, and social issues. They want to design better worlds, and their thinking allows them to do so. Adolescents can also imagine many possible futures for themselves and may try to decide which is best. Feelings about any of these ideals may be strong.

Another characteristic of this stage is **adolescent egocentrism.** Unlike egocentric young children, adolescents do not deny that other people may have different perceptions and beliefs; the adolescents just become very focused on their own ideas. They analyze their own beliefs and attitudes. They reflect on others' thinking as well but often assume that everyone else is as interested as they are in their thoughts, feelings, and behavior. This can lead to what Elkind (1981) calls the sense of an *imaginary audience*—the feeling that everyone is watching. Thus, adolescents believe that others are analyzing them: "Everyone noticed that I wore this shirt twice this week." "The whole class thought my answer was dumb!" "Everybody is going to love my new CD." You can see that social blunders or imperfections in appearance can be devastating if "everybody is watching." Luckily, this feeling of being "on stage" seems to peak in early adolescence by age 14 or 15.

Do We All Reach the Fourth Stage?

As we have just seen, most psychologists agree that there is a level of thinking more sophisticated than concrete operations. But the question of how universal formal-operational thinking actually is, even

Connect & Extend
To your students' thinking
What are the differences (and similarities) between egocentrism in young children and egocentrism in adolescents?

Adolescent Egocentrism: Assumption that everyone else shares one's thoughts, feelings, and concerns.

CHECKPOINT

Piaget's Theory of Cognitive Development

Review

▶ What are the main influences on cognitive development?

▶ What is a scheme?

▶ As children move from sensorimotor to formal-operational thinking, what are the major changes?

Apply

▶ What are the characteristics of concrete-operational thinking? Is Trevor's thinking concrete?

among adults, is a matter of debate. According to Neimark (1975), the first three stages of Piaget's theory are forced on most people by physical realities. Objects really are permanent. The amount of water doesn't change when it is poured into another glass. Formal operations, however, are not so closely tied to the physical environment. They may be the product of experience and of practice in solving hypothetical problems and using formal scientific reasoning. These abilities tend to be valued and taught in literate cultures, particularly in colleges and universities.

Piaget himself (1974) suggested that most adults may be able to use formal-operational thought in only a few areas where they have the greatest experience or interest. So do not expect every student in your junior high or high school class to be able to think hypothetically about all the problems you present. Students who have not learned to go beyond the information given to them are likely to fall by the wayside. Sometimes students find shortcuts for dealing with problems that are beyond their grasp; they may memorize formulas or lists of steps. These

GUIDELINES

Helping Students to Use Formal Operations

Continue to use concrete-operational teaching strategies and materials.

Examples

1. Use visual aids such as charts and illustrations as well as somewhat more sophisticated graphs and diagrams.
2. Compare the experiences of characters in stories to students' experiences.

Give students the opportunity to explore many hypothetical questions.

Examples

1. Have students write position papers, then exchange these papers with the opposing side and debate topical social issues—the environment, the economy, national health insurance.
2. Ask students to write about their personal vision of a utopia; write a description of a universe that has no sex differences; write a description of Earth after humans are extinct.

Give students opportunities to solve problems and reason scientifically.

Examples

1. Set up group discussions in which students design experiments to answer questions.
2. Ask students to justify two different positions on animal rights, with logical arguments for each position.

Whenever possible, teach broad concepts, not just facts, using materials and ideas relevant to the students' lives.

Examples

1. When discussing the Civil War, consider other issues that have divided the United States since then.
2. Use lyrics from popular songs to teach poetic devices, to reflect on social problems, and to stimulate discussion on the place of popular music in our culture.

systems may be helpful for passing tests, but real understanding will take place only if students are able to go beyond this superficial use of memorization—only, in other words, if they learn to use formal-operational thinking. The Guidelines on page 38 may help you support the development of formal operations with your students.

Implications of Piaget's Theory for Teachers

Piaget has taught us that we can learn a great deal about how children think by listening carefully, by paying close attention to their ways of solving problems. If we understand children's thinking, we will be better able to match teaching methods to children's abilities.

Understanding Students' Thinking

The students in any class will vary greatly both in their level of cognitive development and in their academic knowledge. As a teacher, how can you determine whether students are having trouble because they lack the necessary thinking abilities or because they simply have not learned the basic facts? To do this, Case (1985b) suggests you observe your students carefully as they try to solve the problems you have presented. What kind of logic do they use? Do they focus on only one aspect of the situation? Are they fooled by appearances? Do they suggest solutions systematically or by guessing and forgetting what they have already tried? Ask your students how they tried to solve the problem. Listen to their strategies. What kind of thinking is behind repeated mistakes or problems? The students are the best sources of information about their own thinking abilities (Confrey, 1990a).

Matching Strategies to Abilities

An important implication of Piaget's theory for teaching is what Hunt years ago (1961) called "the problem of the match." Students must be neither bored by work that is too simple nor left behind by teaching they cannot understand. According to Hunt, disequilibrium must be kept "just right" to encourage growth. Setting up situations that lead to errors can help create an appropriate level of disequilibrium. When students experience some conflict between what they think should happen (a piece of wood should sink because it is big) and what actually happens (it floats!), they may rethink the situation, and new knowledge may develop.

It is worth pointing out, too, that many materials and lessons can be understood at several levels and can be "just right" for a range of cognitive abilities. Classics such as *Alice in Wonderland*, myths, and fairy tales can be enjoyed at both concrete and symbolic levels. It is also possible for students to be introduced to a topic together, then work individually on follow-up activities matched to their level. Tom Good and Jere Brophy (1997) describe activity cards for three or four ability levels. These cards provide different readings and assignments, but all are directed toward the overall class objectives. One of the cards should be a good "match" for each student.

Connect & Extend
To your students' thinking
Try this test to see if your students can use formal operations by determining, in an organized way, the number of different possibilities that exists within a reasonably limited framework. Ask your students: "How many different outfits can be made with the following clothes: (1) three tops—polo shirt, dress shirt, T-shirt; (2) three pairs of pants—jeans, shorts, slacks; and (3) three jackets—bomber, blazer, jeans jacket?" A student capable of formal operations would begin by laying out the possibilities systematically: first each jacket with the polo shirt and jeans, then each jacket with the polo shirt and shorts, then each jacket with the polo shirt and slacks; then on to the jackets with the dress shirt and jeans, then with the dress shirt and shorts, and so forth. A student at the concrete-operational stage, however, would be much less systematic; he or she might start with favorite clothes and continue in the order of preference. It would not be unusual for a student operating at the concrete level to mention only three outfits, using each garment only once.

Connect & Extend

To the research

Beilin, H. (1992). Piaget's enduring contribution to developmental psychology. *Developmental Psychology, 28,* 191–204 .

ABSTRACT

Piaget's transformation of society's conception of childhood thought and intelligence is described in 4 periods in the history of his research program, which spanned from the 1920s to the 1980s. The account stresses the enduring contribution to developmental psychology of Piaget's constructivism, his description of developmental mechanisms, his cognitivism, his explication of structural and functional analysis, and his addressing of epistemological issues and nontraditional methodologies.

Constructing Knowledge

Piaget's fundamental insight was that individuals *construct* their own understanding; learning is a constructive process. At every level of cognitive development, you will also want to see that students are actively engaged in the learning process. They must be able to incorporate the information you present into their own schemes. To do this, they must act on the information in some way. Schooling must give the students a chance to experience the world. This active experience, even at the earliest school levels, should not be limited to the physical manipulation of objects. It should also include mental manipulation of ideas that arise out of class projects or experiments (Ginsburg & Opper, 1988). For example, after a social studies lesson on different jobs, a primary-grade teacher might show the students a picture of a woman and ask, "What could this person be?" After answers such as "teacher," "doctor," "secretary," "lawyer," "saleswoman," and so on, the teacher could suggest, "How about a daughter?" Answers such as "sister," "mother," "aunt," and "granddaughter" may follow. This should help the children switch dimensions in their classification and center on another aspect of the situation. Next, the teacher might suggest "American," "jogger," or "blonde." With older children, hierarchical classification might be involved: it is a picture of a woman, who is a human being; a human being is a primate, which is a mammal, which is an animal, which is a life form.

All students need to interact with teachers and peers in order to test their thinking, to be challenged, to receive feedback, and to watch how others work out problems. Disequilibrium is often set in motion quite naturally when the teacher or another student suggests a new way of thinking about something. As a general rule, students should act, manipulate, observe, and then talk and/or write (to the teacher and each other) about what they have experienced. Concrete experiences provide the raw materials for thinking. Communicating with others makes students use, test, and sometimes change their thinking abilities.

Discussions about the implications of Piaget's theory often center on the question of whether cognitive development can be accelerated, as you can see in the Point/Counterpoint.

Some Limitations of Piaget's Theory

Piaget taught us that children do not think like adults. His influence on developmental psychology and education has been enormous, even though recent research has not supported all his ideas. Although most psychologists agree with Piaget's insightful descriptions of *how* children think, many disagree with his explanations of *why* thinking develops as it does.

The Trouble with Stages. Some psychologists have questioned the existence of four separate stages of thinking, even though they agree that children do go through the changes that Piaget described (Gelman & Baillargeon, 1983). One problem with the stage model is the lack of consistency in children's thinking. Psychologists reason that if there are separate stages, and if the child's thinking at each stage is based on a particular set of operations, then once the child has mastered the operations, he or she should be somewhat consistent in solving all problems requiring those operations. In other words, once you can conserve, you ought to know that the number of blocks does not change when they are rearranged (conservation of number) and that the weight of a ball of clay does not change when you flatten it (conservation of weight). But it doesn't happen this way. Children can con-

Can Cognitive Development Be Accelerated?

Ever since Piaget described his stages of cognitive development, some people have asked if progress through the stages could be accelerated. More recently, the question has focused on whether we should accelerate learning for preschoolers and young children at risk of academic failure. Can learning be accelerated, and if so, is this a good idea?

▶ **POINT** *Every child deserves a head start.*

Some of the strongest arguments in favor of "speeding up" cognitive development are based on the results of cross-cultural studies of children (studies that compare children growing up in different cultures). These results suggest that certain cognitive abilities are indeed influenced by the environment and education. Children of pottery-making families in one area of Mexico, for example, learn conservation of substance earlier than their peers in families who do not make pottery (Ashton, 1978). Furthermore, children in non-Western cultures appear to acquire conservation operations later than children in Western cultures. It seems likely that factors in the environment contribute to the rate of cognitive development.

But even if cognitive development can be accelerated, is this a good idea? Two of the most vocal (and heavily criticized) advocates of early academic training are Siegfried and Therese Engelmann (1981). In their book, *Give Your Child a Superior Mind*, they suggest that children who learn academic skills as preschoolers will be smarter throughout their school years, are less likely to fail, and are more likely to enjoy school. They contend:

> Children respond to the environment. Their capacity to learn and what they learn depends on what the environment teaches. . . . Instead of relying on the traditional environment that is rich in learning opportunities for the child, we can take the environment a step further and mold it into a purposeful instrument that teaches and that guarantees your child will have a superior mind. (p. 10)

◀ **COUNTERPOINT** *Acceleration is ineffective and may be harmful.*

The position of Piagetian psychologists who attempt to apply his theory to education is that development should not be speeded up. This traditional view has been well summarized by Wadsworth (1978):

> The function of the teacher is not to accelerate the development of the child or speed up the rate of movement from stage to stage. The function of the teacher is to insure that development within each stage is thoroughly integrated and complete. (p. 117)

According to Piaget, cognitive development is based on the self-selected actions and thoughts of the student, not on the teacher's action. If you try to teach a student something the student is not ready to learn, he or she may learn to give the "correct" answer. But this will not really affect the way the student thinks about this problem. Therefore, why spend a long time teaching something at one stage when students will learn it by themselves much more rapidly and thoroughly at another stage?

Today the pressure is on parents and preschool teachers to create "superkids," 3-year-olds who read, write, and speak a second language. David Elkind (1991) asserts that pushing children can be harmful. Elkind believes that preschool children who are given formal instruction in academic subjects often show signs of stress such as headaches. These children may become dependent on adults for guidance. Early focus on "right" and "wrong" answers can lead to competition and loss of self-esteem. Elkind asserts:

> The miseducation of young children, so prevalent in the United States today, ignores well-founded and noncontroversial differences between early education and formal education. As educators, our first task is to reassert this difference and insist on its importance. (p. 31)

serve number a year or two before they can conserve weight. Piagetian theorists have tried to deal with these inconsistencies, but not all psychologists are convinced by their explanations (Case, 1992, 1998; Orlando & Machado, 1996; Siegler, 1991).

Some psychologists have pointed to research on the brain to support Piaget's stage model. Epstein (1978, 1980) observed changes in rates of growth in brain weight and skull size and changes in the electrical activity of the brain between infancy and adolescence. These growth spurts occur at about the same time as prize cooperation and sharing teach these skills early, whereas cultures that encourage competition nurture these abilities in their children (Bakerman et al., 1990; Ceci & Roazzi, 1994; Childs & Greenfield, 1982). The stages observed by Piaget are not necessarily "natural" for all children because to some extent they reflect the expectations and activities of the child's culture (Rogoff & Chavajay, 1995).

A major spokesperson for this **sociocultural theory** (also called *sociohistoric*) was a Russian psychologist who died more than 50 years ago. Lev Semenovich Vygotsky was only 38 when he died of tuberculosis, but he had produced over 100 books and articles. He wrote about language and thought, the psychology of art, learning and development, and educating students with special needs. His work was banned in Russia for many years because he referenced Western psychologists. But in the past 25 years, with the rediscovery of his work, Vygotsky's ideas about language, culture, and cognitive development have become major influences in psychology and education and have provided alternatives to many of Piaget's theories (John-Steiner & Mahn, 1996).

Vygotsky believed that human activities take place in cultural settings and cannot be understood apart from the settings. One of his key ideas was that our specific mental structures and processes can be traced to our interactions with others. These social interactions are more than simple influences on cognitive development—they actually create our cognitive structures and thinking processes (Palincsar, 1998). In fact, "Vygotsky conceptualized development as the transformation of socially shared activities into internalized processes" (John-Steiner & Mahn, 1996, p. 192). We will examine two themes in Vygotsky's writings that explain how social processes form learning and thinking: the social sources of individual thinking and the role of tools in learning and development, especially the tool of language (Wertsch, 1991, Wertsch & Tulviste, 1992).

▲ *Lev Vygotsky, shown here with his daughter, elaborated the sociocultural theory of development. His ideas about language, culture, and cognitive development have become major influences in the fields of psychology and education.*

Sociocultural Theory: Emphasizes role in development of cooperative dialogues between children and more knowledgeable members of society. Children learn the culture of their community (ways of thinking and behaving) through these interactions.

Co-constructed Process: A social process in which people interact and negotiate (usually verbally) to create an understanding or to solve a problem. The final product is shaped by all participants.

The Social Sources of Individual Thinking

Vygotsky assumed that "every function in a child's cultural development appears twice: first, on the social level and later on the individual level; first between people (interpsychological) and then inside the child (intrapsychological)" (1978, p. 57). In other words, higher mental processes appear first between people as they are **co-constructed** during shared activities. Then the processes are internalized by the child and become part of that child's cognitive development. For example, children first use language in activities with others, to regulate the behavior of the others ("No nap!" or "I wanna cookie."). Later, however, the child can regulate her own behavior using private speech ("don't spill"), as you will see in a later section. So, for Vygotsky, social interaction was more than influence, it was the origin of higher mental processes such as problem solving. Consider this example:

> A six-year-old has lost a toy and asks her father for help. The father asks her where she last saw the toy; the child says "I can't remember." He asks a series of questions—did you have it in your room? Outside? Next door? To each question, the child answers, "no." When he says "in the car?" she says "I think so" and goes to retrieve the toy. (Tharp & Gallimore, 1988, p. 14)

Who remembered? The answer is really neither the father nor the daughter, but the two together. The remembering and problem solving was co-constructed—between people—in the interaction. But the child may have internalized strategies to use next time something is lost. At some point, the child will be able to function independently to solve this kind of problem. So, like the strategy for finding the toy, higher functions appear first between a child and a "teacher" before they exist within the individual child (Kozulin, 1990).

Both Piaget and Vygotsky emphasized the importance of social interactions in cognitive development, but Piaget saw a different role for interaction. He believed that interaction encouraged development by creating disequilibrium—cognitive conflict—that motivated change. Thus, Piaget believed that the most helpful interactions were between peers because peers are on an equal basis and can challenge each other's thinking. Vygotsky (1978, 1986, 1987, 1993), on the other hand, suggested that children's cognitive development is fostered by interactions with people who are more capable or advanced in their thinking—people such as parents and teachers (Moshman, 1997; Palinscar, 1998).

Cultural Tools and Cognitive Development

Vygotsky believed that **cultural tools**, including real tools (such as printing presses, rulers, abacus—today, we would add cell phones, computers, calendars, the Internet) and symbolic tools (such as numbers and mathematical systems, Braille and sign language, maps, works of art, signs and codes, and language) play very important roles in cognitive development. For example, as long as the culture provides only Roman numerals for representing quantity, certain ways of thinking mathematically—from long division to calculus—are difficult or impossible. But with a number system that has a zero, fractions, positive and negative values, and an infinite number of numbers, much more is possible. The number system is a cultural tool that supports thinking, learning, and cognitive development. This symbol system is passed from adult to child through formal and informal interactions and teachings.

Vygotsky emphasized the tools that the culture provides to support thinking. He believed that all higher-order mental processes, such as reasoning and problem solving, are *mediated* by (accomplished through and with the help of) psychological tools, such as language, signs, and symbols. Adults teach these tools to children during day-to-day activities and the children internalize them. Then the psychological tools can help students advance their own development (Karpov & Haywood, 1998). The process is something like this: As children engage in activities with adults or more capable peers, they exchange ideas and ways of thinking about or representing concepts—drawing maps, for example, as a way to represent spaces and places. These co-created ideas are internalized by children. Thus, children's knowledge, ideas, attitudes, and values develop through appropriating or "taking for themselves" the ways of acting and thinking provided by their culture and by the more capable members of their group (Kozulin & Presseisen, 1995).

In this exchange of signs and symbols and explanations, children begin to develop a "cultural tool kit" to make sense of and learn about their world (Wertsch, 1991). The kit is filled with physical tools

Cultural Tools: The real tools (computers, scales, etc.) and symbol systems (numbers, language, graphs) that allow people in a society to communicate, think, solve problems, and create knowledge.

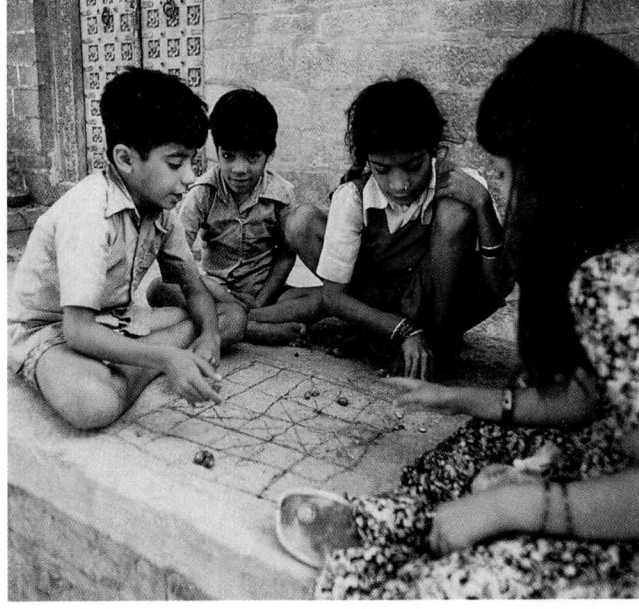

Vygotsky emphasized the tools that particular cultures provide to support thinking, and the idea that children use the tools they're given to construct their own understanding of the physical and social worlds. ▼

such as pencils or paint brushes directed toward the external world and psychological tools such as problem-solving or memory strategies for acting mentally.

Children do not just receive the tools transmitted to them by others, however. Children transform the tools as they construct their own representations, symbols, patterns, and understandings. As we learned from Piaget, children's constructions of meaning are not the same as those of adults. In the exchange of signs and symbols such as number systems, children create their own understandings. These understandings are gradually changed as the children continue to engage in social activities and try to make sense of their world (John-Steiner & Mahn, 1996; Wertsch, 1991).

In Vygotsky's theory, language is the most important symbol system in the tool kit, and it is the one that helps to fill the kit with other tools.

The Role of Language and Private Speech

Language is critical for cognitive development. It provides a means for expressing ideas and asking questions, the categories and concepts for thinking, and the links between the past and the future (Das, 1995). When we consider a problem, we generally think in words and partial sentences. Vygotsky thought that

> the specifically human capacity for language enables children to provide for auxiliary tools in the solution of difficult tasks, to overcome impulsive action, to plan a solution to a problem prior to its execution, and to master their own behavior. (Vygotsky, 1978, p. 28)

Vygotsky placed much more emphasis than Piaget on the role of language in cognitive development. In fact, Vygotsky believed that language in the form of private speech (talking to yourself) guides cognitive development.

Vygotsky's and Piaget's Views Compared. If you have spent much time around young children, you know that they often talk to themselves as they play. Piaget called children's self-directed talk "egocentric speech." He assumed that this egocentric speech is another indication that young children can't see the world through the eyes of others. They talk about what matters to them, without taking into account the needs or interests of their listeners. As they mature, and especially as they have disagreements with peers, Piaget believed, children develop socialized speech. They learn to listen and exchange ideas.

Vygotsky had very different ideas about young children's **private speech.** Rather than being a sign of cognitive immaturity, Vygotsky suggested that these mutterings play an important role in cognitive development by moving children toward self-regulation, the ability to plan, monitor, and guide your own thinking and problem solving.

Vygotsky believed that self-regulation developed in a series of stages. First the child's behavior is regulated by others, usually parents, using language and other signs such as gestures. For example, the parent says, "No!" when the child reaches toward a candle flame. Next the child learns to regulate the behavior of others using the same language tools. The child says, "No!" to another child who is trying to take away a toy, often even imitating the parent's voice tone. Along with learning to use external speech to regulate others, the child begins to use private speech to regulate her own behavior, saying "no" quietly to herself as she is tempted to touch the flame. Finally the child learns to regulate her own behavior by using silent inner speech (Karpov & Haywood, 1998). This series of steps is another example of how higher mental functions appear first between people as they communicate and reg-

Private Speech: Children's self-talk, which guides their thinking and action. Eventually these verbalizations are internalized as silent inner speech.

ulate each others' behavior, and then appear again within the individual as a cognitive process.

So children using private speech are communicating—they are communicating with themselves to guide their behavior and thinking. In any preschool room you might hear 4- or 5-year-olds saying, "No, it won't fit. Try it here. Turn. Turn. Maybe this one!" while they do puzzles. As these children mature, their self-directed speech goes underground, changing from spoken to whispered speech and then to silent lip movements. Finally, the children just "think" the guiding words. The use of private speech peaks at around 5 to 7 years of age and has generally disappeared by 9 years of age. Brighter children seem to make this transition earlier (Bee, 1992).

Vygotsky identified this transition from audible private speech to silent inner speech as a fundamental process in cognitive development. Through this process the child is using language to accomplish important cognitive activities such as directing attention, solving problems, planning, forming concepts, and gaining self-control. Research supports Vygotsky's ideas (Berk & Spuhl, 1995; Bivens & Berk, 1990; Diaz & Berk, 1992; Kohlberg, Yaeger, & Hjertholm, 1969). Children tend to use more private speech when they are confused, having difficulties, or making mistakes. Inner speech not only helps us solve problems but also allows us to regulate our behavior. Have you ever thought to yourself something like, "Let's see, the first step is . . ." or "Where did I use my glasses last?" or "If I work to the end of this page, then I can . . ."? You were using inner speech to remind, cue, encourage, or guide yourself. In a really tough situation, such as taking an important test, you might even find that you return to muttering out loud. Table 2.2 contrasts Piaget's and Vygotsky's theories of private speech. We should note that Piaget accepted many of Vygotsky's arguments and came to agree that language could be used in both egocentric and problem-solving ways (Piaget, 1962).

TABLE 2.2 *Differences between Piaget's and Vygotsky's Theories of Egocentric or Private Speech*

	Piaget	Vygotsky
Developmental Significance	Represents an inability to take the perspective of another and engage in reciprocal communication.	Represents externalized thought; its function is to communicate with the self for the purpose of self-guidance and self-direction.
Course of Development	Declines with age.	Increases at younger ages and then gradually loses its audible quality to become internal verbal thought.
Relationship to Social Speech	Negative; least socially and cognitively mature children use more egocentric speech.	Positive; private speech develops out of social interaction with others.
Relationship to Environmental Contexts	—	Increases with task difficulty. Private speech serves a helpful self-guiding function in situations where more cognitive effort is needed to reach a solution.

Source: From "Development of Private Speech among Low-Income Appalachian Children," by L. E. Berk and R. A. Garvin, 1984, *Developmental Psychology, 20,* p. 272. Copyright © 1984 by the American Psychological Association. Adapted with permission.

CHECKPOINT

Vygotsky's Sociocultural Perspective

Review

▶ Explain how interpsychological development becomes intrapsychological development.

▶ What are the differences between Piaget's and Vygotsky's perspectives on private speech and its role in development?

Apply

▶ Can you trace the origin of one of your problem-solving strategies to social interactions with parents or teachers? How did you learn?

Self-Talk and Learning. Because private speech helps students to regulate their thinking, it makes sense to allow, and even encourage, students to use private speech in school. Insisting on total silence when young students are working on difficult problems may make the work even harder for them. You may notice when muttering increases—this could be a sign that students need help. One approach, called *cognitive self-instruction*, teaches students to use self-talk to guide learning. For example, students learn to give themselves reminders to go slowly and carefully. They "talk themselves through" tasks, saying such things as "Okay, what is it I have to do? . . . Copy the picture with the different lines. I have to go slowly and carefully. Okay, draw the line down, down, good; then to the right, that's it; now . . ." (Meichenbaum, 1977, p. 32).

The Role of Adults and Peers

Language plays another important role in development. Vygotsky believed that cognitive development occurs through the child's conversations and interactions

According to Vygotsky, much of children's learning is assisted or mediated by teachers and tools in their environment, and most of this guidance is communicated through language. ▼

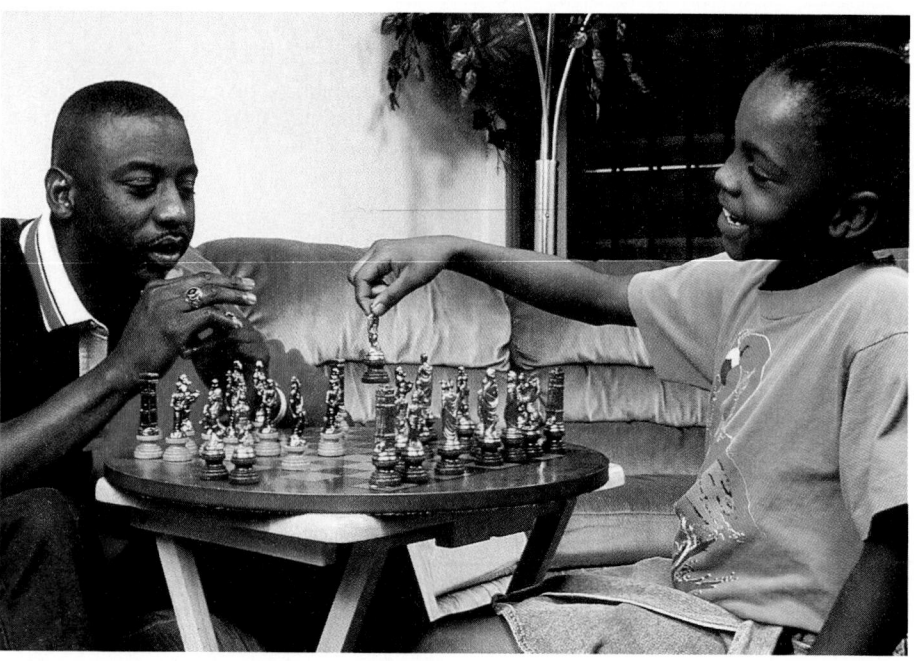

with more capable members of the culture, adults or more able peers. These people serve as guides and teachers, providing the information and support necessary for the child to grow intellectually. The adult listens carefully to the child and provides just the right help to advance the child's understanding. Thus, the child is not alone in the world "discovering" the cognitive operations of conservation or classification. This discovery is assisted or mediated by family members, teachers, and peers. Most of this guidance is communicated through language, at least in Western cultures. In some cultures, observing a skilled performance, not talking about it, guides the child's learning (Rogoff, 1990).

Jerome Bruner called this adult assistance *scaffolding* (Wood, Bruner, & Ross, 1976). The term aptly suggests that children use this help for support while they build a firm understanding that will eventually allow them to solve the problems on their own, as you will see in the next section.

Implications of Vygotsky's Theory for Teachers

There are at least three ways that cultural tools can be passed from one individual to another: imitative learning (where one person tries to imitate the other), instructed learning (where learners internalize the instructions of the teacher and use these instructions to self-regulate), and collaborative learning (where a group of peers strives to understand each other and learning occurs in the process) (Tomasello, Kruger, & Ratner, 1993). Vygotsky was most concerned with instructed learning though direct teaching or through structuring experiences that support another's learning, but his theory supports the other forms of cultural learning as well. Thus, Vygotsky's ideas are relevant for educators who teach directly and also create learning environments (Das, 1995). One major aspect of teaching in either situation is assisted learning.

Assisted Learning

Vygotsky's theory suggests that teachers need to do more than just arrange the environment so that students can discover on their own. He believed that children cannot and should not be expected to reinvent or rediscover knowledge already available in their cultures. Rather, they should be guided and assisted in their learning—so Vygotsky saw teachers, parents, and other adults as central to the child's learning and development (Karpov & Haywood, 1998).

Assisted learning, or guided participation in the classroom, requires **scaffolding**—giving information, prompts, reminders, and encouragement at the right time and in the right amounts, and then gradually allowing the students to do more and more on their own. Teachers can assist learning by adapting materials or problems to students' current levels; demonstrating skills or thought processes; walking students through the steps of a complicated problem; doing part of the problem (for example, in algebra, the students set up the equation and the teacher does the calculations or vice versa); giving detailed feedback and allowing revisions; or asking questions that refocus students' attention (Rosenshine & Meister, 1992). Meichenbaum's cognitive self-instruction described above is an example of assisted learning. Cognitive apprenticeships, reciprocal teaching, and instructional conversations

Assisted Learning: Providing strategic help in the initial stages of learning, gradually diminishing as students gain independence.

Scaffolding: Support for learning and problem solving. The support could be clues, reminders, encouragement, breaking the problem down into steps, providing an example, or anything else that allows the student to grow in independence as a learner.

TABLE 2.3 *Assisted Learning: Strategies to Scaffold Complex Learning*

- *Procedural facilitators.* These provide a "scaffold" to help students learn implicit skills. For example, a teacher might encourage students to use "signal words" such as who, what, where, when, why, and how to generate questions after reading a passage.

- *Modeling use of facilitators.* The teacher, in the above example, might model the generation of questions about the reading.

- *Thinking out loud.* This models the teacher's expert thought processes, showing students the revisions and choices the learner makes in using procedural facilitators to work on problems.

- *Anticipating difficult areas.* During the modeling and presentations phase of instructions, for example, the teacher anticipates and discusses potential student errors.

- *Providing prompt or cue cards.* Procedural facilitators are written on "prompt cards" that students keep for reference as they work. As students practice, the cards gradually become unnecessary.

- *Regulating the difficulty.* Tasks involving implicit skills are introduced by beginning with simpler problems, providing for student practice after each step, and gradually increasing the complexity of the task.

- *Providing half-done examples.* Giving students half-done examples of problems and having them work out the conclusions can be an effective way to teach students how to ultimately solve problems on their own.

- *Reciprocal teaching.* Having the teacher and students rotate the role of teacher. The teacher provides support to students as they learn to lead discussions and ask their own questions.

- *Providing checklists.* Students can be taught self-checking procedures to help them regulate the quality of their responses.

Source: From "Effective Teaching Redux," *ASCD Update,* 32(6), p. 5. Copyright © 1990 by the Association for Supervision and Curriculum Development. Reprinted with permission. All rights reserved.

(Chapter 9) are other examples. Table 2.3 gives examples of strategies that can be used in any lesson.

How can you know what kind of help to give and when to give it? One answer has to do with the student's zone of proximal development.

The Zone of Proximal Development

According to Vygotsky, at any given point in development there are certain problems that a child is on the verge of being able to solve. The child just needs some structure, clues, reminders, help with remembering details or steps, encouragement to keep trying, and so on. Some problems, of course, are beyond the child's capabilities, even if every step is explained clearly. The **zone of proximal development** is the area where the child cannot solve a problem alone, but can be successful under adult guidance or in collaboration with a more advanced peer (Wertsch, 1991). This is the area where instruction can succeed, because real learning is possible.

We can see how Vygotsky's beliefs about the role of private speech in cognitive development fit with the notion of the zone of proximal development. Often, an

Zone of Proximal Development: Phase at which a child can master a task if given appropriate help and support.

adult helps a child to solve a problem or accomplish a task using verbal prompts and structuring. This scaffolding may be gradually reduced as the child takes over the guidance, perhaps first by giving the prompts as private speech and finally as inner speech. Let's move forward to a future day in the life of the girl in the example on page 44 who had lost her toy and listen to her thoughts when she realizes that a schoolbook is missing. They might sound something like this:

> "Where's my math book? Used it in class. Thought I put it in my bookbag after class. Dropped my bag on the bus. That dope Larry kicked my stuff, so maybe . . ."

The girl can now systematically search for ideas about the lost book without help from anyone else.

Assessment. One implication of Vygotsky's zone of proximal development has to do with assessment. Most standard tests simply measure what students can do alone. This is useful information, but may not tell teachers or parents how to help the students learn more. An alternative is dynamic assessment (Spector, 1992) or learning potential assessment (Feuerstein, 1979, 1990). The goal of these approaches is to identify the zone of proximal development by asking a child to solve a problem, and then giving prompts and hints to see how he or she learns, adapts, and uses the guidance. These prompts are systematically increased to see how much support is needed and how the child responds. The teacher watches, listens, and takes careful notes about how the child uses the help and what level of support is necessary, and then applies this information to plan instructional groupings, peer tutoring, learning tasks, assignments, and so on (Grigorenko & Sternberg, 1998).

Teaching. Students should be put in situations where they have to reach to understand, but where support from other students or from the teacher is also available. Sometimes the best teacher is another student who has just figured out the problem, because this student is probably operating in the learner's zone of proximal development. Students should be guided by explanations, demonstrations, and work with other students—opportunities for cooperative learning. Having a student work with someone who is just a bit better at the activity would also be a good idea. In addition, students should be encouraged to use language to organize their thinking and to talk about what they are trying to accomplish. Dialogue and discussion are important avenues to learning (Karpov & Bransford, 1995; Kozulin & Presseisen, 1995). The Guidelines on page 52 give more ideas for applying Vygotsky's ideas.

Clearly, language plays a major role in learning, inside and outside the classroom. Let's look at this human capability more closely.

Connect & Extend
To the research
Grigorenko, E. L., & Sternberg, R. J. (1998). Dynamic testing *Psychological Bulletin, 124,* 75–111.

ABSTRACT
This article evaluatively reviews the literature on dynamic testing, a collection of testing procedures designed to quantify not only the products or even the processes of learning but also the potential to learn. The article considers a variety of approaches to dynamic testing and the strengths and weaknesses of each. Moreover, the literature on each approach is reviewed and analyzed in terms of the extent to which it fulfills the claims made for it. In all of these approaches, testing involves learning at the time of test, rather than just static testing of what has been learned before. It is concluded that dynamic testing has great potential for helping to understand people's potentials but this potential has not yet been realized fully.

CHECKPOINT

Implications of Vygotsky's Theory for Teachers

Review

▶ What is assisted learning, and what role does scaffolding play?

▶ What is a student's zone of proximal development?

Apply

▶ Think of some kinds of scaffolding that would help you learn about Vygotsky.

▶ In the situation at the beginning of the chapter, how would you use peer learning to move students toward an understanding of symbolism?

The Development of Language

All children in every culture master the complicated system of their native language, unless severe deprivation or physical problems interfere. This knowledge is remarkable. At the least, sounds, meanings, words and sequences of words, volume, voice tone, inflection, and turn-taking rules must all be coordinated before a child can communicate effectively in conversations. As you might expect, there are different theories about how people master the complex process of communication.

How Do We Learn Language?

One early view of language development assumed that children learn language by repeating those behaviors that lead to some kind of positive result. The child happens to say, "mmm," in the presence of milk, and the parent says, "Yes, milk, milk," and gives the child a drink. The child learns to say "milk" because it leads to a happy parent and a drink of milk. Children add new words by imitating the sounds they hear and improve their use of language when they are corrected by the adults around them. The trouble with this appealing theory is that many of a child's earliest utterances are not imitations but original creations. And they are unlikely to be rewarded, because they are "incorrect," even though they make sense to the people involved. Examples are such phrases as "paper find," "car mosquito," "tooth-guy" (dentist), or "all gone kitty" (Moshman, Glover, & Bruning, 1987).

In addition, parents rarely correct pronunciation and grammar during the early stages of language development. They are much more likely to respond to the content of a child's remarks (Brown & Hanlon, 1970; Demetras & Post, 1985). Adults caring for children seem continually to adapt their language to stay just ahead of the child. As soon as a child utters identifiable words, adults simplify their language with the child. As the child progresses, adults tend to change their language to stay just a bit more advanced than the child's current level of development, thus encouraging new understanding (Bohannon & Warren-Leubecker, 1989; Fernald, 1993). In order to stretch the child's language development, adults give the kind of support, or scaffolding, that Vygotsky has recommended. By staying slightly more advanced in their language, adults may also create disequilibrium and encourage development as a result.

Even this rich learning environment cannot explain how children learn so much language so quickly and correctly. Think of all the sounds that could be combined in different orders and linked with many different meanings. Why don't children create wild languages or make crazy associations between a sound and a meaning? Why, for example, when their parents say, "Look, a rabbit," do children learn to connect the word *rabbit* with the whole animal, not with the animal's ears, or movements, or size, or fur?

Some psychologists explain this amazing accomplishment by assuming that humans are born with a special capacity for processing, understanding, and creating language (Chomsky, 1965, 1986; Eimas, 1985; Maratsos, 1989). Humans may have built-in biases, rules, and constraints about language that restrict the number of possibilities considered. For example, young children seem to have a constraint specifying that a new label refers to a whole object, not just a part. Another built-in bias leads children to assume that the label refers to a class of similar objects. So the child learning about the rabbit is equipped naturally to assume that *rabbit* refers to the whole animal (not just its ears) and that other similar-looking animals are also rabbits. These built-in constraints simplify language learning (Markman, 1990).

It is likely that many factors—biological and experiential—play a role in language development. The important point is that children develop language as they develop other cognitive abilities by actively trying to make sense of what they hear and by looking for patterns and making up rules to put together the jigsaw puzzle of language. In this process, built-in biases and rules may limit the search and guide the pattern recognition. Reward and correction play a role in helping children learn correct language use, but the child's thinking in putting together the parts of this complicated system are very important (Rosser, 1994).

Language Development in the School Years

By about age 5 or 6, most children have mastered the basics of their native language. What remains for the school-age child to accomplish?

Pronunciation. The majority of 1st graders have mastered most of the sounds of their native language, but a few may remain unconquered. The *j*, *v*, *th*, and *zh* sounds are the last to develop. About 10% of 8-year-olds still have some trouble with *s*, *z*, *v*, *th*, and *zh* (Rathus, 1988). Young children may understand and be able to use many words, but prefer to use the words they can pronounce easily.

Syntax. Children master the basics of word order, or **syntax**, in their native language early. But the more complicated forms, such as the passive voice ("The car was hit by the truck"), take longer to master. By early elementary school, many children can understand the meaning of passive sentences, yet they do not use such constructions in their normal conversations. Other accomplishments during elementary

Syntax: The order of words in phrases or sentences.

"WHEN I SAY 'RUNNED,' YOU KNOW I MEAN 'RAN.' LET'S NOT QUIBBLE."

(© 2000 by Sidney Harris)

school include first understanding and then using complex grammatical structures such as extra clauses, qualifiers, and conjunctions.

Vocabulary and Meaning. The average 6-year-old has a vocabulary of 8,000 to 14,000 words, growing to about 20,000 by age 11. It seems that the time before puberty, especially the preschool years, is a sensitive period for language growth. Research has shown that we can learn much about language after puberty, but that very positive or very negative conditions during the sensitive period before puberty can greatly help or hinder language development (Anglin, 1993; Johnson & Newport, 1989).

In the early elementary years, some children may have trouble with abstract words such as *justice* or *economy.* They may also take statements literally and thus misunderstand sarcasm or metaphor. Fairy tales are understood concretely simply as stories instead of as moral lessons, for example. Many children are in their preadolescent years before they are able to distinguish being kidded from being taunted or before they know that a sarcastic remark is not meant to be taken literally (Gardner, 1982b).

Metalinguistic Awareness. Around the age of 5, students begin to develop **metalinguistic awareness.** This means their understanding about language and how it works becomes explicit. They have knowledge about language itself. They are ready to study and extend the rules that have been implicit—understood but not consciously expressed. This process continues throughout life, as we all become better able to manipulate and comprehend language. Teachers can develop the language abilities and knowledge of their students in a variety of ways.

Language, Literacy, and Teaching

One goal of schooling is the development of language and literacy. Literacy includes oral language as well as reading and writing. Today we know that children know a great deal about written language long before they can read or write in conventional ways:

> A make-believe grocery store in a preschool has a sign announcing the daily special, "APLS BNS 5¢" (apples and bananas 5¢) (Berk, 1996).

> A 4-year-old announces to his mother as they drive into the mall parking lot, "Look Mommy, I can read those letters, M . . . A . . . C . . . Y . . . S—Sears!" (Morrow, 1997).

> A 4-year-old writes a story (a) and a grocery list (b) in Figure 2.3.

These students know a great deal about reading and writing. They know that letters have different forms; that letters are associated with sounds and go together to make words; that words communicate meaning and make sentences; that writing goes from left to right and lists go down the page; and that stories look different from shopping lists. Teachers should strive to build on this emerging literacy understanding (Paris & Cunningham, 1996).

Teachers and Literacy

In its publication *Literacy Development in Early Childhood (Preschool through Grade 3),* the International Reading Association (1995) lists the following basic premises of a sound pre–1st-grade reading program:

Connect & Extend
To research journals
Chall, J. S., & Snow, C. E. (1988). School influences on the reading development of low-income children. *Harvard Education Letter,* 4(1), 1–4. This article talks about classroom factors that make a difference in helping low-income students learn to read. Vocabulary development is an important aspect of successful programs. To develop vocabulary, good programs:

1. Stress vocabulary during content-area instruction as well as during reading, using many materials such as encyclopedias, maps, magazines, comics, and trade books.
2. Place less emphasis on looking up words in the dictionary.
3. Have reading materials at all levels so even the best readers are challenged.
4. Use field trips and other activities to expose students to new vocabulary in context, so students can build background knowledge for understanding the words and any future reading based on the experiences.

FIGURE 2.3

A Story and a Grocery List

          (a) A story   (b) A grocery list

Source: From *Literacy's Beginnings* (2nd ed.) (p. 181), by L. M. McGee and D. J. Richgels, 1990, Boston: Allyn & Bacon. Copyright © 1990 by Allyn & Bacon. Reprinted with permission.

Reading and writing at school should permit children to build upon their existing knowledge of oral and written language.

Learning should take place in a supportive environment where children can build a positive attitude toward themselves and toward language and literacy.

For optimal learning, teachers should involve children actively in many meaningful, functional language experiences, including speaking, listening, writing, and reading.

Teachers of young children should be prepared in ways that acknowledge differences in language and cultural backgrounds, and should emphasize reading as an integral part of language arts as well as the total curriculum.

Teachers can enrich students' language environment by focusing not just on correct or incorrect usage, but on the idea expressed. Probe and extend students' ideas. For example, if a student says, "I writed my name on my picture," the teacher could respond, "You wrote your name above the rocket. Where is your astronaut going?" In this way, the teacher maintains the student's interest and at the same time expands the complexity of the statement and recasts the language to a more mature form (Rice, 1989). Parents who use these strategies have children who make rapid progress in language learning (Farrar, 1990).

Cazden (1988) suggests that word meanings are most easily learned through interactions and conversations with an adult in which the adult introduces new words. For example, when a student complains, "He does that on purpose, just to make me mad!" the teacher might respond, "So you think he is intentionally tripping by your desk just to irritate you? What's your evidence for that conclusion?" Reading aloud is also a potent form of language stimulation. Reading to students often leads to conversations about the pictures or ideas in the books. The importance of

Metalinguistic Awareness: Understanding about one's own use of language.

one-to-one interaction with an adult in developing language abilities has been stressed by many educators and psychologists (Morrow, 1997; Rice, 1989). This is in keeping with Vygotsky's theory of cognitive development.

Partnerships with Families

Especially in the early years, the students' home experiences are central in the development of language and literacy (Roskos & Neuman, 1993; Snow, 1993; Whitehurst et al., 1994). In homes that promote literacy, parents and other adults value reading as a source of pleasure, and there are books and other printed materials everywhere. Parents read to their children, take them to bookstores and libraries, limit the amount of television everyone watches, and encourage literacy-related play such as setting up a pretend school or writing "letters" (Pressley, 1996; Roskos & Neuman, 1998; Sulzby & Teale, 1991). Of course, not all homes provide this literacy-rich environment, but teachers can help, as you will see in the Family and Community Partnerships Guidelines.

FAMILY AND COMMUNITY PARTNERSHIPS

Promoting Literacy

Communicate with families about the goals and activities of your program.

Examples

1. At the beginning of school, send home a description of the goals to be achieved in your class—make sure it is in a clear and readable format.

2. As you start each unit, send home a newsletter describing what students will be studying—give suggestions for home activities that support the learning.

Involve families in decisions about curriculum.

Examples

1. Have planning workshops at times family members can attend—provide child care for younger siblings, but let children and families work together on projects.

2. Invite parents to come to class to read to students, take dictation of stories, tell stories, record or bind books, and demonstrate skills.

Provide home activities to be shared with family members.

Examples

1. Encourage family members to work with children to read and follow simple recipes, play language games, keep diaries or journals for the family, and visit the library. Get feedback from families or students about the activities.

2. Give families feedback sheets and ask them to help evaluate the child's school work.

3. Provide lists of good children's literature available locally—work with libraries, clubs, and churches to identify sources.

Source: From *Literacy Development in the Early Years: Helping Children Read and Write* (3rd ed.) (pp. 68–70), by L. M. Morrow, 1997, Boston: Allyn & Bacon. Copyright © 1997 by Allyn & Bacon. Adapted with permission.

Throughout this text you will read about other ways that teachers can encourage language development for both younger and older students. For example, we will discuss bilingual education in Chapter 5, reciprocal teaching and instructional conversations in Chapter 9, and learning to read and write in Chapter 13.

Summary

A Definition of Development

What are three principles of development?

Theorists generally agree that people develop at different rates, that development is an orderly process, and that development takes place gradually.

What part of the brain is associated with higher mental functions?

The cortex is a crumpled sheet of neurons that serves three major functions: receiving signals from sense organs (such as visual or auditory signals), controlling voluntary movement, and forming associations. The part of the cortex that controls physical motor movement develops or matures first, then the areas that control complex senses such as vision and hearing, and last the frontal lobe that controls higher-order thinking processes.

What is lateralization and why is it important?

Lateralization is the specialization of the two sides, or hemispheres, of the brain. The brain begins to lateralize soon after birth. For most people, the left hemisphere is the major factor in language, and the right hemisphere is prominent in spatial and visual processing. Even though certain functions are associated with certain parts of the brain, the various parts and systems of the brain work together to learn and perform complex activities such as reading and to construct understanding.

Piaget's Theory of Cognitive Development

What are the main influences on cognitive development?

Piaget's theory of cognitive development is based on the assumption that people try to make sense of the world and actively create knowledge through direct experience with objects, people, and ideas. Maturation, activity, social transmission, and the need for equilibrium all influence the way thinking processes and knowledge develop. In response to these influences, thinking processes and knowledge develop through changes in the organization of thought (the development of schemes) and through adaptation—including the complementary processes of assimilation (incorporating into existing schemes) and accommodation (changing existing schemes).

What is a scheme?

Schemes are the basic building blocks of thinking. They are organized systems of actions or thought that allow us to mentally represent or "think about" the objects and events in our world. Schemes may be very small and specific (grasping, recognizing a square), or they may be larger and more general (using a map in a new city). People adapt to their environment as they increase and organize their schemes.

As children move from sensorimotor to formal-operational thinking, what are the major changes?

Piaget believed that young people pass through four stages as they develop: sensorimotor, preoperational, concrete-operational, and formal-operational. In the sensorimotor stage, infants explore the world through their senses and motor activity, and work toward mastering object permanence and performing goal-directed activities. In the preoperational stage, symbolic thinking and logical operations begin. Children in the stage of concrete operations can think logically about tangible situations and can demonstrate conservation, reversibility, classification, and seriation. The ability to perform hypothetico-deductive reasoning, coordinate a set of variables, and imagine other worlds marks the stage of formal operations.

Implications of Piaget's Theory for Teachers

What is the "problem of the match" described by Hunt?

The "problem of the match" is that students must be neither bored by work that is too simple nor left behind by teaching they cannot understand. According to Hunt, disequilibrium must be carefully balanced to encourage growth. Situations that lead to errors can help create an appropriate level of disequilibrium.

What is active learning? Why is Piaget's theory of cognitive development consistent with active learning?

Piaget's fundamental insight was that individuals *construct* their own understanding; learning is a constructive process. At every level of cognitive development, students must be able to incorporate information into their own schemes. To do this, they must act on the information in some way. This active experience, even at the earliest school levels, should include both physical manipulation of objects and mental manipulation of ideas. As a general rule, students should act, manipulate, observe, and then talk and/or write about what they have experienced. Concrete experiences provide the raw materials for thinking. Communicating with others makes students use, test, and sometimes change their thinking abilities.

What are some limitations of Piaget's theory?

Piaget's theory has been criticized because children and adults often think in ways that are inconsistent with the notion of invariant stages. It also appears that Piaget underestimated children's cognitive abilities. Alternative explanations place greater emphasis on students' developing information processing skills and how teachers can enhance their development. Piaget's work is also criticized for overlooking cultural factors in child development.

Vygotsky's Sociocultural Perspective

Explain how interpsychological development becomes intrapsychological development.

Higher mental processes appear first between people as they are co-constructed during shared activities. As children engage in activities with adults or more capable peers, they exchange ideas and ways of thinking about or representing concepts. These co-created ideas are internalized by children. Thus children's knowledge, ideas, attitudes, and values develop through appropriating, or "taking for themselves," the ways of acting and thinking provided by their culture and by the more capable members of their group.

What are the differences between Piaget's and Vygotsky's perspectives on private speech and its role in development?

Vygotsky's sociocultural view asserts that cognitive development hinges on social interaction and the development of language. As an example, Vygotsky describes the role of children's self-directed talk in guiding and monitoring thinking and problem solving, while Piaget suggested that private speech was an indication of the child's egocentrism. Vygotsky, more than Piaget, emphasized the significant role played by adults and more able peers in children's learning. This adult assistance provides early support while students build the understanding necessary to solve problems on their own later.

Implications of Vygotsky's Theory for Teachers

What is assisted learning, and what role does scaffolding play?

Assisted learning, or guided participation in the classroom, requires scaffolding—giving information, prompts, reminders, and encouragement at the right time and in the right amounts, and then gradually allowing the students to do more and more on their own. Teachers can assist learning by adapting materials or problems to students' current levels, demonstrating skills or thought processes, walking students through the steps of a complicated problem, doing part of the problem, giving detailed feedback and allowing revisions, or asking questions that refocus students' attention.

What is a student's zone of proximal development?

At any given point in development there are certain problems that a child is on the verge of being able to solve and others that are beyond the child's capabilities. The zone of proximal development is the area where the child cannot solve a problem alone, but can be successful under adult guidance or in collaboration with a more advanced peer.

The Development of Language

How are humans predisposed to develop language? What role does learning play?

Children develop language as they develop other cognitive abilities by actively trying to make sense of what they hear, looking for patterns, and making up rules. In this process, built-in biases and rules may limit the search and guide the pattern recognition. Reward and correction play a role in helping children learn correct language use, but the child's thought processes are very important. Metalinguistic awareness begins around age 5 or 6 and grows throughout life.

Describe teacher actions and responses that encourage language development.

Teachers have a significant role in helping children develop language ability and knowledge about language. Teachers can focus on effective communication, meaning, comprehension, and respect for language in the classroom. Reading aloud and one-on-one interactions with adults are significant in developing language abilities. Parents can play a key role in promoting literacy at home.

*K*ey Terms

*B*ecoming a Professional

Reflecting on the Chapter

Can you apply the ideas from this chapter on cognitive development to solve the following problems of practice?

Preschool and Kindergarten

▶ A group of vocal parents wants you to introduce workbooks to teach basic arithmetic in your class for 4- and 5-year-olds. They seem to think that "play" with blocks, water, sand, clay, and so on is "wasted time." How would you respond?

Elementary and Middle School

▶ Two very concerned parents want to have a conference with you about their son's "language problems." He is in 1st grade and has some trouble with pronunciation. How would you prepare for the conference?

Junior High and High School

▶ The students in your class persist in memorizing definitions for many of the important abstract concepts in your class. They insist, "That's what you have to do to make a good grade in this class." Even though they can repeat the definitions precisely, they seem to have no conception of what the terms mean; they can't recognize examples of the concept in problems or give their own examples. It is almost as if they don't believe there is any real hope of understanding the ideas. Pick one important, difficult concept in your field, and design a lesson to teach it to students who believe only in memorization.

▶ It seems as if every fourth word from the mouths of your students is *like* or *you know*. Also, their understanding of the material in your class is limited, because they don't know the meaning of many words that you assumed high school students would certainly understand, such as *former* and *latter*. What would you do to encourage language development along with teaching your subject?

Certification Test Requirements

▶ Be clear about the three basic principles of development.

▶ Make sure you understand the elements of Piaget's theory (assimilation, accommodation, equilibration, schemes) and his four stages of cognitive development.

▶ From Vygotsky's theory, be familiar with the ideas of zone of proximal development and assisted learning. Also, be clear about how private speech supports cognitive development.

Your Teaching Portfolio

Think about your philosophy of teaching, a question you will be asked at most job interviews. What do you believe about matching teaching to students' current level of development? Are Piaget's ideas related to "readiness to learn"? What are the roles of direct teaching and discovery in students' learning? Do Piaget and Vygotsky lead you to different philosophies?

Add some ideas for Parent Involvement from this chapter to your **Portfolio**.

Teaching Resources

Adapt Table 2.3, *Assisted Learning: Strategies to Scaffold Complex Learning*, for the grades and subjects you might teach, and add it to your **Teaching Resources** file.

What Would They Do?

Here is how some practicing teachers responded to the teaching situation presented at the beginning of this chapter about teaching abstract concepts such as "symbol."

LINDA GLISSON AND SUE MIDDLETON

Fifth Grade Team Teachers
St. James Episcopal Day School, Baton Rouge, Louisiana

While most eleven-year-olds are in the beginning cognitive stage of understanding abstractions, it seems that these students have not reached that level of readiness. However, with use of controlled instruction designed to guide children from the concrete to the abstract, these students can learn that they actually know more about abstractions and symbolism than they realize.

In order to "listen" to my students' thinking to match my teaching to their level of thinking, I would keep a notepad handy for an entire day to jot down any ideas regarding symbolism that the children might unknowingly express during class time, lunch, and recess. I would then incorporate their personal experiences in a lesson on symbolism before deciding whether to move into the unit on symbolism in poetry.

To begin the lesson, I would have the students use a dictionary to define the word *symbolism* (root word—*symbol*) to discover that it means "something that stands for or represents something else." I would then give them a brief "across the curriculum" exercise in ways they incorporate symbols and symbolism into their thinking every day. For example: (social studies, American history): The American flag is just a piece of cloth. Why then do we recite a pledge to it? Stand at attention when it passes in a parade? What does it stand for? (English, literature—fables and fairy tales): What does the wolf usually represent (stand for)? The lion? The lamb? (Art): What color stands for a glorious summer day? Evil? Goodness and purity? I would continue with math symbols, scientific symbols, and music symbols and lead the students toward contributing other examples such as symbols representing holidays. I would then tell them about their own examples of symbolism that I had recorded. The students' participation in and enthusiasm for the exercises would serve to determine whether they were ready for the material.

MADYA AYALA

High School Teacher of Preperatoria Eugenio Garza Lagüera
Campus Garza Sada, Monterrey, N.L. Mexico

The strategy that the teacher is using in class to explain the symbols is very abstract and does not correspond to the level of a 10-year-old, or that of concrete operations according to Piaget. The teacher is demanding verbal analogy responses, which corresponds to formal operations.

Since the students' experience is concrete, they respond using corporal symbols that they can relate to. Thus, rather than using verbal analogies, I would use visual images, which are more concrete. For example, I would use familiar examples, such as a heart drawn on the blackboard, and then ask the students what the heart represents. I would also take the opportunity to invert this approach. For example, I would ask students to think about the beach, and then ask them to represent it with one symbol.

There will be many different responses (we hope!) to these exercises—it does not matter in poetry—what is important is that the students learn what a symbol or representation is and, perhaps more importantly, that they will have been given the opportunity to develop creativity and critical thinking.

MARY FRANCES DONOHOE

Fifth Grade Teacher
Lawton Chiles Elementary School, Gainesville, Florida

Students who misunderstand an abstract word need redirection and something they can relate to (a concrete word). The first step in this particular case would be to write the word "cymbals" on the overhead or chalkboard and give validity to the students' understanding of that word by stating that these kinds of cymbals are used in orchestras and bands. For example, "I like the beat they give to the music, but actually I was thinking of a different kind of symbol. (Write the word "symbol" on the board and circle it.) Before we discuss symbols, let's talk about friendship."

On the chalkboard or an overhead transparency, I would construct a semantic vocabulary map in order to activate students' background knowledge and engage them in active participation. Ask students what friendship is like for them. Record three or four of their ideas on the semantic map. Then ask them for examples of friendship. Again, record their responses. Finally, ask students to name some symbols of friendship. Illustration of symbols will often motivate even the most reluctant students to become involved. This could be followed by a small group activity:

Step One: Divide the students into groups of three or four and give each group a large sheet of chart paper and a box of colored markers. Then assign different abstract words to each group and ask the groups to do their own sematic maps. Allow approximately 20 minutes for this activity. Hang the completed maps around the room and ask students from each group to explain their words and symbols. Use this as a springboard for an introduction to the unit of poetry.

Step Two: Provide the class with many poetry books. Allow 10 to 20 minutes for them to peruse these books and choose one per student.

Step Three: Encourage students to find examples of symbols in the poems in their books.

Step Four: While the students are in their groups, encourage them to share the symbols they have discovered while the teacher circulates.

Step Five: A spokesperson for each group will provide one or two examples of the group's efforts, which the teacher will record on the chart.

CAROL GROSBERG

Fifth Grade Teacher
Bates School, Wellesley, Massachusetts

It has been my experience that students at the 5th grade level are capable of understanding and actually enjoy learning about homonyms, homophones, and homographs. After giving these students an explanation about the difference between them, I would challenge them to create a list of as many of them as they can. (In order to place a word on the list, they need to understand the meaning and be able to use it correctly in a sentence.)

After I was confident that my students understood the idea of words with multiple meanings, I hope that they would know that a symbol and a cymbal are yet another pair of words that fit into this category. Use of pictures would help students realize that there are objects that can symbolize concepts. Perhaps I would then ask the class to generate a list of others that fall into that category. Assuming the students have had some experience with more simple forms of poetry, it would then be time to teach the district lessons of symbolism in poetry.

DR. NANCY SHEEHAN-MELZACK

Art and Music Teacher
Snug Harbor Community School, Quincy, Massachusetts

Even very young children can recognize symbols *if* the symbol is presented first and the explanation required second. A drawing of an octagon on a pole has always elicited the answer, "A stop sign," whenever I have shown it. Children recognize symbols, but the teacher needs to work from their concrete knowledge to the more abstract concept, and there are a great many symbols in their daily life on which one can draw. It is important in your discussion of symbolism with children to explain that symbols are usually something that a group agrees will stand for an idea or concept. Children as young as 1st graders can recognize traffic sign shapes, letters of the alphabet, and numbers, and further recognize that they stand for directions, sounds, and how many. When they talk about these very common symbols, they can also realize they all use them for the same meaning.

VALERIE A. CHILCOAT

Fifth/Sixth Grade Advanced Academics
Glenmount School, Baltimore, Maryland

Concrete examples of symbolism must come from the students' own world. Street signs, especially those with pictures and not words, are a great example. The writing of the students' own names is a more abstract example of a symbol. Statues, photographs, and drawings are more examples of concrete symbols.

These concrete symbols, however, are not exactly the same as symbolism used in poetry. The link has to be made from the concrete to the abstract. Silly poetry is one way to do this. It is motivating to the students to read or listen to, and it can provide many examples of one thing acting as another. This strategy can also be used in lower grades to simply expose children to poetry containing symbolism.

3

Personal, Social, and Emotional Development

R *eflect on a teacher who helped to shape your sense of who you are—your abilities, aspirations, or values. What did the teacher do or say that influenced you? Do you know someone whose career choice was affected by a teacher?*

Schooling involves more than cognitive development. In this chapter we examine personal, social, and moral development.

We begin with the work of Erik Erikson, whose comprehensive theory provides a framework for studying personal and social development. Next, we explore ideas about how we come to understand others and ourselves. What is the meaning of the self-concept, and how is it shaped? How do our views of others change as we grow? What factors determine our views about morality? What can teachers do to foster such personal qualities as honesty, cooperation, empathy, and self-esteem? We then consider the three major influences on children's personal and social development: families, peers, and schools. Families today have gone through many transitions, and these changes affect the roles of teachers.

We end the chapter by examining several challenges for children—the problems and opportunities of physical development and the many risks that confront students today—such as child abuse, eating disorders, and drugs.

By the time you have completed this chapter, you should be able to:

▶ Describe Erikson's stages of psychosocial development and list several of his theory's implications for teaching.
▶ Suggest how teachers can foster self-esteem in their students.
▶ Describe the child's changing view of friendship.
▶ Describe Kohlberg's stages of moral reasoning and give an example of each.
▶ Evaluate alternatives to Kohlberg's theory.
▶ Explain the factors that encourage cheating and aggression in classrooms and discuss possible responses to each.
▶ Describe a number of challenges and risks that students face today and suggest roles for teachers in helping students respond.

What Would You Do?

One of the girls in your 10th-grade class is desperate for friends. Vanessa seems so lonely and depressed—no one ever joins her at lunch or walks with her to class. She is a reasonably good student, but just doesn't seem to fit in. On several occasions she has tried to join a group by offering help or asking questions, but these initiations never go anywhere. Even when a friendship begins, it never lasts. It seems like Vanessa gets so excited about the possibility of a developing relationship that she pushes the newfound friend away by overwhelming her with attention, showering her with special gifts, pouring out her heart, and sharing her deepest secrets and worries. Then Vanessa always seems to be the one exploited, abandoned, or hurt. Lately her schoolwork is careless and incomplete; she looks tired and pale.

▶ What are your concerns for this student?
▶ How do you think Vanessa feels about herself?
▶ What are some danger signs you might watch for?
▶ How would you help her form some genuine relationships?
▶ Consider the same situation, except the child is a 3rd-grade student.

The Work of Erikson

Erik Erikson proposed a theory of psychosocial development that describes tasks to be accomplished at different stages of life. ▼

Like Piaget, Erik Erikson did not start out as a psychologist. In fact, Erikson never graduated from high school. He spent his early adult years studying art and traveling around Europe. A meeting with Sigmund Freud in Vienna led to an invitation from Freud to study psychoanalysis. Erikson then emigrated to America to practice his profession and to escape the threat of Hitler.

In his influential *Childhood and Society* (1963), Erikson offered a basic framework for understanding the needs of young people in relation to the society in which they grow, learn, and later make their contributions. His later books, *Identity, Youth, and Crisis* (1968) and *Identity and the Life Cycle* (1980), expanded on his ideas. Although Erikson's approach is not the only explanation of personal and social development, I have chosen it to organize our discussion because Erikson emphasizes the emergence of the self, the search for identity, and the individual's relationships with others throughout life.

After studying child-rearing practices in several cultures, Erikson came to the conclusion that all humans have the same basic needs and that each society must provide in some way for those needs. Emotional changes and their relation to the social environment follow similar patterns in every society. This emphasis on the relationship of culture and the individual led Erikson to propose a **psychosocial** theory of development.

Like Piaget, Erikson saw development as a passage through a series of stages, each with its particular goals, concerns, accomplishments, and dangers. The stages are interdependent: Accomplishments at later stages depend on how conflicts are resolved in the earlier years. At each stage, Erikson suggests, the individual faces a **developmental crisis**. Each crisis involves a conflict between a positive alternative and a potentially unhealthy alternative. The way in which the individual resolves each crisis will have a lasting effect on that person's self-image and view of society.

TABLE 3.1   Erikson's Eight Stages of Psychosocial Development

Stages	Approximate Age	Important Event	Description
1. Basic trust versus basic mistrust	Birth to 12–18 months	Feeding	The infant must form a first loving, trusting relationship with the caregiver or develop a sense of mistrust.
2. Autonomy versus shame/doubt	18 months to 3 years	Toilet training	The child's energies are directed toward the development of physical skills, including walking, grasping, controlling the sphincter. The child learns control but may develop shame and doubt if not handled well.
3. Initiative versus guilt	3 to 6 years	Independence	The child continues to become more assertive and to take more initiative but may be too forceful, which can lead to guilt feelings.
4. Industry versus inferiority	6 to 12 years	School	The child must deal with demands to learn new skills or risk a sense of inferiority, failure, and incompetence.
5. Identity versus role confusion	Adolescence	Peer relationships	The teenager must achieve identity in occupation, gender roles, politics, and religion.
6. Intimacy versus isolation	Young adulthood	Love relationships	The young adult must develop intimate relationships or suffer feelings of isolation.
7. Generativity versus stagnation	Middle adulthood	Parenting/Mentoring	Each adult must find some way to satisfy and support the next generation.
8. Ego integrity versus despair	Late adulthood	Reflection on and acceptance of one's life	The culmination is a sense of acceptance of oneself as one is and a sense of fulfillment.

Source: From *Psychology* (5th ed.), by L. A. Lefton, 1994, Boston: Allyn & Bacon. Copyright © 1994 by Allyn & Bacon. Reprinted with permission.

An unhealthy resolution of problems in the early stages can have potential negative repercussions throughout life, although sometimes damage can be repaired at later stages. We will look briefly at all eight stages in Erikson's theory—or, as he called them, the "eight ages of man." Table 3.1 presents the stages in summary form.

The Preschool Years: Trust, Autonomy, and Initiative

Erikson identifies *trust versus mistrust* as the basic conflict of infancy. In the first months of life, babies begin to find out whether they can depend on the world around them. According to Erikson, the infant will develop a sense of trust if its needs for food and care are met with comforting regularity and responsiveness from caregivers. In this first year, infants are in Piaget's sensorimotor stage and are just beginning to learn that they are separate from the world around them. This realization is part of what makes trust so important: infants must trust the aspects of their world that are beyond their control (Bretherton & Waters, 1985; Isabella & Belsky, 1991).

Psychosocial: Describing the relation of the individual's emotional needs to the social environment.

Developmental Crisis: A specific conflict whose resolution prepares the way for the next stage.

Children need opportunities to learn things for themselves in order to develop a sense of initiative. ▶

Connect & Extend

To your thinking

What do you think Erikson's reply would be to the following questions?

a. Do you recommend following a rigid feeding schedule for infants?

b. Isn't it possible to spoil an infant by picking it up whenever it cries?

c. Should you help a child do things before the child reaches the point of frustration?

d. What advice would you give a parent who tends to be overprotective and consistently curtails a child's exploration?

e. If a child is attempting to do something, isn't it helpful to show the child the right way or a better way to do it?

f. Isn't it possible that a child will become conceited if he or she is consistently praised for accomplishments?

g. Do you think adolescents should be treated as adults before the law? Do you think it's fair to have more lenient punishments for juveniles than for adults?

Autonomy: Independence.

Initiative: Willingness to begin new activities and explore new directions.

Industry: Eagerness to engage in productive work.

Erikson's second stage, **autonomy** *versus shame and doubt*, marks the beginning of self-control and self-confidence. Young children are capable of doing more and more on their own. They must begin to assume important responsibilities for self-care such as feeding, toileting, and dressing. During this period parents must tread a fine line; they must be protective—but not overprotective. If parents do not maintain a reassuring, confident attitude and do not reinforce the child's efforts to master basic motor and cognitive skills, children may begin to feel shame; they may learn to doubt their abilities to manage the world on their own terms. Erikson believes that children who experience too much doubt at this stage will lack confidence in their own powers throughout life.

For Erikson, the next stage of "initiative adds to autonomy the quality of undertaking, planning, and attacking a task for the sake of being active and on the move" (Erikson, 1963, p. 255). But with **initiative** comes the realization that some activities are forbidden. At times, children may feel torn between what they want to do and what they should (or should not) do. The challenge of this period is to maintain a zest for activity and at the same time understand that not every impulse can be acted on. Again, adults must tread a fine line, this time in providing supervision without interference. If children are not allowed to do things on their own, a sense of guilt may develop; they may come to believe that what they want to do is always "wrong." The Guidelines at the top of page 67 suggest ways of encouraging initiative.

Elementary and Middle School Years: Industry versus Inferiority

In the early school years, students are developing what Erikson calls a sense of **industry.** They are beginning to see the relationship between perseverance and the pleasure of a job completed. The crisis at this stage is *industry versus inferiority.* For children in modern societies, the school and the neighborhood offer a new set of challenges that must be balanced with those at home. Interaction with peers becomes increasingly important as well. The child's ability to move between these

GUIDELINES

Encouraging Initiative in Preschool Children

Encourage children to make and to act on choices.

Examples

1. Have a free-choice time when children can select an activity or game.
2. As much as possible, avoid interrupting children who are very involved in what they are doing.
3. When children suggest an activity, try to follow their suggestions or incorporate their ideas into ongoing activities.
4. Offer positive choices: instead of saying, "You can't have the cookies now," ask, "Would you like the cookies after lunch or after naptime?"

Make sure that each child has a chance to experience success.

Examples

1. When introducing a new game or skill, teach it in small steps.
2. Avoid competitive games when the range of abilities in the class is great.

Encourage make-believe with a wide variety of roles.

Examples

1. Have costumes and props that go along with stories the children enjoy. Encourage the children to act out the stories or make up new adventures for favorite characters.
2. Monitor the children's play to be sure no one monopolizes playing "teacher," "Mommy," "Daddy," or other heroes.

Be tolerant of accidents and mistakes, especially when children are attempting to do something on their own.

Examples

1. Use cups and pitchers that make it easy to pour and hard to spill.
2. Recognize the attempt, even if the product is unsatisfactory.
3. If mistakes are made, show students how to clean up, repair, or redo.

worlds and to cope with academics, group activities, and friends will lead to a growing sense of competence. Difficulty with these challenges can result in feelings of inferiority. The Guidelines below give ideas for encouraging industry.

GUIDELINES

Encouraging Industry

Make sure that students have opportunities to set and work toward realistic goals.

Examples

1. Begin with short assignments, then move on to longer ones. Monitor student progress by setting up progress checkpoints.
2. Teach students to set reasonable goals. Write down goals and have students keep a journal of progress toward goals.

Give students a chance to show their independence and responsibility.

Examples

1. Tolerate honest mistakes.
2. Delegate to students tasks such as watering class plants, collecting and distributing materials, monitoring the computer lab, grading homework, keeping records of forms returned, and so on.

Provide support to students who seem discouraged.

Examples

1. Use individual charts and contracts that show student progress.
2. Keep samples of earlier work so students can see their improvements.
3. Have awards for most improved, most helpful, most hardworking.

Adolescence: The Search for Identity

The central issue for adolescents is the development of an **identity** that will provide a firm basis for adulthood. The individual has been developing a sense of self since infancy. But adolescence marks the first time that a conscious effort is made to answer the now-pressing question "Who am I?" The conflict defining this stage is *identity versus role confusion.*

Identity refers to the organization of the individual's drives, abilities, beliefs, and history into a consistent image of self. It involves deliberate choices and decisions, particularly about work, values, ideology, and commitments to people and ideas (Marcia, 1987; Penuel & Wertsch, 1995). If adolescents fail to integrate all these aspects and choices, or if they feel unable to choose at all, role confusion threatens.

Identity Statuses. James Marcia has suggested that there are four alternatives for adolescents as they confront their identity choices (Marcia, 1980, 1991, 1994). The first is **identity achievement**. This means that after considering the realistic options, the individual has made choices and is pursuing them. It appears that few students achieve this status by the end of high school; students who attend college may take a bit longer to decide. But even during college, about 80% of students change their majors at least once. And some adults may achieve a firm identity at one period in their lives, only to reject that identity and achieve a new one later. So identity, once achieved, may not be unchanging for everyone (Stephen, Fraser, & Marcia, 1992; Waterman, 1992).

Identity foreclosure describes the situation of adolescents who do not experiment with different identities or consider a range of options, but simply commit themselves to the goals, values, and lifestyles of others, usually their parents but sometimes cults or extremist groups. **Identity diffusion**, on the other hand, occurs when individuals reach no conclusions about who they are or what they want to do with their lives; they have no firm direction. Adolescents experiencing identity diffusion may have struggled unsuccessfully to make choices, or they may have avoided thinking seriously about the issues at all. They may be apathetic and withdrawn, with little hope for the future, or they may be openly rebellious. They may try to block out contact with parents or teachers by listening to music through headphones or sleeping (Berger & Thompson, 1995; Kroger, 1995).

Finally, adolescents in the midst of struggling with choices are experiencing what Erikson called a moratorium. Erikson used the term **moratorium** to describe a delay in the adolescent's commitment to personal and occupational choices. This delay is very common, and probably healthy, for modern adolescents. Erikson believed that adolescents in complex societies have an *identity crisis* during moratorium. Today, the period is no longer referred to as a crisis because, for most people, the experience is a gradual exploration rather than a traumatic upheaval (Grotevant, 1998).

Table 3.2 summarizes some characteristics of the different statuses. Both identity achievement and moratorium are considered healthy alternatives. The natural tendency of adolescents to "try on" identities, experiment with lifestyles, and commit to causes is an important part of establishing a firm identity. But adolescents who can't get past either the identity diffusion or foreclosure stage have difficulties

Connect & Extend
To what you know

Relate this information to concepts you learned in Chapter 2. For example, what aspects of formal-operational thought are helpful (or perhaps necessary) in achieving identity formation? Can you think of people who seem to have established their identity but who do not seem to have achieved the formal-operational stage? Is identity formation necessarily a conscious process?

Connect & Extend
To your own philosophy

Do you agree with either of these positions? What would Erikson say about each?

a. In order to establish their identity, adolescents need to separate themselves from their parents so they can discover who they are, other than being their parents' children. If parents are very strict and controlling, children have to give so much energy to establishing the separation that they don't have the time and effort to give to defining their own identity. For this reason, parents and teachers of adolescents would be more helpful if they were lenient with teenagers.

b. Adolescents are similar to large 2-year-olds in that they are egocentric and exhibit out-of-bounds behavior. They derive a sense of security from knowing that there are limits they must observe. They are in a transition stage with no clear-cut standards of behavior, since they are neither child nor adult. For this reason, parents and teachers of adolescents should be strict and impose rules to help a teenager make the transition more easily and safely.

Identity: The complex answer to the question, "Who am I?"

Identity Achievement: Strong sense of commitment to life choices after free consideration of alternatives.

Identity Foreclosure: Acceptance of parental life choices without consideration of options.

Identity Diffusion: Uncenteredness; confusion about who one is and what one wants.

Moratorium: Identity crisis; suspension of choices because of struggle.

TABLE 3.2 *Characteristics of the Four Identity Statuses: How Do Adolescents Differ Based on Their Progress toward Identity Achievement?*

	Foreclosure	Diffusion	Moratorium	Achievement
Attitude toward parents	Loving and respectful	Withdrawn	Trying to distance self	Loving and caring
Self-esteem	Low (easily affected by others)	Low	High	High
Ethnic identity	Strong	Medium	Medium	Strong
Prejudice	High	Medium	Medium	Low
Moral stage	Preconventional or conventional	Preconventional or conventional	Postconventional	Postconventional
Dependence	Very dependent	Dependent	Self-directed	Self-directed
Cognitive processes	Simplifies complex issues; refers to others and to social norms for opinions and decisions	Complicates simple issues; refers to others in both personal and ideological choices	Thoughtful; procrastinates, especially in decisions; avoids referring to others' opinions or to social norms	Thoughtful; makes decisions by both seeking new information and considering others' opinions
College	Very satisfied	Variable	Most dissatisfied (likely to change major)	High grades
Relations with others	Stereotyped	Stereotyped or isolated	Intimate	Intimate

Source: From *The Developing Person through Childhood and Adolescence* (p. 583), by K. S. Berger and R. A. Thompson, 1995, New York: Worth. Copyright © 1995 by Worth Publishers. Reprinted with permission.

adjusting. For example, identity-diffused adolescents and young adults often give up, trust their lives to fate, or go along with the crowd, so they are more likely to abuse drugs (Archer & Waterman, 1990). Foreclosed adolescents tend to be rigid, intolerant, dogmatic, and defensive (Frank, Pirsch, & Wright, 1990). Schools that give adolescents experiences with community service, real-world work, internships, and mentoring foster identity formation (Cooper, 1998). The Guidelines on page 70 suggest other approaches.

Beyond the School Years

The crises of Erikson's stages of adulthood all involve the quality of human relations. The first of these stages is *intimacy versus isolation.* Intimacy in this sense refers to a willingness to relate to another person on a deep level, to have a relationship based on more than mutual need. Someone who has

CHECKPOINT

The Work of Erikson

Review

▶ Why is Erikson's theory considered a psychosocial perspective?

▶ What are Erikson's stages of psychosocial development?

Apply

▶ How might an adolescent experiencing identity foreclosure answer the question, "Why did you choose that major?"

▶ How might Vanessa's difficulties in making friends (described at the beginning of this chapter) influence her identity achievement?

GUIDELINES

Supporting Identity Formation

Give students many models for career choices and other adult roles.

Examples

1. Point out models from literature and history. Have a calendar with the birthdays of eminent women, minority leaders, or people who made a little-known contribution to the subject you are teaching. Briefly discuss the person's accomplishments on his or her birthday.
2. Invite guest speakers to describe how and why they chose their professions. Make sure all kinds of work and workers are represented.

Help students find resources for working out personal problems.

Examples

1. Encourage them to talk to school counselors.
2. Discuss potential outside services.

Be tolerant of teenage fads as long as they don't offend others or interfere with learning.

Examples

1. Discuss the fads of earlier eras (neon hair, powdered wigs, love beads).
2. Don't impose strict dress or hair codes.

Give students realistic feedback about themselves.

Examples

1. When students misbehave or perform poorly, make sure they understand the consequences of their behavior—the effects on themselves and others.
2. Give students model answers or show them other students' completed projects so they can compare their work to good examples.
3. Since students are "trying on" roles, keep the roles separate from the person. You can criticize behavior without criticizing the student.

---

not achieved a sufficiently strong sense of identity tends to fear being overwhelmed or swallowed up by another person and may retreat into isolation.

The conflict at the next stage is *generativity versus stagnation*. **Generativity** extends the ability to care for another person and involves caring and guidance for the next generation and for future generations. While generativity frequently refers to having and nurturing children, it has a broader meaning. Productivity and creativity are essential features.

The last of Erikson's stages is *integrity versus despair*, coming to terms with death. Achieving **integrity** means consolidating your sense of self and fully accepting its unique and now unalterable history. Those unable to attain a feeling of fulfillment and completeness sink into despair.

With Erikson's theory of psychosocial development as a framework, we can now examine several aspects of personal and social development that are issues throughout childhood and adolescence.

◥ Understanding Ourselves and Others

Generativity: Sense of concern for future generations.

Integrity: Sense of self-acceptance and fulfillment.

What is self-concept? How do we come to understand other people and ourselves? How do we develop a sense of right and wrong—and do these beliefs affect our behavior? You will see that these areas follow patterns similar to those noted in Chapter 2 for cognitive development. Children's understandings of themselves are concrete at first, and then become more abstract. Early views of self and friends are based on immediate behaviors and appearances. Children assume that others share their feelings and perceptions. Their thinking about themselves and others is simple, segmented, and rule-bound, not flexible or integrated into organized systems. In time, children are able to think abstractly about internal processes—beliefs, intentions, values, and motivations. With these developments in abstract thinking, knowledge of self, others, and situations can incorporate more abstract qualities (Berk, 2000; Harter, 1998).

Self-Concept: Our perceptions about ourselves.

Self-Esteem: The value each of us places on our own characteristics, abilities, and behaviors.

Self-Concept and Self-Esteem

When you considered Vanessa's situation at the beginning of this chapter, was the idea of self-concept part of your analysis? The term *self-concept* is part of our everyday conversation. We talk about people who have a "low" self-concept or individuals whose self-concept is not "strong," as if self-concept were fluid levels in a car or a muscle to be developed. These actually are misuses of the term. In psychology, **self-concept** generally refers to "the composite of ideas, feelings, and attitudes people have about themselves" (Hilgard, Atkinson, & Atkinson, 1979, p. 605). We could consider self-concept to be our attempt to explain ourselves to ourselves, to build a scheme (in Piaget's terms) that organizes our impressions, feelings, and attitudes about ourselves. But this model or scheme is not permanent, unified, or unchanging. Our self-perceptions vary from situation to situation and from one phase of our lives to another.

Self-concept and self-esteem are often used interchangeably, even though they have distinct meanings. Self-concept is a cognitive structure—a belief about who you are. **Self-esteem** is an affective reaction—an evaluation of who you are. If people evaluate themselves positively—if they "like what they see"—we say that they have high *self-esteem* (Pintrich & Schunk, 1996).

The Structure of Self-Concept. The model shown in Figure 3.1 suggests that the general view of self is made up of other, more specific concepts, including the nonacademic self-concept, self-concept in English, and self-concept in mathematics. Recent research indicates that self-concept for artistic abilities is another separate area (Vispoel, 1995). These self-concepts at the second level are themselves made up of more specific, separate conceptions of the self, such as conceptions about physical ability, appearance, relations with peers, and relations with family (particularly parents) (Byrne & Shavelson, 1996). These conceptions are based on many experiences and events such as: sports performance; assessment of body, skin, or hair; friendships; artistic abilities; contributions to community groups, and so on.

The hierarchical structure of self-concept shown in Figure 3.1 on page 72 is strongest for early adolescents. Older adolescents and adults seem to have separate, specific self-concepts, but these are not necessarily integrated into an overall self-concept. Perhaps young adolescents, faced with the challenges of different academic subjects in school and the "life task" of forming an identity, try to integrate across their many "selves" to achieve that identity. Adults are not actively involved in *all* the academic domains (math, science, social studies) and can define themselves in terms of their current interests and activities, so self-concept is more situation-specific in adults (Byrne & Worth Gavin, 1996; Pintrich & Schunk, 1996).

One important way self-concept affects learning in school is through course selection. Think back to high school. When you had a chance to choose courses, did you pick your worst subjects—those where you felt least capable? Probably not. Herbert Marsh and Alexander Yeung (1997) examined how 246 boys in early high school in Sydney, Australia chose their courses. Academic self-concept for a particular subject (mathematics, science, etc.) was the most important predictor of course selection—more important than previous grades in the subject or overall

Connect & Extend
To the research
Byrne, B. M., & Worth Gavin, D. A. (1996). The Shavelson model revisited: Testing for structure of academic self-concept across pre-, early, and late adolescents. *Journal of Educational Psychology, 88,* 215–229.

FIGURE 3.1

Structure of Self-Concept

Students have many separate but sometimes related concepts of themselves. The overall sense of self appears to be divided into at least three separate, but slightly related, self-concepts—English, mathematics, and nonacademic.

Source: From "Self-Concept: Its Multifaceted, Hierarchical Structure," by H. W. Marsh and R. J. Shavelson, 1985, *Educational Psychologist, 20,* p. 114. Copyright © 1985 Lawrence Erlbaum Associates, Inc. Adapted with permission of the publisher and the authors.

self-concept. In fact, having a positive self-concept in a particular subject was an even bigger factor in selecting courses when self-concept in other subjects was low. The courses selected in high school put students on a path toward the future, so self-concepts about particular academic subjects can be life-changing influences.

How Self-Concept Develops. The self-concept evolves through constant self-evaluation in different situations. Children and adolescents are continually asking themselves, in effect, "How am I doing?" They gauge the verbal and nonverbal reactions of significant people—parents and other family members in the early years and friends, schoolmates, and teachers later—to make judgments (Harter, 1998). Students compare their performance with their own standards and with the performances of peers. Students compare their performance in math to their performance in English and science, for example, to form self-concepts in these areas. If math is their best subject, their math self-concept may be the most positive, even if their actual performance in math is poor. But social comparisons are influential, too. Students' self-concepts in math are also shaped by how their performance compares to that of other students in their math classes (Marsh, 1994). Students who are strong in math in an average school feel better about their math skills than

Connect & Extend

To the research

Marsh, H. W., Chessor, D., Craven, R., & Roche, L. (1995). The effects of gifted and talented programs on academic self-concept: The big fish strikes again. *American Educational Research Journal, 32,* 285–321.

students of equal ability in high-achieving schools do. Marsh (1990) calls this the "Big-Fish-Little-Pond Effect." Participation in a gifted and talented program seems to have an opposite "Little-Fish-in-a-Big-Pond" effect—students who participate in gifted programs, compared to similar students who remain in regular classes, tend to show *declines* in academic self-concepts over time, but no changes in nonacademic self-concepts (Marsh, Chessor, Craven, & Roche, 1995).

School Life and Self-Esteem

We turn now to self-esteem—the students' evaluations and feelings about themselves. For teachers, there are at least two questions to ask about self-esteem: (1) How does self-esteem affect a student's behavior in school? (2) How does life in school affect a student's self-esteem?

In answer to the first question, it appears that students with higher self-esteem are somewhat more likely to be successful in school (Marsh, 1990), although the strength of the relationship varies greatly, depending on the characteristics of the students and the research methods used (Ma & Kishor, 1997; Marsh & Holmes, 1990). In addition, higher self-esteem is related to more favorable attitudes toward school, more pos-

▲ *Although it is not certain whether one is the cause of the other, high self-esteem and favorable school experiences seem to be closely related.*

itive behavior in the classroom, and greater popularity with other students (Cauley & Tyler, 1989; Metcalfe, 1981; Reynolds, 1980). Of course, as we discussed in Chapter 1, knowing that two variables are related (correlated) does not tell us that one is causing the other. It may be that high achievement and popularity lead to self-esteem, or vice versa. In fact, it probably works both ways (Marsh, 1987; Shavelson & Bolus, 1982).

What about the second question of how school affects self-esteem—is school important? A study that followed 322 6th-grade students for two years would say yes. Hoge, Smit, and Hanson (1990) found that students' satisfaction with the school, their sense that classes were interesting and that teachers cared, and teacher feedback and evaluations influenced students' self-esteem. In physical education, teachers' opinions were especially powerful in shaping students' conceptions of their athletic abilities. Being placed in a low-ability group or being held back in school seems to have a negative impact on students' self esteem, but learning in collaborative and cooperative settings seems to have a positive effect (Covington, 1992; Deci & Ryan, 1985). Interestingly, special programs such as "Student of the Month" or admission to advanced math classes had little effect on self-esteem. (Relate this to the "Big-Fish-Little-Pond Effect.")

Over 100 years ago, William James (1890) suggested that self-esteem is determined by how *successful* we are in accomplishing tasks or reaching goals we *value*. If a skill or accomplishment is *not* important, incompetence in that area doesn't threaten self-esteem. Susan Harter (1990) has found evidence that James was right. Children who believe an activity is important and who feel capable in that area have higher self-esteem than students who think the activity is important, but question their competence. Students must have legitimate success on tasks that matter to them. The way individuals explain their successes or failures also is important. Students must attribute their successes to their own actions, not to luck or to special assistance, in order to build self-esteem.

Connect & Extend
To your teaching
William Glasser talks about self-concept in terms of failure and success identities. Loneliness, apathy, and withdrawal or delinquency characterizes the "failure identity"; the "success identity" is characterized by the ability to give and receive love, and the feeling of doing something that is important to self or others. (Glasser, W. [1969]. *Schools without failure.* New York: Harper and Row.) Given these characteristics, what kind of experience can a teacher provide to help a student change from a failure identity to a success identity, that is, develop a more positive self-concept?

TABLE 3.3 Suggestions for Encouraging Self-Esteem

1. Value and accept all pupils, for their attempts as well as their accomplishments.
2. Create a climate that is physically and psychologically safe for students.
3. Become aware of your own personal biases (everyone has some biases) and expectations.
4. Make sure that your procedures for teaching and grouping students are really necessary, not just a convenient way of handling problem students or avoiding contact with some students.
5. Make standards of evaluation clear; help students learn to evaluate their own accomplishments.
6. Model appropriate methods of self-criticism, perseverance, and self-reward.
7. Avoid destructive comparisons and competition; encourage students to compete with their own prior levels of achievement.
8. Accept a student even when you must reject a particular behavior or outcome. Students should feel confident, for example, that failing a test or being reprimanded in class does not make them "bad" people.
9. Remember that positive self-concept grows from success in operating in the world *and* from being valued by important people in the environment.
10. Encourage students to take responsibility for their reactions to events; show them that they have choices in how to respond.
11. Set up support groups or "study buddies" in school and teach students how to encourage each other.
12. Help students set clear goals and objectives; brainstorm about resources they have for reaching their goals.
13. Highlight the value of different ethnic groups—their cultures and accomplishments.

Sources: Information from "Improving Students' Self-Esteem," by J. Canfield, 1990, *Educational Leadership, 48*(1), pp. 48–50; *Teacher Behavior and Student Self-Concept*, by M. M. Kash and G. Borich, 1978, Menlo Park, CA: Addison-Wesley; "The Development of Self-Concept," by H. H. Marshall, 1989, *Young Children, 44*(5), pp. 44–51.

Teachers' feedback, grading practices, evaluations, and communication of caring for students can make a difference in how students feel about their abilities in particular subjects. But the greatest increases in self-esteem probably come when students grow more competent in areas they value—including the social areas that become so important in adolescence. *Thus, a teacher's greatest challenge is to help students achieve important understandings and skills.* Given this responsibility, what can teachers do? The recommendations in Table 3.3 are a beginning.

Gender, Ethnicity, and Self-Esteem

Younger children tend to have positive and optimistic views of themselves. In one study, over 80% of the 1st graders surveyed thought they were the best students in class. As they mature, students become more realistic, but many are not accurate judges of their own abilities (Paris & Cunningham, 1996). In fact, some students suffer from "illusions of incompetence"—they seriously underestimate their own competence (Phillips & Zimmerman, 1990). Gender and ethnic stereotypes can play roles here.

Gender and Self-Esteem. In the elementary grades, girls and boys have comparable perceptions of their own abilities. By 9th grade and continuing through high school, on average, girls gradually lower their perceptions of their own abilities compared to boys (Cole, Martin, Peeke, Seroczynski, & Fier, 1999; Phillips & Zimmerman, 1990). The American Association of University Women (1991) noted similar trends. Girls, aged 8 and 9, reported feeling confident, assertive, and authoritative about themselves. But they emerged from adolescence with a poor

Connect & Extend
To the research

American Association of University Women (1991). *Shortchanging girls, shortchanging America.* Washington, DC: AAUW. This report of a nationwide poll to assess the self-esteem, educational experiences, interest in math and science, and career aspirations of boys and girls ages 9 to 15 is available from the American Association of University Women Sales Office, P.O. Box 251, Annapolis Junction, MD 20701-0251.

self-image, constrained views of their future and their place in society, and much less confidence about themselves and their abilities. Other studies indicate that for most ethnic groups (except African Americans), males are more confident about their abilities in school, particularly in math and science. Differences between males and females generally are small but consistent across studies (Grossman & Grossman, 1994; Kling, Hyde, Showers, & Buswell, 1999). Put these results together with the findings by Marsh and Yeung (1997) that specific academic self-concept influences course selection. Many women and ethnic minority students make decisions about courses that forever limit their options in life, and often these decisions are not based on ability but instead on "illusions of incompetence."

Personal and Collective Self-Esteem. To this point we have discussed self-esteem as a purely individual characteristic. A number of psychologists have suggested that there is another basis for self-worth and identity called the *collective self*, or the self as a member of a family, peer group, ethnic heritage, class, or team (Wright & Taylor, 1995). Perhaps our self-esteem is influenced by both individual qualities and by **collective self-esteem**—a sense of the worth of the groups to which we belong. When students are faced with daily reminders, subtle or blatant, that their ethnic or family group has less status and power, the basis for collective self-esteem can erode.

Some early research on children's perceptions seemed to indicate that ethnic minority group children internalized negative stereotypes. When confronted with a light-skinned and a dark-skinned doll, African American children tended to choose the light-skinned doll as prettier and better on a number of dimensions (Clark & Clark, 1939). Similar findings were reported for Mexican American children (Weiland & Coughlin, 1979), Chinese American children (Aboud & Skerry, 1984), and Canadian Native children (Corenblum & Annis, 1987). However, many of these studies didn't ask the children *why* they preferred the light-skinned dolls. Some psychologists suggest that the children are simply indicating that they understand the power and status differences that surround them. The children do not think less of themselves—their self-esteem is high—but they know that majority group members tend to have more wealth and power (Spencer & Markstrom-Adams, 1990).

For all students, pride in family and community is part of the foundation for a stable identity and collective self-esteem. Because ethnic-minority students are members of both a majority culture and a subculture, it is sometimes difficult for them to establish a clear identity. Values, learning styles, and communication patterns of the students' subculture may be inconsistent with the expectations of the school and the larger society. Embracing the values of mainstream culture may seem to require rejecting ethnic values. Ethnic minority students have to "sift through two sets of cultural values and identity options" to achieve a firm identity, so they may need more time to explore possibilities (Markstrom-Adams, 1992, p. 177). In the process of establishing identity, individuals may pass through several stages (Frable, 1997):

▶ being unaware of, denying, or devaluing ethnic identity;

▶ being challenged by conflicts and discrimination to confront and examine ethnicity;

▶ immersion in a particular ethnic or racial consciousness;

▶ appreciation of ethnicity;

▶ integration of ethnicity into a full and complex bicultural identity.

Special efforts to encourage **ethnic pride** are particularly important so students examining their identities do not get the message that differences are deficits (Spencer & Markstrom-Adams, 1990). Each of us has an ethnic heritage. When

Collective Self-Esteem: Beliefs about the worth of the groups you belong to.

Ethnic Pride: A positive self-concept about one's racial or ethnic heritage.

majority adolescents are knowledgeable and secure about their own heritage, they are also more respectful of the heritage of others. Thus, exploring the ethnic roots of all students should foster both self-esteem and acceptance of others (Rotherham-Borus, 1994).

There is a particular aspect of ethnic heritage and pride that affects schooling—language. In Chapter 5 we will examine bilingual education in greater depth. But while we are talking about self-esteem, consider the results of a study of the impact of heritage language on personal and collective self-esteem by Stephen Wright and Donald Taylor (1995). These researchers found that when Canadian Native (Inuit) children were educated in their heritage language for the first three years of school, they had more positive personal and collective self-esteem than the Canadian Native children in the same school who received second-language instruction (English or French) from kindergarten on. When schools value the language of all students, ethnic pride and collective self-esteem may be enhanced.

▲ *Collective self-esteem is a sense of the worth of groups to which we belong. Ethnic pride must be encouraged so that students do not feel that their ethnic group is in any way deficient.*

One very important group membership for all students is their family. A study by John Fantuzzo, Gwendolyn Davis, and Marika Ginsburg (1995) capitalized on the power of families to improve students' self-esteem. The Family and Community Partnerships Guidelines list the strategies from their study that proved effective in increasing self-esteem and mathematics achievement for the 4th- and 5th-grade African American urban-school students who participated.

The Self and Others

As we seek our own identity and form images of ourselves, we are also seeking and forming ways to understand the "significant others" around us. Children learn to see themselves as separate and to see others as separate people as well, with their own identities. How do we learn to interpret what others are thinking and feeling?

FAMILY AND COMMUNITY PARTNERSHIPS

Building Self-Esteem

1. Work with families to co-create methods for family involvement. Offer a range of possible participation methods. Make sure the plans are realistic and fit the lives of the families.

2. Maintain regular home–school contact through telephone calls or notes. If a family has no telephone, identify a contact person (relative or friend) who can take messages. If literacy is a problem, use pictures, symbols, and codes for written communication.

3. Make all communications positive, emphasizing growth, progress, and accomplishments.

4. With the families, design family–student celebrations of the student's efforts and successes (a movie, special meal, trip to the park or library, going out for ice cream or pizza).

5. On a regular basis, send home a note in word or picture form that describes the student's progress. Ask families to indicate how they celebrated the success and to return the note.

6. Follow up with a telephone call to discuss progress, answer questions, solicit family suggestions, and express appreciation for the families' contributions.

7. Encourage families to visit the classroom.

Source: Adapted from "Effects of Parent Involvement in Isolation or in Combination with Peer Tutoring on Student Self-Concept and Mathematics Achievement," by J. Fantuzzo, G. Davis, and M. Ginsburg, 1995, *Journal of Educational Psychology, 87,* pp. 272–281.

Intention. Around the age of 2, children have a sense of intention, at least of their own intentions. They will announce, "I wanna peanut butter sandwich." They can say firmly, "I didn't break it on purpose!" By 2 or 3 years old, children extend the understanding of intention to others. Older preschoolers who get along well with their peers are able to separate intentional from unintentional actions and react accordingly. For example, they will not get angry when another child accidentally knocks over their block tower. But aggressive children have more trouble assessing intention. They are likely to attack anyone who topples their tower, even accidentally (Berk, 2000; Dodge & Somberg, 1987). As children mature, they are more able to assess and consider the intentions of others.

Taking the Perspective of Others. Very young children don't understand that other people have different feelings and experiences. But this **perspective-taking ability** develops over time until it is quite sophisticated in adults. Robert Selman (1980) has developed a stage model to describe the development of perspective-taking. As children mature and move toward formal-operational thinking, they take more information into account. They realize that different people can react differently to the same situation. Sometime between the ages of 10 to 15, most children develop the ability to analyze the perspectives of several people involved in a situation from the viewpoint of an objective bystander. Finally, older adolescents and adults can even imagine how different cultural or social values would influence the perceptions of the bystander. Even though children move through these stages, there can be great variation among children of the same age. Students who have difficulty taking the perspective of others may feel little remorse when they mistreat peers or adults. Some coaching in perspective-taking from the teacher might help (Berk, 2000).

Connect & Extend
To the news

The June 3, 1996 issue of *U.S. News and World Report* had a cover story titled "How to Raise a Moral Child: Let's Hear It for Honesty, Self-Discipline, and Empathy" (pp. 52–59). This is an interesting mix of research and opinion and a good discussion starter.

CHECKPOINT

Understanding Ourselves and Others

Review

▶ What are the similarities and differences between self-concept and self-esteem?

▶ How does self-concept change as children develop?

▶ How do perspective-taking skills change as students mature?

Apply

▶ How might Vanessa's experiences with peers influence her self-concept, given her age?

Moral Development

If you have spent time with young children, you know that there is a period when you can say, "Eating in the living room is not allowed!" and get away with it. For young children, rules simply exist. Piaget (1965) called this the state of **moral realism**. At this stage, the child of 5 or 6 believes that rules about conduct or rules about how to play a game are absolute and can't be changed. If a rule is broken, the child believes that the punishment should be determined by how much damage is done, not by the intention of the child or by other circumstances. So accidentally breaking three cups is worse than intentionally breaking one, and in the child's eyes, the punishment for the three-cup offense should be greater.

As children interact with others, develop perspective-taking abilities, and see that different people have different rules, there is a gradual shift to a **morality of cooperation**. Children come to understand that people make rules and people can

Perspective-Taking Ability: Understanding that others have different feelings and experiences.

Moral Realism: Stage of development wherein children see rules as absolute.

Morality of Cooperation: Stage of development wherein children realize that people make rules and people can change them.

Moral Reasoning: The thinking process involved in judgments about questions of right and wrong.

Moral Dilemmas: Situations in which no choice is clearly and indisputably right.

change them. When rules are broken, both the damage done and the intention of the offender are taken into account. These developmental changes and others are reflected in Kohlberg's theory of moral development, based in part on Piaget's ideas.

Kohlberg's Stages of Moral Development

Lawrence Kohlberg (1963, 1975, 1981) proposed a detailed sequence of stages of **moral reasoning,** or judgments about right and wrong. He divided moral development into three levels: (1) preconventional, where judgment is based solely on a person's own needs and perceptions; (2) conventional, where the expectations of society and law are taken into account; and (3) postconventional, where judgments are based on abstract, more personal principles that are not necessarily defined by society's laws. Each of these three levels is then subdivided into stages, as shown in Table 3.4.

Kohlberg has evaluated the moral reasoning of both children and adults by presenting them with **moral dilemmas,** or hypothetical situations in which people

---

TABLE 3.4 *Kohlberg's Theory of Moral Reasoning*

Level 1. Preconventional Moral Reasoning

Judgment is based on personal needs and others' rules.

Stage 1	Punishment–Obedience Orientation	
	Rules are obeyed to avoid punishment. A good or bad action is determined by its physical consequences.	
Stage 2	Personal Reward Orientation	
	Personal needs determine right and wrong. Favors are returned along the lines of "You scratch my back, I'll scratch yours."	

Level 2. Conventional Moral Reasoning

Judgment is based on others' approval, family expectations, traditional values, the laws of society, and loyalty to country.

Stage 3	Good Boy–Nice Girl Orientation	
	Good means "nice." It is determined by what pleases, aids, and is approved by others.	
Stage 4	Law and Order Orientation	
	Laws are absolute. Authority must be respected and the social order maintained.	

Level 3. Postconventional Moral Reasoning

Stage 5	Social Contract Orientation	
	Good is determined by socially agreed-upon standards of individual rights. This is a morality similar to that of the U.S. Constitution.	
Stage 6[*]	Universal Ethical Principle Orientation	
	Good and right are matters of individual conscience and involve abstract concepts of justice, human dignity, and equality.	

*In later work Kohlberg questioned whether Stage 6 exists separately from Stage 5.

Source: From "The Cognitive-Developmental Approach to Moral Education," by L. Kohlberg, 1975, *Phi Delta Kappan, 56,* p. 671. Adapted by permission of the *Journal of Philosophy.*

---

must make difficult decisions. Subjects are asked what the person who is caught in the dilemma should do, and why.

One of the most commonly used moral dilemmas can be summarized as follows: A man's wife is dying. There is one drug that could save her, but it is very expensive, and the druggist who invented it will not sell it at a price low enough for the man to buy it. Finally, the man becomes desperate and considers stealing the drug for his wife. What should he do, and why?

At level 1 (preconventional), the child's answer might be, "It is wrong to steal because you might get caught." This answer reflects the child's basic egocentrism. The reasoning might be: "What would happen to me if I stole something? I might get caught and punished."

At level 2 (the conventional level), the subject is able to look beyond the immediate personal consequences and consider the views, and especially the approval, of others. Laws, religious or civil, are very important and are regarded as absolute and unalterable. One answer stressing adherence to rules is, "It is wrong to steal because it is against the law." Another answer, placing high value on loyalty to family and loved ones but still respecting the law, is, "It's right to steal because the man means well—he's trying to help his wife. But he will still have to pay the druggist when he can or accept the penalty for breaking the law."

At level 3 (the postconventional level), an answer might be, "It is not wrong to steal because human life must be preserved. The worth of a human life is greater than the worth of property." This response considers the underlying values that might be involved in the decision. Abstract concepts are no longer rigid, and, as the name of this level implies, principles can be separated from conventional values. A person reasoning on this level understands that what is considered right by the majority may not be considered right by an individual in a particular situation. Rational, personal choice is stressed.

Moral reasoning is related to both cognitive and emotional development. As we have seen, abstract thinking becomes increasingly important in the higher stages of moral development, as children move from decisions based on absolute rules to decisions based on abstract principles such as justice and mercy. The ability to see another's perspective, to judge intentions, and to imagine alternative bases for laws and rules also enters into judgments at the higher stages.

Alternatives to Kohlberg's Theory

Kohlberg's stage theory has been criticized, first, because the stages do not seem in reality to be separate, sequenced, and consistent. People often give reasons for moral choices that reflect several different stages simultaneously. Or a person's choices in one instance may fit one stage and his or her decisions in a different situation may reflect another stage. When asked to reason about helping someone else versus meeting their own needs, both children and adolescents reason at higher levels than when they are asked to reason about breaking the law or risking punishment (Eisenberg et al., 1987; Sobesky, 1983). Also, Kohlberg emphasized cognitive reasoning about morality, but overlooked other aspects of moral maturity, such as character and virtue, that operate to solve moral problems in everyday life (Walker & Pitts, 1998).

Social Conventions versus Moral Issues. Another criticism is that Kohlberg's theory does not differentiate between social conventions and true moral issues until the higher stages of moral reasoning. Social conventions are the social rules and expectations of a particular group or society—for example, "It is rude to

Connect & Extend
To your teaching
For a concise discussion of the research on moral development, see Nucci, L. (1987). Synthesis of research on moral development. *Educational Leadership, 44*(5), 86–92. Nucci's article is a nice contrast to Kohlberg's analysis of moral development. Nucci suggests that even young children can distinguish between conventions and moral issues. Conventions are rules and expectations that vary from one group to the next, such as dating practices, "politeness" norms, or rules about talking in study hall. Moral issues have to do with such actions as physically or psychologically hurting others, stealing, lying, any activity that would be "wrong" even if there were no rule or law forbidding it. One goal of moral education should be to help children differentiate between the norms and conventions of their culture and universal moral concerns for justice, fairness, and human welfare. To help children understand these distinctions, Nucci suggests: (1) Moral education should focus on issues of justice and human welfare. (2) These concerns should be integrated into the curriculum, not taught as separate programs. (3) Moral discussion promotes moral development when students are at slightly different levels of moral development, are allowed to disagree about solutions to moral dilemmas, and really listen to each other, trying to understand, expand on, or refute each other's opinions. (4) Cooperative goal structures encourage moral development. (5) Firm, fair, flexible classroom management practices contribute to moral development.

eat with your hands." Such behavior is not morally wrong, it is just socially inappropriate—in some cultures or situations it is acceptable to eat with your hands (in fact, try eating potato chips with a fork!). True moral issues, on the other hand, involve the rights of individuals, the general welfare of the group, or the avoidance of harm. "Stealing" would be wrong, even if there were no "rule" against it; stealing is wrong, not rude. Children as young as 3 can distinguish between social conventions and moral issues. They know, for example, that being noisy in school would be fine *if* there were no rule requiring quiet, but that it would not be right to hit another child, even if there were no rule against it. So even very young children can reason based on moral principles that are not tied to social conventions and rules (Nucci, 1987; Smetana & Braeges, 1990; Turiel, 1983).

Cultural Differences in Moral Reasoning. Another criticism of Kohlberg's stage theory is that stages 5 and 6 in moral reasoning are biased in favor of Western, male values that emphasize individualism. In cultures that are more family-centered or group-oriented, the highest moral value might involve putting the opinions of the group before decisions based on individual conscience. There has been much disagreement over the "highest" moral stage. Kohlberg himself questioned the applicability of stage 6. Few people other than trained philosophers reason naturally or easily at this level. Kohlberg (1984) suggested that for all practical purposes, stages 5 and 6 might be combined.

The Morality of Caring

One of the most hotly debated criticisms of Kohlberg's theory is that the stages are biased in favor of males and do not represent the way moral reasoning develops in women. Because the stage theory was based on a longitudinal study of men only, it is very possible that the moral reasoning of women and the stages of women's development are not adequately represented (Gilligan, 1982; Gilligan & Attanucci, 1988). Carol Gilligan (1982) has proposed a different sequence of moral development, an "ethic of care." Gilligan suggests that individuals move from a focus on self-interests to moral reasoning based on commitment to specific individuals and relationships, and then to the highest level of morality based on the principles of responsibility and care for all people.

The highest stage in Kohlberg's theory of moral development involves decisions based on universal principles of justice and fairness. Reasoning based on caring for others and maintaining relationships is scored at a lower level. Many of Kohlberg's early studies of moral reasoning found that most men progressed to stages 4 and 5 by adulthood, while most women "stayed" at stage 3. This makes it appear as if women are morally challenged. But recent studies find few significant differences between men and women, or boys and girls, in their level of moral reasoning as measured by Kohlberg's procedures (Eisenberg, Martin, & Frabes, 1996; Thoma, 1986).

In order to study moral reasoning as it actually happens in real life, and to get an idea about the basis for decisions, Walker and his colleagues (Walker, 1991; Walker, Pitts, Hennig, & Matsuba 1995) asked children, adolescents, and adults to describe a personal moral problem and analyze a traditional moral dilemma. For both types of problems, males and females revealed both a morality of caring and a concern with justice. Andrew Garrod and his colleagues (1990) used fables to study the moral reasoning of 1st, 3rd, and 5th graders and found that both boys and girls tended to adopt a care orientation. There were no differences between the moral reasoning of boys and girls in the 1st and 3rd grades. However, a few 5th-grade

Connect & Extend
To your teaching
In a classroom discussion about stealing, the teacher finds that many students express the opinion that it is all right to steal if you don't get caught. How should a teacher respond? Would the race, culture, gender, or socioeconomic status of the student influence the teacher's response?

Carol Gilligan has challenged traditional conceptions of moral development with her work on the "ethic of care." ▼

TABLE 3.5 *Using "Caring for Strangers and the World" as a Teaching Theme*

As part of a unit on "Caring for Strangers and the World," high school students examine the issue of crime in several classes. In every class, the study of aspects of crime would be continually tied to the theme of caring and to discussions of safety, responsibility, trust in each other and in the community, and commitment to a safer future.

Subject	Elements
Mathematics	Statistics: Gather data on the location and rates of crimes, ages of offenders, and costs of crime to society. Is there a correlation between severity of punishment and incidence of crime? What is the actual cost of a criminal trial?
English and Social Studies	Read *Oliver Twist*. Relate the characters to their social and historical context. What factors contributed to crime in 19th century England?
	Read popular mysteries. Are they literature? Are they accurate depictions of the criminal justice system?
Science	Genetics: Are criminal tendencies heritable? Are there sex differences in aggressive behavior? Are women less competent than men in moral reasoning (and why did some social scientists think so)? How would you test this hypothesis?
Arts	Is graffiti art really art?

Source: From "Teaching Themes of Care," by N. Noddings, 1995, *Phi Delta Kappan, 76*, pp. 675–679. Copyright © 1995 by Phi Delta Kappan. Reprinted with permission of Phi Delta Kappan and the author.

boys (but no girls) suggested solutions involving violence or tricks. So justice and caring seem to be important bases for moral reasoning for both genders. Even though men and women both seem to value caring and justice, there is some evidence that in everyday life, women feel more guilty about violating caring norms (being inconsiderate or untrustworthy) and men feel more guilty when they show violent behaviors (fighting or damaging property) (Williams & Bybee, 1994). Women are somewhat more likely to use a care orientation, but both men and women *can* use both orientations (Skoe, Pratt, Matthews, & Curror, 1996).

Caring for students and helping students learn to care has become a theme for many educators. For example, Nel Noddings (1995) urged that "themes of care" be used to organize the curriculum. Possible themes include "Caring for Self," "Caring for Family and Friends," and "Caring for Strangers and the World." Using the theme of "Caring for Strangers and the World," there could be units on crime, war, poverty, tolerance, ecology, or technology. Table 3.5 shows how a focus on crime and caring for strangers could be integrated into several high school classes.

Connect & Extend
To professional journals
See the May, 1995 issue of *Phi Delta Kappan* for a special section on the schools and caring. Nel Noddings' article is included, as well as an article by Joyce Epstein about family–school partnerships to create caring schools.

Moral Behavior

As people move toward higher stages of moral reasoning, they also evidence more sharing, helping, and defending of victims of injustice. This relationship between moral reasoning and moral behavior is not very strong, however (Berk, 2000). Many other factors besides reasoning affect behavior. Two important influences on moral behavior are internalization and modeling.

Most theories of moral behavior assume that young children's moral behavior is first controlled by others through direct instruction, supervision, rewards and punishments, and correction. But in time, children **internalize** the moral rules and

Internalize: Process whereby children adopt external standards as their own.

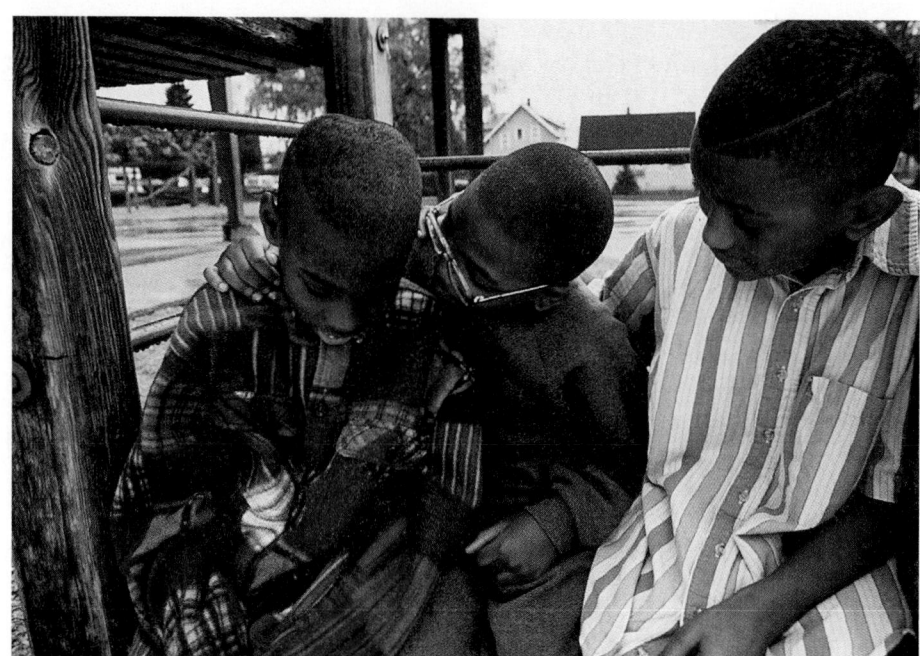

▲ *Over time, children learn to internalize moral principles such as compassion and justice and adopt them for themselves.*

principles of the authority figures who have guided them; that is, children adopt the external standards as their own. If children are given reasons they can understand when they are corrected—particularly reasons that highlight the effects of actions on others—then they are more likely to internalize moral principles. They learn to behave morally even when "no one is watching" (Berk, 2000; Hoffman, 1988).

A second important influence on the development of moral behavior is modeling. Children who have been consistently exposed to caring, generous adult models will tend to be more concerned for the rights and feelings of others (Lipscomb, MacAllister, & Bregman, 1985). Let's consider several moral issues that arise in classrooms.

Connect & Extend
To your own philosophy
Moral action does not necessarily follow directly from moral judgment. But is it necessary for moral judgment to precede moral action? That is, can a person behave in a moral way even if he or she cannot make a cognitive statement about how one "should" behave?

Cheating. Early research indicates that cheating seems to have more to do with the particular situation than with the general honesty or dishonesty of the individual (R. Burton, 1963). A student who cheats in math class is probably more likely to cheat in other classes, but may never consider lying to a friend or taking candy from the store. Most students will cheat if the pressure to perform well is great and the chances of being caught are slim.

There are some individual differences in cheating. Most studies of older and college-age students find that males are more likely to cheat than females; lower achieving students are more likely to cheat than higher achievers, students focusing on performance goals (making good grades, looking smart) as opposed to learning goals are likely to cheat; and college students in engineering, business, and science are more likely to cheat than students in the arts and humanities (Davis, Grover, Becker, & McGregor, 1992; Newstead, Franklyn-Stokes, & Armstead, 1996). Students also are particularly likely to cheat when they are behind or "cramming for tests."

The implications for teachers are straightforward. To prevent cheating, try to avoid putting students in high-pressure situations. Make sure they are well prepared

Aggression: Bold, direct action that is intended to hurt someone else or take property; unprovoked attack.

for tests, projects, and assignments so they can do reasonably well without cheating. Focus on learning and not on grades. Make extra help available for those who need it. Be clear about your policies in regard to cheating, and enforce them consistently. Help students resist temptation by monitoring carefully during testing.

Aggression. **Aggression**, intentionally trying to harm others, should not be confused with assertiveness, which means affirming or maintaining a legitimate right. As Helen Bee (1981) explains, "A child who says, 'That's my toy!' is showing assertiveness. If he bashes his playmate over the head to reclaim it, he has shown aggression" (p. 350).

Modeling plays an important role in the expression of aggression (Bandura, Ross, & Ross, 1963). Children who grow up in homes filled with harsh punishment and family violence are more likely to use aggression to solve their own problems (Emery, 1989; Holden & Ritchie, 1991).

One very real source of aggressive models is found in almost every home in America—television. In the United States, 82% of TV programs have at least some violence. The rate for children's programs is especially high—an average of 32 violent acts per hour, with cartoons being the worst. And in over 70% of the violent scenes, the violence goes unpunished (Mediascope, 1996; Waters, 1993). Aggressive children tend to believe that violence will be rewarded, and they use aggression to get what they want. They are more likely to believe that violent retaliation is acceptable: "It's OK to shove people when you're mad" (Egan, Monson, & Perry, 1998). Seeing violent acts go unpunished on television probably affirms and encourages these beliefs.

Most children spend more time watching television than they do in any other activity except sleep (Timmer, Eccles, & O'Brien, 1988). You can reduce the negative effects of TV violence by stressing three points with your students: Most people do not behave in the aggressive ways shown on television; the violent acts on TV are not real, but are created by special effects and stunts; and there are better ways to resolve conflicts—these are the ways most real people use to solve their problems (Huessmann, Eron, Klein, Brice, & Fischer, 1983). Also, avoid using TV viewing as a reward or punishment because that makes television even more attractive to children (Slaby, et al., 1995). But television is not the only source of violent models. Many popular films and video games are also filled with graphic depictions of violence, often performed by the "hero." Students growing up in the inner cities see gangs and drug deals. Newspapers, magazines, and the radio are filled with stories of murders, rapes, and robberies. In some preschools the children don't play "Mommy" and "Daddy"; they pretend to sell "nickel bags" of heroin (really bags of ground-up chalk) to their playmates.

In addition to being surrounded by violence and believing that violent "pay back" is appropriate when you are insulted or harmed, some children, particularly boys, have difficulty reading the intentions of others (Zelli, Dodge, Lochman, & Laird, 1999). As we saw earlier, they assume the another child "did it on purpose" when their block tower is toppled, they are pushed on the bus, or some other mistake is made. Retaliation follows and the cycle of aggression continues. Sandra Graham (1996) has successfully experimented with approaches that help aggressive, 5th- and 6th-grade African American boys become better judges of others' intentions. Strategies include engaging in role play, participating in group discussions of personal experiences, interpreting social cues from photographs, playing pantomime games, making videos, and writing endings to unfinished stories. The boys in the 12-session training group showed clear improvement in reading the intentions of others and responding with less aggression.

Connect & Extend
To your own philosophy
What about the endless hours spent in front of the television? Are we simply robbing our children of time to play by letting them be entertained? Marie Winn has written a thought-provoking book on this subject: *The Plug-In Drug* (New York: Viking, 1985).

Connect & Extend
To the research
Galen, B. R., & Underwood, M. K. (1997). A developmental investigation of social aggression among children. *Developmental Psychology, 33,* 589–600.
ABSTRACT
Social aggression consists of actions directed at damaging another's self-esteem, social status, or both, and includes behaviors such as facial expressions of disdain, cruel gossiping, and the manipulation of friendship patterns. In Study 1, 4th, 7th, and 10th graders completed the Social Behavior Questionnaire; only boys viewed physical aggression as more hurtful than social aggression, and girls rated social aggression as more hurtful than did boys. In the first phase of Study 2, girls participated in a laboratory task in which elements of social aggression were elicited and reliably coded. In the second phase of Study 2, another sample of participants (elementary, middle, and high school boys and girls) viewed samples of socially aggressive behaviors from these sessions. Girls rated the aggressor as more angry than boys, and middle school and high school participants viewed the socially aggressive behaviors as indicating more dislike than elementary school children.

Moral Development

Review

▶ What are the key differences among the preconventional, conventional, and postconventional levels of moral reasoning?

▶ Describe Gilligan's levels of moral reasoning.

▶ What influences moral behavior?

Apply

▶ How can teachers encourage moral behavior and caring?

▶ How might Vanessa's teacher support Vanessa's attempts to make and keep friends?

Victims. While some students tend to be bullies, other children are victims. Studies from Europe and the United States indicate that about 10% of children are chronic victims—the constant targets for physical or verbal attacks. These victims tend to have low self-esteem and they feel anxious, lonely, insecure, and unhappy. They often are prone to crying and withdrawal; when attacked, generally they won't defend themselves. Recent research suggests that victims may blame themselves for their situation. They believe that they are rejected because they have character flaws that they cannot change or control—no wonder they are depressed and helpless! The situation is worse for young adolescent victims whose peers seem to have little sympathy for them. Children who have been chronic victims through elementary and middle school are more depressed and more likely to attempt suicide as young adults (Graham, 1998; Hodges & Perry, 1999). In

GUIDELINES

Dealing with Aggression and Encouraging Cooperation

Present yourself as a nonaggressive model.

Examples

1. Do not use threats of aggression to win obedience.
2. When problems arise, model nonviolent conflict-resolution strategies (see Chapter 12).

Ensure that your classroom has enough space and appropriate materials for every student.

Examples

1. Prevent overcrowding.
2. Make sure prized toys or resources are plentiful.
3. Remove or confiscate materials that encourage personal aggression, such as toy guns.

Make sure students do not profit from aggressive behaviors.

Examples

1. Comfort the victim of aggression and ignore the aggressor.
2. Use reasonable punishment, especially with older students.

Teach directly about positive social behaviors.

Examples

1. Incorporate lessons on social ethics/morality through reading selections and discussions.
2. Discuss the effects of antisocial actions such as stealing, bullying, and spreading rumors.

Provide opportunities for learning tolerance and cooperation.

Examples

1. Emphasize the similarities among people rather than the differences.
2. Set up group projects that encourage cooperation.

Coach victimized children to be more assertive.

1. Provide models and encouragement—role play appropriate self defense.
2. Build self-esteem by building skills and knowledge.
3. Seek help for students who seem especially isolated and victimized.

the past years we have seen tragic consequences when tormented students turned guns on their tormentors in schools in the United States.

There is a second kind of victim—highly emotional and hot-tempered students who seem to provoke aggressive reactions from their peers. This group, about 10 to 15% of students, is rejected by almost all peers and has few friends (Pellegrini, Bartini, & Brooks, 1999). The Guidelines on page 84 may give you ideas for handling aggression and encouraging cooperation.

Socialization: Family, Peers, and Teachers

Socialization is the process by which the mature members of a society, such as parents and teachers, influence the beliefs and behaviors of children, enabling them to fully participate in and contribute to the society. In this section we will consider three of the most important influences on the development and socialization of children: family, peers, and teachers.

American Families Today

The most appropriate expectation to have about your students' families is no expectation at all. Today in the United States, about 70% of the women with school-aged children are employed (U.S. Bureau of the Census, 1997). Given the number of children who live in single-parent homes (about 25%) and the number of homes where both parents work, your students are likely to be alone or unsupervised much of the time outside school. In fact, the growing number of these *latchkey children* has prompted many schools to offer before- and after-school programs.

Increasingly, students today have only one or no sibling, or they may be part of **blended families,** with stepbrothers or stepsisters who move in and out of their lives. Some of your students may live with an aunt, with grandparents, with one parent, in foster or adoptive homes, or with an older brother or sister. The best advice is to drop the phrases "your parents" and "your mother and father" and to speak of "your family" when talking to students.

Children of Divorce. The divorce rate in the United States is the highest in the world, almost double that of the second-ranked nation, Sweden (Nielsen, 1993). And as too many of us know from experiences in our own families, separation and divorce are stressful events for all participants, even under the best circumstances. The actual separation of the parents may have been preceded by years of conflict in the home or may come as a shock to all, including friends and children. During the divorce itself, conflict may increase as property and custody rights are being decided.

After the divorce, more changes may disrupt the children's lives. Today, as in the past, the mother is most often the custodial parent, but the number of father-headed households is increasing and is now between 9 and 14% (Hetherington & Stanley-Hagan, 1997). The parent who has custody may have to move to a less-expensive home, find new sources of income, go to work for the first time, or work longer hours. For the child, this can mean leaving behind important friendships in the old neighborhood or school, just when support is needed the most. It may mean having just one parent, who has less time than ever to be with the children. About two-thirds of parents remarry and half of them divorce again, so there are more adjust-

Connect & Extend
To the research
Graham, S. (1998). Self-blame and peer victimization in middle school: An attributional analysis. *Developmental Psychology, 34,* 587–599.

ABSTRACT
Relations between characterological versus behavioral self-blaming attributions for victimization and maladjustment were examined in middle school students. Respondents completed a questionnaire that assessed self-perceptions of victim status, attributions for hypothetical incidents of victimization, and feelings of loneliness, social anxiety, and low self-worth. They also completed peer nomination procedures measuring perceptions of victimization in others, as well as peer acceptance and rejection. Self-perceived victimization was associated with characterological self-blame, loneliness, anxiety, and low self-worth. Peer-perceived victimization, in contrast, was related to acceptance and rejection. The data suggest that self-views are more predictive of the intrapersonal consequences of victimization (loneliness, anxiety, and low self-worth), whereas peer views are more predictive of interpersonal consequences (peer acceptance and rejection).

Socialization: The ways in which members of a society encourage positive development for the immature individuals of the group.

Blended Families: Parents, children, and stepchildren merged into families through remarriages.

Connect & Extend

To your students

For a concise discussion of the effects of divorce on children and suggestions for ways that teachers can help their students cope with divorce, see Clarke-Stewart, K. A. (1989). Single-parent families: How bad for the children? *NEA Today, 7*(6), 60–64.

ments ahead for the children (Furstenburg & Cherlin, 1991; Nelson, 1993). In some divorces there are few conflicts, ample resources, and the continuing support of friends and extended family. But divorce is never easy for anyone.

Effects of Divorce. The first two years after the divorce seem to be the most difficult period for both boys and girls. During this time, children may have problems in school, lose or gain an unusual amount of weight, develop difficulties sleeping, and so on. They may blame themselves for the breakup of their family or hold unrealistic hopes for a reconciliation (Hetherington, 1989; Pfeffer, 1981). Long-term adjustment is also affected. Boys tend to show a higher rate of behavioral and interpersonal problems at home and in school than either girls in general or boys from intact families. Girls may have trouble in their dealings with males. They may become more sexually active or have difficulties trusting males. However, living with one fairly content, if harried, parent may be better than living in a conflict-filled situation with two unhappy parents. And adjustment to divorce is an indi-

GUIDELINES

Helping Children of Divorce

Take note of any sudden changes in behavior that might indicate problems at home.

Examples

1. Be alert to physical symptoms such as repeated headaches or stomach pains, rapid weight gain or loss, fatigue or excess energy.
2. Be aware of signs of emotional distress such as moodiness, temper tantrums, difficulty in paying attention or concentrating.
3. Let parents know about the students' signs of stress.

Talk individually to students about their attitude or behavior changes. This gives you a chance to find out about unusual stress such as divorce.

Examples

1. Be a good listener. Students may have no other adult willing to hear their concerns.
2. Let students know you are available to talk, and let the student set the agenda.

Watch your language to make sure you avoid stereotypes about "happy" (two-parent) homes.

Examples

1. Simply say "your families" instead of "your mothers and fathers" when addressing the class.
2. Avoid statements such as "We need volunteers for room mother" or "Your father can help you."

Help students maintain self-esteem.

Examples

1. Recognize a job well done.
2. Make sure the student understands the assignment and can handle the workload. This is not the time to pile on new and very difficult work.
3. The student may be angry with his or her parents, but may direct the anger at teachers. Don't take the student's anger personally.

Find out what resources are available at your school.

Examples

1. Talk to the school psychologist, guidance counselor, social worker, or principal about students who seem to need outside help.
2. Consider establishing a discussion group, led by a trained adult, for students going through a divorce.

Be sensitive to both parents' rights to information.

Examples

1. When parents have joint custody, both are entitled to receive information and attend parent-teacher conferences.
2. The noncustodial parent may still be concerned about the child's school progress. Check with your principal about state laws regarding the noncustodial parent's rights.

vidual matter; some children respond with increased responsibility, maturity, and coping skills (Amato, Loomis, & Booth, 1995; Berk, 2000). See the Guidelines on page 86 for ideas about how to help students in these situations.

Peer Relationships

Peer relationships play a significant role in healthy personal and social development. There is strong evidence that adults who had close friends as children have higher self-esteem and are more capable of maintaining intimate relationships than adults who spent lonely childhoods. The characteristics of friends and the quality of the friendships matter too. Having stable, supportive relationships with friends who are socially competent and mature enhances social development, especially during difficult times such as parents' divorce or transition to new schools (Hartup & Stevens, 1999). Adults who were rejected as children tend to have more problems, such as dropping out of school or committing crimes (Coie et al., 1995; Coie & Dodge, 1998). Friendships are central to students' lives. When there has been a falling-out or an argument, when one child is not invited to a sleep-over, when rumors are started and pacts are made to ostracize someone, the results can be devastating to the children involved. Even when students begin to mature and know intellectually that rifts will soon be healed, they may still be emotionally crushed by temporary trouble in the friendship.

▲ *Peer relationships in the school years appear to play a significant role in self-esteem, success in school, and success in adult life.*

A teacher should be aware of how each student gets along with the group. Are there outcasts? Do some students play the bully role? Careful adult intervention can often correct such problems, especially at the middle elementary-school level.

A book published in 1998 caused a national debate when it claimed that peers, not parents, were the major forces shaping the personalities and behaviors of children. The Point/Counterpoint on page 88 examines this controversy.

New Roles for Teachers

When we consider the high rate of divorce and the power of peer relationships for children, we see that teachers today are dealing with issues that once stayed outside the walls of the school. The first and most important task of the teacher is to educate, but student learning suffers when there are problems with personal and social development.

Teachers are sometimes the best source of help for students facing emotional or interpersonal problems. When students have chaotic and unpredictable home lives, they need a caring, firm structure in school. They need teachers who set clear limits, are consistent, enforce rules firmly but not punitively, respect students, and show genuine concern. As a teacher, you can be available to talk

CHECKPOINT

Socialization: Family, Peers, and Teachers

Review

▶ What challenges face children whose parents are divorced?

▶ Why are peer relations important?

Apply

▶ As Vanessa's teacher, would you involve her family in dealing with her social problems?

▶ How would you decide what to do?

Parents and Peers

A few years ago, Judith Rich Harris published a book that shocked most parents and many psychologists. *The Nurture Assumption: Why Children Turn Out the Way They Do; Parents Matter Less Than You Think and Peers Matter More* (1998) questioned the commonly held belief that parents are the major influences on their children. Her book and the subsequent controversy that rippled through talk shows and the popular press raised some important questions. Just how much influence do families have on their children compared to the possibly powerful effects of peers? How powerful are other factors such as inborn temperament?

▶ **POINT** *Parents matter less than you think.*

Contemporary behavioral genetics has established clearly that personality traits as well as abilities have a genetic component, but genes explain only about half of the variation. Harris's book challenges the deeply held belief that parents account for the other half of the influence. Carol Tavris, a social psychologist and textbook author, writing a review of Harris's book, summarized five sets of findings that question the impact of parents—the nurture assumption: (1) No child-rearing style seems to predict children's personalities outside the home. Besides, the way parents treat children often depends on the children—more permissive with cooperative children but strict with defiant ones, for example. (2) Even when parents treat their children the same way, the children often turn out much different. For instance, most children of troubled parents suffer no lasting damage, but some grow up troubled themselves. (3) There is no correlation between the personality traits of adopted children and their adoptive parents. (4) Whether children are raised by two parents or one, in day care or at home, by gay parents or heterosexual, seems to have no impact on the children's personality.

(5) Parents' behavior seems to affect children mostly when the children are with their parents (which may be why so many parents can't believe teachers' accounts of their children's misbehavior in school). According to Tavris, Harris changed the discussion from nature (genes) and nurture (parents) to the older question of heredity and environment, and then documented the powerful role of one aspect of the environment—peer culture—in children's development. "Parents have long lamented the apparent cruelty of children and the obsessive conformity of teenagers, but Harris argues, they have missed the point. Children's attachment to their peer groups is not irrational, it's essential" (Tavris, 1998, p. 14). Attachment to peers, not parents, is essential for human survival. To see the power of peers, we have to look at situations where the values and interests of parents clash with those of peers, then see whose influence dominates. In these comparisons, peers

about personal problems without requiring that your students do so. One of my student teachers gave a boy in her class a journal entitled "Very Hard Thoughts" so that he could write about his parents' divorce. Sometimes he talked to her about the journal entries, but at other times he just recorded his feelings. The student teacher was very careful to respect the boy's privacy about his writings. What can teachers do to encourage personal and social growth in school? The Guidelines on page 90 give some other ideas.

*C*hallenges for Children

In the next few pages we examine a number of challenges children face as they mature. The first is as old as the human species—growing up—meeting the challenges of physical development. The remaining challenges are all too modern and have put students at great risk today. We will end by considering just a few of these risks.

usually win. Tavris claims, for example, that differences between black and white achievement vanish when you take peer culture into account. And the contribution of parents to the environmental influence on children's personality? About zero according to Harris, once heredity is taken into account. Harris's conclusions have been criticized, but many well-known psychologists, such as neuroscientist Robert Sapolsky of Stanford, say that her work is based on solid science (Begley, 1998).

◄ COUNTERPOINT *Parents are pivotal.*
Other psychologists disagree. Sharon Begley (1998) interviewed several prominent psychologists for an article in Newsweek. Here are a few quotes. Frank Farley, Temple University, and then President of the American Psychological Association, a group that had presented Harris an award for her work said, "She's all wrong. She is taking an extreme position based on a limited set of data. Her thesis is absurd on the face, but consider what might happen if parents believe this stuff! Will it free some to mistreat their kids, since it doesn't matter? Will it tell parents who are tired after a long day that they needn't bother even paying attention to their kid since 'it doesn't matter'?" According to Wendy Williams of Cornell, "There are many, many good studies that show parents can affect how children turn out in both cognitive abilities and behavior. By taking such an extreme position, Harris does a tremendous disservice." Jerome Kagan of Harvard said simply, "I am embarrassed for psychology." Kagan cited one of his own studies as evidence that parents matter. He studied shy children whose parents either overprotected them or pushed them to interact with others. Children who were encouraged to play, even though they were shy, became far less fearful—so parental behaviors interacted with temperament to affect the children's personality. Also, John Gottman of the University of Washington cited evidence from his intervention studies teaching parents how to talk and listen to their children with behavior problems. Parents who learned a new way of interacting have clear effects on their children. Finally, some psychologists questioned Harris's interpretations of the twin studies because the number of these studies is too small to warrant Harris's conclusions.

Perhaps the best lesson from this debate is that parents are not the sole source of influence—positive or negative—on their children. Harris said that she wrote the book "to lighten the burden of guilt and blame placed on the parents of 'problem children.'" Peers, other adults, and teachers all have a role to play, especially when children are away from their parents. Teachers have a chance to help shape a peer culture that can make a difference for their students.

Physical Development

For most children, at least in the early years, growing up means growing bigger, stronger, more coordinated. It also can be frightening, disappointing, exciting, and puzzling.

The Preschool Years. Preschool children are very active. Their **gross-motor skills,** control of the large muscles, improve greatly over the years from ages 2 to 5, as you can see in Table 3.6 on page 91. Between ages 2 and about 4 or 5, preschoolers' muscles grow stronger, their balance improves, and their center of gravity moves lower, so they are able to run, jump, climb, and hop. Most of these movements develop naturally if the child has normal physical abilities and the opportunity to play. Children with physical problems, however, may need special training to develop these skills. For young children, physical activity can be an end in itself. It is fun just to improve. But preschoolers may literally run till they drop. They need periods of rest scheduled after physical exertion.

Fine-motor skills such as tying shoes or fastening buttons, which require the coordination of small movements, also improve greatly during the preschool years,

Gross-Motor Skills: Voluntary body movements that involve the large muscles.

Fine-Motor Skills: Voluntary body movements that involve the small muscles.

GUIDELINES

Supporting Personal and Social Development

Help students examine the kinds of dilemmas they are currently facing or will face in the near future.

Examples

1. In elementary school, discuss sibling rivalries, teasing, stealing, prejudice, treatment of new students in the class, and behavior toward handicapped classmates.
2. In high school, discuss cheating, letting friends drive when they are intoxicated, conforming to be more popular, and protecting a friend who has broken a rule.

Help students see the perspectives of others.

Examples

1. Ask a student to describe his or her understanding of the views of another, then have the other person confirm or correct the perception.
2. Have students exchange roles and try to "become" the other person in a discussion.

Help students make connections between expressed values and actions.

Examples

1. Follow a discussion of "What should be done?" with "How would you act? What would be your first step? What problems might arise?"
2. Help students see inconsistencies between their values and their own actions. Ask them to identify inconsistencies, first in others, then in themselves.

Safeguard the privacy of all participants.

Examples

1. Remind students that in a discussion they can "pass" and not answer questions.
2. Intervene if peer pressure is forcing a student to say more than he or she wants to.
3. Don't reinforce a pattern of telling "secrets."

Make sure students are really listening to each other.

Examples

1. Keep groups small.
2. Be a good listener yourself.
3. Recognize students who pay careful attention to each other.

Make sure that as much as possible your class reflects concern for moral issues and values.

Examples

1. Make clear distinctions between rules based on administrative convenience (keeping the room orderly) and rules based on moral issues.
2. Enforce standards uniformly. Be careful about showing favoritism.

Source: From "What Criteria Should Public School Moral Education Programs Meet?" by J. W. Eiseman, 1981, *The Review of Education*, 7, pp. 226–227. Adapted with permission.

as shown in Table 3.6. Children need to work with large paintbrushes, fat crayons, large pieces of drawing paper, and soft clay or playdough to accommodate their developing skills. During this time, children will begin to show a preference for their right or left hand. Most students, about 85% during this time, will prefer their right hand, but those who prefer their left should not be forced to change. This means that there must be a good supply of left-handed scissors for preschool classes.

Elementary School. During the elementary-school years, physical development is fairly steady for most children. They become taller, leaner, and stronger, so they are better able to master sports and games. There is tremendous variation, however. A particular child can be much larger or smaller than average and still be perfectly healthy. Because children at this age are very aware of physical differences but are not the most tactful people, you may hear comments such as "You're too little to be in 5th grade. What's wrong with you?" or "How come you're so fat?"

TABLE 3.6 *Motor Skills Improve throughout the Preschool Years*

Approximate Age	Gross-Motor Skills	Fine-Motor Skills
Birth to 3 years	Sits and crawls; walks; begins to run	Picks up, grasps, stacks, and releases objects
3 to 4.5 years	Walks up and down stairs; jumps with both feet; throws ball	Holds crayon; uses utensils; buttons; copies shapes
4.5 to 6 years	Skips; rides two-wheel bicycle; catches ball; plays sports	Uses pencil; makes representational drawings; cuts with scissors; prints letters

Throughout elementary school, many of the girls are likely to be as large as or larger than the boys in their classes. Between the ages of 11 and 14, girls are, on the average, taller and heavier than boys of the same age (Tanner, 1990). The size discrepancy can give the girls an advantage in physical activities, although some girls may feel conflict over this and, as a result, downplay their physical abilities.

Adolescence. **Puberty** marks the beginning of sexual maturity. It is not a single event, but a series of changes involving almost every part of the body. The outcome of the changes is the ability to reproduce. The sex differences in physical development we saw during the later elementary years become even more pronounced at the beginning of puberty. Generally, girls begin puberty about two years ahead of boys and reach their final height by age 16; most boys continue growing until about age 18. For the typical North American and European girl, the adolescent growth spurt begins with breast development between the ages of 10 and 11 and continues for about three years. While this is the average time frame for girls, the actual range is from 9 to 16 years. Eighty percent of American girls have their first menstrual period between the ages of 11 and 14. For the typical boy, the growth spurt begins between the ages of 12 and 13. When the growth spurt is at its peak, boys can grow 4 inches and 26 pounds in a single year, girls 3.5 inches and 20 pounds.

The physical changes of adolescence have significant effects on the individual's identity. Psychologists have been particularly interested in the academic, social, and emotional differences between adolescents who mature early and those who mature later. Early maturation seems to have certain special advantages for boys. The early maturers' taller, broader-shouldered body type fits the cultural stereotype for the male ideal. Early-maturing boys are more likely to enjoy high social status; they tend to be popular and to be leaders. On the other hand, boys who mature late have an especially difficult time (Kaplan, 1984). However, some studies show that in adulthood, males who matured later tend to be more creative, tolerant, and perceptive. Perhaps the trials and anxieties of maturing late teach some boys to be better problem solvers (Brooks-Gunn, 1988; Seifert & Hoffnung, 1991).

For girls, these effects are reversed. Maturing way ahead of classmates can be a definite disadvantage. Being larger than everyone else in the class is not a valued characteristic for girls in many cultures (Simmons & Blyth, 1987). A girl who begins to mature early probably will be the first in her peer group to start the changes of puberty. This can be very upsetting to some girls, especially if they have not been prepared for the changes or if friends tease them. Later-maturing girls seem to have fewer problems, but they may worry that something is wrong with them. All students can benefit from knowing that the "normal" range in rates of maturation is great and that there are advantages for both early and late maturers. The Guidelines give a few ideas for dealing with physical differences in the classroom.

Puberty: The period in early adolescence when individuals begin to reach physical and sexual maturity.

GUIDELINES

Dealing with Differences in Growth and Development

Do not call unnecessary attention to physical differences among students.

Examples

1. Avoid seating arrangements that are obviously based on height, but try to seat smaller students so they can see and participate in class activities.
2. Avoid games that call attention to differences in height, size, or strength.
3. Don't use or allow students to use nicknames based on physical traits.

Help students obtain factual information on differences in physical development.

Examples

1. Set up science projects on sex differences in growth rates.
2. Have readings and discussions that focus on differences between early and late maturers. Make sure that you present the positives and the negatives of each.

3. Find out the school policy on sex education and on informal guidance for students. Some schools, for example, encourage teachers to talk to girls who are upset about their first menstrual period, while other schools expect teachers to send the girls to talk to the school nurse.
4. Give the students models in literature or in their community of high-achieving individuals who do not fit the ideal physical stereotypes.

Accept that concerns about appearance and the opposite sex will occupy much time and energy for adolescents.

Examples

1. Allow students a few moments at the end of class to socialize.
2. Deal with some of these issues in curriculum-related materials.

At the same time that they are negotiating the physical transitions from childhood through adolescence, students must navigate the social and academic transitions of schooling. These changes can be uplifting, devastating, or anywhere in between for a child.

Navigating Transitions

Do you remember your first day of school? I remember getting my list of required school supplies (Big Chief tablet, #2 pencils, . . .). I bought them at the Rexall drug store that gave a free milk shake with your school supply purchase. By the time my daughter started school, the free milk shakes were gone—we all were watching our cholesterol. The transition to 1st grade is a critical time, one that can begin a journey toward life-long learning.

Young Children: Starting School. Between the ages of 5 and 7 when most children start school, cognitive development is proceeding rapidly. Children can process more information faster and their memory spans are increasing. They are moving from preoperational to concrete operational thinking. As these internal changes progress, the children are spending hours every weekday in the new physical and social world of school. They must now reestablish Erikson's stages of psychosocial development in the unfamiliar school setting. They must learn to trust new adults, act autonomously in this more complex situation, and initiate actions in ways that fit the new rules of school. At the same time, the new psychosocial challenge of industry versus inferiority looms large. The child must master new skills and work toward new goals, while being compared to others and risking failure.

The way children cope with these challenges has implications for the rest of their school experience. Two of the best predictors of dropping out of school are low grade point average by the 3rd grade and being held back in one of the primary grades (Paris & Cunningham, 1996). Children who do well in the 1st grade are on their way to achievement, while those who flounder are on a path toward difficulty. The achievement test score differences among students from high and low socioeconomic groups in 1st grade are relatively small, but by the 6th grade the differences have tripled. "How well students do in the primary grades matters more for their future success than does their school performance at any other time" (Entwisle & Alexander, 1998, p. 354).

What is this important world of school like for children? First, school requires new social roles—children must fit into the group and learn to be students. These new roles do not come easily or automatically for every child. Also, evaluation is built into school and success is not guaranteed. The basis for reward and recognition changes as children move from their families to school. In families, children generally are compared to themselves in terms of growth and development (remember, "Oh, you've gotten so much bigger since last fall!"). In school, however, children are compared to each other and someone is always bigger, faster, smarter—or so it seems (Entwisle & Alexander, 1998). In addition, different student characteristics are noticed—such as social class and ethnicity—that may not have mattered before because they were shared by family members.

As you will see in Chapter 10, teachers' judgments and expectations can have powerful effects on students. Too often ethnic and social class differences between teachers and students set the stage for miscommunication and lowered expectations. These negative cycles of lowered expectations and lowered achievement begin in the 1st grade and accumulate. By 3rd grade, children's performance on achievement tests stabilizes and predicts future achievement quite well (Butler, Marsh, Sheppard, & Sheppard, 1985).

What can be done to make the transition to school positive? Research points to a few answers. First, quality preschool and full-day kindergarten experiences are critical for helping children, especially children from low-income homes, to do well in 1st grade. Children who achieve in 1st grade do better in later grades, so the time to make a difference is early. Programs such as Reading Recovery and Success for All are based on early and intensive intervention. Continuity helps children become successful students, so staying in the same school for kindergarten and 1st grade, with the same peers and teachers can be helpful. In Chapter 12, you will learn about teaching students directly how to accomplish school rules and procedures. Teachers, administrators, families, and community leaders can work together to make the transition to school positive for all children (Mangione & Speth, 1998; Paris & Cunningham, 1996).

Students in the Middle Grades: Another Transition. There are many different age configurations in schools today, but most students move from elementary to middle school or junior high between the 5th and 7th grades—a time developmental psychologists call "early adolescence" (Sandrock, 1996). Again, cognitive processes are expanding as the students develop capabilities for abstract thinking and for understanding the perspectives of others. But even greater changes are taking place in the students' physical development as they approach puberty. The students bring their new cognitive abilities and their changing bodies to the psychosocial task of identity—exploring possible selves. Who am I? Who do I want to become and who

▲ *Between the ages of 5 and 7, when most children are entering school, cognition is developing rapidly. The transition to 1st grade is a critical time—one that can begin a journey toward life-long learning.*

do I fear becoming? During the middle grades, students are more likely to describe themselves in terms of psychological and social traits such as "moody," "loyal," or "depressed" and political or religious orientation such as Jewish, Muslim, Christian, conservative, or libertarian. Their sense of self becomes more differentiated, so they know that they have many capabilities and limitations. Quite a bit is going on.

And the world is changing, too. The Carnegie Council on Adolescent Development's (1995) report, *Great Transitions: Preparing Adolescents for a New Century*, describes five changes that create a complex context for growing up today. First, as we saw earlier, the number of divorces and working parents in many countries means that young adolescents spend less time with adults and more time with peers or watching television. Second, the job future for many adolescents is grim as the world shifts to a knowledge-based economy, where a high school degree is not enough to earn a good salary. Why work hard in school if you will have the same dead-end job offered to a school drop-out? Third, adolescents go through puberty earlier and assume adult roles later than previous generations. It is a strain, to say the least, to be sexually mature but socially restricted for a long time. Fourth, adolescents are surrounded by media—television, films, videos, and music—that influence their expectations, fears, and values. And finally, the world has become more diverse. About one-third of American adolescents today are of non-European descent.

So, with developing minds and identities and bodies, the young adolescent must navigate the transition to the middle grades in an uncertain world. What are the results? One of the most common findings is that overall self-concept and self-esteem decline in early adolescence, as do assessments of competence in academic and nonacademic areas. Just after a transition to a new school, especially the transition to junior high school, students' self-concepts seem to become more negative and less stable. During the middle school or junior high years, students grow more self-conscious (remember, adolescent egocentrism and Elkind's imaginary audience discussed in Chapter 2). At this age, feelings of self-worth are more closely tied to physical appearance and social acceptance, so these years can be exceedingly difficult for students such as Vanessa, described at the opening of this chapter (Wigfield, Eccles, & Pintrich, 1996). When young adolescents move from being the most mature and highest status students in a small, familiar elementary school to being the bottom of the chain in a large, impersonal junior high school, there may be negative consequences (Graber & Brooks-Gunn, 1996; Lord, Eccles, & McCarthy, 1993; Meece, 1997; Wigfield, Eccles, MacIver, Rueman, & Midgley, 1991).

What can teachers do to make these transitions easier for middle grade students? The middle school movement is one attempt to structure schools to meet the needs of this developmental period. Some of the features of middle grade schools are interdisciplinary teams of teachers who work with a "pod" or cohort of students; integrated curricula that take into account the personal concerns of the students and build learning tasks around these concerns; advisory programs that pair every student with a teacher/advisor; and special-interest exploratory classes such as photography or computers. One more element relates to you, the teacher. Middle grade schools should have teachers who are knowledgeable about and like young adolescents (Muth & Alvermann, 1999).

Children and Youth at Risk

It is a difficult time to become an adult. Many of the challenges children face threaten their safety as well as their personal and social development. We will consider only a few of the risks that students encounter. Teachers can play a role in helping students cope with these situations. In the first area—child abuse—teachers have legal responsibilities to consider.

Child Abuse. Accurate information about the number of abused children in the United States is difficult to find; most experts agree that an enormous number of cases go unreported (Children's Defense Fund, 1994). In 1996, 3.1 million cases were reported, an increase of 132% over the level in the 1980s. It is sad to type this paragraph when I revise this book, because the number of cases of child abuse have to be increased each time I revise. About half of all abusive parents could change their destructive behavior patterns if they received help and support. Without assistance, probably only about 5% of abusing parents improve (Starr, 1979). Of course, parents are not the only people who abuse children. Siblings, other relatives, and even teachers have been responsible for the physical and sexual abuse of children.

As a teacher, you must alert your principal, school psychologist, or school social worker if you suspect abuse. In all 50 states of the United States, in the District of Columbia and the U.S. territories, the law requires certain professionals, often including teachers, to report suspected cases of child abuse. The legal definition of abuse has been broadened in many states to include neglect and failure to provide proper care and supervision. Most laws also protect teachers who report suspected neglect in good faith (Beezer, 1985). Be sure that you understand the laws in your state or province on this important issue as well as your own moral responsibility. At least five children die of abuse or neglect each day in the United States, in many cases because no one would "get involved" (Thompson & Wyatt, 1999). Table 3.7 on page 96 lists possible indicators of abuse.

It has always been difficult to navigate the adolescent years, but today the waters seem more dangerous than ever. We will touch on only a few challenges.

Teenage Sexuality and Pregnancy. By age 15, about half of all African American men have had sexual intercourse; half of all Hispanic and White men by age 17. For women, the ages are a bit higher. Half of all African American women have had intercourse by age 17 and half of all Hispanic and White women by age 18 (Michael, Gagnon, Laumann, & Kolata, 1994). About 40% of boys and 30% of girls have had their first sexual intercourse by 9th grade (U.S. Department of Health and Human Services, 1997). The emotional impact of these early sexual experiences may have repercussions in the school, both for the students involved and for fellow students who hear about the experiences. One consequence of this early sexual activity is unexpected and unwanted pregnancy. Each year, more than one million teenage girls become pregnant—30,000 of them are younger than 15 years old. By age 18, one quarter of all girls in the United States have been pregnant at least once (DeRidder, 1993; Scarr, Weinberg, & Levine, 1986). The adolescent pregnancy rate in the United States is the highest among industrialized societies (Rice, 1999).

A remarkable number of American adolescents have little information, or indeed the wrong information, about birth control. For example, about one-half of the adolescent girls who become pregnant do so in their first six months of sexual activity; often, they haven't decided yet what to do about birth control, partly because they don't expect anything to happen so quickly. It can! Some adults fear that giving adolescents accurate information about sex will encourage them to experiment. Research indicates that the main effect of providing the facts appears to be fewer unwanted pregnancies (Brooks-Gunn & Furstenberg, 1989; DeRidder, 1993).

Eating Disorders. Adolescents going through the changes of puberty are very concerned about their bodies. This has always been true, but today, the emphasis on

Connect & Extend
To the research
Peterson, M. P. (1993). Physical and sexual abuse among school children: Prevalence and prevention. *Educational Psychology Review, 5,* 63–86. Bear, T., Schenk, S., & Buckner, L. (1993). Supporting victims of child abuse. *Educational Leadership, 50*(4), 44.

Connect & Extend
To the research
DeRidder, L. M. (1993). Teenage pregnancy: Etiology and educational interventions. *Educational Psychology Review, 5,* 87–107.

TABLE 3.7 *Indicators of Child Abuse*

The following are some of the signs of abuse. Not every child with these signs is abused, but these indicators should be investigated.

	Physical Indicators	Behavioral Indicators	
Physical Abuse	• Unexplained bruises (in various stages of healing), welts, human bite marks, bald spots • Unexplained burns, especially cigarette burns or immersion-burns (glovelike) • Unexplained fractures, lacerations, or abrasions	• Self-destructive • Withdrawn and aggressive—behavioral extremes • Uncomfortable with physical contact • Arrives at school early or stays late, as if afraid	• Chronic runaway (adolescents) • Complains of soreness or moves uncomfortably • Wears clothing inappropriate to weather, to cover body
Physical Neglect	• Abandonment • Unattended medical needs • Consistent lack of supervision • Consistent hunger, inappropriate dress, poor hygiene • Lice, distended stomach, emaciation	• Regularly displays fatigue or listlessness, falls asleep in class • Steals food, begs from classmates • Reports that no caretaker is at home	• Frequently absent or tardy • Self-destructive • School dropout (adolescents)
Sexual Abuse	• Torn, stained, or bloodied underclothing • Pain or itching in genital area • Difficulty walking or sitting • Bruises or bleeding in external genitalia • Venereal disease • Frequent urinary or yeast infections	• Withdrawn, chronic depression • Excessive seductiveness • Role reversal, overly concerned for siblings • Poor self-esteem, self-devaluation, lack of confidence • Peer problems, lack of involvement • Massive weight change	• Suicide attempts (especially adolescents) • Hysteria, lack of emotional control • Sudden school difficulties • Inappropriate sex play or premature understanding of sex • Threatened by physical contact, closeness • Promiscuity

Source: From "Supporting Victims of Child Abuse," by T. Bear, S. Schenk, and L. Buckner, 1993, *Educational Leadership, 50*(4), p. 44. Copyright © 1993 by the Association for Supervision and Curriculum Development. Reprinted with permission. All rights reserved.

Bulimia: Eating disorder characterized by overeating, then getting rid of the food by self-induced vomiting or laxatives.

Anorexia Nervosa: Eating disorder characterized by very limited food intake.

fitness and appearance makes adolescents even more likely to worry about how their bodies "measure up." For some, the concern becomes excessive. One consequence is eating disorders such as **bulimia** (binge eating) and **anorexia nervosa** (self-starvation), both of which are much more common in females than in males. Bulimics often binge, eating an entire gallon of ice cream or a whole cake. Then, to avoid gaining weight, they force themselves to vomit, or they use strong laxatives, to purge themselves of the extra calories. Bulimics tend to maintain a normal weight, but their digestive systems can be permanently damaged.

Anorexia is an even more dangerous disorder, for anorexics refuse to eat or eat practically nothing while often exercising obsessively. In the process they may lose 20 to 25% of their body weight, and some (about 5 to 10%) literally starve themselves to death. Anorexic students may appear pale, have brittle fingernails, and have fine dark hairs developing all over their bodies. They are easily chilled because they have so little fat to insulate their bodies. They often are depressed, insecure, moody, and lonely. Girls may stop having their menstrual period. These eating disorders often begin in adolescence and are becoming more common—about 1% of adolescent girls become anorexic. These students usually require professional help—don't ignore the warning signs (Harris, 1991). Again, a teacher may be the person who begins the chain of help for students with these tragic problems.

Drug Abuse. Modern society makes growing up a very confusing process. Notice the messages from films and billboards. "Beautiful," popular people drink alcohol and smoke cigarettes with little concern for their health. We have over-the-counter drugs for almost every common ailment. Coffee wakes us up, and a pill helps us sleep. And then we tell students to "say no!" to drugs.

For many reasons, not just because of these contradictory messages, drug use has become a problem for students. Accurate statistics are hard to find, but estimates from the National Center for Education Statistics indicate that 92% of high school seniors report some experience with alcohol—66% using it in the past month. About 20% of seniors are daily smokers, and 30% have tried at least one illegal drug. Throughout the mid-1900s, drug use among 12- to 18-year-olds gradually increased (Lerner & Galambos, 1998).

What can be done about drug use among our students? First, we should distinguish between experimentation and abuse. Many students try something at a party but do not become regular users. The best way to help students who have trouble saying no appears to be through peer programs that teach how to say no assertively. The successful programs also teach general social skills and build self-esteem, are located in schools but run by community agencies, give intensive caring adult attention to individual students, and provide opportunities for work experiences (Lerner & Galambos, 1998). Also, the older students are when they experiment with drugs, the more likely they are to make responsible choices, so helping younger students say no is a clear benefit.

Suicide. Figure 3.2 on page 98 shows a steady climb in the number of suicides among males during adolescence. This suicide rate has tripled in the past 30 years.

Suicide often comes as a response to life problems—problems that parents and teachers sometimes dismiss. There are many warning signs that trouble is brewing. Watch for changes in eating or sleeping habits, weight, grades, disposition, activity level, or interest in friends. Students at risk sometimes suddenly give away prized possessions such as stereos, CDs, clothing, or pets. They may seem depressed or hyperactive and may say things

CHECKPOINT

Challenges for Children

Review

▶ How do students develop physically during the elementary years?

▶ Describe the worlds of the late-maturing adolescent boy and girl.

▶ What are key transitions for students?

▶ What are some danger signs of child abuse, eating disorders, and potential for suicide?

Apply

▶ How might you assess the physical and emotional risks Vanessa faces?

FIGURE 3.2

Suicide Rates among Adolescents

Between the age of 10 and the end of adolescence, the suicide rate for males increases dramatically. There is a much smaller increase for females.

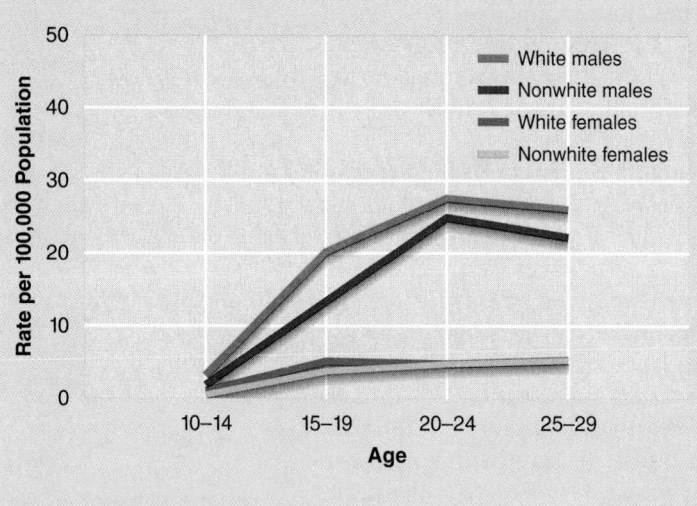

Source: U.S. Bureau of the Census, 1998.

like "Nothing matters anymore," "You won't have to worry about me anymore," or "I wonder what dying is like." They may start missing school or quit doing work. It is especially dangerous if the student not only talks about suicide, but also has a plan for acting.

If you suspect that there is a problem, talk to the student directly. One feeling shared by many people who attempt suicide is that no one really takes them seriously. "A question about suicide does not provoke suicide. Indeed, teens (and adults) often experience relief when someone finally cares enough to ask" (Range, 1993, p. 145). Be realistic, not poetic, about suicide. Ask about specifics, and take the student seriously. Also, be aware that teenage suicides often occur in clusters. After one student acts or when stories about a suicide are reported in the media, other teens are more likely to copy the suicide (Lewinsohn, Rohde, & Seeley, 1994). Table 3.8 lists common myths and facts about suicide.

This has been a brief, selective look at the needs of children. As we saw earlier, educators and psychologists are concerned about providing a developmentally appropriate education for preschool students. All students, whatever their age, require an education that fits their physical, cognitive, personal, and social levels of development.

TABLE 3.8 *Myths and Facts about Suicide*

Myth:	People who talk about suicide don't kill themselves.
Fact:	Eight out of ten people who commit suicide tell someone that they're thinking about hurting themselves before they actually do it.
Myth:	Only certain types of people commit suicide.
Fact:	All types of people commit suicide—male and female, young and old, rich and poor, country people and city people. It happens in every racial, ethnic, and religious group.
Myth:	When a person talks about suicide, you should change the subject to get his or her mind off it.
Fact:	You should take them seriously. Listen carefully to what they are saying. Give them a chance to express their feelings. Let them know you are concerned. And help them get help.
Myth:	Most people who kill themselves really want to die.
Fact:	Most people who kill themselves are confused about whether they want to die. Suicide is often intended as a cry for help.

Source: From *Changing Bodies, Changing Lives: A Book for Teens on Sex and Relationships* (p. 142), by R. Bell, 1980, New York: Random House.

$\mathcal{S}$ummary

The Work of Erikson

Why is Erikson's theory considered a psychosocial perspective?

Erikson was interested in the ways that individuals developed psychologically to become active and contributing members of society. He believed that all humans have the same basic needs and that each society must accommodate those needs. Erikson's emphasis on the relationship between society and the individual is a psychosocial theory of development—a theory that connects personal development (psycho) the social environment (social).

What are Erikson's stages of psychosocial development?

Erikson believed that people go through eight life stages between infancy and old age, each of which involves a central crisis. Adequate resolution of each crisis leads to greater personal and social competence and a stronger foundation for solving future crises. In the first two stages, an infant must develop a sense of trust over mistrust and a sense of autonomy over shame and doubt. In early childhood, the focus of the third stage is on developing initiative and avoiding feelings of guilt. In the child's elementary school years, the fourth stage involves achieving a sense of industry and avoiding feelings of inferiority. In the fifth stage, identity versus role confusion, adolescents consciously attempt to solidify their identity. According to Marcia, these efforts may lead to identity achievement, foreclosure, diffusion, or moratorium. Erikson's three stages of adulthood involve struggles to achieve intimacy, generativity, and integrity.

Understanding Ourselves and Others

Distinguish between self-concept and self-esteem.

Both self-concept and self-esteem are beliefs about the self. Self-concept is our attempt to explain ourselves to ourselves, to build a scheme that organizes our impressions, feelings, and attitudes about ourselves. But this model is not fixed or permanent. Our self-perceptions vary from situation to situation and from one phase of our lives to another. Self-esteem is an affective reaction—an evaluation of who you are. If people evaluate themselves positively—if they "like what they see"—we say that they have high self-esteem. Self-concept and self-esteem are often used interchangeably, even though they have distinct meanings. Self-concept is a cognitive structure and self-esteem is an affective evaluation.

How do self-concept and self-esteem change as children develop?

Self-concept (definition of self) and self-esteem (valuing of self) become increasingly complex, differentiated, and abstract as we mature. Self-concept evolves through constant self-reflection, social interaction, and experiences in and out of school. Students develop a self-concept by comparing themselves to personal (internal) standards and social (external) standards. The self-esteem of middle and junior high school students becomes more tied to physical appearance and social acceptance. High self-esteem is related to better overall school experience, both academically and socially. Gender and ethnic stereotypes are significant factors as well. Teachers can have a profound effect on students' self-concept and self-esteem.

How do perspective-taking skills change as students mature?

An understanding of intentions develops as children mature, but aggressive students often have trouble understanding the intentions of others. Social perspective-taking also changes as we mature. Young children believe that everyone has the same thoughts and feelings they do. Later, they learn that others have separate identities and therefore separate feelings and perspectives on events.

Moral Development

What are the key differences among the preconventional, conventional, and postconventional levels of moral reasoning?

Lawrence Kohlberg's theory of moral development includes three levels: (1) a preconventional level, where judgments are based on self-interest; (2) a conventional level, where judgments are based on traditional family values and social expectations; and (3) a postconventional level, where judgments are based on more abstract and personal ethical principles. Kohlberg has evaluated the moral reasoning of both children and adults by presenting them with moral dilemmas, or hypothetical situations in which people must make difficult decisions. Critics suggest that Kohlberg's view does not account for possible sex differences in moral reasoning or differences between moral reasoning and moral behavior.

Describe Gilligan's levels of moral reasoning.

Carol Gilligan has suggested that because Kohlberg's stage theory was based on a longitudinal study of men only, it is very possible that the moral reasoning of women and the stages of women's development are not adequately represented. She has proposed a different sequence of moral development, an "ethic of care." Gilligan believes that individuals move from a focus on self-interests to moral reasoning based on commitment to specific individuals and relationships, and then to the highest level of morality based on the principles of responsibility and care for all people. There is some evidence that in everyday life, women feel more guilty about violating caring norms (being inconsiderate or untrustworthy) and men feel more guilty when they show violent behaviors (fighting or damaging property). Women are somewhat more likely to use a care orientation, but studies also show that both men and women *can* use both orientations.

What influences moral behavior?

Others first control young children's moral behavior through direct instruction, supervision, rewards and punishments, and correction. In time, children internalize the moral rules and principles of the authority figures who have guided them; that is, children adopt the external standards as their own. If children are given reasons they can understand when they are corrected—particularly reasons that highlight the effects of actions on others—then they are more likely to internalize moral principles. A second important influence on the development of moral behavior is modeling. Children who have been consistently exposed to caring, generous adult models will tend to be more concerned for the rights and feelings of others. The world and the media provide many negative models of behavior. Some schools have adopted programs to increase students' capacity to care for others. Cheating and aggression are two common behavior problems in the schools that involve moral issues.

Socialization: The Home and the School

What challenges face children whose parents are divorced?

During the divorce itself, conflict may increase as property and custody rights are being decided. After the divorce, the custodial parent may have to move to a less expensive home, find new sources of income, go to work for the first time, or work longer hours. For the child, this can mean leaving behind important friendships in the old neighborhood or school just when support is needed the most, having only one parent who has less time than ever to be with the children, or adjusting to new family structures when parents remarry.

Why are peer relations important?

Peer relationships play a significant role in healthy personal and social development. There is strong evidence that adults who had close friends as children have higher self-esteem and are more capable of maintaining intimate relationships than adults who spent lonely childhoods. Adults who were rejected as children tend to have more problems, such as dropping out of school or committing crimes.

Challenges for Children

How do students develop physically during the elementary years?

During the preschool years there is rapid development of children's gross- and fine-motor skills. During the elementary school years, physical development is fairly steady. Children become taller, leaner, and stronger, so they are better able to master sports and games. There is tremendous variation, however. A particular child can be much larger or smaller than average and still be perfectly healthy. Throughout elementary school, many of the girls are likely to be as large as or larger than the boys in their classes. Between the ages of 11 and 14, girls are, on the average, taller and heavier than boys of the same age.

Describe the worlds of the late-maturing adolescent boy and girl.

Early maturation seems to have certain special advantages for boys. The early maturers' taller, broader-shouldered body type fits the cultural stereotype for the male ideal. Early-maturing boys are more likely to enjoy high social status; they tend to be popular and to be leaders. For girls, these effects are reversed. Being larger than everyone else in the class is not a valued characteristic for girls in many cultures. A girl who begins to mature early probably will be the first in her peer group to start the changes of puberty. This can be very upsetting to some girls. Later-maturing girls seem to have fewer problems, but they may worry that something is wrong with them. All students

can benefit from knowing that the "normal" range in rates of maturation is great and that there are advantages for both early and late maturers.

What are key transitions for students?

Transition to kindergarten or 1st grade requires new social roles—children must fit into the group and learn to be students. Evaluation is built into school and success is not guaranteed. The basis for reward and recognition changes as children move from their families to school. In school, children are compared to each other. Different student characteristics are noticed—ones that may not have mattered before because they were shared by family members. How well students do in the primary grades matters more for their future success than does their school performance at any other time. The next transition is to middle school, just as students are undergoing great physical and cognitive changes. Just after a transition to a new school, especially the transition to junior high school, students' self-concepts seem to become more negative and less stable. When young adolescents move from being the most mature and highest status students in a small, familiar elementary school to being the bottom of the chain in a large, impersonal junior high school, there may be negative consequences.

What are some danger signs of child abuse, eating disorders, and potential for suicide?

Signs of abuse or neglect include unexplained bruises, burns, bites, or other injuries and fatigue, depression, frequent absences, poor hygiene, inappropriate clothing, problems with peers and many others (see Table 3.7). Teachers must report suspected cases of child abuse and can be instrumental in helping students cope with other risks as well. Anorexic students may appear pale, have brittle fingernails, and have fine dark hairs developing all over their bodies. They are easily chilled because they have so little fat to insulate their bodies. They often are depressed, insecure, moody, and lonely. Girls may stop having their menstrual period. Students at risk of suicide may show changes in eating or sleeping habits, weight, grades, disposition, activity level, or interest in friends. They sometimes suddenly give away prized possessions such as stereos, CDs, clothing, or pets. They may seem depressed or hyperactive and may start missing school or quit doing work. It is especially dangerous if the student not only talks about suicide, but also has a plan for action.

Key Terms

aggression, p. 83
anorexia nervosa, p. 96
autonomy, p. 66
blended families, p. 85
bulimia, p. 96
collective self-esteem, p. 75
developmental crisis, p. 64
ethnic pride, p. 75
fine-motor skills, p. 89
generativity, p. 70

gross-motor skills, p. 89
identity, p. 68
identity achievement, p. 68
identity diffusion, p. 68
identity foreclosure, p. 68
industry, p. 66
initiative, p. 66
integrity, p. 70
internalize, p. 81
moral dilemmas, p. 78

moral realism, p. 77
moral reasoning, p. 78
morality of cooperation, p. 77
moratorium, p. 68
perspective-taking ability, p. 77
psychosocial, p. 64
puberty, p. 91
self-concept, p. 71
self-esteem, p. 71
socialization, p. 85

Becoming a Professional

Reflecting on the Chapter

Can you apply the ideas from this chapter on personal/social development to solve the following problems of practice?

Preschool and Kindergarten

▶ Elise and Donis have always been two of the most cooperative students in your 4-year-old group. But both will soon have new babies in their families, and as the time draws nearer, they are becoming more and more disruptive. What would you do?

Elementary and Middle School

▶ You notice a fairly dramatic change in one of your students. This boy seems very tired and anxious, and he is not doing his homework. The situation has gone on for a few weeks now. How would you approach this problem?

Junior High and High School

▶ Several of your junior high school students are afraid to go to gym class

because a gang of students has been extorting money and personal possessions. What steps would you take to end this situation?

▶ You hear from one of your students that a group of seniors has a small "business" selling college application essays. What would you do?

Certification Test Requirements

▶ Be clear about the difference between self-esteem and self-concept.

▶ Make sure you understand the elements of Kohlberg's theory and his three stages of moral reasoning, as well as Gilligan's alternative theory.

▶ Understand the range of family structures today.

▶ Be familiar with indicators of child abuse and neglect and your legal responsibilities.

Your Teaching Portfolio

Think about your philosophy of teaching, a question you will be asked at

most job interviews. What do you believe about teaching values and moral behavior? How can you support the development of genuine and well-founded self-esteem in your students? (Consult Table 3.3 for ideas.)

Add some ideas for parent involvement from this chapter to your **Portfolio**.

Teaching Resources

Adapt Table 3.5, *Using "Caring for Strangers and the World" as a Teaching Theme*, for the grades and subjects you might teach and add it to your **Teaching Resources** file.

Add Table 3.7, *Indicators of Child Abuse*, to your **Teaching Resources** file.

What Would They Do?

Here is how some practicing teachers responded to the teaching situation presented at the beginning of this chapter about Vanessa, a student with few friends.

MARÍA ELENA RAMOS

Third Grade Teacher
Instituto San Roberto, Monterrey, N.L. Mexico

After telling the school's psychologist to call Vanessa in, I would invite her to have lunch with me and involve her in interesting activities in class that would include only her and make these activities seem interesting to others. Later I would let her be in charge of these activities as the organizer. The activities' characteristics should involve personal feelings, decisions, attitudes, and traits, which would provide the other students with the opportunitiy to get know her better.

STEWART GILL

Former Eighth Grade Teacher and Guidance Counselor
Hudson City School District, Hudson, New York

Vanessa could use someone to talk with who would be steadfast and noncritical, so I would use the drop in grades as a reason to meet with her. I would ask her to meet with me regularly to work on improving her performance in class. Since Vanessa seems to talk freely, I would expect that her feelings would come out readily. This would give her a sounding board for her frustrations and let her experience acceptance from an ally whom she could trust.

Since Vanessa doesn't seem to "fit in" with her classmates, I would also direct her to biographical literature describing some of the many successful individuals who were regarded as misfits in their early years.

If Vanessa did not respond positively, but seemed deeply depressed, I would involve as many others as I could think of, including parents, counselors, and other teachers.

CONSTANCE CARTER, MARY PHILLIPS, AND DIANE BATTY

Orono High School, Orono, Maine

We've all had students like Vanessa in our classes. Our concerns for her would be that in spite of being a reasonably good student, it might not be enough to compensate for losing out on the social aspect of school. Social issues are very important, almost a matter of life or death for students at this age. Vanessa might go overboard trying to come up with friends and make poor choices simply to impress peers.

With a student like this, teachers should watch for certain warning signals such as absences from school and decreased quality of work. If Vanessa feels like a failure already, a drop in her grades will only make her feel more like one. Listen for talk about feelings of helplessness, of "not fitting in." Other danger signs might be low affect, weight loss, or a drop in personal care. Watch her demeanor in class and in the halls.

A student like this might substitute risk-taking attempts, especially if she feels that academic risk-taking hasn't worked for her. She might substitute more dangerous risk-taking attempts, such as substance abuse or delinquent activities, to impress other students.

Many schools have resources available to help students like Vanessa. Our school has a student assistance team, which is a group of faculty that meets with students who are having difficulty surviving: The team takes a supportive, not a punitive, standpoint. We would encourage Vanessa to get involved in peer groups to develop healthy friendships and to keep in touch with a guidance counselor. Extracurricular activities can also be a wonderful way to develop self-esteem and a sense of belonging in students who otherwise feel cut off from school life.

A student like this might benefit from developing a one-on-one relationship with a counselor who could serve as her advocate. A job at school, even being responsible for one simple errand a day, can be an excellent way to encourage a student's feeling of worthiness. If Vanessa can be helped to feel that her presence each day at school is important, that her being there made the day better, it could have a very positive impact on her life.

SUSAN B. STRAUSS

Principal
Lincoln High School, Lincoln, Rhode Island

Any time a student's work, attitude, or appearance show a continuing change from their regular appearance and routine, it is a "heads-up" notice for concern. Her neediness of others may be an indicator of problems at home—a dysfunctional family, neglect, or abuse. A student such as Vanessa, who relies on others for her feelings of self-worth, may start to question whether there is any point to trying to get good grades, keeping up a good appearance, or even, at the extreme, living at all. It is likely that Vanessa has very negative feelings about herself, and probably doubts that she has any value to anyone.

Whenever a student displays behaviors that are attention-seeking, it is because something is missing and/or wrong in his or her own life. These described behaviors are, in themselves, "danger signs," and having been alerted by them, I would be sure to monitor Vanessa for any increasing displays of the behaviors already observed, as well as being watchful for any signs of withdrawal, self-inflicted injury, or radical mood swings. Utilizing a strategy of collegial brainstorming for student support, I would contact the student's guidance counselor to arrange a meeting of Vanessa's teachers as well as the school social worker and psychologist. Have her behaviors been observed in all classes? Is there any other student who seems to take a genuine interest in Vanessa? Is there a teacher with whom Vanessa has bonded? Such a meeting can help to focus on what the observable behaviors have been and to identify a variety of creative options to help address the issue. It is also an opportunity for the social worker to determine if a social history is needed. At the classroom level, I would seek out the assistance of peer leaders—students, who by their nature, have an interest in helping others—and find ways to provide for cooperative learning activities that will, through the natural classroom learning environment, offer nonthreatening opportunities for interaction.

THOMAS O'DONNELL

Social Studies Chairperson, Grades 7–12
Malden High School, Malden, Massachusetts

The concerns are Vanessa's self-image and interpersonal relationships. I would turn to adjustment personnel, guidance personnel, and parents to alert them and have them use their expertise.

I might try counseling her one-on-one if I felt confident and comfortable under the circumstances. Seating arrangements and cooperative learning situations might help Vanessa develop some relationships. I might encourage her to join extracurricular activities where she can make contributions and form some attachments.

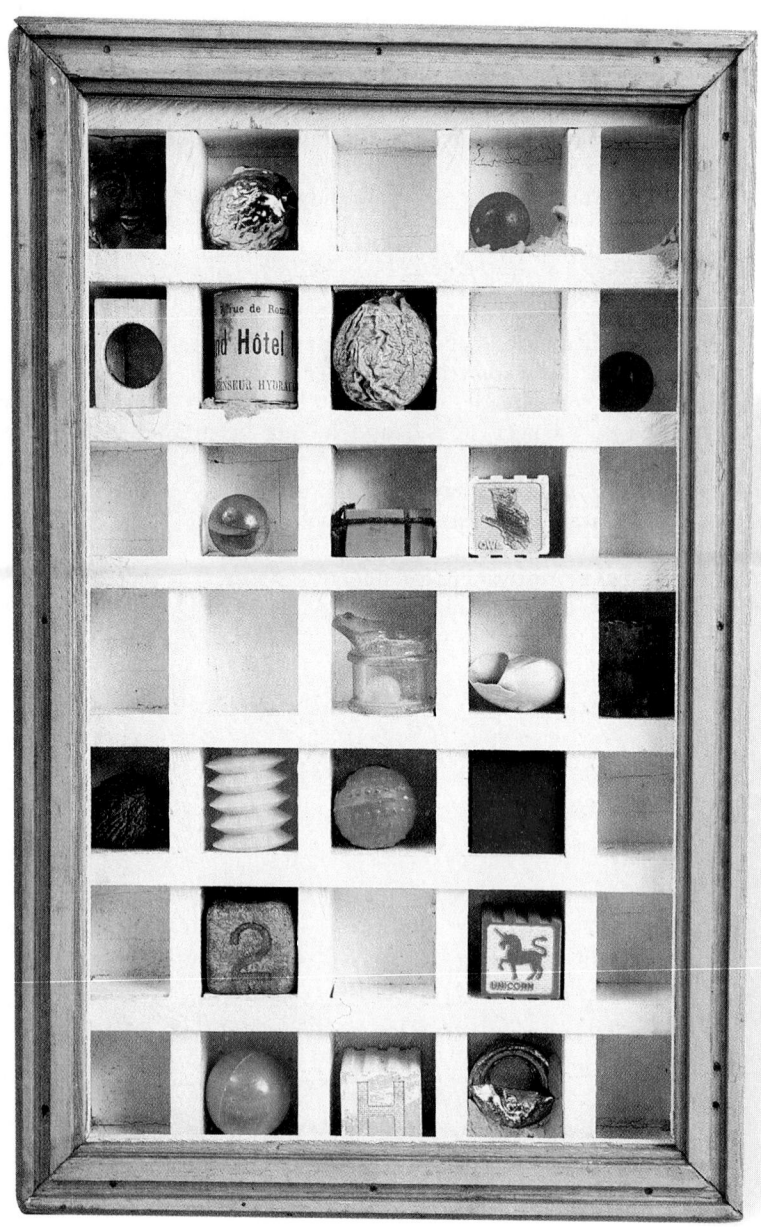

Learner Differences

*H*ave you ever had the experience of being the only one in a group who had trouble doing something? How would you feel if every day in school you faced the same kind of difficulty, while everyone else seemed to find the work easier than you? What kind of support and teaching would you need to keep trying?

So far we have talked little about individuals. We have discussed principles of development that apply to everyone—stages, processes, conflicts, and tasks. Our development as human beings is similar in many ways, but not in every way. Even among members of the same family, there are marked contrasts in appearance, interests, abilities, and temperament.

We will begin our discussion of individual differences in learning with a look at the names and labels that have been applied to some students. Then we turn to an extended examination of intellectual abilities, which vary so greatly from individual to individual and have proved so difficult to define and measure. How can teachers work with such a wide range of abilities? Is ability grouping a good answer? What are the special needs of the gifted and how can teachers encourage creativity in all students? How do individual cognitive styles and learning preferences affect learning?

Recent changes in federal legislation mean that you probably will have at least one exceptional student in your class, whatever grade you teach. We explore both the prevalent and less frequently occurring learning problems students may have. As we discuss each problem area, we will consider how a teacher might recognize problems, seek help from school and community resources, and plan instruction based on individuals' needs. By the time you have completed this chapter, you should be able to:

▶ Discuss the potential problems in categorizing and labeling students.
▶ Begin to develop a personal concept of intelligence.
▶ Discuss how you might recognize and teach students who are gifted.
▶ Adapt lessons for students with varying learning styles.
▶ Discuss the implications of the Individuals with Disabilities Act for your teaching.
▶ List indicators of hearing, vision, language, and behavior problems, as well as indicators of specific learning disabilities.

What Would You Do?

Stuffed in your (undersized) mail box in the school office is a large, official-looking envelope. There seems to be one in almost every box. Inside are computer printouts with the results of the fall testing, including scores on a group test of intelligence for all the 7th- and 8th-grade students in your advisory section. Also in your box are notes from two parents who must have already heard that the test results are in. They want to meet with you to see their child's scores, and especially, as one parent put it, "To find out how smart Jason really is." You look at the printouts and at the notes, wondering what you should do with the results.

▶ How will you use this information?

▶ What do the intelligence test scores tell you about your students?

▶ How would you respond to the notes from the parents? Will you share the scores with the parents?

Language and Labeling

When labels take precedence over individual characteristics, the labels themselves constitute a handicap. Stereotypes about people who use wheelchairs might interfere with recognition of this girl's other characteristics and her individuality. ▼

Every child is a distinctive collection of talents, abilities, and limitations. In that sense they all are "exceptional." But some students are called exceptional because they have learning disabilities or problems and require special services to reach their potential. **Exceptional students** may have learning disabilities, communication disorders, emotional or behavioral disorders, mental retardation, physical disabilities, impaired vision or difficulties hearing, autism, traumatic brain injury, or special abilities and talents. Even though we will use these terms throughout the chapter, a caution is in order: Labeling students is a controversial issue.

A label does not tell which methods to use with individual students. For example, few specific "treatments" automatically follow from a "diagnosis" of mental retardation; many different teaching strategies and materials are appropriate. Further, the labels can become self-fulfilling prophecies. Everyone—teachers, parents, classmates, and even the students themselves—may see a label as a stigma that cannot be changed. Finally, labels are mistaken for explanations, as in, "Mitchell gets into fights because he has a behavior disorder." "How do you know he has a behavior disorder?" "Because he gets into fights."

On the other hand, some educators argue that for younger students, at least, being labeled as "special" protects the child. For example, if classmates know a student has mental retardation (sometimes called a cognitive disability), they will be more willing to accept his or her behaviors. Of course, labels still open doors to some special programs, useful information, special technology and equipment, or financial assistance. Labels probably both stigmatize and help students (Heward & Orlansky, 1992; Keogh & MacMillan, 1996).

This caution also applies to many of the common descriptions heard in schools every day. Today many people object to labels such as "mentally retarded student" or "at-risk student" because describing a complex person with one or two words implies that the condition labeled is the most important aspect of the person. Actually the individual has many abilities, and to focus on the disability is to misrepresent the individual. An alternative is "person-first" language or speaking of "students with mental retardation" or "students placed at risk." Here the emphasis is on the students first, not on the special challenges they face. Figure 4.1 summarizes examples of person-first language.

One more distinction in language is important. A **disability** is just what the word implies—an inability to do something specific such as see or walk. A **handicap** is a disadvantage in certain situations. Some disabilities lead to handicaps, but not in all contexts. For example, being blind (a visual disability) is a handicap if you want to drive a car. But blindness is not a handicap when you are

CHECKPOINT

Language and Labeling

Review

▶ What are the advantages and problems with labels?

▶ What is person-first language?

▶ Distinguish between a disability and a handicap.

Apply

▶ Do your professors use person-first language?

FIGURE 4.1

Examples of Person-First Language
Here are some ways to be sure your language puts the student first.

Examples of Person-First Language

A student with a disability	NOT ➡	A disabled student
Children receiving special education	NOT ➡	Special education children
A man who has cerebral palsy	NOT ➡	A cerebral palsy sufferer
A child with a specific learning disability	NOT ➡	A learning disabled child
The boy with Down syndrome	NOT ➡	The Down syndrome boy
People who are physically disabled	NOT ➡	Physically disabled people
She has epilepsy	NOT ➡	She is epileptic

◆◆◆◆◆

Avoid Using Stigmatizing Terminology (Examples)

Afflicted with . . .	Hare lip	Retardate
Crippled	Hearing impaired	Trainable mentally retarded
Deviant	Mute	Victimized by . . .
Handicapped	Orthopedically impaired	

Source: Adapted from *Child and Adolescent Development for Educators* (p. 392), by J. L. Meece, 1997, New York: McGraw-Hill. Copyright © 1997 McGraw-Hill Companies. Adapted with permission.

Exceptional Students: Students who have abilities or problems so significant that the students require special education or other services to reach their potential.

Disability: The inability to do something specific such as walk or hear.

Handicap: A disadvantage in a particular situation, sometimes caused by a disability.

composing music or talking on the telephone. Stephen Hawking, the greatest living physicist, sufferers from Lou Gehrig's disease and no longer can walk or talk. He once said that he is lucky that he became a theoretical physicist "because it is all in the mind. So my disability has not been a serious handicap." It is important that we do not *create* handicaps for people by the way we react to their disabilities. Some educators have suggested that we drop the word "handicap" altogether because the source of the word is demeaning. *Handicap* came from the phrase "cap-in-hand," used to describe people with disabilities who once were forced to beg just to survive (Hardman, Drew, & Egan, 1999).

In the next section we consider a concept that has provided the basis for many labels—intelligence.

*I*ndividual Differences in Intelligence

Because the concept of intelligence is so important in education, so controversial, and so often misunderstood, we will spend quite a few pages discussing it. Let us begin with a basic question.

What Does Intelligence Mean?

The idea that people vary in what we call **intelligence** has been with us for a long time. Plato discussed similar variations over 2,000 years ago. Most early theories about the nature of intelligence involved one or more of the following three themes: (1) the capacity to learn; (2) the total knowledge a person has acquired; and (3) the ability to adapt successfully to new situations and to the environment in general.

In this century, there has been considerable controversy over the meaning of intelligence. In 1986 at a symposium on intelligence, 24 psychologists offered 24 different views about the nature of intelligence (Neisser et al., 1996; Sternberg & Detterman, 1986). Over half of the experts mentioned higher-level thinking processes such as abstract reasoning, problem solving, and decision making as important aspects of intelligence, and they added metacognition or knowledge of self to earlier views. But they disagreed about the structure of intelligence—whether it is a single ability or many separate abilities (Gustafsson & Undheim, 1996, Sternberg & Kaufman, 1998).

Intelligence: One Ability or Many? Some theorists believe intelligence is a basic ability that affects performance on all cognitively oriented tasks from computing mathematical problems to writing poetry or solving riddles. Evidence for this position comes from correlational evaluations of intelligence tests. In study after study, moderate to high positive correlations are found among all the different tests that are designed to measure separate intellectual abilities (Lohman, 1989; McNemar, 1964). What could explain these results?

Charles Spearman (1927) suggested there is one mental attribute, which he called *g* or *general intelligence*, that is used to perform any mental test, but that each test also requires some specific abilities in addition to *g*. For example, memory for a series of numbers probably involves both *g* and some specific ability for immediate recall of what is heard. Spearman assumed that individuals vary in both general intelligence and specific abilities, and that together these factors determine performance on mental tasks. A current version of the general plus specific abilities theory is John Carroll's (1993) work identifying a few broad abilities (such as learning and memory, visual perception, verbal fluency) and at least 70 specific abilities. The most widely accepted view today is that intelligence, like self-concept, has many facets and is a hierarchy of abilities, with general ability at the top and more specific abilities at lower levels of the hierarchy (Sternberg, 1998). General ability may be related to the maturation and functioning of the frontal lobe of the brain, while specific abilities may be connected to other parts of the brain (Byrnes & Fox, 1998).

Multiple Intelligences. In spite of the correlations among the various tests of different abilities, some psychologists insist that there are several separate "primary mental abilities." Years ago, Thurstone (1938) listed verbal comprehension, memory, reasoning, ability to visualize spatial relationships, numerical ability, word fluency, and perceptual speed as the major mental abilities underlying intellectual tasks. J. P. Guilford (1988) and Howard Gardner (1983) are the most prominent modern proponents of the concept of multiple cognitive abilities.

According to Gardner's (1983, 1993c) theory of **multiple intelligences**, there are at least eight separate intelligences: linguistic (verbal), musical, spatial, logical-mathematical, bodily-kinesthetic (movement), interpersonal (understanding others), intrapersonal (understanding self), and naturalist (observing and understanding natural and human-made patterns and systems) (see Figure 4.2 on page 110). Gardner stresses that there may be more kinds of intelligence—eight is not a magic number. At a recent meeting of the American Psychological Association, I heard him speculate that there may be a ninth—*existential intelligence* or the ability to ask big questions about the meaning of life (Gardner, 1999). He bases his notion of separate abilities in part on evidence that brain damage (from a stroke, for example) often interferes with functioning in one area, such as language, but does not affect functioning in other areas. Also, individuals may excel in one of these eight or nine areas but have no remarkable abilities in the other seven. Still, these "separate abilities" may not be so separate after all. Recent evidence linking musical and spatial abilities has prompted Gardner to consider that there may be connections among the intelligences (Gardner, 1998). Stay tuned for more developments.

What are these intelligences? Gardner (1998, 1999) contends that an intelligence is the ability to solve problems and create products or outcomes that are valued by a culture. Varying cultures and eras of history place different values on the eight intelligences. A naturalist intelligence is critical in farming cultures, whereas verbal and mathematical intelligences are important in technological cultures. In addition, Gardner believes that intelligence has a biological basis. Intelligence "is a biological and psychological potential; that potential is capable of being realized to a greater or lesser extent as a consequence of the experiential, cultural, and motivational factors that affect a person" (1998, p. 62). Some critics suggest that Gardner's multiple intelligences are really multiple talents (Sternberg, 1985). But Gardner rejects the distinction between talent and intelligence. He believes that our common notion of intelligence "is simply a certain set of talents in the linguistic and/or logical-mathematical spheres" (1998, p. 63).

Gardner (1998) has identified a number of myths and misconceptions about multiple intelligence theory and schooling. One is that intelligences are the same as learning styles (Gardner doesn't believe that people actually have consistent learning styles). Another misconception is that multiple intelligence theory disproves the idea of *g*. Gardner does not deny the existence of a general ability, but does question how useful *g* is as an explanation for human achievements.

▲ *Howard Gardner's theory of multiple intelligences proposes that there are several kinds of intelligences, and that they may be affected by culture, biology, and other factors.*

Multiple Intelligences: In Gardner's theory of intelligence, a person's eight separate abilities: logical-mathematical, verbal, musical, spatial, bodily-kinesthetic, interpersonal, intrapersonal, and naturalist.

FIGURE 4.2

Eight Intelligences

Howard Gardner's theory of multiple intelligences suggests that there are eight kinds of human abilities. An individual might have strengths or weaknesses in one or several areas.

Intelligence	End States	Core Components
Logical-mathematical	Scientist Mathematician	Sensitivity to, and capacity to discern, logical or numerical patterns; ability to handle long chains of reasoning.
Linguistic	Poet Journalist	Sensitivity to the sounds, rhythms, and meanings of words; sensitivity to the different functions of language.
Musical	Composer Violinist	Abilities to produce and appreciate rhythm, pitch, and timbre; appreciation of the forms of musical expressiveness.
Spatial	Navigator Sculptor	Capacities to perceive the visual-spatial world accurately and to perform transformations on one's initial perceptions.
Bodily-kinesthetic	Dancer Athlete	Abilities to control one's body movements and to handle objects skillfully.
Interpersonal	Therapist Salesman	Capacities to discern and respond appropriately to the moods, temperaments, motivations, and desires of other people.
Intrapersonal	Person with detailed, accurate self-knowledge	Access to one's own feelings and the ability to discriminate among them and draw on them to guide behavior; knowledge of one's own strengths, weaknesses, desires, and intelligence.
Naturalist	Botanist Farmer Hunter	Abilities to recognize plants and animals, to make distinctions in the natural world, to understand systems and define categories (perhaps even categories of intelligence).

Source: From "Multiple Intelligences Go to School," by H. Gardner and T. Hatch, 1989, *Educational Researcher, 18*(8), Figure p. 6. Copyright © 1989 by the American Educational Research Association. Reprinted with permission of the publisher. "Are There Additional Intelligences? The Case for the Naturalist, Spiritual, and Existential Intelligences," by H. Gardner (in press) in J. Kane (Ed.), *Educational Information and Transformation,* Saddle River, NJ: Prentice-Hall, Inc.

Multiple Intelligences Go to School. An advantage of the perspective is that it expands teachers' thinking about abilities and avenues for teaching, but the theory has been misused. Some teachers embrace a simplistic version of Gardner's theory. They include every "intelligence" in every lesson, no matter how inappropriate. Table

TABLE 4.1 *Misuses and Applications of Multiple Intelligence Theory*

Recently Howard Gardner described these negative and positive applications of his theory. The quotes are his words on the subject.

Misuses:

1. **Trying to teach all concepts or subjects using all intelligences:** "There is no point in assuming that every subject can be effectively approached in at least seven ways, and it is a waste of effort and time to attempt to do this."

2. **Assuming that it is enough just to apply a certain intelligence, no matter how you use it:** For bodily-kinesthetic intelligence, for example, "random muscle movements have nothing to do with the cultivation of the mind."

3. **Using an intelligence as a background for other activities,** such as playing music while students solve math problems. "The music's function is unlikely to be different from that of a dripping faucet or humming fan."

4. **Mixing intelligences with other desirable qualities:** For example, interpersonal intelligence "is often distorted as a license for cooperative learning," and intrapersonal intelligence "is often distorted as a rationale for self-esteem programs."

5. **Direct evaluation or even grading of intelligences without regard to context:** "I see little point in grading individuals in terms of how 'linguistic' or how 'bodily-kinesthetic' they are."

Good uses:

1. **The cultivation of desired capabilities:** "Schools should cultivate those skills and capabilities that are valued in the community and in the broader society."

2. **Approaching a concept, subject matter, discipline in a variety of ways:** Schools try to cover too much. "It makes far more sense to spend a significant amount of time on key concepts, generative ideas, and essential questions and to allow students to become familiar with these notions and their implications."

3. **The personalization of education:** "At the heart of the MI perspective—in theory and in practice—inheres in taking human difference seriously."

Source: "Reflections on Multiple Intelligences: Myths and Messages," by H. Gardner, 1998. In A. Woolfolk (Ed.), *Readings in Educational Psychology* (2nd ed.) (pp. 64–66), Boston: Allyn & Bacon. Copyright © 1998 by Phi Delta Kappan.

4.1 lists some misuses and positive applications of Gardner's work and Figure 4.3 on page 112 is an example of a lesson plan that appropriately incorporates multiple intelligences.

Many teachers and schools have embraced Gardner's ideas. However, there is not yet strong research evidence that adopting a multiple intelligences approach will enhance learning. In one of the few carefully designed evaluations, Callahan, Tomlinson, and Plucker (1997) found no significant gains in either achievement or self-concept for students who participated in START, a multiple intelligences approach to identifying and promoting talent in students who were at risk of failing. Learning is still hard work, even if there are multiple paths to knowledge.

Emotional Intelligence. We all know people who are academically or artistically talented, but unsuccessful. They have problems in school, in relationships, and on the job, but can't improve the situations. According to some psychologists, the source of the difficulties may be a lack of **emotional intelligence (EQ)**, defined as a

Emotional Intelligence (EQ): Abilities to monitor your own and others' feelings and emotions, and to use this information to guide thinking and actions.

Individual Differences in Intelligence   **111**

FIGURE 4.4

Sternberg's Triarchic Theory of Intelligence

Sternberg suggests that intelligent behavior is the product of applying thinking strategies, handling new problems creatively and quickly, and adapting to contexts by selecting and reshaping our environment.

	ANALYTIC Componential Intelligence	CREATIVE Experiential Intelligence	PRACTICAL Contextual Intelligence
Definition	Ability to think abstractly, process information; verbal abilities.	Ability to formulate new ideas and combine unrelated facts; creativity—ability to deal with novel situations and make new solutions automatic.	Ability to adapt to a changing environment and shape the environment to make the most of opportunities—problem solving in specific situations.
Examples	Solving analogies or syllogisms, learning vocabulary.	Diagnosing a problem with a car engine; finding resources for a new project.	Taking your telephone off the hook or putting a "do not disturb" sign on the door to limit distractions while studying.

Insight: The ability to deal effectively with novel situations.

Automaticity: The result of learning to perform a behavior or thinking process so thoroughly that the performance is automatic and does not require effort.

Tacit Knowledge: Knowing how rather than knowing that—knowledge that is more likely to be learned during everyday life than through formal schooling.

Mental Age: In intelligence testing, a score based on average abilities for that age group.

Intelligence Quotient (IQ): Score comparing mental and chronological ages.

Deviation IQ: Score based on statistical comparison of individual's performance with the average performance of others in that age group.

the persistent correlations among all types of mental tests. People who are effective in selecting good problem-solving strategies, monitoring progress, and moving to a new approach when the first one fails are more likely to be successful on all types of tests. Metacomponents may be a modern-day version of Spearman's *g*.

The second part of Sternberg's triarchic theory, *creative/experiential intelligence*, involves coping with new experiences. Intelligent behavior is marked by two characteristics: (1) **insight,** or the ability to deal effectively with novel situations, and (2) **automaticity**—the ability to become efficient and automatic in thinking and problem solving. Thus intelligence involves solving new problems as well as quickly turning new solutions into routine processes that can be applied without much cognitive effort.

The third part of Sternberg's theory, *practical /contextual intelligence*, highlights the importance of choosing to live and work in a context where success is likely, adapting to that context, and reshaping it if necessary. Here, culture is a major factor in defining successful choice, adaptation, and shaping. What works in one cultural group will not work in another. For example, abilities that make a person successful in a rural farm community may be useless in the inner city or at a country club in the suburbs. People who are successful often seek situations in which their abilities will be valuable, then work hard to capitalize on those abilities and compensate for any weaknesses. Thus, intelligence in this third sense involves practical matters such as career choice or social skills.

Practical intelligence is made up mostly of action-oriented **tacit knowledge.** This tacit knowledge is more likely to be learned during everyday life than through formal schooling and "takes the form of 'knowing how' rather than 'knowing that'" (Sternberg, Wagner, Williams, & Horvath, 1995, p. 916). Recently, however, Sternberg and his colleagues have designed a program for developing practical intelligence for school success by teaching students effective strategies for reading, writing, homework, and test taking (Sternberg & Kaufman, 1998; Williams et al., 1996).

How Is Intelligence Measured?

Connect & Extend
To history

For a concise discussion of the history of intelligence testing and the major theories of intelligence, see Chapter 3 of Sattler, J. (1992). *Assessment of children* (3rd ed. rev.). San Diego: Jerome Sattler Publisher.

Even though psychologists do not agree about what intelligence is, they do agree that intelligence, as measured by standard tests, is related to learning in school. Why is this so? It has to do in part with the way intelligence tests were first developed.

Binet's Dilemma. In 1904, Alfred Binet was confronted with the following problem by the minister of public instruction in Paris: How can students who will need special teaching and extra help be identified early in their school careers, before they fail in regular classes? Binet was also a political activist, very concerned with the rights of children. He believed that having an objective measure of learning ability could protect students from poor families who might be forced to leave school because they were the victims of discrimination and assumed to be slow learners.

Binet and his collaborator Theophile Simon wanted to measure not merely school achievement, but the intellectual skill students needed to do well in school. After trying many different tests and eliminating items that did not discriminate between successful and unsuccessful students, Binet and Simon finally identified 58 tests, several for each age group from 3 to 13. Binet's tests allowed the examiner to determine a **mental age** for a child. A child who succeeded on the items passed by most 6-year-olds, for example, was considered to have a mental age of 6, whether the child was actually 4, 6, or 8 years old.

Connect & Extend
To other chapters

The deviation IQ score takes into account variations in performance at different ages by calculating individual deviation from the age-group average. This idea is discussed more fully in Chapter 14.

The concept of **intelligence quotient,** or **IQ,** was added after Binet's test was brought to the United States and revised at Stanford University to give us the Stanford-Binet test. An IQ score was computed by comparing the mental-age score to the person's actual chronological age. The formula was

$$\text{Intelligence Quotient} = \text{Mental Age}/\text{Chronological Age} \times 100$$

The early Stanford-Binet has been revised four times, most recently in 1986 (Thorndike, Hagen, & Sattler, 1986). The practice of computing a mental age has proven to be problematic because IQ scores calculated on the basis of mental age do not have the same meaning as children get older. To cope with this problem, the concept of **deviation IQ** was introduced. The deviation IQ score is a number that tells exactly how much above or below the average a person scored on the test, compared to others in the same age group.

This boy is trying to arrange the red and white blocks so that they match the pattern in the booklet. His performance is timed. This subtest of the Wechsler Intelligence Scale for children assesses spatial ability. ▼

Group versus Individual IQ Tests. The Stanford-Binet is an individual intelligence test. It has to be administered to one student at a time by a trained psychologist and takes about two hours. Most of the questions are asked orally and do not require reading or writing. A student usually pays closer attention and is more motivated to do well when working directly with an adult. Psychologists also have developed group tests that can be given to whole classes or schools. Compared to an individual test, a group test is much *less* likely to yield an accurate picture of any one person's abilities. When students take tests in a group, they may do poorly because they do not understand the instructions, because their pencils break, because other students distract them, or because they do not shine on paper-and-pencil tests. *As a teacher, you should be very wary of IQ scores based on group tests.*

What Does an IQ Score Mean?

Most intelligence tests are designed so that they have certain statistical characteristics. For example, the average score is 100; 50% of the people from the general population who take the tests will score 100 or above, and 50% will score below 100. About 68% of the general population will earn IQ scores between 85 and 115. Only about 16% of the population will receive scores below 85, and only 16% will score above 115. Note, however, that these figures hold true for White, native-born Americans whose first language is Standard English. Whether IQ tests should even be used with ethnic minority-group students is hotly debated. The Guidelines below will help you interpret IQ scores realistically.

Intelligence and Achievement. Intelligence test scores predict achievement in schools quite well, at least for large groups. For example, the correlation is about .65 between school achievement and scores on a popular individual intelligence test, the revised Wechsler Intelligence Scale for Children (WISC-III) (Sattler, 1992). This isn't surprising because the tests were designed to predict school achievement. Remember, Binet threw out test items that did not discriminate between good and poor students.

Do people who score high on IQ tests achieve more in life? Here the answer is less clear. There is evidence that *g*, or general intelligence, correlates with "real-world

GUIDELINES

Interpreting IQ Scores

Check to see if the score is based on an individual or a group test. Be wary of group test scores.

Examples

1. Individual tests include the Wechsler Scales (WPPSI, WISC-III, WAIS-III, WAIS Abbreviated), the Stanford-Binet, the McCarthy Scales of Children's Abilities, the Woodcock-Johnson Psycho-Educational Battery, the Kaufman Assessment Battery for Children, the Kaufman Adolescent and Adult Intelligence Test (KAIT), and the Das-Naglieri Cognitive Assessment System.

2. Group tests include the Lorge-Thorndike Intelligence Tests, the Analysis of Learning Potential, the Kuhlman-Anderson Intelligence Tests, the Otis-Lennon Mental Abilities Tests, and the School and College Ability Tests (SCAT).

Remember that IQ tests are only estimates of general aptitude for learning.

Examples

1. Ignore small differences in scores among students.

2. Bear in mind that even an individual student's scores may change over time for many reasons, including measurement error.

3. Be aware that a total score is usually an average of scores on several kinds of questions. A score in the middle or average range may mean that the student performed at the average on every kind of question or that the student did quite well in some areas (for example, on verbal tasks) and rather poorly in other areas (for example, on quantitative tasks).

Remember that IQ scores reflect a student's past experiences and learning.

Examples

1. Consider these scores to be predictors of school abilities, not measures of innate intellectual abilities.

2. If a student is doing well in your class, do not change your opinion or lower your expectations just because one score seems low.

3. Be wary of IQ scores for minority students and for students whose first language was not English. Even scores on "culture-free" tests are lower for students placed at risk.

academic, social, and occupational accomplishments" (Ceci, 1991), but there is great debate about the size and meaning of these correlations (*Current Directions in Psychological Science*, 1993; McClelland, 1993). People with higher intelligence-test scores tend to complete more years of school and to have higher-status jobs. However, when the number of years of education is held constant, IQ scores and school achievement are not highly correlated with income and success in later life. Other factors such as motivation, social skills, emotional intelligence, and luck may make the difference (Goleman, 1995; Neisser et al., 1996; Sternberg & Wagner, 1993).

Intelligence: Heredity or Environment? Nowhere has the nature-versus-nurture debate raged so hard as in the area of intelligence. Should intelligence be seen as a potential, limited by our genetic makeup? Or does intelligence simply refer to an individual's current level of intellectual functioning, as fed and influenced by experience and education? In fact, it is almost impossible to separate intelligence "in the genes" from intelligence "due to experience." Today, most psychologists believe that *differences in intelligence are due to both heredity and environment, probably in about equal proportions for children*. "Genes do not fix behavior. Rather they establish a range of possible reactions to the range of possible experiences that the environment can provide" (Weinberg, 1989, p. 101). And environmental influences include everything from the health of a child's mother during pregnancy to the amount of lead in the child's home to the quality of teaching a child receives.

As a teacher, it is especially important for you to realize that cognitive skills, like any other skills, are always improvable. *Intelligence is a current state of affairs*, affected by past experiences and open to future changes. Even if intelligence is a limited potential, the potential is still quite large, and a challenge to all teachers. For example, Japanese and Chinese students know much more mathematics than American students, but their intelligence test scores are quite similar. This superiority in math probably is related to differences in the way mathematics is taught and studied in the three countries and to the self-motivation skills of many Asian students (Baron, 1998; Stevenson & Stigler, 1992).

CHECKPOINT

Individual Differences in Intelligence

Review

▶ What is *g*?

▶ What is Gardner's view of intelligence and his position on *g*?

▶ What are the elements of Sternberg's theory of intelligence?

▶ How is intelligence measured, and what does an IQ score mean?

Apply

▶ What will you tell Jason's parents about the meaning and uses of intelligence test scores?

▶ Explain your personal definition of intelligence.

▶ Give an original example of each of Gardner's eight intelligences.

Ability Differences and Teaching

In this section we consider how you might handle differences in academic ability in your classes. Is ability grouping a solution to the challenge of ability differences? The expressed goal of ability grouping is to make teaching more appropriate for students. As we will see, this does not always happen.

Connect & Extend
To the research
Slavin, R. E. (1990). Achievement effects of ability grouping in secondary schools: A best-evidence synthesis. *Review of Educational Research, 60,* 471–500.

Connect & Extend
To the research
A review of the research on ability grouping is: "Organizing Classes by Ability" (1987, July). *Harvard Education Letter, 3*(4), 1–4.

For a comprehensive review of research on the effects of between- and within-class ability grouping on the achievement of elementary school students, see Slavin, R. E. (1987). Ability grouping and student achievement in elementary schools: A best-evidence synthesis. *Review of Educational Research, 57,* 293–336.

For an examination of how tracking has persisted nationally in the middle grades, see Braddock, J. H. (1990). Tracking the middle grades: National patterns of grouping for instruction. *Phi Delta Kappan, 71,* 445–452.

Between-Class Ability Grouping

When whole classes are formed based on ability, the process is called **between-class ability grouping** or tracking, a common practice in secondary schools and some elementary schools as well. Most high schools have "college prep" courses and "general" courses or high-, middle-, and low-ability classes in a particular subject. Although this seems on the surface to be an efficient way to teach, research has consistently shown that segregation by ability may benefit high-ability students, but it causes problems for low-ability students (Garmon, Nystrand, Berends, & LePore, 1995; Good & Marshall, 1984; Slavin, 1987, 1990).

Low-ability classes seem to receive lower-quality instruction in general. Teachers tend to emphasize lower-level objectives and routine procedures, with less academic focus. Often there are more student behavior problems and, along with these problems, increased teacher stress and decreased enthusiasm. These differences in instruction and the teachers' negative attitudes may mean that low expectations are communicated to the students. Attendance may drop along with self-esteem. The lower tracks often have a disproportionate number of minority-group and economically disadvantaged students, so ability grouping, in effect, becomes segregation in school. Possibilities for friendships become limited to students in the same ability range. Assignments to classes are often made on the basis of group IQ tests instead of tests in the subject area itself. However, group IQ tests are not good guides for what someone is ready to learn in a particular subject area (Corno & Snow, 1986; Garmon, Nystrand, Berends, & LePore, 1995; Kulik & Kulik, 1982; Slavin, 1987, 1990).

There are two exceptions to the general finding that between-class ability grouping leads to lower achievement. The first is found in honors or gifted classes, where high-ability students tend to perform better than comparable students in regular classes. The second exception is the **nongraded elementary school** and the related **Joplin Plan.** In these arrangements, students are grouped by ability in particular subjects, regardless of their age or grade. A reading class might therefore have students from several grades, all working on the same level on reading. This cross-grade grouping seems to be effective for students of all abilities as long as the grouping allows teachers to give more direct instruction to the groups. When cross-age grouping is used to implement individualized instruction, the effects are much less positive (Gutierrez & Slavin, 1992).

Within-Class Ability Grouping

A second method, **within-class ability grouping,** clustering students by ability within the same class, is another story. Many elementary school classes are grouped for reading, and some are grouped for math, even though there is no clear evidence that this approach is superior to other approaches. If you use homogeneous small groups in your class, the

---

CHECKPOINT

Ability Differences and Teaching

Review

> What are the problems with between-class ability grouping?

> What are the alternatives available for grouping in classes?

Apply

> If you have a wide range of academic abilities in your class, what are your options in grouping students for learning?

GUIDELINES

Grouping by Achievement

Form and reform groups on the basis of students' *current performance* in the subject being taught.

Examples

1. Use scores on the most recent reading assessments to establish reading groups, and rely on current math performance to form math groups.
2. Change group placement frequently when students' achievement changes.

Discourage comparisons between groups and encourage students to develop a whole-class spirit.

Examples

1. Don't seat groups together outside the context of their reading or math group.
2. Avoid naming ability groups—save the names for mixed-ability or whole-class teams.

Group by ability for one or, at the most, two subjects.

Examples

1. Make sure there are many lessons and projects that mix members from the groups.
2. Experiment with learning strategies in which cooperation is stressed (described in Chapters 9 and 11).

3. Keep the number of groups small (two or three at most) so that you can provide as much direct teaching as possible—leaving students alone for too long leads to less learning.

Make sure teachers, methods, and pace are adjusted to fit the needs of the group.

Examples

1. Organize and teach groups so that low-achieving students get appropriate extra instruction—not just the same material again.
2. Experiment with alternatives to grouping. There are alternatives to within-class grouping that appear more effective for some subjects. DeWayne Mason and Tom Good (1993) found that supplementing whole-class instruction in math with remediation and enrichment for students when they needed it worked better than dividing the class into two ability groups and teaching these groups separately.

Guidelines above should make the approach more effective (Good & Brophy, 1997; Slavin, 1987).

What should teachers do when they have highly intelligent or talented students? We turn to this question next.

Creativity, Giftedness, and Talent

Creative, gifted, talented—these are terms we use every day to describe people with extraordinary abilities. You saw in the section on multiple intelligences earlier in this chapter that Gardner sees little difference between intelligence and talent. Gardner also has written extensively about creativity; he defines the creative individual as "a person who regularly solves problems, fashions products, or defines new questions in a domain in a way that is initially considered novel but that ultimately becomes accepted in a particular cultural setting" (Gardner, 1993a, p. 35). The notion of solving problems that are important for a particular culture is also part of his definition of intelligence. So creativity, talent, and intelligence are related; they allow us to solve important problems (Robinson & Clinkenbeard, 1998). Let's look first at creativity.

Between-Class Ability Grouping: System of grouping in which students are assigned to classes based on their measured ability or their achievements.

Nongraded Elementary School/ The Joplin Plan: Arrangement wherein students are grouped by ability in particular subjects, regardless of their ages or grades.

Within-Class Ability Grouping: System of grouping in which students in a class are divided into two or three groups based on ability in an attempt to accommodate student differences.

Creativity

Most psychologists agree that there is no such thing as "all-purpose creativity"; people are creative *in a particular area*. But to be creative, the "invention" must be intended. An accidental spilling of paint that produces a novel design is not creative unless the artist recognizes the potential of the "accident" or uses the spilling technique intentionally to create new works (Weisberg, 1993). Although we frequently associate the arts with **creativity,** any subject can be approached in a creative manner.

Creativity and Cognition. Having a rich store of knowledge in an area is the basis for creativity, but something more is needed. For many problems, that "something more" is the ability to break set—**restructuring** the problem to see things in a new way, which leads to a sudden insight. Often this happens when a person has struggled with a problem or project, then sets it aside for a while. Some psychologists believe that time away from the problem allows for *incubation,* a kind of unconscious working through the problem. It is more likely that leaving the problem for a time interrupts rigid ways of thinking so you can restructure your view of the situation (Gleitman, Fridlund, & Reisberg, 1999). So it seems that creativity requires extensive knowledge, flexibility, and the continual reorganizing of ideas. Motivation and persistence play important roles in the creative process.

Assessing Creativity. How shall we assess creativity? One answer has been to equate creativity with divergent thinking. **Divergent thinking** is the ability to propose many different ideas or answers. **Convergent thinking** is the more common ability to identify only one answer.

E. P. Torrance has developed two types of creativity tests, verbal and graphic (Torrance, 1972; Torrance & Hall, 1980). In the verbal test, you might be instructed to think up as many uses as possible for a tin can or asked how a particular toy might be changed to make it more fun. On the graphic test, you might be given 30 circles and asked to create 30 different drawings, each drawing including at least one circle (Sattler, 1992). Figure 4.5 shows the creativity of an 8-year-old girl in completing this task.

Responses to all these tasks are scored for *originality, fluency,* and *flexibility,* three aspects of divergent thinking. *Originality* is usually determined statistically. To be original, a response must be given by fewer than 5 or 10 people out of every 100 who take the test. *Fluency* is the number of different responses. *Flexibility* is generally measured by the number of different categories of responses. For instance, if you drew 30 circle pictures, but each was a face, your fluency score might be high, but your flexibility score would be quite low. Of the three measures, fluency—the number of responses—is the best predictor of divergent thinking, but there is more to real-life creativity than divergent thinking (Bjorklund, 1989).

Teachers are not always the best judges of creativity. In fact, Torrance (1972) reports data from a 12-year follow-up study indicating no relationship between teachers' judgments of their students' creative abilities and the actual creativity these students revealed in their adult lives. A few possible indicators of creativity in your students are curiosity, concentration, adaptability, high energy, humor (sometimes bizarre), independence, playfulness, nonconformity, risk taking, attraction to the complex and mysterious, willingness to fantasize and daydream, intolerance for boredom, and inventiveness (Sattler, 1992).

Creativity in the Classroom. Today's and tomorrow's complex problems require creative solutions. How can teachers promote creative thinking? All too often, in the crush of day-to-day classroom life, teachers stifle creative ideas without realizing what they are doing. Teachers are in an excellent position to encourage or discourage creativity through their acceptance or rejection of the unusual and imaginative. "Individuals who ultimately make creative breakthroughs tend from their earliest days to be explorers, innovators, and tinkers. . . . Often this adventurousness is interpreted as insubordination, though more fortunate tinkerers receive from teachers or peers some form of encouragement for their experimentation" (Gardner, 1993a, pp. 32–33).

▲ *Although we frequently associate the arts with creativity, it can also refer to a creative or imaginative approach to solving a problem.*

The Brainstorming Strategy. In addition to encouraging creativity through everyday interactions with students, teachers can try **brainstorming**. The basic tenet of brainstorming is to separate the process of creating ideas from the process of evaluating them because evaluation often inhibits creativity (Osborn, 1963). Evaluation, discussion, and criticism are postponed until all possible suggestions have been made. In this way, one idea inspires others; people do not withhold potentially creative solutions out of fear of criticism. John Baer (1997, p. 43) gives these rules for brainstorming:

1. Defer judgment.

2. Avoid ownership of ideas. When people feel that an idea is "theirs," egos sometimes get in the way of creative thinking. They are likely to be more defensive later when ideas are critiqued, and they are less willing to allow their ideas to be modified.

3. Feel free to "hitchhike" on other ideas. This means that it's okay to borrow elements from ideas already on the table, or to make slight modifications of ideas already suggested.

4. Encourage wild ideas. Impossible, totally unworkable ideas may lead someone to think of other, more possible, more workable ideas. It's easier to take a wildly imaginative bad idea and tone it down to fit the constraints of reality than to take a boring bad idea and make it interesting enough to be worth thinking about.

Individuals as well as groups may benefit from brainstorming. In writing this book, for example, I have sometimes found it helpful to list all the different topics that could be covered in a chapter, then leave the list and return to it later to evaluate the ideas.

Creativity: Imaginative, original thinking or problem solving.

Restructuring: Conceiving of a problem in a new or different way.

Divergent Thinking: Coming up with many possible solutions.

Convergent Thinking: Narrowing possibilities to a single answer.

Brainstorming: Generating ideas without stopping to evaluate them.

TABLE 4.2   Characteristics and Problems of Students with Special Gifts and Talents

Domains	Differentiating Characteristics	Problems
Cognitive (thinking)	Extraordinary quantity of information, unusual retentiveness	Boredom with regular curriculum; impatience with waiting for group
	High level of language development	Perceived as showoff by children of the same age
	Persistent, goal-directed behavior	Perceived as stubborn, willful, uncooperative
	Unusual capacity for processing information	Resent being interrupted; perceived as too serious; dislike for routine and drill
Affective (feeling)	Unusual sensitivity to the expectations and feelings of others	Unusually vulnerable to criticism of others; high level of need for success and recognition
	Keen sense of humor—may be gentle or hostile	Use of humor for critical attack on others, resulting in damage to interpersonal relationships
	Unusual emotional depth and intensity	Unusual vulnerability; problem focusing on realistic goals for life's work
	Advanced levels of moral judgment	Intolerance of and lack of understanding from peer group, leading to rejection and possible isolation
Physical (sensation)	Unusual discrepancy between physical and intellectual development	Comfortable expressing themselves only in mental activity, resulting in a limited development both physically and mentally
	Low tolerance for lag between standards and athletic skills	Refusal to take part in any activities where they do not excel, limiting experience with otherwise pleasurable, constructive physical activities
Intuitive	Early involvement and concern for intuitive knowing and metaphysical ideas and phenomena	Ridiculed by peers; not taken seriously by elders; considered weird or strange
	Creativity apparent in all areas of endeavor	Seen as deviant; become bored with mundane tasks; may be viewed as troublemaker
Societal	Strongly motivated by self-actualization needs	Frustration of not feeling challenged; loss of unrealized talents
	Leadership	Lack of opportunity to use social ability constructively may result in its disappearance from child's repertoire or its being turned into a negative characteristic (e.g., gang leadership)
	Solutions to social and environmental problems	Loss to society if these traits are not allowed to develop with guidance and opportunity for meaningful involvement

Source: From *Human Exceptionality: Society, School, and Family* (6th ed.) by M. L. Hardman, C. J. Drew, & M. W. Egan, 1999, Boston: Allyn & Bacon. Copyright © 1999 by Allyn & Bacon. Original source: From *Growing Up Gifted* (5th ed.) by B. Clark, 1979, Upper Saddle River, NJ: Prentice-Hall, Inc. Copyright © 1979 Prentice-Hall, Inc.

▶ Who learns easily and rapidly?

▶ Who uses a lot of common sense and practical knowledge?

▶ Who retains easily what he or she has heard?

▶ Who knows about many things that the other children don't?

▶ Who uses a large number of words easily and accurately?

IQ tests are still seen as a reliable predictor of academic giftedness; however, there may also be other ways for students to demonstrate their special abilities.

▶ Who recognizes relations and comprehends meanings?

▶ Who is alert and keenly observant and responds quickly?

Based on Renzulli and Reis's (1991) definition of giftedness, we might add:

▶ Who is persistent and highly motivated on some tasks?

▶ Who is creative, often has unusual ideas, or makes interesting connections?

Giftedness and Formal Testing. The best single predictor of academic giftedness is still the individual IQ test, but these tests are costly and time-consuming—and far from perfect. Group achievement and intelligence tests tend to underestimate the IQs of very bright children. Group tests may be appropriate for screening, but they are not appropriate for making placement decisions. Many psychologists recommend a *case study* approach to identifying gifted students. This means gathering many kinds of information, test scores, grades, examples of work, projects and portfolios, letters or ratings from teachers, self-ratings, and so on (Renzulli & Reis, 1991; Sisk, 1988). Especially for recognizing artistic talent, experts in the field can be called in to judge the merits of a child's creations. Science projects, exhibitions, performances, auditions, and interviews are all possibilities. Creativity tests such as those described earlier may identify some children not picked up by other measures, particularly minority students who may be at a disadvantage on the other types of tests (Maker, 1987).

Teaching Gifted Students. Some educators believe that gifted students should be *accelerated*—moved quickly through the grades or through particular subjects. Other educators prefer *enrichment*—giving the students additional, more sophisticated, and more thought-provoking work, but keeping them with their age-mates in school. Actually, both may be appropriate (Torrance, 1986).

Many people object to acceleration, but most careful studies indicate that truly gifted students who begin primary, elementary, junior high, high school, college, or

Creativity, Giftedness, and Talent   **125**

even graduate school early do as well as, and usually better than, nongifted students who are progressing at the normal pace. Social and emotional adjustment does not appear to be impaired. Gifted students tend to prefer the company of older playmates and may be miserably bored if kept with children of their own age. Skipping grades may not be the best solution for a particular student, but it does not deserve the bad name it has received (Jones & Southern, 1991; Kulik & Kulik, 1984; Richardson & Benbow, 1990). An alternative to skipping grades is to accelerate students in one or two particular subjects or allow concurrent enrollment in advanced placement courses, but keep them with peers for most classes (Robinson & Clinkenbeard, 1998). For students who are extremely advanced intellectually (for example, those scoring 160 or higher on an individual intelligence test), the only practical solution may be to accelerate their education (Gross, 1992; Keogh & MacMillan, 1996).

Teaching methods for gifted students should encourage abstract thinking (formal-operational thought), creativity, reading of high-level and original texts, and independence, not just the learning of greater quantities of facts. One approach that does *not* seem promising with gifted students is cooperative learning in mixed ability groups. Gifted students tend to learn more when they work in groups with other high ability peers (Fuchs, Fuchs, Hamlett, & Karns, 1998; Robinson & Clinkenbeard, 1998).

In working with gifted and talented students, a teacher must be imaginative, flexible, and unthreatened by the capabilities of these students. The teacher must ask: What do these children need most? What are they ready to learn? Who can help me to challenge them?

CHECKPOINT

Creativity, Giftedness, and Talent

Review

▶ What is creativity, and how is it assessed?

▶ What are the characteristics of gifted students?

▶ Is acceleration a useful approach with gifted students?

Apply

▶ Think of a time that you solved a problem in a creative way. What helped you see a different approach?

▶ If you had two students in your class who were way ahead of the others in their understanding, how would you help them learn?

Answers might come from faculty members at nearby colleges, retired professionals, books, museums, or older students. Strategies might be as simple as letting the child do math with the next grade. Other options are summer institutes; courses at nearby colleges; classes with local artists, musicians, or dancers; independent research projects; selected classes in high school for younger students; honors classes; and special-interest clubs (Mitchell, 1984).

Cognitive and Learning Styles

In this section we examine individual differences that have very little to do with intelligence but can influence students' learning in school. These differences have been called *cognitive styles* or *learning styles*. Be aware that you may hear these terms used interchangeably. In general, educators prefer the term *learning styles*, and include many kinds of differences in this broad category. Psychologists tend to prefer the term *cognitive styles*, and to limit their discussion to differences in the ways people process information (Bjorklund, 1989).

Cognitive Styles

The notion of **cognitive styles** is fairly new. It grew out of research on how people perceive and organize information from the world around them. Differences in cognitive style have to do with "characteristic modes of perceiving, remembering, thinking, problem solving, and decision making, reflective of information-processing regularities that develop . . . around underlying personality trends" (Messick, 1994, p. 122) and not with intelligence. For example, certain individuals respond very quickly in most situations. Others are more reflective and slower to respond, even though both types of people may be equally knowledgeable about the task at hand.

Connect & Extend
To your teaching
When students fail a grade or a course, they are often "recycled" through the same material on the assumption that repetition will produce learning. Use the concept of cognitive style to argue against this practice.

Field Dependence and Field Independence. In the early 1940s, Herman Witkin became intrigued by the observation that certain airline pilots would fly into a bank of clouds and fly out upside down, without realizing that they had changed position. His research on how people separate one factor from the total visual field identified the cognitive styles of field dependence and field independence (Davis, 1991; Witkin, Moore, Goodenough, & Cox, 1977).

People who are **field dependent** tend to perceive a pattern as a whole, not separating one element from the total visual field. They have difficulty focusing on one aspect of a situation, picking out important details, analyzing a pattern into different parts, or monitoring their use of strategies to solve problems. They tend to work well in groups, have a good memory for social information, and prefer subjects such as literature and history. **Field-independent** people, on the other hand, are more likely to monitor their own information processing. They perceive separate parts of a total pattern and are able to analyze a pattern according to its components. They are not as attuned to social relationships as field-dependent people, but they do well in math and science, where their analytical abilities pay off.

Although you will not necessarily be able to determine all the variations in your students' cognitive styles, you should be aware that students approach problems in different ways. Some may need help learning to pick out important features and to ignore irrelevant details. They may seem lost in less-structured situations and need clear, step-by-step instructions. Other students may be great at organizing but less sensitive to the feelings of others and not as effective in social situations.

Impulsive and Reflective Cognitive Styles. Another aspect of cognitive style is impulsivity versus reflectiveness. An **impulsive** student works very quickly but makes many mistakes. The more **reflective** student, on the other hand, works slowly and makes fewer errors. As with field dependence/independence, impulsive and reflective cognitive styles are not highly related to intelligence within the normal range. However, as children grow older, they generally become more reflective, and for school-age children, being more reflective does seem to improve performance on school tasks such as reading (Kogan, 1983; Smith & Caplan, 1988).

Students can learn to be more reflective, however, if they are taught specific strategies. One that has proved successful in many situations is **self-instruction**, described in Chapter 2. This approach capitalizes on the beneficial use of private speech described by Vygotsky (Meichenbaum, 1986). Another possibility is learning scanning strategies. For example, students taking multiple-choice tests might be encouraged to cross off each alternative as they consider it, so that no possibilities will be ignored. They might work in pairs and talk about why each possibility is right or wrong. In math classes, impulsive children need to be given specific strategies for checking their work. Just slowing down is not enough. These students must

Cognitive Styles: Different ways of perceiving and organizing information.

Field Dependence: Cognitive style in which patterns are perceived as wholes.

Field Independence: Cognitive style in which separate parts of a pattern are perceived and analyzed.

Impulsive: Characterized by cognitive style of responding quickly but often inaccurately.

Reflective: Characterized by cognitive style of responding slowly, carefully, and accurately.

Self-Instruction: Talking oneself through the steps of a task.

be taught effective strategies for solving the problem at hand by considering each reasonable alternative. I have also encountered several bright students who seem too reflective. They turn 30 minutes of homework into an all-night project.

Learning Styles and Preferences

Learning styles are approaches to learning and studying. Although many different learning styles have been described, one theme that unites most of the styles is differences between deep and surface approaches to processing information in learning situations (Snow, Corno, & Jackson, 1996). Individuals who have a *deep-processing approach* to learning see the learning materials or activities as a means for understanding some underlying concepts or meanings. These students tend to learn for the sake of learning and are less concerned about how their performance is evaluated, so motivation plays a role as well. Students who take a *surface-processing* approach focus on memorizing the learning materials, not understanding them. These students tend to be motivated by rewards, grades, external standards, and the desire to be evaluated positively by others. Of course, the situation can encourage deep or surface processing, but there is evidence that individuals have tendencies to approach learning situations in characteristic ways (Pintrich & Schrauben, 1992; Tait & Entwistle, 1998).

Since the late 1970s a great deal has been written about differences in students' learning preferences (Dunn, 1987; Dunn & Dunn, 1978, 1987; Gregorc, 1982; Keefe, 1982). Workshops and in-service training sessions around the country focus on this topic. Learning preferences are usually called *learning styles* in these workshops, but I believe preference is a more accurate label. **Learning preferences** are individual preferences for particular learning modes and environments. They could be preferences for where, when, with whom, or with what lighting, food, or music you like to study. Think for a minute about how you learn best. I like to study and write during large blocks of time, late at night. I usually make some kind of commitment or deadline every week so that I have to work under pressure in long stretches to finish the work before that deadline. Then I take a day off. When I plan or think, I have to see my thinking in writing. I have a colleague who draws diagrams of relationships when she listens to a speaker or plans a paper. You may be similar or very different, even though we all work effectively.

There are a number of instruments for assessing students' learning preferences—for example, *The Learning Style Inventory* (Renzulli & Smith, 1978), *The Learning Style Inventory* (Dunn, Dunn, & Price, 1984), and the *Learning Style Profile* (Keefe & Monk, 1986). Be aware, however, that tests of learning style lack evidence of reliability and validity. This led Snider (1990) to conclude, "People are different, and it is good practice to recognize and accommodate individual differences. It is also good practice to present information in a variety of ways through more than one modality, but it is not wise to categorize learners and prescribe methods solely on the basis of tests with questionable technical qualities. . . . The idea of learning styles is appealing, but a critical examination of this approach should cause educators to be skeptical" (p. 53).

It may be too much to expect the teacher to provide every student with his or her preferred setting and support for learning. But the teacher can make options available. Having quiet, private corners as well as large tables for working; comfortable cushions as well as straight chairs; brightly lighted desks along with darker areas; headphones for listening to music as well as earplugs; structured as well as open-ended assignments; information available from films and tapes as well as in books—all these options will allow students to work and learn in their preferred mode at least some of the time.

Will making these alterations lead to greater learning? Here the answer is not clear. Results of some research indicate that students learn more when they study in their preferred setting and manner (Dunn, Beaudry, & Klavas, 1989; Dunn & Dunn, 1987). There is some evidence that very bright students need less structure and prefer quiet, solitary learning (Torrance, 1986). But before you try to accommodate all your students' learning styles, remember that students, especially younger ones, may not be the best judges of how they should learn. Sometimes students, particularly poorer students, prefer what is easy and comfortable; real learning can be hard and uncomfortable. Sometimes students prefer to learn in a certain way because they have no alternatives; it is the only way they know how to approach the task. These students may benefit from developing new—and perhaps more effective—ways to learn (Weinstein & McCombs, in press).

Thus far we have focused mostly on teachers' responses to the varying abilities and styles of students. For the rest of the chapter we will consider several problems that can interfere with learning. It is important for all teachers to be aware of these issues because laws and policy changes over the past 25 years expand teachers' responsibilities working with all students.

CHECKPOINT

Cognitive and Learning Styles

Review

▶ Distinguish between cognitive style and learning preference.

▶ What are the advantages and disadvantages of matching teaching to individual learning styles?

Apply

▶ Are you more field dependent or field independent? How do you know?

Changes in the Law: Integration, Mainstreaming, and Inclusion

In 1975 a law was passed that began revolutionary changes in the education of children with disabilities. The Education for All Handicapped Children Act (Public Law 94–142) required states to provide "a free, appropriate public education for every child between the ages of 3 and 21 (unless state law does not provide free public education to children 3 to 5 or 18 to 21 years of age) regardless of how, or how seriously, he may be handicapped." In 1986, PL 99–457 extended the requirement for a free, appropriate education to all children ages 3 to 5 with handicaps, even in states that do not have public schooling for children this age. Also in the mid-1980s, some special educators and educational policymakers suggested that regular and special education should be merged so that regular teachers would have to take even more responsibility for the education of exceptional students. This movement is called the **regular education initiative.**

In 1990, PL 94–142 was amended by the **Individuals with Disabilities Education Act (IDEA).** This legislation replaced the word "handicapped" with "disabled," and expanded the services for students with disabilities. Also in 1990, the **Americans with Disabilities Act (ADA)** extended civil rights protection in employment, transportation, public accommodations, state and local government, and telecommunications to people with disabilities.

Connect & Extend
To other chapters

Remember in Chapter 2 we saw that there is little evidence that people are either "right-brained" or "left-brained." For people who have normal intact brains, both hemispheres are involved in all learning tasks, even if one side may be more or less involved at any given moment. Poets write in words but paint images and patterns with their verse. Sculptors often plan analytically, think logically, and perform calculations as they sculpt (Caine & Caine, 1991). It is possible that researchers will trace certain learning problems to aspects of hemispheric specialization, but the evidence is not yet conclusive. In fact, some preliminary research indicates that the front-to-back functioning of the brain may be as important as left/right functioning in understanding learning disabilities (Jordan & Goldsmith-Phillips, 1994).

Connect & Extend
To the research

See the January 1992 issue of *Elementary School Journal* for ten articles on mainstreaming.

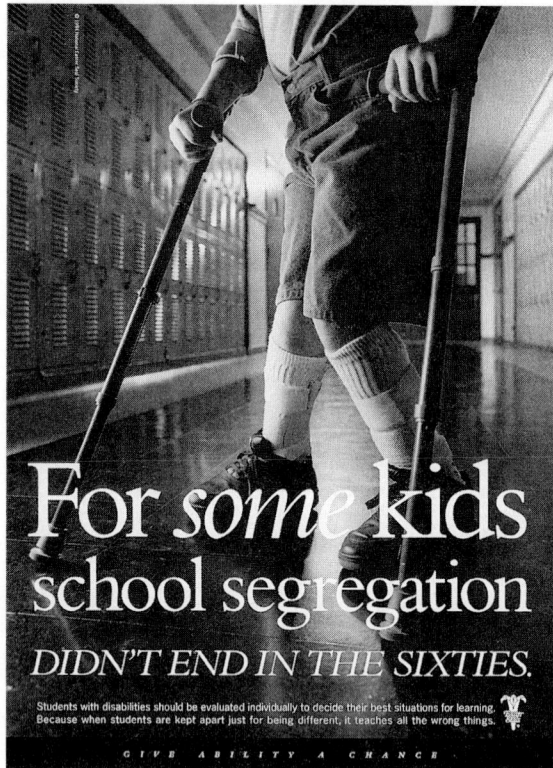

For *some* kids
school segregation
DIDN'T END IN THE SIXTIES.

Students with disabilities should be evaluated individually to decide their best situations for learning.
Because when students are kept apart just for being different, it teaches all the wrong things.

GIVE ABILITY A CHANCE

▲ *The latter portion of the 20th century has seen the doors of the general education system open to students of all abilities.*

Least Restrictive Placement: Placement of each child in as normal an educational setting as possible.

Mainstreaming: Teaching children with disabilities in regular classes for part or all of their school day.

Full Inclusion: The integration of all students, including those with severe disabilities, into regular classes.

Individualized Education Program (IEP): Annually revised program for an exceptional student, detailing present achievement level, goals, and strategies, drawn up by teachers, parents, specialists, and (if possible) student.

Let's examine the requirements in these laws. There are three major points of interest to teachers: the concept of "least restrictive placement"; the individualized education program (IEP); and the protection of the rights of students with disabilities and their parents.

Least Restrictive Placement

The laws require states to develop procedures for educating each child in the **least restrictive placement**—a setting that is as normal as possible. Earlier interpretations of this requirement led to **mainstreaming**—bringing exceptional students into general educational settings when the students could meet expectations for that setting—for example, allowing them to participate in recess or art or music (Friend & Bursuck, 1996). In most schools students with severe disabilities were not integrated into regular classes; but in some districts there is a movement toward **full inclusion**—integrating all students, even those with severe disabilities, into regular classes. Advocates of inclusion believe that students with disabilities can benefit from involvement with their nondisabled peers and should be educated with them in their regular home-district school, even if doing so means changes in educational requirements, special aids, services, and training or consultation for the regular teaching staff (Stainback & Stainback, 1992). However, some researchers caution that inclusion classrooms are not the best placement for every child. For example, Naomi Zigmond and her colleagues (1995) report that only about half of the students with learning disabilities in their study of six full-inclusion elementary schools were able to benefit. As you can see in the Point/Counterpoint, inclusion is a hotly debated issue.

Individualized Education Program

The drafters of the laws recognized that each student is unique and may need a specially tailored program to make progress. The **Individualized Education Program**, or **IEP**, is written by a team that includes the student's teacher or teachers, a qualified school psychologist or special education supervisor, the parent(s) or guardian(s), and (when possible) the student. The program must be updated each year and must state in writing:

1. The student's present level of functioning.
2. Goals for the year and short-term measurable instructional objectives leading to those goals.
3. A list of specific services to be provided to the student and details of when those services will be initiated.
4. A description of how fully the student will participate in the regular school program.
5. A schedule telling how the student's progress toward the objectives will be evaluated and approximately how long the services described in the plan will be needed.

Is Full Inclusion a Reasonable Approach to Teaching Exceptional Students?

In his booklet entitled *Inclusion: Issues of educating students with disabilities in regular educational settings*, Michael Hardman (1994) summarizes the arguments for and against full inclusion.

▶ **POINT** *Full inclusion makes sense.*

Supporters of full inclusion, such as Marsha Forest, believe that:

All children need to learn with and from other children. . . . All children need to belong and feel wanted. . . . All children need to have fun and enjoy noise and laughter in their lives. . . . All children need to take risks and fall and cry and get hurt. . . . All children need to be in real families and real schools and real neighborhoods. (p. 403)

These opportunities are limited in special class placements. No matter how good the teaching, students with disabilities will never learn to cope with the world outside their special classroom if they are not allowed to live in that world. Furthermore, many researchers believe that special education has failed. For example, only 56% of students in special education earn a high school diploma, and only 21% of these graduates go on to pursue any kind of post-secondary education. Segregation away from the mainstream, in special classes, robs students with disabilities of the opportunity to learn to participate fully in society, robs students without disabilities of the opportunity to develop understanding and acceptance of the disabled, and increases the likelihood that individuals with disabilities will be stigmatized.

◀ **COUNTERPOINT** *Full inclusion will not work.*

Just because a student with a disability is physically present in a class does not mean that student feels a sense of belonging. Students with disabilities can be just as socially isolated and alone in a regular class as they would be in a "special" class across the hall or across the state. Children can be cruel, and they may not necessarily provide opportunities for their peers who have disabilities to "have fun and enjoy noise and laughter in their lives." Furthermore, many researchers believe that special education has been quite successful. Seventy-seven percent of parents of students with disabilities are satisfied with the education programs of their children (Harris, 1989). In fact, parents of children with disabilities are more satisfied with the public schools than are parents of school-age children in general (Robert Wood Johnson, 1988). And special classes cannot be held responsible for low graduation and high drop-out rates among special education students. Ninety-two percent of all students with disabilities spend at least some of their time in regular classes already. Shouldn't these classes be held responsible too?

Finally, can we really expect regular teachers who are already overburdened with responsibilities for low-achieving students, students coping with family crises, and students who speak little or no English to also handle the wide range of disabilities that could confront them? Regular educators are unprepared, unsupported, and unable to handle all these challenges at once. The idea that extra support and consultation will be provided is good in theory, but will it actually come to pass in practice? Albert Shanker, President of the American Federation of Teachers (AFT), speaking to members of his union during an AFT conference, *Inclusion: Where We Stand*, said the following:

I do believe very large numbers of students now separated into special education could be included and integrated into regular classes and it would be beneficial. . . . [But] We must put the brakes on the helter-skelter, even tumultuous rush toward full inclusion so that everyone involved—parents, school boards, legislators, Congress, and even the Clinton administration—can develop a policy based on what is best for all children in our public schools. . . . Full inclusion is becoming more widely practiced based on budgetary and social motivation and not on what most Americans think classrooms ought to be about, which is education. (Inclusive Education Programs, 1994, p. 1+)

6. Beginning at age 16 (and as young as 14 for some students), a statement of needed transitional services to move the student toward further education or work in adult life.

Figure 13.3 on page 504 is an excerpt from the IEP of a 9-year-old girl with mild retardation.

The Rights of Students and Families

Several stipulations in these laws protect the rights of parents and students. Schools must have procedures for maintaining the confidentiality of school records. Testing practices must not discriminate against students from different cultural backgrounds. Parents have the right to see all records relating to the testing, placement, and teaching of their child. If they wish, parents may obtain an independent evaluation of their child. Parents may bring an advocate or representative to the meeting at which the IEP is developed. Students whose parents are unavailable must be assigned a surrogate parent to participate in the planning. Parents must receive written notice (in

FAMILY AND COMMUNITY PARTNERSHIPS

Productive Conferences

Plan and prepare for a productive conference.

Examples

1. Have a clear purpose and gather the needed information. If you want to discuss student progress, have work samples.

2. Send home a list of questions and ask families to bring the information to the conference.

Sample questions from Friend and Bursuck (1996) are:

1. What is your child's favorite class activity?

2. Does your child have worries about any class activities? If so, what are they?

3. What are your priorities for your child's education this year?

4. What questions do you have about your child's education in my class this year?

5. How could we at school help make this the most successful year ever for your child?

6. Are there any topics you want to discuss at the conference that I might need to prepare for? If so, please let me know.

7. Would you like other individuals to participate in the conference? If so, please give me a list of their names.

8. Is there particular school information you would like me to have available? If so, please let me know.

During the conference, create and maintain an atmosphere of collaboration and respect.

Examples

1. Arrange the room for private conversation. Put a sign on your door to avoid interruptions. Meet around a conference table for better collaboration. Have tissues available.

2. Address families as "Mr." and "Ms.," not "Mom" and "Dad" or "Grandma." Use students' names.

3. Listen to families' concerns and build on their ideas for their children.

After the conference, keep good records and follow up on decisions.

Examples

1. Make notes to yourself and keep them organized.

2. Summarize any actions or decisions in writing and send a copy to the family and any other teachers or professionals involved.

3. Communicate with families on other occasions, especially when there is good news to share.

TABLE 4.3 *How Many Are There? Children with Disabilities in United States Schools*

During the 1992–1993 school year, there were over 4,500,000 students with disabilities in U.S. schools. As you can see in this table, about 35% of them were taught in regular classrooms.

Disability	Number	Percentage of Identified Students	Percentage Taught in Regular Classrooms
Specific learning disability	2,369,385	51.1	24.7
Communication disorders	1,000,154	21.6	85.5
Mental retardation	533,715	11.5	5.1
Emotional or behavioral disorders	402,668	8.7	15.8
Severe/multiple disabilities	103,215	2.2	6.2
Other health impairments	66,054	1.4	35.3
Deaf or hard of hearing	60,896	1.3	27.0
Physical disabilities	52,291	1.1	32.4
Low vision or blindness	23,811	0.5	39.6
Autism	15,527	0.3	4.7
Traumatic brain injury	3,903	0.1	7.8
Deaf-blindness	1,425	0.0	5.8
All disabilities	4,633,674	100.0	34.9

Source: U.S. Department of Education (1994).

their native language) before any evaluation or change in placement is made. Finally, parents have the right to challenge the program developed for their child, and are protected by due process of law. If you have conferences with your student's family, following the suggestions in the Family and Community Partnerships Guidelines can make the meetings more effective.

Whom will you meet in these conferences? If you look at Table 4.3, you see that certain problems are more prevalent. We turn now to the challenges your students may face.

Prevalent Problems and Mild Disabilities

Teachers are more likely to encounter students with certain disabilities. As you can see in Table 4.3, these higher-incidence groups are children with learning disabilities, communication disorders, mental retardation, and emotional or behavioral disorders. With recent changes in the laws and new, more inclusive policies, you are likely to have children from all these categories in your classes.

Almost one-half of all students receiving some kind of special education services in the public schools are diagnosed as having learning disabilities. This is by far the largest category of students with disabilities.

Connect & Extend
To your students
Students with AIDS can have many of the problems discussed in this chapter: mental retardation, attention-deficit/hyperactiviy disorder, seizures, neurological impairments similar to cerebral palsy, behavior disorders, and so on. Most states have policies that emphasize the education of children with AIDS in the regular classroom.

Connect & Extend
To your teaching
Dolgins, J., Myers, M., Flynn, P. A., & Moore, J. (1984, February). How do we help the learning disabled? *Instructor*, 29–36.

Allow assignments to be typed, taped, or dictated.

Have material to be copied or directions on the child's desk rather than on the board.

Increase the time allowed or decrease the amount of writing.

Omit handwriting as a criterion for evaluating reports.

Construct tests that require minimal writing, such as multiple-choice, matching.

Tape selections that a child cannot read but can comprehend.

Provide opportunities for group projects, peer tutoring, contracts, and/or learning centers.

Write summaries of reading assignments.

Decrease the number of spelling words required at one time.

To increase exposure, use spelling words that are also required in reading or science.

Avoid spelling as a criterion for evaluating assignments.

Require fewer math problems for an assignment.

Allow the use of calculators or other manipulative aids.

Provide concrete examples.

Learning Disability: Problem with acquisition and use of language; may show up as difficulty with reading, writing, reasoning, or math.

Learning Disabilities

How do you explain a student who struggles to read, write, spell, or learn math, even though he or she is not mentally retarded, emotionally disturbed, or educationally deprived and has normal vision, hearing, and language capabilities? One explanation is that the student has a **learning disability**. This is a relatively new and controversial category of exceptional students. There is no fully agreed upon definition. A recent text on learning disabilities lists a dozen definitions (Hallahan, Kauffman, & Lloyd, 1999). The National Joint Committee on Learning Disabilities (1989), a group of parents and professionals, proposes the following definition:

> Learning disabilities is a general term that refers to a heterogeneous group of disorders manifested by significant difficulties in the acquisition and use of listening, speaking, reading, writing, reasoning, or mathematical abilities. These disorders are intrinsic to the individual, presumed to be due to central nervous system dysfunction, and may occur across the life span. (p. 1)

This definition eliminates references to older terms such as *brain injury* or *minimal brain dysfunction*, and indicates that learning disabilities may pose a lifelong challenge. Most definitions agree that students with learning disabilities are at least average in intelligence, but have significant academic problems and perform significantly below what would be expected.

Some educators and psychologists believe the learning disability label is overused and abused. They suggest that many of the students called learning disabled are really slow learners in average schools, average learners in high-achieving schools, students with second-language problems, or students who are behind in their work because they are absent or changed schools often (Gartner & Lipsky, 1987).

Student Characteristics. Students with learning disabilities are not all alike. The most common characteristics are specific difficulties in one or more academic areas; poor coordination; problems paying attention; hyperactivity and impulsivity; problems organizing and interpreting visual and auditory information; disorders of thinking, memory, speech, and hearing; and difficulties making and keeping friends (Hallahan & Kauffman, 2000). As you can see, many students with other disabilities (such as attention deficit disorder) and many normal students may have some of the same characteristics. To complicate the situation even more, not all students with learning disabilities will have these problems, and few will have all of the problems. One student may be three years behind in reading but above grade level in math, while another student may have the opposite strengths and weaknesses and a third may have problems with organizing and studying that affect almost all subject areas.

Most students with learning disabilities have difficulties reading. Table 4.4 lists some of the most common problems and signs. These difficulties appear to be caused by problems with relating sounds to letters that make up words, making spelling hard as well (Stanovich, 1991). Math, both computation and problem solving, is the second most common problem for students with learning disabilities. The writing of some of these students is virtually unreadable, and their spoken language can be halting and disorganized. Students with learning disabilities often lack effective ways to approach academic tasks. They don't know how to focus on the relevant information, get organized, apply learning strategies and study skills, change strategies when one isn't working, or evaluate their learning. They tend to be passive learners, in part because they don't know *how* to learn. Working independently is especially trying, so homework and seatwork are often left incomplete (Hallahan, Kauffman, & Lloyd, 1999).

TABLE 4.4 *Reading Habits and Errors of Students with Learning Disabilities*

Do any of your students show these signs? They could be indications of learning disabilities.

Poor Reading Habits
- Frequently loses his or her place
- Jerks head from side to side
- Expresses insecurity by crying or refusing to read
- Prefers to read with the book held within inches from face
- Shows tension while reading; such as reading in a high-pitched voice, biting lips, and fidgeting

Word Recognition Errors
- Omitting a word (e.g., "He came to the park," is read, "He came to park")
- Inserting a word (e.g., "He came to the [beautiful] park")
- Substituting a word for another (e.g., "He came to the *pond*")
- Reversing letters or words (e.g., *was* is read *saw*)
- Mispronouncing words (e.g., *park* is read *pork*)
- Transposing letters or words (e.g., "The dog ate fast," is read, "The dog fast ate")
- Not attempting to read an unknown word by breaking it into familiar units
- Slow, laborious reading, less than 20 to 30 words per minute

Comprehension Errors
- Recalling basic facts (e.g., cannot answer questions directly from a passage)
- Recalling sequence (e.g., cannot explain the order of events in a story)
- Recalling main theme (e.g., cannot give the main idea of a story)

Source: From *Child and Adolescent Development for Educators* (p. 400), by J. L. Meece, 1997, New York: McGraw-Hill. Copyright © 1997 by McGraw-Hill Companies. Adapted with permission.

Connect & Extend
To the research
Chapman, J. W. (1989). Learning disabled children's self-concepts. *Review of Educational Research, 58,* 347–371.

From the abstract: Studies of learning-disabled (LD) children's self-concepts show that LD students have lower self-concepts than nonhandicapped students. Greater decrements occur for academic self-concept than for general self-concept. Significant variations in results were found as a function of the group LD students were compared with, and the instruments used (the Piers-Harris scale or the Student's Perception of Ability Scale). For most LD children, decrements in self-concept occur by grade 3 and remain fairly stable through high school. Mainstreamed settings did not lead to higher self-concepts than segregated settings. But unplaced LD students clearly had lower self-concepts than LD students who were receiving remedial assistance.

Connect & Extend
To other chapters
The concept of learned helplessness will be discussed again in Chapter 5 as one explanation for the lower achievement of children of poverty and again in Chapter 9 as a factor influencing motivation.

Early diagnosis is important so that students with learning disabilities do not become terribly frustrated and discouraged. The students themselves do not understand why they are having such trouble, and they may become victims of **learned helplessness.** This condition was first identified in learning experiments with animals. The animals were put in situations where they received punishment (electric shocks) that they could not control. Later, when the situation was changed and they could have escaped the shocks or turned them off, the animals didn't even bother trying (Seligman, 1975). They had learned to be helpless victims. Students with learning disabilities may also come to believe that they cannot control or improve their own learning. This is a powerful belief. The students never exert the effort to discover that they can make a difference in their own learning, so they remain passive and helpless.

Students with learning disabilities may also try to compensate for their problems and develop bad learning habits in the process, or they may begin avoiding certain subjects out of fear of not being able to handle the work. To prevent these things from happening, the teacher should refer the students to the appropriate professionals in the school as early as possible.

Learned Helplessness: The expectation, based on previous experiences with a lack of control, that all one's efforts will lead to failure.

Teaching Students with Learning Disabilities. There is also controversy over how best to help these students. A promising approach seems to be to emphasize study skills and methods for processing information in a given subject such as reading or math. Many of the principles of cognitive learning from Chapters 7 and 8 can be applied to help all students improve their attention, memory, and problem-solving abilities (Sawyer, Graham, & Harris, 1992). *The Kansas Learning Strategies Curriculum* is one example of this approach (Deshler & Schumaker, 1986). No set of teaching techniques will be effective for every child. You should work with the special education teachers in your school to design appropriate instruction for individual students. Table 4.5 summarizes problem areas and the most effective teaching approaches for students with learning disabilities across the life span.

TABLE 4.5 *Learning Disabilities across the Life Span*

Learning disabilities are not limited to the school years. This table lists the problems that may occur during different phases of life and the treatments that have the strongest support from research or from expert teachers in the field.

	Preschool	Grades K–1	Grades 2–6	Grades 7–12	Adult
Problem Areas	Delay in developmental milestones (e.g., walking) Receptive language Expressive language Visual perception Auditory perception Short attention span Hyperactivity	Academic readiness skills (e.g., alphabet knowledge, quantitative concepts, directional concepts, etc.) Receptive and expressive language Visual and auditory perception Gross and fine motor skills Attention/Hyperactivity Social skills	Reading skills Arithmetic skills Written expression Verbal expression Receptive language Attention span Hyperactivity Social-emotional	Reading skills Arithmetic skills Written expression Verbal expression Listening skills Study skills (metacognition) Social-emotional delinquency	Reading skills Arithmetic skills Written expression Verbal expression Listening skills Study skills Social-emotional
Treatments with Most Research and/or Expert Support	Direct instruction in language skills Behavioral management Parent training	Direct instruction in academic and language areas Behavioral management Parent training	Direct instruction in academic areas Behavioral management Self-control training Parent training	Direct instruction in academic areas Tutoring in subject areas Direct instruction in learning strategies (study skills) Self-control training Curriculum alternatives	Direct instruction in academic areas Tutoring in subject (college) or job area Compensatory instruction (i.e., using aids such as tape recorder, calculator, computer, dictionary)

Source: From *Students with Learning Disabilities* (5th ed.) (p. 50), by C. D. Mercer, 1997, Saddle River, NJ: Prentice-Hall Inc. Copyright © 1997 by Prentice-Hall Inc. Adapted with permission.

Hyperactivity and Attention Disorders

You have probably heard and may even have used the term **hyperactivity.** The notion is a modern one; there were no hyperactive children 50 to 60 years ago. Today, if anything, the term is applied too often and too widely. Many student teachers in my program have classes with 5 or 6 students diagnosed as "hyperactive" and in one class there are 10 students with that diagnosis. Actually, hyperactivity is not one particular condition; it is "a set of behaviors—such as excessive restlessness and short attention span—that are quantitatively and qualitatively different from those of children of the same sex, mental age, and SES [socioeconomic status]" (O'Leary, 1980, p. 195).

Characteristics of Hyperactivity and Attention Disorders. Today most psychologists agree that the main problem for children labeled hyperactive is directing and maintaining attention, not simply controlling their physical activity. The American Psychiatric Association has established a diagnostic category called **attention-deficit/hyperactivity disorder (ADHD)** to identify children with this problem. Table 4.6 lists some indicators of ADHD used by this group.

> **Hyperactivity:** Behavior disorder marked by atypical, excessive restlessness and inattentiveness.
>
> **Attention-Deficit/Hyperactivity Disorder:** Current term for disruptive behavior disorders marked by overactivity, excessive difficulty sustaining attention, or impulsiveness.

TABLE 4.6 *Indicators of ADHD: Attention-Deficit/ Hyperactivity Disorder*

Do any of your students show these signs? They could be indications of ADHD.

Problems with *Inattention*
- Fails to give close attention to details or makes careless mistakes
- Has difficulty sustaining attention in tasks or play activities
- Does not seem to listen when spoken to directly
- Does not follow through on instructions and fails to finish schoolwork (not due to oppositional behavior or failure to understand instructions)
- Has difficulty organizing tasks or activities
- Avoids, dislikes, or is reluctant to engage in tasks that require sustained mental effort (such as schoolwork or homework)
- Loses things necessary for tasks or activities
- Is easily distracted by extraneous stimuli
- Is forgetful in daily activities

Problems with *Impulse Control*
- Blurts out answers before questions have been completed
- Has difficulty awaiting his/her turn
- Interrupts or intrudes on others in conversations or games

Hyperactivity
- Fidgets with hands or feet or squirms in seat
- Leaves seat in classroom or in other situations in which remaining seated is expected
- Runs about or climbs excessively in situations in which it is inappropriate (in adolescents may be limited to subjective feelings of restlessness)
- Has difficulty playing or engaging in leisure activities quietly
- Talks excessively
- Acts as if "driven by a motor" and cannot remain still

Source: From *Diagnostic Statistical Manual of Mental Disorders* (DSM-IV) (pp. 83–84), 1994, Washington DC: American Psychiatric Association. Copyright © 1994 American Psychiatric Association. Adapted with permission.

MIKE SMITH reprinted by permission of United Features Syndicate, Inc.

▲ *Are we overusing drugs?*

Children with ADHD are not only more physically active and inattentive than other children; they also have difficulty responding appropriately and working steadily toward goals (even their own goals); and they may not be able to control their behavior on command, even for a brief period. The problem behaviors are generally evident in all situations and with every teacher. It is difficult to know how many children should be classified as hyperactive. The most common estimate is 3–5% of the elementary school population, but some estimates are as high as 20% (Friend & Bursuck, 1996). More boys than girls are identified as hyperactive. Just a few years ago, most psychologists thought that ADHD diminished as children entered adolescence, but now there are some researchers who believe that the problems can persist into adulthood (Hallowell & Ratey, 1994). Adolescence—with the increased stresses of puberty, transition to middle or high school, more demanding academic work, and more engrossing social relationships—can be an especially difficult time for students with ADHD.

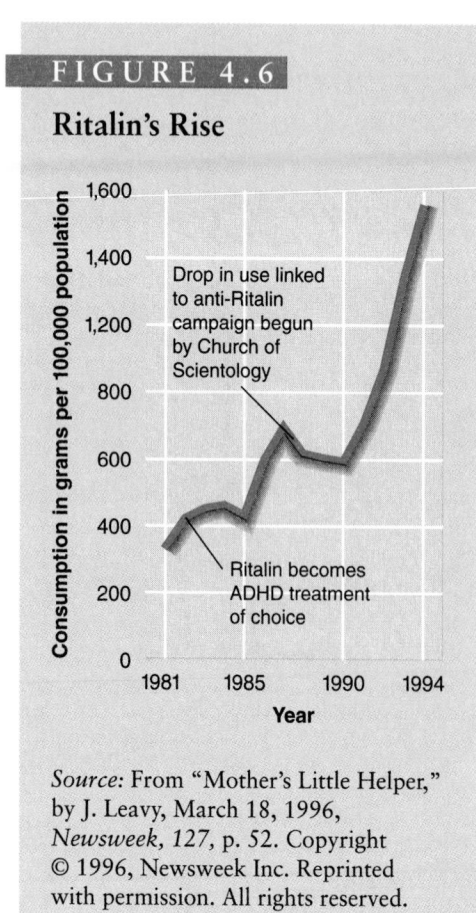

FIGURE 4.6

Ritalin's Rise

Consumption in grams per 100,000 population

Drop in use linked to anti-Ritalin campaign begun by Church of Scientology

Ritalin becomes ADHD treatment of choice

Year

Source: From "Mother's Little Helper," by J. Leavy, March 18, 1996, *Newsweek, 127,* p. 52. Copyright © 1996, Newsweek Inc. Reprinted with permission. All rights reserved.

Treatment and Teaching for Students with ADHD. Today there is an increasing reliance on drug therapy for ADHD. According to a *Newsweek* headline (Leavy, 1996), 1.3 million American children take Ritalin—a 250% increase since 1990, as you can see in Figure 4.6. Ritalin and other prescribed drugs such as Dexedrine and Cylert are stimulants, but in particular dosages they tend to have paradoxical effects on many children with ADHD: Short-term effects include possible improvements in social behaviors such as cooperation, attention, and compliance. Research suggests that about 80% of children with ADHD are more manageable when on medication. But for many there are negative side effects such as increased heart rate and blood pressure, interference with growth rate, insomnia, weight loss, and nausea (Friend & Bursuck, 1996; Panksepp, 1998; Weiss & Hechtman, 1993). In addition, little is known about the long-term effects of drug therapy. There also is no evidence that the drugs lead to improvement in academic learning or peer relationships, two areas where children with ADHD have great problems. Because students appear to improve dramatically in their behavior, parents and teachers, relieved to see change, may assume the problem has been cured. It hasn't. The students still need special help in learning.

The methods that have proved most successful in helping students with attention deficits are based on the behavioral principles described in Chapter 6. Long assignments may overwhelm students with attention deficits, so give them a few problems or paragraphs at a time with clear consequences for completion. One promising approach combines instruction in learning and memory strategies with motivational training. The goal is to give students the "skill and will" to improve their achievement (Paris, 1988). Students learn how and when to apply learning strategies and study skills. They are also encouraged to be persistent and to see themselves as "in control" (Reid & Borkowski, 1987). These methods should be thoroughly tested with the student before drugs are used. Even if students in your class are on medication, it is critical that they also learn the academic and social skills they will need to survive. Again, this will not happen by itself, even if behavior improves with medication (Kneedler, 1984).

Communication Disorders

Communication skills are an important component of a student's IEP. In many cases adaptations are available to help students with communication deficits participate in general education settings. ▼

Language is a complex learned behavior. Language disorders may arise from many sources, because so many different aspects of the individual are involved in learning language. A child with a hearing impairment will not learn to speak normally. A child who hears inadequate language at home will learn inadequate language. Children who are not listened to, or whose perception of the world is distorted by emotional problems, will reflect these problems in their language development. Because speaking involves movements, any impairment of the motor functions involved with speech can cause language disorders. And because language development and thinking are so interwoven, any problems in cognitive functioning can affect ability to use language.

Speech Impairments. Students who cannot produce sounds effectively for speaking are considered to have a **speech impairment**. About 5% of school-age children have some form of speech impairment. Articulation problems and stuttering are the two most common problems.

Articulation disorders include substituting one sound for another (*thunthine* for *sunshine*), distorting a sound (*shoup* for *soup*), adding a sound (*ideer* for *idea*), or omitting sounds (*po-y* for *pony*) (Smith, 1998). Keep in mind, however, that most children are 6 to 8 years old before they can successfully pronounce all English sounds in normal conversation. The sounds of the consonants *l, r, y, s,* and *z* and the consonant blends *sh, ch, zh,* and *th* are the last to be mastered. Also, there are dialect differences based on geography that do not represent articulation problems. A child in your class from New England might say "ideer" for "idea" but have no speech impairment.

Stuttering generally appears between the ages of 3 and 4. It is not yet clear what causes stuttering, but it can cause embarrassment and anxiety for the sufferer. In about 50% of cases, stuttering disappears during early adolescence (Wiig, 1982). If stuttering continues more than a year or so, the child should be referred to a speech therapist. Early intervention is critical (Onslow, 1992).

Voicing problems, a third type of speech impairment, include speaking with an inappropriate pitch, quality, or loudness or in a monotone (Hallahan & Kauffman, 2000). A student with any of these problems should be referred to a speech therapist. Recognizing the problem is the first step. Be alert for students whose pronunciation,

Speech Impairment: Inability to produce sounds effectively for speaking.

Articulation Disorders: Any of a variety of pronunciation difficulties, such as the substitution, distortion, or omission of sounds.

Stuttering: Repetitions, prolongations, and hesitations that block flow of speech.

Voicing Problems: Inappropriate pitch, quality, loudness, or intonation.

TABLE 4.7 *Encouraging Language Development*

- Talk about things that interest children.
- Follow the children's lead. Reply to their initiations and comments. Share their excitement.
- Don't ask too many questions. If you must, use questions such as *how did/do . . . , why did/do . . . ,* and *what happened . . .* that result in longer explanatory answers.
- Encourage children to ask questions. Respond openly and honestly. If you don't want to answer a question, say so and explain why. (*I don't think I want to answer that question; it's very personal.*)
- Use a pleasant tone of voice. You need not be a comedian, but you can be light and humorous. Children love it when adults are a little silly.

- Don't be judgmental or make fun of children's language. If you are overly critical of children's language or try to catch and correct all errors, they will stop talking to you.
- Allow enough time for children to respond.
- Treat children with courtesy by not interrupting when they are talking.
- Include children in family and classroom discussions. Encourage participation and listen to their ideas.
- Be accepting of children and of their language. Hugs and acceptance can go a long way.
- Provide opportunities for children to use language and to have that language work for them to accomplish their goals.

Source: From *Language Disorders: A Functional Approach to Assessment and Intervention* (2nd ed.) (p. 416), by R. E. Owens, Jr., 1995, Boston: Allyn & Bacon. Copyright © 1995 by Allyn & Bacon. Reprinted with permission.

loudness, voice quality, speech fluency, expressive range, or rate is very different from that of their peers. Pay attention also to students who seldom speak. Are they simply shy, or do they have difficulties with language?

Language Disorders. Language differences are not necessarily language disorders. Students with language disorders are those who are markedly deficient in their ability to understand or express language, compared with other students of their own age and cultural group (Owens, 1995). Students who seldom speak, who use few words or very short sentences, or who rely only on gestures to communicate should be referred to a qualified school professional for observation or testing. Table 4.7 gives ideas for promoting language development for all students.

Mental Retardation

According to the American Association on Mental Deficiency (AAMD Ad Hoc Committee on Terminology and Classification, 1992, p. 5), **mental retardation** refers to:

> substantial limitations in present intellectual functioning. It is characterized by significantly subaverage intellectual functioning existing concurrently with related limitations in two or more of the following applicable adaptive skill areas: communication, self-care, home living, social skills, community use, self-direction, health and safety, functional academics, leisure, and work. Mental retardation manifests before age 18.

Mental Retardation: Significantly below-average intellectual and adaptive social behavior, evident before age 18.

Intellectual function is usually measured by IQ tests with a cutoff score of 70 to 75 as one indicator of retardation. But an IQ score below the 70 to 75 range is *not* enough to diagnose a child as having mental retardation. There must also be problems with adaptive behavior, day-to-day independent living, and social functioning. This caution is especially important when interpreting the scores of students from different cultures. Defining retardation based on test scores alone can create what some critics call "6-hour retardates"—students who are seen as retarded only for the part of the day they attend school.

Only about 1 to 1.5% of the population fit the AAMD's definition of retarded in both intellectual functioning and adaptive behavior (Hallahan & Kauffman, 2000). For years, retardation was further divided into mild, moderate, severe, and profound levels, with each level keyed to a particular range of IQ scores. Most school districts still use this system. However, the IQ ranges are not perfect predictors of individuals' abilities to function, so the AAMR now recommends a classification scheme based on the amount of support that a person requires to function at his or her highest level. Table 4.8 summarizes this new classification system.

As a regular teacher, you may not have contact with children needing extensive or pervasive support unless your school is participating in a full inclusion program for exceptional students (described earlier in this chapter), but you probably will work with children with mild retardation. In the early grades, these students may simply learn more slowly than their peers. They need more time and more practice

---

TABLE 4.8   AAMR Classification Scheme for Mental Retardation

This new scheme for classification is based on the level of support a student would need to function as completely as possible.

Intermittent	Supports on an "as needed basis." Characterized by episodic nature, person not always needing the support(s), or short-term supports needed during life-span transitions (e.g., job loss or an acute medical crisis). Intermittent supports may be high or low intensity when provided.
Limited	An intensity of supports characterized by consistency over time and time-limited but not of an intermittent nature, may require fewer staff members and less cost than more intense levels of support (e.g., time-limited employment training or transitional supports during the school-to-adult period).
Extensive	Supports characterized by regular involvement (e.g., daily) in at least some environments (such as work or home) and not time-limited (e.g., long-term home living support).
Pervasive	Supports characterized by their constancy, high intensity, provided across environments; potential life-sustaining nature. Pervasive supports typically involve more staff members and intrusiveness than do extensive or time-limited supports.

Source: From *Mental Retardation: Definition, Classification, and Systems of Support,* by AAMR Ad Hoc Committee on Terminology and Classification, 1992. Washington, DC: American Association on Mental Retardation. Copyright © 1992 by American Association on Mental Retardation. Reprinted with permission.

GUIDELINES

Teaching Students with Mild Retardation

1. Determine readiness: however little a child may know, he or she is ready to learn a next step.

2. State and present objectives simply.

3. Base specific learning objectives on an analysis of the child's learning strengths and weaknesses.

4. Present material in small, logical steps. Practice extensively before going on to the next step.

5. Work on practical skills and concepts based on the demands of adult life.

6. Do not skip steps. Students with average intelligence can form conceptual bridges from one step to the next, but children with retardation need every step and bridge made explicit. Make connections for the student. Do not expect him or her to "see" the connections.

7. Be prepared to present the same idea in many different ways.

8. Go back to a simpler level if you see the student is not following.

9. Be especially careful to motivate the student and maintain attention.

10. Find materials that do not insult the student. A junior high boy may need the low vocabulary of "See Spot run" but will be insulted by the age of the characters and the content of the story.

11. Focus on a few target behaviors or skills so you and the student have a chance to experience success. Everyone needs positive reinforcement.

12. Be aware that students with retardation must overlearn, repeat, and practice more than children of average intelligence. They must be taught how to study, and they must frequently review and practice their newly acquired skills in different settings.

13. Pay close attention to social relations. Simply including students with retardation in a regular class will not guarantee that they will be accepted or that they will make and keep friends.

to learn and have difficulty transferring learning from one setting to another or putting small skills together to accomplish a more complex task. The Guidelines above list suggestions for teaching students with below-average general intelligence.

Learning goals for many students with mental retardation between the ages of 9 and 13 include basic reading, writing, arithmetic, learning about the local environment, social behavior, and personal interests. In junior and senior high school, the emphasis is on vocational and domestic skills, literacy for living (using the telephone book; reading signs, labels, and newspaper ads; completing a job application), job-related behaviors such as courtesy and punctuality; health self-care; and citizenship skills. Today there is a growing emphasis on **transition programming**—preparing the student to live and work in the community. As you saw earlier in the chapter, the law requires that schools design an IEP, or individualized educational program, for every disabled child. An ITP, or individualized transition plan, may be part of the IEP for students with retardation (Hallahan & Kauffman, 2000).

Emotional or Behavioral Disorders

Transition Programming:
Gradual preparation of exceptional students to move from high school into further education or training, employment, or community involvement.

Students with emotional and behavioral disorders can be among the most difficult to teach in a regular class. Behavior becomes a problem when it deviates so greatly from what is appropriate for the child's age group that it significantly interferes with the child's own growth and development and/or the lives of others. Clearly, deviation implies a difference from some standard, and standards of behavior differ from one situation, age group, culture, and historical period to another. Thus, what passes for team spirit in the football bleachers might be seen as disturbed behavior in a bank or restaurant. In addition, the deviation must be more than a temporary response to stressful events; it must be consistent across time and in different situations.

Connect & Extend
To other chapters
In Chapter 12, you will find ideas for dealing with mild to moderate behavior problems.

Quay and Peterson (1987) describe six dimensions of emotional/behavioral disorders. Children who have *conduct disorders* are aggressive, destructive, disobedient, uncooperative, distractible, disruptive, and persistent. They have been corrected and punished for the same misbehavior countless times. The adults and even the other children in their lives dislike many of these children. The most successful strategies for helping these children are the behavior management approaches described in Chapter 6. These students need very clear rules and consequences, consistently enforced. The future is not promising for students who never learn to control their behavior and who also fail academically. Waiting for the students to "outgrow" their problems is seldom effective (O'Leary & Wilson, 1987).

Children who are extremely anxious, withdrawn, shy, depressed, and hypersensitive, who cry easily and have little confidence, are said to have an *anxiety-withdrawal disorder*. These children have few social skills and consequently very few friends. The most successful approaches with them appear to involve the direct teaching of social skills (Gresham, 1981).

The third category is *attentional problems immaturity*. Characteristics include a short attention span, frequent daydreaming, little initiative, messiness, and poor coordination. If an immature student is not too far behind others in the class, she or he may respond to the behavior management strategies described in Chapter 6. But if these approaches fail or if the problem is severe, you should consult the school psychologist, guidance counselor, or another mental health professional. Related to this dimension is the category of *motor excess*. These students are restless and tense; they seem unable to sit still or stop talking. You can see that these children share many characteristics of ADHD.

The fifth category of behavior disorders is *socialized aggression*. Students in this group are often members of gangs. They may steal or vandalize because their peer culture expects it.

Finally, some students exhibit *psychotic behavior*. You are not likely to work with many of these students. Their behavior may be bizarre, and they may express very far-fetched ideas. These six categories are very general. If you are concerned about the behavior of one of your students, it is best to consult the school psychologist or guidance counselor.

Because students with emotional and behavioral disorders frequently break rules and push the limits, teachers often find themselves disciplining the students. Be aware that there have been court rulings on disciplining students with serious emotional problems (Yell, 1990). The Guidelines on page 144 may help when you are faced with these situations.

CHECKPOINT

Prevalent Problems and Mild Disabilities

Review

▶ What is a learning disability?

▶ What is ADHD and how is it handled in school?

▶ What are the most common communication disorders?

Apply

▶ How would you teach the concept of "safety" to a student with mild retardation?

GUIDELINES

Disciplining Students with Emotional Problems

Be careful not to violate due process rights of students—students and parents must know the behaviors expected and the consequences for misbehavior.

Examples

1. Communicate expectations clearly and in writing.
2. Ask parents and students to sign a copy of the classroom rules.
3. Post rules and consequences in class and on a class Web page.

Be very careful with severe punishments that remove students from class for a long time. These constitute a change in the child's educational program (IEP) and require due process.

Examples

1. Suspensions of more than 10 days require due process.
2. Prolonged periods of time-out (in-school suspension) may require due process.

Punishments for students with severe emotional problems must serve a clear educational purpose.

Examples

1. Give a rationale for punishment or correction that ties an action to student's learning or the learning of others in the class.
2. Use written behavior contracts that include a rationale.

Make sure the rule and the punishment are reasonable.

Examples

1. Consider the student's age and physical condition.

2. Does the punishment match the offense and the way others in the class are treated?
3. Do other teachers handle similar situations in the same way?
4. Try less intrusive punishments first. Be patient. Move to more severe actions only when less severe procedures fail.

Keep good records and work collaboratively so all involved are informed.

Examples

1. Document the punishment of all students in a journal or log. List what precipitated the punishment, what procedures were used, how long the punishment lasted, the results, modifications to the punishment, and new results.
2. Note meetings with families, special education teachers, and the principal.
3. Make any changes involving management plans with families and other teachers.

Always use positive consequences in conjunction with negative ones.

Examples

1. If students lose points for breaking rules, give them ways to regain points through positive behavior.
2. Recognize genuine accomplishment and small steps—don't say, "Well it's about time you . . . ."

▼ Less Prevalent Problems and More Severe Disabilities

In this section we meet students with more severe disabilities. In your first years of teaching you may encounter only a few of these students, but you still can make a difference in their lives.

Orthopedic Devices: Devices such as braces and wheelchairs that aid people with physical disabilities.

Health Impairments

Some students must have special **orthopedic devices** such as braces, special shoes, crutches, or wheelchairs to participate in a normal school program. If the school has the necessary architectural features, such as ramps, elevators, and accessible rest rooms, and if teachers allow for the physical limitations of students, little needs to be done to alter the usual educational program. Two other health impairments you may encounter are cerebral palsy and seizure disorders.

Cerebral Palsy and Multiple Disabilities. Damage to the brain before or during birth or during infancy can cause a child to have difficulty moving and coordinating his or her body. The problem may be very mild, so the child simply appears a bit clumsy, or so severe that voluntary movement is practically impossible. The most common form of **cerebral palsy** is characterized by **spasticity** (overly tight or tense muscles). Many children with cerebral palsy also have secondary handicaps (Kirk, Gallagher, & Anastasiow, 1993). In the classroom, these secondary handicaps are the greatest concern—and these are generally what the regular teacher can help with most. For example, many children with cerebral palsy also have visual impairments, speech problems, or mild mental retardation. The strategies described in this chapter should prove helpful in such situations.

Seizure Disorders (Epilepsy). A seizure is a cluster of behaviors that occurs in response to abnormal neurochemical activities in the brain (Hardman, Drew, & Egan, 1999). The effects of the seizure depend on where the discharge of energy starts in the brain and how far it spreads. People with **epilepsy** have recurrent seizures, but not all seizures are the result of epilepsy; temporary conditions such as high fevers or infections can also trigger seizures. Seizures take many forms and differ with regard to the length, frequency, and movements involved. A partial or absence seizure involves only a small part of the brain, whereas a generalized or tonic-clonic seizure includes much more of the brain.

Most **generalized seizures** (once called *grand mal*) are accompanied by uncontrolled jerking movements that ordinarily last two to five minutes, possible loss of bowel or bladder control, and irregular breathing, followed by a deep sleep or coma. On regaining consciousness, the student may be very weary, confused, and in need of extra sleep. Most seizures can be controlled by medication. If a student has a seizure accompanied by convulsions in class, the teacher must take action so the student will not be injured. The major danger to a student having such a seizure is getting hurt by striking a hard surface during the violent jerking. Do not try to restrain the child's movements; you can't stop the seizure once it starts. Lower the child gently to the floor, away from furniture or walls. Move hard objects away. Turn the child's head gently to the side, put a soft coat or blanket under the student's head, and loosen any tight clothing. Never put anything in the student's mouth. Find out from the student's parents how the seizure is usually dealt with. If one seizure follows another and the student does not regain consciousness in between or if the seizure goes on for more than 10 minutes, get medical help right away (Hallahan & Kauffman, 2000).

Not all seizures are dramatic. Sometimes the student just loses contact briefly. The student may stare, fail to respond to questions, drop objects, and miss what has been happening for 1 to 30 seconds. These were once called *petit mal*, but they are now referred to as **absence seizures** and can easily go undetected. If a child in your class appears to daydream frequently, does not seem to know what is going on at times, or cannot remember what has just happened when you ask, you should consult the school psychologist or nurse. The major problem for students with absence seizures is that they miss the continuity of the class interaction—these seizures can occur as often as 100 times a day. If their seizures are frequent, students will find the lessons confusing. Question these students to be sure they are understanding and following the lesson. Be prepared to repeat yourself periodically.

Cerebral Palsy: Condition involving a range of motor or coordination difficulties due to brain damage.

Spasticity: Overly tight or tense muscles, characteristic of some forms of cerebral palsy.

Epilepsy: Disorder marked by seizures and caused by abnormal electrical discharges in the brain.

Generalized Seizure: A seizure involving a large portion of the brain.

Absence Seizure: A seizure involving only a small part of the brain that causes a child to lose contact briefly.

Speech Reading: Using visual cues to understand language.

Sign Language: Communication system of hand movements that symbolize words and concepts.

Finger Spelling: Communication system that "spells out" each letter with a hand position.

Low Vision: Vision limited to close objects.

Educationally Blind: Needing Braille materials in order to learn.

Deaf and Hard of Hearing

You will hear the term, "hearing impaired," to describe these students, but the deaf community and researchers object to the term "hearing impaired," so I will use their preferred terms, deaf and hard of hearing. Signs of hearing problems are turning one ear toward the speaker, favoring one ear in conversation, or misunderstanding conversation when the speaker's face cannot be seen. Other indications include not following directions, seeming distracted or confused at times, frequently asking people to repeat what they have said, mispronouncing new words or names, and being reluctant to participate in class discussions. Take note particularly of students who have frequent earaches, sinus infections, or allergies.

In the past, educators have debated whether oral or manual approaches are better for children who are deaf or hard of hearing. Oral approaches involve **speech reading** (also called lip reading) and training students to use whatever limited hearing they may have. Manual approaches include **sign language** and **finger spelling**. Research indicates that children who learn some manual method of communicating perform better in academic subjects and are more socially mature than students who are exposed only to oral methods. Today, the trend is to combine both approaches (Hallahan & Kauffman, 2000). Technological innovations such as teletypewriters in homes and public phones and the many avenues of communication through e-mail and the Internet have expanded communication possibilities for all people with hearing problems.

Low Vision and Blindness

In the United States only about 1 child in 1,000 has visual impairments so serious that special educational services are needed. Most of this group needing special services is classified as having **low vision.** This means they can read with the aid of a magnifying glass or large-print books. A small group of students, about 1 in every 2,500, is **educationally blind.** These students must use hearing and touch as the predominant learning channels (Kirk, Gallagher, & Anastasiow, 1993).

Students who have difficulty seeing often hold books either very close to or very far from their eyes. They may squint, rub their eyes frequently, or complain that their eyes burn or itch. The eyes may actually be swollen, red, or encrusted. Students with vision problems may misread material on the chalkboard, describe their vision as being blurred, be very sensitive to light, or hold their heads at an odd angle (De Mott, 1982). Any of these signs should be reported to a qualified school professional.

Special materials and equipment that help these students to function in regular classrooms include large-print typewriters; variable-speed tape recorders (allowing teachers

CHECKPOINT

Less Prevalent Problems and More Severe Disabilities

Review

▶ How can schools accommodate the needs of physically disabled students?

▶ How would you handle a seizure in class?

▶ What are some signs of hearing and visual impairment?

Apply

▶ What accommodations could you make in your classroom for students with hearing or vision problems?

to make time-compressed tape recordings, which speed up the rate of speech without changing the voice pitch); special calculators; the abacus; three-dimensional maps, charts, and models; and special measuring devices. For students with visual problems, the quality of the print is often more important than the size, so watch out for hard-to-read handouts and ditto sheets. The Instructional Materials Reference Center of the American Printing House for the Blind (1839 Frankfort Avenue, Louisville, KY 40206) has catalogs of instructional materials for students with visual impairments.

The arrangement of the room is also an issue. Students with visual problems need to know where things are, so consistency matters—a place for everything and everything in its place. Leave plenty of space for moving around the room and make sure to monitor possible obstacles and safety hazards such as trash cans in aisles and open cabinet doors. If you rearrange the room, give students with visual problems a chance to learn the new layout. Make sure the students have a buddy for fire drills or other emergencies (Friend & Bursuck, 1996).

If you decide that students in your class might benefit from special services, the first step is making a referral. How would you begin? Table 4.9 guides you through the referral process. In Chapter 13, when we discuss effective teaching, we will look at more ways to reach all your students.

TABLE 4.9 *Making a Referral*

---

1. Contact the student's parents. It is very important that you discuss the student's problems with the parents *before* you refer.

2. Before making a referral, check *all* the student's school records. Has the student ever:

   - had a psychological evaluation?
   - qualified for special services?
   - been included in other special programs (e.g., for disadvantaged children; speech or language therapy)?
   - scored far below average on standardized tests?
   - been retained?

   Do the records indicate:

   - good progress in some areas, poor progress in others?
   - any physical or medical problem?
   - that the student is taking medication?

3. Talk to the student's other teachers and professional support personnel about your concern for the student. Have other teachers also had difficulty with the student? Have they found ways of dealing successfully with the student? Document the strategies that you have used in your class to meet the student's educational needs. Your documentation will be useful as evidence that will be helpful to or be required by the committee of professionals who will evaluate the student. Demonstrate your concern by keeping written records. Your notes should include items such as:

   - exactly what you are concerned about
   - why you are concerned about it
   - dates, places, and times you have observed the problem
   - precisely what you have done to try to resolve the problem
   - who, if anyone, helped you devise the plans or strategies you have used
   - evidence that the strategies have been successful or unsuccessful

   Remember that you should refer a student only if you can make a convincing case that the student may have a handicapping condition and probably cannot be served appropriately without special education. Referral for special education begins a time-consuming, costly, and stressful process that is potentially damaging to the student and has many legal ramifications.

Source: From *What Should I Know about Special Education? Answers for Classroom Teachers,* by P. L. Pullen & J. M. Kauffman, 1987. Copyright © 1987 PRO-ED, Austin, Texas. Reprinted by permission.

Summary

Language and Labeling

What are the advantages of and problems with labels?

Labels and diagnostic classifications of exceptional students can easily become both stigmas and self-fulfilling prophecies, but they can also open doors to special programs and help teachers develop appropriate instructional strategies.

What is person-first language?

"Person-first" language ("students with mental retardation," "students placed at risk," etc.) is an alternative to labels that describe a complex person with one or two words, implying that the condition labeled is the most important aspect of the person. With person-first language, the emphasis is on the students first, not on the special challenges they face.

Distinguish between a disability and a handicap.

A disability is an inability to do something specific such as see or walk. A handicap is a disadvantage in certain situations. Some disabilities lead to handicaps, but not in all contexts. Teachers must avoid imposing handicaps on disabled learners.

Individual Differences in Intelligence

What is g?

Spearman suggested there is one mental attribute, which he called g or *general intelligence*, that is used to perform any mental test, but that each test also requires some specific abilities in addition to g. Spearman assumed that individuals vary in both general intelligence and specific abilities, and that together these factors determine performance on mental tasks. A current version of the general plus specific abilities theory is Carroll's work identifying a few broad abilities (such as learning and memory,

visual perception, verbal fluency) and at least 70 specific abilities.

What is Gardner's view of intelligence and his position on g?

Gardner contends that an intelligence is a biological and psychological potential to solve problems and create products or outcomes that are valued by a culture. These intelligences are realized to a greater or lesser extent as a consequence of the experiential, cultural, and motivational factors. There are at least eight separate intelligences: linguistic, musical, spatial, logical-mathematical, bodily-kinesthetic, interpersonal, intrapersonal (these last two are similar to the idea of emotional intelligence), naturalist, and perhaps existential. Gardner does not deny the existence of a general ability, but does question how useful g is as an explanation for human achievements.

What are the elements in Sternberg's theory of intelligence?

Sternberg's triarchic theory of intelligence is a cognitive process approach to understanding intelligence that has three parts: analytic, creative, and practical. Analytic/componential intelligence involves the mental processes that lead to more or less intelligent behavior. These processes are defined in terms of components: metacomponents, performance components, and knowledge-acquisition components. Creative/experiental intelligence involves coping with new experiences through insight, or the ability to deal effectively with novel situations, and automaticity, or the ability to become efficient and automatic in thinking and problem solving. The third part is practical/contextual intelligence—choosing to live and work in a context where success is likely, adapting to that context, and reshaping it if necessary. Practical intelligence is made up mostly of action-oriented tacit knowledge learned during everyday life rather than for mal schooling.

How is intelligence measured and what does an IQ score mean?

Intelligence is measured through individual tests (Stanford-Binet, Wechsler, Woodcock-Johnston, etc.) and group tests (Lorge-Thorndike, Analysis of Learning Potential, Otis-Lennon Mental Abilities Tests, School and College Ability Tests, etc.). Compared to an individual test, a group test is much less likely to yield an accurate picture of any one person's abilities. The average score is 100; 50% of the people from the general population who take the tests will score 100 or above, and 50% will score below 100. About 68% of the general population will earn IQ scores between 85 and 115. Only about 16% of the population will receive scores below 85, and only 16% will score above 115. These figures hold true for White, native-born Americans whose first language is Standard English. Intelligence predicts success in school, but is less predictive of success in life when level of education is taken into account.

Ability Differences and Teaching

What are the problems with between-class ability grouping?

Academic ability groupings can have both disadvantages and advantages for students and teachers. For low-ability students, however, between-class ability grouping generally has a negative effect on achievement, social adjustment, and self-esteem. Low-ability classes seem to receive lower-quality instruction in general. Teachers tend to emphasize lower-level objectives and routine procedures, with less academic focus. Often there are more student behavior problems and, along with these problems, increased teacher stress and decreased enthusiasm. Low expectations may be communicated to the students. Attendance may drop along with self-esteem. The lower tracks often have a disproportionate number of minority-group and economically disadvantaged students, so ability grouping, in effect, becomes segregation in school.

What are the alternatives available for grouping in classes?

Cross-age grouping by subject can be an effective way to deal with ability differences in a school. Within-class ability grouping, if handled sensitively and flexibly, can have positive effects, but alternatives such as cooperative learning are also possible.

Creativity, Giftedness, and Talent

What is creativity and how is it assessed?

Creativity is a process that involves independently restructuring problems to see things in new, imaginative ways. Creativity is difficult to measure, but tests of divergent thinking can assess originality, fluency, and flexibility. Originality is usually determined statistically. To be original, a response must be given by fewer than 5 or 10 people out of every 100 who take the test. Fluency is the number of different responses. Flexibility is measured by the number of different categories of responses. Teachers can encourage creativity by providing opportunities for play, using brainstorming techniques, and accepting divergent ideas.

What are the characteristics of gifted students?

Terman and colleagues found that gifted children were larger, stronger, and healthier than the norm. They were more emotionally stable than their peers and became better-adjusted adults than the average. Gifted students learn easily and rapidly and retain what they have learned; use common sense and practical knowledge; know about many things that the other children don't; use a large number of words easily and accurately; recognize relations and comprehend meaning; are alert and keenly observant and respond quickly; are persistent and highly motivated on some tasks; and are creative or make interesting connections.

Is acceleration a useful approach with gifted students?

Many people object to acceleration, but most careful studies indicate that truly gifted students who are accelerated do as well as, and usually better than, nongifted students who are progressing at the normal pace. Gifted students tend to prefer the company of older playmates and may be bored if kept with children their own age. Skipping grades may not be the best solution for a particular student, but for students who are extremely advanced intellectually (with a score of 160 or higher on an individual intelligence test), the only practical solution may be to accelerate their education.

Cognitive and Learning Styles

Distinguish between cognitive style and learning preference.

Cognitive styles are characteristic modes of perceiving, remembering, thinking, problem solving, and decision making. They reflect information-processing regularities that develop around underlying personality trends. Field dependence versus field independence and impulsive versus reflective cognitive styles are examples of these differences. Learning preferences are individual preferences for particular learning modes and environments. They could be preferences for where, when, with whom, or with what lighting, food, or music you like to study. While cognitive styles and learning preferences are not related to intelligence or effort, they may affect school performance.

What are the advantages and disadvantages of matching teaching to individual learning styles?

Results of some research indicate that students learn more when they study in their preferred setting and manner. But sometimes students, particularly poorer students, prefer what is easy and comfortable; real learning can be hard and uncomfortable. Sometimes students prefer to learn in a certain way because they have no alternatives; it is the only way they know how to approach the task. These students may benefit from developing new—and perhaps more effective—ways to learn.

Changes in the Law: Integration, Mainstreaming, and Inclusion

Describe the main legal requirements that pertain to students with disabilities.

Public Law 94–142 (1975) requires that each exceptional learner or student with special needs be educated in the least restrictive environment according to an individualized education program. The law also protects the rights of students with special needs and their parents. Public Law 99–457 extends the 94–142 law to preschool-age children, and IDEA, the Individuals with Disabilities Act, extends services to include transition programming for exceptional learners 16 years old and older. The regular education initiative calls for regular classroom teachers to receive training in teaching exceptional learners.

Prevalent Problems and Mild Disabilities

What is a learning disability?

Specific learning disabilities involve significant difficulties in the acquisition and use of listening, speaking, reading, writing, reasoning, or mathematical abilities. These disorders are intrinsic to the individual, presumed to be the result of central nervous system dysfunction, and may occur across the life span. Students with learning disabilities may become victims of learned helplessness when they come to believe that they cannot control or improve their own learning and therefore cannot succeed. A focus on learning strategies often helps students with learning disabilities.

What is ADHD and how is it handled in school?

Attention deficit-hyperactivity disorder (ADHD) is the term used to describe individuals of any age with hyperactivity and attention difficulties. Use of medication to address ADHD is controversial, but currently on the rise. About 80% of children with ADHD are more manageable when on medication, but for many there are negative side effects such as increased heart rate and blood pressure, interference with growth rate, insomnia, weight loss, and nausea. In addition, little is known about the long-term effects of drug therapy. There also is no evidence that the drugs lead to improvement in academic learning or peer relationships, two areas where children with ADHD have great problems. Two promising approaches are behavior modification and techniques that combine instruction in learning and memory strategies with motivational training.

What are the most common communication disorders?

Common communication disorders include speech impairments (articulation disorders, stuttering, and voicing problems) and oral language disorders.

Less Prevalent Problems and More Severe Disabilities

How can schools accommodate the needs of physically disabled students?

If the school has the necessary architectural features, such as ramps, elevators, and accessible rest rooms, and if teachers allow for the physical limitations of students, little needs to be done to alter the usual educational program. Identifying a peer to help with movements and transitions can be useful.

How would you handle a seizure in class?

Do not restrain the child's movements. Lower the child gently to the floor, away from furniture or walls. Move hard objects away. Turn the child's head gently to the side, put a soft coat or blanket under the student's head, and loosen any tight clothing. Never put anything in the student's mouth. Find out from the student's parents how the seizure is usually dealt with.

If one seizure follows another and the student does not regain consciousness in between or if the seizure goes on for more than 10 minutes, get medical help right away.

What are some signs of hearing and visual impairment?

Signs of hearing problems are turning one ear toward the speaker, favoring one ear in conversation, or misunderstanding conversation when the speaker's face cannot be seen. Other indications include not following directions, seeming distracted or confused at times, frequently asking people to repeat what they have said, mispronouncing new words or names, and being reluctant to participate in class discussions. Take note particularly of students who have frequent earaches, sinus infections, or allergies. Holding books very close or far away, squinting, rubbing eyes, misreading the chalkboard, and holding the head at an odd angle are possible signs of visual problems.

*K*ey Terms

Becoming a Professional

Reflecting on the Chapter

Can you apply the ideas from this chapter on cognitive development to solve the following problems of practice?

Preschool and Kindergarten

▸ A little girl in your kindergarten class seldom speaks. When she does, she usually says only a word or two. She seems to understand when others talk, but almost never responds verbally. How would you approach this situation?

Elementary and Middle School

▸ The school psychologist tells you that one of your students is going to start taking medication designed to "calm him down." What would you want to know? How would you respond?

▸ The principal tells you that she is assigning two more students to your class because you are "new, and have more training in full inclusion than the older teachers." One student has mild retardation and has problems making friends. The other is blind. How will you respond to the principal's decision? How would you prepare your class and modify your teaching for these students?

Junior High and High School

▸ A student in your fifth-period class is failing. When you look at your grade book, you see that it is the written work that is giving the student trouble. Multiple-choice test scores and class participation are fine. But his writing is hardly legible and very disorganized. Sentences are started and never finished. Ideas fly in and out like frightened birds. How would you identify the source of the problem?

▸ How would you adapt your teaching to accommodate a student with a hearing impairment in your biology lab class?

Certification Test Requirements

▸ Know the difference between a handicap and a disability.

▸ Know the mean of standardized IQ tests and the range in which most people score.

▸ Be familiar with Gardner's theory of multiple intelligences.

▸ Know the effects of between-class ability grouping and the alternative for in-class grouping.

▸ Be aware of the alternatives for teaching gifted students, including acceleration.

▸ Be familiar with the basic requirements of PL 94–142, PL 99–457, and IDEA.

▸ Understand the differences between cognitive styles and learning styles/preferences and how to make accommodations for differences in the classroom.

Your Teaching Portfolio

▸ Use Table 4.7 to generate ideas for developing students' language and add these to your **Portfolio**.

▸ For your **Portfolio**, develop a lesson plan that appropriately uses Gardner's work on multiple intelligences—see Figure 4.3 for ideas.

▸ Add Table 4.9, *Making a Referral*, to your **Portfolio**.

Teaching Resources

Add Tables 4.2, 4.3, 4.4, 4.5, 4.6, 4.7, and 4.8 to your file of **Teaching Resources**.

TEACHERS' CASEBOOK

What Would They Do?

Here is how some practicing teachers responded to the teaching situation presented at the beginning of this chapter about discussing IQ scores with parents.

KELLY L. HOY

Third Grade Teacher
Faber Elementary School, Dunellen, New Jersey

Disclosing individual information about standardized tests is always a ticklish problem. Of course, parents want to know as much as they can about their children, but there are dangers of misinterpreting or misusing information, categorizing and stereotyping children, and individual comparisons. I would be very careful about disclosing the specifics of IQ test scores to parents.

I certainly would meet with the parents who have written to explain the reasons for IQ testing in our school. Tests are aids to teachers to help us understand how to deal more effectively with our students—to challenge them, to help them, and to have high, but realistic expectations of them. For those parents who persist in wanting to know the results of an IQ test, in an individual conference I would sketch the meaning of IQ and emphasize the notion of multiple intelligences. I would avoid simple numbers and gross indices such as "your child has an IQ of 115." Rather, I would focus on the strengths of the student as I discussed the student's intelligence profile. All of my explanations would be in general terms, such as "your child is better than most of his peers in coping with new experiences, but about average in solving abstract word problems." Again, I would emphasize the positive and use other results to provide suggestions to parents about what they could do to help in areas in which the student seemed less advanced.

This real problem is a challenge because it forces me to do what I should be doing anyway—assessing each student as an individual to determine how strong the academic challenge should be and how much support is needed. The problem compels me to look for strengths while identifying areas where the child may need special help. I believe this process is fundamental to good teaching.

JEFF D. HORTON

Seventh–Twelfth Grade Teacher
Colton School, Colton, Washington

For the most part, intelligence testing can give some information about groups of students. It also can tell where individual students are positioned compared to a group. However, these tests are usually not a good instrument for determining how "smart" a student is or can be.

When presenting intelligence test scores to parents, it is important to be clear about what the information does and does not say. Parents should also be informed that they will be comparing their son(s) or daughter(s) score(s) against a group, not against individual students. This point is very important. Often teachers will be asked to compare one student's work with that of another student. This should never be done. Each student is unique and has a variety of abilities and limitations. Teachers must look at the individual abilities, skills, and knowledge of the student being assessed, as well as that student's effort in the subject(s) being taught. If the parent wants to see the actual scores, it may be wise to have the school's counselor or an administrator available to help explain the results.

THOMAS W. NEWKIRK

Eighth Grade English Teacher
Hamilton Heights Middle School, Arcadia, Indiana

Reports in regard to the success of my students and especially of my advisory students are important and deserve my full attention. Hopefully such reports, together with my own observations and the observations of my colleagues, give me insight in helping my students realize their potential. Obviously, the more information I have, the more insight I am likely to have, and I would try to avoid basing any judgment on a single observation or report.

When I met with the parents to discuss their child's achievement, I would review the types of questions asked on the test, share my own opinions based upon daily observations, and emphasize that test results are only one measure of intelligence.

AMY NEAL

Ninth Grade Teacher
Katy High School, Katy, Texas

After I read the test results, I would call each parent. I would arrange a time for them to come to the school to meet with me and their child's guidance counselor. At that meeting, we would discuss the results of the test and the validity of the test. I would explain to the parents that as a special education teacher, I use intelligence tests as a guide to a student's intellectual ability, but the scores are not a measure of "how smart a student really is."

ELIZABETH CHOUINARD

Fourth Grade Teacher
MacGregor Elementary School, Houston, Texas

How smart is Jason? Can a standardized intelligence test give an accurate measure? From my personal experiences with standardized tests, I can say that they are not always accurate. One child might have an advantage over another because he or she has been exposed to that test's format before taking it, and the other child has not. Some students might score high on an intelligence test because they have been trained to use effective test-taking strategies. The students who have not been trained in these test-taking straegies would be at a great disadvantage and their test scores would reflect this.

A third concern is the actual test administration. Although the test would likely be administered using explicit directions, there is no way to ensure that test validity is being maintained. People giving the test could interpret the directions differently, they could follow the directions casually, or they could disregard them altogether. The obvious result would be intelligence scores that are not true reflections of the students involved. In addition, there are numerous emotional and physical factors that could affect test results, including amount of sleep the night before the test, awareness of the importance of the test, and whether there was adequate light in the test area, among others. The test results may not legitimately reflect the child's intelligence level.

With this in mind, I would cautiously analyze the test results and compare them to other information on the child, such as performance on other tests and classroom experiences. I would share the test results with parents of the children involved. However, I would caution them about possible sources of error in testing. I would also share other pertinent information with the parents that might present a more accurate rating of their child's intelligence level.

Culture and Community

ere there students in your junior or senior high school who spoke a different language or who were from a different racial or ethnic group than yours? How did you feel about these "different" students? Were they ever the butt of jokes in your group? Are you prepared to dedicate yourself to teaching their children and the children of other racial or ethnic groups who may seem even more unlike you?

The face of American classrooms is changing. In this chapter we examine the many cultures that form the fabric of our society. We begin by tracing the schools' responses to different ethnic and cultural groups and consider the concept of multicultural education. With a broad conception of culture as a basis, we then examine three important dimensions of every student's identity: social class, ethnicity, and gender. For each dimension, we will explore the experiences of the various groups in the schools, possible differences in achievement and learning styles, and explanations for the lower achievement of some groups. Then we turn to a consideration of language and bilingual education. The last section of the chapter presents three general principles for teaching every student.

By the time you have completed this chapter you should be able to:

▶ Compare the notion of the melting pot with views about multicultural education.
▶ Define *culture* and list the various groups that make up your own cultural identity.
▶ Explain why the school achievement of low-income students often falls below that of middle- and upper-income students.
▶ Give examples of conflicts and compatibilities between home and school cultures.
▶ Describe the school's role in the development of gender differences.
▶ Describe effective teaching in bilingual classrooms.
▶ Incorporate multicultural concepts into your teaching.
▶ Give examples of culturally relevant pedagogy.

What Would You Do?

You teach in a fairly homogeneous primary school. In fact, most of your kindergarten–1st grade students are middle or upper-middle class and White. In January, a new student joins your class—the daughter of an African American professor who recently moved to the nearby college. After a few weeks, you notice that the new student is not being included in many activities. She sits alone in the library and plays alone at recess. Then one day you overhear two of your higher achieving girls talking about their "White Girls Club."

▶ Would you investigate to learn more about this "Club?" How?

▶ If you found that your students had created a club that excluded non-White students, what would you do?

▶ If you teach older students, what would you do about student groups that define themselves by who *cannot* be members?

Today's Multicultural Classrooms

Connect and Extend
To professional journals
Multicultural Education (1992, special issue). *Educational Leadership, 49*(4).

Who are the students in American classrooms today? Here are a few statistics:

▶ One in four Americans under the age of 18 lives in poverty. For children under age 3, the number is one in three.

▶ The number of children in poverty in the United States is almost 50% higher than in *any other developed Western nation* and 5 to 8 times higher than in many prominent industrialized nations.

▶ Nearly 50% of all African American children are poor.

▶ One in three children lives with a single parent, usually a working mother.

▶ Fifteen percent of the children entering school in 1986 were immigrants who spoke little or no English; 10% had poorly educated or illiterate parents.

▶ By the year 2020, about 46% of all students in the United States will be students of color, many the children of new immigrants.

▶ By 2050, there will be no majority race or ethnicity in the United States; every American will be a member of a minority group (Banks, 1997; Grant & Sleeter, 1989; Halford, 1999; McLoyd, 1998; Payne & Biddle, 1999; *Teacher Magazine*, April 1991).

Individuals, Groups, and Society

Melting Pot: A metaphor for the absorption and assimilation of immigrants into the mainstream of society so that ethnic differences vanish.

Cultural Deficit Model: A model that explains the school achievement problems of ethnic minority students by assuming that their culture is inadequate and does not prepare them to succeed in school.

Multicultural Education: Education that teaches the value of cultural diversity.

Since the beginning of the 20th century, a flow of immigrants has entered the United Kingdom, Western Europe, Canada, Australia, the United States, and many other developed countries. These new immigrants were expected to assimilate—that is, to enter the cultural **melting pot** and become like those who had arrived earlier. For years, the goal of American schools was to be the fire under the melting pot. Immigrant children who spoke different languages and had different religious and cultural heritages were expected to come to the schools, master standard English, and learn to become mainstream Americans.

In the 1960s and 1970s, some educators suggested that minority group and poor students had problems in school because they had not fully "melted" or assimilated into mainstream American life. The students were described as "culturally disadvantaged" or "culturally handicapped." The assumption of this **cultural deficit model** was that the students' home culture was inferior because it had not prepared them to fit into the schools. Today most people reject the idea of cultural deficits. They believe that no culture is deficient, but rather that there may be incompatibilities between the student's home culture and the expectations of the school.

Also during the 1960s and 1970s, there was growing concern for civil and human rights and an increasing sense among many ethnic groups that they did not want to assimilate completely into mainstream American society. Rather, they wanted to maintain their culture and identity while still being a respected part of the larger society. Multiculturalism was the goal.

Today there are many definitions of and disagreements about multiculturalism. In an interview for *Educational Leadership* (Halford, 1999), Ronald Takaki states that multiculturalism in the United States is simply "serious scholarship that includes all American peoples" (p. 9) and acknowledges that "when we look around us, we realize that not all of us came from Europe. Many came from Africa and Latin America, and others were already here in North America" (p. 9).

Multicultural education is one response to the increasing diversity of the school population as well as to the growing demand for equality for all groups. A narrow definition of multicultural education is the expansion of educational curricula and activities to include the perspectives, histories, accomplishments, and concerns of non-European people (Hilliard, 1991/92). A broader conception of multicultural education is "a reform movement designed to make some major changes in the education of students" (Banks, 1999, p. 1). An examination of the alternative approaches to multicultural education is beyond the scope of an educational psychology text, but be aware that there is no general agreement about the "best" approach.

James Banks (1999) suggests that multicultural education has five dimensions, as shown in Figure 5.1 on page 158. Many people are familiar only with the dimension of *content integration*, using examples and content from a variety of cultures when teaching a subject. Because they believe that multicultural education is simply a change in curriculum, many people assume that it is irrelevant for subjects such as science and mathematics. But if you consider the other four dimensions—helping students understand how knowledge is influenced by beliefs, reducing prejudice, creating social structures in schools that support learning and development for all students, and using teaching methods that reach all students—then you will see that this view of multicultural education is relevant to all subjects and all students.

Multicultural education rejects the idea of the melting pot. According to the multicultural ideal, America should be transformed into a society that values diversity (Banks, 1997, 1999; Sleeter, 1995). Let's take a closer look at the differences that make up the mosaic of cultural diversity.

American Cultural Diversity

In this text we take a broad interpretation of culture and multicultural education, so we will examine social class, race, ethnicity, and gender as aspects of diversity. We begin with a look at the meaning of culture. Many people associate this concept with the "cultural events" section of the newspaper—art galleries, museums,

Connect and Extend
To professional journals
The following paragraphs are quoted with permission from *Education Week* from Debra Viadero (1990), "Battle over multicultural education rises in intensity," *Education Week, 10*(13), November 28, pp. 1, 11, 13:

While the ethnic-studies approach is meant to embrace a number of ethnic groups, it is talked about most often in relation to Afrocentric curricula. In their most commonly envisioned form, Afrocentric programs are embodied in the model used in the Portland public schools since 1989. School officials commissioned scholars to write "baseline essays" on the contributions of African and American Blacks in six fields of study: art, language, mathematics, science, social studies, and music. Teachers are now expected to "infuse" that information throughout their teaching. Similar essays will be developed over the next few years on Hispanics, American Indians, Asians, and Pacific Islanders.

"We're recognizing that most education programs use a European lens to view the world," says Carolyn M. Leonard, coordinator of the Portland district's program. "We're saying, 'I'm using another lens to view the world and my way of looking at it is different than yours.'"

Connect and Extend
To the research
See *Educational Psychology Review*, March 1992, for two articles on multicultural education: Garcia, E. E. (1992). "Hispanic" children: Theoretical, empirical, and related policy issues, pp. 69–94; Yee, A. H. (1992). Asians as stereotypes and students: Misperceptions that persist, pp. 95–132.

Connect and Extend
To professional journals
Dealing with Diversity (1989, special section). *Educational Leadership, 46*(6), 2–58.

FIGURE 5.1

Banks's Dimensions of Multicultural Education

Multicultural education is more than a change in the curriculum. To make education appropriate for all students, we must consider other dimensions as well. The way the athletics and counseling programs are structured, the teaching method used, lessons about prejudice, perspectives on knowledge—these and many more elements contribute to true multicultural education.

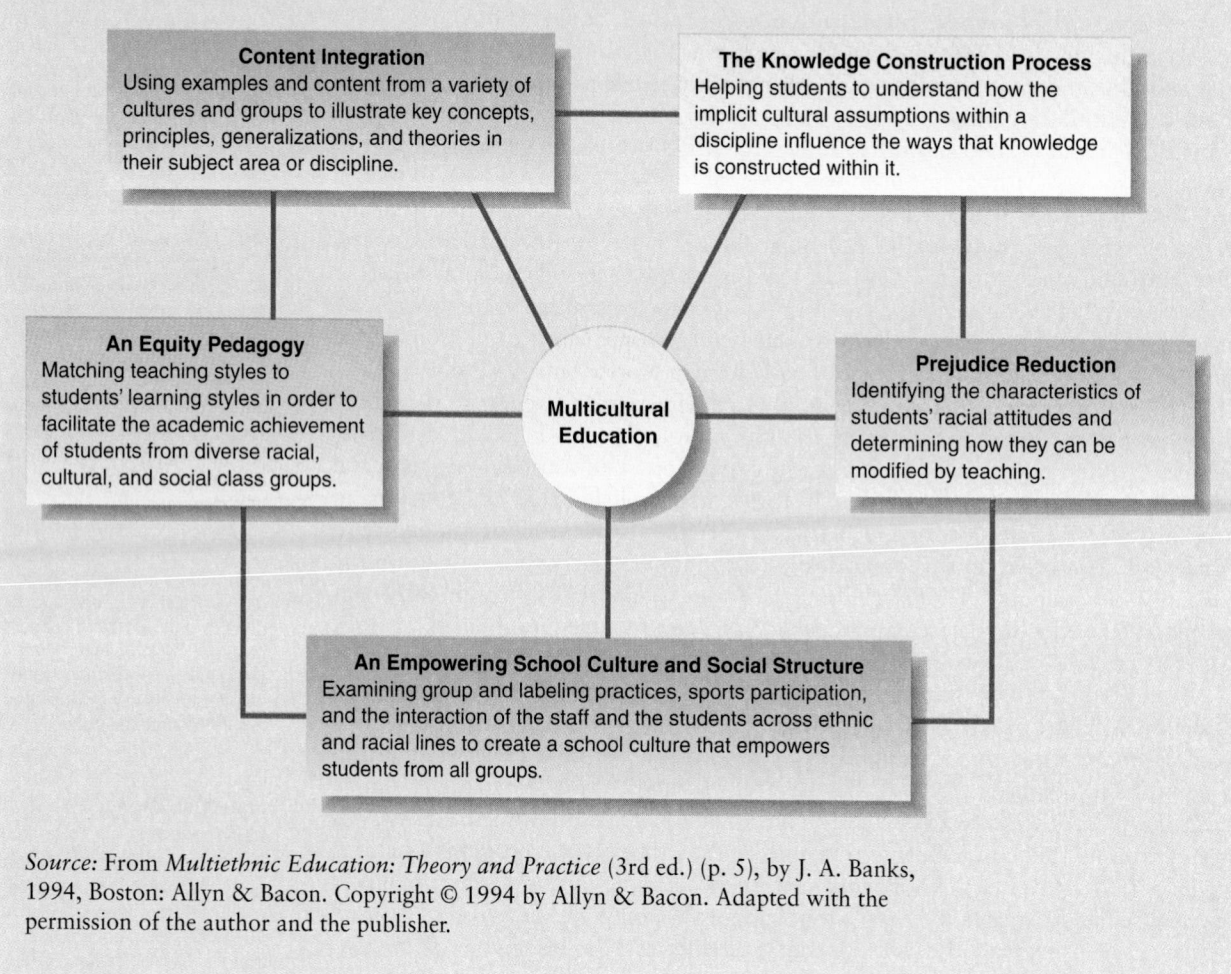

Content Integration
Using examples and content from a variety of cultures and groups to illustrate key concepts, principles, generalizations, and theories in their subject area or discipline.

The Knowledge Construction Process
Helping students to understand how the implicit cultural assumptions within a discipline influence the ways that knowledge is constructed within it.

An Equity Pedagogy
Matching teaching styles to students' learning styles in order to facilitate the academic achievement of students from diverse racial, cultural, and social class groups.

Multicultural Education

Prejudice Reduction
Identifying the characteristics of students' racial attitudes and determining how they can be modified by teaching.

An Empowering School Culture and Social Structure
Examining group and labeling practices, sports participation, and the interaction of the staff and the students across ethnic and racial lines to create a school culture that empowers students from all groups.

Source: From *Multiethnic Education: Theory and Practice* (3rd ed.) (p. 5), by J. A. Banks, 1994, Boston: Allyn & Bacon. Copyright © 1994 by Allyn & Bacon. Adapted with the permission of the author and the publisher.

Shakespeare, classical music, and so on. Culture has a much broader meaning; it embraces the whole way of life of a group of people.

Culture and Group Membership. There are many definitions of **culture**. An article in the 1998 *Annual Review of Psychology* described seven views: Culture as core societal values, as context and customs, as power and social position, as intergroup relations and social identities, as tools and practices, as social capital or wealth, and as psychological capabilities to navigate borders in diverse societies (Cooper & Denner, 1998). Most definitions include the knowledge, rules, traditions, attitudes, and values that guide behavior in a particular group of people (Betancourt & Lopez, 1993). The group creates a culture—a program for living—

Culture: The knowledge, values, attitudes, and traditions that guide the behavior of a group of people and allow them to solve the problems of living in their environment.

and communicates the culture to members. Thus people are members of groups, they are not members of cultures. Groups can be defined along regional, ethnic, religious, racial, gender, social class, or other lines. Each of us is a member of many groups, so we all are influenced by many different cultures. Sometimes the influences are incompatible or even contradictory. For example, if you are a feminist but also a Roman Catholic, you may have trouble reconciling the two different cultures' beliefs about the ordination of women as priests. Your personal belief will be based, in part, on how strongly you identify with each group (Banks, 1994).

There are many different cultures, of course, in every modern country. In the United States, students growing up in a small rural town in the Deep South are part of a cultural group that is very different from that of students in a large urban center or students in a West Coast apartment. In Canada, students living in the suburbs of Toronto certainly differ in a number of ways from students growing up in a Montreal high-rise apartment or on a farm in Quebec. Within those small towns in the Deep South or Quebec, the child of a gas station attendant grows up in a different culture from the child of the town doctor or dentist. Individuals of African, Asian, Hispanic, Native American, or European descent have distinctive histories and traditions. The experiences of males and females are different in most ethnic and economic groups. Everyone living within a particular country shares many common experiences and values, especially because of the influence of the mass media. But other aspects of their lives are shaped by differing cultural backgrounds.

Connect and Extend
To professional journals

For a concise discussion of cultural styles and the possible clashes of styles in classrooms, see Hilliard, A. G., III (1989). Teachers and cultural styles in a pluralistic society. *NEA Today, 7*(6), 65–69. Hilliard notes: "[T]he misunderstanding of behavioral styles leads teachers to mistake achievement in academic areas such as creative expression. . . . Many teachers from Eurocentric cultures have a linear storytelling style. Many African-American children, on the other hand, exhibit a spiraling storytelling style with many departures from an initial point, but a return to make a story whole. Many teachers of these children are unable to follow the children's coherent stories. Some teachers even believe that the children's stories have no coherence at all. Some lose patience with the children and indicate that they are doing badly." (p. 69)

Cautions in Interpreting Cultural Differences. Before we examine the bases for cultural differences, two cautions are necessary. First, we will consider social class, ethnicity, and gender separately, because much of the available research focuses on only one of these variables. Of course, real children are not just African American, or middle class, or female; they are complex beings and members of many groups.

The second caution comes from James Banks (1993), who has written several books on multicultural education:

> Although membership in a gender, racial, ethnic, social-class, or religious group can provide us with important clues about an individual's behavior, it cannot enable us to predict behavior. . . . *Membership in a particular group does not determine behavior but makes certain types of behavior more probable.* (pp. 13–14)

Keep this in mind as you read about characteristics of economically disadvantaged students or Asian Americans or males. The information we will examine reflects tendencies and probabilities. It does not tell you about a specific person. Remember that you will be teaching individual students. Each child is a unique product of many influences, a member of a variety of groups. For example, if a minority group student in your class consistently arrives late, you should not assume that the student's behavior reflects a cultural difference in beliefs about punctuality. It may be that the student has a job before school or must walk a long distance, or even that he or she dreads school.

CHECKPOINT

Today's Multicultural Classrooms

Review

▶ Distinguish between the "melting pot" and multiculturalism.

▶ What is multicultural education?

▶ What is culture?

Apply

▶ What cultural groups affect your identity?

Social Class Differences

Connect and Extend
To professional journals
Knapp, M., Turnbull, B. J., &
Shields, P. M. (1990). New directions for educating children of
poverty. *Educational Leadership,*
48(1), 4–9. *Focus Question:* Contrast traditional approaches for
teaching students at risk of failing
with the newer recommendations
of Knapp and Turnbull. Why should
the new approaches be more
effective?

Connect and Extend
To professional journals
See two issues of *Educational*
Leadership with special sections
on "Reaching for Equity," December
1997/January 1998 (Volume 55,
Number 4) and "Race, Class, and
Culture," April 1999 (Volume 56,
Number 7).

The term used by sociologists for variations in wealth, power, and prestige is **socio-economic status**, or **SES**. In modern societies, levels of wealth, power, and prestige are not always consistent. Some people—for instance, university professors—are members of professions that are reasonably prestigious but provide little wealth or power. Other people have political power though they are not wealthy. No single variable, not even income, is an effective measure of SES. In spite of these inconsistencies, most researchers identify four general levels of SES: upper, middle, working, and lower classes. The main characteristics of these four levels are summarized in Table 5.1.

Social class is a significant dimension of cultural differences, often overpowering other differences such as ethnicity or gender. For example, upper-class Anglo-Europeans, African Americans, and Hispanic Americans typically find that they have more in common with each other than they have with lower-class individuals from their own ethnic groups (Gollnick & Chinn, 1994).

Who Are the Poor?

About one in four Americans under the age of 18 lives in poverty, defined in 1999 by the United States Department of Commerce, Bureau of the Census as an income of $16,530 for a family of four. The United States has the highest rate of poverty for children of all developed nations, as much as five to eight times higher than other industrialized countries. And almost half of these children can be classified as living in deep poverty—in families with incomes 50% below the poverty threshold. As you can see in Figure 5.2, the absolute number of poor children is increasing. By 2020, schools will have to teach 5.4 million more poor students than they taught in 1984 (McLoyd, 1998; Reed & Sautter, 1990).

TABLE 5.1 *Selected Characteristics of Different Social Classes*

	Upper Class	Middle Class	Working Class	Lower Class
Income	$100,000+	$40,000–$100,000 (1/3) $25,000–$39,999 (2/3)	$12,000–$40,000	Below $12,000
Occupation	Corporate, professional, family money	White-collar, skilled blue-collar	Blue-collar	Minimum-wage unskilled labor
Education	Prestigious colleges and professional schools	High school, college, or professional school	High school	High school or less
Home ownership	At least one home	Usually own home	About half own a home	No
Health coverage	Full	Usually	Limited	No
Neighborhoods	Exclusive or comfortable	Comfortable	Modest	Deteriorating
Afford children's college	Easily	Usually	Seldom	No
Political power	National, state, or local	State or local	Limited	No

Source: Information from *Sociology* (4th ed.) (pp. 270–274), by J. J. Macionis, 1993, Saddle River, NJ: Prentice-Hall. Copyright © 1993 by Prentice-Hall.

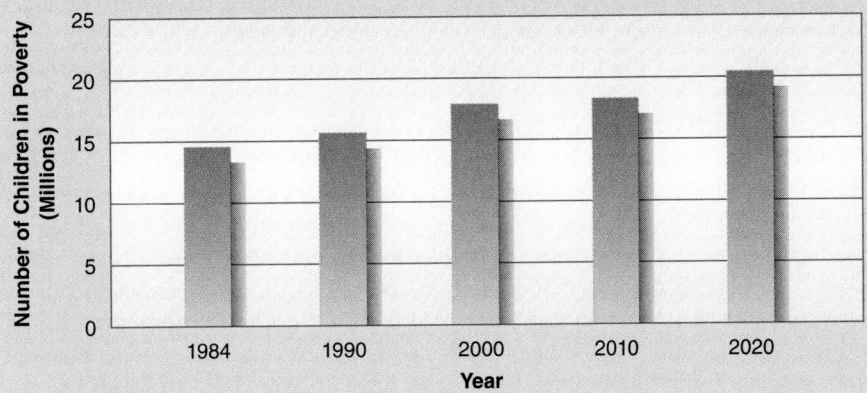

FIGURE 5.2

Projected Number of Children in Poverty

The number of children who live in poverty in the United States grows each year and is projected to reach 20 million by the year 2020.

Source: From "The Changing Nature of the Disadvantaged Population: Current Dimensions and Future Trends," by A. M. Pallas, G. Natriello, and E. L. McDill, 1989, *Educational Researcher, 18* (5), Figure p. 19. Copyright © 1989 by the American Educational Research Association. Reprinted with permission of the publisher.

The majority of these poor children, about 65%, are White, because the total number of poor White families is greater than any other ethnic group. But even though the total number of poor African American and Hispanic American children is smaller than the number of poor White children, the percentages are higher. About 40% of all Hispanic American children and 47% of all African American children live in poverty. Compare this to an overall poverty rate of 22% for all children in the United States. In addition, over half (60%) of all single mothers with preschool children live in poverty (U.S. Bureau of the Census, 1997). Too often, these mothers lack education and job skills, so they have little hope of moving out of poverty.

SES and Achievement

There are many relationships between SES and school performance. For example, it is well documented that high-SES students of all ethnic groups show higher average levels of achievement on test scores and stay in school longer than low-SES students (Alwin & Thornton, 1984; Conger, Conger, & Elder, 1997; McLoyd, 1998). Poverty during a child's preschool years appears to have the greatest negative impact. Unfortunately, families with young children are the most likely to be poor because young parents have the lowest paying jobs or no jobs at all (Bronfenbrenner, McClelland, Wethington, Moen, & Ceci, 1996). And the longer the child is in poverty, the stronger the impact on achievement. For example, even when we take into account parents' education, the chance that children will be retained in grades

Connect and Extend
To professional journals
Teaching the Children of Poverty (1991, special section). *Phi Delta Kappan, 73*(4), 282–310.

Socioeconomic Status (SES): Relative standing in the society based on income, power, background, and prestige.

or placed in special education increases by 2 to 3% for every year the children live in poverty (Sherman, 1994).

What are the effects of low socioeconomic status that might explain the lower school achievement of these students? Many factors maintain a cycle of poverty. Poor health care for mother and child, limited resources, family stress, interruptions in schooling, exposure to violence, overcrowding, homelessness, discrimination, and other factors lead to school failures, low-paying jobs—and another generation born in poverty. Garcia (1991) and McLoyd (1998) describe other possible explanations. Let's take a closer look at each of them.

Poor Health Care. Families in poverty have less access to good prenatal and infant health care and nutrition. Over half of all adolescent mothers receive no prenatal care at all. Poor mothers and adolescent mothers are more likely to have premature babies, and prematurity is associated with many cognitive and learning problems. Children in poverty are more likely to be exposed to legal drugs (nicotine, alcohol) and illegal drugs (cocaine, heroin) before birth. Children whose mothers take drugs during pregnancy can have problems with organization, attention, and language skills. Children who live in older houses with lead paint and lead-soldered pipes, which exist in many inner city areas, have greater concentrations of lead in their blood. This lead poisoning is associated with lower school achievement and long-term neurological impairment (McLoyd, 1998).

Connect and Extend
To other chapters
The concepts of teacher expectation effects and self-fulfilling prophecies are very important in a consideration of cultural differences in the classroom. These concepts are discussed fully in Chapter 11.

Low Expectations—Low Self-Esteem. Because low-SES students may wear old clothes, speak ungrammatically, or be less familiar with books and school activities, teachers and other students may assume that these students are not bright. The teacher may avoid calling on them to protect them from the embarrassment of giving wrong answers or because they make the teacher uncomfortable. The children come to believe that they aren't very good at schoolwork (Elrich, 1994). The following true story shows how powerful this effect on self-esteem can be. Terrence Quinn, principal of an elementary school in New York, spends his mornings serving coffee and doughnuts in a welfare hotel six blocks from his school, trying to convince parents to send their children to school.

> Last spring, Jacqueline, a 6th-grader who had lived at the hotel, was selected as the school's valedictorian. One month before the official announcement, she entered Quinn's office and asked to speak to him in private. "Can someone on welfare actually be the valedictorian?" she asked. Quinn reassured Jacqueline, a youngster who has overcome many obstacles. . . . Why should a child such as Jacqueline feel so humiliated and ashamed of her predicament? (Reed & Sautter, 1990, p. K2)

Connect and Extend
To other chapters
The concept of learned helplessness was discussed in Chapter 4 as one explanation for the lower achievement of students with learning disabilities and will be discussed again in Chapter 10 as a factor influencing motivation.

Learned Helplessness. Low-SES children may be the victims of learned helplessness, described in the previous chapter. That is, low-SES students (or any students who fail continually) may come to believe that doing well in school is impossible. Many of their friends and relatives never finished school, so it seems normal to quit. In fact, about one-fourth of children from poor families drop out of school (Bennett, 1995). Without a high school diploma, these students find few rewards awaiting them in the work world. Many available jobs barely pay a living wage. If the head of a family of three works full time at the minimum wage, the family's income will still be below the poverty line (Reed & Sautter, 1990). Low-SES children, particularly those who also encounter racial discrimination, "become convinced that it is difficult if not impossible for them to advance in the mainstream by doing well in school" (Goleman, 1988).

Peer Influences and Resistance Cultures. Some researchers have suggested that low-SES students may become part of a **resistance culture**. To members of this culture, making it in school means selling out and trying to act "middle class." In order to maintain their identity and their status within the group, low-SES students must reject the behaviors that would make them successful in school—studying, cooperating with teachers, even coming to class (Bennett, 1995; Ogbu, 1987, 1997). John Ogbu linked identification in a resistance culture to poor Hispanic American, Native American, and African American groups, but similar reactions have been noted for poor White students both in the United States and in England (Willis, 1977). This is not to say that all low-SES students resist achievement. Adolescents whose parents value academic achievement tend to select friends who also share those values (Berndt & Keefe, 1995) and many young people are high achievers in spite of their economic situation or negative peer influences (O'Connor, 1997).

Tracking. Another explanation for the lower achievement of many low-SES students is that these students experience **tracking** and therefore have a different academic socialization; that is, they are actually taught differently (Oakes, 1990). If they are tracked into "low-ability" or "general" classes, they may be taught to memorize and be passive. Their classes may be low-level and teacher-dominated. Middle-class students are more likely to be encouraged to think and create in their classes (Anyon, 1980). When low-SES students receive an inferior education, their academic skills are inferior and their life chances are limited. Adam Gamoran (1987) found that the achievement differences between low-track and high-track students were greater than the differences between high school dropouts and graduates. In an interview with Marge Scherer (1993), Jonathan Kozol described the cruel predictive side of tracking:

> [T]racking is so utterly predictive. The little girl who gets shoved into the low reading group in 2nd grade is very likely to be the child who is urged to take cosmetology instead of algebra in the 8th grade, and most likely to be in vocational courses, not college courses, in the 10th grade, if she hasn't dropped out by then. (p. 8)

If tracking can have such profound effects, why not eliminate it altogether? As you can see in the Point/Counterpoint on page 164, the issue may not be that simple.

Childrearing Styles. The oldest explanation for the academic problems of low-SES children is that their home environment does not give them the head start in school provided by middle- and upper-class homes. Schools tend to value and expect the behaviors more often taught in middle-class homes. For example, studies have shown that middle-class mothers talk more; give more verbal guidance; help their children understand the causes of events, make plans, and anticipate consequences; direct their children's attention to the relevant details of a problem; and, rather than impose solutions, encourage children to solve problems themselves (Hess & Shipman, 1965; L. Hoffman, 1984; Willerman, 1979). Contrast these two interactions as a mother works with a child on a puzzle:

"No, that piece goes here!"

"What shape is that piece? Can you find a spot that is straight like the piece? Yes, that's straight, but look at the color. Does the color match? No? Look again for a straight, red piece. Yes—try that one. Good for you! You finished the corner."

By assisting their children in these ways, mothers are actually following Vygotsky's advice to provide intellectual support, or scaffolding, in the children's zone of proximal development, as we discussed in Chapter 2. You can see how the second

Connect and Extend
To professional journals
For a discussion of possible clashes between the culture of the school and the culture of the Black adolescent, see "'The burden of 'acting white'" (1987, November). *Harvard Education Letter, 3*(6), 6.

Connect and Extend
To other chapters
Related information on the effects of ability grouping and tracking appears in Chapter 4.

Connect and Extend
To the research
For a description and evaluation of a program for at-risk children that avoids the use of a "pull out" orientation by using regrouping and tutoring, see Slavin, R. E., Madden, N. A., Karweit, N. L., Livermon, B. J., & Dolan, L. (1990). Success for all: First-year outcomes of a comprehensive plan for reforming urban education. *American Educational Research Journal, 27,* 255–278.

Resistance Culture: Group values and beliefs about refusing to adopt the behaviors and attitudes of the majority culture.

Tracking: Assignment to different classes and academic experiences based on achievement.

Is Tracking an Effective Strategy?

Tracking students into different classes or strands (college prep, vocational, remedial, gifted, etc.) has been standard procedure in many schools for a long time, but does it work? Critics say tracking is harmful while supporters claim it is useful, even though it presents challenges.

▶ POINT *Tracking is harmful and should be eliminated.*

According to Tom Loveless, writing in the April 1999 issue of *Educational Leadership,*

> Prominent researchers and prestigious national reports have argued that tracking stands in the way of equal educational opportunity. (p. 28)

Loveless goes on to cite the work of Braddock and Slavin (1993); Carnegie Council on Adolescent Development (1989); Oakes (1985); and Wheelock (1992)—all of whom make the argument against tracking. What is the basis for these claims? Surprisingly, the evidence is not clear or direct. For example, a few well-done and carefully designed studies found that tracking increases the gap between high and low achievers by depressing the achievement of low-track students and boosting the achievement of high track students (Gamoran, 1987; Kerckhoff, 1986). And Gamoran also found that the achievement gap between low-and high-track students is greater than the gap between students who drop

out of school and students who graduate. Because low-income students and students of color are overrepresented in the lower tracts, they suffer the greatest harm from tracking and should benefit the most from the elimination of tracking (Oakes, 1990). Is this likely?

◀ COUNTERPOINT *Eliminating tracking will hurt many students.*

Researchers who have looked closely at tracking believe that tracking may be harmful for some students some of the time, but not for all students and not all of the time. First, as most people agree, tracking seems to have positive effects for the high-track students. Gifted programs, honors classes, and advanced placement classes seem to work (Fuchs, Fuchs, Hamlett, & Karns, 1998; Robinson & Clinkenbeard, 1998). No one, especially parents, wants to eliminate the positive effects of these programs. And the chance of being assigned to a high track is 10% greater for African American students (Gamoran & Mare, 1989), so detracking could be a special disservice to these students.

What would happen if schools were detracked? Loveless (1999) identifies some possible hidden costs. First, results of a large national study suggest that when low-track 10th graders are assigned to heterogeneous classes rather than low tracks, they gain about 5 percentage points

in achievement. So far, so good. But average students lose 2 percentage points when put into heterogeneous classes and high-ability students lose about 5 points.

> The achievement gap is indeed narrowed, but apparently at the expense of students in regular and high tracks, representing about 70% of 10th graders in the United States. (Loveless, 1999, p. 29)

Another consequence of detracking is *bright flight*—the withdrawal of the brightest students from the schools. Both African American and White parents distrust mixed ability classes to meet the needs of their children (Public Agenda Foundation, 1994).

In some classes, using a mixed ability structure seems to hinder the achievement of all students. For example, students in heterogeneous algebra classes don't learn as much as students in tracked classes—whatever the ability level of the students (Epstein & MacIver, 1992). And James Kulik's meta-analysis of student self-esteem found that students in low-track classes did *not* have lower self-esteem than students in heterogeneous classes.

So what is the answer? As usual, it is more complicated than simply detracking versus tracking. Careful attention to every student's achievement may mean different answers at different times.

approach is more likely to encourage learning concepts (straight, shape, color, corner, match) and problem solving. Hess and McDevitt (1984) studied mothers and children over an eight-year period and found evidence that this "teaching as opposed to telling" style, often used by middle-class mothers, is related to higher achievement test scores for children ages 4 through 12. These differences in parental interaction styles may account for some of the differences among children from various SES groups.

You should be wary, however, of prejudging families based on their socioeconomic status. Recent research indicates that higher control parenting is linked to better grades for Asian and African American students (Glasgow, Dornbusch, Troyer, Steinberg, & Ritter, 1997). Parenting that is strict and directive, with clear rules and consequences, combined with high levels of warmth and emotional support, is associated with higher academic achievement for inner-city children (Jarrett, 1995). Differences in cultural values and in the danger of neighborhoods may make more parental control useful and appropriate.

Home Environment and Resources. Recent research has focused on the home and neighborhood resources of families—books, computers, libraries, trips, museums, and so on. These home and neighborhood resources seem to have the greatest impact on children's achievement when school is not in session—during the summer or before students enter school. For example, Entwisle, Alexander, and Olson (1997) found that low-SES and high-SES students made comparable gains in reading and math when schools were open, but the low SES students lost ground during summer while the high SES students continued to improve academically. Another study found that lack of emotional support and cognitive stimulation in the home accounted for one-third to one-half of the disadvantages in verbal, reading, and math skills of poor children in a national study (Korenman, Miller, & Sjaastad, 1995).

Again, not all low-income families lack resources. Many of these families provide rich learning environments for their children. When parents of any SES level support and encourage their children—by reading to them, providing books and educational toys, taking the children to the library, making time and space for learning—the children tend to become better, more enthusiastic readers (Morrow, 1983; Peng & Lee, 1992; Shields, Gordon, & Dupree, 1983). White (1982) found that the actual behaviors of the parents were more predictive of their children's school achievement than income level or parents' occupation.

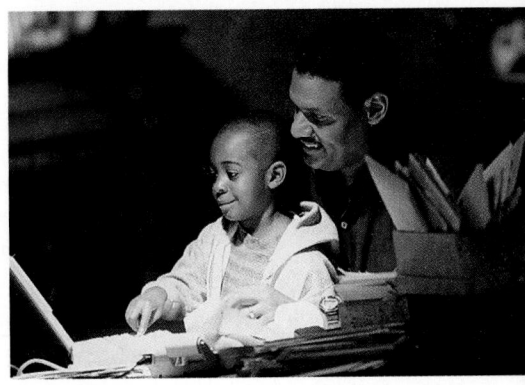

▲ *When families stress the value of reading, studying, and learning, their children are usually at an advantage in school.*

CHECKPOINT

Social Class Differences

Review

▶ What is SES?

▶ What is the relationship between SES and school achievement?

Apply

▶ What changes might you need to make in your classroom to help low-SES students succeed?

Ethnic and Racial Differences

Ethnicity is used to refer to "groups that are characterized in terms of a common nationality, culture, or language" (Betancourt & Lopez, 1993, p. 631). This shared sense of identity may be based on geography, religion, race, or language. We all have some ethnic heritage, whether our background is Italian, Jewish, Ukrainian, Hmong, Chinese, Japanese, Navajo, Hawaiian, Puerto Rican, Cuban, Hungarian, German, African, or Irish—to name only a few. **Race**, on the other hand, is defined as "a category composed of men and women who share biologically transmitted traits that are defined as socially significant" such as skin color or hair texture (Macionis, 1991, p. 308). Depending on the traits you measure and the theory you follow, there are between 3 and 300 races. In effect, race is a label people apply to themselves and to others based on appearances. There are no biologically pure races (Betancourt & Lopez, 1993).

Ethnicity: A cultural heritage shared by a group of people.

Race: A group of people who share common biological traits that are seen as self-defining by the people of the group.

Sociologists sometimes use the term **minority group** to label a group of people that receives unequal or discriminatory treatment. Strictly speaking, however, the term refers to a numerical minority compared to the total population. Referring to particular racial or ethnic groups as "minorities" is technically incorrect in some situations, because in certain places the "minority" group is actually the majority, for example, African Americans in Chicago or Mississippi. So the practice of referring to people as "minorities" because of their racial or ethnic heritage has been criticized because it is misleading—sometimes the "minority" is the "majority."

The Changing Demographics: Cultural Differences

Between 1981 and 1990, the number of immigrants entering the United States was the largest ever. Results of the 1997 census, shown in Table 5.2, reveal that the number of ethnic Americans has increased substantially. By the year 2020, almost half of the population of the country will be from African American, Asian, Latina/Latino, or other ethnic groups.

Ricardo Garcia (1991) compares culture to an iceberg. One-third of the iceberg is visible; the rest is hidden and unknown. The visible signs of culture, such as costumes and marriage traditions, represent only a small portion of the differences among cultures. Many of the differences are "below the surface." They are implicit, unstated, even unconscious biases and beliefs. Each cultural group teaches its members certain "lessons" about living (Casanova, 1987; Kagan, 1983).

Cultures differ in rules for conducting interpersonal relationships, for example. In some groups listeners give a slight affirmative nod of the head and perhaps an occasional "uh huh" to indicate they are listening carefully. But members of other cultures listen without giving acknowledgment, or with eyes downcast, as a sign of respect. In some cultures high-status individuals initiate conversations and ask the questions, and low-status individuals only respond. In other cultures, the pattern is reversed.

Cultural influences are widespread and pervasive. Some psychologists even suggest that culture defines intelligence. For example, physical grace is essential in Balinese social life, so the ability to master physical movements is a mark of intelligence in that culture. Manipulating words and numbers is important in Western societies, so in these cultures such skills are indicators of intelligence (Gardner, 1983).

TABLE 5.2 *Results of the 1997 Census for Selected Ethnic Groups*

Group	Total Number	Percent of Total Population
African American	32 million	12%
Asian	9 million	3.5%
Native American	2.0 million	0.77%
Hispanic	28 million	11%

Source: U.S. Bureau of the Census, 1997.

The visible signs of cultural differences represent only a small portion of the differences among cultures. Many are "below the surface" and have more to do with beliefs and attitudes about life.

Cultural Conflicts. The above are just a few areas where cultures may teach different lessons about living. The differences may be very obvious, such as holiday customs, or they may be very subtle, such as how to get your turn in conversations. The more subtle and unconscious the difference, the more difficult it is to change or even recognize (Casanova, 1987). Cultural conflicts are usually about below-the-surface differences, because when subtle cultural differences meet, misunderstandings are common. Thus, the members of a different culture may be misperceived as rude, slow, or disrespectful.

For example, Erickson and Shultz (1982) studied school counselors working with both students from the same culture and students from different cultures. The researchers found that the culturally different students did not nod and say "uh huh" as they listened to the counselors. Not having received this expected feedback, the counselors assumed that the culturally different students had not understood, and so the counselors repeated their remarks in simpler form. Again no nod, so the counselors simplified and repeated once more. When the students were interviewed afterwards, many said that the counselors had made them feel stupid. In fact, the counselors had decided that these students were not very bright. Neither participant realized that a subtle cultural difference in how to listen was probably to blame for the impressions. In contrast, when students and counselors shared the same background, discussions proceeded smoothly, without the cycles of simplifying and repeating. The students knew the counselors' tacit rules for listening, because both counselor and student had learned from the same teacher—their common culture.

Cultural Compatibility. Not all cultural differences lead to clashes, however. A study comparing mothers in the People's Republic of China, Chinese American mothers, and Caucasian American mothers found dramatic differences in beliefs about motivation and the value of education (Hess, Chih-Mei, & McDevitt, 1987). For example, the mothers from the Republic of China attributed school failure to lack of effort more often than the Caucasian American mothers. The Chinese

Connect and Extend
To the research

In the Chinese tradition, achievement is seen as dependent more on concentration, effort, and persistence than on talent. Centuries ago, Xu Gan, a revered Chinese scholar, said, "Will is the teacher of study and talent is the follower of study. If a person has no talent, [achievement] is possible. But if a person has no will, it is not worth talking about study" (Hess, Chih-Mei, & McDevitt, 1987, p. 180).

Nine-year old Linda Brown, the plaintiff in Brown v. Topeka Board of Education. ▼

The Legacy of Discrimination

When we considered explanations for why low-SES students have trouble in school, we listed the low expectations and biases of teachers and fellow students. This has been the experience of many ethnic minority students as well. Imagine that the child described below is your own. What would you do?

> Almost forty years ago, in the city of Topeka, Kansas, a minister walked hand in hand with his seven-year-old daughter to an elementary school four blocks from their home. Linda Brown wanted to enroll in the 2nd grade, but the school refused to admit her. Instead, public school officials required her to attend another school two miles away. This meant that she had to walk six blocks to a bus stop, where she sometimes waited half an hour for the bus. In bad weather, Linda Brown would be soaking wet by the time the bus came; one day she became so cold at the bus stop that she walked back home. Why, she asked her parents, could she not attend the school only four blocks away? (Macionis, 1991, p. 307)

Her parents' answer to this question, with the help of other concerned families, was to file a suit challenging the school policy. You know the outcome of *Brown v. the Board of Education of Topeka*. "Separate but equal" schools for Black children were declared inherently unequal. Even though segregation in schools became illegal in 1954, about two-thirds of all African American students still attend schools where members of minority groups make up at least 50% of the student body. For about one-third of all Black students, this figure is over 90% (Schofield, 1991). This is because segregation in housing and neighborhoods persists and because some areas have drawn school boundary lines deliberately to separate school enrollments along racial lines (Calmore, 1986; Kantor & Lowe, 1995).

Years of research on the effects of desegregation have mostly shown that legally mandated integration is not a quick solution to the detrimental effects of centuries of racial inequality. Too often, minority group students are resegregated in low-ability tracks even in integrated schools. Simply putting people in the same building does not mean that they will come to respect each other or even that they will experience the same quality of education (Pettigrew, 1998; Schofield, 1991). But when minority group students are moved into high quality schools with a substantial proportion of middle-class peers and when these integrations start in early elementary school, the ethnic minority students benefit. They are more likely to achieve higher grades, attend integrated colleges, and earn more money as adults than comparable students who stayed in segregated schools. The quality of the school probably is the major factor influencing these positive outcomes (Schofield, 1995; Wells & Crain, 1994).

What is the legacy of unequal treatment and discrimination? Part of the testimony during the *Brown v. Board of Education* case in the 1950s was that when African American children in a study were asked to pick the more attractive or smarter doll, they usually chose a White doll and rejected a Black one. This test was repeated in 1990 with the same results (Pine & Hilliard, 1990).

Continuing Prejudice. The word *prejudice* is closely related to the word *prejudge*. **Prejudice** is a rigid and irrational generalization—a prejudgment—about an entire category of people (Macionis, 1994). Prejudice may be positive or negative; that is, you can have positive as well as negative irrational beliefs about a group, but the word usually refers to negative attitudes. Prejudice may target people in partic-

Connect and Extend
To other chapters
This issue was considered in Chapter 3 when ethnic pride was discussed.

Connect and Extend
To professional journals
Pine, G. J., & Hilliard, A. G., III (1990). Rx for racism: Imperatives for America's schools. *Phi Delta Kappan, 71,* 593–600.

Doonesbury

BY GARRY TRUDEAU

ular racial, ethnic, religious, political, geographic, or language groups, or it may be directed toward the sex or sexual orientation of the individual. Racial prejudice is pervasive. A 1991 survey by the National Opinion Research Center found that even though racial attitudes had improved somewhat since 1970, most of the groups surveyed felt at least some prejudice against all the other groups. For example, 78% of non-Hispanic Americans (Whites, Blacks, and Asian Americans) agreed with the statement that Hispanic Americans prefer to live off welfare, and 55% believed that Hispanic Americans are less intelligent. The results were virtually the same when Whites were asked their opinions of African Americans. The United States is a racist society, and this racism is not confined to one group (Clark, Anderson, Clark, & Williams, 1999).

The Development of Prejudice. There are many theories about how and why prejudice develops, but "no framework has yet been proposed that provides a complete explanation of prejudice" (Duckitt, 1992, p. 1182). Current explanations combine personal and social factors. Extreme prejudice may develop as part of an **authoritarian personality**—a person who rigidly conforms to conventional values and believes that society is naturally competitive, with the "better" people rightly reaping the rewards (Duckitt, 1992, 1994; Macionis, 1994). A related source of prejudice is the human tendency to divide the social world into two categories—*us* and *them* or the *in-group* and the *out-group*. These divisions may be made on the basis of race, religion, sex, age, ethnicity, or even athletic team membership. We tend to see members of the out-group as inferior and different from us, but similar to each other—"they all look alike" (Lambert, 1995). The "White Girls Club" described at the beginning of this chapter (based on a real incident in my town) is an example of the potential cruelty of in-groups.

But prejudice is more than a personality trait or a tendency to form in-groups—it is also a set of cultural values. Children learn about valued traits and characteristics from their families, friends, teachers, and the world around them. For years, most of the models presented in books, films, television, and advertising were middle- and upper-class European Americans. People of different ethnic and racial backgrounds were seldom the "heroes" (Gerbner, Gross, Signorelli, & Morgan, 1986). This is changing.

Prejudice is difficult to combat because it can be part of our thinking processes. You saw in Chapter 2 that children develop *schemas*—organized bodies of knowledge—about objects, events, and actions. We have schemas that organize our knowledge about drinking from a straw, people we know, the meaning of words,

Prejudice: Prejudgment, or irrational generalization about an entire category of people.

Authoritarian Personality: Rigidly conforming to the belief that society is naturally competitive, with "better" people reaping its rewards.

and so on. We can also form schemas about groups of people. If I were to ask you to list the traits most characteristic of college freshman, politicians, African Americans, Asian Americans, athletes, Buddhists, lesbians, or members of the National Rifle Association, you probably could generate a list. That list would show that you have a **stereotype**—a schema—that organizes what you know about the group (Wyler, 1988).

As with any schema, we use our stereotype to make sense of the world. You will see in Chapter 7 that having a schema allows you to process information more quickly and efficiently, but it also allows you to distort information to make it fit your schema better (Macrae, Milne, & Bodenhausen, 1994). This is the danger in racial and ethnic stereotypes. We notice information that confirms or agrees with our stereotype—our schema—and miss or dismiss information that does not fit. For example, if a juror has a negative stereotype of Asian Americans and is listening to evidence in the trial of an Asian American, the juror may interpret the evidence more negatively. The juror may actually forget testimony in favor of the defendant but remember more damaging testimony. Information that fits the stereotype is even processed more quickly (Anderson, Klatzky, & Murray, 1990; Baron, 1998).

Continuing Discrimination. Prejudice consists of attitudes, feelings, and beliefs (usually negative) about an entire category of people. **Discrimination** is unequal treatment of particular categories of people. Clearly, ethnic Americans face prejudice and discrimination in subtle or blatant ways every day. One of the most discouraging findings I encountered while writing this chapter is that only 4% of the scientists, engineers, and mathematicians in the United States are either African American or Hispanic American—whereas more than 20% of the total population is from one of these groups. Even though their attitudes toward science and math are more favorable than those of White students, Black and Hispanic students begin to lose out in science and math as early as elementary school. They are chosen less often for gifted classes and acceleration or enrichment programs. They are more likely to be tracked into "basic skills" classes. As they progress through junior high, high school, and college, their paths take them farther and farther out of the pipeline that produces our scientists. If they do persist and become scientists or engineers, they, along with women, will still be paid less than Whites for the same work (National Science Foundation, 1988; Oakes, 1990).

There is another problem caused by stereotypes and prejudice that can undermine academic achievement—stereotype threat.

Stereotype Threat

Stereotype: Schema that organizes knowledge or perceptions about a category.

Discrimination: Treating particular categories of people unequally.

Stereotype Threat: The extra emotional and cognitive burden that your performance in an academic situation might confirm a stereotype that others hold about you.

Stereotype threat is "a social psychological predicament rooted in the prevailing American image of African Americans as intellectually inferior" (Aronson & Fried, in press). The basic idea is that when stereotyped individuals are in situations where the stereotype applies, they bear an extra emotional and cognitive burden. The burden is the possibility of confirming the stereotype, either in the eyes of others or in their own eyes. Thus when girls are asked to solve complicated mathematics problems, for example, they are at risk of confirming widely held stereotypes that girls are inferior to boys in mathematics. It is not necessary that the individual even believe the stereotype. All that matters is that the person is *aware* of the stereotype and *cares about performing* well enough to disprove its unflattering implications (Aronson, Lustina, Good, Keough, Steele, & Brown, 1999). What are the results of stereotype threat? Recent research provides answers that should interest all teachers.

Short-Term Effects: Test Performance. In the short run, the fear that you might confirm a negative stereotype can induce test anxiety and undermine performance. In a series of experiments, Joshua Aronson, Claude Steele, and their colleagues have demonstrated that when African American or Latino college students are put in situations that induce stereotype threat, their performance suffers (Aronson & Salinas, 1998; Aronson, Steele, Salinas, & Lustina, 1999; Steele & Aronson, 1995). For example, African American and White undergraduate subjects in an experiment at Stanford University were told that the test they were about to take would precisely measure their verbal ability. A similar group of subjects was told that the purpose of the test was to understand the psychology of verbal problem solving and not to asses individual ability. As shown in Figure 5.4, when the test was presented as diagnostic of verbal ability, the African American students solved about half as many problems as the White students. In the non-threat situation, the two groups solved about the same number of problems. Other studies found that anxiety and distraction were the main problems. The African American students were more likely to be thinking about the stereotypes as they tried to work.

Long-Term: Disidentification. As we will see in Chapter 10, students often develop self-defeating strategies to protect their self-esteem about academics. They

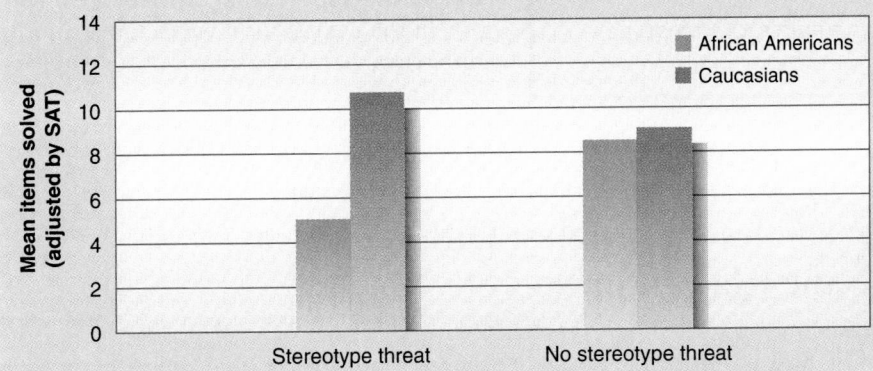

FIGURE 5.4

The Impact of Stereotype Threat on College Students' Standardized Test Performance

When African American college students were told that they were taking a test that would diagnose their verbal ability (stereotype threat), they solved about one-half as many problems as another group of African American students who were not told the test would assess ability. The performance of Caucasian students was not affected by the threat conditions.

Source: From "The Effect of Stereotype Threat on the Standardized Test Performance of College Students," by J. Aronson, C. M. Steele, M. F. Salinas, and M. J. Lustina, 1998. In E. Aronson (Ed.), *Readings about the Social Animal* (8th ed.) (p. 407), New York: Freeman. Adapted with permission.

withdraw, claim to not care, exert little effort—they *disidentify* or psychologically disengage from success in the domain and claim "math is for nerds" or "school is for losers." There is evidence that African Americans are more likely than Whites to disidentify with academics (Major & Schmader, 1998; Ogbu, 1997). Once students define academics as "uncool," it is unlikely they will exert the effort needed for real learning.

Combating Stereotype Threat. Stereotypes are pervasive and difficult to change. Rather than wait for changes, it may be better to acknowledge that these images exist, at least in the eyes of many, and give students ways of coping with the stereotypes. In Chapter 10 we will discuss test anxiety and how to overcome the negative effects of anxiety. Many of those strategies are appropriate for helping students resist stereotype threat.

Aronson and Fried (in press) demonstrated the powerful effects of changing beliefs about intelligence. In their study, African American and White undergraduates were asked to write letters to "at-risk" middle school students to encourage them to persist in school. Some of the undergraduates were given evidence that intelligence is *improveable* and encouraged to communicate this information to their pen pals. Others were given information about multiple intelligences, but not told that these multiple abilities can be improved. The middle school students were not real, but the process of writing persuasive letters about improving intelligence proved powerful. The African American college students, and the White students to a lesser extent, who were encouraged to believe that intelligence can be improved had higher grade point averages and reported greater enjoyment of and engagement in school when contacted at the end of the next school quarter. Thus, believing that intelligence can be improved might inoculate students against stereotype threat.

In the next section we examine another difference that is the source of stereotypes—gender.

Connect and Extend
To the research
The May 1988 issue of *The Elementary School Journal* (Vol. 88, No. 5) is entirely devoted to articles about minority students in the schools.

CHECKPOINT

Ethnic and Racial Differences

Review

▶ Distinguish between ethnicity and race.

▶ How can ethnicity affect school performance?

▶ Distinguish between prejudice, discrimination, and stereotype threat.

Apply

▶ How could you as a teacher counteract stereotype threat for your students?

Females and Males: Differences in the Classroom

Connect and Extend
To the research
For a lively debate on the terminology of gender and sex, see the March 1993 issue of *Psychological Science*.

While I was proofreading this very page for a previous edition, riding cross-country on a train, the conductor stopped beside my seat. He said, "I'm sorry, dear, for interrupting your homework, but do you have a ticket?" I had to smile at his (I'm sure unintended) sexism. I doubt that he made the same comment to the man across the aisle writing on his legal pad. Like racial discrimination, messages of sexism can be subtle. In this section we will examine how men and women are socialized and the role of teachers in providing an equitable education for both sexes.

Gender-Role Identity

Men and women are different. Years of research on personality indicates that men on *average* are more assertive and have slightly higher self-esteem than women. Women are more extroverted, anxious, trusting, and tender-minded (Feingold, 1994). There also appear to be some differences in verbal and spatial abilities between the sexes. The origins and meanings of these differences are hotly debated. Gender-role identity is part of the discussion.

The word *gender* usually refers to judgments about masculinity and femininity, judgments that are influenced by culture and context. In contrast, *sex* refers to biological differences (Deaux, 1993). **Gender-role identity** is the image each individual has of himself or herself as masculine or feminine in characteristics—a part of self-concept. People with a "feminine" identity would rate themselves high on characteristics usually associated with females, such as "sensitive" or "warm," and low on characteristics traditionally associated with males, such as "forceful" and "competitive." Most people see themselves in gender-typed terms, as high on *either* masculine or feminine characteristics. Some children and adults, however, are more **androgynous**—they rate themselves high on *both* masculine and feminine traits. They can be assertive or sensitive, depending on the situation. Having either a masculine or an androgynous identity is associated with higher self-esteem than having a feminine identity, possibly because feminine characteristics are not as valued (Bem, 1974; Boldizar, 1991).

How do gender-role identities develop? It is likely that biology plays a role. Very early, hormones affect activity level and aggression, with boys tending to prefer active, rough, noisy play. Play styles lead young children to prefer same-sex play partners with similar styles, so by age 4, children spend three times as much play time with same-sex playmates as with opposite sex playmates and by age 6 the ratio is 11 to 1 (Benenson, 1993; Maccoby, 1990). Of course, these are averages and individuals do not always fit the average. In addition, many other factors—social and cognitive—affect gender-role identity.

Both parents play more roughly and vigorously with sons than they do with daughters. Parents tend to touch male infants more at first; later, they keep male toddlers at a greater distance than females (Jacklin, DiPietro, & Maccoby, 1984). Parents are more likely to react positively to assertive behavior on the part of their sons and emotional sensitivity in their daughters (Fagot & Hagan, 1991; Lytton & Romney, 1991). Through their interactions with family, peers, teachers, and the environment in general, children begin to form **gender schemas**, or organized networks of knowledge about what it means to be male or female (see Figure 5.5 on page 176). Gender schemas help the children make sense of the world and guide their behavior. So a young girl whose schema for "girls" includes "girls play with dolls and not with trucks" or "girls can't be scientists" will pay attention to, remember, and interact more with dolls than trucks, and she may avoid science activities (Liben & Signorella, 1993; Martin & Little, 1990).

Gender-Role Stereotyping in the Preschool Years.
Different treatment of the sexes and gender-role stereotyping

Gender schemas often have become barriers to success when boys and girls avoid activities not associated with their gender. Recognizing these potential barriers has allowed children's choices to become less gender-driven. ▼

FIGURE 5.5

Gender Schema Theory

According to *gender schema theory*, children and adolescents use gender as an organizing theme to classify and understand their perceptions about the world.

Society's beliefs about the traits of females and males → Gender Schema

Gender Schema → Influences processing of social information

Gender Schema → Influences self-esteem (only behavior or attitudes consistent with gender schema are acceptable)

Connect and Extend
To the research
Lytton, H., & Romney, D. M. (1991). Parents' sex-related differential socialization of boys and girls: A meta-analysis. *Psychological Bulletin, 109*, 267–296.

Connect and Extend
To real life
Do you consider commercials an influence on the development of sex roles?

continue in early childhood. Researchers have found that boys are given more freedom to roam the neighborhood, and they are not protected for as long a time as girls from potentially dangerous activities such as playing with sharp scissors or crossing the street alone. Parents quickly come to the aid of their daughters, but are more likely to insist that their sons handle problems themselves (Block, 1983; Fagot, Hagan, Leinbach, & Kronsberg, 1985). Thus, independence and initiative seem to be encouraged more in boys than in girls.

Many of my student teachers are surprised when they hear young children talk about gender roles. Even in this era of great progress toward equal opportunity of the sexes, a preschool girl is more likely to tell you she wants to become a secretary than to say she wants to be an engineer. After she had given a lecture on the dangers of sex stereotyping in schools, a colleague of mine brought her young daughter to her college class. The students asked the little girl, "What do you want to be when you grow up?" The child immediately replied, "A doctor," and her professor/mother beamed with pride. Then the girl whispered to the students in the front row, "I really want to be a nurse, but my Mommy won't let me." Actually, this is a common reaction for young children. Preschoolers tend to have more stereotyped notions of sex roles than older children, and all ages seem to have more rigid and traditional ideas about male occupations than about what females do (Martin, 1989).

Gender Bias in the Curriculum. During the elementary school years, children continue to learn about what it means to be male or female. Unfortunately, schools often foster these **gender biases** in a number of ways. Most of the textbooks produced for the early grades before 1970 portrayed both males and females in sexually stereotyped roles. In a study of 2,760 stories in 134 books from 16 publishers, a group called *Women on Words and Images* (1975) found that there were four times more stories about male characters than about females. Females tended to be shown in the home, behaving passively and expressing fear or incompetence. Males were usually more dominant and adventurous; they often rescued the females.

Gender Biases: Different views of males and females, often favoring one gender over the other.

In recent years textbook publishers have recognized these problems to some extent and established guidelines to prevent them. It still makes sense to check your teaching materials for such stereotypes, however. When Purcell and Stewart (1990) used the same design as *Women on Words and Images* to analyze 62 elementary readers, they found that the numbers of male and female characters were about equal. Girls were shown in a wide range of activities, but were still portrayed as more helpless than boys. Despite new publishers' guidelines, problems have not disappeared entirely. When Scott O'Dell was looking for a publisher for his *Island of the Blue Dolphins*, he was told by several editors that he needed to make a small change—turn this story of a girl's courageous fight for survival into a story about a boy. O'Dell refused, and the book went on to win a Newbery Award for children's literature (Powell, Garcia, & Denton, 1985; Sadker, Sadker, & Klein, 1991).

Sex Discrimination in Classrooms. There has been quite a bit of research on teachers' treatment of male and female students. One of the best documented findings of the past 25 years is that teachers interact more with boys than with girls. This is true from preschool to college. Teachers ask more questions of males, give males more feedback (praise, criticism, and correction), and give more specific and valuable comments to boys. As girls move through the grades, they have less and less to say. By the time students reach college, men are twice as likely to initiate comments as women (Bailey, 1993; Sadker & Sadker, 1994, 1986b; Serbin & O'Leary, 1975; Wingate, 1986). The effect of these differences is that from preschool through college, girls, on the average, receive 1,800 fewer hours of attention and instruction than boys (Sadker, Sadker, & Klein, 1991). Of course, these differences are not evenly distributed. Some boys, generally high-achieving White students, receive more than their share. Minority group boys, like girls, tend to receive much less attention from the teacher.

The imbalances of teacher attention given to boys and girls are particularly dramatic in science classes. In one study, boys were questioned on the subject matter 80% more often than girls (Baker, 1986). Boys also dominate the use of equipment in science labs, often dismantling the apparatus before the girls in the class have a chance to perform the experiments (Rennie & Parker, 1987).

Stereotypes are perpetuated in many ways, some obvious, some subtle. Guidance counselors, parents, and teachers often do not protest at all when a bright girl says she doesn't want to take any more math or science courses, but when a boy of the same ability wants to forget about math or science, they will object. In these subtle ways, students' stereotyped expectations for themselves can be reinforced (Sadker & Sadker, 1994).

Sex Differences in Mental Abilities

From infancy through the preschool years, most studies find few differences between boys and girls in overall mental and motor development or in specific abilities. During the school years and beyond, psychologists find no differences in general intelligence on the standard measures—these tests have been designed and standardized to minimize sex differences. However, scores on some tests of specific abilities show sex differences. In the concluding article of a special issue on sex differences in cognition in the journal *Learning and Individual Differences*, Diane Halpern (1996) summarized the research:

> The data presented here and in other sources clearly show that there are some areas of cognition in which there are no male-female differences, others where the differences are small, and others where the differences are large, some favor-

Connect and Extend
To the research
Purcell, P., & Stewart, L. (1990). Dick and Jane in 1989. *Sex Roles, 22,* 177–185. This study replicates analyses of textbooks and children's books conducted in the 1970s. *Focus Question:* What evidence of sexism, if any, remains in texts today?

Connect and Extend
To the research
Are females socialized to select or not select scientific careers? See Ware, N. C., & Lee, V. E. (1988). Sex differences in choice of college student majors. *American Educational Research Journal, 25,* 593–614.

Brief abstract: The process of choosing a scientific major was examined in a nationally representative sample of male and female college students of above-average ability. Women who were attending a four-year college, who reported having been influenced by high school teachers and guidance counselors in making plans for college, and who placed a high priority upon aspects of their future family and personal lives were less likely to major in science than their female peers. High socioeconomic status, positive assessments of their high schools, and attending a four-year college predicted science majoring for men.

Connect and Extend
To the research
Linn, M.C., & Hyde, J.S. (1989). Gender, mathematics, and science. *Educational Researcher, 18,* 17–27.

Connect and Extend
To professional journals
See Latham, A. S. (1998). Gender differences on assessments. *Educational Leadership, 55*(4), 88–89.

Connect and Extend
To the research
In contrast to the Maccoby and Jacklin (1974) findings of almost two decades ago, recent findings are showing decreasing achievement differences between males and females, even in mathematics. Articles on this subject include Linn, M. C., & Hyde, J. S. (1989). Gender, mathematics, and science. *Educational Researcher, 118*, 17–28. Also Marsh, H. W. (1989). Sex differences in the development of verbal and mathematics constructs: The high school and beyond study. *American Educational Research Journal, 26*, 191–225. Differences persist between academically gifted males and females in mathematics reasoning. See Mills, C. J., Ablard, K. E., & Stumpf, H. (1993). Gender differences in academically talented young students' mathematical reasoning: Patterns across age and subskills. *Journal of Educational Psychology, 85*, 340–346.

ing females and some favoring males. The "on-the-average" differences show that females excel in reading comprehension, production of written and oral language, and computation (to name a few); whereas the constellation of mathematical, mechanical, and visual information processing is often accomplished either more accurately or more quickly by males. In addition we know that there is much overlap between the sexes in these ability areas, and everyone can improve in any area with appropriate education and practice. (p. 75)

Also, the scores of males tend to be more variable in general, so there are more males than females with very high *and* very low scores on tests (Willingham & Cole, 1997).

There is a caution, however. In most studies of sex differences, race and socioeconomic status are not taken into account. When racial groups are studied separately, African American females outperform African American males in high school mathematics; there is little or no difference in the performance of Asian American girls and boys in math or science (Grossman & Grossman, 1994; Yee, 1992).

What is the basis for the differences? The answers are complex. For example, males on average are better on tests that require mental rotation of a figure in space, prediction of the trajectories of moving objects, and navigating. Some researchers argue that evolution has favored these skills in males (Buss, 1995; Geary, 1995; 1999) but others relate these skills to males' more active play styles and to their participation in athletics (Linn & Hyde, 1989; Newcombe & Baenninger, 1990; Stumpf, 1995).

When Oakes (1990) analyzed the reasons why only 15% of the scientists, engineers, and mathematicians in the United States are women, she concluded that academically qualified girls choose not to take advanced science and math courses in high school. Thus, they don't develop their abilities in this area. In the process, they limit their college and career choices because colleges require applicants to possess some proficiency in mathematics and many jobs also demand abilities in this area. Recent patterns are changing as girls take more mathematics classes.

CHECKPOINT

Women and Men: Differences in the Classroom

Review

▶ What is gender-role identity?

▶ How do gender-role identities develop?

▶ Are there sex differences in cognitive abilities?

Apply

▶ How can teachers promote gender equity in classrooms?

Eliminating Gender Bias

There is some evidence that teachers treat girls and boys differently in mathematics classes. For example, some elementary school teachers spend more academic time with boys in math and with girls in reading. In one study, high school geometry teachers directed most of their questions to boys, even though the girls asked questions and volunteered answers more often. Several researchers have found that some teachers tend to accept wrong answers from girls, saying, in effect, "Well, at least you tried." But when boys give the wrong answer, the teachers are more likely to say, "Try harder! You can figure this out." These messages, repeated time and again, can convince girls that they just aren't cut out for mathematics ("Girls' Math Achievement," 1986; Horgan, 1995). If you are like a few of the student teachers I have supervised who "really hate math," please don't pass this attitude on to your students. You may have been the victim of sex discrimination yourself.

Patricia Casserly of the Educational Testing Service studied 20 high schools where no sex differences in mathematics performance were found. Even though the schools were not alike in all ways, they shared several common features. The teachers had strong backgrounds in mathematics, engineering, or science, not just in general education. They were enthusiastic about mathematics. The brightest students, male and female, were grouped together for instruction in math, and there was heavy emphasis on reasoning in the classes (Kolata, 1980). The activities used to teach math may make a difference as well. Elementary age girls may do better in math if they learn in cooperative as opposed to competitive activities. Certainly it makes sense to balance both cooperative and competitive approaches so that students who learn better each way have equal opportunities (Fennema & Peterson, 1988). The Guidelines below provide additional ideas about avoiding sexism in your teaching. Some are taken from Rop (1997/8).

Connect and Extend
To professional journals
Sadker, D. (1998). Gender equity: still knocking at the classroom door. *Educational Leadership*, *56*(7), 22–27.

GUIDELINES

Avoiding Sexism in Teaching

Check to see if textbooks and other materials you are using present an honest view of the options open to both males and females.

Examples

1. Are both males and females portrayed in traditional and nontraditional roles at work, at leisure, and at home?
2. Discuss your analyses with students, and ask them to help you find sex role biases in other materials—magazine advertising, TV programs, news reporting, for example.

Watch for any unintended biases in your own classroom practices.

Examples

1. Do you group students by sex for certain activities? Is the grouping appropriate?
2. Do you call on one sex or the other for certain answers—boys for math and girls for poetry, for example?
3. Monitor your metaphors. Ask students to "tackle the problem" and also to "cook up a solution."

Look for ways in which your school may be limiting the options open to male or female students.

Examples

1. What advice is given by guidance counselors to students in course and career decisions?
2. Is there a good sports program for both girls and boys?

3. Are girls encouraged to take advanced placement courses in science and mathematics? Boys in English and foreign languages?

Use gender-free language as much as possible.

Examples

1. Do you speak of "law-enforcement officer" and "mail carrier" instead of "policeman" and "mailman"?
2. Do you name a committee "head" instead of a "chairman"?

Provide role models.

Examples

1. Assign articles in professional journals written by female research scientists or mathematicians.
2. Have recent female graduates who are majoring in science, math, engineering or other technical fields come to class to talk about college.
3. Create electronic mentoring programs for both male and female students to connect them with adults working in areas of interest to the students.

Make sure all students have a chance to do complex, technical work.

Examples

1. Experiment with same-sex lab groups so girls do not always end up as the secretaries, boys as the technicians.
2. Rotate jobs in groups or randomly assign responsibilities.

Language Differences in the Classroom

In the classroom, quite a bit happens through language. Communication is at the heart of teaching, but as we have seen in this chapter, culture affects communication. In this section, we will examine two kinds of language differences—dialect differences and bilingualism.

Dialects

A **dialect** is a language variation spoken by a particular ethnic, social, or regional group and is an element of the group's collective identity (Ogbu, 1999). The rules for a language define how words should be pronounced, how meaning should be expressed, and the ways the basic parts of speech should be put together to form sentences. Dialects appear to differ in their rules in these areas, but it is important to remember that these differences are not errors. Each dialect within a language is just as logical, complex, and rule-governed as the standard form of the language (often called **standard speech**). An example of this is the use of the double negative. In Standard English the redundancy of the double negative is not allowed. But in many dialects, such as Black American English, just as in many other languages (for instance, Russian, French, Spanish, and Hungarian), the double negative is required by the grammatical rules. To say "I don't want anything" in Spanish, you must literally say, "I don't want nothing," or "No quiero nada."

Dialects and Pronunciation. Another area in which nonstandard dialects differ from Standard English is pronunciation, which can lead to spelling problems. In Black American English and in Southern dialects, for instance, there is less attention paid to pronouncing the ends of words than in Standard English. A lack of attention to final consonants, such as *s*, can lead to failure to indicate possession, third-person singular verbs, and plurals in the standard way. So *John's book* might be *John book*, and words such as *thinks*, *wasps*, and *lists* may be difficult to pronounce. When endings are not pronounced, there are more *homonyms* (words that sound alike but have different meanings) in the student's speech than the unknowing teacher may expect; *spent* and *spend* might sound alike, for example. Even without the confusions caused by dialect differences, there are many homonyms in English. Usually, special attention is given to words such as these when they come up in the spelling lesson. If teachers are aware of the special homonyms in student dialects, they can teach these differences directly.

Dialects and Teaching. What does all of this mean for teachers? How can they cope with linguistic diversity in the classroom? First, they can be sensitive to their own possible negative stereotypes about children who speak a different dialect. Taylor (1983) found that teachers who held negative attitudes toward "Black English" gave lower ratings for reading comprehension to students using that dialect, even when the accuracy of the students' performance was the same as that of Standard English speakers. Second, teachers can ensure comprehension by repeating instructions using different words and by asking students to paraphrase instructions or give examples.

Dialect: Rule-governed variation of a language spoken by a particular group.

Standard Speech: The most generally accepted and used form of a given language.

Bilingualism: Speaking two languages fluently.

English as a Second Language (ESL): Designation for programs and classes to teach English to students who are not native speakers of English.

Limited English Proficiency (LEP): Descriptive term for students who have limited mastery of English.

But what about the use of home language in the classroom? While the various dialects of a language may be equally logical, complex, and rule-governed, should teachers make learning easier for children by teaching in the dialect of the majority of students? To do this would show respect for the children's language, but the children would be robbed of the opportunity to learn the standard speech of the dominant culture. Being able to communicate effectively in standard speech allows adults to take advantage of many social and occupational opportunities.

The best teaching approach seems to be to focus on understanding the children and to accept their dialect as a valid and correct language system, but to teach as an alternative the standard form of English (or whatever the dominant language is in your country). For example, Lisa Delpit (1995) describes Martha Demientieff, a Native Alaskan teacher of Athabaskan children in a small village. The teacher's goal is for her students to become fluent in both their dialect, which she calls "Heritage English," and the "Formal English" of employers and others outside the village. She explains to her students that people outside the village will judge them by the way they talk and write. She goes on to explain:

> We have to feel sorry for them because they have only one way to talk. We're going to learn two ways to say things. . . . One will be our Heritage way. The other will be Formal English. Then when we go to get jobs, we'll be able to talk like those people who only know and can only listen to one way. Maybe after we get the jobs we can help them to learn how it feels to have another language, like ours, that feels so good. We'll talk like them when we have to, but we'll always know our way is best. (p. 41)

Learning the standard speech is easy for most children whose original language is a dialect, as long as they have good models, clear instruction, and opportunities for authentic practice. The Guidelines on page 182 give other ideas.

Bilingualism

Bilingualism is a topic that sparks heated debates and touches many emotions. One reason is the changing demographics discussed earlier in this chapter. In the past 10 years there has been a 65% increase in the number of Spanish speaking students and almost a 100% increase in students who speak Asian languages. In some states almost one-fourth of all students speak a first language other than English—usually Spanish (Gersten, 1996a). By 2050, about one-fourth of the United States population is expected to be Latina/o (Yetman, 1999).

Two terms that you will see associated with bilingualism are **English as a second language (ESL)**, describing classes for students whose primary language is not English, and **limited English proficiency (LEP)**, referring to students whose English skills are limited.

What Does Bilingualism Mean? There are disagreements about the meaning of *bilingualism*. Some definitions focus exclusively on a language-based meaning: Bilingual people, or bilinguals, speak two languages. But this limited definition minimizes the significant problems that bilingual students face. Consider the words of these two students:

> A 9th-grade boy, who recently arrived in California from Mexico: "There is so much discrimination and hate. Even from other kids from Mexico who have been here longer. They don't treat us like brothers. They hate even more. It makes

Connect and Extend
To the research
Harvard Graduate School of Education (1991, November/December). Kids who speak Spanish: Schools that help them learn. *Harvard Education Newsletter, 7*(6), 1–4. *Focus Question:* What are the characteristics of schools that help Spanish-speaking students learn?

Connect and Extend
To professional journals
Menkart, D. J. (1999). Deepening the meaning of heritage months. *Educational Leadership, 56*(7), 19–21; This article discusses how to get past foods and festivals to increase students' understandings of heritage.

Connect and Extend
To the research
Commins, N. L., & Miramontes, O. B. (1989). Received and actual linguistic components: A descriptive study of four low-achieving Hispanic bilingual students. *American Educational Research Journal, 26,* 427–443.

Brief abstract: This ethnographic study investigated four Hispanic bilingual students perceived to have limited language abilities. The study provided data on the students' language use and abilities in a variety of settings. The data indicated that the organization of instruction limited the students' abilities to demonstrate their full range of competence in their two languages and that teachers interpreted their lack of English structural proficiency and lack of vocabulary in Spanish as a lack of conceptual ability. Observed over a variety of contexts, however, students showed the ability to use language as a vehicle for effective self-expression both socially and cognitively.

GUIDELINES

Dialects in the Classroom

1. Become familiar with features of the students' dialect. This will allow you to understand students better and to distinguish a reading miscue (a non-comprehension feature) from a comprehension error. Students should not be interrupted during the oral reading process. Correction of comprehension features is best done after the reading segment.

2. Allow students to listen to a passage or story first. This can be done in two ways: (a) finish the story and then ask comprehension questions, or (b) interrupt the story at key comprehension segments and ask students to predict the outcome.

3. Use predictable stories, which can be familiar episodes in literature, music, or history. They can be original works or experiential readers.

4. Use visual aids to enhance comprehension. Visual images, whether pictures or words, will aid word recognition and comprehension.

5. Use "cloze procedure" deletions to focus on vocabulary and meaning. Cloze procedures are selected deletions of words from a passage in order to focus on a specific text feature. *Examples:* (a) The little red hen found an ear of corn. The little red _____ said, "Who will dry the ear of _____?" (vocabulary focus) (b) Today I feel like a (*noun*). (grammar focus) (c) There was a (*pain*) in the pit of his stomach. (semantic focus)

6. Allow students to retell the story or passage in various speech styles. Have students select different people to whom they would like to retell the story (family member, principal, friend), and assist them in selecting synonyms most appropriate to each audience. This allows both teacher and student to become language authorities.

7. Integrate reading, speaking, and writing skills whenever possible.

8. Use the computer (if available) as a time-on-task exercise. The computer can effectively assist in teaching the reading techniques of skimming (general idea), scanning (focused reference), reading for comprehension (mastery of total message), and critical reading (inference and evaluation).

9. Teach students directly how to switch between home and school dialects.

10. Give practice with feedback and correction in using school dialect. All learning takes practice.

Source: From *Comprehensive Multicultural Education, Theory and Practice* (2nd ed.) (pp. 234–235), by C. I. Bennett. Copyright © 1990 by Allyn & Bacon. "Beyond Language: Ebonics, Proper English, and Identity in a Black-American Speech Community," by J. U. Ogbu, *American Educational Research Journal, 36,* p. 178. Adapted with permission.

them feel more like natives. They want to be American. They don't want to speak Spanish to us; they already know English and how to act. If they are with us, other people will treat them more like wetbacks, so they try to avoid us." (Olsen, 1988, p. 36)

A 10th-grade Chinese-American girl who had been in America for several years: "I don't know who I am. Am I the good Chinese daughter? Am I an American teenager? I always feel I am letting my parents down when I am with my friends because I act so American, but I also feel that I will never really be an American. I never feel really comfortable with myself anymore." (Olsen, 1988, p. 30)

The experiences of these two students show that there is more to being bilingual than just speaking two languages. You must also be able to move back and forth between two cultures while still maintaining a sense of your own identity (Hakuta & Garcia, 1989). Being bilingual and bicultural means mastering the knowledge necessary to communicate in two cultures as well as dealing with potential discrimination. As a teacher, you will have to help your students learn all these skills.

Monolinguals: Individuals who speak only one language.

Becoming Bilingual. Higher degrees of bilingualism are correlated with increased cognitive abilities in such areas as concept formation, creativity, knowledge of the workings of language, and cognitive flexibility. These findings seem to hold as long as there is no stigma attached to being bilingual and as long as students are not expected to abandon their first language to learn English (Galambos & Goldin-Meadow, 1990; Garcia, 1992; Hakuta & Garcia, 1989; Ricciardelli, 1992).

Learning a second language does not interfere with understanding in the first language. In fact, the more proficient the speaker is in the first language, the faster she or he will master a second language (Cummins, 1984, 1994). If children learn two languages simultaneously as toddlers, there is a period between ages 2 and 3 when they progress more slowly because they have not yet figured out that they are learning two different languages. They may mix up the grammar of the two. But researchers believe that by age 4, if they have enough exposure to both languages, they get things straight and speak as well as native **monolinguals** (Baker, 1993; Reich, 1986). The earlier we learn a second language, the more our pronunciation is near-native. After adolescence it is difficult to learn a new language without speaking with an accent (Anderson & Graham, 1994).

Proficiency in a second language has two separate aspects: face-to-face communication (known as "contextualized language skills") and academic uses of language such as reading and doing grammar exercises ("decontextualized language skills") (Snow, 1987). It takes students about two to three years in a good-quality program to be able to communicate face-to-face in a second language, but mastering decontextualized, academic language skills in the new language takes five to seven years. So students who seem in conversation to "know" a second language may still have great difficulty with complex schoolwork in that language (Cummins, 1994; Ovando, 1989).

Bilingual Education. Virtually everyone agrees that all citizens should learn the official language of their country. But when and how should instruction in that language begin? Here the debate is bitter at times, but it is clear the United States has not solved the problem. For example, "Spanish-speaking students—*even when taught and tested in Spanish*—still score at the [bottom] 32nd percentile in relation to a national comparison group (taught and tested in English)" (Goldenberg, 1996, p. 353).

Is it better to teach non–English-speaking and limited-English-proficiency students to read first in their native language or to begin reading instruction in English? Do these children need some oral lessons in English before reading instruction can be effective? Should other subjects, such as mathematics and social studies, be taught in the primary (home) language until the children are fluent in English? On these questions there are two basic positions, which have given rise to two contrasting teaching approaches, one that focuses on making the *transition* to English as quickly as possible and the other that attempts to *maintain* or improve the native language and use the native language as the primary teaching language until English skills are more fully developed.

Proponents of the first approach—*transition*—believe that English ought to be introduced as early

Connect and Extend
To real life
Is the increasing cultural plurality of the United States making the learning of foreign languages (namely, Spanish) more important in U.S. schools than was the case in the past?

Connect and Extend
To the research
Filmore, L. W., & Valadez, C. (1986). Teaching bilingual learners. In M. Wittrock (Ed.), *Handbook of research on teaching* (3rd ed.) (pp. 648–685). New York: Macmillan.

Teachers in today's bilingual classrooms must help students learn skills to communicate in more than one culture. ▼

Connect and Extend
To professional journals
Thomas, W. P., & Collier, V. P.
(1998). Two languages are better
than one. *Educational Leadership,
55*(4), 23–27. This article makes
the case that native and non-
native speakers of English benefit
greatly from learning together in
two languages.

as possible; they argue that valuable learning time is lost if students are taught in their native language. Most bilingual programs today follow this line of thinking. Proponents of native-language maintenance instruction, however, raise four important issues (Gersten, 1996b; Goldenberg, 1996; Hakuta & Garcia, 1989). First, children who are forced to try to learn math or science in an unfamiliar language are bound to have trouble. What if you had been forced to learn fractions or biology in a second language that you had studied for only a semester? Some psychologists believe students taught by this approach may become **semilingual,** inadequate speakers of both languages. Second, students may get the message that their home languages (and therefore, their families and cultures) are second class. You saw the seeds of these feelings in the stories of the two students at the beginning of this section. Third, the academic content (math, science, history, etc.) that students learn in their native language is learned—they do not forget the knowledge and skills when they are able to speak English.

Fourth is what Kenji Hakuta (1986) calls a "paradoxical attitude of admiration and pride for school-attained bilingualism on the one hand and scorn and shame for home-brewed immigrant bilingualism on the other" (p. 229). Ironically, by the time students have mastered academic English and let their home language deteriorate, they reach secondary school and are encouraged to learn a second language. Had both the home language and English been developed all along, they would already be fluent in two languages without having to take French I or Introductory Spanish. Hakuta (1986) suggests that the goals of the educational system could be the development of *all students* as functional bilinguals.

The *maintenance approach* to teaching advocates using the child's native language for some subject teaching while simultaneously developing English proficiency. Supporters believe that children have a right to be proficient speakers of their native language and to become fully competent speakers of the dominant language of their country. One new approach to reaching this goal is to create classes that mix students who are learning a second language with students who are native speakers. The goal is for both groups to become fluent in both languages (Snow, 1986). My daughter spent a summer in such a program in Quebec and has been ahead in every French class ever since. For truly effective bilingual education, we will need many bilingual teachers. If you have a competence in another language, you might want to develop it fully for your teaching.

CHECKPOINT

Language Differences in the Classroom

Review

▶ What are the origins of language differences in the classroom?

▶ What is bilingual education?

Apply

▶ How should teachers deal with different dialects in the classroom?

Semilingual: Not proficient in any language; speaking one or more languages inadequately.

Research on Bilingual Programs. It is difficult to separate politics from practice in the debate about bilingual education. It is clear that high quality bilingual education programs can have positive results. Students improve in the subjects that were taught in their native language, in their mastery of English, and in self-esteem as well (Crawford, 1997; Hakuta & Gould, 1987; Wright & Taylor, 1995). English as a second language (ESL) programs seem to have positive effects on reading comprehension (Fitzgerald, 1995). But attention today is shifting from debate about general approaches to a focus on effective teaching strategies. As you will see many times in this book, a combination of clarity of learning goals and direct instruction in needed skills—including learning strategies and tactics, teacher- or peer-guided practice leading to independent practice, authentic and engaging tasks, opportunities for interaction and conversation that are academically focused, and warm encouragement from the teacher—seems to be effective (Chamot & O'Malley, 1996; Gersten, 1996b, Goldenberg, 1996). Table 5.3 is a set of constructs for promoting learning and language acquisition that capture many of these methods for effective instruction. We will revisit these ideas in later chapters.

We have dealt with a wide range of differences in this chapter. How can teachers provide an appropriate education for all their students? One response is to make the classroom compatible with the students' cultural heritage. Such a classroom is described as being culturally compatible.

TABLE 5.3 *Ideas for Promoting Learning and Language Acquisition*

Effective teaching for students in bilingual and ESL classrooms combines many strategies—direct instruction, mediation, coaching, feedback, modeling, encouragement, challenge, and authentic activities.

1. Structures, frameworks, scaffolds, and strategies
   - Provide support to students by "thinking aloud," building on and clarifying input of students
   - Use visual organizers, story maps, or other aids to help students organize and relate information
2. Relevant background knowledge and key vocabulary concepts
   - Provide adequate background knowledge to students and informally assess whether students have background knowledge
   - Focus on key vocabulary words and use consistent language
   - Incorporate students' primary language meaningfully
3. Mediation/feedback
   - Give feedback that focuses on meaning, not grammar, syntax, or pronunciation
   - Give frequent and comprehensible feedback
   - Provide students with prompts or strategies
   - Ask questions that press students to clarify or expand on initial statements
   - Provide activities and tasks that students can complete
   - Indicate to students when they are successful
   - Assign activities that are reasonable, avoiding undue frustration
   - Allow use of native language responses (when context is appropriate)
   - Be sensitive to common problems in second language acquisition
4. Involvement
   - Ensure active involvement of all students, including low-performing students
   - Foster extended discourse
5. Challenge
   - Implicit (cognitive challenge, use of higher-order questions)
   - Explicit (high but reasonable expectations)
6. Respect for—and responsiveness to—cultural and personal diversity
   - Show respect for students as individuals, respond to things students say, show respect for culture and family, and possess knowledge of cultural diversity
   - Incorporate students' experiences into writing and language arts activities
   - Link content to students' lives and experiences to enhance understanding
   - View diversity as an asset, reject cultural deficit notions

Source: From "Literacy Instruction for Language-Minority Students: The Transition Years," by R. Gersten, 1996, *The Elementary School Journal, 96,* pp. 241–242. Copyright © 1996 by the University of Chicago Press. Adapted with permission.

Creating Culturally Compatible Classrooms

The goal of creating **culturally compatible classrooms** is to eliminate racism, sexism, and ethnic prejudice while providing equal educational opportunities for all students. Roland Tharp (1989) states that "two decades of data on cultural issues in classroom interactions and school outcomes have accumulated. When schools are changed, children's experiences and achievement also change" (p. 349). Tharp outlines several dimensions of classrooms that can be tailored to fit the needs of students. Three dimensions are social organization, learning style, and sociolinguistics.

Social Organization

Connect and Extend
To your teaching
McCarty, T. L., Wallace, S., & Lynch, R. H. (1989, February). Inquiry-based curriculum development in a Navajo school. *Educational Leadership, 46*(5), 66–71.

Tharp (1989) states that "a central task of educational design is to make the organization of teaching, learning, and performance compatible with the social structures in which students are most productive, engaged, and likely to learn" (p. 350). Social structure or social organization in this context means the ways people interact to accomplish a particular goal. For example, the social organization of Hawaiian society depends heavily on collaboration and cooperation. Children play together in groups of friends and siblings, with older children often caring for the younger ones. When cooperative work groups of four or five boys and girls were established in Hawaiian classrooms, student learning and participation improved. The teacher worked intensively with one group while the children in the remaining groups helped each other. But when the same structure was tried in a Navajo classroom, students would not work together. These students are socialized to be more solitary and not to play with the opposite sex. By setting up same-sex working groups of only two or three Navajo students, teachers encouraged them to help each other.

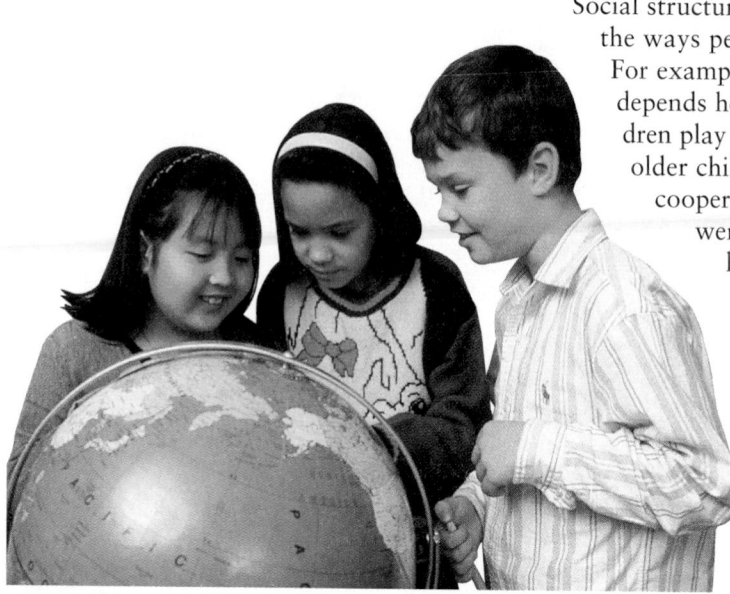

▲ *A major goal of creating culturally compatible classrooms is to encourage mutual respect among students from all backgrounds.*

Culturally Compatible Classrooms: Classrooms in which procedures, rules, grouping strategies, attitudes, and teaching methods do not cause conflicts with the students' culturally influenced ways of learning and interacting.

Learning Styles

Some psychologists have found ethnic group differences in students' cognitive styles. You may remember from the previous chapter that cognitive styles are the ways that individuals typically process information. The following are a few examples.

Possible Differences. Results of some research suggest that Mexican Americans tend to be field dependent, preferring holistic, concrete, social approaches to learning. Because being field independent is related to achievement in mathematics, the tendency to be field dependent may interfere with performance in mathematics if it is taught in the usual abstract, analytical way (Buenning & Tollefson, 1987). Other researchers have suggested that Hispanic American students are more oriented toward family and group loyalty and are less individualistic. This may mean that these students prefer cooperative activities and dislike being made to compete with fellow students (Garcia, 1992; Vasquez, 1990).

Bennett (1999) summarizes research that suggests the learning styles of African Americans may be inconsistent with teaching approaches in most schools. Some of the characteristics of this learning style are a visual/global rather than a verbal/analytic approach; a preference for reasoning by inference rather than formal logic; a focus on people and relationships; a preference for energetic involvement in several activities simultaneously rather than routine, step-by-step learning; a tendency to approximate numbers, space and time; and a greater dependence on nonverbal communication. To capitalize on these learning styles, Hale-Benson (1986) recommends the following strategies with young African American children:

Use appropriate nonverbal cues, gestures, and eye contact.

Allow equal "talking time" for teacher and students.

Emphasize small-group learning and hands-on contact with the teacher.

Use a variety of learning activities that include movement, games, poetry, and music.

Native Americans also appear to have a more global, visual style of learning. For example, Navajo students prefer hearing a story all the way through to the end before discussing parts of the story. Teachers who stop to ask questions seem odd to these students and interrupt the learning process (Tharp, 1989). Also, these students sometimes show strong preferences for learning privately, through trial and error, rather than having their mistakes made public (Vasquez, 1990).

There has been little research on the learning styles of Asian Americans, perhaps because they are seen as "successful minorities." As we discussed earlier, many of the values and attitudes taught by some Asian cultures, such as respect for teachers, hard work, and persistent effort, can support academic achievement. Some educators suggest that Asian children tend to value teacher approval and to work well in structured, quiet learning environments where there are clear goals and social support (Manning & Baruth, 1996). But there are dangers in stereotyping Asian and Asian American students as quiet, hardworking, and passive. Suzuki (1983) suggests that this practice "tends to reinforce conformity and stifle creativity. Asian and Pacific American students, therefore, frequently do not develop the ability to assert and express themselves verbally and are channeled in disproportionate numbers into the technical/scientific fields. As a result, many Asian and Pacific American students undergo traumatic family/school discontinuities, suffer from low self-esteem, are overly conforming, and have their academic and social development narrowly circumscribed" (p. 9).

Suzuki's cautions are echoed by many critics of the research on ethnic differences in learning styles (Yee, 1992).

Cautions about Learning Styles Research. In considering this research on learning styles, you should keep two points in mind. First, the validity of some of the learning styles research has been strongly questioned, as we saw in the previous chapter. Second, there is a heated debate today about whether identifying ethnic group differences in learning styles and preferences is a dangerous, racist, sexist exercise. In our society we are quick to move from the notion of "difference" to the idea of "deficit." Information about the "typical" learning styles of a given ethnic group can become just one more basis for stereotyping, as mentioned above (Gordon, 1991; O'Neil, 1990a). I have included the information about learning style differences because I believe that, used sensibly, this information can help you better understand your students.

Connect and Extend
To professional journals
O'Neil, J. (1990). Link between style, culture proves divisive. *Educational Leadership, 48*(2), 8.
Focus Question: Why do some educators argue against linking learning styles to cultural differences?

It is dangerous and incorrect, however, to assume that every individual in a group shares the same learning style. The best advice for teachers is to be sensitive to individual differences in all your students and to make available alternative paths to learning. Never prejudge how a student will learn best on the basis of assumptions about the student's ethnicity or race. Get to know the individual.

Sociolinguistics

Sociolinguistics is the study of "the courtesies and conventions of conversation across cultures" (Tharp, 1989, p. 351). A knowledge of sociolinguistics will help you understand why communication sometimes breaks down in classrooms. The classroom is a special setting for communicating; it has its own set of rules for when, how, to whom, about what subject, and in what manner to use language. Sometimes the sociolinguistic skills of students do not fit the expectations of teachers.

Participation Structures. In order to be successful, students must know the communication rules; that is, they must understand the pragmatics of the classroom—when, where, and how to communicate. This is not such an easy task. As class activities change, rules change. Sometimes you have to raise your hand (during the teacher's presentation), but sometimes you don't (during storytime on the rug). Sometimes it is good to ask a question (during discussion), but other times it isn't so good (when the teacher is reprimanding you). The differing activity rules are called **participation structures**. These structures define appropriate participation for each class activity. Most classrooms have many different participation structures.

To be competent communicators in the classroom, students sometimes have to read very subtle, nonverbal cues telling them which participation structures are currently in effect. For example, in one classroom, when the teacher stood in a particular area of the room, put her hands on her hips, and leaned forward at the waist, the children in the class were signaled to "stop and freeze," look at the teacher, and anticipate an announcement (Shultz & Florio, 1979).

Sources of Misunderstandings. Some children are simply better than others at reading the classroom situation because the participation structures of the school match the structures they have learned at home. The communication rules for most school situations are similar to those in middle-class homes, so children from these homes often appear to be more competent communicators. They know the unwritten rules. Students from different cultural backgrounds may have learned participation structures that conflict with the behaviors expected in school. For example, one study found that the home conversation style of Hawaiian children is to chime in with contributions to a story. In school, however, this overlapping style is seen as "interrupting." When the teachers in one school learned about these differences and made their reading groups more like their students' home conversation groups, the young Hawaiian children in their classes improved in reading (Au, 1980; Tharp, 1989).

The source of misunderstanding can be a subtle sociolinguistic difference, such as how long the teacher waits to react to a student's response. White and Tharp (1988) found that when Navajo students in one class paused in giving a response, their Anglo teacher seemed to think that they were finished speaking. As a result, the teacher often unintentionally interrupted students. In another study, researchers found that Pueblo Indian students participated twice as much in classes where teachers waited longer to react. Waiting longer also helps girls to participate more freely in math and science classes (Grossman & Grossman, 1994).

Connect and Extend
To the research
See Cultural differences in the classroom (1988, March). *Harvard Education Letter, 2*(2), 1–4. This article describes the KEEP program and Shirley Heath's project in the Piedmont Carolinas and offers four conclusions:

1. Interaction is the key to learning, and language is the key to interaction. "When teachers in both projects became aware of specific communication and interaction skills children were developing in their homes, they adapted classroom practice to build on these skills. In addition, teachers specifically demonstrated respect for the language of their students" (p. 3).

2. Academic standards and teacher expectations for students should not be lowered. Standard English skills were still emphasized in both projects but without devaluing the children's own dialect.

3. Schools can work with local colleges, parents, and other community members to learn more about students' home cultures.

4. By attending to students' cultures teachers can expand and improve their teaching skills. The new ways of teaching developed in the two projects proved helpful for all the students in the classes, not just those from different cultures.

Sociolinguistics: The study of the formal and informal rules for how, when, about what, to whom, and how long to speak in conversations within cultural groups.

Participation Structures: The formal and informal rules for how to take part in a given activity.

It seems that even students who speak the same language as their teachers may still have trouble communicating, and thus learning school subjects, if their knowledge of pragmatics does not fit the school situation. What can teachers do? Especially in the early grades, you should make communication rules for activities clear and explicit. Do not assume students know what to do. Use cues to signal students when changes occur. Explain and demonstrate appropriate behavior. I have seen teachers show young children how to use their "inside voice," "six-inch voice," or "whisper voice." One teacher said and then demonstrated, "If you have to interrupt me while I'm working with other children, stand quietly beside me until I can help you." Be consistent in responding to students. If students are supposed to raise their hands, don't call on those who break the rules. In these ways you teach students how to learn in school.

Culturally Relevant Pedagogy

In the last 20 years, several researchers have focused on teachers who are especially successful with students of color and students in poverty (Bennett, 1999; Delpit, 1995; Ladson-Billings, 1994, 1995; Moll, Amanti, Neff, & Gonzalez, 1992). The work of Gloria Ladson-Billings (1990, 1992, 1995) is a good example. For three years she studied excellent teachers in a California school district that served an African American community. In order to select the teachers, she asked parents and principals for nominations. Parents nominated teachers who respected the parents, created enthusiasm for learning in their children, and understood their children's need to operate successfully in two different worlds—the home community and the White world beyond. Principals nominated teachers who had few discipline referrals, high attendance rates, and high standardized test scores. Ladson-Billings was able to examine in depth 8 of the 9 teachers who were nominated by *both parents and principals*.

Based on her research, Ladson-Billings developed a conception of teaching excellence that encompasses but goes beyond considerations of sociolinguistics or social organizations. She uses the term **culturally relevant pedagogy** to describe teaching that rests on three propositions.

Students Must Experience Academic Success. "Despite the current social inequities and hostile classroom environments, students must develop their academic skills. The ways those skills are developed may vary, but all students need literacy, numeracy, technological, social, and political skills in order to be active participants in a democracy" (Ladson-Billings, 1995, p. 160).

Develop/Maintain Their Cultural Competence. As they become more academically skilled, students still retain their cultural competence. "Culturally relevant teachers utilize students'culture as a vehicle for learning" (Ladson-Billings, 1995, p. 161). For example, one teacher used "non-offensive" rap music to teach about literal and figurative meaning, rhyme, alliteration, and onomatopoeia in poetry. Another brought in a community expert known for her sweet potato pies to work with students. Follow-up lessons included investigations of George Washington Carver's sweet potato research, numerical analyses of taste tests, marketing plans for selling pies, and research on the educational preparation needed to become a chef.

Develop a Critical Consciousness to Challenge the Status Quo. In addition to developing academic skills while retaining cultural competence, excellent

Culturally Relevant Pedagogy: Excellent teaching for students of color that includes academic success, developing/maintaining cultural competence, and critical consciousness to challenge the status quo.

Creating Culturally Compatible Classrooms

Review

▶ What are the elements of a culturally compatible classroom?

▶ What is culturally relevant pedagogy?

Apply

▶ How do participation structures affect students' access to learning in classrooms?

▶ How can you move "beyond the basics" in teaching all your students?

teachers help students "develop a broader sociopolitical consciousness that allows them to critique the social norms, values, mores, and institutions that produce and maintain social inequities" (Ladson-Billings, 1995, p. 162). For example, in one school students were upset that their textbooks were out of date. They mobilized to investigate the funding formulas that allowed middle-class students to have newer books, wrote letters to the newspaper editor to challenge these inequities, and updated their texts with current information from other sources.

Ladson-Billings (1995) noted that many people have said her three principles "are just good teaching." She agrees that she is describing good teaching, but questions "why so little of it seems to be occurring in classrooms populated by African American students" (p. 159).

Bringing It All Together: Teaching Every Student

The goal of this chapter is to give you a sense of the diversity in today's and tomorrow's schools and to help you meet the challenges of teaching in a multicultural classroom. How will you understand and build on all the cultures of your students? How will you deal with many different languages? Here are three general teaching principles to guide you in finding answers to these questions.

Know Your Students. Nothing you read in a chapter on cultural differences will teach you enough to understand the lives of all your students. If you can take other courses in college or read about other cultures, I encourage you to do it. But reading and studying are not enough. You should get to know your students' families and communities. Elba Reyes, a successful bilingual teacher for special needs children describes her approach:

> Usually I find that if you really want to know a parent, you get to know them on their own turf. This is key to developing trust and understanding the parents' perspective. First, get to know the community. Learn where the local grocery store is and what the children do after school. Then schedule a home visit at a time that is convenient for the parents. . . . The home environment is not usually as ladened with failure. I sometimes observed the child being successful in the home, for example, riding a bicycle or helping with dinner. (Bos & Reyes, 1996, p. 349)

Try to spend time with students and parents on projects outside school. Ask parents to help in class or to speak to your students about their jobs, their hobbies, or the history and heritage of their ethnic group. In the elementary grades, don't wait until a student is in trouble to have the first meeting with a family member. Watch and listen to the ways that your students interact in large and small groups. Have students write to you, and write back to them. Eat lunch with one or two students. Spend some nonteaching time with them.

Respect Your Students. From knowledge ought to come respect for your students' learning strengths—for the struggles they face and the obstacles they overcome. For a child, genuine acceptance is a necessary condition for developing self-esteem. Self-esteem and pride are important accomplishments of the school years. Sometimes the self-image and occupational aspirations of minority children actually decline in their early years in public school, probably because of the emphasis on majority culture values, accomplishments, and history. By presenting the accomplishments of particular members of an ethnic group or by bringing that group's culture into the classroom (in the form of literature, art, music, or any cultural knowledge), teachers can help students maintain a sense of pride in their cultural group. This integration of culture must be more than the "tokenism" of sampling ethnic foods or wearing costumes. Students should learn about the socially and intellectually important contributions of the various groups. There are many excellent references that provide background information, history, and teaching strategies for different groups of students (e.g., Banks, 1997, 1999; Bennett, 1999; Ladson-Billings, 1995).

Connect and Extend
To professional journals
Midobuche, E. (1999). Respect in the classroom: Reflections of a Mexican-American educator. *Educational Leadership, 56*(7), 80–83. The story of the early school experiences of a Spanish-speaking child in an all-English world.

Teach Your Students. The most important thing you can do for your students is teach them to read, write, speak, compute, think, and create. Too often, goals for low-SES or minority group students have focused exclusively on basic skills. Students are taught words and sounds, but the meaning of the story is supposed to come later. Knapp, Turnbull, and Shields (1990) make these suggestions:

Focus on meaning and understanding from beginning to end—for example, by orienting instruction toward comprehending reading passages, communicating important ideas in written text, or understanding the concepts underlying number facts.

Balance routine skill learning with novel and complex tasks from the earliest stages of learning.

Provide context for skill learning that establishes clear reasons for needing to learn the skills.

Influence attitudes and beliefs about the academic content areas as well as skills and knowledge.

Eliminate unnecessary redundancy in the curriculum (e.g., repeating instruction in the same mathematics skills year after year). (p. 5)

And finally, teach students directly about how to be students. In the early grades this could mean directly teaching the courtesies and conventions of the classroom: how to get a turn to speak, how and when to interrupt the teacher, how to whisper, how to get help in a small group, how to give an explanation that is helpful. In the later grades it may mean teaching the study skills that fit your subject. You can ask students to learn "how we do it in school" without violating principle number two above—respect your students. Ways of asking questions around the kitchen table at home may be different from ways of asking questions in school, but students can learn both ways, without deciding that either way is superior. The Guidelines on page 192 give more ideas.

GUIDELINES

Culturally Relevant Teaching

Experiment with different grouping arrangements to encourage social harmony and cooperation.

Examples

1. Try "study buddies" and pairs.
2. Organize heterogeneous groups of four or five.
3. Establish larger teams for older students.

Provide a range of ways to learn material to accommodate a range of learning styles.

Examples

1. Give students verbal materials at different reading levels.
2. Offer visual materials—charts, diagrams, models.
3. Provide tapes for listening and viewing.
4. Set up activities and projects.

Teach classroom procedures directly, even ways of doing things that you thought everyone would know.

Examples

1. Tell students how to get the teacher's attention.
2. Explain when and how to interrupt the teacher if students need help.
3. Show which materials students can take and which require permission.
4. Demonstrate acceptable ways to disagree with or challenge another student.

Learn the meaning of different behaviors for your students.

Examples

1. Ask students how they feel when you correct or praise them. What gives them this message?

2. Talk to family and community members and other teachers to discover the meaning of expressions, gestures, or other responses that are unfamiliar to you.

Emphasize meaning in teaching.

Examples

1. Make sure students understand what they read.
2. Try storytelling and other modes that don't require written materials.
3. Use examples that relate abstract concepts to everyday experiences; for instance, relate negative numbers to being overdrawn in your checkbook.

Get to know the customs, traditions, and values of your students.

Examples

1. Use holidays as a chance to discuss the origins and meaning of traditions.
2. Analyze different traditions for common themes.
3. Attend community fairs and festivals.

Help students detect racist and sexist messages.

Examples

1. Analyze curriculum materials for biases.
2. Make students "bias detectives," reporting comments from the media.
3. Discuss the ways that students communicate biased messages about each other and what should be done when this happens.
4. Discuss expressions of prejudice such as anti-Semitism.

Summary

Today's Multicultural Classrooms

Distinguish between the "melting pot" and multiculturalism.

Statistics point to increasing cultural diversity in American society. Old views—that minority group members and immigrants should lose their cultural distinctiveness and assimilate completely in the American "melting pot" or be regarded as culturally deficient—are being replaced by new emphases on multiculturalism, equal educational opportunity, and the celebration of cultural diversity.

What is multicultural education?

According to the multicultural ideal, America should be transformed into a society that values diversity. James

Banks suggests that multicultural education has five dimensions: integrating content, helping students understand how knowledge is influenced by beliefs, reducing prejudice, creating social structures in schools that support learning and development for all students, and using teaching methods that reach all students.

What is culture?

There are many conceptions of culture, but most include the knowledge, rules, traditions, attitudes, and values that guide behavior in a particular group of people—culture is a program for living. Everyone is a member of many cultural groups, defined in terms of geographic region, nationality, ethnicity, race, gender, social class, and religion. Membership in a particular group does not determine behavior or values but makes certain values and kinds of behavior more likely. Wide variations exist within each group.

Social Class Differences

What is SES?

Socioeconomic status (SES) is a term used by sociologists for variations in wealth, power, and prestige. Socioeconomic status is determined by several factors—not just income—and often overpowers other cultural differences. The majority of children in poverty are White, but a disproportionate number of African American and Hispanic American children live in poverty.

What is the relationship between SES and school achievement?

Socioeconomic status and academic achievement are closely related. Low-SES students may suffer from inadequate health care, teachers' lowered expectations of them, low self-esteem, learned helplessness, participation in resistance cultures, school tracking, and understimulating childrearing styles and home environments. A striking finding is that low-SES children lose academic ground outside school over the summer while higher-SES children continue to advance.

Ethnic and Racial Differences

Distinguish between ethnicity and race.

Ethnicity (culturally transmitted behavior) and race (biologically transmitted physical traits) are socially significant categories people use to describe themselves and others. Minority groups (either numerically or historically unempowered) are rapidly increasing in population.

How can ethnicity affect school performance?

Conflicts between groups can arise from differences in culture-based beliefs, values, and expectations. Students in some cultures learn attitudes and behaviors that are more consistent with school expectations. Differences among ethnic groups in cognitive and academic abilities are largely the legacy of racial segregation and continuing prejudice and discrimination.

Distinguish among prejudice, discrimination, and stereotype threat.

Prejudice is a rigid and irrational generalization—a prejudgment—about an entire category of people. Prejudice may target people in particular racial, ethnic, religious, political, geographic, or language groups, or it may be directed toward the sex or sexual orientation of the individual. Discrimination is unequal treatment of particular categories of people. Stereotype threat is the extra emotional and cognitive burden that your performance in an academic situation might confirm a stereotype that others hold about you.

Women and Men: Differences in the Classroom

What is gender-role identity?

Gender-role identity is the image each individual has of himself or herself as masculine or feminine in characteristics—a part of self-concept. People with a "feminine" identity would rate themselves high on characteristics usually associated with females, such as "sensitive" or "warm," and low on characteristics traditionally associated with males, such as "forceful" and "competitive." Most people see themselves in gender-typed terms; however, some children and adults are more androgynous—they rate themselves high on *both* masculine and feminine traits.

How do gender-role identities develop?

Biology (hormones) plays a role, as does the differential behavior of parents and teachers toward male and female children. Through their interactions with family, peers, teachers, and the environment in general, children begin to form gender schemas, or organized networks of knowledge about what it means to be male or female. Research shows that gender-role stereotyping begins in the preschool years and continues through gender bias in the school curriculum and sex discrimination in the classroom. Teachers often unintentionally perpetuate these problems.

Are there sex differences in cognitive abilities?

Some measures on IQ and SAT tests have shown sex-linked differences, especially in verbal and spatial abilities and mathematics. Research on the causes of these differences has been inconclusive, except to indicate that academic socialization and teachers' treatment of male and female students in mathematics classes do play a role. Teachers can use many strategies for reducing gender bias.

Language Differences in the Classroom

What are the origins of language differences in the classroom?

Language differences among students include dialects, bilingualism, and culture-based communication styles. Dialects are not inferior languages and should be respected, but Standard English should be taught for academic contexts.

What is bilingual education?

Bilingual students speak a first language other than English, learn English as a second language, may have some degree of limitation in English proficiency, and also must often struggle with social adjustment problems relating to biculturalism. While there is much debate over the best way to help bilingual students master English, studies show it is best if they are not forced to abandon their first language. The more proficient students are in their first language, the faster they will master the second. Mastering academic language skills in any new language takes five to seven years.

Creating Culturally Compatible Classrooms

What are the elements of a culturally compatible classroom?

Culturally compatible classrooms are free of racism, sexism, and ethnic prejudice and provide equal educational opportunities for all students. Dimensions of classroom life that can be modified to that end are social organization, learning style formats, and participation structures. Teachers, however, must avoid stereotypes of culture-based learning styles and must not assume that every individual in a group shares the same style. Communication may break down in classrooms because of differences in sociolinguistic styles and skills. Teachers can directly teach appropriate participation structures and be sensitive to culture-based communication rules.

What is culturally relevant pedagogy?

Gloria Ladson-Billings developed a conception of teaching excellence that encompasses considerations of sociolinguistics or social organizations, but goes beyond them. She uses the term *culturally relevant pedagogy* to describe teaching that rests on three propositions: Students must experience academic success, develop/maintain their cultural competence, and develop a critical consciousness to challenge the status quo.

Bringing It All Together: Teaching Every Student

How can teachers create classroom environments in which all students can learn?

To help create compatible multicultural classrooms, teachers must know and respect all their students, have high expectations of them, and teach them what they need to know to succeed.

Key Terms

Becoming a Professional

Reflecting on the Chapter

Can you apply the ideas from this chapter on culture and community to solve the following problems of practice?

Elementary and Middle School

▶ Several of your students are from a public housing project in the district and clearly have fewer advantages than the other students in your class. You are concerned that the "project" students never seem to work or play with the others in the class. What would you do?

▶ Every year the number of non–English-speaking students in your class increases. This year there are four different language groups represented—and you know only about five words in each language. The school's resources are very limited. Pick one topic and tell how you would teach it to accommodate the limited English proficiency of your students.

Junior High and High School

▶ One day you notice that the males are doing most of the talking in your classes, particularly the advanced classes. Just out of curiosity, you start to note each day how many girls and boys make contributions and ask questions. You are really surprised to see that your first impression was correct. What would you do to encourage more participation on the part of your female students?

▶ For some reason, this year there have been several racial incidents in your school. Each incident seems a bit nastier and more dangerous than the one before. What would you do in your classes to improve the situation?

Certification Test Requirements

▶ Know the basic dimensions of multicultural education.

▶ Know the difference between prejudice and discrimination.

▶ Be familiar with the three propositions of culturally relevant pedagogy.

▶ Be familiar with research on differences in how teachers interact with male and female students.

Your Teaching Portfolio

What is your stance on multicultural education? On tracking? Add these ideas in your philosophy of teaching statement for your **Portfolio**.

Include ideas for the integration of multicultural material in your **Portfolio**.

Teaching Resources

Add Table 5.4 to your **Teaching Resources** file.

Use the Family and Community Partnerships Guidelines to brainstorm ideas for family involvement in helping your students "take their learning home."

What Would They Do?

Here is how some practicing teachers responded to the teaching situation presented at the beginning of this chapter about the "White Girls Club."

CAROLYN ELY PARHAM

Second Grade Teacher
Conway Elementary School, Ladue (St. Louis), Missouri

My first priority would be to build lessons into the curriculum relating to respecting and appreciating differences in people. At the set age level in this situation, one specific example would be to read out loud the book *Tacky* and the sequel, *Three Cheers for Tacky*, by Helen Lester. After reading, a discussion could be held centering around differences in people. Numerous "What Makes Me Special?" activities could be planned. One such activity could be a Reader/Writer workshop about this topic. For this young group of children, a class picture book could be created with each child illustrating a page of characteristics that make him/her special. Upon completion of the class book, each child could be invited to share his or her page. Another activity could be to initiate a Star of the Week bulletin board where each child's unique interests and hobbies are displayed during their assigned week. Exposure to these types of activities should increase awareness that everyone is different in some way, but THAT is exactly what makes each of us special!

Throughout the day, I would involve the new student in the various class activities, perhaps even asking her to "star" in a few of our lessons (i.e., choose the student to answer a question, erase the whiteboard during a lesson, use her name during a story, etc.). As needed, I would revisit these topics throughout the remainder of the year during "class" meetings. At these sessions, I would pose challenging situations, without names, encouraging the class to solve the problem. For example: Today at recess I saw a student sitting alone on the playground. How would you feel if that child were you? What would you do if you saw another child sitting alone? What would you do to help the child? Another example: I heard about a club today at school; however, not everyone can belong. Is that fair? How would you feel if there were a boys club? A 2nd grade club? Should there be clubs at school that everyone is not invited to join? Why or why not?

Finally, if the above suggestions do not eliminate the "exclusive" behavior in some of my students, I would speak to them individually. At this point, I would involve their parents and the school counselor.

REV. EDWARD MELI, MSC

Teacher, Sacred Heart High School
Hagita, Alotou, Milne Bay Province, Papua New Guinea
(Answered as if a White child joined my secondary class of Papua New Guinea students.)

On learning about the "Milne Bay Girls Club" and the new student's apparent loneliness and isolation, I would conduct an investigation of the club. I would interview the leader of the club to find out about the membership criteria. If I found that the club was created to exclude non-Milne Bay students, then I would encourage the club to change the criteria for membership to include any student regardless of nationality or colour.

I would explain to them that every human is a person with dignity, freedom, and the right to be respected. The club would be doing a great service to someone who really needs that sense of acceptance and comfort in a new learning environment. I would encourage this club to take the new student in as a member and be a support group for her. I'd encourage the group to work toward unity because they have a common goal: to learn.

JENNIFER HUDSON THOMAS

Armidale High School, Armidale, Australia

In students so young, such discriminatory values must emanate from home or community attitudes. Perhaps there would be value in quietly assessing the attitude of the general community toward racial and cultural differences. Having done this, I would adopt a "flanking action" to increase the knowledge and understanding of all involved in this situation to ensure the attitudinal change required for the successful inclusion and acceptance of my new student. This could be done by:

▶ Involving the parents and the broader community, if possible, in a knowledge-gathering and information-sharing program on value differences in society.

- Launching into teaching a unit on diversity with my class, touching on the similarities and differences of ethnic, religious, social, and disability groups.

- Investigating, unobtrusively, the individual strengths of my new student, and using these to demonstrate to the class that she is a greatly valued class member and contributor.

- Utilizing group instruction and cooperative learning during class time in as many learning areas as possible, rotating my new student through different group combinations, ensuring that her role within the group encourages sharing and interaction.

- Demonstrating at all times that I value, appreciate, and include her like everyone else in all class activities.

With older students, a more direct approach may be more appropriate, utilizing a case study/role-playing approach ranging across many personal relationships/situations and in which individual feelings are openly discussed within the group.

PAM GASKILL

2nd Grade Teacher
Riverside Elementary, Dublin, Ohio

Although at first glance this appears to be a difficult situation, it can in fact be a wonderful opportunity to help students gain some valuable insights into tolerance and understanding of others. It is very likely that these students have had little or no contact with others who are different from them and their behavior is more a result of insensitivity than of mean-spiritedness. My first step would be to put an immediate stop to the "White Girls Club" by telling the girls that groups that exclude others are not acceptable at our school because they hurt other people's feelings. I would then initiate a series of activities with all the students in the class that would help them to begin to develop an awareness of similarities and differences between people, an appreciation for the differences, and sensitivity toward the feelings of others.

Peter Spier's book, *People*, provides an excellent starting point for a discussion of attributes shared by all humans. Each page contains colorful cartoon-like illustrations that help young children to compare a different feature of "being human." For example, one page acknowledges that while all people have hair (or noses, eyes, hair, skin, language, clothing, and so forth), there are many variations. In this context, when children are asked to think of something that is different about themselves that makes them a special person, they typically respond openly and comfortably. We make sure that each child not only feels valued for the special person she is, but also begins to understand that each of her classmates is special as well.

Besides using this situation as the "teachable moment" for a study of diversity, it would also be helpful to assign carefully selected small groups to work together on class projects, making sure to place the excluded student with others who are likely to be kind and accepting. Praise of the group's positive behavior should encourage others to behave in a similar manner. Since all of the class shares the common experiences described above, references to the feelings of others and celebration of our differences should be meaningful and helpful if reminders are needed. Hopefully, we will not only resolve the issue of one student being excluded, but raise the entire class's sensitivity to the feelings of others and acceptance of their differences.

KELLY HOY

Third Grade
Faber Elementary School, Dunellen, NJ

I would take quick action if this were my class. First, I would talk to the students about the "White Girls Club" to see what was really happening. I would not make an issue of the comment, but I would use it as an opportunity to talk informally with the students in question. The comment might be simple chatter of a couple of students or it might signal the emergence of an exclusionary group or club. At any rate, I would want to structure the social relations of the class to get the new student more involved and interacting with her classmates. The fact that the she is not being included in many activities, sits alone in the library, and plays alone is reason enough for concern. I can and will structure recess so that she is more involved and central to the activities. I would also ask the new girl to join with a few hand-picked students to help me after school with a project or two so that I could again encourage constructive interaction.

I also periodically do what I call "Lessons in Life" with my students, which revolve around problems of right and wrong. I create a scenario in which a student is being treated unfairly. I break the class into groups and have them assume the problem personally, ask them how they would feel in that situation, and what is the right thing do. We then formulate a lesson for life. My students respond well to this and they do know what is right and wrong.

The current situation, however, presents a natural learning opportunity in which the issues of tolerance, sensitivity, diversity, and democracy could be taught. The third-grade students that I teach are ready to learn and talk about such issues; in fact, these are the kind of problems that a social studies unit can be built around. This situation is a way to help students grow and become more sensitive to people of different races and beliefs. I would not be heavy-handed or unduly upset, but rather I see this incident as a chance to teach democracy and values in a natural way.

Behavioral Views
of Learning

*A*re you one of those people whose blood pressure goes up when it is taken in the doctor's office? Have you ever worn something new and received so many compliments that you found yourself wearing that outfit often? What happens when you tell a joke and no one laughs? Are you more or less likely to tell the joke in the future? If you see someone severely reprimanded for reading a newspaper in class, are you more or less likely to read the paper in that class? Does learning have an influence on your answers to these questions? We will spend the next four chapters looking at learning and its applications.

We begin this chapter with a general definition of learning that takes into account the opposing views of different theoretical groups. We will highlight one group, the behavioral theorists, in this chapter, another major group, the cognitive theorists, in Chapters 7 and 8, and then look at current sociocultural and social cognitive views in Chapter 9.

Our discussion in this chapter will focus on three behavioral learning processes: contiguity, classical conditioning, and operant conditioning, with the greatest emphasis on the last process. After examining the implications of applied behavior analysis for teaching, we look at two recent directions in behavioral approaches to learning—self-management and cognitive behavior modification.

By the time you have completed this chapter, you should be able to:

▶ Define learning.
▶ Compare contiguity, classical conditioning, and operant conditioning, and give examples of each.
▶ Give examples of four different kinds of consequences that can follow any behavior and the effect each is likely to have on future behavior.
▶ Select a common academic or behavior problem and design an intervention based on applied behavior analysis.
▶ Apply group consequences, token economies, and contingency contracts appropriately in your classroom.
▶ Compare self-management and cognitive behavior modification.

What Would You Do?

You were hired in January to take over the class of a teacher who moved away. This is a great district and a terrific school. If you do well, you might be in line for a full-time opening next fall. As you are introduced around the school, you get a number of sympathetic looks and many—too many—offers of help: "Let me know if I can do anything for you."

As you walk toward the class, you begin to understand why so many teachers volunteered their help. You hear the screaming when you are still halfway down the hall. "Give it back, it's MINE!" "No way—come and get it!" "I hate you." A crashing sound follows as a table full of books hits the floor. The first day is a nightmare. Evidently the previous teacher had no management system—no order. Several students walk around the room while you are talking to the class, interrupt you when you are working with a group, torment the class goldfish, and open their lunches (or those of other students) for a self-determined, mid-morning snack. Others listen, but ask a million questions off the topic. Simply taking roll and introducing the first activity takes an hour. You end the first day exhausted and discouraged, losing your voice and your patience.

▶ How would you approach the situation?

▶ Which problem behaviors would you tackle first?

▶ Would giving rewards or administering punishments be useful in this situation? Why or why not?

Understanding Learning

When we hear the word *learning*, most of us think of studying and school. We think about subjects or skills we intend to master, such as algebra, Spanish, chemistry, or karate. But learning is not limited to school. We learn every day of our lives. Babies learn to kick their legs to make the mobile above their cribs move, teenagers learn the lyrics to all their favorite songs, middle-aged people like me learn to change their diet and exercise patterns, and every few years we all learn to find a new style of dress attractive when the old styles (the styles we once loved) go out of fashion. This last example shows that learning is not always intentional. We don't try to like new styles and dislike old; it just seems to happen that way. We don't intend to become nervous when we see the dentist fill a syringe with Novocain or when we step onto a stage, yet many of us do. So what is this powerful phenomenon called learning?

Learning: A Definition

Learning: Process through which experience causes permanent change in knowledge or behavior.

In the broadest sense, **learning** occurs when experience causes a relatively permanent change in an individual's knowledge or behavior. The change may be deliberate or unintentional, for better or for worse. To qualify as learning, this change must be brought about by experience—by the interaction of a person with his or her environment. Changes simply caused by maturation, such as growing taller or turning gray, do not qualify as learning. Temporary changes resulting from illness, fatigue, or hunger are also excluded from a general definition of learning. A person who has gone without food for two days does not learn to be hungry, and a person who is ill does not learn to run more slowly. Of course, learning plays a part in how we respond to hunger or illness.

Our definition specifies that the changes resulting from learning are in the individual's knowledge or behavior. While most psychologists would agree with this statement, some tend to emphasize the change in knowledge, others the change in behavior. Cognitive psychologists, who focus on changes in knowledge, believe learning is an internal mental activity that cannot be observed directly. As you will see in the next chapter, cognitive psychologists studying learning are interested in unobservable mental activities such as thinking, remembering, and solving problems (Schwartz & Reisberg, 1991).

The psychologists discussed in this chapter, on the other hand, favor **behavioral learning theories.** The behavioral view generally assumes that the outcome of learning is change in behavior and emphasizes the effects of external events on the individual. Some early behaviorists such as J. B. Watson took the radical position that because thinking, intentions, and other internal mental events could not be seen or studied rigorously and scientifically, these "mentalisms," as he called them, should not even be included in an explanation of learning. Before we look in depth at behavioral explanations of learning, let's step into an actual classroom and note the possible results of learning.

Learning Is Not Always What It Seems

Elizabeth was beginning her first day of solo teaching. After weeks of working with her cooperating teacher in an eighth-grade social studies class, she was ready to take over. As she moved from behind the desk to the front of the room, she saw another adult approach the classroom door. It was Mr. Ross, her supervisor from college. Elizabeth's neck and facial muscles suddenly became very tense and her hands trembled.

"I've stopped by to observe your teaching," Mr. Ross said. "This will be my first of six visits. I tried to reach you last night to tell you."

Elizabeth tried to hide her reaction, but her hands trembled as she gathered the notes for the lesson.

"Let's start today with a kind of game. I will say some words, then I want you to tell me the first words you can think of. Don't bother to raise your hands. Just say the words out loud, and I will write them on the board. Don't all speak at once, though. Wait until someone else has finished to say your word. Okay, here is the first word: Slavery."

"Civil War." "Lincoln." "Freedom." "Emancipation Proclamation." The answers came very quickly, and Elizabeth was relieved to see that the students understood the game.

"All right, very good," she said. "Now try another one: South."

"South Carolina." "South Dakota." "South Street Seaport," "No, the Confederacy, you dummy." "*Gone with the Wind*." "Clark Gable." With this last answer, a ripple of laughter moved across the room.

"Clark Gable!" Elizabeth sighed dreamily. "*Gone with the Wind* was on television last week." Then she laughed too. Soon all the students were laughing. "Okay, settle down," Elizabeth said. "Here is another word: North."

"Bluebellies." The students continued to laugh. "Yellowbellies." "Bellydancers." More laughter and a few appropriate gestures.

"Just a minute," Elizabeth pleaded. "These ideas are getting a little off base!"

Behavioral Learning Theories: Explanations of learning that focus on external events as the cause of changes in observable behaviors.

"Off base? Baseball," shouted the boy who had first mentioned Clark Gable. He stood up and started throwing balls of paper to a friend in the back of the room, simulating the style of Roger Clemens.

"The Atlanta Braves." "No, the Mets." "Shea Stadium." "Hot dogs." "Popcorn." "Home videos." "*Gone with the Wind*." "Clark Gable." The responses now came too fast for Elizabeth to stop them. For some reason, the Clark Gable line got an even bigger laugh the second time around, and Elizabeth suddenly realized she had lost the class.

"Okay, since you know so much about the Civil War, close your books and take out a pen," Elizabeth said, obviously angry. She passed out the worksheet that she had planned as a cooperative, open-book project. "You have 20 minutes to finish this test!"

"You didn't tell us we were having a test!" "This isn't fair!" "We haven't even covered this stuff yet!" "I didn't do anything wrong!" There were moans and disgusted looks, even from the most mellow students. "I'm reporting you to the principal; it's a violation of students' rights!"

This last comment hit hard. The class had just finished discussing human rights as preparation for this unit on the Civil War. As she listened to the protests, Elizabeth felt terrible. How was she going to grade these "tests"? The first section of the worksheet involved facts about events during the Civil War, and the second section asked students to create a news-style program interviewing ordinary people touched by the war.

"All right, all right, it won't be a test. But you do have to complete this worksheet for a grade. I was going to let you work together, but your behavior this morning tells me that you are not ready for group work. If you can complete the first section of the sheet working quietly and seriously, you may work together on the second section." Elizabeth knew that her students would like to work together on writing the script for the news interview program.

It appears, on the surface at least, that very little learning of any sort was taking place in Elizabeth's classroom. In fact, Elizabeth had some good ideas; but she also made some mistakes in her application of learning principles. We will return to this episode later in the chapter to analyze various aspects of what took place. To get

Does public speaking make you feel anxious or relaxed? What experiences taught you to feel this way? ▶

us started, three events can be singled out, each possibly related to a different learning process.

First, Elizabeth's hands trembled when her college supervisor entered the room. Second, the students were able to associate the words *Carolina* and *Dakota* with the word *South*. Third, one student continued to disrupt the class with inappropriate responses. The three learning processes represented are classical conditioning, contiguity, and operant conditioning. In the following pages we will examine these three kinds of learning, starting with contiguity.

CHECKPOINT

Understanding Learning

Review

 Define learning.

Apply

 Locate examples of the three learning processes from your life this week.

Early Explanations of Learning: Contiguity and Classical Conditioning

One of the earliest explanations of learning came from Aristotle (384–322 B.C.). He said that we remember things together (1) when they are similar, (2) when they contrast, and (3) when they are *contiguous*. This last principle is the most important, because it is included in all explanations of *learning by association*. The principle of **contiguity** states that whenever two or more sensations occur together often enough, they will become associated. Later, when only one of these sensations (a **stimulus**) occurs, the other will be remembered too (a **response**) (Rachlin, 1991; Wasserman & Miller, 1997).

Some results of contiguous learning were evident in Elizabeth's class. When she said "South," students associated the words "Carolina" and "Dakota." They had heard these words together many times. Other learning processes may also be involved when students learn these phrases, but contiguity is a factor. Contiguity also plays a major role in another learning process best known as *classical conditioning*.

Pavlov's Dilemma and Discovery: Classical Conditioning

Classical conditioning focuses on the learning of *involuntary* emotional or physiological responses such as fear, increased heartbeat, salivation, or sweating, which are sometimes called **respondents** because they are automatic responses to stimuli. Through the process of classical conditioning, humans and animals can be trained to react involuntarily to a stimulus that previously had no effect—or a very different effect—on them. The stimulus comes to *elicit*, or bring forth, the response automatically.

Classical conditioning was discovered by Ivan Pavlov, a Russian physiologist, in the 1920s. In his laboratory, Pavlov was plagued by a series of setbacks in his experiments on the digestive system of dogs. He was trying to determine how long it took a dog to secrete digestive juices after it had been fed, but the intervals of time kept changing. At first, the dogs salivated in the expected manner while they were being fed. Then the dogs began to salivate as soon as they saw the food. Finally, they

Contiguity: Association of two events because of repeated pairing.

Stimulus: Event that activates behavior.

Response: Observable reaction to a stimulus.

Classical Conditioning: Association of automatic responses with new stimuli.

Respondents: Responses (generally automatic or involuntary) elicited by specific stimuli.

Neutral Stimulus: Stimulus not connected to a response.

Unconditioned Stimulus (US): Stimulus that automatically produces an emotional or physiological response.

Unconditioned Response (UR): Naturally occurring emotional or physiological response.

Conditioned Stimulus (CS): Stimulus that evokes an emotional or physiological response after conditioning.

Conditioned Response (CR): Learned response to a previously neutral stimulus.

Generalization: Responding in the same way to similar stimuli.

Discrimination: Responding differently to similar, but not identical stimuli.

Extinction: Gradual disappearance of a learned response.

salivated as soon as they saw the scientist enter the room. The white coats of the experimenters and the sound of their footsteps all *elicited* salivation. Pavlov decided to make a detour from his original experiments and examine these unexpected interferences in his work.

In one of his first experiments, Pavlov began by sounding a tuning fork and recording a dog's response. As expected, there was no salivation. At this point, the sound of the tuning fork was a **neutral stimulus** because it brought forth no salivation. Then Pavlov fed the dog. The response was salivation. The food was an **unconditioned stimulus (US)** because no prior training or "conditioning" was needed to establish the natural connection between food and salivation. The salivation was an **unconditioned response (UR)**, again because it occurred automatically—no conditioning required.

Using these three elements—the food, the salivation, and the tuning fork—Pavlov demonstrated that a dog could be conditioned to salivate after hearing the tuning fork. He did this by contiguous pairing of the sound with food. At the beginning of the experiment, he sounded the fork and then quickly fed the dog. After Pavlov repeated this several times, the dog began to salivate after hearing the sound but before receiving the food. Now the sound had become a **conditioned stimulus (CS)** that could bring forth salivation by itself. The response of salivating after the tone was now a **conditioned response (CR)**.

Generalization, Discrimination, and Extinction

Pavlov's work also identified three other processes in classical conditioning: *generalization*, *discrimination*, and *extinction*. After the dogs learned to salivate in response to hearing one particular sound, they would also salivate after hearing similar tones that were slightly higher or lower. This process is called **generalization** because the conditioned response of salivating generalized or occurred in the presence of similar stimuli. Pavlov could also teach the dogs **discrimination**—to respond to one tone but not to others that are similar—by making sure that food always followed only one tone, not any others. **Extinction** occurs when a conditioned stimulus (a particular tone) is presented repeatedly but is not followed by the unconditioned stimulus (food). The conditioned response (salivating) gradually fades away and finally is "extinguished"—it disappears altogether.

Pavlov's findings and those of other researchers who have studied classical conditioning have implications for teachers. It is possible that many of our emotional reactions to various situations are learned in part through classical conditioning. For example, Elizabeth's trembling hands when she saw her college supervisor might be traced to previous unpleasant experiences. Perhaps she had been embarrassed during past evaluations of her performance, and now just the thought of being observed elicits a pounding heart and

GUIDELINES

Applying Classical Conditioning

Associate positive, pleasant events with learning tasks.

Examples

1. Emphasize group competition and cooperation over individual competition. Many students have negative emotional responses to individual competition that may generalize to other learning.

2. Make division drills fun by having students decide how to divide refreshments equally, then letting them eat the results.

3. Make voluntary reading appealing by creating a comfortable reading corner with pillows, colorful displays of books, and reading props such as puppets (see Morrow & Weinstein, 1986, for more ideas).

Help students to risk anxiety-producing situations voluntarily and successfully.

Examples

1. Assign a shy student the responsibility of teaching two other students how to distribute materials for map study.

2. Devise small steps toward a larger goal. For example, give ungraded practice tests daily, and then weekly, to students who tend to "freeze" in test situations.

3. If a student is afraid of speaking in front of the class, let the student read a report to a small group while seated, then read it while standing, then give the report from notes instead of reading it verbatim. Next, move in stages toward having the student give a report to the whole class.

Help students recognize differences and similarities among situations so they can discriminate and generalize appropriately.

Examples

1. Explain that it is appropriate to avoid strangers who offer gifts or rides but safe to accept favors from adults when parents are present.

2. Assure students who are anxious about taking college entrance exams that this test is like all the other achievement tests they have taken.

---

sweaty palms. Remember that emotions and attitudes as well as facts and ideas are learned in classrooms. This emotional learning can sometimes interfere with academic learning. Procedures based on classical conditioning also can be used to help people learn more adaptive emotional responses, as the Guidelines above suggest.

Operant Conditioning: Trying New Responses

So far we have concentrated on the automatic conditioning of involuntary responses such as salivation and fear. Clearly, not all human learning is so automatic and unintentional. Most behaviors are not *elicited* by stimuli, they are *emitted* or voluntarily enacted. People actively "operate" on their environment to produce different kinds of consequences. These deliberate actions are called **operants**. The learning process involved in operant behavior is called **operant conditioning** because we learn to behave in certain ways as we operate on the environment.

The Work of Thorndike and Skinner

Edward Thorndike and B. F. Skinner both played major roles in developing knowledge of operant conditioning. Thorndike's (1913) early work involved cats that he

Operants: Voluntary (and generally goal-directed) behaviors emitted by a person or an animal.

Operant Conditioning: Learning in which voluntary behavior is strengthened or weakened by consequences or antecedents.

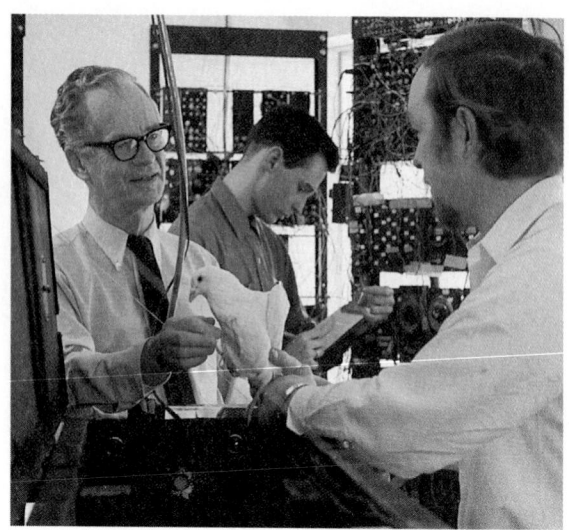

▲ *B. F. Skinner's work on operant conditioning changed the way we think about consequences and learning.*

placed in problem boxes. To escape from the box and reach food outside, the cats had to pull out a bolt or perform some other task; they had to act on their environment. During the frenzied movements that followed the closing of the box, the cats eventually made the correct movement to escape, usually by accident. After repeating the process several times, the cats learned to make the correct response almost immediately. Thorndike decided, on the basis of these experiments, that one important law of learning was the law of effect: Any act that produces a satisfying effect in a given situation will tend to be repeated in that situation. Because pulling out a bolt produced satisfaction (access to food), cats repeated that movement when they found themselves in the box again.

Thorndike thus established the basis for operant conditioning, but the person generally thought to be responsible for developing the concept is B. F. Skinner (1953). Skinner began with the belief that the principles of classical conditioning account for only a small portion of learned behaviors. Many human behaviors are operants, not respondents. Classical conditioning describes only how existing behaviors might be paired with new stimuli; it does not explain how new operant behaviors are acquired.

Behavior, like response or action, is simply a word for what a person does in a particular situation. Conceptually, we may think of a behavior as sandwiched between two sets of environmental influences: those that precede it (its **antecedents**) and those that follow it (its **consequences**) (Skinner, 1950). This relationship can be shown very simply as antecedent–behavior–consequence, or A–B–C. As behavior is ongoing, a given consequence becomes an antecedent for the next ABC sequence. Research in operant conditioning shows that operant behavior can be altered by changes in the antecedents, the consequences, or both. Early work focused on consequences, often using rats or pigeons as subjects.

Types of Consequences

According to the behavioral view, consequences determine to a great extent whether a person will repeat the behavior that led to the consequences. The type and timing of consequences can strengthen or weaken behaviors. We will look first at consequences that strengthen behavior.

Connect and Extend
To real life
To become aware of the prevalence of reinforcement in daily life, keep a log, noting every time you give or receive reinforcement. Look for positive and negative reinforcement and also record the kind of schedule operating. Another possibility is to note reinforcement and schedules in a field placement classroom or even in college classes. What examples of reinforcement are present in your education classes?

Reinforcement. While **reinforcement** is commonly understood to mean "reward," this term has a particular meaning in psychology. A **reinforcer** is any consequence that strengthens the behavior it follows. So, by definition, *reinforced behaviors increase in frequency or duration.* Whenever you see a behavior persisting or increasing over time, you can assume the consequences of that behavior are reinforcers for the individual involved. The reinforcement process can be diagrammed as follows:

CONSEQUENCE		EFFECT
Behavior → Reinforcer	→	Strengthened or repeated behavior

We can be fairly certain that food will be a reinforcer for a hungry animal, but what about people? It is not clear why an event acts as a reinforcer for an individual, but there are many theories about why reinforcement works. For example, some psychologists suggest that reinforcers satisfy needs, while other psychologists believe that reinforcers reduce tension or stimulate a part of the brain (Rachlin, 1991). Whether the consequences of any action are reinforcing probably depends on the individual's perception of the event and the meaning it holds for her or him. For example, students who repeatedly get themselves sent to the principal's office for misbehaving may be indicating that something about this consequence is reinforcing for them, even if it doesn't seem desirable to you.

Reinforcers are those consequences that strengthen the associated behavior (Skinner, 1953, 1989). There are two types of reinforcement. The first, called **positive reinforcement**, occurs when the behavior produces a new stimulus. Examples include a peck on the red key producing food for a pigeon, wearing a new outfit producing many compliments, or falling out of your chair producing cheers and laughter from classmates.

Notice that positive reinforcement can occur even when the behavior being reinforced (falling out of a chair) is not "positive" from the teacher's point of view. In fact, positive reinforcement of inappropriate behaviors occurs unintentionally in many classrooms. Teachers help maintain problem behaviors by inadvertently reinforcing them. For example, Elizabeth may have unintentionally reinforced problem behavior in her class by laughing the first time the boy answered, "Clark Gable." The problem behavior may have persisted for other reasons, but the consequence of Elizabeth's laughter could have played a role.

When the consequence that strengthens a behavior is the *appearance* (addition) of a new stimulus, the situation is defined as positive reinforcement. In contrast, when the consequence that strengthens a behavior is the *disappearance* (subtraction) of a stimulus, the process is called **negative reinforcement**. If a particular action leads to stopping, avoiding, or escaping an **aversive** situation, the action is likely to be repeated in a similar situation. A common example is the car seatbelt buzzer. As soon as you attach your seatbelt, the irritating buzzer stops. You are likely to repeat this action in the future because the behavior made an aversive stimulus disappear. Consider students who continually "get sick" right before a test and are sent to the nurse's office. The behavior allows the students to escape aversive situations—tests—so getting "sick" is being maintained, in part, through negative reinforcement. It is negative because the stimulus (the test) disappears; it is reinforcement because the behavior that caused the stimulus to disappear (getting "sick") increases or repeats. It is also possible that classical conditioning plays a role. The students may have been conditioned to experience unpleasant physiological reactions to tests.

The "negative" in negative reinforcement does not imply that the behavior being reinforced is necessarily negative. The meaning is closer to that of "negative" numbers—something is subtracted. Associate positive and negative reinforcement with adding or subtracting something following a behavior.

Punishment. Negative reinforcement is often confused with punishment. The process of reinforcement (positive or negative) always involves strengthening behavior. **Punishment**, on the other hand, involves *decreasing or suppressing behavior*. A behavior followed by a "punisher" is *less* likely to be repeated in similar situations in the future. Again, it is the effect that defines a consequence as punishment, and different people have different perceptions of

Connect and Extend
To real life
How can the principles of conditioning help explain the difficulty many people experience when they try to stop smoking? Outline a program for the reduction or elimination of smoking behavior.

Connect and Extend
To real life
Positive reinforcement: Praise for good grades, bonus points on tests, a class pizza party when everyone makes above 85 on the weekly spelling test. *Negative reinforcement:* Removing a stone from your shoe; calling on a child who is madly waving his hand and shouting, "I know, I know!"(you are negatively reinforced because the noise stops); wearing a certain pair of shoes on trips to avoid aching feet; saying "I'm really sorry" to your spouse to avoid his or her anger. *Presentation punishment:* Running extra laps; reprimands; bad grades; corporal punishment. *Removal punishment:* Fines; being grounded; missing recess; not being allowed to go on the field trip; getting fired.

Connect and Extend
To your teaching
Recall an instance of punishment that you have experienced at some time during your life. What were your feelings when you were being punished? List the feelings. (Negative feelings, such as embarrassment, resentment, hurt, anger, etc., probably will account for 90% of the responses.) Does the punishment work? What are some other negative effects of punishment? If punishment is ineffective and also produces negative side effects, why do so many teachers rely on it so much?

Antecedents: Events that precede an action.

Consequences: Events that follow an action.

Reinforcement: Use of consequences to strengthen behavior.

Reinforcer: Any event that follows a behavior and increases the chances that the behavior will occur again.

Positive Reinforcement: Strengthening behavior by presenting a desired stimulus after the behavior.

Negative Reinforcement: Strengthening behavior by removing an aversive stimulus when the behavior occurs.

Aversive: Irritating or unpleasant.

Punishment: Process that weakens or suppresses behavior.

Presentation Punishment: Decreasing the chances that a behavior will occur again by presenting an aversive stimulus following the behavior; also called Type I punishment.

Removal Punishment: Decreasing the chances that a behavior will occur again by removing a pleasant stimulus following the behavior; also called Type II punishment.

what is punishing. One student may find suspension from school punishing, while another student wouldn't mind at all. The process of punishment is diagrammed as follows:

	CONSEQUENCE		EFFECT
Behavior	→ Punisher	→	Weakened or decreased behavior

Like reinforcement, punishment may take one of two forms. The first type has been called Type I punishment, but this name isn't very informative, so I use the term **presentation punishment.** It occurs when the appearance of a stimulus following the behavior suppresses or decreases the behavior. When teachers assign demerits, extra work, running laps, and so on, they are using presentation punishment. I call the other type of punishment (Type II punishment) **removal punishment** because it involves removing a stimulus. When teachers or parents take away privileges after

---

FIGURE 6.1

Kinds of Reinforcement and Punishment

Negative reinforcements and punishment are often confused. It may help you to remember that reinforcement is always associated with increases in behaviors, and punishment always involves decreasing or suppressing behavior.

	Behavior Encouraged	**Behavior Suppressed**
Stimulus Presented	**POSITIVE REINFORCEMENT** ("Reward") Example: high grades	**PRESENTATION PUNISHMENT** ("Type I" Punishment) Example: after school detention
Stimulus Removed or Withheld	**NEGATIVE REINFORCEMENT** ("Escape") Example: excused from chores	**REMOVAL PUNISHMENT** ("Type II" Punishment) Example: no TV for a week

---

a young person has behaved inappropriately, they are applying removal punishment. With both types, the effect is to decrease the behavior that led to the punishment. Figure 6.1 summarizes the processes of reinforcement and punishment.

Reinforcement Schedules

When people are learning a new behavior, they will learn it faster if they are reinforced for every correct response. This is a **continuous reinforcement schedule**. Then, when the new behavior has been mastered, they will maintain it best if they are reinforced intermittently rather than every time. An **intermittent reinforcement schedule** helps students to maintain skills without expecting constant reinforcement.

There are two basic types of intermittent reinforcement schedules. One—called an **interval schedule**—is based on the amount of time that passes between reinforcers. The other—a **ratio schedule**—is based on the number of responses learners give between reinforcers. Interval and ratio schedules may be either *fixed* (predictable) or *variable* (unpredictable). Table 6.1 summarizes the five possible reinforcement schedules (the continuous schedule and the four kinds of intermittent schedules).

Summarizing the Effects of Reinforcement Schedules

Speed of performance depends on control. If reinforcement is based on the number of responses you give, then you have more control over the reinforcement: The

Continuous Reinforcement Schedule: Presenting a reinforcer after every appropriate response.

Intermittent Reinforcement Schedule: Presenting a reinforcer after some but not all responses.

Interval Schedule: Length of time between reinforcers.

Ratio Schedule: Reinforcement based on the number of responses between reinforcers.

TABLE 6.1 *Reinforcement Schedules*

Schedule	Definition	Example	Response Pattern	Reaction When Reinforcement Stops
Continuous	Reinforcement after every response	Turning on the television	Rapid learning of response	Very little persistence; rapid disappearance of response
Fixed-interval	Reinforcement after a set period of time	Weekly quiz	Response rate increases as time for reinforcement approaches, then drops after reinforcement	Little persistence; rapid drop in response rate when time for reinforcement passes and no reinforcer appears
Variable-interval	Reinforcement after varying lengths of time	Pop quizzes	Slow, steady rate of responding; very little pause after reinforcement	Greater persistence; slow decline in response rate
Fixed-ratio	Reinforcement after a set number of responses	Piece work Bake sale	Rapid response rate; pause after reinforcement	Little persistence; rapid drop in response rate when expected number of responses are given and no reinforcer appears
Variable-ratio	Reinforcement after a varying number of responses	Slot machines	Very high response rate; little pause after reinforcement	Greatest persistence; response rate stays high and gradually drops off

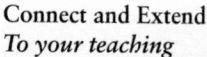

Stimulus Control: Capacity for the presence or absence of antecedents to cause behaviors.

Cueing: Providing a stimulus that "sets up" a desired behavior.

Prompt: A reminder that follows a cue to make sure the person reacts to the cue.

faster you accumulate the correct number of responses, the faster the reinforcement will come. A teacher who says, "As soon as you complete these ten problems correctly, you may go to the student lounge," can expect higher rates of performance than a teacher who says, "Work on these ten problems for the next 20 minutes. Then I will check your papers and those with ten correct may go to the lounge."

Persistence in performance depends on predictability. Continuous reinforcement and both kinds of fixed reinforcement (ratio and interval) are quite predictable. We come to expect reinforcement at certain points and are generally quick to give up when the reinforcement does not meet our expectations. To encourage persistence of response, variable schedules are most appropriate. In fact, if the schedule is gradually changed until it becomes very "lean"—meaning that reinforcement occurs only after many responses or a long time interval—then people can learn to work for extended periods without any reinforcement at all. Just watch gamblers playing slot machines to see how powerful a lean reinforcement schedule can be.

Reinforcement schedules influence how persistently we will respond when reinforcement is withheld. What happens when reinforcement is completely withdrawn?

Extinction. In classical conditioning, we saw that the conditioned response was extinguished (disappeared) when the conditioned stimulus appeared but the unconditioned stimulus did not follow (tone, but no food). In operant conditioning, a person or an animal will not persist in a certain behavior if the usual reinforcer is withheld. The behavior will eventually be extinguished (stop). For example, if you go for a week without selling even one magazine door-to-door, you may give up. Removal of reinforcement altogether leads to extinction. The process may take a while, however, as you know if you have tried to extinguish a child's tantrums by withholding your attention. Often the child wins—you give up ignoring and instead of extinction, intermittent reinforcement occurs. This, of course, may encourage even more persistent tantrums in the future.

Antecedents and Behavior Change

In operant conditioning, antecedents—the events preceding behaviors—provide information about which behaviors will lead to positive consequences and which to negative. Skinner's pigeons learned to peck for food when a light was on, but not to bother when the light was off, because no food followed pecking when the light was off. In other words, they learned to use the antecedent light as a cue to discriminate the likely consequence of pecking. The pigeons' pecking was under **stimulus control,** controlled by the discriminative stimulus of the light. You can see that this idea is related to discrimination in classical conditioning, but here we are talking about voluntary behaviors such as pecking, not reflexes such as salivating.

We all learn to discriminate—to read situations. When should you ask to borrow your roommate's car, after a major disagreement or after you both have had a great time at a party? The antecedent cue of a school principal standing in the hall helps students discriminate the probable consequences of running or attempting to break into a locker. We often respond to such antecedent cues without fully realizing that they are influencing our behavior. But teachers can use cues deliberately in the classroom.

Cueing. By definition, **cueing** is the act of providing an antecedent stimulus just before a particular behavior is to take place. Cueing is particularly useful in setting the stage for behaviors that must occur at a specific time but are easily forgotten. In working with young people, teachers often find themselves correcting behaviors after the fact. For example, they may ask students, "When are you going to start remembering to . . . ?" Such reminders often lead to irritation. The mistake is already made, and the young person is left with only two choices, to promise to try harder or to say, "Why don't you leave me alone?" Neither response is very satisfying. Presenting a nonjudgmental cue can help prevent these negative confrontations. When a student performs the appropriate behavior after a cue, the teacher can reinforce the student's accomplishment instead of punishing the student's failure.

Prompting. Sometimes students need help in learning to respond to a cue in an appropriate way so the cue becomes a discriminative stimulus. One approach is to provide an additional cue, called a **prompt,** following the first cue. There are two principles for using a cue and a prompt to teach a new behavior (Becker, Engelmann, & Thomas, 1975). First, make sure the environmental stimulus that you want to become a cue occurs immediately before the prompt you are using, so students will learn to respond to the cue and not rely only on the prompt. Second, fade the prompt as soon as possible so students do not become dependent on it.

An example of cueing and prompting is providing students with a checklist or reminder sheet. Figure 6.2 on page 212 is a checklist for the steps in peer tutoring. Working in pairs is the cue; the checklist is the prompt. As students learn the procedures, the teacher may stop using the checklist, but may remind the students of the steps. When no written or oral prompts are necessary, the students have learned to respond appropriately to the environmental cue of working in pairs—they have learned how to behave in tutoring situations. However, the teacher should continue to monitor the process, recognize good work, and correct mistakes. Before a tutoring session, the teacher might ask students to close their eyes and "see" the checklist, focusing on each step. As students work, the teacher could listen to their interactions and continue to coach students as they improve their tutoring skills.

Connect and Extend
To real life
Examples of stimulus control: I found myself (more than once) about to turn into my old office parking lot, even after my department had been moved to a new building across town. The old cues kept me heading automatically to the old office. Another example is the supposedly true story of a getaway car driver in a bank robbery who sped through town, only to be caught by the police when she dutifully stopped at a red light. The stimulus of the red light had come to have automatic control.

Connect and Extend
To your teaching
Suggest the cues or prompts you would use to elicit the following behaviors: (1) the class looks at you to hear your directions; (2) the students open their books to the assigned page when the bell rings; (3) the students give you their full attention when you are making an important point; and (4) a student walks instead of running to the door when the dismissal bell rings.

CHECKPOINT

Operant Conditioning: Trying New Responses

Review

▶ What defines a consequence as a reinforcer? As a punisher?

▶ How are negative reinforcement and punishment different?

▶ How can you encourage persistence in a behavior?

▶ What is the difference between a prompt and a cue?

Apply

▶ How might you use reinforcement and punishment to improve the situation described at the beginning of the chapter?

▶ In what kinds of situations is cueing helpful?

FIGURE 6.2

Written Prompts: A Peer-Tutoring Checklist

By using this checklist, students are reminded how to be effective tutors. As they become more proficient, the checklist may be less necessary.

 Remember to…

 _____ 1. Have the lesson ready.

 _____ 2. Talk clearly.

 _____ 3. Be friendly.

 _____ 4. Tell the student when he is right.

 _____ 5. Correct mistakes. STOP! Give the right answer. Have the student do it.

 _____ 6. Praise good work!

 _____ 7. Make the lesson fun.

 _____ 8. Do not give TOO MUCH help.

 _____ 9. Fill out the daily sheet.

 _____ 10. Can you add a suggestion?

Source: From *Achieving Educational Excellence: Behavior Analysis for School Personnel* (Figure, p. 89), by B. Sulzer-Azaroff and G. R. Mayer, 1994, San Marcos, CA: Western Image, P.O. Box 427. Copyright © 1994 by Beth Sulzer-Azaroff and G. Roy Mayer. Reprinted by permission of the authors.

*A*pplied Behavior Analysis

Connect and Extend
To your teaching

Mr. Stevens is a 2nd-grade teacher. He has only been teaching for a few weeks and is having problems. He has a class of 25 overeager children who consistently blurt and yell out their answers instead of waiting and raising their hands. He finds it difficult to respond to each student. He is pleased with their eagerness but needs a calmer setting. What would you do if you were Mr. Stevens?

Applied behavior analysis is the application of behavioral learning principles to change behavior. The method is sometimes called **behavior modification,** but this term has negative connotations for many people and is often misunderstood (Alberto & Troutman, 1990; Kaplan, 1991).

Ideally, applied behavior analysis requires clear specification of the behavior to be changed, careful measurement of the behavior, analysis of the antecedents and reinforcers that might be maintaining inappropriate or undesirable behavior, interventions based on behavioral principles to change the behavior, and careful measurement of changes. In research on applied behavior analysis, an ABAB design is common. That is, researchers take a baseline measurement of the behavior (A), then apply the intervention (B), then stop the intervention to see if the behavior goes back to the baseline level (A), and then reintroduce the intervention (B).

In classrooms, teachers usually cannot follow all the ABAB steps, but they can do the following:

1. Clearly specify the behavior to be changed and note the current level. For example, if a student is "careless," does this mean 2, 3, 4, or more computation errors for every 10 problems?

2. Plan a specific intervention using antecedents, consequences, or both. For example, offer the student one extra minute of computer time for every problem completed with no errors.

3. Keep track of the results, and modify the plan if necessary.

Let's consider some specific methods for accomplishing step 2—the *intervention*.

Methods for Encouraging Behaviors

As we discussed earlier, to encourage behavior is to reinforce it. There are several specific ways to encourage existing behaviors or teach new ones. These include praise, the Premack principle, shaping, and positive practice.

Reinforcing with Teacher Attention. Based on early work such as that of Madsen, Becker, and Thomas (1968) demonstrating that teachers can improve student behavior by ignoring rule-breakers and praising students who are following the rules, many psychologists advised teachers to "accentuate the positive"—liberally praise students for good behavior while ignoring mistakes and misbehavior. This *praise-and-ignore approach* can be helpful, but we should not expect it to solve all classroom management problems. Several studies have shown that disruptive behaviors persist when teachers use positive consequences (mostly praise) as their only classroom management strategy (Pfiffner, Rosen, & O'Leary, 1985; Rosen, O'Leary, Joyce, Conway, & Pfiffner, 1984).

There is a second consideration in using praise. The positive results found in research occur when teachers carefully and systematically praise their students. Unfortunately, praise is not always given appropriately and effectively. Merely "handing out compliments" will not improve behavior. To be effective, praise must (1) be contingent on the behavior to be reinforced, (2) specify clearly the behavior being reinforced, and (3) be believable (O'Leary & O'Leary, 1977). In other words, the praise should be sincere recognition of a well-defined behavior so students understand what they did to warrant the recognition. Teachers who have not received special training often violate these conditions (Brophy, 1981). Ideas for using praise effectively, based on Brophy's extensive review of the subject, are presented in the Guidelines on page 214.

Some psychologists have suggested that teachers' use of praise tends to focus students on learning to win approval rather than on learning for its own sake. Perhaps the best advice is to be aware of the potential dangers of the overuse or misuse of praise and to navigate accordingly.

Applied Behavior Analysis: The application of behavioral learning principles to understand and change behavior.

Behavior Modification: Systematic application of antecedents and consequences to change behavior.

Connect and Extend
To your teaching
When a teacher decides to begin ignoring a behavior that he or she wants to extinguish, there is frequently an increase in the behavior for a short time before it decreases. How do you explain this phenomenon?

Praise can be an effective technique for class management and the encouragement of learning if it is used only as a sincere recognition of well-defined behavior; teachers should not be in the habit of simply "handing out compliments." ▼

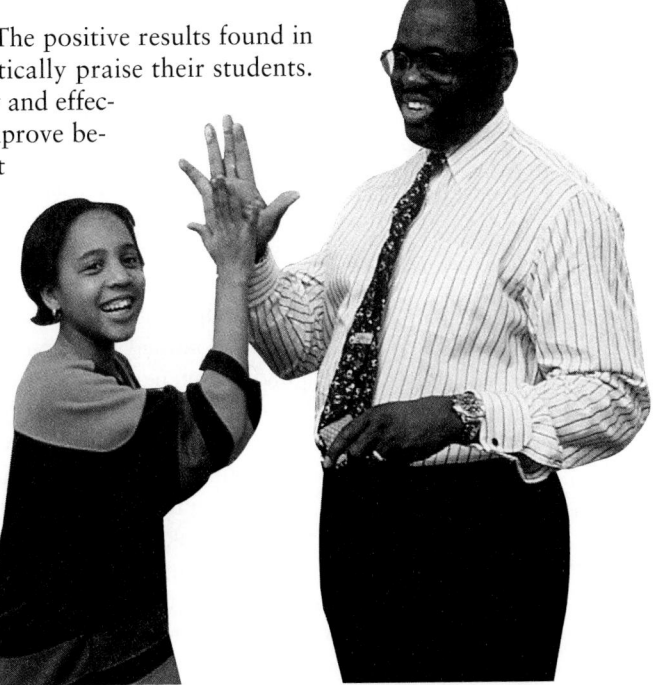

GUIDELINES

Using Praise Appropriately

Be clear and systematic in giving praise.

Examples

1. Make sure praise is tied directly to appropriate behavior.
2. Make sure the student understands the specific action or accomplishment that is being praised. Say, "You returned this poster on time and in good condition," not, "You were very responsible."

Recognize genuine accomplishments.

Examples

1. Reward the attainment of specified goals, not just participation.
2. Do not reward uninvolved students just for being quiet and not disrupting the class.
3. Tie praise to students' improving competence or to the value of their accomplishment. Say, "I noticed that you double-checked all your problems. Your score reflects your careful work."

Set standards for praise based on individual abilities and limitations.

Examples

1. Praise progress or accomplishment in relation to the individual student's past efforts.

2. Focus the student's attention on his or her own progress, not on comparisons with others.

Attribute the student's success to effort and ability so the student will gain confidence that success is possible again.

Examples

1. Don't imply that the success may be based on luck, extra help, or easy material.
2. Ask students to describe the problems they encountered and how they solved them.

Make praise really reinforcing.

Examples

1. Don't attempt to influence the rest of the class by singling out some students for praise. This tactic frequently backfires, since students know what's really going on. In addition, you risk embarrassing the student you have chosen to praise.
2. Don't give undeserved praise to students simply to balance failures. It is seldom consoling and calls attention to the student's inability to earn genuine recognition.

Selecting Reinforcers: The Premack Principle. In most classrooms, there are many readily available reinforcers other than teacher attention, such as the chance to talk to other students or feed the class animals. However, teachers tend to offer these opportunities in a rather haphazard way. Just as with praise, by making privileges and rewards directly contingent on learning and positive behavior, the teacher may greatly increase both learning and desired behavior.

A helpful guide for choosing the most effective reinforcers is the Premack principle, named for David Premack (1965). According to the **Premack principle**, a high-frequency behavior (a preferred activity) can be an effective reinforcer for a low-frequency behavior (a less-preferred activity). This is sometimes referred to as "Grandma's rule": first do what I want you to do, then you may do what you want to do. Elizabeth used this principle in her class when she told them they could work together on their Civil War news program after they quietly completed the first section of the worksheet on their own.

If students didn't have to study, what would they do? The answers to this question may suggest many possible reinforcers. For most students, talking, moving around the room, sitting near a friend, being exempt from assignments or tests, reading magazines, or playing games are preferred activities. The best way to determine appropriate reinforcers for your students may be to watch what they do in their free time.

Premack Principle: Principle stating that a more-preferred activity can serve as reinforcer for a less-preferred activity.

For the Premack principle to be effective, the low-frequency (less preferred) behavior must happen first. In the following dialogue, notice how the teacher loses a perfect opportunity to use the Premack principle:

Students: Oh, no! Do we have to work on grammar again today? The other classes got to discuss the film we saw in the auditorium this morning.

Teacher: But the other classes finished the lesson on sentences yesterday. We're almost finished too. If we don't finish the lesson, I'm afraid you'll forget the rules we reviewed yesterday.

Students: Why don't we finish the sentences at the end of the period and talk about the film now?

Teacher: Okay, if you promise to complete the sentences later.

"HEY, WAIT A MINUTE! YOU'RE CLEANING ERASERS AS A PUNISHMENT? I'M CLEANING ERASERS AS A REWARD!"

(© 1991 Tony Saltzman)

Discussing the film could have served as a reinforcer for completing the lesson. As it is, the class may well spend the entire period discussing the film. Just as the discussion becomes fascinating, the teacher will have to end it and insist that the class return to the grammar lesson.

Some teachers use questionnaires such as the one in Table 6.2 to identify effective reinforcers for their students. Remember, what works for one student may not be right for another. And students can get "too much of a good thing"; reinforcers can lose their potency if they are overused.

Shaping. What happens when students continually fail to gain reinforcement because they simply cannot perform a skill in the first place? Consider these examples:

▶ A 4th-grade student looks at the results of the latest mathematics test. "No credit on almost half of the problems again because I made one dumb mistake in each problem. I hate math!"

▶ A 10th-grade student tries each day to find some excuse for avoiding the softball game in gym class. The student cannot catch a ball and now refuses to try.

TABLE 6.2 *What Do You Like? Reinforcement Ideas from Students*

Name _____ Grade _____ Date _____

Please answer all the questions as completely as you can.

1. The school subjects I like best are:
2. Three things I like most to do in school are:
3. If I had 30 minutes' free time at school each day to do what I really liked it, it would be:
4. My two favorite snacks are:
5. At recess I like most to (three things):
6. If I had $1 to spend on anything, I would buy:
7. Three jobs I would enjoy in the class are:
8. The two people I most like to work with in school are:
9. At home I really enjoy (three things):

Source: From *Modification of Child and Adolescent Behavior* (3rd ed.) (pp. 281–283), by G. Blackman and A. Silberman, 1979, Belmont, CA: Wadsworth. Copyright © 1979 by Wadsworth Publishing Co. Reprinted with permission.

Shaping: Reinforcing each small step of progress toward a desired goal or behavior.

Successive Approximations: Small components that make up a complex behavior.

Task Analysis: System for breaking down a task hierarchically into basic skills and subskills.

Positive Practice: Practicing correct responses immediately after errors.

In both situations the students are receiving no reinforcement for their work because the end product of their efforts is not good enough. A safe prediction is that the students will soon learn to dislike the class, the subject, and perhaps the teacher and school in general. One way to prevent this problem is the strategy of **shaping,** also called **successive approximations.** Shaping involves reinforcing progress instead of waiting for perfection.

In order to use shaping, the teacher must break down the final complex behavior the student is expected to master into a number of small steps. One approach identifying the small steps is **task analysis,** originally developed by R. B. Miller (1962) to help the armed services train personnel. Miller's system begins with a definition of the final performance requirement, what the trainee (or student) must be able to do at the end of the program or unit. Then the steps that will lead to the final goal are specified. The procedure simply breaks skills and processes down into subskills and subprocesses.

Consider an example of task analysis in which students must write a position paper based on library research. If the teacher assigned the position paper without analyzing the task in this way, what could happen? Some of the students might not know how to do computer searching. They might search through one or two encyclopedias, then write a summary of the issues based only on the encyclopedia articles. Another group of students might know how to use computers, tables of contents, and indexes, but have difficulty reaching conclusions. They might hand in lengthy papers listing summaries of different ideas. Another group of students might be able to draw conclusions, but their written presentations might be so confusing and grammatically incorrect that the teacher could not understand what they were trying to say. Each of the groups would have failed in fulfilling the assignment, but for different reasons.

A task analysis gives a picture of the logical sequence of steps leading toward the final goal. An awareness of this sequence can help teachers make sure that students have the necessary skills before they move to the next step. In addition, when students have difficulty, the teacher can pinpoint problem areas.

Krumboltz and Krumboltz (1972) have described the following three methods of shaping: (1) reinforce each subskill, (2) reinforce improvements in accuracy, and (3) reinforce longer and longer periods of performance or participation.

Many behaviors can be improved through shaping, especially skills that involve persistence, endurance, increased accuracy, greater speed, or extensive practice to master. Because shaping is a time-consuming process, however, it should not be used if success can be attained through simpler methods such as cueing.

Positive Practice. A strategy for helping students replace one behavior with another is **positive practice.** This approach is especially appropriate for dealing with academic errors. When students make a mistake, they must correct it as soon as possible and practice the correct response (Gibbs & Luyben, 1985; Kazdin, 1984). The same principle can be applied when students break classroom rules. Instead of being punished, the student might be required to practice the correct alternative action.

The Guidelines on page 217 summarize approaches encouraging positive behavior.

Coping with Undesirable Behavior

No matter how successful you are at accentuating the positive, there are times when you must cope with undesirable behavior, either because other methods fail or because the behavior itself is dangerous or calls for direct action. For this pur-

Connect and Extend
To the classroom
Examples of negative reinforcement: A 10th-grade teacher tells her class that those students who turn in sloppy, careless work will have to use their free-choice time to redo it. A 1st-grade teacher tells an angry boy that he must sit by the tree until he feels able to rejoin the kickball game without arguing.

GUIDELINES

Encouraging Positive Behaviors

Make sure you recognize positive behavior in ways that students value.

Examples

1. When presenting class rules, set up positive consequences for following rules as well as negative consequences for breaking rules.

2. Recognize honest admissions of mistakes by giving a second chance: "Because you admitted that you copied your paper from a book, I'm giving you a chance to rewrite it."

3. Offer desired rewards for academic efforts, such as extra recess time, exemptions from homework or tests, or extra credit on major projects.

When students are tackling new material or trying new skills, give plenty of reinforcement.

Examples

1. Find and comment on something right in every student's first life drawing.

2. Reinforce students for encouraging each other. "French pronunciation is difficult and awkward at first. Let's help each other by eliminating all giggles when someone is brave enough to attempt a new word."

After new behaviors are established, give reinforcement on an unpredictable schedule to encourage persistence.

Examples

1. Offer surprise rewards for good participation in class.

2. Start classes with a short, written extra-credit question. Students don't have to answer, but a good answer will add points to their total for the semester.

3. Make sure the good students get compliments for their work from time to time. Don't take them for granted.

Use cueing to help establish new behaviors.

Examples

1. Put up humorous signs in the classroom to remind students of rules.

2. At the beginning of the year, as students enter class, call their attention to a list on the board of the materials they should have with them when they come to class.

Make sure all students, even those who often cause problems, receive some praise, privileges, or other rewards when they do something well.

Examples

1. Review your class list occasionally to make sure all students are receiving some reinforcement.

2. Set standards for reinforcement so that all students will have a chance to be rewarded.

Establish a variety of reinforcers.

Examples

1. Let students suggest their own reinforcers or choose from a "menu" of reinforcers with "weekly specials."

2. Talk to other teachers or parents about ideas for reinforcers.

Use the Premack principle to identify effective reinforcers.

Examples

1. Watch what students do with their free time.

2. Notice which students like to work together. The chance to work with friends is often a good reinforcer.

---

pose, negative reinforcement, satiation, reprimands, and punishment all offer possible solutions.

Negative Reinforcement. Recall the basic principle of negative reinforcement: If an action stops or avoids something unpleasant, then the action is likely to occur again in similar situations. Negative reinforcement was operating in Elizabeth's classroom. When she gave in to the moans and complaints of her class and canceled the test, her behavior was being negatively reinforced. She escaped the unpleasant student comments by changing her assignment.

Satiation: Requiring a person to repeat a problem behavior past the point of interest or motivation.

Reprimands: Criticisms for misbehavior; rebukes.

Response Cost: Punishment by loss of reinforcers.

Social Isolation: Removal of a disruptive student for 5 to 10 minutes.

Time Out: Technically, the removal of all reinforcement. In practice, isolation of a student from the rest of the class for a brief time.

Negative reinforcement may also be used to enhance learning. To do this, you place students in mildly unpleasant situations so they can "escape" when their behavior improves. Consider these examples:

Teacher to a 3rd-grade class: "When the supplies are put back in the cabinet and each of you is sitting quietly, we will go outside. Until then, we will miss our recess."

High school teacher to a student who seldom finishes in-class assignments: "As soon as you complete the assignment, you may join the class in the auditorium. But until you finish, you must work in the study hall."

Actually, a true behaviorist might object to calling these examples of negative reinforcement because too much student thinking and understanding is required to make them work. Teachers cannot treat students like lab animals, delivering a mild shock to their feet until they give a right answer, then turning off the shock briefly. But teachers can make sure that unpleasant situations improve when student behavior improves.

You may wonder why the examples above are not considered punishment. Surely staying in during recess or not accompanying the class to a special program is punishing. But the focus in each case is on strengthening specific behaviors (putting away supplies or finishing in-class assignments). The teacher strengthens (reinforces) the behaviors by removing something aversive *as soon as the desired behaviors occur.* Because the consequence involves removing or "subtracting" a stimulus, the reinforcement is negative.

Negative reinforcement also gives students a chance to exercise control. Missing recess and staying behind in study hall are unpleasant situations, but in each case the students retain control. As soon as they perform the appropriate behavior, the unpleasant situation ends. In contrast, punishment occurs after the fact, and a student cannot so easily control or terminate it.

There are several rules for negative reinforcement: Describe the desired change in a positive way. Don't bluff. Make sure you can enforce your unpleasant situation. Follow through despite complaints. Insist on action, not promises. If the unpleasant situation terminates when students promise to be better next time, you have reinforced making promises, not making changes (Krumboltz & Krumboltz, 1972; O'Leary, 1995).

Connect and Extend
To the classroom
Satiation: A 6th-grade teacher discovered one of his students making paper airplanes during an independent work time. He gave that student a stack of paper and told her to continue making airplanes until the stack of paper was gone. The student thought it was great fun for the first 10 minutes, but then she got weary and wanted to stop. After this experience, this student made better use of her independent work times.

Satiation. Another way to stop problem behavior is to insist that students continue the behavior until they are tired of doing it. This procedure, called **satiation,** should be applied with care. Forcing students to continue some behaviors may be physically or emotionally harmful or even dangerous.

An example of an appropriate use of satiation is related by Krumboltz and Krumboltz (1972). In the middle of a 9th-grade algebra class, the teacher suddenly noticed four students making all sorts of unusual motions. In response to persistent teacher questioning, the students finally admitted they were bouncing imaginary balls. The teacher pretended to greet this idea with enthusiasm and suggested the whole class do it. At first, there was a great deal of laughing and joking. After a minute this stopped, and one student even quit. The teacher, however, insisted that all the students continue. After 5 minutes and a number of exhausted sighs, the teacher allowed the students to stop. No one bounced an imaginary ball in that class again.

Teachers also may allow students to continue some action until they stop by themselves, if the behavior is not interfering with the rest of the class. A teacher can do this by simply ignoring the behavior. Remember that responding to an ignorable behavior may actually reinforce it.

In using satiation, a teacher must take care not to give in before the students do. It is also important that the repeated behavior be the one you are trying to end. If the algebra teacher above had insisted that the students write, "I will never bounce imaginary balls in class again" 500 times, the students would have become satiated with writing rather than with bouncing balls.

Reprimands. In the *Junction Journal*, my daughter's elementary-school newspaper, I read the following lines in a story called "Why I Like School," written by a 4th grader: "I also like my teacher. She helps me understand and learn. She is nice to everyone. . . . I like it when she gets mad at somebody, but she doesn't yell at them in front of the class, but speaks to them privately."

A study by Dan O'Leary and his associates examined the effectiveness of soft, private **reprimands** versus loud, public reprimands in decreasing disruptive behavior (O'Leary, Kaufman, Kass, & Drabman, 1970). Reprimanding a problem student quietly so that only the student can hear seems to be much more effective. When the teacher in the study spoke to offenders loudly enough for the entire class to hear, the disruptions increased or continued at a constant level. Some students enjoy public recognition for misbehavior. If reprimands are not used too often, and if the classroom is generally a positive, warm environment, then students usually respond quickly (Kaplan, 1991; Van Houten & Doleys, 1983).

Response Cost. The concept of **response cost** is familiar to anyone who has ever paid a fine. For certain infractions of the rules, people must lose some reinforcer (money, time, privileges, pleasures). In a class, the concept of response cost may be applied in a number of ways. The first time a student breaks a class rule, the teacher gives a warning. The second time, the teacher makes a mark beside the student's name in the grade book. The student loses 2 minutes of recess for each mark accumulated. For older students, a certain number of marks might mean losing the privilege of working in a group or going on a class trip.

Social Isolation. One of the most controversial behavioral methods for decreasing undesirable behavior is the strategy of **social isolation,** often called **time out** from reinforcement. The process involves removing a highly disruptive student from the classroom for 5 to 10 minutes. The student is placed in an empty, uninteresting room alone. It seems likely that the factor that actually decreases behavior is the punishment of brief isolation from other people (O'Leary & O'Leary, 1976). A trip to the principal's office or confinement to a chair in the corner of the regular classroom does not have the same effect as sitting alone in an empty room.

Some Cautions. Punishment in and of itself does not lead to any positive behavior. Thus, whenever you consider the use of pun-

Connect and Extend
To the classroom

Soft reprimands: During reading in Miss McCormick's 1st-grade class, she noticed that Kenny wasn't concentrating on his book. She was working with a group at the time and could have called out, "Kenny, you'd better get back to work. You're not concentrating," but she decided this would embarrass him as well as disturb the concentration of others. Instead, Miss McCormick walked over to him, asked him a couple of questions about the story, and asked him to let her know how the story ended. She achieved her goal without causing embarrassment, and she provided Kenny with an impetus and motive to concentrate on his story again.

Connect and Extend
To the classroom

What are some forms of punishment used in the public schools? In the long run, does the punishment decrease or extinguish the behavior for which it is given? Think of times when punishment (according to the teacher's view) is experienced by the student as reinforcement.

CHECKPOINT

Applied Behavior Analysis

Review

▶ What are the steps in applied behavior analysis?

▶ How can the Premack principle help you identify reinforcers?

▶ When is shaping an appropriate approach?

▶ What are some of the possible side effects of punishment?

Apply

▶ How could you use applied behavioral analysis to change one of your behaviors such as exercising or studying?

GUIDELINES

Using Punishment

Try to structure the situation so you can use negative reinforcement rather than punishment.

Examples

1. Allow students to escape unpleasant situations (completing additional workbook assignments, weekly tests of math facts) when they reach a level of competence.
2. Insist on actions, not promises. Don't let students convince you to change the terms of the agreement.

Be consistent in your application of punishment.

Examples

1. Avoid inadvertently reinforcing the behavior you are trying to punish. Keep confrontations private, so that students don't become heroes for standing up to the teacher in a public showdown.
2. Let students know in advance the consequences of breaking the rules by posting major class rules for younger students or outlining rules and consequences in a course syllabus for older students.
3. Tell students they will receive only one warning before punishment is given. Give the warning in a calm way, then follow through.
4. Make punishment as unavoidable and immediate as is reasonably possible.

Focus on the students' actions, not on the students' personal qualities.

Examples

1. Reprimand in a calm but firm voice.
2. Avoid vindictive or sarcastic words or tones of voice. You might hear your own angry words later when students imitate your sarcasm.
3. Stress the need to end the problem behavior instead of expressing any dislike you might feel for the student.

Adapt the punishment to the infraction.

Examples

1. Ignore minor misbehaviors that do not disrupt the class, or stop these misbehaviors with a disapproving glance or a move toward the student.
2. Don't use homework as a punishment for misbehaviors such as talking in class.
3. When a student misbehaves to gain peer acceptance, removal from the group of friends can be effective, because this is really time out from a reinforcing situation.
4. If the problem behaviors continue, analyze the situation and try a new approach. Your punishment may not be very punishing, or you may be inadvertently reinforcing the misbehavior.

ishment, you should make it part of a two-pronged attack. The first goal is to carry out the punishment and suppress the undesirable behavior. The second goal is to make clear what the student should be doing instead and to provide reinforcement for those desirable actions. Thus, while the problem behaviors are being suppressed, positive alternative responses are being strengthened. The Guidelines above give ideas for using punishment for positive purposes.

Behavioral Approaches to Teaching and Management

The behavioral approach to learning has made several important contributions to instruction, including systems for specifying learning objectives (we will look at this topic in Chapter 13 when we discuss planning and teaching), mastery learning techniques, and class management systems such as group consequences, token economies, and contingency contracts. These approaches are useful when the goal is to learn *explicit information* or change *behaviors* and when the material is *sequential* and *factual*. As an example of a teaching approach, let's consider mastery learning.

Mastery Learning

Mastery learning is based on the assumption that given enough time and the proper instruction, most students can master any learning objective (Bloom, 1968; Guskey & Gates, 1986). To use the mastery approach, a teacher must break a course down into small units of study. Each unit might involve mastering several specific objectives. "Mastery" usually means a score of 80 to 90% on a test or other assessment. The teacher informs the students of the objectives and the criteria for meeting each. Students who do not reach the minimum level of mastery or who reach this minimum but want to improve their performance (thus raising their grade) can recycle through the unit. When they are ready, they take another form of the unit test.

The challenge in mastery learning is providing the appropriate extra help for students who don't attain mastery. There are many possibilities. Students can work with peer tutors or aides inside or outside class or they can get extra help from their team members in cooperative groups. If no extra time or staff is available, mastery learning can be adapted to a regular class time frame. For example, after explaining the mastery approach, the teacher teaches the lessons, then gives an ungraded assessment to determine students' levels of understanding. Those who have reached the mastery level are given enrichment activities such as independent or group work, computer simulations, research projects, or creative problems to solve. Those who need more help work with the teacher on corrective instruction (Block & Anderson, 1975). The Keller Plan, also called the Personalized System of Instruction (PSI), is a form of mastery learning used most often in college (Sherman, Ruskin, & Semb, 1982).

Mastery learning makes the most sense when the focus is key concepts or skills that serve as a foundation for later learning. In mathematics, for example, some students will fall farther and farther behind if they have to move from addition of fractions to more advanced topics before they ever really understand addition. By the time they reach division of fractions, they are lost. Mastery learning has been successful when students get the extra time and support they need to learn—especially through corrective instruction outside class or inside class from peer tutors or cooperative learning group members (Guskey, 1990; Kulick, Kulick, & Bangert-Drowns, 1990; Shuell, 1996). The effects of the Block and Anderson (1975) remediation/enrichment in-class model are less clear cut and probably depend on the quality of the remediation possible using class time alone (Ellis & Fouts, 1993).

There are problems with the mastery learning approach. Teachers must have a variety of materials to allow students to recycle through objectives they failed to meet the first time. Usually, just repeating the same materials won't help. It is also important to have several assessments for each unit. In practice, mastery learning has not helped to erase achievement differences among students, as some proponents have hoped. Individual differences in achievement persist, unless the teacher holds back the faster students while the slower ones catch up—a practice that makes little sense (Arlin, 1984). Left to work at their own pace, some students will learn much more and leave a unit with much better understanding than others. Some will work much harder to take advantage of the learning opportunities. (Grabe & Latta, 1981). Some will be frustrated instead of encouraged by the chance to recycle ("You mean I have to do it *again*?").

Mastery Learning: Teaching approach—students must learn one unit and pass a test at a specified level before moving to the next unit.

Connect and Extend
To the research

Fulk, C. L., & Smith, P. J. (1995). Students' perceptions of teachers' instructional and management adaptations for students with learning or behavior problems. *The Elementary School Journal, 95,* 409–419.

Abstract: Students from grades 1–6 were interviewed individually and asked 4 "yes" or "no" questions about the following adaptations for some students: (1) easier work, (2) harder work, (3) rewards for good behavior, and (4) extra chances or different rules. The majority of responses (69%) were positive, with students favoring both academic and behavioral adaptations when needed. However, most 1st, 5th, and 6th graders were opposed to some students getting more difficult work, and first graders also opposed differential handling of behavior problems.

Many of the systematic applications of behavioral principles focus on classroom management. We will look at three: group consequences, token economies, and contingency contracts.

Group Consequences

A teacher can base reinforcement for the class on the cumulative behavior of all members of the class, usually by adding each student's points to a class or a team total. The **good behavior game** is an example of this approach. A class is divided into two teams. Specific rules for good behavior are cooperatively developed. Each time a student breaks one of the rules, that student's team is given a mark. The team with the fewest marks at the end of the period receives a special reward or privilege (longer recess, first to lunch, and so on). If both teams earn fewer than a preestablished number of marks, both teams receive the reward. Most studies indicate that even though the game produces only small improvements in academic achievement, it can produce definite improvements in the behaviors listed in the good behavior rules.

You can also use **group consequences** without dividing the class into teams; that is, you can base reinforcement on the behavior of the whole class. Wilson and Hopkins (1973) conducted a study using group consequences to reduce noise levels. Radio music served effectively as the reinforcer for students in a home economics class. Whenever noise in the class was below a predetermined level, students could listen to the radio; when the noise exceeded the level, the radio was turned off. Given the success of this simple method, such a procedure might be considered in any class where music does not interfere with the task at hand.

▲ *Consequences for breaking rules are posted in this classroom, so they serve as reminders about appropriate behavior. Did the students participate in creating these rules?*

However, caution is needed in group approaches. The whole group should not suffer for the misbehavior or mistakes of one individual if the group has no real influence over that person (Epanchin, Townsend, & Stoddard, 1994; Jenson, Sloane, & Young, 1988). I saw an entire class break into cheers when the teacher announced that one boy was transferring to another school. The chant "No more points! No more points!" filled the room. The "points" referred to the teacher's system of giving one point to the whole class each time anyone broke a rule. Every point meant 5 minutes of recess lost. The boy who was transferring had been responsible for many losses. He was not very popular to begin with, and the point system, though quite effective in maintaining order, had led to rejection and even greater unpopularity.

Peer pressure in the form of support and encouragement, however, can be a positive influence. Group consequences are recommended for situations in which students care about the approval of their peers. If the misbehavior of several students seems to be encouraged by the attention and laughter of other students, then group consequences could be helpful. Teachers might show students how to give support and constructive feedback to classmates. If a few students seem to enjoy sabotaging the system, those students may need separate arrangements.

Token Reinforcement Programs

Often it is difficult to provide positive consequences for all the students who deserve them. A **token reinforcement system** can help solve this problem by allowing all students to earn tokens for both academic work and positive classroom behavior. The tokens may be points, checks, holes punched in a card, chips, play money, or anything else that is easily identified as the student's property. Periodically the students exchange the tokens they have earned for some desired reward (Martin & Pear, 1992).

Depending on the age of the student, the rewards could be small toys, school supplies, free time, special class jobs, or other privileges. When a "token economy," as this kind of system is called, is first established, the tokens should be given out on a fairly continuous schedule, with chances to exchange the tokens for rewards often available. Once the system is working well, however, tokens should be distributed on an intermittent schedule and saved for longer periods of time before they are exchanged for rewards.

Another variation is to allow students to earn tokens in the classroom and then exchange them for rewards at home. These plans are very successful when parents are willing to cooperate. Usually a note or report form is sent home daily or twice a week. The note indicates the number of points earned in the preceding time period. The points may be exchanged for minutes of television viewing, access to special toys, or private time with parents. Points can also be saved up for larger rewards such as trips. Do not use this procedure, however, if you suspect the child might be severely punished for poor reports.

Token reinforcement systems are complicated and time-consuming. Generally, they should be used in only three situations: to motivate students who are completely uninterested in their work and have not responded to other approaches; to encourage students who have consistently failed to make academic progress; and to deal with a class that is out of control. Some groups of students seem to benefit more than others from token economies. Students with mental retardation, children who have failed often, students with few academic skills, and students with behavior problems all seem to respond to the concrete, direct nature of token reinforcement.

Before you try a token system, you should be sure that your teaching methods and materials are right for the students. Sometimes class disruptions or lack of motivation indicate that teaching practices need to be changed. Maybe the class rules are unclear or are enforced inconsistently. Maybe the text is too easy or too hard. Maybe the pace is wrong. If these problems exist, a token system may improve the situation temporarily, but the students will still have trouble learning the academic material (Jenson, Sloane, & Young, 1988).

Contingency Contract Programs

In a **contingency contract** program, the teacher draws up an individual contract with each

---

Good Behavior Game: Arrangement where a class is divided into teams and each team receives demerit points for breaking agreed-upon rules of good behavior.

Group Consequences: Rewards or punishments given to a class as a whole for adhering to or violating rules of conduct.

Token Reinforcement System: System in which tokens earned for academic work and positive classroom behavior can be exchanged for some desired reward.

Contingency Contract: A contract between the teacher and an individual student specifying what the student must do to earn a particular privilege or reward.

CHECKPOINT

Behavioral Approaches to Teaching and Management

Review

▶ What is mastery learning?

▶ Describe the managerial strategies of group consequences, token programs, and contracts.

Apply

▶ How could you use one of these management approaches to handle the situation described at the beginning of the chapter?

---

student, describing exactly what the student must do to earn a particular privilege or reward. In some programs, students participate in deciding on the behaviors to be reinforced and the rewards that can be gained. The negotiating process itself can be an educational experience, as students learn to set reasonable goals and abide by the terms of a contract.

FIGURE 6.3

A Contingency Contract for Completing Assignments

The teacher and student agree on the due dates for each assignment, marking them in blue on the chart. Each time an assignment is turned in, the date of completion is marked in black on the chart. As long as the actual completion line is above the planned completion line, the student earns free time or other contracted rewards.

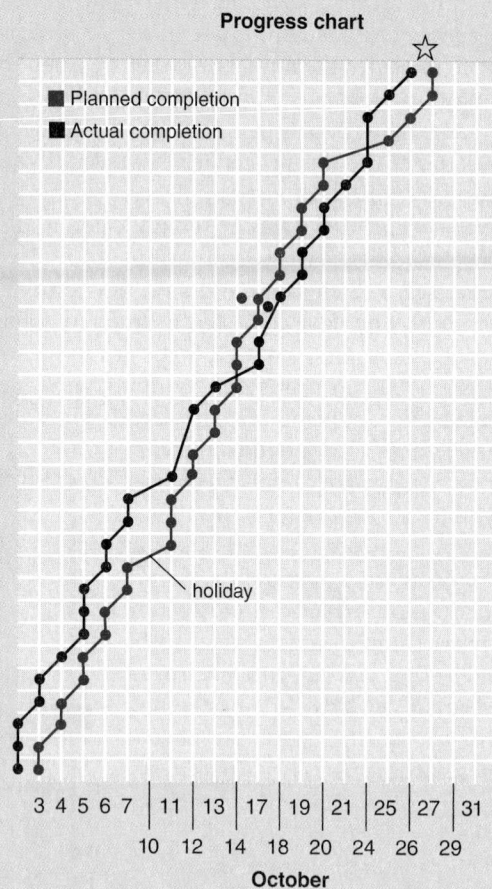

Source: From *Achieving Educational Excellence: Behavior Analysis for School Personnel* (Figure, p. 89), by B. Sulzer-Azaroff and G. R. Mayer, 1994, San Marcos, CA: Western Image, P.O. Box 427. Copyright © 1994 by Beth Sulzer-Azaroff and G. Roy Mayer. Reprinted with permission.

An example of a contract for completing assignments that is appropriate for intermediate and upper-grade students is presented in Figure 6.3 on page 224. This chart serves as a contract, assignment sheet, and progress record. Something like this might even help you keep track of assignments and due dates in your college classes.

The few pages devoted here to token reinforcement and contingency contracts can offer only an introduction to these programs. If you want to set up a large-scale reward program in your classroom, you should probably seek professional advice. Often the school psychologist, counselor, or principal can help. In addition, remember that, applied inappropriately, external rewards can undermine the students' motivation to learn (Deci, 1975; Lepper & Greene, 1978).

Self-Management: Use of behavioral learning principles to change your own behavior.

Recent Approaches: Self-Regulation and Cognitive Behavior Modification

The most recent application of behavioral views of learning emphasizes **self-management**—helping students gain control of their own learning. As you will see throughout this book, the role of students in their own learning is a major concern of psychologists and educators today. This concern is not restricted to any one group or theory. Different areas of research and theory all converge on one important idea, that responsibility and the ability to learn rest within the student. No one can learn for someone else (Manning & Payne, 1996; Winne, 1995; Zimmerman, 1990; Zimmerman & Schunk, 1989).

One reason that behavioral psychologists became interested in self-management is that students taught with classic behavioral methods seldom generalized their learning to new situations. For example, in my dissertation research I found that inattentive students could learn to pay excellent attention to lessons in a small group, but when they returned to the regular classroom, they did not take their new skill back with them (Woolfolk & Woolfolk, 1974). Many behavioral psychologists decided that generalization would be encouraged if students became partners in the behavior change procedures. About this same time, Donald Meichenbaum (1977) was having success teaching impulsive students to "talk themselves through" tasks, so there was evidence that students could benefit from what Meichenbaum termed "cognitive behavior modification" (Manning, 1991).

Self-Management

If one goal of education is to produce people who are capable of educating themselves, then students must learn to manage their own lives, set their own goals, and provide their own reinforcement. In adult life, rewards are sometimes vague and goals often take a long time to reach. Think how many small steps are required to complete an education and find your first job. Life is filled with tasks that call for this sort of self-management (Kanfer & Gaelick, 1986).

Students may be involved in any or all of the steps in implementing a basic behavior change program. They may help set goals, observe their own work, keep records of it, and evaluate their own performance. Finally, they can select and deliver reinforcement. Such involvement can help students master all the steps so they can perform these tasks in the future (Kaplan, 1991).

Connect and Extend
To the classroom

Self-management can be used to encourage social behavior. This self-recording form is taken from Jenson, W. R., Sloane, H. N., & Young, K. R. (1988). *Applied behavior analysis in education: A structured teaching approach.* Englewood Cliffs, NJ: Prentice-Hall, p. 272.

SOCIAL SKILLS PRACTICE CARD
Name _____
Date _____
Things to remember:
Use your new skill. Take this card with you and mark it when you use the social skill.
Social Skill: _____

	How many times?				
Where?	1	2	3	4	5
1. In class					
2. On the playground					
3. At lunch					
4. At home					
5. Other					

Connect and Extend
To other chapters

Concern with self-management is not restricted to any one group or theory. Psychologists who study Vygotsky's ideas about cognitive development (Chapter 2) are involved, as are cognitive psychologists interested in learning strategies (Chapters 7 and 8) and motivational psychologists pointing to self-regulation as a critical factor in motivation (Chapters 10 and 11).

Connect and Extend
To real life

A study conducted by Mark Morgan (1985. Self-monitoring of attained subgoals in private study. *Journal of Educational Psychology, 77*, 623–630) combined goal setting, self-recording, and self-evaluation. Morgan taught self-monitoring strategies to all the education students in the required educational psychology course at his college. The students who set specific short-term objectives for each study unit and monitored their progress toward the objectives outperformed the students who simply monitored study time, even though the students who monitored their time actually spent more hours studying!

Connect and Extend
To your teaching

There is one student in your class who is never prepared to do his work. He doesn't have a pencil, has misplaced his book, left his homework at home, doesn't understand the assignment, forgot to buy notebook paper, and so on. The result of all this is that he seldom hands in his homework assignments. How would you approach this problem? Develop several alternative strategies, such as reward and punishment, shaping, or self-management.

Self-Reinforcement: Providing yourself with positive consequences, contingent on accomplishing a particular behavior.

Goal Setting. It appears that the goal-setting phase is very important in self-management (Pintrich & Schunk, 1996; Reeve, 1996). In fact, some research suggests that setting specific goals and making them public may be the critical elements of self-management programs. For example, S. C. Hayes and his colleagues identified college students who had serious problems with studying and taught them how to set specific study goals. Students who set goals and announced them to the experimenters performed significantly better on tests covering the material they were studying than students who set goals privately and never revealed them to anyone (Hayes, Rosenfarb, Wulfert, Munt, Korn, & Zettle, 1985).

Higher standards tend to lead to higher performance (McLaughlin & Gnagey, 1981). Unfortunately, student-set goals have a tendency to become lower and lower. Teachers can help students maintain high standards by monitoring the goals set and reinforcing high standards. In one study, a teacher helped 1st-grade students raise the number of math problems they set for themselves to work on each day by praising them whenever they increased their objective by 10%. The students maintained their new, higher work standards, and the improvements even generalized to other subjects (Price & O'Leary, 1974).

Recording and Evaluating Progress. Students may also participate in the recording and evaluation phases of a behavior change program. Some examples of behaviors that are appropriate for self-recording are the number of assignments completed, time spent practicing a skill, number of books read, and number of times out of seat without permission. Tasks that must be accomplished without teacher supervision, such as homework or private study, are also good candidates for self-monitoring. Students keep a chart, diary, or checklist recording the frequency or duration of the behaviors in question.

A progress record card can help older students break down assignments into small steps, determine the best sequence for completing the steps, and keep track of daily progress by setting goals for each day. The record card itself serves as a prompt that can be faded out (Jenson, Sloane, & Young, 1988). Because cheating on records is a potential problem, especially when students are rewarded for improvements, intermittent checking by the teacher plus bonus points for accurate recording may be helpful (Hundert & Bucher, 1978).

Self-evaluation is somewhat more difficult than simple self-recording because it involves making a judgment about quality. Very few studies have been conducted in this area, but it appears that students can learn to evaluate their behavior with reasonable accuracy (Rhode, Morgan, & Young, 1983). One key seems to be periodically checking students' self-evaluations and giving reinforcement for accurate judgments. Older students may learn accurate self-evaluation more readily than younger students. Again, bonus points can be awarded when the teachers' and students' evaluations match (Kaplan, 1991). I have worked with one teacher who found that his 8th-grade science class could learn to give themselves fair and accurate grades when he used such a system.

Self-Reinforcement. The last step in self-management is **self-reinforcement.** There is some disagreement, however, as to whether this step is actually necessary. Some psychologists believe that setting goals and monitoring progress alone are sufficient and that self-reinforcement adds nothing to the effects (Hayes et al., 1985). Others believe that rewarding yourself for a job well done can lead to higher levels of performance than simply setting goals and keeping track of progress (Bandura, 1986). If you are willing to be tough and really deny yourself something you want until your goals are reached, then perhaps the promise of the reward can provide extra incentive for work. With that in mind, you may want to think of some way to reinforce yourself when you finish reading this chapter. A similar approach helped me write the chapter in the first place.

At times, families can be enlisted to help their children develop self-management abilities. Working together, teachers and parents can focus on a few goals and, at the same time, support the growing independence of the students. The Family and Community Partnerships Guidelines give some ideas.

Sometimes, teaching students self-management can solve a problem for teachers and provide fringe benefits as well. For example, the coaches of a competitive swim team with members aged 9 to 16 were having difficulty persuading swimmers to maintain high work rates. Then the coaches drew up four charts indicating the training program to be followed by each member and posted the charts near the pool. The swimmers were given the responsibility of recording their numbers of laps and completion of each training unit. Because the recording was public, swimmers could see their own progress and that of others, give and receive congratulations, and keep accurate track of the work units completed. Work output increased by 27%. The coaches also liked the system because swimmers could begin to work immediately without waiting for instructions (McKenzie & Rushall, 1974).

FAMILY AND COMMUNITY PARTNERSHIPS

Student Self-Management

Introduce the system to parents and students in a positive way.

Examples

1. Invite family participation and stress possible benefits to all family members.
2. Consider starting the program just with volunteers.
3. Describe how you use self-management programs yourself.

Help families and students establish reachable goals.

Examples

1. Have examples of possible self-management goals for students such as starting homework early in the evening, or keeping track of books read.
2. Show families how to post goals and keep track of progress. Encourage everyone in the family to work on a goal.

Give families ways to record and evaluate their child's progress (or their own).

Examples

1. Divide the work into easily measured steps.

2. Provide models of good work where judgments are more difficult, such as in creative writing.
3. Give families a record form or checklist to keep track of progress.

Encourage families to check the accuracy of student records from time to time, and help their children to develop forms of self-reinforcement.

Examples

1. Have many checkups when students are first learning, and fewer later.
2. Have siblings check one another's records.
3. Where appropriate, test the skills that students are supposed to be developing at home and reward students whose self-evaluations match their test performances.
4. Have students brainstorm ideas with their families for rewarding themselves for jobs well done.

Cognitive Behavior Modification:
Procedures based on both behavioral and cognitive learning principles for changing your own behavior by using self-talk and self-instruction.

Self-Instruction: Talking oneself through the steps of a task.

Cognitive Behavior Modification and Self-Instruction

Self-management generally means getting students involved in the basic steps of a behavior change program. **Cognitive behavior modification** adds an emphasis on thinking and self-talk. For this reason, many psychologists consider cognitive behavior modification more a cognitive than a behavioral approach. I present it here because it serves as a bridge to Chapters 7 and 8 on cognitive learning.

As noted in Chapter 2, there is a stage in cognitive development when young children seem to guide themselves through a task using private speech. They talk to themselves, often repeating the words of a parent or teacher. In cognitive behavior modification, students are taught directly how to use **self-instruction.** Meichenbaum (1977) outlined the steps:

1. An adult model performs a task while talking to him- or herself out loud (cognitive modeling).
2. The child performs the same task under the direction of the model's instructions (overt, external guidance).
3. The child performs the task while instructing him- or herself aloud (overt, self-guidance).
4. The child whispers the instructions to him- or herself as he/she goes through the task (faded, overt self-guidance).
5. The child performs the task while guiding his/her performance via private speech (covert self-instruction). (p. 32)

Brenda Manning and Beverly Payne (1996) list four skills that can increase student learning: *listening, planning, working,* and *checking.* How might cognitive self-instruction help students develop these skills? One possibility is to use personal booklets or class posters that prompt students to "talk to themselves" about these skills. For example, one 5th-grade class designed a set of prompts for each of the four skills and posted the prompts around the classroom. The prompts for listening included "Does this make sense?" "Am I getting this?" "I need to ask a question now before I forget." "Pay attention!" "Can I do what he's saying to do?" Planning prompts were, "Do I have everything together?" "Do I have my friends tuned out for right now?" "Let me get organized first." "What order will I do this in?" "I know this stuff!" Posters for these and the other two skills, working and checking, are shown in Figure 6.4. Part of the power of this process is in getting students involved in thinking about and creating their own guides and prompts. Having the discussion and posting the ideas makes students more self-aware and in control of their own learning.

Actually, cognitive behavior modification as it is practiced by Meichenbaum and others has many more components than just teaching students to use self-instruction. Meichenbaum's methods also include dia-

C H E C K P O I N T

Recent Approaches: Self-Regulation and Cognitive Behavior Modification

Review

 What are the steps in self-management?

Apply

 How could you use the elements of self-management to study in this course?

FIGURE 6.4

Posters to Remind Students to "Talk Themselves Through" Listening, Planning, Working, and Checking in School

These four posters were designed by a 5th-grade class to help them remember to use self-instruction. Some of the reminders reflect the special world of these preadolescents.

Poster 1

While Listening:
1. Does this make sense?
2. Am I getting this?
3. I need to ask a question now before I forget.
4. Pay attention.
5. Can I do what he's saying to do?

Poster 3

While Working:
1. Am I working fast enough?
2. Stop staring at my girlfriend and get back to work.
3. How much time is left?
4. Do I need to stop and start over?
5. This is hard for me, but I can manage okay.

Poster 2

While Planning:
1. Do I have everything together?
2. Do I have my friends tuned out for right now?
3. Let me get organized first.
4. What order will I do this in?
5. I know this stuff!

Poster 4

While Checking:
1. Did I finish everything?
2. What do I need to recheck?
3. Am I proud of this work?
4. Did I write all the words? Count them.
5. I think I finished. I organized myself. Did I daydream too much?

Source: From *Self-Talk for Teachers and Students: Metacognitive Strategies for Personal and Classroom Use* (p. 125), by B. H. Manning and B. D. Payne, 1996, Boston: Allyn & Bacon. Copyright © 1996 by Allyn & Bacon. Adapted by permission.

logue and interaction between teacher and student, modeling, guided discovery, motivational strategies, feedback, careful matching of the task with the student's developmental level, and other principles of good teaching. The student is even involved in designing the program (Harris, 1990; Harris & Pressley, 1991). Given all this, it is no surprise that students do seem to generalize the skills developed with cognitive behavior modification to new learning situations (Harris, Graham, & Pressley, in press).

Problems and Issues

The preceding sections provide an overview of several strategies for changing classroom behavior. However, you should be aware that these strategies are tools that may be used responsibly or irresponsibly. What, then, are some issues you should keep in mind?

Criticisms of Behavioral Methods

Properly used, the strategies in this chapter can be effective tools to help students learn academically and grow in self-sufficiency. Effective tools, however, do not automatically produce excellent work. The indiscriminate use of even the best tools can lead to difficulties. Critics of behavioral methods point to two basic problems that may arise.

Some psychologists fear that rewarding students for all learning will cause them to lose interest in learning for its own sake (Deci, 1975; Deci & Ryan, 1985; Kohn, 1993, 1996; Lepper & Greene, 1978; Lepper, Keavney, & Drake, 1996; Ryan & Deci, 1996). Studies have suggested that using reward programs with students who are already interested in the subject matter may, in fact, cause students to be less interested in the subject when the reward program ends, as you can see in the Point/Counterpoint. In addition, there is some evidence that praising students for being intelligent when they succeed can undermine their motivation if they do not perform as well the next time. After they fail, students who had been praised for being smart may be less persistent and enjoy the task less compared to students who had been praised earlier for working hard (Mueller & Dweck, 1998).

Just as you must take into account the effects of a reward system on the individual, you must also consider the impact on other students. Using a reward program

POINT ▼ COUNTERPOINT

Should Students Be Rewarded for Learning?

For years educators and psychologists have debated whether students should be rewarded for school work and academic accomplishments. In the early 1990s, Paul Chance and Alfie Kohn exchanged opinions in several issues of *Phi Delta Kappan* (March 1991; November 1992; June, 1993). Then, Judy Cameron and W. David Pierce (1996) published an article on reinforcement in the *Review of Educational Research* that precipitated extensive criticisms and rebuttals in the same journal from Mark Lepper, Mark Keavney, Michael Drake, Alfie Kohn, Richard Ryan, and Edward Deci. Many of the same people exchanged opinions in the November 1999 issue of *Psychological Bulletin*. What are the arguments?

▶ **POINT** *Students are punished by rewards.*

Alfie Kohn (1993) argues that "Applied behaviorism, which amounts to saying, 'do this and you'll get that,' is essentially a technique for controlling people. In the classroom it is a way of doing things *to* children rather than working *with* them" (p. 784). He contends that rewards are ineffective because when the praise and prizes stop, the behaviors stop too. After analyzing 128 studies of extrinsic rewards, Edward Deci, Richard Koestner, and Richard Ryan (1999) concluded that "tangible rewards tend to have a substantial effect on intrinsic motivation, with the limiting conditions we have specified. Even when tangible rewards are offered as indicators of good performance, they typically decrease intrinsic motivation for interesting activities" (pp. 658-659).

The problem with rewards does not stop here. According to Kohn, rewarding students for learning actually makes them less interested in the material:

All of this means that getting children to think about learning as a way to receive a sticker, a gold star, or a grade—or even worse, to get money or a toy *for* a grade, which amounts to an extrinsic motivator for an extrinsic motivator—is likely to turn learning from an end into a means. Learning becomes something that must be gotten through in order to receive the reward. Take the depressingly pervasive program by which children receive certificates for pizzas when they have read a certain number of books. John Nicholls of the University of Illinois comments, only half in jest, that the likely consequence of this program is "a lot of fat kids who don't like to read." (p. 785)

◀ **COUNTERPOINT** *Learning should be rewarding.*

According to Paul Chance (1993):

Behavioral psychologists in particular emphasize that we learn by *acting on* our environment.

or giving one student increased attention may have a detrimental effect on the other students in the classroom. Is it possible that other students will learn to be "bad" in order to be included in the reward program? Most of the evidence on this question suggests that using individual adaptations such as reward programs does not have any adverse effects on students who are not participating if the teacher believes in the program and explains the reasons for using it to the nonparticipating students. After interviewing 98 students in grades 1 through 6, Cindy Fulk and Paula Smith (1995) concluded that "Teachers may be more concerned about equal treatment of students than students are" (p. 416). If the conduct of some students does seem to deteriorate when their peers are involved in special programs, many of the same procedures discussed in this chapter should help them return to previous levels of appropriate behavior (Chance, 1992, 1993).

Ethical Issues

The ethical questions related to the use of the strategies described in this chapter are similar to those raised by any process that seeks to influence people. What are the goals? How do these goals fit with those of the school as a whole? Might students be rewarded for the "wrong" thing, though it seems "right" at first? By what criteria

---

As B.F. Skinner put it: "[People] act on the world, and change it, and are changed in turn by the consequences of their actions." Skinner, unlike Kohn, understood that people learn best in a responsive environment. Teachers who praise or otherwise reward student performance provide such an environment. . . . If it is immoral to let students know they have answered questions correctly, to pat students on the back for a good effort, to show joy at a student's understanding of a concept, or to recognize the achievement of a goal by providing a gold star or a certificate—if this is immoral, then count me a sinner. (p. 788)

Do rewards undermine interest? In their review of research, Cameron and Pierce (1994) concluded, "When tangible rewards (e.g., gold star, money) are offered contingent on performance on a task [not just on participation] or are delivered unexpectedly, intrinsic motivation is maintained" (p. 49). In a later review of research, Eisenberg, Pierce, and Cameron (1999) added that "Reward procedures requiring specific high task performance convey a task's personal or social significance, increasing intrinsic motivation" (p. 677). Even psychologists such as Edward Deci and Mark Lepper who suggest that rewards might undermine intrinsic motivation agree that rewards can also be used positively. When rewards provide students with information about their growing mastery of a subject or when the rewards show appreciation for a job well done, then the rewards bolster confidence and make the task more interesting to the students, especially students who lacked ability or interest in the task initially. Nothing succeeds like success. If students master reading or mathematics with the support of rewards, they will not forget what they have learned when the praise stops. Would they have learned without the rewards? Some would, but some might not. Would you continue working for a company that didn't pay you, even though you liked the work? Will freelance writer Alfie Kohn, for that matter, lose interest in writing because he gets paid fees and royalties?

Source: From "Sticking Up for Rewards," by P. Chance, June 1993, *Phi Delta Kappan,* pp. 787–790. Copyright © 1993 by *Phi Delta Kappan.* Reprinted with permission of Phi Delta Kappan and the author. From "Rewards versus Learning: A Response to Paul Chance," by A. Kohn, June 1993, *Phi Delta Kappan,* p. 783 and 785. Copyright © 1993 by Alfie Kohn. Reprinted from *Phi Delta Kappan* with the author's permission.

Problems and Issues

Review

 What are the main criticisms of behavioral approaches?

Apply

 Is it ever appropriate to reward students for learning? Why or why not?

should strategies be chosen? What effect will a strategy have on the individuals involved? Is too much control being given to the teacher, or to a majority?

Goals. The strategies described in this chapter could be applied exclusively to teaching students to sit still, raise their hands before speaking, and remain silent at all other times (Winett & Winkler, 1972). This certainly would be an unethical use of the techniques. It is true that a teacher may need to establish some organization and order, but stopping with improvements in conduct will not ensure academic learning. On the other hand, in some situations, reinforcing academic skills may lead to improvements in conduct. Whenever possible, emphasis should be placed on academic learning. Academic improvements generalize to other situations more successfully than do changes in classroom conduct.

Strategies. Punishment can have negative side effects: It can serve as a model for aggressive responses, and it can encourage negative emotional reactions. Punishment is unnecessary and even unethical when positive approaches, which have fewer potential dangers, might work as well. When simpler, less-restrictive procedures fail, then more complicated procedures should be tried.

A second consideration in the selection of a strategy is the impact of the strategy on the individual student. For example, some teachers arrange for students to be rewarded at home with a gift or activities based on good work in school. But if a student has a history of being severely punished at home for bad reports from school, a home-based reinforcement program might be very harmful to that student. Reports of unsatisfactory progress at school could lead to increased abuse at home.

Summary

Understanding Learning

Define learning.

Although theorists disagree about the definition of learning, most would agree that learning occurs when experience causes a change in a person's knowledge or behavior. Behavioral theorists emphasize the role of environmental stimuli in learning and focus on behavior—observable responses. Behavioral learning processes include contiguity learning, classical conditioning, and operant conditioning.

Early Explanations of Learning: Contiguity and Classical Conditioning

How does a neutral stimulus become a conditioned stimulus?

In classical conditioning, which was discovered by Pavlov, a previously neutral stimulus is repeatedly paired with a stimulus that evokes an emotional or physiological response. Later, the previously neutral stimulus alone evokes the response—that is, the neutral stimulus is conditioned to bring forth a con-

ditioned response. The neutral stimulus has become a conditioned stimulus.

Discriminate between generalization and discrimination.

Conditioned responses are subject to the processes of generalization and discrimination. After animals or people learn to respond to one particular stimulus, they may also have similar responses to other stimuli that are similar to the original one. This process is called generalization because the conditioned response has generalized or occurred in the presence of similar stimuli. Discrimination is learning to make distinctions—to respond to one stimulus but not to others that are similar.

Operant Conditioning: Trying New Responses

What defines a consequence as a reinforcer? As a punisher?

In operant conditioning, a theory of learning developed by B. F. Skinner, people learn through the effects of their deliberate responses. For an individual, the effects of consequences following an action may serve as reinforcement or punishment. A consequence is defined as a reinforcer if it strengthens or maintains the response that brought it about, while a consequence is defined as a punishment if it decreases or suppresses the response that brought it about.

How are negative reinforcement and punishment different?

Negative reinforcement is often confused with punishment. The process of reinforcement (positive or negative) always involves strengthening behavior. The focus of negative reinforcement is strengthening specific behaviors (putting away supplies or finishing in-class assignments, etc.). The teacher strengthens (reinforces) the behaviors by removing something aversive *as soon as the desired behaviors occur*. Because the consequence involves removing or "subtracting" a stimulus, the reinforcement is negative. Punishment, on the other hand, involves *decreasing or suppressing behavior*. A behavior followed by a "punisher" is *less* likely to be repeated in similar situations in the future. Negative reinforcement also gives students a chance to exercise control. As soon as they perform the appropriate behavior, the unpleasant situation ends. In contrast, punishment occurs after the fact, and a student cannot so easily control or terminate it.

How can you encourage persistence in a behavior?

The scheduling of reinforcement influences the rate and persistence of responses. Ratio schedules (based on the number of responses) encourage higher rates of response, and variable schedules (based on varying numbers of responses or varying time intervals) encourage persistence of responses.

What is the difference between a prompt and a cue?

A cue is an antecedent stimulus just before a particular behavior is to take place. A prompt is an additional cue following the first cue. There are two principles for using a cue and a prompt to teach a new behavior. First, make sure the environmental stimulus that you want to become a cue occurs immediately before the prompt you are using, so students will learn to respond to the cue and not rely only on the prompt. Second, fade the prompt as soon as possible so students do not become dependent on it.

Applied Behavior Analysis

What are the steps in applied behavior analysis?

Applied behavior analysis provides teachers with methods for encouraging positive behaviors and coping with undesirable ones. The steps are: (1) Clearly specify the behavior to be changed and note the current level. (2) Plan a specific intervention using antecedents, consequences, or both. (3) Keep track of the results, and modify the plan if necessary.

How can the Premack principle help you identify reinforcers?

The Premack principle states that a high-frequency behavior (a preferred activity) can be an effective reinforcer for a low-frequency behavior (a less-preferred activity). This is sometimes referred to as "Grandma's rule": first do what I want you to do, then you may do what you want to do. The best way to determine appropriate reinforcers for your students may be to watch what they do in their free time. For most students, talking, moving around the room, sitting near a friend, being exempt from assignments or tests, reading magazines, or playing games are preferred activities.

When is shaping an appropriate approach?

There are many behaviors that can be improved through shaping, especially skills that involve persistence, endurance, increased accuracy, greater speed, or extensive practice to master. Because shaping is a time-consuming process, however, it should not be used if success can be attained through simpler methods such as cueing. Teachers can use shaping to help students develop new responses a little at a time, so shaping is useful for building complex skills or working toward difficult goals.

What are some cautions in using punishment?

Negative reinforcement, satiation, and forms of punishment—such as reprimands, response cost, and social isolation—can also help change behavior but must be used with caution. Punishment in and of itself does not lead to any positive behavior. Thus, whenever you consider the use of punishment, you should make it part of a two-pronged attack. The first goal is to carry out the punishment and suppress the undesirable behavior. The second goal is to make clear what the student should be doing instead and to provide reinforcement for those desirable actions. Thus, while the problem behaviors are being suppressed, positive alternative responses are being strengthened.

Behavioral Approaches to Teaching and Management

What is mastery learning?

To use mastery learning, a teacher must break a course down into small units of study. Each unit might involve mastering several specific objectives. "Mastery" usually means a score of 80 to 90% on a test or other assessment. The teacher informs the students of the objectives and the criteria for meeting each. Students who do not reach the minimum level of mastery or who reach this minimum but want to improve their performance (thus raising their grade) can recycle through the unit. When they are ready, they take another form of the unit test.

Describe the managerial strategies of group consequences, token programs, and contracts.

Using group consequences involves basing reinforcement for the whole class on the behavior of the whole class. In token programs, students earn tokens for both academic work and positive classroom behavior. The tokens may be points, checks, holes punched in a card, chips, play money, or anything else that is easily identified as the student's property. Periodically the students exchange the tokens they have earned for some desired reward. In a contingency contract program, the teacher draws up an individual contract with each student, describing exactly what the student must do to earn a particular privilege or reward. In some programs, students participate in deciding on the behaviors to be reinforced and the rewards that can be gained. A teacher must use these programs with caution, emphasizing learning and not just "good" behavior.

Recent Approaches: Self-Regulation and Cognitive Behavior Modification

What are the steps in self-management?

Students can apply behavior analysis on their own to manage their own behavior. Teachers can encourage the development of self-management skills by allowing students to participate in setting goals, keeping track of progress, evaluating accomplishments, and selecting and giving their own reinforcements. Teachers can also use cognitive behavior modification, a behavior change program described by Meichenbaum in which students are directly taught how to use self-instruction.

Problems and Issues

What are the main criticisms of behavioral approaches?

The misuse or abuse of behavioral learning methods is unethical. Critics of behavioral methods also point out the danger that reinforcement could decrease interest in learning by overemphasizing rewards and could have a negative impact on other students. Guidelines do exist, however, for helping teachers use behavioral learning principles appropriately and ethically.

Key Terms

Becoming a Professional

Reflecting on the Chapter

Can you apply the ideas from this chapter on learning to solve the following problems of practice?

Preschool and Kindergarten

▶ A student in your class is terrified of the class's pet guinea pigs. The child won't get close to the cages and wants you to "give them away." How would you help the child overcome this fear?

Elementary and Middle School

▶ You want your students to improve their time management and self-management abilities so they will be prepared for the increased demands of school next year. What would you do?

Junior High and High School

▶ You have been assigned an emotionally disturbed student. She seemed fine at first, but now you notice that when she encounters difficult work, she often interrupts or teases other students. How would you work with this student and the class to improve the situation?

▶ It takes you 10 minutes to get your class to settle down after the bell rings. Analyze this situation. What could be maintaining this problem? What could you do?

Certification Test Requirements

▶ Know the difference between reinforcement and punishment and between negative reinforcement and punishment.

▶ Be aware of the criticisms of behavior modification.

▶ Be familiar with token programs and contingency contracts.

▶ Know the cautions in using punishment.

Your Teaching Portfolio

What is your stance on using extrinsic reinforcement and punishment in teaching? Be prepared to answer questions about these issues in your interviews.

Use Table 6.2 to generate ideas for appropriate reinforcers for students you will teach and include these ideas in your **Portfolio**.

Teaching Resources

Add Figures 6.2, 6.3, and 6.4 to your **Teaching Resources** file.

What Would They Do?

Here is how some practicing teachers responded to the teaching situation presented at the beginning of this chapter about a class out of control.

RICHARD T. SMITH

Fifth Grade Teacher
Harrison Middle School, Yarmouth, Maine

The fact that the other teachers know that this is a tough class and you are in for a challenge is probably a good thing. People are offering help and understand that as a new teacher you may need it, so look at it as a challenge and ask for the help you need. Every school has experienced teachers and teachers with great classroom management skills. Talk to these teachers and find a style and a system that works for you.

Most teachers want to have a positive effect on their students. The more difficult the class, the more they need a role model, or calm force in their lives. If you remember that these kids need you and your expertise, you will have an easier time keeping your patience.

Begin "Day Two" with a class meeting, with all students sitting quietly in a circle. The teacher begins with a tennis ball in her hand. The teacher has the ball so she has the floor—she explains her expectation of her students in order to conduct a class. The ball is passed and each student is given a chance to explain what he or she needs from fellow classmates and the teacher. After everybody has spoken, they begin to make a list of classroom expectations, consequences, and privileges. You know what the kids expect and they know what to expect from you. These rules should be photocopied and taped to their desks, reminding students of behaviors, rewards, and consequences.

Discipline is something all kids need and it does not have to be negative. Being a role model to kids and letting them know what you value is important. As a teacher you need to convey your value system to your students. "You get what you tolerate." This is true in all aspects of life, including the classroom. If you don't tolerate students speaking out, then they will not. If you don't tolerate students saying "I hate you," they will not. Stick with your consequences. Be consistent!

I believe that if this teacher looks at the situation as a challenge; seeks help from experienced teachers; establishes ground rules, expectations and rewards and punishments with the students, she will end her second day, and many days to follow, still exhausted, still losing her voice, but encouraged!

KATHLEEN CONROY

Third Grade Teacher
Rancho Canada Elementary School, Lake Forest, California

If I were hired in January to take over a class that had no management system, I would start the class as if it were day one with my own system of rules, expectations, and consequences. We would create the needed classroom expectations together so that students felt part of this process. Then we would go through how to enforce these expectations. I would put up a colored chart with our class-created rules, and another corresponding chart with the consequences if rules are broken. I would put up all the students' names and newly assigned numbers on a series of different colored cards, and explain that this system of behavior is a reward system. If all the rules are followed, then they earn different privileges by collecting stamps for being on task. These would be passed out on a daily or weekly basis. The reward aspect is a motivator. Students choose their privilege from a posted list that includes the amount of stamps needed next to each reward or privilege. Examples would be things as small as a water pass, to lunch with the teacher, a homework pass, and so on. Therefore, students will want to try hard to follow the management rules to seek the rewards of their choice.

KATIE CHURCHILL

Third Grade Teacher
Oriole Parke Elementary School, Chicago, Illinois

I believe that it is extremely important to be firm when entering a new classroom. I would enter the classroom the next morning and make the students aware that I will enforce classroom rules and expectations and that I will contact parents if any behavior problems persist. I would have my students help me choose a set of classroom rules that are reasonable so the rules will have more meaning to the students. I would make it clear that the students are in charge of their own behavior and consequences. The students will know exactly what is expected of them and what will happen if they disobey any of the rules. I would consistently follow through with the prescribed consequences. I also would keep the students busy with material that interests them. Finally, I would encourage good behavior in the classroom through positive reinforcement.

CAREY PERKSON

Second Grade Teacher
Brown School, Natick, Massachusetts

Establishing an environment in the classroom conducive to learning is vitally important. Although a previous teacher may or may not have had classroom rules, it would be necessary for me to communicate to the students what the expectations are for the remainder of the school year. Working in conjunction with the students, we would develop a set of class rules that everyone agrees to.

I would discuss with the students the reasons for having rules that we could uphold and at the same time respect one another with. Making the students an integral part of the decision-making process is important in gaining their trust and respect. The students need to understand that I value them as well as their individual ideas. Together as a classroom community we would establish a set of rules.

My philosophy has always been to be firm but fair, ensuring that students know they will be given every opportunity to be successful.

ANNE WORTH

Fourth Grade Teacher
Clardy School, Kansas City, Missouri

After the first day of agony, it is obvious that something needs changing before any learning can occur. Have the students share their ideas about what rules are necessary at school and what a working classroom sounds and looks like. Try to call only on those who raise their hands and compliment those who do follow the rules. Before you begin this discussion say, "I think it is important that we establish the rules we will follow together, so for the next ten minutes we will share ideas about school rules. Please raise your hand to be called on so that everyone gets a chance to share." The time limit will keep this from getting away from the teacher. When the list is complete, or if the list needs additions, the teacher can add some basics.

Using a behavior tool such as marbles in a jar, the teacher can set up a system instantly. Tell the class that when each of the rules is followed, a marble will be dropped in the jar. When the jar is full there will be 15 minutes of free time. Drop a marble each time something good happens in the class. Hopefully by the end of the day or the next there will be a reward and you can begin to control the class and do some teaching.

BRENDA MILLER

Second Grade Teacher
Yucca Elementary School, Alamogordo, New Mexico

I would introduce this class to a reward system using classroom "bucks" and a "store" of items to be open each Friday. I would ask parents for various items to be sold in the store, such as toys, pencils, notepads, markers, and toiletries. I would describe the behaviors I expected to see and reward each good behavior with a "buck."

I believe rewards would be more useful at first because most children see discipline as negative, and this class has already seen too much negativism. After my reward system was established I would enlist the help of my students to determine the classroom rules. The key to the reward system's working is to be consistent, generous, and fair. I would price my items higher in the store and give "bucks" away often in reinforcement of good behavior. On the day of store I would have two students (different each week) be the shopkeepers. This reward system teaches responsibility, math, cooperation, and communication. I use this in my second grade classroom with much success.

237

Cognitive Views
of Learning

*W*hat makes a lesson easy to learn and remember? Think about the classes that you are taking this semester. What have you studied in the last two or three days that you expect to remember next week? Next year? What is different about the memorable information? Did you learn it in a different way?

In this chapter we turn from behavioral theories of learning to the cognitive perspective. This means a shift from "viewing the learners and their behaviors as products of incoming environmental stimuli" to seeing the learners as "sources of plans, intentions, goals, ideas, memories, and emotions actively used to attend to, select, and construct meaning from stimuli and knowledge from experience" (Wittrock, 1982, pp. 1–2). We will begin with a discussion of the general cognitive approach to learning and memory and the importance of knowledge in learning. To understand memory, we will consider a widely accepted cognitive model, information processing, which suggests that information moves through three different storage systems. We will briefly consider an alternative to the three-store model of memory—depth of processing. Next we will explore metacognition, a field of study that may provide insights into individual and developmental differences in learning. Then we turn to ideas about how teachers can help their students become more knowledgeable. By the time you have completed this chapter, you should be able to:

▶ Discuss the role of knowledge in learning.
▶ Describe two models of human information processing—the three-store model and levels of processing.
▶ Define declarative, procedural, and conditional knowledge.
▶ Give examples of the roles of perception and attention in learning.
▶ Explain how schemas and scripts influence learning and remembering.
▶ Explain the role of metacognition in learning and remembering.
▶ Discuss individual differences in working and long-term memory.
▶ Describe the stages in the development of cognitive skills.

What Would You Do?

The students in your senior history classes seem to equate understanding with memorizing. They prepare for each unit test by memorizing the exact words of the textbook. Even the best students seem to think that flash cards are the only learning strategy possible. In fact, when you try to get them to think about history by reading some original sources, debating issues in class, or examining art and music from the time period you are studying, they rebel. "Will this be on the test?" "Why are we looking at these pictures—will we have to know who painted them and when?" "What's this got to do with history?" Even the students who participate in the debates seem to use words and phrases straight from the textbook without knowing what they are saying.

▶ What do these students "know" about history? What are their beliefs and expectations, and how do these affect their learning?

▶ Why do you think they insist on using the rote memory approach?

▶ How would you teach your students to learn in this new way?

▶ How will these issues affect the grade levels you will teach?

Connect & Extend
To life

Consider these proverbs about memory taken from Klatzky, R. L. (1984). *Memory and awareness: An information processing perspective.* New York: Freeman, p. 122.

On Learning

Learning teacheth more in one year than experience in twenty. (Roger Ascham)

What we have to learn to do, we learn by doing. (Aristotle)

On Memory

The true art of memory is the art of attention. (Samuel Johnson)

A man's memory may almost become the art of continually varying and misrepresenting his past, according to his interests in the present. (George Santayana)

On Forgetting

The mind is slow in unlearning what it has been long in learning. (Seneca)

Soon learnt, soon forgotten. (Proverb)

Out of sight, out of mind. (Proverb)

An injury is much sooner forgotten than an insult. (Lord Chesterfield)

On Aging

I am too old to learn. (Shakespeare, *King Lear*)

No one is so old that he cannot still learn something. (German proverb)

An old dog will learn no new tricks. (Thomas D'Urfey)

Connect & Extend
To other chapters

Two different models of instruction based on principles of cognitive learning—Bruner's discovery learning and Ausubel's expository teaching—are described in Chapter 8.

Elements of the Cognitive Perspective

The cognitive perspective is both the oldest and the youngest member of the psychological community. It is old because discussions of the nature of knowledge, the value of reason, and the contents of the mind date back at least to the ancient Greek philosophers (Hernshaw, 1987). From the late 1800s until a few decades ago, however, cognitive studies fell from favor and behaviorism thrived. Then, research during World War II on the development of complex human skills, the computer revolution, and breakthroughs in understanding language development all stimulated a resurgence in cognitive research. Evidence accumulated indicating that people do more than simply respond to reinforcement and punishment. For example, we plan our responses, use strategies to help us remember, and organize the material we are learning in our own unique ways (Miller, Galanter, & Pribram, 1960; Shuell, 1986). With the growing realization that learning is an active mental process, educational psychologists became interested in how people think, learn concepts, and solve problems (e.g., Ausubel, 1963; Bruner, Goodnow, & Austin, 1956).

Interest in concept learning and problem solving soon gave way, however, to interest in how knowledge is represented in the mind and particularly how it is remembered. Remembering and forgetting became major topics for investigation in cognitive psychology in the 1970s and 1980s, and the information processing model of memory dominated research.

Today, there are other models of memory besides information processing. In addition, many cognitive theorists have a renewed interest in learning, thinking, and problem solving. The **cognitive view of learning** can best be described as a generally agreed-upon philosophical orientation. This means that cognitive theorists share basic notions about learning and memory. Cognitive theorists believe, for example, that learning is the result of our attempts to make sense of the world. To do this, we use all the mental tools at our disposal. The ways we think about situations, along with our knowledge, expectations, feelings, and interactions with others and the environment, influence how and what we learn (Anderson, 1995a, b; Bandura, 1986; Farnham-Diggory, 1994; Piaget, 1963).

Comparing Cognitive and Behavioral Views

The cognitive and behavioral views differ in their assumptions about what is learned. In the cognitive view, knowledge is learned, and changes in knowledge make changes in behavior possible. In the behavioral view, the new behaviors themselves are learned (Shuell, 1986). Both behavioral and cognitive theorists believe reinforcement is important in learning, but for different reasons. The strict behaviorist maintains that reinforcement strengthens responses; cognitive theorists see reinforcement as a source of feedback about what is likely to happen if behaviors are repeated—as a source of information.

The cognitive view sees people as active learners who initiate experiences, seek out information to solve problems, and reorganize what they already know to achieve new insights. In fact, learning within this perspective is seen as "transforming significant understanding we already have, rather than simple acquisitions written on blank slates" (Greeno, Collins, & Resnick, 1996, p. 18). Instead of being passively influenced by environmental events, people actively choose, practice, pay attention, ignore, reflect, and make many other decisions as they pursue goals. Older cognitive views emphasized the *acquisition* of knowledge, but newer approaches stress its *construction* (Anderson, Reder, & Simon, 1996; Greeno, Collins, & Resnick, 1996; Mayer, 1996).

Differences between behavioral and cognitive views are also apparent in the methods each group has used to study learning. Much of the work on behavioral learning principles has been with animals in controlled laboratory settings. The goal is to identify a few general laws of learning that apply to all higher organisms (including humans, regardless of age, intelligence, or other individual differences). Cognitive psychologists, on the other hand, study a wide range of learning situations. Because of their focus on individual and developmental differences in cognition, they have not sought general laws of learning. This is one of the reasons that there is no single cognitive model or theory of learning representative of the entire field.

▲ *The cognitive view sees learning as an active process in which learners, rather than simply "receiving" knowledge, seek new information to solve problems and reorganize what they already know to achieve new insights.*

The Importance of Knowledge in Learning

Knowledge is the outcome of learning. When we learn a name, the history of cognitive psychology, or the rules of tennis, we know something new. However, knowledge is more than the end product of previous learning; it also guides new learning. The cognitive approach suggests that one of the most important elements in the learning process is what the individual brings to the learning situation. What we already know "is a scaffold that supports the construction of all future learning" (Alexander, 1996, p. 89)—it determines to a great extent what we will pay attention to, perceive, learn, remember, and forget (Greeno, Collins, & Resnick, 1996; Shuell, 1986).

A study by Recht and Leslie (1988) shows the importance of knowledge in understanding and remembering new information. These psychologists identified junior high school students who were either very good or very poor readers. They tested the students on their knowledge of baseball and found that knowledge of baseball was not related to reading ability. So the researchers were able to identify

Cognitive View of Learning: A general approach that views learning as an active mental process of acquiring, remembering, and using knowledge.

four groups of students: *good readers/high baseball knowledge, good readers/low baseball knowledge, poor readers/high baseball knowledge, and poor readers/low baseball knowledge.* Then all the subjects read a passage describing a baseball game and were tested in a number of ways to see if they understood and remembered what they had read.

The results demonstrated the power of knowledge. Poor readers who knew baseball remembered more than good readers with little baseball knowledge and almost as much as good readers who knew baseball. Poor readers who knew little about baseball remembered the least of what they had read. Thus a good basis of knowledge can be more important than good learning strategies in understanding and remembering—but extensive knowledge plus good strategies is even better.

General and Specific Knowledge. The cognitive perspective on knowledge "emphasizes understanding of concepts and theories in different subject matter domains [such as math or history] and general cognitive abilities, such as reasoning, planning, solving problems, and comprehending language" (Greeno, Collins, & Resnick, 1996, p. 16). So, there are different kinds of knowledge. Some is **domain-specific knowledge** that pertains to a particular task or subject. For example, knowing that the shortstop plays between second and third base is specific to the domain of baseball. Some knowledge, on the other hand, is general—it applies to many different situations. For example, **general knowledge** about how to read or write or use a word processor is useful in and out of school. Of course, there is no absolute line between general and domain-specific knowledge. When you were first learning to read, you may have studied specific facts about the sounds of letters. At that time, knowledge about letter sounds was specific to the domain of reading. But now you can use both knowledge about sounds and the ability to read in more general ways (Alexander, 1992; Schunk, 2000).

Declarative, Procedural, and Conditional Knowledge. Another way of categorizing knowledge is as declarative, procedural, or conditional (Paris & Cunningham, 1996; Paris, Lipson, & Wixson, 1983). **Declarative knowledge** is "knowledge that can be declared, usually in words, through lectures, books, writing, verbal exchange, Braille, sign language, mathematical notation, and so on" (Farnham-Diggory, 1994, p. 468). Declarative knowledge is "knowing that" something is the case. The history students in the opening "What Would You Do?" situation were focusing exclusively on declarative knowledge about history. The range of declarative knowledge is tremendous. You can know very specific facts (the atomic weight of gold is 196.967), or generalities (leaves of some trees change color in autumn), or personal preferences (I don't like lima beans), or rules (to divide fractions, invert the divisor and multiply). Small units of declarative knowledge can be organized into larger units; for example, principles of reinforcement and punishment can be organized in your thinking into a theory of behavioral learning (Gagné, Yekovich, & Yekovich, 1993).

Procedural knowledge is "knowing how" to do something such as divide fractions or clean a carburetor—procedural knowledge must be demonstrated. Notice that repeating the rule "to divide fractions, invert the divisor and multiply" shows *declarative* knowledge—the student can state the rule. But to show *procedural* knowledge, the student must act. When faced with a fraction to divide, the student must divide correctly. Students demonstrate procedural knowledge when they translate a passage into Spanish or correctly categorize a geometric shape or craft a coherent paragraph.

Domain-Specific Knowledge: Information that is useful in a particular situation or that applies only to one specific topic.

General Knowledge: Information that is useful in many different kinds of tasks; information that applies to many situations.

Declarative Knowledge: Verbal information; facts; "knowing that" something is the case.

Procedural Knowledge: Knowledge that is demonstrated when we perform a task; "knowing how."

TABLE 7.1 *Kinds of Knowledge*

	General Knowledge	Domain-Specific Knowledge
Declarative	Hours the library is open Rules of grammar	The definition of "hypotenuse" The lines of the poem "The Raven"
Procedural	How to use your word processor How to drive	How to solve an oxidation-reduction equation How to throw a pot on a potter's wheel
Conditional	When to give up and try another approach When to skim and when to read carefully	When to use the formula for calculating volume When to rush the net in tennis

Conditional knowledge is "knowing when and why" to apply your declarative and procedural knowledge. Given many kinds of math problems, it takes conditional knowledge to know when to apply one procedure and when to apply another to solve each. It takes conditional knowledge to know when to read every word in a text and when to skim. For many students, conditional knowledge is a stumbling block. They have the facts and can do the procedures, but they don't seem to apply what they know at the appropriate time.

Table 7.1 shows that we can combine our two systems for describing knowledge. Declarative, procedural, and conditional knowledge can be either general or domain-specific.

To be used, knowledge must be remembered. What do we know about memory?

CHECKPOINT

Elements of the Cognitive Perspective

Review

▶ Contrast cognitive and behavioral views of learning in terms of what is learned and the role of reinforcement.

▶ How does knowledge affect learning?

Apply

▶ What do you already know that will help you in learning the material in this chapter?

The Information Processing Model of Memory

There are a number of theories of memory, but the most common are the **information processing** explanations (Hunt & Ellis, 1999; Sternberg, 1999). We will use this well-researched framework for examining learning and memory.

An Overview of the Model

Information processing views of memory use the computer as a model. Like the computer, the human mind takes in information, performs operations on it to change its form and content, stores the information, retrieves it when needed, and generates responses to it. Thus, processing involves gathering and representing information, or *encoding*; holding information, or *storage;* and getting at the information when needed, or *retrieval*. The whole system is guided by *control processes* that determine how and when information will flow through the system.

Conditional Knowledge: "Knowing when and why" to use declarative and procedural knowledge.

Information Processing: Human mind's activity of taking in, storing, and using information.

The Gestalt principles are valid explanations of certain aspects of perception, but they are not the whole story. There are two other kinds of explanations in information processing theory for how we recognize patterns and give meaning to sensory events. The first is called *feature analysis*, or **bottom-up processing** because the stimulus must be analyzed into features or components and assembled into a meaningful pattern "from the bottom up." For example, a capital letter A consists of two relatively straight lines joined at a 45-degree angle and a horizontal line (—) through the middle. Whenever we see these features, or anything close enough, including, A, *A*, **A**, *A*, A, and *A*, we recognize an A (Anderson, 1995a). This explains how we are able to read words written in other people's handwriting.

If all perception relied on feature analysis, learning would be very slow. Luckily, humans are capable of another type of perception based on knowledge and expectation often called **top-down processing**. To recognize patterns rapidly, in addition to noting features, we use what we already know about the situation—what we know about words or pictures or the way the world generally operates. For example, you would not have seen the marks above as the letter A if you had no knowledge of the Roman alphabet. So, what you know also affects what you are able to perceive.

The Role of Attention.
If every variation in color, movement, sound, smell, temperature, and so on had to be perceived, life would be impossible. By paying attention to certain stimuli and ignoring others, we select from all the possibilities what we will process. But **attention** is a limited resource. We can pay attention to only one cognitively demanding task at time (Anderson, 1995a). For example, there was a time when I was learning to drive when I couldn't listen to the radio and drive at the same time. After some practice, I could listen, but I had to turn the radio off when traffic was heavy. After years of practice, I can plan a class or talk on the phone as I drive (I have a "hands-free" model). This is because many processes that initially require attention and concentration become automatic with practice. Actually, **automaticity** probably is a matter of degree; we are not completely automatic, but rather more or less automatic in our performances depending on how much practice we have had and the situation. For example, even experienced drivers might become very attentive and focused during a blinding blizzard (Anderson, 1995a).

Attention and Teaching.
The first step in learning is paying attention. Students cannot process something that they do not recognize or perceive. Many factors in the classroom influence student attention. Eye-catching or startling displays or actions can draw attention at the beginning of a lesson. A teacher might begin a science lesson on air pressure by blowing up a balloon until it pops. Bright colors, underlining, highlighting of written or spoken words, calling students by name, surprise events, intriguing questions, variety in tasks and teaching methods, and changes in voice level, lighting, or pacing can all be used to gain attention. And students have to maintain attention—they have to stay focused on the important features of the learning situation. The Guidelines on page 247 offer additional ideas for capturing and maintaining students' attention.

Working Memory

Once noticed and transformed into patterns of images or sounds (or perhaps other types of sensory codes), the information in sensory memory is available for further processing. **Working memory** is the "workbench" of the memory system, the interface component of memory where

Connect & Extend
To the research

Flavell (1985) described four aspects of attention in developing children:

1. *Controlled:* Develop longer attention spans and ability to focus on important details, ignoring minor ones.

2. *Tailored to task:* Older children focus attention on most difficult material being learned (Berk 1994).

3. *Directive:* They develop a feel for cues (teacher's voice, gestures) telling them when/how to direct their attention.

4. *Self-monitoring:* They learn to decide if they are using the right strategy, and to change if it's not working.

Teachers must first be able to gain and maintain their students' attention, especially in learning situations that may be less inherently interesting. Lessons might be introduced with an eye-catching or startling display to "grab" students. ▼

GUIDELINES

Gaining and Maintaining Attention

Use signals.

Examples

1. Develop a signal that tells students to stop what they are doing and focus on you. Some teachers move to a particular spot in the room, flick the lights, or play a chord on the class piano.

2. Avoid distracting behaviors such as tapping a pencil that interfere with both signals and attention to learning.

3. Give short, clear directions before, not during, transitions.

Make sure the purpose of the lesson or assignment is clear to students.

Examples

1. Write the goals or objectives on the board and discuss them with students before starting. Ask students to summarize or restate the goals.

2. Explain the reasons for learning, and ask students for examples of how they will apply their understanding of the material.

3. Tie the new material to previous lessons—show an outline or map of how the new topic fits with previous and upcoming material.

Emphasize variety, curiosity, and surprise.

Examples

1. Arouse curiosity with questions such as "What would happen if . . . ?"

2. Create shock by staging an unexpected event such as a loud argument just before a lesson on communication.

3. Alter the physical environment by changing the arrangement of the room or moving to a different setting.

4. Shift sensory channels by giving a lesson that requires students to touch, smell, or taste.

5. Use movements, gestures, and voice inflection—walk around the room, point, and speak softly and then more emphatically. (My husband has been known to jump up on his desk to make an important point in his college classes!)

Ask questions and provide frames for answering.

Examples

1. Ask students why the material is important, how they intend to study, and what strategies they will use.

2. Give students self-checking or self-editing guides that focus on common mistakes or have them work in pairs to improve each other's work—sometimes it is difficult to pay attention to your own errors.

---

new information is held temporarily and combined with knowledge from long-term memory. Working memory is like the workspace or screen of a computer—its *content* is activated information—what you are thinking about at the moment. For this reason, some psychologists consider the working memory to be synonymous with "consciousness" (Sweller, van Merrienboer, & Paas, 1998).

Capacity, Duration, and Contents of Working Memory. Working memory *capacity* is limited—something many of your professors seem to forget as they race through a lecture. In early experimental situations based on the information processing model, it appeared that the capacity of working memory was only about five to nine separate new items at once (Miller, 1956). This limitation holds true to some degree in everyday life. It is quite common to remember a new phone number after looking it up, as you walk across the room to make the call. But what if you have two phone calls to make in succession? Two new phone numbers (14 digits) probably cannot be stored simultaneously.

Bottom-Up Processing: Perceiving based on noticing separate defining features and assembling them into a recognizable pattern.

Top-Down Processing: Perceiving based on the context and the patterns you expect to occur in that situation.

Attention: Focus on a stimulus.

Automaticity: The ability to perform thoroughly learned tasks without much mental effort.

Working Memory: The information that you are focusing on at a given moment.

Remember—put in your working memory—that we are discussing the recall of *new information*. In daily life we certainly can hold more than five to nine bits of information at once. While you are dialing that seven-digit phone number you just looked up, you are bound to have other things "on your mind"—in your memory—such as how to use a telephone, whom you are calling, and why. You don't have to pay attention to these things; they are not new knowledge. Some of the processes, such as dialing the phone, have become automatic. However, because of the working memory's limitations, if you were in a foreign country and were attempting to use an unfamiliar telephone system, you might very well have trouble remembering the phone number because you were trying to figure out the phone system at the same time. Even a few bits of new information can be too much to remember if the new information is very complex or unfamiliar or if you have to integrate several elements to make sense of a situation (Sweller, van Merrienboer, & Paas, 1998).

Some psychologists argue that working memory is limited not by the number of bits of information it can store, but by the amount of information we can hold in an articulatory loop. The **articulatory loop** is a rehearsal system of about 1.5 seconds. Baddeley (1986) suggests that we can hold as much in working memory as we can rehearse (repeat to ourselves) in 1.5 seconds. The seven-digit telephone number fits this limitation.

No matter how the capacity of working memory is defined, by number of bits or by the amount you can keep in the articulatory (rehearsal) loop, it is clear that the *duration* of information is short, about 5 to 20 seconds. This is why working memory has been called *short-term* memory. It may seem to you that a memory system with a 20-second time limit is not very useful, but without this system, you would have already forgotten what you read in the first part of this sentence before you came to these last few words. This would clearly make understanding sentences difficult.

The *contents* of information in working memory may be in the form of images that resemble the perceptions in sensory memory, or the information may be structured more abstractly, based on meaning. Some recent theories suggest that there are actually two working-memory systems: one for language-based information and another for nonverbal, spatial, visual information (Baddeley, 1986; 1998; Jurden, 1995).

Maintenance rehearsal—going over something several times—can be an effective way to remember, or memorize, larger amounts of information such as lines in a play, at least temporarily. Whether the information will be remembered long into the future depends on other factors as well. ▼

Retaining Information in Working Memory. Because information in working memory is fragile and easily lost, it must be kept activated to be retained. Activation is high as long as you are focusing on information, but activation decays or fades quickly when attention shifts away. Holding information in working memory is like keeping all the plates spinning on top of poles in a circus act. The performer gets one plate spinning, moves to the next, and the next, but has to return to the first before it slows down too much and falls off the pole. If we don't keep the information "spinning" in working memory—keep it activated—it will "fall off" (Anderson, 1995a, b). When activation fades, forgetting follows, as shown in Figure 7.3. To keep information activated in

FIGURE 7.3

Working Memory

Information in working memory can be kept activated through maintenance rehearsal or transferred into long-term memory by being connected with information in long-term memory (elaborative rehearsal).

working memory for longer than 20 seconds, most people keep rehearsing the information mentally.

There are two types of rehearsal (Craik & Lockhart, 1972). **Maintenance rehearsal** involves repeating the information in your mind—in the articulatory loop. As long as you repeat the information, it can be maintained in working memory indefinitely. Maintenance rehearsal is useful for retaining something you plan to use and then forget, such as a phone number.

Elaborative rehearsal involves connecting the information you are trying to remember with something you already know, with information from long-term memory. For example, if you meet someone at a party whose name is the same as your brother's, you don't have to repeat the name to keep it in memory, you just have to make the association. This kind of rehearsal not only retains information in working memory but helps move information from short-term to long-term memory. Rehearsal is thus an "executive control process" that affects the flow of information through the information processing system.

The limited capacity of working memory can also be somewhat circumvented by the control process of **chunking.** Because the number of bits of information, not the size of each bit, is a limitation for working memory, you can retain more information if you can group individual bits of information. For example, if you have to remember the six digits 3, 5, 4, 8, 7, and 0, it is easier to put them together into three chunks of two digits each (35, 48, 70) or two chunks of three digits each (354, 870). With these changes, there are only two or three bits of information rather than six to hold at one time. Chunking helps you remember a telephone number or a social security number (Bruning, Schraw, & Ronning, 1999).

Forgetting. Information may be lost from working memory through interference or decay (see Figure 7.3). Interference is fairly straightforward: Remembering new information interferes or gets confused with remembering old information.

Maintenance Rehearsal: Keeping information in working memory by repeating it to yourself.

Elaborative Rehearsal: Keeping information in working memory by associating it with something else you already know.

Chunking: Grouping individual bits of data into meaningful larger units.

The new thought replaces the old one. As new thoughts accumulate, old information is lost from working memory. Information is also lost by time **decay.** If you don't continue to pay attention to information, the activation level decays (weakens) and finally drops so low that the information cannot be reactivated—it disappears altogether.

Forgetting is very useful. Without forgetting, people would quickly overload their working memories and learning would cease. Also, it would be a problem if you remembered permanently every sentence you ever read. Finding a particular bit of information in all that sea of knowledge would be impossible. It is helpful to have a system that provides temporary storage.

Long-Term Memory

Working memory holds the information that is currently activated, such as a telephone number you have just found and are about to dial. **Long-term memory** holds the information that is well learned, such as all the other telephone numbers you know. Well-learned information is said to be high in memory strength or *durability* (Anderson, 1995b).

Capacity and Duration of Long-Term Memory. There are a number of differences between working and long-term memory, as you can see in Table 7.2. Information enters working memory very quickly. To move information into long-term storage requires more time and a bit of effort. Whereas the capacity of working memory is limited, the capacity of long-term memory appears to be, for all practical purposes, unlimited. In addition, once information is securely stored in long-term memory, it can remain there permanently. Theoretically, we should be able to remember as much as we want for as long as we want. Of course, the problem is to find the right information when it is needed. Our access to information in working memory is immediate because we are thinking about the information at that very moment. But access to information in long-term memory requires time and effort. Recently, some psychologists have suggested that there are not two separate memory stores (working and long-term). Rather, working memory is the part of long-term memory that works on (processes) currently activated information—so working memory is more about processing than storage (Baddeley, 1998).

TABLE 7.2 *Working and Long-Term Memory*

Type of Memory	Input	Capacity	Duration	Contents	Retrieval
Working	Very fast	Limited	Very brief: 5–20 sec.	Words, images, ideas, sentences	Immediate
Long-Term	Relatively slow	Practically unlimited	Practically unlimited	Propositional networks, schemata, productions, episodes, perhaps images	Depends on representation and organization

Source: From *Comprehension and Learning: A Conceptual Framework for Teachers,* by F. Smith, 1975, New York: Holt, Rinehart, and Winston. Copyright © Holt, Rinehart, and Winston. Adapted with permission of the author.

Contents of Long-Term Memory. Allan Paivio (1971, 1986; Clark & Paivio, 1991) suggests that information is stored in long-term memory as either visual images or verbal units, or both. Psychologists who agree with this point of view believe that information coded both visually and verbally is easiest to learn (Mayer & Sims, 1994). This may be one reason why explaining an idea with words and representing it visually in a figure, as we do in textbooks, has proved helpful to students. For example, Diana and Webb (1997) found that using maps such as the one in Figure 7.4 along with written text helped sixth-grade students to remember more about Ancient Greece. Paivio's ideas have some support, but critics contend that the capacity of the brain is not large enough to store all the images we have seen or can imagine. They suggest that many images are actually stored as verbal codes and then translated into visual information when an image is needed (Schunk, 2000).

Most cognitive psychologists distinguish three categories of long-term memory: semantic, episodic, and procedural.

Connect & Extend
To the research
Clark, J. M., & Paivio, A. (1991). Dual coding theory and education. *Educational Psychology Review, 3,* 149–210. This is a current statement of the dual coding theory.

Connect & Extend
To real life
Why would drawing pictures of events or objects facilitate learning?

FIGURE 7.4

A Geographic Map That Supports Learning about Ancient Greece

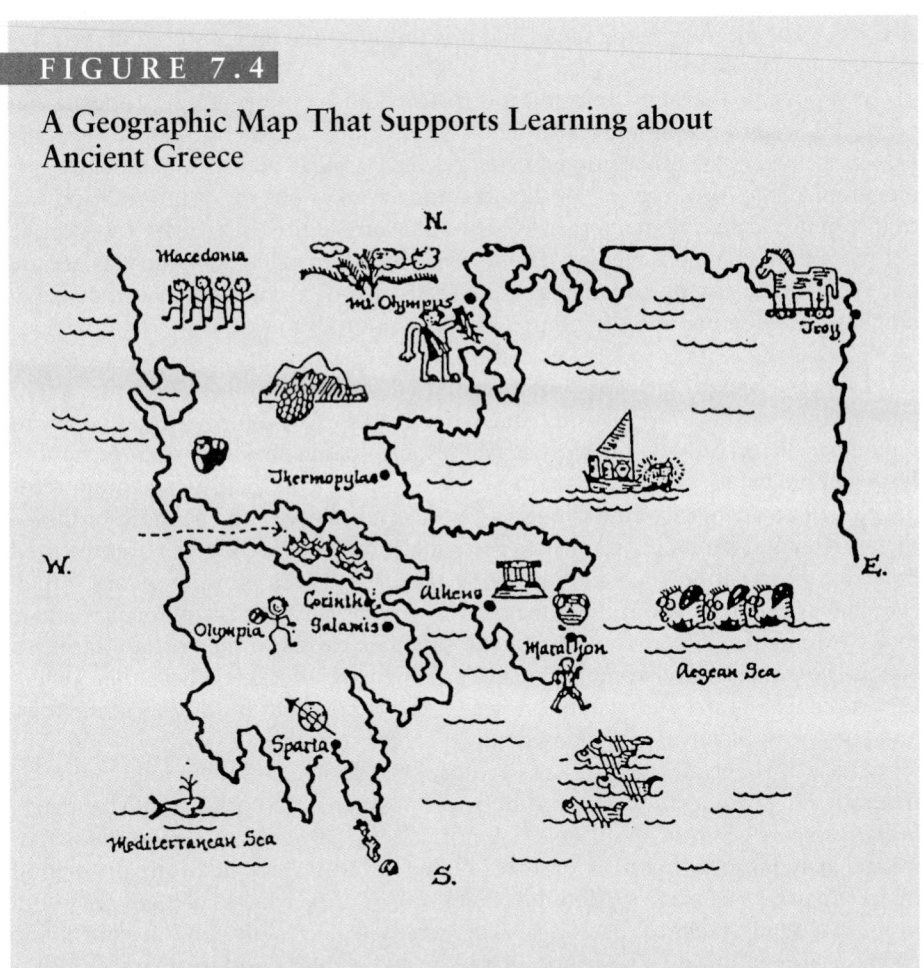

Sources: From "Using Geographic Maps in the Classroom: The Conjoint Influence of Individual Differences and Dual Coding on Learning Facts," by E. M. Diana and J. M. Webb, 1997, *Learning and Individual Differences, 9,* p. 200. Map from *The World and Its People, Europe, Africa, Asia, and Australia.* Silver Burdett Co. 1984. Reprinted with permission.

Semantic memory is memory for meaning. These memories are stored as *propositions*, *images*, and *schemas*. Because these are very important concepts for teaching, we will spend some extra time on them.

Propositions and Propositional Networks. A *proposition* is the smallest unit of knowledge that can be judged true or false. The statement, "Ida borrowed the antique tablecloth" has two propositions:

1. Ida borrowed the tablecloth.

2. The tablecloth is an antique.

Propositions that share information, such as the two above that share information about the tablecloth (Ida borrowed the tablecloth and the tablecloth is an antique) are linked in what cognitive psychologists call **propositional networks**. It is the meaning, not the exact words or word order, that is stored in the network. The same propositional network would apply to these sentences: "The antique tablecloth was borrowed by Ida," or "Ida borrowed the tablecloth, which was an antique." The meaning is the same, and it is this *meaning* that is stored in memory as a set of relationships.

It is possible that most information is stored and represented in propositional networks. When we want to recall a bit of information, we may translate its meaning (as represented in the propositional network) into familiar phrases and sentences, or mental pictures. Also, because of the network, recall of one bit of information can trigger or *activate* recall of another. We are not aware of these networks, for they are not part of our conscious memory (Anderson, 1995a). In much the same way, we are not aware of underlying grammatical structure when we form a sentence in our own language; we don't have to diagram a sentence in order to say it.

Images. **Images** are representations based on *perceptions*—on the structure or appearance of the information (Anderson, 1995a). As we form images we try to remember or recreate the physical attributes and spatial structure of information. For example, when asked how many windowpanes are in their living room, most people call up an image of the windows "in their mind's eye" and count the panes— the more panes, the longer it takes to respond. If the information were represented only in a proposition such as "my living room has seven window panes," then everyone would take about the same time to answer, whether the number was one or 24 (Mendell, 1971). However, as we saw earlier, researchers don't agree on exactly how images are stored in memory. Some psychologists believe that images are stored as pictures, others believe we store propositions in long-term memory and convert to pictures in working memory when necessary.

There probably are features of each process involved—some picture copying memory and some memory for verbal or propositional descriptions of the image. Seeing images "in your mind's eye" is not exactly the same as seeing the actual image. It is more difficult to perform complicated transformations on mental images than on real images (Matlin & Foley, 1997). Nevertheless, images are useful in making many practical decisions such as how a sofa might look in your living room or how to line up a golf shot. Images may also be helpful in abstract reasoning. Physicists, such as Faraday and Einstein, report creating images to reason about complex new problems (Gagné, Yekovich, & Yekovich, 1993).

Schemas. Propositions and images are fine for representing single ideas and relationships, but often our knowledge about a topic combines images and proposi-

Semantic Memory: Memory for meaning.

Propositional Network: Set of interconnected concepts and relationships in which long-term knowledge is held.

Images: Representations based on the physical attributes—the appearance—of information.

tions. "In order to deal with the fact that much of our knowledge seems integrated, psychologists have developed the idea of a schema" (Gagné, Yekovich, & Yekovich, 1993, p. 81). **Schemas** (sometimes called *schemata*) are abstract knowledge structures that organize vast amounts of information. A schema (the singular form) is a pattern or guide for understanding an event, concept, or skill. Figure 7.5 is a partial representation of a schema for knowledge about an "antique."

The schema tells you what features are typical of a category, what to expect. The schema is like a pattern, specifying the "standard" relationships in an object or situation. The pattern has "slots" that are filled with specific information as we apply the schema in a particular situation. And schemas are individual. For example, my schema of an antique is less richly developed than the schema of an antique collector. You encountered the very similar concept of scheme in the discussion of Piaget's theory of cognitive development in Chapter 2.

Schemata (singular, **Schema**): Basic structures for organizing information; concepts.

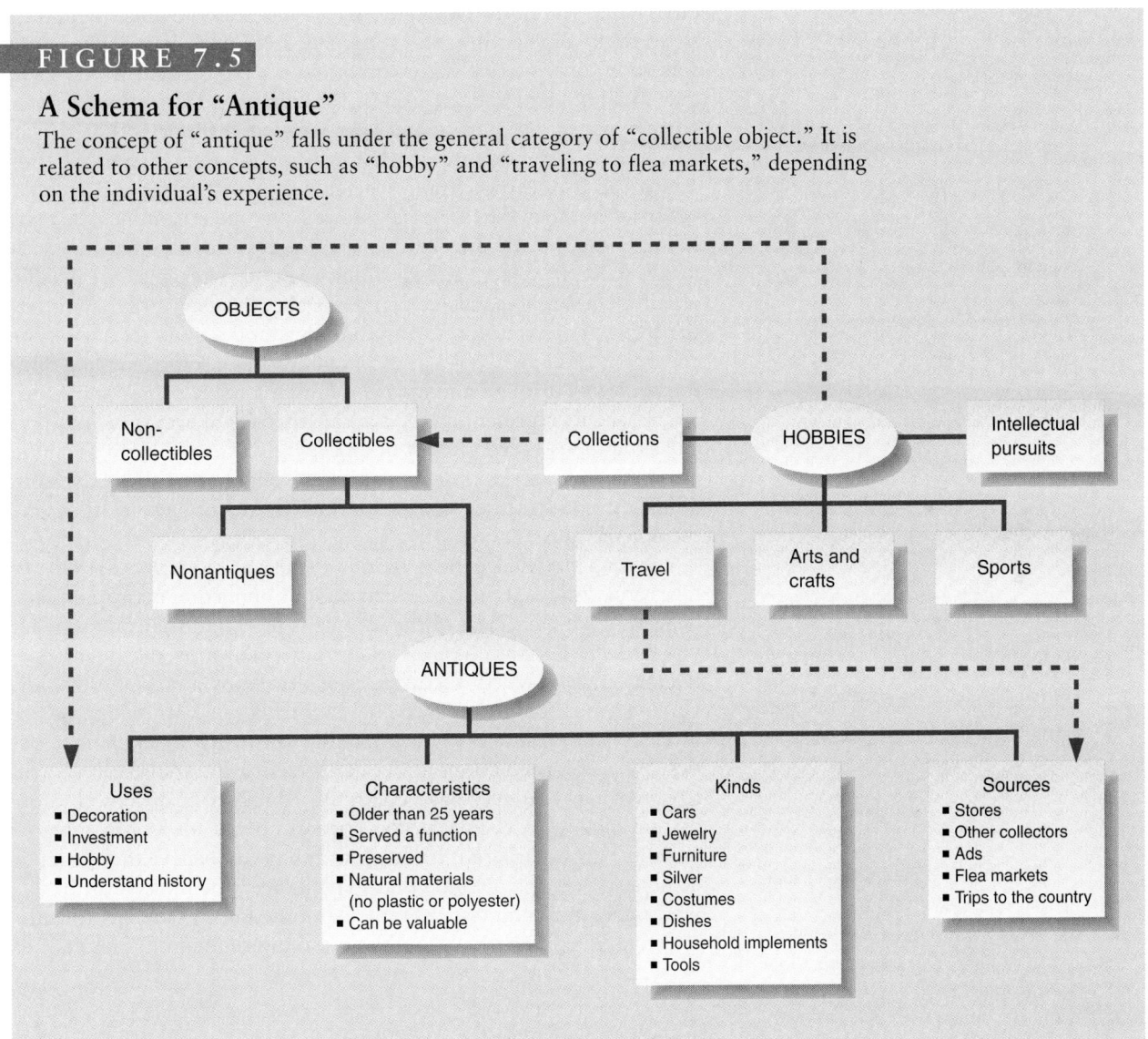

FIGURE 7.5

A Schema for "Antique"

The concept of "antique" falls under the general category of "collectible object." It is related to other concepts, such as "hobby" and "traveling to flea markets," depending on the individual's experience.

Connect & Extend
To real life
How can schemas about differences among individuals, groups, and social contexts determine how new information about people and situations is interpreted?

When you hear the sentence, "Ida borrowed the antique tablecloth," you know even more about it than the two propositions. This is because you have schemas about borrowing, tablecloths, antiques, and maybe even Ida herself. You know without being told, for example, that the lender does not have the tablecloth now, because it is in Ida's possession, and that Ida has an obligation to return the tablecloth to the lender (Gentner, 1975). None of this information is explicitly stated, but it is part of our schema for understanding the meaning of "borrow." Other schemas allow you to infer that the cloth is not plastic (if it is a real antique) and that Ida has probably invited guests for a meal. Your schema about Ida may even allow you to predict how promptly the cloth will be returned and in what condition.

Another type of schema, a **story grammar** (sometimes called a schema for text or story structure) helps students to understand and remember stories (Gagné, Yekovich, & Yekovich, 1993; Rumelhart & Ortony, 1977). A story grammar could be something like this: murder discovered, search for clues, murderer's fatal mistake identified, trap set to trick suspect into confessing, murderer takes bait . . . mystery solved! In other words, a story grammar is a typical general structure that could fit many specific stories. To comprehend a story, we select a schema that seems appropriate. Then we use this framework to decide which details are important, what information to seek, and what to remember. It is as though the schema is a theory about what should occur in the story. The schema guides us in "interrogating" the text, filling in the specific information we expect to find so that the story makes sense. If we activate our "murder mystery schema" we may be alert for clues or a murderer's fatal mistake (Resnick, 1981). Without the appropriate schema, trying to understand a story, textbook, or classroom lesson is a very slow, difficult process, something like finding your way through a new town without a map.

A schema representing the typical sequence of events in an everyday situation is called a **script** or an *event schema*. Children as young as 3 have basic scripts for the familiar events in their lives (Nelson, 1986). A kindergartner's script for "lunch" might be something like the one in Figure 7.6.

Storing knowledge of the world in schemas and scripts has advantages and disadvantages. A schema can be applied in many contexts, depending on what part of the schema is relevant. You can use what you know about antiques, for example, to plan trips, decide if a particular article is worth the price asked, or enjoy a museum display. Having a well-developed schema about Ida lets you recognize her (even as her appearance changes), remember many of her characteristics, and make predictions about her behavior. But it also allows you to be wrong. You may have incorporated incorrect or biased information into your schema of Ida. For example, if Ida is a member of an ethnic group different from yours and if you believe that group is dishonest, you may assume that Ida will keep the tablecloth. In this way, racial and ethnic stereotypes can function as schemas for misunderstanding individuals and for racial discrimination (Sherman & Bessenoff, 1999).

Episodic Memory. Memory for information tied to a particular place and time, especially information about the events or episodes of

FIGURE 7.6

"Lunchtime" Script

This script is typical of ones generated by children 5 or 6 years of age. Younger children give scripts that are less detailed and that contain fewer main acts.

First you play outside for a while.

⬇

When the teacher calls your name, you go in.

⬇

You get your lunchbox and sit down.

⬇

You eat.

⬇

You throw away your trash.

⬇

You get ready for your nap.

Source: From *Child Development* (2nd ed.), by L. E. Berk, 1991, Boston: Allyn & Bacon. Copyright © 1991 by Allyn & Bacon. Reprinted with permission.

your own life, is called **episodic memory**. Episodic memory is about events we have experienced, so we often can explain *when* the event happened. In contrast, we usually can't describe when we acquired a semantic memory. For example, you may have a difficult time remembering when you developed semantic memories for the meaning of the word "injustice," but you can easily remember a time that you felt unjustly treated. Episodic memory also keeps track of the order of things, so it is also a good place to store jokes, gossip, or plots from films.

Procedural Memory. Memory for how to do things is called **procedural memory**. It may take a while to learn a procedure—such as how to ski, serve a tennis ball, or factor an equation—but once learned, this knowledge tends to be remembered for a long time. Procedural memories are represented as *condition-action rules*, sometimes called productions. **Productions** specify what to do under certain conditions: If A occurs, then do B. A production might be something like, "If you want to snow ski faster, lean back slightly," or "If your goal is to increase student attention and a student has been paying attention a bit longer than usual, then praise the student." People can't necessarily state all their condition-action rules, but they act on them nevertheless. The more practiced the procedure, the more automatic the action (Anderson, 1995a).

Storing and Retrieving Information in Long-Term Memory

Just what is done to "save" information permanently—to create semantic, episodic, or procedural memories? How can we make the most effective use of our practically unlimited capacity to learn and remember? *The way you learn information in the first place*—the way you process it at the outset—seems to affect its recall later. One important requirement is that you integrate new material with information already stored in long-term memory as you construct an understanding. Here *elaboration*, *organization*, and *context* play a role.

Elaboration is the addition of meaning to new information through its connection with already existing knowledge. In other words, we apply our schemas and draw on already existing knowledge to construct an understanding and frequently change our existing knowledge in the process. We often elaborate automatically. For example, a paragraph about an historic figure in ancient Rome tends to activate our existing knowledge about that period; we use the old knowledge to understand the new.

Material that is elaborated when first learned will be easier to recall later. First, as we saw earlier, elaboration is a form of rehearsal. It keeps the information activated in working memory long enough to have a chance for permanent storage in long-term memory. Second, elaboration builds extra links to existing knowledge. The more one bit of information or knowledge is associated with other bits, the more routes there are to follow to get to the original bit. To put it another way, you have several "handles," or retrieval cues, by which you can recognize or "pick up" the information you might be seeking (Schunk, 2000). Psychologists have also found that the more precise and sensible the elaborations, the easier recall will be (Bransford, Stein, Vye, Franks, Auble, Mezynski, & Perfetto, 1982; Stein, Littlefield, Bransford, & Persampieri, 1984).

The more students elaborate new ideas, the more they "make them their own," the deeper their understanding and the better their memory for the knowledge. We help students to elaborate when we ask them to translate information into their own

Connect & Extend
To your teaching
See the Teachers' Casebook for practicing teachers' ideas about how to help students retain and retrieve information.

Story Grammar: Typical structure or organization for a category of stories.

Script: Schema or expected plan for the sequence of steps in a common event such as buying groceries or ordering take-out pizza.

Episodic Memory: Long-term memory for information tied to a particular time and place, especially memory of the events in a person's life.

Procedural Memory: Long-term memory for how to do things.

Productions: The contents of procedural memory; rules about what actions to take, given certain conditions.

Elaboration: Adding and extending meaning by connecting new information to existing knowledge.

words, create examples, explain to a peer, draw or act out the relationships, or apply the information to solve new problems. Of course, if students elaborate new information by making incorrect connections or developing misguided explanations, these misconceptions will be remembered too.

Organization is a second element of processing that improves learning. Material that is well organized is easier to learn and to remember than bits and pieces of information, especially if the information is complex or extensive. Placing a concept in a structure will help you learn and remember both general definitions and specific examples. The structure serves as a guide back to the information when you need it. For example, Table 7.1 organizes information about types of knowledge; Table 7.2 gives an organized view of the capacity, duration, contents, and retrieval of information from working and long-term memory; and Figure 7.5 organizes my (limited) knowledge about antiques.

Context is a third element of processing that influences learning. Aspects of physical and emotional context—places, rooms, how we are feeling on a particular day, who is with us—are learned along with other information. Later, if you try to remember the information, it will be easier if the current context is similar to the original one. This has been demonstrated in the laboratory. Students who learned material in one type of room performed better on tests taken in a similar room than they did on tests taken in a very different-looking room (Smith, Glenberg, & Bjork, 1978). So studying for a test under "testlike" conditions may result in improved performance. Of course, you can't always go back to the same or a similar place in order to recall something. But you can picture the setting, the time of day, and your companions, and you may eventually reach the information you seek.

Levels of Processing Theories. Craik and Lockhart (1972) first proposed their **levels of processing theory** as an alternative to short-/long-term memory models, but levels of processing is particularly related to the notion of elaboration described above. Craik and Lockhart suggested that what determines how long information is remembered is *how completely* the information is analyzed and connected with other information. The more completely information is processed, the better are our chances of remembering it. For example, according to the levels of processing theory, if I ask you to sort pictures of dogs based on the color of their coats, you might not remember many of the pictures later. But if I ask you to rate each dog on how likely it is to chase you as you jog, you probably would remember more of the pictures. To rate the dogs, you must pay attention to details in the pictures, relate features of the dogs to characteristics associated with danger, and so on. This rating procedure requires "deeper" processing and more focus on the *meaning* of the features in the photos.

Retrieving Information from Long-Term Memory. When we need to use information from long-term memory, we search for it. Sometimes the search is conscious, as when you see a friend approaching and search for her name. At other times locating and using information from long-term memory is automatic, as when you dial a telephone or solve a math problem without having to search for each step. Think of long-term memory as a huge shelf full of tools and supplies ready to be brought to the workbench of working memory to accomplish a task. The shelf (long-term memory) stores an incredible amount, but it may be hard to find what you are looking for quickly. The workbench (working memory) is small, but anything on it is immediately available. Because it is small, however, supplies (bits of

Organization: Ordered and logical network of relations.

Context: The physical or emotional backdrop associated with an event.

Levels of Processing Theory: Theory that recall of information is based on how deeply it is processed.

information) sometimes are lost when the workbench overflows or when one bit of information covers (interferes with) another (E. Gagné, 1985).

The size of the memory network is huge, but only one small area is activated at any one time. Only the information we are currently thinking about is in working memory. Information is retrieved in this network through the **spread of activation.** When a particular proposition or image is active—when we are thinking about it— other closely associated knowledge can be activated as well, and activation can spread through the network (Anderson, 1993; Gagné, Yekovich, & Yekovich, 1993). Thus, as I focus on the propositions, "I'd like to go for a drive to see the fall leaves," related ideas such as, "I should rake leaves," and "The car needs an oil change," come to mind. As activation spreads from the "car trip" to the "oil change," the original thought, or active memory, disappears from working memory because of the limited space. So **retrieval** from long-term memory is partly through the spreading of activation from one bit of knowledge to related ideas in the network. We often use this spreading in reverse to retrace our steps in a conversation, as in, "Before we got onto the topic of where to get the oil changed, what were we talking about? Oh yes, seeing the leaves." The learning and retrieving processes of long-term memory are diagrammed in Figure 7.7.

In long-term memory the information is still available, even when it is not activated, even when you are not thinking about it at the moment. If spreading activation does not "find" the information we seek, then we might still come up with the answer through **reconstruction,** a problem-solving process that makes use of logic, cues, and other knowledge to *construct* a reasonable answer by filling in any missing parts. Sometimes reconstructed recollections are incorrect. For example, in 1932,

Spread of Activation: Retrieval of pieces of information based on their relatedness to one another. Remembering one bit of information activates (stimulates) recall of associated information.

Retrieval: Process of searching for and finding information in long-term memory.

Reconstruction: Recreating information by using memories, expectations, logic, and existing knowledge.

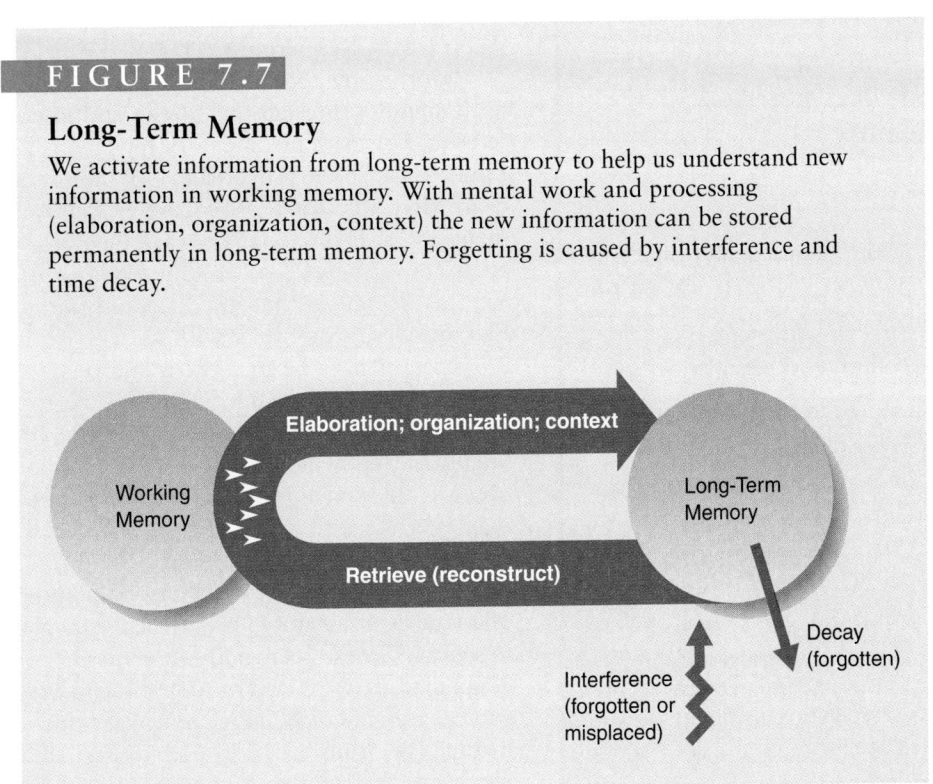

FIGURE 7.7

Long-Term Memory

We activate information from long-term memory to help us understand new information in working memory. With mental work and processing (elaboration, organization, context) the new information can be stored permanently in long-term memory. Forgetting is caused by interference and time decay.

F. C. Bartlett conducted a series of famous studies on remembering stories. He read a complex, unfamiliar Native-American tale to students at England's Cambridge University and, after various lengths of time, asked the students to recall the story. Students' recalled stories were generally shorter than the original and were translated into the concepts and language of the Cambridge student culture. The story told of a seal hunt, for instance, but many students remembered a "fishing trip," an activity closer to their experiences and more consistent with their schemas.

One area where reconstructed memory can play a major role is eyewitness testimony. Elizabeth Loftus and her colleagues have conducted a number of studies showing that misleading questions or other information during questioning can affect memory. For example, in a classic study, Loftus and Palmer (1974) showed subjects slides of a car wreck. Later, the experimenters asked some subjects, "How fast were the cars going when they *hit* each other?" while other subjects who saw the same slides were asked, "How fast were the cars going when they *smashed* into each other?" The difference in verbs was enough to bias the subjects' memories—the "hit" subjects estimated the cars were traveling an average of 34 miles per hour, but the "smashed" subjects estimated almost 41 miles per hour. And one week later, 32% of the "smashed" subjects remembered seeing broken glass at the scene of the wreck, while only 14% of the "hit" subjects remembered glass. (There was no broken glass visible in any of the slides.)

Forgetting and Long-Term Memory. Information lost from working memory truly disappears. No amount of effort will bring it back. But information stored in long-term memory may be available, given the right cues. Some people believe that nothing is ever lost from long-term memory; however, research casts doubts on this assertion (Schwartz & Reisberg, 1991).

Information appears to be lost from long-term memory through time decay and **interference**. For example, memory for Spanish–English vocabulary decreases for about 3 years after a person's last course in Spanish, then stays level for about 25 years, then drops again for the next 25 years. One explanation for this decline is that neural connections, like muscles, grow weak without use. After 25 years, it may be that the memories are still somewhere in the brain, but they are too weak to be reactivated (Anderson, 1995a, b). Finally, newer memories may interfere with or obscure older memories, and older memories may interfere with memory for new material. Even with decay and interference, long-term memory is remarkable. In a review of almost 100 studies of memory for knowledge taught in school, George Semb and John Ellis (1994) concluded that, "contrary to popular belief, students retain much of the knowledge taught in the classroom" (p. 279). It appears that teaching strategies that encourage student

CHECKPOINT

The Information Processing Model of Memory

Review

▶ Compare declarative, procedural, and conditional knowledge.

▶ Give two explanations for perception.

▶ How is information retained in working memory?

▶ How is information represented in long-term memory and what role do schemas play?

▶ What learning processes improve long-term memory?

▶ Why do we forget?

Apply

▶ A child from a large city has trouble understanding and remembering a story about endangered species in a national park. Explain this situation using information processing theory.

engagement and lead to higher levels of *initial* learning (such as frequent reviews and tests, elaborated feedback, high standards, mastery learning, and active involvement in learning projects) are associated with longer retention. The Guidelines below give applications of information processing for teaching.

GUIDELINES

Using Information Processing Ideas in the Classroom

Make sure you have the students' attention.

Examples

1. Develop a signal that tells students to stop what they are doing and focus on you. Make sure students respond to the signal—don't let them ignore it. Practice using the signal.

2. Move around the room, use gestures, and avoid speaking in a monotone.

3. Begin a lesson by asking a question that stimulates interest in the topic.

4. Regain the attention of individual students by walking closer to them, using their names, or asking them a question.

Help students separate essential from nonessential details and focus on the most important information.

Examples

1. Summarize instructional objectives to indicate what students should be learning. Relate the material you are presenting to the objectives as you teach: "Now I'm going to explain exactly how you can find the information you need to meet Objective One on the board—determining the tone of the story."

2. When you make an important point, pause, repeat, ask a student to paraphrase, note the information on the board in colored chalk, or tell students to highlight the point in their notes or readings.

Help students make connections between new information and what they already know.

Examples

1. Review prerequisites to help students bring to mind the information they will need to understand new material: "Who can tell us the definition of a quadrilateral? Now, what is a rhombus? Is a square a quadrilateral? Is a square a rhombus? What did we say yesterday about how you can tell? Today we are going to look at some other quadrilaterals."

2. Use an outline or diagram to show how new information fits with the framework you have been developing. For example, "Now that you know the duties of the FBI, where would you expect to find it in this diagram of the branches of the U.S. government?"

3. Give an assignment that specifically calls for the use of new information along with information already learned.

Provide for repetition and review of information.

Examples

1. Begin the class with a quick review of the homework assignment.

2. Give frequent, short tests.

3. Build practice and repetition into games, or have students work with partners to quiz each other.

Present material in a clear, organized way.

Examples

1. Make the purpose of the lesson very clear.

2. Give students a brief outline to follow. Put the same outline on an overhead so you can keep yourself on track. When students ask questions or make comments, relate these to the appropriate section of the outline.

3. Use summaries in the middle and at the end of the lesson.

Focus on meaning, not memorization.

Examples

1. In teaching new words, help students associate the new word to a related word they already understand: "*Enmity* is from the same base as *enemy*. . . ."

2. In teaching about remainders, have students group 12 objects into sets of 2, 3, 4, 5, 6, and ask them to count the "leftovers" in each case.

$\mathcal{M}$etacognition, Regulation, and Individual Differences

Connect & Extend
To the research
See the entire issue of *Learning and Individual Differences* (1996, #4) on individual differences in metacognition.

One question that intrigues many cognitive psychologists is why some people learn and remember more than others. For those who hold an information processing view, part of the answer lies in the executive control processes shown in Figure 7.1. **Executive control processes** guide the flow of information through the information processing system. We have already discussed a number of control processes, including attention, maintenance rehearsal, elaborative rehearsal, organization, and elaboration. These executive control processes are sometimes called *metacognitive skills*, because the processes can be intentionally used to regulate cognition.

Metacognitive Knowledge and Regulation

This young woman using an electronic organizer might be a good analogy for the metacognitive processes. In both cases, the individual sets goals, makes plans, organizes activities, decides what procedure is needed next, selects procedures from several choices, monitors the effect of making the choice, and returns to the menu if the results are unsatisfactory. ▼

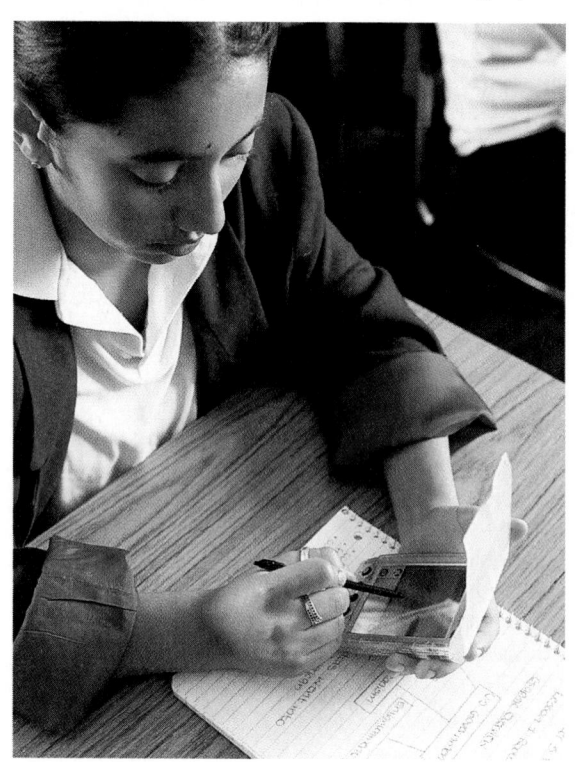

Donald Meichenbaum and his colleagues describe **metacognition** as people's "awareness of their own cognitive machinery and how the machinery works" (Meichenbaum, Burland, Gruson, & Cameron, 1985, p. 5). Metacognition literally means cognition about cognition—or knowledge about knowing. This knowledge is used to monitor and regulate cognitive processes such as reasoning, comprehension, problem solving, learning, and so on (Metcalfe & Shimamura, 1994). Because people differ in their metacognitive knowledge and skills, they differ in how well and how quickly they learn (Brown, Bransford, Ferrara, & Campione, 1983; Morris, 1990).

Metacognition involves three kinds of knowledge: declarative knowledge about yourself as a learner, the factors that influence your learning and memory, and the skills, strategies, and resources needed to perform a task—knowing *what* to do; procedural knowledge or knowing *how* to use the strategies; and conditional knowledge to ensure the completion of the task—knowing *when* and *why* to apply the procedures and strategies (Brunning, Schraw, & Ronning, 1999). Metacognition is the strategic application of this declarative, procedural, and conditional knowledge to accomplish goals and solve problems (Schunk, 2000).

Metacognitive knowledge is used to regulate thinking and learning (Brown, 1987; Nelson, 1996). There are three essential skills that allow us to do this: planning, monitoring, and evaluation. *Planning* involves deciding how much time to give to a task, which strategies to use, how to start, what resources to gather, what order to follow, what to skim and what to give intense attention to, and so on. *Monitoring* is the on-line awareness of "how I'm doing." Monitoring entails asking, "Is this making sense? Am I trying to go too fast? Have I studied enough?" *Evaluation* involves making judgments about the processes and outcomes of thinking and learning. Should I change strategies? Get help? Give up for now? Is this paper (painting, model, poem, plan, etc.) finished?

Of course, we don't have to be metacognitive all the time. Some actions become routine. Metacognition is most useful when tasks are challenging, but not too difficult. Then planning, monitoring, and evaluation can be helpful. And even when we are planning, monitoring, and evaluating, these processes are not necessarily conscious. Especially in adults, these processes can be automatic or implicit—we may use them without being aware of our efforts. Experts in a field may plan, monitor, and evaluate as second nature; they have difficulty describing their metacognitive knowledge and skills (Bargh & Chartrand, 1999; Reder, 1996).

Individual Differences in Metacognition

Some differences in metacognitive abilities are the result of development. As children grow older they are more able to exercise executive control and use strategies. For example, they are more able to determine if they have understood instructions (Markman, 1977, 1979) or if they have studied enough to remember a set of items (Flavell, Friedrichs, & Hoyt, 1970). Metacognitive abilities begin to develop around ages 5 to 7 and improve throughout school (Flavell, 1985; Flavell, Green, & Flavell, 1995; Garner, 1990). In her work with first and second graders, Nancy Perry found that asking students two questions helped them become more metacognitive. The questions were "What did you learn about yourself as a reader/writer today?" and "What did you learn that you can do again and again and again?" When teachers asked these questions regularly during class, even young students demonstrated fairly sophisticated levels of metacognitive understanding and action (Perry et al., 2000).

Not all differences in metacognitive abilities have to do with age or maturation. There is great variability even among students of the same developmental level, but these differences do not appear to be related to intellectual abilities. In fact, superior metacognitive skills can compensate for lower levels of ability, so these metacognitive skills can be especially important for students who often have trouble in school (Swanson, 1990).

Some individual differences in metacognitive abilities are probably caused by biological differences or by variations in learning experiences. Students can vary greatly in their ability to attend selectively to information in their environment. In fact, many students diagnosed as learning disabled actually have attention disorders (Hallahan & Kauffman, 2000), particularly with long tasks (Pelham, 1981). Attention is also influenced by the individual and cultural differences we examined in Chapters 4 and 5, such as learning abilities and preferences, cognitive styles, and cultural background. Students who are field dependent, for example, have difficulty perceiving elements in a pattern and tend to focus on the whole.

Individual Differences and Working Memory

As you might expect, there are both developmental and individual differences in working memory. Let's examine a few.

Developmental Differences. Research indicates that young children have very limited working memories, but their memory span improves with age. It is not clear whether these differences are the result of changes in memory *capacity* or improvements in *strategy* use. Case (1985a & b) suggests that the total amount of "space" available for processing information is the same at each age, but young children must use quite a bit of this space to remember how to execute basic operations, such as reaching for a toy, finding the right word for an object, or counting. Using a new operation takes up a large portion of the child's working memory. Once an operation

Connect & Extend
To your teaching
E. Bondy (1989) describes the importance of metacognitive processes, particularly monitoring comprehension, and lists nine suggestions for educators. *Highlights:* (1) Have students keep a daily learning log. (2) Demonstrate and discuss appropriate metacognitive activity (such as estimating difficulty of task, setting goals, choosing a strategy). (3) Provide opportunities for feedback. (4) Provide instruction in self-questioning. (5) Teach students to summarize material. (6) Teach students to rate their comprehension (i.e., "I understand well," "I sort of understand," "I don't understand"). (7) Use model of learning as framework for planning instruction. (8) Teach students how to study. (9) Teach students to think aloud and systematically solve problems. [Thinking about thinking. In *Annual editions: Educational psychology* (pp. 83–86). Guilford, CT: Duskin.]

Executive Control Processes: Processes such as selective attention, rehearsal, elaboration, and organization that influence encoding, storage, and retrieval of information in memory.

Metacognition: Knowledge about our own thinking processes.

is mastered, however, there is more working memory available for short-term storage of new information. Biology may play a role too. As the brain and neurological system of the child mature, processing may become more efficient so that more working-memory space is available.

As children grow older, they develop more effective strategies for remembering information. Most children spontaneously discover rehearsal around age 5 or 6. Siegler (1991) describes a 9-year-old boy who witnessed a robbery, then mentally repeated the license number of the getaway car until he could give the number to the police. Younger children can be taught to rehearse, and will use the strategy effectively as long as they are reminded. But they will not apply the strategy spontaneously. Children are 10 to 11 years old before they have adult-like working memories.

According to Case (1985a, 1985b), young children often use reasonable, but incorrect, strategies for solving problems because of their limited memories. They try to simplify the task by ignoring important information or skipping steps to reach a correct solution. This puts less strain on memory. For example, when comparing quantities, young children may consider only the height of the water in a glass, not the diameter of the glass, because this approach demands less of their memory. According to Case, this explains young children's inability to solve the classic Piagetian conservation problem. (See Figure 2.2 on page 35.)

There are several developmental differences in how students use organization, elaboration, and knowledge to process information in working memory. Around age 6, most children discover the value of using *organizational strategies* and by 9 or 10 they use these strategies spontaneously. So, given the following words to learn:

couch, orange, rat, lamp, pear, sheep, banana, rug, pineapple, horse, table, dog

an older child or an adult might organize the words into three short lists of furniture, fruit, and animals. Younger children can be taught to use organization to improve memory, but they probably won't apply the strategy unless they are reminded. Children also become more able to use elaboration as they mature, but this strategy is developed late in childhood. Creating images or stories to remember ideas is more likely for older elementary school students and adolescents (Siegler, 1991).

Individual Differences. Besides developmental differences, there are other individual variations in working memory. Some people seem to have more efficient working memories than others (Cariglia-Bull & Pressley, 1990; Di Vesta & Di Cintio, 1997; Jurden, 1995), and differences in working memory may be associated with giftedness in math and verbal areas. For example, subjects in one research study were asked to remember lists of numbers, the locations of marks on a page, letters, and words (Dark & Benbow, 1991). Subjects who excelled in mathematics remembered numbers and locations significantly better than subjects talented in verbal areas. The verbally talented subjects, on the other hand, had better memories for words. Based on these results, Dark and Benbow believe that basic differences in information processing abilities play a role in the development of mathematical and verbal talent.

Individual Differences and Long-Term Memory

The major individual difference that affects long-term memory is knowledge. When students have more *domain-specific declarative* and *procedural knowledge*, they are better at learning and remembering material in that domain (Alexander, 1997).

Think what it is like for you to read a very technical textbook in an area you know little about. Every line is difficult. You have to stop and look up words or turn back to read about concepts you don't understand. It is hard to remember what you are reading because you are trying to understand and remember at the same time. But with a good basis of knowledge, learning and remembering become easier; the more you know, the easier it is to know more. This is true in part because having knowledge improves strategy use. Another factor is related to developing domain knowledge and remembering it—interest. Pat Alexander and her colleagues point out that to develop expert understanding and recall in a domain requires the "continuous interplay of skill (i.e., knowledge) and thrill (i.e., interest)" (Alexander, Kulikowich, & Schulze, 1994, p. 334).

Now that we have examined the information processing explanation of how knowledge is represented and remembered, let's turn to the really important question: How can teachers support the development of knowledge?

CHECKPOINT

Metacognition, Regulation, and Individual Differences

Review

▶ What are the three metacognitive skills?

▶ Describe some individual differences in metacognition.

▶ How can using better metacognitive strategies improve children's memories?

Apply

▶ Give some examples of your own metacognitive abilities.

Becoming Knowledgeable: Some Basic Principles

Understanding a concept such as "antique" involves *declarative knowledge* about characteristics and images and *procedural knowledge* about how to apply rules to categorize specific antiques. We will discuss the development of declarative and procedural knowledge separately, but keep in mind that real learning is holistic and interrelated.

Development of Declarative Knowledge

Within the information processing perspective, to learn declarative knowledge is really to integrate new ideas with existing knowledge and construct an understanding. For example, a teacher says: "In vitro experiments show vitamin C increases the formation of white blood cells."

Students may ignore the phrase *in vitro* because they have no existing schemas for making sense of it. But through *spreading of activation* the concepts of "white blood cells" and "vitamin C" cue the retrieval of prior knowledge such as "vitamin C fights colds," "viruses cause colds," and "white blood cells destroy viruses." Using this prior knowledge about colds, viruses, and vitamin C, along with the new information that vitamin C increases the formation of white blood cells, the students may infer that "vitamin C fights colds *because* it increases the formation of the white blood cells." This information was neither in their long-term memories nor in the teacher's statement, but it was constructed by the students as they elaborated on and

Connect & Extend
To your teaching
Smith, S. M. (1985). A method for teaching name mnemonics. *Teaching of Psychology, 12,* 156–158. In small groups, students create keyword mnemonics for each other's names. The name mnemonics are then presented to the whole class.

organized their understanding of vitamin C. The resulting elaborated, reorganized network of knowledge includes the students' interpretations of the new information from the teacher in addition to their constructions and inferences (Gagné, Yekovich, & Yekovich, 1993). Let's examine factors that support the construction of declarative knowledge.

As you have seen, people learn best when they have a good base of knowledge in the area they are studying. With many well-elaborated schemas and scripts to guide them, new material makes more sense, and there are many possible networks for connecting new information with old. But students don't always have a good base of knowledge. In the early phases of learning, students of any age must grope around the landscape a bit, searching for landmarks and direction. Even experts in an area must use some learning strategies when they encounter unfamiliar material or new problems (Alexander, 1996, 1997; Garner, 1990; Perkins & Salomon, 1989; Shuell, 1990).

What are some possible strategies? When information has little inherent meaning, **rote memorization** techniques may provide the basic building blocks for other learning.

Rote Memorization. Very few things need to be learned by rote. The greatest challenge teachers face is to help students think and understand, not just memorize. Unfortunately, many students, including those in the scenario opening this chapter, see memorizing and learning as the same thing (Iran-Nejad, 1990). However, there are times when we have to memorize something word-for-word, such as lines in a song, poem, or play.

If you must memorize, how would you do it? If you have tried to memorize a list of items that are all similar to one another, you may have found that you tended to remember items at the beginning and at the end of the list but forgot those in the middle. This is called the **serial-position effect**. **Part learning**, breaking the list into smaller segments, can help prevent this effect, because breaking a list into several shorter lists means there will be fewer middle items to forget.

Another strategy for memorizing a long selection or list is the use of **distributed practice**. A student who studies Hamlet's soliloquy intermittently throughout the weekend will probably do much better than a student who tries to memorize the entire speech on Sunday night. Studying for an extended period, rather than for briefer periods with rest time in between, is called **massed practice**. Distributed practice gives time for deeper processing and the chance to move information into long-term memory (Mumford, Costanza, Baughman, Threlfall, & Fleishman, 1994).

Next we examine *mnemonic strategies*, which build in meaning by connecting what is to be learned with established words or images.

Mnemonics. **Mnemonics** are systematic procedures for improving memory. Many of these mnemonic strategies use imagery (Atkinson et al., 1999; Levin, 1993; McCormick & Levin, 1987).

The **loci method** derives its name from the plural of the Latin word *locus*, meaning "place." To use loci, you must first imagine a very familiar place, such as your own house or apartment, and pick out particular locations. Every time you have a list to remember, the same locations serve as "pegs" to "hang" memories. Simply place each item from your list in one of these locations. For instance, let's say you want to remember to buy milk, bread, butter, and cereal at the store. Imagine a giant bottle of milk blocking the entry hall, a lazy loaf of bread sleeping on the living room couch, a stick of butter melting all over the dining room table, and cereal covering the kitchen floor. When you want to remember the items, all you have to do is take an imaginary walk through your house. Other **peg-type mnemonics** use a standard list of words (one is bun, two is shoe . . .) as pegs.

If you need to remember information for long periods of time, an acronym may be the answer. An **acronym** is a form of abbreviation—a word formed from the first letter of each word in a phrase, for example HOMES to remember the Great Lakes (Huron, Ontario, Michigan, Erie, Superior). Another method forms phrases or sentences out of the first letter of each word or item in a list, for example, Every Good Boy Does Fine to remember the lines on the G clef—E, G, B, D, F. Because the words must make sense as a sentence, this approach also has some characteristics of **chain mnemonics**, methods that connect the first item to be memorized with the second, the second item with the third, and so on. In one type of chain method, each item on a list is linked to the next through some visual association or story. Another chain-method approach is to incorporate all the items to be memorized into a jingle such as "i before e except after c."

The mnemonic system that has been most extensively applied in teaching is the **keyword method.** The approach has two stages. To remember a foreign word, for example, you first choose an English word, preferably a concrete noun, that sounds like the foreign word or a part of it. Next, you associate the meaning of the foreign word with the English word through an image or sentence. For example, the Spanish word *carta* (meaning "letter") sounds like the English word "cart." Cart becomes the keyword: You imagine a shopping cart filled with letters on its way to the post office, or you make up a sentence such as "The cart full of letters tipped over" (Pressley, Levin, & Delaney, 1982). Figure 7.8 on page 266 offers another example of this method, this time used to learn English vocabulary.

One problem, however, is that the keyword method does not work well if it is difficult to identify a keyword for a particular item. Many words and ideas that students need to remember do not lend themselves to associations with keywords (Hall, 1991; Pressley, 1991). Also, vocabulary learned with keywords may be more easily forgotten than vocabulary learned in other ways, especially if students are given keywords and images instead of being asked to supply the words and images. When the teacher provides the memory links, these associations may not fit the students' existing knowledge and may be forgotten or confused later, so remembering suffers (Wang & Thomas, 1995; Wang, Thomas, & Ouelette, 1992). Younger students have some difficulty forming their own images. For them, memory aids that rely on auditory cues—rhymes such as "Thirty days hath September . . ." seem to work better.

Many teachers use a mnemonic system to quickly learn their students' names. Until we have some knowledge to guide learning, it may help to use some rote memorization and mnemonic approaches to build vocabulary and facts. Not all educators agree, as is noted in the Point/Counterpoint on page 267.

Making It Meaningful. Perhaps the best single method for helping students learn is to make each lesson as meaningful as possible. Meaningful lessons are presented in vocabulary that makes sense to the students. New terms are clarified through ties with more familiar words and ideas. Meaningful lessons are also well organized, with clear connections between the different

"HOW MANY TIMES MUST I TELL YOU—IT'S 'CAT' BEFORE 'TEMPLE' EXCEPT AFTER 'SLAVE.'"

(By permission of Bo Brown. From Phi Delta Kappan)

New information will be more meaningful to students, and thus will be learned more readily, if they can connect it to knowledge that they already have. This student has made a model of an elbow using materials he is familiar with such as balloons and construction paper. ▼

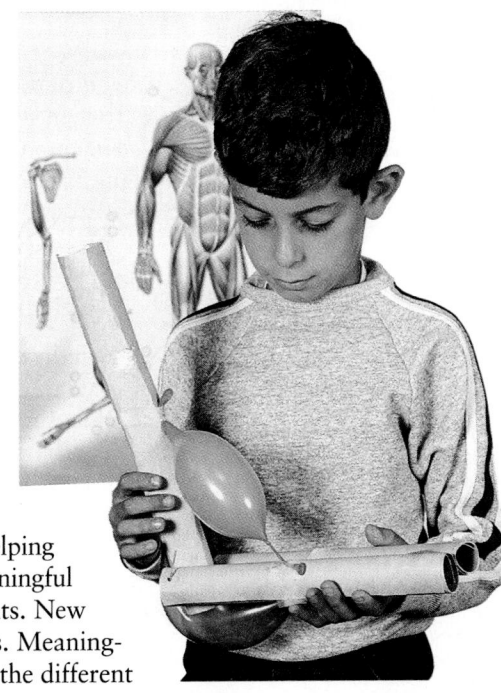

FIGURE 7.8

Using the Keyword Method to Learn English Vocabulary

Here the keyword is "purse." It is a concrete noun that sounds like "persuade" (the vocabulary word to be learned). The keyword, definition, and vocabulary word are linked in an image.

Source: From "Mnemonic versus Nonmnemonic Vocabulary—Learning Strategies for Children," by J. R. Levin, C. B. McCormick, G. E. Miller, J. K. Berry, and M. Pressley, 1982, *American Educational Research Journal, 19,* pp. 121–136. Copyright © 1982 by the American Educational Research Association. Reprinted with permission.

Connect & Extend
To your teaching

What is the memory strategy used in each of the following examples?

a. In order to help children remember the symbol for the number eight, the teacher makes a snowman out of the figure 8 while telling a story about the snowman with eight buttons who lives for eight days.

b. To remember that Bismarck is the capital of North Dakota, a student imagines N.D. on a biscuit.

c. To help students remember how to spell "separate," the teacher says, "There is a rat in separate."

d. A student lists the products of Alabama so that the first letters spell CAPS—for cotton, apples, paper products, and soybeans.

e. Columbus sailed the ocean blue in fourteen hundred and ninety-two.

f. To remember a grocery list, Mrs. Tarent imagines cheese on her TV, limes on the sofa, milk on the table, beans in the wicker basket, and tomatoes on the stove.

g. The teacher uses a time line to show the major events before, during, and after the Vietnam War.

h. Students are asked to compare their present home chores with chores they might have if they lived during Civil War times.

elements of the lesson. Finally, meaningful lessons make natural use of old information to help students understand new information through examples or analogies.

The importance of meaningful lessons is emphasized in an example presented by Smith (1975). Consider the three lines below:

1. KBVODUWGPJMSQTXNOGMCTRSO
2. READ JUMP WHEAT POOR BUT SEEK
3. KNIGHTS RODE HORSES INTO WAR

Begin by covering all but the first line. Look at it for a second, close the book, and write down all the letters you remember. Then repeat this procedure with the second and third lines. Each line has the same number of letters, but the chances are great that you remembered all the letters in the third line, a good number of letters in the second line, and very few in the first line. The first line makes no sense. There is no way to organize it in a brief glance. Working memory is simply not able to process all that unfamiliar information quickly. The second line is more meaningful. You do not have to see each letter because your long-term memory brings prior knowledge of spelling rules and vocabulary to the task. The third line is the most meaningful. Just a glance and you can probably remember all of it because you bring to this task prior knowledge not only of spelling and vocabulary but

What's Wrong with Memorizing?

For years students have relied on memorization to learn vocabulary, procedures, steps, names, and facts. Is this a bad idea?

▶ **POINT** *Rote memorization creates inert knowledge.*

Years ago William James (1912) described the limitations of rote learning by telling a story about what can happen when students memorize but do not understand:

> A friend of mine, visiting a school, was asked to examine a young class in geography. Glancing at the book, she said: "Suppose you should dig a hole in the ground, hundreds of feet deep, how should you find it at the bottom—warmer or colder than on top?" None of the class replying, the teacher said: "I'm sure they know, but I think you don't ask the question quite rightly. Let me try." So, taking the book, she asked: "In what condition is the interior of the globe?" And received the immediate answer from half the class at once. "The interior of the globe is in a condition of igneous fusion." (p. 150)

The students had memorized the answer, but they had no idea what it meant. Perhaps they didn't understand the meaning of "interior," "globe," or "igneous fusion." At any rate, the knowledge was useful to them only when they were answering test questions, and only then when the questions were phrased ex-

actly as they had been memorized. Students often resort to memorizing the exact words of definitions when they have no hope for actually understanding the terms or when teachers count off for definitions that are not exact.

Most recently, Howard Gardner has been a vocal critic of rote memorization and a champion of "teaching for understanding." In an interview in *Phi Delta Kappan* (Siegel & Shaughnessy, 1994), Gardner says:

> My biggest concern about American education is that even our better students in our better schools are just going through the motions of education. In *The Unschooled Mind*, I review ample evidence that suggests an absence of understanding—the inability of students to take knowledge, skills, and other apparent attainments and apply them successfully in new situations. In the absence of such flexibility and adaptability, the education that the students receive is worth little. (pp. 563–564)

◀ **COUNTERPOINT** *Rote memorization can be effective.*

Memorization may not be such a bad way to learn new information that has little inherent meaning, such as foreign language vocabulary. Alvin Wang, Margaret Thomas, and Judith Ouellette (1992) compared learning Tagalog (the national language of the Philippines) using either rote memorization or the keyword approach. The keyword method is a way of cre-

ating connections and meaning for associating new words with existing words and images. In their study, even though the keyword method led to faster and better learning initially, long-term forgetting was *greater* for students who had used the keyword method than for students who had learned by rote memorization.

There are times when students must memorize and we do them a disservice if we don't teach them how. Every discipline has its own terms, names, facts, and rules. As adults, we want to work with physicians who have memorized the correct names for the bones and organs of the body or the drugs needed to combat particular infections. Of course, they can look up some information or research certain conditions, but they have to know where to start. We want to work with accountants who give us accurate information about the new tax codes, information they probably had to memorize because it changes from year to year in ways that are not necessarily rational or meaningful. We want to deal with computer sales people who have memorized their stock and know exactly which printers will work with our computer. Just because something was learned through memorization does not mean it is inert knowledge. The real question, as Gardner points out above, is whether you can *use* the information flexibly and effectively to solve new problems.

also of rules about syntax and probably some historical information about knights (they didn't ride in tanks). This sentence is meaningful because you have existing schemas for assimilating it. It is relatively easy to associate the words and meaning with other information already in long-term memory (Sweller, van Merrienboer, & Paas, 1998).

The challenge for teachers is to make lessons less like learning the first line and more like learning the third line. Although this may seem obvious, think about the times when *you* have read a sentence in a text or heard an explanation from a professor that might just as well have been KBVODUWGPJMSQTXNOGMCTRSO. But remember, attempts to change the ways that students are used to learning—moving from memorizing to meaningful activities as in the opening "What Would You Do?" situation, are not always greeted with student enthusiasm. Students may be concerned about their grades; at least when memorization gains an A, they know what is expected. Meaningful learning is riskier and more challenging. In Chapters 8, 9, and 13 we will examine a variety of ways in which teachers can support meaningful learning and understanding.

The Instructional Events Model. Robert Gagné (1977; Gagné & Driscoll, 1988) has proposed a well-developed theory of instruction based on the information processing model of learning. Table 7.3 shows Gagné's phases of learning and the "instructional events" associated with each phase.

As you can see, in the instructional events model, the first step in learning, and the first challenge for the teacher, is to gain the students' attention. The next step is to set an expectancy for learning by letting the students know the goals of the lesson and perhaps arousing their curiosity or providing other motivation for learning (we will talk more about this in Chapters 10 and 11). When the students are paying attention and have the right expectations, they need to be reminded of what they already know that is related to the material to be learned. With this prior knowledge in their working memories, they are ready to make connections between new and old information. Now it is time to present the new material, highlighting the important aspects or key features. At this point the students should have the new material in their short-term or working memories, so they are ready to process the information and move it to long-term memory. The teacher's role now is to provide learning guidance, such as explanations and examples or a guided-discovery exercise.

But learning does not stop here. In Gagné's model, students have to demonstrate, both to the teacher and to themselves, that they really understand the mate-

---

TABLE 7.3 *Gagné's Phases of Learning and the Instructional Events That Support Learning at Each Phase*

Description	Learning Phase	Instructional Event
Preparation for learning	1. Attention; alertness	Gain learner's attention through unusual event, question, or change of stimulus
	2. Expectancy	Inform the learner of the objective; activate motivation
	3. Retrieval (of relevant information and/or skills) to working memory	Stimulate recall of prior knowledge
Acquisition and performance	4. Selective perception of stimulus features	Present material; highlight distinctive features
	5. Encoding; storage in long-term memory	Provide learning guidance
	6. Retrieval and responding	Elicit performance
	7. Reinforcement	Provide informative feedback
Transfer of learning	8. Cueing retrieval	Assess performance
	9. Generalizing	

Source: From *Learning and Instruction: Theory into Practice*, (3rd ed.) (p. 125), by M. E. Gredler, 1997, Saddle River, NJ: Prentice Hall, Inc. Copyright © 1997 by Prentice-Hall, Inc. Reprinted with permission.

---

rial. The students must respond in some way. These responses allow the teacher to check the students' understanding and provide reinforcement or corrections or both. Finally, to ensure that they can retrieve and apply their new knowledge readily, students should practice in a variety of situations. Reviews at the end of the lesson, week, and unit encourage transfer by extending practice over time.

Becoming an Expert: Development of Procedural and Conditional Knowledge

Experts in a particular field have a wealth of domain-specific knowledge, that is, knowledge that applies specifically to their area or domain. They not only have *declarative knowledge* (facts and verbal information), but they also have at their command considerable *procedural knowledge*, an understanding of how to perform various cognitive activities. And they know when and why to apply their understandings; that is, they have *conditional knowledge*, so they can manipulate their declarative and procedural knowledge to solve problems.

Another characteristic distinguishes experts from novices. Much of the expert's declarative knowledge has become "proceduralized," that is, incorporated into routines that can be applied automatically without making many demands on working memory. Skills that are applied without conscious thought are called **automated basic skills**. An example is shifting gears in a standard transmission car. At first you had to think about every step, but as you became more expert (if you did), the procedure became automatic. But not all procedures (sometimes called *cognitive skills*) can be automatic, even for experts in a particular domain. For example, no matter how expert you are in driving, you still have to consciously watch the traffic around you. This kind of conscious procedure is called a **domain-specific strategy**. Automated basic skills and domain-specific strategies are learned in different ways (Gagné, Yekovich, & Yekovich, 1993).

Automated Basic Skills. Most psychologists identify three stages in the development of an automated skill: *cognitive, associative,* and *autonomous* (Anderson, 1995b; Fitts & Posner, 1967). At the **cognitive stage,** when we are first learning, we rely on declarative knowledge and general problem-solving strategies to accomplish our goal. For example, to learn to assemble a bookshelf, we might try to follow steps in the instruction manual, putting a check beside each step as we complete it to keep track of progress. At this stage we have to "think about" every step and perhaps refer back to the pictures of parts to see what a "4- inch metal bolt with lock nut" looks like. The load on working memory is heavy. There can be quite a bit of trial-and-error learning at this stage when, for example, the bolt we chose doesn't fit.

At the **associative stage,** individual steps of a procedure are combined, or "chunked" into larger units. We reach for the right bolt and put it into the right hole. One step smoothly cues the next. With practice, the associative stage moves to the **autonomous stage,** where the whole procedure can be accomplished without much attention. So if you assemble enough bookshelves, you can have a lively conversation as you do, paying little attention to the assembly task. This movement from the cognitive to the associative to the autonomous stage holds for the development of basic cognitive skills in any area, but science, medicine, chess, and mathematics have been most heavily researched.

What can teachers do to help their students pass through these three stages and become more expert? In general, it appears that two factors are critical: *prerequisite knowledge* and *practice with feedback*. First, if students don't have the essential

Automated Basic Skills: Skills that are applied without conscious thought.

Domain-Specific Strategies: Consciously applied skills to reach goals in a particular subject or problem area.

Cognitive Stage: The initial learning of an automated skill when we rely on general problem-solving approaches to make sense of steps or procedures.

Associative Stage: Individual steps of a procedure are combined or "chunked" into larger units.

Autonomous Stage: Final stage in the learning of automated skills. The procedure is fine-tuned and becomes "automatic."

CHECKPOINT

Becoming Knowledgeable: Some Basic Principles

Review

▶ Describe three ways to develop declarative knowledge.

▶ Describe some procedures for developing procedural knowledge.

Apply

▶ How would you use the keyword method to teach the exports of foreign countries?

prior knowledge (schemas, skills, etc.), the load on working memory will be too great. In order to compose a poem in a foreign language, for example, you must know some of the vocabulary and grammar of that language, and you must have some understanding of poetry forms. To learn the vocabulary, grammar, *and* forms as you also try to compose the poem would be too much.

Second, practice with feedback allows you to form associations, recognize cues automatically, and combine small steps into larger condition-action rules or *productions*. Even from the earliest stage, some of this practice should include a simplified version of the whole process in a real context. Practice in real contexts helps students learn not only *how* to do a skill but also *why* and *when* (Collins, Brown, & Newman, 1989; Gagné, Yekovich, & Yekovich, 1993). Of course, as every athletic coach knows, if a particular step, component, or process is causing trouble, that element might be practiced alone until it is more automatic, and then put back into the whole sequence, to lower the demands on working memory (Anderson, Reder, & Simon, 1996).

Domain-Specific Strategies. As we saw earlier, some procedural knowledge, such as monitoring the traffic while you drive, is not automatic because conditions are constantly changing. Once you decide to change lanes, the maneuver may be fairly automatic, but the decision to change lanes was conscious, based on the traffic

FAMILY AND COMMUNITY PARTNERSHIPS

Organizing Learning

Give families specific strategies to help their children practice and remember.

Examples

1. Develop "super learner" homework assignments that include material to be learned and a "parent coaching card" with a description of a simple memory strategy—appropriate for the material—that parents can teach their child.

2. Provide a few comprehension check questions so a family member can review reading assignments and check the child's understanding.

3. Describe the value of distributed practice and give family members ideas for how and when to work skills practice into home conversations and projects.

Ask family members to share their strategies for organizing and remembering.

Examples

1. Create a family calendar.

2. Encourage planning discussions in which family members help students break large tasks into smaller jobs, identify goals, and find resources.

Discuss the importance of attention in learning.

Examples

1. Encourage families to create study spaces for children away from distractions.

2. Make sure parents know the purpose of homework assignments.

conditions around you. Domain-specific strategies are these consciously applied skills of organizing thoughts and actions to reach a goal. To support this kind of learning, teachers need to provide opportunities for practice in many different situations—for example, practice reading with newspapers, package labels, magazines, books, letters, operating manuals, and so on. In the next chapter's discussion of problem solving and study strategies, we will examine other ways to help students develop domain-specific strategies. For now, let's turn to a consideration of how students can develop strategies for learning outside school.

Learning Outside School

The last several sections of this chapter have described many ideas for helping students become knowledgeable—memory strategies, mnemonics, metacognitive skills such as planning or monitoring comprehension, and cognitive skills. Some students have an advantage in school because they learn these strategies and skills at home. The Family and Community Partnerships Guidelines on page 270 give ideas for working with families to give all your students more support and practice developing these skills.

Summary

Elements of the Cognitive Perspective

Contrast cognitive and behavioral views of learning in terms of what is learned and the role of reinforcement.

Cognitive learning theorists focus on the human mind's active attempts to make sense of the world. In the cognitive view, knowledge is learned, and changes in knowledge make changes in behavior possible. In the behavioral view, the new behaviors themselves are learned. Both behavioral and cognitive theorists believe reinforcement is important in learning, but for different reasons. The strict behaviorist maintains that reinforcement strengthens responses; cognitive theorists see reinforcement as a source of feedback about what is likely to happen if behaviors are repeated—as a source of information.

How does knowledge affect learning?

The cognitive approach suggests that one of the most important elements in the learning process is what the individual brings to the learning situation.

Knowledge is the outcome of learning and the power of knowledge is the driving element in learning. What we already know determines to a great extent what we will pay attention to, perceive, learn, remember, and forget.

The Information Processing Model of Memory

Compare declarative, procedural, and conditional knowledge.

Declarative knowledge is knowledge that can be declared, usually in words or other symbols. Declarative knowledge is "knowing that" something is the case. Small units of declarative knowledge can be organized into larger units. Procedural knowledge is "knowing how" to do something; procedural knowledge must be demonstrated. Conditional knowledge is "knowing when and why" to apply your declarative and procedural knowledge.

Give two explanations for perception.

The Gestalt principles are valid explanations of certain aspects of perception, but there are two other kinds of explanations in information processing theory for how we recognize patterns and give meaning to sensory events. The first is called feature analysis, or bottom-up processing, because the stimulus must be analyzed into features or components and assembled into a meaningful pattern. The second type of perception, top-down processing, is based on knowledge and expectation. To recognize patterns rapidly, in addition to noting features, we use what we already know about the situation.

How is information retained in working memory?

To keep information activated in working memory for longer than 20 seconds, people use maintenance rehearsal (mentally repeating the information in the articulatory loop) and elaborative rehearsal (connecting the information you are trying to remember with information from long-term memory). This kind of rehearsal not only retains information in working memory but helps move information from short-term to long-term memory. The limited capacity of working memory can also be somewhat circumvented by the control process of chunking.

How is information represented in long-term memory and what role do schemas play?

Long-term memory seems to hold an unlimited amount of information permanently. Information may be part of our semantic, episodic, or procedural memories. In long-term memory, bits of information may be stored and interrelated in terms of propositional networks and in schemas (such as story grammars and scripts) that are data structures that allow us to represent large amounts of complex information, make inferences, and understand new information.

What learning processes improve long-term memory?

The way you learn information in the first place affects its recall later. One important requirement is to integrate new material with information already stored in long-term memory using elaboration, organization, and context. Elaboration is the addition of meaning to new information through its connection with already existing knowledge. Material that is well organized is easier to learn and to remember, especially if the information is complex or extensive. Aspects of physical and emotional context are learned along with other information. Another view of memory is the levels of processing theory, in which recall of information is determined by how completely it is processed.

Why do we forget?

Information lost from working memory truly disappears, but information stored in long-term memory may be available, given the right cues. Information appears to be lost from long-term memory through time decay (neural connections, like muscles, grow weak without use) and interference (newer memories may interfere with or obscure older memories, and older memories may interfere with memory for new material).

Metacognition, Regulation, and Individual Differences

What are the three metacognitive skills?

The three metacognitive skills used to regulate thinking and learning are planning, monitoring, and evaluation. Planning involves deciding how much time to give to a task, which strategies to use, how to start, and so on. Monitoring is the on-line awareness of "how I'm doing." Evaluation involves making judgments about the processes and outcomes of thinking and learning and acting on those judgments.

Describe some individual differences in metacognition.

As children develop cognitively, they are more able to exercise executive control and use strategies. Also, some individual differences in metacognitive abilities probably are caused by biological differences or by variations in learning experiences. Students can vary greatly in their ability to attend selectively to information in their environment, plan, and execute strategies.

How can using better metacognitive strategies improve children's memories?

Younger children can be taught to use organization to improve memory, but they probably won't apply the strategy unless they are reminded. Children also become more able to use elaboration as they mature, but this strategy is developed late in childhood. Creating images or stories to remember ideas is more likely for older elementary school students and adolescents.

Becoming Knowledgeable: Some Basic Principles

Describe three ways to develop declarative knowledge.

Declarative knowledge develops as we integrate new information with our existing understanding. The least effective way to accomplish this is rote memorization, which can best be improved by part learning and distributed practice. Mnemonics as memorization aids include peg-type approaches such as the loci method, acronyms, chain mnemonics, and the keyword method. The best way to learn and remember is to understand and use information. Making the information to be remembered meaningful is important and often is the greatest challenge for teachers.

Describe some procedures for developing procedural knowledge.

Automated basic skills and domain-specific strategies—two types of procedural knowledge—are learned in different ways. There are three stages in the development of an automated skill: cognitive (following steps or directions guided by declarative knowledge), associative (combining individual steps into larger units), and autonomous (where the whole procedure can be accomplished without much attention). Prerequisite knowledge and practice with feedback help students move through these stages. Domain-specific strategies are consciously applied skills of organizing thoughts and actions to reach a goal. To support this kind of learning, teachers need to provide opportunities for application in many different situations.

◣ *Key* Terms

Becoming a Professional

Reflecting on the Chapter

Can you apply the ideas from this chapter on cognitive views of learning to solve the following problems of practice?

Preschool and Kindergarten

▶ The 1st-grade teachers believe that the kindergarten teachers could do a better job of preparing their students to "pay attention" in class. As a kindergarten teacher, what would you do? How would you justify your plans to the 1st-grade teachers?

Elementary and Middle School

▶ Several students in your class are recent immigrants and have limited knowledge of the kinds of experiences described in your basal reader series (county fairs, zoos, trips to the beach, shopping malls, etc.). The students speak and read English, but still have difficulty understanding and remembering what they read. What would you do?

Junior High and High School

▶ You have reached a very complicated chapter in your text—one that is difficult for students every year. How would you make the highly abstract concepts (such as sovereignty and jurisprudence) understandable for your students?

Certification Test Requirements

▶ Understand the role of prior knowledge in learning.

▶ Know what a schema is and how schemas affect attention, learning, and remembering.

▶ Know how metacognitive skills impact learning and remembering.

▶ Be familiar with some common mnemonic strategies.

Your Teaching Portfolio

Use the section on the differences between behavioral and cognitive approaches to learning to refine your teaching philosophy. How will you answer the job interview question, "What is your theory of learning and why?"

Teaching Resources

Use the section on mnemonics to generate ideas for helping your students learn key vocabulary in science or social studies subjects and include these ideas in your **Teaching Resources** file.

Are there maps such as the one in Figure 7.4 that would help your students learn important relationships?

What Would They Do?

Here is how some practicing teachers responded to the teaching situation presented at the beginning of this chapter about history students intent on memorizing.

MARK SMITH

Ninth–Twelfth Grade Teacher
Medford High School, Medford, Massachusetts

The students in this class have always used memorization, and although they have probably been somewhat successful in the past, there comes a point where learners must get into higher-level thinking. Because this is a senior history class and many of these students will be heading off to college, they must be taught different ways of learning and thinking. Knowing facts and giving information is nice, but they also need to be able to reason what happens, why it is important, and what other things came about as a result of the information.

A critical piece of learning is being able to debate a topic and do so with a convincing argument. If I were the teacher in this class and the students were so worried about tests and grades, I would add more oral presentations and writing assignments that make the students think about the facts and try to analyze the information. A solution would be to give them the facts and information on the test and have them develop their own thoughts about why it is important or relate it to some other topic they had studied. Knowing facts and details in history is not as important as understanding how they affected the present and why the past is important for today and tomorrow.

MADYA AYALA

High School Teacher of Preperatoria Eugenio Garza Lagüera
Campus Garza Sada, Monterrey, N.L. Mexico

I observe that there are two existing conflicts. First, the students' available cognitive strategies (memorizing) don't fit the assigned task (higher-level thinking). Second, the students can't see connections between current situations and past events. For the first conflict I would use cognitive strategies such as mind mapping, schemas, comparative tables, and other advanced organizers that would enable students to learn the material.

Second, I recommend establishing a relation between past and present realities by focusing students' attention on an important event from the past and asking them to link it to an international, national, local, or even a social problem that is happening in school. Drama is a very interesting way of involving students because it gives them the opportunity to feel and experience any historic action. They could represent what "really" happens in making decisions and living the consequences. On the other hand they can change the facts and analyze how history could have changed if different decisions had been made. This is an active and constructivist approach.

The above allows students to make connections between the past and their present experiences, thus encouraging significant learning. It would be very interesting if they could make predictions about present social problems (short term) and the decisions they would make to solve the problems, and then predict how the decisions would affect the future.

ASHLEY DODGE

Ninth and Tenth Grade Teacher
Los Angeles Unified School District, Los Angeles, California

These students are obviously using strategies that have worked for them in the past (memorization and regurgitation of facts and dates), but they have not developed any critical thinking skills. Many students are very successful with these techniques up to a certain point. They become obsessed with learning only what is necessary to pass the class. At times it has seemed to me that they are attempting to conserve their energy for other things. Their insistence on using the rote memory approach may stem from unimaginative teachers in their past who have relied on tests of only facts and dates. These students may have received very good grades in the past, and thus now equate this type of learning with succeeding academically.

In order to give these students the opportunity to see history as something more than a time line, I would announce to the class that for the next unit, there would be no test. Instead, we would create projects reflective of the era. Perhaps we would produce a play, a fashion show with period clothing, or a festival. Some students may wish to construct a city at the time being studied, focusing on the differences in the city as it was then compared to now. The students would need to use the information in the text to incorporate their ideas into their projects, but it would not need to be memorized. They would be graded on both the originality and the quality of their work, and the project grade would count as two unit grades.

Because I believe that it is important to give students reasonable assurance of success, especially when attempting something so foreign, I would try to give examples of successful similar projects, and to offer as much guidance and time as necessary. This requires a lot more personal time and energy on my part than simply lecturing on the text, but students are generally appreciative when they see a teacher working with them. In my experience students have worked very hard on these projects and have been pleased with the results.

MITCHELL D. KLETT

Twelfth Grade Teacher
A.C. New Middle School, Springs, Texas

Apparently, these students know historical events, including dates and places, but they don't comprehend the implications of these events to today's world. They seem to equate superficial knowledge with comprehension and conceptual understanding. Their beliefs indicate that the events in the past are "history" and of little or no relevance to the world today or specifically to their world. Their learning consists of surface knowledge and rote memorization, probably because they've experienced history as a series of disjointed, sequential events.

Students need to understand that the events of the past have a profound influence on the world today. The adage, "those who don't know history are doomed to repeat it,"

rings true. As their teacher, I would emphasize cause-and-effect relationships throughout history and compare them with one another. By focusing on the causes of specific events, such as revolutions caused by economic rifts, students can better understand the cyclic nature of these types of revolutions. Events such as the French Revolution and the Russian Revolution could be examined through inquiry learning, group discussion, or role playing. Students could be given the opportunity to explore the nature of revolutions and apply what they have learned to new situations. An example topic could be: Third World countries have increasing populations and diminishing resources—what will happen as the rift between the haves and the have-nots is increased?

THOMAS O'DONNELL

Social Studies Chairperson, Grades 7–12
Malden High School, Malden, Massachusetts

These students "know" history as a set of factual events that happened in the past. Although much bias, prejudice, and myth have crept into the "known" history, the students don't realize this. Since they believe history is only a set of facts, they expect to learn them, know them, and be tested accordingly.

If their school experience has brought success through rote learning, it is logical for them to continue this approach to learning.

To help students break out of rote thinking I would test them on comprehension and assess them on that basis. Once they realize what the goal is, they will switch their approach in order to achieve success. I would also teach them to recognize any word in the reading that assumes "a truth" or accepts only one explanation of events. Finally, I would train students to ask Who? What? Where? How? and Why? for all situations.

Complex Cognitive
Processes

hink of a concept you learned lately in a class. How did you learn it? If you learned from a text or a teacher, were there examples provided? What kinds? Do you understand the concept well enough to define it in your own words? Can you apply it to solve a problem?

In the previous chapter we focused on the development of knowledge—how people make sense of and remember information and ideas. In this chapter we will focus on understanding and problem solving. We will be concerned with the implications of cognitive theories for the day-to-day practice of teaching, particularly for the development of students' thinking and understanding.

Because the cognitive perspective is a philosophical orientation and not a unified theoretical model, teaching methods derived from it are varied. In this chapter, we will first examine three important areas in which cognitive theorists have made suggestions for learning and teaching: concept learning, problem solving, and learning strategies and tactics. Finally, we will explore the question of how to encourage the transfer of learning from one situation to another to make learning more useful.

By the time you have completed this chapter, you should be able to:

▶ Design a lesson for teaching a key concept in your subject area.
▶ Describe the steps in solving complex problems and explain the role of problem representation.
▶ Give examples of algorithms and heuristics for problem solving.
▶ Apply new learning strategies and tactics to prepare for tests and assignments in your current courses.
▶ List three ways a teacher might encourage positive transfer of learning.

What Would You Do?

You have just finished reading the journals and projects from the discovery lesson on magnets, and you are depressed. In almost every working group, only one or two students seemed to "get it." The rest just drew pictures that were vaguely related to the unit or copied from the readings (or from the students who got it). You had taken the activities from a good "hands-on" science book and you thought the objectives and directions were clear. You know many students will be upset with the grades you are about to give.

▶ What might have happened to make this lesson so unsuccessful?

▶ What will you do now with these projects?

▶ How could you make similar discovery activities more productive in the future?

The Importance of Understanding

Connect and Extend
To the field

"The greatest enemy of understanding is coverage. As long as you are determined to cover everything, you actually ensure that most kids are not going to understand." Howard Gardner in Brandt, R. (1993). On teaching for understanding: A Conversation with Howard Gardner. *Educational Leadership, 50*(7), 7.

The previous chapter examined basic learning and memory processes such as attention, knowledge representation, remembering, and forgetting. In this chapter we consider complex cognitive processes that lead to understanding. Understanding is more than memorizing. It is more than retelling in your own words. Howard Gardner (1993b) defines understanding as:

> the capacity to take knowledge, skills, and concepts and apply them appropriately in new situations. If someone only parrots back what he or she has been taught, we do not know whether the individual understands. If that person applies the knowledge promiscuously, regardless of whether it is appropriate, then I would not say he or she understands either. . . . But if that person knows where to apply and where not to apply, and can do it to new situations, he or she understands. (p. 2)

So understanding involves appropriately *transforming* and *using* knowledge, skills, and ideas. These understandings are considered "higher-level cognitive objectives" in a commonly used system of educational objectives (Bloom, Engelhart, Frost, Hill, & Krathwohl, 1956).

In the following sections we will explore what is known about different aspects of thinking: learning concepts, solving problems, using learning strategies, and how teachers can support these paths to understanding. We begin with a discussion of the building blocks of understanding—concepts.

Learning and Teaching about Concepts

Concept: A general category of ideas, objects, people, or experiences whose members share certain properties.

Most of what we know about the world involves concepts and relations among concepts (Schwartz & Reisberg, 1991). But what exactly is a concept? A **concept** is a category used to group similar events, ideas, objects, or people. When we talk about a particular concept such as *student*, we refer to a category of people who are similar to one another—they all study a subject. The people may be old or young, in school or not; they may be studying baseball or Bach, but they can all be categorized as students. Concepts are abstractions. They do not exist in the real world. Only individual examples of concepts exist. Concepts help us organize vast amounts of information into manageable units. For instance, there are about 7.5 million distinguishable differences in colors. By categorizing these colors into some dozen or so groups, we manage to deal with this diversity quite well (Bruner, 1973).

Views of Concept Learning

Traditionally, psychologists have assumed that members of a category share a set of **defining attributes,** or distinctive features. For example, books all contain pages that are bound together in some way (but what about electronic "books?"). The defining attributes theory of concepts suggests that we recognize specific examples by noting key required features.

Since about 1970, however, these long-popular views about the nature of concepts have been challenged (Benjafield, 1992). Although some concepts, such as equilateral triangle, have clear-cut defining attributes, most concepts do not. Take the concept of *party*. What are the defining attributes? You might have difficulty listing these attributes, but you probably recognize a party when you see or hear one (unless, of course we are talking about political parties, or the other party in a lawsuit, where the sound might not help you recognize the "party"). What about the concept of *bird*? Your first thought might be that birds are animals that fly. But is an ostrich a bird? What about a penguin?

Prototypes and Exemplars. According to critics of the traditional view of concept learning, we have in our minds a prototype of a party and a bird—an image that captures the essence of each concept. A **prototype** is the best representative of its category. For instance, the best representative of the "birds" category for many North Americans might be a robin (Rosch, 1973). Other members of the category may be very similar to the prototype (sparrow) or similar in some ways but different in others (chicken, ostrich). At the boundaries of a category, it may be difficult to determine if a particular instance really belongs. For example, is a telephone a piece of "furniture"? Is an elevator a "vehicle"? Is an olive a "fruit"? Whether something fits into a category is a matter of degree. Thus, categories have fuzzy boundaries and **graded membership** (Schwartz & Reisberg, 1991). Some events, objects, or ideas are simply better examples of a concept than others.

Another explanation of concept learning suggests that we identify members of a category by referring to exemplars. **Exemplars** are our actual memories of specific birds, parties, furniture, and so on that we use to compare with an item in question to see if that item belongs in the same category as our exemplar. For example, if you see a strange steel-and-stone bench in a public park, you may compare it to the sofa in your living room to decide if the uncomfortable-looking creation is still for sitting or if it has crossed a fuzzy boundary into "sculpture."

Prototypes probably are built from experiences with many exemplars. This happens naturally because episodic memories of particular events tend to blur together over time, creating an average or typical sofa prototype from all the sofa exemplars you have experienced (Schwartz & Reisberg, 1991).

Concepts and Schemas. In addition to prototypes and exemplars, there is a third element involved when we recognize a concept—our schematic knowledge related to the concept. How do we know that counterfeit money is not "real" money, even though it perfectly fits our "money" prototype and exemplars? We know

Connect and Extend
To your teaching
According to Piaget, a person cannot think in abstract terms until the stage of formal operations is reached. How then can a child learn abstract concepts such as "yesterday" and "happy"?

"CITY CHILDREN HAVE TROUBLE WITH THE CONCEPT OF HARVEST."
(© Martha Campbell—From Phi Delta Kappan)

Defining Attributes: Distinctive features shared by members of a category.

Prototype: Best representative of a category.

Graded Membership: The extent to which something belongs to a category.

Exemplar: A specific example of a given category that is used to classify an item.

because of its history. It was printed by the "wrong" people. So our understanding of the concept of money is connected with concepts of crime, forgery, the federal treasury, and many others.

Strategies for Teaching Concepts

Connect and Extend
To the research
Tennyson, R. D., & Cocchiarella, M. M. (1986). An empirically based instructional design theory for teaching concepts. *Review of Educational Research, 56*, 40–71.
Abstract: An instructional design theory views concept learning as a two-phase process: (a) formation of conceptual knowledge, and (b) development of procedural knowledge. Two fundamental components of the proposed theoretical model are content structure variables and instructional design variables. A rational combination of these components provides the means for the selection of one of four basic instructional design strategies. The theoretical model is described with reference to instructional methods and cognitive processes.

Most of the current approaches to teaching concepts still rely heavily on the traditional analysis of defining attributes. Interest is growing, however, in the prototypes view of concept learning, partly because children first learn many concepts in the real world from the best examples or prototypes, pointed out by adults (Tennyson, 1981). The teaching of concepts can combine both distinctive features and prototypes.

One approach to teaching about concepts is called *concept attainment*—a way of helping students construct an understanding of specific concepts and practice thinking skills such as hypothesis testing (Joyce & Weil, 1996; Klausmeier, 1992).

An Example Concept-Attainment Lesson. Here is how a 5th-grade teacher helped his students learn about a familiar concept and practice thinking skills at the same time (Eggen & Kauchak, 1996, pp. 105–107). The teacher began a lesson by saying that he had an idea in mind and wanted students to "figure out what it is." He placed two signs on a table—"Examples" and "Nonexamples." Then he placed an apple in front of the "Examples" sign and a rock in front of the "Nonexamples" sign. He asked his students, "What do you think the idea might be?" "Things we eat" was the first suggestion. The teacher wrote "HYPOTHESES" on the board and, after a brief discussion of the meaning of "hypotheses," listed "things we eat" under this heading. Next he asked for other hypotheses—"living things" and "things that grow on plants" came next. After some discussion about plants and living things, the teacher brought out a tomato for the "Examples" side and a carrot for the "Nonexamples." Animated reconsideration of all the hypotheses followed these additions and a new hypothesis—"red things"—was suggested. Through discussion of more examples (peach, squash, orange) and nonexamples (lettuce, artichoke, potato), the students narrowed their hypothesis to "things with seeds in the parts you eat." The students had "constructed" the concept of "fruit"—foods with seeds in the edible parts (or, a more advanced definition, any engorged ovary, such as a pea pod, nut, tomato, pineapple, or the edible part of the plant developed from a flower).

Connect and Extend
To your teaching
Can abstract concepts be taught through the use of prototypes?

Lesson Components. Whatever strategy you use for teaching concepts, you will need four components in any lesson: examples and nonexamples, relevant and irrelevant attributes, the name of the concept, and a definition (Joyce & Weil, 1996). In addition, visual aids such as pictures, diagrams, or maps can improve learning of many concepts (Anderson & Smith, 1987).

Examples are essential in teaching concepts. More examples are needed in teaching complicated concepts and in working with younger or less able students. Both examples and nonexamples (sometimes called *positive* and *negative instances*) are necessary to make the boundaries of the category clear. Thus a discussion of why a bat (nonexample) is not a bird will help students define the boundaries of the bird concept.

The identification of relevant and irrelevant attributes is another aspect of teaching concepts. The ability to fly, as we've seen, is not a relevant attribute for classifying animals as birds. Even though many birds fly, some birds do not (ostrich, penguin), and some nonbirds do (bats, flying squirrels). The ability to fly would have to be included in a discussion of the bird concept, but students should understand that flying does not define an animal as a bird.

The name of the concept is important for communicating, but it is somewhat arbitrary. Simply learning a label does not mean the person understands the concept, although the label is necessary for the understanding. In the example above, students probably already used the "fruit" name, but may not have understood that tomatoes, squash, and avocados are fruits.

A definition makes the nature of the concept clear. A good definition has two elements: a reference to any more *general category* that the new concept falls under, and a statement of the new concept's *defining attributes* (Klausmeier, 1976). For example, a fruit is food (general category) with seeds in the edible parts (defining attributes). An equilateral triangle is a plane, a simple, closed figure (general category), with three equal sides and three equal angles (defining attributes). This kind of definition helps place the concept in a schema of related knowledge.

In teaching some concepts, "a picture is worth a thousand words"—or at least a few hundred. Seeing and handling specific examples, or pictures of examples, helps young children learn concepts. For students of all ages, the complex concepts in history, science, and mathematics can often be illustrated in diagrams or graphs. For example, Anderson and Smith (1983) found that when their students just read about the concept of light, only 20% could understand the role of reflected light in our ability to see objects. But when the students worked with diagrams such as the one in Figure 8.1, almost 80% understood the concept.

FIGURE 8.1

Understanding Complex Concepts
Illustrations can help students grasp a difficult concept.

Q. When sunlight strikes the tree it helps the boy to see the tree. How does it do this?

A. Some of the light bounces (is reflected) off the tree and goes to the boy's eyes.

Source: From *The Educator's Handbook: A Research Perspective*, edited by V. Richardson-Koehler, 1987, Reading MA: Addison-Wesley Educational Publishers, Inc. Copyright © 1987 by Addison-Wesley Educational Publishers. Reprinted with permission.

Undergeneralization: Exclusion of some true members from a category; limiting a concept.

Overgeneralization: Inclusion of nonmembers in a category; over-extending a concept.

Concept Mapping: Student's diagram of his or her understanding of a concept.

Connect and Extend
To your teaching
How can a teacher determine if a student has learned a concept?

Lesson Structure. The fruit lesson above is an example of good concept teaching for several reasons. First, it appears that it is more effective to examine examples and nonexamples *before* discussing attributes or definitions (Joyce & Weil, 1996). Start your concept lesson with prototypes, or best examples, to help the students establish the category. The teacher above began with the classic fruit example, an apple, then moved to less typical examples such as tomatoes and squash. These examples show the wide range of possibilities the category includes and the variety of irrelevant attributes within a category. This information helps students avoid focusing on an irrelevant attribute as a defining feature. Including fruits that have one seed or many, have a sweet taste or not, are different colors, and have thick or thin skin, will prevent **undergeneralization,** or the exclusion of some foods from their rightful place in the category *fruit.*

Nonexamples should be very close to the concept, but miss by one or just a few critical attributes. For instance, sweet potatoes and rhubarb are not fruits, even though sweet potatoes are sweet and rhubarb is used to make pies. Including nonexamples will prevent **overgeneralization,** or the inclusion of substances that are not fruits.

After the students seem to have grasped the concept under consideration, it is useful to ask them to think about the ways that they formed and tested their hypotheses. Some students may consider one example at a time, while other students may work with several simultaneously. Some older students may make systematic tests and eliminate one hypothesis at a time, keeping written records, while others are more global and scattered. Thinking back helps students develop their metacognitive skills and shows them that different people approach problems in different ways (Joyce & Weil, 1996). Table 8.1 summarizes the stages of concept teaching.

Extending and Connecting Concepts. Once students have a good sense of a concept, they should use it. This might mean doing exercises, solving problems,

---

TABLE 8.1 *Phases of the Concept Attainment Model*

There are three main phases in concept attainment teaching. First the teacher presents examples/nonexamples and students identify the concept, then the teacher checks for understanding, and finally students analyze their thinking strategies.

Phase One: Presentation of Data and Identification of Concept	Phase Two: Testing Attainment of the Concept	Phase Three: Analysis of Thinking Strategies
Teacher presents labeled examples.	Students identify additional unlabeled examples as yes or no.	Students describe thoughts.
Students compare attributes in positive and negative examples.	Teacher confirms hypotheses, names concept, and restates definitions according to essential attributes.	Students discuss role of hypotheses and attributes.
Students generate and test hypotheses.	Students generate examples.	Students discuss type and number of hypotheses.
Students state a definition according to the essential attributes.		

Source: From *Models of Teaching*, (5th ed.) (p. 173), by B. R. Joyce and M. Weil, 1996, Boston: Allyn & Bacon. Copyright © 1996 by Allyn & Bacon. Reprinted with permission.

---

writing, reading, explaining, or any other activity that requires them to apply their new understanding. This will connect the concept into the students' web of related schematic knowledge. One approach that you may see in some texts and workbooks for students above the primary grades is **concept mapping** (Novak & Musonda, 1991). Students "diagram" their understanding of the concept, as Amy has in Figure 8.2. Amy's map shows a reasonable understanding of the concept of *molecule*, but also indicates that Amy holds one misconception. She thinks that there is no space between the molecules in solids.

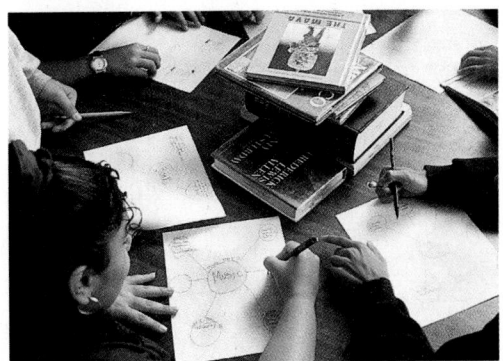

▲ *Concept maps require students to draw a diagram of their understanding of a particular concept. Maps can be used to organize information, take notes, assess understanding, and make thinking visible.*

FIGURE 8.2

Amy's Molecule

Amy, an eighth grader, has drawn a map to represent her understanding of the concept of "molecule." Her concept includes one misconception—that there is no space between molecules in solids.

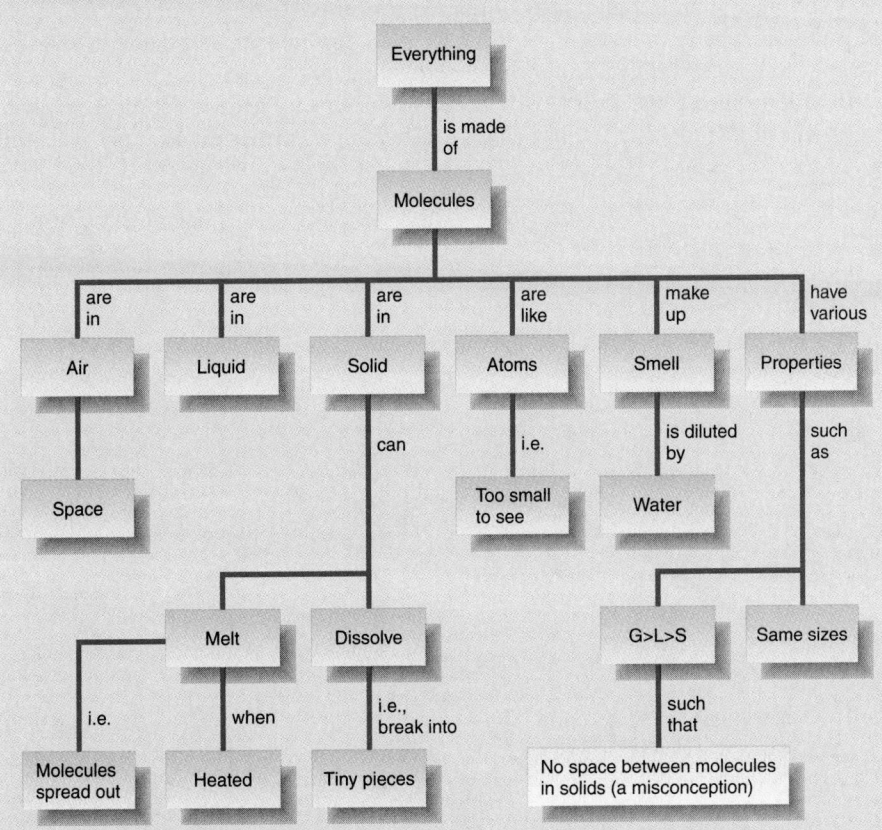

Source: From "A Twelve-Year Longitudinal Study of Science Concept Learning," by J. D. Novak and D. Musonda, 1991, *American Educational Resource Journal,* 28, figure p. 137. Copyright © 1991 by the American Educational Research Association. Reprinted by permission of the publisher.

Teaching Concepts through Discovery

Jerome Bruner's early research on thinking (Bruner, Goodnow, & Austin, 1956) stirred his interest in educational approaches that encourage concept learning and the development of thinking. Bruner's work emphasized the importance of understanding the structure of a subject being studied, the need for active learning as the basis for true understanding, and the value of inductive reasoning in learning.

Structure and Discovery. Subject structure refers to the fundamental ideas, relationships, or patterns of the field—the essential information. Because structure does not include specific facts or details about the subject, the essential structure of an idea can be represented simply as a diagram, set of principles, or formula. According to Bruner, learning will be more meaningful, useful, and memorable for students if they focus on understanding the structure of the subject being studied. For example, if you learned the concepts *figure, plane, simple, closed, quadrilateral, isosceles,* and *scalene,* you would be on your way to understanding one aspect of geometry. But how do these terms relate to one another? If you can place the terms into a coding system such as the one in Figure 8.3, you will have a better understanding of the basic structure of this part of geometry.

A **coding system** is a hierarchy of related concepts. At the top of the coding system is the most general concept, in this case *plane, simple, closed figure.* More specific concepts are arranged under the general concept.

In order to grasp the structure of information, Bruner believes, students must be active—they must identify key principles for themselves rather than simply accepting

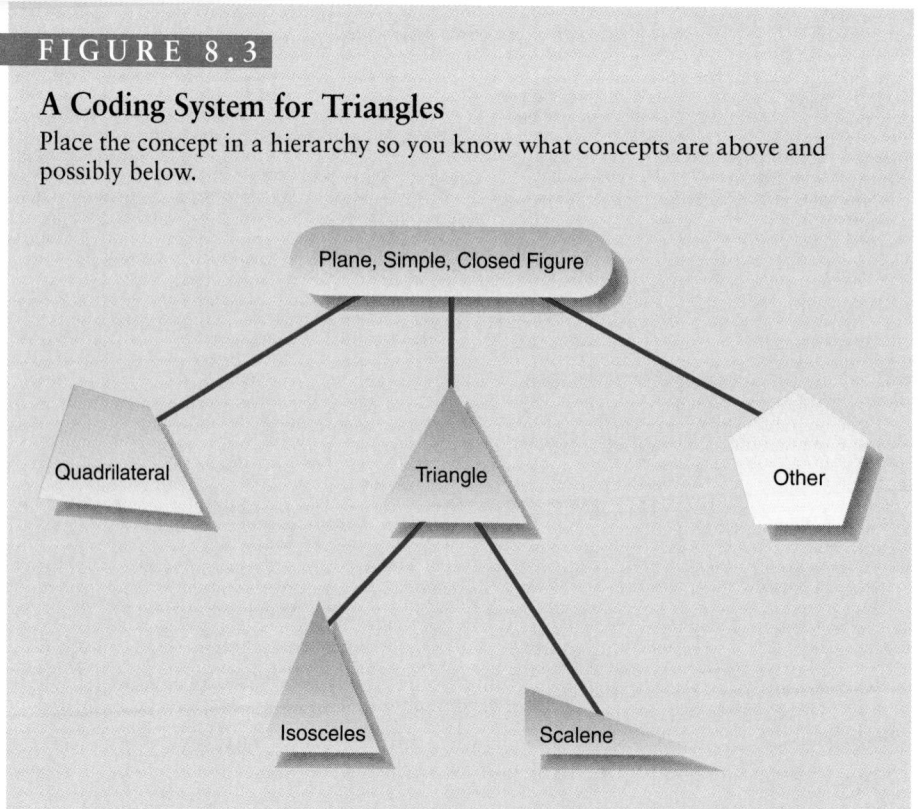

FIGURE 8.3

A Coding System for Triangles
Place the concept in a hierarchy so you know what concepts are above and possibly below.

teachers' explanations. This process has been called discovery learning. In **discovery learning,** the teacher presents examples and the students work with the examples until they discover the interrelationships—the subject's structure. Thus, Bruner believes that classroom learning should take place through **inductive reasoning,** that is, by using specific examples to formulate a general principle. For instance, if students are presented with enough examples of triangles and nontriangles, they will eventually discover what the basic properties of any triangle must be. Encouraging inductive thinking in this way is sometimes called the **eg-rule method,** from the Latin e.g., meaning "for example." The concept attainment lesson on fruit above used this approach.

Discovery in Action. An inductive approach requires **intuitive thinking** on the part of students. Bruner suggests that teachers can nurture this intuitive thinking by encouraging students to make guesses based on incomplete evidence and then to confirm or disprove the guesses systematically (Bruner, 1960). After learning about ocean currents and the shipping industry, for example, students might be shown old maps of three harbors and asked to guess which one became a major port. Then students could check their guesses through systematic research. Unfortunately, educational practices often discourage intuitive thinking by punishing wrong guesses and rewarding safe but uncreative answers.

Notice that in Bruner's discovery learning, a teacher organizes the class so that the students learn through their own active involvement. A distinction is usually made between discovery learning, in which the students work on their own to a very great extent, and **guided discovery,** in which the teacher provides some direction. Unguided discovery is appropriate for preschool children, but in a typical elementary or secondary classroom, unguided activities usually prove unmanageable and unproductive. For these situations, guided discovery is preferable. Students are presented with intriguing questions, baffling situations, or interesting problems: Why does the flame go out when we cover it with a jar? Why does this pencil seem to bend when you put it in water? What is the rule for grouping these words together? Instead of explaining how to solve the problem, the teacher provides the appropriate materials and encourages students to make observations, form hypotheses, and test solutions. Feedback must be given at the optimal moment, when students can either use it to revise their approach or take it as encouragement to continue in the direction they've chosen. The Guidelines on page 286 should help you apply Bruner's suggestions.

Discovery learning appears to have many advantages, but even Bruner believes that it is not appropriate in every situation. The Point/Counterpoint on page 287 examines the pros and cons of this approach.

Teaching Concepts through Exposition

David Ausubel's (1963, 1977) view of concept learning offers an interesting contrast to that of Bruner. According to Ausubel, people acquire knowledge primarily through reception rather than through discovery. Concepts, principles, and ideas are presented and understood, not discovered. As you saw in Chapter 7, the more organized and focused the presentation, the more thoroughly the person will learn.

Ausubel stresses what is known as **meaningful verbal learning**—verbal information, ideas, and relationships among ideas, taken together. Rote memorization is not considered meaningful learning, because material learned by rote is not *connected* with existing knowledge. Ausubel has proposed his **expository teaching** model to encourage meaningful rather than rote reception learning. (Here, exposition means

Discovery Learning: Bruner's approach, in which students work on their own to discover basic principles.

Inductive Reasoning: Formulating general principles based on knowledge of examples and details.

Eg-Rule Method: Teaching or learning by moving from specific examples to general rules.

Intuitive Thinking: Making imaginative leaps to correct perceptions or workable solutions.

Guided Discovery: An adaptation of discovery learning, in which the teacher provides some direction.

Meaningful Verbal Learning: Focused and organized relationships among ideas and verbal information.

Expository Teaching: Ausubel's method—teachers present material in complete, organized form, moving from broadest to more specific concepts.

Connect and Extend
To other chapters
What characteristics of cognitive development would support the statement that expository teaching is more appropriate for the secondary than the elementary level?

GUIDELINES

Applying Bruner's Ideas

Present both examples and nonexamples of the concepts you are teaching.

Examples

1. In teaching about mammals, include people, kangaroos, whales, cats, dolphins, and camels as examples, and chickens, fish, alligators, frogs, and penguins as nonexamples.
2. Ask students for additional examples and nonexamples.

Help students see connections among concepts.

Examples

1. Ask questions such as these: What else could you call this apple? (Fruit.) What do we do with fruit? (Eat.) What do we call things we eat? (Food.)
2. Use diagrams, outlines, and summaries to point out connections.

Pose a question and let students try to find the answer.

Examples

1. How could the human hand be improved?
2. What is the relation between the area of one tile and the area of the whole floor?

Encourage students to make intuitive guesses.

Examples

1. Instead of giving a word's definition, say, "Let's guess what it might mean by looking at the words around it."
2. Give students a map of ancient Greece and ask where they think the major cities were.
3. Don't comment after the first few guesses. Wait for several ideas before giving the answer.
4. Use guiding questions to focus students when their discovery has led them too far astray.

explanation, or the setting forth of facts and ideas.) In this approach, teachers present materials in a carefully organized and sequenced form, and students thus receive the most usable material in the most efficient way. Ausubel does agree with Bruner that people learn by organizing new information into hierarchies or coding systems. Ausubel calls the general concept at the top of the system the *subsumer*, because all other concepts are subsumed under it, as in Figure 8.3. However, Ausubel believes

Expository teaching methods present information to learners in an organized, "finished" form, rather than having them discover it themselves. ▶

Deductive Reasoning: Drawing conclusions by applying rules or principles; logically moving from a general rule or principle to a specific solution.

Is Discovery Learning Effective?

Most psychologists and educators agree that students must make sense of information in order to learn and remember it. Simply memorizing lists and facts leads to superficial understanding and rapid forgetting. When students struggle with perplexing problems, test possible solutions, and finally discover for themselves the fundamental structure of a key concept, they are more likely to understand and remember the information. But critics of discovery learning raise some important questions. Is discovery learning an effective method?

▶ **POINT** *Discovery learning matches cognitive development.*
Educators favoring discovery learning note that this approach is consistent with the ways that people learn and develop. For example, Jerome Bruner (1966, 1971) identified three stages of cognitive growth, similar to the stages identified by Piaget. Bruner believes that children move from an *enactive* stage to an *iconic* stage and finally to a *symbolic* stage. In the enactive stage (similar to Piaget's sensorimotor stage), the child represents and understands the world through actions—to understand something is to manipulate it, taste it, throw it, break it, and so on. At the iconic stage, the child represents the world in images—appearances dominate. This stage corresponds to Piaget's preoperational thinking, in which the higher the water level, the more

water there must be in the glass, because that's what appears to be true. At the final level, the child is able to use abstract ideas, symbols, language, and logic to understand and represent the world. Actions and images can still be used in thinking, but they do not dominate.

Discovery learning allows students to move through these three stages as they encounter new information. First the students manipulate and act on materials; then they form images as they note specific features and make observations; and finally they abstract general ideas and principles from these experiences and observations. Because they have experienced each stage of representation, Bruner believes, the students will have a better understanding of the topic. When students are motivated and really participate in the discovery project, discovery learning leads to superior learning (Strike, 1975).

◀ **COUNTERPOINT** *Discovery learning is impractical.*
In theory, discovery learning seems ideal, but in practice there are problems. To be successful, discovery projects often require special materials and extensive preparations. And these preparations can't guarantee success. For example, a discovery lesson on the effects of light on plants takes many hours and often falls flat because the plants grown in darkness and those grown in light don't always behave as they should—many fac-

tors other than light affect growth (Anderson & Smith, 1987).

In order to benefit from a discovery situation, students must have basic knowledge about the problem and must know how to apply problem-solving strategies. Without this knowledge and skill, they will flounder and grow frustrated. Instead of learning from the materials, they may simply play with them. The brightest students may make some discoveries, while the others lose interest or just wait passively for someone else to complete the project. Instead of benefiting from a teacher's organized explanation, these "nondiscovering" students may get an inadequate explanation from a fellow student who can't quite communicate his or her discoveries. Everyone may grow frustrated as the teacher seems to withhold the solutions and explanations needed.

Critics believe that discovery learning is so inefficient and so difficult to organize successfully that other methods are preferable. This seems especially true for lower-ability students. Discovery methods may make too many demands on these students, because they lack the background knowledge and problem-solving skills needed to benefit. Some research has shown that discovery methods are ineffective and even detrimental for lower-ability students (Corno & Snow, 1986; Slavin, Karweit, & Madden, 1989).

---

that learning should progress, not inductively as Bruner recommends, but deductively: from the general to the specific, or from the rule or principle to examples. The approach using **deductive reasoning** is sometimes called the **rule-eg method**.

Advance Organizers. Optimal learning generally occurs when there is a potential fit between the student's schemas and the material to be learned. To make this fit more likely, a lesson following Ausubel's strategy always begins with an **advance organizer**. This is an introductory statement of a relationship or a high-level concept

Rule-Eg Method: Teaching or learning by moving from general principles to specific examples.

Advance Organizer: Statement of inclusive concepts to introduce and sum up material that follows.

Connect and Extend
To life

The following advance organizer is taken from Joyce, B., & Weil, M. (1988). *Models of teaching* (3rd ed.). Englewood Cliffs, NJ: Prentice-Hall, pp. 70–71.

A guide, beginning a tour of an art museum with a group of high school students, says, "I want to give you an idea that will help you understand the paintings and sculpture we are about to see. The idea is simply that art, although it is a personal expression, reflects in many ways the culture and times in which it was produced. This may seem obvious to you at first when you look at the difference between Oriental and Western art. However, it is also true that, within each culture, as the culture changes, so the art will change—and that is why we can speak of periods of art. The changes are often reflected in the artists' techniques, subject matter, colors, and style. Major changes are often reflected in the forms of art that are produced." In the tour that follows, as the students look at paintings and sculpture, the guide points out to them the differences.

broad enough to encompass all the information that will follow. The function of advance organizers is to provide scaffolding or support for the new information. Textbooks often contain advance organizers—the chapter overviews in this book are examples. The organizers can serve three purposes: They direct your attention to what is important in the coming material; they highlight relationships among ideas that will be presented; and they remind you of relevant information you already have.

In general, advance organizers fall into one of two categories, *comparative* and *expository* (Joyce & Weil, 1996; Mayer, 1984). Each fulfills an important function. Comparative organizers *activate* (bring into working memory) already existing schemas. They remind you of what you already know, but may not realize is relevant. A comparative advance organizer for a history lesson on revolutions might be a statement that contrasts military uprisings with the physical and social changes involved in the Industrial Revolution; you could also compare the common aspects of the French, English, Mexican, Russian, Iranian, and American revolutions (Salomon & Perkins, 1989).

In contrast, *expository organizers* provide *new* knowledge that students will need to understand the upcoming information. An expository organizer is thus a statement of a subsumer, a definition of a general concept. In an English class, you might begin a large thematic unit on rites of passage in literature with a very broad statement of the theme and why it has been so central in literature—something like, "A central character coming of age must learn to know himself or herself, often makes some kind of journey of self-discovery, and must decide what in the society is to be accepted and what rejected."

The general conclusion of research on advance organizers is that they do help students learn, especially when the material to be learned is quite unfamiliar, complex, or difficult (Corkill, 1992; Mayer, 1984; Shuell, 1981b), if two conditions are met. First, to be effective, the organizer must be understood by the students. This was demonstrated dramatically in a study by Dinnel and Glover (1985). They found that instructing students to paraphrase an advance organizer—which, of course, requires them to understand its meaning—increased the effectiveness of the organizer.

Second, the organizer must really be an organizer: It must indicate relations among the basic concepts and terms that will be used. In other words, a true organizer isn't just a statement of historical or background information or an outline of the material. No amount of student processing can make a bad organizer more effective. Concrete models, diagrams, or analogies seem to be especially good organizers (Mayer 1983a, 1984).

Steps in an Expository Lesson. After presenting an advance organizer, the next step in a lesson using Ausubel's approach is to present content in terms of basic similarities and differences, using specific examples. To learn any new material, students must see not only the similarities between the material presented and what they already know but also the differences so that interference—the confusion of old and new material—can be avoided.

CHECKPOINT

Learning and Teaching about Concepts

Review

▶ Distinguish between prototypes and exemplars.

▶ What are the four elements needed in concept teaching?

▶ What are the key characteristics of Bruner's discovery learning?

▶ What are the stages of Ausubel's expository teaching?

Apply

▶ What are the defining attributes of the concept of "cup"? What attributes are irrelevant?

It is often helpful in an expository lesson to ask students to supply similarities and differences themselves. In a grammar lesson, you might ask, "What are the differences between the way commas and semicolons are used?" Or suppose in teaching the coming-of-age theme in literature, you choose *The Diary of Anne Frank* and *The Adventures of Huckleberry Finn* as the basic material for the unit. As the students read the first book, you might ask them to compare the central character's growth, state of mind, and position in society with characters from other novels, plays, and films. When the class moves on to the second book, you can start by asking students to compare Anne Frank's inner journey with Huck Finn's trip down the Mississippi. As comparisons are made, whether within a single class lesson or during an entire unit, it is useful to underscore the goal of the lesson and occasionally to repeat the advance organizer (with amendments and elaborations).

Along with the comparisons, specific examples must come into play. You can see that the best way to point out similarities and differences is with examples. There must be specific examples of comma and semicolon usage; the specific elements of Huck Finn's and Anne Frank's dilemmas must be clear. Finally, when all the material has been presented, ask students to discuss how the examples can be used to expand on the original advance organizer. The phases of expository teaching are summarized in Figure 8.4.

Expository teaching is more developmentally appropriate for students at or above later elementary school, that is, around the 5th or 6th grade (Luiten, Ames, & Ackerson, 1980). The Guidelines below should help you follow the main steps in expository teaching.

FIGURE 8.4

Phases of Expository Teaching

Advance organizer → Present content in terms of similarities and differences using specific examples → Relate content back to organizer

GUIDELINES

Applying Ausubel's Ideas

Use advance organizers.

Examples

1. English: Shakespeare used the social ideas of his time as a framework for his plays—*Julius Caesar*, *Hamlet*, and *Macbeth* dealt with concepts of natural order, a nation as the human body, etc.
2. Social studies: Geography dictates economy in preindustrialized regions or nations.
3. History: Important concepts during the Renaissance were symmetry, admiration of the classical world, the centrality of the human mind.

Use a number of examples.

Examples

1. In mathematics class, ask students to point out all the examples of right angles that they can find in the room.

2. In teaching about islands and peninsulas, use maps, slides, models, postcards.

Focus on both similarities and differences.

Examples

1. In a history class, ask students to list the ways in which the North and South were alike and different before the Civil War.
2. In a biology class, ask students how they would transform spiders into insects or an amphibian into a reptile.

$\mathcal{P}$roblem Solving

"Educational programs," Robert Gagné has written, "have the important ultimate purpose of teaching students to solve problems—mathematical and physical problems, health problems, social problems, and problems of personal adjustment" (1977, p. 177). A **problem** has an initial state—the current situation, a goal—the desired outcome, and a path for reaching the goal, including operations or activities that move you toward the goal. Problem solvers often have to set and reach subgoals as they move toward the final solution. For example, if your goal is to drive to the beach, but at the first stop sign you skid through the intersection, you may have to reach a subgoal of fixing your brakes before you can continue toward the original goal (Schunk, 2000). Also, problems can range from well-structured to ill-structured, depending on how clear-cut the goal is and how much structure is provided for solving the problem. Most arithmetic problems are well-structured but finding the right college major is ill-structured—many different solutions and paths to solutions are possible.

Problem solving is usually defined as formulating new answers, going beyond the simple application of previously learned rules to achieve a goal. Problem solving is what happens when no solution is obvious—when, for example, you can't afford new brakes for that car that skidded on the way to the beach (Mayer & Wittrock, 1996). Some psychologists suggest that most human learning involves problem solving (Anderson, 1993).

Connect and Extend
To history
You might want to note that, although interest in problem solving is great today, many of the early ideas of John Dewey are consistent with the recent emphasis on teaching students to be effective problem solvers.

Problem Solving: General or Domain-Specific?

There is an interesting debate about problem solving. Some psychologists believe that effective problem-solving strategies are specific to the problem area. That is, the problem-solving strategies in mathematics are unique to math, the strategies in art are unique to art, and so on. Becoming an expert problem solver in an area requires that you master the strategies of the area. The other side of the debate claims that there are some general problem-solving strategies that can be useful in many areas.

There is evidence for both sides of the argument. In fact, it appears that people move between general and specific approaches, depending on the situation and their level of expertise. Early on, when we know little about a problem area or domain, we may rely on general learning and problem-solving strategies to make sense of the situation. As we gain more domain-specific knowledge (particularly procedural knowledge about how to do things in the domain), we consciously apply the general strategies less; our problem solving becomes more automatic. But if we encounter a problem outside our current knowledge, we may return to relying on general strategies to attack the problem (Alexander, 1992, 1996; Perkins & Salomon, 1989; Shuell, 1990).

Let's consider general problem-solving strategies first. Think of a general problem-solving strategy as a beginning point, a broad outline. Such strategies usually have five stages (Derry, 1991; Derry & Murphy, 1986; Gallini, 1991; Gick, 1986). John Bransford and Barry Stein (1993) use the acronym IDEAL to identify the five steps:

Problem: Any situation in which you are trying to reach some goal and must find a means to do so.

Problem Solving: Creating new solutions for problems.

I   Identify problems and opportunities.

D   Define goals and represent the problem.

E   Explore possible strategies.

A   Anticipate outcomes and Act.

L   Look back and Learn.

We will examine each of these steps because they are found in many approaches to problem solving.

Identifying: Problem Finding

The first step, identifying that a problem exists and treating the problem as an opportunity, begins the process. This is not always straightforward. There is a story describing tenants who were angry about the slow elevators in their building. Consultants hired to "fix the problem" reported that the elevators were no worse than average and that improvements would be very expensive. Then one day, as the building supervisor watched people waiting impatiently for an elevator, he realized that the problem was not slow elevators but the fact that people were bored; they had nothing to do while they waited. When the boredom problem was identified and seen as an opportunity to improve the "waiting experience," the simple solution of installing a mirror by the elevator on each floor eliminated complaints.

Identifying the problem is a critical first step. Research indicates that people often hurry through this important step and "leap" to naming the first problem that comes to mind ("the elevators are too slow!"). Experts in a field are more likely to spend time carefully considering the nature of the problem (Bruning, Schraw, & Ronning, 1999). Finding a solvable problem and turning it into an opportunity is the process behind many successful inventions, such as the ball point pen, garbage disposal, appliance timer, alarm clock, self-cleaning oven, and thousands of others.

Once a solvable problem is identified, what next?

Defining Goals and Representing the Problem

Let's take a real problem: The machines designed to pick tomatoes are damaging the tomatoes. What to do? If we represent the problem as a faulty machine design, then the goal is to improve the machine. But if we represent the problem as a faulty design of the tomatoes, then the goal is to develop a tougher tomato. The problem-solving process follows two entirely different paths, depending on which representation and goal are chosen (Bransford & Stein, 1993). To represent the problem and set a goal, you have to focus attention on relevant information, understand the words of the problem, and activate the right *schema* to understand the whole problem.

Focusing Attention. Representing the problem often requires finding the relevant information and ignoring the irrelevant details. For example, consider the following problem adapted from Sternberg & Davidson (1982):

> If you have black socks and white socks in your drawer, mixed in the ratio of four to five, how many socks will you have to take out to make sure of having a pair the same color?

What information is relevant to solving this problem? Did you realize that the information about the four-to-five ratio of black socks to white socks is irrelevant? As long as you have only two different colors of socks in the drawer, you will have to remove only three socks before two of them have to match.

Understanding the Words. The second task in representing a story problem is **linguistic comprehension,** understanding the meaning of each sentence (Mayer, 1983a, b, 1992). Take, for example, the following sentence from an algebra story problem:

The riverboat's rate in still water is 12 miles per hour more than the rate of the river current.

This is a *relational proposition*. It describes the relationship between two rates, that of the riverboat and that of the current. Here is another sentence from a story problem:

The cost of the candy is $2.75 per pound.

This is an *assignment proposition*. It simply assigns a value to something, in this case the cost of one unit of candy. Research shows that relational propositions are harder to understand and remember than assignment propositions. If you misunderstand the meaning of individual statements in a problem, you will have a hard time representing the whole problem correctly and setting a goal.

The main stumbling block in representing many word problems is the students' understanding of *part-whole relations* (Cummins, 1991). Students have trouble figuring out what is part of what, as evident in this dialogue between a teacher and a 1st grader:

Teacher:	Pete has three apples. Ann also has some apples. Pete and Ann have nine apples altogether. How many apples does Ann have?
Student:	Nine.
Teacher:	Why?
Student:	Because you just said so.
Teacher:	Can you retell the story?
Student:	Pete had three apples. Ann also had some apples. Ann had nine apples. Pete also has nine apples. (Adapted from De Corte & Verschaffel, 1985, p. 19)

The student interprets "altogether" (the whole) as "each" (the parts).

Understanding the Whole Problem. The third task in representing a problem is to assemble all the relevant information and sentences into an accurate understanding or translation of the total problem. Even if you understand every sentence, you may still misunderstand the problem as a whole. Consider this example:

Two train stations are 50 miles apart. At 2 P.M. one Saturday afternoon two trains start toward each other, one from each station. Just as the trains pull out of the stations, a bird springs into the air in front of the first train and flies ahead to the front of the second train. When the bird reaches the second train it turns back and flies toward the first train. The bird continues to do this until the trains meet. If both trains travel at the rate of 25 miles per hour and the bird flies at 100 miles per hour, how many miles will the bird have flown before the trains meet? (Posner, 1973)

Your interpretation of the problem is called a *translation* because you translate the problem into a schema that you understand. If you translate this as a *distance*

Connect and Extend
To other chapters
Piaget (Chapter 2) identified children's difficulties with part-whole relations years ago when he asked questions such as, "There are six daisies and two daffodils; are there more daisies or flowers?" Young children usually answer, "Daisies!"

Linguistic Comprehension:
Understanding of the meaning of sentences in word problems.

problem and set a goal ("I have to figure out how far the bird travels before it meets the oncoming train and turns around, then how far it travels before it has to turn again, and finally add up all the trips back and forth . . ."), then you have a very difficult task on your hands. But there is a better way to structure the problem. You can represent it as a question of *time* and focus on the time the bird is in the air. The solution could be stated like this:

> The trains are going the same speed so they will meet in the middle, 25 miles from each station. This will take *one hour* because they are traveling 25 mph. In an hour, the bird will cover 100 miles because it is flying at 100 miles per hour. Easy!

Research shows that students can be too quick to decide what a problem is asking. The subjects in one study made their decisions about how to categorize standard algebra problems after reading only the first few sentences of a problem (Hinsley, Hayes, & Simon, 1977). Once a problem is categorized—"Aha, it's a distance problem!"—a particular schema is activated. The schema directs attention to relevant information and sets up expectations for what the right answer should look like (Robinson & Hayes, 1978).

When students do not have the necessary schemas to represent problems, they often rely on surface features of the situation and represent the problem incorrectly, as in the student who wrote "15 + 24 = 39" as the answer to the question, "Joan has 15 bonus points and Louise has 24. How many more does Louise have?" This student saw two numbers and the word "more," so he applied the *add to get more* procedure. When students use the wrong schema, they overlook critical information, use irrelevant information, and may even misread or misremember critical information so that it fits the schema. Errors in representing the problem and difficulties in solving it are the results. But when students use the proper schema for representing a problem, they are less likely to be confused by irrelevant information or tricky wording, such as *more* in a problem that really requires *subtraction* (Resnick, 1981). Figure 8.5 on page 294 gives examples of different ways students might represent a simple mathematics problem.

Translation and Schema Training. How can students improve translation and schema selection? To answer this question, we often have to move from general to area-specific problem-solving strategies because schemas are specific to content areas. In mathematics, for example, it appears that students benefit from seeing many different kinds of example problems worked out correctly for them. The common practice of showing students a few examples, then having students work many problems on their own, is less effective. Especially when problems are unfamiliar or difficult, worked-out examples are helpful (Cooper & Sweller, 1987). The most effective examples seem to be those that *do not* require students to integrate several sources of information, such as a diagram and a set of statements about the problem. This kind of attention splitting may put too much strain on the working memory. When students are learning, worked examples should deal with one source of information at a time (Marcus, Cooper, & Sweller, 1996). Ask students to compare examples. What is the same about each solution? What is different? Why? The same procedures may be effective in areas other than mathematics. Adrienne Lee and Laura Hutchinson (1998) found that undergraduate students learned more when they had examples of chemistry problem solutions that were annotated to show an expert problem solver's thinking at critical steps. Asking students to reflect on the examples helped too, so explanation and reflection can make worked examples more effective.

How else might students develop the schemas they will need to represent problems in a particular subject area? Mayer (1983b) has recommended giving students

FIGURE 8.5

Four Different Ways to Represent a Problem

A teacher asks, "How many wildlife stamps will Jane need to fill her book if there are three empty pages and each page holds 30 stamps?" The teacher gives the students supplies such as squared paper, number lines, and place-value frames and encourages them to think of as many ways as possible to solve the problem. Here are four different solutions, based on four different but correct representations:

JIM:
30
30
+30
90

JOE:

90 stamps

MARIAH:

tens	ones
I I I	
I I I	
I I I	

90 stamps

PHYLLIS:

30   30   30

90 stamps

Source: From *Essentials of Classroom Teaching: Elementary Mathematics* (pp. 123–124) by J. E. Schwartz and C. A. Riedesel, 1994, Boston: Allyn & Bacon. Copyright © 1994 by Allyn & Bacon. Reprinted by permission.

Connect and Extend
To your teaching
Guidelines for encouraging problem solving in children:

1. Provide problems, not just solutions.
2. Encourage viewing problems from different angles.
3. Make sure students have necessary background information.
4. Make sure students understand the problem.
   • Make accurate and useful representation
   • Math: ensure linguistic comprehension, use problem schemas
   • Understand through associations and analogies
5. Help students tackle the problem systematically.
   • Verbalize
   • Describe and compare
   • Practice with worked-out examples
   • Watch for "bugs" in math

practice in the following: (1) Recognizing and categorizing a variety of problem types; (2) representing problems—either concretely in pictures, symbols, or graphs, or in words; and (3) selecting relevant and irrelevant information in problems.

The Results of Problem Representation. There are two main outcomes of the problem representation stage of problem solving, as shown in Figure 8.6. If your representation of the problem suggests an immediate solution, your task is done. In the language of the cognitive scientist, you have activated the right schema and the solution is apparent because it is part of the schema. In one sense, you haven't really solved a new problem, you have simply recognized the new problem as a "disguised" version of an old problem that you already know how to solve. This has been called **schema-driven problem solving**, a kind of matching between the situation and your store of systems for dealing with different problems (Gick, 1986). In terms of Figure 8.6, you have taken the *schema-activated route* and have proceeded directly to a solution. But what if you have no existing way of solving the problem or if your activated schema fails? Time to search for a solution!

Exploring Possible Solution Strategies

If you do not have existing schemas that suggest an immediate solution, then you must take the *search-based route* indicated in Figure 8.6. Obviously, this path is not

Diagram of the Problem-Solving Process

There are two paths to a solution. In the first, the correct schema is activated and the solution is apparent. But if no schema is available, searching and testing may become the path to a solution.

Source: From "Problem-Solving Strategies," by M. L. Gick, 1986, *Educational Psychologist, 21,* p. 101. Copyright © 1986 by Lawrence Erlbaum Associates, Inc. Adapted with permission of the publisher and the author.

as efficient as activating the right schema, but sometimes it is the only way. In conducting your search for a solution, you have available two general kinds of procedures, algorithmic and heuristic.

Algorithms. An **algorithm** is a step-by-step prescription for achieving a goal. It usually is domain-specific; that is, it is tied to a particular subject area. In solving a problem, if you choose an appropriate algorithm and implement it properly, a right answer is guaranteed. Unfortunately, students often apply algorithms haphazardly. They try first this, then that. They may even happen on the right answer, but not understand how they found it. For some students, applying algorithms haphazardly could be an indication that formal operational thinking and the ability to work through a set of possibilities systematically, as described by Piaget, is not yet developed.

In math classes you probably experienced some success applying algorithms. As long as you were careful in your computations, you were able to solve even complicated problems. Later, if you were given geometry proofs to verify or equations to differentiate, you soon discovered that there were no algorithms guaranteeing a solution. At that point, if you did not learn some heuristics, you probably bailed out of math classes as soon as possible.

Heuristics. A **heuristic** is a general strategy that might lead to the right answer. Because many of life's problems (careers, relationships, etc.) are not straightforward and have ill-defined problem statements and no apparent algorithms, the discovery or development of effective heuristics is important. Let's examine a few.

In **means-ends analysis,** the problem is divided into a number of intermediate goals or subgoals and then a means of solving each is figured out. For example, writing a 20-page term paper can loom as an insurmountable problem for some students. They would be better off breaking this task into several intermediate goals, such as

Schema-Driven Problem Solving: Recognizing a problem as a "disguised" version of an old problem for which one already has a solution.

Algorithm: Step-by-step procedure for solving a problem; prescription for solutions.

Heuristic: General strategy used in attempting to solve problems.

Means-Ends Analysis: Heuristic in which a goal is divided into subgoals.

▲ *One of the advantages of having students work in groups in problem-solving situations is that they will be called on to explain their proposed solutions to one another. Putting solutions into words usually improves problem solving.*

Connect and Extend
To the research

Vosniadou, S., & Schommer, M. (1988). Explanatory analogies can help children acquire information from expository text. *Journal of Educational Psychology, 80,* 524–536. This article describes the results of an experiment in which analogies were used to help young children learn new information from science texts. For example, "an infection is like a war," "a stomach is like a blender," etc. Results showed that children in the analogy condition communicated more information than those in the control condition. Implication: Analogies can facilitate learning.

selecting a topic, locating sources of information, reading and organizing the information, making an outline, and so on. As they attack a particular intermediate goal, they may find that other goals arise. For example, locating information may require that they find someone to refresh their memory about using the library computer search system. Keep in mind that psychologists have yet to discover an effective heuristic for students who are just starting their term paper the night before it is due.

A second aspect of means-ends analysis is *distance reduction*, or pursuing a path that moves directly toward the final goal. People tend to look for the biggest difference between the current state of affairs and the goal and then search for a strategy that reduces the difference. We resist taking detours or making moves that are indirect as we search for the quickest way to reach the goal. So when you realize that reaching the goal of completing a term paper may require a detour of relearning the library computer search system, you may resist at first because you are not moving directly and quickly toward the final goal (Anderson, 1993).

Some problems lend themselves to a **working-backward strategy,** in which you begin at the goal and move back to the unsolved initial problem. Working backward is sometimes an effective heuristic for solving geometry proofs. It can also be a good way to set intermediate deadlines ("Let's see, if I have to submit this chapter in three weeks, then it has to be in the mail by the 28th, so I should have a first draft by the 11th").

Another useful heuristic is **analogical thinking** (Copi, 1961), which limits your search for solutions to situations that have something in common with the one you currently face. When submarines were first designed, for example, engineers had to figure out how battleships could determine the presence and location of vessels hidden in the depths of the sea. Studying how bats solve an analogous problem of navigating in the dark led to the invention of sonar.

Analogical reasoning can lead to faulty problem solving too. When they were first learning to use a word processor, some people used the analogy of the typewriter and failed to take advantage of the features of a computer. It seems that people need knowledge in both the problem domain and the analogy domain in order to use an analogy effectively (Gagné, Yekovich, & Yekovich, 1993).

Putting your problem-solving plan into words and giving reasons for selecting it can lead to successful problem solving (Cooper & Sweller, 1987; Lee & Hutchinson, 1998). You may have discovered the effectiveness of this **verbalization** process accidentally, when a solution popped into your head as you were explaining a problem to someone else. Gagné and Smith (1962) found that when 9th- and 10th-grade students were instructed to state a reason for each step they were taking, they were much more successful in solving the problem than students who did not state reasons.

Anticipating, Acting, and Looking Back

After representing the problem and exploring possible solutions, the next step is to select a solution and *anticipate the consequences*. For example, if you decide to solve the damaged tomato problem by developing a tougher tomato, how will consumers react? If you take time to learn a new graphics program to enhance your term paper (and your grade), will you still have enough time to finish the paper?

After you choose a solution strategy and implement it, evaluate the results by checking for evidence that confirms or contradicts your solution. Many people tend to stop working before reaching the best solution and simply accept an answer that works in some cases. In mathematical problems, evaluating the answer might mean applying a checking routine, such as adding to check the result of a subtraction problem or, in a long addition problem, adding the column from bottom to top instead of top to bottom. Another possibility is estimating the answer. For example, if the computation was 11×21, the answer should be around 200, since 10×20 is 200. A student who reaches an answer of 2,311 or 23 or 562 should quickly realize these cannot be correct. Estimating an answer is particularly important when students rely on calculators or computers, because they cannot go back and spot an error in the figures.

Factors That Hinder Problem Solving

Consider the following situation:

> You enter a room. There are two ropes suspended from the ceiling. You are asked by the experimenter to tie the two ends of the ropes together and assured that the task is possible. On a nearby table are a few tools, including a hammer and pliers. You grab the end of one of the ropes and walk toward the other rope. You immediately realize that you cannot possibly reach the end of the other rope. You try to extend your reach using the pliers but still cannot grasp the other rope. What can you do? (Maier, 1933)

Functional Fixedness. This problem can be solved by using an object in an unconventional way. If you tie the hammer or the pliers to the end of one rope and start swinging it like a pendulum, you will be able to catch it while you are standing across the room holding the other rope, as shown in Figure 8.7. You can use the weight of the tool to make the rope come to you instead of trying to stretch the rope. People often fail to solve this problem, because they seldom consider unconventional uses for materials that have a specific function. This difficulty is called **functional fixedness** (Duncker, 1945). Problem solving requires seeing things in new ways. In

Connect and Extend
To your teaching
A student was given the problem "Find the value of *x* and *y* that solves both equations":
$8x + 4y = 28$ $4x + 2y = 10$
The student quickly responded $x = 2$, $y = 3$, correctly addressing the first problem, but neglecting to check the solution on the second. How could you help the student be more reflective?

FIGURE 8.7

Overcoming Functional Fixedness
In the two-string problem, the subject must set one string in motion in order to tie both strings together.

Working-Backward Strategy: Heuristic in which one starts with the goal and moves backward to solve the problem.

Analogical Thinking: Heuristic in which one limits the search for solutions to situations that are similar to the one at hand.

Verbalization: Putting your problem-solving plan and its logic into words.

Functional Fixedness: Inability to use objects or tools in a new way.

Response Set: Rigidity; tendency to respond in the most familiar way.

Insight: Sudden realization of a solution.

your everyday life, you may often exhibit functional fixedness. Suppose a screw on a dresser-drawer handle is loose. Will you spend 10 minutes searching for a screwdriver? Or will you think to use another object not necessarily designed for this function, such as a ruler edge or a dime?

Response Set. Another block to effective problem solving is **response set.** Consider the following:

> In each of the four matchstick arrangements below, move only one stick to change the equation so that it represents a true equality such as V = V.
>
> $$V = VII \quad VI = XI \quad XII = VII \quad VI = II$$

You probably figured out how to solve the first example quite quickly. You simply move one matchstick from the right side over to the left to make VI = VI. Examples two and three can also be solved without too much difficulty by moving one stick to change the V to an X or vice versa. But the fourth example (taken from Raudsepp & Haugh, 1977) probably has you stumped. To solve this problem you must change your response set or switch schemas, because what has worked for the first three problems will not work this time. The answer here lies in changing from Roman numerals to Arabic numbers and using the concept of square root. By overcoming response set, you can move one matchstick from the right to the left to form the symbol for square root; the solution reads $\sqrt{1} = I$, which is simply the symbolic way of saying that the square root of 1 equals 1.

The Importance of Flexibility. Functional fixedness and response set point to the importance of flexibility in understanding problems. If you get started with an inaccurate or inefficient representation of the true problem, it will be difficult—or at least very time-consuming—to reach a solution (Wessells, 1982). Sometimes it is helpful to "play" with the problem. Ask yourself: "What do I know? What do I need to know to answer this question? Can I look at this problem in other ways?" Try to think conditionally rather than rigidly and divergently rather than convergently. Ask, "What could this be?" instead of "What is it?" (Benjafield, 1992).

If you open your mind to multiple possibilities, you may have what the Gestalt psychologists called an insight. **Insight** is the sudden reorganization or reconceptualization of a problem that clarifies the problem and suggests a feasible solution. The supervisor described earlier, who suddenly realized that the problem in his building was not slow elevators but impatient, bored tenants, had an insight that allowed him to reach the solution of installing mirrors by the elevators.

Effective Problem Solving: What Do the Experts Do?

Most psychologists agree that effective problem solving is based on an ample store of knowledge about the problem area. In order to solve the matchstick problem, for example, you had to understand Roman and Arabic numbers as well as the concept of square root. You also had to know that the square root of 1 is 1. Let's take a moment to examine this expert knowledge.

Expert Knowledge. The modern study of expertise began with investigations of chess masters (Simon & Chase, 1973). Results indicated that masters can quickly recognize about 50,000 different arrangements of chess pieces. They can look at one

Connect and Extend
To your teaching

The following five heuristics that might help students solve college math problems are from Schoenfeld, A. H. (1979). Explicit heuristic training as a variable in problem solving performance. *Journal for Research in Mathematics Education, 10,* 173–187.

1. Draw a diagram, if possible.

2. If the problem has an "N" that takes on integer values, try substituting numbers such as 1, then 2, then 3, then 4 for the "N," and look for a pattern in the results.

3. If you are trying to prove a statement, for example, "If X is true, then Y is true," try proving the contrapositive, "If X is false, then Y is false," or try assuming the statement you want to prove is false and look for a contradiction.

4. Try solving a similar problem with fewer variables.

5. Try to set up subgoals.

of these patterns for a few seconds and remember where every piece on the board was placed. It is as though they have a "vocabulary" of 50,000 patterns. Michelene Chi (1978) demonstrated that 3rd- through 8th-grade chess experts had a similar ability to remember chess piece arrangement. For all the masters, patterns of pieces are like words. If you were shown any word from your vocabulary store for just a few seconds, you would be able to remember every letter in the word in the right order (assuming you could spell the word).

But a series of letters arranged randomly is hard to remember, as you saw in Chapter 7. An analogous situation holds for chess masters. When chess pieces are placed on a board randomly, masters are no better than average players at remembering the positions of the pieces. The master's memory is for patterns that make sense or could occur in a game.

A similar phenomenon occurs in other fields. There may be an intuition about how to solve a problem based on recognizing patterns and knowing the "right moves" for those patterns. Experts in physics, for example, organize their knowledge around central principles, whereas beginners organize their smaller amounts of physics knowledge around the specific details stated in the problems. For instance, when asked to sort physics problems from a textbook in any way they wanted, novices sorted based on superficial features such as the kind of apparatus mentioned—a lever or a pulley—while the experts grouped problems according to the underlying physics principle needed to solve the problem, such as Boyle's or Newton's laws (Hardiman, Dufresne, & Mestre, 1989).

In addition to representing a problem very quickly, experts know what to do next. They have a large store of productions or condition-action schemas about what action to take in various situations. Thus, the steps of understanding the problem and choosing a solution happen simultaneously and fairly automatically (Ericsson & Smith, 1991). Of course, this means that they must have many, many schemas available. A large part of becoming an expert is simply acquiring a great store of *domain knowledge* or knowledge that is particular to a field (Alexander, 1992). To do this, you must encounter many different kinds of problems in that field, see problems solved by others, and practice solving many yourself. Some estimates are that it takes 10 years or 10,000 hours of study to become an expert in most fields (Simon, 1995).

Experts' rich store of knowledge is *elaborated* and *well practiced*, so that it is easy to retrieve from long-term memory when needed (Anderson, 1993). Experts can use their extensive knowledge to *organize* information for easier learning and retrieval. Compared to 4th-graders with little knowledge of soccer, 4th-graders who were soccer experts learned and remembered far more new soccer terms, even though the abilities of the two groups to learn and remember nonsoccer terms were the same. The soccer experts organized and clustered the soccer terms to aid in recall (Schneider & Bjorklund, 1992). Even very young children who are experts on a topic can use strategies to organize their knowledge. To get an example of the use of category knowledge about dinosaurs, I called my nephews, Lucas and Geoffrey (4 and 3 years old at the time), who promptly ran down the list of large and small plant- and meat-eating dinosaurs, from the well-known stegosaurus (large, plant eater) to the less familiar ceolophysis (small, meat eater).

With organization comes planning and monitoring. Experts spend more time analyzing problems, drawing diagrams, breaking large problems down into subproblems, and making plans. While a novice might begin immediately—writing equations for a physics problem or drafting the first paragraph of a paper, experts plan out the whole solution and often make the task simpler in the process. As they work, experts monitor progress, so time is not lost pursuing dead ends or weak ideas (Gagné et al., 1993).

Chi, Glaser, and Farr (1988) summarize the superior capabilities of experts. Experts (1) perceive large, meaningful patterns in given information, (2) perform tasks quickly and with few errors, (3) deal with problems at a deeper level, (4) hold more information in short- and long-term memories, (5) take a great deal of time to analyze a given problem, and (6) are better at monitoring their performance. When the area of problem solving is fairly well defined, such as chess or physics or computer programming, then these skills of expert problem solvers hold fairly consistently. But when the problem-solving area is less well-defined and has fewer clear underlying principles, such as problem solving in economics or psychology, then the differences between experts and novices are not as clear-cut (Alexander, 1992). The Guidelines give some ideas for helping students become expert problem solvers.

Expert Teachers. Studies of expert teachers identify many of the characteristics described above. Expert teachers have a sense of what is typical in classrooms, of what to expect during certain activities or times of the day. Many of their teaching routines have become automatic—they don't even have to think about how to distribute materials, take roll, move students in and out of groups, or assign grades. This gives the teachers more mental and physical energy for being creative and focusing on their students' progress. For example, one study found that expert math

GUIDELINES

Problem Solving

Ask students if they are sure they understand the problem.

Examples

1. Can they separate relevant from irrelevant information?
2. Are they aware of the assumptions they are making?
3. Encourage them to visualize the problem by diagramming or drawing it.
4. Ask them to explain the problem to someone else. What would a good solution look like?

Encourage attempts to see the problem from different angles.

Examples

1. Suggest several different possibilities yourself, and then ask students to offer some.
2. Give students practice in taking and defending different points of view on an issue.

Help students develop systematic ways of considering alternatives.

Examples

1. Think out loud as you solve problems.

2. Ask, "What would happen if . . . ?"
3. Keep a list of suggestions.

Teach heuristics.

Examples

1. Ask students to explain the steps they take as they solve problems.
2. Use analogies to solve the problem of limited parking in the downtown area. How are other "storage" problems solved?
3. Use the working backward strategy to plan a party.

Let students do the thinking; don't just hand them solutions.

Examples

1. Offer individual problems as well as group problems, so that each student has the chance to practice.
2. Give partial credit if students have good reasons for "wrong" solutions to problems.
3. If students are stuck, resist the temptation to give too many clues. Let them think about the problem overnight.

teachers could go over the previous day's work with the class in two or three minutes, compared to 15 minutes for novices (Leinhardt, 1986).

Expert teachers work from integrated sets of principles instead of dealing with each new event as a new problem. They look for patterns revealing similarities in situations that seem quite different at first glance. Experts focus more than beginners on analyzing a problem and mentally applying different principles to develop a solution. In one study of solutions to discipline problems, the expert teachers spent quite a bit of time framing each problem, forming questions, deciding what information was necessary, and considering alternatives (Swanson, O'Conner, & Cooney, 1990).

Expert teachers have a deep and well-organized knowledge of the subjects they teach. They can improvise explanations and create new examples on the spot. They can turn students' confusion into understanding by helping the students organize and expand on what they know. Expert teachers are not bound by their plans, but can follow the needs of the students (Borko & Livingston, 1989; Sabers, Cushing, & Berliner, 1991; Tochon & Munby, 1993). And, as we saw in Chapter 1, expert teachers also know a great deal about their students, the curriculum, teaching strategies, and ways to make the curriculum understandable and accessible to the students.

Novice Knowledge. Studies of the differences between experts and novices in particular areas have revealed some surprising things about how novices understand and misunderstand a subject. Physics again provides many examples. Most beginners approach physics with a great deal of misinformation, partly because many of their intuitive ideas about the physical world are wrong. Most elementary school children believe that light helps us see by brightening the area around objects. They do not realize that we see an object because the light is reflected by the object to our eyes. This concept does not fit with the everyday experience of turning on a light and "brightening" the dark area. Researchers from the Elementary Science Project at Michigan State University found that even after completing a unit on light in which materials explicitly stated the idea of reflected light and vision, most 5th-grade students— about 78%—continued to cling to their intuitive notions. But when new materials were designed that directly confronted the students' misconceptions, only about 20% of the students failed to understand (Eaton, Anderson, & Smith, 1984).

It seems quite important for science teachers to understand their students' intuitive models of basic concepts. If the students' intuitive model includes misconceptions and inaccuracies, then the students are likely to develop inadequate or misleading representations of a problem. (You should note that some researchers don't use the term "misconception," but refer to *naïve* or *intuitive conceptions* to describe students' beginning knowledge in an area.) In order to learn new information and solve problems, students must sometimes "unlearn" common sense ideas (Joshua & Dupin, 1987). Changing your intuitive ideas about concepts involves

Connect and Extend
To the research
Joshua, S., & Dupin, J. J. (1988). Taking into account student conceptions in instructional strategy: An example in physics. *Cognition and Instruction, 5,* 193–222.

Abstract: Several studies have emphasized the predominant influence of students' conceptions in the learning process in physics. But, more often than not, these conceptions are somehow considered in a negative way, as "errors." This article describes taking students' conceptions as an active basis for scientific reasoning in real class situations with groups approximately 12 and 14 years old.

The subject matter taught was basic electricity. The article shows how preinstruction conceptions were actually used (or not used) by the students to explain the electricity phenomena, and how these conceptions subsequently changed, increasing in internal consistency, without moving closer to scientific conceptions. Analogical explanation helped overcome this situation.

CHECKPOINT

Problem Solving

Review

▶ What are the steps in the general problem-solving process?

▶ Why is the representation stage of problem solving so important?

▶ Describe factors that can interfere with problem solving.

▶ What are the differences between expert and novice knowledge in a given area?

▶ How do misconceptions interfere with learning?

Apply

▶ What are some common misconceptions about being an expert?

Connect and Extend
To your teaching
Brainstorm about intuitive models in other fields besides science and mathematics. What are some common misconceptions about cultural differences, history, government, or educational psychology?

motivation too. Pintrich, Marx, and Boyle (1993) suggest that four conditions are necessary for people to change basic concepts: (1) Students have to be dissatisfied with the current concept; that is, their existing concept must be seen as inaccurate, incomplete, or not useful. (2) Students must understand the new concept. (3) The new concept must be plausible—it must fit in with what the students already know. (4) The new concept must be fruitful—it must be seen as useful in solving problems or answering questions.

*B*ecoming an Expert Student: Learning Strategies and Study Skills

Connect and Extend
To other chapters
The guidelines for study skills apply to everyone who wishes to become an expert learner and involve the metacognitive abilities and executive control processes discussed in Chapter 7.

As we saw in Chapter 7, the way something is learned in the first place greatly influences how readily we remember and how appropriately we can apply the knowledge later. First, students must be *cognitively engaged* in order to learn—they have to focus attention on the relevant or important aspects of the material. Second, they have to *invest effort*, make connections, elaborate, translate, organize, and reorganize in order to *think and process deeply*—the greater the practice and processing, the stronger the learning. Finally, students must *regulate and monitor* their own learning—keep track of what is making sense and notice when a new approach is needed. The emphasis today is on helping students develop effective learning strategies and tactics that *focus attention and effort, process information deeply, and monitor understanding*. Some students will develop good strategies for organizing and learning on their own, but most need help.

Learning Strategies and Tactics

Connect and Extend
To other chapters
See Chapter 7 for a discussion of declarative, procedural, and conditional knowledge.

Learning strategies are ideas for accomplishing learning goals, a kind of overall plan of attack. **Learning tactics** are the specific techniques that make up the plan (Derry, 1989). Your strategy for learning the material in this chapter might include the tactics of using mnemonics to remember key terms, skimming the chapter to identify the organization, and then writing answers to possible essay questions. Your use of strategies and tactics reflects metacognitive knowledge.

Fortunately, teaching these strategic skills has become a high priority in education, and several important principles have been identified.

Learning Strategies: General plans for approaching learning tasks.

Learning Tactics: Specific techniques for learning, such as using mnemonics or outlining a passage.

1. Students must be exposed to a number of *different strategies*, not only general learning strategies but also very specific tactics, such as the graphic strategies described later in this chapter.

2. Students should be taught *conditional knowledge* about when, where, and why to use various strategies (Pressley, 1986). Although this may seem obvious, teachers often neglect this step, either because they do not realize its significance or because they assume students will make inferences on their own. A strategy is more likely to be maintained and employed if students know when, where, and why to use it.

3. Students may know when and how to use a strategy, but unless they also *develop the desire to employ these skills*, general learning ability will not improve. Several learning strategy programs (Borkowski, Johnston, & Reid, 1986; Dansereau, 1985) include a motivational training component. In Chapters 10 and 11 we look more closely at this important issue of motivation.

TABLE 8.2 *Examples of Learning Tactics*

	Examples	Use When?
Tactics for Learning Verbal Information	1. Attention Focusing	
	• Making outlines, underlining	With easy, structured materials; for good readers
	• Looking for headings and topic sentences	For poorer readers; with more difficult materials
	2. Schema Building	
	• Story grammars	With poor text structure, goal is to encourage active comprehension
	• Theory schemas	
	• Networking and mapping	
	3. Idea Elaboration	
	• Self-questioning	To understand and remember specific ideas
	• Imagery	
Tactics for Learning Procedural Information	1. Pattern Learning	
	• Hypothesizing	To learn attributes of concepts
	• Identifying reasons for actions	To match procedures to situations
	2. Self-instruction	
	• Comparing own performance to expert model	To tune, improve complex skills
	3. Practice	
	• Part practice	When few specific aspects of a performance need attention
	• Whole practice	To maintain and improve skill

Source: Based on "Putting Learning Strategies to Work," by S. Derry, 1989, *Educational Leadership, 47*(5), pp. 5–6.

4. *Direct instruction in schematic knowledge* is often an important component of strategy training. In order to identify main ideas—a critical skill for a number of learning strategies—you must have an appropriate schema for making sense of the material. Table 8.2 summarizes several tactics for learning declarative (verbal) knowledge and procedural skills (Derry, 1989).

Deciding What Is Important. You can see from the first entry in Table 8.2, that learning begins with focusing attention—deciding what is important. But distinguishing the main idea from less important information is not always easy. Often students focus on the "seductive details" or the concrete examples, perhaps because they are more interesting (Dole, Duffy, Roehler, & Pearson, 1991; Gardner, Brown, Sanders, & Menke, 1992). You may have had the experience of remembering a joke or an intriguing example from a lecture, but not being clear about the larger point the professor was trying to make. Finding the central idea is especially difficult if you lack prior knowledge in an area and the amount of new information provided is extensive. Teachers can give students practice using signals in texts such as headings, bold words, outlines, or other indicators to identify key concepts and main ideas. Teaching students to summarize material can be helpful too.

Summaries. Creating summaries can help students learn, but students have to be taught how to summarize (Byrnes, 1996; Dole et al., 1991; Palincsar & Brown, 1984). Jeanne Ormrod (1999, p. 333) summarizes these suggestions for helping students create summaries:

▶ Begin doing summaries of short, easy, well-organized readings. Introduce longer, less organized, and more difficult passages gradually.

▶ For each summary, ask students to
  • find or write a *topic sentence* for each paragraph or section,
  • identify *big ideas* that cover several specific points,
  • find some *supporting information* for each big idea, and
  • delete any *redundant information* or unnecessary details.

▶ Ask students to compare their summaries and discuss what ideas they thought were important and why—what's their evidence?

Two other study strategies that are based on identifying key ideas are *underlining* texts and *taking notes*.

Underlining and Highlighting.

Do you underline or highlight key phrases in textbooks? Are my words turning yellow or pink at this very moment? What about outlining or taking notes? Underlining and note taking are probably two of the most commonly used strategies among college students. Yet few students receive any instruction in the best ways to take notes or underline, so it is not surprising that many students use ineffective strategies.

One common problem is that students underline or highlight too much. It is far better to be selective. In studies that limit how much students can underline—for example, only one sentence per paragraph—learning has improved (Snowman, 1984). In addition to being selective, you also should actively transform the information into your own words as you underline or take notes. Don't rely on the words of the book. Note connections between what you are reading and other things you already know. Draw diagrams to illustrate relationships. Finally, look for organizational patterns in the material and use them to guide your underlining or note taking (Irwin, 1991; Kiewra, 1988).

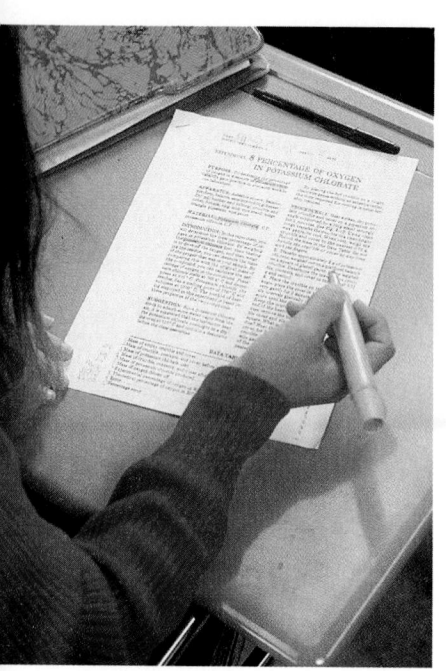

▲ *One common problem students have in studying is underlining or highlighting too much. Studies that limit how much students are allowed to highlight correlate this strategy with higher learning.*

Taking Notes.

As you sit in class, filling your notebook with words or furiously trying to keep up with a lecturer, you may wonder if taking notes makes a difference. The answer appears to be yes—taking notes serves at least two important functions:

▶ Taking notes focuses attention during class and helps encode information so it has a chance of making it to long-term memory. In order to record key ideas in your own words, you have to translate, connect, elaborate, and organize. Even if students don't review notes before a test, taking them in the first place appears to aid learning, especially for those who lack prior knowledge in an area. Of course, if taking notes distracts you from actually listening to and making sense of the lecture, then note taking may not be effective (DiVesta & Gray, 1972, Kiewra, 1989; van Meter, Yokoi, & Pressley, 1994).

▶ Notes provide extended external storage that allows you to return and review. Students who use their notes to study tend to perform better on tests, especially if they take many high quality notes—more is better as long as you are capturing *key ideas*, *concepts*, and *relationships*, not just intriguing details (Kiewra, 1985, 1989).

In an extensive interview study of 252 college students, Peggy van Meter, Linda Yokoi, and Mike Pressley (1994) concluded that understanding is served when students use note taking to focus attention on important ideas and construct a representation in the notes that reflects the organization of the lecture. As the course progresses, the expert student matches notes to their anticipated use and makes modifications in strategies after tests or assignments; uses personal codes to flag material that is unfamiliar or difficult; fills in holes by consulting relevant sources (including other students in the class); records information verbatim only when a verbatim response will be required; and generally is strategic about taking and using notes.

To help students organize their note taking, some teachers provide matrices or maps, such as the one in Figure 8.8. When students are first learning to use these maps, you might fill in some of the spaces for them. If you use maps and matrices with your students, you might encourage them to exchange their filled-in maps and explain their thinking to each other.

Connect and Extend

To your teaching

Weinstein, C., Ridley, D. S., Dahl, T., & Weber, E. S. (1988/1989). Helping students develop strategies for effective learning. *Educational Leadership, 46*(4), 17–19.

The authors give many examples of elaboration strategies.

What is the main idea of this story?

If this principle were not true, what would that imply?

What does this remind me of?

How could I use this information in the project I am working on?

How could I represent this in a diagram?

How do I feel about the author's opinion?

How could I put this in my own words?

What might be an example of this?

If I were going to interview the author, what would I ask her?

How does this apply to my life?

FIGURE 8.8

A Map to Guide Note Taking

The compare/contrast map below allows students to organize their listening or reading as they consider two ideas, concepts, time periods, authors, experiments, theories, and so on.

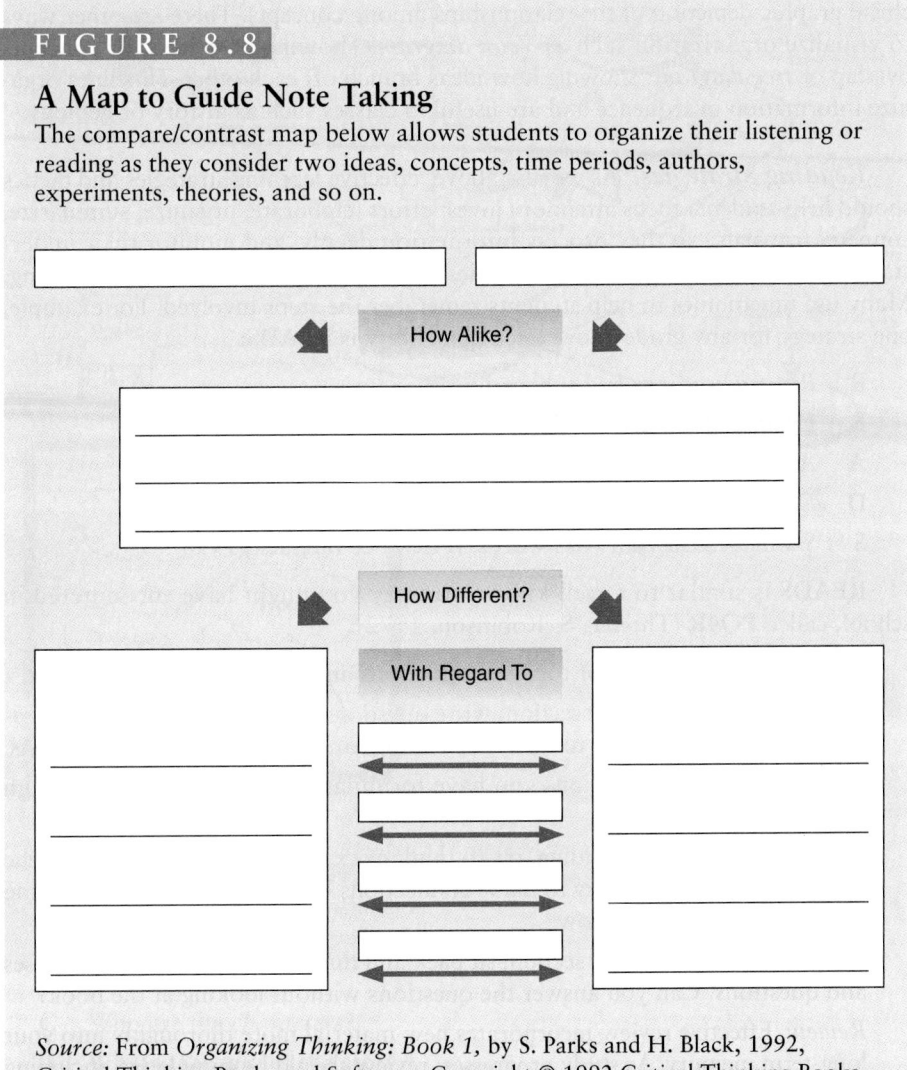

Source: From *Organizing Thinking: Book 1,* by S. Parks and H. Black, 1992, Critical Thinking Books and Software. Copyright © 1992 Critical Thinking Books and Software. Reprinted with permission.

A challenge for all learners and educators is to be sure that knowledge acquired in school will be applicable to real-life situations or problems. ▶

What Is Worth Learning? First you must answer the question "What is worth learning?" The learning of basic skills such as reading, writing, computing, cooperating, and speaking will definitely transfer to other situations, because these skills are necessary for later work both in and out of school—writing job applications, reading novels, paying bills, working on a team, locating and evaluating health care services, among others. All later learning depends on positive transfer of these basics to new situations.

Teachers must also be aware of what the future is likely to hold for their students, both as a group and as individuals. What will society require of them as adults? As a child growing up in Texas in the 1950s and 1960s, I studied nothing about computers, even though my father was a computer systems analyst; yet now I spend hours at my Mac. Computer programming and word processing were not part of my high school curriculum, but learning to use a slide rule was taught. Now calculators and computers have made this skill obsolete. Undoubtedly changes as extreme and unpredictable as these await the students you will teach. For this reason, the general transfer of principles, attitudes, learning strategies, and problem solving will be just as important to these students as the specific transfer of basic skills.

How Can Teachers Help? To have something to transfer, students must first learn and understand. Students will be more likely to transfer information to new situations if they have been actively involved in the learning process. They must be encouraged to form abstractions that they will apply later. For example, Salomon and Perkins (1989) give this advice for teaching history:

> [The] history teacher can introduce direct discussion of contemporary events. To provoke forward-reaching transfer, the teacher can select an episode in history and encourage students to seek contemporary analogs. To provoke backward-

ing concepts that asks students to form hypotheses about why particular examples are members of a category and what that category (concept) might be.

What are the key characteristics of Bruner's discovery learning?

In discovery learning, the teacher presents examples and the students work with the examples until they discover the interrelationships—the subject's structure. Bruner believes that classroom learning should take place through inductive reasoning, that is, by using specific examples to formulate a general principle. Encouraging inductive thinking in this way is sometimes called the eg-rule method.

What are the stages of Ausubel's expository teaching?

Ausubel believes that learning should progress deductively: from the general to the specific, or from the rule or principle to examples. After presenting an advance organizer, the next step in a lesson using Ausubel's approach is to present content in terms of basic similarities and differences, using specific examples. Finally, when all the material has been presented, ask students to discuss how the examples can be used to expand on the original advance organizer.

Problem Solving

What are the steps in the general problem-solving process?

Problem solving is both general and domain-specific. The five stages of problem solving are: identifying the problem (and perhaps seeing the problem as an opportunity); understanding the problem through representation and setting goals; exploring possible solutions; anticipating possible consequences of the strategies and then implementing one strategy; and evaluating the results and learning from the results. Bransford and Stein use the acronym IDEAL to identify

the five steps: Identify the problem, Define goals and represent the problem, Explore possible strategies, Anticipate outcomes and Act, Look back and Learn.

Why is the representation stage of problem solving so important?

A critical element in solving problems in school is representing the problem accurately, showing understanding of both the whole problem and its discrete elements. Schema training may improve this ability. The problem-solving process follows entirely different paths, depending on what representation and goal are chosen. If your representation of the problem suggests an immediate solution, the task is done, the new problem is recognized as a "disguised" version of an old problem with a clear solution. But if there is no existing way of solving the problem or if the activated schema fails, then students must search for a solution. The application of algorithms and heuristics—such as means-ends analysis, analogical thinking, working backward, and verbalization—may help students solve problems.

Describe factors that can interfere with problem solving.

Factors that hinder problem solving include functional fixedness or rigidity (response set). These disallow the flexibility needed to represent problems accurately and to have insight into solutions.

What are the differences between expert and novice knowledge in a given area?

Expert problem solvers have a rich store of declarative, procedural, and conditional knowledge. They organize this knowledge around general principles or patterns that apply to large classes of problems. They work faster, remember relevant information, and monitor their progress better than novices. The same is true for expert teachers. Accomplishing many class-

room tasks has become automatic, so that routines are smooth. Less class time is wasted. Experts have a rich store of well-organized knowledge about the many specific situations of teaching.

How do misconceptions interfere with learning?

If the students' intuitive model includes misconceptions and inaccuracies, then the students are likely to develop inadequate or misleading representations of a problem. In order to learn new information and solve problems, students must sometimes "unlearn" common sense ideas.

Becoming an Expert Student: Learning Strategies and Study Skills

Distinguish between learning strategies and tactics.

Learning strategies are ideas for accomplishing learning goals, a kind of overall plan of attack. Learning tactics are the specific techniques that make up the plan. A strategy for learning might include several tactics such as mnemonics to remember key terms, skimming to identify the organization, and then writing answers to possible essay questions. Use of strategies and tactics reflects metacognitive knowledge.

What key functions do learning strategies play?

Learning strategies help students *become cognitively engaged*—focus attention on the relevant or important aspects of the material. Second, they encourage students to *invest effort*, make connections, elaborate, translate, organize, and reorganize in order to *think and process deeply*—the greater the practice and processing, the stronger the learning. Finally, strategies help students *regulate and monitor* their own learning—keep track of what is making sense and notice when a new approach is needed.

Describe some procedures for developing learning strategies.

Expose students to a number of different strategies, not only general learning strategies but also very specific tactics, such as the graphic strategies. Teach conditional knowledge about when, where, and why to use various strategies. Develop motivation to use the strategies and tactics by showing students how their learning and performance can be improved. Provide direct instruction in content knowledge needed to use the strategies.

Teaching for Transfer

Distinguish between specific and general transfer.

Specific transfer occurs when a rule, fact, or skill learned in one situation is applied in another, very similar situation; for example, applying rules of punctuation to write a job application letter. General transfer involves applying to new problems the principles and attitudes learned in other, often dissimilar situations.

Distinguish between low-road and high-road transfer.

Transfer involving spontaneity and automaticity in familiar situations has been called low-road transfer. High-road transfer involves reflection and conscious application of abstract knowledge to new situations. Teachers can promote thinking and learning skills by teaching for mastery and for the positive, general transfer of knowledge. In addition, teachers can help students transfer learning strategies by teaching strategies directly, providing practice with feedback, and then expanding the application of the strategies to new and unfamiliar situations.

Key Terms

Becoming a Professional

Reflecting on the Chapter

Can you apply the ideas from this chapter on complex cognitive processes to solve the following problems of practice?

Preschool and Kindergarten

- Several students in your class still have trouble discriminating between simple shapes. What would you do to help them understand?

Elementary and Middle School

- Students in your class are having a really hard time with the concepts of heat and energy. What would you do?

Junior High and High School

- Students in your math class can solve problems for homework, but get confused on tests that cover several chapters. They don't seem to know when to apply one procedure and when to use another. How would you help them?

- You decide to give an essay test that requires original thinking and creativity. Your students perform very badly and protest loudly that the test is "unfair." They want to use the definitions and facts they have so carefully memorized. What would you do?

Certification Test Requirements

- Know the basic features of concept teaching.

- Know the five common steps in problem solving.

- Be familiar with the notion of intuitive or naïve conceptions.

- Be familiar with a range of learning strategies and tactics.

Your Teaching Portfolio

Use Table 8.2 plus the section titled *Learning Strategies and Tactics* to generate ideas for appropriate learning strategies and tactics for the students you will teach and include these ideas in your **Portfolio**.

Teaching Resources

Add Figures 8.5 "Four Different Ways to Represent a Problem," 8.8 "A Map To Guide Note Taking," 8.9 "A Map to Organize Studying and Learning," and Table 8.2 to your file of **Teaching Resources**.

Use the Family and Community Partnerships Guidelines to brainstorm ideas for family involvement in helping your students "take their learning home."

What Would They Do?

Here is how some practicing teachers responded to the teaching situation presented at the beginning of this chapter about a discovery lesson that went wrong.

MARIA CIRMIA

Fifth Grade Teacher
Hillside School, Needham, Massachusetts

This is a struggle many teachers have had to face. Often, we wonder where we went wrong. Although it's important for teachers to consider improvements that could be made to any lesson, it is not necessary for them to do this alone. What I have found to be most beneficial is to involve my students in this process as well. It is important for them to know that I am a student and learner just like them, constantly striving to improve on my teaching practices and the curriculum I have to teach.

I would hand back the graded lessons and projects and would encourage my students to discuss with me in an open forum how they feel they did on their finished projects. I am always honest about their performance and achievements and urge them to reflect on their own efforts, difficulties, and feelings of success. I would let them know that I am questioning the assignment itself and need their help to improve on it for future classes. In a way, they are the best source for this information because they experienced the assignment firsthand.

We would discuss how the lesson could be approached differently and if directions, criteria, and expectations were clear enough to follow. This is their opportunity to help me rewrite the assignment. It's also a way to model self-evaluation, which is an important tool for students and teachers to utilize, because it aids in the learning process, helps build on prior knowledge, and enables us to move forward in our work. Many students will want the opportunity to redo the assignment because of their personal investment. They'll be more productive and will have a healthier attitude toward their own learning.

JAN ANDREWS

Teaching Principal, Years Four–Seven
Dulacca State School, Dulacca QLD 4255, Australia

I do not believe that the failure of the lesson could be the fault of the science book but that the approach was new to the students and they were unable to adapt themselves to it successfully. The projects would not be marked but handed back to the students. Those who "got it" would have their projects and journals used as examples. I would explain to the students the process that I had intended them to go through and what I expected them to "discover." Then I would take the class through simple exercises that would help them when next participating in a discovery lesson (e.g., brainstorming, how to question what you see, how to draw conclusions, how to write up what you've discovered, working as a group, and some "guided" discovery lessons). Finally I would implement another discovery lesson and use the projects and journals from that to grade the students.

KATE McMENEMY

Fifth Grade Teacher
St. Ignatius Primary School, Grove Crescent, Toowong, Australia

Many aspects of this lesson could have contributed to students' poor reports.

A. With a graded report as an outcome, one lesson (particularly a discovery lesson) is not adequate. Guided discovery would be more effective. I have found that the students' excitement in being involved in a scientific experiment overpowers their interest in sticking to the procedure.

B. It may well be that the students were not skilled in group work. My students need to display adequate signs of social skills, cooperation, teamwork, and interest in working as a group before I consider using this form of learning. Then they are given practice in group roles and group processes.

C. Rather than marking the projects, I would consider an apology for my lack of leadership and hence their lack of success. Following proper preparation they would repeat the experiment with myself now knowing they are aware of the procedures both in science experiments and in teamwork.

WENDY MEREFIELD-WARD

Teacher-Librarian
Payne Road State School, The Gap QLD 4061, Australia

1. Why was it so unsuccessful? I would ask myself the following questions:
   - ▶ Did I clearly and concisely communicate what I wanted to all of the students?
   - ▶ Did the students have enough experience with group work to cope with the task?
   - ▶ Were the groups effective in size and composition?
   - ▶ Did the tasks include a variety of learning experiences to cater to differing learning styles?
   - ▶ Were the students given enough time and resources to complete the task?
   - ▶ Was the task interesting and relevant?

   Find the negatives in the answers and address them.
2. What should we do with the projects?
   - ▶ The unsuccessful projects could be shared as a problem—let's solve them together.
   - ▶ We could view the projects as part of the process, not the end product.
   - ▶ We could ask the "successful" students to explain how they put it all together—sometimes children can communicate with their age group more effectively than the teacher can.
3. For future productivity:
   - ▶ Build your knowledge of the students—their abilities, experiences, and learning styles.
   - ▶ Incorporate an "multiple intelligences" approach to provide a variety of learning experiences.
   - ▶ Plan the task and the groups so that members will be compatible and use their different abilities.
   - ▶ Keep the tasks relevant to the students.

JENNIFER HUDSON THOMAS

Armidale High School, Armidale, Australia

It is fairly obvious that the science material that I chose did not engage the learners, no matter how well it was researched, presented, and taught. It would seem that it was fairly purposeless learning for this group of students. How discouraging! Maybe it is time to negotiate with the class the science topics that they are interested in pursuing. With choice and ownership for their learning on their side, meaningful and productive units of work could then be developed. Following the successful completion of a number of student-chosen science topics, my confidence and that of the students may allow a return to the more abstract and challenging learning required to understand magnetism.

Social Cognitive and Constructivist Views of Learning

hat have you heard about cognitive apprenticeships? Inquiry? Cooperative learning? Reciprocal teaching? What comes to mind when you hear these terms?

For the past three chapters we have analyzed different aspects of learning. We considered behavioral and information processing explanations of what people learn and how they learn it. We have examined complex cognitive processes such as concept learning and problem solving. These explanations of learning focus on the individual and what is happening in his or her "head." But recent perspectives on learning have called attention to two other aspects of learning that are critical—social and cultural factors. In this chapter we look at the role of other people and the cultural context in learning.

Two general theoretical frames include social and cultural factors as major elements: social learning/social cognitive views and sociocultural constructivist theories. Rather than debating the merits of each approach, we will consider the contributions of different models of instruction, grounded in different theories of learning. Don't feel that you must choose the "best" approach—there is no such thing. The goal of all the different models is to create situations in which students learn, understand, and remember. Even though theorists argue about which model is best, most excellent teachers learn from all the approaches and apply them as appropriate.

By the time you have completed this chapter, you should be able to:

► Summarize the elements of social cognitive theory.
► Describe situations in which a teacher might use modeling.
► Explain three constructivist perspectives on learning.
► Incorporate inquiry, problem based-learning, and cooperative groups into your teaching.
► Design lessons that include instructional conversations and apprenticeships in thinking.

What Would You Do?

You have finally landed a job teaching English and writing in a high school. Over the summer, you plan your World Literature course, pick books you really enjoyed in high school, and add some new selections that relate to recent films. The first day of class, you discover that a number of students appear to have limited English proficiency. You make a mental note to meet with them to determine how much and what kind of reading they can handle. To get a sense of the class's interest, you ask them to write a "review" of the last book they read, as if they were on TV doing a "Book Beat" program. There is a bit of grumbling, but the students seem to be writing, so you take a few minutes to try to talk with one of the students who has trouble with English.

That night you look over the "book reviews." Either the students are giving you a hard time, or no one has read anything lately. Two students try to write about the Bible, but they refuse to "review" it. Several mention a text from another class, but their reviews are one sentence evaluations—usually containing the words "lame" or "useless" (often misspelled). If the paragraphs are any indication, these students can't put four sentences together and stay on the same topic. In stark contrast are the papers of three students—they are a pleasure to read, worthy of publication in the school literary magazine (if there were one), and reflect a fairly sophisticated understanding of some good literature.

▶ How would you adapt your plans for this group?

▶ What will you do tomorrow?

▶ What teaching approaches do you think will work with this class?

▶ How will you work with the three students who are more advanced?

Social Processes in Learning

When you consider the English class above, do you think about social and cultural influences on the students' learning? Reading and books seem to have very different meanings for various students in the class. And the students probably have seen different models of reading in their lives outside school. In the following pages we will discuss how people learn through interactions with others and how observation, modeling, dialogue, and culture affect learning. Understanding the role of social processes in learning has become increasingly important in educational psychology. As Carol Goodenow (1992) noted almost a decade ago:

> Education is fundamentally a social and interpersonal process. Although individuals can and do learn many things through isolated observation of the world around them, personal experimentation and experience, and solitary reading, for the most part what we term education (i.e., "schooling") occurs in the company of others. (p. 177)

The first perspective we will examine that adds social considerations to an explanation of learning is the work of Albert Bandura (1977, 1986, 1997). In the early 1960s he demonstrated that people can learn by observing the actions and consequences of others.

Social Learning Theory: Theory that emphasizes learning through observation of others.

Social Cognitive Theory: Theory that adds concern with cognitive factors such as beliefs, self-perceptions, and expectations to social learning theory.

Social Learning and Social Cognitive Theories

In Chapter 6 we discussed behavioral views of learning. Bandura's early work on learning was grounded in behavioral principles of reinforcement and punishment. But Bandura challenged and expanded behavioral conceptions of learning by adding social factors. He believed that the traditional behavioral views of learning were accurate—but incomplete. Behavioral views give only a partial explanation of learning and overlook important elements, particularly the social influences on learning. Bandura's early work focused on social *behaviors*, particularly the behaviors of others. For this reason, the earlier work was labeled **social learning theory** and was considered a *neobehavioral* approach (Bandura, 1977).

To explain some limitations of the behavioral model, Bandura distinguishes between the *acquisition of knowledge* (learning) and the *observable performance based on that knowledge* (behavior). In other words, Bandura suggests that we all may know more than we show. An example is found in one of Bandura's early studies (1965). Preschool children saw a film of a model kicking and punching an inflatable "Bobo" doll. One group saw the model rewarded for the aggression, another group saw the model punished, and a third group saw no consequences. When they were moved to a room with the doll, the children who had seen the punching and kicking reinforced on the film were the most aggressive toward the doll. Those who had seen the attacks punished were the least aggressive. But when the children were promised rewards for imitating the model's aggression, all of them demonstrated that they had learned the behavior. Thus incentives can affect performance. Even though learning may have occurred, it may not be demonstrated until the situation is right or there are incentives to perform. This might explain why some students don't perform the "bad behaviors" such as swearing or smoking that they all see modeled by their peers. For these students, personal consequences may discourage performing the behaviors. Also, children may have learned how to write the alphabet, but perform badly because their limited fine motor coordination makes neat writing impossible—their performance is not an indication of their learning. Students may have learned how to simplify fractions, but perform badly on a test because they are anxious or ill or have misread the problem.

Recently, Bandura has focused on cognitive factors such as beliefs, self-perceptions, and expectations, so his theory is now called a **social cognitive theory.** Social cognitive theory distinguishes between enactive and vicarious learning. *Enactive learning* is learning by doing and experiencing the consequences of your actions. This may sound like operant conditioning all over again, but it is not, and the difference has to do with the role of consequences. Proponents of operant conditioning believe that consequences strengthen or weaken behavior. In enactive learning, however, consequences are seen as providing information. Our interpretations of the consequences create expectations, influence motivation, and shape beliefs (Schunk, 2000). We will see many examples of enactive learning—learning by doing—later in the chapter when we consider inquiry, problem-based learning, cognitive apprenticeships, and other approaches.

Vicarious learning is learning by observing others. People and animals can learn merely by observing another person or animal learn, and this fact challenges the behaviorist idea that cognitive factors are unnecessary in an explanation of learning. If people can learn by watching, they must be focusing their attention, constructing

▲ *Albert Bandura expanded on behavioral theories to develop the social cognitive theory of learning.*

images, remembering, analyzing, and making decisions that affect learning. Thus much is going on mentally before performance and reinforcement can even take place.

One important factor in both the earlier and the more recent versions of Bandura's theory is the role of observation in learning.

Connect and Extend
To real life
Other examples of learning through observation include: learning how to kiss by watching TV and movies; avoiding air travel after witnessing a plane wreck; cheating on a test after seeing someone else cheat without getting caught.

Learning by Observing Others

Through **observational learning** we learn not only how to perform a behavior but also what will happen to us in specific situations if we do perform it. Observation can be a very efficient learning process. The first time children hold hairbrushes, cups, or tennis rackets, they usually brush, drink, or swing as well as they can, given their current muscle development and coordination. Let's take a closer look at how observational learning occurs. Bandura (1986) notes that there are four important elements to be considered in observational learning. They are *paying attention, retaining information or impressions, producing behaviors,* and *being motivated* to repeat the behaviors.

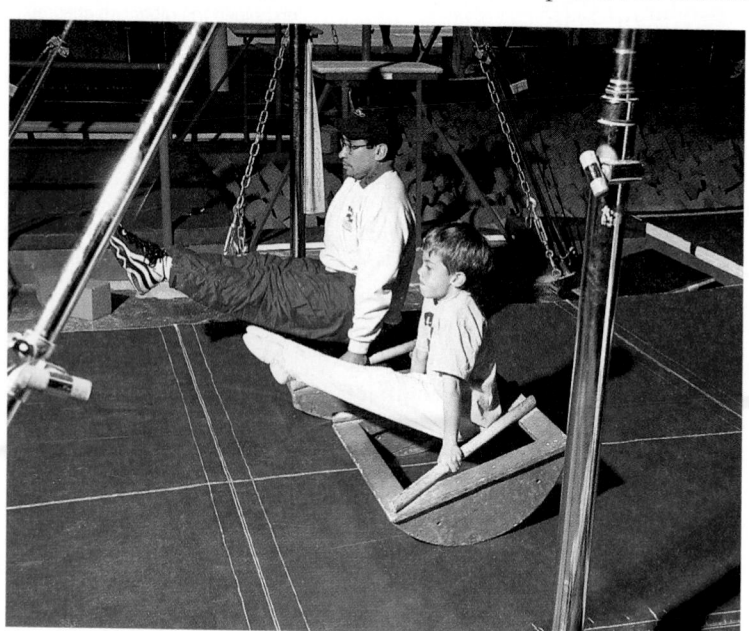

▲ *Social cognitive theories of learning consider the importance of learning by doing and learning by observing others.*

Attention. In order to learn through observation, we have to pay attention. In teaching, you will have to ensure students' attention to the critical features of the lesson by making clear presentations and highlighting important points. In demonstrating a skill (for example, threading a sewing machine or operating a lathe), you may need to have students look over your shoulder as you work. Seeing your hands from the same perspective as they see their own directs their attention to the right features of the situation and makes observational learning easier.

Retention. In order to imitate the behavior of a model, you have to remember it. This involves mentally representing the model's actions in some way, probably as verbal steps ("Hwa-Rang, the eighth form in Tae Kwan Do karate, is a palm-heel block, then a middle riding stance punch, then . . ."), or as visual images, or both. Retention can be improved by mental rehearsal (imagining imitating the behavior) or by actual practice. In the retention phase of observational learning, practice helps us remember the elements of the desired behavior, such as the sequence of steps.

Production. Once we "know" how a behavior should look and remember the elements or steps, we still may not perform it smoothly. Sometimes we need a great deal of practice, feedback, and coaching about subtle points before we can reproduce the behavior of the model. In the production phase, practice makes the behavior smoother and more expert.

Motivation and Reinforcement. As mentioned earlier, social learning theory distinguishes between acquisition and performance. We may acquire a new skill or behavior through observation, but we may not perform that behavior until there is

Observational Learning: Learning by observation and imitation of others.

some motivation or incentive to do so. Reinforcement can play several roles in observational learning. If we anticipate being reinforced for imitating the actions of a model, we may be more motivated to pay attention, remember, and reproduce the behaviors. In addition, reinforcement is important in maintaining learning. A person who tries a new behavior is unlikely to persist without reinforcement (Barton, 1981; Ollendick, Dailey, & Shapiro, 1983). For example, if an unpopular student adopted the dress of the "in" group but was greeted with teasing and ridicule, it is unlikely that the imitation would continue.

Bandura identifies three forms of reinforcement that can encourage observational learning. First, of course, the observer may reproduce the behaviors of the model and receive direct reinforcement, as when a gymnast successfully executes a front flip/round-off combination and the coach/model says, "Excellent!"

But the reinforcement need not be direct—it may be **vicarious reinforcement**. The observer may simply see others reinforced for a particular behavior and then increase his or her production of that behavior. For example, if you compliment two students on the attractive illustrations in their lab reports, several other students who observe your compliments may turn in illustrated lab reports next time. Most TV ads hope for this kind of effect. People in commercials become deliriously happy when they drive a particular car or drink a specific juice, and the viewer is supposed to do the same; the viewer's behavior is reinforced vicariously by the actors' obvious pleasure. Punishment can also be vicarious: You may slow down on a stretch of highway after seeing several people get speeding tickets there.

The final form of reinforcement is self-reinforcement, or controlling your own reinforcers. This sort of reinforcement is important for both students and teachers. We want our students to improve not because it leads to external rewards but because the students value and enjoy their growing competence. And as a teacher, sometimes self-reinforcement is all that keeps you going.

Factors That Influence Observational Learning. What causes an individual to learn and perform modeled behaviors and skills? Several factors play a role, as shown in Table 9.1 on page 326. The developmental level of the observer makes a difference in learning. As children grow older, they are able to focus attention for longer periods of time, use memory strategies to retain information, and motivate themselves to practice. A second influence is the status of the model. Children are more likely to imitate the actions of others who seem competent, powerful, and prestigious, so parents, teachers, older siblings, Barney, athletes, action heroes, rock stars, or film personalities may serve as models, depending on the age and interests of the child. Third, by watching others, we learn about what behaviors are appropriate for people like ourselves, so models who are seen as similar are more readily imitated. All students need to see successful, capable models who look and sound like them, no matter what their ethnicity, socioeconomic status, or sex.

The last three influences involve goals and expectations. If observers expect that certain actions of models will lead to particular outcomes (such as particular practice regimens leading to improved athletic performance) and the observers value those outcomes or goals, then the observers are more likely to pay attention to the models and try to reproduce their behaviors. Finally, observers are more likely to learn from models if the observers have a high level of **self-efficacy**—that is, if they believe they are capable of doing the actions needed to reach the goals, or at least of learning how to do so (Bandura, 1997; Pintrich & Schunk, 1996). We will discuss goals, expectations, and self-efficacy in greater depth in Chapters 10 and 11 on motivation.

Connect and Extend
To other chapters
Sense of self-efficacy is discussed more fully in Chapter 10, as is the related concept of teacher efficacy. Background: Two books by Bandura about self-efficacy: Bandura, A. (1997). *Self-efficacy: The exercise of control.* New York: Freeman. Bandura, A. (Ed.). (1995). *Self-efficacy in changing societies.* New York: Cambridge University Press.

Vicarious Reinforcement: Increasing the chances that we will repeat a behavior by observing another person being reinforced for that behavior.

Self-Efficacy: A person's sense of being able to deal effectively with a particular task.

TABLE 9.1 *Factors That Affect Observational Learning*

Characteristic	Effects on Modeling
Developmental Status	Improvements with development include longer attention and increased capacity to process information, use strategies, compare performances with memorial representations, and adopt intrinsic motivators.
Model Prestige and Competence	Observers pay greater attention to competent, high-status models. Consequences of modeled behaviors convey information about functional value. Observers attempt to learn actions they believe they will need to perform.
Vicarious Consequences	Consequences to models convey information about behavioral appropriateness and likely outcomes of actions. Valued consequences motivate observers. Similarity in attributes or competence signals appropriateness and heightens motivation.
Outcome Expectations	Observers are more likely to perform modeled actions they believe are appropriate and will result in rewarding outcomes.
Goal Setting	Observers are likely to attend to models who demonstrate behaviors that help observers attain goals.
Self-efficacy	Observers attend to models when they believe they are capable of learning or performing the modeled behavior. Observation of similar models affects self-efficacy ("If they can do it, I can too").

Source: From *Learning Theories: An Education Perspective* (3rd ed.) (p. 121), by D. H. Schunk, 2000, Saddle River, NJ: Prentice-Hall, Inc. Copyright © 2000 by Prentice-Hall, Inc. Adapted with permission.

Observational Learning in Teaching

There are five possible outcomes of observational learning: directing attention, encouraging existing behaviors, changing inhibitions, teaching new behaviors and attitudes, and arousing emotions. Let's look at each of these as they occur in classrooms.

The "ripple effect" noted in observational learning can be a benefit to teachers if their responses to rule-breaking are noticed by other students. ▼

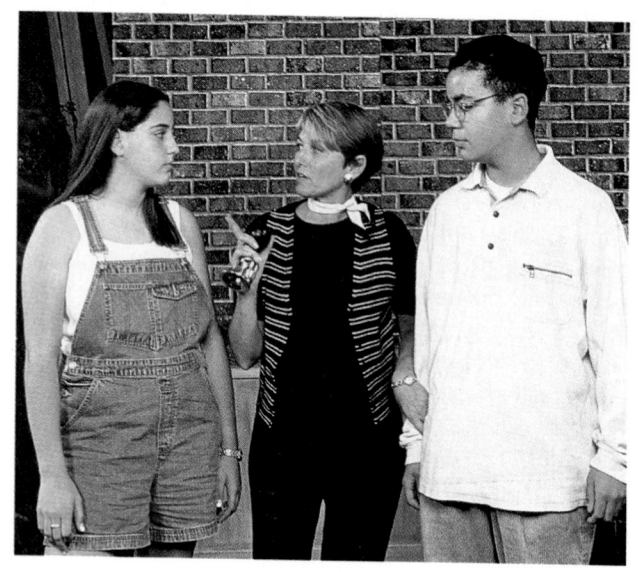

Directing Attention. By observing others, we not only learn about actions, but we also notice the objects involved in the actions. For example, in a preschool class, when one child plays enthusiastically with a toy that has been ignored for days, many other children may want to have the toy, even if they play with it in different ways or simply carry it around. This happens, in part, because the children's attention has been drawn to that particular toy.

Fine-Tuning Already-Learned Behaviors. All of us have had the experience of looking for cues from other people when we find ourselves in unfamiliar situations. Observing the behavior of others tells us which of our already-learned behaviors to use: the proper fork for eating the salad, when to leave a gathering, what kind of language is appropriate, and so on. Adopting the dress and grooming styles of TV idols is another example of this kind of effect.

Strengthening or Weakening Inhibitions. If class members witness one student breaking a class rule and getting away with it, they may learn that undesirable consequences do not always follow rule breaking. The class may be less inhibited in the future about breaking this rule. If the rule breaker is a well-liked, high-status class leader, the effect of the modeling may be even more pronounced. One psychologist has called this phenomenon the **ripple effect** (Kounin, 1970). The ripple effect can work for the teacher's benefit. When the teacher deals effectively with a rule breaker, especially a class leader, the idea of breaking this rule may be inhibited for the other students viewing the interaction. This does not mean that teachers must reprimand each student who breaks a rule, but once a teacher has called for a particular action, following through is an important part of capitalizing on the ripple effect.

Teaching New Behaviors. **Modeling** has long been used, of course, to teach dance, sports, and crafts, as well as skills in subjects such as home economics, chemistry, and shop. Modeling can also be applied deliberately in the classroom to teach mental skills and to broaden horizons—to teach new ways of thinking. Teachers serve as models for a vast range of behaviors, from pronouncing vocabulary words, to reacting to the seizure of a student with epilepsy, to being enthusiastic about learning. For example, a teacher might model sound critical thinking skills by thinking "out loud" about a student's question. Or a high school teacher concerned about girls who seem to have stereotyped ideas about careers might invite women with nontraditional jobs to speak to the class.

What is this son learning by observing his father? ▼

"Dad, can you read?"

© The New Yorker Collection 1990
Peter Steiner from cartoonbank.com.
All rights reserved.

Modeling, when applied deliberately, can be an effective and efficient means of teaching new behavior (Bandura, 1986; Schunk, 1987). Studies indicate that modeling can be most effective when the teacher makes use of all the elements of observational learning described in the previous section, especially reinforcement and practice.

Models who are the same age as the students may be particularly effective. For example, Schunk and Hanson (1985) compared two methods for teaching subtraction to 2nd graders who had difficulties learning this skill. One group of students observed other 2nd graders learning the procedures, then participated in an instructional program on subtraction. Another group of students watched a teacher's demonstration, then participated in the same instructional program. Of the two groups, the students who observed peer models learning not only scored higher on tests of subtraction after instruction, but also gained more confidence in their own ability to learn. For students who doubt their own abilities, a good model is a low-achieving student who keeps trying and finally masters the material (Schunk, 2000).

Arousing Emotion. Finally, through observational learning people may develop emotional reactions to situations they have never experienced personally, such as flying or driving. A child who watches a friend fall from a swing and break an arm may become fearful of swings. Students may be anxious when they are assigned to a certain teacher because they've heard frightening stories about how "mean" that teacher is. Note that hearing and reading about a situation are also forms of observation. Some terrible examples of modeling occur with "copy cat killings" in schools. When frightening things happen to people who are similar in age or circumstances to your students, they may need to talk about their emotions. The Guidelines on page 328 will give you some ideas about using observational learning in the classroom.

Ripple Effect: "Contagious" spreading of behaviors through imitation.

Modeling: Changes in behavior, thinking, or emotions that occur through observing another person—a model.

GUIDELINES

Using Observational Learning

Model behaviors and attitudes you want your students to learn.

Examples

1. Show enthusiasm for the subject you teach.

2. Be willing to demonstrate both the mental and the physical tasks you expect the students to perform. I once saw a teacher sit down in the sandbox while her 4-year-old students watched her demonstrate the difference between "playing with sand" and "throwing sand."

3. When reading to students, model good problem solving. Stop and say, "Now let me see if I remember what happened so far," or "That was a hard sentence. I'm going to read it again."

4. Model good problem solving—think out loud as you work through a difficult problem.

Use peers, especially class leaders, as models.

Examples

1. In group work, pair students who do well with those who are having difficulties.

2. Ask students to demonstrate the difference between "whispering" and "silence—no talking."

Make sure students see that positive behaviors lead to reinforcement for others.

Examples

1. Point out the connections between positive behavior and positive consequences in stories.

2. Be fair in giving reinforcement. The same rules for rewards should apply to the problem students as to the good students.

Enlist the help of class leaders in modeling behaviors for the entire class.

Examples

1. Ask a well-liked student to be friendly to an isolated, fearful student.

2. Let high-status students lead an activity when you need class cooperation or when students are likely to be reluctant at first. Popular students can model dialogues in foreign-language classes or be the first to tackle dissection procedures in biology.

Reciprocal Determinism

In social cognitive theory both internal and external factors are important. Environmental events, personal factors, and behaviors are seen as interacting in the process of learning. Personal factors (beliefs, expectations, attitudes, and knowledge), the physical and social environment (resources, consequences of actions, other people, and physical settings), and behavior (individual actions, choices, and verbal statements) all influence and are influenced by each other. Bandura calls this interaction of forces **reciprocal determinism.**

> In the social cognitive view people are neither driven by inner forces nor automatically shaped and controlled by external stimuli. Rather, human functioning is explained in terms of a model of triadic reciprocality in which behavior, cognitive and other personal factors, and environmental events all operate as interacting determinants of each other. (Bandura, 1986, p. 18)

Think for a minute about the power of reciprocal determinism in human interactions. If personal factors, behaviors, and the environment are in constant interaction, then cycles of events are progressive and self-perpetuating. For example, a new student walks into class late. The student has a tattoo and several visible pierced body parts. The student is actually anxious and hopes to do better at this new school, but the teacher's initial reaction to the late entry and dramatic appearance is a bit hostile. The student feels insulted and responds in kind, so the teacher

Reciprocal Determinism: An explanation of behavior that emphasizes the mutual effects of the individual and the environment on each other.

begins to form expectations about the student, is more vigilant and less trusting, and the student decides that this school will be just as worthless as his previous one—so why bother to try. The teacher sees the student's disengagement, invests less effort in teaching him, and on and on.

Social cognitive theories study the impact of social factors on individuals—the direction of the influence is from social processes outside the learner to the mind inside the learner. But there are other perspectives on learning that include a much wider range of social processes, such as cultural and historical factors, and focus on constructions of knowledge that occur between people, not just within them. Many of these ideas began in anthropology or sociology and have been brought into educational psychology to help us get a more complete picture of learning. Because these are very influential theories, we will spend the rest of the chapter learning more about them.

CHECKPOINT

Social Learning and Social Cognitive Theories

Review

▶ Distinguish between social learning and social cognitive theories.

▶ Distinguish between enactive and vicarious learning.

▶ What are the elements of observational learning?

▶ What is reciprocal determinism?

Apply

▶ Describe how observational learning and modeling might be used to help the students described at the beginning of the chapter write better book reviews.

Constructivism and Situated Learning

Consider this situation:

A young child who has never been to the hospital is in her bed in the pediatric wing. The nurse at the station down the hall calls over the intercom above the bed, "Hi Chelsea, how are you doing? Do you need anything?" The girl looks puzzled and does not answer. The nurse repeats the question with the same result. Finally, the nurse says emphatically, "Chelsea, are you there? Say something!" The little girl responds tentatively, "Hello wall—I'm here."

Chelsea encountered a new situation—a talking wall. The wall is persistent. It sounds like a grown-up wall. She shouldn't talk to strangers, but she is not sure about walls. She uses what she knows and what the situation provides to *construct* meaning and to act. Constructivist theories of learning focus on how people make meaning.

Constructivist Views of Learning

Constructivism, "a vast and woolly area in contemporary psychology, epistemology, and education" (Von Glaserfeld, 1997, p. 204), is a broad term used by philosophers, curriculum designers, psychologists, educators, and others. Most people who use the term emphasize "the learner's contribution to meaning and learning through both individual and social activity" (Bruning, Schraw, & Ronning, 1999, p. 215). Constructivist perspectives are grounded in the research of Piaget, Vygotsky, the Gestalt psychologists, Bartlett, and Bruner as well as the educational philosophy of John Dewey, to mention just a few intellectual roots.

Connect and Extend
To the research
Marshall, H. H. (Ed.) (1992). *Redefining student learning: Roots of educational change.* Norwood, NJ: Ablex.

Constructivism: View that emphasizes the active role of the learner in building understanding and making sense of information.

There is no one constructivist theory of learning. Most of the theories in cognitive science include some kind of constructivism because these theories assume that individuals construct their own cognitive structures as they interpret their experiences in particular situations (Palincsar, 1998). There are constructivist approaches in science and mathematics education, in educational psychology and anthropology, and in computer-based education. But even though many psychologists and educators use the term "constructivism," they often mean very different things (Marshall, 1996; Phillips, 1997). Some constructivist views focus on how individuals make meaning; others emphasize the *shared, social construction of knowledge* (Driscoll, 1994; Iran-Nejad, 1990; Perkins, 1991; Spiro, Feltovich, Jacobson, & Coulson, 1991; Tobin, 1990; von Glaserfeld, 1990; Wittrock, 1992). In fact, one way to organize constructivist views is to talk about two forms of constructivism: psychological and social (Palincsar, 1998; Phillips, 1997).

Psychological/Individual Constructivism. Psychological constructivists "are concerned with how *individuals* build up certain elements of their cognitive or emotional apparatus" (Phillips, 1997, p. 153). These constructivists are interested in individual knowledge, beliefs, self-concept, or identity, so they are sometimes called *individual* constructivists; they all focus on the inner psychological life of people. Using these standards, the most recent information processing theories are constructivist (Mayer, 1996). Information processing approaches to learning regard the human mind as a symbol processing system. This system converts sensory input into symbol structures (propositions, images, or schemas), and then processes (rehearses or elaborates) those symbol structures so knowledge can be held in memory and retrieved. The outside world is seen as a source of input, but once the sensations are perceived and enter working memory, the important work is assumed to be happening "inside the head" of the individual (Schunk, 2000; Vera & Simon, 1993).

Even though information processing theorists talk about meaning and knowledge construction, many psychologists believe that information processing is "trivial constructivism" because the individual's only constructive contribution is to build accurate representations of the outside world (Derry, 1992; Garrison, 1995; Marshall, 1996). In contrast, Piaget's psychological constructivist perspective is less concerned with "correct" representations and more interested in meaning as constructed by the individual. As we saw in Chapter 2, Piaget proposed a sequence of cognitive stages that all humans pass through. Thinking at each stage builds on and incorporates previous stages as it becomes more organized and adaptive and less tied to concrete events. Piaget's special concern was with logic and the construction of universal knowledge that cannot be learned directly from the environment—knowledge such as conservation or reversibility (Miller, 1993). Such knowledge comes from reflecting on and coordinating our own cognitions or thoughts, not from mapping external reality. Piaget saw the social environment as an important factor in development, but did not believe that social interaction was the main mechanism for changing thinking (Moshman, 1997).

Vygotsky's Social Constructivism. As you also saw in Chapter 2, Vygotsky believed that social interaction, cultural tools, and activity shape individual development and learning. By participating in a broad range of activities with others, learners appropriate (internalize or take for themselves) the outcomes produced by working together; "they acquire new strategies and knowledge of the world and culture" (Palincsar, 1998, pp. 351–352). Some theorists categorize Vygotsky as a psychological constructivist because he was primarily interested in development

▲ *Psychological constructivist theories pay particular attention to the inner psychological life of people and their unique conceptions of the world.*

within the individual (Moshman, 1997; Phillips, 1997). But because his theory relies heavily on social interactions and the cultural context to explain learning, most psychologists classify Vygotsky as a social constructivist (Palincsar, 1998, Prawat, 1996). In a sense, he is both. One advantage of his theory of learning is that it gives us a way to consider both the psychological and the social—he bridges both camps. For example, Vygotsky's concept of the zone of proximal development—the area where a child can solve a problem with the help (scaffolding) of an adult or more able peer—has been called a place where culture and cognition create each other (Cole, 1985). Culture creates cognition when the adult uses tools and practices from the culture (language, maps, computers, looms, or music) to steer the child toward goals the culture values (reading, writing, weaving, dance). Cognition creates culture as the adult and child together generate new practices and problem solutions to add to the cultural group's repertoire (Serpell, 1993).

The term *constructivism* is sometimes used to talk about how public knowledge is created. Although this is not our main concern in educational psychology, it is worth a quick look.

Sociological Constructivism. Sociological constructivists (sometimes called *constructionists*) do not focus on individual learning. Their concern is how public knowledge in disciplines such as science, math, economics, or history is constructed. Beyond this kind of academic knowledge, sociological constructivists also are interested in how common-sense ideas, everyday beliefs, and commonly held understandings about the world are communicated to new members of a sociocultural group (Gergen, 1997; Phillips, 1997). Questions raised might include who determines what constitutes history or the proper way to behave in public or how to get elected class president. All of knowledge is socially constructed, and, more important, some people have more power than others do in defining what constitutes such knowledge. Relationships between and among teachers, students, families, and the community are the central issues. Collaboration to understand diverse viewpoints is encouraged and traditional bodies of knowledge often are challenged (Gergen, 1997). Vygotsky's theory, with its attention to how cognition creates culture, has some elements in common with sociological constructivism.

These different perspectives on constructivism raise some general questions and disagree on the answers. These questions can never be fully resolved, but different theories tend to favor different positions.

How Is Knowledge Constructed?

One tension among different approaches to constructivism is based on *how* knowledge is constructed. Moshman (1982) describes three explanations.

1. *The realities and truths of the external world direct knowledge construction.* Individuals *reconstruct* outside reality by building accurate mental representations such as propositional networks, concepts, cause-and-effect patterns, and condition-action production rules that reflect "the way things really are." Information processing holds this view of knowledge as an entity that is constructed in one situation and applied in another (Cobb & Bowers, 1999).

2. *Internal processes such as Piaget's organization, assimilation, and accommodation direct knowledge construction.* New knowledge is abstracted from old knowledge. Knowledge is not a mirror of reality, but rather an abstraction that grows and

Connect and Extend
To the research
The 2000 Yearbook of the National Society for the Study of Education (NSSE) is devoted to the examination of constructivism. Phillips, D. C. (Ed.) (2000). *Constructivism in education: Opinions and second opinions on controversial issues.* Chicago, IL: University of Chicago Press.

Constructivism and Situated Learning **331**

TABLE 9.2 *How Knowledge Is Constructed*

Type	Assumptions about Learning and Knowledge	Example Theories
External Direction	Knowledge is acquired by constructing a representation of the outside world. Direct teaching, feedback, and explanation affect learning. Knowledge is accurate to the extent that it reflects the "way things really are" in the outside world.	Information processing
Internal Direction	Knowledge is constructed by transforming, organizing, and reorganizing previous knowledge. Knowledge is not a mirror of the external world, even though experience influences thinking and thinking influences knowledge. Exploration and discovery are more important than teaching.	Piaget
Both External and Internal Direction	Knowledge is constructed based on social interactions and experience. Knowledge reflects the outside world as filtered through and influenced by culture, language, beliefs, interactions with others, direct teaching, and modeling. Guided discovery, teaching, models, and coaching as well as the individual's prior knowledge, beliefs, and thinking affect learning.	Vygotsky

develops with cognitive activity. Knowledge is not true or false; it just grows more internally consistent and organized with development.

3. *Both external and internal factors direct knowledge construction.* Knowledge grows through the *interactions* of internal (cognitive) and external (environmental and social) factors. Vygotsky's description of cognitive development through the appropriation and use of cultural tools such as language is consistent with this view (Bruning, Schraw, & Ronning, 1999). Another example is Bandura's theory of reciprocal interactions between people, behaviors, and environments (Schunk, 2000). Table 9.2 summarizes the three general explanations about how knowledge is constructed.

Is the World Knowable?

Most constructivists believe that people cannot perceive the world directly, but must filter it through their understandings, like Chelsea did when she answered the wall. But some perspectives, such as information processing, assume the world is knowable. There is an objective reality "out there," and an individual can grasp it, even though knowledge constructions are personal and may include misconceptions about how the world operates. For example, young children sometimes construct a subtraction procedure that says, "subtract the smaller number from the larger number, no matter which number in a problem is on top." Other constructivists, including Piaget and Vygotsky, don't talk about accurate conceptions but instead about logical or sound interpretations. Still, they believe that we can know about the world because knowledge construction is a rational process and some constructions are better than others—more logical, justifiable, or defensible, for example (Moshman, 1997).

Many of the more extreme constructivist perspectives, on the other hand, do not assume that the world is knowable. These theorists, often called **radical constructivists**, suggest that all knowledge is individually constructed within cultural and

Radical Constuctivism: Theory of knowledge and learning asserting that all knowledge is individually constructed and equally valid.

social contexts. Radical constructivists are not concerned with accurate, "true" representations of the world.

> Radical constructivists hold that we live in a relativistic world that can only be understood from individually unique perspectives, which are constructed through experimental activity in the social/physical world. No individual's viewpoint thus constructed should be viewed as inherently distorted or less correct than another's, although it is certainly true that one individual perspective can be more useful than another. (Derry, 1992, p. 415)

A difficulty with this position is that, when pushed to the extreme of relativism, all knowledge and beliefs are equal because all are constructed. There are problems with this thinking for educators. First, teachers have a professional responsibility to emphasize some values, such as honesty or justice, over others such as bigotry. All beliefs are not equal. As teachers we ask students to work hard to learn. If learning cannot advance understanding because all understandings are equally good, then, as David Moshman (1997) notes, "we might just as well let students continue to believe whatever they believe" (p. 230). Also, it appears that some knowledge, such as counting and one-to-one correspondence, is not constructed but universal. Knowing one-to-one correspondence is part of being human (Geary, 1995; Schunk, 2000).

Knowledge: Situated or General?

A final question that cuts across many constructivist perspectives is whether knowledge is internal, general, and transferable or bound to the time and place in which it is constructed. Psychologists who emphasize the social construction of knowledge and **situated learning** affirm Vygotsky's notion that learning is inherently social and embedded in a particular cultural setting (Cobb & Bowers, 1999). What is true in one time and place—such as the "fact" before Columbus's time that the earth was flat—becomes false in another time and place. Particular ideas may be useful within a specific **community of practice**, such as fifteenth century navigation, but useless outside that community. What counts as new knowledge is determined in part by how well the new idea fits with current accepted practice. Over time, the current practice may be questioned and even overthrown, but until such major shifts occur, current practice will shape what is considered useful.

Situated learning emphasizes that the real world is not like studying in school. It is more like an apprenticeship where novices, with the support of an expert guide and model, take on more and more responsibility until they are able to function independently. For those who take a situated learning view, this explains learning in factories, around the dinner table, in high school halls, in street gangs, in the business office, and on the playground.

Situated learning is often described as "enculturation," or adopting the norms, behaviors, skills, beliefs, language, and attitudes of a particular community. The community might be mathematicians or gang members or writers or students in your 8th-grade class or soccer players—any group that has particular ways of thinking and doing. Knowledge is seen *not* as individual cognitive structures but as a creation of the community over time. The practices of the community—the ways of interacting and getting things done, as well as the tools the community has created—constitute the knowledge of that community. Learning means becoming more able to participate in those practices and use the tools (Cognition and Technology Group at Vanderbilt University, 1990, 1993; Derry, 1992; Garrison, 1995; Greeno, Collins, & Resnick, 1996).

Connect and Extend
To the research
Background: Gardner, H. (1991). *The unschooled mind: How children think and how schools should teach.* New York: Basic Books. Gardner, H. (1993). *Educating the unschooled mind: A science and public policy seminar.* Washington, DC: American Educational Research Association. Brandt, R. (1993). On teaching for understanding: A Conversation with Howard Gardner. *Educational Leadership, 50*(7), 4–7.

Situated Learning: The idea that skills and knowledge are tied to the situation in which they were learned and difficult to apply in new settings.

Community of Practice: Social situation or context in which ideas are judged useful or true.

At the most basic level, "situated learning . . . emphasizes the idea that much of what is learned is specific to the situation in which it is learned" (Anderson, Reder, & Simon, 1996, p. 5). Thus, some would argue, learning to do calculations in school may help students do more school calculations, but may not help them balance a checkbook, because the skills can be applied only in the context in which they were learned, namely school (Lave, 1988; Lave & Wenger, 1991).

There is evidence that much learning is tied to the situation in which it was learned. But it also appears that knowledge and skills can be applied across contexts that were not part of the initial learning situation, as when you use your ability to read and calculate to do your income taxes, even though income tax forms were not part of your high school curriculum (Anderson, Reder, & Simon, 1996). So learning that is situated in school does not have to be doomed or irrelevant. As you saw in Chapter 8, a major question in educational psychology and education in general concerns *specific* and *general* knowledge and the *transfer* of knowledge from one situation to another. How can you encourage this transfer? Help is on the way in the next section.

Common Elements of Constructivist Perspectives

Connect and Extend
To professional journals
Special issue on Authentic Learning: *Educational Leadership*, April 1993. There are 25 articles in this issue—everything from an interview with Howard Gardner to descriptions of Civil War reenactments.

We have looked at some areas of disagreement among the constructivist perspectives, but what about areas of agreement? Even though there is no single constructivist theory, many constructivist approaches recommend:

▶ complex, challenging learning environments and authentic tasks;

▶ social negotiation and shared responsibility as a part of learning;

▶ multiple representations of content;

▶ understanding that knowledge is constructed; and

▶ student-centered instruction (Driscoll, 1994; Marshall, 1992).

Before we discuss particular teaching approaches, let's look more closely at these dimensions of constructivist teaching.

Constructivist approaches may involve, among other things, authentic or real-life tasks, social negotiation, and shared responsibility as part of learning. ▼

Complex Learning Environments and Authentic Tasks. Constructivists believe that students should not be given stripped down, simplified problems and basic skills drills, but instead should encounter **complex learning environments** that deal with "fuzzy," ill-structured problems. The world beyond school presents few simple problems or step-by-step directions, so schools should be sure that *every* student has experience solving complex problems. Complex problems are not simply difficult ones. Complex problems have many parts. There are multiple, interacting elements in the problems and multiple solutions are possible. There is no one right way to reach a conclusion, and each solution may bring a new set of problems. These complex problems should be embedded in authentic tasks and activities, the kinds of situations that students will face as they apply what they are learning to the real world (J. S. Brown, 1990; Needles & Knapp, 1994; Resnick, 1987). Students may need support as they work on these complex problems, helping them find resources, keeping track of their progress, breaking larger problems down into smaller ones, and so on. This aspect of constructivist approaches is consistent with situated learning in emphasizing learning in *situations* where the learning will be applied.

Social Negotiation. Many constructivists share Vygotsky's belief that higher mental processes develop through **social negotiation** and interaction, so collaboration in learning is valued. The Language Development and Hypermedia Group (1992) suggests that a major goal of teaching is to develop students' abilities to establish and defend their own positions while respecting the positions of others and working together to negotiate or co-construct meaning. To accomplish this exchange, students must talk and listen to each other. It is a challenge for children in cultures that are individualistic and competitive, such as the United States, to adopt what has been called an **intersubjective attitude** about negotiation and joint construction of meaning. An intersubjective attitude is a commitment to build shared meaning by finding common ground and exchanging interpretations.

Multiple Representations of Content. When students encounter only one model, one analogy, one way of understanding complex content, they often oversimplify as they try to apply that one approach to every situation. I saw this happen in my educational psychology class when six students were presenting an example of guided discovery learning. The students' presentation was a near copy of a guided discovery demonstration I had given earlier in the semester, but with some major misconceptions. My students knew only one way to represent discovery learning. Resources for the class should have provided **multiple representations of content** (guided discovery) using different analogies, examples, and metaphors.

Rand Spiro and his colleagues (1991) suggest that "revisiting the same material, at different times, in rearranged contexts, for different purposes, and from different conceptual perspectives is essential for attaining the goals of advanced knowledge acquisition" (p. 28). This idea is consistent with Jerome Bruner's (1966) **spiral curriculum**, a structure for teaching that introduces the fundamental structure of all subjects—the "big ideas"—early in the school years, then revisits the subjects in more and more complex forms over time.

Understanding the Knowledge Construction Process. Throughout this text you have encountered the concept of metacognition—knowledge of your own mental processes and how you learn. Constructivist approaches often go beyond helping students understand their own metacognitive processes to making them aware of their own role in constructing knowledge (Cunningham, 1992). The assumptions we make, our beliefs, and experiences shape what each of us comes to "know" about the world. Different assumptions and different experiences lead to different knowledge. Constructivists stress the importance of understanding the knowledge construction process so that students

Social Negotiation: Aspect of learning process that relies on collaboration with others and respect for different perspectives.

Intersubjective Attitude: A commitment to build shared meaning with others by finding common ground and exchanging interpretations.

Multiple Representations of Content: Considering problems using various analogies, examples, and metaphors.

Spiral Curriculum: Bruner's structure for teaching that introduces the fundamental structure of all subjects early in the school years, then revisits the subjects in more and more complex forms over time.

Connect and Extend
To the research
Confrey, J. (1990). What constructivism implies for teaching. In R. Davis, C. Maher, & N. Noddings (Eds.), *Constructivist views on the teaching and learning of mathematics* (pp. 107–122). Monograph 4 of the National Council of Teachers of Mathematics, Reston, VA.

CHECKPOINT

Constructivism and Situated Learning

Review

▶ Describe three kinds of constructivism.

▶ In what ways do constructivist views differ about knowledge sources, accuracy, and generality?

▶ What are four common elements in most constructivist views of learning?

Apply

▶ Explain how a constructivist approach might be used to help the students described at the beginning of the chapter write better book reviews.

Inquiry Learning: Approach in which the teacher presents a puzzling situation and students solve the problem by gathering data and testing their conclusions.

will be aware of the influences that shape their thinking; thus they will be able to choose, develop, and defend positions in a self-critical way while respecting the positions of others.

Student-Centered Instruction. "While there are several interpretations of what [constructivist] theory means, most agree that it involves a dramatic change in the focus of teaching, putting the students' own efforts to understand at the center of the educational enterprise" (Prawat, 1992, p. 357). Student-centered instruction does not mean that the teacher abandons responsibility for instruction. Because the design of teaching is a central issue in this book, we will spend the rest of this chapter discussing examples of student-centered instruction.

Applications of Constructivist and Situated Perspectives on Learning

In this section we will examine four specific teaching approaches that put the student at the center: inquiry and problem-based learning, cooperative learning, dialogue and instructional conversations, and cognitive apprenticeships.

Inquiry and Problem-Based Learning

John Dewey described the basic **inquiry learning** format in 1910. There have been many adaptations of this strategy, but the form usually includes these elements (Pasch, Sparks-Langer, Gardner, Starko, & Moody, 1991).

The teacher presents a puzzling event, question, or problem. The students:

▶ formulate hypotheses to explain the event or solve the problem;

▶ collect data to test the hypotheses;

▶ draw conclusions; and

▶ reflect on the original problem and the thinking processes needed to solve it.

Examples of Inquiry. In one kind of inquiry, teachers present a problem and students ask yes/no questions to gather data and test hypotheses. This allows the teacher to monitor students' thinking and guide the process. Here is an example:

1. *Teacher presents discrepant event* (after clarifying ground rules). The teacher blows softly across the top of an 8½" x 11" sheet of paper, and the paper rises. She tells students to figure out why it rises.
2. *Students ask questions* to gather more information and to isolate relevant variables. Teacher answers only "yes" or "no." Students ask if temperature is important (no). They ask if the paper is of a special kind (no). They ask if air pressure has anything to do with the paper rising (yes). Questions continue.
3. *Students test causal relationships.* In this case, they ask if the nature of the air on top causes the paper to rise (yes). They ask if the fast movement of the air results in less pressure on the top (yes). Then they test out the rule with other materials—for example, thin plastic.
4. *Students form a generalization* (principle): "If the air on the top moves faster than the air on the bottom of a surface, then the air pressure on top is lessened, and the object rises." Later lessons expand students' understanding of the principles and physical laws through further experiments.

Connect and Extend
To your teaching

John Cronin lists these four common misconceptions about authentic learning:

Misconception #1: If you can't take 'em to Spain, they might as well not learn Spanish at all. The fact that living with native speakers is the best way to learn Spanish does not make using the language in classroom conversations a poor alternative. Look for the small and obvious ways to make learning more authentic—especially if you can't take 'em to Spain.

Misconception #2: If you don't have your chef's license, then you'll have to starve. You don't need special training or materials to create authentic instruction. Good teachers have been doing it for years.

Misconception #3: If it isn't real fun, then it isn't real. Important learning and valuable life skills are not always fun to learn or fun to use. Self-discipline is part of growing up authentically.

Misconception #4: If you want to learn to play the piano, you must start with mastering Chopin. Not all learning has to be complicated; some important life skills are simple. From Cronin, J. F. (1993). Four misconceptions about authentic learning. *Educational Leadership,* *50*(7), 78–80.

5. The teacher leads students in a discussion of their thinking processes. What were the important variables? How did you put the causes and effects together? and so on. (Pasch et al., 1991, pp. 188–189)

Shirley Magnusson and Annemarie Palincsar have developed a teachers' guide for planning, implementing, and assessing different phases of inquiry science units (Palincsar, Magussson, Marano, Ford, & Brown, 1998). The model, called *Guided Inquiry Supporting Multiple Literacies* or GIsML, is shown in Figure 9.1.

The teacher first identifies a curriculum area and some general guiding questions, puzzles, or problems. For example, an elementary teacher chooses communication as the area and asks this general question: "How and why do humans and animals communicate?" Next, several specific focus questions are posed. "How do

FIGURE 9.1

A Model to Guide Teacher Thinking about Inquiry-Based Science Instruction

The straight lines show the sequence of phases in instruction and the curved lines show cycles that might be repeated during instruction.

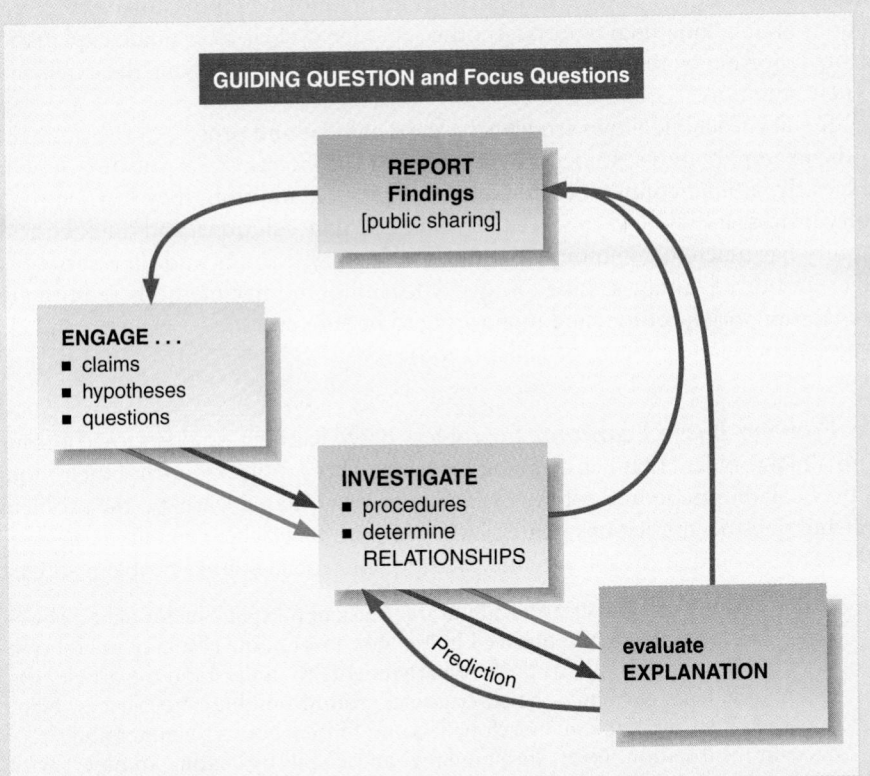

Source: From "Designing a Community of Practice: Principles and Practices of the GIsML Community," by A. S. Palincsar, S. J. Magnuson, N. Marano, D. Ford, and N. Brown, 1998, *Teaching and Teacher Education, 14,* p. 12. Adapted with permission.

whales communicate? How do gorillas communicate? The focus questions have to be carefully chosen to guide students toward important understandings. One key idea in understanding animal communication is the relationship between the animal's structures, survival functions, and habitat. Animals have specific *structures* such as large ears or echo-locators, that *function* to find food or attract mates or identify predators, and these structures and functions are related to the animals' *habitats*. So focus questions must ask about animals with different structures for communication, different functional needs for survival, and different habitats. Questions about animals with the same kinds of structures or the same habitats would not be good focus points for inquiry (Magnusson & Palincsar, 1995).

The next phase is to engage students in the inquiry, perhaps by playing different animal sounds, having students make guesses and claims about communication, and asking the students questions about their guesses and claims. Then the students conduct both first-hand and second-hand investigations. *First-hand investigations* are direct experiences and experiments, for example, measuring the size of bats' eyes and ears in relation to their bodies (using pictures or videos—not real bats!). In *second-hand investigations*, students consult books, the Internet, interviews with experts, and so on to find specific information or get new ideas. As part of investigating, the students begin to identify patterns. The curved line in Figure 9.1 shows that cycles can be repeated. In fact, students might go through several cycles of investigation, pattern identification, and reporting results before moving on to constructing explanations and making final reports. Another possible cycle is to evaluate explanations before reporting by making and then checking predictions, applying the explanation to new situations.

Inquiry teaching allows students to learn content and process at the same time. In the examples above, students learned about the effects of air pressure, how airplanes fly, animal communication, and habitats. In addition, they learned the inquiry process itself—how to solve problems, evaluate solutions, and think critically. Inquiry has much in common with guided discovery learning and shares its advantages and disadvantages. Like discovery learning, inquiry methods require great preparation, organization, and monitoring to be sure everyone is engaged and challenged (Kindsvatter, Wilen, & Ishler, 1988).

Problem-Based Learning. In **problem-based learning**, students are confronted with a real problem that has meaning for them. This problem launches their inquiry as they collaborate to find solutions. In true problem-based learning, the problem is real and the students' actions matter. For example, one teacher capitalized on current affairs to encourage student reading, writing, and social studies problem solving:

> Cathie's elementary class learned about the Alaskan oil spill. She brought a newspaper article to class that sequenced in logbook fashion the events of the oil spill in Prince William Sound. To prepare her students to understand the article, she had her students participate in several background-building experiences. First, they used a world map, an encyclopedia, and library books to gather and share relevant information. Next, she simulated an oil spill by coating an object with oil. By then, the class was eager to read the article. (Espe, Worner, & Hotkevich, 1990, p. 45)

Problem-Based Learning: Methods that provide students with realistic problems that don't necessarily have "right" answers.

After they read and discussed the newspaper article, the teacher asked the class to imagine how the problem might have been prevented. Students had to explain and support their proposed solutions. The next week the students read another newspaper article about how people in their state were helping with the cleanup efforts in Alaska. The teacher asked if the students wanted to help, and they replied with an enthusiastic "Yes!" The students designed posters and made speeches requesting donations of clean towels to be used to clean the oil-soaked animals in Prince William Sound. The class sent four large bags of towels to Alaska to help in the cleanup. The teacher's and the students' reading, writing, research, and speaking were directed toward solving a real-life problem (Espe, Worner, & Hotkevich, 1990). Other authentic problems that might be the focus for student projects are pollution in local rivers, student conflicts in school, raising money for class projects, or building a playground for young children. The teacher's role in problem-based learning is summarized in Table 9.3.

Some problems are not authentic in the sense that they affect the students' lives, but they are engaging. For example, the Cognition and Technology Group at Vanderbilt University (CTGV, 1990, 1993) has developed a videodisc-based learning environment that focuses on mathematics instruction for the 5th and 6th grades. The series, called *The Adventures of Jasper Woodbury*, presents students with complex situations that require problem finding; subgoal setting; and the application of mathematics, science, history, and literature concepts to solve problems. Even though the situations are complex and lifelike, the problems can be solved using data embedded in the stories presented. For example, in one adventure, Jasper sets out in a small motorboat, headed to Cedar Creek to inspect an old cruiser he is thinking of buying. Along the way Jasper has to consult maps, use his marine radio, deal with fuel and repair problems, buy the cruiser, and finally determine if he has enough fuel and time to sail his purchase home before sundown. Often the adventures have real-life follow-up problems that build on the knowledge

TABLE 9.3 *The Teacher's Role in Problem-Based Learning*

Phase	Teacher Behavior
Phase 1 Orient students to the problem	Teacher goes over the objectives of the lesson, describes important logistical requirements, and motivates students to engage in self-selected problem-solving activity.
Phase 2 Organize students for study	Teacher helps students define and organize study tasks related to the problem.
Phase 3 Assist independent and group investigation	Teacher encourages students to gather appropriate information, conduct experiments, and search for explanations and solutions.
Phase 4 Develop and present artifacts and exhibits	Teacher assists students in planning and preparing appropriate artifacts such as reports, videos, and models and helps them share their work with others.
Phase 5 Analyze and evaluate the problem-solving process	Teacher helps students to reflect on their investigations and the processes they used.

Source: From *Classroom Instruction and Management* (p. 161), by R. I. Arends, New York: McGraw-Hill. Copyright © 1997 McGraw Hill. Reprinted with permission.

developed. For example, after designing a playground for a hypothetical group of children in one Jasper adventure, students can tackle building a real playhouse for a preschool class.

There are 12 different adventures. Research indicates that students as young as 4th grade and as old as high school can work with the adventures (CTGV, 1990). Students are highly motivated as they work in groups to solve the problems; even group members with limited math skills can contribute to the solutions because they might notice key information in the videotape or suggest innovative ways to approach the situation.

The Vanderbilt group calls its problem-based approach **anchored instruction.** The *anchor* is the rich, interesting situation. This anchor provides a focus—a reason for setting goals, planning, and using mathematical tools to solve problems. The intended outcome is to develop knowledge that is useful and flexible, not inert. Inert knowledge is information that is memorized but seldom applied (CTVG, 1996; Whitehead, 1929).

Group Work and Cooperation in Learning

The terms *group learning* and *cooperative learning* often are used as if they meant the same thing. Actually, group work is simply several students working together— they may or may not be cooperating.

Working in Groups. Many activities can be completed in groups. For example, students can work together in conducting local surveys. How do people feel about the plan to build a new mall that will bring more shopping and more traffic? Would the community support or oppose the building of a nuclear power plant? If students must learn 10 new definitions in a biology class, why not let students divide up the terms and definitions and teach one another? Be sure, however, that everyone in the group can handle the task. Sometimes a group effort ends with one or two students doing the work of the entire group.

Group work can be useful, but true **cooperative learning** requires much more than simply putting students in groups, as you will see in the next few pages.

Beyond Groups to Cooperation. Collaboration and cooperative learning have a long history in American education. In the early 1900s, John Dewey criticized the use of competition in education and encouraged educators to structure schools as democratic learning communities. These ideas fell from favor in the 1940s and 1950s, replaced by a resurgence of competition. In the 1960s, there was a swing back to individualized and cooperative learning structures, stimulated in part by concern for civil rights and interracial relations (Webb & Palincsar, 1996).

Today, evolving constructivist perspectives on learning fuel interest in collaboration and cooperative learning. As you saw above, two characteristics of constructivist teaching are *complex*, *real-life learning environments* and *social interaction*. As educators focus on learning in real contexts, "there is a heightened interest in situations where elaboration, interpretation, explanation, and argumentation are integral to the activity of the group and where learning is supported by other individuals" (Webb & Palincsar, 1996, p. 844).

Different constructivist approaches favor cooperative learning for different reasons. Information processing theorists point to the value of group discussion in helping participants rehearse, elaborate, and expand their knowledge. As group members question and explain, they have to organize their knowledge, make con-

Connect and Extend
To your teaching

Cooperative learning (1986, September). *Harvard Education Letter, 2*(5), 4–6. This article describes STAD and the approach of Roger and David Johnson. One advantage of cooperative learning, as noted by Nel Noddings of Stanford University, is that "children solve problems at a more thoughtful, deliberate pace than they do when working as a class. Without any teacher to approve or reject a proposed solution, they debate strategies for some time." Noting how often children in groups call out, "Wait, wait!" Noddings wonders how many would like to slow down the pace of full-class instruction so they could feel that they really understood.

Connect and Extend
To the research

Slavin, R. R. (1991). Synthesis of research on cooperative learning. *Educational Leadership, 48*(5), 71–82. *Focus Question:* When is cooperative learning most effective, and with which students?

Connect and Extend
To professional journals

Cooperative Learning (1990, special section). *Educational Leadership, 47*(4), 4–67, and Cooperative Learning (1991, special section). *Educational Leadership, 48*, 71–95.

Anchored Instruction: A type of problem-based learning that uses a complex interesting situation as an anchor for learning.

Cooperative Learning: Arrangement in which students work in mixed-ability groups and are rewarded on the basis of the success of the group.

TABLE 9.4 *Different Forms of Cooperative Learning for Different Purposes*

Different forms of cooperative learning (Elaboration, Piagetian, and Vygotskian) fit different purposes, need different structures, and have their own potential problems and possible solutions.

Considerations	Elaboration	Piagetian	Vygotskian
Group size	Small (2–4)	Small	Dyads
Group composition	Heterogeneous/homogeneous	Heterogeneous	Heterogeneous
Tasks	Rehearsal/integrative	Exploratory	Skills
Teacher role	Facilitator	Facilitator	Model/guide
Potential problems	Poor help-giving	Inactive	Poor help-giving
	Unequal participation	No cognitive conflict	Providing adequate time/dialogue
Averting Problems	Direct instruction in help-giving	Structuring controversy	Direct instruction in help-giving
	Modeling help-giving		Modeling help-giving
	Scripting interaction		

Source: From "Learning from Peers: Beyond the Rhetoric of Positive Results," by A. M. O'Donnell and J. O'Kelly, 1994, *Educational Psychology Review*, 6, p. 327. Copyright © 1999 by Plenum Publishing Corporation. Reprinted with permission.

nections, and review—all processes that support information processing and memory. Advocates of a Piagetian perspective suggest that the interactions in groups can create the cognitive conflict and disequilibrium that lead an individual to question his or her understanding and try out new ideas—or, as Piaget (1985) said, "to go beyond his current state and strike out in new directions" (p. 10). Constructivists who favor Vygotsky's theory suggest that social interaction is important for learning because higher mental functions such as reasoning, comprehension, and critical thinking originate in social interactions and are then internalized by individuals. Children can accomplish mental tasks with social support before they can do them alone. Thus cooperative learning provides the social support and scaffolding that students need to move learning forward. Table 9.4 summarizes the functions of cooperative learning from different constructivist perspectives, and describes some of the elements of each kind of group.

To benefit from the dimensions of cooperative learning listed in Table 9.4, groups must *be cooperative*—all members must participate. But, as any teacher or parent knows, cooperation is not automatic when students are put into groups. Angela O'Donnell and Jim O'Kelly, colleagues of mine at Rutgers University, describe a teacher who claimed to be using "cooperative learning" by asking students to work in pairs on a paper, each writing one part. Unfortunately, the teacher allowed no time to work together and provided no guidance or preparation in cooperative social skills. Students got a grade for their individual part and a group grade for the whole project. One student received an A for his part, but a C for the group project because his partner earned an F—he never turned in any work. So one student was punished with a C for a situation he could not control while the other was rewarded with a C for doing no work at all. This was not cooperative learning—it wasn't even group work (O'Donnell & O'Kelly, 1994).

Connect and Extend
To other chapters

The need for belonging is the third level of Maslow's hierarchy, discussed in Chapter 10. The need to maintain relationships is strong. I was reminded of this when my daughter was reprimanded by her 4th-grade teacher for passing notes during class. Liz's explanation was that there had been a fight during lunch, ". . . and we had to work it out!"

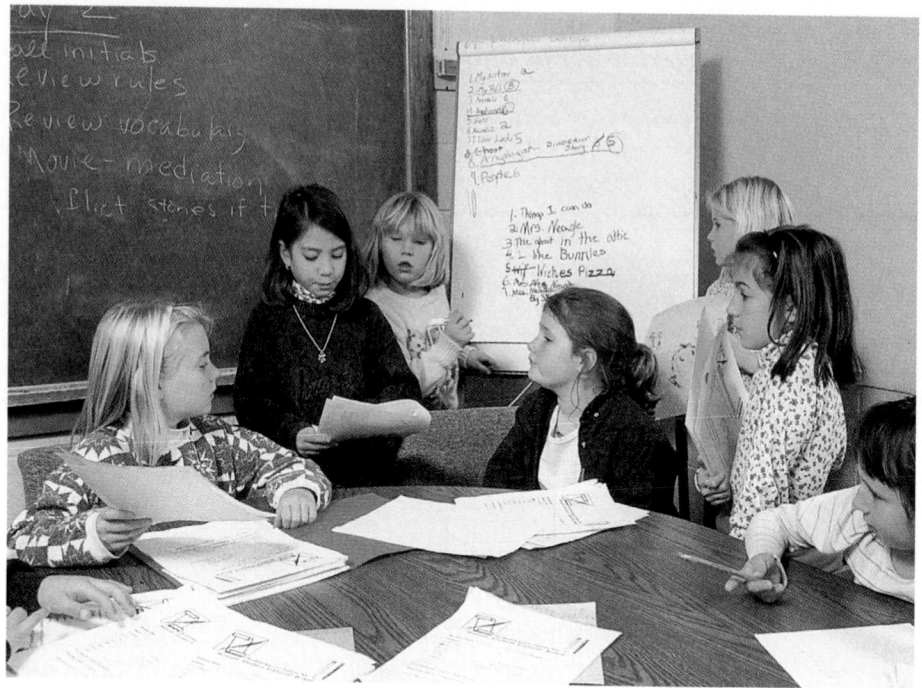

In order to benefit from cooperative learning, groups of students must truly be working together, not just "next to" one another. ▶

Let's look at what can go wrong with cooperative learning—then we can consider how to avoid these problems.

What Can Go Wrong: Misuses of Group Learning. Without careful planning and monitoring by the teacher, group interactions can hinder learning and reduce rather than improve social relations in classes. For example, if there is pressure in a group for conformity—perhaps because rewards are being misused or one student dominates the others—interactions can be unproductive and unreflective. Misconceptions might be reinforced or the worst, not the best, ideas may be combined to construct a superficial understanding (Battistich, Solomon, & Delucci, 1993). Also, the ideas of low status students may be ignored or even ridiculed while the contributions of high status students are accepted and reinforced, regardless of the merit of either set of ideas (Anderson, Holland, & Palincsar, 1997; Cohen, 1986). Mary McCaslin and Tom Good (1996) list several other disadvantages of group learning:

▶ Students often value the process or procedures over the learning. Speed and finishing take precedence over thoughtfulness and learning.

▶ Rather than challenging and correcting misconceptions, students support and reinforce misunderstandings.

▶ Socializing and interpersonal relationships may take precedence over learning.

▶ Students may simply shift dependency from the teacher to the "expert" in the group—learning is still passive and what is learned can be wrong.

▶ Status differences may be increased rather than decreased. Some students learn to "loaf" because the group progresses with or without their contributions. Others are even more convinced that they are helpless to understand without the support of the group.

The next sections examine how teachers can avoid these problems and encourage true cooperation.

Making Cooperative Learning Work

David and Roger Johnson (1999) list five elements that define true cooperative learning groups:

- Face-to-face interaction
- Positive interdependence
- Individual accountability
- Collaborative skills
- Group processing

Students *interact face-to-face* and close together, not across the room. Group members experience *positive interdependence*—they need each other for support, explanations, and guidance. Even though they work together and help each other, members of the group must ultimately demonstrate learning on their own—they are held *individually accountable* for learning, often through individual tests or other assessments. *Collaborative skills* are necessary for effective group functioning. Often these skills, such as giving constructive feedback, reaching consensus, and involving every member, must be taught and practiced before the groups tackle a learning task. Finally, members monitor *group processes* and relationships to make sure the group is working effectively and to learn about the dynamics of groups. They take time to ask, "How are we doing as a group? Is everyone working together?"

Setting Up Cooperative Groups. How large should a cooperative group be? The answer depends on your learning goals. If the purpose is for the group members to review, rehearse information, or practice, 4 to 5 or 6 students is about the right size. But if the goal is to encourage each student to participate in discussions, problem solving, or computer learning, then groups of 2 to 4 members work best. Also, in setting up cooperative groups, it often makes sense to balance the number of boys and girls. Some research indicates that when there are just a few girls in a group, they tend to be left out of the discussions unless they are the most able or assertive members. By contrast, when there are only one or two boys in the group, they tend to dominate and be "interviewed" by the girls unless these boys are less able than the girls or are very shy. In general, for very shy and introverted students, individual learning may be a better approach (O'Donnell & O'Kelly, 1994; Webb, 1985; Webb & Palincsar, 1996). Whatever the case, teachers must monitor groups to make sure everyone is contributing and learning.

In practice, the effects of learning in a group vary, depending on what actually happens in the group and who is in it. If only a few people take responsibility for the work, these people will learn, but the nonparticipating members probably will not. Students who ask questions, get answers, and attempt explanations are more likely to learn than students whose questions go unasked or unanswered. In fact, there is evidence that the more a student provides elaborated, thoughtful explanations to other students in a group, the more the *explainer* learns. Giving good explanations appears to be even more important for learning than receiving explanations (Webb & Palincsar, 1996). In order to explain, you have to organize the information, put it into your own words, think of examples and analogies (which connect the information to things you already know), and test your understanding by answering questions. These are excellent learning strategies (King, 1990; O'Donnell & O'Kelly, 1994).

Some teachers assign roles to students to encourage cooperation and full participation. Several roles are described in Table 9.5 on page 344. If you use roles, be

TABLE 9.5 *Possible Student Roles in Cooperative Learning Groups*

Depending on the purpose of the group and the age of the participants, having these assigned roles might help students cooperate and learn. Of course, students may have to be taught how to enact each role effectively, and roles should be rotated so students can participate in different aspects of group learning.

Role	Description
Encourager	Encourages reluctant or shy students to participate
Praiser/Cheerleader	Shows appreciation of other's contributions and recognizes accomplishments
Gate Keeper	Equalizes participation and makes sure no one dominates
Coach	Helps with the academic content, explains concepts
Question Commander	Makes sure all students' questions are asked and answered
Checker	Checks the group's understanding
Taskmaster	Keeps the group on task
Recorder	Writes down ideas, decisions, and plans
Reflector	Keeps group aware of progress (or lack of progress)
Quiet Captain	Monitors noise level
Materials Monitor	Picks up and returns materials

Source: From *Cooperative Learning*, by S. Kagan, 1994, San Clemente, CA: Kagan Cooperative Learning, 1 (800) WEE CO-OP. Copyright © 1994 by Kagan Cooperative Learning. Adapted with permission.

sure that the roles support learning. In groups that focus on practice, review, or mastery of basic skills, roles should support persistence, encouragement, and participation. In groups that focus on higher-order problem solving or complex learning, roles should encourage thoughtful discussion, sharing of explanations and insights, probing, brainstorming, and creativity. Make sure that you don't communicate to students that the major purpose of the groups is simply to do the procedures—the roles. Roles are supports for learning, not ends in themselves (Woolfolk Hoy & Tschannen-Moran, 1999).

Jigsaw. An early format for cooperative learning that emphasizes high interdependence is **jigsaw**. Each group member is given part of the material to be learned by the whole group and becomes an "expert" on his or her piece. Students have to teach each other, so everyone's contribution is important. A more recent version, Jigsaw II, adds expert groups where the students who have the same material from each learning group confer to make sure they understand their assigned part and then plan ways to teach the information to their learning group members. Next, students return to their learning groups, bringing their expertise to the sessions. In the end, students take an individual test covering all the material and earn points for their learning team score. Teams can work for rewards or simply for recognition (Slavin, 1995).

Jigsaw: A cooperative structure in which each member of a group is responsible for teaching other members one section of the material.

Judy Pitts (1992) describes a lesson about how to do library research that has a jigsaw format. The overall project for each group is to educate the class about a different country. Groups have to decide what information to present and how to make it interesting for their classmates. In the library, each group member is responsible for mastering a particular resource (*Readers' Guide, NewsBank*, reference sets, almanacs, etc.) and teaching other group members, if the need arises. Students learning about each resource meet first in expert groups to be sure all the "teachers" know how to use the resource.

In this class, students confront complex, real-life problems, and not simplified worksheets. They learn by doing and by teaching others. The students must take positions and argue for them—how should our group educate the class about Turkey, for example—while being open to the ideas of others. They may encounter different representations of the same information—graphs, databases, maps, interviews, or encyclopedia articles—and have to integrate information from different sources. This lesson exemplifies many of the characteristics of constructivist approaches. But the most important characteristic of the lesson is that students have a good chance of learning how to do library research by actually doing it.

Reciprocal Questioning. Another cooperative approach can be used with a wide range of ages and subjects. **Reciprocal questioning** requires no special materials or testing procedures. After a lesson or presentation by the teacher, students work in pairs or triads to ask and answer questions about the material (King, 1990, 1994). The teacher provides question stems (see Figure 9.2), then students are taught how to develop specific questions on the lesson material using the generic question stems. The students create questions, then take turns asking and answering. This process has proved more effective than traditional discussion groups because it seems to encourage deeper thinking about the material. Questions such as those on the "Prompt Cards" in Figure 9.2 on page 346, which encourage students to make connections between the lesson and previous knowledge or experience, seems to be the most helpful.

Scripted Cooperation. Donald Dansereau and his colleagues have developed a method for learning in pairs called **scripted cooperation**. Students work together on almost any task, including reading a selection of text, solving math problems, or editing writing drafts. In reading, for example, both partners read a passage, then one student gives an oral summary. The other partner comments on the summary, noting omissions or errors. Next, the partners work together to elaborate on the information—create associations, images, mnemonics, ties to previous work, examples, analogies, and so on. The partners switch roles of summarizer and listener for the next section of the reading, and then continue to take turns until they finish the assignment (Dansereau, 1985, O'Donnell & O'Kelly, 1994).

There are many other forms of cooperative learning. In Chapter 11 you will find methods that emphasize increasing motivation through teamwork and interteam competition. Spencer Kagan (1994) has written extensively on the subject and developed many formats.

Another constructivist approach that relies heavily on interaction is instructional conversations.

Reciprocal Questioning: Approach where groups of two or three students ask and answer each other's questions after a lesson or presentation.

Scripted Cooperation: A learning strategy in which two students take turns summarizing material and criticizing the summaries.

Connect and Extend
To the research
King, A. (1990). Enhancing peer interaction and learning in the classroom through reciprocal questioning. *American Educational Research Journal, 27*, 664–687.

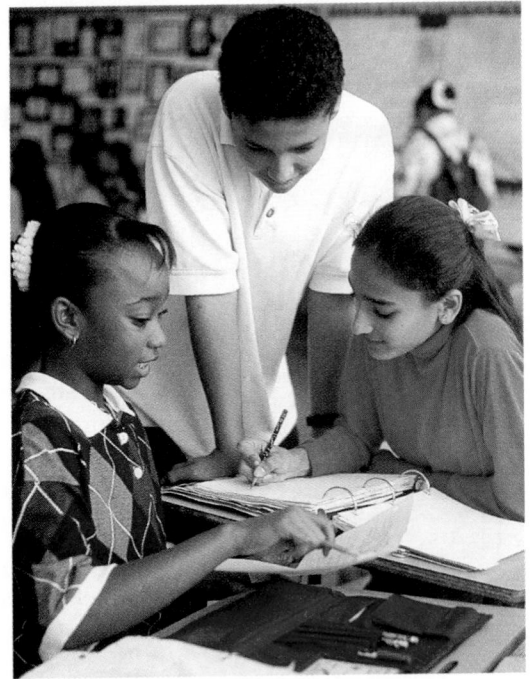

▲ *Reciprocal questioning techniques encourage students to ask and answer probing questions.*

FIGURE 9.2

Reciprocal Questioning Prompt Cards to Guide Dialogue

After studying materials or participating in a lesson, pairs of students use the "Prompt Cards" below to develop questions and then share answers.

Comprehension Questions

Describe ... in your own words.

What does ... mean?

Why is ... important?

Connection Questions

Explain why ... and how ...

How are ... and ... similar?... different?

How could ... be used to ... ?

How does ... tie in with ... that we learned before?

Source: From "Guiding Knowledge Construction in the Classroom: Effects of Teaching Children How to Question and How to Explain," by A. King, 1994, *American Educational Research Journal, 31,* p. 345. Copyright © 1994 by the American Educational Research Association. Adapted with permission.

Dialogue and Instructional Conversations

Connect and Extend
To professional resources
For more information on instructional conversations, including examples of class transcripts and instruments to assess instructional conversations, contact: Dissemination Center, National Center for Research on Cultural Diversity and Second Language Learning, Center for Applied Linguistics, 1118 22nd Street NW, Washington, DC 20037.

One implication of Vygotsky's theory of cognitive development is that important learning and understanding require interaction and conversation. Students need to grapple with problems in their zone of proximal development, and they need the scaffolding provided by interaction with a teacher or other students. Instructional conversations provide these opportunities. **Instructional conversations** are *instructional* because they are designed to promote learning, but they are *conversations*, not lectures or traditional discussions. Here is a segment of conversation from a literature group in a bilingual 3rd-grade classroom (Moll & Whitmore, 1993). The conversation shows how the participants mediate each other's learning through dialogue about the shared experience.

T: *Sylvester and the Magic Pebble.* What did you think about this story?
Rita: I think they cared a lot for him.
T: What do you mean? You mean his parents?
Rita: Yes.
T: What made you think that when you read the story?
Rita: Because they really worried about him.
T: Who else wants to share something? I'd like to hear everybody's ideas. Then we can decide what we want to talk about. Sarah?
Sarah: I think he got the idea of it when he was little, or maybe one of his friends got lost or something?

Instructional Conversation: Situation in which students learn through interactions with teachers and/or other students.

T: What do you mean, he got the idea?

Sarah: He got the idea for his parents to think that Sylvester got lost.

T: You're talking about where William Steig might have gotten his ideas.

Sarah: Yes.

T: That maybe something like this happened to him or someone he knew. A lot of times authors get their ideas from real life things, don't they? Jon, what did you think about this story?

Jon: It was like a moral story. It's like you can't wish for everything. But, in a sense, everything happened to him when he was panicking.

T: When did you think he panicked?

Jon: Well, when he saw the lion, he started to panic.

Richard: And he turned himself into a rock.

Jon: Yeah. He said, "I wish I were a rock."

T: Right. And it happened, didn't it?

Richard: It was stupid of him.

T: So maybe he wasn't thinking far enough ahead? What would you have wished instead of a rock? (pp. 24–25)

The conversation continues as the students contribute different levels of interpretation of the story. The teacher notes these interpretations in her summary: "Look at all the different kinds of things you had to say. Rita talked about the characters in the story and what they must be feeling. Sarah took the author's point of view. And you saw it as a particular kind of story, Jon, a moral story."

In instructional conversations, the teacher's goal is to keep everyone cognitively engaged in a substantive discussion. In the above conversation, the teacher takes almost every other turn. As the students become more familiar with this learning approach, we would expect them to talk more among themselves with less teacher talk. These conversations do not have to be long. Even taking up lunch money can be an opportunity for an instructional conversation.

> During the first few minutes of the day, Ms. White asked how many children wanted hot lunches that day. Eighteen children raised their hands. Six children were going to eat cold lunches. Ms. White asked, "How many children are going to eat lunch here today?"
>
> By starting with 18 and counting on, several children got to the answer of 24. One child got out counters and counted out a set of 18 and another set of 6. He then counted all of them and said "24."
>
> Ms. White then asked, "How many more children are eating hot lunch than are eating cold lunch?"
>
> Several children counted back from 18 to 12. The child with the blocks matched 18 blocks with 6 blocks and counted the blocks left over.
>
> Ms. White asked the children who volunteered to tell the rest of the class how they got the answer. Ms. White continued asking for different solutions until no one could think of a new way to solve the problem. (Peterson, Fennema, & Carpenter, 1989, p. 45)

This teacher is creating an environment in which students can make sense of mathematics and use mathematics to make sense of the world. To accomplish these goals, teaching begins with the student's current understanding. Teachers can capitalize on the natural use of counting strategies to see how many different ways students can solve a problem. The emphasis is on mathematical thinking, not on math "facts" or on learning the one best (teacher's) way to solve the problem. The teacher is a guide, helping students construct their own understandings through dialogue (Putnam & Borko, 1997). Table 9.6 on page 348 summarizes the elements of productive instructional conversations.

TABLE 9.6 Elements of the Instructional Conversation

Good instructional conversations must have elements of both instruction and conversation.

Instruction

1. *Thematic focus.* Teacher selects a theme on which to focus the discussion and has a general plan for how the theme will unfold, including how to "chunk" the text to permit optimal exploration of the theme.

2. *Activation and use of background knowledge.* Teacher either "hooks into" or provides students with pertinent background knowledge necessary for understanding a text, weaving the information into the discussion.

3. *Direct teaching.* When necessary, teacher provides direct teaching of a skill or concept.

4. *Promotion of more complex language and expression.* Teacher elicits more extended student contributions by using a variety of elicitation techniques: invitation to expand, questions, restatements, and pauses.

5. *Promotion of bases for statements or positions.* Teacher promotes students' use of text, pictures, and reasoning to support an argument or position, by gently probing: "What makes you think that?" or "Show us where it says _____."

Conversation

6. *Fewer "known-answer" questions.* Much of the discussion centers on questions for which there might be more than one correct answer.

7. *Responsiveness to student contributions.* While having an initial plan and maintaining the focus and coherence of the discussion, teacher is also responsive to students' statements and the opportunities they provide.

8. *Connected discourse.* The discussion is characterized by multiple, interactive, connected turns; succeeding utterances build on and extend previous ones.

9. *Challenging, but non-threatening, atmosphere.* Teacher creates a challenging atmosphere that is balanced by a positive affective climate. Teacher is more collaborator than evaluator and students are challenged to negotiate and construct the meaning of the text.

10. *General participation, including self-selected turns.* Teacher does not hold exclusive right to determine who talks; students are encouraged to volunteer or otherwise influence the selection of speaking turns.

Source: From *Instructional Conversations and Their Classroom Application* (p. 7), by Claude Goldenberg, 1991, Santa Cruz, CA and Washington, DC: National Center for Research on Cultural Diversity and Second Language Learning. Copyright © 1991 by National Center for Research on Cultural Diversity and Second Language Learning. Reprinted with permission.

Cognitive Apprenticeships

Over the centuries, apprenticeships have proved to be an effective form of education. By working alongside a master and perhaps other apprentices, young people have learned many skills, trades, and crafts. Apprenticeships are powerful teaching and learning opportunities and can be beneficial to both master and apprentice. More knowledgeable guides provide models, demonstrations, and corrections, as well as a personal bond that is motivating. The performances required of the learner are real and important and grow more complex as the learner becomes more competent (Collins, Brown, & Holum, 1991; Collins, Brown, & Newman, 1989). In addition, both the new comers to learning and the old timers contribute to the community of practice by mastering and remastering skills—and sometimes improving these skills in the process (Lave & Wenger, 1991).

Allan Collins and his colleagues (1989) suggest that knowledge and skills learned in school have become too separated from their use in the world beyond school. To correct this imbalance, some educators recommend that schools adopt many of the features of apprenticeships. But rather than learning to sculpt or dance or build a cabinet, apprenticeships in school would focus on cognitive objectives such as reading comprehension, writing, or mathematical problem solving. There are many cognitive apprenticeship models, but most share six features:

▶ Students observe an expert (usually the teacher) *model* the performance.

▶ Students get external support through *coaching* or tutoring (including hints, feedback, models, and reminders).

▶ Students receive conceptual *scaffolding*, which is then gradually faded as the student becomes more competent and proficient.

▶ Students continually *articulate* their knowledge—putting into words their understanding of the processes and content being learned.

▶ Students *reflect* on their progress, comparing their problem solving to an expert's performance and to their own earlier performances.

▶ Students are required to *explore* new ways to apply what they are learning—ways that they have not practiced at the master's side.

As students learn, they are challenged to master more complex concepts and skills and to perform them in many different settings (Roth & Bowen, 1995; Shuell, 1996).

How can teaching provide **cognitive apprenticeships?** In the Key School, an inner-city public elementary school in Indianapolis, Indiana, students of different ages work side-by-side for part of every day on a "pod" designed to have many of the qualities of an apprenticeship. The pods might focus on a craft or a discipline. Examples include gardening, architecture, and "making money." Many levels of expertise are evident in the students of different ages, so students can move at a comfortable pace, but still have the model of a master available. Community volunteers, including many parents, visit to demonstrate a skill that is related to the pod topic.

Another successful example of cognitive apprenticeships is the reciprocal teaching approach.

An Example of a Cognitive Apprenticeship: Reciprocal Teaching

The goal of **reciprocal teaching** is to help students understand and think deeply about what they read (Palincsar, 1986; Palincsar & Brown, 1984, 1989). To accomplish this goal, students in small reading groups learn four strategies: *summarizing* the content of a passage, *asking a question* about the central point, *clarifying* the difficult parts of the material, and *predicting* what will come next. These are strategies that skilled readers apply almost automatically, but poor readers seldom do—or they don't know how. To use the strategies effectively, poorer readers need direct instruction, modeling, and practice in actual reading situations.

Cognitive Apprenticeship: A relationship in which a less experienced learner acquires knowledge and skills under the guidance of an expert.

Reciprocal Teaching: A method, based on modeling, to teach reading comprehension strategies.

▲ *Annemarie Palincsar's research has focused attention on strategies that improve reading comprehension.*

Connect and Extend
To the research
Rosenshine, B., & Meister, C. (1994). Reciprocal teaching: A review of the research. *Review of Educational Research, 64,* 479–530.

First, the teacher introduces these strategies, perhaps focusing on one strategy each day. The teacher explains and models each strategy and encourages students to practice. Next, the teacher and the students read a short passage silently. Then the teacher again provides a model by summarizing, questioning, clarifying, and predicting based on the reading. Everyone reads another passage, and the students gradually begin to assume the teacher's role. Often the students' first attempts are halting and incorrect. But the teacher gives clues, guidance, encouragement, support in doing parts of the task (such as providing question stems), and models (what Bruner might call "scaffolding") to help the students master these strategies. The goal is for students to learn to apply these strategies independently as they read so they can make sense of text.

Reciprocal Teaching in Action. Let's look at some examples of reciprocal teaching in action. The first example is an early lesson. Here the teacher is guiding one member of a reading group as he tries to formulate a question about the central point in a passage on spiders ("When the Student Becomes the Teacher," 1986, p. 6):

Text: Spinner's mate is much smaller than she, and his body is dull brown. He spends most of his time sitting at one side of her web.
Charles: (No question)
Teacher: What's this paragraph about?
Charles: Spinner's mate. How do spinner's mate . . .
Teacher: That's good. Keep going.
Charles: How do spinner's mate is smaller than . . . . How am I going to say that?
Teacher: Take your time with it. You want to ask a question about spinner's mate and what he does, beginning with the word "how."
Charles: How do they spend most of his time sitting?
Teacher: You're very close. The question would be, "How does spinner's mate spend most of his time?" Now, you ask it.
Charles: How does spinner's mate spend most of his time?

After a while, students are usually able to take more and more responsibility for the teaching. In the following example, Laura shows how much progress she has made after about 12 lessons ("When the Student Becomes the Teacher," 1986, p. 6):

Text: The second oldest form of salt production is mining. Unlike early methods that made the work extremely dangerous and difficult, today's methods use special machinery, and salt mining is easier and safer. The old expression "back to the salt mine" no longer applies.
Laura: Name two words that often describe mining salt in the old days.
Kim: Back to the salt mines?
Laura: No. Angela?
Angela: Dangerous and difficult.
Laura: Correct. This paragraph is all about comparing the old mining of salt and today's mining of salt.
Teacher: Beautiful!
Laura: I have a prediction to make.
Teacher: Good.
Laura: I think it might tell when salt was first discovered . . . well, it might tell what salt is made of and how it's made.
Teacher: OK. Can we have another teacher?

Applying Reciprocal Teaching. Research on reciprocal teaching has shown some dramatic results. Although reciprocal teaching seems to work with almost any age student, most of the research has been done with younger adolescents who can read aloud fairly accurately, but who are far below average in reading comprehension. After 20 hours of practice with this approach, many students who were in the bottom quarter of their class moved up to the average or above average level on tests of reading comprehension. Based on the results of several studies, Palincsar has identified three guidelines for effective reciprocal teaching (Palincsar & Brown, 1984; "When the Student Becomes the Teacher," 1986):

1. *Shift gradually.* The shift from teacher control to student responsibility must be gradual.

2. *Match demands to abilities.* The difficulty of the task and the responsibility must match the abilities of each student and grow as these abilities develop.

3. *Diagnose thinking.* Teachers should carefully observe the "teaching" of each student for clues about how the student is thinking and what kind of instruction the student needs.

In reciprocal teaching, Annemarie Palincsar and Ann Brown have made four significant contributions to education. First, they remind us that procedures for fostering and monitoring comprehension must be taught—not all students develop these strategies on their own. Second, Palincsar and Brown focused attention on 4 rather than 40 or more strategies, as some sources have suggested. Third, they emphasized practicing these 4 strategies in the context of actual reading—reading literature and reading texts. Finally, they refined and developed the idea of scaffolding and gradually moving the student toward independent and fluid reading comprehension (Rosenshine & Meister, 1994).

With a consideration of reciprocal teaching, we are moving toward instructional approaches that emphasize social interaction and students' active construction of meaning.

Cognitive Apprenticeships in Thinking

Many educational psychologists believe that good thinking can and should be developed in school. But clearly, teaching thinking entails much more than the standard classroom practices of answering "thought" questions at the end of the chapter or participating in teacher-led discussions. What else is needed? One approach has been to focus on the development of *thinking skills*, either through stand-alone programs that teach skills directly, or through indirect methods that embed development of thinking in the regular curriculum.

Stand-Alone Programs for Developing Thinking. There are many different programs that teach thinking skills directly. A resource book for educators (Costa, 1985) lists over 15 different programs, including *de Bono's CoRT* system; *Odyssey: A Curriculum for Thinking*; *Winocur's Project Impact*; *Lipman's Philosophy for Children*; and *Meeker's SOI*. In these programs students learn skills such as comparing, ordering, classifying, and making inferences. The advantage of these **stand-alone thinking skills programs** is that students do not need extensive subject matter knowledge to master the skills. Students who have had trouble with the traditional curriculum may achieve success—and perhaps an enhanced sense of self-efficacy—through these programs. As you saw in Chapter 8, encouraging students to transfer knowledge and skills to new situations is a challenge for all teachers (Mayer & Wittrock, 1996; Prawat, 1991). The disadvantage is that the general skills often are not used outside the program unless teachers make a concerted

Connect and Extend
To your own philosophy
Can different formats, such as lecture or seatwork, be used in the service of different models, such as direct instruction or constructivist approaches?

Connect and Extend
To professional resources
The following description of the Odyssey program is abridged from the *Human Intelligence International Newsletter* (1985, winter). Odyssey: A curriculum for thinking, p. 9:
Odyssey, which can be introduced between grades 4 and 8, includes six books:

Foundations of Reasoning, the introductory book. It teaches the basic concepts that are developed in other Odyssey books: processes for gathering, organizing, and interpreting information in systematic and critical ways.

Understanding Language. This book helps students extend their analytical skills to vocabulary, sentences, and paragraphs.

Verbal Reasoning. Students learn how to recognize, analyze, produce, and evaluate assertions and arguments.

Problem Solving. Teaches students graphic representation and simulation of problem statements, use of trial and error, and ways to think through the implications of a solution.

Decision Making. How to gather and sort information along the dimensions of relevance, consistency, and credibility.

Inventive Thinking. Designs as descriptions, comparisons, and experimentation; ways to evaluate, improve, and invent designs.

Stand-Alone Thinking Skills Programs: Programs that teach thinking skills directly without need for extensive subject matter knowledge.

Connect and Extend
To the research

Adams, M. J. (1989). Thinking skills curricula. *Educational Psychologist, 24,* 25–27. This article addresses the explosion of interest in the teaching of thinking. What content or processes should a thinking skills curriculum include? How should it be organized? In what ways would such a curriculum differ in force or effect from thoughtful delivery of conventional school topics? This article concludes that the direct teaching of thinking offers an important complement to conventional school regimen for all students, and is invaluable for those with scholastic difficulties.

Connect and Extend
To the research

Perkins, D., Jay, E., & Tishman, S. (1993). New conceptions of thinking: From ontology to education. *Educational Psychologist, 28,* 67–85; see also Tishman, S., Perkins, D., and Jay, E. (1995). *The thinking classroom: Learning and teaching in a culture of thinking.* Boston: Allyn and Bacon.

"WE DID THAT LAST YEAR— HOW COME WE HAVE TO DO IT AGAIN THIS YEAR?"

(© W. A. VANSELOW—From Phi Delta Kappan.*)*

effort to show students how to apply the skills in specific subjects, as you can see in the Point/Counterpoint discussion.

Developing Thinking in Every Class. Another way to develop students' thinking is to provide cognitive apprenticeships in analysis, problem solving, and reasoning through the regular lessons of the curriculum. David Perkins and his colleagues (Perkins, Jay, & Tishman, 1993) propose that teachers do this by creating a *culture of thinking* in their classrooms. This means that there is a spirit of inquisitiveness and critical thinking, a respect for reasoning and creativity, and an expectation that students will learn and understand. In such a classroom, education is seen as *enculturation,* a broad and complex process of acquiring knowledge and understanding consistent with Vygotsky's theory of mediated learning. We all learned language by being a member of a particular cultural group. We also learned ways of interacting, norms of appropriate behavior, and many other complicated rules and procedures through living in a culture that supports certain knowledge and values. Just as our home culture taught us lessons about the use of language, the culture of a classroom can teach lessons about thinking by giving us *models* of good thinking; providing *direct instruction* in thinking processes; and encouraging *practice* of those thinking processes through *interactions* with others.

Let's consider how this might happen in a classroom described by Perkins, Jay, and Tishman (1993).

Suppose an 8th-grade teacher wants her students to learn how to construct explanations that involve *multiple causes.* The class is studying the agriculture of eastern Asia, specifically the important rice crops. The teacher introduces a lesson by *modeling* good thinking about multiple causes:

> Have you noticed that the roses in the park bloomed early this year? I'm asking myself why. What factors caused these early blooms? I recall it was a warm winter. That was probably an important factor. But certainly there are other factors involved—probably some hidden ones—and I know it is important to search for them. In fact, now that I have stopped to think, I remember that we had very heavy rains in March. This may be a factor too. (Perkins, Jay, & Tishman, 1993, p. 80)

After providing this model, the teacher points out other effects that have multiple causes such as winning a football game or staying healthy. Next, the teacher gives straightforward, *direct instruction* about how to analyze causes, such as considering how causal factors may work together or separately. She teaches the students to draw diagrams that depict multiple causes. Then she gives the students *practice* in analyzing multiple causes by asking them to diagram the causes involved in rice growth

Should Schools Teach Critical Thinking and Problem Solving?

The question of whether schools should focus on process or content, problem-solving skills or core knowledge, higher-order thinking skills or academic information has been debated for years. Some educators suggest that students must be taught how to think and solve problems, while other educators assert that students cannot learn to "think" in the abstract. They must be thinking about something—some content. Should teachers focus on knowledge or thinking?

▶ **POINT** *Problem solving and higher-order thinking can and should be taught.*

An article in the April, 28, 1995, issue of the *Chronicle of Higher Education* makes this claim:

> Critical thinking is at the heart of effective reading, writing, speaking, and listening. It enables us to link together mastery of content with such diverse goals as self-esteem, self-discipline, multicultural education, effective cooperative learning, and problem solving. It enables all instructors and administrators to raise the level of their own teaching and thinking. (p. A-71)

How can students learn to think critically? Some educators recommend teaching thinking skills directly with widely used techniques such as the Productive Thinking Program or CoRT (Cognitive Research Trust). Other researchers argue that learning computer programming languages such as LOGO will improve students' minds and teach them how to think logically. For example, Papert (1980) believes that when children learn through discovery how to give instructions to computers in LOGO, "powerful intellectual skills are developed in the process" (p. 60). Finally, because expert readers automatically apply certain metacognitive strategies, many educators and psychologists recommend directly teaching novice or poor readers how to apply these strategies. Michael Pressley's Good Strategy User model and Palincsar and Brown's (1984) reciprocal teaching approach are successful examples of direct teaching of metacognitive skills. Research on these approaches generally shows improvements in achievement and comprehension for students of all ages who participate (Pressley, Barkowski, & Schneider, 1987; Rosenshine & Meister, 1994).

◀ **COUNTERPOINT** *Thinking and problem-solving skills do not transfer.*

According to E. D. Hirsch, a vocal critic of critical thinking programs:

> But whether such direct instruction of critical thinking or self-monitoring *does* in fact improve performance is a subject of debate in the research community. For instance, the research regarding critical thinking is not reassuring. Instruction in critical thinking has been going on in several countries for over a hundred years. Yet researchers found that students from nations as varied as Israel, Germany, Australia, the Philippines, and the United States, including those who have been taught critical thinking continue to fall into logical fallacies. (1996, p. 136)

The CoRT program has been used in over 5,000 classrooms in 10 nations. But Polson and Jeffries (1985) report that "after 10 years of widespread use we have no adequate evidence concerning . . . the effectiveness of the program" (p. 445). In addition, Mayer and Wittrock (1996) note that field studies of problem solving in real situations show that people often fail to apply the mathematical problem-solving approaches they learn in school to actual problems encountered in the grocery store or home.

Even though educators have been more successful in teaching metacognitive skills, critics still caution that there are times when such teaching hinders rather than helps learning. Robert Siegler (1993) suggests that teaching self-monitoring strategies to low-achieving students can interfere with the students' development of adaptive strategies. Forcing students to use the strategies of experts may put too much burden on working memory as the students struggle to use an unfamiliar strategy and miss the meaning or content of the lesson. For example, rather than teach students strategies for figuring out words from context, it may be helpful for students to focus on learning more vocabulary words.

and how the causes work together or separately to produce rice. The teacher stimulates their thinking by suggesting that the students cast a wide net and consider many factors such as weather, soil, insects, and farming practices. One student's diagram is presented in Figure 9.3 on page 354.

FIGURE 9.3

A Multicasual Analysis of Factors Affecting Rice Growth

Students are taught how to use the *and/or* convention to diagram causes that work together (*and*) or separately (*or*) to produce an effect; in this case, the growth of rice.

Source: From "Epistemic Forms and Epistemic Games: Structures and Strategies to Guide Inquiry," by A. Collins and W. Ferguson, 1993, *Educational Psychologist,* 28, p. 35. Adapted by permission of the publisher and the authors.

When the students finish their diagrams, the teacher asks them to discuss their analysis with a partner. She guides the *interaction* with questions such as "How did you identify causes?" "Was it hard to figure out if causes worked together or alone?" "What questions can you invent about this multifactor causal analysis game?" "Can you envision other situations where you could use this kind of causal analysis?"

In this lesson, the four factors of modeling, direct instruction, practice, and interaction help students become expert members of the thinking community.

The Language of Thinking. How many words can you find in the above lesson that describe aspects of thinking? A quick look finds "search," "asking why," "hidden factors," "analyze," "identify," "figure out," "envision," "effects," "causes," and "invent." My computer's thesaurus just found over 100 more words when I highlighted "thinking." The language of thinking consists of natural language terms that refer to mental processes and mental products—"words like *think, believe, guess, conjecture, hypothesis, evidence, reasons, estimate, calculate, suspect, doubt,* and *theorize*—to name just a few" (Tishman, Perkins, & Jay, 1995, p. 8).

Connect and Extend
To what you know
List all the different words related to thinking that you hear during one of your college classes. You might contrast the "thinking language" in a class that seems to challenge you to think with a class that focuses on skills and facts.

The classroom should be filled with a clear, precise, and rich vocabulary of thinking. Rather than saying, "What do you think about Jamie's answer?" the teacher might ask questions that expand thinking such as, "What evidence can you give to refute or support Jamie's answer?" "What assumptions is Jamie making?" "What are some alternative explanations?" Students surrounded by a rich language of thinking are more likely to think deeply about thinking. Students learn more when they engage in talk that is interpretive and that analyzes and gives explanations. Talk that just describes but doesn't explain, give reasons, identify parts, make a case, defend a position, or evaluate evidence is less helpful in learning (Palincsar, 1998).

Critical Thinking. **Critical thinking** skills are useful in almost every life situation—even in evaluating the media ads that constantly bombard us. To evaluate the claim that 99 out of 100 dentists prefer a particular brand of toothpaste, you must consider such questions as: Which dentists were polled? How were they chosen? Was the toothpaste company involved in the polling process? If so, how could this bias the results of the poll? Or when you see a group of gorgeous people extolling the virtues of a particular brand of orange juice as they frolic in skimpy bathing suits, you must decide if sex appeal is a relevant factor in choosing a fruit drink. Psychologists have not been able to agree on the skills that constitute critical thinking, but Table 9.7 provides a representative list of skills.

No matter what approach you use to develop critical thinking, it is important to follow up with additional practice. One lesson is not enough. For example, if your class examined a particular historical document to determine if it reflected bias or propaganda, you should follow up by analyzing other written historical

Connect and Extend
To professional journals
Educational Leadership (1988, April), Vol. 45, No. 7, has a special section called "Teaching Thinking Throughout the Curriculum."

Connect and Extend
To the research
Greeno, J. G. (1989). A perspective on thinking. *American Psychologist, 44,* 134–141.
Abbreviated abstract: Research on general thinking abilities—productive, higher-order, critical, and creative thinking—has progressed slowly compared with the rapid progress in the study of cognitive structures and procedures. Three framing assumptions for the study of thinking are proposed, involving situated cognition, personal and social epistemologies, and conceptual competence; topics in the psychology of thinking are discussed in relation to the assumptions.

TABLE 9.7 *Examples of Critical Thinking Skills*

Defining and Clarifying the Problem

1. Identify central issues or problems.
2. Compare similarities and differences.
3. Determine which information is relevant.
4. Formulate appropriate questions.

Judging Information Related to the Problem

5. Distinguish among fact, opinion, and reasoned judgment.
6. Check consistency.
7. Identify unstated assumptions.
8. Recognize stereotypes and clichés.
9. Recognize bias, emotional factors, propaganda, and semantic slanting.
10. Recognize different value systems and ideologies.

Solving Problems/Drawing Conclusions

11. Recognize the adequacy of data.
12. Predict probable consequences.

Source: From "California Assesses Critical Thinking," by P. Kneedler. In A. Costa (Ed.), *Developing Minds: A Resource Book for Teaching Thinking,* p. 277. Copyright © 1985 by the Association for Supervision and Curriculum Development and the author. Reprinted with permission. All rights reserved.

Critical Thinking: Evaluating conclusions by logically and systematically examining the problem, the evidence, and the solution.

documents, contemporary advertisements, or news stories. Until thinking skills become overlearned and relatively automatic, they are not likely to be transferred to new situations. Instead, students will use these skills only to complete the lesson in social studies, not to evaluate the claims made by friends, politicians, toy manufacturers, or diet plans. What else is needed to apply good thinking?

Many of the new standards for teaching, such as the National Council of Teachers of Mathematics' *Curriculum and Evaluation Standards for School Mathematics* (NCTM, 1989) and the American Association for the Advancement of Science's *Benchmarks for Science Literacy* (AAAS, 1993) are based on constructivist attempts to develop thinking. Efforts to reform and restructure schools often are attempts to apply constructivist perspectives on teaching and learning to the curriculum and organization of entire schools. Not all reforms are met with approval by families or the community. Many teachers using nontraditional approaches to learning find that they must explain these approaches to students' families. The Family and Community Partnerships Guidelines give ideas for communicating with parents about innovative constructivist teaching and learning.

Looking Back at Learning

For the past four chapters we have examined different aspects of learning. We considered behavioral, information processing, social cognitive, constructivist, and situated explanations of what people learn and how they learn it. As a summary of the different theories of learning, Table 9.8 on page 358 presents several of these perspectives on learning. Rather than debating the merits of each approach, consider their contributions to understanding learning and improving teaching. Don't feel that you must choose the "best" approach—there is no such thing. Chemists, biologists, and nutritionists rely on different theories to explain and improve health. Different views of learning can be used together to create productive learning environments. Behavioral theory helps us understand the role of cues in setting the stage for behaviors and the role of consequences and practice in encouraging or dis-

FAMILY AND COMMUNITY PARTNERSHIPS

Communicating about Innovations

Be confident and honest.

Examples

1. Write out your rationale for the methods you are using—consider likely objections and craft your responses.

2. Admit mistakes or oversights—explain what you have learned from them.

Treat parents as equal partners.

Examples

1. Listen carefully to parents' objections, take notes, and follow up on requests or suggestions—remember, you both want the best for the child.

2. Give parents the telephone number of an administrator who will answer their questions about a new program or initiative.

3. Invite families to visit your room or assist in the project in some way.

Communicate effectively.

Examples

1. Use plain language and avoid jargon. If you must use a technical term, define it in accessible ways. Use your best teaching skills to educate parents about the new approach.

2. Encourage local newspapers or television stations to do stories about the "great learning" going on in your classroom or school.

3. Create a lending library of articles and references about the new strategies.

Have examples of projects and assignments available for parents when they visit your class.

Examples

1. Encourage parents to try math activities. If they have trouble, show them how your students (and their child) are successful with the activities and highlight the strategies the students have learned.

2. Keep a library of students' favorite activities to demonstrate for parents.

Develop family involvement packages.

Examples

1. Once a month, send families, via their children, descriptions and examples of the math, science, or language to be learned in the upcoming unit. Include activities children can do with their parents.

2. Make the family project count, for example, as a homework grade.

Source: From "Addressing Parents' Concerns over Curriculum Reform," by M. Meyer, M. Delgardelle, and J. Middleton, 1996, *Educational Leadership, 53*(7), p. 57. Copyright © 1996 by the Association for Supervision and Curriculum Development. Adapted with permission. All rights reserved.

couraging behaviors. But much of humans' lives and learning is more than behaviors. Language and higher-order thinking requires complex information processing and memory—something the cognitive models of the thinker-as-computer have helped us understand. And what about the person as a creator and constructor of knowledge, not just a processor of information? Here, constructivist perspectives have much to offer.

TABLE 9.8 *Four Views of Learning*

There are variations within each of these views of learning that differ in emphasis. There is also an overlap in constructivist views.

	Behavioral	Cognitive — Information Processing	Constructivist — Psychological/ Individual	Constructivist — Social/ Situated
	Skinner	J. Anderson	Piaget	Vygotsky
Knowledge	Fixed body of knowledge to acquire	Fixed body of knowledge to acquire	Changing body of knowledge, individually constructed in social world	Socially constructed knowledge
	Stimulated from outside	Stimulated from outside	Built on what learner brings	Built on what participants contribute, construct together
		Prior knowledge influences how information is processed		
Learning	Acquisition of facts, skills, concepts	Acquisition of facts, skills, concepts, and strategies	Active construction, restructuring prior knowledge	Collaborative construction of socially defined knowledge and values
	Occurs through drill, guided practice	Occurs through the effective application of strategies	Occurs through multiple opportunities and diverse processes to connect to what is already known	Occurs through socially constructed opportunities
Teaching	Transmission Presentation (Telling)	Transmission Guide students toward more "accurate" and complete knowledge	Challenge, guide thinking toward more complete understanding	Co-construct knowledge with students
Role of Teacher	Manager, supervisor	Teach and model effective strategies	Facilitator, guide	Facilitator, guide Co-participant
	Correct wrong answers	Correct misconceptions	Listen for student's current conceptions, ideas, thinking	Co-construct different interpretation of knowledge; listen to socially constructed conceptions
Role of Peers	Not usually considered	Not necessary but can influence information processing	Not necessary but can stimulate thinking, raise questions	Ordinary part of process of knowledge construction
Role of Student	Passive reception of information	Active processor of information, strategy user	Active construction (within mind)	Active co-construction with others and self
	Active listener, direction-follower	Organizer and reorganizer of information	Active thinker, explainer, interpreter, questioner	Active thinker, explainer, interpreter, questioner
		Rememberer		Active social participator

Source: From *Reconceptualizing Learning for Restructured Schools* by H. H. Marshall. Paper presented at the Annual Meeting of the American Educational Research Association, April 1992. Copyright © Hermine H. Marshall. Adapted with permission.

Summary

Social Learning and Social Cognitive Theories

Distinguish between social learning and social cognitive theories.

Social learning theory was an early neobehavioral theory that expanded behavioral views of reinforcement and punishment. In behavioral views, reinforcement and punishment directly affect behavior. In social learning theory, seeing another person, a model, reinforced or punished can have similar effects on the observer's behavior. Social cognitive theory expands social learning theory to include cognitive factors such as beliefs, expectations, and perceptions of self.

Distinguish between enactive and vicarious learning.

Enactive learning is learning by doing and experiencing the consequences of your actions. *Vicarious learning* is learning by observing, which challenges the behaviorist idea that cognitive factors are unnecessary in an explanation of learning. If people can learn by watching, they must be focusing their attention, constructing images, remembering, analyzing, and making decisions that affect learning. Thus much is going on mentally before performance and reinforcement can even take place.

What are the elements of observational learning?

The elements are *paying attention, retaining information or impressions, producing behaviors*, and *being motivated* to repeat the behaviors. In order to learn through observation, we have to pay attention to aspects of the situation that will help us learn. In order to imitate the behavior of a model, you have to retain the information. This involves mentally representing the model's actions in some way, probably as verbal steps. In the production phase, practice makes the behavior smoother and more expert. Sometimes we need a great deal of practice, feedback, and coaching about subtle points before we can reproduce the behavior of the model. Finally, motivation shapes observational learning through incentives and reinforcement. We may acquire a new skill or behavior through observation, but we may not perform that behavior until there is some motivation or incentive to do so. Reinforcement can play several roles in observational learning including focusing attention, encouraging reproduction or practice, and supporting maintenance of the new learning.

What is reciprocal determinism?

Environmental events, personal factors and behaviors interact in the process of learning. Personal factors (beliefs, expectations, attitudes, and knowledge), the physical and social environment (resources, consequences of actions, other people, and physical settings), and behavior (individual actions, choices, and verbal statements) all influence and are influenced by each other.

Constructivism and Situated Learning

Describe three kinds of constructivism.

Psychological constructivists are concerned with how *individuals* make sense of their worlds. These constructivists might be interested in individual knowledge, beliefs, self-concept, or identity, so they are sometimes called *individual* constructivists; they all focus on the inner psychological life of people. Piaget is an example of an individual constructivist. *Social* constructivists believe that social interaction, cultural tools, and activity shape individual development and learning. By participating in a broad range of activities with others, learners appropriate (take for themselves) the outcomes produced by working together; they acquire new strategies and knowledge of their world. Most psychologists classify Vygotsky as a social constructivist. Finally, sociological constructivists are interested in how public knowledge in disciplines such as science, math, economics, or history is constructed as well as how everyday beliefs and commonly held understandings about the world are communicated to new members of a sociocultural group.

In what ways do constructivist views differ about knowledge sources, accuracy, and generality?

Constructivists debate whether knowledge is constructed by mapping external reality, by adapting and changing internal understandings, or by an interaction of external forces and internal understandings. Most psychologists posit a role for both internal and external factors, but differ in how much they emphasize one or the other. Some constructivists argue that the world is knowable and that humans can construct accurate, logical, or warranted models of reality. Others argue that all constructions are equally valid and correct, even though some may be more useful than others. Also, there is discussion about whether knowledge can be constructed in one situation and applied to another or whether knowledge is so specific and tied to the context in which it was learned that it cannot be used successfully in another context. Situated learning emphasizes the latter view—the importance of physical and social contexts in learning.

What are some common elements in most constructivist views of learning?

Even though there is no single constructivist theory, many constructivist approaches recommend complex, challenging learning environments and authentic tasks; social negotiation and shared responsibility as a part of learning; multiple representations of content; understanding that knowledge is constructed; and student-centered instruction.

Applications of Constructivist and Situated Perspectives on Learning

Distinguish between inquiry and problem-based learning.

There have been many adaptations of inquiry, but the strategy begins when the teacher presents a puzzling event, question, or problem. The students then formulate hypotheses to explain the event or solve the problem; collect data to test the hypotheses; draw conclusions; and reflect on the original problem and the thinking processes needed to solve it. Problem-based learning may follow a similar path, but the learning begins with an authentic problem—one that matters to the students. The goal is to learn math or science or history or some other important subject while seeking a real solution to the problem.

Describe five elements that define true cooperative learning.

Students *interact face-to-face* and close together, not across the room. Group members experience *positive interdependence*—they need each other for support, explanations, and guidance. Even though they work together and help each other, members of the group must ultimately demonstrate learning on their own—they are held *individually accountable* for learning, often through individual tests or other assessments. If necessary, the *collaborative skills* important for effective group functioning, such as giving constructive feedback, reaching consensus, and involving every member, are taught and practiced before the groups tackle a learning task. Finally, members monitor *group processes* and relationships to make sure the group is working effectively and to learn about the dynamics of groups.

Describe six features that most cognitive apprenticeship approaches share.

There are many cognitive apprenticeship models, but most share six features: Students observe an expert (usually the teacher) *model* the performance. Students get external support through *coaching* or tutoring (including hints, feedback, models, and reminders). Students receive conceptual *scaffolding*, which is then gradually faded as the student becomes more competent and proficient. Students continually *articulate* their knowledge—putting into words their understanding of the processes and content being learned. Students *reflect* on their progress, comparing their problem solving to an expert's performance and to their own earlier performances. Students are required to *explore* new ways to apply what they are learning—ways that they have not practiced at the master's side.

Describe the use of dialogue in reciprocal teaching.

The goal of reciprocal teaching is to help students understand and think deeply about what they read. To accomplish this goal, students in small reading groups learn four strategies: *summarizing* the content of a passage, *asking a question* about the central point, *clarifying* the difficult parts of the material, and *predicting* what will come next. These strategies are practiced in a classroom dialogue about the readings. In these dialogues, teachers first take a central role, but as the discussion progresses, the students take more and more control.

What is meant by thinking as enculturation?

Enculturation is a broad and complex process of acquiring knowledge and understanding consistent with Vygotsky's theory of mediated learning. We all learned language, norms of appropriate behavior, and many other complicated rules by being a member of a particular cultural group. Just as our home culture taught us lessons about the use of language, the culture of a classroom can teach lessons about thinking by giving us *models* of good thinking; providing *direct instruction* in thinking processes; and encouraging *practice* of those thinking processes through *interactions* with others.

Looking Back at Learning

What do different views of learning add to our understanding?

Rather than debating the merits of each approach, consider their contributions to understanding learning and improving teaching. Different views of learning can be used together to create productive learning environments. Behavioral theory helps us understand the role of cues in setting the stage for behaviors and the role of consequences in encouraging or discouraging behaviors. But much of humans' lives and learning is more than behaviors. Language and higher-order thinking require complex information processing and memory—something the cognitive models of the thinker-as-computer helped us understand. And what about the person as a creator and constructor of knowledge, not just a processor of information? Here, constructivist perspectives have much to offer.

*K*ey Terms

Becoming a Professional

Reflecting on the Chapter

Can you apply the ideas from this chapter on social cognitive and constructivist views of learning to solve the following problems of practice?

Preschool and Kindergarten

▶ One of your students is very fearful of taking risks or attempting any task that does not have a right answer. The child tries to tell other students "the right way" to do everything. How would you help the student tolerate uncertainty and take risks in her thinking?

Elementary and Middle School

▶ How would you help 3rd-grade students understand negative numbers?

▶ You want to use cooperative learning with your students, but they are used to individual work. How would you begin?

Junior High and High School

▶ Your school librarian wants to help all the history classes learn to use the print and database resources in the library. How would you take advantage of this opportunity?

▶ Brainstorm ways to "understand your students' understanding" in a particular content area. What would you do before, during, and after a class to make your students' knowledge and thinking processes visible to both you and them?

Certification Test Requirements

▶ Know elements of observational learning.

▶ Know the five common teaching recommendations shared by most constructivist views.

▶ Be able to recognize examples of inquiry, problem-based learning, cognitive apprenticeships, and instructional conversations.

Your Teaching Portfolio

Use Table 9.8 to think about your own philosophy of learning. Would you incorporate elements from different theoretical approaches into your personal conception of learning?

Teaching Resources

Use the Family and Community Partnerships Guidelines to brainstorm ideas for how you would explain your teaching innovations to families. Experiment by drafting a "Newsletter."

Add Table 9.5, "Possible Student Roles in Cooperative Learning Groups," Table 9.6, "Elements of an Instructional Conversation," and Figure 9.2, "Reciprocal Questioning Prompt Cards to Guide Dialogue" to your **Teaching Resources** file.

What Would They Do?

Here is how some practicing teachers responded to the teaching situation presented at the beginning of this chapter about the awful "book reviews."

MARK H. SMITH

Teacher, Grades Nine–Twelve
Medford High School, Medford, Massachusetts

Experience is the best teacher. In an ideal world you can plan your course with what you think would be great material and be ready with a curriculum to meet the level you expect. But reality sets in when you see the true level of the class. High standards and expectations are great goals but they must be reasonable for the students in your class. The education profession is one that needs constant flexibility and adjustment to situations. Students learn in different ways and teachers who can adapt to classes and curricula have a better chance of succeeding.

Because this class has many different levels it will be important to find some common ground that will interest them as well as get them involved in learning. It will probably be a good idea to do different activities and even let the three top students help teach some of the others. It will not be easy to get everybody on the same page and you will probably have to spend lots of time planning, but with patience and effort you can find the level that fits and get the students to respond.

Although the teacher in this story was new, the same things apply to any teacher who must constantly adapt to courses, classes, and curricula. Teaching is not an exact science, and without flexibility and adjustments to situations, teachers cannot do their job well.

THOMAS W. NEWKIRK

Eighth Grade Teacher
Hamilton Heights Middle School, Arcadia, Indiana

It would be wonderful from the outset to have a class enthralled with world literature, but you are more likely to have a class frustrated with the prospect of reading another "lame" book. Therefore, it is important to find books with themes relevant to my students. Fortunately, on the reading list there are already some selections related to recent films, and probably there are some selections related to music, television, or even commercials. The more connections I can make between the literature and my students' lives, the more likely I am to motivate them.

While three students in the class demonstrate a sophisticated understanding of literature, every student in the class can bring a fresh insight into a discussion and be recognized for his or her contribution. In addition to class discussion, individual and group projects can be designed to encourage students to respond to the material. Considering the diversity of the class, I would evaluate student achievement with grading contracts that challenge students performing at different levels.

JEFF D. HORTON

Seventh–Tenth Grade Teacher
Colton School, Colton, Washington

This teacher may have set himself or herself up for problems from the start by assuming that all the students would be at the same learning level. Since this is clearly not the case, the course was delivered to a narrow range of students, and the majority are probably frustrated. The teacher needs to take another approach, though perhaps not abandon his or her original goals.

It appears that most of the students need some form of reteaching of the skills this teacher feels are necessary to complete the original plans. The teacher must determine which skills and knowledge are necessary for the students to successfully complete the course, and then assess the students in those areas. Once this is completed the teacher can develop several units that address those needs. This may take several days, but it is not wasted time. It will make life for all much easier in the long run.

Another problem may be the materials that the teacher planned to use. I do believe that students need to be introduced to the "classics" in literature. However, teachers are self-motivated to read and study these writings. We must remember that most students do not feel the same way. The teacher in this scenario must present the "classics" in a way that will hold the students' interest. Instead of reading a whole book, pick out parts that reflect the writing style or message of the author. Then present other parts of the book using other teaching tools. There are movies available that are presented in a more current style that will appeal to students. Whatever the teaching tool used, there must always be a learning activity connected to it.

Having students that excel in a subject is always rewarding to a teacher. It makes us feel that we have accomplished what we are setting out to do. These three students can help a teacher convey the skills and knowledge to the rest of the class. They should be required to complete all the assignments and activities along with the class. However, they will do this quickly while others struggle. The teacher should try to use them to help in conveying the material to the other students. Students that are finding the work easy could be used to help others by reviewing their work and offering suggestions on how to improve it. They could also offer the teacher some suggestions as to how to make the material more interesting to the rest of the class.

MICHAEL J. ELLIS

Tenth and Eleventh Grade English Teacher
Quincy High School, Quincy, Massachusetts

The problem here is one of mistaken assumption. The teacher has anticipated a certain level of ability and a certain degree of past knowledge, both of which seem to be abundantly lacking in this case. Obviously, the students are unfamiliar with the review as a literary form. Starting tomorrow, I'd begin teaching that. The first thing the students need to see is a well-written review, something they can begin to pattern their own responses on. Fortunately, I have three excellent examples already in hand, passed in by my own students. In the next class, I would have those three students read their reviews aloud and I'd pass out copies of them to the class. A discussion of what made those three papers so good would not only be instructive to the group, but would also positively reinforce the work done by those three students.

It seems the purpose behind the curriculum for this class is to expose the students to a wide array of great literature. That is a noble goal. In teaching, however, nobility must frequently give way to practicality. A teacher's first duty is to guide his students in the acquisition of necessary skills. Sometimes having them read Dickens isn't the best way to do that. The curriculum worked up over the summer will probably work well with the three standouts in the class. I'd try splintering them off from the rest. This can be a logistical nightmare and it effectively doubles your prep time for the class, but it's the best way to be sure that the students of a particular ability level don't stagnate while you cater to another group.

With the rest of the class, it's time to shift on the fly and ditch the original reading list. Emphasizing longer novels in a class dominated by poor readers is nothing less than a suicide attempt spread over 40 weeks. If you rely instead on shorter selections and young adult fiction titles with catchy plot lines, then you've at least given yourself a fighting chance at a class that actually finishes the books. It's also never a bad idea to throw video material into the mix. My first year of teaching I showed an episode of the *Mighty Morphin Power Rangers* to two classes of tenth graders, knowing they'd despise it. Kids can always write more effectively on things they hate than on things they like. The reviews they passed in were, from a technical standpoint, the best paragraphs most of them had ever written. That assignment really helped to etch the proper paragraph format in a lot of their minds. You can never allow yourself to forget that it's the skill itself, and not the means you use to convey it, that is ultimately most important.

Motivation: Issues and Explanations

hy are you reading this chapter? Are you curious about motivation and interested in the topic? Or is there a test in your near future? Do you need this course to earn a teaching certificate or to graduate? Maybe you believe that you have a good chance to do well in this class, and that belief keeps you working. Perhaps it is some combination of these reasons. What motivates you to study motivation?

Most educators agree that motivating students is one of the critical tasks of teaching. We begin with the question "What is motivation?" and examine many of the answers that have been proposed. This leads to a discussion of intrinsic and extrinsic motivation and four general theories of motivation: behavioral, humanistic, cognitive, and sociocultural.

The remainder of the chapter examines more closely several personal factors that frequently appear in discussions of motivation: goal orientations; interests and emotions, including curiosity and anxiety; and self-schemas including the important concept of self-efficacy. In Chapter 11 we will complete the picture with an examination of the external factors that can affect motivation to learn in school.

By the time you have completed this chapter, you should be able to:

▶ Give examples of intrinsic and extrinsic motivation and motivation to learn.
▶ Define the concept of motivation from the behavioral, humanistic, cognitive, and sociocultural points of view.
▶ List Maslow's seven levels of needs and give a classroom example of each.
▶ Discuss the possible motivational effects of success and failure and how these effects relate to beliefs about ability.
▶ Set motivating goals for yourself and your students.
▶ Describe the roles of interests and emotions in motivation.
▶ Explain the relationship between self-efficacy, self-determination, and motivation.
▶ Describe the characteristics of mastery-oriented, failure-avoiding, and failure-accepting students.

What Would You Do?

For some reason this year, many of the students in your middle school classes seem defeated about learning. They look at an assignment and protest, "This is too long (too hard, too much)!" "We can't do this by tomorrow (Monday, next week)!" Because they don't exert much effort, of course, they prove themselves right every time—they can't do the work. Neither pep talks nor punishments for incomplete work are making a dent in the students' defeatist attitudes. And the "I can'ts" seem contagious. Even the better students are starting to drag their feet, protest longer assignments, and invest minimal effort in class. You suspect some students have started to cheat on tests to save their sinking grades. A few teachers blame the negative attitudes on students from "projects" who are in school this year because the other middle school in the district was closed and those students had to be redistributed. A cloud of despair seems to be hovering over the whole school. You are starting to dread Mondays.

▶ Are these students "unmotivated"?

▶ Why might they be so pessimistic about learning?

▶ What could you do to change the attitudes in your class?

▶ How can you save your own sinking motivation?

▶ How will these issues affect the grades you will teach?

What Is Motivation?

Connect and Extend
To the research
For a thorough discussion of the many terms and concepts related to motivation, see Murphy, P. K., & Alexander, P. A. (2000). A motivated exploration of motivation terminology. *Contemporary Educational Psychology, 25,* 3–53.

Motivation is usually defined as an internal state that arouses, directs, and maintains behavior. Psychologists studying motivation have focused on five basic questions (Graham & Weiner, 1996; Pintrich, Marx, & Boyle, 1993):

1. *What choices do people make about their behavior?* Why do some students, for example, focus on their homework while others watch television?

2. *How long does it take to get started?* Why do some students who chose to do their homework start right away, while others procrastinate?

3. *What is the intensity or level of involvement?* Once the book bag is opened, is the student absorbed and focused or just going through the motions?

4. *What causes a person to persist or to give up?* Will a student read the entire Shakespeare assignment or just a few pages?

5. *What is the individual thinking and feeling during the activity?* Is the student enjoying Shakespeare or worrying about an upcoming test?

Meeting Some Students

Answering these questions about real students in classrooms is a challenge. As you will see in this chapter and the next, there are many factors that influence motivation. To get a sense of the complexity, let's step into a middle school general science classroom and survey the motivational problems that might confront you as the teacher. The student profiles are taken from Stipek (1998).

Motivation: An internal state that arouses, directs, and maintains behavior.

The assignment: "In your lab notebook, describe the procedures for tomorrow's chemistry experiment. Indicate all the materials you will need and how you will set up the apparatus." As soon as you finish your instructions, the hands go up. "Do we have to write in paragraphs or can we outline?" "Do we have to draw the apparatus or just describe it?" "Can we work together?" Some students begin right away, while others wait for answers to these questions. A few students seem to be in another world.

Hopeless Henry won't even start the assignment—as usual. He just keeps saying, "I don't understand," or "This is too hard." When you try to help him, he answers your questions correctly, but then says he "guessed" and he "doesn't really know." Henry causes no management problems because he spends most of his time staring into space, but he is falling farther and farther behind. Harry has trouble with question 2 above (getting started) and with question 5—during the activity he feels defeated and helpless.

Safe Sarah checks with you about every step—she wants to be perfect. You once gave her bonus points for doing an excellent color drawing of the apparatus, and now she produces a work of art for lab every time. But Sarah never takes any chances. She does well in science, but plans to take only the required science courses so she won't risk getting a B. If it isn't required or on the test, Sarah isn't interested. In terms of the five questions above, Sarah makes good choices (1), gets started right away (2), and persists (3). But she is not really engaged and takes little pleasure in the work (4 and 5).

Satisfied Sam on the other hand, is interested in this project. In fact, he knows more than you do about it. Evidently he has set up a lab in his garage and spends hours reading about chemistry and performing experiments. But his overall grade in your class is between B– and C+ because when you were studying biology, Sam couldn't have cared less. He was satisfied with the C he could get on tests without even trying. Homework didn't interest him. His only participation was to make jokes about the illustrations in the text. Judging by his standardized test scores, Sam could do much better. In terms of the five questions about motivation, as long as he is following his own choices, Sam is prompt in getting started, engaged, persistent, and enjoys the task.

Defensive Diana doesn't have her lab manual—again. You tell her that she may share with another student. Then Diana pretends to be working, but she spends most of her time making fun of the assignment or trying to get answers from other students when your back is turned. She wants everyone to know that she "isn't really trying." That way, if her grades are low she has an excuse. She is afraid to try because if she makes an effort and fails, she fears that everyone will know she is "dumb." In terms of the five questions above, Diana makes poor choices, procrastinates, avoids engagement, and gives up easily because she is so concerned about how others will judge her.

Anxious Amy is a good student in most subjects, but she freezes on science tests. She seems fine in group projects and doing her homework, but "forgets" everything she knows when she has to answer questions in class or take a test. Her parents are scientists and expect her to become one too, but her prospects for this future look dim. Amy's problems have to do with question 5 above—what she thinks and how she feels as she works. Her worry and anxiety may lead her to make poor choices and procrastinate, which only makes her more anxious at test time.

Each student presents a different motivational challenge, yet you have to teach the entire class. In the next few pages we will look more closely at the meaning of motivation so we can better understand these students.

Connect and Extend
To your teaching
Hopeless Henry is an example of a student experiencing *learned helplessness,* discussed later in the chapter.

Connect and Extend
To your teaching
Safe Sarah is an example of a student who is motivated by *extrinsic* factors, sets *performance goals,* fears *failure,* and views *ability as fixed.* She is also a (successful) *failure-avoiding student.* All these concepts will be discussed later in the chapter.

Connect and Extend
To your teaching
Satisfied Sam is an example of a student motivated by *intrinsic* factors. He set *learning goals* in his areas of interest, but just wants to perform "OK" in other areas. These concepts are discussed later in the chapter.

Connect and Extend
To your teaching
Defensive Diana is an example of a student who is motivated by *extrinsic* factors, sets *performance goals,* fears *failure,* and views *ability as fixed.* She is also a *failure-avoiding student.* Because she avoids work, she may soon become a *failure-accepting student.* All of these concepts will be discussed later in the chapter.

Connect and Extend
To your teaching
Anxious Amy is an example of a student experiencing debilitating *anxiety,* discussed later in the chapter.

Connect and Extend
To the research

Weiner, B. (1990). History of motivational research in education. *Journal of Educational Psychology, 82,* 616–622.

Focus Questions: How are the behavioral and cognitive views of learning reflected in the various theories of motivation? What is the current conception of motivation?

We all know how it feels to be motivated, to move energetically toward a goal. We also know what it is like to work hard, even if we are not fascinated by the task. What energizes and directs our behavior? The explanation could be drives, needs, incentives, fears, goals, social pressure, self-confidence, interests, curiosity, beliefs, values, expectations, and more. Some psychologists have explained motivation in terms of personal *traits* or individual characteristics. Certain people, so the theory goes, have a strong need to achieve, a fear of tests, or an enduring interest in art, so they behave accordingly. They work hard to achieve, avoid tests, or spend hours in art galleries. Other psychologists see motivation more as a *state*, a temporary situation. If, for example, you are reading this paragraph because you have a test tomorrow, you are motivated (at least for now) by the situation. Of course, the motivation we experience at any given time usually is a combination of trait and state. You may be studying because you value learning *and* because your professor often gives pop quizzes. As you can see, some explanations of motivation rely on internal, personal factors such as needs, interests, curiosity, and enjoyment. Other explanations point to external, environmental factors—rewards, social pressure, punishment, and so on.

"WHAT DO I GET FOR JUST NEATNESS?"

(© Glenn Bernhardt)

Motivation that stems from factors such as interest or curiosity is called **intrinsic motivation.** Intrinsic motivation is the natural tendency to seek out and conquer challenges as we pursue personal interests and exercise capabilities (Deci & Ryan, 1985; Reeve, 1996). When we are intrinsically motivated, we do not need incentives or punishments, because *the activity itself is rewarding.* James Raffini (1996) states simply that intrinsic motivation is "what motivates us to do something when we *don't have* to do anything (p. 3). Satisfied Sam studies chemistry outside school simply because he loves the activity; no one makes him do it.

In contrast, when we do something in order to earn a grade or reward, avoid punishment, please the teacher, or for some other reason that has very little to do with the task itself, we experience **extrinsic motivation.** We are not really interested in the activity for its own sake; we care only about what it will gain us. Safe Sarah works for the grade; she has little interest in the subject itself.

It is impossible to tell just by looking if a behavior is intrinsically or extrinsically motivated. The essential difference between the two types of motivation is the student's reason for acting, that is, whether the **locus of causality** for the action (the location of the cause) is internal or external—inside or outside the person. Students who read or practice their backstroke or paint may be reading, stroking, or painting because they freely chose the activity based on personal interests (*internal locus* of causality/intrinsic motivation), or because someone or something else outside is influencing them (*external locus* of causality/ extrinsic motivation) (Reeve, 1996).

Is your motivation for reading this page intrinsic or extrinsic? Is your locus of causality internal or external? As you try to answer this question, you proba-

A basic question in motivation is "Where does it come from—within or outside the individual?" Why does this girl raise her hand in class—because she is interested in the subject or because she wants to earn a good grade? The answer is probably more complicated than either alternative. ▼

bly realize that the dichotomy between intrinsic and extrinsic motivation is too simple—too all-or-nothing. Our activities fall along a continuum from fully *self-determined* (internal locus of causality/intrinsic motivation) to fully *determined by others* (external locus of causality/extrinsic motivation). For example, students may freely choose to work hard on activities that they don't find particularly enjoyable because they know the activities are important in reaching a valued goal—such as spending hours studying educational psychology in order to become a good teacher. Is this intrinsic or extrinsic motivation? Actually, it is in between—the person is freely choosing to accept outside causes such as certification requirements and then tries to get the most benefit from the requirements. The person has *internalized an external cause.*

In school, both intrinsic and extrinsic motivation are important. Many activities are, or could be, interesting to students. Teaching can create intrinsic motivation by stimulating the students' curiosity and making them feel more competent as they learn. But you know this won't work all the time. Did you find long division or grammar inherently interesting? Was your curiosity piqued by the states and their capitals? If teachers count on intrinsic motivation to energize all their students all of the time, they will be disappointed. There are situations when incentives and external supports are necessary. Teachers must encourage and nurture intrinsic motivation while making sure that extrinsic motivation supports learning (Brophy, 1988; Deci, Koestner, & Ryan, 1999; Ryan & Deci, 1996). To do this, they need to know about the factors that influence motivation.

C H E C K P O I N T

What Is Motivation?

Review

▷ Define motivation.

▷ What is the difference between intrinsic and extrinsic motivation?

▷ How does locus of causality apply to motivation?

Apply

▷ It is sometimes suggested that one way of improving education would be to pay students for successful school achievement. What would be the likely effects of doing this?

Four General Approaches to Motivation

Motivation is a vast and complicated subject encompassing many theories. Some theories were developed through work with animals in laboratories. Others are based on research with humans in situations that used games or puzzles. Some theories grow out of the work done in clinical or industrial psychology. Our examination of the field will be selective; otherwise we would never finish the topic.

Behavioral Approaches to Motivation

Behaviorists explain motivation with concepts such as "reward" and "incentive." A **reward** is an attractive object or event supplied as a consequence of a particular behavior. For example, Safe Sarah was rewarded with bonus points when she drew an excellent diagram. An **incentive** is an object or event that encourages or discourages behavior. The promise of an A+ was an incentive to Sarah. Actually receiving

Intrinsic Motivation: Motivation associated with activities that are their own reward.

Extrinsic Motivation: Motivation created by external factors like rewards and punishments.

Locus of Causality: The location—internal or external—of the cause of behavior.

Reward: An attractive object or event supplied as a consequence of a behavior.

Incentive: An object or event that encourages or discourages behavior.

Humanistic View: Approach to motivation that emphasizes personal freedom, choice, self-determination, and striving for personal growth.

Hierarchy of Needs: Maslow's model of seven levels of human needs, from basic physiological requirements to the need for self-actualization.

Self-Actualization: Fulfilling one's potential.

Deficiency Needs: Maslow's four lower-level needs, which must be satisfied first.

Being Needs: Maslow's three higher-level needs, sometimes called growth needs.

The comfort provided by her mother will help meet this girl's needs for safety and belonging—which are included in Maslow's hierarchy of needs. ▼

the grade was a reward. Thus, according to the behavioral view, an understanding of student motivation begins with a careful analysis of the incentives and rewards present in the classroom.

If we are consistently reinforced for certain behaviors, we may develop habits or tendencies to act in certain ways. For example, if a student is repeatedly rewarded with affection, money, praise, or privileges for earning letters in baseball, but receives little recognition for studying, the student will probably work longer and harder on perfecting her fastball than on understanding geometry. Providing grades, stars, stickers, and so on for learning—or demerits for misbehavior—is an attempt to motivate students by extrinsic means of incentives, rewards, and punishments. Of course, in any individual case, many other factors will affect how a person behaves.

Humanistic Approaches to Motivation

The **humanistic view** is sometimes referred to as "third-force" psychology because it developed in the 1940s as a reaction against the two forces dominant at that time: behaviorism and Freudian psychoanalysis. Humanistic interpretations of motivation emphasize such intrinsic sources of motivation as a person's needs for "self-actualization" (Maslow, 1968, 1970), the inborn "actualizing tendency" (Rogers & Freiberg, 1994), or the need for "self-determination" (Deci, Vallerand, Pelletier, & Ryan, 1991). These theories have in common a belief that people are continually motivated by the inborn need to fulfill their potential. So, from the humanistic perspective, to motivate students means to encourage their inner resources—their sense of competence, self-esteem, autonomy, and self-actualization (Reeve, 1996). Maslow's theory is a very influential humanistic explanation of motivation.

Maslow's Hierarchy. Abraham Maslow has had a great impact on psychology in general and on the psychology of motivation in particular. Maslow (1970) suggested that humans have a **hierarchy of needs** ranging from lower-level needs for survival and safety that must be met first to higher-level needs for **self-actualization.** Self-actualization is Maslow's term for self-fulfillment, the realization of personal potential. Figure 10.1 is a diagram of Maslow's model.

Maslow (1968) called the four lower-level needs—survival, safety, belonging, and self-esteem—**deficiency needs.** When these needs are satisfied, the motivation for fulfilling them decreases. He labeled the three higher-level needs—intellectual achievement, aesthetic appreciation, and self-actualization—**being needs.** When they are met, a person's motivation does not cease; instead, it increases to seek further fulfillment. For example, the more successful you are in your efforts to know and understand, the harder you are likely to strive for even greater knowledge and understanding. Unlike the deficiency needs, being needs can never be completely filled. The motivation to achieve them is endlessly renewed.

Maslow's theory has been criticized for the very obvious reason that people do not always appear to behave as the theory would predict. Most of us move back and forth among different types of needs and may even be motivated by many different needs at the same time. Some people deny themselves safety or friendship in order to achieve knowledge, understanding, or greater self-esteem.

Criticisms aside, Maslow's theory does give us a way of looking at the whole person, whose physical, emotional, and intellectual needs are all interrelated. This has important implications for education. Students who come to

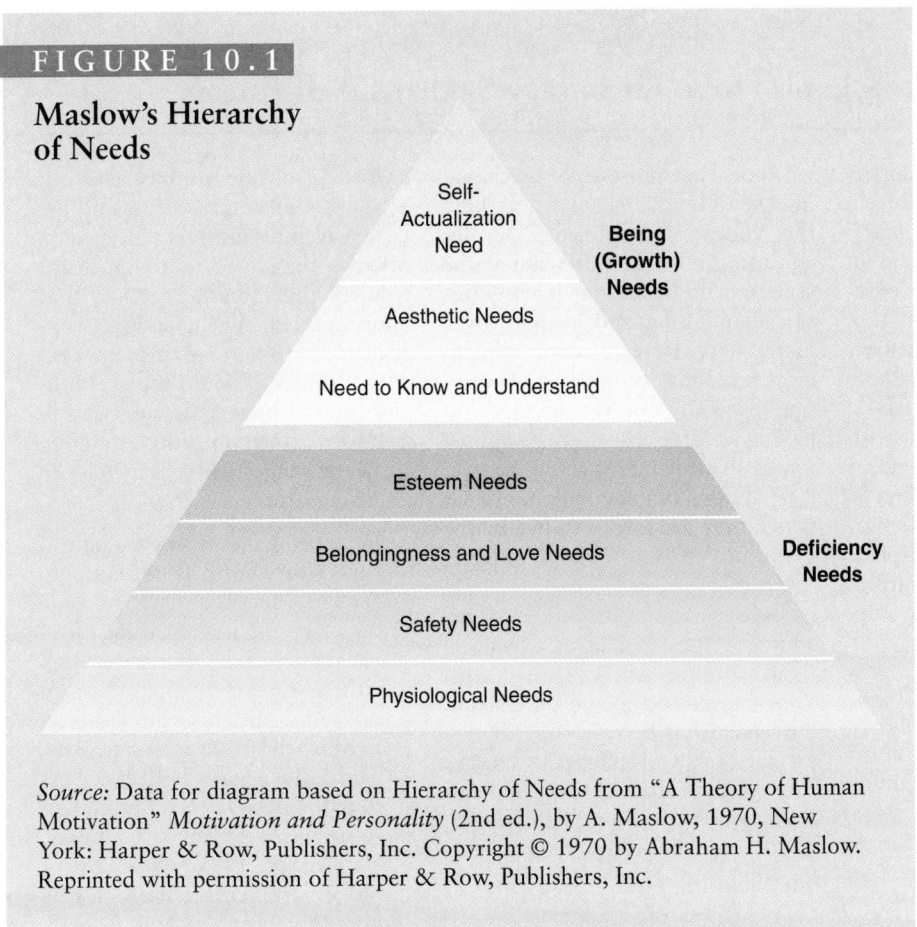

FIGURE 10.1

Maslow's Hierarchy of Needs

Self-Actualization Need

Being (Growth) Needs

Aesthetic Needs

Need to Know and Understand

Esteem Needs

Belongingness and Love Needs

Deficiency Needs

Safety Needs

Physiological Needs

Source: Data for diagram based on Hierarchy of Needs from "A Theory of Human Motivation" *Motivation and Personality* (2nd ed.), by A. Maslow, 1970, New York: Harper & Row, Publishers, Inc. Copyright © 1970 by Abraham H. Maslow. Reprinted with permission of Harper & Row, Publishers, Inc.

school hungry, sick, or hurt are unlikely to be motivated to seek knowledge and understanding. A child whose feelings of safety and sense of belonging are threatened by divorce may have little interest in learning to divide fractions. If the classroom is a fearful, unpredictable place and students seldom know where they stand, they are likely to be more concerned with security and less with learning. Maslow's hierarchy can provide other insights into students' behavior. Students' desires to fill lower-level needs may at times conflict with a teacher's desire to have them achieve higher-level goals. Belonging to a social group and maintaining self-esteem within that group, for example, are important to students. If doing what the teacher says conflicts with group rules, students may choose to ignore the teacher's wishes or even defy the teacher.

One current reflection of the humanistic perspective is the "self-esteem movement," a controversial approach to meeting students' needs for dignity and self-esteem. The Point/Counterpoint on page 372 explores this issue.

Cognitive Approaches to Motivation

In many ways, cognitive theories of motivation also developed as a reaction to the behavioral views. Cognitive theorists believe that behavior is determined by our thinking, not simply by whether we have been rewarded or punished for the

What Should Schools Do to Encourage Students' Self-Esteem?

James Beane (1991) begins his article "Sorting Out the Self-Esteem Controversy" with this statement: "In the '90s, the question is not whether schools should enhance students' self-esteem, but how they propose to do so" (p. 25). The attempts to improve students' self-esteem have taken three main forms: personal development activities such as sensitivity training; self-esteem programs where the curriculum focuses directly on improving self-esteem; and structural changes in schools that place greater emphasis on cooperation, student participation, community involvement, and ethnic pride.

▶ POINT *The self-esteem movement has problems.*

Attempts to encourage self-esteem directly through sensitivity training or self-esteem courses have not proven very successful. As Beane notes, "Saying 'I like myself and others' in front of a group is not the same as actually feeling that way, especially if I am only doing it because I am supposed to. Being nice has a place in enhancing self-esteem, but it is not enough" (p. 26). Many of the self-esteem courses are commercial packages—costly for schools but without solid evidence that they make a difference for students (Crisci, 1986; Leming, 1981).

Sensitivity training and self-esteem courses share a common conceptual problem. They assume that we encourage self-esteem by changing the individual's beliefs, making the young person work harder against the odds. But what if the student's environment is truly unsafe, debilitating, and unsupportive? Some people have overcome tremendous problems, but to expect everyone to do so "ignores the fact that having positive self-esteem is almost impossible for many young people, given the deplorable conditions under which they are forced to live by the inequities in our society" (Beane, 1991, p. 27).

Because many attempts to encourage self-esteem have been superficial, commercial, and filled with "pop psychology," the self-esteem movement has become an easy target for critics in magazine articles such as "Education: Doing Bad and Feeling Good" (*Time*, February 5, 1990) and "The Trouble with Self-Esteem" (*U.S. News and World Report*, April 2, 1990).

◀ COUNTERPOINT *The self-esteem movement has promise.*

Beyond the "feel-good psychology" of some aspects of the self-esteem movement is a basic truth: "Self-esteem is a central feature of human dignity and thus an inalienable human entitlement. As such, schools and other agencies have a moral obligation to help build it and avoid debilitating it" (Beane, 1991, p. 28). If we view self-esteem accurately as a product of our thinking and our actions—our values, ideas, and beliefs as well as our interactions with others—then we see a significant role for the school. Practices that allow authentic participation, cooperation, problem solving, and accomplishment should replace policies that damage self-esteem, such as tracking and competitive grading.

Beane suggests four principles to guide educators:

First, being nice is surely a part of this effort, but it is not enough. Second, there is a place for some direct instruction regarding affective matters, but this is not enough either. Self-esteem and affect are not simply another school subject to be placed in set-aside time slots. Third, the negative affect of "get tough" policies is not a promising route to self-esteem and efficacy. This simply blames young people for problems that are largely not of their own making. Fourth, since self-perceptions are powerfully informed by culture, comparing self-esteem across cultures without clarifying cultural differences is distracting and unproductive. (pp. 29–30)

behavior in the past (Schunk, 1996; Stipek, 1998). Behavior is initiated and regulated by plans (Miller, Galanter, & Pribram, 1960), goals (Locke & Latham, 1990), schemas (Ortony, Clore, & Collins, 1988), expectations (Vroom, 1964), and attributions (Weiner, 1992). One of the central assumptions in cognitive approaches is that people respond not to external events or physical conditions such as hunger, but rather to their interpretations of these events. You may have had the experience of being so involved in a project that you missed a meal, not realizing you were hungry until you noticed the time. Food deprivation did not automatically motivate you to seek food.

Cognitive theories emphasize intrinsic motivation. People are seen as active and curious, searching for information to solve personally relevant problems. Bernard Weiner's attribution theory is a good example.

Attribution Theory. This cognitive explanation of motivation begins with the assumption that we all ask "Why?" in our attempts to understand our successes and failures. Students may ask themselves, "Why did I flunk my midterm?" "What's wrong with my essay?" "Why did I do so well this grading period?" Students may *attribute* their successes and failures to ability, effort, mood, knowledge, luck, help, interest, clarity of instructions, the interference of others, unfair policies, and so on. **Attribution theories** of motivation describe how the individual's explanations, justifications, and excuses influence motivation.

Bernard Weiner is one of the main educational psychologists responsible for relating attribution theory to school learning (Weiner, 1979, 1986, 1992, 1994a, b; Weiner & Graham, 1989). According to Weiner, most of the attributed causes for successes or failures can be characterized in terms of three dimensions:

1. *locus* (location of the cause internal or external to the person),
2. *stability* (whether the cause stays the same or can change), and
3. *responsibility* (whether the person can control the cause).

Every cause for success or failure can be categorized on these three dimensions. For example, luck is external (locus), unstable (stability), and uncontrollable (responsibility). Table 10.1 shows some common attributions for success or failure on a test.

Weiner believes that these three dimensions have important implications for motivation. The *internal/external locus*, for example, seems to be closely related to feelings of self-esteem (Weiner, 1980). If success or failure is attributed to internal factors, success will lead to pride and increased motivation, whereas failure will diminish self-esteem. The *stability* dimension seems to be closely related to expecta-

Connect and Extend
To the research
Graham, S. (1991). A review of attribution theory in achievement contexts. *Educational Psychology Review, 3,* 5–39. This article reviews several major principles of attribution theory as they relate to achievement strivings, including the antecedents to particular self-ascriptions, the emotional consequences of causal attributions for success and failure, help seeking and help giving, peer acceptance and rejection, achievement evaluation, and attributional process in African American populations.

TABLE 10.1 *Weiner's Theory of Causal Attribution*

There are many explanations students can give for why they fail a test. Below are eight reasons representing the eight combinations of locus, stability, and responsibility in Weiner's model of attributions.

Dimension Classification	Reason for Failure
Internal-stable-uncontrollable	Low aptitude
Internal-stable-controllable	Never studies
Internal-unstable-uncontrollable	Sick the day of the exam
Internal-unstable-controllable	Did not study for this particular test
External-stable-uncontrollable	School has hard requirements
External-stable-controllable	Instructor is biased
External-unstable-uncontrollable	Bad luck
External-unstable-controllable	Friends failed to help

Source: From *Human Motivation: Metaphors, Theories and Research* (p. 253), by B. Weiner, 1992, Newbury Park, CA: Sage Publications. Copyright © 1992 by Sage Publications. Adapted with permission.

Attribution Theories: Descriptions of how individuals' explanations, justifications, and excuses influence their motivation and behavior.

Connect and Extend
To your teaching

What are the implications of attribution theories of motivation? Consider the following, taken from "Why can't Susie and Johnny do math?" (1987, July). *Harvard Education Letter, 3*(4), 6–7.

Dale Schunk identified 40 elementary school children who were having trouble with subtraction, divided them into four groups, and set them to working . . . A monitor . . . checked . . . groups A, B, and C every 8 minutes. To each child in the A group she commented, "You've been working hard." To children in the B group she said, "You need to work hard." Children in the C group got no comment at all, and children in the D group had contact with the proctor only when she read them instructions.

The results were unambiguous: youngsters who were told that they had been working hard completed 63% more problems than their fellows. They got three times as many subtraction problems right on the test that followed the training.

Connect and Extend
To the research

Blumenfeld, P. C., Pintrich, P. R., & Hamilton, V. L. (1986). Children's concepts of ability, effort, and conduct. *American Educational Research Journal, 23*, 95–104.

Brief abstract: Children's self-perceptions of ability may reflect assessments of their effort and good conduct as well as academic performance. In a study of 158 2nd and 6th graders, ability was generally linked to effort and effort to conduct, but not ability to conduct, in either ratings or judgment criteria. Children generally used absolute standards in judging ability and did so almost exclusively in judging effort and conduct. The results suggest that children's judgments of ability, effort, and conduct are interrelated but distinguishable.

tions about the future. If, for example, students attribute their failure to stable factors such as the difficulty of the subject, they will expect to fail in that subject in the future. But if they attribute the outcome to unstable factors such as mood or luck, they can hope for better outcomes in the future.

The *responsibility* dimension is related to emotions such as anger, pity, gratitude, or shame (Weiner, 1994a). If we feel responsible for our failures, we may feel guilt; if we feel responsible for successes, we may feel proud. Failing at a task we cannot control can lead to shame or anger toward the person or institution in control, while succeeding at uncontrollable tasks leads to feeling lucky or grateful.

When failure is attributed to lack of ability and ability is considered *uncontrollable*, the sequence of motivation is:

Failure → Lack of Ability → Uncontrollable → Not Responsible → Shame, Embarrassment → Withdraw → Performance Declines

When failure is attributed to lack of effort, the sequence is:

Failure → Lack of Effort → Controllable → Responsible → Guilt → Engagement → Performance Improves

Also, feeling in control of your own learning seems to be related to choosing more difficult academic tasks, putting out more effort, and persisting longer in school work (Schunk, 1996; Weiner, 1994a, b). On the negative side, continuing discrimination against women, people of color, and individuals with special needs can affect these individuals' perceptions of their own ability to control their lives (Beane, 1991). If people feel that they are not in control of their own lives, their self-esteem is likely to be diminished. Weiner's locus and responsibility dimensions are closely related to Deci's concept of *locus of causality*.

Attributions in the Classroom.

When usually successful students fail, they often make internal, controllable attributions: They misunderstood the directions, lacked the necessary knowledge, or simply did not study hard enough, for example. When students see themselves as capable and attribute failure to lack of effort or insufficient knowledge—controllable causes—they usually focus on strategies for succeeding next time. This is an adaptive, mastery-oriented response, one that often leads to achievement, pride, and a greater feeling of control (Ames, 1992).

The greatest motivational problems arise when students attribute failures to stable, uncontrollable causes. Such students may seem resigned to failure, depressed, helpless—what we generally call "unmotivated" (Weiner, 1994a, b; Weiner, Russell, & Lerman, 1978). These students respond to failure by focusing even more on their own inadequacy; their attitudes toward schoolwork may deteriorate even further (Ames, 1992). Apathy is a logical reaction to failure if students believe the causes are stable, unlikely to change, and beyond their control. In addition, students who view their failures in this light are less likely to seek help—they believe nothing and no one can help (Ames & Lau, 1982).

Teacher Actions and Student Attributions.

How do students determine the causes of their successes and failures? The behaviors of their teachers are cues. When teachers assume that student failure is attributable to forces beyond the students' control, they tend to respond with sympathy and to avoid giving punishments. If, however, the failures are attributed to a controllable factor such as lack of effort, the teacher's response is more likely to be anger, and punishments may follow. These tendencies seem to be consistent across time and cultures (Weiner, 1986).

What do students make of these reactions from their teachers? Sandra Graham (1991, 1996) gives some surprising answers. There is evidence that when teachers respond to students' mistakes with pity, praise for a "good try," or unsolicited help, the students are more likely to attribute their failure to an uncontrollable cause—usually lack of ability. For example, Graham and Barker (1990) asked subjects of various ages to rate the effort and ability of two boys on a videotape. On the tape was a teacher circulating around the class while students worked. The teacher stopped to look at the two boys' papers, did not comment to the first boy, but said to the second, "Let me give you a hint. Don't forget to carry your tens." The second boy had not asked for help and did not appear to be stumped by the problem. All the age groups watching the tapes, even the youngest, perceived the helped boy as lower in ability than the boy who did not get help. It is as if the subjects read the teacher's behavior as saying, "You poor child, you just don't have the ability to do this hard work, so I will help."

Does this mean that teachers should be critical and withhold help? Of course not! But it is a reminder that "praise as a consolation prize" for failing (Brophy, 1985) or oversolicitous help can give unintended messages. Graham (1991) suggests that many minority group students could be the victims of well-meaning pity from teachers. Seeing the very real problems that the students face, teachers may "ease up" on requirements so the students will "experience success" and "feel good about themselves." But a subtle communication may accompany the pity, praise, and extra help: "You don't have the ability to do this, so I will overlook your failure." Graham says, "The . . . pertinent question for blacks is whether their own history of academic failure makes them more likely to be the targets of sympathetic feedback from teachers and thus the recipients of low-ability cues" (1991, p. 28). This kind of sympathetic feedback, even if well-intended, can be a subtle form of racism.

Connect and Extend
To your teaching
Read Clifford, M. M. (1990). Students need challenge, not easy success. *Educational Leadership* 48(1), 22–26. Evaluate Clifford's claim that students need some experience with failure. For whom is this experience most needed?

Expectancy x Value Theories. Theories that take into account both the behaviorists' concern with the effects or outcomes of behavior and the cognitivists' interest in the impact of individual thinking can be characterized as **expectancy x value theories**. This means that motivation is seen as the product of two main forces, the individual's expectation of reaching a goal and the value of that goal to him or her. In other words, the important questions are, "If I try hard, can I succeed?" and "If I succeed, will the outcome be valuable or rewarding to me?" Motivation is a product of these two forces, because if either factor is zero, there is no motivation to work toward the goal. For example, if I believe I have a good chance of making the basketball team (high expectation), and if making the team is very important to me (high value), then my motivation should be strong. But if either factor is zero (I believe I haven't a prayer of making the team, or I couldn't care less about playing basketball), then my motivation will be zero, too. Bandura's self-efficacy, discussed later in this chapter, is an example of an expectancy x value approach to motivation (Feather, 1982; Pintrich & Schunk, 1996).

Connect and Extend
To your teaching
Based on expectancy theory, predict the level of motivation in each of the following:

a. Perceived probability of success under minimum effort is high; incentive value is high.

b. Perceived probability of success under maximum effort is high; incentive value is moderate.

c. Perceived probability of success under maximum effort is low; incentive value is moderate.

Sociocultural Conceptions of Motivation

Sociocultural views of motivation emphasize participation in communities of practice. People engage in activities to maintain their identities and their interpersonal relations within the community. Thus, students are motivated to learn if they are members of a classroom or school community that values learning. To learn is to participate in the life of the community. Just as we learn to speak and dress and conduct

Expectancy x Value Theories: Explanations of motivation that emphasize individuals' expectations for success combined with their valuing of the goal.

Sociocultural Views of Motivation: Perspectives that emphasize participation, identities, and interpersonal relations within communities of practice.

ourselves in restaurants or shopping malls by being socialized—watching and learning from more capable members of the culture—we also learn to be students by watching and learning from members of our community. In other words, we learn by the company we keep (Greeno, Collins, & Resnick, 1996).

The concept of identity is central in sociocultural views of motivation. When we see ourselves as soccer players, or sculptors, or engineers, or teachers, or psychologists, we have an identity within a group. Part of our socialization is moving from legitimate peripheral participation to central participation in that group. **Legitimate peripheral participation** means that beginners are genuinely involved in the work of the group, even if their abilities are undeveloped and their contributions are small. The novice weaver learns to dye wool before spinning and weaving and the novice teacher learns to tutor one child before working with the whole group. Each task is a piece of the real work of the expert. The identities of the novice and the expert are bound up in their participation in the community. They are motivated to learn the values and practices of the community to keep their identity as community members (Lave & Wenger, 1991).

Some classrooms are intentionally structured as learning communities. For example, Brown and Campione (1996) developed learning communities for middle school students around research projects in science. Scardamalia and Bereiter (1996) designed a learning community using a computer system called CSILE—Computer-Supported Intentional Learning Environment—that encourages collaboration among students about questions, hypotheses, and findings. The challenge in these approaches is to be sure that all students are fully participating members of

TABLE 10.2 *Four Views of Motivation*

	Behavioral	Humanistic	Cognitive	Sociocultural
Source of Motivation	Extrinsic	Intrinsic	Intrinsic	Intrinsic
Important Influences	Reinforcers, rewards, incentives, and punishers	Need for self-esteem, self-fulfillment, and self-determination	Beliefs, attributions for success and failure, expectations	Engaged participation in learning communities; maintaining identity through participation in activities of group
Key Theorists	Skinner	Maslow Deci	Weiner Graham	Lave Wenger

the community, because motivation comes from identity and identity comes from legitimate participation.

The behavioral, humanistic, cognitive, and sociocultural approaches to motivation are summarized in Table 10.2 on page 376. These theories differ in their answers to the question, "What is motivation?" but each contributes in its own way toward a comprehensive understanding of human motivation.

To organize the many ideas about motivation in a way that is useful for teaching, let's examine three broad areas. Most contemporary explanations of motivation include a discussion of goals, interests and emotions, and self-perceptions (Murphy & Alexander, 2000). We will look closely at each of these areas—with an emphasis on implications for teaching and learning.

Goal Orientation and Motivation

A **goal** is an outcome or attainment an individual is striving to accomplish (Locke & Latham, 1990). When students strive to read a chapter or make a 4.0 GPA, they are involved in *goal-directed behavior*. In pursuing goals, students are generally aware of some current condition (I haven't even opened my book), some ideal condition (I have read and understood every page), and the discrepancy between the current and ideal situations. Goals motivate people to act in order to reduce the discrepancy between "where they are" and "where they want to be." Goal setting is usually effective for me. In addition to the routine tasks, such as eating lunch, which will happen without much attention, I often set goals for each day. For example, today I intend to finish this chapter, exercise, and send a gift to my daughter for her new apartment. Having decided to do these things, I will feel uncomfortable if I don't complete the list.

According to Locke and Latham (1990), there are four main reasons why goal setting improves performance. First, goals direct our attention to the task at hand. (Every time my mind wanders from this chapter, my goal of finishing helps direct my attention back to the writing.) Second, goals mobilize effort. (The harder the goal, to a point, the greater the effort.) Third, goals increase persistence. (When we have a clear goal, we are less likely to be distracted or to give up until we reach the goal.) Finally, goals promote the development of new strategies when old strategies fall short. For example, if your goal is making an A and you don't reach that goal on your first quiz, you might drop the strategy of reading the text over and over and try a new study approach for the next quiz, such as explaining the key points to a friend.

Connect and Extend
To the research
Ames, C. (1992). Classrooms: Goals, structures, and student motivation. *Journal of Educational Psychology, 84*, 261–271. This article integrates many concepts about goals and provides a frame for the next chapter in this text. For an elaboration of Ames's ideas, see Blumenfeld, P. C. (1992). Classroom learning and motivation: Clarifying and expending goal theory. *Journal of Educational Psychology, 84*, 272–281.

Types of Goals

The types of goals we set influence the amount of motivation we have to reach them. Goals that are specific, moderately difficult, and likely to be reached in the near future tend to enhance motivation and persistence (Pintrich & Schunk, 1996; Stipek, 1996). Specific goals provide clear standards for judging performance. If performance falls short, we keep going. For example, I have decided to "finish this chapter" instead of deciding to "work on the book." Because it is clear when I am finished (the chapter is in the mail), I know when I have met the goal. Anything short of having the chapter in the mail means "keep working" (looks like another late night!). Moderate difficulty provides a challenge, but not an unreasonable one.

Legitimate Peripheral Participation: Genuine involvement in the work of the group, even if your abilities are undeveloped and contributions are small.

Goal: What an individual strives to accomplish.

I can finish this chapter if I stay with it. Finally, goals that can be reached fairly soon are not likely to be pushed aside by more immediate concerns. Groups such as Alcoholics Anonymous show they are aware of the motivating value of short-term goals when they encourage their members to stop drinking "one day at a time."

Four Kinds of Goals. Educational psychologists have written about many *goal orientations*—learning goals, performance goals, work-avoidance goals, and social goals—to name only four categories (Murphy & Alexander, 2000). The most common distinction in research on students' goals is between learning goals (also referred to as task goals or mastery goals) and performance goals (also called ability goals or ego goals). The point of a **learning goal** is to improve, to learn, no matter how many mistakes you make or how awkward you appear. Students who set learning goals tend to seek challenges and persist when they encounter difficulties. Nicholls and Miller (1984) call these students **task-involved learners** because they are concerned with mastering the task and are not worried about how their performance "measures up" compared to others in the class. We often say that these people "get lost in their work." In addition, task-involved learners are more likely to seek appropriate help, use deeper cognitive processing strategies, and apply better study strategies (Butler & Neuman, 1995; Young, 1997).

The second kind of goal is a **performance goal.** Students with performance goals care about demonstrating their ability to others. They may be focused on getting good test scores and grades or they may be more concerned with winning and beating other students (Wolters, Yu, & Pintrich, 1996). Students whose goal is outperforming others may do things to look smart, such as reading easy books in order to "read the most books" (Young, 1997). If winning is impossible, they may adopt defensive, failure-avoiding strategies like Defensive Diana described earlier—they pretend not to care, make a show of "not really trying," or cheat (Jagacinski & Nicholls, 1987; Pintrich & Schunk, 1996). The evaluation of their performance by others, not what they learn or how hard they try, is what matters. Nicholls and Miller (1984) refer to these students as **ego-involved learners** because they are preoccupied with themselves. Deborah Stipek (1996) lists these behaviors as indicative of a student who is ego-involved with classwork:

▶ Cheats/copies from classmates' papers.

▶ Seeks attention for good performance.

▶ Only works hard on graded assignments.

▶ Is upset by and hides papers with low grades.

▶ Compares grades with classmates.

▶ Chooses tasks that are most likely to result in positive evaluations.

▶ Is uncomfortable with assignments that have unclear evaluation criteria.

Some students don't want to learn or to look smart; they just want to avoid work. These students try to complete assignments and activities as quickly as possible without exerting much effort (Schunk & Pintrich, 1996). Nicholls called these students **work-avoidant learners**—they feel successful when they don't have to try hard, when the work is easy, or when they can "goof off."

A final category of goals becomes more important as students get older—**social goals.** As students move into adolescence, their social networks change to include more peers. Nonacademic activities such as athletics, dating, and "hanging out" compete with schoolwork (Urdan & Maehr, 1995). Social goals include a wide variety of needs and motives with different relationships to learning—some help,

Connect and Extend
To your teaching
Are students with learning goals more likely to (1) be internal or external in locus of control; (2) have internal, stable or internal, unstable attributions; (3) be failure-avoiders or success-seekers?

Learning Goal: A personal intention to improve abilities and understand, no matter how performance suffers.

Task-Involved Learners: Students who focus on mastering the task or solving the problem.

Performance Goal: A personal intention to seem competent or perform well in the eyes of others.

Ego-Involved Learners: Students who focus on how well they are performing and how they are judged by others.

Work-Avoidant Learners: Students who don't want to learn or to look smart, but just want to avoid work.

Social Goals: A wide variety of needs and motives to be connected to others or part of a group.

but some hinder learning. For example, adolescents' goal of maintaining friendly relations in a cooperative learning group can get in the way of learning when group members don't challenge wrong answers or misconceptions because they are afraid to hurt members' feelings (Anderson, Holland, & Palincsar, 1997). Certainly, pursuing goals such as having fun with friends or avoiding being labeled a "nerd" can get in the way of learning. But goals of bringing honor to your family or team by working hard can support learning (Urdan & Maehr, 1995).

We talk about goals in separate categories, but students have to coordinate their goals so they can make decisions about what to do and how to act. As noted above, some-times social and academic goals are incompatible. For example, academic failure may be interpreted positively by some minority group students because noncompliance with the majority culture's norms and standards is seen as an accomplishment. Thus it would be impossible to simultaneously succeed in both school and the peer group (Ogbu, 1987; Wentzel, 1999). And succeeding in the peer group is important. The need for social relationships is basic and strong for most people.

▲ *If this girl's goal is to improve and not worry about mistakes, she may attempt more difficult pieces and welcome criticism. If her goal is to simply look good, she may avoid difficulty and criticism.*

The Need for Relatedness. Relatedness is the need to establish close emotional bonds and attachments with others and reflects the desire to be emotionally connected to the important people in our lives (Ryan, 1991). When teachers and parents are responsive and demonstrate that they care about the children's interests and well-being, the children show high intrinsic motivation. But, when children are denied the interpersonal involvement they seek from adults—when adults, for example, are unresponsive to their needs—the children lose intrinsic motivation (Grolnick, Ryan, & Deci, 1991). In addition, emotional and physical problems—ranging from eating disorders to suicide—are more common among people who lack social relationships (Baumeister & Leary, 1995).

Relatedness has two components, involvement and autonomy support. Involvement is the degree to which teachers and parents are interested in and knowledgeable about their children's activities and experiences and devote time to them. When students feel a sense of belonging and personal support from their teachers, they are more interested in class work and find it more valuable (Goodnow, 1993; Stipek, 1996). Autonomy support is the degree to which teachers and parents encourage children to make their own choices rather than applying pressure to control the children's behavior. When teachers and parents show high involvement and autonomy support, children show greater competence, academic achievement, and responsibility, as well as less aggression (Grolnick & Ryan, 1989; Grolnick, Ryan, & Deci, 1991).

Feedback and Goal Acceptance

Besides having specific, challenging, attainable learning goals, focusing on the task, and creating supportive social relationships, there are two additional factors that make goal-setting in the classroom effective. The first is *feedback*. In order to be motivated by a discrepancy between "where you are" and "where you want to be," you must have an accurate sense of where you are and how far you have to go. When feedback tells a student that current efforts have fallen short of the goal, the student can exert more effort or even try another strategy. When feedback tells the student that the goal is reached or exceeded, the student should feel satisfied and

Goal Orientation and Motivation

Review

▶ What kinds of goals are the most motivating?

▶ Describe learning, performance, work-avoidant, and social goals.

▶ What makes goal setting effective in the classroom?

Apply

▶ A teacher says to the class, "I want all of you to study hard so you can make good scores on the state tests next spring." Predict the effects of this goal-setting statement. Are students likely to be motivated by the goal? Why or why not?

competent—competent enough perhaps to set a higher goal for the future. There is evidence that feedback emphasizing progress is the most effective. In one study, feedback to adults emphasized either that they had accomplished 75% of the standards set or that they had fallen short of the standards by 25%. When the feedback highlighted accomplishment, the subjects' self-confidence, analytic thinking, and performance were all enhanced (Bandura, 1997).

The second factor affecting motivation to pursue a goal is *goal acceptance*. When students accept the goals set by their teachers or establish their own goals, then the power of goal setting to motivate learning can be tapped. But if students reject goals set by others or refuse to set their own goals, then motivation will suffer. Generally, students are more willing to adopt the goals of others if the goals seem realistic, reasonably difficult, and meaningful (Erez & Zidon, 1984) and if good reasons are given for the value of the goals. Goal acceptance might be greater (and goals more appropriate) if you work with students' families to identify and monitor the goals. The Family and Community Partnerships Guidelines give some ideas.

FAMILY AND COMMUNITY PARTNERSHIPS

Setting Goals

Understand family goals for children.

Examples

1. In an informal setting, around a coffee pot or snacks, meet with families individually or in small groups to listen to what they want for their children.

2. Mail out questionnaires or send response cards home with students, asking what skills the families believe their children most need to work on. Pick one goal for each child and develop a plan for working toward the goal both inside and outside school. Share the plan with the families and ask for feedback.

Identify student and family interests that can be related to goals.

Examples

1. Ask a member of the family to share a skill or hobby with the class.

2. Identify "family favorites"—favorite foods, music, vacations, sports, colors, activities, hymns, movies, games, snacks, recipes, memories. Tie class lessons to interests.

Give families a way to track progress toward goals.

Examples

1. Provide simple "progress charts" or goal cards that can be posted on the refrigerator.

2. Ask for feedback (and mean it) about parents' perceptions of your effectiveness in helping students reach goals.

Goals: Lessons for Teachers

Students are more likely to work toward goals that are clear, specific, reasonable, moderately challenging, and attainable within a relatively short period of time. If teachers focus on student performance, high grades, and competition, they may encourage students to set performance goals. This will undermine the students' ability to learn and become task-involved (Anderman & Maehr, 1994). Students may not yet be expert at setting their own goals or keeping the goal in mind, so encouragement and accurate feedback are necessary. If you use any reward or incentive systems, be sure the goal you set is to *learn and improve* in some area, not just to perform well or look smart. And be sure the goal is not too difficult.

Most people are more motivated when they are involved with tasks that give them a chance to form positive relationships with others. Students, like adults, are unlikely to stick with tasks or respond well to teachers who make them feel insecure or incompetent. They are less likely to take responsibility for learning if they believe that the teacher doesn't really care about them.

Interests and Emotions

How do you feel about learning? Excited, bored, curious, fearful? Today, researchers emphasize that learning is not only about the *cold cognition* of reasoning and problem solving. Learning and information processing also are influenced by emotion, so *hot cognition* plays a role in learning as well (Miller, 1993; Pintrich, Marx, & Boyle, 1993). Students are more likely to pay attention to, learn, and remember events, images, and readings that provoke emotional responses (Alexander & Murphy, 1998; Cowley & Underwood, 1998; Reisberg & Heuer, 1992) or that are related to their personal interests (Renninger, Hidi, & Krapp, 1992). How can we use these findings to support learning in school?

Students' interest in and excitement about what they're learning is one of the most important factors in education. ▼

Tapping Interests

When Walter Vispoel and James Austin (1995) asked over 200 middle school students to rate reasons for their successes and failures in different school subjects, lack of interest in the topic received the highest rating as an explanation for failures. Interest was second only to effort as a choice for explaining successes. It seems logical that learning experiences should be related to the interests of the students. And interests increase when students feel competent, so even if students are not initially interested in a subject or activity, they may develop interests as they experience success (Stipek, 1996).

One source of interest is fantasy. For example, Cordova and Lepper (1996) found that students learned more math facts during a computer exercise when they were challenged, as captains of star ships, to navigate through space by solving math problems. The students got to name their ships, stock the (imaginary) galley with their favorite snacks, and name all the crew members after their friends. The Guidelines on page 382 give other ideas.

GUIDELINES

Building on Students' Interests

Relate content objectives to student experiences.

Examples

1. With a teacher in another school, establish pen pals across the classes. Through writing letters, students exchange personal experiences, photos, drawings, written work, and ask and answer questions ("Have you learned cursive writing yet?" "What are you doing in math now?" "What are you reading?"). Letters can be mailed in one large mailer to save stamps.

2. Identify classroom experts for different assignments or tasks. Who knows how to use the computer for graphics? How to search the Net? How to cook? How to use an index?

3. Have a "Switch Day" when students exchange roles with a school staff or support person. Students must research the role by interviewing their staff member, prepare for the job, dress the part for the day they take over, and then evaluate their success after the switch.

Identify student interests, hobbies, and extracurricular activities that can be incorporated into class lessons and discussions.

Examples

1. Have students design and conduct interviews and surveys to learn about each other's interests.

2. Keep the class library stocked with books that connect to students' interests and hobbies.

Support instruction with humor, personal experiences, and anecdotes that show the human side of the content.

Examples

1. Share your own hobbies, interests, and favorites.

2. Tell students there will be a surprise visitor; then dress up as the author of a story and tell about "yourself" and your writing.

Source: Adapted from *150 Ways to Increase Intrinsic Motivation in the Classroom,* by J. P. Raffini, 1996, Boston: Allyn & Bacon. Copyright © 1996 by Allyn & Bacon.

However, there are cautions that need to be addressed in responding to students' interests. Ruth Garner (1992) and her colleagues found that the presence of "seductive details" can hinder learning. Seductive details are interesting bits of information that are not central to the learning, but distract from it. Some examples might be interesting puzzles or other manipulatives that don't connect with important learning objectives but are intriguing to students or details about the life of a scientist that do not help you understand her theories. So, if you dress up like the author of the book, as described in the Guidelines, make sure that the details you share about "your" life are connected to your teaching objectives for students' reading.

Arousal: Excitement and Anxiety in Learning

Just as we all know how it feels to be motivated, we all know what it is like to be aroused. **Arousal** involves both psychological and physical reactions—changes in brain wave patterns, blood pressure, heart rate, and breathing rate. We feel alert, wide-awake, even excited. To understand the effects of arousal on motivation, think of two extremes. The first is late at night. You are trying for the third time to understand a required reading, but you are so sleepy. Your attention drifts as your eyes droop, even though you have not finished the assignments for tomorrow. You decide to go to bed and get up early to study (a plan that you know seldom works). At the

Arousal: Physical and psychological reactions causing a person to be alert, attentive, wide awake.

FIGURE 10.2

Arousal and Quality of Performance

On a simple or well-practiced task, the best performance occurs when arousal is moderately high. But on a complex task, lower arousal leads to better performance—as long as the arousal isn't *too* low.

other extreme, imagine that you have a critical test tomorrow—one that determines whether you will get into the school you want. You feel tremendous pressure from everyone to do well. You know that you need a good night's sleep, but you are wide awake. In the first case, arousal is too low and in the second, too high.

There appears to be an optimum level of arousal for most activities, as shown in Figure 10.2 (Yerkes & Dodson, 1908). Generally speaking, a higher level of arousal is helpful on simple tasks such as sorting laundry, but lower levels of arousal are better for complex tasks such as taking the GRE. Let's look for a moment at how to increase arousal by arousing curiosity.

Curiosity: Novelty and Complexity. Over 30 years ago, psychologists suggested that individuals are naturally motivated to seek novelty, surprise, and complexity (Berlyne, 1966). Research on teaching has found that variety in teaching approaches and tasks can support learning (Brophy & Good, 1986; Stipek, 1996). For younger students, the chance to manipulate and explore objects relevant to what is being studied may be the most effective way to keep curiosity stimulated. For older students, well-constructed questions, logical puzzles, and paradoxes can have the same effect. Example: Ranchers in an area killed the wolves on their land. The following spring they noticed that the deer population was much smaller. How could this be, since wolves hunt the deer and fewer wolves should mean more deer? In searching for a solution, students learn about ecology and the balance of nature: Without wolves to eliminate the weaker and sicker deer, the deer population expanded so much that the winter food supply could not sustain the deer herds. Many deer died of starvation.

George Lowenstein (1994) suggests that curiosity arises when attention is focused on a gap in knowledge. "Such information gaps produce the feeling of deprivation labeled *curiosity*. The curious person is motivated to obtain the missing information to reduce or eliminate the feeling of deprivation" (p. 87). This idea is similar to Piaget's concept of disequilibrium, discussed in Chapter 2, and has a

Connect and Extend
To the research
Meece, J. L., Wigfield, A., & Eccles, J. (1990). Predictors of math anxiety and its influence on young adolescents' course enrollment intentions and performance in mathematics. *Journal of Educational Psychology, 92,* 6–70. This study found that math anxiety was most directly related to students' math ability perceptions, performance expectancies, and value perceptions. Students' performance expectancies predicted subsequent math grades, whereas their value perception predicted course enrollment intentions.

number of implications for teaching. First, students need some base of knowledge before they can experience gaps in knowledge leading to curiosity. Second, students must be aware of the gaps in order for curiosity to result. Asking students to make guesses and then providing feedback can be helpful. Also, mistakes, properly handled, can stimulate curiosity by pointing to missing knowledge. Finally, the more we learn about a topic, the more curious we may become about that subject. As Maslow (1970) predicted, fulfilling the need to know and understand increases, not decreases, the need to know more.

As we discussed earlier, sometimes arousal is too high, not too low. Because classrooms are places where students are tested and graded, anxiety can become a factor in classroom motivation.

Anxiety in the Classroom.

At one time or another, everyone has experienced **anxiety,** or "general uneasiness, a sense of foreboding, a feeling of tension" (Hansen, 1977, p. 91). The effects of anxiety on school achievement are clear. "From the time of the earliest work on this problem, starting with the pioneering work of Yerkes and Dodson (1908), to the present day, researchers have consistently reported a negative correlation between virtually every aspect of school achievement and a wide range of anxiety measures" (Covington & Omelich, 1987, p. 393). Anxiety can be both a cause and an effect of school failure—students do poorly because they are anxious, and their poor performance increases their anxiety. Anxiety probably is both a trait and a state. Some students tend to be anxious in many situations (*trait anxiety*), but some situations are especially anxiety-provoking (*state anxiety*) (Covington, 1992).

Anxiety seems to have both cognitive and affective components. The cognitive side includes worry and negative thoughts—thinking about how bad it would be to fail and worrying that you will, for example. The affective side involves physiological and emotional reactions such as sweaty palms, upset stomach, racing heartbeat, or fear (Schunk, 2000; Zeidner, 1995).

In the classroom, the conditions surrounding a test can influence the performance of highly anxious individuals. For example, Hill and Eaton (1977) found that very anxious 5th and 6th graders worked as quickly and accurately as their less-anxious classmates when there was no time limit for solving arithmetic problems. With a time limit, however, the very anxious students made three times as many errors as their classmates, spent about twice as much time on each problem, and cheated twice as often as the less-anxious group. Whenever there are pressures to perform, severe consequences for failure, and competitive comparisons among students, anxiety may be encouraged (Wigfield & Eccles, 1989).

How Does Anxiety Interfere with Achievement?

Sigmund Tobias (1985) suggests a model to explain how anxiety interferes with learning and test performance at three points in the learning and performance cycle. When students are learning new material, they must pay attention to it. Highly anxious students evidently divide their attention between the new material and their preoccupation with how nervous they are feeling. Instead of concentrating on a lecture or on what they are reading, they keep noticing the tight feelings in their chest, thinking, "I'm so tense, I'll never understand this stuff!" Much of their attention is taken up with negative thoughts about performing poorly, being criticized, and feeling embarrassed. From the beginning, anxious students may miss much of the information they are supposed to learn because their thoughts are focused on their own worries (Hill & Wigfield, 1984; Paulman & Kennelly, 1984).

But the problems do not end here. Even if they are paying attention, many anxious students have trouble learning material that is somewhat disorganized

Anxiety: General uneasiness, a feeling of tension.

and difficult—material that requires them to rely on their memory. Unfortunately, much material in school could be described this way. Anxious students may be more easily distracted by irrelevant or incidental aspects of the task at hand. They seem to have trouble focusing on the significant details (Hill & Wigfield, 1984). In addition, many highly anxious students have poor study habits. Simply learning to be more relaxed will not automatically improve these students' performance; their learning strategies and study skills must be improved as well (Naveh-Benjamin, 1991).

Finally, anxious students often know more than they can demonstrate on a test. They may lack critical test-taking skills, or they may have learned the materials but "freeze and forget" on tests. Thus anxiety can interfere at one or all three points: attention, learning, and testing (Naveh-Benjamin, McKeachie, & Lin, 1987).

C H E C K P O I N T

Interests and Emotions

Review

▶ Do interests and emotions affect learning?

▶ What is the role of arousal in learning?

▶ How does anxiety interfere with learning?

Apply

▶ How would you use students' interests in sports or films to motivate learning?

▶ Name some sources of anxiety in typical classroom situations.

Coping with Anxiety. When students face stressful situations such as tests, they can use three kinds of coping strategies: *problem solving, emotional management,* and *avoidance.* Problem-focused strategies might include planning a study schedule, borrowing good notes, or finding a protected place to study. Emotion-focused strategies are attempts to reduce the anxious feelings, for example, by using relaxation exercises or describing the feelings to a friend. Of course, the latter might become an avoidance strategy, along with going out for pizza or suddenly launching an all out desk-cleaning attack (can't study until you get organized!). Different strategies are helpful at different points—for example, problem solving before and emotion management during an exam. Different strategies fit different people and situations (Zeidner, 1995).

Teachers should help highly anxious students to set realistic goals, because these individuals often have difficulty making wise choices. They tend to select either extremely difficult or extremely easy tasks. In the first case, they are likely to fail, which will increase their sense of hopelessness and anxiety about school. In the second case, they will probably succeed on the easy tasks, but they will miss the sense of satisfaction that could encourage greater effort and ease their fears about schoolwork. Anxious students may need a good deal of guidance in choosing both short- and long-term goals. Goal cards, progress charts, or goal-planning journals may help here.

Interests and Emotions: Lessons for Teachers

You need to work at keeping the level of arousal right for the task at hand. If students are going to sleep, energize them by introducing variety, piquing their curiosity, surprising them, or giving them a brief chance to be physically active. Learn about their interests and incorporate interests into lessons and assignments. If arousal is too great, follow the Guidelines on page 386 for dealing with anxiety.

GUIDELINES

Coping with Anxiety

Use competition carefully.

Examples

1. Monitor activities to make sure no students are being put under undue pressure.
2. During competitive games, make sure all students involved have a reasonable chance of succeeding.
3. Experiment with cooperative learning activities.

Avoid situations in which highly anxious students will have to perform in front of large groups.

Examples

1. Ask anxious students questions that can be answered with a simple yes or no, or some other brief reply.
2. Give anxious students practice in speaking before smaller groups.

Make sure all instructions are clear. Uncertainty can lead to anxiety.

Examples

1. Write test instructions on the board or on the test itself instead of giving them orally.
2. Check with students to make sure they understand. Ask several students how they would do the first question, exercise, or sample question on a test. Correct any misconceptions.
3. If you are using a new format or starting a new type of task, give students examples or models to show how it is done.

Avoid unnecessary time pressures.

Examples

1. Give occasional take-home tests.
2. Make sure all students can complete classroom tests within the period given.

Remove some of the pressures from major tests and exams.

Examples

1. Teach test-taking skills; give practice tests; provide study guides.
2. Avoid basing most of a report-card grade on one test.
3. Make extra-credit work available to add points to course grades.
4. Use different types of items in testing because some students have difficulty with particular formats.

Develop alternatives to written tests.

Examples

1. Try oral, open-book, or group tests.
2. Have students do projects, organize portfolios of their work, make oral presentations, or create a finished product.

Self-Schemas

Thus far, we have talked about goals, interests, and emotions, but there is another factor that must be considered in explaining motivation. What do students believe about themselves? Let's start with a basic question—What do they believe about ability?

Beliefs about Ability

As you saw when we discussed attribution theory, some of the most powerful attributions affecting motivation in school are beliefs about *ability*. By examining these beliefs and how they affect motivation, we will understand why some people set inappropriate, unmotivating goals; why some students adopt self-defeating strategies; and why some students seem to give up altogether.

Adults use two basic concepts of ability. An **entity view of ability** assumes that ability is a *stable, uncontrollable* trait—a characteristic of the individual that cannot be changed. According to this view, some people have more ability than others, but the amount each person has is set. An **incremental view of ability,** on the other hand, suggests that ability is unstable and controllable—"an ever-expanding repertoire of skills and knowledge" (Dweck & Bempechat, 1983, p. 144). By hard work, study, or practice, knowledge can be increased and thus ability can be improved. Thus in Table 10.1, ability changes from being stable and uncontrollable, to unstable and controllable.

Young children tend to hold an exclusively incremental view of ability (Nicholls & Miller, 1984). Through the early elementary grades, most students believe that effort is the same as intelligence. Smart people try hard and trying hard makes you smart. If you fail, you aren't smart and you didn't try hard; if you succeed, you must be a smart, hard worker (Stipek, 1998). Children are age 11 or 12 before they can differentiate among effort, ability, and performance. About this time, they come to believe that someone who succeeds without working at all must be really smart. This is when beliefs about ability begin to influence motivation (Anderman & Maehr, 1994).

Students who hold an entity (unchangeable) view of intelligence tend to set performance goals. They seek situations where they can look smart and protect their self-esteem. Like Safe Sarah, they keep doing what they can do well without expending too much effort or risking failure, because either one—working hard or failing—indicates (to them) low ability. To work hard but still fail would be a devastating blow to their sense of competence.

Another protective strategy is to make a point of not trying at all, as in the example of defensive Diana described earlier. If you don't try and fail, no one can accuse you of being dumb. Just before a test a student might say, "I didn't study at all!" or "All I want to do is pass." Then, any grade above passing is a success. Procrastination is another self-protective strategy. Low grades do not imply low ability if the student can claim, "I did okay considering I didn't start the term paper until last night." Some evidence suggests that blaming anxiety for poor test performance can also be a self-protective strategy (Covington & Omelich, 1987). Of course, even though these strategies may help students avoid the negative implications of failure, very little learning is going on.

Incremental theorists, in contrast, tend to set learning goals and seek situations in which they can improve their skills, since improvement means getting smarter. Failure is not devastating; it simply indicates more work is needed. Ability is not threatened. Incremental theorists tend to set moderately difficult goals, the kind we have seen are the most motivating.

One of the most powerful influences on motivation to achieve is another kind of belief—self-efficacy.

Beliefs about Self-Efficacy

Albert Bandura (1986, 1997) suggests that critical sources of motivation are predictions about possible outcomes of behavior. "Will I succeed or fail? Will I be liked or laughed at?" We imagine future consequences based on past experiences and our observations of others. These predictions are affected by **self-efficacy**—our beliefs about our personal competence or effectiveness *in a given area*. Bandura (1997) defines self-efficacy as "beliefs in one's capabilities to organize and execute the courses of action required to produce given attainments" (p. 3).

Entity View of Ability: Belief that ability is a fixed characteristic that cannot be changed.

Incremental View of Ability: Belief that ability is a set of skills that can be changed.

Self-Efficacy: Beliefs about personal competence in a particular situation.

Self-Efficacy, Self-Concept, and Self-Esteem. Most people assume self-efficacy is the same as self-concept or self-esteem, but it isn't. Self-efficacy is distinct from other conceptions of self, in that it involves judgments of capabilities *specific to a particular task*. So self-efficacy is future-oriented, "a context-specific assessment of competence to perform a specific task" (Pajares, 1997, p. 15). Self-concept is a more global construct that contains many perceptions about the self, including self-efficacy. Self-concept is developed as a result of external and internal comparisons, using other people or other aspects of the self as frames of reference. But self-efficacy focuses on your ability to successfully accomplish a particular task with no need for comparisons—the question is whether *you* can do it, not whether others would be successful (Marsh, Walker, & Debus, 1991). Also, self-efficacy beliefs are strong predictors of behavior, but self-concept has weaker predictive power (Bandura, 1997).

Compared to self-esteem, self-efficacy is concerned with judgments of personal capabilities; self-esteem is concerned with judgments of self-worth. There is no direct relationship between self-esteem and self-efficacy. It is possible to feel highly efficacious in one area and still not have a high level of self-esteem, or vice versa. For example, I have very low self-efficacy for singing, but my self-esteem is not affected, probably because my life does not require singing. But if my self-efficacy for teaching a particular class started dropping after several bad experiences, I know my self-esteem would suffer.

Sources of Self-Efficacy. Bandura identified four sources of self-efficacy expectations: mastery experiences, physiological and emotional arousal, vicarious experiences, and social persuasion. **Mastery experiences** are our own direct experiences—the most powerful source of efficacy information. Successes raise efficacy beliefs, while failures lower efficacy. Level of arousal affects self-efficacy, depending on how the arousal is interpreted. As you face the task, are you anxious and worried (lowers efficacy) or excited and "psyched" (raises efficacy) (Bandura, 1997; Pintrich & Schunk, 1996).

In **vicarious experiences**, accomplishments are modeled by someone else. The more closely the student identifies with the model, the greater the impact on self-efficacy. When the model performs well, the student's efficacy is enhanced, but when the model performs poorly, efficacy expectations decrease. Although mastery experiences generally are acknowledged as the most influential source of efficacy beliefs in adults, Keyser and Barling (1981) found that children (6th graders in this study) rely more on modeling as a source of self-efficacy information.

Social persuasion may be a "pep talk" or specific performance feedback. Social persuasion alone can't create enduring increases in self-efficacy, but a persuasive boost in self-efficacy can lead a student to make an effort, attempt new strategies, or try hard enough to succeed (Bandura, 1982). Social persuasion can counter occasional setbacks that might have instilled self-doubt and interrupted persistence. The potency of persuasion depends on the credibility, trustworthiness, and expertise of the persuader (Bandura, 1986).

Efficacy and Motivation. Greater efficacy leads to greater effort and persistence in the face of setbacks. Self-efficacy also influences motivation through goal setting. If we have a high sense of efficacy in a given area, we will set higher goals, be less afraid of failure, and find new strategies when old ones fail. If our sense of efficacy is low, however, we may avoid a task altogether or give up easily when problems arise (Bandura, 1993, 1997; Zimmerman, 1995).

Self-efficacy and attributions affect each other. If success is attributed to internal or controllable causes such as ability or effort, then self-efficacy is enhanced.

Mastery Experiences: Our own direct experiences—the most powerful source of efficacy information.

Vicarious Experiences: Accomplishments that are modeled by someone else.

Social Persuasion: A "pep talk" or specific performance feedback—one source of self-efficacy.

But if success is attributed to luck or the intervention of others, then self-efficacy may not be strengthened. And efficacy affects attributions too. People with a strong sense of self-efficacy for a given task ("I'm good at math") tend to attribute their failures to lack of effort ("I should have double-checked my work"). But people with a low sense of self-efficacy ("I'm terrible at math") tend to attribute their failures to lack of ability ("I'm just dumb"). So having a strong sense of self-efficacy for a certain task encourages controllable attributions and controllable attributions increase self-efficacy. You can see that if a student held an entity view (ability cannot be changed) and a low sense of self-efficacy, motivation would be destroyed when failures were attributed to lack of ability ("I just can't do this and I'll never be able to learn") (Bandura, 1997; Pintrich & Schunk, 1996).

There is evidence that a high sense of self-efficacy supports motivation, even when the efficacy is unrealistically high. Children and adults who are optimistic about the future, believe that they can be effective, and have high expectations are more mentally and physically healthy, less depressed, and more motivated to achieve (Flammer, 1995). After examining almost 140 studies of motivation, Sandra Graham concluded that these qualities characterize many African Americans. She found that the African Americans studied had strong self-concepts and high expectations, even in the face of difficulties (Graham, 1994, 1995).

Research on self-efficacy and achievement suggests that performance in school is improved and self-efficacy is increased when students (a) adopt short-term goals so it is easier to judge progress; (b) are taught to use specific learning strategies such as outlining or summarizing that help them focus attention; and (c) receive rewards based on performance, not just engagement, because performance rewards signal increasing competence (Graham & Weiner, 1996).

▲ *Students' beliefs about their own ability to succeed influence achievement. These beliefs are affected in one way or another by family, teachers, and others.*

Teacher Efficacy. Much of my own research has focused on a particular kind of self-efficacy—sense of efficacy in teaching (Hoy & Woolfolk, 1990, 1993; Tschannen-Moran, Woolfolk Hoy, & Hoy, 1998; Woolfolk & Hoy, 1990; Woolfolk, Rosoff, & Hoy, 1990). **Teaching efficacy,** a teacher's belief that he or she can reach even difficult students to help them learn, appears to be one of the few personal characteristics of teachers that is correlated with student achievement. Self-efficacy theory predicts that teachers with a high sense of efficacy work harder and persist longer even when students are difficult to teach, in part because these teachers believe in themselves and in their students.

We have found that prospective teachers tend to increase in their personal sense of efficacy as a consequence of completing student teaching. Teachers' sense of personal efficacy is higher in schools where the other teachers and administrators have high expectations for students and where teachers receive help from their principals in solving instructional and management problems (Hoy & Woolfolk, 1993). Another important conclusion from our research is that efficacy grows from real success with students, not just from the moral support or cheerleading of professors and colleagues. Any experience or training that helps you succeed in the day-to-day tasks of teaching will give you a foundation for developing a sense of efficacy in your career.

The perception of control is a significant element in having a sense of efficacy. Sense of control is also an element in a current humanistic theory of motivation—self-determination.

Teaching Efficacy: A teacher's belief that he or she can reach even the most difficult students and help them learn.

Self-Determination

Self-determination is the need to experience choice and control in what we do and how we do it. It is the desire to have our own wishes, rather than external rewards or pressures, determine our actions (Deci & Ryan, 1985; Deci, Vallerand, Pelletier, & Ryan, 1991). People strive to be in charge of their own behavior. They constantly struggle against pressure from external controls such as the rules, schedules, deadlines, orders, and limits imposed by others. Sometimes even help is rejected so that the individual can remain in command (deCharms, 1976, 1983).

To capture the difference between self- and other-determination, Richard deCharms used the metaphor of people as "origins" and "pawns." Origins perceive themselves as the origin or source of their intention to act in a certain way. As pawns, people see themselves as powerless participants in a game controlled by others. When people feel like pawns, play becomes work, leisure feels like obligation, and intrinsic motivation becomes extrinsic motivation (Lepper & Greene, 1978). For example, you may have had the experience of deciding to wash the car or clean your room, only to have your motivation dampened by a parent who insists that you tackle the chore. Your chance to be an origin seems spoiled by outside attempts at control. You don't want to wash the car anymore because your sense of self-determination is taken away.

DeCharms was struck by his observation that students are too little governed by their own intrinsic motivation and too powerless over external controls and demands. As origins, students are active and responsible, but as pawns, they are passive and they take little responsibility for schoolwork. To deal with the issue, deCharms developed programs to help teachers support student self-determination. The programs emphasized the setting of realistic goals, personal planning of activities to reach the goals, personal responsibility for actions, and feelings of self-confidence. Results of some studies show that when students feel more like origins and less like pawns, they have higher self-esteem, feel more competent and in charge of their learning, score higher on standardized tests, and are absent less (deCharms, 1976; Ryan & Grolnick, 1986).

Self-Determination in the Classroom. Classroom environments that support student self-determination and autonomy are associated with greater student interest, sense of competence, creativity, conceptual learning, and preference for challenge. These relationships appear to hold from 1st grade through graduate school (Ryan & Grolnick, 1986; Williams, Wiener, Markakis, Reeve, & Deci, 1993). When students can make choices, they are more likely to believe that the work is important, even if it is not "fun." Thus, they tend to internalize educational goals and take them as their own. Ruth Garner (1998) sums up the value of self-determination: "It is through this self determination, measured though it might be, that wise teachers allow each of their students to guide them to what the students find particularly enjoyable and worth learning" (p. 236).

Controlling environments tend to improve performance only on rote recall tasks. When students are pressured to perform, they often seek the quickest, easiest solution. One discomforting finding, however, is that both students and parents seem to prefer more controlling teachers, even though the students learn more when their teachers support autonomy (Flink, Boggiano, & Barrett, 1990). Assuming you are willing to risk going against popular images, how can you support student autonomy? One answer is to focus on *information*, not *control*, in your interactions with students.

Self-Determination: The need to experience choice and control in what we do and how we do it.

Information and Control. Many things happen to students throughout the school day. They are praised or criticized, reminded of deadlines, assigned grades, given choices, lectured about rules, and on and on. **Cognitive evaluation theory** (Deci & Ryan, 1985; Deci, Vallerand, Pelletier, & Ryan, 1991) explains how these events can influence the students' intrinsic motivation by affecting their sense of self-determination and competence. According to this theory, all events have two aspects, controlling and informational. If an event is highly controlling, that is, if it pressures students to act or feel a certain way, then students will experience less control and their *intrinsic motivation* will be diminished. If, on the other hand, the event provides information that increases the students' sense of competence and efficacy, then intrinsic motivation will increase. Of course, if the information provided makes students feel less competent, it is likely that motivation will decrease.

For example, a teacher might praise a student by saying, "Good for you! You got an A because you finally followed my instructions correctly." This is a highly controlling statement, giving the credit to the teacher and thus undermining the student's sense of self-determination and intrinsic motivation. The teacher could praise the same work by saying, "Good for you! Your understanding of the author's use of metaphors has improved tremendously. You earned an A." This statement provides information about the student's growing competence and should increase intrinsic motivation.

What can teachers do to support student autonomy? An obvious first step is to limit their controlling messages to their students and make sure the information they provide highlights students' growing competence. Unfortunately, when teachers are under pressure and "controlled" by the school administration, they are likely to treat students the same way. In one study, teachers told to "make sure" their students performed well in solving problems were more critical and gave students more hints and less time for independent work than teachers who were told that their job was to "help" the students learn how to solve the problems themselves. And the students of the pressured teachers actually performed worse (Boggiano, Flink, Shields, Seelbach, & Barrett, 1995). The Guidelines on page 392 give ideas about how to support students' self-determination and autonomy.

Learned Helplessness

Whatever the label, most theorists agree that a sense of efficacy, control, or self-determination is critical if people are to feel intrinsically motivated. When people come to believe that the events and outcomes in their lives are mostly uncontrollable, they have developed **learned helplessness** (Seligman, 1975). To understand the power of learned helplessness, consider this experiment (Hiroto & Seligman, 1975): Subjects receive either solvable or unsolvable puzzles. In the next phase of the experiment, all subjects are given a series of solvable puzzles. The subjects who struggled with unsolvable problems in the first phase of the experiment usually solve significantly fewer puzzles in the second phase. They have learned that they cannot control the outcome, so why should they even try?

Learned helplessness appears to cause three types of deficits: motivational, cognitive, and affective. Students who feel hopeless will be unmotivated and reluctant to attempt work. Like Helpless Henry described earlier, they expect to fail, so why should they even try—thus motivation suffers. Because they are pessimistic about learning, these students miss opportunities to practice and improve skills and abilities, so they develop cognitive deficits. Finally, they often suffer from affective problems such as depression, anxiety, and listlessness (Alloy & Seligman, 1979). Once

Connect and Extend
To other chapters
The concept of learned helplessness was first introduced in Chapter 4 during the discussion of learning disabilities. Learned helplessness is also an issue for at-risk students, as described in Chapter 5. Consider the many factors in a classroom that might lead to learned helplessness, including physical or cognitive disabilities, racial prejudice, sex-role stereotyping, poverty, and so on.

Cognitive Evaluation Theory: Suggests that events affect motivation through the individual's perception of the events as controlling behavior or providing information.

Learned Helplessness: The expectation, based on previous experiences with a lack of control, that all one's efforts will lead to failure.

GUIDELINES

Supporting Self-Determination and Autonomy

Allow and encourage students to make choices.

Examples

1. Design several different ways to meet a learning objective (e.g., a paper, a compilation of interviews, a test, a news broadcast) and let students choose one. Encourage them to explain the reasons for their choice.

2. Appoint student committees to make suggestions about streamlining procedures such as caring for class pets or distributing equipment.

3. Provide time for independent and extended projects.

Help students plan actions to accomplish self-selected goals.

Examples

1. Experiment with goal cards. Students list their short- and long-term goals and then record 3 or 4 specific actions that will move them toward the goals. Goal cards are personal—like credit cards.

2. Encourage middle and high school students to set goals in each subject area, record them in a goal book or on a floppy disk, and check progress toward the goals on a regular basis.

Hold students accountable for the consequences of their choices.

Examples

1. If students choose to work with friends and do not finish a project because too much time was spent socializing, grade the project as it deserves and help the students see the connection between lost time and poor performance.

2. When students choose a topic that captures their imagination, discuss the connections between their investment in the work and the quality products that follow.

Provide rationales for limits, rules, and constraints.

Examples

1. Explain reasons for rules.

2. Respect rules and constraints in your own behavior.

Acknowledge that negative emotions are valid reactions to teacher control.

Examples

1. Communicate that it is okay (and normal) to feel bored waiting for a turn, for example.

2. Communicate that sometimes important learning involves frustration, confusion, weariness.

Use noncontrolling, positive feedback.

Examples

1. See poor performance or behavior as a problem to be solved, not a target of criticism.

2. Avoid controlling language, "should," "must," "have to."

Source: Adapted from *150 Ways to Increase Intrinsic Motivation in the Classroom,* by J. P. Raffini, 1996, Boston: Allyn & Bacon, and *Motivating Others: Nurturing Inner Motivational Resources* (pp. 29–31), by J. Reeve, 1996, Boston: Allyn & Bacon. Copyright © 1996 by Allyn & Bacon.

Mastery-Oriented Students: Students who focus on learning goals because they value achievement and see ability as improvable.

Failure-Avoiding Students: Students who avoid failure by sticking to what they know, by not taking risks, or by claiming not to care about their performance.

established, it is very difficult to reverse the effects of learned helplessness. As we saw in Chapters 4 and 5, learned helplessness is a particular danger for students with learning disabilities and students who are the victims of discrimination.

Self-Worth

What are the connections between attributions for success and failure, and beliefs about ability, self-efficacy, and self-worth? Covington and his colleagues suggest that these factors come together in three kinds of motivational sets: *mastery-oriented, failure-avoiding,* and *failure-accepting,* as shown in Table 10.3 (Covington, 1992; Covington & Omelich, 1984, 1987).

TABLE 10.3 *Mastery-Oriented, Failure-Avoiding, and Failure-Accepting Students*

	Attitude toward Failure	Goals Set	Attributions	View of Ability	Strategies
Mastery-Oriented	Low fear of failure	Learning goals: moderately difficult and challenging	Effort, use of right strategy, sufficient knowledge is cause of success	Incremental; improvable	Adaptive strategies; e.g., try another way, seek help, practice/study more
Failure-Avoiding	High fear of failure	Performance goals; very hard or very easy	Lack of ability is cause of failure	Entity; set	Self-defeating strategies; e.g., make a feeble effort, pretend not to care
Failure-Accepting	Expectation of failure; depression	Performance goals or no goals	Lack of ability is cause of failure	Entity; set	Learned helplessness; likely to give up

Mastery-oriented students tend to value achievement and see ability as improvable (an incremental view), so they focus on learning goals in order to increase their skills and abilities. They are not fearful of failure, because failing does not threaten their sense of competence and self-worth. This allows them to set moderately difficult goals, take risks, and cope with failure constructively. They generally attribute success to their own effort, and thus they assume responsibility for learning and have a strong sense of self-efficacy. They perform best in competitive situations, learn fast, have more self-confidence and energy, are more aroused, welcome concrete feedback (it does not threaten them), and are eager to learn "the rules of the game" so that they can succeed. All of these factors make for persistent, successful learning (Alderman, 1985; McClelland, 1985; Morris, 1991).

Failure-avoiding students tend to hold an entity view of ability, so they set performance goals. They lack a strong sense of their own competence and self-worth separate from their performance. In other words, they feel only as smart as their last test grade, so they never develop a solid sense of self-efficacy. In order to feel competent, they must protect themselves (and their self-images) from failure. If they have been generally successful, they may avoid failure simply by taking few risks and "sticking with what they know." If, on the other hand, they have experienced some successes but also a good bit of failure, they may adopt the strategies we discussed earlier—

CHECKPOINT

Self-Schemas

Review

▶ How do beliefs about ability affect motivation?

▶ What is self-efficacy, and how is it different from other self-schemas?

▶ What are the sources of self-efficacy, and how does efficacy affect motivation?

▶ How does self-determination affect motivation?

▶ How does self-worth influence motivation?

Apply

▶ Explain how beliefs about the nature of ability might be associated with students' self-protective, self-defeating behaviors such as procrastination or not trying.

▶ Describe the development of learned helplessness. What kinds of goals would a student set if the student felt helpless?

Failure-Accepting Students: Students who believe their failures are due to low ability and there is little they can do about it.

procrastination, feeble efforts, setting very low or ridiculously high goals, or claiming not to care. Both Safe Sarah and Defensive Diana are failure-avoiding students.

Unfortunately, as we have seen, failure-avoiding strategies are self-defeating, generally leading to the very failure the students were trying to avoid. If failures continue and excuses wear thin, the students may finally decide that they are incompetent. This is what they feared in the first place, but they come to accept it. Their sense of self-worth and self-efficacy deteriorate. They give up and thus become **failure-accepting students.** They are convinced that their problems are due to low ability, and they can no longer protect themselves from this conclusion. As we saw earlier, those students who attribute failure to low ability and believe ability is set are likely to become depressed, apathetic, and helpless. Like Hopeless Henry, they have little hope for change.

Teachers may be able to prevent some failure-avoiding students from becoming failure-accepting by helping them to find new and more realistic goals. Also, some students may need support in aspiring to higher levels in the face of sexual or ethnic stereotypes about what they "should" want or what they "should not" be able to do well. This kind of support could make all the difference. Instead of pitying or excusing these students, teachers can teach them how to learn and then hold them accountable.

Guidelines

Encouraging Self-Efficacy and Self-Worth

Emphasize students' progress in a particular area.

Examples

1. Return to earlier material in reviews and show how "easy" it is now.
2. Encourage students to improve projects when they have learned more.
3. Keep examples of particularly good work in portfolios.

Make specific suggestions for improvement, and revise grades when improvements are made.

Examples

1. Return work with comments noting what the students did right, what they did wrong, and why they might have made the mistakes.
2. Experiment with peer editing.
3. Show students how their revised, higher grade reflects greater competence and raises their class average.

Stress connections between past efforts and past accomplishments.

Examples

1. Have individual goal-setting and goal-review conferences with students, in which you ask students to reflect on how they solved difficult problems.

2. Confront self-defeating, failure-avoiding strategies directly.

Set learning goals for your students, and model a mastery orientation for them.

Examples

1. Recognize progress and improvement.
2. Share examples of how you have developed your abilities in a given area and provide other models of achievement who are similar to your students—no supermen or superwomen whose accomplishments seem unattainable.
3. Read stories about students who overcame physical, mental, or economic challenges.
4. Don't excuse failure because a student has problems outside school. Help the student succeed inside school.

Self-Schemas: Lessons for Teachers

If students believe they lack the ability to deal with higher mathematics, they will probably act on this belief even if their actual abilities are well above average. These students are likely to have little motivation to tackle trigonometry or calculus, because they expect to do poorly in these areas. If students believe that failing means they are stupid, they are likely to adopt many self-protective, but also self-defeating, strategies. Just telling students to "try harder" is not particularly effective. Students need real evidence that effort will pay off, that setting a higher goal will not lead to failure, that they can improve, and that abilities can be changed. They need authentic mastery experiences. The Guidelines on page 394 provide ideas for encouraging self-efficacy and self-worth.

Summary

What Is Motivation?

Define motivation.

Motivation is an internal state that arouses, directs, and maintains behavior. The study of motivation focuses on how and why people initiate actions directed toward specific goals, how intensively they are involved in the activity, how persistent they are in their attempts to reach these goals, and what they are thinking and feeling along the way. Explanations of motivation include both personal and environmental factors as well as intrinsic and extrinsic sources of motivation.

What is the difference between intrinsic and extrinsic motivation?

Intrinsic motivation is the natural tendency to seek out and conquer challenges as we pursue personal interests and exercise capabilities—it is motivation to do something when we don't have to. Extrinsic motivation is based on factors not related to the activity itself. We are not really interested in the activity for its own sake; we care only about what it will gain us.

How does locus of causality apply to motivation?

The essential difference between intrinsic and extrinsic motivation is the person's reason for acting, that is, whether the locus of causality for the action (the location of the cause) is internal or external—inside or outside the person. If the locus in internal, the motivation is intrinsic and if the locus is external the motivation is extrinsic. Most motivation has elements of both.

Four General Approaches to Motivation

What are the key factors in motivation according to a behavioral viewpoint? A humanistic viewpoint? A cognitive viewpoint? A sociocultural viewpoint?

Behaviorists tend to emphasize extrinsic motivation caused by incentives, rewards, and punishment. Humanistic views stress the intrinsic motivation created by the need for personal growth, fulfillment, and self-determination. Cognitive views stress a person's active search for meaning, understanding, and competence, and the power of the individual's attributions and interpretations. Sociocultural views emphasize legitimate engaged participation and identity within a community.

Distinguish between deficiency needs and being needs in Maslow's theory.

Maslow called four lower-level needs—survival, safety, belonging, and self-esteem—deficiency needs. When these needs are satisfied, the motivation for fulfilling them decreases. He labeled the three higher-level needs—intellectual achievement, aesthetic appreciation, and self-actualization—being needs. When they are met, a person's motivation does not cease; instead, it increases to seek further fulfillment.

What are the three dimensions of attributions in Weiner's theory?

According to Weiner, most of the attributed causes for successes or failures can be characterized in terms of three dimensions: *locus* (location of the cause internal or external to the person), *stability* (whether the cause stays the same or can change), and *responsibility* (whether the person can control the cause). The greatest motivational problems arise when students attribute failures to stable, uncontrollable causes. These students may seem resigned to failure, depressed, helpless—what we generally call "unmotivated."

What are expectancy x value theories?

Expectancy x value theories suggest that motivation to reach a goal is the product of our expectations for success and the value of the goal to us. If either is zero, our motivation is zero also.

What is legitimate peripheral participation?

Legitimate peripheral participation means that beginners are genuinely involved in the work of the group, even if their abilities are undeveloped and their contributions are small. The identities of the novice and the expert are bound up in their participation in the community. They are motivated to learn the values and practices of the community to keep their identity as community members.

Goal Orientation and Motivation

What kinds of goals are the most motivating?

Goals increase motivation if they are specific, moderately difficult, and able to be reached in the near future.

Describe learning, performance, work-avoidant, and social goals.

A learning goal is the intention to gain knowledge and master skills. Students who set learning goals tend to seek challenges and persist when they encounter difficulties. A performance goal is the intention to get good grades or to appear smarter or more capable than others. Students who set performance goals are preoccupied with themselves and how they appear. Work-avoidant learners simply want to find the easiest way to handle the situation. Students with social goals can be supported or hindered in their learning, depending on the specific goal (i.e., have fun with friends or bring honor to the family).

What makes goal setting effective in the classroom?

In order for goal setting to be effective in the classroom, students need accurate feedback about their progress toward goals and they must accept the goals set. Generally, students are more willing to adopt goals that seem realistic, reasonably difficult, and meaningful and if good reasons are given for the value of the goals.

Interests and Emotions

Do interests and emotions affect learning?

Learning and information processing are influenced by emotion. Students are more likely to pay attention to, learn, and remember events, images, and readings that provoke emotional responses or that are related to their personal interests. However, there are cautions in responding to students' interests. "Seductive details," interesting bits of information that are not central to the learning, can hinder learning.

What is the role of arousal in learning?

There appears to be an optimum level of arousal for most activities. Generally speaking, a higher level of arousal is helpful on simple tasks, but lower levels of arousal are better for complex tasks. When arousal is too low, teachers can stimulate curiosity by pointing out gaps in knowledge or using variety in activities. Severe anxiety is an example of arousal that is too high for optimal learning.

How does anxiety interfere with learning?

Anxiety can be the cause or the result of poor performance; it can interfere with attention to, learning of, and retrieval of information. Many anxious students need help in developing effective test-taking and study skills.

Self-Schemas

How do beliefs about ability affect motivation?

When people hold an entity theory of ability, that is, they believe that ability is fixed, they tend to set performance goals and strive to protect themselves from failure. When they believe ability is improvable (an incremental theory), however, they tend to set learning goals and handle failure constructively.

What is self-efficacy and how is it different from other self-schemas?

Self-efficacy is distinct from other self-schemas in that it involves judgments of capabilities *specific to a particular task*. Self-concept is a more global construct that contains many perceptions about the self, including self-efficacy. Self-concept is developed as a result of external and internal comparisons, using other people or other aspects of the self as frames of reference. Compared to self-esteem, self-efficacy is concerned with judgments of personal capabilities; self-esteem is concerned with judgments of self-worth.

What are the sources of self-efficacy and how does efficacy affect motivation?

Four sources of efficacy expectations are mastery experiences (direct experiences), level of arousal as you face the task, vicarious experiences (accomplishments are modeled by someone else), and social persuasion (a "pep talk" or specific performance feedback). Greater efficacy leads to greater effort and persistence in the face of setbacks. Efficacy also influences motivation through goal setting. People with a high sense of efficacy in a given area set higher goals, are less afraid of failure, and find new strategies when old ones fail. If sense of efficacy is low, however, people may avoid a task altogether or give up easily when problems arise.

How does self-determination affect motivation?

When students experience self-determination, they are intrinsically motivated—they are more interested in their work, have a greater sense of self-esteem, and learn more. Whether students experience self-determination depends in part on if the teacher's communications with students provide information or seek to control them. In addition, teachers must acknowledge the students' perspective, offer choices, provide rationales for limits, and treat poor performance as a problem to be solved rather than a target for criticism.

How does self-worth influence motivation?

Mastery-oriented students tend to value achievement and see ability as improvable, so they focus on learning goals in order to increase their skills and abilities. They are not fearful of failure, because failing does not threaten their sense of competence and self-worth. This allows them to take risks and cope with failure constructively. A low sense of self-worth seems to be linked with the failure-avoiding and failure-accepting strategies intended to protect the individual from the consequences of failure. These strategies may seem to help in the short term, but are damaging to motivation and self-esteem in the long run.

Key Terms

anxiety, p. 384
arousal, p. 382
attribution theories, p. 373
being needs, p. 370
cognitive evaluation theory, p. 391
deficiency needs, p. 370
ego-involved learners, p. 378
entity view of ability, p. 387
expectancy x value theories, p. 375
extrinsic motivation, p. 368
failure-accepting students, p. 394
failure-avoiding students, p. 393
goal, p. 377

hierarchy of needs, p. 370
humanistic view, p. 370
incentive, p. 369
incremental view of ability, p. 387
intrinsic motivation, p. 368
learned helplessness, p. 391
learning goal, p. 378
legitimate peripheral participation, p. 376
locus of causality, p. 368
mastery experience, p. 388
mastery-oriented students, p. 393
motivation, p. 366

performance goal, p. 378
reward, p. 369
self-actualization, p. 370
self-determination, p. 390
self-efficacy, p. 387
social goals, p. 378
social persuasion, p. 388
sociocultural view of motivation, p. 375
task-involved learners, p. 378
teaching efficacy, p. 389
vicarious experience, p. 388
work-avoidant learners, p. 378

Becoming a Professional

Reflecting on the Chapter

Can you apply the ideas from this chapter on motivation to solve the following problems of practice?

Preschool and Kindergarten

▶ How could you help young students build a foundation for self-efficacy in school?

Elementary and Middle School

▶ Several of your students seem to have given up in science. They almost expect to fail. This is especially troubling because a number of the students are girls who believe that "girls are no good in science." What would you do?

▶ How would you respond to mistakes without communicating to students that their mistakes are the result of low ability? You also want to avoid being unrealistic about what they can do or implying that the material is "easy."

Junior High and High School

▶ You are the faculty advisor for the student newspaper. Your students have grand ideas for stories and features, but they seem to run out of steam and never quite finish. The production of the paper is always last-minute and rush, rush. How would you help the students stay motivated and work steadily?

▶ As the time to take the PSAT nears, a few of your students are becoming so anxious that you wonder if they will make it through the test. What can you do to help them?

Certification Test Requirements

▶ Be clear about the kinds of goals that are most motivating.

▶ Make sure you understand the difference between intrinsic and extrinsic motivation.

▶ Understand the elements of attribution theory.

▶ Know ways to enhance self-efficacy in students.

Your Teaching Portfolio

Think about your philosophy of teaching, a question you will be asked at most job interviews. What do you believe about motivating hard-to-reach students? How can you support the development of genuine and well-founded self-efficacy in your students? (Consult the Guidelines for ideas.)

Add some ideas for parent involvement from this chapter to your **Portfolio**.

Teaching Resources

Adapt all the Guidelines from the chapter for the age group you plan to teach.

TEACHERS' CASEBOOK

What Would They Do?

Here is how some practicing teachers responded to the teaching situation presented at the beginning of this chapter about the middle school students who give up before they start.

THOMAS W. NEWKIRK

Eighth Grade Teacher
Hamilton Heights Middle School, Arcadia, Indiana

If things are not going well in the classroom, I remember three important lessons my students have taught me. First, humor is often important in presenting a lesson. For example, students are morely likely to build strong transitions between their ideas after they see me wobbling on an imaginary rope bridge from one detail to another.

The second lesson is that variety is important in planning curriculum. Maybe a lesson doesn't need to be taught in the classroom. Perhaps it can be taught in the cafeteria or on the football field. Maybe someone else—a parent or a member of the community—can teach the lesson. Maybe the lesson can be taught by listening to a recording or by viewing a film rather than by reading one more assignment.

I have also learned my students' attitudes are likely to be a reflection of my own. From the beginning of the year my students learn the emphasis is on what we can do: "I can't" receives short shrift. They know I am enthusiastic not only about what I teach but also about what they achieve.

Remembering these lessons, I have dispelled many clouds of despair before they've overwhelmed my classes.

PEGGY MCDONNELL

Sixth Grade Teacher
West Park School, Moscow, Idaho

It appears that the students in this middle school class have lost the motivation to work in school. Have they also lost the motivation to excel on the basketball court, in the video arcade, or on their rollerblades? If not, it may help to see what rewards they reap from their efforts outside of school. Are these rewards all external? Probably not—many are intrinsic, such as the feelings of well-being and success. Outside of school, these students are striving to meet higher, often self-imposed standards. What can we as educators, do to parallel this in our classrooms?

First and foremost we can provide a sense of relevance to our assignments, an attachment to real-life situations and problems. If we are teaching about percentages, we should be taking students "shopping" to calculate sales prices. If we are exploring classification in science, we can visit a pet store or greenhouse to classify the animals or plants. We need to make the subjects we share with our students come alive by providing material in a variety of ways. We should also be giving students choices that allow them to share their understanding of subject matter in various ways. This would offer more opportunities for success.

Educators have made great strides in developing "shared-decision making models" in schools. In such models teachers share decision-making power with administrators. Somehow, many of us have left the students out of this process. Although we realize how much harder we work when we have an investment in a process, we tend to deny our students that right. This middle school class needs a project that they can plan and develop as a group and execute as a group to see if they can benefit from this model. It appears that the students need to have some ownership of their activities and that they need to help set the standards for performance.

JEFF HOVERMILL

Seventh–Twelfth Grade Teacher
Seabury Hall School, Makawao, Idaho

I would try to improve the environment for learning in the classroom by fostering intrinsic motivation in the students. I would look for topics in which the students are interested and incorporate those themes into assignments and activities. Keeping class fresh and interesting is particularly important in the middle grades. A wide variety of activities and assignments help to keep the students involved and motivated. I try to use such activities as group work, films, field trips, projects, speakers, drill and practice, and interdisciplinary themes to introduce assignments.

Some of their projects should have varying levels of difficulty. Students should have the option of selecting from the entire list the projects that most appeal to them and are more realistic in terms of meeting their goals. This is one way to help students experience success without having them feel they have been "tracked" into different ability levels. I also choose assignments of varying lengths, in different educational settings, and ones which will involve different learning styles.

Getting to know the students outside of the classroom is another way to demonstrate concern and model motivational behaviors. Participating with or observing students in extracurricular activities outside of class often enhances motivation inside of class. When a teacher expresses enough interest in the students to be a club sponsor or athletic coach and attends plays or recitals in which students are involved, this attention is often reciprocated with increased effort in the classroom.

Decreased motivation to learn can be a contagious inhibitor to learning in school. If students are apathetic and feel that the locus of causality for success in school is extrinsic to them and that they cannot succeed even if they do try, it will be very difficult to motivate them to learn. Careful attention by the teacher to the students' needs can help to alleviate decreased motivation. Helping the students to meet realistic goals and develop intrinsic reasons for learning will increase academic success and in turn increase self-esteem and motivation. Group and individual affect among the students within the classroom should also be improved by this attention, which in turn provides a better environment for learning.

NICOLE DEPALMA COBB AND
SANDRA T. MCNEICE

Eighth Grade Teachers
Sterling Middle School, Quincy, Massachusetts

In a situation where the students seem defeated about learning, we must ask ourselves if the current curriculum fits the children and the times. We must remember the power of connecting their high interest and curiosity to our curriculum. Assuming that we have developed our curriculum to fit our students' needs and we still find there is a motivation problem, we must try to adopt certain strategies. In order to tap into the inner motivation of the students, groupings of students could be used to brainstorm about the current conflicts facing the class. We can entice students by modeling the inquiry process. To encourage our students to be vested and have a sense of ownership, inner motivation could also be stimulated by peer tutorials, educational games, project-based learning, oral presentations, videos or photo montages, student-peer teaching drama, newspaper or community magazine work, and the use of interdisciplinary connections.

Motivation, Teaching, and Learning

hen you are facing a difficult task, what do you do? How do you handle distractions? Are there activities that you have no trouble doing—that you have to "make yourself quit"? What are they? Are you more motivated when you are a member of a team and others are counting on you or when you are on your own?

In the previous chapter we saw that motivation is an extremely complex concept. Many factors seem to affect the goals we choose and our energy and persistence in working toward them. We saw that goals, needs, beliefs, attributions, expectations, and anxiety can all affect motivation.

How do we put all this information together in teaching? How do we create environments, situations, and relationships that encourage motivation? These are the questions we will address in the next several pages. First we consider how the influences on motivation discussed in the previous chapter come together to support motivation to learn. Then we examine how motivation is influenced by the academic work of the class, the value of the work, and the setting in which the work must be done. Having considered the task and the setting, we turn to a very important influence on student motivation—the teacher. Finally, we discuss a number of strategies for developing motivation as a constant state in your classroom and as a permanent trait in your students.

By the time you have completed this chapter, you should be able to:

▶ Define motivation to learn.
▶ Explain how the ambiguity and risk of the learning task affect motivation.
▶ Discuss how the value of a task affects motivation to learn.
▶ Describe the characteristics of classrooms that support students' autonomy.
▶ Explain how evaluation procedures and grouping arrangements, particularly cooperative learning, can influence motivation.
▶ Describe potential effects of teachers' expectations on students.
▶ Devise a strategy for teaching your subject to an uninterested student.

What Would You Do?

On the first day of your orientation for your new position as a 4th grade teacher you are handed a long list of competencies and topics that could be covered on the 4th grade proficiency test in the spring. You learn that your new school is on a State list of districts being monitored because the test scores from previous years have been so low. You agree that many of the topics on the test list are important, but your school seems to have no plan for teaching other than drill and practice on facts and skills that might be on the test.

▶ How will you arouse students' curiosity and interests about the topics and tasks that will be tested?

▶ How will you establish the value of learning these skills and facts?

▶ How will you get students engaged in real learning about the topics?

▶ What more do you need to know to prepare your students for this big test?

Motivation to Learn in School

Teachers are concerned about developing a particular kind of motivation in their students—the motivation to learn. Jere Brophy (1988) describes student **motivation to learn** as "a student tendency to find academic activities meaningful and worthwhile and to try to derive the intended academic benefits from them. Motivation to learn can be construed as both a general trait and a situation-specific state" (pp. 205–206).

Many elements make up the motivation to learn. These include planning, concentration on the goal, metacognitive awareness of what you intend to learn and how you intend to learn it, the active search for new information, clear perceptions of feedback, pride and satisfaction in achievement, and no anxiety or fear of failure (Johnson & Johnson, 1985). Motivation to learn thus involves more than wanting or intending to learn. It includes the quality of the student's mental efforts. For example, reading the text 10 times may indicate persistence, but motivation to learn implies more thoughtful, active study strategies, such as summarizing, elaborating the basic ideas, outlining in your own words, drawing graphs of the key relationships, and so on (Brophy, 1988).

It would be wonderful if all our students came to us filled with the motivation to learn, but they don't. And even if they did, work in school might still seem boring or unimportant to some students. As teachers, we have three major goals. The first is to get students productively involved with the work of the class; in other words, to create a *state* of motivation to learn. The second and longer-term goal is

CHECKPOINT

Motivation to Learn in School

Review

▶ Define motivation to learn.

Apply

▶ What motivates you?

TABLE 11.1 *Building a Concept of Motivation to Learn*

Motivation to learn is encouraged when the sources of motivation are intrinsic, the goals are personally challenging, and the individual is focused on the task, has a mastery orientation, attributes successes and failures to controllable causes, and believes ability can be improved.

	Optimum Characteristics of Motivation to Learn	Characteristics That Diminish Motivation to Learn
Source of Motivation	INTRINSIC: Personal factors such as needs, interests, curiosity, enjoyment	EXTRINSIC: Environmental factors such as rewards, social pressure, punishment
Type of Goal Set	LEARNING GOAL: Personal satisfaction in meeting challenges and improving; tendency to choose moderately difficult and challenging goals	PERFORMANCE GOAL: Desire for approval for performance in others' eyes; tendency to choose very easy or very difficult goals
Type of Involvement	TASK-INVOLVED: Concerned with mastering the task	EGO-INVOLVED: Concerned with self in others' eyes.
Achievement Motivation	Motivation to ACHIEVE: mastery orientation	Motivation to AVOID FAILURE: prone to anxiety
Likely Attributions	Successes and failures attributed to CONTROLLABLE effort and ability	Success and failures attributed to UNCONTROLLABLE causes
Beliefs about Ability	INCREMENTAL VIEW: Belief that ability can be improved through hard work and added knowledge and skills	ENTITY VIEW: Belief that ability is a stable, uncontrollable trait

to develop in our students the *trait* of being motivated to learn so they will be able "to educate themselves throughout their lifetime" (Bandura, 1993, p. 136). And finally, we want our students to be cognitively engaged—to think deeply about what they study. In other words, we want them to be *thoughtful* (Blumenfeld, Puro, & Mergendoller, 1992).

In the previous chapter we examined the roles of intrinsic and extrinsic motivation, attributions, goals, interests, emotions, and self-schemas in motivation. Table 11.1 shows how each of these factors contributes to motivation to learn. The central questions in this chapter are: What can teachers do to encourage and support motivation to learn? How can teachers use knowledge about attributions, goals, interests, beliefs, and self-schemas to increase motivation to learn? To organize our discussion, we will use the TARGETT model.

*O*n TARGETT for Learning

Carol Ames (1990, 1992) has identified six areas where teachers make decisions that can influence student motivation to learn: the nature of the *task* that students are asked to do, the *autonomy* students are allowed in working, how students are *recognized* for their accomplishments, *grouping* practices, *evaluation* procedures, and the scheduling of *time* in the classroom. Epstein (1989) coined the acronym TARGET to organize these areas of possible teacher influence. We will add *teacher expectations* to the model, so ours will be a TARGETT for motivation to learn as shown in Table 11.2 on page 404. In the following pages we will examine each of these areas more closely.

Connect and Extend
To professional journals
Ames, C. (1992). Classrooms: Goals, structures, and student motivation. *Journal of Educational Psychology, 84,* 261–271.

Motivation to Learn: The tendency to find academic activities meaningful and worthwhile and to try to benefit from them.

TABLE 11.2   *The TARGETT Model for Supporting Student Motivation to Learn*

Teachers make decisions in many areas that can influence motivation to learn. The TARGETT acronym highlights task, autonomy, recognition, grouping, evaluation, time, and teacher expectations.

TARGETT Area	Focus	Objectives	Examples of Possible Strategies
Task	How learning tasks are structured—what the student is asked to do	Enhance intrinsic attractiveness of learning tasks Make learning meaningful	Encourage instruction that relates to students' backgrounds and experience Avoid payment (monetary and other) for attendance, grades, or achievement Foster goal setting and self-regulation
Autonomy/Responsibility	Student participation in learning/school decisions	Provide optimal freedom for students to make choices and take responsibility	Give alternatives in making assignments Ask for student comments on school life—and take them seriously Encourage students to take initiatives and evaluate their own learning Establish leadership opportunities for *all* students
Recognition	The nature and use of recognition and reward in the school setting	Provide opportunities for *all* students to be recognized for learning Recognize *progress* in goal attainment Recognize challenge seeking and innovation	Foster "personal best" awards Reduce emphasis on "honor rolls" Recognize and publicize a wide range of school-related activities of students
Grouping	The organization of school learning and experiences	Build an environment of acceptance and appreciation of all students Broaden the range of social interaction, particularly of at-risk students Enhance social skills development	Provide opportunities for cooperative learning, problem solving, and decision making Encourage multiple group membership to increase range of peer interaction Eliminate ability-grouped classes
Evaluation	The nature and use of evaluation and assessment procedures	Grading and reporting processes Practices associated with use of standardized tests Definition of goals and standards	Reduce emphasis on social comparisons of achievement Give students opportunities to improve their performance (e.g., study skills, classes) Establish grading/reporting practices that portray student progress in learning Encourage student participation in the evaluation process
Time	The scheduling of the school day	Allow the learning task and student needs to dictate scheduling Provide opportunities for extended and significant student involvement in learning tasks	Allow students to *progress at their own rate* whenever possible Encourage flexibility in the scheduling of learning experiences Give teachers greater control over time usage through, for example, block scheduling
Teacher Expectations	Beliefs and predictions about students' abilities	Hold appropriate but high expectations for all students Communicate that you expect growth	Give all students the chance to revise and improve their work Monitor who gets which opportunities Make sure materials show diversity in achievement

Source: From "Reinventing Schools for Early Adolescents: Emphasizing Task Goals," by M. L. Maehr and E. M. Anderman, 1993, *The Elementary School Journal, 93*, pp. 604–605. Copyright © 1993 by The University of Chicago Press. Adapted with permission.

Tasks for Learning

To understand how an **academic task** can affect students' motivation, we need to analyze the task. Tasks can be interesting or boring for students. Tasks have a particular subject content and also involve certain cognitive operations such as *memorize, infer, classify, apply,* and so on. As students work on a task they are learning content and practicing operations. Tasks also vary in terms of how clear-cut or ambiguous they are and how much risk is involved in doing them (Doyle, 1983). Finally, tasks have a certain value to students, determined in part by how authentic and meaningful the tasks are for them. We will look at each of these aspects of tasks more closely.

Task Operations: Risk and Ambiguity. Doyle (1983) has suggested that academic tasks can be categorized by the operations that they require: *memory, routine procedure, comprehension,* and *opinion.* Memory tasks require students to recognize or reproduce something they have encountered before, such as matching states and capitals. Routine procedures involve following steps or rules to solve a problem—using πr^2 to calculate the area of a circle, for example. Comprehension tasks require students to go beyond the information given—by combining several ideas, originating a procedure, or writing in a particular style. Opinion tasks ask students to state a personal preference of belief, such as which character in a story is the bravest. The kind of operation in a task determines how ambiguous and risky the task is, and this, in turn, affects student motivation, as you will soon see.

Some tasks involve less risk than others because failure is unlikely. For example, opinion tasks are very low-risk—there are no right or wrong answers. Simple memory or procedural tasks also involve few risks, because getting the right answer is easy: You just follow the steps. However, the stakes can be very high with longer and more complex memory or procedural tasks. Reciting 100 lines from Shakespeare is risky, especially if you are graded on how well you do, because there is a great deal to memorize.

Academic Tasks: The work the student must accomplish, including the content covered and the mental operations required.

Connect and Extend
To the research
Maehr, M. L., & Anderman, E. M. (1993). Reinventing schools for early adolescents: Emphasizing task goals. *The Elementary School Journal, 93,* 593–610. This article describes how the TARGET model can be used to reform middle schools to support learning goals.

Connect and Extend
To the research
Graham, S., & Golan, S. (1991). Motivational influences on cognition: Task involvement, ego involvement, and depth of information processing. *Journal of Educational Psychology, 83,* 187–194.

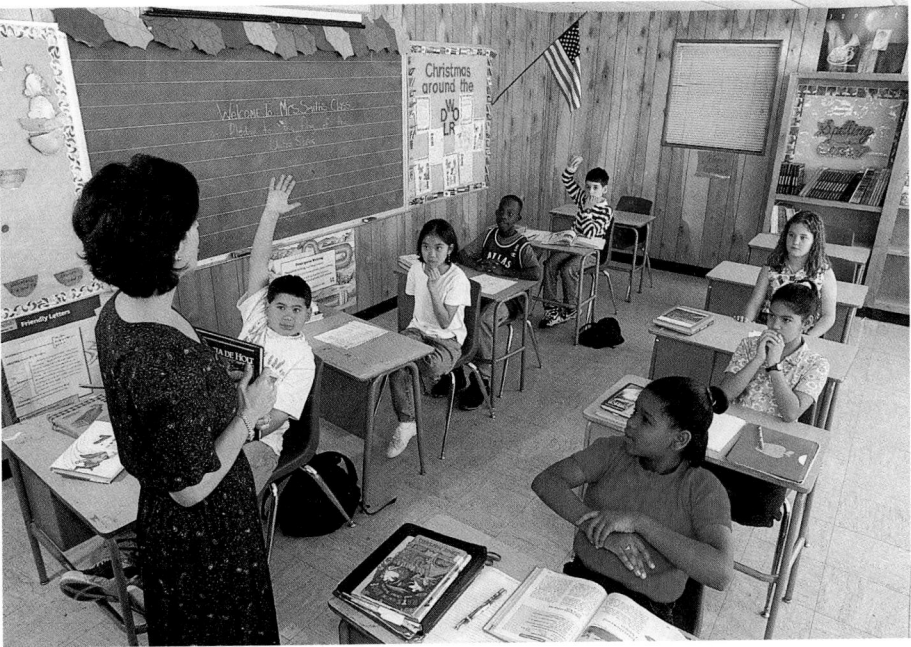

◀ *Students may differ in the degree to which they are willing to take risks—or risk being "wrong"—in classroom activities.*

Connect and Extend
To the research

Nolen, S. B. (1988). Reasons for studying: Motivational orientations and study strategies. *Cognition and Instruction, 5,* 269–288.

Brief Abstract: This study of 8th graders explored the relationship among (a) individual differences in three motivational or goal orientations and (b) valuing and use of study strategies. Task orientation was positively correlated with both valuing and use of strategies requiring deep processing of information. Ego orientation was positively related to valuing and use of surface-level strategies only. Work avoidance was negatively related to valuing and use of both kinds of strategies. Analysis indicated that task orientation, more than perceived ability or knowledge of the value of deep-processing strategies, predicts the spontaneous use of these strategies. The prediction held over four to six weeks, suggesting the importance of individual differences in motivational orientation.

In the same issue are two commentaries on this study:

Lepper, M. R. (1988). Motivational considerations in the study of instruction. *Cognition and Instruction, 5,* 289–310.

Brown, A. L. (1988). Motivation to learn and understand: Taking charge of one's own learning. *Cognition and Instruction, 5,* 311–322.

Another characteristic of tasks is level of *ambiguity*—how straightforward the expected answer is. Opinion and understanding tasks are ambiguous: It is hard to predict the right answer (if there is one) or how to find it. The "right" answer may involve the teacher's opinion. Memory and procedural tasks, on the other hand, are straightforward and unambiguous. If you are reciting a soliloquy from *Hamlet*, the "right" answer is clear, even though the task is difficult. Figure 11.1 summarizes how tasks can be categorized by risk and ambiguity.

What does this have to do with motivation? Most students want to *lower the risk* and *decrease the ambiguity* involved in schoolwork, because their grades are at stake. This is especially true for highly anxious students or those who are trying to avoid failure. Many times teachers plan a complicated *comprehension* task that is both ambiguous and risky. They want their students to think and solve problems. But the students want more guidance. They may ask for models, rules, minimums, or formulas: "How many references do you want?" "How many pages?" "Will we have to know dates and names?" "Give us a model to follow." In other words, students *negotiate the task*. These negotiations can lead to management problems. If the students are very confused, they may become restless, turn to other students for help, get discouraged, or lose interest in the task.

Under this kind of pressure, the teacher often responds by stating the three main points that should be addressed, giving a minimum number of references or a page limit, and providing books that would be helpful. This transforms the *comprehension* task into a *procedural* one. Risk and ambiguity are reduced and motivation may seem to increase, at least temporarily. But the task itself is not as interesting. Doing well on the procedural task is not as rewarding, because achievement does not lead to a sense of increased competence. Thus the results of the "task negotiation" may be a temporary *state* of motivation, but it is motivation to perform, to get the grade, not motivation to learn. And little has been done to foster the long-term

FIGURE 11.1

Ambiguity and Risk Associated with Academic Tasks in Classrooms

Academic tasks can be characterized by their levels of risk and ambiguity. Because students often find high-ambiguity/high-risk tasks very threatening, they need extra support and fewer pressures when completing them.

Source: From "Academic Work," by W. Doyle, 1983, *Review of Educational Research, 53,* Figure p. 183. Copyright © 1983 by the American Educational Research Association. Adapted with permission of the publisher.

development of the *trait* of motivation to learn. Furthermore, because students learn the operations that they practice, these students have learned how to do a procedure—and how to negotiate with teachers (Doyle, 1983). But they probably have not improved the problem-solving or critical-thinking skills that the teacher had intended to develop.

Obviously, some balance is needed. Teachers must make wise choices and then stick with them, even when students try to negotiate changes. Instructions should be clear, but not too restricting. The penalties for taking a risk or making a mistake should not be too great. Finally, tasks must have some value to students. Let's take a closer look now at the value of classroom tasks.

Task Value. As you recall from the previous chapter, many theories suggest that the strength of our motivation in a particular situation is determined by our *expectation* that we can succeed and the *value* of that success to us. We can think of a task as having three kinds of value to the students (Eccles & Wigfield, 1985). **Attainment value** is the importance of doing well on the task. This aspect of value is closely tied to the needs of the individual (for example, the need to be competent, well-liked, etc.) and the meaning of success to that person. For instance, if someone has a strong need to appear smart and believes that a high grade on a test shows you are smart, then the test has high attainment value for that person. A second kind of value is **intrinsic** or **interest value**. This is simply the enjoyment one gets from the activity itself. Some people like the experience of learning. Others enjoy the feeling of hard physical effort or the challenge of solving puzzles. Finally, tasks have **utility value**; that is, they help us achieve a short-term or long-term goal.

You see from our discussion of task value that personal and environmental influences on motivation interact constantly. The task we ask students to accomplish is an aspect of the environment; it is external to the student. But the value of accomplishing the task is bound up with the internal needs, beliefs, and goals of the individual.

Recently there has been a great deal written about the use of authentic tasks in teaching. An **authentic task** is one that has some connection to the real-life problems and situations that students will face outside the classroom, now and in the future. If you ask students to do busywork, to memorize definitions they will never use, to learn the material only because it is on the test, or to repeat work they already understand, then there can be little motivation to learn. But if the tasks are authentic, students are more likely to see the genuine utility value of the work and are also more likely to find the tasks meaningful and interesting.

Problem-based learning is one example of the use of authentic tasks in teaching. According to William Stepien and Shelagh Gallagher (1993), "problem-based learning turns instruction topsy-turvy. Students meet an ill-structured problem before they receive any instruction. In place of covering the curriculum, learners probe deeply into issues searching for connections, grappling with complexity, and using knowledge to fashion solutions" (p. 26). Teachers act as coaches and tutors, asking questions, modeling thinking, helping students organize and monitor their own problem solving.

An example problem presented to one group of 7th and 8th graders in Illinois is, "What should be done about a nuclear waste dump site in our area?" The students soon learn that this real problem is not a simple one. Scientists disagree about the dangers. Environmental activists demand that the materials be removed, even if this bankrupts the company involved—one that employs many local residents. Some members of the state assembly want the material taken out of state, even though no place in the country is licensed to receive the toxic materials. The company believes the safest solution is to leave the materials buried. The students must research the

Connect and Extend
To the research
The January 1988 issue of *Elementary School Journal* is devoted to the topic "Schoolwork and Academic Tasks."

Connect and Extend
To the research
Vispoel, W. P. & Austing, J. R. (1995). Success and failure in junior high school: A critical incident approach to understanding students' attributional beliefs. *American Educational Research Journal, 32,* 377–412.

Connect and Extend
To the research
Lowenstein, G. (1994). The psychology of curiosity: A review and reinterpretation. *Psychological Bulletin, 117,* 75–98. This article connects curiosity to perceived gaps in information.

Connect and Extend
To professional journals
See the special issue on "authentic learning" in the April, 1993 issue of *Educational Leadership.*

Attainment Value: The importance of doing well on a task; how success on the task meets personal needs.

Intrinsic or Interest Value: The enjoyment a person gets from a task.

Utility Value: The contribution of a task to meeting one's goals.

Authentic Task: Tasks that have some connection to real-life problems the students will face outside the classroom.

Problem-Based Learning: Methods that provide students with realistic problems that don't necessarily have "right" answers.

situation, interview parties involved, and develop recommendations to be presented to state experts and community groups. "In problem-based learning students assume the roles of scientists, historians, doctors, or others who have a real stake in the proposed problem. Motivation soars because students realize it's their problem" (Stepien & Gallagher, 1993, p. 26).

Supporting Autonomy and Recognizing Accomplishment

The second area in the TARGETT model involves how much choice and autonomy students are allowed. Choice in schools is not the norm. Children and adolescents spend literally thousands of hours in schools where other people decide what will happen and "where raised hands are sometimes ignored, questions to teachers are fairly frequently brushed aside, and permission to go somewhere else to do something else is quite routinely refused" (Garner, 1998, p. 232). Yet, as we saw in Chapter 10, self-determination and a sense of internal locus of causality are critical to maintaining intrinsic motivation. What can teachers do to support choice without creating chaos?

Calvin and Hobbes   by Bill Watterson

Connect and Extend
To the research
The June 1998 issue of *Educational Psychology Review*, edited by Karen Harris and Pat Alexander, has a series of articles describing models of integrated teaching that include student choice. One article by Ruth Garner (pp. 227–238) describes the power of bounded choices.

Supporting Choices. Like totally unguided discovery or aimless discussions, unstructured or unguided choices can be counterproductive for learning (Garner, 1998). For example, Dyson (1997) found that children became anxious and upset when directed by teachers to draw or write about anything they want in anyway they want. Dyson says that students see this unbounded choice as a "scary void." I know that graduate students in my classes also find it disconcerting if I ask them to design a final project that will determine their grade, just as I panic when I am asked to give a talk on "anything you want." The alternative is bounded choice—giving students a range of options that set valuable tasks for them but also allow them to follow personal interests. The balance must be just right: "too much autonomy is bewildering and too little is boring" (Guthrie et al., 1998, p. 185).

The following description of how a student in a 5th grade class exercised her choices about researching and writing is taken from Guthrie et al. (1998, p. 186). The class was studying the life cycle of the Monarch butterfly. Each child worked in a heterogeneous team and each team had a chrysalis to observe as it grew. The class had organized a library of multilevel expository books, trade books, literary books, reference books, maps, electronic data bases, and other resources. The teacher had taught specific skills that would be needed—using an index, table of contents, setting goals, writing summaries, but the students were able to choose topics and appropriate resources for crafting their own chapter.

On this day, Shawna was formulating a topic for her contribution to the class book on the Monarch's life cycle. She often thought about the different colors that her specimen was turning as it passed through the different phases of metamorphosis. She searched the class library for books to help her choose a topic.

She chose three books. . . . As she studied the table of contents and looked at the pictures of the butterflies, she read that the Monarch's patches of colors on one side of the wing were quite different from on the other side of the wing. . . . She turned to her friend Jane and announced, "Hey, did you know that the coloring on the butterflies' wings helps to protect them when they are sleeping in winter?" With her notes gathered, Shawna was ready to write her chapter about how colors help in the Monarch's life cycle. (Guthrie et al., 1998, p. 186)

Students also can exercise autonomy about how they receive feedback from the teacher or from classmates. Figure 11.2 describes a strategy called "Check it Out" in which students specify the skills that they want to have evaluated in a particular assignment. Over the course of a unit, all the skills have to be "checked out," but students choose when each one is evaluated.

Beyond these ideas, what can teachers do to support student self-determination in everyday interactions? A study by Reeve, Bolt, and Cai (1999) found that, compared to controlling teachers, autonomy-supporting teachers listened more, held instructional materials less, resisted giving solutions to problems, gave fewer directives, and asked more questions about what students wanted to do.

Recognizing Accomplishment. The third TARGETT area is *recognition.* How should students' accomplishments be acknowledged and rewarded? In Chapter

---

FIGURE 11.2

Student Autonomy: Check It Out

Using this technique to support student autonomy, the teacher decides on a set of skills that will be developed over a unit, but the student decides which skill(s) will be evaluated on any given assignment. Over the course of the unit, all the skills have to be "checked out." This student has indicated that she wants the teacher to "check out" her creativity and verb tense.

Source: From *150 Ways to Increase Intrinsic Motivation in the Classroom* (pp. 33–34) by J. P. Raffini, 1996, Boston: Allyn & Bacon. Copyright © 1996 Allyn & Bacon, Inc. Adapted with permission.

Connect and Extend
To the research

Butler, R. (1987). Task-involving and ego-involving properties of evaluation: Effects of different feedback conditions on motivational perceptions, interest, and performance. *Journal of Educational Psychology, 79,* 474–482.

Brief Abstract: Does the impact of information about performance on subsequent intrinsic motivation depend significantly on the degree to which this information promotes a task-involved or an ego-involved motivational orientation? Two hundred 5th- and 6th-grade students were given interesting divergent thinking tasks in each of three sessions. Individual comments, numerical grades, standardized praise, or no feedback were received after Sessions 1 and 2. At Session 3 (post-test), interest, performance, and attributions of effort, outcome, and the impact of evaluation to task-involved causes were highest after receipt of comments. Ego-involved attributions were highest after receipt of grades and praise. These findings support the conceptualization of feedback conditions as task involving (comments), ego involving (grades and praise), or neither (no feedback).

6 we discussed the importance of authentic praise that focuses on progress, growing competence, and independence. But nothing in teaching is simple. At times praise can have paradoxical effects. For example, if two students succeed and the teacher praises only one of them, the message, to older children at least, may be that the praised student had less ability and had to work harder to succeed, thus earning praise. The unpraised student was simply "doing what comes naturally," succeeding based on high ability. So students may use the teacher's praise or criticism as cues about capabilities—praise means I'm not very smart, so when I succeed, I deserve recognition. Criticism means my teacher thinks I'm smart and could do better (Stipek, 1996).

We have also seen that giving students rewards for activities that they already enjoy can undermine intrinsic motivation. Students should be recognized for improving on their own personal best, for tackling difficult tasks, for persistence, and for creativity—not just for performing better than others. The next section explains one way to use personal progress as a basis for recognition in classrooms.

What sort of recognition leads to engagement? One answer comes from a study by Ruth Butler (1987). Students in the 5th and 6th grades were given interesting divergent thinking tasks followed by either individual comments, standardized praise ("very good"), grades, or no feedback. Interest, performance, attributions to effort, and task involvement were higher after personal comments. Ego-involved motivation (the desire to look good or do better than others) was greater after grades and standard praise.

Grouping, Evaluation, and Time

You may remember a teacher who made you want to work hard—someone who made a subject come alive. Or you may remember how many hours you spent practicing as a member of a team, orchestra, choir, or theater troupe. If you do, then you know the motivational power of relationships with other people. David and Roger Johnson (1985) describe the power this way:

> Motivation to learn is inherently interpersonal. It is through interaction with other people that students learn to value learning for its own sake, enjoy the process of learning, and take pride in their acquisition of knowledge and development of skill. Of the interpersonal relationships available in the classroom, peers may be the most influential on motivation to learn. (p. 250)

The ways that students relate to peers are influenced by the goal structure of the activities and tasks created by the teacher.

Grouping and Goal Structures. Students in the classroom function as part of a large group. Johnson and Johnson (1999) have given considerable attention to this in their work on motivation. They have found that motivation can be greatly influenced by the ways we relate to the other people who are also involved in accomplishing a particular goal. Johnson and Johnson have labeled this interpersonal factor the **goal structure** of the task. There are three such structures: cooperative, competitive, and individualistic, as shown in Figure 11.3.

We saw in Chapter 9 that there are many advantages for cooperative goal structures. Several studies have shown that when the task involves complex learning and problem-solving skills, cooperation leads to higher achievement than competition, especially for low-ability students (Johnson & Johnson, 1985; Slavin, 1995). In addition, well-designed **cooperative learning** seems to result in improved ability to see the world from another person's point of view, better relations among

FIGURE 11.3

Different Goal Structures

Each goal structure is associated with a different relationship between the individual and the group. This relationship influences motivation to reach the goal.

	Cooperative	Competitive	Individualistic
Definition	Students believe their goal is attainable only if other students will also reach the goal.	Students believe they will reach their goal if and only if other students do not reach the goal.	Students believe that their own attempt to reach a goal is not related to other students' attempts to reach the goal.
Examples	Team victories—each player wins only if all the team members win: a relay race, a quilting bee, a barn raising, a symphony, a play.	Golf tournament, singles tennis match, a 100-yard dash, valedictorian, Miss America pageant.	Lowering your handicap in golf, jogging, learning a new language, enjoying a museum, losing or gaining weight, stopping smoking.

Source: From *Learning Together and Alone: Cooperation, Competition, and Individualization* (5th ed.), by D. Johnson and R. Johnson, 1999, Boston: Allyn & Bacon. Copyright © 1999 by Allyn & Bacon. Adapted with permission.

different ethnic groups in schools and classrooms, increased self-esteem, greater willingness to help and encourage fellow students, and greater acceptance of students with disabilities and low-achieving students (Slavin, 1995; Stipek, 1996; Webb & Palincsar, 1996). Students learn to set attainable goals and negotiate. They become more altruistic. The interaction with peers that students enjoy so much becomes a part of the learning process. The result? The need for belonging described by Maslow is more likely to be met and motivation is increased.

There are many approaches to peer learning or group learning, as you saw in Chapter 9. Some approaches, such as STAD and TGT, are designed specifically to enhance motivation.

STAD. Robert Slavin and his associates have developed a system for overcoming the disadvantages of the cooperative goal structure (lack of focus, off-task behaviors, unfair division of work) while maintaining its advantages. The system is called **Student Teams–Achievement Divisions,** or **STAD** (Slavin, 1995). Each team has about five members with a mix of abilities, ethnic backgrounds, and sexes. The teacher calculates an **individual learning expectation (ILE)** score, or base score, for each team member. This score represents the student's average level of performance. Details about how to determine the base scores are given in Table 11.3 on page 412.

Students work in their teams to study and prepare for twice-weekly quizzes, but they take the quizzes individually, just as in a regular class. Based on test performance, each team member can earn from one to three points for the group. Table 11.3 shows how points are awarded by comparing each student's current test score to his or her base (ILE) score

Students working in teams can support each others' learning and motivation. Immediate help is available for learning problems, and encouragement can help overcome lagging interest. ▼

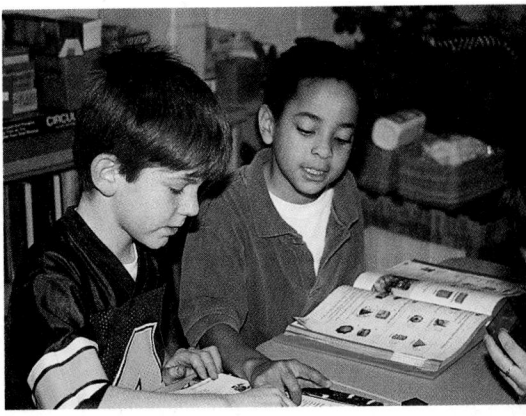

Teams-Games-Tournaments
(TGT): Learning arrangement
in which team members prepare
cooperatively, then meet comparable individuals of competing
teams in a tournament game to
win points for their team.

Connect and Extend
To the research
Slavin, R. R. (1991). Synthesis of
research on cooperative learning.
Educational Leadership, 48(5),
71–82. *Focus Question:* When is
cooperative learning most effective,
and with which students?

Connect and Extend
To other chapters
The need for belonging is the third
level of Maslow's hierarchy, discussed in Chapter 10. The need
to maintain relationships is strong.
I was reminded of this when my
daughter was reprimanded by her
4th-grade teacher for passing
notes during class. Liz's explanation was that there had been a
fight during lunch, "and we had to
work it out!"

Connect and Extend
To the research
For a thorough review of research
on different forms of cooperative
learning, see O'Donnell, A. M., &
O'Kelly, J. (1994). Learning from
peers: Beyond the rhetoric of positive results. *Educational Psychology Review, 6*, 321–350.

Connect and Extend
To your teaching
Design a lesson plan using a cooperative learning format. The assignment should consist of (1) a
description of how to prepare the
class; (2) a summary of the expected results; (3) the topic of the
lesson and the information that
would be given to members of the
groups; and (4) the actual test or
means of assessment that would
be used to determine learning. If
possible, you should actually teach
the lesson in a school classroom.

TABLE 11.3 *Using Individual Learning Expectations*

The idea behind individual learning expectations, or ILEs, is that students ought to be judged in relation to their own abilities and not compared to others. The focus is on improvement, not on comparisons among students.

To calculate an ILE score, the teacher simply averages the student's grades or test scores from previous work. These scores are usually on a 100-point scale. Letter grades can be converted to points based on the school's system—for example, A = 90 points, B = 80 points, and so on. The student's average score is her or his initial base score. The ILE score becomes the standard for judging each student's work.

If the teacher is using the STAD system of cooperative learning, then students earn points for their group based on the following system:

Test Score	Points Earned for Group
A perfect score	3
10 or more points above ILE score	3
5 to 9 points above ILE score	2
4 points below to 4 points above ILE score	1
5 or more points below ILE score	0

(Slavin, 1995). As you can see from the table, every student has an equal chance to contribute the maximum number of points to the team total. Thus, every student, not just the most able or motivated, has reason to work hard. This system avoids the problem of students' unequal contributions to a group project. Every week the group earning the greatest number of points is declared the winner. Team accomplishments should be recognized in a class newsletter or a bulletin board display.

Every few weeks the teams can be changed so that students have a chance to work with many different class members. Every two weeks or so the teacher must recompute each student's ILE score by averaging the old base score with grades on the recent tests. With this system, improvement pays off for all students. Those with less ability can still earn the maximum for their team by scoring 10 or more points above their own base score. Those with greater ability are still challenged because they must score well above their own average or make a perfect score to contribute the maximum to the group total.

TGT. **Teams-Games-Tournaments** or **TGT** is similar to STAD. After the teacher's presentation, students move into their heterogeneous groups to help each other answer problems or questions about the material. Instead of taking written tests, however, each student meets once a week at a "tournament table" with two other students of comparable ability from the other teams. The three students at each tournament table compete, answering questions similar to the problems practiced in their study teams. The winner at each table earns 6 points for his or her team. Each week the participants at the tournament tables are adjusted—the winners are "bumped" up to a higher-ability table to keep the competition fair. This way, every student has the chance to contribute equally to the team's total score (Slavin, 1990).

Research on TGT raises a caution. Bette Chambers and Philip Abrami (1991) found that members of successful teams did learn more than members of unsuccessful teams, but also they were happier about the outcome and rated their ability higher than members of losing teams. For low-achieving students who tend to be anxious, failure-accepting, or helpless, being on a losing team could make matters worse. Chambers and Abrami suggest experimenting with cooperation both within and between teams. For example, the whole class might earn recognition if each team reaches a specified level of learning.

Table 11.2 gave ideas for fostering motivation through peer relations. Besides using cooperative learning, other ideas include allowing time and opportunity for peer interaction in school, using project-based learning, and encouraging the development of teams and "schools within schools."

The nature of the goal structure—cooperative, competitive, or individualistic—has implications for the next two TARGETT areas, *evaluation* and *time*.

Evaluation. The greater the emphasis on competitive evaluation and grading, the more students will focus on performance goals rather than learning goals and the more they will be ego-involved as opposed to task-involved. Students must take tests, answer questions in class, and complete assignments, and they must perform within certain time limits. Doyle (1983) suggests that students look on most classroom work as "an exchange of performance for grades" (p. 181). Grading here refers to more than marks on a report card. It includes both the formal and informal evaluations of teachers.

Of course, not all students are caught up in an exchange of performance for grades. Low-achieving students who have little hope of either "making the grade" or mastering the task may simply want to finish. One study of 1st graders found that low-achieving students made up answers, filled in the page with patterns, or copied from other students, just to get through their seatwork. As one student said when she finished a word/definition matching exercise, "I don't know what it means, but I did it" (Anderson, Brubaker, Alleman-Brooks, & Duffy, 1985, p. 132). On closer examination, the researchers found that the work was much too hard for these students, so they connected words and definitions at random.

How can teachers prevent students from simply focusing on the grade or doing the work "just to get finished"? The most obvious answer is to de-emphasize grades and emphasize learning in the class. Students need to understand the value of the work. Instead of saying, "You will need to know this for the test," tell students how the information will be useful in solving problems they want to solve. Suggest that the lesson will answer some interesting questions. Communicate that understanding is more important than finishing.

Unfortunately, many teachers do not follow this advice. Brophy (1988) reports that when he and several colleagues spent about 100 hours observing how six teachers introduced their lessons, they found that most introductions were routine, apologetic, or unenthusiastic. The introductions described procedures, made threats, emphasized finishing, or promised tests on the material. A few examples are:

"You don't expect me to give you baby work to do every day, do you?"
"My talkers are going to get a third page to do during lunch."
"If you are done by 10 o'clock, you can go outside." (Brophy, 1988, p. 204)

While many teachers are similar to the six Brophy studied, there are exceptions. Hermine Marshall (1987) described a few elementary school teachers who seemed to establish a *learning orientation* in their classrooms. They stressed understanding instead of performing, being graded, or finishing work. Later in the chapter we will examine strategies for establishing such an orientation in your class.

Connect and Extend
To the research
Chambers, B., & Abrami, P. C. (1991). The relationship between student learning outcomes and achievement, causal attributions, and effect. *Journal of Educational Psychology, 83,* 140–146.

Connect and Extend
To your teaching
A recent addition to the list of cooperative learning techniques is Cooperative Integrated Reading and Composition (CIRC). This system supports the traditional approach of using ability-based reading groups. Students are assigned to teams made up of pairs from each reading group in the class. While the teacher works with one reading group, the teams work in their pairs using many of the methods of reciprocal teaching described in Chapter 9—reading aloud, making predictions, asking questions, summarizing, and writing about the stories they are reading. Teams help each other prepare for tests, write and edit work, and often "publish" team books. Teams are rewarded based on the average performance of all their members on all the reading and writing assignments. Thus, there is equal opportunity for success, group support for learning, and individual accountability for final performance. These three elements are characteristic of many cooperative learning strategies (Slavin, 1995).

Do Teachers' Expectations Affect Students' Learning?

The answer to this question is more complicated than it might seem. There are two ways to investigate the question. One is to give teachers unfounded expectations about their students and note if these baseless expectations have any effects. The other approach is to identify the naturally occurring expectations of teachers and study the effects of these expectations. The answer to the question of whether teacher expectations affect student learning depends in part on which approach is taken to study the question.

▶ **POINT** *Teachers' expectations have less effect than we think.*

The original Rosenthal and Jacobson experiment used the first approach—giving teachers groundless expectations and noting the effects. The study was heavily criticized for the experimental and statistical methods used (Elashoff & Snow, 1971; Snow, 1995; Weinberg, 1989). A careful analysis of the results revealed that even though 1st- through 6th-grade students participated in the study, the self-fulfilling prophecy effects were confined mostly to students in grades one and two. In these grades, the effects could be traced to just five students who changed dramatically. When other researchers tried to replicate the study, they did not find evidence of a self-fulfilling prophecy effect, even for children in these lower grades (Claiborn, 1969; Wilkins & Glock, 1973). Critics argued that even if higher expectations do lead to greater learning in the early grades, this does not prove that lower expectations will lead to decreased learning. Besides, the critics pointed out, giving teachers false expectations is an unnatural situation. Several studies found that when teachers did not believe the information they were given, no expectation effects occurred. After reviewing the research on teacher expectations, Raudenbush (1984) concluded that these expectations have only a small effect on student IQ scores (the outcome measure used by Rosenthal and Jacobson) and only in the early years of a new school setting—in the first years of elementary school and then again in the first years of junior high school.

◀ **COUNTERPOINT** *Teachers' expectations can have powerful effects.*

When researchers study the naturally occurring expectations of teachers, they find that teachers do indeed form beliefs about students' capabilities. Many of these beliefs are accurate assessments based on the best available data and are corrected as new information is collected (Good & Brophy, 1997). Even so, some teachers do favor certain students (Babad, 1995; Rosenthal, 1987). For example, in a study of over 400 classrooms in the southwest United States, the Civil Rights Commission (1973) found that Hispanic-American students consistently received less praise and encouragement and fewer positive teacher responses and questions than Anglo-American students. In classes where teachers treat high-achieving students differently from lower-achieving students, the teachers' evaluation of students' ability appears to affect the students' achievement in the class. "Although the importance of teacher expectation effects has sometimes been overstated, it is clear that these effects are important, especially when considered with other teaching abilities" (Good & Brophy, 1994, p. 114). If teachers decide that some students are less able, and if the teachers lack effective strategies for working with lower-achieving students, then students may experience a double threat—low expectations and inadequate teaching. Just how powerful the expectation effect is depends on how differently a teacher treats high- versus low-expectation students.

Connect and Extend
To the research
Is there any reason why teachers should not have high expectations for all of their students? What about the distinction between "high expectations" and "reasonable expectations"?

teacher expects. The Point/Counterpoint examines the debate over the existence of a self-fulfilling prophecy or **Pygmalion effect.**

Two Kinds of Expectation Effects

Actually, two kinds of expectation effects can occur in classrooms. The first is the self-fulfilling prophecy described above. In this situation the teacher's beliefs about the students' abilities have no basis in fact, but student behavior comes to match the initially inaccurate expectation. The second kind of expectation effect occurs when teachers are fairly accurate in their initial reading of students' abilities and respond to students appropriately. So far, so good. There is nothing wrong with forming and acting on accurate estimates of student ability. Indeed, many teachers do this almost automatically. The problems arise when students show some improvement but teachers do not alter their expectations to take account of the improvement. This is called a **sustaining expectation effect,** because the teacher's unchanging expectation sustains the student's achievement at the expected level. The chance to raise expectations, provide more appropriate teaching, and thus encourage greater student achievement is lost. In practice, sustaining effects are more common than self-fulfilling prophecy effects (Cooper & Good, 1983). Withdrawn children provide little information about themselves, so teachers may sustain their expectations about these children for lack of new input (Jones & Gerig, 1994).

Sources of Expectations

There are many possible sources of teachers' expectations (Braun, 1976). Intelligence test scores are an obvious source, especially if teachers do not interpret the scores appropriately. Sex also influences teachers; most teachers expect more behavior problems from boys than from girls. The notes from previous teachers and the medical or psychological reports found in cumulative folders (permanent record files) are another obvious source of expectations. Knowledge of ethnic background also seems to have an influence, as does knowledge of older brothers and sisters. The influence of students' physical characteristics is shown in several studies, indicating that teachers hold higher expectations for attractive students. Previous achievement, socioeconomic class, and the actual behaviors of the student are also often used as sources of information.

Expectations and beliefs focus attention and organize memory, so teachers may pay attention to and remember the information that fits the initial expectations (Fiske, 1993; Hewstone, 1989). Even when student performance does not fit expectations, the teacher may rationalize and attribute the performance to external causes beyond the student's control. For example, a teacher may assume that the low-ability student who did well on a test must have cheated and that the high-ability student who failed must have been upset that day. In both cases, behavior that seems out of character is dismissed. It may take many instances of supposedly uncharacteristic behavior to change the teacher's beliefs about a particular student's abilities. Thus, expectations often remain in the face of contradictory evidence (Brophy, 1982).

Teacher Behavior and Student Reaction

Table 11.4 on page 418 shows six dimensions of teacher communication toward students that may be influenced by expectations. These dimensions include both instructional practices and interpersonal interactions.

Instructional Strategies. As we have seen, different grouping processes may well have a marked effect on students. And some teachers leave little to the imagination; they make their expectations all too clear. For example, Alloway (1984) recorded comments such as these directed to low-achieving groups:

"I'll be over to help you slow ones in a minute."
"The blue group will find this hard."

In these remarks the teacher not only tells the students that they lack ability, but also communicates that finishing the work, not understanding, is the goal.

Connect and Extend
To your own philosophy
Should you read your students' cumulative folders at the beginning of the school year? If so, how can you keep from forming low expectations?

Connect and Extend
To the research
For a complete discussion of teacher expectations and student learning, see Good, T. (1987). Teacher expectations. In D. Berliner & B. Rosenshine (Eds.), *Talks to teachers* (pp. 159–200). New York: Random House.

Pygmalion Effect: Exceptional progress by a student as a result of high teacher expectations for that student; named for mythological king, Pygmalion, who made a statue, then caused it to be brought to life.

Sustaining Expectation Effect: Student performance maintained at a certain level because teachers don't recognize improvements.

Teacher Expectations   **417**

TABLE 11.4 *Six Dimensions of Teaching That Can Communicate Expectations*

Dimension	Students believed to be MORE capable have:	Students believed to be LESS capable have:
Task environment curriculum, procedures, task definition, pacing, qualities of environment	More opportunity to perform publicly on meaningful tasks	Less opportunity to perform publicly, especially on meaningful tasks (supplying alternate endings to a story vs. learning to pronounce a word correctly)
	More opportunity to think	Less opportunity to think, analyze (because much work is aimed at practice)
Grouping practices	More assignments that deal with comprehension, understanding (in higher-ability groups)	Less choice on curriculum assignments—more work on drill-like assignments because they are low achievers
Locus of responsibility for learning	More autonomy (more choice in assignments, fewer interruptions)	Less autonomy (frequent teacher monitoring of work, frequent interruptions)
Feedback and evaluation practices	More opportunity for self-evaluation	Less opportunity for self-evaluation
Motivational strategies	More honest/contingent feedback	Less honest/more gratuitous/less contingent feedback
Quality of teacher relationships	More respect for the learner as an individual with unique interests and needs	Less respect for the learner as an individual with unique interests and needs

Source: From "Teacher Expectations: A Framework for Exploring Classrooms," by T. Good and R. Weinstein. In K. Zumwalt (Ed.), *Improving Teaching* (The ASCD 1986 Yearbook). Copyright © 1986 by the Association for Supervision and Curriculum Development. Reprinted with permission. All rights reserved.

Once teachers assign students to ability groups, they usually assign different learning activities. To the extent that teachers choose activities that challenge students and increase achievement, these differences are probably necessary. Activities become inappropriate, however, when students who are ready for more challenging work are not given the opportunity to try it because teachers believe they cannot handle it. This is an example of a sustaining expectation effect.

If students think their teacher doesn't care what they're doing, they may not care either. ▼

Teacher–Student Interactions. However the class is grouped and whatever the assignments, the quantity and the quality of teacher–student interactions are likely to affect the students. Students who are expected to achieve tend to be asked more and harder questions, to be given more chances and a longer time to respond, and to be interrupted less often than students who are expected to do poorly. Teachers also give these high-expectation students cues and prompts, communicating their belief that the students can answer the question (Allington, 1980; Good & Brophy, 1997; Rosenthal, 1995). Teachers tend to be more encouraging in general toward those students for whom they have high expectations. They smile at these students more often and show greater warmth through such nonverbal responses as leaning toward the students and nodding their heads as the students speak (Woolfolk & Brooks, 1983, 1985). In contrast, with low-expectation students, teachers ask easier questions, allow less time for answering, and are less likely to give prompts.

It appears that feedback and reinforcement are also somewhat dependent on teacher expectations. Good and Brophy (1997) have noted that teachers demand better performance from high-achieving students, are less likely to accept a poor answer from them, and praise them more for good answers. Teachers are more likely to respond with sympathetic acceptance or even praise to inadequate answers from low-achieving students, but to criticize these same students for wrong answers. Even more disturbing, low-achieving students receive less praise than high-achieving students for similar correct answers. When an answer on a test is "almost right," the teacher is more likely to give the benefit of the doubt (and thus the better grade) to high-achieving students (Finn, 1972).

This inconsistent feedback can be very confusing for low-ability students. Imagine how hard it would be to learn if your wrong answers were sometimes praised, sometimes ignored, and sometimes criticized, and your right answers received little recognition (Good 1983a, b).

You may be promising yourself that you will never communicate low expectations to your students, especially now that you know about the dangers involved. Of course, not all teachers form inappropriate expectations or act on their expectations in unconstructive ways (Babad, Inbar, & Rosenthal, 1982). But avoiding the problem may be more difficult than it seems. In general, low-expectation students also tend to be the most disruptive students. (Of course, low expectations can reinforce their desire to disrupt or misbehave.) Teachers may call on these students less, wait a shorter time for their answers, and give them less praise for right answers, partly to avoid the wrong, careless, or silly answers that can cause disruptions, delays, and digressions (Cooper, 1979). The challenge is to deal with these very real threats to classroom management without communicating low expectations to some students or fostering their own low expectations of themselves. And sometimes, low expectations become part of the culture of the school—beliefs shared by teachers and administrators alike (Weinstein, Madison, & Kuklinski, 1995). The Guidelines on page 420 may help you avoid some of these problems.

CHECKPOINT

Teacher Expectations

Review

▶ What are some sources of teacher expectations?

▶ What are the two kinds of expectation effects and how do they happen?

▶ What are the different avenues for communicating teacher expectations?

Apply

▶ How can teacher expectations set up a cycle of expectation and confirmation?

Strategies to Encourage Motivation and Thoughtful Learning

Until four basic conditions are met, no motivational strategies will succeed. Once these requirements are in place, there are many strategies to help students gain confidence, value learning, and stay involved with the task (Brophy, 1988; Lepper, 1988). Let's look at the necessary conditions.

Connect and Extend
To your teaching
Relate the information in Chapter 5 to the discussion in this chapter of the challenges teachers face in helping to motivate all students.

Necessary Conditions in Classrooms

First, the classroom must be relatively organized and free from constant interruptions and disruptions. (Chapter 12 will give you the information you need to make sure this requirement is met.) Second, the teacher must be a patient, supportive person

GUIDELINES

Avoiding the Negative Effects of Teacher Expectations

Use information about students from tests, cumulative folders, and other teachers very carefully.

Examples

1. Some teachers avoid reading cumulative folders at the beginning of the year.
2. Be critical and objective about the reports you hear from other teachers.

Be flexible in your use of grouping strategies.

Examples

1. Review work of students often and experiment with new groupings.
2. Use different groups for different subjects.
3. Use mixed-ability groups in cooperative exercises.

Make sure all the students are challenged.

Examples

1. Don't say, "This is easy, I know you can do it."
2. Offer a wide range of problems, and encourage all students to try a few of the harder ones for extra credit. Find something positive about these attempts.

Be especially careful about how you respond to low-achieving students during class discussions.

Examples

1. Give them prompts, cues, and time to answer.
2. Give ample praise for good answers.
3. Call on low achievers as often as high achievers.

Use materials that show a wide range of ethnic groups.

Examples

1. Check readers and library books. Is there ethnic diversity?
2. If few materials are available, ask students to research and create their own, based on community or family sources.

Make sure that your teaching does not reflect racial, ethnic, or sexual stereotypes or prejudice.

Examples

1. Use a checking system to be sure you call on and include all students.

2. Monitor the content of the tasks you assign. Do boys get the "hard" math problems to work at the board? Do you avoid having students with limited English give oral presentations?

Be fair in evaluation and disciplinary procedures.

Examples

1. Make sure equal offenses receive equal punishment. Find out from students in an anonymous questionnaire whether you seem to be favoring certain individuals.
2. Try to grade student work without knowing the identity of the student. Ask another teacher to give you a "second opinion" from time to time.

Communicate to all students that you believe they can learn—and mean it.

Examples

1. Return papers that do not meet standards with specific suggestions for improvements.
2. If students do not have the answers immediately, wait, probe, and then help them think through an answer.

Involve all students in learning tasks and in privileges.

Examples

1. Use some system to make sure you give each student practice in reading, speaking, and answering questions.
2. Keep track of who gets to do what job. Are some students always on the list while others seldom make it?

Monitor your nonverbal behavior.

Examples

1. Do you lean away or stand farther away from some students? Do some students get smiles when they approach your desk while others get only frowns?
2. Does your tone of voice vary with different students?

who never embarrasses students for mistakes. Everyone in the class should see mistakes as opportunities for learning (Clifford, 1990, 1991). Third, the work must be challenging but reasonable. If work is too easy or too difficult, students will have lit-

TABLE 11.5 *Strategies to Encourage Motivation to Learn*

This table refers to the entire Strategies to Encourage Motivation and Thoughtful Learning section of the text.

Fulfill basic requirements
- Provide an organized class environment
- Be a supportive teacher
- Assign challenging work, but not too difficult
- Make tasks worthwhile

Build confidence and positive expectations
- Begin work at the students' level
- Making learning goals clear, specific, and attainable
- Stress self-comparison, not competition
- Communicate that academic ability is improvable
- Model good problem solving

Show the value of learning
- Connect the learning task to the needs of the students
- Tie class activities to the students' interests

- Arouse curiosity
- Make the learning task fun
- Make use of novelty and familiarity
- Explain connections between present learning and later life
- Provide incentives and rewards, if needed

Help students stay focused on the task
- Give students frequent opportunities to respond
- Provide opportunities for students to create a finished product
- Avoid heavy emphasis on grading
- Reduce task risk without oversimplifying the task
- Model motivation to learn
- Teach learning tactics

tle motivation to learn. They will focus on finishing, not on learning. Finally, the learning tasks must be authentic (Brophy 1983; Brophy & Kher, 1986; Stipek, 1993).

Once these four basic conditions are met, the influences on students' motivation to learn in a particular situation can be summarized in three questions: Can I succeed at this task? Do I want to succeed? What do I need to do to succeed? (Eccles & Wigfield, 1985). As reflected in these questions, we want students to have confidence in their ability so they will approach learning with energy and enthusiasm. We want them to see the value of the tasks involved and work to learn, not just try to get the grade or get finished. We want students to believe that success will come when they apply good learning strategies instead of believing that their only option is to use self-defeating, failure-avoiding, face-saving strategies. When things get difficult, we want students to stay focused on the task, not get so worried about failure that they "freeze." Table 11.5 summarizes the basic requirements and strategies for encouraging student motivation to learn, all of which are discussed at length in the next few pages.

Can I Do It? Building Confidence and Positive Expectations

One of the most important factors in building expectations for success is past success. No amount of encouragement or "cheerleading" will substitute for real accomplishment. To ensure genuine progress:

1. *Begin work at the students' level and move in small steps.* The pace should be brisk, but not so fast that students have to move to the next step before they understand the previous one. This may require assigning different tasks to different students. One possibility is to have very easy and very difficult questions on every test

and assignment, so all students are both successful and challenged. When grades are required, make sure all the students in class have a chance to make at least a C if they work hard.

2. *Make sure learning goals are clear, specific, and possible to reach in the near future.* When long-term projects are planned, break the work into subgoals and help students feel a sense of progress toward the long-term goal. If possible, give students a range of goals at different levels of difficulty and let them choose.

3. *Stress self-comparison, not comparison with others.* Help students see the progress they are making by showing them how to use self-management strategies such as those described in Chapter 6. Give specific feedback and corrections. Tell students what they are doing right as well as what is wrong and *why* it is wrong. Periodically, give students a question or problem that was once hard for them but now seems easy. Point out how much they have improved.

4. *Communicate to students that academic ability is improvable* and specific to the task at hand. In other words, the fact that a student has trouble in algebra doesn't necessarily mean that geometry will be difficult or that he or she is a bad English student. Don't undermine your efforts to stress improvement by displaying only the 100% papers on the bulletin board.

5. *Model good problem solving*, especially when *you* have to try several approaches to get a solution. Students need to see that learning is not smooth and error-free, even for the teacher.

Do I Want to Do It? Seeing the Value of Learning

Teachers can use intrinsic and extrinsic motivation strategies to help students see the value of the learning task. In this process the age of the student must be taken into consideration. For younger children, intrinsic or *interest value* is a greater determinant of motivation than attainment or utility value. Because younger students have a more immediate, concrete focus, they have trouble seeing the value of an activity that is linked to distant goals such as getting a good job—or even preparing for the next grade. Older students, on the other hand, have the cognitive ability to think more abstractly and connect what they are learning now with goals and future possibilities, so *utility value* becomes important to these students (Eccles & Wigfield, 1985).

Attainment and Intrinsic Value. To establish *attainment value*, we must connect the learning task with the needs of the students. First, it must be possible for students to meet their needs for safety, belonging, and achievement in our classes. The classroom should not be a frightening or lonely place. Second, we must be sure that sexual or ethnic stereotypes do not interfere with motivation. For example, if students subscribe to rigid notions of masculinity and femininity, we must make it clear that both women and men can be high achievers in all subjects and that no subjects are the territory of only one sex. It is not "unfeminine" to be strong in mathematics, science, shop, or sports. It is not "unmasculine" to be good in literature, art, music, or French.

There are many strategies for encouraging *intrinsic* (interest) motivation. Several of the following are taken from Brophy (1988).

1. *Tie class activities to student interests* in sports, music, current events, pets, common problems or conflicts with family and friends, fads, television and cinema personalities, or other significant features of their lives (Schiefele, 1991). But be sure you know what you are talking about. For example, if you use a verse from an Alanis Morissette song to make a point, you had better have some knowledge of the music and the performer. When possible, give students choices of research paper or reading topics so they can follow their own interests.

2. *Arouse curiosity.* Point out puzzling discrepancies between students' beliefs and the facts. For example, Stipek (1993) describes a teacher who asked her 5th-grade class if there were "people" on some of the other planets. When the students said yes, the teacher asked if people needed oxygen to breathe. Since the students had just learned this fact, they responded yes to this question also. Then the teacher told them that there is no oxygen in the atmosphere of the other planets. This surprising discrepancy between what the children knew about oxygen and what they believed about life on other planets led to a rousing discussion of the atmospheres of other planets, the kinds of beings that could survive in these atmospheres, and so on. A straight lecture on the atmosphere of the planets might have put the students to sleep, but this discussion led to real interest in the subject.

3. *Make the learning task fun.* Many lessons can be taught through simulations or games. For example, when my daughter was in the 8th grade, all the students in her grade spent three days playing a game her teachers had designed called ULTRA. Students were divided into groups and formed their own "countries." Each country had to choose a name, symbol, national flower, and bird. They wrote and sang a national anthem and elected government officials. The teachers allocated different resources to the countries. To get all the materials needed for the completion of assigned projects, the countries had to establish trade with one another. There was a monetary system and a stock market. Students had to work with their fellow citizens to complete cooperative learning assignments. Some countries "cheated" in their trades with other nations, and this allowed debate about international relations, trust, and war. Liz says she had fun—but she also learned how to work in a group without the teacher's supervision and gained a deeper understanding of world economics and international conflicts.

4. *Make use of novelty and familiarity.* Don't overuse a few teaching approaches or motivational strategies. We all need some variety. Varying the goal structures of tasks (cooperative, competitive, individualistic) can help, as can using different teaching media. When the material being covered in class is abstract or unfamiliar to students, try to connect it to something they know and understand. For example, talk about the size of a large area, such as the Acropolis in Athens, in terms of football fields. Brophy (1988) describes one teacher who read a brief passage from *Spartacus* to personalize the unit on slavery in the ancient world.

> *Instrumental Value.* Sometimes it is difficult to encourage intrinsic motivation, and so teachers must rely on the utility or "instrumental" value of tasks. That is, it is important to learn many skills because they will be needed in more advanced classes or because they are necessary for life outside school.

1. When these connections are not obvious, you should *explain the connections to your students.* Jeanette Abi-Nader (1991) describes one project, the PLAN program, that makes these connections come alive for Hispanic high school students. The three major strategies used in the program to focus students' attention on their future are:

▲ *Learning is more interesting, and motivation is increased, when students feel personally involved and take pride in learning tasks.*

Connect and Extend
To professional journals
Abi-Nader, J. (1991). Creating a vision of the future: Strategies for motivating minority students. *Phi Delta Kappan, 72,* 546–549. *Focus Questions:* Why do minority-group students sometimes find schooling unmotivating? What can be done?

(1) working with mentors and models—often PLAN graduates—who give advice about how to choose courses, budget time, take notes, and deal with cultural differences in college; (2) storytelling about the achievements of former students—sometimes the college term papers of former students are posted on PLAN bulletin boards; and (3) filling the classroom with future-oriented talk such as "When you go to college, you will encounter these situations . . ." or, "You're at a parents' meeting—you want a good education for your children—and you are the ones who must speak up; that's why it is important to learn public speaking skills" (p. 548).

2. In some situations teachers can *provide incentives and rewards for learning* (see Chapter 6). Remember, though, that giving rewards when students are already interested in the activity may undermine intrinsic motivation. If teachers began testing and grading students on their memory of the television programs they watched the previous evening, even television viewing would lose some of its intrinsic appeal (Stipek, 1998).

3. Use *ill-structured problems and authentic tasks* in teaching. Connect problems in school to real problems outside.

What Do I Need to Do to Succeed?
Staying Focused on the Task

When students encounter difficulties, as they must if they are working at a challenging level, they need to keep their attention on the task. If the focus shifts to worries about performance, fear of failure, or concern with looking smart, then motivation to learn is lost. Here are some ideas for keeping the focus on learning.

1. *Give students frequent opportunities to respond* through questions and answers, short assignments, or demonstrations of skills. Make sure you check the students' answers so you can correct problems quickly. You don't want students to practice errors too long. Computer learning programs give students the immediate feedback they need to correct errors before they become habits.

2. When possible, *have students create a finished product.* They will be more persistent and focused on the task when the end is in sight. We all have experienced the power of the need for closure. For example, I often begin a house-painting project thinking I will work for just an hour and then find myself still painting hours later because I want to see the finished product.

3. *Avoid heavy emphasis on grades and competition.* An emphasis on grades forces students to be ego-involved rather than task-involved. Anxious students are especially hard hit by highly competitive evaluation.

4. *Reduce task risk without oversimplifying the task.* When tasks are risky (failure is likely and the consequences of failing are grave), student motivation suffers. For difficult, complex, or ambiguous tasks, provide students with plenty of time, support, resources, help, and the chance to revise or improve work.

5. *Model motivation to learn for your students.* Talk about your interest in the subject and how you deal with difficult learning problems.

6. *Teach the particular learning tactics* that students will need to master the material being studied. Show students how to learn and remember so they won't be forced to fall back on self-defeating strategies or rote memory.

How Do Beginning Teachers Motivate Students?

Timothy Newby (1991) trained classroom observers to record the motivational strategies of 30 first-year elementary-school teachers over a 16-week period. He found that the teachers used about 10 different strategies per hour—half were rewards and punishments. Figure 11.5 gives examples of the four types of strategies used by these beginning teachers. As you can see, commenting on the relevance of the lessons (showing value) accounted for 8% of strategies and building student confidence accounted for 7% of strategies, focusing student attention made up 27%, and rewards and punishments accounted for 58%.

Another interesting finding is that commenting on relevance was positively correlated with students being on task, while using rewards/punishments was negatively correlated. Thus, beginning teachers tended to use less effective strategies more often. It may be that these new teachers turned to extrinsic reinforcement (rewards and punishments) only when it became difficult to keep the students interested in their work. These findings suggest that it is wise to develop a repertoire of strategies in addition to rewards and punishments. The support of families and the community can be helpful as you design strategies for your students. The Family and Community Partnerships Guidelines on page 426 give ideas for working with families.

Connect and Extend
To the research
Newby, T. J. (1991). Classroom motivation: Strategies of first-year teachers. *Journal of Educational Psychology, 83,* 195–200. *Focus Question:* Ask your students to list examples of the four basic motivational strategies used by beginning teachers.

FIGURE 11.5

Motivational Strategies of Beginning Teachers

First-year teachers tend to rely on reward and punishment strategies to motivate students, even though these are not necessarily the most effective approaches.

Reward/Punishment Strategies
Teacher gives verbal reinforcement (praise), provides tangible rewards (extra points), or takes away a privilege (time at recess).

Attention-Focusing Strategies
Teacher waits until all is quiet. Student work groups switch to new locations and tasks at the sound of a bell. Students work on story problem for the first 5 minutes of class.

Confidence-Building Strategies
Teacher explains that it is okay to make mistakes. Teacher states explicit instructions with pertinent examples (listing the critical steps to the assignment on the board, then reviewing each step with the class).

Relevance Strategies
Teacher uses familiar experiences to introduce a subject (playing in the snow for a lesson on how animals prepare for winter). Teacher has a guest relate an experience (a parent describes his or her job).

Source: From "Classroom Motivation: Strategies of First-Year Teachers," by T. J. Newby, 1991, *Journal of Educational Psychology, 83,* pp. 195–200. Copyright © 1991 by the American Psychological Association. Adapted with permission.

Motivation to Learn

Work with families to build confidence and positive expectations.

Examples

1. Avoid comparing one child in a family to another during conferences and discussions with family members.

2. Ask family members to highlight strong points of homework assignments. They might attach a note to assignments describing the three best aspects of the work and one element that could be improved.

Make families partners in showing the value of learning.

Examples

1. Invite family members to the class to demonstrate how they use mathematics or writing in their work.

2. Involve parents in identifying skills and knowledge for the children to learn in school that could be applied at home and prove helpful to the family right now, for example, keeping records on service agencies, writing letters of complaint to department stores or landlords, or researching vacation destinations.

Provide resources that build skill and will for families.

Examples

1. Give family members simple strategies for helping their children improve study skills.

2. Involve older students in a "homework hotline" telephone network for helping younger students with class assignments.

Have frequent celebrations of learning.

Examples

1. Invite families to a "museum" at the end of a unit on dinosaurs. Students create the museum in the auditorium, library, or cafeteria. After visiting the museum, families go to the classroom to examine their child's portfolio for the unit.[1]

2. Place mini-exhibits of student work at local grocery stores, libraries, or community centers.

[1]R. C. Fowler and K. K. Corley (1996). Linking families, building community. *Educational Leadership, 7*(7), 24–26.

Students' Views of Motivation

Let's let the students have the last word on motivation. Two recent studies examined students' beliefs about motivation and fairness. Theresa Thorkildsen and her colleagues interviewed 93 students (grades 2 through 5) from an urban and a suburban elementary school. The interviewers described four approaches to motivation: encouraging focus on the task, praising excellent performance, giving rewards for excellent performance, and giving rewards for high effort. Students were asked a number of questions, including how effective and fair each practice seemed to them. Analyses of the interviews showed that students seemed to hold different personal theories about motivation. One group valued meaningful learning and favored strategies that encourage the desire to understand. Another group valued learning as duty and liked practices that promote effort. A third group favored extrinsic rewards for either effort or good performance. In terms of fairness, 98% of the students thought that encouraging task focus is fair, 85% saw rewarding effort as fair, 50% viewed rewarding performance as fair, and only 30% believed public praise is fair (Thorkildsen, Nolen, & Fournier, 1994).

In a second study, John Nicholls and his colleagues interviewed 128 African American students, 8 boys and 8 girls randomly selected from each grade—1

Connect and Extend

To the research

Thorkildsen, T. A., Nolen, S. B., & Fournier, J. (1994). What is fair? Children's critiques of practices that influence motivation. *Journal of Educational Psychology, 86,* 475–486.

Children (aged 7–12 years) were interviewed about the fairness of selected practices for influencing motivation to learn.

through 8—in an urban school. The focus of the interviews was two types of teaching: collaborative inquiry about controversies, such as why dinosaurs died out, contrasted with traditional presentations of facts about dinosaurs, such as their names and sizes. One conclusion was that older students were more likely than younger students to see collaborative inquiry as fairer and more motivating. In addition, the older the students, the more strongly they agreed that schools should foster motivation and understanding, not just memory for facts (Nicholls, Nelson, & Gleaves, 1995).

What can the results of these studies offer teachers? First, it might be interesting to learn about your own students' theories of motivation and fairness. Second, expect there to be developmental and individual differences among students in their beliefs about these topics. Knowing what your students believe about motivation will help you to apply the TARGETT model and design strategies to encourage motivation to learn.

CHECKPOINT

Strategies to Encourage Motivation and Thoughtful Learning

Review

▷ What are four conditions that must exist in a classroom before any motivational strategies can be successful?

▷ What else can teachers do to motivate students?

▷ What are the most commonly used motivational strategies of beginning teachers?

▷ What can we learn from students about motivation?

Apply

▷ Give an example of a strategy to:
- build student confidence
- show the value of learning
- help students stay focused on the task

Summary

Motivation to Learn in School

Define motivation to learn.

Teachers are interested in a particular kind of motivation—student motivation to learn. Student motivation to learn is both a trait and a state. It involves taking academic work seriously, trying to get the most from it, and applying appropriate learning strategies in the process.

On TARGETT for Learning

What does TARGETT stand for?

TARGETT is an acronym for the seven areas where teachers make decisions that can influence student motivation to learn: the nature of the *task* that students are asked to do, the *autonomy* students are allowed in working, how students are *recognized* for their accomplishments, *grouping* practices, *evaluation* procedures, the scheduling of *time* in the classroom, and the communication of *teacher expectations*.

How do tasks affect motivation?

The tasks that teachers set affect motivation. When students encounter tasks that are related to their interests, stimulate their curiosity, or are connected to real-life situations, the students are more likely to be motivated to learn. Tasks that are difficult and require critical thinking are risky and ambiguous.

What does it mean for students to "negotiate a task?"

Many times teachers plan a complicated *comprehension* task that is both ambiguous and risky. But the students want more guidance, so they ask for models, rules, minimums, or formulas. If the students are very confused, they may become restless, turn to other students for help, get discouraged, or lose interest in the task. Under this kind of pressure, the teacher often responds by transforming the *comprehension* task into a *procedural* one. Risk and ambiguity are reduced and motivation may seem to increase, at least temporarily, but the task itself is not as interesting. So the results of the "task negotiation" may be a temporary *state* of motivation, but it is motivation to perform, to get the grade, not motivation to learn.

What are the three kinds of task value?

Tasks can have attainment, intrinsic, or utility value for students. Attainment value is the importance to the student of succeeding. Intrinsic value is the enjoyment the student gets from the task. Utility value is determined by how much the task contributes to reaching short-term or long-term goals.

Distinguish between bounded and unbounded choices.

Like totally unguided discovery or aimless discussions, unstructured or unguided choices can be counterproductive for learning. The alternative is bounded choice—giving students a range of options that set valuable tasks for them but also allow them to follow personal interests. The balance must be just right so that students are not bewildered by too much choice or bored by too little.

How can recognition undermine motivation and a sense of self-efficacy?

Recognition and reward in the classroom will support motivation to learn if the recognition is for personal progress rather than competitive victories. Praise and rewards should focus on students' growing competence. At times praise can have paradoxical effects. For example, if two students succeed and the teacher praises only one of them, the message, to older children at least, may be that the praised student had less ability and had to work harder to succeed, thus earning praise. The unpraised student was simply "doing what comes naturally," succeeding based on high ability. So students may use the teacher's praise or criticism as cues about capabilities.

What determines whether a goal structure is cooperative, competitive, or individualistic?

How students relate to their peers in the classroom is influenced by the goal structure of the activities. Goal structures can be competitive (I reach my goal only if others do not), individualistic (reaching my goals is unrelated to whether others reach theirs), or cooperative (I reach my goals only if others reach theirs). Cooperative goal structures can encourage motivation and increase learning, especially for low-achieving students.

How does evaluative climate affect goal-setting?

The more competitive the grading, the more students set performance goals and focus on "looking competent"; that is, the more they are ego-involved. When the focus is on performing rather than learning, students often see the goal of classroom tasks as simply finishing, especially if the work is difficult.

What are some effects of time on motivation?

In order to foster motivation to learn, teachers should be flexible in their use of time in the classroom. Students who are forced to move faster or slower than they should or who are interrupted as they become involved in a project are not likely to develop persistence for learning.

Teacher Expectations

What are some sources of teacher expectations?

Sources include intelligence test scores, gender, notes from previous teachers and the medical or psychological reports found in cumulative folders, ethnic background, knowledge of older brothers and sisters, physical characteristics, previous achievement, socioeconomic class, and the actual behaviors of the student.

What are the two kinds of expectation effects and how do they happen?

The first is the self-fulfilling prophecy when the teacher's beliefs about the students' abilities have no basis in fact, but student behavior comes to match the initially inaccurate expectation. The second is a sustaining expectation effect when teachers are fairly accurate in their initial reading of students' abilities and respond to students appropriately. The problems arise when students show some improvement but teachers do not alter their expectations to take account of the improvement. When this happens, the teacher's unchanging expectation can sustain the student's achievement at the expected level. In practice, sustaining effects are more common than self-fulfilling prophecy effects.

What are the different avenues for communicating teacher expectations?

Some teachers tend to treat students differently, depending on their own views of how well the students are likely to do. Differences in treatment toward low-expectation students may include setting less challenging tasks, focusing on lower-level learning, giving fewer choices, providing inconsistent feedback, and communicating less respect and trust. Students may behave accordingly, fulfilling teachers' predictions or staying at an expected level of achievement.

Strategies to Encourage Motivation and Thoughtful Learning

What are four conditions that must exist in a classroom before any motivational strategies can be successful?

Before any strategies to encourage motivation can be effective, four conditions must exist in the classroom. The classroom must be organized and free from constant disruption, the teacher must be a supportive person who never embarrasses students for making mistakes, the work must be neither too easy nor too difficult, and finally, the tasks set for students must be authentic—not busy work.

What else can teachers do to motivate students?

Once these conditions are met, teachers can use strategies that help students feel confident in their abilities to improve (e.g., set challenging but reachable goals, stress self—not other—comparisons, communicate that ability is improvable), strategies that highlight the value of the learning tasks (e.g., tie tasks to student interests, arouse curiosity, show connections to the future and to real-world problems, provide incentives), and strategies that help students stay involved in the learning process without being threatened by fear of failure (e.g., provide opportunities to create a finished product, teach learning tactics, model motivation to learn for students, avoid emphasizing grades, reduce risk without oversimplifying the task).

What are the most commonly used motivational strategies of beginning teachers?

In one study, commenting on the relevance of the lessons (showing value) accounted for 8% of strategies and building student confidence accounted for 7% of strategies, focusing student attention made up 27%, and rewards and punishments accounted for 58%.

Commenting on relevance was positively correlated with students being on task, while using rewards/punishments was negatively correlated. Thus, beginning teachers tended to use less effective strategies more often. These findings do suggest that it is wise to develop a repertoire of strategies in addition to rewards and punishments.

What can we learn from students about motivation?

First, learn about your own students' theories of motivation and fairness.

Second, expect there to be developmental and individual differences among students in their beliefs about these topics. Knowing what your students believe about motivation will help you to apply the TARGETT model and design strategies to encourage motivation to learn.

Key Terms

academic tasks, p. 405
attainment value, p. 407
authentic task, p. 407
cooperative learning, p. 410
goal structure, p. 410
individual learning expectation (ILE), p. 411

intrinsic or interest value, p. 407
motivation to learn, p. 402
problem-based learning, p. 407
Pygmalion effect, p. 416
self-fulfilling prophecy, p. 415
student teams-achievement divisions (STAD), p. 411

sustaining expectation effect, p. 417
teams-games-tournaments (TGT), p. 412
utility value, p. 407

Becoming a Professional

Reflecting on the Chapter

Can you apply the ideas from this chapter on motivation to solve the following problems of practice?

Preschool and Kindergarten

▸ What would you do to help your students develop persistence without discouraging their spontaneity and enthusiasm?

Elementary and Middle School

▸ You are talking to the parents of one of your lower-achieving students. You really like the student, but he seems not to apply himself to the work. Suddenly the boy's mother says, "We think our son is doing badly in your class because you don't like him. You just seem to expect him to fail!" What would you do?

Junior High and High School

▸ You want to prepare your senior classes for the kind of independent work they will face in college, so you assign a research project. As soon as you make the assignment, the questions begin: "How many sources?" "How many pages?" "What exactly do you mean by 'support your conclusions with evidence'?" "What kind of evidence?" How do you make the assignment clear without turning it into a "spoon feeding"?

Certification Test Requirements

▸ Know about the role of choice in motivation.

▸ Understand the difference between a self-fulfilling prophecy and a sustaining expectation effect.

▸ Be familiar with several approaches to cooperative learning.

Your Teaching Portfolio

Use the section on the TARGETT model to refine your teaching philosophy. How will you answer the job interview question "What would you do to motivate difficult to reach students?"

Teaching Resources

Use the TARGETT model (Table 11.2) to generate motivational strategies for the grade you will teach.

Add Table 11.3 (showing how to compute an Individual Learning Expectation) to your **Teaching Resources** file.

Select ideas from Table 11.5 that fit your teaching and copy them into your **Teaching Resources** file.

What Would They Do?

Here is how some practicing teachers responded to the teaching situation presented at the beginning of this chapter about preparing students for proficiency tests.

SANDRA GILL

Sixth Grade Teacher
Hudson Middle School, Hudson, New York

Since the topics on the upcoming proficiency test are important ones, I would use them to form the core of my own curriculum. The curriculum would augment individual assignments with a hefty dose of group challenges in which students would work collaboratively in doing projects involving the examination of the world outside of school. These challenges would culminate in written reports as well as group presentations, incorporating both visual and verbal elements, for classmates and others. I would choose the members of each group based on the personalities and learning styles of the students. The competencies and topics that pertained to the proficiency test would be identified in the plan for each group challenge, and they would be repeated in subsequent challenges in order to reinforce them.

JULIE MOHOK (Currently a doctoral student at Queensland University of Technology)

Classroom Teacher
Ponam Primary School, Manus Island, Papua New Guinea

The first thing I would do is try to understand the situation. Perhaps through conversing with other teachers, and analyzing past records I could quickly learn of the contributing factors to the present low school performance. In addition, I would find out what the reasons are for the school's decision to resort to drill and practice on facts and skills. This may be a situation analysis. This understanding would assist me in planning my teaching for the first few weeks without overtly challenging the school administration.

I would proceed to plan and teach on the principle that learning and developing skills is for usage in the real world and not merely for passing some important test. This may include experiments, simulations, role plays, watching a video clip on a specific topic, etc. These activities should motivate students by arousing curiosity and interest in learning. Drilling and practice of key concepts and skills can follow enjoyable segments. In the process, I would inform the school's administration of my teaching program. Perhaps I might even suggest that they conduct a mid-test within the school to find out if my teaching makes a difference to the students' success rate as they prepare for the big test.

I believe that through active participation, students should be able to master skills and understand topics more clearly. Perhaps by understanding the real value of learning, preparing for the "big" test can be more of an individual challenge. The teacher is only a facilitator.

MARGARET DOOLAN

Year Three
St. Michael's School, Gordonvale QLD 4865, Australia

What a challenge!
The first few weeks would be spent in becoming familiar with my students and the standard of work of each. I would then enlist the help of my teacher-aide and as many parents as possible to help with individual and small-group study. Such helpers would work with those children exhibiting learning difficulties, focusing on areas of difficulty. They would also spend time with the students performing at the highest level, giving them the chance to attempt challenging exercises under supervision. The bulk of the class would be exposed to a variety of exercises that would improve their reading, interpreting, comprehension, and thinking skills.

Throughout the year we would cover all test topics using all forms of information available—books, library visits, excursions, guest speakers, newspapers, computers, and displays. We would read, write, talk, write poems, illustrate, and integrate with science, math, and the arts wherever possible. I would present these topics as normal curriculum learning, without mentioning "test" to the class at this stage.

Finally, in order to prepare the class for the actual test itself, I would obtain copies of previous papers and practice going through them. If necessary to create enthusiasm, I would graph class results (not individual) and attempt to achieve a higher rate of successful answers each time.

The test would be tackled with confidence, not fear, by most of the class at least!

JENNIFER HUDSON THOMAS

Armidale High School, Armidale, Australia

Although the importance of the 4th grade proficiency test cannot be overlooked from both the student's and school's point of view, it should not impede the process of "real" teaching and learning. Developing an enthusiasm for the learning required should be the greatest priority for any group of learners. Listing the mandatory topics to be covered and voting on the order in which these topics will be undertaken will give the learners some ownership of the direction that their learning will take over the year. Further involvement in planning the course and outcomes of such units of work will also increase students' commitment to their learning. Relating the learning within each topic to the real-life situations and interests of the group of learners will also help promote and "sell" the learning required. As the teacher, it will be my responsibility to incorporate as many of the required competencies as often as possible in all learning undertaken. This should ensure that the facts and skills required for that proficiency test become consolidated learning and form the basis of an automatic and well-rehearsed response repertoire. With such a learning background, my students should be able to generalize their skills and approach the proficiency test in the spring with confidence.

Creating Learning Environments

hen you imagine facing 25 or 30 students on the first day of class, what are your concerns? List the management problems that you find most difficult. What are your strengths in dealing with classroom management problems?

This chapter examines the ways that teachers create social and physical environments for learning. We will look at classroom management—one of the main concerns of teachers, particularly beginning teachers.

The very nature of classes, teaching, and students makes good management a critical ingredient of success; we will look at why this is true. Next, we will turn to the goals of classroom management. Successful managers create more time for learning, involve more students, and help students to become self-managing.

A positive learning environment must be established and maintained throughout the year. One of the best ways to do this is to try to prevent problems from occurring at all. But when problems arise—as they always do—an appropriate response is important. What will you do when students challenge you openly in class, when one student asks your advice on a difficult personal problem, or when another withdraws from all participation? We will examine the ways that teachers can communicate effectively with their students in these and many other situations.

By the time you have completed this chapter, you should be able to:

▶ Describe the special managerial demands of classrooms and relate these demands to students of different ages.
▶ Create a list of rules and procedures for a class.
▶ Arrange the physical environment of your classroom to fit your learning goals and teaching methods.
▶ Develop a plan for organizing your first week of teaching.
▶ Explain Kounin's suggestions for preventing management problems.
▶ Describe how you might respond to a student who seldom completes work.
▶ Suggest two different approaches for dealing with a conflict between teacher and student, or between two students.

What Would You Do?

There are students from four different ethnic groups in the middle school "pod" you are working with this year. Last week, the principal added a student with pretty severe emotional/behavioral problems and a student with cerebral palsy to the group as part of an experiment in full inclusion. The boy with cerebral palsy is in a wheelchair and has some difficulties with language and hearing. Each of the four ethnic groups seems to stick together, never making friends with students from "outside." When you ask people to work together for projects, the divisions are strictly on ethnic lines. Many of the subgroups communicate in their native language—one you don't understand—and you assume that often the joke is on you because of the looks and laughs directed your way. Clarise, the emotionally disturbed student, is making matters worse by telling ethnic jokes to anyone who will listen in a voice loud enough to be overheard by half the class. There are rumors of an ambush after school to "teach Clarise a lesson." You agree that she—and the whole class for that matter—needs a lesson, but not this kind.

▶ How would you structure the class to help the students feel more comfortable together?

▶ What are your first goals in working on this problem?

▶ Is conflict negotiation called for here? How would you handle the situation?

▶ How will these issues affect the grade levels you will teach?

The Need for Organization

Connect and Extend
To public opinion
Every year the September issue of *Phi Delta Kappan* contains the *"Annual Phi Delta Kappa/Gallup Poll of the Public's Attitudes Toward the Public Schools."* Questions usually ask respondents to "grade" the schools, identify the problems facing the schools, rate strategies for improvement, and give opinions about current issues such as school choice, home schooling, vouchers, and values.

In 1999, *Phi Delta Kappan* published the 31st annual Gallup Poll of the public's attitude toward public schools. In 1999, as in almost every year since 1969, "lack of discipline" was named as the number one problem facing the schools (Rose & Gallup, 1999). Clearly, the public sees discipline as an important challenge for teachers. In order to understand the role of management in teaching, let's take a closer look at the classroom itself.

The Ecology of Classrooms

The word *ecology* is usually associated with nature. But classrooms are ecological systems, too. The environment of the classroom and the inhabitants of that environment—students and teachers—are constantly interacting. Each aspect of the system affects all others. The characteristics of classrooms, the tasks of teaching, and the needs of students all influence classroom management (Epanchin, Townsend, & Stoddard, 1994).

Characteristics of Classrooms. Classes are particular kinds of environments. They have "distinctive properties affecting participants regardless of how students are organized for learning or what educational philosophy the teacher espouses" (Doyle, 1986, p. 394). Let's look at six of the features described by Doyle.

◀ *While the stereotypical classroom consists of students seated quietly in rows, their hands folded neatly on their desks, the reality is that teachers are often called on to keep track of many different activities at one time.*

Classrooms are *multidimensional*. Many individuals, all with differing goals, preferences, and abilities, must share resources, accomplish various tasks, use and reuse materials without losing them, move in and out of the room, keep track of what is happening, and so on. In addition, actions can have multiple effects. Calling on low-ability students may encourage their participation and thinking but may slow the discussion and lead to management problems if the students cannot answer. Classrooms also are *simultaneous*. Everything happens at once. A teacher explaining a concept must also notice if students are following the explanation, decide whether two whispering youngsters should be ignored or stopped, determine if there is enough time to start the next topic, and decide who should answer the question that Jill just asked. Action is fast-paced and *immediate*. Teachers have literally hundreds of exchanges with students during a single day. In this rapid-fire existence, events are *unpredictable*. Even when plans are carefully made, the overhead projector is in place, and the activities are ready, the lesson can still be interrupted by a burned-out bulb in the projector, a child who suddenly becomes ill, or a loud, angry discussion right outside the classroom.

Because classrooms are *public*, the way the teacher handles these unexpected intrusions is seen and judged by all. Students are always noticing if the teacher is being "fair." Is there favoritism? What happens when a rule is broken? Finally, classrooms have *histories*. The meaning of a particular teacher's or student's actions depends in part on what has happened before. The 15th time a student arrives late requires a different response from the teacher than the first late arrival. In addition, the history of the first few weeks of school affects life in the class all year.

The Basic Task: Gain Their Cooperation.

No productive activity can take place in a group without the cooperation of all members. This obviously applies to classrooms. Even if some students don't participate, they must allow others to do so. (You have probably seen one or two students bring an entire class to a halt.) So the basic management task for teachers is to achieve order and harmony by gaining and maintaining student cooperation in class activities (Doyle, 1986). Given the

Connect and Extend
To your teaching

Many computer programs exist to help teachers manage their own activities inside and outside the classroom. Typical activities include online standard forms, IEPs, student home and school databases, student reports, letters to parents, archiving and locating information, electronic mail, financial planning, and scheduling. Complete classroom management systems and computer-managed instruction (CMI) are also available. For more information see: Bitter, G. G., & Pierson, M. E. (1999). *Using technology in the classroom* (3rd ed.). Boston: Allyn & Bacon.

Connect and Extend
To your own philosophy

Some educators object to the metaphor of teacher as manager. These critics suggest that the image brings with it notions of manipulation and detachment. Is the metaphor of manager an appropriate choice? What other metaphors can you suggest for teachers acting to maintain order and discipline? My research in this area, presented at the annual meeting of AERA in 1993, suggests that images of group leaders (coaches, guides, etc.), problem solvers (physicians, chess players), and nurturers (mother, father, gardeners) are common for beginning teachers.

multidimensional, simultaneous, immediate, unpredictable, public, and historical nature of classrooms, this is quite a challenge.

Gaining student cooperation means much more than dealing effectively with misbehavior. It means planning activities, having materials ready, having developmentally appropriate expectations for behavior and academics, giving clear signals to students, accomplishing transitions smoothly, foreseeing problems and stopping them before they start, selecting and sequencing activities so that flow and interest are maintained, establishing a climate of trust and respect, and much more. Also, different activities require different managerial skills. For example, a new or complicated activity may be a greater threat to classroom organization than a familiar or simple activity.

Age-Related Needs. Obviously, gaining the cooperation of kindergartners is not the same task as gaining the cooperation of high school seniors. Jere Brophy and Carolyn Evertson (1978) have identified four general stages of classroom management, defined by age-related needs. Let's look briefly at each.

During kindergarten and the first few years of elementary school, children are learning how to go to school. They are being socialized into a new role. Direct teaching of classroom rules and procedures is important during this stage. Little learning will take place until the children master these basics.

Children in the middle elementary years are usually familiar with the student role, even if they are not always perfect examples of it. Many school and classroom routines have become relatively automatic. Specific new rules and procedures for a particular activity may have to be taught directly, however. And you may hear the familiar refrain, "My teacher last year didn't do it that way!" Still, at this stage you will spend more time monitoring and maintaining the management system than teaching it directly.

Toward the end of elementary school and the beginning of high school, friendships and status within peer groups take on tremendous importance. Pleasing the teacher may be replaced by pleasing peers. Some students begin to test and defy authority. The management challenges at this stage are to deal productively with these disruptions and to motivate students who are becoming less concerned with teachers' opinions and more interested in their social lives.

By the end of high school, the focus of most students returns to academics. By this time, unfortunately, many of the students with overwhelming behavioral problems have dropped out. At this stage the challenges are to manage the curriculum, fit academic material to students' interests and abilities, and help students become more self-managing in their learning. The first few classes each semester may be devoted to teaching particular procedures for using materials and equipment, or for keeping track of and submitting assignments. But most students know what is expected.

The Goals of Classroom Management

The aim of **classroom management** is to maintain a positive, productive learning environment. But order for its own sake is an empty goal. As we discussed in Chapter 6, it is unethical to use class management techniques just to keep students docile and quiet. What, then, is the point of working so hard to manage classrooms? There are at least three reasons why management is important.

More Time for Learning. As a child, I once used a stopwatch to time the commercials during a TV quiz show. I was amazed to find that half of the program

Classroom Management: Techniques used to maintain a healthy learning environment, relatively free of behavior problems.

was devoted to commercials. Actually, very little quizzing took place. If you used a similar approach in classrooms, timing all the different activities throughout the day, you might be surprised by how little actual teaching takes place. Many minutes each day are lost through interruptions, disruptions, late starts, and rough transitions (Karweit, 1989; Karweit & Slavin, 1981).

Obviously, students will learn only the material they have a chance to learn. Almost every study examining time and learning has found a significant relationship between time spent on content and student learning (Berliner, 1988). In fact, the correlations between content studied and student learning are usually larger than the correlations between specific teacher behaviors and student learning (Rosenshine, 1979). So one important goal of classroom management is to expand the sheer number of minutes available for learning. This is sometimes called **allocated time**.

Simply making more time for learning will not automatically lead to achievement. To be valuable, time must be used effectively. As you saw in the chapters on cognitive learning, the way students process information is a central factor in what they learn and remember. Basically, students will learn what they practice and think about (Doyle, 1983). Time spent actively involved in specific learning tasks is often called **engaged time**, or sometimes **time on task**.

Again, however, engaged time doesn't guarantee learning. Students may be struggling with material that is too difficult or using the wrong learning strategies. When students are working with a high rate of success—really learning and understanding—we call the time spent **academic learning time**. A second goal of class management is to increase academic learning time by keeping students *actively engaged in worthwhile, appropriate learning activities*. Figure 12.1 on page 438 shows how the 1,000+ hours of time mandated for school in most states can become only about 333 hours of quality academic learning time for a typical student.

Access to Learning. Each classroom activity has its own rules for participation. Sometimes these rules are clearly stated by the teacher, but often they are implicit and unstated. Teacher and students may not even be aware that they are following different rules for different activities (Berliner, 1983). The differences are sometimes quite subtle. For example, in a reading group students may have to raise their hands to make a comment, but in a show-and-tell circle in the same class they may simply have to catch the teacher's eye.

As we saw in Chapter 5, the rules defining who can talk; what they can talk about; and when, to whom, and how long they can talk are often called **participation structures**. In order to participate successfully in a given activity, students must understand the participation structure. Some students, however, seem to come to school less able to participate than others. The participation structures they learn at home in interactions with siblings, parents, and other adults do not match the participation structures of school activities (Tharp, 1989). But teachers are not necessarily aware of this conflict. Instead, the teachers see that a child doesn't quite fit in, always seems to say the wrong thing at the wrong time, or is very reluctant to participate, and they are not sure why.

What can we conclude? In order to involve all your students, you must make sure that everyone knows *how* to participate in each specific activity. The key is awareness. What are your rules and expectations? Are they understandable, given your students' cultural backgrounds and home experiences? What unspoken rules or values may be operating? Are you clear and consistent in signaling your students about how to participate? To reach the second goal of good classroom management—giving all students access to learning—you must make sure everyone knows

Allocated Time: Time set aside for learning.

Engaged Time: Time spent actively learning.

Time on Task: Time spent actively engaged in the learning task at hand.

Academic Learning Time: Time when students are actually succeeding at the learning task.

Participation Structures: Rules defining how to participate in different activities.

Connect and Extend
To your teaching
Are there cultural differences in the verbal and nonverbal ways that students show respect, pay attention, and bid for a turn in conversation? How can cultural differences in interaction styles and expectations make classroom management more challenging?

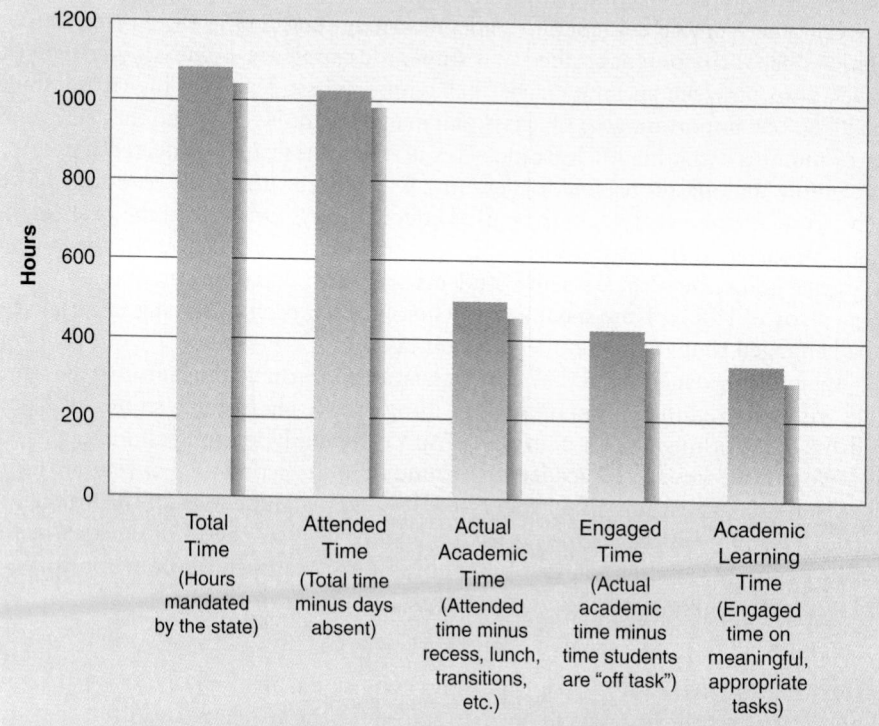

FIGURE 12.1

Who Knows Where the Time Goes?

The over 1,000 hours per year of instruction mandated by most states can represent only 300 or 400 hours of quality academic learning time.

Source: From *Elementary Classroom Management* (2nd ed.), by C. S. Weinstein and A. J. Mignano, Jr., 1997, New York: McGraw-Hill. Copyright © 1997 by The McGraw-Hill Companies. Adapted with permission.

CHECKPOINT

The Need for Organization

Review

▶ What are the challenges of classroom management?

▶ What are the goals of good classroom management?

Apply

▶ Explain how you would increase academic learning time in your classroom.

how to participate in class activities. This means teaching, signaling, and practicing appropriate ways to participate.

Management for Self-Management. The third goal of any management system is to help students become better able to manage themselves. The movement from demanding obedience to teaching self-regulation and self-control is a fundamental shift in discussions of classroom management today (Weinstein, 1999). Tom Savage (1999) says simply, "the most fundamental purpose of discipline is the development of self-control. . . . Academic knowledge and technological skill will be of little consequence if those who possess them lack self-control" (p. 11). Through self-control, students demonstrate *responsibility*—the ability to fulfill their own needs without interfering with the rights and needs of others (Glasser, 1990). Students learn self-control by making choices and dealing with the consequences, setting goals and priorities, managing time, collaborating to learn, mediating disputes and making peace, and developing trusting relations with trustworthy teachers and classmates (Rogers & Frieberg, 1994).

Encouraging **self-management** requires extra time, but teaching students how to take responsibility is an investment well worth the effort. When elementary and secondary teachers have very effective class management systems but neglect to set student self-management as a goal, their students often find that they have trouble working independently after they graduate from these "well-managed" classes.

Self-Management: Management of your own behavior and acceptance of responsibility for your own actions.

$\mathscr{C}$reating a Positive Learning Environment

In making plans for your class, much of what you have already learned in this book should prove helpful. You know, for example, that problems are prevented when individual variations, such as those discussed in Chapters 2, 3, 4, and 5, are taken into account in instructional planning. Sometimes students become disruptive because the work assigned is too difficult. And students who are bored by lessons well below their ability levels may be interested in finding more exciting activities to fill their time.

In one sense, teachers prevent discipline problems whenever they make an effort to motivate students. A student involved in learning is usually not involved in a clash with the teacher or other students at the same time. All plans for motivating students are steps toward preventing problems.

Some Research Results

What else can teachers do to be good managers? For several years, educational psychologists at the University of Texas at Austin studied classroom management quite thoroughly (Emmer, Evertson, & Anderson, 1980; Emmer, Evertson, & Worsham, 2000; Evertson, 1988; Evertson, Emmer, & Worsham, 2000). Their general approach was to study a large number of classrooms, making frequent observations the first weeks of school and less frequent visits later in the year. After several months there were dramatic differences among the classes. Some had very few management problems, while others had many. The most and least effective teachers were identified on the basis of the quality of classroom management and student achievement later in the year.

Next, the researchers looked at their observation records of the first weeks of class to see how the effective teachers got started. Other comparisons were made between the teachers who ultimately had harmonious, high-achieving classes and those whose classes were fraught with problems. On the basis of these comparisons, management principles were developed. The researchers then taught these principles to a new group of teachers; the results were quite positive. Teachers who applied the principles had fewer problems; their students spent more time learning and less time disrupting; and achievement was higher. The findings of these studies formed the basis for two books on classroom management (Emmer et al., 2000; Evertson et al., 2000). Many of the ideas in the following pages are from these books.

Connect and Extend
To other chapters
In Chapter 13 you will learn about the importance of careful planning and clear objectives. Good planning is an important aspect of classroom management.

Connect and Extend
To other chapters
Motivation and classroom management are closely related. The motivational strategies described in Chapters 10 and 11 are good first steps in effective class management.

Connect and Extend
To the research
For a description of a study that tested the Emmer/Evertson management principles along with other approaches, such as reinforcement strategies with adolescents in several schools, see Gottfredson, D. C., Gottfredson, G. D., & Hybl, L. G. (1993). Managing adolescent behavior: A multiyear, multischool study. *American Educational Research Journal, 30,* 179–217. Generally, the application of these principles improved behavior.

Rules and Procedures Required

Procedures: Prescribed steps for an activity.

Rules: Statements specifying expected and forbidden behaviors; dos and don'ts.

At the elementary school level, teachers must lead 20 to 30 students of varying abilities through many different activities each day. Without efficient rules and procedures, a great deal of time is wasted answering the same question over and over. "My pencil broke. How can I do my math?" "I'm finished with my story. What should I do now?" "Steven hit me!" "I left my homework in my locker."

At the secondary school level, teachers must deal daily with over 100 students who use dozens of materials and often change rooms for each class. Secondary school students are also more likely to challenge teachers' authority. The effective managers studied by Emmer, Evertson, and their colleagues had planned procedures and rules for coping with these situations.

Procedures. How will materials and assignments be distributed and collected? Under what conditions can students leave the room? How will grades be determined? What are the special routines for handling equipment and supplies in science, art, or vocational classes? **Procedures** describe how activities are accomplished in classrooms, but they are seldom written down; they are simply the ways of getting things done in class. Carol Weinstein (1996) and Weinstein and Mignano (1997) suggest that teachers establish procedures to cover the following areas:

1. *Administrative routines,* such as taking attendance.
2. *Student movement,* such as entering and leaving or going to the bathroom.
3. *Housekeeping,* such as watering plants or storing personal items.
4. *Routines for accomplishing lessons,* such as how to collect assignments or return homework.
5. *Interactions between teacher and student,* such as how to get the teacher's attention when help is needed.
6. *Talk among students,* such as giving help or socializing.

Classroom rules that are clearly understood by all students can help maintain a classroom environment that is respectful and more conducive to effective learning. ▼

You might use these six areas as a framework for planning your class procedures and routines. The Guidelines on page 441 should help you as you plan.

Rules. **Rules** specify expected and forbidden actions in the class. They are the dos and don'ts of classroom life. Unlike procedures, rules are often written down and posted. In establishing rules, you should consider what kind of atmosphere you want to create. What student behaviors will help you teach effectively? What limits do the students need to guide their behavior? The rules you set should be consistent with school rules, and also in keeping with principles of learning. For example, we know from the research on small group learning that students benefit when they explain work to peers. They learn as they teach. A rule that forbids students to help each other may be inconsistent with good learning principles. Or a rule that says, "No erasures when writing" may make students focus more on preventing mistakes than on communicating clearly in their writing (Burden, 1995; Weinstein & Mignano, 1997).

GUIDELINES

Establishing Class Procedures

Determine procedures for student upkeep of desks, classroom equipment, and other facilities.

Examples

1. Some teachers set aside a cleanup time each day or once a week in self-contained classes.

2. You might demonstrate and have students practice how to push chairs under the desk, take and return materials stored on shelves, sharpen pencils, use the sink or water fountain, assemble lab equipment, and so on.

3. In some classes a rotating monitor is in charge of equipment or materials.

Decide how students will be expected to enter and leave the room.

Examples

1. How will students know what they should do as soon as they enter the room? Some teachers have a standard assignment ("Have your homework out and be checking it over").

2. Under what conditions can students leave the room? When do they need permission?

3. If students are late, how do they gain admission to the room?

4. Many teachers require students to be in their seats and quiet before they can leave at the end of class. The teacher, not the bell, dismisses class.

Establish a signal and teach it to your students.

Examples

1. In the classroom, some teachers flick the lights, sound a chord on a piano or recorder, sound a bell like the "ring bell for service" at a sales counter, move to the podium and stare silently at the class, use a phrase like "Eyes, please," take out their grade books, or move to the front of the class.

2. In the halls, a raised hand, one clap, or some other signal may mean "Stop."

3. On the playground, a raised hand or whistle may mean "Line up."

Set procedures for student participation in class.

Examples

1. Will you have students raise their hands for permission to speak or simply require that they wait until the speaker has finished?

2. How will you signal that you want everyone to respond at once? Some teachers raise a cupped hand to their ear. Others preface the question with "Everyone . . . ."

3. Make sure you are clear about differences in procedures for different activities: reading group, learning center, discussion, teacher presentation, seatwork, film, peer learning group, library, and so forth.

4. How many students at a time can be at the pencil sharpener, teacher's desk, learning center, sink, bookshelves, reading corner, or bathroom?

Determine how you will communicate, collect, and return assignments.

Examples

1. Some teachers reserve a particular corner of the board for listing assignments. Others write assignments in colored chalk. For younger students it may be better to prepare assignment sheets or folders, color-coding them for math workbook, reading packet, and science kit.

2. Some teachers collect assignments in a box or bin; others have a student collect work while they introduce the next activity.

Having a few general rules that cover many specifics is better than listing all the dos and don'ts. But, if specific actions are forbidden, such as chewing gum in class or smoking in the bathrooms, then a rule should make this clear.

Rules for Elementary School. Evertson and her colleagues (2000) give five examples of general rules for elementary school classes:

1. *Be polite and helpful.* This applies to behavior toward adults (including substitute teachers) and children. Examples of polite behavior include waiting your turn, saying "please" and "thank you," and not fighting or calling names.

Connect and Extend
To your teaching
Visit elementary school classes and note the rules posted by different teachers at the same grade level. Identify rules that are common to all or most classes, as well as those that are unusual.

Connect and Extend
To your teaching

What are the differences between procedures and rules? What rewards and penalties are appropriate for the grade levels you will teach?

Connect and Extend
To your teaching

Here are some tips for using consequences taken from Richard Curwin (1992). *Rediscovering hope: Our greatest teaching strategy*. Bloomington, IN: National Educational Service, pp. 79–80.

- Always implement a consequence when a rule is broken.
- Select the most appropriate consequence from the list of alternatives, taking into account the offense, situation, student involved, and the best means of helping that student.
- State the rule and consequence to the offending student. Nothing more need be said.
- Be private. Only the student(s) involved should hear.
- Do not embarrass the student.
- Do not think of the situation as win–lose. This is not a contest. Do not get involved in a power struggle.
- Control your anger. Be calm and speak quietly, but accept no excuses from the student.
- Sometimes it is best to let the student choose the consequence.
- The professional always looks for ways to help the client.

Source: From Richard Curwin. *Rediscovering Hope: Our Greatest Teaching Strategy*, Copyright 1992, pp. 79–80. Permission to excerpt granted by the National Education Service, Bloomington, IN. To obtain a copy, contact the NES at 1-800-733-6786 or FAX 812-336-7790 or e-mail NES@Bluemarble.net. All rights reserved by NES.

2. *Respect other people's property.* This might include picking up litter; returning library books; not marking on walls, desks, or buses; and getting permission before using other people's things.

3. *Listen quietly while others are speaking.* This applies to the teacher and other students, in large-class lessons or small-group discussions.

4. *Do not hit, shove, or hurt others.* Make sure you give clear explanations of what you mean by "hurt." Does this apply to hurt feelings as well as hurt bodies?

5. *Obey all school rules.* This reminds students that all school rules apply in your classroom. Then students cannot claim, for example, that they thought it was okay to chew gum or listen to a radio in your class, even though these are against school rules, "because you never made a rule against it for us."

Whatever the rule, students need to be taught the behaviors that the rule includes and excludes. Examples, practice, and discussion will be needed before learning is complete.

As you've seen, different activities often require different rules. This can be confusing for elementary students until they have thoroughly learned all the rules. To prevent confusion, you might consider making signs that list the rules for each activity. Then, before the activity, you can post the appropriate sign as a reminder. This provides clear and consistent cues about participation structures so all students, not just the "well-behaved," know what is expected. Of course, these rules must be explained and discussed before the signs can have their full effect.

Rules for Secondary School. Emmer and colleagues (2000) suggest six examples of rules for secondary students:

1. *Bring all needed materials to class.* The teacher must specify the type of pen, pencil, paper, notebook, texts, and so on.

2. *Be in your seat and ready to work when the bell rings.* Many teachers combine this rule with a standard beginning procedure for the class, such as a warm-up exercise on the board or a requirement that students have paper with a proper heading ready when the bell rings.

3. *Respect and be polite to everyone.* This covers fighting, verbal abuse, and general troublemaking.

4. *Respect other people's property.* This means property belonging to the school, the teacher, or other students.

5. *Listen and stay seated while someone else is speaking.* This applies when the teacher or other students are talking.

6. *Obey all school rules.* As with the elementary class rules, this covers many behaviors and situations, so you do not have to repeat every school rule for your class. It also reminds the students that you will be monitoring them inside and outside your class. Make sure you know all the school rules. Some secondary students are very adept at convincing teachers that their misbehavior "really isn't against the rules."

Consequences. As soon as you decide on your rules and procedures, you must consider what you will do when a student breaks a rule or does not follow a procedure. It is too late to make this decision after the rule has been broken. For many infractions, the logical consequence is having to go back and "do it right."

TABLE 12.1 *Seven Categories of Penalties for Students*

1. *Expressions of disappointment.* If students like and respect their teacher, then a serious, sorrowful expression of disappointment may cause students to stop and think about their behavior.

2. *Loss of privileges.* Students can lose free time. If they have not completed homework, for example, they can be required to do it during a free period or recess.

3. *Exclusion from the group.* Students who distract their peers or fail to cooperate can be separated from the group until they are ready to cooperate. Some teachers give a student a pass for 10 to 15 minutes. The student must go to another class or study hall, where the other students and teachers ignore the offending student for that time.

4. *Written reflections on the problem.* Students can write in journals, write essays about what they did and how it affected others, or write letters of apology—if this is appropriate. Another possibility is to ask students to describe objectively what they did; then the teacher and the student can sign and date this statement. These records are available if parents or administrators need evidence of the students' behavior.

5. *Detentions.* Detentions can be very brief meetings after school, during a free period, or at lunch. The main purpose is to talk about what has happened. (In high school, detentions are often used as punishments; suspensions and expulsions are available as more extreme measures.)

6. *Visits to the principal's office.* Expert teachers tend to use this penalty rarely, but they do use it when the situation warrants. Some schools require students to be sent to the office for certain offenses, such as fighting. If you tell a student to go to the office and the student refuses, you might call the office saying the student has been sent. Then the student has the choice of either going to the office or facing the principal's penalty for "disappearing" on the way.

7. *Contact with parents.* If problems become a repeated pattern, most teachers contact the student's family. This is done to seek support for helping the student, not to blame the parents or punish the student.

Source: From *Elementary Classroom Management* (2nd ed.), by C. S. Weinstein and A. J. Mignano, Jr., New York: McGraw-Hill. Copyright © 1997 by The McGraw-Hill Companies. Adapted with permission.

Students who run in the hall may have to return to where they started and walk properly. Incomplete papers can be redone. Materials left out should be put back (Charles, 1996). Sometimes consequences are more complicated. In their case studies of four expert elementary school teachers, Weinstein and Mignano (1997) found that the teachers' negative consequences fell into seven categories, as shown in Table 12.1. The main point here is that decisions about penalties (and rewards) must be made early on, so students know before they break a rule or use the wrong procedure what this will mean for them. I encourage my student teachers to get a copy of the school rules and their cooperating teacher's rules, and then plan their own.

Who Sets the Rules and Consequences? In the first chapter I described Ken, an expert teacher who worked with his students to establish a students' and teacher's "Bill of Rights" instead of defining rules. These "rights" cover most situations that might require a "rule" and help the students move toward the goal of becoming self-managing. The rights for one recent year's class are listed in Table 12.2 on page 444. Developing rights and responsibilities rather than rules makes a very important point to students. "Teaching children that something is wrong *because there is a rule against it* is not the same as teaching them that there is a rule against it *because it is wrong,* and helping them to understand why this is so" (Weinstein, 1999, p. 154). Students should understand that the rules are developed so that everyone can work and learn together.

Another kind of planning that affects the learning environment is designing the physical arrangement of the class furniture, materials, and learning tools.

Connect and Extend
To other chapters
See the description of Ken's teaching approach in Chapter 1.

TABLE 12.2 *A Bill of Rights for Students and Teachers*

Students' Bill of Rights

Students in this class have the following rights:

To whisper when the teacher isn't talking or asking for silence.

To celebrate authorship or other work at least once a month.

To exercise outside on days there is no physical education class.

To have 2-minute breaks.

To have healthy snacks during snack time.

To participate in choosing a table.

To have privacy. Get permission to touch anyone else's possessions.

To be comfortable.

To chew gum without blowing bubbles or making a mess.

To make choices about the day's schedule.

To have free work time.

To work with partners.

To talk to the class without anyone else talking.

To work without being disturbed.

Teacher's Bill of Rights

The Teacher has the following rights:

To talk without anyone else talking, moving about, or disturbing the class.

To work without being disturbed.

To have everyone's attention while giving directions.

To punish someone who is not cooperating.

To send someone out of the group or room, or to the office.

Source: From *Elementary Classroom Management* (2nd ed.), by C. S. Weinstein and A. J. Mignano, Jr., New York: McGraw-Hill. Copyright © 1997 by The McGraw-Hill Companies. Adapted with permission.

Planning Spaces for Learning

Connect and Extend
To professional journals
See the September 1998 issue of *Educational Leadership* for several articles on "Realizing a Positive School Climate." There are descriptions of ways to improve school climate through architecture and design, school meetings, cooperative learning, violence prevention, parent involvement, and other approaches.

Spaces for learning should invite and support the activities you plan in your classroom, and they should respect the inhabitants of the space. This respect begins at the classroom door for young children by helping them identify their class—protecting them from the embarrassment and fear of getting lost. One school that has won awards for its architecture paints each classroom door a different bright color, so young children can find their "home" (Herbert, 1998). Once inside, spaces can be created that invite quiet reading, group collaboration, or independent research. If students are to use materials, they should be able to reach them. And learning spaces should be inviting. In an interview with Marge Scherer (1999), Herb Kohl describes how he creates a positive environment in his classes.

> What I do is put up the most beautiful things I know—posters, games, puzzles, challenges—and let the children know these are provocations. These are ways of provoking them into using their minds. You have to create an environment that

makes kids walk in and say, "I really want to see what's here. I would really like to look at this." (p. 9)

In terms of classroom arrangement, there are two basic ways of organizing space: interest areas and personal territories. These are not mutually exclusive; many teachers use a design that combines interest areas and personal territories. Individual students' desks—their territories—are placed in the center, with interest areas in the back or around the periphery of the room. This allows the flexibility needed for both large- and small-group activities. Figure 12.2 shows an elementary classroom that combines interest area and personal territory arrangements.

Interest Areas. The design of interest areas can influence the way the areas are used by students. For example, working with a classroom teacher, Carol Weinstein (1977) was able to make changes in interest areas that helped the teacher meet her objectives of having more girls involved in the science center and having all students experiment more with a variety of manipulative materials. In a second study, changes in a library corner led to more involvement in literature activities throughout the class (Morrow & Weinstein, 1986).

To plan your classroom space, first decide what activities the classroom should accommodate. For example, if you are in a self-contained elementary classroom, you might set up interest areas for reading, arts and crafts, science, and math. If you are teaching one particular subject on the junior or senior high level, you might divide your room into several areas, perhaps for audiovisual activities, small-group instruction, quiet study, and projects.

Next, you are ready to draw several possible floor plans. Use graph paper if possible, and draw to scale. As you work, keep the Guidelines on page 446 in mind.

Personal Territories. Can the physical setting influence teaching and learning in classrooms organized by territories? Adams and Biddle (1970) found that verbal interaction between teacher and students was concentrated in the center front of the classroom and in a line directly up the center of the room. The data were so dramatic that Adams and Biddle coined the term **action zone** to refer to this area of the room. Later research modified this finding. Even though most rooms have an action zone

Action Zone: Area of a classroom where the greatest amount of interaction takes place.

FIGURE 12.2

An Elementary Classroom Arrangement

This 4th-grade teacher has designed a space that allows teacher presentations and demonstrations, small group work, computer interactions, math manipulatives activities, informal reading, art, and other projects without requiring constant rearrangements.

Source: From *Elementary Classroom Management* (2nd ed.), by C. S. Weinstein and A. J. Mignano, Jr., 1997, New York: McGraw-Hill. Copyright © 1997 by The McGraw-Hill Companies. Reprinted with permission.

GUIDELINES

Designing Learning Spaces

Note the fixed features and plan accordingly.

Examples

1. Remember that the audiovisual center and computers need an electrical outlet.
2. Keep art supplies near the sink, small-group work by a blackboard.

Create easy access to materials and a well-organized place to store them.

Examples

1. Make sure materials are easy to reach and visible to students.
2. Have enough shelves so that materials need not be stacked.

Provide students with clean, convenient surfaces for studying.

Examples

1. Put bookshelves next to the reading area, games by the game table.
2. Prevent fights by avoiding crowded work spaces.

Make sure work areas are private and quiet.

Examples

1. Make sure there are no tables or work areas in the middle of traffic lanes; a person should not have to pass through one area to get to another.
2. Keep noisy activities as far as possible from quiet ones. Increase the feeling of privacy by placing partitions, such as bookcases or pegboards, between areas or within large areas.

Arrange things so you can see your students and they can see all instructional presentations.

Examples

1. Make sure you can see over partitions.
2. Design seating so that students can see instruction without moving their chairs or desks.

Avoid dead spaces and "racetracks."

Examples

1. Don't have all the interest areas around the outside of the room, leaving a large dead space in the middle.
2. Avoid placing a few items of furniture right in the middle of this large space, creating a "racetrack" around the furniture.

Provide choices and flexibility.

Examples

1. Establish private cubicles for individual work, open tables for group work, and cushions on the floor for whole-class meetings.
2. Give students a place to keep their personal belongings. This is especially important if students don't have personal desks.

Try new arrangements, then evaluate and improve.

Examples

1. Have a "two-week arrangement," then evaluate.
2. Enlist the aid of your students. They have to live in the room, too, and designing a classroom can be a very challenging educational experience.

where participation is greatest, this area may be on one side, or near a particular learning center (Good, 1983a).

Front-seat location does seem to increase participation for students who are predisposed to speak in class, whereas a seat in the back will make it more difficult to participate and easier to sit back and daydream (Woolfolk & Brooks, 1983). To "spread the action around," Weinstein and Mignano (1997) suggest that teachers move around the room when possible, establish eye contact with students seated far away, and direct comments to students seated at a distance.

Many teachers vary the seating so the same students are not always consigned to the back of the room or to make the arrangement more appropriate for particular objectives and activities. Figure 12.3 is a high school mathematics class with a seating arrangement that allows focus on teacher demonstration as well as small-group work.

Horizontal rows (like the front and back rows in Figure 12.3) share many of the advantages of the traditional row and column arrangements. Both are useful for independent seatwork and teacher, student, or media presentations; they encourage students to focus on the presenter and simplify housekeeping. Horizontal rows also permit students to work more easily in pairs. However, this is a poor arrangement for large-group discussion.

Clusters of four or circle arrangements are best for student interaction. Circles are especially useful for discussions but still allow for independent seatwork. Clusters permit students to talk, help one another, share materials, and work on group tasks. Both arrangements, however, are poor for whole-group presentations and may make class management more difficult.

The fishbowl or stack special formation, where students sit close together near the focus of attention (the back row may even be standing), should be used only for short periods of time, because it is not comfortable and can lead to discipline problems. On the other hand, the fishbowl can create a feeling of group cohesion and is helpful when the teacher wants students to watch a demonstration, brainstorm on a class problem, or see a small visual aid.

Getting Started: The First Weeks of Class

Determining a room design, rules, and procedures are first steps toward having a well-managed class, but how do effective teachers gain students' cooperation in those first critical days and weeks? One study carefully analyzed the first weeks' activities of effective and ineffective elementary teachers, and found striking differences (Emmer, Evertson, & Anderson, 1980).

FIGURE 12.3

A High School Math Classroom

This high school teacher has designed a math classroom that allows teacher presentations and demonstrations as well as small group work. By moving 3 tables, the room can be transformed into 4 horizontal rows for independent work or testing.

Source: From *Elementary Classroom Management* (2nd ed.), by C. S. Weinstein and A. J. Mignano, Jr., 1997, New York: McGraw-Hill. Copyright © 1997 by The McGraw-Hill Companies. Reprinted with permission.

Effective Managers for Elementary Students. In the effective teachers' classrooms, the very first day was well organized. Name tags were ready. There was something interesting for each child to do right away. Materials were set up. The teachers had planned carefully to avoid any last-minute tasks that might take them away from their students. These teachers dealt with the children's pressing concerns first. "Where do I put my things?" "How do I pronounce my teacher's name?" "Can I whisper to my neighbor?" "Where is the bathroom?" The effective teachers had a workable, easily understood set of rules and taught the students the most important rules right away. They taught the rules like any other subject, with lots of explanation, examples, and practice.

Connect and Extend
To your teaching
Five excellent and very practical discussions of classroom management are:

Evertson, C. M., Emmer, E. T., & Worsham, M. E. (2000). *Classroom management for elementary teachers* (5th ed.). Boston: Allyn & Bacon.

Emmer, E. T., Evertson, C. M., Clements, B. S., & Worsham, M. E. (2000). *Classroom management for secondary teachers* (5th ed.). Boston: Allyn & Bacon.

Freiberg, H. J. (Ed.). (1999). *Beyond behaviorism: Changing the classroom management paradigm.* Boston: Allyn & Bacon.

Weinstein, C. S., & Mignano, A. J., Jr. (1997). *Elementary classroom management: Lessons from research and practice.* New York: McGraw-Hill.

Weinstein, C. S. (1996). *Secondary classroom management: Lessons from research and practice.* New York: McGraw-Hill.

Throughout the first weeks, the effective managers continued to spend quite a bit of time teaching rules and procedures. Some used guided practice to teach procedures; others used rewards to shape behavior. Most taught students to respond to a bell or some other signal to gain their attention. These teachers worked with the class as a whole on enjoyable academic activities. They did not rush to get students into small groups or to get them started in readers. This whole-class work gave the teachers a better opportunity to continue monitoring all students' learning of the rules and procedures. Misbehavior was stopped quickly and firmly, but not harshly.

In the poorly managed classrooms, the first weeks were quite different. Rules were not workable; they were either too vague or very complicated. For example, one teacher made a rule that students should "be in the right place at the right time." Students were not told what this meant, so their behavior could not be guided by the rule. Neither positive nor negative behaviors had clear, consistent consequences. After students broke a rule, ineffective managers might give a vague criticism, such as "Some of my children are too noisy," or issue a warning, but not follow through with the threatened consequence.

In the poorly managed classes, procedures for accomplishing routine tasks varied from day to day and were never taught or practiced. Instead of dealing with these obvious needs, ineffective managers spent time on procedures that could have waited. For example, one teacher had the class practice for a fire drill the first day, but left unexplained other procedures that would be needed every day. Students wandered aimlessly and had to ask each other what they should be doing. Often the students talked to one another because they had nothing productive to do. Ineffective teachers frequently left the room. Many became absorbed in paperwork or in helping just one student. They had not made plans for how to deal with late-arriving students or interruptions. One ineffective manager tried to teach students to respond to a bell as a signal for attention, but later let the students ignore it. All in all, the first weeks in these classrooms were disorganized and filled with surprises for teachers and students alike.

Effective Managers for Secondary Students. What about getting started in a secondary school class? It appears that many of the differences between effective and ineffective elementary school teachers hold at the secondary level as well. Again, effective managers focus on establishing rules, procedures, and expectations on the first day of class. These standards for academic work and class behavior are clearly communicated to students and consistently enforced during the first weeks of class. Student behavior is closely monitored, and infractions of the rules are dealt with quickly. In classes with lower-ability students, work cycles are shorter; students are not required to spend long, unbroken periods on one type of activity. Instead, during each period they are moved smoothly through several different tasks. In general, effective teachers carefully follow each student's progress, so students cannot avoid work without facing consequences (Emmer & Evertson, 1982).

CHECKPOINT

Creating a Positive Learning Environment

Review

▶ Distinguish between rules and procedures.

▶ Distinguish between personal territories and interest-area spatial arrangements.

▶ Contrast the first school week of effective and ineffective classroom managers.

Apply

▶ What basic rules would you use for your students and how would you teach them?

▶ How can the physical arrangement of the room promote learning?

With all this close monitoring and consistent enforcement of the rules, you may wonder if effective secondary teachers have to be grim and humorless. Not necessarily. The effective managers in one study also smiled and joked more with their students (Moskowitz & Hayman, 1976). As any experienced teacher can tell you, there is much more to smile about when the class is cooperative. In fact, there is another requirement for getting started, one that was evident in Ken Kowalski's class—establishing a climate of trust and respect that creates a community for learning.

Creating a Learning Community

Nel Noddings (1992, 1995) has written about the need to create caring educational environments where students take more responsibility for governing their school and classroom. As we saw in Chapter 10 when we discussed the need for relatedness, students are more intrinsically motivated when they feel that their teachers care about them (Grolnick, Ryan, & Deci, 1991). Historically, however, American schools have emphasized regulating students' behavior through rules, not through relationships. This is not true in every culture, however. For example, in the book, *Learning to Teach in Two Cultures*, Shimahara and Sakai (1995) observe that the Japanese approach to classroom management emphasizes such interpersonal bonds as emotional ties, relationships, and character. Success of the Japanese system "does not depend on many rules, but on a sense of trust and interdependency between the classroom teacher and his or her students and among the students" (Shimahara & Sakai, 1995, p. 79). One approach to developing this kind of caring and mutually trusting community is David and Roger Johnson's "Three Cs" of school and classroom management.

The Three Cs of Classroom Management

The three Cs for safe and productive schools are cooperative community, constructive conflict resolution, and civic values (Johnson & Johnson, 1999). Classroom management begins by establishing a learning community based on cooperative approaches such as those described in Chapters 9 and 11. At the heart of the community is the idea of positive interdependence—individuals working together to achieve mutual goals. Constructive conflict resolution is essential in the community because conflicts are inevitable and even necessary for learning. Piaget's theory of development and the research on conceptual change teaching tell us that true learning requires cognitive conflict. And individuals trying to exist in groups will have interpersonal conflict—these can lead to learning too. Table 12.3 on page 450 shows how academic and interpersonal conflicts can be positive forces in a learning community. At the end of this chapter we will talk more about conflict resolution in schools.

The last C is civic values—the understandings and beliefs that hold the community together. Values are learned through direct teaching, modeling, literature, group discussions, and the sharing of concerns. Some teachers have a "Concerns Box" where students can put written concerns and comments. The box is opened once a week at a class meeting and the concerns are discussed. Johnson and Johnson (1999) give the example of a class meeting about respect. One student tells her classmates that she felt hurt during recess the day before because no one listened when she was trying to teach them the rules to a new game. The students discussed what it means to be respectful and why respect is important. Then the students shared personal experiences of times when they felt respected versus not respected.

TABLE 12.3 *Academic and Interpersonal Conflict and Learning*

Conflict, if handled well, can support learning. Academic conflicts can lead to critical thinking and conceptual change. Conflicts of interest are unavoidable, but can be handled so no one is the loser.

Academic Controversy	Conflicts of Interest
One person's ideas, information, theories, conclusions, and opinions are incompatible with those of another, and the two seek to reach an agreement.	The actions of one person attempting to maximize benefits prevents, blocks or interferes with another person maximizing her or his benefits.
Controversy Procedure	*Integrative (Problem-Solving) Negotiations*
Research and prepare positions	Describe wants
Present and advocate positions	Describe feelings
Refute opposing position and refute attacks on own position	Describe reasons for wants and feelings
	Take other's perspective
Reverse perspectives	Invent three optional agreements that maximize joint outcomes
Synthesize and integrate best evidence and reasoning from all sides	
	Choose one and formalize agreement

Source: From "The Three Cs of School and Classroom Management," by D. Johnson and R. Johnson, 1999, in H. J. Freiberg (Ed.), *Beyond Behaviorism: Changing the Classroom Management Paradigm* (p. 133), Boston: Allyn & Bacon. Copyright © 1999 by Allyn & Bacon. Adapted by permission.

Getting Started on Community

Here is how a 7th grade teacher described her experiences working with one English class to establish rules and procedures together (Freiberg, 1999, p. 171):

> I began with my first-period class. We started slowly, with my asking them about what it would take for the class to work for them. I then told them what it would take for the class to work for me. I was amazed at the overlap. They wanted to know up front what I expected in terms of tests, quantity and quality of work, late assignments, talking in class, and amount and how often they would have homework, where they could sit, grading and whether classroom participation counted. We talked about the best classes and the worst classes. We talked about respect and the need to respect ideas and each other, to listen to and be willing to be an active participant without [verbally] running over other people in the class or being run over. I talked about "my teacher time" and their "student time." Well, this was five months ago and I am amazed at the level of cooperation. I am well ahead of last year in the curriculum; we have class meetings once a week to see how things are going and adjust as needed. We created a classroom constitution and had a constitutional convention when we felt it needed to be changed. I didn't believe it would make a difference, the students really surprised me with their level of maturity and responsibil-

CHECKPOINT

Creating a Learning Community

Review

▶ What are Johnson and Johnson's 3 Cs of establishing a classroom community?

Apply

▶ How would you introduce the idea of community to the students you will teach?

ity and I surprised myself with my own willingness to change. This has been a great year and I am sorry to see it end and my students leave to another grade level. I am considering asking my principal to move me to eighth grade so I could have the same students again. I have been teaching for fourteen years and this has been my best year. I feel supported by my students and my students told me they feel supported by me.

Maintaining a Good Environment for Learning

A good start is just that—a beginning. Effective teachers build on this beginning. They maintain their management system by preventing problems and keeping students engaged in productive learning activities. We have discussed several ways to keep students engaged. In the chapters on motivation, for example, we considered stimulating curiosity, relating lessons to student interests, encouraging cooperative learning, establishing learning goals instead of performance goals, and having positive expectations. What else can teachers do?

Encouraging Engagement

The format of a lesson affects student involvement. In general, as teacher supervision increases, students' engaged time also increases (Emmer & Evertson, 1981). A study, for example, found that elementary students working directly with a teacher were on task 97% of the time, while students working on their own were on task only 57% of the time (Frick, 1990). This does not mean that teachers should eliminate independent work for students. It simply means that this type of activity usually requires careful monitoring.

When the task provides continuous cues for the student about what to do next, involvement will be greater. Activities with clear steps are likely to be more absorbing, since one step leads naturally to the next. When students have all the materials they need to complete a task, they tend to stay involved (Kounin & Doyle, 1975). If their curiosity is piqued, students will be motivated to continue seeking an answer. And, as you now know, students will be more engaged if they are involved in authentic tasks—activities that have connections to real life.

Of course, teachers can't supervise every student all the time or rely on curiosity. Something else must keep students working on their own. In their study of elementary and secondary teachers, Evertson, Emmer, and their colleagues found that effective class managers at both levels had well-planned systems for encouraging students to manage their own work (Evertson et al., 2000; Emmer et al., 2000). The Guidelines on page 452 are based on their findings.

Prevention Is the Best Medicine

What else can you do to maintain your management system? The ideal way to manage problems, of course, is to prevent them in the first place. In a classic study, Jacob Kounin (1970) examined classroom management by comparing effective teachers, whose classes were relatively free of problems, with ineffective teachers, whose classes were continually plagued by chaos and disruption. Observing both groups in

Connect and Extend
To your teaching
The teacher has divided the class into small groups to work on different aspects of a class assignment. In one group there is a child who is preventing the group from completing its task because of his crazy antics and remarks. How would you set up a program that would encourage the group to take responsibility for getting the student to cooperate?

GUIDELINES

Keeping Students Engaged

Make basic work requirements clear.

Examples

1. Specify and post the routine work requirements for headings, paper size, pen or pencil use, and neatness.

2. Establish and explain rules about late or incomplete work and absences. If a pattern of incomplete work begins to develop, deal with it early; speak with parents if necessary.

3. Make due dates reasonable, and stick to them unless the student has a very good excuse for lateness.

Communicate the specifics of assignments.

Examples

1. With younger students, have a routine procedure for giving assignments, such as writing them on the board in the same place each day. With older students, assignments may be dictated, posted, or given in a syllabus.

2. Remind students of upcoming assignments.

3. With complicated assignments, give students a sheet describing what to do, what resources are available, due dates, and so on. Older students should also be told your grading criteria.

4. Demonstrate how to do the assignment, do the first few questions together, or provide a sample worksheet.

Monitor work in progress.

Examples

1. When you make an assignment in class, make sure each student gets started correctly. If you check only students who raise their hands for help, you will miss those who think they know what to do but don't really understand, those who are too shy to ask for help, and those who don't plan to do the work at all.

2. Check progress periodically. In discussions, make sure everyone has a chance to respond.

Give frequent academic feedback.

Examples

1. Elementary students should get papers back the day after they are handed in.

2. Good work can be displayed in class and graded papers sent home to parents each week.

3. Students of all ages can keep records of grades, projects completed, and extra credits earned.

4. For older students, break up long-term assignments into several phases, giving feedback at each point.

In addition to teaching subjects, teachers must be capable of managing the activities of a group of people: their attention, how they move from one place to another, and how they transition from one activity to another. ▼

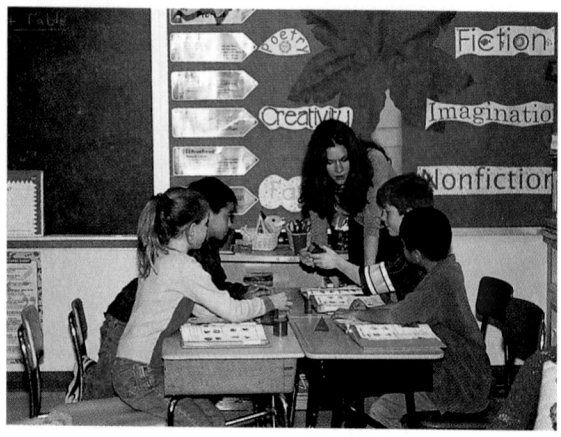

action, Kounin found that they were not very different in the way they handled discipline once problems arose. The difference was that the successful managers were much better at preventing problems. Kounin concluded that effective classroom managers were especially skilled in four areas: *"withitness," overlapping activities, group focusing,* and *movement management* (Doyle, 1977). More recent research confirms the importance of these factors (Emmer & Evertson, 1981; Evertson, 1988).

Withitness. **Withitness** means communicating to students that you are aware of everything that is happening in the classroom, that you aren't missing anything. "With-it" teachers seem to have eyes in the back of their heads. They avoid becoming absorbed or interacting with only a few students, because this encourages the rest of the class to wander. They are always scanning the room, making eye contact with individual students, so the students know they are being monitored (Brooks, 1985).

These teachers prevent minor disruptions from becoming major. They also know who instigated the problem, and they make sure the right people are dealt with. In other words, they do not make what Kounin called *timing errors* (waiting too long before intervening) or *target errors* (blaming the wrong student and letting the real perpetrators escape responsibility for their behavior).

If two problems occur at the same time, effective managers deal with the more serious one first. For example, a teacher who tells two students to stop whispering but ignores even a brief shoving match at the pencil sharpener communicates to students a lack of awareness. Students begin to believe they can get away with almost anything if they are clever (Charles, 1996).

Overlapping and Group Focus. **Overlapping** means keeping track of and supervising several activities at the same time. For example, a teacher may have to check the work of an individual and at the same time keep a small group working by saying, "Right, go on," and stop an incident in another group with a quick "look" or reminder (Burden, 1995; Charles, 1996).

Maintaining a **group focus** means keeping as many students as possible involved in appropriate class activities and avoiding narrowing in on just one or two students. All students should have something to do during a lesson. For example, the teacher might ask everyone to write the answer to a question, then call on individuals to respond while the other students compare their answers. Choral responses might be required while the teacher moves around the room to make sure everyone is participating (Charles, 1996). Some teachers have their students use small blackboards or colored cards for responding in groups. This lets the teacher check for understanding as well. For example, during a grammar lesson the teacher might say, "Everyone who thinks the answer is *have run*, hold up the red side of your card. If you think the answer is *has run*, hold up the green side" (Hunter, 1982). This is one way teachers can ensure that all students are involved and check that they all understand the material.

Movement Management. **Movement management** means keeping lessons and the group moving at an appropriate (and flexible) pace, with smooth transitions and variety. The effective teacher avoids abrupt transitions, such as announcing a new activity before gaining the students' attention or starting a new activity in the middle of something else. In these situations, one-third of the class will be doing the new activity, many will be on the old lesson, several will be asking other students what to do, some will be taking the opportunity to have a little fun, and most will be confused.

Another transition problem Kounin noted is the *slowdown*, or taking too much time to start a new activity. Sometimes teachers give too many directions. Problems also arise when teachers have students work one at a time while the rest of the class waits and watches. Charles (1985, p. 26) gives this example:

> During a science lesson the teacher began, "Row 1 may get up and get their beakers. Row 2 may get theirs. Now Row 3. Now, Row 1 may line up to put some bicarbonate of soda in their beakers. Row 2 may follow them," and so forth. When each row had obtained their bicarbonate of soda the teacher had them go row by row to add water. This left the remainder of the class sitting at their desks with no direction, doing nothing or else beginning to find something with which to entertain themselves.

A teacher who successfully demonstrates withitness, overlapping activities, group focus, and movement management tends to have a class filled with actively engaged

Withitness: According to Kounin, awareness of everything happening in a classroom.

Overlapping: Supervising several activities at once.

Group Focus: The ability to keep as many students as possible involved in activities.

Movement Management: Keeping lessons and the group moving at an appropriate (and flexible) pace, with smooth transitions and variety.

students who do not escape his or her all-seeing eye. This need not be a grim class-room. It is more likely a busy place where students are actively learning and gaining a sense of self-worth rather than misbehaving in order to get attention and achieve status.

Dealing with Discipline Problems

Connect and Extend
To the research
For a description of an extensive research project examining how teachers cope with problem behav-iors, see Brophy, J., & McCaslin, M. (1992). Teachers' reports of how they perceive and cope with prob-lem students. *Elementary School Journal, 93,* 3–68.

Being an effective manager does not mean publicly correcting every minor infraction of the rules. This kind of public attention may actually reinforce the misbehavior, as we saw in Chapter 6. Teachers who frequently correct students do not necessarily have the best behaved classes (Irving & Martin, 1982). The key is to know what is happening and what is important so you can prevent problems. Emmer and col-leagues (2000) and Levin and Nolan (2000) suggest seven simple ways to stop mis-behavior quickly, moving from least to most intrusive:

▶ *Make eye contact* with, or move closer to, the offender. Other nonverbal signals, such as pointing to the work students are supposed to be doing, might be helpful. Make sure the student actually stops the inappropriate behavior and gets back to work. If you do not, students will learn to ignore your signals.

▶ Try *verbal hints* such as "name-dropping" (simply insert the student's name into the lecture), asking the student a question, or making a humorous (not sarcastic) comment such as, "I must be hallucinating. I swear I heard someone shout out an answer, but that can't be because I haven't called on anyone yet!"

▶ You might also ask students *if they are aware* of the negative effects of their actions or send an "I message," described later in the chapter.

▶ If they are not performing a class procedure correctly, *remind the students* of the procedure and have them follow it correctly. You may need to quietly collect a toy, comb, magazine, or note that is competing with the learning activities, while privately informing the students that their possessions will be returned after class.

▶ In a calm, unhostile way, *ask the student to state the correct rule or procedure* and then to follow it. Glasser (1969) proposes three questions: "What are you doing? Is it against the rules? What should you be doing?"

▶ Tell the student in a clear, assertive, and unhostile way to *stop the misbehavior.* (Later in the chapter we will discuss assertive messages to students in more detail.) If students "talk back," simply repeat your statement.

▶ *Offer a choice.* For example, when a student continued to call out answers no matter what the teacher tried, the teacher said, "John, you have a choice. Stop calling out answers immediately and begin raising your hand to answer or move your seat to the back of the room and you and I will have a private discussion later. You decide." (Levin & Nolan, 2000, p. 177).

If you must impose penalties, the Guidelines on page 455, taken from Wein-stein and Mignano (1997, 1996), give ideas about how to do it. The examples are taken from the actual words of the expert teachers described in their book.

Special Problems with Secondary Students

Many secondary students never complete their work. Besides encouraging student responsibility, what else can teachers do to deal with this frustrating problem? Because students at this age have many assignments and teachers have many stu-

GUIDELINES

Imposing Penalties

Delay the discussion of the situation until you and the students involved are calmer and more objective.

Examples

1. Say calmly to a student, "Sit there and think about what happened. I'll talk to you in a few minutes," or, "I don't like what I just saw. Talk to me during your free period today."

2. Say, "I'm really angry about what just happened. Everybody take out journals; we are going to write about this." After a few minutes of writing, the class can discuss the incident.

Impose penalties privately.

Examples

1. Make arrangements with students privately. Stand firm in enforcing arrangements.

2. Resist the temptation to "remind" students in public that they are not keeping their side of the bargain.

3. Move close to a student who must be disciplined and speak so that only the student can hear.

After imposing a penalty, reestablish a positive relationship with the student immediately.

Examples

1. Send the student on an errand or ask him or her for help.

2. Compliment the student's work or give a real or symbolic "pat on the back" when the student's behavior warrants. Look hard for such an opportunity.

Set up a graded list of penalties that will fit many occasions.

Example

1. For not turning in homework: (1) receive reminder; (2) receive warning; (3) hand homework in before close of school day; (4) stay after school to finish work; (5) participate in a teacher-student-parent conference to develop an action plan.

---

dents, both teacher and students may lose track of what has and has not been completed. It often helps to teach students how to use a daily planner. In addition, the teacher must keep accurate records. The most important thing is to enforce the established consequences for incomplete work. Do not pass a student because you know he or she is "bright enough" to pass. Make it clear to these students that the choice is theirs: they can do the work and pass, or they can refuse to do the work and face the consequences.

There is also the problem of students who continually break the same rules, always forgetting materials, for example, or getting into fights. What should you do? Seat these students away from others who might be influenced by them. Try to catch them before they break the rules, but if rules are broken, be consistent in applying established consequences. Do not accept promises to do better next time (Levin & Nolan, 2000). Teach the students how to monitor their own behavior; some of the self-management techniques described in Chapter 6 should be helpful. Finally, remain friendly with the students. Try to catch them in

"THEY'RE TESTING YOU."

(By permission of James Warren. From Phi Delta Kappan.*)*

Connect and Extend
To your teaching

Almost every day in your 6th grade class, Rod talks out of turn and loses the reward for his group. The other group members are giving Rod a difficult time, and the parents of two students have called you to complain that the group reward system is unfair. What would you do to resolve this problem?

CHECKPOINT

Maintaining a Good Environment for Learning

Review

▶ How can teachers encourage engagement?

▶ Explain the factors identified by Kounin that prevent management problems in the classroom.

▶ Describe seven levels of intervention in misbehavior.

Apply

▶ Will you use penalties in your class when students violate rules? What kinds?

Connect and Extend
To your teaching
What is a teacher's responsibility if he or she finds out that a pupil is involved in illegal acts such as selling drugs or stealing?

a good moment so you can talk to them about something other than their rule-breaking.

A defiant, hostile student can pose serious problems. If there is an outbreak, try to get out of the situation as soon as possible; everyone loses in a public power struggle. One possibility is to give the student a chance to save face and cool down by saying, "It's your choice to cooperate or not. You can take a minute to think about it." If the student complies, the two of you can talk later about controlling the outbursts. If the student refuses to cooperate, you can tell him or her to wait in the hall until you get the class started on work, then step outside for a private talk. If the student refuses to leave, send another class member for the assistant principal. Again, follow through. If the student complies before help arrives, do not let him or her off the hook. If outbursts occur frequently, you might have a conference with the counselor, parents, or other teachers. If the problem is an irreconcilable clash of personalities, the student should be transferred to another teacher.

It sometimes is useful to keep records of the incidents by logging the student's name, words and actions, date, time, place, and teacher's response. These records may help identify patterns and can prove useful in meeting with administrators, parents, or special services personnel (Burden, 1995). Some teachers have students sign each entry to verify the incidents.

Violence or destruction of property is a difficult and potentially dangerous problem. The first step is to send for help and get the names of participants and witnesses. Then get rid of any crowd that may have gathered; an audience will only make things worse. Do not try to break up a fight without help. Make sure the school office is aware of the incident; usually the school has a policy for dealing with these situations.

⟆he Need for Communication

Communication between teacher and students is essential when problems arise. Communication is more than "teacher talks—student listens." It is more than the words exchanged between individuals. We communicate in many ways. Our actions, movements, voice tone, facial expressions, and many other nonverbal behaviors send messages to our students. Many times the messages we intend to send are not the messages our students receive.

Message Sent—Message Received

Teacher: Carl, where is your homework?
Carl: I left it in my Dad's car this morning.

Teacher: Again? You will have to bring me a note tomorrow from your father saying that you actually did the homework. No grade without the note.

Message Carl receives: I can't trust you. I need proof you did the work.

Teacher: Sit at every other desk. Put all your things under your desk. Jane and Laurel, you are sitting too close together. One of you move!

Message Jane and Laurel receive: I expect you two to cheat on this test.

A new student comes to Ms. Lincoln's kindergarten. The child is messy and unwashed. Ms. Lincoln puts her hand lightly on the girl's shoulder and says, "I'm glad you are here." Her muscles tense, and she leans away from the child.

Message student receives: I don't like you. I think you are bad.

In all interactions, a message is sent and a message is received. Sometimes teachers believe they are sending one message, but their voices, body positions, choices of words, and gestures may communicate a different message.

Students may hear the hidden message and respond to it. For example, a student may respond with hostility if she or he feels insulted by the teacher (or by another student), but may not be able to say exactly where the feeling of being insulted came from. Perhaps it was in the teacher's tone of voice, not the words actually spoken. In such cases, the teacher may feel attacked for no reason. "What did I say? All I said was. . . ." The first principle of communication is that people respond to what they *think* was said or meant, not necessarily to the speaker's intended message or actual words.

There are many exercises for practicing sending and receiving messages accurately. Students in my classes have told me about one instructor who encourages accurate communication by using the **paraphrase rule**. Before any participant, including the teacher, is allowed to respond to any other participant in a class discussion, he or she must summarize what the previous speaker said. If the summary is wrong, indicating the speaker was misunderstood, the speaker must explain again. The respondent then tries again to paraphrase. The process continues until the speaker agrees that the listener has heard the intended message.

Paraphrasing is more than a classroom exercise. It can be the first step in communicating with students. Before teachers can deal appropriately with any student problem, they must know what the real problem is. A student who says, "This book is really dumb! Why did we have to read it?" may really be saying, "The book was too difficult for me. I couldn't read it, and I feel dumb."

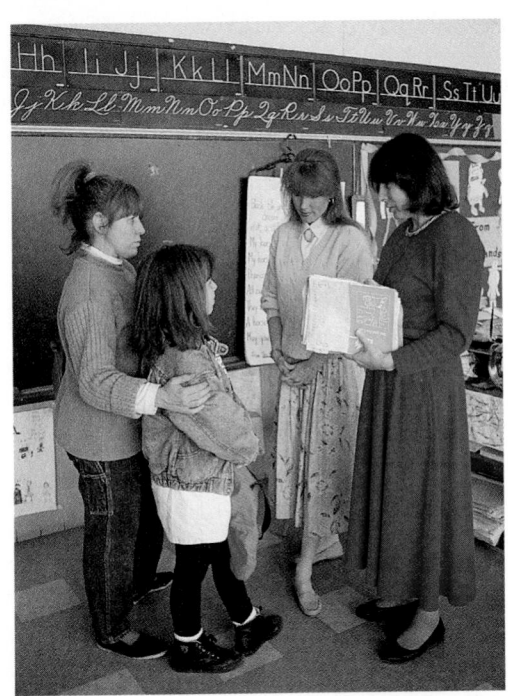

▲ *One of the challenges of managing elementary school students is to deal effectively with disruptive behavior and achieve a positive outcome. In some cases, it might be appropriate to involve a student's family.*

Diagnosis: Whose Problem Is It?

As a teacher, you may find many student behaviors unacceptable, unpleasant, or troubling. It is often difficult to stand back from these problems, take an objective look, and decide on an appropriate response. According to Thomas Gordon (1981), the key to good teacher–student relationships is determining why you are troubled by a particular behavior and whose problem it is. The teacher must begin by asking who "owns" the problem. The answer to this question is critical. If it is really the student's problem, the teacher must become a counselor and supporter,

Paraphrase Rule: Policy whereby listeners must accurately summarize what a speaker has said before being allowed to respond.

helping the student find his or her own solution. But if the teacher "owns" the problem, it is the teacher's responsibility to find a solution through problem solving with the student.

Diagnosing who owns the problem is not always straightforward. Let's look at three troubling situations to get some practice in this skill:

1. A student writes obscene words and draws sexually explicit illustrations in a school encyclopedia.
2. A student tells you that his parents had a bad fight and he hates his father.
3. A student quietly reads a newspaper in the back of the room.

Why are these behaviors troubling? If you cannot accept the student's behavior because it has a serious effect on you as a teacher—if you are blocked from reaching your goals by the student's action—then *you* own the problem. It is your responsibility to confront the student and seek a solution. A teacher-owned problem appears to be present in the first situation described above—the young pornographer—because teaching materials are damaged.

If you feel annoyed by the behavior because it is getting in the student's own way or because you are embarrassed for the child, but the behavior does not directly interfere with your teaching, then it is probably the student's problem. The test question is: Does this student's action tangibly affect you or prevent you from fulfilling your role as a teacher? The student who hates his father would not prevent you from teaching, even though you might wish the student felt differently. The problem is really the student's, and he must find his own solution.

Situation 3 is more difficult to diagnose. I have had lengthy debates in my class about whose problem it is when a student reads a newspaper in class. One argument is that the teacher is not interfered with in any way, so it is the student's problem. Another argument is that teachers might find reading the paper distracting during a lecture, so it is their problem, and they must find a solution. In a gray area such as this, the answer probably depends on how the teacher actually experiences the student's behavior. Having decided who owns the problem, it is time to act.

Counseling: The Student's Problem

Let's pick up the situation in which the student found the reading assignment "dumb." How might a teacher handle this positively?

Student: This book is really dumb! Why did we have to read it?
Teacher: You're pretty upset. This seemed like a worthless assignment to you. [Teacher paraphrases the student's statement, trying to hear the emotions as well as the words.]
Student: Yeah! Well, I guess it was worthless. I mean, I don't know if it was. I couldn't exactly read it.
Teacher: It was just too hard to read, and that bothers you.
Student: Sure, I felt really dumb. I know I can write a good report, but not with a book this tough.
Teacher: I think I can give you some hints that will make the book easier to understand. Can you see me after school today?
Student: Okay.

Empathetic Listening: Hearing the intent and emotions behind what another says and reflecting them back by paraphrasing.

Here the teacher used **empathetic listening** to allow the student to find a solution. (As you can see, this approach relies heavily on paraphrasing.) By trying to hear the student and by avoiding the tendency to jump in too quickly with advice, solutions, criticisms, reprimands, or interrogations, the teacher keeps the communication lines open. Here are a few *unhelpful* responses the teacher might have made:

▶ I chose the book because it is the best example of the author's style in our library. You will need to have read it before your English II class next year. (The teacher justifies the choice; this prevents the student from admitting that this "important" assignment is too difficult.)

▶ Did you really read it? I bet you didn't do the work, and now you want out of the assignment. (The teacher accuses; the student hears, "The teacher doesn't trust me!" and must either defend herself or himself or accept the teacher's view.)

▶ Your job is to read the book, not ask me why. I know what's best. (The teacher pulls rank, and the student hears, "You can't possibly decide what is good for you!" The student can rebel or passively accept the teacher's judgment.)

Empathetic, active listening can be a helpful response when students bring problems to you. You must reflect back to the student what you hear him or her saying. This reflection is more than a parroting of the student's words; it should capture the emotions, intent, and meaning behind them. Sokolove, Garrett, Sadker, and Sadker (1986, p. 241) have summarized the components of active listening: (1) blocking out external stimuli; (2) attending carefully to both the verbal and nonverbal messages; (3) differentiating between the intellectual and the emotional content of the message; and (4) making inferences regarding the speaker's feelings.

When students realize they really have been heard and not evaluated negatively for what they have said or felt, they feel freer to trust the teacher and to talk more openly. Sometimes the true problem surfaces later in the conversation.

Confrontation and Assertive Discipline

Now let's assume a student is doing something that actively interferes with teaching. The teacher decides the student must stop. The problem is the teacher's. Confrontation, not counseling, is required.

"I" Messages. Gordon (1981) recommends sending an **"I" message** in order to intervene and change a student's behavior. Basically, this means telling a student in a straightforward, assertive, and nonjudgmental way what she or he is doing, how it affects you as a teacher, and how you feel about it. The student is then free to change voluntarily, and often does so. Here are two "I" messages:

▶ If you leave your book bags in the aisles, I might trip and hurt myself.

▶ When you all call out, I can't concentrate on each answer, and I'm frustrated.

Assertive Discipline. Lee and Marlene Canter (1992; Canter, 1989) suggest other approaches for dealing with a teacher-owned problem. They call their method **assertive discipline.** Teachers are assertive when they make their expectations clear and follow through with established consequences. Students then have a straightforward choice: they can follow the rules or accept the consequences. Many teachers are ineffective with students because they are either wishy-washy and passive or hostile and aggressive.

The *passive style* can take several forms. Instead of telling the student directly what to do, the teacher tells, or often asks, the student to *try* or to *think about* the

Connect and Extend
To professional debates
Read Canter, L. (1989). Assertive discipline—More than names on the board and marbles in a jar. *Phi Delta Kappan, 71*(1) 41–56. Evaluate Canter's claims for his "assertive discipline" approach. What are the similarities between the criticisms of behavioral approaches to learning and the criticisms of assertive discipline? A special feature on discipline can be found in the 1989 issue of *Educational Leadership, 46*(6) 72–83. This feature presents a debate between supporters and critics of assertive discipline.

"I" Message: Clear, nonaccusatory statement of how something is affecting you.

Assertive Discipline: Clear, firm, unhostile response style.

appropriate action. The passive teacher might comment on the problem behavior without actually telling the child what to do differently: "Why are you doing that? Don't you know the rules?" or "Sam, are you disturbing the class?" Or teachers may clearly state what should happen, but never follow through with the established consequences, giving the students "one more chance" every time. Finally, teachers may ignore behavior that should receive a response or may wait too long before responding.

A *hostile response style* involves different mistakes. Teachers may make "you" statements that condemn the student without stating clearly what the student should be doing: "You should be ashamed of the way you're behaving!" or "You never listen!" or "You are acting like a baby!" Teachers may also threaten students angrily but follow through too seldom, perhaps because the threats are too vague—"You'll be very sorry you did that when I get through with you!"—or too severe. For example, a teacher tells a student in a physical education class that he will have to "sit on the bench for *three weeks*." A few days later the team is short one member and the teacher lets the student play, never returning him to the bench to complete the three-week sentence. Often a teacher who has been passive becomes hostile and explodes when students persist in misbehaving.

In contrast with both the passive and hostile styles, an *assertive response* communicates to the students that you care too much about them and the process of learning to allow inappropriate behavior to persist. Assertive teachers clearly state what they expect. To be most effective, the teachers often look into a student's eyes when speaking and address the student by name. Assertive teachers' voices are calm, firm, and confident. They are not sidetracked by accusations such as "You just don't understand!" or "You don't like me!" Assertive teachers do not get into a debate about the fairness of the rules. They expect changes, not promises or apologies.

Even though many teachers and school administrators have given enthusiastic testimonies about the assertive discipline approach, some educators and psychologists question its effectiveness. The Point/Counterpoint further explores the issue.

Confrontations and Negotiations. If "I" messages or assertive responses fail and a student persists in misbehaving, teacher and student are in a conflict. Several pitfalls now loom. The two individuals become less able to perceive each other's behavior accurately. Research has shown that the angrier you get with another person, the more you see the other as the villain and yourself as an innocent victim. Because you feel the other person is in the wrong, and he or she feels just as strongly that the conflict is all your fault, very little mutual trust is possible. A cooperative solution to the problem is almost impossible. In fact, by the time the discussion has gone on a few minutes, the original problem is lost in a sea of charges, countercharges, and self-defense (Johnson & Johnson, 1994).

There are three methods of resolving a conflict between teacher and student. One is for the teacher to impose a solution. This may be necessary during an emergency, as when a defiant student refuses to go to the hall to discuss a public outbreak, but it is not a good solution for most conflicts. The second method is for the teacher to give in to the student's demands. You might be convinced by a particularly compelling student argument, but again, this should be used sparingly. It is generally a bad idea to be talked out of a position, unless the position was wrong in the first place. Problems arise when either the teacher or the student gives in completely.

Does Assertive Discipline Work?

Lee Canter, the developer of "assertive discipline," describes his observations of effective teachers:

I found that, above all, the master teachers were assertive; that is they taught students how to behave. They established clear rules for the classroom, they communicated those rules to the students, and they taught students how to follow them. (1989, p. 58)

Is assertive discipline effective? There are strong opinions both against and in favor of the approach, as you will see. Researchers are skeptical, but some practitioners are committed to assertive discipline.

▶ POINT *Research results do not support assertive discipline.*

In an article entitled "What research really shows about Assertive Discipline," Gary Render, Je Neil Padilla, and H. Mark Krank (1989) note that very little unbiased information is available about the effectiveness of this approach. Even though reports claim that 500,000 people have been trained in assertive discipline, Render and his colleagues were able to find only 16 systematic studies of assertive discipline. Their analysis of these studies led them to conclude that:

The claims made by Canter (1988) . . . are simply not supported by the existing and available literature. We would agree that Assertive Discipline could be helpful in severe cases where stu-

dents are behaving inappropriately more than 96% of the time, as in the study by Mandlebaum et al. (1983). We would also argue that teachers such as the one in that study would benefit from any intervention. However, we can find no evidence that Assertive Discipline is an effective approach deserving schoolwide or district-wide adoption. (p. 72)

A second criticism of assertive discipline is that while it may stop misbehavior in the short run, the long-term effects on students are damaging. Richard Curwin and Allen Mendler (1988) remind teachers that classroom management systems not only manage behavior, they also teach students lessons about their own self-worth, their ability to act responsibly and solve problems, how much control they have over their own lives, and how to use that control. What lessons are taught by systems such as assertive discipline? "If Richard shapes up after the third mark on the chalkboard because the fourth means a call home to an abusive parent, did the program improve his self-control, or did it simply transfer the inner turmoil of a child caught in a dysfunctional family?" (Curwin & Mendler, 1988, p. 68). This concern is echoed by John Covaleskie (1992): "What helps children become moral is not knowledge of the rules, or even obedience to the rules, but discussions about the reasons for acting in certain ways (p. 56).

◀ COUNTERPOINT *Practitioners know that assertive discipline works.*

In response to the assertion by Render and his colleagues that research does not support assertive discipline, Sammie McCormack (1989) says, "The decision to implement a program should be based on many factors, in addition to research; from a practitioner's standpoint, Assertive Discipline works" (p. 77). McCormack reports the reactions of more than 8,700 teachers from four school districts and a confederation of schools in Oregon. In these schools, 78 to 99% of the teachers saw improvements in student behavior as a consequence of using assertive discipline. McCormack does not explain how these particular samples were selected or if teachers in other schools had different reactions.

In response to Curwin and Mendler's (1988) concerns that classroom management models such as assertive discipline may undermine students' self-worth and sense of responsibility, Lee Canter (1988) notes that several studies have found improvements in both teachers' and students' self-concepts after the introduction of assertive discipline. Further, Canter states that the basis of assertive discipline is giving students choices and that it is through making choices and accepting the consequences that students learn about responsibility.

Gordon recommends a third approach, which he calls the "no-lose method." Here the needs of both the teacher and the students are taken into account in the solution. No one person is expected to give in completely; all participants retain respect for themselves and each other. The no-lose method is a six-step, problem-solving strategy:

1. *Define the problem.* What exactly are the behaviors involved? What does each person want? (Use active listening to help students pinpoint the real problem.)

2. *Generate many possible solutions.* Brainstorm, but remember, don't allow any evaluations of ideas yet.

3. *Evaluate each solution.* Any participant may veto any idea. If no solutions are found to be acceptable, brainstorm again.

4. *Make a decision.* Choose one solution through consensus—no voting. In the end, everyone must be satisfied with the solution.

5. *Determine how to implement the solution.* What will be needed? Who will be responsible for each task? What is the timetable?

6. *Evaluate the success of the solution.* After trying the solution for a while, ask, "Are we satisfied with our decision? How well is it working? Should we make some changes?"

Many of the conflicts in classrooms are between students. These can be important learning experiences for all concerned.

Student Conflicts and Confrontations

Handling conflict is difficult for most of us—for young people it can be even harder. Given the public's concern about violence in schools, it is surprising how little we know about conflicts among students (Rose & Gallup, 1999; Johnson, Johnson, Dudley, Ward, & Magnuson, 1995). There is some evidence that in elementary schools, conflicts most often center on disputes over resources (school supplies, computers, athletic equipment, or toys) and over preferences (which activity to do first or what game to play). Over twenty years ago, a large study of more than 8,000 junior and senior high students and 500 faculty from three major cities concluded that 90% of the conflicts among students are resolved in destructive ways or never resolved at all (DeCecco & Richards, 1974). The few studies since that time have reached similar conclusions. Avoidance, force, and threats seem to be the major strategies for dealing with conflict (Johnson et al., 1995).

Conflicts: Goals and Needs. When people are in conflict, they have two major concerns. The first is to satisfy their needs and meet their goals. This usually is the source of the conflict—the needs or goals of one person or group clash with the needs or goals of others. The second concern is to maintain an appropriate relationship with the other party in the conflict. Both of these concerns can be placed on a continuum from not very important to critically important. Different strategies are called for, depending on the importance of the goals and the relationships, as shown in Table 12.4 (Johnson & Johnson, 1994).

The message here is that different strategies make sense in different situations. Without guidance and practice, however, students may always use the same strategy—they may not be able to fit strategy to situation.

Violence in the Schools. "Interpersonal violence among youth is a growing problem in many communities and schools across this nation" (Lowry, Sleet, Duncan, Powell, & Kolbe, 1995, p. 7). Young people ages 12 to 24 are the most

Connect and Extend
To the research

Parks, C. P. (1995). Gang behavior in the schools: Myth or reality? *Educational Psychology Review, 7,* 41–68.

Abstract: The purpose of this review is to explore the nature of gang behavior in U.S. schools, with a particular focus on the extent to which such behavior affects or exacerbates the larger issue of school violence. An unanticipated finding was the absence of strong empirical support for school gang violence. The evidence does show youth gangs have changed dramatically over the last several decades and have become more violent, largely due to drugs and weapons-carrying. One major impact of this violence on schools has been the dissolving of the school as the "neutral zone," where gang activity ceased. Thus, it appears that the similar "turf" issues of the street gangs have infiltrated the schools. The review explores problems related to school gang violence definitions and literature, trends in school-related gang activity, reasons for gang membership, at-risk youth, and proposed strategies for ameliorating the problem.

TABLE 12.4 Strategies for Managing Conflict

Different situations call for different strategies. But any strategy can be used inappropriately. For example, withdrawing may be used inappropriately to avoid all conflict or appropriately to postpone confrontation until constructive discussions are possible.

Goal Important?	Relationship Important?	Strategy	Appropriate Uses	Inappropriate Uses
No	No	Withdraw	Postpone until constructive discussion is possible	Avoid conflict, hide
No	Yes	Smooth/Give in	When other's needs are more important	Give in just to be liked
Yes	No	Force	Seldom appropriate, perhaps when others' safety is your responsibility	To intimidate, win at all costs, overpower
Yes	Yes	Confront	Resolve conflict—strengthen relationship—protect both parties' goals	Generally appropriate
Moderately	Moderately	Compromise	When mutual sacrifices are required for the common good	When confrontation could satisfy both parties' goals

likely victims of nonfatal violence in American society, and many of these attacks happen on school property. This problem has many causes; it is a challenge for every element of society. What can the schools do?

One answer is prevention. Some Chicano gang members in Chicago reported that they turned to gang activities when their teachers insulted them, called them names, humiliated them publicly, belittled their culture, ignored them in class, or blamed all negative incidents on particular students. The students reported joining gangs for security and to escape teachers who treated them badly or expected little of them because they were Latino (Padilla, 1992; Parks, 1995). Another two-year study in Ohio found that gang members respected teachers who insisted on academic performance in a caring way (Huff, 1989). I once asked a gifted educator in an urban New Jersey high school which teachers were most effective with the really tough students. He said there are two kinds, teachers who can't be intimidated or fooled and expect their students to learn, and teachers who really care about the students. When I asked, "Which kind are you?" he answered "Both!"

Besides prevention, schools can also establish mentoring programs, conflict resolution training, social skills training, more relevant curricula, and parent and community involvement programs (Padilla, 1992; Parks, 1995). One intervention that seems to be helpful is peer mediation.

Peer Mediation. David Johnson and his colleagues (1995) provided conflict resolution training to 227 students in 2nd through 5th grade. Students learned a five-step negotiating strategy:

1. *Jointly define the conflict.* Separate the person from the problem and the actions involved, avoid win–lose thinking, and get both parties' goals clear.

2. *Exchange positions and interests.* Present a tentative proposal and make a case for it; listen to the other person's proposal and feelings; and stay flexible and cooperative.

3. *Reverse perspectives.* See the situation from the other person's point of view and reverse roles and argue for that perspective.

4. *Invent at least three agreements that allow mutual gain.* Brainstorm, focus on goals, think creatively, and make sure everyone has power to invent solutions.

5. *Reach an integrative agreement.* Make sure both sets of goals are met. If all else fails, flip a coin, take turns, or call in a third party—a mediator.

In addition to learning conflict resolution, all students in Johnson and Johnson's study were trained in mediation strategies. The role of the mediator was rotated—every day the teacher chose two students to be the class mediators and to wear the mediators' T-shirts. Johnson and his colleagues found that students learned the conflict resolution and mediation strategies and used them successfully, both in school and at home, to handle conflicts in a more productive way. For details of the strategies, see Johnson and Johnson (1994), Miller, (1994), or Smith (1993).

Peer mediation has also been successful with older students and those with serious problems (Sanchez & Anderson, 1990). In one program, selected gang members were given mediation training, then all members were invited to participate voluntarily in the mediation process, supervised by school counselors. Strict rules governed the process leading to written agreements signed by gang representatives. Sanchez and Anderson (1990) found that gang violence in the school was reduced to a bare minimum—"The magic of the mediation process was communication" (p. 56).

Respect and Protect. One system that has been developed to combat violence in the schools is Respect and Protect from the Johnson Institute, Minneapolis, Minnesota. The program is founded on five ideas: First, everyone is obliged to respect and protect the rights of others. Second, violence is not acceptable. Third, the program targets the violence-enabling behaviors of staff, students, and parents such as denying, rationalizing, justifying, or blaming others for violence. Fourth, there is a clear definition of what constitutes violence that distinguishes two kinds of violence—bully/victim violence and violence that arises from normal conflicts. Finally, the program has both adult-centered prevention that improves the school climate and student-centered interventions that give students choices and clear consequences (Rembolt, 1998). Table 12.5 gives an overview of the levels of choices and consequences.

Connect and Extend
To the research

Johnson, D. W., Johnson, R., Dudley, B., Ward, M., & Magnuson, D. (1995). The impact of peer mediation training on the management of school and home conflicts. *American Educational Research Journal, 32,* 829–844.

Abstract: A peer mediation program in a midwestern, suburban school was examined to determine the types of conflicts that occurred, the strategies students used to resolve their conflicts, and the types of resolutions in both school and home settings. The impact of the peer mediation program on the strategies used to manage conflicts and the resolutions of conflicts was also examined. A significant difference between the types of conflict occurring in the school and in the home was found. The training had significant impact on the strategies students used and the resulting resolutions.

TABLE 12.5   *Respect and Protect*

This table shows measured responses to each level of violence.

Overview of Choices, Consequences, and Contracts Intervention Process

Violence Level	Level One	Level Two	Level Three	Level Four	Level Five
Violation	Rule Violation (Minor infraction)	Misuse of Power (Repeat violation)	Abuse of Power (Serious)	Continued Abuse (Severe)	Pathology (Intractable)
Staff Action	Confront behavior	Confront behavior	Confront behavior	Confront behavior	Confront behavior
	Stop violence	Stop violence	Stop violence	Stop violence	Stop violence
	Deal with problem	Refer to office	Refer to office	Refer to office	Refer to office
	File intervention report	File intervention report	File intervention report	File intervention report	File intervention report
	Review No Violence rule	Try to assess type of conflict	Try to assess type of conflict	Assess type of conflict	Follow psycho-social recommendations
	Suggest anger management, conflict resolution, peer mediation, or class meeting	Evaluate for talk with parent	Parent conference	Do psycho-social evaluation	Hold parent conference
			Suggest parenting program	Hold parent conference	Mandate parenting program
				Mandate parenting program	Suggest intensive therapy or treatment for student
				Suggest family counseling	
Student Consequences	Review of activity for violence	Office referral	Office referral	Office referral	Office referral
	Parent notified (optional)	Life Skills worksheet	Parent notified	Parent notified	Parent notified
	Restitution	Parent notified	Minimum time-out	Maximum time-out	Maximum time-out
	Legal action	Restricted until worksheet finished	Violence Group	Violence Group	Placement into an alternative setting
		Restitution	Anger management	Reconnections	Restitution
		Legal action	Connections	Restitution	Legal action
			Empowerment	Legal action	
			Restitution		
			Legal action		
Contracts*	Verbal Promise	Simple Contract	Turf Contract I	Turf Contract II	Bottom-Line Contract

Students are placed at Levels 1–5 depending on the frequency and severity of their violent behavior. Students may stay at a particular level as the situation warrants. Any violent act that is racial, sexual, involves physical fighting, or is committed against staff results in the student being placed immediately at Level 3 or higher. The program manual provides lists of behaviors that correlate with each level of violence.

Source: From "Making Violence Unacceptable," by C. Rembolt, 1998, *Educational Leadership,* 56(1), p. 36. Copyright © 1998 by *Educational Leadership.* Adapted with permission.

*See source for a complete description of the different contracts.

Communicating with Families about Classroom Management

As we have seen throughout this book, families are important partners in education. This statement applies to classroom management as well. When parents and teachers share the same expectations and support each other, they can create a more positive classroom environment and more time for learning. The Family and Community Partnerships Guidelines give ideas for working with families and the community.

FAMILY AND COMMUNITY PARTNERSHIPS

Classroom Management

Make sure families know the expectations and rules of your class and school.

Examples

1. At a Family Fun Night, have your students do skits showing the rules—how to follow them and what breaking them "looks like" and "sounds like."

2. Make a poster for the refrigerator at home that describes, in a light way, the most important rules and expectations.

3. For older students, give families a list of due dates for the major assignments, along with tips about how to encourage quality work by pacing the effort—avoiding last minute panic.

4. Communicate in appropriate ways—use the family's first language when possible. Tailor messages to the reading level of the home.

Make families partners in recognizing good citizenship.

Examples

1. Send positive notes home when students, especially students who have had trouble with classroom management, work well in the classroom.

2. Give ideas for ways any family, even those with few economic resources, can celebrate accom-plishment—a favorite food; the chance to choose a video to rent; a comment to a special person such as an aunt, grandparent, or minister; the chance to read to a younger sibling.

Identify talents in the community to help build a learning environment in your class.

Examples

1. Have students write letters to carpet and furniture stores asking for donations of remnants to carpet a reading corner.

2. Find family members who can build shelves or room dividers, paint, sew, laminate manipulatives, write stories, repot plants, or network computers.

3. Contact businesses for donations of computers, printers, or other equipment.

Seek cooperation from families when behavior problems arise.

Examples

1. Talk to families over the phone or in their home. Keep good records about the problem behavior.

2. Listen to family members and solve problems with them.

Summary

The Need for Organization

What are the challenges of classroom management?

Classrooms are by nature multidimensional, full of simultaneous activities, fast-paced and immediate, unpredictable, public, and affected by the history of students' and teachers' actions. A manager must juggle all these elements every day. Productive classroom activity requires students' cooperation. Maintaining cooperation is different for each age group. Young students are learning how to "go to school" and need to learn the general procedures of school. Older students need to learn the specifics required for working in different subjects. Working with adolescents requires teachers to understand the power of the adolescent peer group.

What are the goals of good classroom management?

The goals of effective classroom management are to make ample time for learning; improve the quality of time use by keeping students actively engaged; make sure participation structures are clear, straightforward, and consistently signaled; and encourage student self-management, self-control, and responsibility.

Creating a Positive Learning Environment

Distinguish between rules and procedures.

The most effective teachers set rules and establish procedures for handling predictable problems. Rules are the specific dos and don'ts of classroom life. They usually are written down or posted. Procedures cover administrative tasks, student movement, housekeeping, routines for running lessons, interactions between students and teachers, and interactions among students. Rules can be written in terms of rights and students may benefit from participating in establishing these rules.

Consequences should be established for following and breaking the rules and procedures so that the teacher and the students know what will happen.

Distinguish between personal territories and interest-area spatial arrangements.

There are two basic kinds of spatial organization, territorial (the traditional classroom arrangement) and functional (dividing space into interest or work areas). Flexibility is often the key. Access to materials, convenience, privacy when needed, ease of supervision, and a willingness to reevaluate plans are important considerations in the teacher's choice of physical arrangements.

Contrast the first school week of effective and ineffective classroom managers.

Effective classroom managers spent the first days of class teaching basic rules and procedures. Students were occupied with organized, enjoyable activities and learned to function cooperatively in the group. Quick, firm, clear, and consistent responses to infractions of the rules characterized effective teachers. Materials were set up. The teachers had planned carefully to avoid any last-minute tasks that might have taken them away from their students. These teachers dealt with the children's pressing concerns first. They had a workable, easily understood set of rules and taught the students the most important rules right away. They taught the rules like any other subject, with lots of explanation, examples, and practice.

Creating a Learning Community

What are Johnson and Johnson's three Cs of establishing a classroom community?

The three Cs are cooperative community, constructive conflict resolution, and civic values. Classroom management begins by establishing a community based on cooperative learning. At the heart of the community is the idea of positive interdependence—individuals working together to achieve mutual goals. Constructive conflict resolution is essential in the community because conflicts are inevitable and even necessary for learning. The last C is civic values—the understandings and beliefs that hold the community together. Values are learned through direct teaching, modeling, literature, group discussions, and the sharing of concerns.

Maintaining a Good Environment for Learning

How can teachers encourage engagement?

The format of a lesson affects student involvement. In general, as teacher supervision increases, students' engaged time also increases. When the task provides continuous cues for the student about what to do next, involvement will be greater. Activities with clear steps are likely to be more absorbing, because one step leads naturally to the next. Making work requirements clear and specific, providing needed materials, and monitoring activities all add to engagement.

Explain the factors identified by Kounin that prevent management problems in the classroom.

To create a positive environment and prevent problems, teachers must take individual differences into account, maintain student motivation, and reinforce positive behavior. Successful problem preventers are skilled in four areas described by Kounin: "withitness," overlapping, group focusing, and movement management. When penalties have to be imposed, teachers should impose them calmly and privately.

Describe seven levels of intervention in misbehavior.

Teachers can first make eye contact with the student or use other nonverbal signals, then try verbal hints such as simply inserting the student's name into the lecture. Next the teacher asks if the offender is aware of the negative effects of the actions, then reminds the student of the procedure and has her or him follow it correctly. If this does not work, the teacher can ask the student to state the correct rule or procedure and then to follow it, and then moves to telling the student in a clear, assertive, and unhostile way to stop the misbehavior. If this fails too, the teacher can offer a choice—stop the behavior or meet privately to work out the consequences.

The Need for Communication

What is meant by "empathetic listening"?

Communication between teacher and student is essential when problems arise. All interactions between people, even silence or neglect, communicate some meaning. Empathetic, active listening can be a helpful response when students bring problems to teachers. Teachers must reflect back to the students what they hear them saying. This reflection is more than a parroting of words; it should capture the emotions, intent, and meaning behind them.

Distinguish among assertive, passive, and hostile response styles.

The *passive style* can take several forms. Instead of telling the student directly what to do, the teacher simply comments on the behavior, asks the student to *think about* the appropriate action, or threatens but never follows through. In a *hostile response style*, teachers may make "you" statements that condemn the student without stating clearly what the student should be doing. An *assertive response* communicates to the students that the teacher cares too much about them and the process of learning to allow inappropriate behavior to persist. Assertive teachers clearly state what they expect.

What are some options for dealing with student–student and student–teacher conflict?

Students need guidance in resolving conflicts. Different strategies are useful, depending on whether the goal, the relationship, or both are important to those experiencing conflict. It can help to reverse roles and see the situation through the eyes of the other. In dealing with serious problems, prevention and peer mediation might be useful. No matter what the situation, the cooperation of families can help to create a positive learning environment in the classroom and school.

Key Terms

Becoming a Professional

Reflecting on the Chapter

Can you apply the ideas from this chapter on creating learning environments to solve the following problems of practice?

Preschool and Kindergarten

- Your class is larger than ever this year, and it is very difficult to get everyone dressed for play outside. How would you handle the situation?

Elementary and Middle School

- It takes your class 15 minutes to settle down each morning and begin work. What would you do?

- A few students in your class always seem to be out of step with the rest of the class. They call out answers when they shouldn't, interrupt others, and get up and walk around when they should be seated and working. What would you do?

Junior High and High School

- You tell a student to put away a CD player, and she says, "Try and make me!" What would you do?

- One of your students who is bright and able has stopped doing homework. What would you do?

Certification Test Requirements

- Be familiar with Kounin's terms of *"withitness," overlapping activities, group focusing,* and *movement management*.

- Know the basic room arrangements of rows, circles, clusters, and horseshoes and what activities each is best suited for.

- Understand a range of penalties for minor to major misbehaviors.

- Be familiar with alternatives for communicating with students such as empathetic listening, "I" messages, and problem solving.

Your Teaching Portfolio

Think about your philosophy of teaching, a question you will be asked at most job interviews. What is your philosophy of classroom management? What rules will you set and how will you establish them? (Consult the Guidelines for ideas.)

Add some ideas for Parent Involvement from this chapter to your *Portfolio*.

Teaching Resources

Adapt the rules on pages 441–442 for students you will teach.

Add the floorplans from Figures 12.2 and 12.3 to your **Teaching Resources** file.

Add Table 12.5 on graduated responses to school violence to your **Teaching Resources** file.

What Would They Do?

Here is how some practicing teachers responded to the teaching situation presented at the beginning of this chapter about bringing together a class with many conflicts and cliques.

MARY FRANCES DONOHOE

Fifth Grade Teacher
Lawton Chiles Elementary, Gainesville, Florida

Students must learn to respect themselves and others. Respect should be taught, modeled, and practiced throughout the school year. A short daily activity that engages students in reflecting, talking about, and practicing respect constantly reinforces this concept. At the end of each week, students are asked to nominate a citizen of the week. They should give reasons why they have nominated this person and the teacher should respond with positive comments. Students can cast a secret ballot, or the teacher may decide based on his or her observation. The citizen of the week is announced at the end of the day, her name is placed on a recognition board, and she is given a reward commensurate with age. Middle school students like to receive certificates excusing them from a homework assignment.

For example, the allegory *The Terrible Things*, by Eve Bunting, stimulates students' thinking about and understanding prejudice. Early in the school year, I read this to students and encourage them to respond by writing individually, sharing with others at their table, and finally with a whole class discussion.

Each week a quote regarding respect is presented. A short daily activity serves as a reminder that we must respect ourselves and others.

THOMAS W. NEWKIRK

Eighth Grade Teacher
Hamilton Heights Middle School, Arcadia, Indiana

The members of the class need lessons that both celebrate their differences and recognize their similarities. Assigning students to homogeneous groups to report to the class about their cultures may eliminate some misconceptions students have. Assigning students to heterogeneous groups may encourage them to work with people from "outside." Introducing the class to E. L. Konigsburg's *The View from Saturday*, as well as to other notable examples of young adult literature could provide topics for class discussion and could help students understand the contributions each member of the class has to offer. Hopefully these activities would reduce the tension in the classroom and would eliminate the audience for Clarise's ethnic jokes. Certainly Clarise cannot be allowed to make the class uncomfortable for anyone.

The expertise of the special needs instuctors and of the guidance counselors would be needed to help me understand Clarise as well as the boy with language and hearing difficulties. The more I understand the backgrounds of my students, the more able I am to create a classroom where everyone has a role to play.

ANN SANDE

Third Grade Teacher
Henry Viscardi School, Albertson, New York

In order to break down the barriers separating ethnic groups I would assign two children from different groups to perform a desirable task. It might be working together to find information on the computer's encyclopedia or the Internet and reporting it back to the class, or preparing materials for the class science experiments. It would depend on the grade level and the interests of the group. I would assure that the task was one in which the children would meet success together. This is time-consuming but must be done repeatedly with different students in a variety of situations. The children need to "see" each other in new ways and to learn to appreciate each other's strengths and talents beyond preconceived notions.

I would do a theme relating to a group that has suffered injustice. I would allow choice within a predetermined list of topics. One might be a study of the problems of the physically disabled in terms of access or discrimination. Hopefully the students would be able to draw comparisons between the group being studied and other ethnic groups who suffer discrimination and to see the experiences and challenges that each group has in common.

Modeling behavior is critical. When a group of students is speaking in another language and seemingly laughing at me I would "call them on it." I would express my dislike of the behavior in a firm manner and reiterate that it is unacceptable within our class community. By doing so, it gives the students another way and the appropriate language to deal with the objectionable behavior displayed by Clarise. I might also suggest that, as a fun activity, the entire class try to learn a language that is not part of the curriculum; we might learn some American Sign Language together.

STEVEN P. RUDE

Guidance Counselor
John C. Fremont High School, Los Angeles, California

I would request that the school psychologist or special education teacher come to my class to prepare the class for the arrival of their new fellow students. I would also encourage the students with disabilities to explain their own individual differences in their own way. There are many classroom activities that encourage students to explore and acknowledge their own differences, whether it be the color of their skin or the type of disability they possess. I would expect to review the Individual Education Plan for each of the students involved in the transition. Also, it would be helpful to know what behavior interventions work for the emotionally disturbed child and what teaching methods are most effective for the student with cerebral palsy. I would speak with the parents of these children to explore their expectations and past experiences in inclusive settings. There would also need to be teacher's aides available to help the special education students and to assist in communicating with the children who do not speak English. The inclusion of special education students into the classroom is a challenge, but it can ultimately encourage acceptance across all lines, including ethnicities and exceptionalities.

Teaching for Learning

I *n the first chapter of this book I asked you to list the characteris-*
tics of those teachers you found truly outstanding. Consider what
you now know about student learning and suggest why the teacher char-
acteristics you listed might promote learning.

Much of this text has been about learning and learners, with most of
Chapter 9 focused on student-centered teaching strategies. In this chapter
we focus on teachers—their decisions, plans, knowledge, and actions. We
look first at how teachers plan, including how to use taxonomies of learning objectives or themes as a basis for planning. With a sense of how to set
goals and make plans, we move to a consideration of some general teacher-
centered strategies: lecturing, seatwork, homework, questioning, recitation,
and group discussion.

What else do we know about teachers? Are there particular characteristics that distinguish effective from ineffective teachers? Research on whole-
class teaching points to the importance of several factors and we will explore
them as well as the elements of effective teaching in inclusive classrooms.

In the final section of this chapter, we will focus on successful teaching for different subjects—reading, writing, mathematics, and science.
Educational psychologists have studied how people learn these subjects
and identified implications for teaching.

By the time you have completed this chapter you should be able to:

▶ Write instructional objectives for your students using different taxonomies.
▶ Describe situations in which each of the following formats would be
  most appropriate: lecture, seatwork and homework, questioning, and
  group discussion.
▶ Describe a number of characteristics that effective teachers seem to
  share.
▶ List steps that can ensure clarity in presentation.
▶ Compare the teacher's role in direct and constructivist teaching strategies.
▶ Debate the merits of whole-language, code-based, and balanced approaches to reading.

What Would You Do?

Your school district has adopted a whole-language, integrated curriculum approach for grades K through 6. Quite a bit of time and money was spent on workshops for teachers; buying big books and multiple copies of good children's literature; developing manipulatives for mathematics; building comfortable reading corners; making costumes, puppets, and other reading props; designing science projects; and generally supporting the innovations. Students and teachers are mostly pleased with the program. There seems to be more reading and more enjoyment of reading, at least for many children—but some students seem lost. The students' written work is longer and more creative. However, standardized tests indicate a drop in scores. The principal is clearly getting worried—this was her big project and she had to work hard to "sell it" to some members of the PTA and school board. Several parents of students in your class are complaining that they have had to hire tutors or buy commercial programs to teach their children to read.

▶ As a teacher, what would you do about the parents' complaints?

▶ Would you make any changes in your approach?

▶ What information would you need to make good decisions?

▶ Who should be involved in these decisions?

The First Step: Planning

When you thought about how to translate your principal's reading program into units and lessons for your students, you were *planning*. In the past few years, educational researchers have become very interested in teachers' planning. They have interviewed teachers about how they plan, asked teachers to "think out loud" while planning or to keep journals describing their plans, and even studied teachers intensively for months at a time. What have they found?

First, planning influences what students will learn, because planning transforms the available time and curriculum materials into activities, assignments, and tasks for students. When a teacher decides to devote 7 hours to language arts and 15 minutes to science in a given week, the students in that class will learn more language than science. In fact, differences as dramatic as this do occur. Nancy Karweit (1989) reported that in one school the time allocated to mathematics ranged from 2 hours and 50 minutes a week in one class to 5 hours and 55 minutes a week in a class down the hall (Clark & Peterson, 1986; Clark & Yinger, 1988; Doyle, 1983).

Second, teachers engage in several levels of planning—by the year, term, unit, week, and day. All the levels must be coordinated. Accomplishing the year's plan requires breaking the work into terms, the terms into units, and the units into weeks and days. Planning done at the beginning of the year is particularly important, because many routines and patterns are established early. For experienced teachers, unit planning seems to be the most important level, followed by weekly and then daily planning (Clark & Peterson, 1986; Clark & Yinger, 1988).

Third, plans reduce—but do not eliminate—uncertainty in teaching. Even the best plans cannot (and should not) control everything that happens in class—planning must allow flexibility (Calderhead, 1996). There is some evidence that when teachers "overplan"—fill every minute and stick to the plan no matter what—their students do not learn as much as students whose teachers are flexible (Shavelson, 1987). Chris Clark (1983) suggests that beginning teachers should think of their plans as "flexible frameworks for action, as devices for getting started in the right direction, as something to depart from or elaborate on, rather than as rigid scripts" (p. 13). So, don't proceed with a planned new unit if your in-class review shows that many students still don't understand the material in the current unit.

In order to plan creatively and flexibly, teachers need to have wide-ranging knowledge about students, their interests, and abilities; the subjects being taught; alternative ways to teach and assess understanding; working with groups; the expectations and limitations of the school and community; how to apply and adapt materials and texts; and how to pull all this knowledge together into meaningful activities. The plans of beginning teachers sometimes don't work because they lack knowledge about the students or the subject—they can't estimate how long it will take students to complete an activity, for example, or they stumble when asked for an explanation or a different example (Calderhead, 1996).

Finally, there is no one model for effective planning. For experienced teachers, planning is a creative problem-solving process (Shavelson, 1987). Experienced teachers know how to accomplish many lessons and segments of lessons. They know what to expect and how to proceed, so they don't necessarily continue to follow the detailed lesson-planning models they learned during their teacher-preparation programs. Planning is more informal—"in their heads." However, many experienced teachers think it was helpful to learn this detailed system as a foundation (Clark & Peterson, 1986).

No matter how you plan, you must have a learning goal in mind. In the next section we consider the range of goals that you might have for your students.

"AND THEN, OF COURSE, THERE'S THE POSSIBILITY OF BEING JUST THE SLIGHTEST BIT TOO ORGANIZED."

(By permission of Glen Dines. From Phi Delta Kappan.)

◀ Planning involves designing learning goals, making decisions about how to help students achieve them, and assessing their success.

Objectives for Learning

We hear quite a bit today about visions, goals, outcomes, and standards. At a very general, abstract level are the grand goals society may have for graduates of public schools such as, "All children will start school ready to learn," one of the eight goals for U.S. education in *Goals 2000*. However, very general goals are meaningless as potential guidelines for instruction. States may turn these grand goals into standards, such as the South Carolina standard that students will, "Develop the concept of fractions, mixed numbers, and decimals and use models to relate fractions to decimals and to find equivalent fractions." Sometimes the standards are turned into indicators such as "representing equivalent fractions." At this level, the indicators are close to being instructional objectives (Airasian, in press).

An **instructional objective** is a clear and unambiguous description of your educational intentions for your students. Norman Gronlund (2000) defines instructional objectives as "intended learning outcomes . . . the types of performance students are expected to demonstrate at the end of instruction to show that they have learned what was expected of them" (p. 4). Although there are many different approaches to writing objectives, each assumes that the first step in teaching is to decide what changes should take place in the learner—what is the goal of teaching. Objectives written by people with behavioral views focus on observable and measurable changes in the learner. **Behavioral objectives** use terms such as *list*, *define*, *add*, or *calculate*. **Cognitive objectives**, on the other hand, emphasize thinking and comprehension, so they are more likely to include words such as *understand*, *recognize*, *create*, or *apply*. Let's look at one well-developed method of writing specific objectives.

Mager: Start with the Specific. Robert Mager has developed a very influential system for writing instructional objectives. Mager's idea is that objectives ought to describe what students will be doing when demonstrating their achievement and how you will know they are doing it (Mager, 1975). Mager's objectives are generally regarded as *behavioral*. According to Mager, a good objective has three parts. First, it describes the intended student behavior—what must the student do? Second, it lists the conditions under which the behavior will occur—how will this behavior be recognized or tested? Third, it gives the criteria for acceptable performance on the test. Figure 13.1 shows how the system works. This system, with its emphasis on final behavior, requires a very explicit statement. Mager contends that often students can teach themselves if they are given well-stated objectives.

Gronlund: Start with the General. Norman Gronlund (2000) offers a different approach, often used for writing cognitive objectives. He believes that an objective should be stated first in general terms (*understand*, *solve*, *appreciate*, etc.). Then the teacher should clarify by listing a few sample behaviors that would provide evidence that the student has attained the objective. Look at the example in Table 13.1. The goal here really is presenting and defending a research project. The teacher does not want the student to stop with describing, summarizing, answering questions, and so on. Instead, the teacher looks at performance on these sample tasks to decide if the student can effectively present and defend. The teacher could just as well have chosen six different indicators.

Gronlund's emphasis on specific objectives as samples of more general student ability is important. A teacher could never list all the behaviors that might be involved in solving problems in the subject area, but stating an initial, general objec-

Connect and Extend
To your own philosophy
Cuban, L. (1990). Four stories about national goals for American education. *Phi Delta Kappan, 72*(4), 264–314. *Focus Questions:* What should be the goals of American education? Should we have a national agenda that shapes our instructional objectives?

Connect and Extend
To your own philosophy
What is your reaction to the following statement? "Behavioral objectives often may be appropriate for training (an end in itself) but seldom are appropriate for education (which is concerned with understanding)."

Instructional Objective: Clear statement of what students are intended to learn through instruction.

Behavioral Objectives: Instructional objectives stated in terms of observable behaviors.

Cognitive Objectives: Instructional objectives stated in terms of higher-level thinking operations.

FIGURE 13.1

Mager's Three-Part System

Robert Mager believes that a good learning objective has three parts: the student behavior, the conditions under which the behavior will be performed, and the criteria for judging a performance.

Part	Central Question	Example
Student behavior	Do what?	Mark statements with an *F* for fact or an *O* for opinion
Conditions of performance	Under what conditions?	Given an article from a newspaper
Performance criteria	How well?	75% of the statements are correctly marked

Source: From *Preparing Instructional Objectives,* by R. F. Mager, 1975, Fearon, Belmont, CA. Copyright © 1975 by David S. Lake Publishers. Reprinted with permission.

tive makes it clear that the ability to solve problems is the purpose. The most recent research on instructional objectives tends to favor approaches similar to Gronlund's. It seems reasonable to state a few central objectives in general terms and clarify them with samples of specific behaviors, as in Table 13.1 (Hamilton, 1985; Popham, 1993).

TABLE 13.1   *Gronlund's Combined Method for Creating Objectives*

General Objective

Presents and defends the research project before a group.

Specific Examples

1. Describes the project in a well-organized manner.
2. Summarizes the findings and their implications.
3. Uses display materials to clarify ideas and relationships.
4. Answers group members' questions directly and completely.
5. Presents a report that reflects careful planning.
6. Displays sound reasoning ability through presentation and answers to questions.

Source: Adapted from *How to Write and Use Instructional Objectives* (6th ed.) (pp. 74–75), by N. E. Gronlund, 2000, Columbus, OH: Merrill. Copyright © 2000 Merrill Education, Upper Saddle River, NJ.

GUIDELINES

Using Instructional Objectives

Avoid "word magic"—phrases that sound noble and important but say very little, such as "Students will become deep thinkers."

Examples

1. Keep the focus on specific changes that will take place in the students' knowledge of skills.
2. Ask students to explain the meaning of the objectives. If they can't give specific examples of what you mean, the objectives are not communicating your intentions to your students.

Suit the activities to the objectives.

Examples

1. If the goal is the memorization of vocabulary, give the students memory aids and practice exercises.

2. If the goal is the ability to develop well-thought-out positions, consider position papers, debates, projects, or mock trials.
3. If you want students to become better writers, give many opportunities for writing and rewriting.

Make sure your tests are related to your objectives.

Examples

1. Write objectives and rough drafts for tests at the same time—revise these drafts of tests as the units unfold and objectives change.
2. Weight the tests according to the importance of the various objectives and the time spent on each.

Connect and Extend
To your own philosophy
Do you think behavioral objectives are really objectives in themselves, or are they a "means to an end"?

Are Objectives Useful? Providing objectives for students can promote learning with loosely organized and less-structured activities such as lectures, films, and research projects. If the importance of some information is not clear from the learning materials and activities themselves, instructional objectives will probably help focus students' attention and thus increase achievement (Duchastel, 1979). But when the task involves simply getting the gist of the passage or transferring the information to a new situation, it is better to use questions that focus on meaning, inserting the questions right before the passage to be read (Hamilton, 1985).

If the objectives are supplied in advance—and especially if students have a role in designing objectives—both students and teachers will know what the performance criteria are. In thinking about objectives, both teachers and students must consider what is important, what is worth learning. I have found that teachers who have clear, appropriate goals for each student often are successful in helping the students learn. Finally, many school districts still require teachers to complete lesson plans that include learning objectives. The Guidelines above should help you whether you decide to make thorough use of objectives or just prepare them for certain assignments.

Flexible and Creative Plans— Using Taxonomies

Several decades ago, a group of experts in educational evaluation led by Benjamin Bloom set out to improve college and university examinations. The impact of their work has touched education at all levels around the world (Anderson & Sosniak, 1994). Bloom and his colleagues developed a **taxonomy**, or classification system, of educational objectives. Objectives were divided into three domains: cognitive, affective, and psychomotor. A handbook describing the objectives in each area was eventually published. In real life, of course, behaviors from these three domains occur simultaneously. While students are writing (psychomotor), they are also remembering or reasoning (cognitive), and they are likely to have some emotional response to the task as well (affective).

The Cognitive Domain. Six basic objectives are listed in Bloom's taxonomy of the thinking or **cognitive domain** (Bloom, Engelhart, Frost, Hill, & Krathwohl, 1956):

1. *Knowledge:* Remembering or recognizing something without necessarily understanding, using, or changing it.
2. *Comprehension:* Understanding the material being communicated without necessarily relating it to anything else.
3. *Application:* Using a general concept to solve a particular problem.
4. *Analysis:* Breaking something down into its parts.
5. *Synthesis:* Creating something new by combining different ideas.
6. *Evaluation:* Judging the value of materials or methods as they might be applied in a particular situation.

It is common in education to consider these objectives as a hierarchy, each skill building on those below, but this is not entirely accurate (Seddon, 1978). Some subjects, such as mathematics, do not fit this structure very well (Kreitzer & Madaus, 1994). Still, you will hear many references to *lower-level* and *higher-level objectives*, with knowledge, comprehension, and application considered lower level and the other categories considered higher level. As a rough way of thinking about objectives, this can be helpful (Gronlund, 2000).

The taxonomy of objectives can also be helpful in planning assessments because different procedures are appropriate for objectives at the various levels. Gronlund (2000) suggests that factual knowledge objectives can best be measured by true/false, short answer, matching, or multiple-choice tests. Such tests will also work with the comprehension, application, and analysis levels of the taxonomy. For measuring synthesis and evaluation objectives, however, essays, reports, projects, and portfolios are more appropriate. Essay tests will also work at the middle levels of the taxonomy.

Bloom 2001. Bloom's taxonomy guided educators for over 40 years. It is considered one of the most significant educational writings of the 20th century (Anderson & Sosniak, 1994). In 1995, a group of educational researchers met to discuss revising the taxonomy. The outcome of that project (Anderson & Krathwohl, in press) is still developing as I write this sentence, but I can give you some preliminary information. First, the taxonomy revisers have retained the six basic levels, but they have altered the order slightly and changed the names of three to indicate the cognitive processes involved. The six cognitive processes are remembering (knowledge), understanding (comprehension), applying, analyzing, evaluating, and creating (synthesizing). In addition, the revisers have added a new dimension to the taxonomy to recognize that cognitive processes must process something—you have to remember or understand or apply some form of knowledge. If you look at Table 13.2 on page 480 you will see the result. We now have six processes or verbs—the cognitive acts of remembering, understanding, applying, analyzing, evaluating, and creating. These processes act on four kinds of knowledge—factual, conceptual, procedural, and metacognitive.

Consider how this revised taxonomy might suggest objectives for a social studies/language arts class. An objective that targets *analysis of conceptual knowledge* is:

Taxonomy: Classification system.

Cognitive Domain: In Bloom's taxonomy, memory and reasoning objectives.

TABLE 13.2   A Revised Taxonomy in the Cognitive Domain

	The Cognitive Process Dimension					
The Knowledge Dimension	**1. Remember**	**2. Understand**	**3. Apply**	**4. Analyze**	**5. Evaluate**	**6. Create**
A. Factual Knowledge						
B. Conceptual Knowledge						
C. Procedural Knowledge						
D. Metacognitive Knowledge						

Source: From *A Taxonomy of Teaching and Learning: A Revision of Bloom's Taxonomy of Educational Objectives* by L. Anderson & D. Krathwohl (Eds.) (in press), New York: Addison Wesley Longman. Copyright © 2000 by Addison Wesley Longman. Adapted with permission.

After reading an historical account of the battle of the Alamo, students will be able to recognize the author's point of view or bias.

An objective for *evaluating metacognitive knowledge* might be:

Students will reflect on their strategies for identifying the biases of the author.

The Affective Domain. The objectives in the taxonomy of the **affective domain,** or domain of emotional response, run from least committed to most committed (Krathwohl, Bloom, & Masia, 1964). At the lowest level, a student would simply pay attention to a certain idea. At the highest level, the student would adopt an idea or a value and act consistently with that idea. There are five basic objectives in the affective domain.

1. *Receiving:* Being aware of or attending to something in the environment. This is the I'll-listen-to-the-concert-but-I-won't-promise-to-like-it level.

2. *Responding:* Showing some new behavior as a result of experience. At this level a person might applaud after the concert or hum some of the music the next day.

3. *Valuing:* Showing some definite involvement or commitment. At this point a person might choose to go to a concert instead of a film.

4. *Organization:* Integrating a new value into one's general set of values, giving it some ranking among one's general priorities. This is the level at which a person would begin to make long-range commitments to concert attendance.

5. *Characterization by value:* Acting consistently with the new value. At this highest level, a person would be firmly committed to a love of music and demonstrate it openly and consistently.

Like the basic objectives in the cognitive domain, these five objectives are very general. To write specific learning objectives, you must state what students will actually be doing when they are receiving, responding, valuing, and so on. For example, an objective for a nutrition class at the valuing level (showing involvement or com-

Affective Domain: Objectives focusing on attitudes and feelings.

mitment) might be stated: After completing the unit on food contents and labeling, at least 50% of the class will commit to the junk-food boycott project by giving up candy for a month.

How can the teacher in the nutrition example be sure that students have given up candy in support of a junk-food boycott? The best method may be to ask them to report anonymously on their candy consumption; if students have to sign their names to their responses, the process may counteract the desire to reach another affective goal, honesty. Also, if students are graded on their success, this process might really encourage the students to give false reports. In most cases, it is best not to grade the assessment of affective goals. It would be unethical to give students grades for their beliefs and values, even if you asked them to consider other positions or provide evidence for their own conclusions.

The Psychomotor Domain. Until recently, the **psychomotor domain**, or realm of physical ability objectives, has been mostly overlooked by teachers not directly involved with physical education. There are several taxonomies in this domain (e.g., Harrow, 1972; Simpson, 1972) that generally move from basic perceptions and reflex actions to skilled, creative movements. James Cangelosi (1990) provides a useful way to think about objectives in the psychomotor domain as either voluntary muscle capabilities that require endurance, strength, flexibility, agility, or speed, or the ability to perform a specific skill.

Objectives in the psychomotor domain should be of interest to a wide range of educators, including those in fine arts, vocational-technical education, and special education. Many other subjects, such as chemistry, physics, and biology also require specialized movements and well-developed hand and eye coordination. Using lab equipment, the "mouse" on a computer, or art materials means learning new physical skills. Here are two psychomotor objectives:

> Four minutes after completing a one-mile run in eight minutes or under, your heart rate will be below 120.

> Use a computer mouse effectively to "drag and drop" files.

Learning in the psychomotor area means developing a particular performance ability. How do you assess a student's performance? The obvious answer is to ask the student to demonstrate the skill and then observe the student's proficiency. In some cases, the performance of the skill results in a product, so assessment of the product can be substituted for observation of the actual performance. An art student learning to use the potter's wheel, for example, should be able to produce a pot that is symmetrical, stands by itself, and doesn't crack when fired.

When students are actually demonstrating skills or performing, you need a checklist or rating scale to help you focus on the important aspects of the skill being evaluated. A checklist usually gives the measurable dimensions of performance, along with a series of blank spaces for judgments. Table 13.3 on page 482 provides an example. A rating scale generally follows the same plan but has a numerical scale to rate each aspect of performance.

Another View: Planning from a Constructivist Perspective

Traditionally, it has been the teacher's responsibility to do most of the planning for instruction, but new ways of planning are developing. In **constructivist approaches,**

Psychomotor Domain: Physical ability and coordination objectives.

Constructivist Approach: View that emphasizes the active role of the learner in building understanding and making sense of information.

TABLE 13.3 *Checklist to Evaluate Student's Performance of a Two-Arm Press*

The student, stationed in front of a barbell with only a light weight that would offer little resistance, is directed to demonstrate one two-arm press.

Scoring key: (11 points possible) +1 for each blank checked on the following form:

_____ feet properly positioned under the bar throughout the entire lift
_____ proper grip and hand spread
_____ back straight throughout
_____ head facing forward throughout
_____ clean initiated with knees flexed
_____ clean initiated with elbows extended
_____ clean properly executed
_____ pauses with bar just above chest
_____ executes press properly
_____ returns bar to position just above chest and pauses
_____ gently returns bar to floor, flexing knees on the way down

Source: From *Designing Tests for Evaluating Student Achievement* (p. 125) by J. S. Cangelosi, 1990, Reading, MA: Addison Wesley. Copyright © 1990 by Addison Wesley Educational Publishers, Inc. Adapted with permission.

planning is shared and negotiated. The teacher and students together make decisions about content, activities, and approaches. Rather than having specific student behaviors and skills as objectives, the teacher has overarching goals—"big ideas"—that guide planning. These goals are understandings or abilities that the teacher returns to again and again.

An Example of Constructivist Planning. Vito Perrone (1994) has these goals for his secondary history students. He wants his student to be able to:

▶ use primary sources, formulate hypotheses, and engage in systematic study;
▶ handle multiple points of view;
▶ be close readers and active writers; and
▶ pose and solve problems.

The next step in the planning process is to create a learning environment that allows students to move toward these goals in ways that respect their individual interests and abilities. Perrone (1994) suggests identifying "those ideas, themes, and issues that provide the depth and variety of perspective that help students develop significant understandings" (p. 12). For a secondary history course, a theme might be "democracy and revolution," "fairness," or "slavery." In math or music a theme might be "patterns"; in literature, "personal identity" might be the theme. Perrone suggests mapping the topic as a way of thinking about how the theme can generate learning and understanding. An example of a topic map, using the theme of "Immigrants in the United States," is shown in Figure 13.2.

With this topic map as a guide, teacher and students can work together to identify activities, materials, projects, and performances that will support the develop-

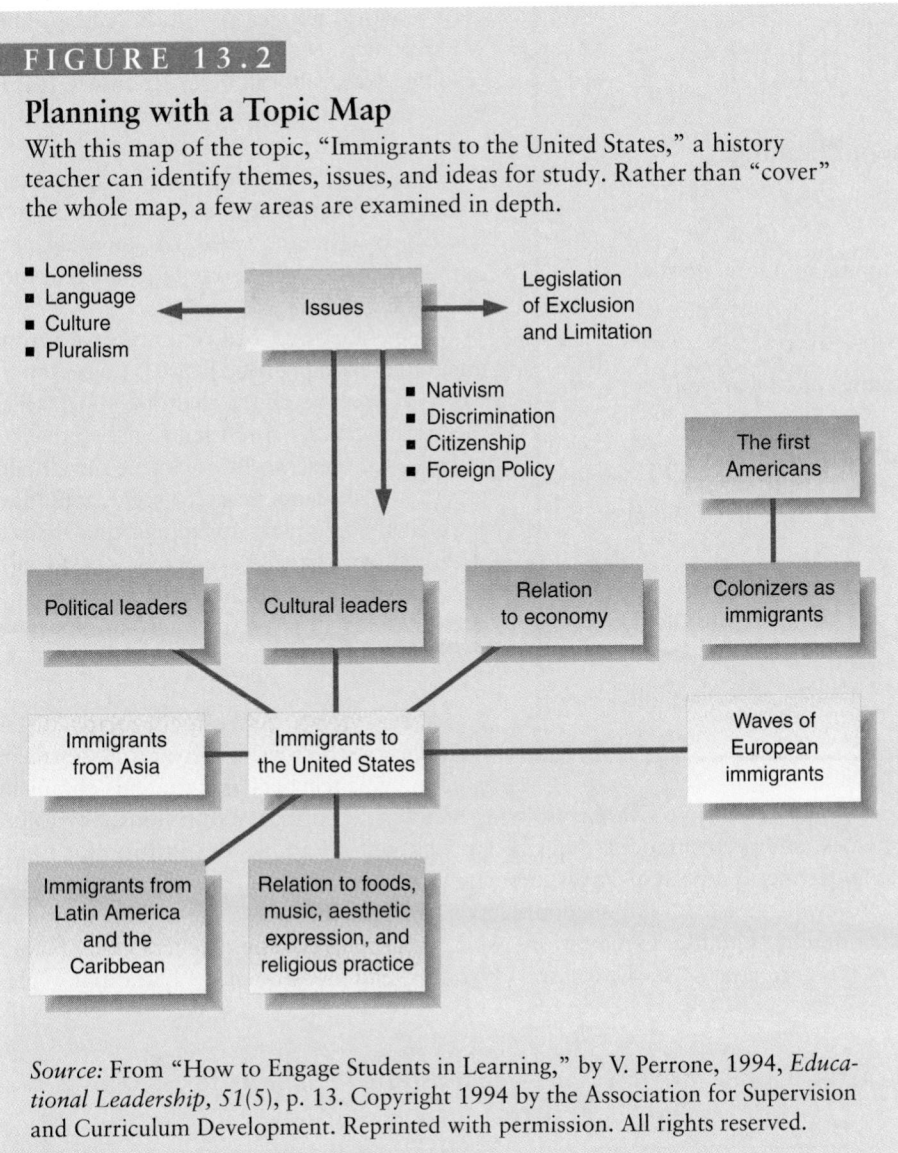

Planning with a Topic Map

With this map of the topic, "Immigrants to the United States," a history teacher can identify themes, issues, and ideas for study. Rather than "cover" the whole map, a few areas are examined in depth.

- Loneliness
- Language
- Culture
- Pluralism

Issues

Legislation of Exclusion and Limitation

- Nativism
- Discrimination
- Citizenship
- Foreign Policy

The first Americans

Political leaders

Cultural leaders

Relation to economy

Colonizers as immigrants

Immigrants from Asia

Immigrants to the United States

Waves of European immigrants

Immigrants from Latin America and the Caribbean

Relation to foods, music, aesthetic expression, and religious practice

Source: From "How to Engage Students in Learning," by V. Perrone, 1994, *Educational Leadership, 51*(5), p. 13. Copyright 1994 by the Association for Supervision and Curriculum Development. Reprinted with permission. All rights reserved.

ment of the students' understanding and abilities—the overarching goals of the class. The teacher spends less time planning specific presentations and assignments and more time gathering a variety of resources and facilitating students' learning. The focus is not so much on students' products as on the processes of learning and the thinking behind the products.

Integrated and Thematic Plans. Perrone's planning map shows a way to use the theme of immigrants to the United States to integrate issues in a history class. Today, teaching with themes and integrated content are major elements in planning and designing lessons and units, from kindergarten (Roskos & Neuman, 1995) through high school (Clarke & Agne, 1997). For example, Elaine Homestead and Karen McGinnis (two middle school teachers) and Elizabeth Pate (a college professor) (1995) designed a unit on "Human Interactions" that included studying racism, world hunger, pollution, and air and water quality. Students researched issues by reading textbooks and outside sources, learning to use databases, interviewing local officials, and inviting guest speakers into class. Students had to develop knowledge in science, mathematics, and social studies. They learned to write and speak persuasively, and in the process, raised money for hunger relief in Africa.

Elementary age students can benefit from integrated planning too. There is no reason to work on spelling skills, then listening skills, then writing skills, and then social studies or science. All these abilities can be developed together if students work to solve authentic problems. Some ideas for integrating themes with younger children are people, friendship, communications, habitats, communities, and patterns. Possibilities for older children are given in Table 13.4.

Review

▶ What are the levels of planning and how do they affect teaching?

▶ What is an instructional objective?

▶ Describe the three taxonomies of educational objectives.

▶ Describe teacher-centered and student-centered planning.

Apply

▶ Identify a cognitive, affective, and psychomotor objective for yourself for this week.

▶ Name a theme that could organize your planning for a grade you might teach.

Assessment. Assessment plans differ within a constructivist classroom. Assessment is ongoing as teachers and students comment on each others' efforts. *Authentic assessment* in the form of exhibitions, portfolios of work, and performances (described in Chapters 14 and 15) substitutes for traditional testing. But perhaps most important, teachers and students share the authority to evaluate work. The students have a responsibility to assess their own and each others' thinking, explanations, and performances. The teachers give up control of "correctness" in the classroom and instead ask students, "Does that expla-

---

TABLE 13.4 *Some Themes for Integrated Planning for Older Children*

Courage	Time and Space
Mystery	Groups and Institutions
Survival	Work
Human Interaction	Motion
Communities of the Future	Cause and Effect
Communication/Language	Probability and Prediction
Human Rights and Responsibilities	Change and Conservation
Identity/Coming of Age	Diversity and Variation
Interdependence	Autobiography

Source: Adapted from *Toward a Coherent Curriculum* by J. A. Beane (Ed.), 1995, Alexandria, VA: Association for Supervision and Curriculum Development; *Interdisciplinary High School Teaching* by J. H. Clarke and R. M. Agne, 1997, Boston: Allyn & Bacon; and *Teaching through Themes* by G. Thompson, 1991, New York: Scholastic. See Thompson for resources and strategies to develop some of these themes in elementary school and Clarke and Agne for ideas at the high school level.

TABLE 13.5 *Checklist to Guide Assessment in Teaching with Themes*

You may want to use this checklist as one of your bases of evaluation for the children's discussions, writing, and projects.

_____ Displays knowledge of content
_____ Uses theme vocabulary
_____ Understands relationships explored in theme
_____ Notes the details of the theme information
_____ Classifies and categorizes theme information
_____ Compares and contrasts books in theme
_____ Assimilates and displays knowledge of books' relationship to theme
_____ Listens to discussions and responds accordingly
_____ Recognizes different curriculum areas explored in theme
_____ Is able to work in groups and individually on activities
_____ Clarifies theme information
_____ Completes projects on a timely basis
_____ Expands theme reading independently

Source: From *Teaching with Themes* (p. 176), by G. Thompson, 1991, New York: Scholastic. Copyright © 1991 by Scholastic, Inc. Reprinted with permission.

nation make sense?" "Does it work to solve the problem?" "Can you improve it?" "Do you agree?" "Why?" Students learn that self-assessment, judgment, and reflection are important parts of learning. Table 13.5 is a checklist that can be used to plan assessment in teaching with themes.

Let's assume you and your students have valuable and interesting plans and learning objectives as well as some appropriate ways to assess learning. What next? You still need to decide what's happening on Monday. You need to design tasks and activities for teaching and learning that are appropriate for the objectives. You have an idea of *what* you want students to understand, but *how* do you teach to encourage understanding?

Formats for Teaching: Teacher Directed

This section describes a variety of general teaching strategies or formats for turning objectives into action in the classroom. These strategies are not complete models of teaching, but rather building blocks that can be used to construct lessons and units. We begin with the strategy many people associate most directly with teaching: lecturing.

Lecturing and Explaining

Some studies have found that teachers' presentations take up one-sixth to one-fourth of all classroom time. High school teachers, of course, lecture more than

TABLE 13.6 *Three Phases in the Lecture Method*

Entry: Preparation for Learning

A. State objectives and rationale.
B. Provide a context for the new material to be presented.
C. Focus attention on key concept, generalization, or principle that encompasses the lecture.

Presentation

A. Sequence content from simpler to complex understandings.
B. Enhance presentation with visual aids.
C. Stimulate attention with verbal and nonverbal behaviors.

Closure: Review of Learning

A. Integrate with students' knowledge and experiences.
B. Transition to next lesson or activity.

Source: From *Dynamics of Effective Teaching* (2nd ed.) (p. 221) by R. Kindsvatter, W. Wilen, and M. Ishler, 1988, 1992, Reading, MA: Addison Wesley. Copyright © 1988 and 1992 by Addison Wesley Educational Publishers Inc. Reprinted with permission.

A lecture format is most appropriate for communicating a large amount of material to many students in a short period of time. ▼

Lecturing: Organized explanation of a topic by a teacher.

Scripted Cooperation: Learning strategy in which two students take turns summarizing material and criticizing the summaries.

teachers in the lower grades. You will probably learn about how to lecture in your methods classes. Many different approaches are available, and the one you choose will depend on your objectives and the subject you are teaching. You will certainly want to keep in mind the age of your students, because the younger your students, the briefer and simpler your explanations should be. You may also want to follow a basic three-part format suggested by Kindsvatter, Wilen, and Ishler (1992), shown in Table 13.6.

Lecturing is appropriate for communicating a large amount of material to many students in a short period of time. The teacher can integrate information from many sources in less time than it would take for the students to integrate all the information themselves. Lecturing is a good method for introducing a new topic, giving background information, and motivating students to learn more on their own. Lecturing also helps students learn to listen accurately and critically and gives the teacher a chance to make on-the-spot changes to help students understand when they are confused (Gilstrap & Martin, 1975; Kindsvatter, Wilen, & Ishler, 1988). Lectures are therefore most appropriate for cognitive and affective objectives at the lower levels of the taxonomies described earlier: for knowledge, comprehension, application, receiving, responding, and valuing.

Scripted cooperation, described in Chapter 9, is one way of incorporating active learning into lectures. Several times during the presentation, the teacher asks students to work in pairs. One person is the summarizer and the other critiques the summary. This gives students a chance to check their understanding, organize their thinking, and translate ideas into their own words. Other possibilities are described in Table 13.7.

TABLE 13.7 *Active Learning and Teacher Presentations*

Here are some ideas for keeping students cognitively engaged in lessons. They can be adapted for many ages.

Question, All Write: Pose a question, ask everyone to jot an answer, then ask, "How many students would be willing to share their thoughts?"

Outcome Sentences: After a segment of presentation, ask students to finish a sentence such as "I learned . . . , I'm beginning to wonder . . . , I was surprised. . . ." Share as above. Students may keep their outcome sentences in a learning log or portfolio.

Underexplain with Learning Pairs: Give a brief explanation, then ask students to work in pairs to figure out the process or idea.

Voting: Ask "How many of you . . ." questions and take a count. "How many of you agree with Raschon?" "How many of you are ready to move on?" "How many of you got 48 on this problem?"

Choral Response: Have the whole class restate in unison important facts and ideas, such as "The environment is one whole system" or "A 10-sided polygon is called a decagon."

Speak-Write: Tell students you will speak briefly, for 3 or 4 minutes. They are to listen, but not take notes. At the end of the time, ask them to write the main ideas, a summary, or questions they have about what you said.

Source: From *Inspiring Active Learning: A Handbook for Teachers* by M. Harmin, 1994, Alexandria, VA: Association for Supervision and Curriculum Development.

The lecture method also has disadvantages. You may find that some students have trouble listening for more than a few minutes at a time and that they simply tune you out. Lecturing puts the students in a passive position. It does much of the cognitive work for the students and may prevent them from asking or thinking of questions. Also, students learn and comprehend at different paces, whereas a lecture proceeds at the lecturer's own pace (Freiberg & Driscoll, 1996; Gilstrap & Martin, 1975). If your objectives include having students solve a problem; develop arguments; write essays, poems, or short stories; create paintings; or evaluate work, then you must go beyond lecturing to methods that require more active student involvement.

Seatwork and Homework

There is little research on the effects of **seatwork**, or independent classroom-desk work, but it is clear that this technique is often overused. In fact, a study found that American elementary students spend 51% of mathematics time in school working alone, while Japanese students spend 26% and Taiwanese students spend only 9% (Stigler, Lee, & Stevenson, 1987). Some educators point to these differences as part of the explanation for Asian students' superiority in mathematics. Seatwork should follow up a lesson and give students supervised practice. It should not be the main mode of instruction.

Making Seatwork and Homework Valuable. There is recent evidence that students who do more homework (and watch less television after school) have higher grades, even when other factors such as gender, grade level, ethnicity, SES,

Seatwork: Independent classroom work.

and amount of adult supervision are taken into consideration (Cooper, Valentine, Nye, & Lindsay, 1999). But just assigning more homework is not necessarily a good idea. The homework must be meaningful extensions of class lessons, not just busywork. The primary focus should be review and practice, not exposure to new material. Unfortunately, many workbook pages and "dittos" do little to support the learning of important objectives. Before you assign work, ask yourself, "Does doing this work help students learn anything that matters?" For example, consider this task, cited in the report of the Commission on Reading of the National Institute of Education (Anderson, Hiebert, Scott, & Wilkinson, 1985):

> Read each sentence. Decide which consonant letter is used the most. Underline it each time.

What's the point? This sort of activity communicates to students that reading isn't very important or useful. Students should see the connection between the seatwork or homework and the lesson. Tell them why they are doing the work. The objectives should be clear, all the materials that might be needed should be provided, and the work should be easy enough that students can succeed on their own. Success rates should be high—near 100%. When seatwork is too difficult, students often resort to guessing or copying just to finish (Anderson, 1985).

Carol Weinstein and Andy Mignano (1997) describe several alternatives to workbooks and dittos, such as reading silently and reading aloud to a partner; writing for a "real" audience; writing letters or journals; transcribing conversations and punctuating them properly; making up problems; working on long-term projects and reports; solving brainteasers and puzzles; and engaging in computer activities. One of my favorites is creating a group story. Two students begin a story on the computer. Then two more add a paragraph. The story grows with each new pair's addition. The students are reading and writing, editing and improving.

Staying Engaged. To benefit from individual or group seatwork or homework, students must stay involved and do the work. The first step toward involvement is getting students started correctly by making sure they understand the assignment. It may help to do the first few questions as a class, to clear up any misconceptions. This is especially important for homework assignments, because students may have no one at home to consult if they have problems with the assignment. A second way to keep students involved is to hold them accountable for completing the work correctly, not just for filling in the page. This means the work should be checked, the students given a chance to correct the errors or revise work, and the results counted toward the class grade (Brophy & Good, 1986). Expert teachers often have ways of correcting homework quickly during the first minutes of class by having students check each other's or their own work.

Seatwork particularly requires careful monitoring. Being available to students doing seatwork is more effective than offering students help before they ask for it. To be available, you should move around the class and avoid spending too much time with one or two students. Short, frequent contacts are best (Brophy & Good, 1986; Rosenshine, 1977).

Sometimes you may be working with a small group while other students do seatwork. In these situations it is especially important for students to know what to do if they need help. One expert teacher described by Weinstein and Mignano (1997) taught students a rule, "Ask three, then me." Students have to consult three classmates before seeking help from the teacher. This teacher also spends time early in the year showing students *how* to help each other—how to ask questions and how to explain.

FAMILY AND COMMUNITY PARTNERSHIPS

Homework

Make sure families know what students are expected to learn.

Examples

1. At the beginning of a unit, send home a list of the main objectives, examples of major assignments, key due dates, a homework "calendar," and a list of resources available free at libraries or on the Internet.

2. Provide a clear, concise description of your homework policy—how homework is counted toward class grades; consequences for late, forgotten, or missing homework, etc.

Help families find a comfortable and helpful role in their child's homework.

Examples

1. Remind families that "helping with homework" means encouraging, listening, monitoring, praising, discussing, brainstorming—not necessarily teaching and never doing the work for their child.

2. Encourage families to set aside a quiet time and place for everyone in the family to study. Make this time a regular part of the daily routine.

3. Have some homework assignments that are fun and involve the whole family—puzzles, family albums, watching a television program together and doing a "review."

4. At parent–teacher conferences, ask families what they need to play a more helpful role in their child's homework.

Solicit and use suggestions from families about homework.

Examples

1. Find out what responsibilities the child has at home—how much time is available for homework.

2. Periodically, have a "homework hotline" for call-in questions and suggestions.

If no one is at home to help with homework, set up other support systems.

Examples

1. Assign study buddies who can be available over the phone.

2. If students have computers, provide lists of Internet help lines.

3. Locate free help in public libraries and make these resources known.

What about monitoring homework? If students get stuck on homework, they need help at home, someone who can scaffold their work without just "giving the answer" (Pressley, 1995). But many parents don't know how to help (Hoover-Dempsey, Bassler, & Burow, 1995). The Family and Community Partnerships Guidelines give ideas for helping parents help with homework.

Recitation and Questioning

Recitation is a common approach to teaching that has been with us for many years (Stodolsky, 1988). Teachers pose questions, students answer. The teacher's questions generally follow some sort of plan to develop a framework for the subject matter involved. The students' answers are often followed by reactions from the teacher, such as praise, correction, or requests for further information. The pattern from the teacher's point of view consists of *structure* (setting a framework), *solicitation* (asking questions), and *reaction* (praising, correcting, and expanding) (Clark et al., 1979). These steps are repeated over and over.

Let us consider the heart of recitation, the soliciting or *questioning* phase, by looking at the different kinds of questions, when to ask them, and how to respond to student answers. Of course, an important goal of teaching should be to encourage

Recitation: Format of teacher questioning, student response, and teacher feedback.

students to ask questions, but for now we will focus on teachers' questions, to make them as helpful as possible for students. Many of the beginning teachers I work with are surprised to discover how valuable good questions can be and how difficult they are to create.

Kinds of Questions. Some educators have estimated that high school teachers ask an average of 395 questions per day (Gall, 1970). What are these questions like? Many can be categorized in terms of Bloom's taxonomy of objectives in the cognitive domain. Table 13.8 offers examples of questions at the different taxonomic levels.

Another way to categorize questioning is in terms of **convergent questions** (only one right answer) or **divergent questions** (many possible answers). Questions about concrete facts are convergent: "Who ruled England in 1540?" "Who wrote the original *Peter Pan*?" Questions dealing with opinions or hypotheses are divergent: "In this story, which character is most like you and why?" "In 100 years, which of the past five presidents will be most admired?"

Quite a bit of space in education textbooks has been devoted to urging teachers to ask a greater number of higher-level (analysis, synthesis, and evaluation) and

---

TABLE 13.8 *Classroom Questions for Objectives in the Cognitive Domain*

Questions can be posed that encourage thinking at every level of Bloom's taxonomy in the cognitive domain. Of course, the thinking required depends on what has gone before in the discussion.

Category	Type of Thinking Expected	Examples
Knowledge (Remembering)	Recalling or recognizing information as learned	Define . . . . What is the capital of . . . ? What did the text say about . . . ?
Comprehension (Understanding)	Demonstrating understanding of the materials; transforming, reorganizing, or interpreting	Explain your own words. . . . Compare. . . . What is the main idea of . . . ? Describe what you saw . . . .
Application (Applying)	Using information to solve a problem with a single correct answer	Which principle is demonstrated in . . . ? Calculate the area of . . . . Apply the rule of . . . to solve. . . .
Analysis (Analyzing)	Critical thinking; identifying reasons and motives; making inferences based on specific data; analyzing conclusions to see if supported by evidence	What influenced the writings of . . . ? Why was Washington, D.C. chosen . . . ? Which of the following are facts and which are opinions . . . ? Based on your experiment, what is the chemical . . . ?
Synthesis (Creating)	Divergent, original thinking; original plan, proposal, design, or story	What's a good name for . . . ? How could we raise money for . . . ? What would the United States be like if the South had won . . . ?
Evaluation (Evaluating)	Judging the merits of ideas, offering opinions, applying standards	Which U.S. senator is the most effective? Which painting do you believe to be better? Why? Why would you favor . . . ?

Source: From "Questioning Skills" by M. Sadker and D. Sadker, in J. Cooper (Ed.), *Classroom Teaching Skills: A Handbook* (3rd ed.) (pp. 143–160), 1986, Boston: D. C. Heath. Copyright © 1986 D. C. Heath. Adapted with permission.

divergent questions. Is this really a better way of questioning? Research has provided several surprises.

Fitting the Questions to the Students. Both high- and low-level questions can be effective (Gall, 1984; Redfield & Rousseau, 1981). Different patterns seem to be better for different students, however. The best pattern for younger students and for lower-ability students of all ages is simple questions that allow a high percentage of correct answers, ample encouragement, help when the student does not have the correct answer, and praise. For high-ability students, the successful pattern includes harder questions at both higher and lower levels and more critical feedback (Berliner, 1987; Good, 1988).

Whatever their age or ability, all students should have some experience with thought-provoking questions and, if necessary, help in learning how to answer them. As we saw in Chapter 8, to master critical thinking and problem-solving skills, students must have a chance to practice the skills. They also need time to think about their answers. But research shows that teachers wait an average of only one second for students to answer (Rowe, 1974). Consider the following slice of classroom life (Sadker & Sadker, 1986a, p. 170):

Teacher:	Who wrote the poem "Stopping by Woods on a Snowy Evening"? Tom?
Tom:	Robert Frost.
Teacher:	Good. What action takes place in the poem? Sally?
Sally:	A man stops his sleigh to watch the woods get filled with snow.
Teacher:	Yes. Emma, what thoughts go through the man's mind?
Emma:	He thinks how beautiful the woods are . . . (She pauses for a second.)
Teacher:	What else does he think about? Joe?
Joe:	He thinks how he would like to stay and watch. (Pauses for a second.)
Teacher:	Yes—and what else? Rita? (Waits half a second.) Come on, Rita, you can get the answer to this. (Waits half a second.) Well, why does he feel he can't stay there indefinitely and watch the woods and the snow?
Sarah:	Well, I think it might be—(Pauses a second.)
Teacher:	Think, Sarah. (Teacher waits for half a second.) All right then—Mike? (Waits again for half a second.) John? (Waits half a second.) What's the matter with everyone today? Didn't you do the reading?

Very little thoughtful responding can take place in this situation. When teachers learn to pose a question, then wait at least 3 to 5 seconds before calling on a student to answer, students tend to give longer answers; more students are likely to participate, ask questions, and volunteer appropriate answers; student comments involving analysis, synthesis, inference, and speculation tend to increase; and the students generally appear more confident in their answers (Berliner, 1987; Rowe, 1974; Sadker & Sadker, 1986a; Tobin, 1987). This seems like a simple improvement in teaching, but 5 seconds of silence is not that easy to handle. It takes practice. You might try asking students to jot down ideas or even discuss the question with another student and formulate an answer together. This makes the wait more comfortable and gives students a chance to think. Of course, if it is clear that students are lost or don't understand the question, waiting longer will not help. When your question is met with blank stares, rephrase the question or ask if anyone can explain the confusion. However, there is some evidence that extending wait times does not affect learning in university classes (Duell, 1994), so with advanced high school students, you might conduct your own evaluation of wait time.

A word about selecting students to answer questions. If you call only on volunteers, then you may get the wrong idea about how well students understand the material. Also, the same people volunteer over and over again. Many expert teachers have some systematic way of making sure that they call on everyone: They pull names from a jar or check names off a list as each student speaks (Weinstein, 1996; Weinstein & Mignano, 1997). Another possibility is to put each student's name on an index card, then shuffle the cards and go through the deck as you call on people. You can use the card to make notes about students' answers or extra help they may need.

Responding to Student Answers. What do you do after the student answers? The most common response, occurring about 50% of the time in most classrooms, is simple acceptance—"OK" or "Uh-huh" (Sadker & Sadker, 1986a). But there are better reactions, depending on whether the student's answer is correct, partially correct, or wrong. If the answer is quick, firm, and correct, simply accept the answer or ask another question. If the answer is correct but hesitant, give the student feedback about *why* the answer is correct: "That's right, Chris, the Senate is part of the legislative branch of government because the Senate. . . ." This allows you to explain the material again. If this student is unsure, others may be confused as well. If the answer is partially or completely wrong but the student has made an honest attempt, you should probe for more information, give clues, simplify the question, review the previous steps, or reteach the material. If the student's wrong answer is silly or careless, however, it is better simply to correct the answer and go on. (Good, 1988; Rosenshine & Stevens, 1986).

Group Discussion

Group discussion is in some ways similar to the recitation strategy described in a previous section, but should be more like the instructional conversations described in Chapter 9 (Tharp & Gallimore, 1991). A teacher may pose questions, listen to student answers, react, and probe for more information, but in a true group discussion, the teacher does not have a dominant role. Students ask questions, answer each other's questions, and respond to each other's answers (Beck, McKeown, Worthy, Sandora, & Kucan, 1996).

There are many advantages to group discussions. The students are directly involved and have the chance to participate. Group discussion helps students learn to express themselves clearly, to justify opinions, and to tolerate different views. Group discussion also gives students a chance to ask for clarification, examine their own thinking, follow personal interests, and assume responsibility by taking leadership roles in the group. Thus, group discussions help students evaluate ideas and synthesize personal viewpoints. Discussions are also useful when students are trying to understand difficult concepts that go against common sense. As we saw in Chapters 8 and 9, many scientific concepts, such as the role of light in vision or Newton's laws of motion, are difficult to grasp because they contradict commonsense notions. By thinking together,

---

CHECKPOINT

Formats for Teaching

Review

▶ Describe the lecture format.

▶ Distinguish between convergent versus divergent and high- versus low-level questions.

▶ What are the uses and disadvantages of group discussion?

Apply

▶ Describe some alternatives to seatwork.

▶ Give examples of convergent and divergent questions in your subject area.

---

challenging each other, and suggesting and evaluating possible explanations, students are more likely to reach a genuine understanding.

Of course, there are disadvantages. Class discussions are quite unpredictable and may easily digress into exchanges of ignorance. Some members of the group may have great difficulty participating and may become anxious if forced to speak. In addition, you may have to do a good deal of preparation to ensure that participants have a background of knowledge on which to base the discussion. And large groups are often unwieldy. In many cases, a few students will dominate the discussion while the others daydream (Kindsvatter, Wilen, & Ishler, 1988). The Guidelines below give some ideas for facilitating a productive group discussion.

We have been looking at instructional planning and some basic teaching formats for whole classes, groups, and individuals. What about the person who is doing the planning—the teacher? What can teachers do to be effective in many different formats?

GUIDELINES

Productive Group Discussions

Invite shy children to participate.

Examples

1. "What's your opinion, Joel?" or "Does anyone have another opinion?"

2. Don't wait until there is a deadly silence to ask shy students to reply. Most people, even those who are confident, hate to break a silence.

Direct student comments and questions back to another student.

Examples

1. "That's an unusual idea, Steve. Kim, what do you think of Steve's idea?"

2. "That's an important question, John. Maura, do you have any thoughts about how you'd answer that?"

3. Encourage students to look at and talk to one another rather than wait for your opinion.

Make sure that you understand what a student has said. If you are unsure, other students may be unsure as well.

Examples

1. Ask a second student to summarize what the first student said; then the first student can try again to explain if the summary is incorrect.

2. "Karen, I think you're saying. . . . Is that right, or have I misunderstood?"

Probe for more information.

Examples

1. "That's a strong statement. Do you have any evidence to back it up?"

2. "Tell us how you reached that conclusion. What steps did you go through?"

Bring the discussion back to the subject.

Examples

1. "Let's see, we were discussing . . . and Sarah made one suggestion. Does anyone have a different idea?"

2. "Before we continue, let me try to summarize what has happened thus far."

Give time for thought before asking for responses.

Examples

"How would your life be different if television had never been invented? Jot down your ideas on paper, and we will share reactions in a minute." After a minute: "Hiromi, will you tell us what you wrote?"

When a student finishes speaking, look around the room to judge reactions.

Examples

1. If other students look puzzled, ask them to describe why they are confused.

2. If students are nodding assent, ask them to give an example of what was just said.

Focus on the Teacher

How would you go about identifying the keys to teaching? You might ask students, principals, college professors of education, or experienced teachers to list the characteristics of good teachers. Or you could do intensive case studies of a few classrooms over a long period. You might observe classrooms, rate different teachers on certain characteristics, and then see which characteristics were associated with teachers whose students either achieved the most or were the most motivated to learn. (To do this, of course, you would have to decide how to assess achievement and motivation.) You could identify teachers whose students, year after year, learned more than students working with other teachers; then you could watch the more successful teachers, and note what they do. You might also train teachers to apply several different strategies to teach the same lesson and then determine which strategy led to the greatest student learning. You could videotape teachers, then ask them to view the tapes and report what they were thinking about as they taught and what influenced their decisions while teaching. You might study transcripts of classroom dialogue to learn what helped students understand.

All these approaches and more have been used to investigate teaching. Often researchers conduct a series of studies by making careful observations and identifying relationships between teaching and learning. The researchers then use these relationships as the basis for developing teaching approaches and testing these approaches in design experiments (Brown, 1992; Greeno, Collins, and Resnick, 1996). Let's examine some of the specific knowledge about teaching gained from these projects.

Characteristics of Effective Teachers

Some of the earliest research on effective teaching focused on the personal qualities of the teachers themselves. Researchers thought that the key to success in teaching must lie in the characteristics of teachers (Medley, 1979). Although this assumption proved incorrect—or at least incomplete—it did teach us some lessons about three teacher characteristics: knowledge, clarity, and warmth.

Effective teachers know how to transform their knowledge into examples, explanations, illustrations, and activities. ▼

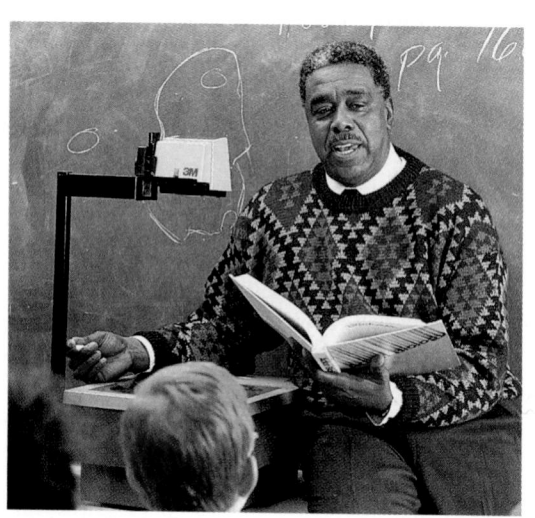

Teachers' Knowledge. Do teachers who know more about their subject have a more positive impact on their students? When we look at teachers' knowledge of facts and concepts, as measured by test scores and college grades, the relationship to student learning is unclear and may be indirect. Teachers who know more facts about their subject do not necessarily have students who learn more. But teachers who know more may make clearer presentations and recognize student difficulties more readily. They are ready for any student questions and do not have to be evasive or vague in their answers. Thus, knowledge is necessary but not sufficient for effective teaching because being more knowledgeable helps teachers be clearer and more organized.

Clarity and Organization. Students discussing a teacher are likely to make statements such as "Oh, she can really explain," or "He's so disorganized!" When Barak Rosenshine and

494   *Chapter 13*   Teaching for Learning

Norma Furst (1973) reviewed about 50 studies of teaching, they concluded that clarity was the most promising teacher behavior for future research on effective teaching. Studies confirm the importance of clarity. Teachers who provide clear presentations and explanations tend to have students who learn more and who rate their teachers more positively (Hines, Cruickshank, & Kennedy, 1985; Land, 1987). Teachers with more knowledge of the subject tend to be less vague in their explanations to the class. The less vague the teacher, the more the students learn (Land, 1987).

Planning for Clarity. Recent research offers guidelines for greater clarity in teaching (Berliner, 1987; Evertson et al., 2000; Hines, Cruickshank, & Kennedy, 1985). When planning a lesson, try to anticipate the problems your students will have with the material. Turn to teachers' manuals and experienced teachers for help with this. You might also do the written parts of the lesson yourself to identify potential problems. Have definitions ready for new terms, and prepare several relevant examples for concepts. Think of analogies that will make ideas easier to understand. Organize the lesson in a logical sequence; include checkpoints that incorporate oral or written questions or problems to make sure the students are following the explanations.

Plan a clear introduction to the lesson. Tell students what they will be learning and how they could approach it. Often teachers are vague about both the "what" and the "how." For example, in a study by Duffy, Roehler, Meloth, and Vavrus (1986), an ineffective reading teacher began her lesson on using context in reading by saying, "Today we are going to learn about context. This skill will help you in your reading" (p. 206). This is a vague and general statement of "what" the students will learn. An effective teacher in the same study began her lesson with an explicit, precise description:

> At the end of today's lesson, you will be able to use the other words in a sentence to figure out the meaning of an unknown word. The skill is one that you use when you come to a word that you don't know and you have to figure out what the word means. (p. 206)

Being precise about "how" to do the work is even harder. One study found that teachers seldom, if ever, explain the cognitive processes they want their students to practice in a seatwork activity. Bright students figure out the right process, but slower students often guess or give up. For example, an *ineffective* teacher might introduce a seatwork activity on words with prefixes by saying, "Here are some words with prefixes. Write the meaning of each in the blanks." An *effective* teacher, on the other hand, would demonstrate how to divide the words into a prefix and a root; how to determine the meaning of the root and the prefix; and how to put the two meanings together to make sense of the whole word (Berliner, 1987).

Clarity during the Lesson. Make clear connections between facts or concepts by using **explanatory links** such as *because*, *if . . . then*, or *therefore*. For example, when a teacher says, "The Northern economy was based on manufacturing and the North had an advantage in the Civil War," students are given two facts, but no connection between them. If there is a relationship between the two ideas, it should be indicated with an explanatory link as in, "The North had an advantage in the Civil War *because* its economy was based on manufacturing." Explanatory links tie ideas together and make them easier to learn (Berliner, 1987). Explanatory links are also helpful in labeling visual material such as graphs, concept maps, or illustrations.

Explanatory Links: Words and phrases such as *because* and *in order to* that specify the relationships between ideas.

In general, stick with your plan and do not digress. Signal transitions from one major topic to another with phrases such as *"The next area . . . ,"* *"Now we will turn to . . . ,"* or *"The second step is . . . ."* You might help students follow the lesson by outlining topics, listing key points, drawing concept maps on the board, or using an overhead projector. Continually monitor the group to see if everyone is following the lesson. Look for confident nods or puzzled stares. You should be able to tell if most students are keeping up.

Throughout the lesson, choose words that are familiar to the students. Define new terms and relate them to what the students already know. Be precise and check often for student understanding. Avoid vague words and ambiguous phrases: steer clear of "the somes"—*something, someone, sometime, somehow;* "the not verys"— *not very much, not very well, not very hard, not very often;* and other unspecific fillers, such as *most, not all, sort of, and so on, of course, as you know, I guess, in fact, or whatever,* and *more or less.* Use specific (and, if possible, colorful) names instead of *it, them,* and *thing.* Also, refrain from using pet phrases such as *you know, like,* and *Okay?* Another idea is to record a lesson on tape to check yourself for clarity.

Warmth and Enthusiasm. As you are well aware, some teachers are much more enthusiastic than others. Some studies have found that ratings of teachers' enthusiasm for their subject are correlated with student achievement gains (Rosenshine & Furst, 1973).Warmth, friendliness, and understanding seem to be the teacher traits most strongly related to student attitudes (Murray, 1983; Ryans, 1960; Soar & Soar, 1979). In other words, teachers who are warm and friendly tend to have students who like them and the class in general. But notice, these are correlational studies. The results do not tell us that teacher enthusiasm causes student learning or that warmth causes positive attitudes, only that the two variables tend to occur together. Teachers trained to demonstrate their enthusiasm have students who are more attentive and involved but not necessarily more successful on tests of content (Gillett & Gall, 1982).

The research we have looked at has identified teacher knowledge, clarity, organization, and enthusiasm as important characteristics of effective teachers. The Guidelines on page 497 summarize the practical implications of this work for the classroom.

The Teacher in Teacher-Centered Instruction

Connect and Extend
To your teaching
If you have observed in a primary grade, would you say that the teacher made use of direct instruction? Why or why not?

Direct Instruction/Explicit Teaching: Systematic instruction for mastery of basic skills, facts, and information.

Active Teaching: Teaching characterized by high levels of teacher explanation, demonstration, and interaction with students.

Much of the research that focused on effective teaching in the 1970s and 1980s pointed toward a model of teaching that was related to improved student learning. Barak Rosenshine calls this approach **direct instruction** (1979) or **explicit teaching** (1986). Tom Good (1983a) uses the term **active teaching** for a similar approach. The direct instruction model fits a specific set of circumstances because it was derived from a particular approach to research. Researchers identified the elements of direct instruction by comparing teachers whose students learned more than expected (based on entering knowledge) with teachers whose students performed at an expected or average level. The researchers focused on teaching as it is—on existing practices in American classrooms. Because the focus was on traditional forms of teaching, the research could not identify successful innovations. Effectiveness was usually defined as average improvement in standardized test scores for a whole class or school. So the results hold for large groups, but not necessarily for every student in the group.

GUIDELINES

Teaching Effectively

Organize your lessons carefully.

Examples

1. Provide objectives that help students focus on the purpose of the lesson.
2. Begin lessons by writing a brief outline on the board, or work on an outline with the class as part of the lesson.
3. If possible, break the presentation into clear steps or stages.
4. Review periodically.

Strive for clear explanations.

Examples

1. Use concrete examples or analogies that relate to the students' own lives. Have several examples for particularly difficult points.

2. Give explanations at several levels so all students, not just the brightest, will understand.
3. Focus on one idea at a time and avoid digressions.

Communicate an enthusiasm for your subject and the day's lesson.

Examples

1. Tell students why the lesson is important. Have a better reason than "This will be on the test" or "You will need to know it next year." Emphasize the value of the learning itself.
2. Be sure to make eye contact with the students.
3. Vary your pace and volume in speaking. Use silence for emphasis.

Even when the average achievement of a group improves, the achievement of some individuals may decline (Brophy & Good, 1986; Good, 1996; Shuell, 1996).

Given these conditions, you can see that direct instruction applies best to the teaching of **basic skills**—clearly structured knowledge and essential skills, such as science facts, mathematics computations, reading vocabulary, and grammar rules (Rosenshine & Stevens, 1986). These skills involve tasks that are relatively unambiguous; they can be taught step-by-step and tested by standardized tests. The teaching approaches described below are not necessarily appropriate for objectives such as helping students to write creatively, solve complex problems, or mature emotionally. Weinert and Helmke (1995) describe direct instruction as having the following features:

> (a) the teacher's classroom management is especially effective and the rate of student interruptive behaviors is very low; (b) the teacher maintains a strong academic focus and uses available instructional time intensively to initiate and facilitate students' learning activities; (c) the teacher insures that as many students as possible achieve good learning progress by carefully choosing appropriate tasks, clearly presenting subject-matter information and solution strategies, continuously diagnosing each student's learning progress and learning difficulties, and providing effective help through remedial instruction. (p. 138)

How would a teacher turn these themes into actions?

Rosenshine's Six Teaching Functions. Rosenshine and his colleagues (Rosenshine, 1988; Rosenshine & Stevens, 1986) have identified six teaching functions based on the research on effective instruction. These could serve as a checklist or framework for teaching basic skills.

1. *Review and check the previous day's work.* Reteach if students misunderstood or made errors.

Basic Skills: Clearly structured knowledge that is needed for later learning and that can be taught step by step.

Connect and Extend
To your teaching

Madeline Hunter gives these examples of instructions a teacher can give to check for student understanding [Hunter, M. (1982). *Mastery teaching*. El Segundo, CA: TIP Publications, p. 60]:

"Look at the first multiple choice question. Decide which answer you would select and when I say 'show me,' place that number of fingers under your chin."

"Make a plus with your fingers if you agree with this statement, a minus if you don't and a zero if you have strong feelings."

Connect and Extend
To the research

Madeline Hunter's approaches have been remarkably popular over the years, but they are not without their critics. See the November 1986 issue of *Elementary School Journal* for five articles on a four-year Madeline Hunter follow-through project. There are findings of quantitative and qualitative analysis, commentaries by Andrew Porter and Bob Slavin, and a response from Madeline Hunter. In general, the findings show some gains in the schools that used the Hunter program, but these gains were not maintained when consultation and support for the teachers were withdrawn in the final year of the program.

2. *Present new material.* Make the purpose clear, teach in small steps, provide many examples and nonexamples.

3. *Provide guided practice.* Question students, give practice problems, and listen for misconceptions and misunderstandings. Reteach if necessary. Continue guided practice until students answer about 80% of the questions correctly.

4. *Give feedback and correctives* based on student answers. Reteach if necessary.

5. *Provide independent practice.* Let students apply the new learning on their own, in seatwork, cooperative groups, or homework. The success rate during independent practice should be about 95%. This means that students must be well prepared for the work by the presentation and guided practice and that assignments must not be too difficult. The point is for the students to practice until the skills become over-learned and automatic—until the students are confident. Hold students accountable for the work they do—check it.

6. *Review weekly and monthly* to consolidate learning. Include some review items as homework. Test often, and reteach material missed on the tests.

These six functions are not steps to be followed in a particular order, but all of them are elements of effective instruction. For example, feedback, review, or reteaching should occur whenever necessary and should match the abilities of the students. There are several other models of direct instruction, but most share the elements presented in Table 13.9. Madeline Hunter's Mastery Teaching (Hunter, 1982) is another example of direct instruction.

Why Does Direct Instruction Work? What aspects of direct instruction might explain its success? Linda Anderson (1989b) suggests that lessons that help students perceive links among main ideas will help them construct accurate understandings. Well-organized presentations, clear explanations, the use of explanatory links, and reviews can all help students perceive connections among ideas. If done well, therefore, a direct instruction lesson could be a resource that students use to construct understanding. For example, reviews activate prior knowledge so the student is ready to understand. Brief, clear presentations and guided practice avoid overloading the students' information processing systems and taxing their working memories. Numerous examples and explanations give many pathways and associations for building networks of concepts. Guided practice can also give the teacher a snapshot of the students' thinking and of their misconceptions, so these can be addressed directly as misconceptions rather than simply as "wrong answers."

Criticisms of Direct Instruction

Critics say that direct instruction is limited to lower-level objectives, and that it is based on traditional teaching methods, ignores innovative models, and discourages students' independent thinking. Some educational psychologists claim that the direct instruction model tells teachers to "do what works" without grounding the suggestions in a theory of student learning. Other critics disagree, saying that direct instruction is based on a theory of student learning—but it is the *wrong* theory. Teachers break material into small segments, present each segment clearly, and reinforce or correct, thus *transmitting* accurate understandings from teacher to student. The student is seen as an "empty vessel" waiting to be filled with knowledge, rather than an active constructor of knowledge (Anderson, 1989a; Berg & Clough,

TABLE 13.9 *The Hunter Mastery Teaching Program: Selected Principles*

Get students set to learn.

- Make the best use of the prime time at the beginning of the lesson.
- Give students a review question or two to consider while you call the roll, pass out papers, or do other "housekeeping" chores. Follow up—listen to their answers, and correct if necessary.
- Create an *anticipatory set* to capture the students' attention. This might be an advance organizer, an intriguing question, or a brief exercise. For example, at the beginning of a lesson on categories of plants you could ask, "How is pumpkin pie similar to cherry pie but different from sweet potato pie?" Answer: Pumpkins and cherries are both fruits, unlike sweet potatoes.
- Communicate the lesson objectives (unless withholding this information for a while is part of your overall plan).

Provide information effectively.

- Determine the basic information and organize it. Use this basic structure as scaffolding for the lesson.
- Present information clearly and simply. Use familiar terms, examples, illustrations.
- Model what you mean. If appropriate, demonstrate or use analogies—"If the basketball Ann is holding were the sun, how far away do you think I would have to hold this pea to represent Pluto . . . ?"

Check for understanding, and give guided practice.

- Ask a question, and have every student signal an answer—"Thumbs up if this statement is true, down if it's false."
- Ask for a choral response: "Everyone, is this a dependent or an independent clause?"
- Sample individual responses: "Everyone, think of an example of a closed system. Jon, what's your example?"

Allow for independent practice.

- Get students started right by doing the first few questions together.
- Make independent practice brief. Monitor responses, giving feedback quickly.

Connect and Extend
To the research

For another perspective, read Berg, C. A., & Clough, M. (1991). Hunter lesson design: The wrong *one for science teaching*. *Educational Leadership, 48*(4), 73–78. *Focus Questions:* Why do Berg and Clough believe that the Hunter design is the wrong one for science teaching? How do students think Hunter would react? Then read Hunter, M. (1991). Hunter design helps achieve the goals of science instruction. *Educational Leadership, 48*(4), 79–81. *Focus Questions:* Evaluate Hunter's defense of her model. Do you agree that the Hunter approach can achieve the goals of science instruction?

Connect and Extend
To your teaching

Here are some ideas for ways to involve all students actively in a lesson. Ask them to:

1. Tell the answer to a neighbor.
2. Summarize the main idea in one or two sentences, writing the summary on a piece of paper and sharing this with a neighbor, or repeat the procedures to a neighbor.
3. Write the answer on a slate, then hold up the slate.
4. Raise their hand if they know the answer (thereby allowing the teacher to check the entire class).
5. Raise their hand if they agree with an answer someone else gave.
6. Raise different colored cards when the answer is a, b, or c.

Taken from Rosenshine, B. (1987). Explicit teaching. In D. Berliner & B. Rosenshine (Eds.), *Talks to teachers* (pp. 75–92). New York: Random House, p. 84.

1991; Davis, Maher, & Noddings, 1990). These criticisms of direct instruction echo the criticisms of behavioral learning theories.

There is ample evidence, however, that direct instruction and explanation can help students learn actively, not passively. For younger and less prepared learners, student-controlled learning without teacher direction and instruction can lead to systematic deficits in the students' knowledge. Without guidance, the understandings that students construct can be incomplete and misleading (Weinert & Helmke, 1995). Deep understanding and fluid performance—whether in dance or mathematical problem solving or reading—require models of expert performance and extensive practice with feedback (Anderson, Reder, & Simon, 1995). Guided and independent practice with feedback are at the heart of the direct instruction model.

What direct instruction cannot do is *ensure* that students understand. If badly done, it may encourage students to memorize and mimic but never to "own" the knowledge. To help students reach this goal, Eleanor Duckworth believes that teachers must pay very close attention to understanding their students' understandings (Meek, 1991). What do we know about good teaching in student-centered instruction? The next section describes this kind of effective teaching.

The Teacher in Student-Centered Instruction

Table 13.10 lists some characteristics of constructivist teaching practices described by Jacqueline Grennon Brooks and M. G. Brooks (1993). These teaching approaches are consistent with constructivist strategies such as those described in Chapter 9— inquiry, cooperative learning, instructional conversations, and cognitive apprenticeships.

TABLE 13.10 *Constructivist Teaching Practices*

Many constructivist practices can be incorporated into any class.

1. Constructivist teachers encourage and accept student autonomy and initiative.
2. Constructivist teachers use raw data and primary sources, along with manipulative, interactive, and physical materials.
3. When framing tasks, constructivist teachers use cognitive terminology such as "classify," "analyze," "predict," and "create."
4. Constructivist teachers allow student responses to drive lessons, shift instructional strategies, and alter content.
5. Constructivist teachers inquire about students' understandings of concepts before sharing their own understandings of those concepts.
6. Constructivist teachers encourage students to engage in dialogue, both with the teacher and with one another.
7. Constructivist teachers encourage student inquiry by asking thoughtful, open-ended questions and encouraging students to ask questions of each other.
8. Constructivist teachers seek elaboration of students' initial responses.
9. Constructivist teachers engage students in experiences that might engender contradictions to their initial hypotheses and then encourage discussion.
10. Constructivist teachers allow wait-time after posing questions.
11. Constructivist teachers provide time for students to discover relationships and create metaphors.

Source: From "Becoming a Constructivist Teacher." In *In Search of Understanding: The Case for Constructivist Classrooms* (pp. 101–118) by J. G. Brooks and M. G. Brooks, 1995, Association for Supervision and Curriculum Development. Copyright © 1995 by ASCD. Reprinted with permission.

Beyond Models to Outstanding Teaching

We have examined two perspectives on good teaching, one that fits direct, explicit teaching and one that is consistent with constructivist approaches. You may hear debates about the merits of these general approaches in many of your education courses. Often the debate about directive versus constructivist approaches is loudest when the students in question are at risk of failing, as you can see in the Point/Counterpoint.

What Is the Best Way to Help Students at Risk of Failing?

There are many ideas and models for teaching low-achieving students—students often referred to as "at risk" for failure. Some recommendations are based on direct instruction and basic skills teaching. Another approach bases its recommendations on cognitive theories of learning, and these recommendations question the value of direct instruction. What are the teaching strategies offered by each approach?

▶ **POINT** *Adapt direct instruction for students' needs.*

Research on effective teachers of low achievers (Ebmeier & Ziomek, 1982; Emmer et al., 2000; Slavin, Karweit, & Madden, 1989) has identified these approaches as helpful:

Break instruction into small steps and provide short activities, chosen and sequenced by the teacher.

Cover material thoroughly and at a moderate pace. Give plenty of practice, immediate clear feedback, and specific praise.

Have students work as a whole class or in groups so the teacher can supervise. Avoid individualized, self-paced, or independent work.

Keep a level of difficulty that guarantees high rates of success.

Ask convergent questions—one correct answer.

Make sure to call on everyone and stay with a student until a question is answered.

Avoid interruptions, open-ended questions, and nonacademic conversations.

Emphasize short, frequent paper-and-pencil exercises, not games, arts, crafts, discovery learning activities, and interest centers. These are less helpful for learning.

◀ **COUNTERPOINT** *Move beyond the basics.*

Educators and psychologists who hold a cognitive view of learning are critical of direct instruction. For example, Barbara Means and Michael Knapp (1991) decry the "basics" approach to teaching low achievers:

A recent summary of critiques of conventional approaches to teaching academic skills to at-risk students, offered by a group of national experts in reading, writing, and mathematics education, concluded that such approaches tend to:

underestimate what students are capable of doing;

postpone more challenging and interesting work for too long— in some cases, forever;

and deprive students of a meaningful or motivating context for learning or for employing the skills that are taught. (pp. 283–284)

What do critics of direct instruction offer in its place? The following are some principles rec-

ommended by Means and Knapp (1991):

Focus on complex, meaningful problems. Keep the level of tasks high enough that the purpose of the task is apparent and makes sense to students.

Embed basic skills instruction in the context of more global tasks such as class record keeping or letter writing.

Make connections with students' out-of-school experience and culture.

Model powerful thinking strategies for students; for example, think aloud as you try to figure out a difficult text passage.

Encourage multiple approaches to academic tasks. Have students describe how they reached their answers.

Provide scaffolding to enable students to accomplish complex tasks; for example, perform the calculations for students as they set up an algebra problem correctly.

Make dialogue the central medium for teaching and learning. Reciprocal teaching is one example. (See Chapter 9.)

In spite of the debates, there is no one best way to teach. Different goals require different methods. Teacher-centered instruction leads to better performance on achievement tests, while the open, informal methods such as discovery learning or inquiry approaches are associated with better performance on tests of creativity, abstract thinking, and problem solving. In addition, the open methods are better for improving attitudes toward school and for stimulating curiosity, cooperation among students, and lower absence rates (Walberg, 1990). According to these conclusions, when the goals of teaching involve problem solving, creativity, understanding, and

Connect and Extend
To your own philosophy
Can different formats, such as lecture or seatwork, be used in the service of different models, such as direct instruction or constructivist approaches?

mastering processes, many approaches besides direct instruction should be effective.

These guidelines are in keeping with Tom Good's conclusion that teaching should become less direct as students mature and when the goals involve affective development and problem solving or critical thinking (Good, 1983a). Of course, every subject, even college English or chemistry, can require some direct instruction. If you are teaching when to use "who" and "whom," or how to set up laboratory apparatus, direct instruction may be the best approach. Noddings (1990) reminds teachers that students may need some direct instruction in how to use various manipulative materials to get the possible benefits from them. Students working in cooperative groups may need guidance, modeling, and practice in how to ask questions and give explanations. And to solve difficult problems, students may need some direct instruction in possible problem-solving strategies. The message for teachers is to match instructional methods to learning goals.

Effective Teaching in Inclusive Classrooms

When you think about teaching in an inclusion classroom, what are your concerns? Do you have enough training? Will you get the support you need from school administrators or specialists? Will working with the students with disabilities take time away from your other responsibilities? These are common questions, and sometimes concerns are justified. But effective teaching for exceptional students does not require a unique set of skills. It is a combination of good teaching practices and sensitivity to all your students. Students with disabilities need to *learn the academic material*, and they need to be *full participants in the day-to-day life of the classroom*.

To accomplish the first goal of academic learning, Larrivee (1985) concluded that effective teachers of mainstreamed students do the following:

1. Use time efficiently by having smooth management routines, avoiding discipline problems, and planning carefully.

2. Ask questions at the right level of difficulty.

3. Give supportive, positive feedback to students, helping them figure out the right answer if they are wrong but on the right track.

To accomplish the second goal of integrating students with disabilities into the day-to-day life of the classroom, Ferguson, Ferguson, and Bogdan (1987) give the following guidelines:

1. Mix students with disabilities into groups with students who do not have special needs. Avoid resegregating the students with disabilities into separate groups.

2. Instead of sending students out for special services such as speech therapy, remedial reading, or individualized instruction, try to integrate the special help into the class setting, perhaps during a time when the other students are working independently too.

3. Make sure your language and behavior toward students with disabilities is a good model for everyone.

4. Teach about differences among people as part of the curriculum. Let students become familiar with aids for individuals with disabilities, such as hearing aids, sign language, communication boards, and so on. And give students many different ways to show their ability—writing, talking, organizing, drawing, diagramming, planning, demonstrating, helping, or performing, for example.

5. Have students work together in cooperative groups or on special projects such as role plays, biographical interviews, or lab assignments.

6. Try to keep similar schedules and activity patterns for all students.

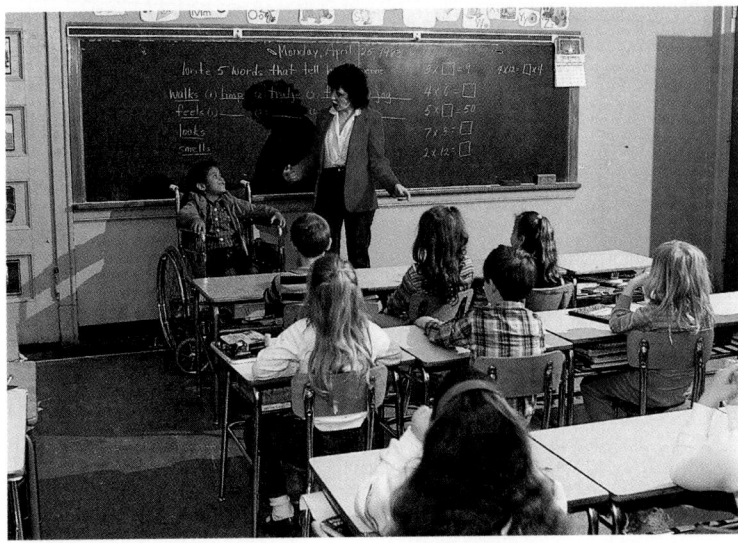

▲ *For a classroom to be truly inclusive, students with disabilities need access to learning academic material, and to full participation in day-to-day classroom activities.*

Working with Individual Students

When students have special needs, they may be referred to specialists such as child study teams, school psychologists, or teachers of students with special needs for evaluation (see Table 4.9 on page 147 for guidelines about referring students for evaluation). The outcome of this process sometimes includes the preparation of an individualized educational program or IEP, as described in Chapter 4. Figure 13.3 on page 504 is an excerpt from the IEP of a 9-year old girl with mild retardation. This section of the plan focuses on one behavior problem and reading. You may help to develop these programs for students in your classes. The programs should provide guidance for you in teaching.

Resource Rooms, Collaborative Consultation, and Cooperative Teaching

Many schools provide additional help for classroom teachers who work with students with disabilities. A **resource room** is a classroom with special materials and equipment and a specially trained teacher. Students may come to the resource room each day for several minutes or several hours and receive instruction individually or in small groups. The rest of the day the students are in regular education classes. Besides working with students directly, a resource teacher may also work with them indirectly by giving the general education teacher ideas, materials, or actual demonstrations of teaching techniques.

Resource Room: Classroom with special materials and a specially trained teacher.

An Excerpt from an Individualized Educational Program (IEP)

This IEP was developed for a 9-year-old girl. This section of the plan focuses on following the teacher's directions and on reading.

Student: _Amy North_   Age: _9_   Grade: _1_   Date: _Oct. 17, 1995_

1. Unique Characteristics or Needs: Noncompliance

Frequently noncompliant with teacher's instructions.

1. **Present Levels of Performance**
Complies with about 50% of teacher requests/commands.

2. **Special Education, Related Services, and Modifications**
Implemented immediately, strong reinforcement for compliance with teacher's instructions (Example: "Sure I will!" plan including precision requests and reinforcer menu for points earned for compliance, as described in The Tough Kid Book, by Rhode, Jenson, and Reavis, 1992); within 3 weeks, training of parents by school psychologist to use precision requests and reinforcement at home.

3. **Objectives (Including Procedures, Criteria, and Schedule)**
Within one month, will comply with teacher requests/commands 90% of the time; compliance monitored weekly by the teacher.

4. **Annual Goals**
Will become compliant with teacher's requests/commands.

2. Unique Characteristics or Needs: Reading

2a. Very slow reading rate   2c. Limited phonics skills
2b. Poor comprehension   2d. Limited sight-word vocabulary

1. **Present Levels of Performance**
2a. Reads stories of approximately 100 words of first-grade level at approximately 40 words per min.
2b. Seldom can recall factual information about stories immediately after reading them.
2c. Consistently confuses vowel sounds, often misidentifies consonants, and does not blend sounds.
2d. Has sight-word vocabulary of approximately 150 words.

2. **Special Education, Related Services, and Modifications**
2a–2c. Direct instruction 30 minutes daily in vowel discrimination, consonant identification, and sound blending; begin immediately, continue throughout schoolyear.
2a & 2d. Sight word drill 10 minutes daily in addition to phonics instruction and daily practice; 10 minutes practice in using phonics and sight-word skills in reading story at her level; begin immediately, continue for schoolyear.

3. **Objectives (Including Procedures, Criteria, and Schedule)**
2a. Within 3 months, will read stories on her level at 60 words per minute with 2 or fewer errors per story; within six months, 80 words with 2 or fewer errors; performance monitored daily by teacher or aide.
2b. Within 3 months will answer oral and written comprehension questions requiring recall of information from stories she has just read with 90% accuracy (e.g., Who is in the story? What happened? When? Why?) and be able to predict probably outcomes with 80% accuracy; performance monitored daily by teacher or aide.
2c. Within 3 months, will increase sight-word vocabulary to 200 words, within 6 months to 250 words, assessed by flash-card presentation.

4. **Annual Goals**
2a–2c. Will read fluently and with comprehension at beginning-second-grade level.

Source: From *Exceptional Learners: Introduction to Special Education* (7th ed.) (p. 37), by D. P. Hallahan and J. M. Kauffman, 1995, Boston: Allyn & Bacon. Copyright © 1995 by Allyn & Bacon. Reprinted with permission.

Increasingly, special and general education teachers are working together, collaborating to assume equal responsibility for the education of students with disabilities. The collaboration may work through consultation, planning, and problem solving about how to teach specific students, or the special education teacher might

FIGURE 13.4

Cooperative and Co-Teaching Approaches

There are many ways for teachers to work together in inclusion classrooms.

One teach, one support   Station teaching   Parallel teaching   Alternative teaching   Team teaching

◖ Teacher   ● Student   ▭ Desk/Table

Source: From *Including Students with Special Needs: A Practical Guide for Classroom Teachers* (p. 87), by M. Friend and W. Bursuck, Boston: Allyn & Bacon. Copyright © 1996 by Allyn & Bacon. Reprinted with permission.

work directly alongside the general education teacher in a class made up of students with and without disabilities. The latter is called **cooperative teaching**. The teachers assume different roles, depending on the age of the students and their needs. For example, in a secondary class the general education teacher might be responsible for academic content, while the special education instructor teaches study skills and learning strategies. In another classroom the general education teacher might deal with core content, while the special teacher provides remediation, enrichment, or re-teaching when necessary. The two teachers might also try team teaching, where each is responsible for different parts of the lesson.

When using cooperative teaching, it is important that general education students and students with disabilities aren't resegregated in the class, with the general education teacher always working with the "general education" students and the special education teacher always working with the "mainstreamed" students. I observed one class in which the students with disabilities worked only with the special education teacher but often looked longingly over their shoulders at the activities of their classmates working with the general education teacher. Rather than integrating the students with disabilities into the class, this cooperative teaching arrangement accentuated their separateness. Figure 13.4 shows different ways to implement cooperative teaching.

Computers and Exceptional Students

Computers have improved the education of exceptional children in countless ways. Given the recordkeeping and program planning needed to meet federal regulations, teachers can use computers to manage instruction. For students who require small steps and many repetitions to learn a new concept, computers are the perfect patient tutors, repeating steps and lessons as many times as necessary. A well-designed computer instructional program is engaging and interactive—two important qualities for

Cooperative Teaching: Collaboration between regular and special education teachers.

students with problems paying attention or with a history of failure that has eroded motivation. For example, a math or spelling program might use images, sounds, and gamelike features to maintain the attention of a student with an attention-deficit disorder. Interactive videodisc programs are being developed to help hearing people use sign language. Many programs do not involve sound, so students with hearing impairments can get the full benefit from the lessons. Students who have trouble reading can use programs that will "speak" a word for them if they touch the unknown word with a light pen or the cursor. With this immediate access to help, the students are much more likely to get the reading practice they need to prevent falling farther and farther behind. Other devices actually convert printed pages and typed texts to spoken words for students who are blind or others who benefit from hearing information.

For the student with a learning disability whose writing can't be read, word processors produce perfect penmanship so the ideas can finally get on paper. Once the ideas are on paper, the student can reorganize and improve the writing without the agony of rewriting by hand (Hallahan & Kauffman, 2000; Hardman, Drew, & Egan, 1996; Reynolds & Birch, 1988).

With these tremendous advances in technology have come new barriers, however. Many computers have graphic interfaces. To manipulate the programs requires precise "mouse movements," as you may remember when you first learned to point and click. These maneuvers are difficult for students with motor problems or visual impairments. And the information available on the Internet often is unusable for students with visual problems. Researchers are working on the problem—trying to devise ways for people to access the information nonvisually, but the adaptations are not perfected yet (Hallahan & Kauffman, 2000).

For gifted students, computers can be a connection with databases and computers in universities, museums, and research labs. Computer networks allow students to work on projects and share information with others across the country. It is also possible to have gifted students write programs for students and teachers. Quite a few principals around the country rely on their students to make the technology in the school work. These are just a few examples of what technology can do. Check with the resource teachers in your district to find out what is available in your school.

In the next section we examine successful teaching in different subjects.

CHECKPOINT

Effective Teaching in Inclusive Classrooms

Review

▶ What characterizes effective teaching for exceptional students?

▶ What resources do teachers have to work effectively with exceptional children?

Apply

▶ What resources do you have to be successful in an inclusion classroom?

Focus on the Subject: Teaching Reading, Mathematics, and Science

It is clear that a teacher's knowledge of the subject is critical for teaching (Borko & Putnam, 1996). Part of that knowledge is pedagogical content knowledge, or knowing how to teach a subject to your particular students (Shulman, 1987). In the last decade, psychologists have made great progress understanding how students learn different subjects (Mayer, 1992). Based on these findings, many approaches have been developed to teach reading, writing, science, mathematics, social studies, and all the other subjects. Many of these approaches reflect the constructivist perspectives described in Chapter 9.

Learning to Read and Write

For years, educators have debated whether students should be taught to read and write through code-based (phonics or skills) approaches that relate letters to sounds and sounds to words or through meaning-based (whole-language, literature-based, emergent literacy) approaches that do not dissect words and sentences into pieces, but instead focus on the meaning of the text (Goodman, 1986; Goodman & Goodman, 1990; Smith, 1994; Stahl & Miller, 1989; Symons, Woloshyn, & Pressley, 1994; Vellutino, 1991).

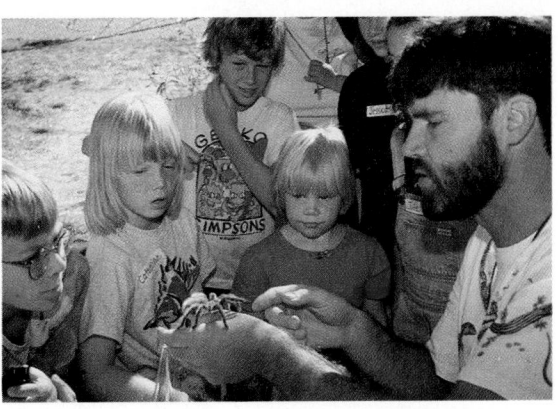

▲ *Contemporary learning theories have sought to understand how students learn different subjects in different ways, and in turn, how teaching methods might be adapted to these differences.*

Whole Language. Advocates of whole-language approaches believe that learning to read is a natural process, very much like mastering your native language. Reading is a kind of guessing game in which students sample words and make predictions and guesses about meaning based on the context of other words in the passage and on their prior knowledge. Thus, words should not be presented out of context, and "sounding out" words and "breaking whole (natural) language into bite-size abstract little pieces" should be avoided (Goodman, 1986, p. 7). Rather, children should be immersed in a print-rich environment, surrounded by books worth reading and adults who read—to the children and for themselves.

Within this **whole-language perspective**, teaching and learning are seen as reciprocal and collaborative. The teacher becomes an astute observer of students, noticing what support or resources they need in order to learn. Teacher and students together make decisions about curriculum. When students write, they write for an audience; their goal is to communicate effectively. Writing is a relevant and meaningful activity. Vygotsky (1978) recognized the importance of authentic writing tasks: "[W]riting should be incorporated into a task that is necessary and relevant for life. Only then can we be certain that it will develop not as a matter of hand and finger habits but as a really new and complex form of speech" (p. 118). David Pearson (1989) makes a similar point: "[We] should ask students to read and write for real reasons (the kind real people in the real world have) rather than fake reasons we give them in school. School is too school-like" (p. 235).

There are many approaches to whole-language learning, but most share an emphasis on authentic tasks and integrated curricula. Clearly, there are many advantages of a whole-language, integrated curriculum approach, but still. . . .

Do Students Need Skills and Phonics? There are now two decades of research demonstrating that skill in recognizing sounds and words supports reading. Advocates of code-based approaches cite research showing that being able to identify many words as you read does not depend on using context to guess meaning. In fact, it is almost the other way around—knowing words helps you make sense of context. Identifying words as you read is a highly automatic process. The more fluent and

Whole-Language Perspective: A philosophical approach to teaching and learning that stresses learning through authentic, real-life tasks. Emphasizes using language to learn, integrating learning across skills and subjects, and respecting the language abilities of student and teacher.

automatic you are in identifying words, the more effective you will be in getting meaning from context (Vellutino, 1991). It is the poorest readers who resort to using context to help them understand meaning (Pressley, 1996).

Many studies support the code-based position. For example, three different groups reported similar findings in the *Journal of Educational Psychology* (December, 1991). Summarizing the results of these investigations, Frank Vellutino states:

> I think it is fair to say that the major theoretical assumptions on which whole-language approaches to instruction are based have simply not been verified in relevant research testing those assumptions. Aside from the fact that there are very sound reasons to reject the "natural" parallel between spoken and written language drawn by whole-language theorists, the research supports the following generalizations: (a) The most basic skill in learning to read is word identification; (b) an adequate degree of fluency in word identification is a basic prerequisite to successful reading comprehension; (c) word identification in skilled readers is a fast-acting, automatic, and in effect modular process that depends little on contextual information for execution; (d) even skilled readers can predict not more than one word out of four in sentence contexts, indicating that the predictive role of context must be extremely limited; (e) because of limited facility in word identification, beginning and poor readers are much more dependent on context than are more advanced readers. (p. 442)

Vellutino goes on to list two more generalizations, that alphabetic coding and awareness of letter sounds are essential skills for acquiring word identification, so some direct teaching of the alphabet and phonics is helpful in learning to read. The best approach probably makes sensible use of both phonics and whole language. After all, we want our students to be fluent *and* enthusiastic readers and writers (Bus & van IJzendoorn, 1999; Pressley, 1998).

Being Sensible about Reading and Writing. The results of high-quality studies, summarized in Table 13.11, suggest that:

▶ Whole-language approaches to reading and writing are most effective in preschool and kindergarten. Whole language gives children a good conceptual basis for reading and writing. The social interactions around reading and writing—reading big books, writing shared stories, examining pictures, discussing meaning—are activities that support literacy and mirror the early home experiences of children who come to school prepared to learn. Whole-language approaches seem to improve students' motivation, interest, and attitude toward reading and help children understand the nature and purposes of reading and writing (Graham & Harris, 1994; Morrow, 1992; Neuman & Roskos, 1992).

▶ Phonemic awareness—the sense that words are composed of separate sounds and that sounds are combined to create words—in kindergarten and 1st grade predicts literacy in later grades. If children do not have phonemic awareness in the early grades, direct teaching can dramatically improve their chances of long-term achievement in literacy. Earlier is better—preschoolers tend to profit more from phonological training than kindergarten or primary grade students (Bus & van IJzendoorn, 1999; Pressley, 1998).

▶ Excellent primary school teachers use both explicit decoding-skills teaching and whole-language instruction. Reading teachers should use a balanced approach rather than stressing either a literature-based whole-language or a skills-first approach (Adams, Trieman, & Pressley, 1998; Bus & van IJzendoorn, 1999; Vellutino, 1991).

TABLE 13.11 *Improving the Reading Achievement of America's Children: CIERA's 10 Research-Based Principles*

CIERA (the Center for the Improvement of Early Reading Achievement) has reviewed the research on learning to read and distilled the best findings into these 10 principles. You can read the expanded version of the principles on their Web site—www.ciera.org— under free information.

1. **Home language and literacy experiences** support the development of key print concepts and a range of knowledge prepares students for school-based learning. Programs that help families initiate and sustain these experiences show positive benefits for children's reaching achievement.

   Examples: Joint reading with a family member, parental modeling of good reading habits, monitoring homework and television viewing.

2. **Preschool programs** are particularly beneficial for children who do not experience informal learning opportunities in their homes. Such preschool experiences lead to improved reading achievement, with some effects lasting through grade 3.

   Examples: Listening to and examining books, saying nursery rhymes, writing messages, and seeing and talking about print.

3. **Skills that predict later reading success** can be promoted in kindergarten and grade 1. The two most powerful of these predictors are letter-name knowledge and phonemic awareness. Instruction in these skills has demonstrated positive effects on primary grade reading achievement, especially when it is coupled with letter-sound instruction.

   Examples: Encourage children to hear and blend sound through oral renditions of rhymes, poems, and songs, as well as writing messages and in journals.

4. **Primary-level instruction** that supports successful reading acquisition is consistent, well-designed, and focused.

   Examples: Systematic word recognition instruction on common, consistent letter-sound relationships and important but often unpredictable high-frequency words, such as *the* and *what;* teaching children to monitor the accuracy of their reading as well as their understanding of texts through strategies such as predicting, inferencing, clarifying misunderstandings, and summarizing; promoting word recognition and comprehension through repeated reading of text, guided reading and writing, strategy lessons, reading aloud with feedback, and conversations about texts children have read.

5. **Primary-level classroom environments** in successful schools provide opportunities for students to apply what they have learned in teacher-guided instruction to everyday reading and writing.

   Examples: Teachers read books aloud and hold follow-up discussions, children read independently every day, and children write stories and keep journals. These events are monitored frequently by teachers, ensuring that time is well spent and that children receive feedback on their efforts. Teachers design and revise these events based on information from ongoing assessment of children's strengths and needs.

6. **Cultural and linguistic diversity** among America's children reflects the variations within their communities and homes. This diversity is manifest in differences in the children's dispositions toward and knowledge about topics, language, and literacy.

   Examples: Effective instruction includes assessment, integration, and extension of relevant background knowledge and the use of texts that recognize diverse backgrounds. Build on the children's language when children are learning to speak, listen to, write, and read English. When teachers capitalize on the advantages of bilingualism or biliteracy, second language reading acquisition is significantly enhanced.

7. **Children who are identified as having reading disabilities** profit from the same sort of well-balanced instructional programs that benefit all children who are learning to read and write, including systematic instruction *and* meaningful reading and writing.

   Examples: Intensive one-on-one or small-group instruction, attention to both comprehension and word recognition processes, thoroughly individualized assessment and instructional planning, and extensive experiences with many types of texts.

8. **Proficient reading in third grade** and above is sustained and enhanced by programs that adhere to four fundamental features:

   Features: (1) deep and wide opportunities to read, (2) acquiring new knowledge and vocabulary, through wide reading and through explicit instruction about networks of new concepts, (3) emphasizing the influence on understanding of kinds of text (e.g., stories versus essays) and the ways writers organize particular texts, and (4) assisting students in reasoning about text.

9. **Professional opportunities** to improve reading achievement are prominent in successful schools and programs.

   Examples: Opportunities for teachers and administrators to analyze instruction, assessment, and achievement; to set goals for improvement; to learn about effective practices; and to participate in ongoing communities that deliberately try to understand both successes and persistent problems.

10. **Entire school staffs,** not just first-grade teachers, are involved in bringing children to high levels of achievement.

    Examples: In successful schools, reading achievement goals are clear, expectations are high, instructional means for attaining goals are articulated, and shared assessments monitor children's progress. Even though they might use different materials and technologies, successful schools maintain a focus on reading and writing and have programs to involve parents in their children's reading and homework. Community partnerships, including volunteer tutoring programs, are common.

If students need help cracking the code—give them what they need. Don't let ideology get in the way. You will just send more students to private tutors—if their families can afford it. But don't forget that reading and writing are for a purpose. Surround students with good literature and create a community of readers and writers. As you saw in Table 13.11, the Center for Early Reading describes 10 principles that capture this balanced approach to teaching.

The above discussion applies to reading and writing in the early grades, but what about the later years when comprehending difficult texts becomes important? Here reciprocal teaching (Chapter 9) and study skills (Chapter 8) can be helpful.

Learning and Teaching Mathematics

Some of the most compelling support for constructivist approaches to teaching comes from mathematics education. Critics of direct instruction believe that traditional mathematics instruction often teaches students an unintended lesson—that they "cannot understand mathematics," or worse, that mathematics doesn't have to make sense, you just have to memorize the formulas. Arthur Baroody and Herbert Ginsburg (1990, p. 62) give this example:

> Sherry, a junior high student, explained that her math class was learning how to convert measurements from one unit to another. The interviewer gave Sherry the following problem:
>
> > To feed data into the computer, the measurements in your report have to be converted to one unit of measurement: feet. Your first measurement, however, is 3 feet 6 inches. What are you going to feed into the computer?
>
> Sherry recognized immediately that the conversion algorithm taught in school applied. . . . However, because she really did not understand the rationale behind the conversion algorithm, Sherry had difficulty in remembering the steps and how to execute them. After some time she came up with an improbable answer (it was less than 3 feet). Sherry knew she was in trouble and became flustered. At this point, the interviewer tried to help by asking her if there was any other way of solving the problem. Sherry responded sharply, "No!" She explained, "That's the way it has to be done." The interviewer tried to give Sherry a hint: "Look at the numbers in the problem, is there another way we can think about them that might help us figure out the problem more easily?" Sherry grew even more impatient, "This is the way I learned in school, so it has to be the way."

Sherry believed that there was only one way to solve a problem. Though Sherry knew that 6 inches was one-half a foot and that the fraction one-half was equivalent to the decimal expression .5, she did not use this knowledge to solve the problem informally and quickly ("3 feet 6 inches is 3½ feet, or 3.5 feet"). Her beliefs prevented her from effectively using her existing mathematical knowledge to solve the problem. Sherry had probably been taught to memorize the steps to convert one measurement to another. How would a constructivist approach teach the same material?

The following excerpt shows how a 3rd-grade teacher, Ms. Coleman, uses a constructivist approach to teach negative numbers. Notice the use of dialogue and the way the teacher asks students to justify and explain their thinking. The class has been considering one problem: $-10 + 10 = ?$ A student, Marta, has just tried to explain, using a number line, why $-10 + 10 = 0$:

Teacher: Marta says that negative ten plus ten equals zero, so you have to count ten numbers to the right. What do you think, Harold?

Connect and Extend
To the research
Another example of how students solve mathematics problems by applying rules is taken from Merseth, K. K. (1993). How old is the shepherd? An essay about mathematics education. *Phi Delta Kappan, 74*, 548–554. Merseth cites findings from research showing that three out of four students will produce some numerical answer to the problem: There are 125 sheep and 5 dogs in a flock. How old is the shepherd? Here is how one child reached an answer. Notice that logic and reasoning play a role: "125 + 5 = 130 . . . this is too big, and 125 − 5 = 120 is still too big . . . while 125/ 5 = 25. That works! I think the shepherd is 25 years old!"

Connect and Extend
To the research
Research: Resnick, L. B. (1989). Developing mathematical knowledge. *American Psychologist, 44*, 162–169.
Brief Abstract: Research has given rise to new ideas about the nature of children's number-knowledge development. This article shows how infants' and preschoolers' implicit protoquantitative reasoning schemas combine with early counting knowledge to produce mathematical concepts of number. It also discusses elementary school children's informal and invented arithmetic, as well as implications for mathematics education.

TABLE 13.12 *A Constructivist Approach to Mathematics: Five Components*

1. Promote students' autonomy and commitment to their answers

   Examples:

   • Question both right and wrong student answers.

   • Insist that students at least try to solve a problem and be able to explain what they tried.

2. Develop students' reflective processes

   Examples:

   • Question students to guide them to try different ways to resolve the problem.

   • Ask students to restate the problem in their own words; to explain what they are doing and why; and to discuss what they mean by the terms they are using.

3. Construct a case history of each student

   Examples:

   • Note general tendencies in the way the student approaches problems, as well as common misconceptions and strengths.

4. If the student is unable to solve a problem, intervene to negotiate a possible solution with the student.

   Examples:

   • Based on the case study and your understanding of how the student is thinking about a problem, guide the student to think about a possible solution.

   • Ask questions such as "Is there anything you did in the last one that will help you here?" or "Can you explain your diagram?"

   • If the student is becoming frustrated, ask more direct, product-oriented questions.

5. When the problem is solved, review the solution

   Examples:

   • Encourage students to reflect on what they did and why.

   • Note what students did well and build confidence.

Source: From "What Constructivism Implies for Teaching," by J. Confrey, 1990, in *Constructivist Views on the Teaching and Learning of Mathematics* by R. Davis, C. Maher, and N. Noddings (Eds.). Monograph 4 of the National Council of Teachers of Mathematics, Reston, VA. Copyright © 1990 National Council of Teachers of Mathematics. Adapted with permission.

Harold: I think it's easy, but I don't understand how she explained it.

Teacher: OK. Does anybody else have a comment or a response to that? Tessa? (Peterson, 1992, p. 165)

As the discussion progresses, Ms. Coleman encourages students to talk directly to each other:

Teacher: You said you don't understand what she is trying to say?

Chang: No.

Teacher: Do you want to ask her?

Chang: What do you mean by counting to the right?

This dialogue reveals three things about learning and teaching in a constructivist classroom: The thinking processes of the students are the focus of attention; one topic is considered in depth rather than attempting to "cover" many topics; and assessment is ongoing and mutually shared by teacher and students.

Jere Confrey (1990b) analyzed an expert mathematics teacher in a class for high school girls who had difficulty with mathematics. Confrey identified five components in a model of this teacher's approach to teaching. These components are summarized in Table 13.12.

Learning Science

We have seen a number of times that by high school many students have "learned" some unfortunate lessons in school. Like Sherry, described in the preceding section, they have learned that math is impossible to understand and you just have to apply

Connect and Extend
To the research

Peterson, P., Fennema, E., & Carpenter, T. (1989). Using knowledge of how students think about mathematics. *Educational Leadership, 46*(4), 42–46.

Connect and Extend
To the research

The May 1993 issue of *Educational Leadership* has over a dozen articles on the changing curriculum, including several on the ways that mathematics education has been changed by the National Council of Teachers of Mathematics (NCME) Curriculum and Evaluation Standards for School Mathematics.

the rules to get the answers. Or they may have developed some misconceptions about the world, such as the belief that the earth is warmer in the summer because it is closer to the sun.

Many educators note that the key to understanding in science is for students to directly examine their own theories and confront the shortcomings (Hewson, Beeth, & Thorley, 1998). Only then can true learning and conceptual change happen. For change to take place, students must go through six stages: initial discomfort with their own ideas and beliefs, attempts to explain away inconsistencies between their theories and evidence presented to them, attempts to adjust measurements or observations to fit personal theories, doubt, vacillation, and finally conceptual change (Nissani & Hoefler-Nissani, 1992). You can see Piaget's notions of assimilation, disequilibrium, and accommodation operating here. Students try to make new information fit existing ideas (assimilation), but when the fit simply won't work and disequilibrium occurs, then accommodation or changes in cognitive structures follow.

The goal of **conceptual change teaching in science** is to help students pass through these six stages of learning. The two central features of conceptual change teaching are:

▶ Teachers are committed to teaching for student understanding rather than "covering the curriculum."

Connect and Extend
To the research
White, B. Y. (1993). TinkerTools: Causal models, conceptual change, and science education. *Cognition and Instruction, 10*, 1–100.

GUIDELINES

Teaching for Conceptual Change

Encourage students to make their ideas explicit.

Examples

1. Ask students to make predictions that might contradict their naïve conceptions.

2. Ask students to state their ideas in their own words, including the attractions and limitations of the ideas for them.

3. Have students explain their ideas using physical models or illustrations.

Help students see the differences among ideas.

Examples

1. Have students summarize or paraphrase each other's ideas.

2. Encourage comparing ideas by presenting and comparing evidence.

Encourage metacognition.

Examples

1. Give a pretest before starting a unit; then have students discuss their own responses to the pretest. Group similar pretest responses together and ask students to discover what is a more general concept underlying the responses.

2. At the end of lessons, ask students: "What did you learn?" "What do you understand?" "What do you believe about the lesson?" "How have your ideas changed?"

Explore the status of ideas. Status is an indication of how much students know and accept ideas and find them useful.

Examples

1. Ask direct questions about how intelligible, plausible, and fruitful an idea is. That is, do you know what the idea means, do you believe it, and can you achieve some valuable outcome using the idea?

2. Plan activities and experiments that support and question the students' ideas such as showing successful applications or pointing out contradictions.

Ask students for justifications of their ideas.

Examples

1. Teach students to use terms such as *logical*, *consistent*, *inconsistent*, and *coherent* in giving justifications.

2. Ask students to share and analyze each other's justifications.

TABLE 13.13 One Teacher's Learning Goals for Conceptual Change Teaching

The teacher in one 5th grade class gives these questions to her students to support their thinking about science.

1. Can you state your own ideas?
2. Can you talk about why you are attracted to your ideas?
3. Are your ideas consistent?
4. Do you realize the limitations of your ideas and the possibility they might need to change?
5. Can you try to explain your ideas using physical models?
6. Can you explain the difference between understanding an idea and believing in an idea?
7. Can you apply intelligible and plausible to your own ideas?

Source: Adapted from "Teaching Science in Fifth Grade: Instructional Goals that Support Conceptual Change," by M. E. Beeth, 1998, *Journal of Research in Science Teaching, 35,* p. 1093.

▶ Students are encouraged to make sense of science using their current ideas—they are challenged to describe, predict, explain, justify, debate, and defend the adequacy of their understanding. Dialogue is key. Only when intuitive ideas prove inadequate can new learning take hold (Anderson & Roth, 1989).

Conceptual change teaching has much in common with cognitive apprenticeships, inquiry learning, and reciprocal teaching described in Chapter 9—with scaffolding and dialogue playing key roles (Shuell, 1996). The Guidelines on page 512, adapted from Hewson, Beeth, and Thorley (1998), give some ideas for teaching for conceptual change.

How would these guidelines look in practice? One answer comes from Michael Beeth's study of a 5th-grade classroom. Table 13.13 is a list of learning goals that the teacher presented to her students. In this classroom, the teacher typically began instruction with a question such as, "Do you have ideas? Can you talk about them? Bring them out into the open? Why do you like your ideas? Why are you attracted to them?" (Beeth, 1998, p. 1095). During her teaching she constantly asked questions that required explanation and justifications. She summarized the students' answers, and sometimes challenged, "But do you really believe what you say?" Studies of the students in the teacher's classroom over the years showed that they had a sophisticated understanding of science concepts.

Criticisms of Constructivist Approaches to Subject Teaching

Constructivist approaches have done much to correct the excesses of tell-and-drill teaching. Some positive outcomes from constructivist teaching are better understanding of the material, greater enjoyment of literature, more positive attitudes toward school, better problem solving, and greater motivation (Harris & Graham, 1996; Palincsar, 1998). But total reliance on constructivist approaches that ignores

Conceptual Change Teaching in Science: A method that helps students understand (rather than memorize) concepts in science by using and challenging the students' current ideas.

direct teaching of skills can be detrimental for some children. For example, Harris and Graham (1996) describe the experiences of their daughter Leah in a whole-language/progressive education school, where the teachers successfully developed their daughter's creativity, thinking, and understanding.

> Skills, on the other hand, have been a problem for our daughter and for other children. At the end of kindergarten, when she had not made much progress in reading, her teacher said she believed Leah had a perceptual problem or a learning disability. Leah began asking what was wrong with her, because other kids were reading and she wasn't. Finally, an assessment was done. (p. 26)

The testing indicated no learning disability, strong comprehension abilities, and poor word attack skills. Luckily, Leah's parents knew how to teach word attack skills. Direct teaching of these skills helped Leah become an avid and able reader in about six weeks.

Leah's experience is not unique. Whole-language and constructivist approaches alone may not work for *all* children (Airasian & Walsh, 1997; Harris & Graham, 1996; Smith, 1994) or all kinds of learning (Weinert & Helmke, 1995). Susan Stodolsky (1988) cautions that constructivist methods may not be equally successful across all subject areas. If students fall behind because they lack specific skills, it would be unethical to withhold teaching and wait for those skills to "develop naturally," simply to be true to a particular philosophy.

Ernst von Glasersfeld (1995), a strong advocate of constructivist teaching in mathematics, believes that it is a misunderstanding of constructivism to say that memorization and rote learning always are useless. "There are, indeed, matters that can and perhaps must be learned in a purely mechanical way" (p. 5). Classrooms that integrate constructivist teaching with needed direct teaching of skills are especially good learning environments for students with special needs. Careful ongoing assessment of each student's abilities, knowledge, and motivations, followed by appropriate support should insure that no students are lost or left behind (Graham & Harris, 1994). In the next two chapters, we look more closely at student assessment.

CHECKPOINT

Focus on the Subject: Teaching Reading, Mathematics, and Science

Review

▶ Describe the debate about learning to read.

▶ Describe constructivist approaches to mathematics and science teaching.

Apply

▶ How would you assess students' conceptions about the science topics you will teach?

Summary

The First Step: Planning

What are the levels of planning and how do they affect teaching?

Teachers engage in several levels of planning—by the year, term, unit, week, and day. All the levels must be coordinated. Accomplishing the year's plan requires breaking the work into terms, the terms into units, and the units into weeks and days. The plan determines how time and materials will be turned into activities for students. There is no single model of planning, but all plans should allow for flexibility.

What is an instructional objective?

An instructional objective is a clear and unambiguous description of your educational intentions for your students. Mager's influential system for writing behavioral objectives states that objectives ought to describe what students will be doing when demonstrating their achievement and how you will know they are doing it. A good objective has three parts—the intended student behavior, the conditions under which the behavior will occur, and the criteria for acceptable performance. Gronlund's alternative approach suggests that an objective should be stated first in general terms, then the teacher should clarify by listing sample behaviors that would provide evidence that the student has attained the objective.

Describe the three taxonomies of educational objectives.

Bloom and others have developed taxonomies categorizing basic objectives in the cognitive, affective, and psychomotor domains. In real life, of course, behaviors from these three domains occur simultaneously. A taxonomy encourages systematic thinking about relevant objectives and ways to evaluate them. Six basic objectives are listed in the cognitive domain: knowledge, comprehension, application, analysis, synthesis, and evaluation. A recent revision of this taxonomy keeps the same cognitive processes, but adds that these processes can act on four kinds of knowledge—factual, conceptual, procedural, and metacognitive.

Describe teacher-centered and student-centered planning.

In teacher-centered approaches, teachers select learning objectives and plan how to get students to meet those objectives. Teachers control the "what" and "how" of learning. In contrast, planning is shared and negotiated in student-centered, or constructivist, approaches. The teacher and students together make decisions about content, activities, and approaches. Rather than having specific student behaviors as objectives, the teacher has overarching goals or "big ideas" that guide planning. Integrated content and teaching with themes are often part of the planning. Assessment of learning is ongoing and mutually shared by teacher and students.

Formats for Teaching

Describe the lecture format.

The teaching format for putting objectives into action should be suited to the objectives. Lecturing is efficient for communicating a large amount of new material to a large group. There are three basic phases a lecture should follow: preparation of students; presentation of content; and review of content. However, lecturing may keep students too passive and ignore individual learning rates. The younger the student, the shorter the presentation should be. Recitation can involve various types of questions, and should fit students' abilities and motivation levels.

Distinguish between convergent and divergent and high-level versus low-level questions.

Convergent questions have only one right answer. Divergent questions have many possible answers. Higher-level questions require analysis, synthesis, and evaluation—students have to think for themselves. Teacher responses to answers should not be too hasty in most cases and should provide appropriate feedback.

What are the uses and disadvantages of group discussion?

Group discussion helps students participate directly, express themselves clearly, justify opinions, and tolerate different views. Group discussion also gives students a chance to ask for clarification, examine their own thinking, follow personal interests, and assume responsibility by taking leadership roles in the group. Thus, group discussions help students evaluate ideas and synthesize personal viewpoints. By thinking together, challenging each other, and suggesting and evaluating possible explanations, students are more likely to reach a genuine understanding. However, discussions are quite unpredictable and may easily digress into exchanges of ignorance. Some members of the group may have great difficulty participating and may become anxious if forced to speak.

Focus on the Teacher

What methods have been used to study teaching?

For years, researchers have tried to unravel the mystery of effective teaching. Researchers have used a variety of methods including classroom observation, case studies, interviews, experimentation with different methods, and other approaches to study teaching in real classrooms. Results of research on teacher characteristics indicate that thorough and expert knowledge of a subject, organization and clarity in presentation, and enthusiasm all play important parts in effective teaching. But no one way of teaching has been found to be right for each class, lesson, or day.

What are the general characteristics of good teaching?

Teacher knowledge of the subject is necessary but not sufficient for effective teaching because being more knowledgeable helps teachers be clearer and more organized; organization and clarity are important characteristics of good teaching. Teachers who provide clear presentations and explanations tend to have students who learn more and who rate their teachers more positively. Clarity begins with planning. Tell students what they will be learning and how they could approach it. During the lesson, avoid vague language, make clear connections between facts or concepts by using explanatory links, and check often for understanding. Finally, teacher warmth, friendliness, and understanding seem to be the traits most strongly related to positive student attitudes.

Contrast teaching in direct and student-centered instruction.

In direct instruction, the teacher gives well-organized presentations, clear explanations, carefully delivered prompts, and feedback. These actions can be resources for students as they construct understanding. In student-centered approaches, the teacher designs authentic tasks, monitors student thinking, ask questions, and prods inquiry. Both kinds of teaching may be appropriate at different times.

Effective Teaching in Inclusive Classrooms

What characterizes effective teaching for exceptional students?

Effective teaching for exceptional students does not require a unique set of skills. It is a combination of good teaching practices and sensitivity to all students. Students with disabilities need to learn the academic material, and they need to be full participants in the day-to-day life of the classroom.

What resources do teachers have to work effectively with exceptional children?

When students have special needs they may be referred to specialists such as child study teams, school psychologists, or teachers of students with special needs for evaluation. The outcome of this process sometimes includes the preparation of an individualized educational program or IEP, as described in Chapter 4, which will have teaching ideas and guidelines. Many schools provide additional help for classroom teachers working with students with disabilities, such as a resource room with special materials and equipment and a specially trained teacher. Increasingly, special and regular educators are working together to teach specific students or the special education teacher might work directly alongside the regular teacher in a class made up of students with and without disabilities.

Focus on the Subject: Teaching Reading, Mathematics, and Science

Describe the debate about learning to read.

Today there is an ongoing debate between advocates of whole-language approaches to reading and writing and balanced approaches that include direct teaching of skills and phonics. Advocates of whole language believe children learn best when they are surrounded by good literature and read and write for authentic purposes. Advocates of a balanced approach cite extensive research indicating that skill in recognizing sounds and words—phonemic awareness—is fundamental in learning to read. Excellent primary teachers use a balanced approach combining authentic reading with skills instruction when needed.

Describe constructivist approaches to mathematics and science teaching.

Constructivist approaches to teaching mathematics and science emphasize deep understanding of concepts (as opposed to memorization), discussion and explanation, and exploration of students' implicit understandings. Many educators note that the key to understanding in science is for students to directly examine their own theories and confront the shortcomings. For change to take place, students must go through six stages: initial discomfort with their own ideas and beliefs, attempts to explain away inconsistencies between their theories and evidence presented to them, attempts to adjust measurements or observations to fit personal theories, doubt, vacillation, and finally conceptual change.

Key Terms

Becoming a Professional

Reflecting on the Chapter

Can you apply the ideas from this chapter on teaching to solve the following problems of practice?

Preschool and Kindergarten

▶ You have a very well-supplied science corner in your class, but your students seldom visit it. When they do, they don't seem to take advantage of the learning possibilities available with the manipulatives. How would you help students benefit from the materials?

Elementary and Middle School

▶ Your cooperating teacher wants a full lesson plan for each subject. What would you include in the plan to make it useful for you?

▶ You are given a math workbook and text series and told that you must use these materials as the basis for your math teaching. What would you do to incorporate these materials into lessons that help students understand mathematical thinking and problem solving?

Junior High and High School

▶ You have been assigned a "developmental" class—25 students who are several years behind their peers. How would you help them become better learners?

▶ Identify three instructional objectives for a lesson in your subject to be used in a mixed-ability 10th-grade class. How would you make these learning objectives clear to your students?

Certification Test Requirements

▶ Be familiar with Bloom's taxonomy in the cognitive domain, including examples of verbs that fit each level of the domain.

▶ Know the differences between convergent and divergent questions and between higher- and lower-level questions.

▶ Be familiar with the teaching functions of direct instruction.

Your Teaching Portfolio

Think about your philosophy of teaching, a question you will be asked at most job interviews.

What is your approach to planning? How will you match teaching approaches to learning goals?

Add some ideas for parent involvement in homework from this chapter to your **Portfolio.**

Teaching Resources

Include a summary of the cognitive, affective, and psychomotor taxonomies in your **Teaching Resources** file.

Add Table 13.2, "A Revised Taxonomy in the Cognitive Domain," to your file.

Include Table 13.7, "Active Learning and Teacher Presentations," in your file.

If you will teach elementary school, include Table 13.11, "Improving Reading: CIERA's 10 Research-Based Principles" in your file.

TEACHERS' CASEBOOK

What Would They Do?

Here is how some practicing teachers responded to the teaching situation presented at the beginning of this chapter about a whole-language program under fire.

KATIE CHURCHILL

Third Grade Teacher
Oriole Parke Elementary School, Chicago, Illinois

If the principal chose to keep the whole-language program intact, then I would integrate another method of teaching into the program. Children require more than one method of teaching to compensate for varied learning needs. I would include phonics within the program as well as more direct instruction to ensure that the children are achieving and learning. In addition, I would assess the students' learning more carefully to track individual progress. Some aspects of the whole-language program are beneficial because the students have shown an increased interest in reading and are writing more creatively. This is an integral part of learning because children need this type of encouragement and motivation to remain interested in school.

REGINA M. LAROSE

Second Grade Teacher
Hillside School, Needham, Massachusetts

The good news in this case is that the children appear to be productive learners with positive attitudes. I would remind parents of this as I respond to their questions and concerns. Parents need to be informed; therefore, I would approach their complaints with an open mind and offer explanations as directly and honestly as I could. Perhaps parent workshops could be held by the school's principal and teachers to further explain goals and to answer questions.

I believe that children are successful when they are offered a balance between an innovative approach and a structured plan for delivering skills. If children were not meeting the standards of a required test, I would take a serious look at my goals and methods. I would scrutinize my plans and make sure that I was offering students suf-

ficient practice in those skills that seem to be the weakest. Because children have different learning styles, a variety of approaches should be used to introduce and practice skills. Discussions with fellow teachers often reveal new techniques that help to stimulate ideas.

After analyzing my program, I would supply my principal with concrete examples of methods that would provide more understanding and practice in the skills that I found lacking. I would include an explanation of these additional lessons in my weekly newsletter to parents.

VALERIE A. CHILCOAT

Fifth/Sixth Grade Advanced Academics
Glenmount School, Baltimore, Maryland

When addressing parent complaints, great care is needed, especially when they concern the decisions made by your administration. If the concern is widespread, I would set up a meeting with the parents that included your administrator. Perhaps other teachers would want to be involved. Discuss in detail with your administrator what you plan to say, and make sure you are clear on the position of the administration.

As a teacher who uses an integrated curriculum, I have much practical experience with the pros and cons of a whole-language approach. As educators, we know that all children do not learn in the same way. That is why I believe that a completely whole-language approach is an inappropriate teaching style. In keeping with the idea of an integrated curriculum, basic language and reading skills can be introduced in conjunction with the standard whole-language approach.

By first evaluating the learning styles of my students, I could discover which of my students learn better whole-to-part and which learn better part-to-whole. I could then provide all students with lessons designed to meet their needs as well as introduce alternative learning strategies to them.

By using an integrated curriculum approach, I believe that students learn and retain more of the major concepts and themes that run throughout the many disciplines. Issues are constantly visited and revisited from different perspectives and through the implementation of the dictaes inherent in the disciplines of reading, math, science, and the social sciences. However, this may not be enough. Basic reading, language, and math skills must also be integrated into the program to best address the needs of all students.

FRANCES D. GARLAND

Third Grade Teacher
Winship School, Boston, Massachusetts

I would speak directly to individual parents about their concerns regarding whole language and lower test scores. While I certainly would validate their complaints, I would also point out that test scores are not the only indicators of progress. Whole-language teachers are kid watchers. Kid watching informs good teaching and provides insight into children's strengths, weaknesses, strategies, and skills. Test scores are only part of the overall assessment process.

During the dialogue with parents, I would invite them to visit my classroom so they could witness a meaning-based learning environment, where children are engaged in real reading and real writing activities. I would also provide some suggestions for them to use at home that would reinforce and support techniques employed in the classroom. I would recommend books for them to read to help them understand the whole-language philosophy, such as *The Foundations of Literacy* (Holdaway) or *Classrooms That Work* (Cunningham, Allington).

14

Standardized Testing

*H*ow *has standardized testing affected your life so far? What opportunities have opened or closed to you based on test scores? Was the process fair? Propose a better way to make these decisions.*

Would it surprise you to learn that published tests, such as the college entrance exams and IQ tests, are creations of the 20th century? In the 19th and early 20th centuries, college entrance was generally based on grades, essays, and interviews. From your own experience, you know that testing has come a long way since then—too far, say some critics. They want to reshape testing as a way of reshaping the curriculum and reforming education. We will explore these new ideas.

In spite of the criticisms, schools still use many standardized tests, so teachers must be knowledgeable about testing. This chapter focuses on preparing for and interpreting standardized tests. Understanding how standardized test scores are determined, what they really mean, and how they can be used (or misused) provides you a framework for ensuring that the tests you give are appropriate.

First, we consider testing in general, including the various methods of interpreting test scores. Then we look at the different kinds of standardized tests used in schools. Finally, we examine the criticisms of testing and the alternatives being proposed. By the time you have completed this chapter, you should be able to do the following:

▶ Calculate mean, median, mode, and standard deviation.
▶ Define percentile ranks, standard deviations, z scores, T scores, and stanine scores.
▶ Explain how to improve reliability and validity in testing.
▶ Interpret the results of achievement, aptitude, and diagnostic tests in a realistic manner.
▶ Take a position on the testing issue and defend your position.
▶ Describe how to prepare students (and yourself) for taking standardized tests.
▶ Explain the strengths and weaknesses of alternative forms of assessment such as portfolios.

What Would You Do?

It is nearing the end of school and the 9th grade achievement test results are finally in. The parents' report form went home last Friday, and Monday morning you get a call from the principal during your planning period. The parents of one of your math students are in the office and have asked to speak with you and the principal immediately. The father is a prominent business-man and the mother is a lawyer. Their daughter received a grade-equivalent score of 11.8 on her standardized math test. The girl has been making Bs and Cs in your class—she seldom completes homework and has trouble with your conceptual approach to math. She just wants to know the "steps" to solve the problems so she can finish. You have tried several times to get the parents to come in to talk about ways to support the girl's learning, but they never seem to have had the time—until today.

You smile as you enter the principal's office, but the parents are not smiling. As soon as you sit down, the father says, "Well, you can see from our daughter's scores that you have been totally wrong in the grades you have given her this year. We thought she was just weak in math, but now it is clear you have something against her! Or maybe you just don't know how to teach math to bright girls."

The mother chimes in, "Yes, we expect you to reconsider her final grades for the year in light of her obvious ability. In fact," she glances at the principal and then glares at you again, "we believe she should get credit for the 10th grade class you teach as well, because she obviously knows the material already."

▶ What would you say to the parents?

▶ What do you need to know about tests to deal with this situation?

▶ How will you approach working with this student?

▶ How will these issues affect the grade levels you will teach?

Evaluation, Measurement, and Assessment

All teaching involves **evaluation**. At the heart of evaluation is judgment, making decisions based on values. In the process of evaluation, we compare information to criteria and then make judgments. Teachers must make all kinds of judgments. "Should we use a different text this year?" "Is this film appropriate for my students?" "Will Sarah do better if she repeats the 1st grade?" "Should Terry get a B– or a C+ on the project?"

Measurement is evaluation put in quantitative terms—the numeric description of an event or characteristic. Measurement tells how much, how often, or how well by providing scores, ranks, or ratings. Instead of saying, "Sarah doesn't seem to understand addition," a teacher might say, "Sarah answered only 2 of the 15 problems correctly in her addition homework." Measurement also allows a teacher to compare one student's performance on one particular task with a standard or with the performances of the other students. When we think of measurement, we often think of paper-and-pencil tests.

Connect and Extend
To your teaching
Both subjective judgments and objective measurements are used in evaluation. Are both equally valid in making educational decisions?

Not all the evaluative decisions made by teachers involve measurement. Some decisions are based on information that is difficult to express numerically: student preferences, information from parents, previous experiences, even intuition. But measurement does play a large role in many classroom decisions, and, when properly done, it can provide unbiased data for evaluations.

Increasingly, evaluation and measurement specialists are using the term **assessment** to describe the process of gathering information about students' learning. Assessment is broader than testing and measurement because it includes all kinds of ways to sample and observe students' skills, knowledge, and abilities. Assessment is "any of a variety of procedures used to obtain information about student performance" (Linn & Gronlund, 2000, p. 32). Assessments can be formal, such as unit tests, or informal, such as observing who emerges as a leader in group work. Assessments can be designed by classroom teachers or by local, state, or national agencies such as school districts or the Educational Testing Service. And today, assessments can go well beyond paper-and-pencil exercises to observations of performances, the development of portfolios, or the creation of artifacts (Linn & Gronlund, 2000; Popham, 1999). In this chapter, we focus on formal assessments designed by groups and agencies outside the classroom. These assessments usually involve testing and the reporting of scores, so we will start by examining two types of tests.

The answers given on any type of test have no meaning by themselves; we must make some kind of comparison to interpret test results. There are two basic types of comparison: In the first, a test score is compared to the scores obtained by other people who have taken the same test. (This is called a norm-referenced comparison.) The second type is criterion-referenced. Here, the comparison is to a fixed standard or minimum passing score.

Evaluation: Decision making about student performance and about appropriate teaching strategies.

Measurement: An evaluation expressed in quantitative (number) terms.

Assessment: Procedures used to obtain information about student performance.

Norm-Referenced Testing: Testing in which scores are compared with the average performance of others.

Norm Groups: A group whose average score serves as a standard for evaluating any student's score on a test.

Norm-Referenced Tests

In **norm-referenced testing**, the people who have taken the test provide the *norms* for determining the meaning of a given individual's score. You can think of a norm as being the typical level of performance for a particular group. By comparing the individual's raw score (the actual number correct) to the norm, we can determine if the score is above, below, or around the average for that group. There are at least three types of **norm groups** (comparison groups) in education—the class or school itself, the school district, and national samples.

Norm-referenced testing compares an individual's score to the average score of others in a larger group. The group could be a particular classroom, school district, or national sample. ▼

Norm-referenced tests cover a wide range of general objectives rather than assessing a limited number of specific objectives. Norm-referenced tests are especially useful in measuring the overall achievement of students who have come to understand complex material by different routes. Norm-referenced tests are also appropriate when only the top few candidates can be admitted to a program.

However, norm-referenced measurement has its limitations. The results of a norm-referenced test do not tell you whether students are ready to move on to more advanced material. For instance, knowing that a student is in the top 3% of the class on a test of algebraic concepts will not tell you if he or she is ready to move on to trigonometry; everyone in the class may have a limited understanding of the algebraic concepts.

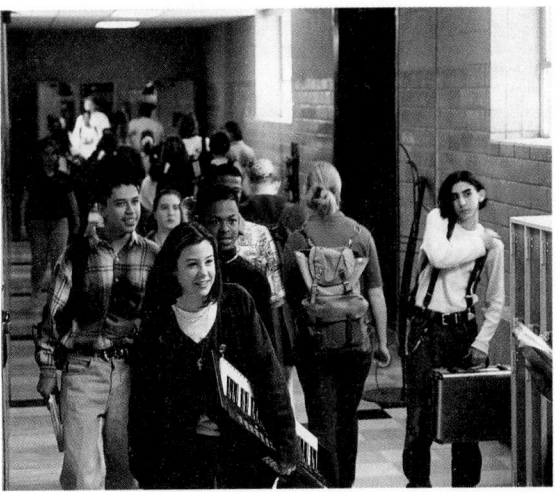

Nor are norm-referenced tests particularly appropriate for measuring affective and psychomotor objectives. To measure individuals' psychomotor learning, you need a clear description of standards. (Even the best gymnast in school performs certain exercises better than others and needs specific guidance about how to improve.) In the affective area, attitudes and values are personal; comparisons among individuals are not really appropriate. For example, how could we measure an "average" level of political values or opinions? Finally, norm-referenced tests tend to encourage competition and comparison of scores. Some students compete to be the best. Others, realizing that being the best is impossible, may compete to be the worst. Either goal has its casualties.

Criterion-Referenced Tests

When test scores are compared, not to those of others, but to a given criterion or standard of performance, this is **criterion-referenced testing.** To decide who should be allowed to drive a car, it is important to determine just what standard of performance is appropriate for selecting safe drivers. It does not matter how your test results compare to the results of others. If your performance on the test was in the top 10% but you consistently ran through red lights, you would not be a good candidate for receiving a license, even though your score was high.

Criterion-referenced tests measure the mastery of very specific objectives. The results of a criterion-referenced test should tell the teacher exactly what the students can and cannot do, at least under certain conditions. For example, a criterion-referenced test would be useful in measuring the ability to add three-digit numbers. A test could be designed with 20 different problems, and the standard for mastery could be set at 17 correct out of 20. (The standard is often somewhat arbitrary and may be based on such things as the teacher's experience.) If two students receive scores of 7 and 11, it does not matter that one student did better than the other because neither met the standard of 17. Both need more help with addition.

In teaching basic skills there are many instances where comparison to a preset standard is more important than comparison to the performance of others. It is not very comforting to know, as a parent, that your child is better in reading than most of the students in class if none of the students is reading at grade level. Sometimes standards for meeting the criterion must be set at 100% correct. You would not like to have your appendix removed by a surgeon who left surgical instruments inside the body *only* 10% of the time.

Criterion-referenced tests are not appropriate for every situation, however. Many subjects cannot be broken down into a set of specific objectives. Moreover, although standards are important in criterion-referenced testing, they can often be arbitrary, as you have already seen. When deciding whether a student has mastered the addition of three-digit num-

---

CHECKPOINT

Evaluation, Measurement, and Assessment

Review

▶ Distinguish among evaluation, measurement, and assessment.

▶ Distinguish between norm-referenced and criterion-referenced tests.

Apply

▶ The doctor tells you that your cholesterol level is above average. What would you like to know about the norm group?

▶ Would you prefer a criterion-referenced or norm-referenced measure of your blood pressure? Why?

TABLE 14.1 *Deciding on the Type of Test to Use*

Norm-referenced tests may work best when you are

- Measuring general ability in certain areas, such as English, algebra, general science, or American history.
- Assessing the range of abilities in a large group.
- Selecting top candidates when only a few openings are available.

Criterion-referenced tests may work best when you are

- Measuring mastery of basic skills.
- Determining if students have prerequisites to start a new unit.
- Assessing affective and psychomotor objectives.
- Grouping students for instruction.

bers comes down to the difference between 16 or 17 correct answers, it seems difficult to justify one particular standard over another. Finally, at times it is valuable to know how the students in your class compare to other students at their grade level both locally and nationally. Table 14.1 offers a comparison of norm-referenced and criterion-referenced tests. You can see that each type of test is well suited for certain situations, but each also has its limitations.

What Do Test Scores Mean?

On the average, more than one million standardized tests are given per school day in classes throughout this country (Lyman, 1986). Most of these are norm-referenced standardized tests. **Standardized tests** are those official-looking pamphlets and piles of forms purchased by school systems and administered to students. More specifically, the tests are called standardized because "the same directions are used for administering them in all classrooms and standard procedures are used for scoring and interpreting them" (Carey, 1994, p. 443). Standard methods of developing items, administering the test, scoring it, and reporting the scores are all implied by the term *standardized test*.

Basic Concepts

In standardized testing the test items and instructions have been tried out to make sure they work and then rewritten and retested as necessary. The final version of the test is administered to a **norming sample,** a large sample of subjects as similar as possible to the students who will be taking the test in school systems throughout the country. This norming sample serves as a comparison group for all students who take the test.

The test publishers provide one or more ways of comparing each student's raw score (number of correct

Over one million standardized tests are given each school day in the United States, on average. ▼

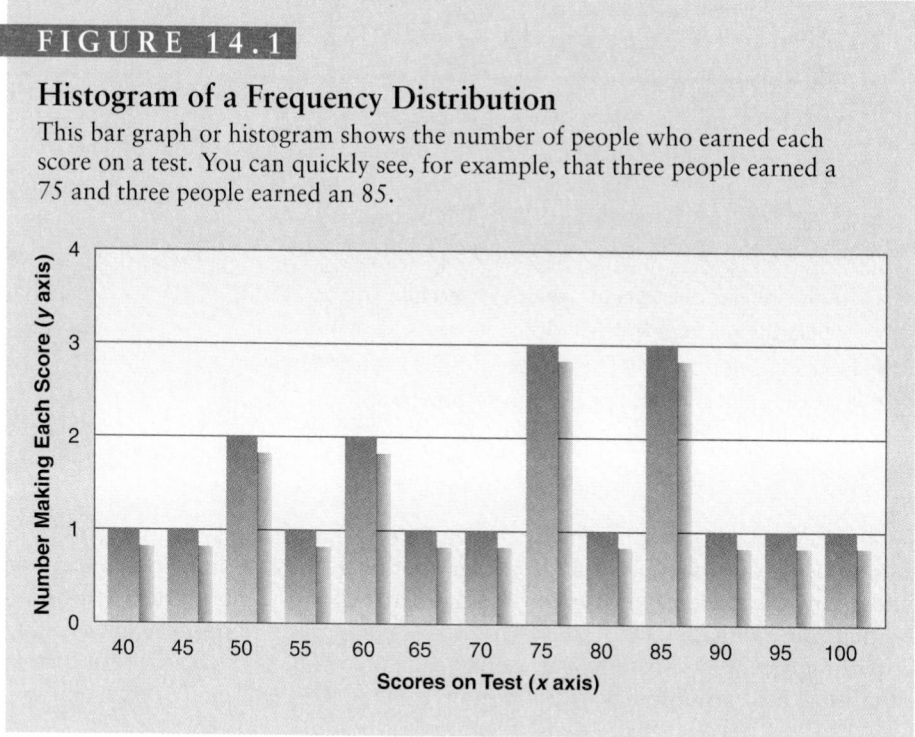

FIGURE 14.1

Histogram of a Frequency Distribution

This bar graph or histogram shows the number of people who earned each score on a test. You can quickly see, for example, that three people earned a 75 and three people earned an 85.

Number Making Each Score (y axis)

Scores on Test (x axis)

answers) with the norming sample. Let's look at some of the measurements on which comparisons and interpretations are based.

Frequency Distributions. A **frequency distribution** is simply a listing of the number of people who obtain each score or fall into each range of scores on a test or other measurement procedure. For example, on a spelling test 19 students made these scores: 100, 95, 90, 85, 85, 85, 80, 75, 75, 75, 70, 65, 60, 60, 55, 50, 50, 45, 40. A graph, in this case a **histogram** (bar graph), of the spelling test scores is shown in Figure 14.1 where one axis (the *x*, or horizontal, axis) indicates the possible scores and the other axis (the *y*, or vertical, axis) indicates the number of subjects who attained each score.

Measurements of Central Tendency and Standard Deviation. You have probably had a great deal of experience with means. A **mean** is simply the arithmetical average of a group of scores. To calculate the mean, you add the scores and divide the total by the number of scores in the distribution. For example, the total of the 19 spelling scores is 1,340, so the mean is 1,340/19, or 70.53. The mean offers one way of measuring **central tendency,** the score that is typical or representative of the whole distribution of scores.

Two other measures of central tendency are the median and the mode. The **median** is the middle score in the distribution, the point at which half the scores are larger and half are smaller. The median of the 19 scores is 75. Nine scores in the distribution are greater than or equal to 75, and nine are less. The **mode** is the score that occurs most often. The distribution in Figure 14.1 actually has two modes, 75 and 85, because each of these scores occurred three times. This makes it a **bimodal distribution.**

Connect and Extend
To your teaching
At a PTA meeting parents were complaining because half of the students in the district scored below the district average on the achievement tests that were given. Is this a valid complaint?

Frequency Distribution: Record showing how many scores fall into set groups.

Histogram: Bar graph of a frequency distribution.

Mean: Arithmetical average.

Central Tendency: Typical score for a group of scores.

Median: Middle score in a group of scores.

Mode: Most frequently occurring score.

Bimodal Distribution: Frequency distribution with two modes.

The measure of central tendency gives a score that is representative of the group of scores, but it does not tell you anything about how the scores are distributed. Two groups of scores may both have a mean of 50 but be alike in no other way. One group might contain the scores 50, 45, 55, 55, 45, 50, 50; the other group might contain the scores 100, 0, 50, 90, 10, 50, 50. In both cases the mean, median, and mode are all 50, but the distributions are quite different.

The **standard deviation** is a measure of how widely the scores vary from the mean. The larger the standard deviation, the more spread out the scores in the distribution. The smaller the standard deviation, the more the scores are clustered around the mean. For example, in the distribution 50, 45, 55, 55, 45, 50, 50, the standard deviation is much smaller than in the distribution 100, 0, 50, 90, 10, 50, 50. Another way of saying this is that distributions with very small standard deviations have less **variability** in the scores.

The standard deviation is relatively easy to calculate if you remember your high school math. It does take time, however. The process is similar to taking an average, but you use square roots. To calculate the standard deviation, you follow these steps:

1. Calculate the mean (written as $\overline{X}$) of the scores.
2. Subtract the mean from each of the scores. This is written as $(X - \overline{X})$.
3. Square each difference (multiply each difference by itself). This is written $(X - \overline{X})^2$.
4. Add all the squared differences. This is written $\Sigma(X - \overline{X})^2$.
5. Divide this total by the number of scores. This is written $\dfrac{\Sigma(X - \overline{X})^2}{N}$.
6. Find the square root. This is written $\sqrt{\dfrac{\Sigma(X - \overline{X})^2}{N}}$, which is the formula for calculating the standard deviation.

Knowing the mean and the standard deviation of a group of scores gives you a better picture of the meaning of an individual score. For example, suppose you received a score of 78 on a test. You would be very pleased with the score if the mean of the test were 70 and the standard deviation were 4. In this case, your score would be 2 standard deviations above the mean, a score well above average.

Consider the difference if the mean of the test had remained at 70 but the standard deviation had been 20. In the second case, your score of 78 would be less than 1 standard deviation from the mean. You would be much closer to the middle of the group, with a score above average, but not high. Knowing the standard deviation tells you much more than simply knowing the **range** of scores. No matter how the majority scored on the tests, one or two students may do very well or very poorly and thus make the range very large.

The Normal Distribution. Standard deviations are very useful in understanding test results. They are especially helpful if the results of the tests form a normal distribution. You may have met the **normal distribution** before. It is the bell-shaped curve, the most famous frequency distribution because it describes many naturally occurring physical and social phenomena. Many scores fall in the middle, giving the curve its puffed appearance. You find fewer and fewer scores as you look out toward the end points, or *tails*, of the distribution. The normal distribution has been thoroughly analyzed by statisticians. The mean of a normal distribution is also its midpoint. Half the scores are above the mean, and half are below it. In a normal distribution, the mean, median, and mode are all the same point.

Connect and Extend
To your teaching
Which math class, A or B, is probably easier to teach, judging from the following standard score results (50 = national average)?

Class A: Mean = 55 SD = 13
Class B: Mean = 53 SD = 4

(Answer: Probably Class B because the range of achievement levels is not as great as in Class A.)

Connect and Extend
To your teaching
What conclusions would you draw about a test with a possible score range from 1 to 50 on which your class mean was 40 with a standard deviation of 3? You gave the same test to another class whose mean was 26 with a standard deviation of 7. How would you characterize the second class? What is the difference between the classes?

Standard Deviation: Measure of how widely scores vary from the mean.

Variability: Degree of difference or deviation from mean.

Range: Distance between the highest and the lowest scores in a group.

Normal Distribution: The most commonly occurring distribution, in which scores are distributed evenly around the mean.

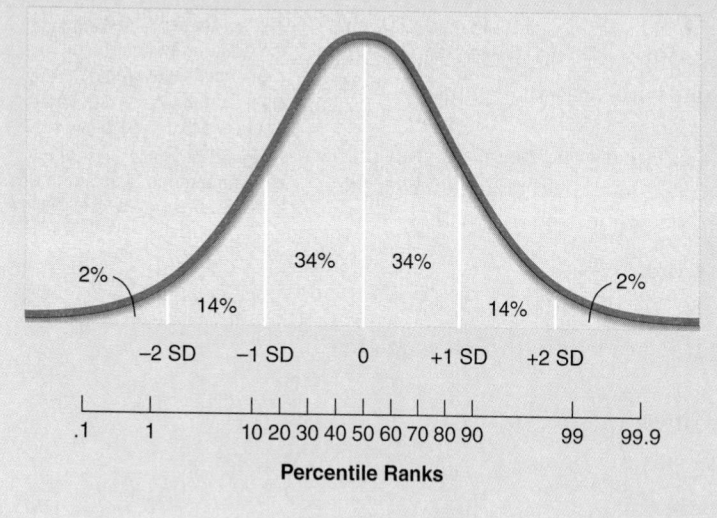

FIGURE 14.2

The Normal Distribution

The normal distribution or bell-shaped curve has certain predictable characteristics. For example, 68% of the scores are clustered within 1 standard deviation below to 1 standard deviation above the mean.

Another convenient property of the normal distribution is that the percentage of scores falling within each area of the curve is known, as you can see in Figure 14.2. A person scoring within 1 standard deviation of the mean obviously has company. Many scores pile up here. In fact, 68% of all scores are located in the area from 1 standard deviation below to 1 standard deviation above the mean. About 16% of the scores are higher than 1 standard deviation above the mean. Of this higher group, only 2% are better than 2 standard deviations above the mean. Similarly, only about 16% of the scores are less than 1 standard deviation below the mean, and of that group only about 2% are worse than 2 standard deviations below. At 2 standard deviations from the mean in either direction, the scorer has left the pack.

The SAT college entrance exam is one example of a normal distribution. The mean of the SAT is 500 and the standard deviation is 100. If you know people who made scores of 700, you know they did very well. Only about 2% of the people who take the test do that well, because only 2% of the scores are better than 2 standard deviations above the mean in a normal distribution.

Types of Scores

Now you have enough background for a discussion of the different kinds of scores you may encounter in reports of results from standardized tests.

Percentile Rank Scores. The concept of ranking is the basis for one very useful kind of score reported on standardized tests, a **percentile rank** score. In percentile ranking, each student's raw score is compared with the raw scores of the students in the norming sample. The percentile rank shows the percentage of students in the norming sample that scored at or below a particular raw score. If a student's score were the same as or better than three-quarters of the students in the norming sample, the student would score in the 75th percentile or have a percentile rank of 75. You can see that this does *not* mean that the student had a raw score of 75 correct answers or even that the student answered 75% of the questions correctly. Rather, the 75 refers to the percentage of people in the norming sample whose scores on the test were equal to or below this student's score. A percentile rank of 50 means that a student has scored as well as or better than 50% of the norming sample and has achieved an average score.

Figure 14.3 illustrates one caution in interpreting percentile scores. Differences in percentile ranks do not mean the same thing in terms of raw score points in the middle of the scale as they do at the fringes. The graph shows Joan's and Alice's percentile scores on the fictitious Test of Excellence in Language and Arithmetic. Both

Percentile Rank: Percentage of those in the norming sample who scored at or below an individual's score.

Grade-Equivalent Score: Measure of grade level based on comparison with norming samples from each grade.

students are about average in arithmetic skills. One equaled or surpassed 50% of the norming sample; the other, 60%. However, because their scores are in the middle of the distribution, this difference in percentile ranks means a raw score difference of only a few points. Their raw scores were actually 75 and 77. In the language test, the difference in percentile ranks seems to be about the same as the difference in arithmetic, since one ranked at the 90th percentile and the other at the 99th. But the difference in their raw scores on the language test is much greater. It takes a greater difference in raw score points to make a difference in percentile rank at the extreme ends of the scale. On the language test the difference in raw scores is about 10 points.

Grade-Equivalent Scores. **Grade-equivalent scores** are generally obtained from separate norming samples for each grade level. The average of the scores of all the 10th graders in the norming sample defines the 10th-grade equivalent score. Suppose the raw-score average of the 10th grade norming sample is 38. Any student who attains a raw score of 38 on that test will be assigned a grade-equivalent score of 10th grade. Grade-equivalent scores are generally listed in numbers such as 8.3, 4.5, 7.6, 11.5, and so on. The whole number gives the grade. The decimals stand for tenths of a year, but they are usually interpreted as months.

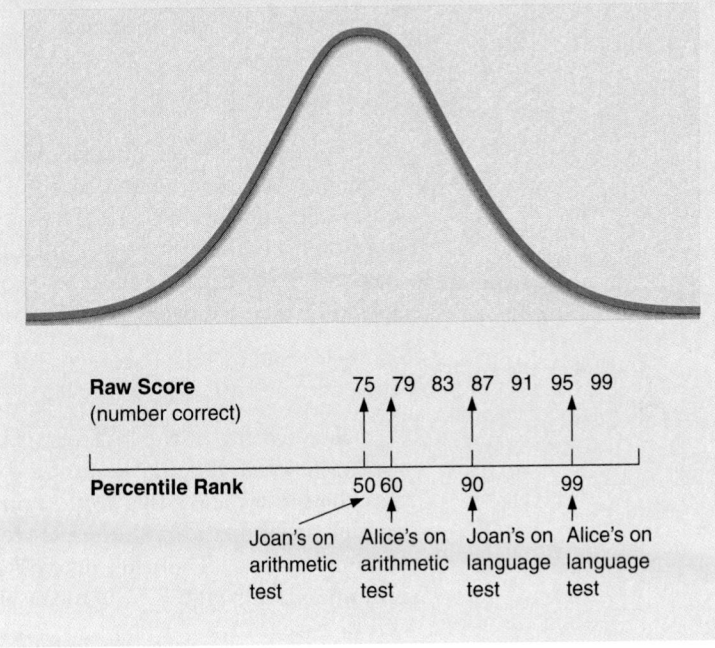

FIGURE 14.3

Percentile Ranking on a Normal Distribution Curve

Percentile scores have different meanings at different places on the scale. For example, a difference of a few raw score points near the mean might translate into a 10-point percentile difference, while it would take 6 or 7 points to make a 10 point percentile difference farther out of the scale.

Raw Score (number correct): 75 79 83 87 91 95 99

Percentile Rank: 50 60 90 99

Joan's on arithmetic test — Alice's on arithmetic test — Joan's on language test — Alice's on language test

Suppose a student with the grade-equivalent score of 10 is a 7th grader. Should this student be promoted immediately? Probably not. Different forms of tests are used at different grade levels, so the 7th grader may not have had to answer items that would be given to 10th graders. The high score may represent superior mastery of material at the 7th-grade level rather than a capacity for doing advanced work. Even though an average 10th grader could do as well as our 7th grader on this particular test, the 10th grader would certainly know much more than this test covered. Also, grade-equivalent score units do not mean the same thing at every grade level. For example, a 2nd grader reading at the 1st-grade level would have more trouble in school than an 11th grader who reads at the 10th-grade level.

Because grade-equivalent scores are misleading and are often misinterpreted, especially by parents, most educators and psychologists strongly believe they should not be used at all. There are several other forms of reporting available that are more appropriate.

Standard Scores. As you may remember, one problem with percentile ranks is the difficulty in making comparisons among ranks. A discrepancy of a certain

Connect and Extend
To your teaching

The Individual Test Record in Figure 14.5 is the 1992 version of the California Achievement Test (CAT). This 5th edition of the CAT does not report grade-equivalent scores, but the same figure in the previous edition of this text shows that the 1985 version of the same CAT test does report grade-equivalent scores. This change may reflect the testing company's recognition that grade-equivalent scores are not appropriate.

number of raw-score points has a different meaning at different places on the scale. With standard scores, on the other hand, a difference of 10 points is the same everywhere on the scale.

Standard scores are based on the standard deviation. A very common standard score is called the *z* **score**. A *z* score tells how many standard deviations above or below the average a raw score is. In the example described earlier, in which you were fortunate enough to get a 78 on a test where the mean was 70 and the standard deviation was 4, your *z* score would be +2, or 2 standard deviations above the mean. If a person were to score 64 on this test, the score would be 1.5 standard deviation units *below* the mean, and the *z* score would be –1.5. A *z* score of 0 would be no standard deviations above the mean—in other words, right on the mean.

To calculate the *z* score for a given raw score, subtract the mean from the raw score and divide the difference by the standard deviation. The formula is:

$$z = \frac{X - \bar{X}}{SD}$$

Because it is often inconvenient to use negative numbers, other standard scores have been devised to eliminate this difficulty. The *T* **score** has a mean of 50 and uses a standard deviation of 10. Thus a *T* score of 50 indicates average performance. If you multiply the *z* score by 10 (which eliminates the decimal) and add 50 (which gets rid of the negative number), you get the equivalent *T* score as the answer. The person whose *z* score was –1.5 would have a *T* score of 35.

First multiply the *z* score by 10: $-1.5 \times 10 = -15$
Then add 50: $-15 + 50 = 35$

The scoring of the SAT test is based on a similar procedure. The mean of the scores is set at 500, and a standard deviation of 100 is used.

Before we leave this section on types of scores, we should mention one other widely used method. **Stanine scores** (the name comes from "standard nine") are standard scores. There are only nine possible scores on the stanine scale, the whole numbers 1 through 9. The mean is 5, and the standard deviation is 2. Each unit from 2 to 8 is equal to half a standard deviation.

Stanine scores provide a method of considering a student's rank, since each of the nine scores includes a specific range of percentile scores in the normal distribution. For example, a stanine score of 1 is assigned to the bottom 4% of scores in a distribution. A stanine of 2 is assigned to the next 7%. Of course, some raw scores in this 7% range are better than others, but they all get a stanine score of 2.

Each stanine score represents a wide range of raw scores. This has the advantage of encouraging teachers and parents to view a student's score in more general terms instead of making fine distinctions based on a few points. Figure 14.4 compares the four types of standard scores we have considered, showing how each would fall on a normal distribution curve.

Interpreting Test Scores

One of the most common problems with the use of tests is misinterpretation of scores. This often happens because of the belief that numbers are precise measurements of a student's ability. No test provides a perfect picture of a person's abilities; a test is only one small sample of behavior. Two factors are important in developing good tests and interpreting results: reliability and validity.

Standard Scores: Scores based on the standard deviation.

***z* Score:** Standard score indicating the number of standard deviations above or below the mean.

***T* Score:** Standard score with a mean of 50 and a standard deviation of 10.

Stanine Scores: Whole number scores from 1 to 9, each representing a wide range of raw scores.

Reliability. If you took a standardized test on Monday, then took the same test again a week later, and you received about the same score each time, you would have reason to believe the test was reliable. If 100 people took the test one day, then repeated it the following week, and the ranking of the individual scores was about the same for both tests, you would be even more certain the test was reliable. (Of course, this assumes that no one looks up answers or studies before the second test.) A reliable test gives a consistent and stable "reading" of a person's ability from one occasion to the next, assuming the person's ability remains the same. A reliable thermometer works in a similar manner, giving you a reading of 100°C each time you measure the temperature of boiling water. Measuring a test's **reliability** in this way, by giving the test on two different occasions, indicates *stability* or *test-retest reliability*. If a group of people takes two equivalent versions of a test and the scores on both tests are comparable, this indicates *alternate-form reliability.*

Reliability can also refer to the internal consistency or the precision of a test. This type of reliability, known as *split-half reliability,* is calculated by comparing performance on half of the test questions with performance on the other half. If, for example, someone did quite well on all the odd-numbered items and not at all well on the even-numbered items, we could assume that the items were not very consistent or precise in measuring what they were intended to measure. The most effective way to improve reliability is to add more items to a test. Generally speaking, longer tests are more reliable than shorter ones.

True Score. All tests are imperfect estimators of the qualities or skills they are trying to measure. There are errors in every testing situation. Sometimes the errors are in your favor and you score higher than your ability might warrant; perhaps you reviewed a key section just before the test. Sometimes the errors go against you—you are sick, sleepy, or focused on the wrong material in your review. But if you could be tested over and over again without becoming tired and without memorizing the answers, your good luck and bad luck would even out, and the average of the test scores would bring you close to a **true score**. In other words, we can think of a student's true score as the mean of all the scores the student would receive if the test were repeated many times.

In reality, however, students take a test only once. That means that the score each student receives is made up of the hypothetical true score plus some amount of error. How can error be reduced so that the actual score can be brought closer to a true score? As you might guess, this returns us to the question of reliability. The more reliable the test, the less error in the score actually obtained. On standardized tests, test

FIGURE 14.4

Four Types of Standard Scores on a Normal Distribution Curve

Using this figure, you can translate one type of standard into another.

	−3 SD	−2 SD	−1 SD	0	+1 SD	+2 SD	+3 SD
Standard deviation				(Mean)			
z scores	−3	−2	−1	0	+1	+2	+3
T scores	20	30	40	50	60	70	80
SAT scores	200	300	400	500	600	700	800
Stanine scores		1 2 3	4	5	6	7 8 9	

Connect and Extend
To your teaching

There are many sources of error in testing: personal (e.g., misreading directions, illness, reviewing wrong material, anxiety); test-related (e.g., unclear directions, excessive length, too-high reading level); and context-related (too-competitive situation, noise, mistakes by test administrator).

Reliability: Consistency of test results.

True Score: Hypothetical average of all of an individual's scores if repeated testing under ideal conditions were possible.

developers take this into consideration and make estimations of how much the students' scores would probably vary if they were tested repeatedly. This estimation is called the **standard error of measurement.** It represents the *standard deviation* of the distribution of scores from our hypothetical repeated testings. Thus a reliable test can also be defined as a test with a small standard error of measurement. In their interpretation of tests, teachers must also take into consideration the margin for error.

Confidence Interval. Never base an opinion of a student's ability or achievement on the exact score the student obtains. Many test companies now report scores using a **confidence interval,** or "standard error band," that encloses the student's actual score. This makes use of the standard error of measurement and allows a teacher to consider the range of scores that might include a student's true score.

Let us assume, for example, that two students in your class take a standardized achievement test in Spanish. The standard error of measurement for this test is 5. One student receives a score of 79 and the other, a score of 85. At first glance, these scores seem quite different. But when you consider the standard error bands around the scores, not just the scores alone, you see that the bands overlap. The first student's true score might be anywhere between 74 and 84 (that is, the actual score of 79 plus and minus the standard error of 5). The second student's true score might be anywhere between 80 and 90. It is crucial to keep in mind the idea of standard error bands when selecting students for special programs. No child should be rejected simply because the obtained score missed the cutoff by one or two points. The student's true score might well be above the cutoff point.

Validity. If a test is sufficiently reliable, the next question is whether it is valid, or more accurately, whether the judgments and decisions based on the test are valid. To have **validity,** the decisions and inferences based on the test must be supported by evidence. This means that validity is judged in relation to a particular use or purpose, that is, in relation to the actual decision being made and the evidence for that decision (Linn & Gronlund, 2000).

There are different kinds of evidence to support a particular judgment. If the purpose of a test is to measure the skills covered in a particular course or unit, then we would hope to see test questions on all the important topics and not on extraneous topics. If this condition is met, we would have *content-related evidence of validity*. Have you ever taken a test that dealt only with a few ideas from one lecture or just a few pages of the textbook? Then decisions based on that test (like your grade) certainly lacked content-related evidence of validity.

Some tests are designed to predict outcomes. The SATs, for example, are intended to predict performance in college. If SAT scores correlate with academic performance in college as measured by, say, grade-point average in the first year, then we have *criterion-related evidence of validity* for the use of the SAT in admissions decisions.

Most standardized tests are designed to measure some psychological characteristic or "construct" such as reasoning ability, reading comprehension, achievement motivation, intelligence, creativity, and so on. It is a bit more difficult to gather *construct-related evidence of validity*, yet this is a very important requirement, probably the most important. Construct-related evidence of validity is gathered over many years. It is indicated by a pattern of scores. For example, older children can answer more questions on intelligence tests than younger children can. This fits with our construct of intelligence. If the average 5-year-old answered as many questions correctly on a test as the average 13-year-old we would doubt that the test really measured intelligence. Construct-related evidence for validity can also be demonstrated when the results of a test correlate with the results of other well-established, valid measures of the same construct.

Today, many psychologists suggest that construct validity is the broadest category and that gathering content- and criterion-related evidence is another way of determining if the test measures the construct it was designed to measure. Twenty years ago Sam Messick (1975) raised two important questions to consider in making any decisions about using a test: Is the test a good measure of the characteristic it is assumed to assess? Should the test be used for the proposed purpose? The first question is about construct validity; the second is about ethics and values (Moss, 1992).

Standardized achievement tests must be chosen so that the items on the test actually measure knowledge gained in the classes. This match is absent more often than we might assume: one group of teachers in St. Louis found that fewer than 10% of the items in their curriculum overlapped in both the textbooks and the standardized tests they were using (Fiske, 1988). Also, students must have the necessary skills to take the test. If students score low on a science test not because they lack knowledge about science, but because they have difficulty reading the questions, do not understand the directions, or do not have enough time to finish, then the test is not a valid measure of science achievement for those students.

A test must be reliable in order to be valid. For example, if, over a few months, an intelligence test yields different results each time it is given to the same child, then by definition it is not reliable. Certainly it couldn't be a valid measure of intelligence because intelligence is assumed to be fairly stable, at least over a short period of time. However, reliability will not guarantee validity. If that intelligence test gave the same score every time for a particular child but didn't predict school achievement, speed of learning, or other characteristics associated with intelligence, then performance on the test would not be a true indicator of intelligence. The test would be reliable—but invalid. The Guidelines on page 534 should help you increase the reliability and validity of the standardized tests you give.

The Guidelines on page 534

CHECKPOINT

What Do Test Scores Mean?

Review

▶ Describe the key features of a standardized test.

▶ What are mean, median, mode, and standard deviation?

▶ Describe different kinds of scores.

▶ What is test reliability?

▶ What is test validity?

Apply

▶ If 10 million people take the SAT, about how many should score between 400 and 600 on the verbal test? Remember, the mean is 500.

▶ Which is better, a percentile score of 75 or a T score of 75? Which is easier to explain to a family member?

▶ Every time you check, your bathroom scale gives you the same weight, but you always weigh more at the doctor's office. Is your scale valid? Is it reliable?

Connect and Extend
To the research
Moss, P. A. (1992). Shifting conceptions of validity in educational measurement: Implications for performance assessment. *Review of Educational Research, 62*, 229–258.

Connect and Extend
To real life
A woman aims her gun at the bull's-eye on a target and shoots five times. All five shots hit in the upper right-hand corner. Is the gun reliable? Is it valid? What are some possible sources of error?

Connect and Extend
To your teaching
If you have access to your own records, locate copies of standardized tests you have taken and interpret the scores as if you were your own teacher.

T ypes of Standardized Tests

Several kinds of standardized tests are used in schools today. If you have seen the cumulative folders that include testing records for individual students over several years, then you know the many ways students are tested in this country. There are three broad categories of standardized tests: achievement, diagnostic, and aptitude (including interest). As a teacher, you will probably encounter achievement and aptitude tests most frequently.

GUIDELINES

Increasing Reliability and Validity

Make sure the test actually covers the content of the unit of study.

Examples

1. Compare test questions to course objectives. Make sure that there is good overlap.
2. Use local achievement tests and local norms when possible.
3. Check to see if the test is long enough to cover all important topics.
4. Are there any difficulties your students experience with the test, such as not enough time, level of reading, and so on? If so, discuss these problems with appropriate school personnel.

Make sure students know how to use all the test materials.

Examples

1. Several days before the testing, do a few practice questions with a similar format.
2. Demonstrate the use of the answer sheets, especially computer-scored answer sheets.
3. Check with new students, shy students, slower students, and students who have difficulty reading to make sure they understand the questions.

4. Make sure students know if and when guessing is appropriate.

Follow instructions for administering the test exactly.

Examples

1. Practice giving the test before you actually use it.
2. Follow the time limits exactly.

Make students as comfortable as possible during testing.

Examples

1. Do not create anxiety by making the test seem like the most important event of the year.
2. Help the class relax before beginning the test, perhaps by telling a joke or having everyone take a few deep breaths. Don't be tense yourself!
3. Make sure the room is quiet.
4. Discourage cheating by monitoring the room. Don't become absorbed in your own paperwork.

Remember that no test scores are perfect.

Examples

1. Interpret scores using bands instead of a single score.
2. Ignore small differences between scores.

"I HATE TAKING A TEST WITHOUT AN ERASER."

(© Martha Campbell)

Achievement Tests: What Has the Student Learned?

The most common standardized tests given to students are **achievement tests.** These are meant to measure how much a student has learned in specific content areas such as reading comprehension, language usage, computation, science, social studies, mathematics, and logical reasoning. There are achievement tests for both individuals (for example, the Wide-Range Achievement Test; Peabody Individual Achievement Test; KeyMath Diagnostic Tests) and groups (the California, Metropolitan, SRA, or Stanford Achievement Tests; the TerraNova [Comprehensive Test of Basic Skills]; and the Iowa Tests). These tests vary in their reliability and validity. Group tests can be used for screening—to identify children who might need further testing or as a basis for grouping students according to achievement levels. Individual achievement tests are given to determine a child's academic level more precisely, or to help diagnose learning problems.

Using Information from a Norm-Referenced Achievement Test. What specific information can teachers expect from achievement test results? Test publishers usually provide individual profiles for each student, showing scores on each subtest. Figure 14.5 is an example of an individual profile for a 5th grader, Ken Allen, on the *California Achievement Test*, Fifth Edition. Note that the Individual Test Record reports the scores in many different ways. At the top of the form, after the identifying information about Ken's grade and birthday, is a list of the various tests—Reading Vocabulary, Reading Comprehension, Total Reading (Vocabulary and Comprehension combined), Language Mechanics, and so on. Beside each test are several different ways of reporting Ken's score:

FIGURE 14.5

An Individual Test Record

Test publishers provide several kinds of report forms for individual students and for entire classes. The form below gives both norm-referenced and criterion-referenced information about a fifth-grade boy.

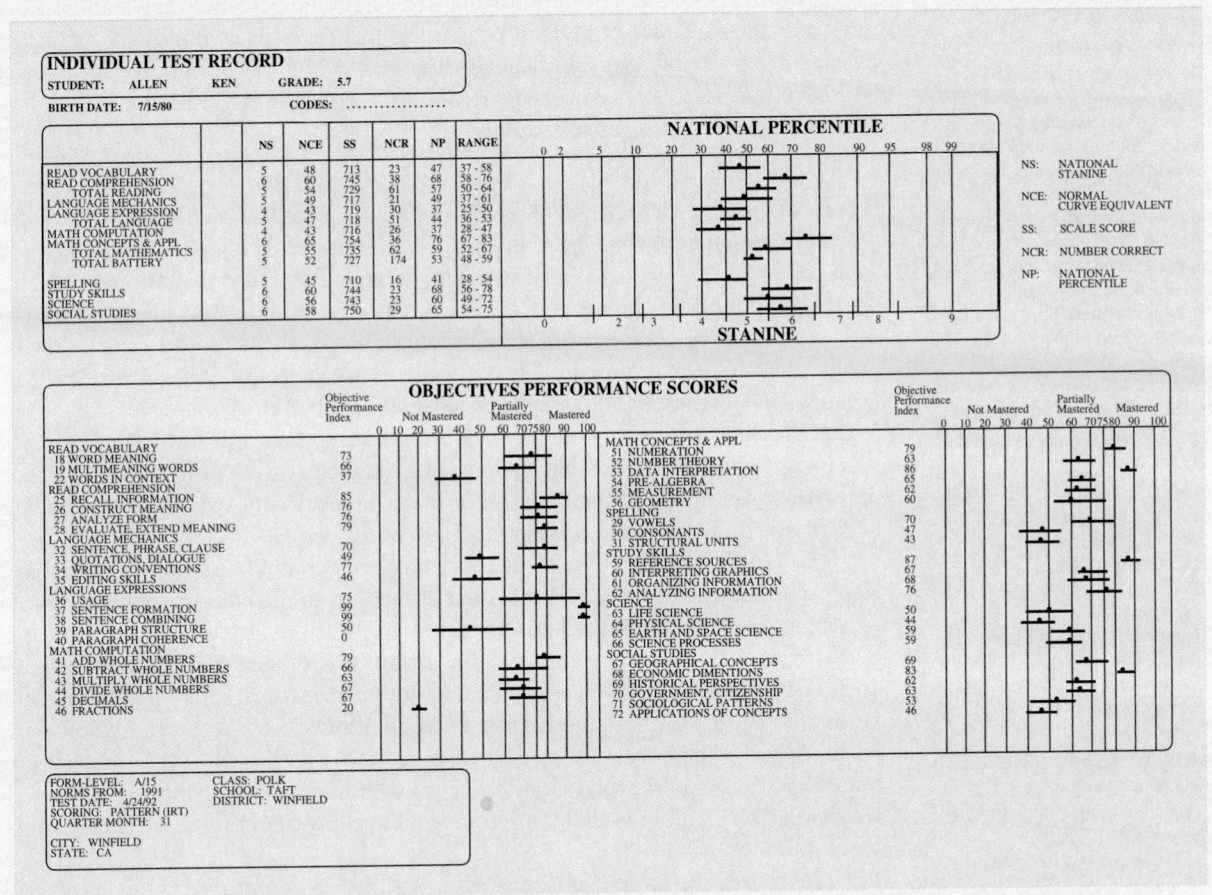

NS: Ken's National Stanine Score (his stanine score based on a national norming sample comparison group).

NCE: Ken's Normal Curve Equivalent Score (a score used mostly for research purposes to evaluate certain compensatory education programs).

SS: Ken's Scale Score. This describes growth in achievement that typically occurs as a student progresses through the grades—the higher the grade the higher the expected scale score.

NCR: Ken's actual number correct—his raw score.

NP: Ken's National Percentile Score, telling us where he stands in relation to students at his grade level across the country.

RANGE: The range of national percentile scores in which Ken's true score is likely to fall. You may remember from our discussion of true scores that this range, or confidence interval, is determined by adding and subtracting the standard error of the test from Ken's actual score. There is a 95% chance that Ken's true score is within this range.

Beside the scores is a graph showing Ken's national percentile and stanine scores, with the standard error bands indicated around the scores. Bands that show any overlap are probably not significantly different. When there is no overlap between bands for two test scores, we can be reasonably certain that Ken's achievement levels in these two areas are actually different.

Interpreting Achievement Test Scores. Let's look at Ken's scores more carefully. In language mechanics he has a stanine score of 5, which is equal to a scale score of 717. This is at the 49th percentile nationally. His true national percentile score is probably in the range from 37 to 61 (that is, plus and minus 1 standard error of measurement from the actual score of 49, so the standard error of the language mechanics test must be 12). By looking at the graph, we can see that Ken's language mechanics and language expression score bands overlap. His achievement in these areas is probably similar, even though there seems to be a difference when you look at the NP scores alone. Comparing language expression with reading comprehension, on the other hand, we see that the bands do not overlap. Ken is stronger in reading comprehension than in language expression.

The profile in Figure 14.5 tells us a number of things. First, we can see that all Ken's scores are within the average range compared to the national norming sample. Ken's highest score is in math concepts and applications. However, this score band overlaps several other score bands, so we cannot say for sure that this is his strongest area. Ken's strength in math concepts and applications raises his total math battery score to a percentile of 59, but his math computation score is significantly lower than his math concepts score (the bands do not overlap). With some work on math computations, Ken would probably improve his overall math performance. We can also see that Ken is weak in spelling. Improving his spelling might improve his vocabulary score and vice versa.

The scores we have just described are all norm-referenced. However, results from standardized tests like the one Ken took can also be interpreted in a criterion-referenced way. The bottom portion of Ken's Individual Test Record in Figure 14.5 breaks down the larger categories of the top section (reading vocabulary, reading comprehension, etc.) and shows criterion-referenced scores that indicate mastered, partially mastered, or not mastered for specific skills. These include reading vocabulary skills such as the use of word meanings and words in context and study skills

Connect and Extend
To your teaching

Choose a partner to role play a parent–teacher conference. Below are two examples of test results that the teacher should interpret to the parent. Each member of the dyad should take the role of the teacher or parent, then reverse the roles. The teacher should interpret the scores to the parent and make judgments or recommendations about the child's future educational experiences. The parent should feel free to ask questions concerning the interpretation and the recommendations.

Terry: 3rd grade, scores based on national norm.

Math Computation: 6.0 (grade-equivalent score)

Math Reasoning: 3.5 (grade-equivalent score)

Reading Vocabulary: 85th percentile

Reading Comprehension: 53rd percentile

Group IQ score: 79 (test was given the day before Terry's birthday)

Bobbie: 10th grade, scores based on local norms

Math Computation: 5 (stanine score)

Math Reasoning: 4 (stanine score)

Reading Vocabulary: 53 (*T* score)

Reading Comprehension: 38 (*T* score)

WISC III Verbal = 121

WISC III Performance = 130

WISC III Total = 125

such as using reference sources and interpreting graphics. The Objective Performance Index score is an estimate of the percentage of all possible items that Ken could be expected to answer correctly in each performance area. In other words, based on his performance on these test items, what percentage of all possible questions in this area (at his level) should he get right? Teachers can use these results to get an idea of Ken's strengths and weaknesses with these specific skills and thus determine his progress toward objectives in a given subject. Be aware, though, that some of these specific skill areas may be measured with only a few items each, and the fewer the items, the more potential problems there can be with reliability.

Diagnostic Tests: What Are the Student's Strengths and Weaknesses?

If teachers want to identify specific learning problems, they may need to refer to results from the various diagnostic tests that have been developed. Most **diagnostic tests** are given to students individually by a highly trained professional. The goal is usually to identify the specific problems a student is having. Achievement tests, both standardized and teacher-made, identify weaknesses in academic content areas such as mathematics, computation, or reading. Individually administered diagnostic tests identify weaknesses in learning processes. There are diagnostic tests to assess the ability to hear differences among sounds, remember spoken words or sentences, recall a sequence of symbols, separate figures from their background, express relationships, coordinate eye and hand movements, describe objects orally, blend sounds to form words, recognize details in a picture, coordinate movements, and many other abilities needed to learn, remember, and communicate learning. Elementary school teachers are more likely than secondary school teachers to receive information from diagnostic tests. High school students are more likely to take aptitude tests.

Aptitude Tests: How Well Will the Student Do in the Future?

Both achievement and aptitude tests measure developed abilities. Achievement tests may measure abilities developed over a short period of time, such as during a week-long unit on map reading, or over a longer period of time, such as a semester. **Aptitude tests** are meant to measure abilities developed over many years and to predict how well a student will do in the future at learning unfamiliar material. The greatest difference between the two types of tests is that they are used for different purposes. Achievement tests measure final performance (and perhaps give grades), and aptitude tests predict how well people will do in particular programs such as college or professional school (Anastasi, 1988).

Scholastic Aptitude. The purpose of a scholastic aptitude test, such as the SAT (Scholastic Assessment Test) or ACT (American College Testing Program) is to predict how well a student is likely to do in college. Colleges use such scores to help decide on acceptances and rejections. The SAT may have seemed like an achievement test to you, measuring what you had learned in high school. Although the test is designed to avoid drawing too heavily on specific high school curricula, the questions are very similar to achievement test questions.

Standardized aptitude tests—such as the SAT, the School and College Ability Tests (SCAT), and the Preliminary Scholastic Assessment Test (PSAT) for younger

Connect and Extend
To your teaching
Some diagnostic tests measure a student's ability in a variety of areas. These tests include the Detroit Test of Learning Aptitude and Part I of the Woodcock-Johnson Psycho-Educational Battery: Tests of Cognitive Ability. Others, however, assess a student's ability in a more specific area. Tests of motor skills include the Bender Gestalt Test and the Purdue Perceptual Motor Survey. For assessing specific areas of perception, commonly used tests include the Wepman Auditory Discrimination Test, the Goldman-Fristoe-Woodcock Test of Auditory Discrimination, the Frostig Developmental Test of Visual Perception, and the Motor-Free Visual Perception Test.

Diagnostic Tests: Individually administered tests to identify special learning problems.

Aptitude Tests: Tests meant to predict future performance.

Connect and Extend

To your teaching

How should a teacher interpret an IQ score that is recorded in a student's cumulative folder? If there is a large discrepancy (in either direction) between the IQ score and the child's performance level in school, which would you be more concerned about? Which would you consider more valid? Why?

students—seem to be reliable in predicting future achievement. Since standardized tests are less open to teacher bias, they may be even fairer predictors of future achievement than high school grades. Indeed, some psychologists believe grade inflation in high schools has made tests such as the SAT even more important. Others believe that the SATs are not good predictors of success in college, particularly for women or members of cultural or ethnic minority groups. The controversy continues.

IQ and Scholastic Aptitude. In Chapter 4 we discussed one of the most influential aptitude tests of all, the IQ test. The IQ test as we know it could well be called a test of scholastic aptitude. Now that you understand the concept of standard deviation, you will be able to appreciate several statistical characteristics of the tests. For example, the IQ score is really a standard score with a mean of 100 and a standard deviation of 15 or 16, depending on the test. Thus about 68% of the general population would score between +1 and −1 standard deviations from the mean, or between about 85 and 115.

A difference of a few points between two students' IQ scores should not be viewed as important. Scores between 90 and 109 are within the average range. In fact, scores between 80 and 119 are considered within the range of low average to high average. To see the problems that may arise, consider the following conversation:

Parent: We came to speak with you today because we are shocked at our son's IQ score. We can't believe he has only a 99 IQ when his sister scored much higher on the same test. We know they are about the same. In fact, Sam has better marks than Lauren did in the 5th grade.

Teacher: What was Lauren's score?

Parent: Well, she did much better. She scored a 103!

Clearly, brother and sister have both scored within the average range. While the standard error of measurement on the WISC-III (Weschler Intelligence Scale for Children, third edition) varies slightly from one age to the next, the average standard error for the total score is 3.2. So the bands around Sam's and Lauren's IQ scores—about 96 to 102 and 100 to 106—are overlapping. Either child could have scored 100, 101, or 102.

Discussing Test Results with Families. At times, you will be expected to explain or describe test results to your students' families. The Family and Community Partnerships Guidelines give some ideas.

*I*ssues in Standardized Testing

Today, many important decisions about students, teachers, and schools are based in part on the results of standardized tests. Test scores may affect "admission" to 1st grade, promotion from one grade to the next, high school graduation, access to special programs, placement in special education classes, teacher certification and tenure, and school funding. Because the decisions affected by test scores are so critical, many educators call this process **high-stakes testing.** By 1991, 47 states had some form of statewide mandated testing for public school students (Ziomek & Maxey, 1993). Some groups are working to increase the role of testing—by establishing a national examination, for example—while others are working to cut back the use of standardized tests in schools (Linn & Gronlund, 2000; Madaus & Kellaghan, 1993).

In the next few pages we will consider two basic questions: What role should testing play in making decisions about people? Do some students have an unfair advantage in taking tests?

The Uses of Testing in American Society

Tests are not simply procedures used in research. Every day, there are many decisions made about individuals that are based on the results of tests. Should Liz be issued a

Connect and Extend
To the research
Madaus, G. F., & Kellaghan, T. (1993). Testing as a mechanism of public policy: A brief history. *Measurement and Evaluation in Counseling and Development, 26,* 6–10.

High-Stakes Testing: Standardized tests whose results have powerful influences when used by school administrators, other officials, or employers to make decisions.

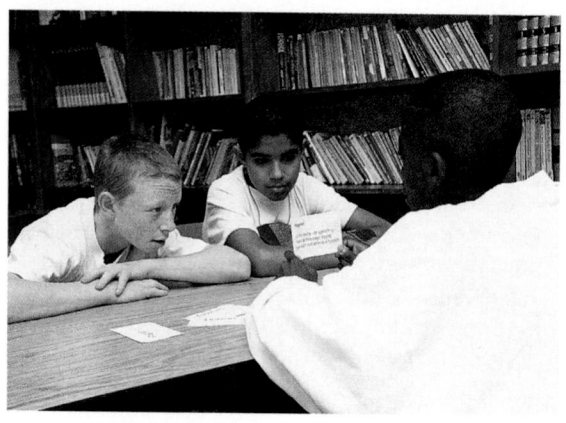

▲ *Standardized tests have become a part of schooling in many states. One challenge for teachers is how to give students the practice they need to learn factual information. These students are quizzing each other to prepare for a test.*

Connect and Extend
To the research

Smith, M. L. (1991). Put to the test: The effects of external testing on teachers. *Educational Researcher, 20*(5), 8–11.

Connect and Extend
To the research

Kirst, M. (1991a). Interview on assessment issues with Lorrie Shepard. *Educational Researcher, 20*(2), 21–23+. Kirst, M. (1991b). Interview on assessment issues with James Popham. *Educational Researcher, 20*(2), 24–27. *Focus Questions:* Summarize Shepard's and Popham's views on assessment. What kind of classroom assessment would each support?

driver's license? How many and which students from the 8th grade would benefit from an accelerated program in science? Who belongs in a remedial class? Who will be admitted to college or professional school? Who will get a teaching certificate? In answering these questions, it is important to distinguish between the quality of the test itself and how the test is used. Even the best instruments can be, and have been, misused. In earlier years, for example, using otherwise valid and reliable individual intelligence tests, many students were inappropriately identified as having mental retardation. The problem was not with the tests, but with the fact that the test score was the only information used to classify students. Much more information must be considered.

Behind all the statistics and terminology are issues related to values and ethics. Who will be tested? What are the consequences of choosing one test over another for a particular purpose with a given group? What is the effect of the testing on the students? How will the test scores of minority group students be interpreted? What do we really mean by intelligence, competence, and scholastic aptitude? Do our views agree with those implied by the tests we use to measure these constructs? How will test results be integrated with other information about the individual to make judgments? Answering these questions requires choices based on values, as well as accurate information about what tests can and cannot tell us. As you can see in the Point/Counterpoint, the debate about testing continues.

Readiness Testing. In 1988, Georgia became the first state to require that children pass a test before moving from kindergarten to 1st grade (Fiske, 1988; Linn, 1986). The test quickly became a symbol of the misuse of tests. Public outcry led to modifications of the policy and spurred many educators to reform the **readiness testing** process. In fact, the uproar over this group-administered, machine-scored, norm-referenced test for kindergarten children "probably did more to advance readiness assessment reform in this country than all other causes combined" (Engel, 1991, p. 41).

Critics of readiness tests (Meisels, 1989; Shepard & Smith, 1989) believe:

1. Group-administered paper-and-pencil tests are inappropriate for preschool children and thus should not be the basis for decisions about school entry. Readiness tests do not have sufficient predicative validity to be used alone to make screening or placement decisions (Linn & Gronlund, 2000).

2. The use of readiness tests narrows the preschool curriculum, making it more academic and less developmentally appropriate.

3. The evidence shows that delaying entry into 1st grade or retaining students in kindergarten is not effective. Students who are retained do no better than similar students who are not held back.

In spite of these criticisms, today almost every state uses testing at the state or district level to determine if a child is "ready" for 1st grade or to place a child in a special "developmental kindergarten" (Kirst, 1991a). Several states, as well as a few test publishers, are trying to develop appropriate ways to determine readiness. Engel (1991) suggests that such procedures could be ongoing assessments about many different aspects of readiness—cognitive, social/emotional, physical, and so on. These assessments would be indirect, that is, they would be completed by adults rather than requiring the children to answer questions directly on paper. The obser-

Readiness Testing: Testing procedures meant to determine if an individual is ready to proceed to the next level of education or training.

To Test or Not to Test?

Student teachers are often astounded by the amount of time they must spend every spring preparing their students for "test week." Schools have been known to abandon innovations such as "whole language" and hands-on science teaching and to adopt drill-and-practice test-based programs in their place, just because test scores fell when these innovations were introduced. Yet there is talk of more, not less, testing and the development of a National Curriculum. Should standardized testing be continued?

▶ POINT *Testing should be stopped.*

Critics of standardized testing state that these tests measure disjointed facts and skills that have no use or meaning in the real world. Often test questions do not match the curriculum of the schools, so the tests can't measure how well students have learned the curriculum. Even so, there is great pressure on teachers to produce high test scores. Teachers' jobs, principals' raises, and even the value of real estate in the school district are affected by the schools' test scores. So teachers find themselves "teaching to the test." Because tests are best at measuring lower-level objectives, facts, and basic skills, these facts and skills become the content of the curriculum. Too often, the results of tests are used to label students as low achievers, and self-fulfilling

prophecies are set into motion. Mary Lee Smith (1991) found the following effects of standardized testing on teachers:

When test scores are made public, teachers often feel embarrassed, angry, or ashamed. They sometimes change students' answers, excuse poor students from taking the test, drill students on the answers, or give unallowed "help" because the pressure for high scores is so great.

Teachers feel alienated from the test process, because when test scores are published, no one takes into account the fact that some of their students live in poverty or are just learning English.

Teachers are concerned that the tests take away valuable teaching time and make their students too anxious. Preparing for, giving, and recovering from the tests took an average of 100 hours of instructional time in the schools Smith studied.

◀ COUNTERPOINT *Tests can provide valuable information.*

Defenders of standardized tests note that it is the responsibility of the school to select an appropriate test. Standardized tests are designed to sample what is typically taught, so the fit with any particular school's curriculum will not be perfect. Thus a standardized test is only one source

of information. To redesign the curriculum so that it matches the test or to make placement decisions based only on a test score is to overuse and misuse the test. No test is reliable and valid enough to serve as the only basis for making important decisions. But tests do provide useful information.

To make good use of test results, Blaine Worthen and Vicki Spandel (1991) suggest the following:

Don't test unless there is an important decision to make. Then choose a good test that will give useful information about the decision.

Never use the test as the only basis for the decision. Supplement with other information, including the teacher's judgment.

Assume every test score is imperfect. Take the score as an estimate.

Know what the test actually measures. Just because it is called a test of reading comprehension does not mean that a test measures everything about reading comprehension.

Know your students. A test of math achievement that uses word problems can be a test of reading comprehension for students whose English is limited.

Don't use test results to compare students or foster competition. Use the results to benefit students.

vations would provide useful information for teaching; they would be conducted in a comfortable natural setting, often as part of the preschool program itself.

Minimum and World-Class Standards. In many studies comparing the United States with other industrialized nations, American students have placed low in academic achievement. For example, in the Third International Mathematics and Science Study (TIMSS), the students in the United States did not do well compared to students from other developed countries. Even though these conclusions have

Connect and Extend
To debates on testing

Background: For an argument that American standards and students are not in crisis, see Berliner, D., & Biddle, B. (1996). *The manufactured crisis: Myths, frauds, and the attack on America's public schools.* White Plains, NY: Longman. For the counterargument, see Ravitch, D. (1995). *National standards in American education: A citizens's guide.* Washington, DC: Brookings Institution.

Connect and Extend
To debates on testing

The cover story for the April 1, 1996 issue of *U. S. News and World Report* was "Dumb and Dumber: The Battle to Raise School Standards." The article describes a recent meeting of 45 governors and the chief executive officers of dozens of major corporations. The purpose of the meeting? To explore ways to bring "world class" standards to American education. Are higher standards necessary?

Connect and Extend
To debates on testing

Two special issues devoted to the standards debate: *Educational Leadership*, March, 1995 and *Phi Delta Kappan*, June, 1995.

Connect and Extend
To your teaching

Find out what the requirements are for certification tests in your state. Check the Web site for the Educational Testing Service: www.ets.org.

Minimum Competency Test: Standardized test meant to determine if students meet minimum requirements to graduate or to proceed in school.

been questioned (Berliner & Biddle, 1997), policymakers are concerned. One suggestion to improve student performance is minimum competency testing. A **minimum competency test** is a standardized test meant to determine whether an individual meets the minimum standard for moving to the next level or graduating. Almost every state in the United States has some kind of high school competency testing program. Some people have even suggested that a national examination would be helpful (O'Neil, 1991).

The push for a national test slowed, replaced by the idea of *national standards* (Lewis, 1995; Ziomek & Maxey, 1993). There are several kinds of standards. *Content standards* define what should be learned in particular subject areas such as mathematics or history. *Performance standards* specify the level or quality of student learning expected. *Opportunity-to-learn standards* describe the conditions and resources necessary to give every student an equal chance to reach the content and performance standards. Finally, you may hear about *world-class standards*, or the level of content and performance expected in other countries.

National educational groups such as the National Council of Teachers of Mathematics (NCTM, 1991) have led the way in establishing standards (Hambleton, 1996; Lewis, 1995; Resnick & Nolan, 1995). At this point, standards are voluntary, but the debate continues about the value of adopting national standards. The public is divided on the standards question. In the 1999 Phi Delta Kappa/Gallup Poll of the Public's Attitude Toward the Public Schools (Rose & Gallup, 1999), 57% of the respondents said current standards were "about right" while 33% said standards were too low (but 43% of people in urban centers felt standards were too low).

Testing Teachers. New models of teacher assessment are in the planning and development stages. For example, the revised National Teachers Examination (NTE) is a battery of tests called the *Praxis Series* and is given in three phases. Early in the prospective teacher's education program, *Praxis I: Academic Skills Assessment* tests basic skills such as reading, writing, and mathematics. A computer-based package is available to remediate any weak areas identified by the test. *Praxis II: Subject Assessments*, given at the end of the undergraduate program, test subject matter knowledge and principles of teaching and learning. *Praxis III: Classroom Performance Assessments* is based on the particular licensing requirements for each participating state. This assessment is conducted by trained local evaluators, mostly through classroom observations. Within each Praxis phase there are several modules from which to choose. States can require any one—or a combination of two or all three—of the Praxis phases for certification (Danielson & Dwyer, 1995; Dwyer & Villegas, 1993).

Like the alternatives to standardized tests we will examine shortly, the Praxis Series and other new teacher tests will make greater use of authentic performances and products. In *Praxis II*, teacher candidates analyze case studies and suggest solutions to teaching problems. In *Praxis III*, teachers might complete a lesson-planning exercise and then be interviewed about what they planned and why. They might be asked to submit a portfolio containing an overview of a unit, details of two consecutive lessons, copies of student handouts, lists of the resources selected for background, a videotape of teaching samples showing both large- and small-group lessons, and other examples of the teacher's actual work. Connecticut is developing a new system for assessing beginning science teachers that also relies on portfolios, including samples of teachers' writing, student work, and videotaped segments of classroom instruction, as shown in Table 14.2. Results of these assessments will be used to determine eligibility for a provisional teaching certificate as well as to pro-

TABLE 14.2 *An Overview of a Science Teaching Portfolio*

These are the entries expected in the portfolio of a beginning science teacher in Connecticut. Decisions about provisional certification as well as suggestions for improvement are based on the portfolio.

Task I—Planning for student learning

- Description of major concepts and goals for a two-week unit.
- Description of student characteristics relevant to learning this unit.
- Day-to-day journal entries for the unit.

Task II—Facilitating student learning

- Description of one student-centered lab activity during the unit.
- Description of one unit's topic dealing with science, technology, and society issues.
- Three 15-minute video segments of lab activity, post-lab discussion, and science-technology-society lesson.

Task III—Evaluation of student learning

- Entire work of three students during the unit.
- Detailed analysis of these students' learning.
- General analysis of whole class work and learning.
- Analysis of teaching and suggestions for future changes.

Source: "Assessing New Science Teachers," by M. S. Lomask, R. L. Pecheone, and J. B. Baron, 1995, *Educational Leadership, 52*(6), p. 63. Copyright © 1995 by Connecticut State Department of Education. Adapted with permission.

vide feedback for continuing professional development (Lomask, Pecheone, & Baron, 1995).

These procedures look promising. Of course, every innovation has its shortcomings. Can these portfolios and performances be evaluated objectively? Will we see an explosion of businesses that specialize in helping teachers build a beautiful portfolio? Will the wealthier teachers and teacher candidates have the best portfolios and videos (Kirst, 1991b)?

In addition to assessing beginning teachers, there is growing interest in setting standards for accomplished teaching. In 1986 the Carnegie Task Force on Teaching as a Profession called for the creation of a National Board for Professional Teaching Standards (NBPTS). This Board will offer experienced teachers advanced certification in more than 30 fields, categorized by subject matter and developmental level of students. Standards in all areas will be grounded in five general propositions about accomplished practice (Yinger, 1998):

▶ Teachers are committed to students and their learning.

▶ Teachers know the subjects they teach and how to teach those subjects to their students.

▶ Teachers are responsible for managing and monitoring student learning.

▶ Teachers think systematically about their practice and learn from experience.

▶ Teachers are members of learning communities.

The process, which relies on portfolio assessment, is voluntary and still being refined. If you become a teacher, assessment awaits you at several points in your career.

Advantages in Taking Tests— Fair and Unfair

Connect and Extend
To debates on testing
Worthen, B. R., & Spanel, V. (1991). Putting the standardized test debate in perspective. *Educational Leadership, 48*(5), 65–70.

In this section we will consider three basic issues: Are standardized tests biased against minority students? Can students gain an advantage on admissions tests through coaching? Can they be taught test-taking skills?

Bias and Fairness in Testing. Are tests such as the individual measures of intelligence or college admissions tests fair assessments for minority group students? This is a complex question. Research on **test bias** shows that most standardized tests predict school achievement equally well across all groups of students. Items that might appear on the surface to be biased against minorities are not necessarily more difficult for minorities to answer correctly (Sattler, 1992). Even though standardized aptitude and achievement tests are not biased against minorities in predicting school performance, many people believe that the tests still can be unfair. Tests may not have *procedural fairness*; that is, some groups may not have an equal opportunity to show what they know on the test: Here are a few examples:

1. The language of the test and the tester is often different from the languages of the students.

2. Answers that support middle-class values are often rewarded with more points.

3. On individually administered intelligence tests, being very verbal and talking a lot is rewarded. This favors students who feel comfortable in that particular situation.

Also, tests may not be fair, because different groups have had different *opportunities to learn* the material tested. The questions asked tend to center on experiences and facts more familiar to the dominant culture than to minority group students.

Concern about cultural bias in testing has led some psychologists to try to develop **culture-fair** or **culture-free tests**. These efforts have not been very successful. On many of the so-called culture-fair tests, the performance of students from lower socioeconomic backgrounds and minority groups has been the same as or worse than their performance on the standard Wechsler and Binet Intelligence scales (Sattler, 1992). The Guidelines might help all your students take tests.

Coaching and Test-Taking Skills. Courses to prepare students for college entrance exams are becoming more popular. As you probably know from experience, both commercial and public school coaching programs are available. In general, research has indicated that short high school training programs yield average gains of 10 points in SAT verbal scores and 15 points in SAT math scores, whereas longer commercial programs show gains of anywhere from 50 to as much as 200 points for some people (Owen, 1985). Kulik, Kulik, and Bangert (1984) analyzed the results of 40 different studies on aptitude and achievement test training and found that there were more substantial gains when students practiced on a parallel form of a test for brief periods. The design of the coaching program, therefore, may be the critical factor.

Two other types of training can make a difference in test scores. One is simple familiarity with the procedures of standardized tests. Students who have extensive

Test Bias: A potential problem with tests in which the content discriminates against a group of students on the basis of gender, SES, race, ethnicity, etc.

Culture-Fair/Culture-Free Test: A test without cultural bias.

GUIDELINES

Becoming an Expert Test-Taker

Use the night before the test effectively.

Examples

1. Study the night before the exam, ending with a final look at a summary of the key points, concepts, and relationships.

2. Get a good night's sleep. If you know you generally have trouble sleeping the night before an exam, try getting extra sleep on several previous nights.

Set the situation so you can concentrate on the test.

Examples

1. Give yourself plenty of time to eat and get to the exam room.

2. Don't sit near a friend. It may make concentration difficult. If your friend leaves early, you may be tempted to do so, too.

Make sure you know what the test is asking.

Examples

1. Read the directions carefully. If you are unsure, ask the instructor or proctor for clarification.

2. Read each question carefully to spot tricky words, such as *not, except, all of the following but one.*

3. On an essay test, read every question first, so you know the size of the job ahead of you and can make informed decisions about how much time to spend on each question.

4. On a multiple-choice test, read every alternative, even if an early one seems right.

Use time effectively.

Examples

1. Begin working right away and move as rapidly as possible while your energy is high.

2. Do the easy questions first.

3. Don't get stuck on one question. If you are stumped, mark the question so you can return to it easily later, and go on to questions you can answer more quickly.

4. If you are unsure about a question, answer it but mark it so you can go back if there is time.

5. On a multiple-choice test, if you know you will not have time to finish, fill in all the remaining questions with the same letter if there is no penalty for guessing.

6. If you are running out of time on an essay test, do not leave any questions blank. Briefly outline a few key points to show the instructor you "knew" the answer but needed more time.

Know when to guess on multiple-choice or true-false tests.

Examples

1. Always guess when only right answers are scored.

2. Always guess when you can eliminate some of the alternatives.

3. Don't guess if there is a penalty for guessing, unless you can confidently eliminate at least one alternative.

4. Are correct answers always longer? shorter? in the middle? more likely to be one letter? more often true than false?

5. Does the grammar give the right answer away or eliminate any alternatives?

Check your work.

Examples

1. Even if you can't stand to look at the test another minute, reread each question to make sure you answered the way you intended.

2. If you are using a machine-scored answer sheet, check occasionally to be sure the number of the question you are answering corresponds to the number of the answer on the sheet.

On essay tests, answer as directly as possible.

Examples

1. Avoid flowery introductions. Answer the question in the first sentence and then elaborate.

2. Don't save your best ideas till last. Give them early in the answer.

3. Unless the instructor requires complete sentences, consider listing points, arguments, and so on by number in your answer. It will help you organize your thoughts and concentrate on the important aspects of the answer.

Learn from the testing experience.

Examples

1. Pay attention when the teacher reviews the answers. You can learn from your mistakes, and the same question may reappear in a later test.

2. Notice if you are having trouble with a particular kind of item; adjust your study approach next time to handle this type of item better.

Issues in Standardized Testing

Review

▶ What are some current issues in testing?

▶ Can students become better test-takers?

Apply

▶ What does high-stakes testing mean? What are some decisions that should *not* be based on standardized test scores?

▶ How would you determine readiness for school?

experience with standardized tests do better than those who do not. Some of this advantage may be the result of greater self-confidence, less tendency to panic, familiarity with different kinds of questions (for example, analogies such as house: garage::———: car), and practice with the various answer sheets (Anastasi, 1988). Even brief orientations about how to take tests can help students who lack familiarity and confidence.

A second type of training that appears to be very promising is instruction in general cognitive skills such as solving problems, carefully analyzing questions, considering all alternatives, noticing details and deciding which are relevant, avoiding impulsive answers, and checking work. These are the kinds of metacognitive and study skills we have discussed before. Training in these skills is likely to generalize to many tasks (Anastasi, 1988).

Connect and Extend
To the research
Kozulin, A., & Falik, L. (1995). Dynamic cognitive assessment of the child. *Current Directions, 4,* 192–195. From the article:

Assumptions of standard intellectual assessment:

1. The manifest level of functioning reveals more or less accurately the child's inner abilities.
2. Unaided performance is the best format for assessment.
3. The goal of testing is to predict future functioning and to classify the child according to his or her level of abilities.

Assumptions of dynamic cognitive assessment:

1. Cognitive processes are highly modifiable. The task of assessment is to ascertain the degree of modifiability rather than the manifest level of functioning.
2. Interactive assessment, which includes a learning phrase, provides better insight into the child's learning capacity than unaided performance.
3. The goal of assessment is to reveal the child's learning potential and to suggest psychoeducational interventions aimed at enhancing and realizing this potential.

Preparing Students for Testing. I recently read about a 6th grade class that used their statewide testing as an opportunity for problem-based learning (Ewy with student authors, 1997). This class read a newspaper article about the upcoming test and the less than stellar performance of the 6th graders in previous years. They took on the following problem: How could they improve their own test scores on the IGAP (Illinois Goal Assessment Program)? The students talked about why the problem was important and how to solve it, generating the problem analysis chart in Figure 14.6. Then they divided into groups to do different tasks: schedule practice times, look for resources, make up questions and interview experts, and set up a tutoring program. The result? The students met or exceeded the state reading, writing, and mathematics goals. When they moved to junior high and had to take the math placement test, these students researched the test. What are the cutoff points, the possible range of scores, and evaluation criteria? Perhaps you can take on a similar problem with your students. The following guidelines might help as part of the program.

New Directions in Standardized Testing

Standardized tests continue to be controversial. In response to dissatisfaction with traditional forms of assessment, new approaches have emerged to deal with some of the most common testing problems.

Assessing Learning Potential

One criticism of traditional forms of intelligence testing is that such tests are merely samples of performance at one particular point in time; they fail to capture the child's

FIGURE 14.6

Taking on "The Test": Problem-Based Learning

Students in a 6th grade classroom produced this chart as they designed a program for improving their own test performance.

Problem Analysis Chart

Problem: How can we improve our performance on the IGAP test in such a way that we (1) keep improving each year, (2) set a good example for our school, (3) make preparing for IGAP more fun?

Our Ideas	Facts We Know	Our Questions	Our Action Plan
• Pay attention in class • Hold fundraiser to get books and computer program • Look at actual IGAP book format • Practice: Use computer games • Get someone who knows how to coach IGAP: teacher, parent, friend, brother/sister • Tackle one subject at a time • Find out who wants to know	• Test on reading, writing, and math • You get better when you practice • You might read questions wrong • Fill in circles • Writing is scored by time, spelling, sentence structure	• When is IGAP? • How long is the test? • How long should we practice? • What should we practice (math, reading, writing)? • How many problems? • How is the test scored (math, reading, writing)? • How much time is given for math, reading, writing? • How did I do on the last IGAP test?	• Ask principal, teacher, tutor • Ask person who made test • Work with teacher to set up schedule • Look for resources for practice • Ask parents and principal to help

Source: Adapted from "Kids Take on 'the Test,'" by C. Ewy & student authors, *Educational Leadership, 54*(4), p. 77. Copyright © 1997 by the Association for Supervision and Curriculum Development. Reprinted with permission. All rights reserved.

potential for future learning. An alternative view of cognitive assessment is based on the assumption that the goal of assessment is to reveal potential for learning and to identify the psychological and educational interventions that will help the person realize this potential. Procedures developed by Joe Campione and Ann Brown give graduated prompts as a child works to solve a problem. The prompts are scripted, beginning with a general hint and ending with a detailed instruction for how find the answer. The way the child uses the prompt and learns within the testing situation gives evidence of learning potential (Kozulin & Falik, 1995).

Reuven Feuerstein's **Learning Propensity Assessment Device** is another attempt to look at the process of learning rather than its product (Feuerstein, 1979; Kozulin & Falik, 1995). The assessment is a battery of 14 different instruments that include reasoning, numerical, verbal, figural, logical, and memory tasks. When necessary, the examiner teaches the child how to solve the problems and then assesses how well the child has benefited from instruction. The outcome of the assessment is not a score but descriptive information about practical teaching methods and materials for working with the child.

Both Feuerstein's and Campione and Brown's techniques reflect Vygotsky's ideas about the zone of proximal development—the range of functioning where a child cannot solve problems independently but can benefit from guidance. Results of these tests offer a thought-provoking and radically different approach to intelligence testing. Rather than focusing on where a child is, these approaches point

Connect and Extend
To the research
Grigorenko, E. L., & Sternberg, R. J. (1998). Dynamic testing. *Psychological Bulletin, 124,* 75–111.

Learning Propensity Assessment Device: Innovative method for testing the student's ability to benefit from teaching, consistent with Vygotsky's theory of cognitive development.

Connect and Extend
To debates on testing

Read At Odds: Performance Assessment (1991, special feature). *Phi Delta Kappan, 72*(9). This feature includes two articles: Cizek, G. J. Innovation or enervation: Performance assessment in perspective, pp. 695–699, and Wiggins, G. A response to Cizek, pp. 700–703. *Focus Questions:* Summarize the two positions on performance assessment expressed by the authors. Which position most closely represents your views? Why?

In many subjects the most reliable test is to demonstrate the ability to produce a finished product. ▶

Connect and Extend
To other chapters

Chapter 15 includes a discussion of alternatives for authentic assessment, including portfolios and exhibitions.

Connect and Extend
To professional journals

Special Section on Authentic Assessment. (1993, February). *Phi Delta Kappan, 74,* 444–479.

Connect and Extend
To the research

For an interesting look at performance assessment, see the report of a conference, "What Works in Performance Assessment?" in the Spring 1993 issue of *Evaluation Comment,* from UCLA's Center for the Study of Evaluation and the National Center for Research on Evaluation, Standards, and Student Testing, Graduate School of Education, 405 Hilgard Ave., Los Angeles, CA 90024-1522.

For a complete discussion of performance assessment, see Hambleton, R. K. (1996). Advances in assessment models, methods, and practices. In D. C. Berliner & R. C. Calfee (Eds.), *Handbook of educational psychology.* New York: Macmillan.

toward where the child could go and give guidance for the journey (Grigorenko & Sternberg, 1998).

Authentic Assessment

As the public and government demanded greater accountability in education in the 1980s and 1990s and as traditional standardized tests became the basis for high-stakes decisions, pressure to do well led many teachers and schools to "teach to the test." This tended to focus student learning on basic skills and facts. Even more troubling, say critics, the traditional tests assess skills that have no equivalent in the real world. Students are asked to solve problems or answer questions they will never encounter again; they are expected to do so alone, without relying on any

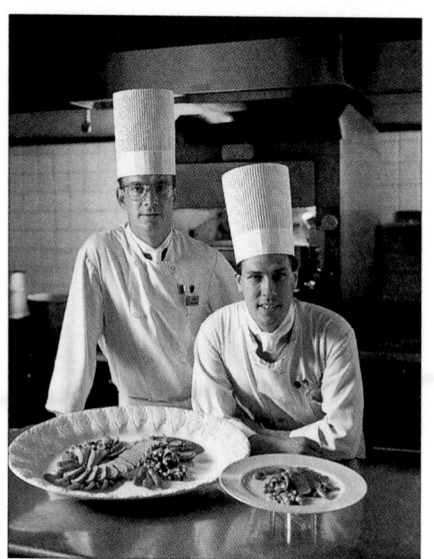

tools or resources and while working under extreme time limits. Real life just isn't like this. Important problems take time to solve and often require using resources, consulting other people, and integrating basic skills with creativity and high-level thinking (Kirst, 1991a; Wolf, Bixby, Glenn, & Gardner, 1991).

In response to these criticisms, the **authentic assessment** movement was born. The goal was to create standardized tests that assess complex, important, real-life outcomes. The approach is also called *direct assessment, performance assessment,* or *alternative assessment.* These terms refer to procedures that are alternatives to traditional multiple-choice standardized tests because they directly assess student performance on "real-life" tasks (Hambleton, 1996; Worthen, 1993). Some states are developing procedures to conduct authentic assessments. For example, in 1990, Kentucky passed the Educational Reform Act. The act identifies six objectives for students, including such goals as applying knowledge from mathematics, the "hard" sciences, arts, humanities, and the social sciences to problems the students will encounter throughout their lives as they become self-sufficient individuals and responsible members of families, work groups, and communities.

Many of the suggestions for improving standardized tests will require new forms of testing, more thoughtful and time-consuming scoring, and perhaps new ways of judging the quality of the tests themselves. Standardized tests of the future may be more like the writing sample you may have submitted for college entrance and less like the multiple-choice college entrance tests you also had to take. Newer tests will feature more **constructed-response formats.** This means that students will create responses (essays, problem solutions, graphs, diagrams), rather than simply selecting the (one and only) correct answer. This will allow tests to measure higher-level and divergent thinking. For example, on the mathematical portion of the revised *Scholastic Assessment Test* students generate their own answers for 20% of the questions. Hand-held calculators are allowed, but not required. In addition, there is a writing test consisting of two-thirds multiple-choice questions and one-third essay.

In the excitement about authentic assessment, it is important to be sensible. Just being different from traditional standardized tests will not guarantee that the alternative tests are better. Many questions have to be answered. Assume, for example, that a new assessment requires students to complete a hands-on science project. If the student does well on one science project, does this mean the student "knows" science and would do well on other projects? One study found that students' performance on three different science tasks was quite variable: a student who did well on the absorbency experiment, for example, might have trouble with the electricity task. Thus, it was hard to generalize about a student's knowledge of science based on just the three tasks. Many more tasks would be needed to get a good sense of science knowledge, but a performance assessment with many different tasks would be expensive and time-consuming (Shavelson, Gao, & Baxter, 1993).

In addition, if high-stakes decisions are based on performance assessments, will teachers begin to "teach to the assessment" by giving students practice in these particular performances? Will being a good writer bias judges in favor of a performance? Will this make performance assessments even more prone to discriminate against some groups? And how will the projects be judged? Will different judges agree on the quality? When researchers examined the results of the 1992 Vermont Portfolio Assessment Program, they found that scorers assessing the same portfolio often gave very different ratings (Kotrez, Stecher, & Diebert, 1993). In other words, will judgments based on alternative assessments be reliable and valid? Will the assessment results generalize to tasks beyond those on the test itself? Will the new assessments have a positive effect on learning (Hambleton, 1997; Moss, 1992)? Because this is a new area, it will take time to develop high-quality alternative assessments for use by whole school districts or states. Until more is known, it may be best to focus on authentic assessment at the classroom level, as we will discuss in the next chapter.

CHECKPOINT

New Directions in Standardized Testing

Review

▶ What is learning potential assessment?

▶ What is authentic assessment?

Apply

▶ How would you judge the reliability and validity of a performance test in which a student was asked to show a knowledge of geometry by designing a tile floor using tiles of different shapes and sizes?

▶ Relate the measurement of learning potential to Vygotsky's theory of zone of proximal development.

Authentic Assessment: Measurement of important abilities using procedures that simulate the application of these abilities to real-life problems.

Constructed-Response Format: Assessment procedures that require the student to create an answer instead of selecting an answer from a set of choices.

Summary

Evaluation, Measurement, and Assessment

Distinguish among evaluation, measurement, and assessment.

In the process of evaluation, we compare information to criteria and then make judgments. Measurement is evaluation put in quantitative terms. Assessment includes measurement, but is broader because it includes all kinds of ways to sample and observe students' skills, knowledge, and abilities.

Distinguish between norm-referenced and criterion-referenced tests.

In norm-referenced tests, a student's performance is compared to the average performance of others. In criterion-referenced tests, scores are compared to a preestablished standard. Norm-referenced tests cover a wide range of general objectives and are appropriate when only the top few candidates can be admitted to a program. However, results of norm-referenced tests do not tell whether students are ready for advanced material, and they are not appropriate for affective and psychomotor objectives. Criterion-referenced tests measure the mastery of very specific objectives—they tell the teacher exactly what the students can and cannot do, but they cannot compare students to others at their grade level either locally or nationally.

What Do Test Scores Mean?

Describe the key features of a standardized test.

Standardized tests are most often norm-referenced. They have been pilot-tested, revised, and then administered in final form to a norming sample, which becomes the comparison group for scoring. Important aspects of measurement in standardized testing are the frequency distribution, the central tendency, and the standard deviation.

What are mean, median, mode, and standard deviation?

The mean (arithmetical average), median (middle score), and mode (most common score) are all measures of central tendency. The standard deviation reveals how scores spread out around the mean. A normal distribution is a frequency distribution represented as a bell-shaped curve. Many scores cluster in the middle; the farther from the midpoint, the fewer the scores. Half the scores are above the mean; half are below.

Describe different kinds of scores.

There are several basic types of standardized test scores: percentile rankings, which indicate the percentage of others who scored at or below an individual's score; grade-equivalent scores, which indicate how closely a student's performance matches average scores for a given grade; and standard scores, which are based on the standard deviation. T and z scores are both common standard scores. A stanine score is a standard score that incorporates elements of percentile rankings.

What is test reliability?

Some tests are more reliable than others; that is, they yield more stable and consistent estimates. Care must be taken in the interpretation of test results. Each test is only a sample of a student's performance on a given day. The score is only an estimate of a student's hypothetical true score. The standard error of measurement takes into account the possibility for error and is one index of test reliability.

What is test validity?

The most important consideration about a test is the validity of the decisions and judgments that are based on the test results. Some of these judgments are more valid than others because there is strong evidence for the interpretations and judgments made. Evidence of validity can be related to content, criterion, or construct. Construct-related evidence for validity is the broadest category and encompasses the other two categories of content and criterion. Tests must be reliable to be valid, but reliability does not guarantee validity.

Types of Standardized Tests

What are three kinds of standardized tests?

Three kinds of standardized tests are used frequently in schools: achievement, diagnostic, and aptitude. Profiles from norm-referenced achievement tests can also be used in a criterion-referenced way to help a teacher assess a student's strengths and weaknesses in a particular subject. Diagnostic tests usually are given individually to elementary school students when learning problems are suspected. Aptitude tests are designed to predict how a student will perform in the future. For example, the Scholastic Assessment Test (SAT) predicts performance in the first year of college.

Issues in Standardized Testing

What are some current issues in testing?

Controversy over standardized testing has focused on the role and interpretation of tests, the validity of readiness tests as a guide for decisions about young children, the usefulness of minimum competency testing, the testing of teachers, and the degree of fairness in testing, including possible bias against minority group students inherent in tests. The way test results are used is a major issue for teachers. Teachers should use results to improve instruction, not to stereotype students or justify lowered expectations.

Can students become better test-takers?

Performance on standardized tests can be improved if students gain experience with this type of testing and are given training in study skills and problem solving. Many students can profit from direct instruction about how to prepare for and take tests. Involving students in designing these test preparation programs can be helpful.

New Directions in Standardized Testing

What is learning potential assessment?

An alternative goal of assessment is to reveal potential for learning and to identify the psychological and educational interventions that will help the individual realize this potential. Procedures give graduated prompts as a child works to solve a problem—beginning with a general hint and ending with a detailed instruction for how to find the answer. The way the child uses the prompt and learns within the testing situation gives evidence of learning potential.

What is authentic assessment?

Authentic assessments are procedures that assess students' abilities to solve important real-life problems, think creatively, and act responsibly. Such approaches assume that assessment should reveal the potential for future learning and help identify interventions for realizing that potential. Standardized tests of the future will be more varied and will use more constructed-response formats, requiring students to generate (rather than select) answers.

Key Terms

achievement tests, p. 534
aptitude tests, p. 537
assessment, p. 523
authentic assessment, p. 548
bimodal distribution, p. 526
central tendency, p. 526
confidence interval, p. 532
constructed-response format, p. 548
criterion-referenced testing, p. 524
culture-fair/culture-free test, p. 544
diagnostic tests, p. 537
evaluation, p. 522
frequency distribution, p. 526
grade-equivalent score, p. 529
high-stakes testing, p. 539

histogram, p. 526
Learning Propensity Assessment Device, p. 547
mean, p. 526
measurement, p. 522
median, p. 526
minimum competency test, p. 542
mode, p. 526
norm group, p. 523
norm-referenced testing, p. 523
normal distribution, p. 527
norming sample, p. 525
percentile rank, p. 528
range, p. 527
readiness testing, p. 540

reliability, p. 531
standard deviation, p. 527
standard error of measurement, p. 532
standard scores, p. 530
standardized tests, p. 525
stanine scores, p. 530
T score, p. 530
test bias, p. 544
true score, p. 531
validity, p. 532
variability, p. 527
z score, p. 530

Becoming a Professional

Reflecting on the Chapter

Can you apply the ideas from this chapter on standardized assessments to solve the following problems of practice?

Preschool and Kindergarten

▶ Your district is considering establishing a 1st grade readiness-testing program. As the lead teacher for the kindergarten, you are asked to speak to the school board about the issue; they are still open to various alternatives. What points would you make?

Elementary and Middle School

▶ Your students seem very nervous about the spring testing. The local paper has carried stories about the school's "low" scores last year, and there is pressure on everyone to do better this time. How would you prepare your students?

Junior High and High School

▶ The parents of one of your students are angry with you because their child was not selected for the accelerated math group. Selection was based on both standardized test scores and class performance. How would you explain the school's decision?

Certification Test Requirements

▶ This chapter describes many concepts that frequently appear on tests for teachers. Be sure you know the difference between norm-referenced and criterion-referenced tests; and the definitions of mean, median, and mode; percentile ranks, stanines, z-scores, grade-equivalent scores, and T-scores (not necessarily the formula but what these scores tell you); reliability and validity; high-stakes testing; test bias, and achievement, diagnostic, and aptitude tests. Be

able to interpret Ken's test results in Figure 14.5.

Your Teaching Portfolio

Think about your philosophy of teaching, a question you will be asked at most job interviews. What do you believe about the uses of testing for children? How would you interpret the test scores of minority group children?

Add some ideas for parent involvement from this chapter to your *Portfolio*.

Using the Guidelines for preparing for a test, prepare a testing guide sheet for the grades you will teach.

Teaching Resources

Add Figure 14.4, "Four Types of Standard Scores on a Normal Distribution Curve," and Figure 14.6, "Taking on 'The Test': Problem-Based Learning," to your **Teaching Resources** file.

TEACHERS' CASEBOOK

What Would They Do?

Here is how some practicing teachers responded to the teaching situation presented at the beginning of this chapter about the parents who want their daughter to skip a grade in math.

MARK H. SMITH

Teacher, Grades Nine through Twelve
Medford High School, Medford, Massachusetts

The only thing that the 11.8 grade-equivalent score that the daughter received on her standardized math test tells us is that she has the ability to do well in high school mathematics. The parents should be more concerned that with the ability shown on the standardized test, she should probably be scoring a lot higher in her math course in school. As students develop and move up to the high school level, courses become more conceptual and there is more of a process than just getting the steps and the answer, especially in mathematics, which is a sequential subject with each course leading into the next one. It is imperative that students get beyond the simple solutions in order to progress to the next level.

I understand that many parents will choose the side of their child over the side of a teacher. This definitely happened in this case, because the parents would not come in to talk about their daughter's learning until they had something they thought would give them ammunition against the teacher. As a teacher all you can do is explain your grading procedure, what the curriculum is, and what is expected of the students in your class. When you have clear and reasonable expectations for all of your students, then it becomes the responsibility of the student to achieve.

It is unrealistic for a parent to expect a teacher to change a grade for a class based on results in a standardized test. It is even more ridiculous to want to skip a course in a sequence because of the results. Although this case did finally get the parents to meet with the teacher, the parents were way off base and the educational system must be explained to them. At the high school level and beyond, the responsibility of learning is geared more toward the student.

THOMAS W. NEWKIRK

Eighth Grade Teacher
Hamilton Heights Middle School, Arcadia, Indiana

The grade a student receives in a class is sometimes not so much a measure of intelligence as it is a measure of performance. Bright students who are disorganized may bring assignments in days past a due date. Bright students who are distracted may not bring assignments in at all. Bright students who have been absent several days may be overwhelmed by the work waiting for them.

The grade a student receives in a class often requires an explanation in order that the students and the parents understand the basis for the evaluation. It is important that the teacher maintain a record of comments and correspondence for parents and teachers to review.

While it is wonderful that the student has a grade-equivalent of 11.8 on the achievement test, her daily class performance does not meet the established standard for an A. Whether a student's achievement test results are high or low, it would be unfair to reconsider a final grade based on one score.

Unless the school has a policy for receiving credit for classes based on achievement tests, the parents and the student should be encouraged to maintain the lines of communication as she enters the 10th grade class.

THOMAS O'DONNELL

Social Studies Chairperson, Grades Seven through Twelve
Malden High School, Malden, Massachusetts

The math achievement the girl took might not be a good device for measuring one's ability to go beyond high school math to the more abstract, conceptual approach needed for college-level math. You must explain your grading system to parents so they understand the needed combination of effort and achievement to achieve top grades.

Since the parent statements include two serious charges against you, make it clear you expect respect from them, but that this issue will have no impact on your work with the student. You must reject their expectations of changing grades and credits.

SUZY L. BOSWELL

Art Teacher, Grades Six through Eight
Pickens County Middle School, Jasper, Georgia

One of the most challenging aspects of a teacher's job is often the task of communicating with the parents. Unfortunately, most parents begin to lose contact with the school system and the children's teachers when their child enters middle school or junior high. Parents may think that they are no longer needed or that their child prefers them to remain anonymous, so as not to embarrass them. However, the motivation and learning process are still very much a shared responsibility of school and home.

Concerned parents such as these who apparently could not seem to find the time until something happens, are at least showing up now. Whatever the reason that finally brings them to school, I think it is important for the teacher to first of all thank the parents for coming in to the school to discuss the education of their child. Make it clear to them that we want them to be involved in their child's education. We know that it is important to the child to have their support. Secondly, we are on the same team and together we can win. We all want the best possible education for the child and we are best able to accomplish that by working together.

The parents did not volunteer their time to listen to a lecture. In this particular case they may actually be coming to the school to give the teacher a lecture and to "set her straight." It may require a great deal of diplomacy to turn this into a positive and productive meeting, but we as teachers deal with unwilling students almost daily and this situation is not any different.

Once the tone is set and the parents are receptive, it may be helpful to explain to them the characteristics of the tests, including the various methods that are used to measure the results of the test. It is important to note that students may have the aptitude to learn and to perform in the classroom and yet simply choose not to apply themselves. Therefore, these students are still not meeting the requirements necessary to earn credit for a particular class.

Their daughter is apparently bright. If she would apply herself in class and do the homework, her grade in class should improve considerably. However, she must realize that it is her responsibility to complete the class requirements in order to earn a higher grade.

In closing, it is important to assure the parents that you do appreciate their concerns and that you are happy to work with them and their daughter to improve her grades. Assure them that working together, we can certainly expect their daughter's performance in school to reflect the abilities indicated in the standardized test score.

Classroom Assessment and Grading

*t*hink back on your report cards and grades over the years. Did you ever receive a grade that was lower than you expected? How did you feel about yourself, the teacher, the subject, and school in general as a result of the lower grade? What could the teacher have done to help you understand and profit from the experience?

In this chapter, we will look at both tests and grades, focusing not only on the effects they are likely to have on students, but also on practical means of developing more efficient methods for testing and grading.

We begin with a consideration of the many types of tests teachers prepare each year and some new approaches to assessment. Then we examine the effects grades are likely to have on students. Because there are so many grading systems, we also spend some time identifying the advantages and disadvantages of one system over another. Finally, we turn to the very important topic of communication with students and parents. How will you justify the grades you give?

By the time you have completed this chapter, you should be able to:

- ▶ Make a plan for testing students on a unit of work.
- ▶ Evaluate tests that accompany textbooks and teachers' manuals.
- ▶ Create multiple-choice and essay test items for your subject area.
- ▶ Describe authentic assessment approaches, including portfolios, performances, exhibitions, and the development of scoring rubrics.
- ▶ Discuss the potential positive and negative effects of grades on students.
- ▶ Give examples of criterion-referenced and norm-referenced grading systems.
- ▶ Assign grades to a hypothetical group of students and defend your decisions in a class debate.
- ▶ Role play a conference with parents who do not understand your grading system or their child's grades.

What Would You Do?

Your school requires that you give letter grades to your class. You can use any method you want, as long as an A, B, C, D, or F appears for each of the subject areas on every student's report card, every grading period. Some teachers are using worksheets, quizzes, homework, and tests. Others are assigning group work and portfolios. A few teachers are individualizing standards by grading on progress and effort more than final achievement. Some are trying contract approaches and experimenting with longer term projects while others are relying almost completely on daily class work. Two teachers who use group work are considering giving credit toward grades for being a "good group member" or competitive bonus points for the top-scoring group. Others are planning to use improvement points for class rewards but not for grades. Your only experience with grading was using written comments and a mastery approach that rated the students as making satisfactory or unsatisfactory progress toward particular objectives. You want a system that is fair and manageable, but also encourages learning, not just performance.

▶ What would be your major graded assignments and projects?

▶ Would you include credit for behaviors such as group participation or effort?

▶ How would you put all the elements together to determine a grade for every student for every marking period? How would you justify your system to the principal and to the parents?

▶ How will these issues affect the grades you will teach?

Formative and Summative Assessment

As a teacher, you may or may not help in designing the grading system for your school or your class. Many school districts have a standard approach to grading. Still, you will have choices about how you use your district's grading system and how you assess your students' learning. Will you give tests? How many? What kinds? Will students do projects or keep portfolios of their work? How will homework influence grades?

There are two general uses or functions for assessment: formative and summative. **Formative assessment** occurs before or during instruction. It has two basic purposes: to guide the teacher in planning and to help students identify areas that need work. In other words, formative assessment helps *form* instruction. Often students are given a formative test prior to instruction, a **pretest** that helps the teacher determine what students already know. Sometimes a test is given during instruction to see what areas of weakness remain so teaching can be directed toward the problem areas. This is generally called a **diagnostic test** but should not be confused with the standardized diagnostic tests of more general learning abilities. A classroom diagnostic test identifies a student's areas of achievement and weakness in a particular subject. Older students are often able to apply the information from diagnostic tests to "reteach" themselves.

Pretests and diagnostic tests are not graded. And since formative tests do not count toward the final grade, students who tend to be very anxious about "real" tests may find this low-pressure practice in test taking especially helpful.

Connect and Extend
To your teaching
What are some specific ways in which formative evaluation can be implemented in the classroom?

Connect and Extend
To the research
For a description of the different models of curriculum-based assessment and ideas for how it can be used with mainstreamed students, see Shapiro, E. S., & Ager, C. (1992). Assessment of special education students in regular education programs: Linking assessment to instruction. *The Elementary School Journal, 92,* 283–296.

A variation of formative measurement is ongoing measurement, often called **data-based instruction** or **curriculum-based assessment (CBA)**. This approach uses frequent "probes," brief tests of specific skills and knowledge drawn from the curriculum, to give a precise picture of a student's current performance. Actually, CBA is not just one approach, but a whole family of approaches for linking teaching and assessment. CBA is "*any* set of measurement procedures that use direct observation and recording of a student's performance in the local curriculum as a basis for gathering information to make instructional decisions" (Deno, 1987, p. 41). This method has been used primarily with students who have learning problems because it provides systematic assessment of both student performance and the teaching methods used. The assessment probes check to see if the difficulty level and the pace of instruction is right for the student. If a student shows inadequate progress on the assessment probes, the teacher should consider modifying or switching instructional strategies or pacing (Shapiro & Ager, 1992).

Summative assessment occurs at the end of instruction. Its purpose is to let the teacher and the students know the level of accomplishment attained. Summative assessment, therefore, provides a *summary* of accomplishment. The final exam is a classic example.

The distinction between formative and summative assessment is based on how the results are used. The same assessment procedure can be used for either purpose. If the goal is to obtain information about student learning for planning purposes, the assessment is formative. If the purpose is to determine final achievement (and help determine a course grade), the assessment is summative.

CHECKPOINT

Formative and Summative Assessment

Review

▶ What are two kinds of classroom assessment?

Apply

▶ What is the most important consideration in deciding whether to use a test that comes with the text for your class?

▲ *Testing is formative or summative depending on what is done with the results: If the results are used to plan future instruction, then it is formative. If they're used to determine a final evaluation of a student, then it is summative.*

ᏉᎧetting the Most from Traditional Assessment Approaches

When most people think of assessment, they usually think of testing. As you will see shortly, teachers today have many other options, but testing is still a significant activity in most classrooms. Let's consider your options for assessing students using the traditional testing approach. In this section we will examine how to plan effective tests, how to evaluate the tests that accompany standard curriculum materials, and how to write your own test questions.

Planning for Testing

Both instruction and assessment are most effective when they are well organized and planned. When

Formative Assessment: Ungraded testing used before or during instruction to aid in planning and diagnosis.

Pretest: Formative test for assessing students' knowledge, readiness, and abilities.

Diagnostic Test: Formative test to determine students' areas of weakness.

Data-Based Instruction: Assessment method using daily probes of specific-skill mastery.

Curriculum-Based Assessment (CBA): Evaluation method using frequent tests of specific skills and knowledge.

Summative Assessment: Testing that follows instruction and assesses achievement.

Connect and Extend
To the research
Dempster, F. (1991). Synthesis of research on reviews and tests. *Educational Leadership, 48*(7), 71–76. *Focus Question:* How can tests and reviews be used to encourage student learning?

Connect and Extend
To the research
Dempster, F. N. (1993). Exposing our students to less should help them learn more. *Phi Delta Kappan, 74,* 432–437.

you have a good plan, you are in a better position to judge the tests provided in teachers' manuals and texts and to write tests yourself.

When to Test? Frank Dempster (1991) examined the research on reviews and tests and reached these useful conclusions for teachers:

1. Frequent testing encourages the retention of information and appears to be more effective than a comparable amount of time spent reviewing and studying the material.

2. Tests are especially effective in promoting learning if you give students a test on the material soon after they learn it, then retest on the material later. The retestings should be spaced farther and farther apart.

3. The use of cumulative questions on tests is a key to effective learning. Cumulative questions ask students to apply information learned in previous units to solve a new problem.

Unfortunately, the curriculum in many schools is so full that there is little time for frequent tests and reviews. Dempster argues that students will learn more if we "teach them less," that is, if the curriculum includes fewer topics, but explores those topics in greater depth and allows more time for review, practice, testing, and feedback (Dempster, 1993).

Judging Textbook Tests. Most elementary and secondary school texts today come complete with supplemental materials such as teaching manuals, handout masters, and ready-made tests. Using these tests can save time, but is this good teaching practice? The answer depends on your objectives for your students, the way you taught the material, and the quality of the tests provided (Airasian, 1996). If the textbook test matches your testing plan and the instruction you actually provided for your students, then it may be the right test to use. Table 15.1 gives key points to consider in evaluating textbook tests.

TABLE 15.1 *Key Points to Consider in Judging Textbook Tests*

The decision to use a textbook test must come *after* a teacher identifies the objectives that he or she taught and now wants to assess.

Textbook tests are designed for the typical classroom, but since few classrooms are typical, most teachers deviate somewhat from the text in order to accommodate their pupils' needs.

The more classroom instruction deviates from the textbook objectives and lesson plans, the less valid the textbook tests are likely to be.

The main consideration in judging the adequacy of a textbook test is the match between its test questions and what pupils were taught in their classes:

• Are questions similar to the teacher's objectives and instructional emphases?

• Do questions require pupils to perform the behaviors they were taught?

• Do questions cover all or most of the important objectives taught?

• Is the language level and terminology appropriate for pupils?

• Does the number of items for each objective provide a sufficient sample of pupil performance?

Source: From *Assessment in the Classroom* (p. 190), by P. Airasian, 1996, New York: McGraw-Hill. Copyright © 1996 by The McGraw-Hill Companies. Adapted with permission.

What if there are no tests available for the material you want to cover, or the tests provided in your teachers' manuals are not appropriate for your students? Then it's time for you to create your own tests. We will consider the two major kinds of tests—objective and essay.

Objective Testing

Multiple-choice questions, matching exercises, true/false statements, and short-answer or fill-in items are all types of **objective testing**. The word "objective" in relation to testing means "not open to many interpretations," or "not subjective." The scoring of these types of items is relatively straightforward compared to the scoring of essay questions because the answers are more clear-cut than essay answers.

Gronlund (1993) suggests that the guiding principle for deciding which item format is best is to "use the item types that provide the most direct measures of student performance specified by the intended learning outcome" (p. 28). In other words, if you want to see how well students can write a letter, have them write a letter, don't ask multiple-choice questions about letters. But if many different item formats will work equally well, then use multiple-choice questions because they are easier to score fairly and can cover many topics. Switch to other formats if writing good multiple-choice items for the material is not possible. For example, if related concepts need to be linked, such as terms and definitions, then a matching item is a better format than multiple-choice. If it is difficult to come up with several wrong answers for a multiple-choice item, try a true/false question instead. Alternatively, ask the student to supply a short answer that completes a statement (fill in the blank). Variety in objective testing can lower students' anxiety because the entire grade does not depend on one type of question that a particular student may find difficult. Here we look closely at the multiple-choice format, because it is the most versatile—and the most difficult to use well.

Using Multiple-Choice Tests. People often assume that multiple-choice items are appropriate only for asking factual questions. But multiple-choice items can test higher-level objectives as well, although writing higher-level items is difficult. A multiple-choice item can assess more than recall and recognition if it requires the student to deal with new material by *applying* or *analyzing* the concept or principle being tested (Gronlund, 1993). For example, the following multiple-choice item is designed to assess students' ability to recognize unstated assumptions, one of the skills involved in analyzing an idea:

> An educational psychology professor states, "A *z* score of +1 on a test is equivalent to a percentile rank of approximately 84." Which of the following assumptions is the professor making?
> 1. The scores on the test range from 0 to 100.
> 2. The standard deviation of the test scores is equal to 3.4.
> 3. The distribution of scores on the test is normal. (correct answer)
> 4. The test is valid and reliable.

Writing Multiple-Choice Questions. All test items require skillful construction, but good multiple-choice items are a real challenge. Some students jokingly refer to multiple-choice tests as "multiple-guess" tests—a sign that these tests are often poorly designed. Your goal in writing test items is to design them so that they measure student achievement, not test-taking and guessing skills.

Connect and Extend
To other chapters
See Chapter 12 for a discussion of Bloom's taxonomy of objectives in the cognitive domain and a recent revision of this taxonomy.

Objective Testing: Multiple-choice, matching, true/false, short-answer, and fill-in tests; scoring answers does not require interpretation.

GUIDELINES

Writing Objective Test Items

The stem should be clear and simple, and present only a single problem. Unessential details should be left out.

Poor

There are several different kinds of standard or derived scores. An IQ score is especially useful because . . .

Better

An advantage of an IQ score is . . .

The problem in the stem should be stated in positive terms. Negative language is confusing. If you must use words such as *not*, *no*, or *except*, underline them or type them in all capitals.

Poor

Which of the following is not a standard score?

Better

Which of the following is NOT a standard score?

Do not expect students to make extremely fine discrimination among answer choices.

Poor

The percentage of area in a normal curve falling between +1 and −1 standard deviations is about:
   a. 66%.   b. 67%.   c. 68%.   d. 69%.

Better

The percentage of area in a normal curve falling between +1 and −1 standard deviations is about:
   a. 14%.   b. 34%.   (c.) 68%.   d. 95%.

As much wording as possible should be included in the stem so that phrases will not have to be repeated in each alternative.

Poor

A percentile score

   a. indicates the percentage of items answered correctly.

   b. indicates the percentage of correct answers divided by the percentage of wrong answers.

   c. indicates the percentage of people who scored at or above a given raw score.

   d. indicates the percentage of people who scored at or below a given raw score.

Better

A percentile score indicates the percentage of

   a. items answered correctly.

   b. correct answers divided by the percentage of wrong answers.

   c. people who scored at or above a given raw score.

   (d.) people who scored at or below a given raw score.

Each alternative answer should fit the grammatical form of the stem, so that no answers are obviously wrong.

Poor

The Stanford-Binet test yields an

   a. IQ score.   c. vocational preference.

   b. reading level.   d. mechanical aptitude.

Connect and Extend

To your teaching

One reason students prefer essay tests is that they can write down something, even if it doesn't answer the question, and receive at least partial credit for the question. Do you think that granting partial credit is a common grading practice among teachers? Considering that essay questions sample only a limited amount of material, does the practice seem commendable or defensible?

The **stem** of a multiple-choice item is the part that asks the question or poses the problem. The choices that follow are called *alternatives*. The wrong answers are called **distractors** because their purpose is to distract students who have only a partial understanding of the material. If there were no good distractors, students with only a vague understanding would have no difficulty in finding the right answer.

The Guidelines above, adapted from Gronlund (1993), should make writing multiple-choice and other objective test questions easier.

Essay Testing

The best way to measure some learning objectives is to require students to create answers on their own. An essay question is appropriate in these cases. The most difficult part of essay testing is judging the quality of the answers, but writing good, clear questions is not particularly easy, either. We will look at writing, administering,

Better

The Stanford-Binet is a test of

(a.) intelligence.　　c. vocational preference.

b. reading level.　　d. mechanical aptitude.

Categorical words such as *always, all, only,* or *never* should be avoided unless they can appear consistently in all the alternatives. Most smart test takers know that categorical answers are usually wrong.

Poor

A student's true score on a standardized test is

a. never equal to the obtained score.

b. always very close to the obtained score.

c. always determined by the standard error of measurement.

d. usually within a band that extends from +1 to −1 standard errors of measurement on each side of the obtained score.

Better

Which one of the statements below would most often be correct about a student's true score on a standardized test?

a. It equals the obtained score.

b. It will be very close to the obtained score.

c. It is determined by the standard error of measurement.

(d.) It could be above or below the obtained score.

You should also avoid including two distractors that have the same meaning. If only one answer can be right and if two answers are the same, then these two must both be wrong. This narrows down the choices considerably.

Poor

The most frequently occurring score in a distribution is called the

a. mode.　　c. arithmetical average.

b. median.　　d. mean.

Better

The most frequently occurring score in a distribution is called the

(a.) mode.　　c. standard deviation.

b. median.　　d. mean.

Avoid using the exact wording found in the textbook. Poor students may recognize the answers without knowing what they mean.

Avoid overuse of *all of the above* and *none of the above*. Such choices may be helpful to students who are simply guessing. In addition, using *all of the above* may trick a quick student who sees that the first alternative is correct and does not read on to discover that the others are correct, too.

Obvious patterns on a test also aid students who are guessing. The position of the correct answer should be varied, as should its length.

and grading essay tests, with most of the specific suggestions taken from Gronlund (1993). We will also consider factors that can bias the scoring of essay questions and ways you can overcome these problems.

Constructing Essay Tests. Because answering takes time, true essay tests cover less material than objective tests. Thus, for efficiency, essay tests should be limited to the assessment of more complex learning outcomes.

An essay question should give students a clear and precise task and should indicate the elements to be covered in the answer. Gronlund suggests the following as an example of an essay question that might appear in an educational psychology course to measure an objective at the *synthesis* level of Bloom's taxonomy in the cognitive domain:

For a course that you are teaching or expect to teach, prepare a complete plan for assessing student achievement. Be sure to include the procedures you would follow, the instruments you would use, and the reasons for your choices.

Stem: The question part of a multiple-choice item.

Distractors: Wrong answers offered as choices in a multiple-choice item.

This question requires students to apply information and values derived from course material to produce a complex new product.

Students should be given ample time for answering. If more than one essay is being completed in the same class period, you may want to suggest time limits for each. Remember, however, that time pressure increases anxiety and may prevent accurate assessment of some students. Whatever your approach, do not try to make up for the limited amount of material an essay test can cover by including a large number of essay questions. It would be better to plan on more frequent testing than to include more than two or three essay questions in a single class period. Combining an essay question with a number of objective items is one way to avoid the problem of limited sampling of course material (Gronlund, 1993).

Evaluating Essays: Dangers. In 1912, Starch and Elliot began a classic series of experiments that shocked educators into critical consideration of subjectivity in testing. These researchers wanted to find out the extent to which teachers were influenced by personal values, standards, and expectations in scoring essay tests. For their initial study, they sent copies of English examination papers written by two high school students to English teachers in 200 high schools. Each teacher was asked to score the papers according to his or her school's standards. A percentage scale was to be used, with 75% as a passing grade.

The results? Neatness, spelling, punctuation, and communicative effectiveness were all valued to different degrees by different teachers. The scores on one of the papers ranged from 64% to 98%, with a mean of 88.2. The average score for the other paper was 80.2, with a range between 50% and 97%. The following year, Starch and Elliot (1913a, b) published similar findings in a study involving history and geometry papers. The most important result of these studies was the discovery that the problem of subjectivity in grading was not confined to any particular subject area. The main difficulties were the individual standards of the grader and the unreliability of scoring procedures.

Certain qualities of an essay may influence grades. Teachers may reward quantity rather than quality in essays. In a series of studies described by Fiske (1981), many high school and college English teachers rated pairs of student essays that were identical in every way but linguistic style. One essay was quite verbose, with flowery language, complex sentences, and passive verbs. The other essay was written in the simple, straightforward language that most teachers claim is the goal for students of writing. The teachers consistently rated the verbose essay higher.

Evaluating Essays: Methods. Gronlund (1993) offers several strategies for grading essays that avoid problems of subjectivity

Connect and Extend
To the research
Writing evaluation: Examining four teachers' holistic and analytic scores. *Elementary School Journal, 90,* 88–95.

CHECKPOINT

Getting the Most from Traditional Assessment Approaches

Review

 How should teachers plan for assessment?

How should teachers plan for assessment?
Describe two kinds of traditional testing.

Apply

Would an objective test or an essay test be more appropriate under the following circumstances?

1. You wish to test the students' knowledge of the terminology used in lab experiments.
2. The test must be given and graded in the two days before the end of the six-week grading period.
3. You want to test the students' ability to present a logical argument.
4. Your aim is to balance subjective judgments with a highly reliable measure.
5. You are seeking to test student understanding of a few major principles.
6. You have limited time to construct the test.

and inaccuracy. When possible, a good first step is to construct a model answer, then you can assign points to its various parts. You might also give points for the organization of the answer and the internal consistency. You can then assign grades such as 1 to 5 or A, B, C, D, and F, and sort the papers into piles by grade. As a final step, skim the papers in each pile to see if they are comparable in quality. These techniques will help ensure fairness and accuracy in grading.

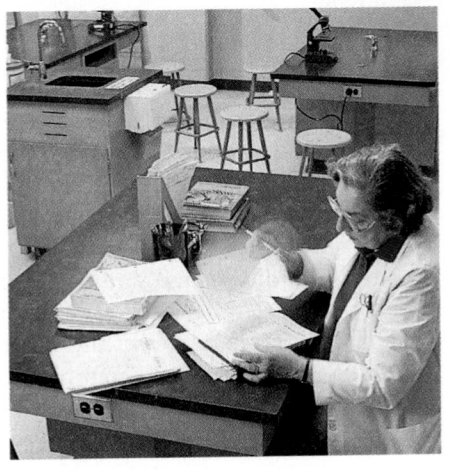

◀ *There are special cautions in evaluating essay tests. The challenges are to be clear with students about the criteria for grading, and then apply those criteria fairly and consistently.*

Connect and Extend
To the research
Cambourne, B., & Turbill, J. (1990). Assessment in whole-language classrooms: Theory into practice. *Elementary School Journal, 90,* 337–349.

When grading essay tests with several questions, it makes sense to grade all responses to one question before moving on to the next. This helps prevent the quality of a student's answer to one question from influencing your reaction to the student's other answers. After you finish reading and scoring the first question, shuffle the papers so that no students end up having all their questions graded first, last, or in the middle.

You may achieve greater objectivity if you ask students to put their names on the back of the paper, so that grading is anonymous. A final check on your fairness as a grader is to have another teacher who is equally familiar with your goals and subject matter grade your tests without knowing what grades you have assigned. This can give you valuable insights into areas of bias in your grading practices.

Now that we have examined both objective and essay testing, we can compare the two approaches. Table 15.2 presents a summary of the important characteristics of each.

TABLE 15.2   *Comparing Objective and Essay Tests*

Objective tests include any tests that ask the student to select the answer from a set of choices (multiple-choice, true/false, matching).

	Selection-Type Items	Essay Questions
Learning Outcomes Measured	Good for measuring outcomes at the knowledge, comprehension, and application levels of learning; inadequate for organizing and expressing ideas.	Inefficient for measuring knowledge outcomes; best for ability to organize, integrate, and express ideas.
Sampling of Content	The use of a large number of items results in broad coverage which makes representative sampling of content feasible.	The use of a small number of items limits coverage which makes representative sampling of content infeasible.
Preparation of Items	Preparation of good items is difficult and time consuming.	Preparation of good items is difficult but easier than selection-type items.
Scoring	Objective, simple, and highly reliable.	Subjective, difficult, and less reliable.
Factors Distorting Scores	Reading ability and guessing.	Writing ability and bluffing.
Probable Effect on Learning	Encourages students to remember, interpret, and use the ideas of others.	Encourages students to organize, integrate, and express their own ideas.

Source: From *How to Make Achievement Tests and Assessments* (5th ed.) (p. 83), by N. E. Gronlund, 1993, Boston: Allyn & Bacon. Copyright © 1993 by Allyn & Bacon. Reprinted with permission.

*I*nnovations in Assessment

Connect and Extend
To other chapters
See Chapter 14 for a discussion of authentic assessment and standardized tests.

We have been considering how to make traditional testing more effective; now let's look at a few new approaches to classroom assessment. One of the main criticisms of standardized tests—that they control the curriculum, emphasizing recall of facts instead of thinking and problem solving—is a major criticism of classroom tests as well. Few teachers would dispute these criticisms. Even if you follow the guidelines we have been discussing, traditional testing can be limiting. What can be done? Should innovations in classroom assessment make traditional testing obsolete? The Point/Counterpoint addresses this question.

One solution that has been proposed to solve the testing dilemma is to apply the concept of authentic assessment to classroom testing.

Connect and Extend
To professional journals
Wiggins, G. (1989). Teaching to the authentic test. *Educational Leadership, 46*(7), 41–47. *Focus Question:* What makes tests "authentic"?

Authentic Classroom Tests

Authentic tests ask students to apply skills and abilities as they would in real life. For example, they might use fractions to enlarge or reduce recipes. Grant Wiggins makes this argument:

> If tests determine what teachers actually teach and what students will study for— and they do—then the road to reform is a straight but steep one: test those capabilities and habits we think are essential, and test them in context. Make [tests]

POINT ▼ COUNTERPOINT

To Test or Not to Test, Part II

We have seen the advantages and disadvantages of standardized tests, but what about classroom testing? Are traditional multiple-choice and essay tests useful in classroom assessment?

▶ **POINT** *Traditional tests are a poor basis for classroom assessment.*

In his article "Standards, Not Standardization: Evoking Quality Student Work," Grant Wiggins (1991) makes a strong case for giving students standards of excellence against which they can judge their accomplishments. But these standards should not be higher scores on multiple-choice tests. When scores on traditional tests become the standard, the message to students is that only right answers matter and the

thinking behind the answers is unimportant. Wiggins notes:

> We do not judge Xerox, the Boston Symphony, the Cincinnati Reds, or Dom Perignon vineyards on the basis of indirect, easy to test, and common indicators. Nor would the workers in those places likely produce quality if some generic, secure test served as the only measure of their success in meeting a standard. Demanding and getting quality, whether from students or adult workers, means framing standards in terms of the work that we undertake and value. And it means framing expectations about that work which make quality a necessity, not an option. Consider:

- the English teacher who instructs peer-editors to mark the place in a student paper where they lost interest in it or found it slapdash and to hand it back for revision at that point;
- the professor who demands that all math homework be turned in with another student having signed off on it, where one earns the grade for one's work *and* the grade for the work that each person (willingly!) countersigned. (p. 22)

In a more recent article, Wiggins continues to argue for assessment that makes sense, that tests knowledge as it is applied in real-world situations. Understanding cannot be measured by tests that ask students to use skills and knowledge out of replicate, within reason, the challenges at the heart of each academic discipline. Let them be—authentic. (1989, p. 41)

Wiggins goes on to say that if our instructional goals for students include the abilities to write, speak, listen, create, think critically, do research, solve problems, or apply knowledge, then our tests should ask students to write, speak, listen, create, think, solve, and apply. How can this happen?

Many educators suggest we look to the arts and sports for analogies to solve this problem. If we think of the "test" as being the recital, exhibition, game, mock court trial, or other performance, then teaching to the test is just fine. All coaches, artists, and musicians gladly "teach" to these "tests" because performing well on these tests is the whole point of instruction. Authentic assessment asks students to perform. The performances may be thinking performances, physical performances, creative performances, or other forms.

It may seem odd to talk of thinking as a performance, but there are many parallels. Serious thinking is risky, because real-life problems are not well defined. Often the outcomes of our thinking are public—others evaluate our ideas. Like a dancer auditioning for a Broadway show, we must cope with the consequences of being evaluated. Like a sculptor looking at a lump of clay, a student facing a difficult problem must experiment, observe, redo, imagine and test solutions, apply both basic skills and inventive techniques, make interpretations, decide how to communicate results to the intended audience, and often accept criticism and improve the solution (Eisner, 1999; Herman, 1997). Table 15.3 on page 566 lists some characteristics of authentic tests.

Authentic Tests: Assessment procedures that test skills and abilities as they would be applied in real-life situations.

Connect and Extend
To professional journals
Aschbacher, P. R., & Winters, L. (1992). *A practical guide to alternative assessment.* Alexandria, VA: Association for Supervision and Curriculum Development.
Aschbacher, P. (1997). New directions in student assessment [Special Issue]. *Theory Into Practice,* 36(4), 194–272.

context. "In other words, we cannot be said to understand something unless we can employ our knowledge wisely, fluently, flexibly, and aptly in particular and diverse contexts" (Wiggins, 1993, p. 200).

◄ COUNTERPOINT *Traditional tests can play an important role.*

Most psychologists and educators would agree with Wiggins that setting clear, high, authentic standards is important, but many also believe that traditional tests are useful in this process. Learning may be more than knowing the right answers, but right answers are important. While schooling is about learning to think and solve problems, it is also about knowledge. Students must have something to think about—facts, ideas, concepts, principles, theories, explanations, arguments, images, opinions. Well-designed traditional tests can evaluate students' knowledge effectively and efficiently (Airasian, 1996; Kirst, 1991b). Some educators believe that traditional testing should play an even greater role than it currently does. Educational policy analysts suggest that American students, compared to students in many other developed countries, lack essential knowledge because American schools emphasize process—critical thinking, self-esteem, problem solving—more than content. In order to teach more about content, teachers will need to determine how well their students are learning the content, and traditional testing provides useful information about content learning.

Tests are also valuable in motivating and guiding students' learning. There is research evidence that frequent testing encourages learning and retention (Nungester & Duchastel, 1982). In fact, students generally learn more in classes with more rather than fewer tests (Dempster, 1991).

Source: From "Standards Not Standardization," by G. Wiggins, 1991, *Educational Leadership,* 48(5), pp. 18–25. Copyright © 1991 by the Association for Supervision and Curriculum Development. Reprinted with permission.

TABLE 15.3 *Characteristics of Authentic Tests*

A. Structure and Logistics

1. Are more appropriately public; involve an audience, a panel, and so on.
2. Do not rely on unrealistic and arbitrary time constraints.
3. Offer known, not secret, questions or tasks.
4. Are more like portfolios or a *season* of games (not one-shot).
5. Require some collaboration with others.
6. Recur—and are *worth* practicing for, rehearsing, and retaking.
7. Make assessment and feedback to students so central that school schedules, structures, and policies are modified to support them.

B. Intellectual Design Features

1. Are "essential"—not needlessly intrusive, arbitrary, or contrived to "shake out" a grade.
2. Are "enabling"—constructed to point the student toward more sophisticated use of the skills or knowledge.
3. Are contextualized, complex intellectual challenges, not "atomized" tasks, corresponding to isolated "outcomes."
4. Involve the student's own research or use of knowledge, for which "content" is a means.
5. Assess student habits and repertoires, not mere recall or plug-in skills.
6. Are *representative* challenges—designed to emphasize *depth* more than breadth.

7. Are engaging and educational.
8. Involve somewhat ambiguous ("ill-structured") tasks or problems.

C. Grading and Scoring Standards

1. Involve criteria that assess essentials, not easily counted (but relatively unimportant) errors.
2. Are graded not on a "curve" but in reference to performance standards (criterion-referenced, not norm-referenced).
3. Involve demystified criteria of success that appear to *students* as inherent in successful activity.
4. Make self-assessment a part of the assessment.
5. Use a multifaceted scoring system instead of one aggregate grade.
6. Exhibit harmony with shared schoolwide aims—a *standard*.

D. Fairness and Equity

1. Ferret out and identify (perhaps hidden) strengths.
2. Strike a *constantly* examined balance between honoring achievement and native skill or fortunate prior training.
3. Minimize needless, unfair, and demoralizing comparisons.
4. Allow appropriate room for student learning styles, aptitudes, and interests.
5. Can be—should be—attempted by *all* students, with the test "scaffolded up," not "dumbed down," as necessary.

Source: From "Teaching to the Authentic Test," by G. W. Wiggins, 1989, *Educational Leadership*, 45(7), p. 44. Copyright © 1989 by the Association of Supervision and Curriculum Development. Reprinted with permission.

Connect and Extend
To professional journals
Paulson, F. L., Paulson, P. R., & Meyer, C. A. (1991). What makes a portfolio a portfolio? *Educational Leadership, 48*(5), 60–63. *Focus Question:* Describe five entries that they might include in portfolios for their students.

Portfolio: A collection of the student's work in an area, showing growth, self-reflection, and achievement.

Exhibition: A performance test or demonstration of learning that is public and usually takes an extended time to prepare.

Performance in Context: Portfolios and Exhibitions

The concern with authentic assessment has led to the development of several new approaches based on the goal of *performance in context*. Instead of circling answers to "factual" questions on nonexistent situations, students are required to solve real problems. Facts are used in a context where they apply—for example, the student uses grammar facts to write a persuasive letter to a software company requesting donations for the class computer center. The following example of a test of performance is taken from the Connecticut Core of Common Learning:

> Many local supermarkets claim to have the lowest prices. But what does this really mean? Does it mean that every item in their store is priced lower, or just some of them? How can you really tell which supermarket will save you the most money? Your assignment is to design and carry out a study to answer this

question. What items and prices will you compare and why? How will you justify the choice of your "sample"? How reliable is the sample, etc.? (Wolf, Bixby, Glenn, & Gardner, 1991, p. 61)

Students completing this "test" will use mathematical facts and procedures in the context of solving a real-life problem. In addition, they will have to think critically and write persuasively.

Portfolios and exhibitions are two new approaches to assessment that require performance in context. With these new approaches, it is difficult to tell where instruction stops and assessment starts because the two processes are interwoven.

Portfolios. According to Paulson, Paulson, and Meyer (1991), a **portfolio** is:

> a purposeful collection of student work that exhibits the student's efforts, progress, and achievements in one or more areas. The collection must include student participation in selecting contents, the criteria for judging merit, and evidence of student self-reflection. (p. 60)

Portfolios often include work in progress, revisions, student self-analyses, and reflections on what the student has learned. For example, one student's self-reflection is presented in Figure 15.1.

Written work or artistic pieces are common contents of portfolios, but students might also include graphs, diagrams, snapshots of displays, peer comments, audio- or videotapes, laboratory reports, and computer programs—anything that demonstrates learning in the area being taught and assessed (Belanoff & Dickson, 1991; Camp, 1990; Wolf, Bixby, Glenn, & Gardner, 1991). The Vermont Mathematics Portfolio, for example, has (a) five to seven of the student's "best pieces," including at least one puzzle, one investigation, one application, and no more than two examples of group work; (b) a letter to the portfolio examiner; and (c) a collection of other pieces of mathematics work (Abruscato, 1993). The Guidelines on page 568 give some ideas for using portfolios in your teaching.

Exhibitions. An **exhibition** is a performance test that has two additional features. First, it is public, so students preparing exhibitions must take the audience

---

FIGURE 15.1

A Student Reflects on Learning: Self-Analysis of Work in a Portfolio

Not only has this student's writing improved, but the student has become a more self-aware and self-critical writer.

> Today I looked at all my 2
> stories in my writing folder
> I read some of my writing since
> September. I noticed that I've
> improved some stuff. Now I edit my
> stories, and revise. Now I use periods,
> quotation mark. Sometimes my stories
> are longer I used to miss pell my
> words and now I look in a
> dictionary or ask a friend and now
> I write exciting and scary stories
> and now I have very good endings.
> Now I use capitals I used to leave out
> words and write short simple stories.

Exhibitions and performances can be used to assess students for mastery of subject matter, communication skills, organization, and effort. ▼

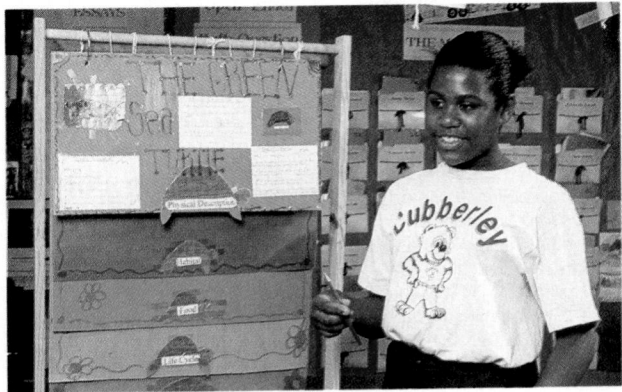

GUIDELINES

Creating Portfolios

Students should be involved in selecting the pieces that will make up the portfolio.

Examples

1. During the unit or semester, ask each student to select work that fits certain criteria, such as "my most difficult problem," "my best work," "my most improved work," or "three approaches to. . . ."
2. For their final submissions, ask students to select pieces that best show how much they have learned.

A portfolio should include information that shows student self-reflection and self-criticism.

Examples

1. Ask students to include a rationale for their selections.
2. Have each student write a "guide" to his or her portfolio, explaining how strengths and weaknesses are reflected in the work included.
3. Include self- and peer critiques, indicating specifically what is good and what might be improved.
4. Model self-criticism of your own productions.

The portfolio should reflect the students' activities in learning.

Examples

1. Include a representative selection of projects, writings, drawings, and so forth.

2. Ask students to relate the goals of learning to the contents of their portfolios.

The portfolio can serve different functions at different times of the year.

Examples

1. Early in the year, it might hold unfinished work or "problem pieces."
2. At the end of the year, it should contain only what the student is willing to make public.

Portfolios should show growth.

Examples

1. Ask students to make a "history" of their progress along certain dimensions and to illustrate points in their growth with specific works.
2. Ask students to include descriptions of activities outside class that reflect the growth illustrated in the portfolio.

Teach students how to create and use portfolios.

Examples

1. Keep models of very well done portfolios as examples, but stress that each portfolio is an individual statement.
2. Examine your students' portfolios frequently, especially early in the year when they are just getting used to the idea. Give constructive feedback.

Connect and Extend
To professional journals

For a positive view of using portfolios as a state-wide assessment process, see Ambruscato, J. (1993). Early results and tentative implications from the Vermont Portfolio Project. *Phi Delta Kappan, 74*, 474–477.

Connect and Extend
To professional journals

For a description of one school's graduation exhibitions and a thoughtful analysis of the use of exhibitions in teaching, see McDonald, J. P. (1993). Three pictures of an exhibition: Warm, cool, and hard. *Phi Delta Kappan, 74*, 480–485.

into account; communication and understanding are essential. Second, an exhibition often requires many hours of preparation, because it is the culminating experience of a whole program of study. Ted Sizer (1984) proposed that "exhibitions of mastery" replace traditional tests in determining graduation or course completion requirements. Grant Wiggins (1989) believes that an exhibition of mastery "is meant to be more than a better test. Like the thesis and oral examination in graduate school, it indicates whether a student has earned a diploma, is ready to leave high school" (p. 47).

Evaluating Portfolios and Performances

Checklists, rating scales, and scoring rubrics are helpful when you assess performances, because assessments of performances, portfolios, and exhibitions are criterion-referenced, not norm-referenced. In other words, the students' products and performances are compared to established public standards, not ranked in relation to other students' work (Cambourne & Turbill, 1990; Wiggins, 1991). For example,

FIGURE 15.2

Three Ways of Rating an Oral Presentation

Numerical Rating Scale

Directions: Indicate how often the pupil performs each of these behaviors while giving an oral presentation. For each behavior circle **1** if the pupil **always** performs the behavior, **2** if the pupil **usually** performs the behavior, **3** if the pupil **seldom** performs the behavior, and **4** if the pupil **never** performs the behavior.

Physical Expression

A. Stands straight and faces audience.

    1 2 3 4

B. Changes facial expression with change in the tone of the presentation.

    1 2 3 4

Graphic Rating Scale

Directions: Place an **X** on the line which shows how often the pupil did each of the behaviors listed while giving an oral presentation.

Physical Expression

A. Stands straight and faces the audience.

    always   usually   seldom   never

B. Changes facial expressions with change in tone of the presentation.

    always   usually   seldom   never

Descriptive Rating Scale

Directions: Place an **X** on the line at the place which best describes the pupil's performance on each behavior.

Physical Expression

A. Stands straight and faces audience.

stands straight, always looks at audience	weaves, fidgets, eyes roam from audience to ceiling	constant, distracting movements, no eye contact with audience

B. Changes facial expressions with change in tone of the presentation.

matches facial expressions to content and emphasis	facial expressions usually appropriate, occasional lack of expression	no match between tone and facial expression; expression distracts

Source: From *Assessment in the Classroom* (p. 153), by P. W. Airasian, 1996, New York: McGraw-Hill. Copyright © by The McGraw-Hill Companies. Adapted with permission.

Figure 15.2 gives three alternatives—numerical, graphic, and descriptive—for rating an oral presentation.

> **Scoring Rubrics:** Rules that are used to determine the quality of a student performance.

Scoring Rubrics. A checklist or rating scale gives specific feedback about elements of a performance. **Scoring rubrics** are rules that are used to determine the quality of a student performance (Mabry, 1999). For example, a rubric describing an excellent oral presentation might be:

> Pupil consistently faces audience, stands straight, and maintains eye contact; voice projects well and clearly; pacing and tone variation appropriate; well-organized; points logically and completely presented; brief summary at end. (Airasian, 1996, p. 155)

It is often helpful to have students join in the development of rating scales and scoring rubrics. When students participate, they are challenged to decide what quality work looks or sounds like in a particular area. They know in advance what is expected. As students gain practice in designing and applying scoring rubrics, their work and their learning often improve. Figure 15.3 is an evaluation form for self- and peer assessment of contributions to cooperative learning groups.

Performance assessment requires careful judgment on the part of teachers and clear communication to students about what is good and what needs improving. In

---

FIGURE 15.3

Self- and Peer Evaluation of Group Learning

STUDENT SELF- AND PEER EVALUATION FORM

This form will be used to assess the members of your learning group. Fill one form out on yourself. Fill one form out on each member of your group. During the group discussion, give each member the form you have filled out on them. Compare the way you rated yourself with the ways your groupmates have rated you. Ask for clarification when your rating differs from the ratings given you by your groupmates. Each member should set a goal for increasing his or her contribution to the academic learning of all group members.

Person Being Rated: _____

Write the number of points earned by the group member:
(4 = Excellent, 3 = Good, 2 = Poor, 1 = Inadequate)

___ On time for class.

___ Arrives prepared for class.

___ Reliably completes all assigned work on time.

___ Work is of high quality.

___ Contributes to groupmates' learning daily.

___ Asks for academic help and assistance when it is needed.

___ Gives careful step-by-step explanations (doesn't just tell answers).

___ Builds on others' reasoning.

___ Relates what is being learned to previous knowledge.

___ Helps draw a visual representation of what is being learned.

___ Voluntarily extends a project.

Source: From "The Role of Cooperative Learning in Assessing and Communicating Student Learning," by D. W. Johnson and R. T. Johnson. In *ASCD 1996 Yearbook: Communicating Student Learning* (p. 41), T. Guskey (Ed.). Copyright © 1996 by the Association for Supervision and Curriculum Development. Reprinted with permission. All rights reserved.

GUIDELINES

Developing a Rubric

1. *Look at models:* Show students examples of good and not-so-good work. Identify the characteristics that make the good ones good and the bad ones bad.

2. *List criteria:* Use the discussion of models to begin a list of what counts in quality work.

3. *Articulate gradations of quality:* Describe the best and worst levels of quality, then fill in the middle levels based on your knowledge of common problems and the discussion of not-so-good work.

4. *Practice on models:* Have students use the rubrics to evaluate the models you gave them in Step. 1.

5. *Use self- and peer-assessment:* Give students their task. As they work, stop them occasionally for self- and peer-assessment.

6. *Revise:* Always give students time to revise their work based on the feedback they get in Step 5.

7. *Use teacher assessment:* Use the same rubric students used to assess their work yourself.

Step 1 may be necessary only when you are asking students to engage in a task with which they are unfamiliar. Steps 3 and 4 are useful but time-consuming; you can do these on your own, especially when you've been using rubrics for a while. A class experienced in rubric-based assessment can streamline the process so that it begins with listing criteria, after which the teacher writes out the gradations of quality, checks them with the students, makes revisions, then uses the rubric for self-, peer, and teacher assessment.

some ways the approach is similar to the clinical method first introduced by Binet to assess intelligence: It is based on observing the student perform a variety of tasks and comparing his or her performance to a standard. Just as Binet never wanted to assign a single number to represent the child's intelligence, teachers who use authentic assessments do not try to assign one score to the student's performance. Even if rankings, ratings, and grades have to be given, these judgments are not the ultimate goals—improvement of learning is. The above Guidelines for developing rubrics are taken from Goodrich (1997).

Reliability, Validity, Generalizability, and Equity. Because judgment plays such a central role in evaluating performances, issues of reliability, validity, and equity are critical considerations. As we saw in the previous chapter, judges assessing the Vermont Portfolios often have not agreed on ratings, so reliability may not be adequate. When raters are experienced and scoring rubrics are well developed and refined, however, reliability may improve (Herman & Winters, 1994; LeMahieu, Gitomer, & Eresh, 1993). Some of this improvement in reliability occurs because a rubric focuses the raters' attention on a few dimensions of the work and gives limited scoring levels to choose from. If scorers can give only a rating of 1, 2, 3, or 4, they are more likely to agree than if they could score based on a 100-point scale. So the rubrics may achieve reliability not because they capture underlying agreement among raters, but because the rubrics limit options and thus limit variability in scoring (Mabry, 1999).

In terms of validity, there is some evidence that students who are classified as "master" writers on the basis of portfolio assessment are judged less capable using standard writing assessment. Which form of assessment is the best reflection of enduring qualities? There is so little research on this question, it is hard to say (Herman & Winters, 1994). In addition, when rubrics are developed to assess specific tasks, the results of applying the rubric may not predict performance on anything

Review

▶ What is authentic assessment?

▶ Describe portfolios and exhibitions.

Apply

▶ How would you assure reliability, validity, and equity in your use of authentic assessment tasks?

▶ How can checklists and rating scales be used to assess student portfolios and exhibitions?

except very similar tasks, so what do we actually know about students' learning more generally (Haertel, 1999; Herman, 1997)?

Equity is an issue in all assessment and no less so with performances and portfolios. With a public performance there could be bias effects based on a student's appearance and speech or the student's access to expensive audio, video, or graphic resources. Performance assessments have the same potential as other tests to discriminate unfairly against students who are not wealthy or who are culturally different (McDonald, 1993). And the extensive group work, peer editing, and out-of-class time devoted to portfolios means that some students may have access to more extensive networks of support and outright help. Many students in your classes will have families with sophisticated computer graphics and desktop publishing capabilities. Others may have little support from home. These differences can be sources of bias and inequity.

Effects of Grades and Grading on Students

Connect and Extend
To your own philosophy
Classroom evaluation is frequently referred to as the "grading game." What aspects of grading resemble a game from the student's point of view?

There is some evidence that high standards, a competitive class atmosphere, and a large percentage of lower grades are associated with increased absenteeism and dropout rates (Moos & Moos, 1978). This seems especially likely with disadvantaged students (Wessman, 1972). Highly competitive classes may be particularly hard on anxious students or students who lack self-confidence. So, while high standards and competition do tend generally to be related to increased academic learning, it is clear that a balance must be struck between high standards and a reasonable chance to succeed.

Effects of Failure

It may sound as though low grades and failure should be avoided in school. But the situation is not that simple. After reviewing many years of research on the effects of failure from several perspectives, Margaret Clifford (1990, 1991) concluded that failure can have both positive and negative effects on subsequent performance, depending on the situation and the personality of the students involved.

For example, one study required subjects to complete three sets of problems. On the first set, the experimenters arranged for subjects to experience either zero, 50, or 100% success. On the second set, it was arranged for all subjects to fail completely. On the third set of problems, the experimenters merely recorded how well the subjects performed. Those who had succeeded only 50% of the time before the failure experience performed the best. It appears that a history of complete failure or 100% success may be bad preparation for learning to cope with failure, something we must all learn. Some level of failure may be helpful for most students, especially if teachers help the students see connections between hard work and improvement. Efforts to protect students from failure and to guarantee success may be counterproductive. Clifford (1990) gives this advice to teachers:

> It is time for educators to replace easy success with challenge. We must encourage students to reach beyond their intellectual grasp and allow them the privilege of learning from mistakes. There must be a tolerance for error-making in every classroom, and gradual success rather than continual success must become the yardstick by which learning is judged. (p. 23)

The more able your students, the more challenging and important it will be to help them learn to "fail successfully" (Foster, 1981).

So far, we have been talking about the effects of failing a test or perhaps a course. But what about the effect of failing an entire grade—that is, of being "held back"? Almost 20% of seniors have repeated at least one grade since kindergarten, usually in the earlier grades (Kelly, 1999). Some researchers believe that being held back injures students' self-esteem and increases the chances that they will drop out of school (Grissom & Smith, 1989; Roderick, 1994). In their view, students generally do better academically when promoted. Other researchers have found some advantage for more emotionally immature children of average or above average ability who are retained in 1st, 2nd, or 3rd grade (Kelly, 1999; Pierson & Connell, 1992), but the advantage may not last. In one study that followed many students for several years, children who could have been retained, but who were promoted, did about as well as similar children who were held back, and sometimes better (Reynolds, 1992).

No matter what, students who have trouble should get help, whether they are promoted or retained. Just covering the same material again in the same way won't solve the students' academic or social problems. As Jeannie Oakes (1999) has said, "No sensible person advocates social promotion as it is currently framed—simply passing incompetent students on to the next grade" (p. 8). The best approach may be to promote the students along with their peers, but to give them special remediation during the summer or the next year (Mantzicopoulos & Morrison, 1992; Shepard & Smith, 1989). An even better approach would be to prevent the problems before they occur by providing extra resources such as tutoring, as happens in the Reading Recovery program or Slavin's Success for All (Oakes, 1999).

Effects of Feedback

The results of several studies of feedback fit well with the notion of "successful" or constructive failure. These studies have concluded that it is more helpful to tell students *why* they are wrong so they can learn more appropriate strategies (Bangert-Drowns, Kulik, Kulik, & Morgan, 1991). Students often need help figuring out why their answers are incorrect. Without such feedback, they are likely to make the same mistakes again. Yet this type of feedback is rarely given. In one study, only about 8% of the teachers noticed a consistent type of error in a student's arithmetic computation and informed the student (Bloom & Bourdon, 1980).

What are the identifying characteristics of effective written feedback? With older students (late elementary through high school), written comments are most helpful when they are personalized and when they provide constructive criticism.

Connect and Extend
To professional journals
Harvard Graduate School of Education. (1999, January/February). Retention vs. social promotion: Schools search for alternatives. *Harvard Education Newsletter*, *15*(1), 1–3. *Focus Question:* What are the effects of retention on students? Can you propose alternatives?

Connect and Extend
To professional journals
Two studies and a synthesis of research on grade retention: Mantzicopolous, P., & Morrison, D. (1992). Kindergarten retention: Academic and behavioral outcomes through the end of second grade. *American Educational Research Journal, 29*, 182–198. Pierson, L. H., & Connell, J. P. (1992). Effect of grade retention on self-system processes, school engagement, and academic performance. *Journal of Educational Psychology, 84*, 300–307. Shepard, L. A., & Smith, M. L. (1990). Synthesis of research on grade retention. *Educational Leadership, 47*(8), 84–88.

Connect and Extend
To your own philosophy
What are some of your experiences in receiving feedback on papers and tests? Is it fair to give a student less than an A without indicating where improvement needs to be made?

Connect and Extend
To other chapters
See Chapter 6 for a discussion of how to use praise effectively. These guidelines apply to written feedback as well.

This means the teacher should make specific comments on errors or faulty strategies, but balance this criticism with suggestions about how to improve, and with comments on the positive aspects of the work (Butler & Nisan, 1986; Elawar & Corno, 1985). Working with 6th grade teachers, Elawar and Corno (1985) found that feedback was dramatically improved when the teachers used these four questions as a guide: "What is the key error? What is the probable reason the student made this error? How can I guide the student to avoid the error in the future? What did the student do well that could be noted?" (p. 166). Here are some examples of teachers' written comments that proved helpful (Elawar & Corno, 1985, p. 164):

> Juan, you know how to get a percent, but the computation is wrong in this instance. . . . Can you see where? (Teacher has underlined the location of errors.)

> You know how to solve the problem—the formula is correct—but you have not demonstrated that you understand how one fraction multiplied by another can give an answer that is smaller than either ($\frac{1}{2} \times \frac{1}{2} = \frac{1}{4}$).

These comments should help students correct errors and should recognize good work, progress, and increasing skill.

Grades and Motivation

Is there really a difference between working for a grade and working to learn? The answer depends in part on how a grade is determined. As a teacher, you can use grades to motivate the kind of learning you intend students to achieve in your course. If you test only at a simple but detailed level of knowledge, you may force students to choose between higher aspects of learning and a good grade. But when a grade reflects meaningful learning, working for a grade and working to learn become the same thing. Finally, while high grades may have some value as rewards or incentives for meaningful engagement in learning, low grades generally do not encourage greater efforts. Students receiving low grades are more likely to withdraw, blame others, decide that the work is "dumb," or feel responsible for the low grade but helpless to make improvements. Rather than give a failing grade, you might consider the work incomplete and give students support in revising or improving. Maintain high standards and give students a chance to reach them (Guskey, 1994). The Guidelines summarize the effects grades can have on students.

CHECKPOINT

Effects of Grades and Grading on Students

Review

▶ How can failure support learning?

▶ Which is better, social promotion or being "held back"?

▶ Can feedback, including grades, promote learning and motivation?

Apply

▶ How would you assess the value of the feedback you are getting in your college classes?

Minimizing the Detrimental Effects of Grades

Avoid reserving high grades and high praise for answers that conform to your ideas or to those in the textbook.

Examples

1. Give extra points for correct and creative answers.
2. Withhold your opinions until all sides of an issue have been explored.
3. Reinforce students for disagreeing in a rational, productive manner.
4. Give partial credit for partially correct answers.

Make sure each student has a reasonable chance to be successful, especially at the beginning of a new task.

Examples

1. Pretest students to make sure they have prerequisite abilities.
2. When appropriate, provide opportunities for students to retest to raise their grades, but make sure the retest is as difficult as the original.
3. Consider failing efforts as "incomplete" and encourage students to revise and improve.

Balance written and oral feedback.

Examples

1. Consider giving short, lively written comments with younger students and more extensive written comments with older students.

2. When the grade on a paper is lower than the student might have expected, be sure the reason for the lower grade is clear.
3. Tailor comments to the individual student's performance; avoid writing the same phrases over and over.
4. Note specific errors, possible reasons for errors, ideas for improvement, and work done well.

Make grades as meaningful as possible.

Examples

1. Tie grades to the mastery of important objectives.
2. Give ungraded assignments to encourage exploration.
3. Experiment with performances and portfolios.

Base grades on more than just one criterion.

Examples

1. Use essay questions as well as multiple-choice items on a test.
2. Grade oral reports and class participation.

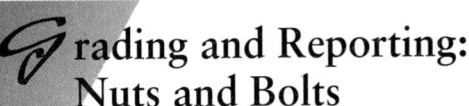

Grading and Reporting: Nuts and Bolts

Connect and Extend
To your own philosophy
What would school be like for students if all testing were eliminated? Would most students still be motivated to learn and complete assignments?

In determining a final grade, the teacher must make a major decision. Should a student's grade reflect the amount of material learned and how well it has been learned, or should the grade reflect the student's status in comparison with the rest of the class? In other words, should grading be criterion-referenced or norm-referenced?

Criterion-Referenced versus Norm-Referenced Grading

In **criterion-referenced grading**, the grade represents a list of accomplishments. If clear objectives have been set for the course, the grade may represent a certain number of objectives met satisfactorily. When a criterion-referenced system is used, criteria for each grade generally are spelled out in advance. It is then up to the student to

Criterion-Referenced Grading: Assessment of each student's mastery of course objectives.

Connect and Extend
To professional journals
Hills, J. R. (1991). Apathy concerning grading and testing. *Phi Delta Kappan, 72*(7), 540–545.

earn the grade she or he wants to receive. Theoretically, in this system all students can achieve an A if they reach the criteria.

In **norm-referenced grading**, the major influence on a grade is the student's standing in comparison with others who also took the course. If a student studies very hard and almost everyone else does too, the student may receive a disappointing grade, perhaps a C.

Criterion-Referenced Systems.

Criterion-referenced grading has the advantage of relating judgments about a student to the achievement of clearly defined instructional goals. Some school districts have developed reporting systems where report cards list objectives along with judgments about the student's attainment of each. Reporting is done at the end of each unit of instruction. The elementary school report card shown in Figure 15.4 demonstrates the relationship between assessment and the goals of the unit.

Norm-Referenced Systems.

One common type of norm-referenced grading is called **grading on the curve**. In grading on the curve, the middle of the normal distribution or "average" performance becomes the anchor on which grading is based. In other words, teachers look at the average level of performance, assign what they consider an "average grade" for this performance, and then grade superior performances higher and inferior performances lower.

Connect and Extend
To your teaching
A useful way of increasing the frequency of testing and students' motivation to study is by giving "pop quizzes." But how can pop quizzes be given in a way that is not overly anxiety-producing? One answer: make them count as special incentives or bonus points.

Connect and Extend
To your own philosophy
What type of grading orientation, norm-referenced or criterion-referenced, would be best understood by parents? Which would parents generally favor? Would the choices vary depending on the grade level concerned?

If grading were done strictly on the normal curve, there would be an equal number of As and Fs, a larger number of Bs and Ds, and an even larger number of Cs. The grades would have to form a bell-shaped curve. For example, a teacher might decide to give 10% As and Fs, 20% Bs and Ds, and 40% Cs. This is a very strict interpretation of grading on the curve, and will discourage students who work hard, but always perform below average.

Grading on the curve can be done with varying levels of precision. The simplest approach is to rank-order the students' raw scores on a test and use this ranked list of scores as the basis for assigning grades. Knowing that two-thirds of the scores in a normal distribution should be in the middle, you might bracket off the middle two-thirds of the scores and plan to give those students Cs (or Bs, if you believed B was an average grade for the class in question). Some people prefer to use the middle one-third of the students rather than the middle two-thirds as the basis for the average grade. Based on this second approach, grades for the following scores might be:

Middle One-Third Assigned Cs

A	B	C	D	F

92 | 91 91 90 83 80 78 76 | 72 68 65 61 57 54 53 49 | 48 47 46 43 38 36 | 29 29

In this example the distance between one letter grade and another is sometimes one point! Given the amount of error in testing, this assignment of grades is probably not fair. You can correct some of these problems by introducing common sense into the process. For example, you may believe the following grade assignment is fairer:

Adjusted Grades

A	B	C	D	F

92 91 91 90 | 83 80 78 76 72 | 68 65 61 57 54 53 | 49 48 47 46 43 38 36 | 29 29

Norm-Referenced Grading: Assessment of students' achievement in relation to one another.

Grading on the Curve: Norm-referenced grading that compares students' performance to an average level.

FIGURE 15.4

A Criterion-Referenced Report Card

This is one example of a criterion-referenced report card. Other forms are possible, but all criterion-referenced reports indicate student progress toward specific goals.

LINCOLN ELEMENTARY SCHOOL
GRADE 5

Student _____ Teacher _____ Principal _____Muriel Simms_____ Quarter 2 3 4

E = Excellent   S = Satisfactory   P = Making Progress   N = Needs improvement

READING PROGRAM

Materials Used: _____
_____
_____

____ Reads with understanding
____ Is able to write about what is read
____ Completes reading group work accurately and on time
____ Shows interest in reading

Reading Skills
____ Decodes new words
____ Understands new words

Independent Reading Level
Below/At Grade Level/Above

LANGUAGE ARTS

____ Uses oral language effectively
____ Listens carefully
____ Masters weekly spelling

Writing skills
____ Understands writing as process
____ Creates a rough draft
____ Makes meaningful revisions
____ Creates edited, legible final draft

Editing skills
____ Capitalizes
____ Punctuates
____ Uses complete sentences
____ Uses paragraphs
____ Demonstrates dictionary skills

Writing skill level:
Below/At Grade Level/Above

MATHEMATICS

Problem Solving
____ Solves teacher-generated problems
____ Solves self-/student-generated problems
____ Can create story problems

Interpreting Problems
____ Uses appropriate strategies
____ Can use more than one strategy
____ Can explain strategies in written form
____ Can explain strategies orally

Math Concepts
Understands Base Ten
Beginning/Developing/Sophisticated
Multiplication, Basic facts
Beginning/Developing/Sophisticated
2 digit Multiplication
Beginning/Developing/Sophisticated
Division
Beginning/Developing/Sophisticated
Geometry
Beginning/Developing/Sophisticated

Overall Math Skill Level:
Beginning/Developing/Sophisticated

Attitude/Work Skills
____ Welcomes a challenge
____ Persistent
____ Takes advantage of learning from others
____ Listens to others
____ Participates in discussion

It Figures
Is working on: _____

Goals: _____
Is working on achieving goal:
_____

SOCIAL STUDIES

____ Understands subject matter
____ Shows curiosity and enthusiasm
____ Contributes to class discussions
____ Uses map skills
____ Demonstrates control of reading skills by interpreting text
Topics covered: individual cultures, Columbus–first English colonies

SCIENCE

____ Shows curiosity about scientific subject matter
____ Asks good scientific questions
____ Shows knowledge of scientific method
____ Uses knowledge of scientific method to help set up and run experiment(s)
____ Makes good scientific observations
____ Has researched scientific topic(s)
Topic(s) _____

I Wonder
Is currently working on _____
_____

WORKING SKILLS

____ Listens carefully
____ Follows directions
____ Works neatly and carefully
____ Checks work
____ Completes work on time
____ Uses time wisely
____ Works well independently
____ Works well in a group
____ Takes risks in learning
____ Welcomes a challenge

HOMEWORK

____ Self-selects homework
____ Completes work accurately
____ Completes work on time

PRESENTATIONS/PROJECTS
_____
_____

HUMAN RELATIONS

____ Shows courtesy
____ Respects rights of others
____ Shows self-control
____ Interacts well with peers
____ Shows a cooperative and positive attitude in class
____ Shows a cooperative attitude when asked to work with other students
____ Is willing to help other students
____ Works well with other adults (subs, student teacher, parents, etc.)

Attendance

	1st	2nd	3rd	4th
Present				
Absent				
Tardy				

Placement for next year:

TABLE 15.4 *Comparing Norm-Referenced and Criterion-Referenced Standards for Grading*

Norm-referenced systems use the performance of the rest of the class as the standard for determining grades. Criterion-referenced systems use standards of subject mastery and learning to determine grades.

Grade	Criterion-referenced	Norm-referenced
A	Firm command of knowledge domain High level of skill development Exceptional preparation for later learning	Far above class average
B	Command of knowledge beyond the minimum Advanced development of most skills Has prerequisites for later learning	Above class average
C	Command of only the basic concepts of knowledge Demonstrated ability to use basic skills Lacks a few prerequisites for later learning	At the class average
D	Lacks knowledge of some fundamental ideas Some important skills not attained Deficient in many of the prerequisites for later learning	Below class average
F	Most of the basic concepts and principles not learned Most essential skills cannot be demonstrated Lacks most prerequisites needed for later learning	Far below class average

Source: From "Developing a Personal Grading Plan," by D. A. Frisbie and K. K. Waltmen, 1992, *Educational Measurement: Issues and Practices*, p. 37. Copyright © 1992 by the National Council on Measurement in Education. Reprinted with permission.

In this case the instructor has used the natural gaps in the range of scores to locate boundaries between grades. Between the A and B categories are 7 points, between the B and C, 4 points, and so on. Even though this may seem fairer, many educators encourage teachers to avoid grading on the curve because this approach determines in advance that students must compete for the few good grades available (Guskey, 1994; Kohn, 1996).

Table 15.4 compares descriptions of a student's performance using criterion-referenced and norm-referenced standards and suggests a way to translate these descriptions into grades.

Preparing Report Cards

Connect and Extend
To professional journals
For a summary of the considerations in developing a grading plan, see Frisbie, D. A., & Waltmen, K. K. (1992). Developing a personal grading plan. *Educational Measurement: Issues and practices* (pp. 35–42). Washington, DC: National Council on Measurement in Education.

Whatever grading system you use, you will undoubtedly give several tests and you will probably assign homework or projects. Let's assume your unit assessment plan includes two short tests (mostly multiple-choice questions with one essay), homework, a portfolio, and a unit test. If you use a criterion-referenced system for testing and grading, how will you convert scores on these individual performances to the overall indications of mastery on a report card such as that in Figure 15.4? What about using a norm-referenced system? How do you combine results from individual tests and assignments to yield a final distribution of scores for the unit grade?

Let us consider criterion-referenced grading first. If you adopt this system, you cannot average or combine test scores or homework grades mathematically. Since each test and assignment measures the mastery of a particular objective (or set of objectives), it would be meaningless to average, say, the students' mastery of addition of two-digit numbers with their mastery of measurement with a ruler, although both might be objectives in arithmetic. On the report card, the various objectives are listed and the student's level of proficiency in each is indicated.

Norm-referenced grading is a different story. In order to assign grades, the teacher must merge all the scores from tests and other assignments into one final score. Final grades are based on how each student's final score compares with that of the rest of the students. But the usual procedure of simply adding up all the scores and averaging the total is often not appropriate, and it can be misleading. For example, assume two students took two tests. The tests are equally important in the overall unit. The students' scores are shown below (from Chase, 1978, p. 328).

	Test 1 Class mean = 30 Standard deviation = 8	Test 2 Class mean = 50 Standard deviation = 16	Total Raw score
Leslie	38	50	88
Jason	30	66	96

If we compute an average or rank the students based on their totals, Jason will be ahead of Leslie. But if we look at the class mean and standard deviation for each test, we see a different picture. On one test, Leslie's score was 1 standard deviation above the mean, and on the other her score was at the mean; Jason's record is exactly the same.

If these two tests are really equally important, Jason and Leslie have identical records in relation to the rest of the class on these tests. To compare students' performances on several tests, the scores for each must be converted to a standard scale such as a T score. As you may recall from Chapter 14, a T mean is automatically 50 and the standard deviation is 10. Most teachers do not calculate T scores for all their students, but the example illustrates the importance of using common sense in grading. Gross totals do not always reflect how well one student is doing in relation to others in the class.

The Point System

One popular system for combining grades from many assignments is a point system. Each test or assignment is given a certain number of total points, depending on its importance. A test worth 40% of the grade could be worth 40 points. A paper worth 20% could be worth 20 points. Points are then awarded on the test or paper based on specific criteria. An A+ paper, one that meets all the criteria, could be given the full 20 points; an average paper might be given 10 points. If tests of comparable importance are worth the same number of points, are equally difficult, and cover a similar amount of material, we can expect to avoid some of the problems encountered with Jason and Leslie, when the means and standard deviations of two supposedly comparable tests varied so greatly.

Let us assume a grade book indicates the scores shown in Table 15.5 on page 580. How would you assign grades to students for this unit? The most common way is to find the total number of points for each student and rank the students. Assign

TABLE 15.5 *Points Earned on Five Assignments*

Student	Test 1 20% 20 points	Test 2 20% 20 points	Unit Test 30% 30 points	Homework 15% 15 points	Portfolio 15% 15 points	Total
Amy	10	12	16	6	7	___
Lee	12	10	14	7	6	___
Luis	20	19	30	15	13	___
Wayne	18	20	25	15	15	___
Étienne	6	5	12	4	10	___
Frieda	10	12	18	10	9	___
Grace	13	11	22	11	10	___
Houston	7	9	12	5	6	___
Isaac	14	16	26	12	12	___
Liz	20	18	28	10	15	___
Peter	19	20	25	11	12	___
Linda	14	12	20	13	9	___
Melody	15	13	24	8	10	___
Ned	8	7	12	8	6	___
Olivia	11	12	16	9	10	___
Rob	7	8	11	4	8	___

grades by looking for natural gaps of several points or imposing a curve (a certain percentage of As, Bs, and so on).

Percentage Grading

There is another approach to assigning grades to a group of students such as those in Table 15.5. Using **percentage grading** the teacher can assign grades based on how much knowledge each student has mastered—what percentage of the total knowledge he or she understands. To do this, the teacher might score tests and other classwork with percentage scores (based on how much is correct—50%, 85%, etc.) and then average these scores to reach a course score. These scores can then be converted into letter grades according to predetermined cutoff points. Any number of students can earn any grade. This procedure is very common; you may have experienced it yourself as a student. Let us look at it more closely, because it has some frequently overlooked problems.

The grading symbols of A, B, C, D, and F are probably the most popular means of reporting at the present time. School systems often establish equivalent percentage categories for each of these symbols. The percentages vary from school district to school district, but two typical ones are as follows:

90–100% = A; 80–89% = B; 70–79% = C; 60–69% = D; below 60% = F
94–100% = A; 85–93% = B; 76–83% = C; 70–75% = D; below 70% = F

As you can see, although both districts have an A to F five-point grading system, the average achievement required for each grade is different.

Percentage Grading: System of converting class performances to percentage scores and assigning grades based on predetermined cutoff points.

Can we really say what is the total amount of knowledge available in, for example, 8th grade science? Are we sure we can accurately measure what percentage of this body of knowledge each student has attained? To use percentage grading appropriately, we would have to know exactly what there was to learn and exactly how much of that each student had learned. These conditions are seldom met, even though teachers use the cutoff points to assign grades as if measurement were so accurate that a one-point difference was meaningful: "In spite of decades of research in educational and psychological measurement, which has produced more defensible methods, the concept [of percentage grading], once established, has proved remarkably resistant to change" (Zimmerman, 1981, p. 178).

Any grading system prescribed or suggested by the school can be influenced by particular concerns of the teacher. So don't be fooled by the seeming security of absolute percentages. Your own grading philosophy will continue to operate, even in this system. Because there is more concern today with specifying objectives and criterion-referenced assessment, especially at the elementary grade levels, several alternative methods for evaluating student progress against predetermined criteria have evolved. We will look at one: the contract system.

The Contract System and Grading Rubrics

When applied to the whole class, the **contract system** indicates the type, quantity, and quality of work required for each number or letter grade in the system. Rubrics describe the performance expected for each level. Students agree, or "contract," to work for particular grades by meeting the specified requirements and performing at the level specified. For example, the following standards might be established:

F: Not coming to class regularly or not turning in the required work.

D: Coming to class regularly and turning in the required work on time.

C: Coming to class regularly, turning in the required work on time, and receiving a check mark on all assignments to indicate they are satisfactory.

B: Coming to class regularly, turning in the required work on time, and receiving a check mark on all assignments except at least three that achieve a check-plus, indicating superior achievement.

A: As above, plus a successful oral or written report on one of the books listed for supplementary reading.

This example calls for more subjective judgment than would be ideal. However, contract systems reduce student anxiety about grades. The contract system can be applied to individual students, in which case it functions much like an independent study plan.

Unfortunately, the system can lead to overemphasis on the quantity of work. Teachers may be too vague about the standards that differentiate acceptable from unacceptable work. This is where scoring rubrics for each assignment can be helpful. If clear and well-developed rubrics describe the performances expected for each assignment, and if students learn to use the rubrics to evaluate their own work, then quality, not quantity, will be at the center of grading. A teacher can modify the contract system by including a **revise option**. For example, a check mark might be worth 75 points and a check-plus 90 points; a check-plus earned after revision could be worth 85 points—more than a check, but less than a check-plus earned the first time

Connect and Extend
To your own philosophy
How would you solve the following problem?—You are using a contract system in one of your classes. One of the requirements for an A is "to write a book report." However, some students are reporting on books that you think they read last year, and some are handing in short, superficial reports. How can you structure the contract system so that the students will do a better quality of work?

Connect and Extend
To other chapters
See Chapter 6 for a discussion of behavior management contracts.

Contract System: System in which each student works for a particular grade according to agreed-upon standards.

Revise Option: In a contract system, the chance to revise and improve work.

around. This system allows students to improve their work, but also rewards getting it right the first time. Some quality control is possible, because students earn points not just for quantity but also for quality. In addition, the teacher may be less reluctant to judge a project unsatisfactory because students can improve their work (King, 1979). But beware, if a school system requires a five-point grading scale and all students contract for and achieve the highest grade (before or after revising), the teacher will wish that the principal had been consulted about the system before the grades came out. The Guidelines give ideas for using any grading system in a fair and reasonable way.

Grading on Effort and Improvement

Grading on effort and improvement is not really a complete grading system but rather a theme that can run through most grading methods. Should teachers grade students based on how much they learn or on the final level of learning? One problem with using improvement as a standard for grading is that the best students improve the least, because they are already the most competent. Do you want to penalize these students because they knew quite a bit initially, and the teaching and testing have limited how much learning they can demonstrate? After all, unless you assign extra work, these students will run out of things to do.

One solution is to use the **individual learning expectation** (**ILE**) system described on page 412. With this system students earn improvement points on tests or assignments for scoring above their personal base (average) score or for making a perfect score. The teacher can count these improvement points when figuring a final grade or simply use them as a basis for giving other classroom rewards.

Many teachers try to include some judgment of effort in final grades, but effort is difficult to assess. Are you certain your perception of each student's effort is correct? Clement (1978) suggests a system for including a judgment about effort in the final grade called the **dual marking system**. Students are assigned two grades. One, usually a letter, indicates the actual level of achievement. The other, a number, indicates the relationship of the achievement to the student's ability and effort. For example, a grade of B could be qualified as follows (Clement, 1978, p. 51):

B1: Outstanding effort, better achievement than expected, good attitude

B2: Average effort, satisfactory in terms of ability

B3: Lower achievement than ability would indicate, poor attitude

Of course, this system assumes that the teacher can adequately judge true ability and effort. A grade of D1, D2, or F2 could be quite insulting. A grade of A3 or F1 should

---

CHECKPOINT

Grading and Reporting: Nuts and Bolts

Review

▶ Describe two kinds of grading.

▶ What is the point system?

▶ Describe some alternatives to traditional grading.

▶ What are some sources of bias in grading?

Apply

▶ What grading systems are you experiencing right now in your college classes?

▶ What are the advantages and disadvantages of contract grading? percentage grading? grading on the curve?

GUIDELINES

Using Any Grading System

Explain your grading policies to students early in the course and remind them of the policies regularly.

Examples

1. Give older students a handout describing the assignments, tests, grading criteria, and schedule.
2. Explain to younger students in a low-pressure manner how their work will be evaluated.

Set reasonable standards.

Examples

1. Discuss workload and grading standards with more experienced teachers.
2. Give a few formative tests to get a sense of your students' abilities before you give a graded test.
3. Take tests yourself first to gauge the difficulty of the test and to estimate the time your students will need.

Base your grades on as much objective evidence as possible.

Examples

1. Plan in advance how and when you will test.
2. Keep a portfolio of student work. This may be useful in student or parent conferences.

Be sure students understand test directions.

Examples

1. Outline the directions on the board.
2. Ask several students to explain the directions.
3. Go over a sample question first.

Correct, return, and discuss test questions as soon as possible.

Examples

1. Have students who wrote good answers read their responses for the class; make sure they are not the same students each time.

2. Discuss why wrong answers, especially popular wrong choices, are incorrect.
3. As soon as students finish a test, give them the answers to questions and the page numbers where answers are discussed in the text.

As a rule, do not change a grade.

Examples

1. Make sure you can defend the grade in the first place.
2. DO change any clerical or calculation errors.

Guard against bias in grading.

Examples

1. Ask students to put their names on the backs of their papers.
2. Use an objective point system or model papers when grading essays.

Keep pupils informed of their standing in the class.

Examples

1. Write the distribution of scores on the board after tests.
2. Schedule periodic conferences to go over work from previous weeks.

Give students the benefit of the doubt. All measurement techniques involve error.

Examples

1. Unless there is a very good reason not to, give the higher grade in borderline cases.
2. If a large number of students miss the same question in the same way, revise the question for the future and consider throwing it out for that test.

Source: From *Problems in Middle and High School Teaching: A Handbook for Student Teachers and Beginning Teachers* (pp. 182–187), by A. M. Drayer, 1979, Boston: Allyn & Bacon. Copyright © 1979 by Allyn & Bacon. Adapted by permission of the author and publisher.

Individual Learning Expectation (ILE): Personal average score.

Dual Marking System: System of assigning two grades, one reflecting achievement, the other effort, attitude, and actual ability.

not be possible. But the system does have the advantage of recognizing hard work and giving feedback about a seeming lack of effort. An A2 or B2 might tell very bright students: "You're doing well, but I know you could do better." This could help the students to expect more of themselves and not slip by on high ability. The overall grade—A, B, C—still reflects achievement and is not changed (or biased) by teachers' subjective judgment of effort.

Cautions: Being Fair

The attributions a teacher makes about the causes of student successes or failures can affect the grades that students receive. Teachers are more likely to give higher grades for effort (a controllable factor) than for ability (an uncontrollable factor). Lower grades are more likely when teachers attribute a student's failure to lack of effort instead of lack of ability (Weiner, 1979). It is also possible that grades can be influenced by a **halo effect**—that is, by the tendency to view particular aspects of a student based on a general impression, either positive or negative. As a teacher, you may find it difficult to avoid being affected by positive and negative halos. A very pleasant student who seems to work hard and causes little trouble may be given the benefit of the doubt (B– instead of C+), whereas a very difficult student who seems to refuse to try might be a loser at grading time (D instead of C–).

*B*eyond Grading: Communication

No number or letter grade conveys the totality of a student's experience in a class or course. Both students and teachers sometimes become too focused on the end point—the grade. But children and adolescents spend the majority of their waking hours for many months of the year in school, where teachers are the relevant adults. This gives teachers the opportunity and the responsibility to know their students as people.

Conferences with parents will be more successful if the teacher is able to use effective communication skills. Listening is an important element. ▼

Conferences with parents are often expected of teachers in elementary school and can be equally important in junior high and high school. Clearly, the more skilled teachers are at communicating, the more effective they will be at conducting these conferences. Listening and problem-solving skills such as those discussed in Chapter 12 can be particularly important. When you are dealing with parents or students who are angry or upset, make sure you really hear the concerns of the participants, not just their words. The atmosphere should be friendly and unrushed. Any observations about the student should be as factual as possible, based on observation or information from assignments. Information gained from a student or a parent should be kept confidential. The Family and Community Partnerships Guidelines offer some helpful ideas for planning and conducting conferences.

An important federal law, the Buckley Amendment, may affect you as a teacher. Also called the Family Educational Rights and Privacy Act of 1974 and the Educational Amendments Act of 1974, this law states that all educational agencies must make test results and any other information in students' records available to the students and/or their parents. If the records contain information students or parents believe is incorrect, they can challenge such entries and have the information removed if they win the challenge. This means that the information in a student's records must be based on firm, defensible evidence. Tests must be valid and reliable. Your grades must be justified by thorough assessment and observation. Comments and anecdotes about students must be accurate and fair.

CHECKPOINT

Beyond Grading: Communication

Review

 How can communication with families support learning?

Apply

 Evaluate a parent conference you have seen.

Formative and Summative Assessment

What are two kinds of classroom assessment?

Most teachers must assess students and assign grades. Many schools have established policies about testing and grading practices, but individual teachers decide how these practices will be carried out. In the classroom, assessment may be formative (ungraded, diagnostic) or summative (graded). Formative assessment helps form instruction, and summative assessment summarizes students' accomplishments.

Getting the Most from Traditional Assessment Approaches

How should teachers plan for assessment?

Assessment requires planning. Learning is supported by frequent testing using cumulative questions that ask students to apply and integrate knowledge. With the goals of assessment in mind, teachers are in a better position to design their own tests or evaluate the tests provided by textbook publishers.

Describe two kinds of traditional testing.

Two traditional formats for testing are the objective test and the essay test. Objective tests, which can include multiple-choice, true/false, fill-in, and matching items, should be written with specific guidelines in mind. Writing and scoring essay questions requires careful planning, in addition to criteria to discourage bias in scoring. Essay tests are susceptible to biases such as grading essays higher when they are longer or written in elaborate prose.

Innovations in Assessment

What is authentic assessment?

Critics of traditional testing believe that teachers should use authentic tests and other authentic assessment procedures. Authentic assessment requires students to perform tasks and solve problems that are similar to the real-life performances that will be expected of them outside of school.

Describe portfolios and exhibitions.

Portfolios and exhibitions are two examples of authentic assessment. A portfolio is a collection of the student's work, sometimes chosen to represent growth or improvement or sometimes featuring "best work." Exhibitions are public performances of the student's understandings. With portfolios and exhibitions there is an emphasis on performing real-life tasks in meaningful contexts. Evaluating alternative assessments requires judgment and attention to validity, reliability, generalizability, and equity, just as with all assessment.

Effects of Grades and Grading on Students

How can failure support learning?

Students need experience in coping with failure, so standards must be high enough to encourage effort. Occasional failure can be positive if appropriate feedback is provided. Students who never learn how to cope with failure and persist in learning may give up quickly when their first efforts are unsuccessful.

Which is better, social promotion or being "held back"?

Simply retaining or promoting a student who is having difficulty will not guarantee that the student will learn. Unless the student is very young or emotionally immature compared to others in the class, the best approach may be to promote, but provide extra support such as tutoring or summer school sessions.

Can feedback, including grades, promote learning and motivation?

Written or oral feedback that includes specific comments on errors or faulty strategies, but balances this criticism with suggestions about how to improve, along with comments on the positive aspects of the work, increases learning. Grades can encourage students' motivation to learn if they are tied to meaningful learning.

Grading and Reporting: Nuts and Bolts

Describe two kinds of grading.

Grading can be either criterion-referenced or norm-referenced. Criterion-referenced report cards usually indicate how well each of several objectives has been met by the individual student. One popular norm-referenced system is grading on the curve, based on a ranking of students in relation to the average performance level.

What is the point system?

Tests and papers are often scored on a point system. Many schools use percentage grading systems, but the difficulty of the tests and the scoring criteria often influence the results. The difference between a B and a C may only be a matter of one or two points on paper, but the effect of the difference can be large for a student.

Describe some alternatives to traditional grading.

Alternatives to traditional grading are the contract, ILE, and dual marking approaches. Whatever system you use, you will have to decide whether you want to grade on effort, improvement, or some combination and whether you want to limit the number of good grades available.

What are some sources of bias in grading?

Many factors besides quality of work can influence grades: the teacher's beliefs about the student's ability or effort or the student's general classroom behavior, for example.

Beyond Grading: Communication

How can communication with families support learning?

Not every communication from the teacher needs to be tied to a grade. Communication with students and parents can be important in helping a teacher understand students and present effective instruction by creating a consistent learning environment. Students and parents have a legal right to see all the information in the students' records, so the contents of files must be appropriate, accurate, and supported by evidence.

Key Terms

authentic tests, p. 564
contract system, p. 581
criterion-referenced grading, p. 575
curriculum-based assessment (CBA), p. 557
data-based instruction, p. 557
diagnostic test, p. 556
distractors, p. 560

dual marking system, p. 582
exhibition, p. 567
formative assessment, p. 556
grading on the curve, p. 576
halo effect, p. 583
individual learning expectation (ILE), p. 582
norm-referenced grading, p. 576

objective testing, p. 559
percentage grading, p. 580
portfolio, p. 567
pretest, p. 556
revise option, p. 581
scoring rubrics, p. 569
stem, p. 560
summative assessment, p. 557

Becoming a Professional

Reflecting on the Chapter

Can you apply the ideas from this chapter on classroom assessment and grading to solve the following problems of practice?

Preschool and Kindergarten

▶ The parents of several children in your class want a report about how their daughters and sons are "progressing" in preschool. How would you respond to their requests? What kind of assessment and reporting would be helpful for your young students?

Elementary and Middle School

▶ During a parent–teacher conference, a mother and father accuse you of playing favorites and giving their child low grades "just because he's different." How would you respond?

Junior High and High School

▶ Several students are very unhappy with the grades on their term projects. They come to you for an explanation and to try to get you to raise their grades. What would you do?

▶ Your school requires percentage grading, but you would prefer a different system. How would you make a case for your alternative?

Certification Test Requirements

▶ Know the differences between formative and summative assessments.

▶ Understand the characteristics of authentic assessment.

▶ Be familiar with different ways of determining grades.

▶ Know the requirements of the Buckley law.

Your Teaching Portfolio

Think about your philosophy of teaching. What do you believe about testing and grading? How will you assign grades? (Consult the Guidelines for ideas.)

Develop a grading plan for the grade level you want to teach and add it to your **Portfolio**.

Add some ideas for parent involvement from this chapter to your **Portfolio**.

Teaching Resources

Adapt the Guidelines for developing rubrics for the age group you plan to teach.

Add Table 15.1, "Key Points to Consider in Judging Textbook Tests," and Table 15.3, "Characteristics of Authentic Tests," to your **Teaching Resources** file.

Add Figure 15.2, "Three Ways of Rating an Oral Presentation," and Figure 15.3, "Self and Peer Evaluation of Group Learning," to your **Teaching Resources** file.

What Would They Do?

Here is how some practicing teachers responded to the teaching situation presented at the beginning of this chapter about setting up a system to give letter grades.

KATIE CHURCHILL

Third Grade Teacher
Oriole Parke Elementary School, Chicago, Illinois

I would use a combination of assessment tools to evaluate my students. Using a rubric that students and parents alike are familiar with provides an easy-to-follow and understand grading system. The rubric needs to remain in a focal area in the classroom as a constant reminder to the students of what their expectations are.

By differentiating instruction consistently to cover all learning styles and modalities, the students would hopefully become more involved and invested in their own learning and, as a result, produce better quality work and exceed expectations.

Several factors would play a part in obtaining a particular letter grade. The letter grade would be earned through a combination of group work, completing objectives, and following the rubric quidelines for quality work.

MADYA AYALA

High School Teacher of Preperatoria Eugenio Garza Lagüera
Campus Garza Sada, Monterrey, N.L. Mexico

I think it is important to assess a cross-section of student work. First, portfolios can be a useful way to gather various types of work throughout the year. Using a portfolio, a teacher can then attach a letter grade to student progress and achievement. It is important to grade children not only on progress, but also on their understanding of material. I would use meaningful, written assessments to test for retention and understanding of my students' knowledge. Finally, I would grade various projects and experiments so that the students who are better project-based learners will be graded fairly. I also like the idea of using a rubric system to grade students on writing or projects.

Under a rubric system, a teacher allocates a certain number of points to each content area. It is then easy to attach a letter grade based on the number of points received.

Feedback for the progress is very useful to reach objectives, although the teacher should also evaluate the achievement of the students. She already uses qualitative values as satisfactory or unsatisfactory progress. If the school's politics demand grading with letters, I would not forget about feedback; this is an important strategy that all the teachers must do to supervise the students' performance, besides giving the opportunity to develop critical thinking, strategic thinking, metacognition, etc. I would teach the students to supervise their own performance and that of others (of course, depending on age and how long the school term lasts).

My strategy would be:

Training:

▶ Teach them to elaborate criteria.
▶ Make them aware of the difference between feedback and grading.
▶ Train them in feedback.
▶ Train them in giving value to certain tasks related to criteria, considering the teacher's guide.

When the training finishes:

▶ The evaluation criteria are made by the group with teacher assistance.
▶ Students and teacher give feedback to one another in different tasks.
▶ Students and teacher grade the tasks.

KATIE PIEL

Kindergarten–Sixth Grade Teacher
West Park School, Moscow, Idaho

Grades have always been a debatable issue in K–12 classrooms. I will speak from the point of view of an elementary K–6 teacher. I have been faced with the same situation cited above. Like most educators, I would enjoy the freedom to be able to select the assessment and evaluation criteria that best suits both my teaching style and the learning style of my students each year. However, this is not the case, as "A–F" grades are still widely used. In this situation I would review the National Standards, the State Guidelines, and the School District Curriculum Goals. That review would assure me that my curriculum is aligned. I would establish a curriculum for the grading period based on acceptable academic behaviors established by the National, State, and District Guidelines. Then I would clearly spell out the expectations or criteria for each grade. For example, in social science to earn the grade of "A," *all* the listed criteria must be satisfactorily accomplished. In math, to earn a "B," 4/5 of the listed criteria must be satisfactorily met. A grade of "C" in science is earned when 3/5 of the expectations are satisfactorily completed. These standards, criteria, expectations, or rubric must be clearly delineated for the learner, the parent, and the administrator before the grading period begins. Students should be given the latitude to express achievement in different ways like group projects, daily class work, tests, and individual projects. All students would be held accountable for demonstrating their own learning. With each teacher grading on a different standard, the teachers must also take on the responsibility of collaborating with their peers. Communicating to other teachers the skills a student can be expected to bring with him or her to the next level is crucial.

AIMEE FREDETTE

Second Grade Teacher
Fisher Elementary School, Walpole, Massachusetts

I believe that students are not all smart in the same ways. I give the students a variety of ways to demonstrate their knowledge. I also focus on the students' ability to take their knowledge and integrate it into other subject areas across the curriculum.

I use a student portfolio for each child, compiled throughout the year and used to show growth and development. Each time I correct papers I choose a couple of pieces of work that each child has done. I put these papers in the portfolio folder. I try to choose a variety of work, not necessarily their "prize work." At the end of the year the children receive the entire folder to keep.

I individualize the grades for each student. Each child is compared only to himself or herself, using work samples from the portfolio. In order to do this type of assessment, teachers need the support of the school administration. To justify the portfolio type assessment I use, I would simply show the administration or parents the "proof" (the students' actual work) of what a particular student was able to do. Growth and development can be demonstrated more concretely by holding a work sample from September in one hand and a work sample from December in the other.

ALLAN OSBORNE

Assistant Principal
Snug Harbor Community School, Quincy, Massachusetts

Any grading system should consider a student's progress and effort. Grading systems also should be individualized to account for a student's unique strengths and weaknesses. Thus, a mainstreamed special education student should not be held to the same expectations as a gifted student.

The final grade for each marking period should be based on a number of variables. Although tests and quizzes are important methods of ascertaining what has been learned, students should be given the opportunity to demonstrate knowledge through other vehicles as well. For this reason I would ask students to complete long-term projects that demonstrate knowledge in a practical, real-life way. In calculating a final grade for the term, I would place a greater emphasis on assignments that demonstrated practical knowledge on a topic.

Although group assignments can be an important learning experience, I would be reluctant to place too much emphasis on a group project grade. As we all know, each member of the group does not participate equally, and thus, a group grade does not reflect the contribution of each individual member.

The most critical aspect of any successful grading system is that it is fair. Fairness dictates that students and their parents be given information in advance about class requirements and expectations, along with a description of grading criteria. A system that is fair can be easily justified. It is also important to keep accurate and detailed records of student progress. In addition to recording grades on tests, quizzes, and projects, anecdotal records describing a student's typical performance should be kept. These records can be valuable if a report card grade is questioned.

Glossary

Absence Seizure: A seizure involving only a small part of the brain that causes a child to lose contact briefly.

Academic Learning Time: Time when students are actually succeeding at the learning task.

Academic Tasks: The work the student must accomplish, including the mental operations required, the resources provided, and the product expected.

Accommodation: Altering existing schemes or creating new ones in response to new information.

Achievement Tests: Standardized tests measuring how much students have learned in a given content area.

Acronym: Technique for remembering names, phrases, or steps by using the first letter of each word to form a new, memorable word.

Action Zone: Area of a classroom where the greatest amount of interaction takes place.

Active Teaching: Teaching characterized by high levels of teacher explanation, demonstration, and interaction with students.

Adaptation: Adjustment to the environment.

Adolescent Egocentrism: Assumption that everyone else shares one's thoughts, feelings, and concerns.

Advance Organizer: Statement of inclusive concepts to introduce and sum up material that follows.

Affective Domain: Objectives focusing on attitudes and feelings.

Affective Education: Education focusing on emotional growth.

Aggression: Bold, direct action that is intended to hurt someone else or take property; unprovoked attack.

Algorithm: Step-by-step procedure for solving a problem; prescription for solutions.

Allocated Time: Time set aside for learning.

Americans with Disabilities Act (ADA): Legislation prohibiting discrimination against persons with disabilities in employment, transportation, public access, local government, and telecommunications.

Analogical Thinking: Heuristic in which one limits the search for solutions to situations that are similar to the one at hand.

Anchored Instruction: A type of problem-based learning that uses a complex interesting situation as an anchor for learning.

Androgynous: Having some typically male and some typically female characteristics apparent in one individual.

Anorexia Nervosa: Eating disorder characterized by very limited food intake.

Antecedents: Events that precede an action.

Anxiety: General uneasiness, a feeling of tension.

Applied Behavior Analysis: The application of behavioral learning principles to understand and change behavior.

Aptitude Tests: Tests meant to predict future performance.

Arousal: Physical and psychological reactions causing a person to be alert, attentive, wide awake.

Articulation Disorders: Any of a variety of pronunciation difficulties, such as the substitution, distortion, or omission of sounds.

Articulatory Loop: A memory rehearsal system of about 1.5 seconds.

Assertive Discipline: Clear, firm, unhostile response style.

Assessment: Procedures used to obtain information about student performance.

Assimilation: Fitting new information into existing schemes.

Assisted Learning: Providing strategic help in the initial stages of learning, gradually diminishing as students gain independence.

Associative Stage: Individual steps of a procedure are combined or "chunked" into larger units.

Attainment Value: The importance of doing well on a task; how success on the task meets personal needs.

Attention: Focus on a stimulus.

Attention-Deficit/Hyperactive Disorder: Current term for disruptive behavior disorders marked by overactivity, excessive difficulty sustaining attention, or impulsiveness.

Attribution Theories: Descriptions of how individuals' explanations, justifications, and excuses influence their motivation and behavior.

Authentic Assessment: Measurement of important abilities using procedures that simulate the application of these abilities to real-life problems.

Authentic Task: Tasks that have some connection to real-life problems the students will face outside the classroom.

Authentic Tests: Assessment procedures that test skills and abilities as they would be applied in real-life situations.

Authoritarian Personality: Rigidly conforming to the belief that society is naturally competitive, with "better" people reaping its rewards.

Automated Basic Skills: Skills that are applied without conscious thought.

Automaticity: The result of learning to perform a behavior or thinking process so thoroughly that the performance is automatic and does not require effort.

Autonomous Stage: Final stage in the learning of automated skills. The procedure is fine-tuned and becomes "automatic."

Autonomy: Independence.

Aversive: Irritating or unpleasant.

Basic Skills: Clearly structured knowledge that is needed for later learning and that can be taught step by step.

Behavior Modification: Systematic application of antecedents and consequences to change behavior.

Behavioral Learning Theories: Explanations of learning that focus on external events as the cause of changes in observable behaviors.

Behavioral Objectives: Instructional objectives stated in terms of observable behaviors.

Being Needs: Maslow's three higher-level needs, sometimes called growth needs.

Between-Class Ability Grouping: System of grouping in which students are assigned to classes based on their measured ability or their achievements.

Bilingualism: Speaking two languages fluently.

Bimodal Distribution: Frequency distribution with two modes.

Blended Families: Parents, children, and stepchildren merged into families through remarriages.

Bottom-Up Processing: Perceiving based on noticing separate defining features and assembling them into a recognizable pattern.

Brainstorming: Generating ideas without stopping to evaluate them.

Bulimia: Eating disorder characterized by overeating, then getting rid of the food by self-induced vomiting or laxatives.

CAPS: A strategy that can be used in reading literature: *Characters, Aim* of story, *Problem, Solution.*

Case Study: Intensive study of one person or one situation.

Central Tendency: Typical score for a group of scores.

Cerebral Palsy: Condition involving a range of motor or coordination difficulties due to brain damage.

Certification Tests: In many states, teachers are required to take standardized tests, such as the Praxis series designed by the Educational Testing Service, in order to be certified or licensed as a teacher.

Chain Mnemonics: Memory strategies that associate one element in a series with the next element.

Chunking: Grouping individual bits of data into meaningful larger units.

Classical Conditioning: Association of automatic responses with new stimuli.

Classification: Grouping objects into categories.

Classroom Management: Techniques used to maintain a healthy learning environment, relatively free of behavior problems.

Co-constructed Process: A social process in which people interact and negotiate (usually verbally) to create an understanding or to solve a problem. The final product is shaped by all participants.

Coding System: A hierarchy of ideas or concepts.

Cognitive Apprenticeship: A relationship in which a less experienced learner acquires knowledge and skills under the guidance of an expert.

Cognitive Behavior Modification: Procedures based on both behavioral and cognitive learning principles for changing your own behavior by using self-talk and self-instruction.

Cognitive Development: Gradual orderly changes by which mental processes become more complex and sophisticated.

Cognitive Domain: In Bloom's taxonomy, memory and reasoning objectives.

Cognitive Evaluation Theory: Suggests that events affect motivation through the individual's perception of the events as controlling behavior or providing information.

Cognitive Monitoring: Monitoring of our thinking and learning strategies.

Cognitive Objectives: Instructional objectives stated in terms of higher-level thinking operations.

Cognitive Stage: The initial learning of an automated skill when we rely on general problem-solving approaches to make sense of steps or procedures.

Cognitive Styles: Different ways of perceiving and organizing information.

Cognitive View of Learning: A general approach that views learning as an active mental process of acquiring, remembering, and using knowledge.

Collective Monologue: Form of speech in which children in a group talk but do not really interact or communicate.

Collective Self-Esteem: Beliefs about the worth of the groups you belong to.

Community of Practice: Social situation or context in which ideas are judged useful or true.

Compensation: The principle that changes in one dimension can be offset by changes in another.

Complex Learning Environments: Problems and learning situations that mimic the ill-structured nature of real life.

Components: In an information-processing view, basic problem-solving processes underlying intelligence.

Concept: A general category of ideas, objects, people, or experiences whose members share certain properties.

Concept Mapping: Student's diagram of his or her understanding of a concept.

Conceptual Change Teaching in Science: A method that helps students understand (rather than memorize) concepts in science by using and challenging the students' current ideas.

Concrete Operations: Mental tasks tied to concrete objects and situations.

Conditional Knowledge: "Knowing when and why" to use declarative and procedural knowledge.

Conditioned Response (CR): Learned response to a previously neutral stimulus.

Conditioned Stimulus (CS): Stimulus that evokes an emotional or physiological response after conditioning.

Confidence Interval: Range of scores within which an individual's particular score is likely to fall.

Consequences: Events that follow an action.

Conservation: Principle that some characteristics of an object remain the same despite changes in appearance.

Constructed-Response Format: Assessment procedures that require the student to create an answer instead of selecting an answer from a set of choices.

Constructivism (also **Constructivist Approach**): View that emphasizes the active role of the learner in building understanding and making sense of information.

Context: The physical or emotional backdrop associated with an event.

Contiguity: Association of two events because of repeated pairing.

Contingency Contract: A contract between the teacher and an individual student specifying what the student must do to earn a particular privilege or reward.

Continuous Reinforcement Schedule: Presenting a reinforcer after every appropriate response.

Contract System: System in which each student works for a particular grade according to agreed-upon standards.

Convergent Questions: Questions that have a single correct answer.

Convergent Thinking: Narrowing possibilities to a single answer.

Cooperative Integrated Reading and Composition (CIRC): Cooperative learning technique in which pairs of students from each reading group work together on reading and writing projects, then teams are rewarded on the basis of their work.

Cooperative Learning: Arrangement in which students work in mixed-ability groups and are rewarded on the basis of the success of the group.

Cooperative Teaching: Collaboration between regular and special education teachers.

Correlations: Statistical descriptions of how closely two variables are related.

Creativity: Imaginative, original thinking or problem solving.

Criterion-Referenced Grading: Assessment of each student's mastery of course objectives.

Criterion-Referenced Testing: Testing in which scores are compared to a set performance standard.

Critical Thinking: Evaluating conclusions by logically and systematically examining the problem, the evidence, and the solution.

Cueing: Providing a stimulus that "sets up" a desired behavior.

Cultural Deficit Model: A model that explains the school achievement problems of ethnic minority students by assuming that their culture is inadequate and does not prepare them to succeed in school.

Cultural Tools: The real tools (computers, scales, etc.) and symbol systems (numbers, language, graphs) that allow people in a society to communicate, think, solve problems, and create knowledge.

Culturally Compatible Classrooms: Classrooms in which procedures, rules, grouping strategies, attitudes, and teaching methods do not cause conflicts with the students' culturally influenced ways of learning and interacting.

Culturally Relevant Pedagogy: Excellent teaching for students of color that includes academic success, developing/maintaining cultural competence, and critical consciousness to challenge the status quo.

Culture: The knowledge, values, attitudes, and traditions that guide the behavior of a group of people and allow them to solve the problems of living in their environment.

Culture-Fair/Culture-Free Test: A test without cultural bias.

Curriculum-Based Assessment (CBA): Evaluation method using frequent tests of specific skills and knowledge.

Data-Based Instruction: Assessment method using daily probes of specific-skill mastery.

Decay: The weakening and fading of memories with the passage of time.

Decentering: Focusing on more than one aspect at a time.

Declarative Knowledge: Verbal information; facts; "knowing that" something is the case.

Deductive Reasoning: Drawing conclusions by applying rules or principles; logically moving from a general rule or principle to a specific solution.

Deficiency Needs: Maslow's four lower-level needs, which must be satisfied first.

Defining Attributes: Distinctive features shared by members of a category.

Descriptive Studies: Studies that collect detailed information about specific situations, often using observation, surveys, interviews, recordings, or a combination of these methods.

Development: Orderly, adaptive changes we go through from conception to death.

Developmental Crisis: A specific conflict whose resolution prepares the way for the next stage.

Deviation IQ: Score based on statistical comparison of individual's performance with the average performance of others in that age group.

Diagnostic Tests: There are two types: (1) formative tests to determine students' areas of weakness, and (2) individually administered tests to identify special learning problems.

Dialect: Rule-governed variation of a language spoken by a particular group.

Direct Instruction/Explicit Teaching: Systematic instruction for mastery of basic skills, facts, and information.

Disability: The inability to do something specific such as walk or hear.

Discovery Learning: Bruner's approach, in which students work on their own to discover basic principles.

Discrimination (in learning): Responding differently to similar, but not identical stimuli.

Discrimination: Treating particular categories of people unequally.

Disequilibrium: In Piaget's theory, the "out-of-balance" state that occurs when a person realizes that his or her current ways of thinking are not working to solve a problem or understand a situation.

Distractors: Wrong answers offered as choices in a multiple-choice item.

Distributed Practice: Practice in brief periods with rest intervals.

Divergent Questions: Questions that have no single correct answer.

Divergent Thinking: Coming up with many possible solutions.

Domain-Specific Knowledge: Information that is useful in a particular situation or that applies only to one specific topic.

Domain-Specific Strategies: Consciously applied skills to reach goals in a particular subject or problem area.

Dual Marking System: System of assigning two grades, one reflecting achievement, the other effort, attitude, and actual ability.

Educational Psychology: The discipline concerned with teaching and learning processes; applies the methods and theories of psychology and has its own as well.

Educationally Blind: Needing Braille materials in order to learn.

Eg-Rule Method: Teaching or learning by moving from specific examples to general rules.

Ego-Involved Learners: Students who focus on how well they are performing and how they are judged by others.

Egocentric: Assuming that others experience the world the way you do.

Elaboration: Adding and extending meaning by connecting new information to existing knowledge.

Elaborative Rehearsal: Keeping information in working memory by associating it with something else you already know.

Emotional Intelligence (EQ): Abilities to monitor your own and others' feelings and emotions, and to use this information to guide thinking and actions.

Empathetic Listening: Hearing the intent and emotions behind what another says and reflecting them back by paraphrasing.

Engaged Time: Time spent actively learning.

English as a Second Language (ESL): Designation for programs and classes to teach English to students who are not native speakers of English.

Entity View of Ability: Belief that ability is a fixed characteristic that cannot be changed.

Epilepsy: Disorder marked by seizures and caused by abnormal electrical discharges in the brain.

Episodic Memory: Long-term memory for information tied to a particular time and place, especially memory of the events in a person's life.

Equilibration: Search for mental balance between cognitive schemes and information from the environment.

Ethnic Pride: A positive self-concept about one's racial or ethnic heritage.

Ethnicity: A cultural heritage shared by a group of people.

Ethnography: A descriptive approach to research that focuses on life within a group and tries to understand the meaning of events to the people involved.

Evaluation: Decision making about student performance and about appropriate teaching strategies.

Exceptional Students: Students who have abilities or problems so significant that the students require special education or other services to reach their potential.

Executive Control Processes: Processes such as selective attention, rehearsal, elaboration, and organization that influence encoding, storage, and retrieval of information in memory.

Exemplar: A specific example of a given category that is used to classify an item.

Exhibition: A performance test or demonstration of learning that is public and usually takes an extended time to prepare.

Expectancy x Value Theories: Explanations of motivation that emphasize individuals' expectations for success combined with their valuing of the goal.

Experimentation: Research method in which variables are manipulated and the effects recorded.

Expert Teachers: Experienced, effective teachers who have developed solutions for common classroom problems. Their knowledge of teaching process and content is extensive and well organized.

Explanatory Links: Words and phrases such as *because* and *in order to* that specify the relationships between ideas.

Expository Teaching: Ausubel's method—teachers present material in complete, organized form, moving from broadest to more specific concepts.

Extinction: Gradual disappearance of a learned response.

Extrinsic Motivation: Motivation created by external factors like rewards and punishments.

Failure-Accepting Students: Students who believe their failures are due to low ability and there is little they can do about it.

Failure-Avoiding Students: Students who avoid failure by sticking to what they know, by not taking risks, or by claiming not to care about their performance.

Field Dependence: Cognitive style in which patterns are perceived as wholes.

Field Independence: Cognitive style in which separate parts of a pattern are perceived and analyzed.

Fine-Motor Skills: Voluntary body movements that involve the small muscles.

Finger Spelling: Communication system that "spells out" each letter with a hand position.

Formal Operations: Mental tasks involving abstract thinking and coordination of a number of variables.

Formative Assessment: Ungraded testing used before or during instruction to aid in planning and diagnosis.

Frequency Distribution: Record showing how many scores fall into set groups.

Full Inclusion: The integration of all students, including those with severe disabilities, into regular classes.

Functional Fixedness: Inability to use objects or tools in a new way.

Gender Biases: Different views of males and females, often favoring one gender over the other.

Gender-Role Identity: Beliefs about characteristics and behaviors associated with one sex as opposed to the other.

Gender Schemas: Organized networks of knowledge about what it means to be male or female.

General Knowledge: Information that is useful in many different kinds of tasks; information that applies to many situations.

Generalization: Responding in the same way to similar stimuli.

Generalized Seizure: A seizure involving a large portion of the brain.

Generativity: Sense of concern for future generations.

Gestalt: German for pattern or whole; Gestalt theorists hold that people organize their perceptions into coherent wholes.

Gifted Student: A very bright, creative, and talented student.

Goal-Directed Actions: Deliberate actions toward a goal.

Goal Structure: The way students relate to others who are also working toward a particular goal.

Good Behavior Game: Arrangement where a class is divided into teams and each team receives demerit points for breaking agreed-upon rules of good behavior.

Grade-Equivalent Score: Measure of grade level based on comparison with norming samples from each grade.

Graded Membership: The extent to which something belongs to a category.

Grading on the Curve: Norm-referenced grading that compares students' performance to an average level.

Gross-Motor Skills: Voluntary body movements that involve the large muscles.

Group Consequences: Rewards or punishments given to a class as a whole for adhering to or violating rules of conduct.

Group Discussion: Conversation in which the teacher does not have the dominant role; students pose and answer their own questions.

Group Focus: The ability to keep as many students as possible involved in activities.

Guided Discovery: An adaptation of discovery learning, in which the teacher provides some direction.

Halo Effect: The tendency for a general impression of a person to influence our perception of any aspect of that person.

Handicap: A disadvantage in a particular situation, sometimes caused by a disability.

Heuristic: General strategy used in attempting to solve problems.

Hierarchy of Needs: Maslow's model of seven levels of human needs, from basic physiological requirements to the need for self-actualization.

High-Road Transfer: Application of abstract knowledge learned in one situation to a different situation.

High-Stakes Testing: Standardized tests whose results have powerful influences when used by school administrators, other officials, or employers to make decisions.

Histogram: Bar graph of a frequency distribution.

Holistic Scoring: Evaluation of a piece of written work as a whole, without separate grades for individual elements.

Humanistic View: Approach to motivation that emphasizes personal freedom, choice, self-determination, and striving for personal growth.

Hyperactivity: Behavior disorder marked by atypical, excessive restlessness and inattentiveness.

Hypothetico-Deductive Reasoning: A formal-operations problem-solving strategy in which an individual begins by identifying all the factors that might affect a problem and then deduces and systematically evaluates specific solutions.

"I" Message: Clear, nonaccusatory statement of how something is affecting you.

Identity (in cognitive development): Principle that a person or object remains the same over time.

Identity (in personal/social development): The complex answer to the question, "Who am I?"

Identity Achievement: Strong sense of commitment to life choices after free consideration of alternatives.

Identity Diffusion: Uncenteredness; confusion about who one is and what one wants.

Identity Foreclosure: Acceptance of parental life choices without consideration of options.

Images: Representations based on the physical attributes—the appearance—of information.

Impulsive: Characterized by cognitive style of responding quickly but often inaccurately.

Incentive: An object or event that encourages or discourages behavior.

Incremental View of Ability: Belief that ability is a set of skills that can be changed.

Individual Learning Expectation (ILE): Constantly recomputed average score in a subject.

Individualized Education Program (IEP): Annually revised program for an exceptional student, detailing present achievement level, goals, and strategies, drawn up by teachers, parents, specialists, and (if possible) student.

Individuals with Disabilities Education Act (IDEA): Amendment to PL 94–142.

Inductive Reasoning: Formulating general principles based on knowledge of examples and details.

Industry: Eagerness to engage in productive work.

Information Processing: Human mind's activity of taking in, storing, and using information.

Initiative: Willingness to begin new activities and explore new directions.

Inquiry Learning: Approach in which the teacher presents a puzzling situation and students solve the problem by gathering data and testing their conclusions.

Insight (in problem solving): Sudden realization of a solution.

Insight (in Sternberg's theory of intelligence): The ability to deal effectively with novel situations.

Instructional Conversation: Situation in which students learn through interactions with teachers and/or other students.

Instructional Objective: Clear statement of what students are intended to learn through instruction.

Integrity: Sense of self-acceptance and fulfillment.

Intelligence: Ability or abilities to acquire and use knowledge for solving problems and adapting to the world.

Intelligence Quotient (IQ): Score comparing mental and chronological ages.

Interference: The process that occurs when remembering certain information is hampered by the presence of other information.

Intermittent Reinforcement Schedule: Presenting a reinforcer after some but not all responses.

Internalize: Process whereby children adopt external standards as their own.

Intersubjective Attitude: A commitment to build shared meaning with others by finding common ground and exchanging interpretations.

Interval Schedule: Length of time between reinforcers.

Intrinsic Motivation: Motivation associated with activities that are their own reward.

Intrinsic or Interest Value: The enjoyment a person gets from a task.

Intuitive Thinking: Making imaginative leaps to correct perceptions or workable solutions.

Jigsaw: A cooperative structure in which each member of a group is responsible for teaching other members one section of the material.

Keyword Method: System of associating new words or concepts with similar-sounding cue words and images.

KWL Plus: A strategy to guide reading and inquiry: Before—What do I already *know*? What do I *want* to know? After—What have I *learned*?

Lateralization: The specialization of the two hemispheres (sides) of the brain cortex.

Learned Helplessness: The expectation, based on previous experiences with a lack of control, that all one's efforts will lead to failure.

Learning: Process through which experience causes permanent change in knowledge or behavior.

Learning Disability: Problem with acquisition and use of language; may show up as difficulty with reading, writing, reasoning, or math.

Learning Goal: A personal intention to improve abilities and understand, no matter how performance suffers.

Learning Preferences: Preferred ways of studying and learning, such as using pictures instead of text, working with other people versus alone, learning in structured or in unstructured situations, and so on.

Learning Propensity Assessment Device: Innovative method for testing the student's ability to benefit from teaching, consistent with Vygotsky's theory of cognitive development.

Learning Strategies: General plans for approaching learning tasks.

Learning Styles: Characteristic approaches to learning and studying.

Learning Tactics: Specific techniques for learning, such as using mnemonics or outlining a passage.

Least Restrictive Placement: Placement of each child in as normal an educational setting as possible.

Lecturing: Organized explanation of a topic by a teacher.

Legitimate Peripheral Participation: Genuine involvement in the work of the group, even if your abilities are undeveloped and contributions are small.

Levels of Processing Theory: Theory that recall of information is based on how deeply it is processed.

Limited English Proficiency (LEP): Descriptive term for students who have limited mastery of English.

Linguistic Comprehension: Understanding of the meaning of sentences in word problems.

Loci Method: Technique of associating items with specific places.

Locus of Causality: The location—internal or external—of the cause of behavior.

Long-Term Memory: Permanent store of knowledge.

Low-Road Transfer: Spontaneous and automatic transfer of highly practiced skills.

Low Vision: Vision limited to close objects.

Mainstreaming: Teaching children with disabilities in regular classes for part or all of their school day.

Maintenance Rehearsal: Keeping information in working memory by repeating it to yourself.

Massed Practice: Practice for a single extended period.

Mastery Experiences: Our own direct experiences—the most powerful source of efficacy information.

Mastery Learning: Teaching approach—students must learn one unit and pass a test at a specified level before moving to the next unit.

Mastery-Oriented Students: Students who focus on learning goals because they value achievement and see ability as improvable.

Maturation: Genetically programmed, naturally occurring changes over time.

Mean: Arithmetical average.

Meaningful Verbal Learning: Focused and organized relationships among ideas and verbal information.

Means-Ends Analysis: Heuristic in which a goal is divided into subgoals.

Measurement: An evaluation expressed in quantitative (number) terms.

Median: Middle score in a group of scores.

Melting Pot: A metaphor for the absorption and assimilation of immigrants into the mainstream of society so that ethnic differences vanish.

Memory Strength: The durability of a memory; if information is well learned, it is more durable.

Mental Age: In intelligence testing, a score based on average abilities for that age group.

Mental Retardation: Significantly below-average intellectual and adaptive social behavior, evident before age 18.

Metacognition: Knowledge about our own thinking processes.

Metalinguistic Awareness: Understanding about one's own use of language.

Minimum Competency Test: Standardized test meant to determine if students meet minimum requirements to graduate or to proceed in school.

Minority Group: A group of people who have been socially disadvantaged—not always a minority in actual numbers.

Mnemonics: Techniques for remembering; also, the art of memory.

Mode: Most frequently occurring score.

Modeling: Changes in behavior, thinking, or emotions that occur through observing another person—a model.

Monolinguals: Individuals who speak only one language.

Moral Dilemmas: Situations in which no choice is clearly and indisputably right.

Moral Realism: Stage of development wherein children see rules as absolute.

Moral Reasoning: The thinking process involved in judgments about questions of right and wrong.

Morality of Cooperation: Stage of development wherein children realize that people make rules and people can change them.

Moratorium: Identity crisis; suspension of choices because of struggle.

Motivation: An internal state that arouses, directs, and maintains behavior.

Motivation to Learn: The tendency to find academic activities meaningful and worthwhile and to try to benefit from them.

Movement Management: Keeping lessons and the group moving at an appropriate (and flexible) pace, with smooth transitions and variety.

Multicultural Education: Education that teaches the value of cultural diversity.

Multiple Intelligences: In Gardner's theory of intelligence, a person's eight separate abilities: logical-mathematical, verbal, musical, spatial, bodily-kinesthetic, interpersonal, intrapersonal, and naturalist.

Multiple Representations of Content: Considering problems using various analogies, examples, and metaphors.

Myelination: The process by which neural fibers are coated with a fatty sheath called myelin that makes message transfer more efficient.

Negative Correlation: A relationship between two variables in which a high value on one is associated with a low value on the other. Example: height and distance from top of head to the ceiling.

Negative Reinforcement: Strengthening behavior by removing an aversive stimulus when the behavior occurs.

Neo-Piagetian Theories: More recent theories that integrate findings about attention, memory, and strategy use with Piaget's insights about children's thinking and the construction of knowledge.

Neutral Stimulus: Stimulus not connected to a response.

Nongraded Elementary School/The Joplin Plan: Arrangement wherein students are grouped by ability in particular subjects, regardless of their ages or grades.

Norm Groups: A group whose average score serves as a standard for evaluating any student's score on a test.

Norm-Referenced Grading: Assessment of students' achievement in relation to one another.

Norm-Referenced Testing: Testing in which scores are compared with the average performance of others.

Normal Distribution: The most commonly occurring distribution, in which scores are distributed evenly around the mean.

Norming Sample: Large sample of students serving as a comparison group for scoring standardized tests.

Object Permanence: The understanding that objects have a separate, permanent existence.

Objective Testing: Multiple-choice, matching, true/false, short-answer, and fill-in tests; scoring answers does not require interpretation.

Observational Learning: Learning by observation and imitation of others.

Operant Conditioning: Learning in which voluntary behavior is strengthened or weakened by consequences or antecedents.

Operants: Voluntary (and generally goal-directed) behaviors emitted by a person or an animal.

Operations: Actions a person carries out by thinking them through instead of literally performing the actions.

Organization (in Piaget's theory): Ongoing process of arranging information and experience into mental systems or categories.

Organization (in information processing): Ordered and logical network of relations.

Orthopedic Devices: Devices such as braces and wheelchairs that aid people with physical disabilities.

Overgeneralization: Inclusion of nonmembers in a category; overextending a concept.

Overlapping: Supervising several activities at once.

Overlearning: Practicing a skill past the point of mastery.

Paraphrase Rule: Policy whereby listeners must accurately summarize what a speaker has said before being allowed to respond.

Part Learning: Breaking a list of rote learning items into shorter lists.

Participant Observation: A method for conducting descriptive research in which the researcher becomes a participant in the situation in order to better understand life in that group.

Participation Structures: The formal and informal rules for how to take part in a given activity.

Peg-Type Mnemonics: Systems of associating items with cue words.

Percentage Grading: System of converting class performances to percentage scores and assigning grades based on predetermined cutoff points.

Percentile Rank: Percentage of those in the norming sample who scored at or below an individual's score.

Perception: Interpretation of sensory information.

Performance Goal: A personal intention to seem competent or perform well in the eyes of others.

Personal Development: Changes in personality that take place as one grows.

Perspective-Taking Ability: Understanding that others have different feelings and experiences.

Physical Development: Changes in body structure and function over time.

Portfolio: A collection of the student's work in an area, showing growth, self-reflection, and achievement.

Positive Correlation: A relationship between two variables in which the two increase or decrease together. Example: calorie intake and weight gain.

Positive Practice: Practicing correct responses immediately after errors.

Positive Reinforcement: Strengthening behavior by presenting a desired stimulus after the behavior.

PQ4R: A method for studying text that involves six steps: Preview, Question, Read, Reflect, Recite, Review.

Prejudice: Prejudgment, or irrational generalization about an entire category of people.

Premack Principle: Principle stating that a more-preferred activity can serve as reinforcer for a less-preferred activity.

Preoperational: The stage before a child masters logical mental operations.

Presentation Punishment: Decreasing the chances that a behavior will occur again by presenting an aversive stimulus following the behavior; also called Type I punishment.

Pretest: Formative test for assessing students' knowledge, readiness, and abilities.

Principle: Established relationship between factors.

Private Speech: Children's self-talk, which guides their thinking and action. Eventually these verbalizations are internalized as silent inner speech.

Problem: Any situation in which you are trying to reach some goal and must find a means to do so.

Problem-Based Learning: Methods that provide students with realistic problems that don't necessarily have "right" answers.

Problem Solving: Creating new solutions for problems.

Procedural Knowledge: Knowledge that is demonstrated when we perform a task; "knowing how."

Procedural Memory: Long-term memory for how to do things.

Procedures: Prescribed steps for an activity.

Productions: The contents of procedural memory; rules about what actions to take, given certain conditions.

Prompt: A reminder that follows a cue to make sure the person reacts to the cue.

Propositional Network: Set of interconnected concepts and relationships in which long-term knowledge is held.

Prototype: Best representative of a category.

Psychomotor Domain: Physical ability and coordination objectives.

Psychosocial: Describing the relation of the individual's emotional needs to the social environment.

Puberty: The period in early adolescence when individuals begin to reach physical and sexual maturity.

Punishment: Process that weakens or suppresses behavior.

Pygmalion Effect: Exceptional progress by a student as a result of high teacher expectations for that student; named for mythological king, Pygmalion, who made a statue, then caused it to be brought to life.

Race: A group of people who share common biological traits that are seen as self-defining by the people of the group.

Radical Constructivism: Theory of knowledge and learning asserting that all knowledge is individually constructed and equally valid.

Random: Without any definite pattern; following no rule.

Range: Distance between the highest and the lowest scores in a group.

Ratio Schedule: Reinforcement based on the number of responses between reinforcers.

Readiness Testing: Testing procedures meant to determine if an individual is ready to proceed to the next level of education or training.

READS: A five-step reading strategy: *Review* headings; *Examine* boldface words; *Ask*, "What do I expect to learn?"; *Do* it—Read; *Summarize* in your own words.

Reciprocal Determinism: An explanation of behavior that emphasizes the mutual effects of the individual and the environment on each other.

Reciprocal Questioning: Approach where groups of two or three students ask and answer each other's questions after a lesson or presentation.

Reciprocal Teaching: A method, based on modeling, to teach reading comprehension strategies.

Recitation: Format of teacher questioning, student response, and teacher feedback.

Reconstruction: Recreating information by using memories, expectations, logic, and existing knowledge.

Reflective (as a cognitive style): Characterized by cognitive style of responding slowly, carefully, and accurately.

Reflective (in teaching): Thoughtful and inventive. Reflective teachers think back over situations to analyze what they did and why and to consider how they might improve learning for their students.

Regular Education Initiative: An educational movement that advocates giving regular education teachers, not special education teachers, responsibility for teaching mildly (and sometimes moderately) handicapped students.

Reinforcement: Use of consequences to strengthen behavior.

Reinforcer: Any event that follows a behavior and increases the chances that the behavior will occur again.

Reliability: Consistency of test results.

Removal Punishment: Decreasing the chances that a behavior will occur again by removing a pleasant stimulus following the behavior; also called Type II punishment.

Reprimands: Criticisms for misbehavior; rebukes.

Resistance Culture: Group values and beliefs about refusing to adopt the behaviors and attitudes of the majority culture.

Resource Room: Classroom with special materials and a specially trained teacher.

Respondents: Responses (generally automatic or involuntary) elicited by specific stimuli.

Response: Observable reaction to a stimulus.

Response Cost: Punishment by loss of reinforcers.

Response Set: Rigidity; tendency to respond in the most familiar way.

Restructuring: Conceiving of a problem in a new or different way.

Retrieval: Process of searching for and finding information in long-term memory.

Reversibility: A characteristic of Piagetian logical operations—the ability to think through a series of steps, then mentally reverse the steps and return to the starting point; also called *reversible thinking*.

Reversible Thinking: Thinking backward, from the end to the beginning.

Revise Option: In a contract system, the chance to revise and improve work.

Reward: An attractive object or event supplied as a consequence of a behavior.

Ripple Effect: "Contagious" spreading of behaviors through imitation.

Rote Memorization: Remembering information by repetition without necessarily understanding the meaning of the information.

Rule-Eg Method: Teaching or learning by moving from general principles to specific examples.

Rules: Statements specifying expected and forbidden behaviors; dos and don'ts.

Satiation: Requiring a person to repeat a problem behavior past the point of interest or motivation.

Scaffolding: Support for learning and problem solving. The support could be clues, reminders, encouragement, breaking the problem down into steps, providing an example, or anything else that allows the student to grow in independence as a learner.

Schema-Driven Problem Solving: Recognizing a problem as a "disguised" version of an old problem for which one already has a solution.

Schemata (singular, Schema): Basic structures for organizing information; concepts.

Schemes: Mental systems or categories of perception and experience.

Scoring Rubrics: Rules that are used to determine the quality of a student performance.

Script: Schema or expected plan for the sequence of steps in a common event such as buying groceries or ordering take-out pizza.

Scripted Cooperation: Learning strategy in which two students take turns summarizing material and criticizing the summaries.

Seatwork: Independent classroom work.

Self-Actualization: Fulfilling one's potential.

Self-Concept: Our perceptions about ourselves.

Self-Determination: The need to experience choice and control in what we do and how we do it.

Self-Efficacy: A person's expectation that he or she would deal effectively with a particular task. A future-oriented judgment.

Self-Esteem: The value each of us places on our own characteristics, abilities, and behaviors.

Self-Fulfilling Prophecy: A groundless expectation that is confirmed because it has been expected.

Self-Instruction: Talking oneself through the steps of a task.

Self-Management: Management of your own behavior and acceptance of responsibility for your own actions.

Self-Management (in behavioral learning theory): Use of behavioral learning principles to change your own behavior.

Self-Regulated Learners: Learners who have a combination of academic learning skills and self-control that makes learning easier; they have the *skill* and the *will* to learn.

Self-Reinforcement: Providing yourself with positive consequences, contingent on accomplishing a particular behavior.

Semantic Memory: Memory for meaning.

Semilingual: Not proficient in any language; speaking one or more languages inadequately.

Semiotic Function: The ability to use symbols—language, pictures, signs, or gestures—to represent actions or objects mentally.

Sensorimotor: Involving the senses and motor activity.

Sensory Memory: System that holds sensory information very briefly.

Serial-Position Effect: The tendency to remember the beginning and the end but not the middle of a list.

Seriation: Arranging objects in sequential order according to one aspect, such as size, weight, or volume.

Shaping: Reinforcing each small step of progress toward a desired goal or behavior.

Short-Term Memory: Working memory, holding a limited amount of information briefly.

Sign Language: Communication system of hand movements that symbolize words and concepts.

Situated Learning: The idea that skills and knowledge are tied to the situation in which they were learned and difficult to apply in new settings.

Skinner Box: Experimental chamber designed to isolate stimulus-response connections.

Social Cognitive Theory: Theory that adds concern with cognitive factors such as beliefs, self-perceptions, and expectations to social learning theory.

Social Development: Changes over time in the ways we relate to others.

Social Goals: A wide variety of needs and motives to be connected to others or part of a group.

Social Isolation: Removal of a disruptive student for 5 to 10 minutes.

Social Learning Theory: Theory that emphasizes learning through observation of others.

Social Negotiation: Aspect of learning process that relies on collaboration with others and respect for different perspectives.

Social Persuasion: A "pep talk" or specific performance feedback—one source of self-efficacy.

Socialization: The ways in which members of a society encourage positive development for the immature individuals of the group.

Sociocultural Theory: Emphasizes role in development of cooperative dialogues between children and more knowledgeable members of society. Children learn the culture of their community (ways of thinking and behaving) through these interactions.

Sociocultural Views of Motivation: Perspectives that emphasize participation, identities, and interpersonal relations within communities of practice.

Socioeconomic Status (SES): Relative standing in the society based on income, power, background, and prestige.

Sociolinguistics: The study of the formal and informal rules for how, when, about what, to whom, and how long to speak in conversations within cultural groups.

Spasticity: Overly tight or tense muscles, characteristic of some forms of cerebral palsy.

Speech Impairment: Inability to produce sounds effectively for speaking.

Speech Reading: Using visual cues to understand language.

Spiral Curriculum: Bruner's structure for teaching that introduces the fundamental structure of all subjects early in the school years, then revisits the subjects in more and more complex forms over time.

Spread of Activation: Retrieval of pieces of information based on their relatedness to one another. Remembering one bit of information activates (stimulates) recall of associated information.

Stand-Alone Thinking Skills Programs: Programs that teach thinking skills directly without need for extensive subject matter knowledge.

Standard Deviation: Measure of how widely scores vary from the mean.

Standard Error of Measurement: Hypothetical estimate of variation in scores if testing were repeated.

Standard Scores: Scores based on the standard deviation.

Standard Speech: The most generally accepted and used form of a given language.

Standardized Tests: Tests given, usually nationwide, under uniform conditions and scored according to uniform procedures.

Stanine Scores: Whole number scores from 1 to 9, each representing a wide range of raw scores.

Statistically Significant: Not likely to be a chance occurrence.

Stem: The question part of a multiple-choice item.

Stereotype: Schema that organizes knowledge or perceptions about a category.

Stereotype Threat: The extra emotional and cognitive burden that your performance in an academic situation might confirm a stereotype that others hold about you.

Stimulus: Event that activates behavior.

Stimulus Control: Capacity for the presence or absence of antecedents to cause behaviors.

Story Grammar: Typical structure or organization for a category of stories.

Student Teams–Achievement Divisions (STAD): Cooperative learning with heterogeneous groups and elements of competition and reward.

Stuttering: Repetitions, prolongations, and hesitations that block flow of speech.

Subjects: People or animals studied.

Successive Approximations: Small components that make up a complex behavior.

Summative Assessment: Testing that follows instruction and assesses achievement.

Sustaining Expectation Effect: Student performance maintained at a certain level because teachers don't recognize improvements.

Syntax: The order of words in phrases or sentences.

T-Score: Standard score with a mean of 50 and a standard deviation of 10.

Tacit Knowledge: Knowing how rather than knowing that—knowledge that is more likely to be learned during everyday life than through formal schooling

Task Analysis: System for breaking down a task hierarchically into basic skills and subskills.

Task-Involved Learners: Students who focus on mastering the task or solving the problem.

Taxonomy: Classification system.

Teaching Efficacy: A teacher's belief that he or she can reach even the most difficult students and help them learn.

Teaching Portfolio: A depiction of you as a teacher, usually including a curriculum vitae, statement of teaching philosophy, examples of your teaching plans and activities, example assignments and tests, students' work, and even videos or CD excerpts of teaching.

Teams-Games-Tournaments (TGT): Learning arrangement in which team members prepare cooperatively, then meet comparable individuals of competing teams in a tournament game to win points for their team.

Test Bias: A potential problem with tests in which the content discriminates against a group of students on the basis of gender, SES, race, ethnicity, etc.

Theory: Integrated statement of principles that attempts to explain a phenomenon and make predictions.

Time on Task: Time spent actively engaged in the learning task at hand.

Time Out: Technically, the removal of all reinforcement. In practice, isolation of a student from the rest of the class for a brief time.

Token Reinforcement System: System in which tokens earned for academic work and positive classroom behavior can be exchanged for some desired reward.

Top-Down Processing: Perceiving based on the context and the patterns you expect to occur in that situation.

Tracking: Assignment to different classes and academic experiences based on achievement.

Transfer: Influence of previously learned material on new material.

Transition Programming: Gradual preparation of exceptional students to move from high school into further education or training, employment, or community involvement.

Triarchic Theory of Intelligence: A three-part description of the mental abilities (thinking processes, coping with new experiences, and adapting to context) that lead to more or less intelligent behavior.

True Score: Hypothetical average of all of an individual's scores if repeated testing under ideal conditions were possible.

Unconditioned Response (UR): Naturally occurring emotional or physiological response.

Unconditioned Stimulus (US): Stimulus that automatically produces an emotional or physiological response.

Undergeneralization: Exclusion of some true members from a category; limiting a concept.

Utility Value: The contribution of a task to meeting one's goals.

Validity: Degree to which a test measures what it is intended to measure.

Variability: Degree of difference or deviation from mean.

Verbalization: Putting your problem-solving plan and its logic into words.

Vicarious Experiences: Accomplishments that are modeled by someone else.

Vicarious Reinforcement: Increasing the chances that we will repeat a behavior by observing another person being reinforced for that behavior.

Voicing Problems: Inappropriate pitch, quality, loudness, or intonation.

Volition: Will power; self-discipline.

Whole-Language Perspective: A philosophical approach to teaching and learning that stresses learning through authentic, real-life tasks. Emphasizes using language to learn, integrating learning across skills and subjects, and respecting the language abilities of student and teacher.

Within-Class Ability Grouping: System of grouping in which students in a class are divided into two or three groups based on ability in an attempt to accommodate student differences.

Withitness: According to Kounin, awareness of everything happening in a classroom.

Work-Avoidant Learner: Students who don't want to learn or to look smart, but just want to avoid work.

Working-Backward Strategy: Heuristic in which one starts with the goal and moves backward to solve the problem.

Working Memory: The information that you are focusing on at a given moment.

z-Score: Standard score indicating the number of standard deviations above or below the mean.

Zone of Proximal Development: Phase at which a child can master a task if given appropriate help and support.

References

AAMD Ad Hoc Committee on Terminology and Classification. (1992). *Mental retardation: Definition, classification, and systems of support* (9th ed.). Washington, DC: American Association on Mental Retardation.

Abi-Nader, J. (1991). Creating a vision of the future: Strategies for motivating minority students. *Phi Delta Kappan, 72,* 546–549.

Aboud, F., & Skerry, S. (1984). The development of ethnic identification: A critical review. *Journal of Cross-Cultural Psychology, 15,* 3–34.

Abruscato, J. (1993). Early results and tentative implications from the Vermont Portfolio Project. *Phi Delta Kappan, 74,* 474–477.

Adams, M. J., Treiman, R., & Pressley, M. (1998). Reading, writing, and literacy. In I. Sigel & A. Renninger (Eds.), *Handbook of child psychology: Child psychology in practice* (Vol. 4, pp. 275–355). New York: Wiley.

Adams, R. S., & Biddle, B. J. (1970). *Realities of teaching: Exploration with videotape.* New York: Holt, Rinehart, & Winston.

Airasian, P. W. (1996). *Assessment in the classroom.* New York: McGraw-Hill.

Airasian, P. W. (in press). Types, uses, and critiques of objectives. In L. Anderson & D. Krathwohl (Eds.), *A taxonomy of teaching and learning: A revision of Bloom's taxonomy of educational objectives.* New York: Addison, Wesley, Longman.

Airasian, P. W., & Walsh, M. E. (1997). Constructivist cautions. *Phi Delta Kappan, 78,* 444–449.

Alberto, P., & Troutman, A. C. (1990). *Applied behavior analysis for teachers: Influencing student performance* (3rd ed.). Columbus, OH: Merrill.

Alderman, M. K. (1985). Achievement motivation and the preservice teacher. In M. Alderman & M. Cohen (Eds.), *Motivation theory and practice for preservice teachers* (pp. 37–49). Washington, DC: ERIC Clearinghouse on Teacher Education.

Alexander, P. (in press). Stages and phases of domain learning: The dynamics of subject-matter knowledge, strategy knowledge, and motivation. In C. Weinstein & B. McCombs (Eds.), *Strategic learning: Skill, will, and self-regulation.* Mahwah, NJ: Lawrence Erlbaum Associates.

Alexander, P. A. (1992). Domain knowledge: Evolving themes and emerging concerns. *Educational Psychologist, 27,* 33–51.

Alexander, P. A. (1995). Superimposing a situation-specific and domain-specific perspective on an account of self-regulated learning. *Educational Psychologist, 30,* 189–194.

Alexander, P. A. (1996). The past, present, and future of knowledge research: A reexamination of the role of knowledge in learning and instruction. *Educational Psychologist, 31,* 89–92.

Alexander, P. A. (1997). Mapping the multidimensional nature of domain learning: The interplay of cognitive, motivational, and strategic forces. *Advances in Motivation and Achievement, 10,* 213–250.

Alexander, P. A., & Jetton, T. L. (1996). The role of importance and interest in the processing of text. *Educational Psychology Review, 8,* 89–121.

Alexander, P. A., Kulikowich, J. M., & Schulze, S. K. (1994). How subject-matter knowledge affects recall and interest. *American Educational Research Journal, 31,* 313–337.

Alexander, P. A., & Murphy, P. K. (1998). The research base for APA's Learner-Centered Psychological Principles. In N. Lambert & B. McCombs (Eds.), *How students learn: Reforming schools through learner-centered education.* Washington, DC: American Psychological Association.

Allington, R. (1980). Teacher interruption behaviors during primary-grade oral reading. *Journal of Educational Psychology, 71,* 371–377.

Alloway, N. (1984). *Teacher expectations.* Paper presented at the meetings of the Australian Association for Research in Education, Perth, Australia.

Alloy, L. B., & Seligman, M. E. P. (1979). On the cognitive component of learned helplessness and depression. *The Journal of Learning and Motivation, 13,* 219–276.

Alwin, D., & Thornton, A. (1984). Family origins and schooling processes: Early versus late influence of parental characteristics. *American Sociological Review, 49,* 784–802.

Amato, L. F., Loomis, L. S., & Booth, A. (1995). Parental divorce, marital conflict, and offspring well-being during early adulthood. *Social Forces, 73,* 895–915.

American Association for the Advancement of Science (AAAS). (1993). *Benchmarks for science literacy.* Washington, DC: Author.

American Association of University Women (AAUW). (1991). *Shortchanging girls, shortchanging America.* Washington, DC: Author.

Ames, C. (1990). Motivation: What teachers need to know. *Teachers College Record, 91,* 409–421.

Ames, C. (1992). Classrooms: Goals, structures, and student motivation. *Journal of Educational Psychology, 84,* 261–271.

Ames, R., & Lau, S. (1982). An attributional analysis of student help-seeking in academic settings. *Journal of Educational Psychology, 74,* 414–423.

Anastasi, A. (1988). *Psychological testing* (6th ed.). New York: Macmillan.

Anderman, E. M., & Maehr, M. L. (1994). Motivation and schooling in the middle grades. *Review of Educational Research, 64,* 287–310.

Anderson, C. W., & Roth, K. J. (1989). Teaching for meaningful and self-regulated learning of science. In J. Brophy (Ed.), *Advances in research on teaching* (Vol. 1, pp. 265–306). Greenwich, CT: JAI Press.

Anderson, C. W., & Smith, E. L. (1983, April). *Children's conceptions of light and color: Developing the concept of unseen rays.* Paper presented at the annual meeting of the American Educational Research Association, Montreal.

Anderson, C. W., & Smith, E. L. (1987). Teaching science. In V. Richardson-Koehler (Ed.), *Educators' handbook: A research perspective* (pp. 84–111). New York: Longman.

Anderson, C. W., Holland, J. D., & Palincsar, A. S. (1997). Canonical and sociocultural approaches to research and reform in science education: The story of Juan and his group. *The Elementary School Journal, 97,* 359–384.

Anderson, J. R. (1993). Problem solving and learning. *American Psychologist, 48,* 35–44.

Anderson, J. R. (1995a). *Cognitive psychology and its implications* (4th ed.). New York: Freeman.

Anderson, J. R. (1995b). *Learning and memory*. New York: John Wiley & Sons.

Anderson, J. R., Reder, L. M., & Simon, H. A. (1995). Applications and misapplication of cognitive psychology to mathematics education. Unpublished manuscript. [www document] URL http://www.psy.cmu.edu/~mm4b/misapplied.html

Anderson, J. R., Reder, L. M., & Simon, H. A. (1996). Situated learning and education. *Educational Researcher, 25,* 5–11.

Anderson, L. M. (1985). What are students doing when they do all that seatwork? In C. Fisher & D. Berliner (Eds.), *Perspectives on instructional time* (pp. 189–202). New York: Longman.

Anderson, L. M. (1989a). Learners and learning. In M. Reynolds (Ed.), *Knowledge base for beginning teachers* (pp. 85–100). New York: Pergamon.

Anderson, L. M. (1989b). Classroom instruction. In M. Reynolds (Ed.), *Knowledge base for beginning teachers* (pp. 101–116). New York: Pergamon.

Anderson, L. M., Brubaker, N. L., Alleman-Brooks, J., & Duffy, G. G. (1985). A qualitative study of seatwork in first-grade classrooms. *Elementary School Journal, 86,* 123–140.

Anderson, L. W., & Krathwohl, D. R. (Eds.). (2001). *A Taxonomy for Learning, Teaching, and Assessing: A Revision of Bloom's Taxonomy of Educational Objectives*. New York: Addison, Wesley, Longman.

Anderson, L. W., & Sosniak, L. A. (Eds.). (1994). *Bloom's Taxonomy: A forty-year retrospective*. Ninety-third yearbook for the National Society for the Study of Education: Part II. Chicago: University of Chicago Press.

Anderson, P. J., & Graham, S. M. (1994). Issues in second-language phonological acquisition among children and adults. *Topics in Language Disorders, 14,* 84–100.

Anderson, R., Hiebert, E., Scott, J., & Wilkinson, I. (1985). *Becoming a nation of readers: The report of the commission on reading*. Washington, DC: National Institute of Education.

Anderson, S. M., Klatzky, R. L., & Murray, J. (1990). Traits and social stereotypes: Efficiency differences in social information processing. *Journal of Personality and Social Psychology, 59,* 192–201.

Anglin, J. M. (1993). Vocabulary development: A morphological analysis. *Monographs of the Society for Research in Child Development, 58*(10, Serial No. 238).

Anyon, J. (1980). Social class and the hidden curriculum of work. *Journal of Education, 162,* 67–92.

APA Board of Educational Affairs. (1995). *Learner-centered psychological principles: A framework for school redesign and reform*. Washington, DC: American Psychological Association.

Archer, S. L., & Waterman, A. S. (1990). Varieties of identity diffusions and foreclosures: An exploration of the subcategories of the identity statuses. *Journal of Adolescent Research, 5,* 96–111.

Arlin, M. (1984). Time, equality, and mastery learning. *Review of Educational Research, 54,* 65–86.

Armbruster, B. B., & Anderson, T. H. (1981). Research synthesis on study skills. *Educational Leadership, 39,* 154–156.

Armstrong, L. S. (1991, January 16). Racial, ethnic prejudice still prevalent, survey finds. *Education Week,* 7.

Aronson, J., & Fried, C. B. (in press). Reducing the effects of stereotype threat on African American college students: The role of theories of intelligence. *Journal of Experimental Social Psychology*.

Aronson, J., Lustina, M. J., Good, C., Keough, K., Steele, C. M., & Brown, J. (1999). When White men can't do math: Necessary and sufficient factors in stereotype threat. *Journal of Experimental Social Psychology, 35,* 2946.

Aronson, J., & Salinas, M. F. (1998). Stereotype threat, attributional ambiguity, and Latino underperformance. Unpublished manuscript, University of Texas at Austin.

Aronson, J., Steele, C. M., Salinas, M. F., & Lustina, M. J. (1999). The effect of stereotype threat on the standardized test performance of college students. In E. Aronson (Ed.), *Readings About the Social Animal* (8th ed.). New York: Freeman.

Artman, L., & Cahan, S. (1993). Schooling and the development of transitive inference. *Developmental Psychology, 29,* 753–759.

Aschbacher, P. (1997). New directions in student assessment [Special issue]. *Theory Into Practice, 36*(4), 194–272.

Ashton, P. T. (1978). Cross-cultural Piagetian research: An experimental perspective. *Harvard Educational Review* (Reprint Series No. 13).

Association for Supervision and Curriculum Development. (1990). Effective teaching redux. *ASCD Update, 32*(6), 5.

Association for Supervision and Curriculum Development. (1991). Issue. *ASCD Update, 33*(3), 7.

Atkinson, R. C., & Shiffrin, R. M. (1968). Human memory: A proposed system and its control processes. In K. Spence & J. Spence (Eds.), *The psychology of learning and motivation* (Vol. 2). New York: Academic Press.

Atkinson, R. K., Levin, J. R., Kiewra, K. A., Meyers, T., Atkinson, L. A., Renandya, W. A., & Hwang, Y. (1999). Matrix and mnemonic text-processing adjuncts: Comparing and combining their components. *Journal of Educational Psychology, 91,* 242–257.

Au, K. H. (1980). Participation structures in a reading lesson with Hawaiian children: Analysis of a culturally appropriate instructional event. *Anthropology and Education Quarterly, 11,* 91–115.

Ausubel, D. P. (1963). *The psychology of meaningful verbal learning*. New York: Grune and Stratton.

Ausubel, D. P. (1977). The facilitation of meaningful verbal learning in the classroom. *Educational Psychologist, 12,* 162–178.

Babad, E. Y. (1995). The "Teachers' Pet" phenomenon, students' perceptions of differential behavior, and students' morale. *Journal of Educational Psychology, 87,* 361–374.

Babad, E. Y., Inbar, J., & Rosenthal, R. (1982). Pygmalion, Galatea, and the Golem: Investigations of biased and unbiased teachers. *Journal of Educational Psychology, 74,* 459–474.

Baddeley, A. D. (1986). *Working memory*. Oxford, UK: Clarendon Books.

Baddeley, A. (1998). *Human memory: Theory and practice* (Rev. ed.). Boston: Allyn & Bacon.

Baer, J. (1997). *Creative teachers, creative students*. Boston: Allyn & Bacon.

Bailey, S. M. (1993). The current status of gender equity research in American Schools. *Educational Psychologist, 28,* 321–339.

Baillargeon, R., & DeVos, J. (1991. Object permanence in young infants: Further evidence. *Child Development, 62,* 1227–1246.

Baker, C. (1993). *Foundations of bilingual education and bilingualism*. Clevedon, England: Multilingual Matters.

Baker, D. (1986). Sex differences in classroom interaction in secondary science. *Journal of Classroom Interaction, 22,* 212–218.

Bakerman, R., Adamson, L. B., Koner, M., & Barr, R. G. (1990). !Kung infancy: The social context of object exploration. *Child Development, 61,* 794–809.

Bandura, A. (1965). Influence of models' reinforcement contingencies on the acquisition of imitative responses. *Journal of Personality and Social Psychology, 1,* 589–595.

Bandura, A. (1977). *Social learning theory*. Englewood Cliffs, NJ: Prentice-Hall.

Bandura, A. (1982). Self-efficacy mechanisms in human agency. *American Psychologist, 37,* 122–147.

Bandura, A. (1986). *Social foundations of thought and action*. Englewood Cliffs, NJ: Prentice-Hall.

Bandura, A. (1993). Perceived self-efficacy in cognitive development and functioning. *Educational Psychologist, 28,* 117–148.

Bandura, A. (1997). *Self-efficacy: The exercise of control*. New York: Freeman.

Bandura, A., Ross, D., & Ross, S. A. (1963). Vicarious reinforcement and imitative learning. *Journal of Abnormal and Social Psychology, 67,* 601–607.

Bangert-Drowns, R. L., Kulik, C. C., Kulik, J. A., & Morgan, M. (1991). The instructional effect of feedback in test-like events. *Review of Educational Research, 61,* 213–238.

Banks, J. A. (1993). Multicultural education: Characteristics and goals. In J. Banks & C. McGee Banks (Eds.), *Multicultural education: Issues and perspectives* (2nd ed.) (pp. 2–26). Boston: Allyn & Bacon.

Banks, J. A. (1993). Multicultural education: Development, dimensions, and challenges. *Phi Delta Kappan, 75*, 22–28.

Banks, J. A. (1994). *Multiethnic education: Theory and practice.* Boston: Allyn & Bacon.

Banks, J. A. (1997). *Teaching strategies for ethnic studies* (6th ed.). Boston: Allyn & Bacon.

Banks, J. A. (1999). *An introduction to multicultural education* (2nd ed.). Boston: Allyn & Bacon,

Bargh, J. A., & Chartrand, T. L. (1999). The unbearable automaticity of being. *American Psychologist, 54*, 462–479.

Baron, R. A. (1998). *Psychology* (4th ed.). Boston: Allyn & Bacon.

Baroody, A. R., & Ginsburg, H. P. (1990). Children's learning: A cognitive view. In R. Davis, C. Maher, & N. Noddings (Eds.), *Constructivist views on the teaching and learning of mathematics* (pp. 51–64). Monograph 4 of the National Council of Teachers of Mathematics, Reston, VA.

Bartlett, F. C. (1932). *Remembering: A study in experimental and social psychology.* New York: Macmillan.

Barton, E. J. (1981). Developing sharing: An analysis of modeling and other behavioral techniques. *Behavior Modification, 5*, 386–398.

Battistich, V., Solomon, D., & Delucci, K. (1993). Interaction processes and student outcomes in cooperative groups. *Elementary School Journal, 94*, 19–32.

Baumeister, R. F., & Leary, M. R. (1995). The need to belong: Desire for interpersonal attachments as a fundamental human motivation. *Psychological Bulletin, 117*, 497–529.

Beane, J. A. (1991). Sorting out the self-esteem controversy. *Educational Leadership, 49*(1), 25–30.

Beane, J. A. (1995). (Ed.). *Toward a coherent curriculum.* Alexandria, VA: Association for Supervision and Curriculum Development.

Bear, T., Schenk, S., & Buckner, L. (1993). Supporting victims of child abuse. *Educational Leadership, 50*(4), 44.

Beck, I. L., McKeown, M. G., Worthy, J., Sandora, C. A., & Kucan, L. (1996). Questioning the author: A yearlong classroom implementation to engage students with text. *The Elementary School Journal, 96*, 385–414.

Becker, W. C., Engelmann, S., & Thomas, D. R. (1975). *Teaching 1: Classroom management.* Chicago: Science Research Associates.

Bee, H. (1981). *The developing child* (3rd ed.). New York: Harper & Row.

Bee, H. (1992). *The developing child* (6th ed.). New York: Harper & Row.

Beeth, M. E. (1998). Teaching science in fifth grade: Instructional goals that support conceptual change. *Journal of Research in Science Teaching, 35*, 1091–1101.

Beezer, B. (1985). Reporting child abuse and neglect: Your responsibilities and your protections. *Phi Delta Kappan, 66*, 434–436.

Begley, S. (1998, September 7). The parent trap. *Newsweek, 132*(10), 52–59.

Belanoff, P., & Dickson, M. (1991). *Portfolios: Process and product.* Portsmouth, NH: Heinemann, Boynton/Cook.

Bem, S. L. (1974). The measurement of psychological androgyny. *Journal of Consulting and Clinical Psychology, 42*, 155–162.

Benbow, C. P., & Minor, L. L. (1986). Mathematically talented males and females and achievement in the high school sciences. *American Educational Research Journal, 23*, 425–436.

Benbow, C. P., & Stanley, J. C. (1980). Sex differences in mathematical ability: Fact or artifact? *Science, 210*, 1262–1264.

Benbow, C. P., & Stanley, J. C. (1983a). Sex differences in mathematical abilities: More facts. *Science, 222*, 1029–1031.

Benbow, C. P., & Stanley, J. C. (1983b). Differential course-taking hypothesis revisited. *American Educational Research Journal, 20*, 469–473.

Benenson, J. F. (1993). Greater preference among females than males for dyadic interaction in early childhood. *Child Development, 64*, 544–555.

Benjafield, J. G. (1992). *Cognition.* Englewood Cliffs, NJ: Prentice-Hall.

Bennett, C. I. (1995). *Comprehensive multicultural education: Theory and practice* (3rd ed.). Boston: Allyn & Bacon.

Bennett, C. I. (1999). *Comprehensive multicultural education: Theory and practice* (4th Ed.). Boston: Allyn & Bacon.

Berg, C. A., & Clough, M. (1991). Hunter lesson design: The wrong one for science teaching. *Educational Leadership, 48*(4), 73–78.

Berger, K. S., & Thompson, R. A. (1995). *The developing person through childhood and adolescence.* New York: Worth.

Berk, L. E. (1993). *Infants, children, and adolescents.* Boston: Allyn & Bacon.

Berk, L. E. (1994). *Child development* (3d ed.). Boston: Allyn & Bacon.

Berk, L. E. (1996). *Infants, children, and adolescents* (2nd ed.). Boston: Allyn & Bacon.

Berk, L. E. (1997). *Child development* (4th ed.). Boston: Allyn & Bacon.

Berk, L. E. (1999). *Infants, children, and adolescents* (3rd ed.). Boston: Allyn & Bacon.

Berk, L. E., & Spuhl, S. T. (1995). Maternal interaction, private speech, and task performance in preschool children. *Early Childhood Research Quarterly, 10*, 145–169.

Berliner, D. (1983). Developing concepts of classroom environments: Some light on the T in studies of ATI. *Educational Psychologist, 18*, 1–13.

Berliner, D. (1987). But do they understand? In V. Richardson-Koehler (Ed.), *Educators' handbook: A research perspective* (pp. 259–293). New York: Longman.

Berliner, D. (1988). Simple views of effective teaching and a simple theory of classroom instruction. In D. Berliner & B. Rosenshine (Eds.), *Talks to teachers* (pp. 93–110). New York: Random House.

Berliner, D. (1992).Telling the stories of educational psychology. *Educational Psychologist, 27*, 143–152.

Berliner, D., & Biddle, B. (1997). *The manufactured crisis: Myths, frauds, and the attack on America's public schools.* White Plains: Longman.

Berlyne, D. (1966). Curiosity and exploration. *Science, 153*, 25–33.

Berndt, T. J., & Keefe, K. (1995). Friends' influence on adolescents' adjustment to school. *Child Development, 66*, 1312–1329.

Betancourt, H., & Lopez, S. R. (1993). The study of culture, ethnicity, and race in American psychology. *American Psychologist, 48*, 629–637.

Bivens, J. A., & Berk, L. E. (1990). A longitudinal study of elementary school children's private speech. *Merrill-Palmer Quarterly, 36*, 443–463.

Bjorklund, D. F. (1989). *Children's thinking: Developmental function and individual differences.* Pacific Grove, CA: Brooks/Cole.

Block, J. H. (1983). Differential premises arising from differential socialization of the sexes: Some conjectures. *Child Development, 54*, 1335–1354.

Block, J. H., & Anderson, L. W. (1975). *Mastery learning in classroom instruction.* New York: Macmillan.

Bloom, B. (1994). Reflections on the development and use of the taxonomy. In L. Anderson & L. Sosniak (Eds.), *Bloom's taxonomy: A forty-year retrospective.* Ninety-third yearbook for the National Society for the Study of Education: Part II (pp. 1–8). Chicago: University of Chicago Press.

Bloom, B. S. (1968). *Learning for mastery. Evaluation Comment, 1(2).* Los Angeles: University of California, Center for the Study of Evaluation of Instructional Programs.

Bloom, B. S., Engelhart, M. D., Frost, E. J., Hill, W. H., & Krathwohl, D. R. (1956). *Taxonomy of educational objectives. Handbook I: Cognitive domain.* New York: David McKay.

Bloom, R., & Bourdon, L. (1980). Types and frequencies of teachers' written instructional feedback. *Journal of Educational Research, 74,* 13–15.

Blumenfeld, P. C., Puro, P., & Mergendoller, J. R. (1992). Translating motivation into thoughtfulness. In H. Marshall (Ed.), *Redefining student learning: Roots of educational change* (pp. 207–240). Norwood, NJ: Ablex.

Boggiano, A. K., Flink, C., Shields, A., Seelbach, A., & Barrett, M. (1993). Use of techniques promoting students' self-determination: Effects on students' analytic problem-solving skills. *Motivation and Education, 17,* 319–336.

Bohannon, J. N., III, & Warren-Leubecker, A. (1989). Theoretical approaches to language acquisition. In J. Berko Gleason (Ed.), *The development of language* (pp. 167–223). Columbus, OH: Merrill.

Boldizar, J. P. (1991). Assessing sex typing and androgyny in children: The children's sex inventory. *Developmental Psychology, 27,* 505–515.

Borko, H., & Putnam, R. (1996). Learning to teach. In D. Berliner & R. Calfee (Eds.), *Handbook of educational psychology* (pp. 673–708). New York: Macmillan.

Borko, H. (1989). Research on learning to teach: Implications for graduate teacher preparation. In A. Woolfolk (Ed.), *Research perspectives on the graduate preparation of teachers* (pp. 69–87). Boston: Allyn & Bacon.

Borko, H., & Livingston, C. (1989). Cognition and improvisation: Differences in mathematics instruction by expert and novice teachers. *American Educational Research Journal, 26,* 473–498.

Borkowski, J. G., Johnston, M. B., & Reid, M. K. (1986). Metacognition, motivation, and the transfer of control processes. In S. J. Ceci (Ed.), *Handbook of cognition: Social and neurological aspects of learning disabilities.* Hillsdale, NJ: Erlbaum.

Bos, C. S., & Reyes, E. I. (1996). Conversations with a Latina teacher about education for language-minority students with special needs. *The Elementary School Journal, 96,* 344–351.

Braddock, J., II, & Slavin, R. E. (1993). Why ability grouping must end: Achieving excellence and equity in American education. *Journal of Intergroup Relations, 20*(2), 51–64.

Brandt, R. (1994). On making sense: A conversation with Magdalene Lampert. *Educational Leadership, 51*(5), 26–32.

Brandt, R. (1993). On teaching for understanding: A conversation with Howard Gardner. *Educational Leadership, 50*(7), 4–7.

Bransford, J. D., & Stein, B. S. (1993). *The IDEAL problem solver: A guide for improving thinking, learning, and creativity* (2nd ed.). New York: Freemen.

Bransford, J. D., Stein, B. S., Vye, N. J., Franks, J. J., Auble, P. M., Mezynski, K. J., & Perfetto, G. A. (1982). Differences in approaches to learning: An overview. *Journal of Experimental Psychology: General, 111,* 390–398.

Braun, C. (1976). Teacher expectation: Sociopsychological dynamics. *Review of Educational Research, 46*(2), 185–212.

Bredo, E. (1994). Reconstructing educational psychology: Situated cognition and Deweyian pragmatism. *Educational Psychologist, 29,* 23–36.

Bretherton, I., & Waters, E. (1985). Growing points of attachment theory and research. *Monographs of the Society for Research in Child Development, 50* (1, 2, Serial No. 209).

Bronfenbrenner, U., McClelland, P., Wethington, E., Moen, P., & Ceci, S. (1996). *The state of Americans: This generation and the next.* New York: Free Press.

Brookhart, S. M., & Freeman, D. J. (1992). Characteristics of entering teacher candidates. *Review of Educational Research, 62,* 37–60.

Brooks, D. (1985). Beginning the year in junior high: The first day of school. *Educational Leadership, 42,* 76–78.

Brooks, J. G., & Brooks, M. G. (1993). Becoming a constructivist teacher. In Association for Supervision and Curriculum Development (ASCD) (Ed.), *In search of understanding: The case for constructivist classrooms.* Alexandria, VA: ASCD.

Brooks-Gunn, J. (1988). The impact of puberty and sexual activity upon the health and education of adolescent boys and girls. *Peabody Journal of Education, 64,* 88–113.

Brooks-Gunn, J., & Furstenberg, F. F., Jr. (1989). Adolescent sexual behavior. *American Psychologist, 44,* 2249–2257.

Brophy, J. E. (1981). Teacher praise: A functional analysis. *Review of Educational Research, 51,* 5–21.

Brophy, J. E. (1982, March). *Research on the self-fulfilling prophecy and teacher expectations.* Paper presented at the annual meeting of the American Educational Research Association, New York.

Brophy, J. E. (1983). Conceptualizing student motivation to learn. *Educational Psychologist, 18,* 200–215.

Brophy, J. E. (1985). Teacher-student interaction. In J. Dusek (Ed.), *Teacher expectancies.* Hillsdale, NJ: Erlbaum.

Brophy, J. E. (1988). On motivating students. In D. Berliner & B. Rosenshine (Eds.), *Talks to teachers* (pp. 201–245). New York: Random House.

Brophy, J. E., & Evertson, C. (1978). Context variables in teaching. *Educational Psychologist, 12,* 310–316.

Brophy, J. E., & Good, T. (1986). Teacher behavior and student achievement. In M. Wittrock (Ed.), *Handbook of research on teaching* (3rd ed.) (pp. 328–375). New York: Macmillan.

Brophy, J. E., & Kher, N. (1986). Teacher socialization as a mechanism for developing student motivation to learn. In R. Feldman (Ed.), *Social psychology applied to education* (pp. 256–288). New York: Cambridge University Press.

Brown, A. (1987). Metacognition, executive control, self-regulation, and other more mysterious mechanisms. In F. Weinert & R. Kluwe (Eds.), *Metacognition, motivation, and understanding* (pp. 65–116). Hillside, NJ: Erlbaum.

Brown, A. L. (1992). Design experiments: Theoretical and methodological challenges in creating complex interventions in classroom settings. *Journal of the Learning Sciences, 2,* 141–178.

Brown, A. L., Bransford, J., Ferrara, R., & Campione, J. (1983). Learning, remembering, and understanding. In P. Mussen (Ed.), *Handbook of child psychology* (Vol. 3). New York: Wiley.

Brown, A. L., & Campione, J. C. (1996). Psychological theory and the design of innovative learning environments: On procedures, principles, and systems. In L. Schauble & R. Glaser (Eds.), *Innovations in learning: New environments for education* (pp. 289–325). Mahwah, NJ: Lawrence Erlbaum Associates.

Brown, J. S., & Burton, R. R. (1979). Diagnostic models for procedural bugs in basic mathematical skills. *Cognitive Science, 2,* 155–192.

Brown, R., & Hanlon, C. (1970). Derivational complexity and order of acquisition in child speech. In J. M. Hays (Ed.), *Cognition and the development of language.* New York: Wiley.

Bruner, J. S. (1966). *Toward a theory of instruction.* New York: Norton.

Bruner, J. S. (1971). *The relevance of education.* New York: Norton.

Bruner, J. S. (1973). *Beyond the information given: Studies in the psychology of knowing.* New York: Norton.

Bruner, J. S., Goodnow, J. J., & Austin, G. A. (1956). *A study of thinking.* New York: Wiley.

Bruning, R. H., Schraw, G. J., & Ronning, R. R. (1999). *Cognitive psychology and instruction* (3rd ed.). Columbus, OH: Merrill.

Buenning, M., & Tollefson, N. (1987). The cultural gap hypothesis as an explanation for the achievement patterns of Mexican-American students. *Psychology in the Schools, 14,* 264–271.

Burden, P. R. (1995). *Classroom management and discipline: Methods to facilitate cooperation and instruction.* White Plains, NY: Longman.

Burton, N. W., & Jones, L. V. (1982). Recent trends in achievement levels of black and white youth. *Educational Research, 11,* 10–14.

Burton, R. V. (1963). The generality of honesty reconsidered. *Psychological Review, 70,* 481–499.

Bus, A. G., & van Ijzendoorn, M. H. (1999). Phonological awareness and early reading: a meta-analysis of experimental training studies. *Journal of Educational Psychology, 91,* 403–414.

Buss, D. M. (1995). Psychological sex differences: Origin through sexual selection. *American Psychologist, 50,* 164–168.

Butler, R. (1987). Task-involving and ego-involving properties of evaluation: Effects of different feedback conditions on motivational perceptions, interest, and performance. *Journal of Educational Psychology, 79,* 474–482.

Butler, R., & Neuman, O. (1995). Effects of task and ego achievement goals on help-seeking behaviors and attitudes. *Journal of Educational Psychology, 87,* 261–271.

Butler, R., & Nisan, M. (1986). Effects of no feedback, task-related comments, and grades on intrinsic motivation and performance. *Journal of Educational Psychology, 78,* 210–224.

Butler, S. R., Marsh, H. W., Sheppard, M. J., & Sheppard, J. L. (1985). Seven-year longitudinal study of the early prediction of reading achievement. *Journal of Educational Psychology, 77,* 349–361.

Byrne, B. M., & Shavelson, R. J. (1996). On the structure of social self-concept for pre-, early, and late adolescents: A test of the Shavelson model. *Journal of Personality and Social Psychology, 70,* 599–613.

Byrne, B. M., & Worth Gavin, D. A. (1996). The Shavelson model revisited: Testing for structure of academic self concept across pre-, early, and late adolescents. *Journal of Educational Psychology, 88,* 215–229.

Byrnes, J. P. (1996). *Cognitive development and learning in instructional contexts.* Boston: Allyn & Bacon.

Byrnes, J. P., & Fox, N. A. (1998). The educational relevance of research in cognitive neuroscience. *Educational Psychology Review, 10,* 297–342.

Caine, R. N., & Caine, G. (1991). *Making connections: Teaching and the human brain.* Alexandria, VA: Association for Supervision and Curriculum Development.

Calderhead, J. (1996). Teacher: Beliefs and knowledge. In D. Berliner & R. Calfee (Eds.), *Handbook of educational psychology* (pp. 709–725). New York: Macmillan.

Calderhead, J., & Robson, M. (1991). Images of teaching: Student teachers' early conceptions of classroom practice. *Teaching and Teacher Education, 7,* 1–8.

Calfee, R. (1992), Refining educational psychology: The case of the missing links. *Educational Psychologist, 27,* 163–176.

Callahan, C. M., Tomlinson, C. A., & Plucker, J. (1997). *Project STATR using a multiple intelligences model in identifying and promoting talent in high-risk students.* Storrs, CT: National Research Center for Gifted and Talented. University of Connecticut Technical Report.

Calmore, J. A. (1986). National housing policy and black America: Trends, issues, and implications. In *The state of black America 1986* (pp. 115–149). New York: National Urban League.

Cambourne, B., & Turbill, J. (1990). Assessment in whole-language classrooms: Theory into practice. *Elementary School Journal, 90,* 337–349.

Cameron, J., & Pierce, W. D. (1994). Reinforcement, reward, and intrinsic motivation: A meta-analysis. *Review of Educational Research, 64,* 363–423.

Cameron, J., & Pierce, W. D. (1996). The debate about rewards and intrinsic motivation: Protests and accusations do not alter the results. *Review of Educational Research, 66,* 39–52.

Camp, R. (1990, Spring). Thinking together about portfolios. *The Quarterly of the National Writing Project, 27,* 8–14.

Campbell, F. A., & Ramey, C. T. (1994). Effects of early intervention on intellectual and academic achievement: A follow-up study of children from low-income families. *Child Development, 65,* 684–698.

Campbell, F. A., & Ramey, C. T. (1995). Cognitive and school outcomes for high-risk African-American students at middle adolescence: Positive effects of early interventions. *American Educational Research Journal, 32,* 743–772.

Campbell, L., Campbell, B., & Dickinson, D. (1999). *Teaching and learning through multiple intelligences* (2nd ed.). Boston: Allyn & Bacon.

Canfield, J. (1990). Improving students' self-concepts. *Educational Leadership, 48*(1), 48–50.

Cangelosi, J. S. (1990). *Designing tests for evaluating student achievement.* New York: Longman.

Canter, L. (1988). Let the educator beware: A response to Curwin and Mendler. *Educational Leadership, 46*(2), 71–73.

Canter, L. (1989). Assertive discipline—More than names on the board and marbles in a jar. *Phi Delta Kappan, 71*(1), 41–56.

Canter, L., & Canter, M. (1992). *Lee Canter's Assertive Discipline: Positive behavior management for today's classroom.* Santa Monica: Lee Canter and Associates.

Carey, L. M. (1994). *Measuring and evaluating school learning* (2nd ed.). Boston: Allyn & Bacon.

Cariglia-Bull, T., & Pressley, M. (1990). Short-term memory differences between children predict imagery effects when sentences are read. *Journal of Experimental Child Psychology, 49,* 384–398.

Carnegie Council on Adolescent Development. (1995). *Great transitions: Preparing adolescents for a new century.* New York: Carnegie Corporation of New York.

Carnegie Forum on Education and the Economy. (1986). *A nation prepared: Teachers for the 21st century.* Washington, DC: Author.

Carnegie Foundation for the Advancement of Teaching (1987). *1987 national survey of public school teachers.* Princeton, NJ: Author.

Carroll, J. (1993). *Human cognitive abilities: A survey of factor analytic studies.* Cambridge, England: Cambridge University Press.

Carter, K. (1984). Do teachers understand principles of writing tests? *Journal of Teacher Education, 35,* 57–60.

Casanova, U. (1987). Ethnic and cultural differences. In V. Richardson-Koehler (Ed.), *Educators' handbook: A research perspective* (pp. 370–393). New York: Longman.

Case, R. (1985a). *Intellectual development: Birth to adulthood.* New York: Academic Press.

Case, R. (1985b). A developmentally-based approach to the problem of instructional design. In R. Glaser, S. Chipman, & J. Segal (Eds.), *Teaching thinking skills* (Vol. 2, pp. 545–562). Hillsdale, NJ: Erlbaum.

Case, R. (1992). *The mind's staircase: Exploring the conceptual underpinnings of children's thought and knowledge.* Mahwah, NJ: Lawrence Erlbaum.

Case, R. (1998). The development of conceptual structures. In D. Kuhn & R. S. Siegler (Eds.), *Handbook of child psychology: Vol. 2: Cognition, perception, and language* (pp. 745–800). New York: Wiley.

Cauley, K., & Tyler, B. (1989). The relationship of self-concept to prosocial behavior in children. *Early Childhood Research Quarterly, 4,* 51–60.

Cazden, C. B. (1988). *Classroom discourse: The language of teaching and learning.* Portsmouth, NH: Heinemann.

Ceci, S. J. (1991). How much does schooling influence intelligence and its cognitive components? A reassessment of the evidence. *Developmental Psychology, 27,* 703–720.

Ceci, S. J., & Roazzi, A. (1994). The effects of context on cognition: Postcards from Brazil. In R. J. Sternberg (Ed.), *Mind in context* (pp. 74–101). New York: Cambridge University Press.

Chambers, B., & Abrami, P. C. (1991). The relationship between student team learning outcomes and achievement, causal attributions, and affect. *Journal of Educational Psychology, 83,* 140–146.

Chamot, A. U., & O'Malley, J. M. (1996). The Cognitive Academic Language Learning Approach: A model for linguistically diverse classrooms. *The Elementary School Journal, 96,* 259–274.

Chance, P. (1991). Backtalk: a gross injustice. *Phi Delta Kappan, 72,* 803.

Chance, P. (1992). The rewards of learning. *Phi Delta Kappan, 73,* 200–207.

Chance, P. (1993). Sticking up for rewards. *Phi Delta Kappan, 74,* 787–790.

Chapman, M., Zahn-Waxler, C., Cooperman, G., & Iannotti, R. (1987). Empathy and responsibility in the motivation of children's helping. *Developmental Psychology, 23,* 140–145.

Charles, C. M. (1985). *Building classroom discipline: From models to practice* (2nd ed.). New York: Longman.

Charles, C. M. (1996). *Building classroom discipline* (5th ed.). White Plains, NY: Longman.

Chase, C. I. (1978). *Measurement for educational evaluation* (2nd ed.). Reading, MA: Addison-Wesley.

Chi, M. T. H. (1978). Knowledge structures and memory development. In R. Siegler (Ed.), *Children's thinking: What develops?* (pp. 73–96). Hillsdale, NJ: Erlbaum.

Chi, M. T. H., Glaser, R., & Farr, M. (Eds.) (1988). *The nature of expertise.* Hillsdale, NJ: Erlbaum.

Chi, M. T. H., & Koeske, R. D. (1983). Network representation of a child's dinosaur knowledge. *Developmental Psychology, 19,* 29–39.

Children's Defense Fund. (1994). *The state of America's children: Yearbook 1994.* Washington, DC: Author.

Childs, C. P., & Greenfield, P. M. (1982). Informal modes of learning and teaching: The case of Zinacanteco weaving. In N. Warren (Ed.), *Advances in cross-cultural psychology* (Vol. 2, pp. 269–316). London: Academic Press.

Chomsky, N. (1965). *Aspects of a theory of syntax.* Cambridge, MA: MIT Press.

Chomsky, N. (1986). *Knowledge of language: Its nature, origin, and use.* New York: Praeger.

Civil Rights Commission. (1973). *Teacher and students: Differences in teacher interactions with Mexican-American and Anglo students.* Washington, DC: Government Printing Office.

Cizek, G. J. (1991). Innovation or enervation: Performance assessment in perspective. *Phi Delta Kappan, 72*(9), 695–699.

Claiborn, W. L. (1969). Expectancy effects in the classroom: A failure to replicate. *Journal of Education Psychology, 60,* 377–383.

Clark, C. M. (1983). Personal communication.

Clark, C. M., & Peterson, P. L. (1986). Teachers' thought processes. In M. Wittrock (Ed.), *Handbook of research on teaching* (3rd ed.) (pp. 255–296). New York: Macmillan.

Clark, C. M., & Yinger, R. (1988). Teacher planning. In D. Berliner & B. Rosenshine (Eds.), *Talks to teachers* (pp. 342–365). New York: Random House.

Clark, C. M., Gage, N. L., Marx, R. W., Peterson, P. L., Staybrook, N. G., & Winnie, P. H. (1979). A factorial experiment on teacher structuring, soliciting, and reacting. *Journal of Educational Psychology, 71,* 534–550.

Clark, D. L., & Astuto, T. A. (1994). Redirecting reform: Challenges to popular assumptions about teachers and students. *Phi Delta Kappan, 75,* 512–520.

Clark, J. M., & Paivio, A. (1991). Dual coding theory and education. *Educational Psychology Review, 3,* 149–210.

Clark, K., & Clark, M. (1939). The development of consciousness of self and the emergence of racial identification in Negro preschool children. *Journal of Social Psychology, 10,* 591–599.

Clark, R., Anderson, N. B., Clark, V. R., & Williams, D. R. (1999). Racism as a stressor for African Americans. *American Psychologist, 54,* 805–816.

Clarke, J. H., & Agne, R. M. (1997). *Interdisciplinary high school teaching.* Boston: Allyn & Bacon.

Clement, S. L. (1978). Dual marking system: Simple and effective. *American Secondary Education, 8,* 49–52.

Clifford, M. M. (1984a). Educational psychology. In *Encyclopedia of Education* (pp. 413–416). New York: Macmillan.

Clifford, M. M. (1990). Students need challenge, not easy success. *Educational Leadership, 48*(1), 22–26.

Clifford, M. M. (1991). Risk taking: Empirical and educational considerations. *Educational Psychologist, 26,* 263–298.

Cobb, P., & Bowers, J. (1999). Cognitive and situated learning: Perspectives in theory and practice. *Educational Researcher, 28*(2), 4–15.

Cognition and Technology Group at Vanderbilt. (1990). Anchored instruction and its relations to situated cognition. *Educational Researcher, 19*(6) 2–10.

Cognition and Technology Group at Vanderbilt. (1991). Some thoughts about constructivism and instructional design. *Educational Technology, 31*(5), 16–18.

Cognition and Technology Group at Vanderbilt. (1993). Anchored instruction and situated learning revisited. *Educational Technology, 33*(3), 52–70.

Cognition and Technology Group at Vanderbilt. (1996). Looking at technology in context: A framework for understanding technology and educational research. In D. Berliner & R. Calfee (Eds.), *Handbook of educational psychology* (pp. 807–840). New York: Macmillan.

Cohen, E. G. (1986). *Designing groupwork: Strategies for the heterogeneous classroom.* New York: Teachers College Press.

Coie, J. D., & Dodge, K. A. (1998). Aggression and antisocial behavior. In N. Eisenberg (Ed.), *Handbook of child psychology: Vol. 3. Social, emotional, and personality development* (5th ed.) (pp. 779–862). New York: Wiley.

Coie, J. D., Terry, R., Lenox, K., Lochman, J., & Hyman, C. (1995). Childhood peer rejection and aggression as predictors of stable patterns of adolescent disorder. *Development and Psychopathology, 7,* 697–714.

Cole, D. A., Martin, J. M., Peeke, L. A., Seroczynski, A. D., & Fier, J. (1999). Children's over- and underestimation of academic competence: A longitudinal study of gender differences, depression, and anxiety. *Child Development, 70,* 459–473.

Cole, M. (1985). The zone of proximal development: Where culture and cognition create each other. In J. V. Wertsch (Ed.), *Culture, communication, and cognition: Vygotskian perspectives* (pp. 146–161). Cambridge: Cambridge University Press.

Coles, R. (1990, September). Teachers who made a difference. *Instructor,* 58–59.

Collins, A., Brown, J. S., & Holum, A. (1991). Cognitive apprenticeship: Making thinking visible. *American Educator, 15*(3), 38–39.

Collins, A., Brown, J. S., & Newman, S. E. (1989). Cognitive apprenticeship: Teaching the crafts of reading, writing, and mathematics. In L. B. Resnick (Ed.), *Knowing, learning, and instruction: Essays in honor of Robert Galser* (pp. 453–494). Hillsdale, NJ: Lawrence Erlbaum.

Collins, A., & Ferguson, W. (1993). Epistemic forms and epistemic games: Structures and strategies to guide inquiry. *Educational Psychologist, 28,* 35.

Confrey, J. (1990a). A review of the research on students' conceptions in mathematics, science, and programming. *Review of Research in Education, 16,* 3–56.

Confrey, J. (1990b). What constructivism implies for teaching. In R. Davis, C. Maher, & N. Noddings (Eds.), *Constructivist views on the teaching and learning of mathematics* (pp. 107–122). Monograph 4 of the National Council of Teachers of Mathematics, Reston, VA.

Conger, R. D., Conger, K. J., & Elder, G. (1997). Family economic hardship and adolescent academic performance: Mediating and moderating processes. In G. Duncan & J. Brooks-Gunn (Eds.), *Consequences of growing up poor* (pp. 288–310). New York: Russell Sage Foundation

Conley, S. (1991). Review of research on teacher participation in school decision making. *Review of Research in Education, 17,* 225–266.

Cooke, B. L., & Pang, K. C. (1991). Recent research on beginning teachers: Studies of trained and untrained novices. *Teaching and Teacher Education, 7,* 93–110.

Cooper, C. R. (1998). *The weaving of maturity: Cultural perspectives on adolescent development.* New York: Oxford University Press.

Cooper, C. R., & Denner, J. (1998). Theories linking culture and psychology: Universal and community-specific processes. In J. T. Spence, J. M. Darley, & D. J. Foss (Eds.), *Annual review of psychology* (pp. 559–584). Palo Alto, CA: Annual Reviews.

Cooper, G., & Sweller, J. (1987). Effects of schema acquisition and rule automation on mathematical problem-solving transfer. *Journal of Educational Psychology, 79,* 347–362.

Cooper, H. M. (1979). Pygmalion grows up: A model for teacher expectation communication and performance influence. *Review of Educational Research, 49,* 389–410.

Cooper, H. M., & Good, T. (1983). *Pygmalion grows up: Studies in the expectation communication process.* New York: Longman.

Cooper, H. M, Valentine, J. C., Nye, B., & Kindsay, J. J. (1999). Relationships between five after-school activities and academic achievement. *Journal of Educational Psychology, 91,* 369–683.

Copi, I. M. (1961). *Introduction to logic.* New York: Macmillan.

Cordova, D. I., & Lepper, M. R. (1996). Intrinsic motivation and the process of learning: Beneficial effects of contextualization, personalization, and choice. *Journal of Educational Psychology, 88,* 715–730.

Corenblum, B., & Annis, R. C. (1987). Racial identity and preference among Canadian Indian and White children: Replication and extension. *Canadian Journal of Behavioural Science, 19,* 254–265.

Corkill, A. J. (1992). Advance organizers: Facilitators of recall. *Educational Psychology Review, 4,* 33–67.

Corno, L. (1992). Encouraging students to take responsibility for learning and performance. *The Elementary School Journal, 93,* 69–84.

Corno, L. (1995). Comments on Winne: Analytic and systemic research are both needed. *Educational Psychologist, 30,* 201–206.

Corno, L., & Snow, R. E. (1986). Adapting teaching to individual differences in learners. In M. Wittrock (Ed.), *Handbook of research on teaching* (3rd ed.) (pp. 605–629). New York: Macmillan.

Corwin, R. (1981). Patterns of organizational control and teacher militancy: Theoretical continuities in the idea of "loose coupling." In A. Kerckhoff (Ed.), *Research in the sociology of education and socialization* (Vol. 2, pp. 261–291). Greenwich, CT: JAI Press.

Costa, A. L. (Ed.). (1985). *Developing minds: A resource book for teaching thinking.* Alexandria, VA: Association for Supervision and Curriculum Development.

Covaleskie, J. F. (1992). Discipline and morality: Beyond rules and consequences. *The Educational Forum, 56*(2), 56–60.

Covington, M. V. (1992). *Making the grade: A self-worth perspective on motivation and school reform.* New York: Holt, Rinehart, & Winston.

Covington, M. V., & Omelich, C. L. (1984). An empirical examination of Weiner's critique of attribution research. *Journal of Educational Psychology, 76,* 1214–1225.

Covington, M. V., & Omelich, C. L. (1987). "I knew it cold before the exam": A test of the anxiety-blockage hypothesis. *Journal of Educational Psychology, 79,* 393–400.

Cowley, G., & Underwood, A. (1998, June 15). Memory. *Newsweek, 131*(24), 48–54.

Craik, F. I. M., & Lockhart, R. S. (1972). Levels of processing: A framework for memory research. *Journal of Verbal Learning and Verbal Behavior, 11,* 671–684.

Crawford, J. (1997). *Best evidence: Research foundations of the Bilingual Education Act.* Washington, DC: National Clearinghouse for Bilingual Education.

Crisci, P. E. (1986). The Quest National Center: A focus on prevention of alienation. *Phi Delta Kappan, 67,* 440–442.

Cronin, J. F. (1993). Four misconceptions about authentic learning. *Educational Leadership, 50*(7), 78–80.

Cummins, D. D. (1991). Children's interpretation of arithmetic word problems. *Cognition and Instruction, 8,* 261–289.

Cummins, J. (1984). *Bilingualism and special education.* San Diego: College Hill Press.

Cummins, J. (1994). *The acquisition of English as a second language.* In K. Spangenberg-Urbschat & R. Prichard (Eds.), *Kids come in all languages: Reading instruction for ESL students* (pp. 36–62). Newark, DE: International Reading Association.

Cunningham, D. J. (1992) Beyond educational psychology: Steps toward an educational semiotic. *Educational Psychology Review, 4,* 165–194.

Current Directions in Psychological Science. (1993). Special Section: Controversies, 2, 1–12.

Curwin, R. L., & Mendler, A. N. (1988). Packaged discipline programs: Let the buyer beware. *Educational Leadership, 46*(2), 68–71.

Danielson, C., & Dwyer, C. (1995). How Praxis III supports beginning teachers. *Educational Leadership, 52*(6), 66–67.

Dansereau, D. F. (1985). Learning strategy research. In J. Segal, S. Chipman, & R. Glaser (Eds.), *Thinking and learning skills. Vol. I: Relating instruction to research.* Hillsdale, NJ: Erlbaum.

Dark, V. J., & Benbow, C. P. (1991). Differential enhancement of working memory with mathematical versus verbal precocity. *Journal of Educational Psychology, 83,* 48–60.

Das, J. P. (1995). Some thoughts on two aspects of Vygotsky's work. *Educational Psychologist, 30,* 93–97.

Davidson, J. (1982). The group mapping activity for instruction in reading and thinking. *Journal of Reading, 26,* 52–56.

Davis, J. K. (1991). Educational implications of field-dependence—independence. In S. Wapner & J. Demick (Eds.), *Field-dependence—independence: Cognitive styles across the life span* (pp. 149–176). Hillsdale, NJ: Lawrence Erlbaum.

Davis, R. B., Maher, C. A., & Noddings, N. (Eds.). (1990). Constructivist views on the teaching and learning of mathematics. *Monograph 4 of the National Council of Teachers of Mathematics,* Reston, VA.

Davis, S. F., Grover, C. A., Becker, A. H., & McGregor, L. N. (1992). Academic dishonesty: Prevalence, determinants, techniques, and punishments. *Teaching of Psychology, 9,* 16–20.

De Corte, E., & Verschaffel, L. (1985). Beginning first graders' initial representation of arithmetic word problems. *Journal of Mathematical Behavior, 4,* 3021.

De Corte, E., Greer, B., & Verschaffel, L. (1996). Mathematics learning and teaching. In D. Berliner & R. Calfee (Eds.), *Handbook of educational psychology* (pp. 491–549). New York: Macmillan.

De Mott, R. M. (1982). Visual impairments. In N. Haring (Ed.), *Exceptional children and youth.* Columbus, OH: Charles E. Merrill.

Deaux, K. (1993). Commentary: Sorry, wrong number: A reply to Gentile's call. *Psychological Science, 4,* 125–126.

DeCecco, J., & Richards, A. (1974). *Growing pains: Uses of school conflicts.* New York: Aberdeen.

deCharms, R. (1976). *Enhancing motivation.* New York: Irvington.

deCharms, R. (1983). Intrinsic motivation, peer tutoring, and cooperative learning: Practical maxims. In J. Levine & M. Wang (Eds.), *Teacher and student perceptions: Implications for learning* (pp. 391–398). Hillsdale, NJ: Erlbaum.

Deci, E. L. (1975). *Intrinsic motivation.* New York: Plenum.

Deci, E. L., Koestner, R., & Ryan, R. M. (1999). A meta-analytic review of experiments examining the effects of extrinsic rewards on intrinsic motivation. *Psychological Bulletin, 125,* 627–668.

Deci, E. L., & Ryan, R. M. (1985). *Intrinsic motivation and self-determination in human behavior.* New York: Plenum.

Deci, E. L., Vallerand, R. J., Pelletier, L. G., & Ryan, R. M. (1991). Motivation and education: The self-determination perspective. *Educational Psychologist, 26,* 325–346.

Delpit, L. (1995). *Other people's children: Cultural conflict in the classroom.* New York: The New York Press.

Dembo, M. H. (1994). *Applying educational psychology* (5th ed.). New York: Longman.

Demetras, M. J., & Post, K. N. (1985, April). *Negative feedback in mother-child dialogues.* Paper presented at the biennial meeting of the Society for Research in Child Development, Toronto.

Dempster, F. N. (1991). Synthesis of research on reviews and tests. *Educational Leadership, 48*(7), 71–76.

Dempster, F. N. (1993). Exposing our students to less should help them learn more. *Phi Delta Kappan, 74,* 432–437.

Deno, S. L. (1987). Curriculum-based measurement. *Teaching Exceptional Children, 20,* 41.

DeRidder, L. M. (1993). Teenage pregnancy: Etiology and educational interventions. *Educational Psychology Review, 5,* 87–107.

Derry, S. J. (1989). Putting learning strategies to work. *Educational Leadership, 47*(5) 4–10.

Derry, S. J. (1991). Strategy and expertise in solving word problems. In C. McCormick, G. Miller, & M. Pressley (Eds.), *Cognitive strategies research: From basic research to educational applications.* New York: Springer-Verlag.

Derry, S. J. (1992). Beyond symbolic processing: Expanding horizons for educational psychology. *Journal of Educational Psychology, 84,* 413–419.

Derry, S. J., & Murphy, D. A. (1986). Designing systems that train learning ability: From theory to practice. *Review of Educational Research, 56,* 1–39.

Deshler, D. D., & Schumaker, J. B. (1986). Learning strategies: An instructional alternative for low-achieving adolescents. *Exceptional Children, 52,* 583–590.

Dewey, J. (1910). *How we think.* Boston: D. C. Heath.

Diana, E. M., & Webb, J. M. (1997). Using geographic maps in classroom: The conjoint influence of individual differences and dual coding on learning facts. *Learning and Individual Differences, 9,* 195–214.

Diaz, R. M., & Berk, L. E. (Eds.). (1992). *Private speech: From social interaction to self-regulation.* Hillsdale, NJ: Erlbaum.

Dinnel, D., & Glover, J. A. (1985). Advance organizers: Encoding manipulations. *Journal of Educational Psychology, 77,* 514–522.

DiVesta, F. J., & Di Cintio, M. J. (1997). Interactive effects of working memory span and text comprehension on reading comprehension and retrieval. *Learning and Individual Differences, 9,* 215–231.

DiVesta, F. J., & Gray, G. S. (1972). Listening and notetaking. *Journal of Educational Psychology, 63,* 8–14.

Doctorow, M., Wittrock, M. C., & Marks, C. (1978). Generative processes in reading comprehension. *Journal of Educational Psychology, 70,* 109–118.

Dodge, K. A., & Somberg, D. R. (1987). Hostile attributional biases among aggressive boys are exacerbated under conditions of threats to the self. *Child Development, 58,* 213–224.

Dole, J. A., Duffy, G. G., Roehler, L. R., & Pearson, P. D. (1991). Moving from the old to the new: Research on reading comprehension instruction. *Review of Educational Research, 61,* 239–264.

Doyle, W. (1977). The uses of nonverbal behaviors: Toward an ecological model of classrooms. *Merrill-Palmer Quarterly, 23,* 179–192.

Doyle, W. (1983). Academic work. *Review of Educational Research, 53,* 159–200.

Doyle, W. (1986). Classroom organization and management. In M. C. Wittrock (Ed.), *Handbook of research on teaching* (3rd ed.) (pp. 392–431). New York: Macmillan.

Driscoll, M. P. (1994). *Psychology of learning for instruction.* Boston: Allyn & Bacon.

Duchastel, P. (1979). Learning objectives and the organization of prose. *Journal of Educational Psychology, 71,* 100–106.

Duckitt, J. (1992). Psychology and prejudice: A historical analysis and integrative framework. *American Psychologist, 47,* 1182–1193.

Duckitt, J. (1994). *The social psychology of prejudice.* Westport, CN: Praeger.

Duell, O. K. (1994). Extended wait time and university student achievement. *American Educational Research Journal, 31,* 397–414.

Duffy, G., Roehler, L. R., Meloth, M. S., & Vavrus, L. G. (1986). Conceptualizing instructional explanation. *Teaching and Teacher Education, 2,* 197–214.

Duncker, K. (1945). On solving problems. *Psychological Monographs, 58*(5, Whole No. 270).

Dunkin, M. J., & Biddle, B. J. (1974). *The study of teaching.* New York: Holt, Rinehart & Winston.

Dunn, K., & Dunn, R. (1978). *Teaching students through their individual learning styles.* Reston, VA: National Council of Principals.

Dunn, K., & Dunn, R. (1987). Dispelling outmoded beliefs about student learning. *Educational Leadership, 44*(6), 55–63.

Dunn, R. (1987). Research on instructional environments: Implications for student achievement and attitudes. *Professional School Psychology, 2,* 43–52.

Dunn, R., Beaudry, J. S., & Klavas, A. (1989). Survey of research on learning styles. *Educational Leadership, 47*(7), 50–58.

Dunn, R., Dunn, K., & Price, G. E. (1984). *Learning Style Inventory.* Lawrence, KS: Price Systems.

Dweck, C. S. (1986). Motivational processes affecting learning. *American Psychologist, 41,* 1040–1047.

Dweck, C. S., & Bempechat, J. (1983). Children's theories on intelligence: Consequences for learning. In S. Paris, G. Olson, & W. Stevenson (Eds.), *Learning and motivation in the classroom* (pp. 239–256). Hillsdale, NJ: Erlbaum.

Dwyer, C. A., & Villegas, A. M. (1993, January). *Guiding conceptions and assessment principles for the Praxis Series: Professional assessments for beginning teachers.* Princeton, NJ: Educational Testing Service.

Dyson, A. H. (1997). *Writing superheroes: Contemporary childhood, popular culture, and classroom literacy.* New York: Teachers College Press.

Eaton, J. F., Anderson, C. W., & Smith, E. L. (1984). Students' misconceptions interfere with science learning: Case studies of fifth-graders. *Elementary School Journal, 84,* 365–379.

Eccles, J., & Wigfield, A. (1985). Teacher expectations and student motivation. In J. Dusek (Ed.), *Teacher expectancies* (pp. 185–226). Hillsdale, NJ: Erlbaum.

Educational Testing Service (ETS). (1992). *The second international assessment of educational progress.* Princeton, NJ: Author.

Egan, S. K., Monson, T. C., & Perry, D. G. (1998). Social-cognitive influences on change in aggression over time. *Developmental Psychology, 34,* 996–1006.

Eggen, P. D., & Kauchak, D. P. (1996). *Strategies for teachers: Teaching content and thinking skills* (3rd ed.) Boston: Allyn & Bacon.

Eimas, P. D. (1985). The perception of speech in early infancy. *Scientific American, 252,* 46–52.

Eiseman, J. W. (1981). What criteria should public school moral education programs meet? *The Review of Education, 7,* 213–230.

Eisenberg, N., Martin, C. L., & Fabes, R. A. (1996). Gender development and gender effects. In D. Berliner & R. Calfee (Eds.), *Handbook of educational psychology* (pp. 358–396). New York: Macmillan.

Eisenberg, N., & Miller, P. A. (1987). The relation of empathy to prosocial and related behaviors. *Psychological Bulletin, 101,* 91–119.

Eisenberg, N., Shell, R., Pasernack, J., Lennon, R., Beller, R., & Mathy, R. M. (1987). Prosocial development in middle childhood: A longitudinal study. *Developmental Psychology, 23,* 712–718.

Eisenberg, R., Pierce, W. D., & Cameron, J. (1999). Effects of rewards on intrinsic motivation—Negative, neutral, and positive: Comment on Deci, Koestner, and Ryan (1999). *Psychological Bulletin, 125,* 677–691.

Eisner, E. W. (1999). The uses and limits of performance assessments. *Phi Delta Kappan, 80,* 658–660.

Elashoff, J. D., & Snow, R. E. (1971). *Pygmalion reconsidered.* Worthington, OH: Charles A. Jones.

Elawar, M. C., & Corno, L. (1985). A factorial experiment in teachers' written feedback on student homework: Changing teacher behavior a little rather than a lot. *Journal of Educational Psychology, 77,* 162–173.

Elkind, D. (1981). Obituary—Jean Piaget (1896–1980). *American Psychologist, 36,* 911–913.

Elkind, D. (1989). Developmentally appropriate education for 4-year-olds. *Theory Into Practice, 28*(1), 47–52.

Elkind, D. (1991). Formal education and early childhood education: An essential difference. In K. M. Cauley, F. Linder, & J. H. MacMillan (Eds.), *Annual Editions: Educational Psychology 91/92* (pp. 27–37). Guilford, CT: Duskin.

Ellis, A. K., & Fouts, J. T. (1993). *Research on educational innovations.* Princeton, NJ: Eye on Education.

Elrich, M. (1994). The stereotype within. *Educational Leadership, 51*(8), 12–15.

Emery, R. E. (1989). Family violence. *American Psychologist, 44,* 321–328.

Emmer, E. T., & Evertson, C. M. (1981). Synthesis of research on classroom management. *Educational Leadership, 38,* 342–345.

Emmer, E. T., & Evertson, C. M. (1982). Effective classroom management at the beginning of the school year in junior high school classes. *Journal of Educational Psychology, 74,* 485–498.

Emmer, E. T., Evertson, C. M., & Anderson, L. M. (1980). Effective classroom management at the beginning of the school year. *Elementary School Journal, 80,* 219–231.

Emmer, E. T., Evertson, C., Clements, B., & Worsham, M. (1997). *Classroom management for secondary teachers* (4th ed.). Boston: Allyn & Bacon.

Emmer, E. T., Evertson, C. M., & Worsham, M. E. (2000). *Classroom management for secondary teachers* (5th ed.). Boston: Allyn & Bacon.

End of innocence. (1991, Summer). *Newsweek* [Special Edition, How Kids Grow], 62–64.

Engel, P. (1991). Tracking progress toward the school readiness goal. *Educational Leadership, 48*(5), 39–42.

Engelmann, S., & Englemann, T. (1981). *Give your child a superior mind.* New York: Simon & Schuster.

Entwisle, D. R., & Alexander, K. L. (1998). Facilitating the transition to first grade: The nature of transition and research on factors affecting it. *The Elementary School Journal, 98,* 351–364.

Entwisle, D. R., Alexander, K., & Olson, L. (1997). *Children, schools, and inequality.* Boulder, CO: Westview Press.

Epanchin, B. C., Townsend, B., & Stoddard, K. (1994). *Constructive classroom management: Strategies for creating positive learning environments.* Pacific Grove, CA: Brooks/Cole.

Epstein, H. (1978). Growth spurts during brain development: Implications for educational policy and practice. In J. Chall & A. Mirsky (Eds.), *Education and the brain. The seventy-seventh yearbook of the National Society for the Study of Education, Part II* (pp. 343–370). Chicago: University of Chicago Press.

Epstein, H. (1980). EEG developmental stages. *Developmental Psychobiology, 13,* 629–631.

Epstein, J. L. (1989). Family structure and student motivation. In R. E. Ames & C. Ames (Eds.), *Research on motivation in education: Vol 3. Goals and cognitions* (pp. 259–295). New York: Academic Press.

Epstein, J. L. (1995). School/Family/Community partnerships: Caring for the children we share. *Phi Delta Kappan, 76,* 701–712.

Epstein, J. L., & MacIver, D. J. (1992). *Opportunities to learn: Effects on eighth graders of curriculum offerings and instructional approaches.* (Report No. 34). Baltimore: Center for Research on Elementary and Middle Schools, Johns Hopkins University.

Erez, M., & Zidon, I. (1984). Effects of goal acceptance on the relationship of goal difficulty to performance. *Journal of Applied Psychology, 69,* 69–78.

Erickson, F., & Shultz, J. (1982). *The counselor as gatekeeper: Social interaction in interviews.* New York: Academic Press.

Ericsson, K. A., & Smith, J. (Eds.) (1991). *Toward a general theory of expertise.* Cambridge, UK: Cambridge University Press.

Erikson, E. H. (1963). *Childhood and society* (2nd ed.). New York: Norton.

Erikson, E. H. (1968). *Identity, youth, and crisis.* New York: Norton.

Erikson, E. H. (1980). *Identity and the life cycle* (2nd ed.). New York: Norton.

Espe, C., Worner, C., & Hotkevich, M. (1990). Whole language—What a bargain. *Educational Leadership, 47*(6), 45.

Estes, W. K. (1993). Concepts, categories, and psychological science. *Psychological Science, 4,* 143–153.

Evertson, C. M. (1988). Managing classrooms: A framework for teachers. In D. Berliner & B. Rosenshine (Eds.), *Talks to teachers* (pp. 54–74). New York: Random House.

Evertson, C. M., Emmer, E. T., Clements, B. S., & Worsham, M. E. (1997). *Classroom management for elementary teachers* (4th ed.). Boston: Allyn & Bacon.

Evertson, C. M., Emmer, E. T., & Worsham, M. E. (2000). *Classroom management for elementary teachers* (5th ed.). Boston: Allyn & Bacon.

Ewy, C. & student authors. (1997). Kids take on "the test." *Educational Leadership, 54*(4), 76–78.

Fagot, B. I., & Hagan, R. (1991). Observations of parent reactions to sex-stereotyped behaviors: Age and sex effects. *Child Development, 62,* 617–628.

Fagot, B. I., Hagan, R., Leinbach, M. D., & Kronsberg, S. (1985). Differential reactions to assertive and communicative acts of toddler boys and girls. *Child Development, 56,* 1499–1505.

Fantuzzo, J., Davis, G., & Ginsburg, M. (1995). Effects of parent involvement in isolation or in combination with peer tutoring on student self-concept and mathematics achievement. *Journal of Educational Psychology, 87,* 272–281.

Farnaham-Diggory, S. (1994). Paradigms of knowledge and instruction. *Review of Educational Research, 64,* 463–477.

Farrar, M. J. (1990). Discourse and the acquisition of grammatical morphemes. *Journal of Child Language, 17,* 607–624.

Feather, N. T. (1982). *Expectations and actions: Expectancy-value models in psychology.* Hillsdale, NJ: Lawrence Erlbaum.

Feiman-Nemser, S. (1983). Learning to teach. In L. Shulman & G. Sykes (Eds.), *Handbook of teaching and policy* (pp. 150–170). New York: Longman.

Feingold, A. (1994). Gender differences in personality: A meta-analysis. *Psychological Bulletin, 116,* 429–456.

Fennema, E., & Peterson, P. (1988). Effective teaching for boys and girls: The same or different? In D. Berliner & B. Rosenshine (Eds.), *Talks to teachers* (pp. 111–127). New York: Random House.

Fennema, E., & Sherman, J. (1977). Sex-related differences in mathematics achievement, spatial visualization and affective factors. *American Educational Research Journal, 14*(1), 51–71.

Ferguson, D. L., Ferguson, P. M., & Bogdan, R. C. (1987). If mainstreaming is the answer, what is the question? In V. Richardson-Koehler (Ed.), *Educators' handbook: A research perspective* (pp. 394–419). New York: Longman.

Fernald, A. (1993). Approval and disapproval: Infant responsiveness to vocal affect in familiar and unfamiliar languages. *Child Development, 64,* 657–674.

Feuerstein, R. (1979). *The dynamic assessment of retarded performers: The Learning Potential Assessment Device, theory, instruments, and techniques.* Baltimore: University Park Press.

Feuerstein, R. (1990). The theory of structural cognitive modifiability. In B. Presseisen (Ed.), *Learning and thinking styles: Classroom interaction* (pp. 68–134). Washington, DC: National Education Association.

Fielding, L. G., & Pearson, P. D. (1994). Synthesis of research: Reading comprehension: What works. *Educational Leadership, 51*(5), 62–68.

Finn, J. (1972). Expectations and the educational environment. *Review of Educational Research, 42,* 387–410.

Fiske, E. B. (1981, October 27). Teachers reward muddy prose, study finds. *New York Times,* p. C1.

Fiske, E. B. (1988, April 10). America's test mania. *New York Times* (Education Life Section), pp. 16–20.

Fiske, S. T. (1993). Social cognition and social perception. *Annual Review of Psychology, 44,* 155–194.

Fitts, P. M., & Posner, M. I. (1967). *Human performance.* Belmont, CA: Brooks Cole.

Fitzgerald, J. (1995). English-as-a-second-language learners' cognitive reading process: A review of the research in the United States. *Review of Educational Research, 62*, 145–190.

Flammer, A. (1995). Developmental analysis of control beliefs. In A. Bandura, (Ed.). *Self-efficacy in changing societies* (pp. 69–113). New York: Cambridge University Press.

Flavell, J. H. (1985). *Cognitive development* (2nd ed.). Englewood Cliffs, NJ: Prentice-Hall.

Flavell, J. H., Friedrichs, A. G., & Hoyt, J. D. (1970). Developmental changes in memorization processes. *Cognitive Psychology, 1*, 324–340.

Flavell, J. H., Green, F. L., & Flavell, E. R. (1995). Young children's knowledge about thinking. *Monographs of the Society for Research in Child Development, 60*(1) (Serial No. 243).

Flink, C. F., Boggiano, A. K., & Barrett, M. (1990). Controlling teaching strategies: Undermining children's self-determination and performance. *Journal of Personality and Social Psychology, 59*, 916–924.

Floden, R. E., & Klinzing, H. G. (1990). What can research on teacher thinking contribute to teacher preparation? A second opinion. *Educational Researcher, 19*(4), 15–20.

Forest, M. (1991). It's about relationships. In L. Meyer, C. Peck, & L. Brown (Eds.), *Critical issues in the lives of people with disabilities* (pp. 399–408). Baltimore: Paul H. Brookes.

Foster, J. D. (1991). The role of accountability in Kentucky's Educational Reform Act of 1990. *Educational Leadership, 48*(5), 34–36.

Foster, W. (1981, August). *Social and emotional development in gifted individuals.* Paper presented at the Fourth World Conference on Gifted and Talented, Montreal.

Fox, L. H. (1981). Identification of the academically gifted. *American Psychologist, 36*, 1103–1111.

Frable, D. E. S. (1997). Gender, Racial, ethnic, and class identities. In J. T, Spence, J. M. Darley, & D. J. Foss (Eds.) *Annual Review of Psychology* (pp. 139–162). Palo Alto, CA: Annual Reviews.

Frank, S. J., Pirsch, L. A., & Wright, V. C. (1990). Late adolescents' perceptions of their parents: Relationships among deidealization, autonomy, relatedness, and insecurity and implications for adolescent adjustment and ego identity status. *Journal of Youth and Adolescence, 19*, 571–588.

Frederiksen, N. (1984). Implications of cognitive theory for instruction in problem solving. *Review of Educational Research 54*, 363–407.

Freiberg, H. J. (1999). Sustaining the paradigm. In H. J. Freiberg (Ed.), *Beyond behaviorism: Changing the classroom management paradigm* (pp. 164–173). Boston: Allyn & Bacon

Freiberg, H. J. (Ed.). (1999). *Beyond behaviorism: Changing the classroom management.* Boston: Allyn & Bacon.

Freiberg, H. J., & Driscoll, A. (1996). *Universal teaching strategies* (2nd ed.). Boston: Allyn & Bacon.

Freud, S. (1959). Creative writers and daydreaming. In J. Strachey (Ed.), *The standard edition of the complete psychological works of Sigmund Freud* (Vol. 9). London: Hogarth Press.

Frick, T. W. (1990). Analysis of patterns in time: A method of recording and quantifying temporal relations in education. *American Educational Research Journal, 27*, 180–204.

Friend, M., & Bursuck, W. (1996). *Including students with special needs: A practical guide for classroom teachers.* Boston: Allyn & Bacon.

Frisbie, D. A., & Waltmen, K. K. (1992). Developing a personal grading plan. *Educational Measurement: Issues and practices* (pp. 35–42). Washington, DC: National Council on Measurement in Education.

Fromberg, D. P., & Driscoll, M. (1985). *The successful classroom: Management strategies for regular and special education teachers.* New York: Teachers College Press.

Fuchs, L. S., Fuchs, D., Hamlett, C. L., & Karns, K. (1998). High-achieving students' interactions and performance on complex mathematical tasks as a function of homogeneous and heterogeneous pairings. *American Educational Research Journal, 35*, 227–268.

Fulk, C. L., & Smith, P. J. (1995). Students' perceptions of teachers' instructional and management adaptations for students with learning or behavior problems. *The Elementary School Journal, 95*, 409–419.

Fuller, F. G. (1969). Concerns of teachers: A developmental conceptualization. *American Educational Research Journal, 6*, 207–226.

Furstenberg, F. F., & Cherlin, A. J. (1991). *Divided families.* Cambridge: Harvard University Press.

Gage, N. L. (1991). The obviousness of social and educational research results. *Educational Researcher, 20*(A), 10–16.

Gagné, E. D. (1985). *The cognitive psychology of school learning.* Boston: Little Brown.

Gagné, E. D., Yekovich, C. W., & Yekovich, F. R. (1993). *The cognitive psychology of school learning* (2nd ed.). New York: HarperCollins.

Gagné, R. M. (1977). *The conditions of learning* (3rd ed.). New York: Holt, Rinehart & Winston.

Gagné, R. M. (1985). *The conditions of learning and theory of instruction* (4th ed.). New York: Holt, Rinehart & Winston.

Gagné, R. M., & Driscoll, M. P. (1988). *Essentials of learning for instruction* (2nd ed.). Englewood Cliffs, NJ: Prentice-Hall.

Gagné, R. M., & Smith, E. (1962). A study of the effects of verbalization on problem solving. *Journal of Experimental Psychology, 63*, 12–18.

Gaines, S. O., & Reed, E. S. (1995). Prejudice: From Allport to DuBois. *American Psychologist, 50*, 96–103.

Galambos, S. J., & Goldin-Meadow, S. (1990). The effects of learning two languages on metalinguistic development. *Cognition, 34*, 1–56.

Gall, M. D. (1970). The use of questions in teaching. *Review of Educational Research, 40*, 707–721.

Gall, M. D. (1984). Synthesis of research on teachers' questioning. *Educational Leadership, 41*, 40–47.

Gallini, J. K. (1991). Schema-based strategies and implications for instructional design in strategy training. In C. McCormick, G. Miller, & M. Pressley (Eds.), *Cognitive strategies research: From basic research to educational applications.* New York: Springer-Verlag.

Gamoran, A., & Mare, R. D. (1989). Secondary school detracking and educational inequity: Compensation, reinforcement, or neutrality? *American Journal of Education, 106*(3), 385–415.

Garcia, E. E. (1992). "Hispanic" children: Theoretical, empirical, and related policy issues. *Educational Psychology Review, 4*, 69–94.

Garcia, R. L. (1991). *Teaching in a pluralistic society: Concepts, models, and strategies.* New York: HarperCollins.

Garcia, T., & Pintrich, P. (1994). Regulating motivation and cognition in the classroom: The role of self-schemas and self-regulatory strategies. In B. J. Zimmerman & D. Schunk (Eds.), *Self-regulation of learning and performance: Issues and educational applications* (pp. 127–153). Hillsdale, NJ: Erlbaum.

Gardner, H. (1982a). *Art, mind, and brain: A cognitive approach to creativity.* New York: Basic Books.

Gardner, H. (1982b). *Developmental psychology* (2nd ed.). Boston: Little, Brown.

Gardner, H. (1983). *Frames of mind: The theory of multiple intelligences.* New York: Basic Books.

Gardner, H. (1991). *The unschooled mind: How children think and how schools should teach.* New York: Basic Books.

Gardner, H. (1993a). *Creating minds: An anatomy of creativity seen through the lives of Freud, Einstein, Picasso, Stravinsky, Elliot, Graham, and Gandhi.* New York: Basic Books.

Gardner, H. (1993b). *Educating the unschooled mind: A science and public policy seminar.* Washington, DC: American Educational Research Association.

Gardner, H. (1993c). *Multiple intelligences: The theory in practice.* New York: Basic Books.

Gardner, H. (1998). Reflections on multiple intelligences: Myths and messages. In A. Woolfolk (Ed.), *Readings in educational psychology* (2nd ed.) (pp. 61–67). Boston: Allyn & Bacon.

Gardner, H. (1999, August). *Who owns intelligence?* Invited address at the Annual Meeting of the American Psychological Association, Boston.

Gardner, H., & Hatch, T. (1989). Multiple intelligences go to school. *Educational Researcher, 18*(8), 4–10.

Gardner, R., Brown, R., Sanders, S. & Menke, D. J. (1992). "Seductive details" in learning from text. In K. A. Renninger, S. Hidi, & A. Krapp (Eds.), *The role of interest in learning and development* (pp. 239–254). Hillsdale, NJ: Erlbaum.

Gargarian, G. (1996). The art of design. In Y. Kafai & M. Resnick (Eds.), *Constructivism in practice: Designing, thinking, and learning in a digital world* (pp. 125–160). Mahwah, NJ: Erlbaum.

Garmon, A., Nystrand, M., Berends, M., & LePore, P. C. (1995). An organizational analysis of the effects of ability grouping. *American Educational Research Journal, 32*, 687–715.

Garmoran, A. (1987). The stratification of high school learning opportunities. *Sociology of Education, 60*, 135–155.

Garner, R. (1990). When children and adults do not use learning strategies: Toward a theory of settings. *Review of Educational Psychology, 60*, 517–530.

Garner, R. (1992). Learning from school tests. *Educational Psychologist, 27*, 53–63.

Garner, R. (1998). Choosing to learn and not-learn in school. *Educational Psychology Review, 10*, 227–238.

Garrison, J. (1995). Deweyan pragmatism and the epistemology of contemporary social constructivism. *American Educational Research Journal, 32*, 716–741.

Garrod, A., Beal, C., & Shin, P. (1990). The development of moral orientation in elementary school children. *Sex Roles, 22*, 13–27.

Gartner, A., & Lipsky, D. K. (1987). Beyond special education: Toward a quality system for all students. *Harvard Educational Review, 57*, 367–395.

Geary, D. C. (1995). Reflections of evolution and culture in children's cognition: Implications for mathematical development and instruction. *American Psychologist, 50*, 24–37.

Geary, D. C. (1995). Sexual selection and sex differences in spatial cognition. *Learning and Individual Differences, 7*, 289–303.

Geary, D. C. (1998). What is the function of mind and brain? *Educational Psychologist, 10*, 377–388.

Geary, D. C. (1999). Evolution and developmental sex differences. *Current Directions in Psychological Science, 8*, 115–120.

Gelman, R. (1979). Preschool thought. *American Psychologist, 34*, 900–905.

Gelman, R., & Baillargeon, R. (1983). A review of some Piagetian concepts. In P. Mussen (Ed.), *Carmichael's manual of child psychology. Vol. 3: Cognitive development* (E. Markman & J. Flavell, Volume Eds.). New York: Wiley.

Gelman, R., Meck, E., & Merkin, S. (1986). Young children's numerical competence. *Cognitive Development, 1*, 1–29.

Gelman, S. A., & Ebeling, K. S. (1989). Children's use of nonegocentric standards in judgments of size. *Child Development, 60*, 920–932.

Gentner, D. (1975). Evidence for the psychological reality of semantic components: The verbs of possession. In D. Norman & D. Rumelhart (Eds.), *Explorations in cognition* (pp. 211–246). San Francisco: Freeman.

Gerbner, G., Gross, L. Signorelli, N., & Morgan, M. (1986). *Television's mean world: Violence Profile No. 14–15.* Philadelphia: Annenberg School of Communication, University of Pennsylvania.

Gergen, K. J. (1997). Constructing constructivism: Pedagogical potentials. *Issues in Education: Contributions from Educational Psychology, 3*, 195–202.

Gersten, R. (1996a). The language-minority students in transition: Contemporary instructional research. *The Elementary School Journal, 96*, 217–220.

Gersten, R. (1996b). Literacy instruction for language-minority students: The transition years. *The Elementary School Journal, 96*, 217–220.

Giaconia, R. M., & Hedges, L. V. (1982). Identifying features of effective open education. *Review of Educational Research, 52*, 579–602.

Gibbs, J. W., & Luyben, P. D. (1985). Treatment of self-injurious behavior: Contingent versus noncontingent positive practice overcorrection. *Behavior Modification, 9*, 3–21.

Gick, M. L. (1986). Problem-solving strategies. *Educational Psychologist, 21*, 99–120.

Gick, M. L., & Holyoak, K. L. (1983). Schema induction and analogical transfer. *Cognitive Psychology, 15*, 1–38.

Gillett, M., & Gall, M. (1982, March). *The effects of teacher enthusiasm on the at-task behavior of students in the elementary grades.* Paper presented at the annual meeting of the American Educational Research Association, New York.

Gilligan, C. (1982). *In a different voice: Psychological theory and women's development.* Cambridge, MA: Harvard University Press.

Gilligan, C., & Attanucci, J. (1988). Two moral orientations: Gender differences and similarities. *Merrill-Palmer Quarterly, 34*, 223–237.

Gilstrap, R. L., & Martin, W. R. (1975). *Current strategies for teachers: A resource for personalizing education.* Pacific Palisades, CA: Goodyear.

Ginsburg, H., & Opper, S. (1988). *Piaget's theory of intellectual development* (3rd ed.). Englewood Cliffs, NJ: Prentice-Hall.

Girls' math achievement: What we do and don't know. (1986, January). *Harvard Education Letter, 2*(1), 1–5.

Glaser, R. (1981). The future of testing: A research agenda for cognitive psychology and psychometrics. *American Psychologist, 36*, 923–936.

Glasgow, K. L., Dornbusch, S. M., Troyer, L., Steinberg, L., & Ritter, P. L. (1997). Parenting styles, adolescents' attributions, and educational outcomes in nine heterogeneous high schools. *Child Development, 68*, 507–523.

Glasser, W. (1969). *Schools without failure.* New York: Harper & Row.

Glasser, W. (1990). *The quality school: Managing students without coercion.* New York: Harper & Row.

Gleitman, H., Fridlund, A. J., & Reisberg, D. (1999). *Psychology* (5th ed.). New York: Norton.

Goldenberg, C. (1996). The education of language-minority students: Where are we, and where do we need to go? *The Elementary School Journal, 96*, 353–361.

Goleman, D. (1988, April 10). An emerging theory on blacks' I.Q. scores. *New York Times* (Education Life Section), pp. 22–24.

Goleman, D. (1995). *Emotional intelligence.* New York: Bantam.

Gollnick, D. A., & Chinn, P. C. (1994). *Multicultural education in a pluralistic society* (4th ed.). New York: Merrill.

Good, T. L. (1983a). Classroom research: A decade of progress. *Educational Psychologist, 18*, 127–144.

Good, T. L. (1983b). Research on classroom teaching. In L. Shulman & G. Sykes (Eds.), *Handbook of teaching and policy* (pp. 42–80). New York: Longman.

Good, T. L. (1988). Teacher expectations. In D. Berliner & B. Rosenshine (Eds.), *Talks to teachers* (pp. 159–200). New York: Random House.

Good, T. L. (1996). Teaching effects and teacher evaluation. In J. Sikula (Ed.) *Handbook of research on teacher education* (pp. 617–665). New York: Macmillan.

Good, T. L., & Brophy, J. E. (1994). *Looking in classrooms* (6th ed.). New York: HarperCollins.

Good, T. L., & Brophy, J. E. (1997). *Looking in classrooms* (7th ed.). New York: Longman.

Good, T. L., Grouws, D., & Ebmeier, H. (1983). *Active mathematics teaching.* New York: Longman.

Good, T. L., & Marshall, S. (1984). Do students learn more in heterogeneous or homogeneous groups? In P. Peterson, L. C. Wilkinson, & M. Hallinan (Eds.), *The social context of instruction: Group organization and group processes* (pp. 15–38). Orlando, FL: Academic Press.

Good, T. L., & Weinstein, R. (1986). Schools make a difference: Evidence, criticisms, and new directions. *American Psychologist, 41,* 1090–1097.

Goodenow, C. (1992). Strengthening the links between educational psychology and the study of social contexts. *Educational Psychologist, 27,* 177–196.

Goodenow, C. (1993). Classroom belonging among early adolescents: Relationships to motivation and achievement. *Journal of Early Adolescence, 13,* 21–43.

Goodman, K. S. (1986). *What's whole in whole language: A parent-teacher guide.* Portsmouth, NH: Heinemann.

Goodman, Y. M., & Goodman, K. S. (1990). Vygotsky in a whole-language perspective. In L. Moll (Ed.), *Vygotsky and education: Instructional implications and applications of sociohistorical psychology* (pp. 223–250). New York: Cambridge University Press.

Goodrich, H. (1997). Understanding rubrics. *Educational Leadership, 54(4),* 14–17.

Gordon, E. W. (1991). Human diversity and pluralism. *Educational Psychologist, 26,* 99–108.

Gordon, T. (1974). *Teacher effectiveness training.* New York: Peter H. Wyden.

Gordon, T. (1981). Crippling our children with discipline. *Journal of Education, 163,* 228–243.

Grabe, M., & Latta, R. M. (1981). Cumulative achievement in a mastery instructional system: The impact of differences in resultant achievement motivation and persistence. *American Educational Research Journal, 18,* 7–14.

Graber, J. A, & Brooks-Gunn, J. (1996). Transitions and turning points: Navigating the passage from childhood through adolescence. *Developmental Psychology, 32,* 768–776.

Graham, S., & Weiner, B. (1996). Theories and principles of motivation. In D. Berliner & R. Calfee (Eds.), *Handbook of educational psychology* (pp. 63–84). New York: Macmillan.

Graham, S. (1991). A review of attribution theory in achievement contexts. *Educational Psychology Review, 3,* 5–39.

Graham, S. (1994). Motivation in African Americans. *Review of Educational Research, 64,* 55–117.

Graham, S. (1995). Narrative versus meta-analytic reviews of race differences in motivation. *Review of Educational Research, 65,* 509–514.

Graham, S. (1996). How causal beliefs influence the academic and social motivation of African-American children. In G. G. Brannigan (Ed.), *The enlightened educator: Research adventures in the schools* (pp. 111–126). New York: McGraw-Hill.

Graham, S. (1998). Self-blame and peer victimization in middle school: An attributional analysis. *Developmental Psychology, 34,* 587–599.

Graham, S., & Barker, G. (1990). The downside of help: An attributional developmental analysis of helping behavior as a low ability cue. *Journal of Educational Psychology, 82,* 7–14.

Graham, S., & Golan, S. (1991). Motivational influences on cognition: Task involvement, ego involvement, and depth of information processing. *Journal of Educational Psychology, 83,* 187–194.

Graham, S., & Guskey, T. R. (1990). Cooperative mastery learning strategies. *The Elementary School Journal, 91,* 33–42.

Graham, S., & Harris, K. R. (1994). The effects of whole language on children's writing: A review of literature. *Educational Psychologist, 29,* 187–192.

Graham, S., & Harris, K. R. (1994). The effects of whole language on children's writing: A review of the literature. *Educational Psychologist, 29,* 187–192.

Grant, C. A., & Sleeter, C. E. (1989). Race, class, gender, exceptionality, and educational reform. In J. Banks & C. McGee Banks (Eds.), *Multicultural education: Issues and perspectives* (pp. 49–66). Boston: Allyn & Bacon.

Greeno, J. G., Collins, A. M., & Resnick, L. B. (1996). Cognition and learning. In D. Berliner & R. Calfee (Eds.), *Handbook of educational psychology* (pp. 15–46). New York: Macmillan.

Greenough, W. T., Black, J. E., & Wallace, C. S. (1987). Experience and brain development. *Child Development, 58,* 539–559.

Gregorc, A. F. (1982). *Gregorc Style Delineator: Development, technical, and administrative manual.* Maynard, MA: Gabriel Systems.

Gresham, F. (1981). Social skills training with handicapped children. *Review of Educational Research, 51,* 139–176.

Grigorenko, E. L., & Sternberg, R. J. (1998). Dynamic testing. *Psychological Bulletin, 124,* 75–111.

Grinder, R. E. (1981). The "new" science of education: Educational psychology in search of a mission. In F. H. Farley & N. J. Gordon (Eds.), *Psychology and education: The state of the union* (pp. 354–366). Berkeley, CA: McCutchan.

Grissom, J. B., & Smith, L. A. (1989). Repeating and dropping out of school. In L. Shepard & M. Smith (Eds.), *Flunking grades: Research and policies on retention* (pp. 34–63). Philadelphia: Falmer Press.

Grolnick, W. S., & Ryan, R. M. (1989). Parent styles associated with children's self-regulation and competence in school. *Journal of Educational Psychology, 81,* 143–154.

Grolnick, W. S., Ryan, R. M., & Deci, E. L. (1991) Inner resources for school achievement: Motivational mediators of children's perceptions of their parents. *Journal of Educational Psychology, 83,* 508–517.

Gronlund, N. E. (1993). *How to make achievement tests and assessments* (5th ed.). Boston: Allyn & Bacon.

Gronlund, N. E. (2000). *How to write and use instructional objectives* (6th ed.). Columbus: OH: Merrill.

Gross, M. U. M. (1992). The use of radical acceleration in cases of extreme intellectual precocity. *Gifted Child Quarterly, 36,* 91–99.

Grossman, H., & Grossman, S. H. (1994). *Gender issues in education.* Boston: Allyn & Bacon.

Grotevant, H. D. (1998). Adolescent development in family contexts. In N. Eisenberg (Ed.), *Handbook of child psychology: Vol 3. Social, emotional, and personality development* (5th ed.) (pp. 1097–1149). New York: Wiley.

Guilford, J. P. (1988). Some changes in the Structure-of-Intellect model. *Educational and Psychological Measurement, 48,* 1–4.

Guitierrez, R., & Slavin, R. E. (1992). Achievement effects of the nongraded elementary school: A best evidence synthesis. *Review of Educational Research, 62,* 333–376.

Guskey, T. R. (1994). Making the grade: What benefits students? *Educational Leadership, 52(2),* 14–21.

Guskey, T. R., & Gates, S. L. (1986). Synthesis of research on mastery learning. *Education Leadership, 43,* 73–81.

Gustafsson, J-E., & Undheim, J. O. (1996) Individual differences in cognitive functioning. In D. Berliner & R. Calfee (Eds.), *Handbook of educational psychology* (pp. 186–242). New York: Macmillan.

Guthrie, J. T., Cox, K. E., Anderson, E., Harris, K., Mazzoni, S., & Rach, L. (1998). Principles of integrated instruction for engagement in reading. *Educational Psychology Review, 10,* 227–238.

Guttmacher (Alan) Institute. (1991). *Issues in brief* (Vol. 11, No. 2). Washington, DC: Author.

Haertel, E. H. (1999). Performance assessment and educational reform. *Phi Delta Kappan, 80,* 662–666.

Hakuta, K. (1986). *Mirror of language: The debate on bilingualism.* New York: Basic Books.

Hakuta, K., & Garcia, E. E. (1989). Bilingualism and education. *American Psychologist, 44,* 374–379.

Hakuta, K., & Gould, L. J. (1987). Synthesis of research on bilingual education. *Educational Leadership, 44(6),* 38–45.

Hale-Benson, J. E. (1986). *Black children: Their roots, culture, and learning styles* (rev. ed.). Baltimore: Johns Hopkins University Press.

Halford, J. M. (1999). A different mirror: A conversation with Ronald Takaki. *Educational Leadership, 56(7),* 8–13.

Hall, J. W. (1991). More on the utility of the keyword method. *Journal of Educational Psychology, 83,* 171–172.

Hallahan, D. P., & Kauffman, J. M. (2000). *Exceptional learners: Introduction to special education* (8th ed.). Boston: Allyn & Bacon.

Hallahan, D. P., Kauffman, J. M., & Lloyd, J. W. (2000). *Introduction to learning disabilities* (4th ed.). Boston: Allyn & Bacon.

Hallowell, E. M., & Ratey, J. J. (1994). *Driven to distraction*. New York: Pantheon Books.

Halpern, D. F. (1996). Changing data, changing minds: What the data on cognitive sex differences tell us and what we hear. *Learning and Individual Differences, 8*, 73–82.

Hambleton, R. K. (1996). Advances in assessment models, methods, and practices. In D. C. Berliner & R. C. Calfee (Eds.), *Handbook of educational psychology* (pp. 899–925). New York: Macmillan.

Hamilton, R. J. (1985). A framework for the evaluation of the effectiveness of adjunct questions and objectives. *Review of Educational Research, 55*, 47–86.

Hansen, R. A. (1977). Anxiety. In S. Ball (Ed.), *Motivation in education*. New York: Academic Press.

Hardiman, P. T., Dufresne, R., & Mestre, J. P. (1989). The relation between problem categorization and problem solving among experts and novices. *Memory & Cognition, 17*, 627–638.

Hardman, M. L. (1994). *Inclusion: Issues of educating students with disabilities in regular educational settings*. A booklet to accompany Hardman, M. L., Drew, C. J., Egan, M. W., & Wolf, B. (1993). *Human exceptionality: Society, school, and family* (4th ed.). Boston: Allyn & Bacon.

Hardman, M. L., Drew, C. J., & Egan, M. W. (1996). *Human exceptionality: Society, school, and family* (5th ed.). Boston: Allyn & Bacon.

Hardman, M. L., Drew, C. J., & Egan, M. W. (1999*). Human exceptionality: Society, school, and family* (6th ed.). Boston: Allyn & Bacon.

Harmin, M. (1994). *Inspiring active learning: A handbook for teachers*. Alexandria, VA: Association for Supervision and Curriculum Development.

Harris, J. R. (1998). *The nurture assumption: Why children turn out the way they do; parents matter less than you think and peers matter more*. New York: Free Press.

Harris, K. R. (1990). Developing self-regulated learners: The role of private speech and self-instruction. *Educational Psychologist, 25*, 35–50.

Harris, K. R., & Graham, S. (1996). Memo to constructivist: Skills count too. *Educational Leadership, 53*(5), 26–29.

Harris, K. R., Graham, S., & Pressley, M. (1991). Cognitive-behavioral approaches in reading and written language: Developing self-regulated learners. In N. N. Singh & I. L. Beale (Eds.), *Learning disabilities: Nature, theory, and treatment* (pp. 415–451). New York: Springer-Verlag.

Harris, K. R., Graham, S., & Pressley, M. (in press). Cognitive strategies in reading and written language. In N. Singhh & I. Beale (Eds.), *Current perspectives in learning disabilities: Nature, theory, and treatment*. New York: Springer-Verlag.

Harris, K. R., & Pressley, M. (1991). The nature of cognitive strategy instruction: Interactive strategy construction. *Exceptional Children, 57*, 392–404.

Harris, L. (1989, June). *The ICD survey III: A report card on special education*. New York: Louis Harris & Associates.

Harris, R. T. (1991). Anorexia nervosa and bulimia nervosa in female adolescents. *Nutrition Today, 26*(2), 30–34.

Harrison, A. O., Wilson, M. N., Pine, C. J., & Buriel, R. (1990). Family ecologies of ethnic minority children. *Child Development, 61*, 347–362.

Harrow, A. J. (1972). *A taxonomy of the psychomotor domain: A guide for developing behavior objectives*. New York: David McKay.

Harter, S. (1990). Issues in the assessment of self-concept of children and adolescents. In A. LaGreca (Ed.), *Through the eyes of a child* (pp. 292–325). Boston: Allyn & Bacon.

Harter, S. (1998). The development of self-representations. In N. Eisenberg (Ed.), *Handbook of child psychology: Vol 3. Social, emotional, and personality development* (5th ed.) (pp. 553–618). New York: Wiley.

Hartup, W. W., & Stevens, N. (1999). Friendships and adaptation across the lifespan. *Current Directions in Psychological Science, 8*, 76–79.

Hayes, J. R., Waterman, D. A., & Robinson, C. S. (1977). Identifying relevant aspects of a problem text. *Cognitive Science, 1*, 297–313.

Hayes, S. C., Rosenfarb, I., Wulfert, E., Munt, E. D., Korn, Z., & Zettle, R. D. (1985). Self-reinforcement effects: An artifact of social standard setting? *Journal of Applied Behavior Analysis, 18*, 201–214.

Herbert, E. A. (1998). Design matters: How school environment affects children. *Educational Leadership, 56*(1), 69–71.

Herman, J. (1997). Assessing new assessments: How do they measure up? *Theory Into Practice, 36*, 197–204.

Herman, J. L., Aschbacher, P. R., & Winters, L. (1992). *A practical guide to alternative assessment*. Alexandria, VA: Association for Supervision and Curriculum Development.

Herman, J., & Winters. L. (1994). Portfolio research: A slim collection. *Educational Leadership, 52*(2), 48–55.

Hernshaw, L. S. (1987). *The shaping of modern psychology: A historical introduction from dawn to present day*. London: Routledge & Kegan Paul.

Hess, R., & McDevitt, T. (1984). Some cognitive consequences of maternal intervention techniques. A longitudinal study. *Child Development, 55*, 1902–1912.

Hess, R., Chih-Mei, C., & McDevitt, T. M. (1987). Cultural variation in family beliefs about children's performance in mathematics: Comparisons among People's Republic of China, Chinese-American, and Caucasian-American families. *Journal of Educational Psychology, 79*, 179–188.

Hess, R. D., & Shipman, V. C. (1965). Early experience and the socialization of cognitive modes in children. *Child Development, 36*, 869–886.

Hetherington, E. M. (1989). Coping with family transitions: Winners, losers, and survivors. *Child Development, 60*, 1–14.

Hetherington, E. M., & Stanley-Hagan, M. M. (1997). The effects of divorce on fathers and their children. In M. Lamb (Ed.), *The role of the father in child development* (pp. 191–211). New York: Wiley.

Heward, W. L., & Orlansky, M. D. (1992). *Exceptional children* (4th ed.). Columbus, OH: Charles E. Merrill.

Hewson, P. W., Beeth, M. E., & Thorley, N. R. (1998). Teaching for conceptual change. In B. J. Fraserr & K. G. Tobin (Eds.), *International handbook of science education* (pp. 199–218). New York: Kluwer.

Hewstone, M. (1989). Changing stereotypes with disconfirming information. In D. Bar-Tal, C. Graumann, A. Kruglanski, & W. Stroebe (Eds.), *Stereotyping and prejudice: Changing conceptions* (pp. 207–223). New York: Springer-Verlag.

Hilgard, E. R., Atkinson, R. L., & Atkinson, R. C. (1979). *Introduction to psychology* (7th ed.). New York: Harcourt Brace Jovanovich.

Hill, K. T., & Eaton, W. O. (1977). The interaction of test anxiety and success-failure experiences in determining children's arithmetic performance. *Developmental Psychology, 13*, 205–211.

Hill, K. T., & Wigfield, A. (1984). Test anxiety: A major educational problem and what can be done about it. *Elementary School Journal, 85*, 105–126.

Hilliard, A. G. (1991/1992). Why we must pluralize curriculum. *Educational Leadership, 49*(4), 12–16.

Hines, C. V., Cruickshank, D. R., & Kennedy, J. J. (1982, March). *Measures of teacher clarity and their relationships to student achievement and satisfaction*. Paper presented at the annual meeting of the American Educational Research Association, New York.

Hines, C. V., Cruickshank, D. R., & Kennedy, J. J. (1985). Teacher clarity and its relation to student achievement and satisfaction. *American Educational Research Journal, 22*, 87–99.

Hinsley, D., Hayes, J. R., & Simon, H. A. (1977). From words to equations. In P. Carpenter & M. Just (Eds.), *Cognitive processes in comprehension*. Hillsdale, NJ: Erlbaum.

Hiroto, D. S., & Seligmen, M. E. P. (1975). Generality of learned helplessness in man. *Journal of Personality and Social Psychology, 31,* 311–327.

Hirsch, E. D., Jr. (1996). *The schools we need—and why we don't have them.* New York: Doubleday.

Hodges, E. V. E., & Perry, D. G. (1999). Personal and interpersonal antecedents and consequences of victimization by peers. *Journal of Personality and Social Psychology, 76,* 677–685.

Hodgkinson, H. L. (1985). *All one system: Demographics of education, kindergarten through graduate school.* Washington, DC: Institute of Educational Leadership.

Hoffman, L. W. (1984). Work, family, and the socialization of the child. In R. Parke (Ed.), *Review of child development research* (Vol. 7) (pp. 223–282). Chicago: University of Chicago Press.

Hoffman, M. L. (1988). Moral development. In M. Bornstein & M. Lamb (Eds.), *Developmental psychology: An advanced textbook* (2nd ed.) (pp. 497–548). Hillsdale, NJ: Erlbaum.

Hoge, D. R., Smit, E. K., & Hanson, S. L. (1990). School experiences predicting changes in self-esteem of sixth- and seventh-grade students. *Journal of Educational Psychology, 82,* 117–126.

Holden, G. W., & Ritchie, K. L. (1991). Linking extreme marital discord, child rearing practices, and child behavior problems: Evidence from battered women. *Child Development, 62,* 311–327.

Holmes, C. T., (1989). Grade-level retention effects: A meta analysis of research studies. In L. Shepard & M. Smith (Eds.), *Flunking grades: Research and policies on retention* (pp. 16–33). Philadelphia: Falmer Press.

Hoover-Dempsey, K. V., Bassler, O. C., & Burow, R. (1995). Parents' reported involvement in students' homework: Strategies and practices. *The Elementary School Journal, 95,* 435–450.

Horgan, D. D. (1995). *Achieving gender equity: Strategies for the classroom.* Boston: Allyn & Bacon.

Howard, K. (1990, Spring). Making the writing portfolio real. *The Quarterly of the National Writing Project, 27,* 4–8.

Hoy, W. K., & Woolfolk, A. E. (1990). Organizational socialization of student teachers. *American Educational Research Journal, 27,* 279–300.

Hoy, W. K., & Woolfolk, A. E. (1993). Teachers' sense of efficacy and the organizational health of schools. *Elementary School Journal, 93,* 355–372.

Huessman, L. R., Eron, L. D., Klein, R., Brice, P., & Fischer, P. (1983). Mitigating the imitation of aggressive behaviors by changing children's attitudes about media violence. *Journal of Personality and Social Psychology, 44,* 899–910.

Huff, C. R. (1989). Youth gangs and public policy. *Crime & Delinquency, 35,* 524–537.

Hundert, J., & Bucher, B. (1978). Pupil's self-scored arithmetic performance: A practical procedure for maintaining accuracy. *Journal of Applied Behavior Analysis, 11,* 304.

Hunt, J. McV. (1961). *Intelligence and experience.* New York: Ronald.

Hunt, R. R., & Ellis, H. C. (1999). *Fundamentals of cognitive psychology* (6th ed.). New York: McGraw-Hill College.

Hunter, M. (1982). *Mastery teaching.* El Segundo, CA: TIP Publications.

Hyde, J. S., Fennema, E., & Lamon, S. J. (1990). Gender differences in mathematical performance: A meta-analysis. *Psychological Bulletin, 107,* 139–155.

IIS Report. (1990). Water Mill, NY: Educational Products Information Exchange Institute.

Inclusive Education Programs. (1994, February). AFT President calls inclusion "fad." *Inclusive Education Programs: Advice on Educating Students with Disabilities in Regular Settings.* LRP Publications, 1+.

International Reading Association (IRA). (1985). *Literacy development.* Newark, DE: Author.

Iran-Nejad, A. (1990). Active and dynamic self-regulation of learning processes. *Review of Educational Research, 60,* 573–602.

Iran-Nejad, A., Marsh, G. E., & Clements, A. C. (1992). The figure and ground of constructive brain functioning: Beyond explicit memory processes. *Educational Psychologist, 27,* 473–492.

Iran-Najad, A., Wittrock, M. C., & Hidi, S. (Eds.). (1992, Fall). Brain and education [Special issue]. *Educational Psychologist, 27*(4).

Irving, O., & Martin, J. (1982). Withitness: The confusing variable. *American Educational Research Journal, 19,* 313–319.

Irwin, J. W. (1991). *Teaching reading comprehension* (2nd ed.). Boston: Allyn & Bacon.

Isabella, R., & Belsky, J. (1991). Interactional synchrony and the origins of infant-mother attachment: A replication study. *Child Development, 62,* 373–384.

Jacklin, C. N., Dipietro, J. A., & Maccoby, E. E. (1984). Sex-typing behavior and sex-typing pressure in child-parent interactions. *Sex Roles, 13,* 413–425.

Jagacinski, C. M., & Nicholls, J. G. (1987). Competence and affect in task involvement and ego involvement: The impact of social comparison information. *Journal of Educational Psychology, 76,* 107–114.

James, W. (1890). *The principles of psychology* (Vol. 2). New York: Henry Holt.

James, W. (1912). *Talks to teachers on psychology: And to students on some of life's ideals.* New York: Holt.

Jarrett, R. (1995). Growing up poor: The family experiences of socially mobile youth in low-income African American neighborhoods. *Journal of Adolescent Research, 10,* 111–135.

Jenson, W. R., Sloane, H. N., & Young, K. R. (1988). *Applied behavior analysis in education: A structured teaching approach.* Englewood Cliffs, NJ: Prentice-Hall.

Jimenez, R. T., & Gersten, R. (1999). Lessons and dilemmas derived from the literacy instruction of two Latina/o teachers. *American Educational Research Journal, 36,* 265–302.

John-Steiner, V., & Mahn, H. (1996). Sociocultural approaches to learning and development: A Vygotskian framework. *Educational Psychologist, 31,* 191–206.

Johnson, D. W. (1993). *Reaching out: Interpersonal effectiveness and self-actualization* (5th ed.). Boston: Allyn & Bacon.

Johnson, D. W., & Johnson, R. (1985). Motivational processes in cooperative, competitive, and individualistic learning situations. In C. Ames & R. Ames (Eds.), *Research on motivation in education. Vol. 2: The classroom milieu* (pp. 249–286). New York: Academic Press.

Johnson, D. W., & Johnson, R. (1994). *Learning together and alone: Cooperation, competition, and individualization* (4th ed.). Boston: Allyn & Bacon.

Johnson, D. W., & Johnson, R. (1999). *Learning together and alone: Cooperation, competition, and individualization* (5th ed.). Boston: Allyn & Bacon.

Johnson, D. W., & Johnson, R. (1999). The three Cs of school and classroom management. In H. J. Freiberg (Ed.), *Beyond behaviorism: Changing the classroom management paradigm* (pp. 119–144). Boston: Allyn & Bacon.

Johnson. D. W., & Johnson, R. T. (1996). The role of cooperative learning in assessing and communicating student learning. In T. Guskey (Ed.), *ASCD 1996 Yearbook: Communicating student learning* (pp. 25–46). Alexandria, VA: Association for Supervision and Curriculum Development.

Johnson, D. W., Johnson, R., Dudley, B., Ward, M., & Magnuson, D. (1995). The impact of peer mediation training on the management of school and home conflicts. *American Educational Research Journal, 32,* 829–844.

Johnson, J. S., & Newport, E. L. (1989). Critical period effects in second language learning: The influence of maturational state on the acquisition of English as a second language. *Cognitive Psychology, 21,* 60–69.

Jones, E. D., & Southern, W. T. (1991). Conclusions about acceleration: Echoes of a debate. In W. Southern & E. Jones (Eds.), *The academic acceleration of gifted children* (pp. 223–228). New York: Teachers College Press.

Jones, M. G., & Gerig, T. M. (1994). Silent sixth-grade students: Characteristics, achievement, and teacher expectations. *Elementary School Journal, 95,* 169–182.

Jones, V. F., & Jones, L. S. (1995). *Comprehensive classroom management: Creating positive learning environments* (4th ed.). Boston: Allyn & Bacon.

Jordan, N., & Goldsmith-Phillips, J. (1994). *Assessment of learning disabilities.* Boston: Allyn & Bacon.

Joshua, S., & Dupin, J. J. (1987). Taking into account students' conceptions in instructional strategy: An example in physics. *Cognition and Instruction, 4,* 117–135.

Joyce, B., & Weil, M. (1996). *Models of teaching* (5th ed.). Boston: Allyn & Bacon.

Jurden, F. H. (1995). Individual differences in working memory and complex cognition. *Journal of Educational Psychology, 87,* 93–102.

Kagan, D. (1992). Implications of research on teacher belief. *Educational Psychologist, 27,* 65–90.

Kagan, S. (1983). Social orientation among Mexican-American children: A challenge to traditional classroom structures. In E. Garcia (Ed.), *The Mexican-American child: Language, cognition, and social development.* Tempe, AZ: Center for Bilingual Education.

Kagan, S. (1994). *Cooperative learning.* San Juan Capistrano, CA: Kagan Cooperative Learning.

Kanfer, F. H., & Gaelick, L. (1986). Self-management methods. In F. Kanfer & A. Goldstein (Eds.), *Helping people change: A textbook of methods* (3rd ed.). New York: Pergamon.

Kantor, H., & Lowe, R. (1995). Class, race, and the emergence of federal education policy: From the New Deal to the Great Society. *Educational Researcher, 24*(3), 4–11.

Kaplan, B. (1984). *Development and growth.* Hillsdale, NJ: Erlbaum.

Kaplan, J. S. (1991). *Beyond behavior modification* (2nd ed.). Austin, TX: Pro-Ed.

Karpov, Y. V., & Bransford, J. D. (1995). L. S. Vygotsky and the doctrine of empirical and theoretical learning. *Educational Psychologist, 30,* 61–66.

Karpov, Y. V., & Haywood, H. C. (1998). Two ways to elaborate Vygotsky's concept of mediation implications for instruction. *American Psychologist, 53,* 27–36

Karweit, N. (1989). Time and learning: A review. In R. E. Slavin (Ed.), *School and classroom organization* (pp. 69–95). Hillsdale, NJ: Erlbaum.

Karweit, N., & Slavin, R. (1981). Measurement and modeling choices in studies of time and learning. *American Educational Research Journal, 18,* 157–171.

Kazdin, A. E. (1984). *Behavior modification in applied settings.* Homewood, IL: Dorsey Press.

Keefe, J. W. (1982). Assessing student learning styles: An overview. In *Student learning styles and brain behavior.* Reston, VA: National Association of Secondary School Principals.

Keefe, J. W., & Monk, J. S. (1986). *Learning style profile examiner's manual.* Reston, VA: National Association of Secondary School Principals.

Keith, T. Z. (1982). Time spent on homework and high school grades: A large-sample path analysis. *Journal of Educational Psychology, 74,* 248–253.

Kelly, K. (1999). Retention vs. social promotion: Schools search for alternatives. *Harvard Education Letter, 15*(1), 1–3.

Keogh, B. K., & MacMillan, D. L. (1996). Exceptionality. In D. Berliner & R. Calfee (Eds.), *Handbook of educational psychology* (pp. 311–330). New York: Macmillan.

Kerckhoff, A. C. (1986). Effects of ability grouping in British secondary schools. *American Sociological Review, 51,* 842–858.

Keyser, V., & Barling, J. (1981). Determinants of children's self-efficacy beliefs in an academic environment. *Cognitive Therapy and Research, 5,* 29–40.

Kiewra, K. A. (1985). Investigating notetaking and review: A depth of processing alternative. *Educational Psychologist, 20,* 23–32.

Kiewra, K. A. (1988). Cognitive aspects of autonomous note taking: Control processes, learning strategies, and prior knowledge. *Educational Psychologist, 23,* 39–56.

Kiewra, K. A. (1989). A review of note-taking: The encoding storage paradigm and beyond. *Educational Psychology Review, 1,* 147–172.

Kindsvatter, R., Wilen, W., & Ishler, M. (1988). *Dynamics of effective teaching.* New York: Longman.

Kindsvatter, R., Wilen, W., & Ishler, M. (1992). *Dynamics of effective teaching* (2nd ed.). New York: Longman.

King, A. (1990). Enhancing peer interaction and learning in the classroom through reciprocal questioning. *American Educational Research Journal, 27,* 664–687.

King, A. (1994). Guiding knowledge construction in the classroom: Effects of teaching children how to question and how to explain. *American Educational Research Journal, 31,* 338–368.

King, G. (1979, June). Personal communication. University of Texas at Austin.

Kintsch, E. (1990). Macroprocesses and microprocesses in the development of summarization skills. *Cognition and Instruction, 7,* 161–195.

Kirk, S., Gallagher, J. J., & Anastasiow, N. J. (1993). *Educating exceptional children* (7th ed.). Boston: Houghton Mifflin.

Kirst, M. (1991a). Interview on assessment issues with Lorrie Shepard. *Educational Researcher, 20*(2), 21–23.

Kirst, M. (1991b). Interview on assessment issues with James Popham. *Educational Researcher, 20*(2), 24–27.

Klausmeier, H. J. (1976). Instructional design and the teaching of concepts. In J. Levin & V. Allen (Eds.), *Cognitive learning in children: Theories and strategies* (pp. 191–218). New York: Academic Press.

Klausmeier, H. J. (1992). Concept learning and concept teaching. *Educational Psychologist, 27,* 267–286.

Kling, K. C., Hyde, J. S., Showers, C. J., & Buswell, B. N. (1999). Gender differences in self-esteem: A meta-analysis. *Psychological Bulletin, 125,* 470–500.

Knapp, M., Turnbull, B. J., & Shields, P. M. (1990). New directions for educating children of poverty. *Educational Leadership, 48*(1), 4–9.

Kneedler, P. (1985). California assesses critical thinking. In A. Costa (Ed.), *Developing minds: A resource book for teaching thinking* (pp. 276–280). Alexandria, VA: Association for Supervision and Curriculum Development.

Kogan, N. (1983). Stylistic variation in childhood and adolescence: Creativity, metaphor, and cognitive style. In P. Mussen (Ed.), *Handbook of child psychology* (4th ed.) (Vol. 3, pp. 630–706). New York: Wiley.

Kohlberg, L. (1963). The development of children's orientations toward moral order: Sequence in the development of moral thought. *Vita Humana, 6,* 11–33.

Kohlberg, L. (1975). The cognitive-developmental approach to moral education. *Phi Delta Kappan, 56,* 670–677.

Kohlberg, L. (1981). *The philosophy of moral development.* New York: Harper & Row.

Kohlberg, L. (1984). *Essays on moral development.* San Francisco: Harper & Row.

Kohlberg, L., Yaeger, J., & Hjertholm, E. (1969). Private speech: Four studies and a review of theories. *Child Development, 39,* 691–736.

Kohn, A. (1991). Caring kids: The role of the schools. *Phi Delta Kappan, 72,* 496–506.

Kohn, A. (1993). Rewards versus learning: A response to Paul Chance. *Phi Delta Kappan, 74,* 783–787.

Kohn, A. (1996). By all available means: Cameron and Pierce's defense of extrinsic motivators. *Review of Educational Research, 66,* 1–4.

Kolata, G. B. (1980). Math and sex: Are girls born with less ability? *Science, 210,* 1234–1235.

Kolb, G., & Whishaw, I. Q. (1998). Brain plasticity and behavior. In J. T. Spence, J. M. Darley, & D. J. Foss (Eds.), *Annual Review of Psychology* (pp. 43–64). Palo Alto, CA: Annual Reviews

Korenman, S., Miller, J., & Sjaastad, J. (1995). Long-term poverty and child development in the United States: Results from the NLSY. *Children and Youth Services Review, 17,* 127–155.

Kotrez, D., Stecher, B., & Diebert, E. (1993). *The reliability of scores from the 1992 Vermont Portfolio Assessment Program.* CSE Technical Report 355. Los Angeles: UCLA Center for the Study of Evaluation.

Kounin, J. S. (1970). *Discipline and group management in classrooms.* New York: Holt, Rinehart & Winston.

Kounin, J. S., & Doyle, P. H. (1975). Degree of continuity of a lesson's signal system and task involvement of children. *Journal of Educational Psychology, 67,* 159–164.

Kozulin, A. (1990). *Vygotsky's psychology: A biography of ideas.* Cambridge, MA: Harvard University Press.

Kozulin, A., & Falik, L. (1995). Dynamic cognitive assessment of the child. *Current Directions, 4,* 192–195.

Kozulin, A., & Presseisen, B. Z. (1995). Mediated learning experience and psychological tools: Vygotsky's and Feuerstein's perspectives in a study of student learning. *Educational Psychologist, 30,* 67–75.

Krathwohl, D. R., Bloom, B. S., & Masia, B. B. (1964). *Taxonomy of educational objectives. Handbook II: Affective domain.* New York: David McKay.

Kreitzer, A. E., & Madaus, G. F. (1994). Empirical investigations of the hierarchical structure of the taxonomy. In L. W. Anderson & L. A. Sosniak (Eds.), *Bloom's taxonomy: A forty-year retrospective.* Ninety-third yearbook for the National Society for the Study of Education: Part II (pp. 64–81). Chicago: University of Chicago Press.

Kroger, J. (1995). The differentiation of "firm" and "developmental" foreclosure identity statuses: A longitudinal study. *Journal of Adolescent Research, 10,* 317–337.

Krumboltz, J. D., & Krumboltz, H. B. (1972). *Changing children's behavior.* Englewood Cliffs, NJ: Prentice-Hall.

Kulik, C. C., & Kulik, J. A. (1982). Effects of ability grouping on secondary school students: A meta-analysis of evaluation findings. *American Educational Research Journal, 19,* 415–428.

Kulik, C. L., Kulik, J. A., & Bangert-Drowns, R. L. (1990). Effectiveness of mastery learning programs: A meta-analysis. *Review of Educational Research, 60,* 265–299.

Kulik, J. A., & Kulik, C. C. (1984). Effects of accelerated instruction on students. *Review of Educational Research, 54,* 409–425.

Kulik, J. A., Kulik, C. C., & Bangert, R. L. (1984, April). Effects of practice on aptitude and achievement test scores. *American Educational Research Journal, 21,* 435–447.

Kupersmidt, J. B., Coie, J. D., & Dodge, K. A. (1990). The role of poor peer relations in the development of disorder. In S. Asher & J. Coie (Eds.), *Peer rejection in childhood* (pp. 274–305). New York: Cambridge.

Ladson-Billings, G. (1990). Like lightning in a bottle: Attempting to capture the pedagogical excellence of successful teachers of Black students. *Qualitative Studies in Education, 3,* 335–344.

Ladson-Billings, G. (1992). Culturally relevant teaching: The key to making multicultural education work. In C.A. Grant (Ed.), *Research and multicultural education* (pp. 106–121). London: Falmer Press.

Ladson-Billings, G. (1994). *The dream keepers.* San Francisco: Jossey Bass.

Ladson-Billings, G. (1995). But that is just good teaching! The case for culturally relevant pedagogy. *Theory Into Practice, 34,* 161–165.

Lake, K., & Kafka, K. (1996). Reporting methods in grades K–8. In T. Guskey (Ed.), *ASCD 1996 Yearbook: Communicating student learning* (pp. 90–118). Alexandria, VA: Association for Supervision and Curriculum Development.

Lambert, (1995). Stereotypes and social judgment: The consequences of group variability. *Journal of Personality and Social Psychology, 68,* 388–403.

Land, M. L. (1987). Vagueness and clarity. In M. Dunkin (Ed.), *The international encyclopedia of teaching and teacher education* (pp. 392–397). New York: Pergamon.

Langer, E. J. (1993). A mindful education. *Educational Psychologist, 28,* 43–51.

Language Development and Hypermedia Group (1992). "Open" software design: A case study. *Educational Technology, 32,* 43–55.

Languis, M. L., & Miller, D. C. (1992). Luria's theory of brain functioning: A model for research in cognitive psychophysiology. *Educational Psychologist, 27,* 493–512.

Larrivee, B. (1985). *Effective teaching behaviors for successful mainstreaming.* New York: Longman.

Lave, J. (1988). *Cognition in practice: Mind, mathematics, and culture in everyday life.* New York: Cambridge University Press.

Lave, J., & Wenger, E. (1991). *Situated learning: Legitimate peripheral participation.* Cambridge, MA: Cambridge University Press.

Leavy, J. (1996, March 18). Mother's little helper. *Newsweek, 127,* 51–56.

Lee, A. Y., & Hutchinson, L. (1998). Improving learning from examples through reflection. *Journal of Experimental Psychology: Applied, 4,* 187–210.

Lefton, L. A. (1994). *Psychology* (5th ed.). Boston: Allyn & Bacon.

Leinhardt, G. (1986). Expertise in mathematics teaching. *Educational Leadership, 43,* 28–33.

Leinhardt, G. (1988). Situated knowledge and expertise in teaching. In J. Calderhead (Ed.), *Teachers' professional learning* (pp. 146–168). London: Farmer Press.

LeMahieu, P., Gitomer, D. H., & Eresh, J. T. (1993). *Portfolios in large-scale assessment: Difficult but not impossible.* Unpublished manuscript, University of Delaware.

Leming, J. S. (1981). Curriculum effectiveness in value/moral education. *Journal of Moral Education, 10,* 147–164.

Lepper, M. (1995, August). *Intrinsic motivation and the process of learning.* Paper presented at the American Psychological Association, New York.

Lepper, M. R. (1988). Motivational considerations in the study of instruction. *Cognition and Instruction, 5,* 289–309.

Lepper, M. R., & Greene, D. (1978). *The hidden costs of rewards: New perspectives on the psychology of human motivation.* Hillsdale, NJ: Erlbaum.

Lepper, M. R., Keavney, M., & Drake, M. (1996). Intrinsic motivation and extrinsic reward: A commentary on Cameron and Pierce's meta-analysis. *Review of Educational Research, 66,* 5–32.

Lerner, R. M., & Galambos, N. L. (1998). Adolescent development: Challenges and opportunities for research, programs, and policies. In J. T. Spence, J. M. Darley, & D. J. Foss (Eds.), *Annual Review of Psychology* (pp. 413–446). Palo Alto, CA: Annual Reviews.

Levin, J. R. (1985). Educational applications of mnemonic pictures: Possibilities beyond your wildest imagination. In A. A. Sheikh (Ed.), *Imagery in the educational process* (pp. 63–87). Farmingdale, NY: Baywood.

Levin, J. R. (1994). Mnemonic strategies and classroom learning: A twenty-year report card. *Elementary School Journal, 94,* 235–254.

Levin, J. R., McCormick, C. B., Miller, G. E., Kessler, J., & Pressley, M. (1981). *Mnemonic versus nonmnemonic vocabulary learning strategies for children.* Report from the Project on Studies in Language: Reading and Communication. University of Wisconsin.

Levin, J. R., & Nolan, J. F. (1996). *Principles of classroom management: A professional decision-making model.* Boston: Allyn & Bacon.

Levin, J. R., & Nolan, J. F. (2000). *Principles of classroom management: A professional decision-making model.* Boston: Allyn & Bacon.

Lewinsohn, P. M., Rohde, P., & Seeley, J. R. (1994). Psychological risk factors for future attempts. *Journal of Consulting and Clinical Psychology, 62,* 297–305.

Lewis, A. C. (1995). An overview of the standards movement. *Phi Delta Kappan, 76,* 744–750.

Liben, L. S., & Signorella, M. L. (1993). Gender-schematic processing in children: The role of initial interpretations of stimuli. *Developmental Psychology, 29*, 141–149.

Lindsay, P. H., & Norman, D. A. (1977). *Human information processing: An introduction to psychology* (2nd ed.). New York: Academic Press.

Linn, M. C., & Hyde, J. S. (1989). Gender, mathematics, and science. *Educational Researcher, 18*, 17–27.

Linn, R. L. (1986). Educational testing and assessment: Research needs and policy issues. *American Psychologist, 41*, 1153–1160.

Linn, R. L., & Gronlund, N. E. (2000). *Measurement and assessment in education* (8th ed.). Columbus, OH: Merrill.

Lipscomb, T. J., MacAllister, H. A., & Bregman, N. J. (1985). A developmental inquiry into the effects of multiple models on children's generosity. *Merrill-Palmer Quarterly, 31*, 335–344.

Locke, E. A., & Latham, G. P. (1990). *A theory of goal setting and task performance.* Englewood Cliffs, NJ: Prentice-Hall.

Loftus, E., & Palmer, J. C. (1974). Reconstruction of automobile destruction: An example of the interaction between language and memory. *Journal of Verbal Learning and Verbal Behavior, 13*, 585–589.

Lohman, D. L. (1989). Human intelligence: An introduction to advances in theory and research. *Review of Educational Research, 59*, 333–374.

Lomask, M. S., Pecheone, R. L., & Baron, J. B. (1995). Assessing new science teachers. *Educational Leadership, 52*(6), 62–65.

Lord, S., Eccles, J., & McCarthy, K. (1994). Surviving the junior high school transition: Family processes and self-perceptions as protective factors. *Journal of Early Adolescence, 14*, 162–199.

Lortie, D. (1975). *Schoolteachers: A sociological study.* Chicago: University of Chicago Press.

Lortie, D. (1977). The balance of control and autonomy in elementary school teaching. In D. Erickson (Ed.), *Educational organization and administration* (pp. 335–371). Berkeley, CA: McCutchan.

Loveless, T. (1999). Will tracking reform promote social equity? *Educational Leadership, 56*(7), 28–32.

Lowenstein, G. (1994). The psychology of curiosity: A review and reinterpretation. *Psychological Bulletin, 117*, 75–98.

Lowry, R., Sleet, D., Duncan, C., Powell, K., & Kolbe, L. (1995). Adolescents at risk for violence. *Educational Psychology Review, 7*, 7–40.

Luiten, J., Ames, W., & Ackerson, G. (1980). A meta-analysis of the effects of advance organizers on learning and retention. *American Educational Research Journal, 17*, 211–218.

Lyman, H. B. (1986). *Test scores and what they mean* (4th ed.). Englewood Cliffs, NJ: Prentice-Hall.

Lytton, H., & Romney, D. M. (1991). Parents' sex-related differential socialization of boys and girls: A meta-analysis. *Psychological Bulletin, 109*, 267–296.

Ma, X., & Kishor, N. (1997). Attitude toward self, social factors, and achievement in mathematics: A meta-analytic review. *Educational Psychology Review, 9*, 89–120.

Mabry, L. (1999). Writing to the rubrics: Lingering effects of traditional standardized testing on direct writing assessment. *Phi Delta Kappan, 80*, 673–679.

Maccoby, E. E. (1990). Gender and relationships. *American Psychologist, 45*, 513–520.

Maccoby, E. E., & Martin, J. A. (1983). Socialization in the context of the family: Parent–child interactions. In E. M. Hetherington (Ed.), *Handbook of child psychology: Vol. 4, Socialization, personality, and social development* (4th ed.) (pp. 1–101). New York: Wiley.

Macionis, J. J. (1991). *Sociology* (3rd ed.). Englewood Cliffs, NJ: Prentice-Hall.

Macionis, J. J. (1994). *Sociology* (4th ed.). Englewood Cliffs, NJ: Prentice-Hall.

Macrae, C. N., Milne, A. B., & Bodenhausen, C. V. (1994). Stereotypes as energy-saving devices: A peek inside the cognitive toolbox. *Journal of Personality and Social Psychology, 66*, 37–47.

Madaus, G. F., & Kellaghan, T. (1993). Testing as a mechanism of public policy: A brief history. *Measurement and Evaluation in Counseling and Development, 26*, 6–10.

Madsen, C. H., Becker, W. C., & Thomas, D. R. (1968). Rules, praise, and ignoring: Elements of elementary classroom control. *Journal of Applied Behavior Analysis, 1*, 139–150.

Madsen, C. H., Becker, W. C., Thomas, D. R., Koser, L., & Plager, E. (1968). An analysis of the reinforcing function of "sit down" commands. In R. K. Parker (Ed.), *Readings in educational psychology.* Boston: Allyn & Bacon.

Maehr, M. L., & Anderman, E.M. (1993). Reinventing schools for early adolescents: Emphasizing task goals. *The Elementary School Journal, 93*, 593–610.

Mager, R. (1975). *Preparing instructional objectives* (2nd ed.). Palo Alto, CA: Fearon.

Magusson, S. J., & Palincsar, A. S. (1995). The learning environment as a site of science reform. *Theory Into Practice, 34*, 43–50.

Maier, N. R. F. (1933). An aspect of human reasoning. *British Journal of Psychology, 24*, 144–155.

Major, B., & Schmader, T. (1998), Coping with stigma through psychological disengagement. In J. Swim & C. Stangor (Eds.), *Stigma: The target's perspective* (pp. 219–241). New York: Academic Press.

Maker, C. J. (1987). Gifted and talented. In V. Richardson-Koehler (Ed.), *Educators' handbook: A research perspective* (pp. 420–455). New York: Longman.

Mandlebaum, L. H., Russell, S. C., Krouse, J., & Gonter, M. (1983). Assertive discipline: An effective classwide behavior management program. *Behavior Disorders, 8*(4), 258–264.

Mangione, P. L., & Speth, T. (1998). The transition to elementary school: A framework for creating early childhood continuity through home, school, and community partnerships. *The Elementary School Journal, 98*, 381–397.

Manning, B. H. (1991). *Cognitive self-instruction of classroom processes.* Albany, NY: State University of New York Press.

Manning, B. H., & Payne, B. D. (1996). *Self-talk for teachers and students: Metacognitive strategies for personal and classroom use.* Boston: Allyn & Bacon.

Manning, M. L., & Baruth, L. G. (1996). *Multicultural education of children and adolescents* (2nd ed.). Boston: Allyn & Bacon.

Mantzicopolos, P., & Morrison, D. (1992). Kindergarten retention: Academic and behavioral outcomes through the end of second grade. *American Educational Research Journal, 29*, 182–198.

Maratsos, M. P. (1989). Innateness and plasticity in language acquisition. In M. L. Rice & R. L. Schiefelbusch (Eds.), *The teachability of language* (pp. 105–125). Baltimore, MD: Brooks/Cole.

Marcia, J. E. (1980). Ego identity development. In J. Adelson (Ed.), *The handbook of adolescent psychology* (pp. 159–187). New York: Wiley.

Marcia, J. E. (1987). The identity status approach to the study of ego identity development. In T. Honess & K. Yardley (Eds.), *Self and identity: Perspectives across the life span* (pp. 161–171). London: Routledge & Kagan Paul.

Marcia, J. E. (1991). Identity and self development. In R. Lerner, A. Peterson, & J. Brooks-Gunn (Eds.), *Encyclopedia of Adolescence* (Vol. 1). New York: Garland.

Marcia, J. E. (1994). The empirical study of ego identity. In H. Bosma, T. Graafsma, H. Grotebanc, & D. DeLivita (Eds.), *The identity and development.* Newbury Park, CA: Sage.

Marcus, N., Cooper, M., & Sweller, J. (1996). Understanding instructions. *Journal of Educational Psychology, 88*, 49–63.

Markman, E. M. (1977). Realizing that you don't understand: A preliminary investigation. *Child Development, 48*, 986–992.

Markman, E. M. (1979). Realizing that you don't understand: Elementary school children's awareness of inconsistencies. *Child Development, 50*, 643–655.

Markman, E. M. (1990). Constraints children place on word meanings. *Cognitive Science, 14*, 57–77.

Markstrom-Adams, C. (1992). A consideration of intervening factors in adolescent identity formation. In G. R. Adams, R. Montemayor, and T. Gullotta (Eds.), *Advances in adolescent development: Vol. 4. Adolescent identity formation* (pp. 173-192). Newbury Park, CA: Sage.

Marsh, H. W. (1987). The big-fish-little-pond effect on academic self-concept. *Journal of Educational Psychology, 79,* 280–295.

Marsh, H. W. (1990). Influences of internal and external frames of reference on the formation of math and English self-concepts. *Journal of Educational Psychology, 82,* 107–116.

Marsh, H. W. (1993). The multidimensional structure of academic self-concept: Invariance over gender and age. *American Educational Research Journal, 30,* 841–860.

Marsh, H. W. (1994). Using the National Longitudinal Study of 1988 to evaluate theoretical models of self-concept: The Self-Description Questionnaire. *Journal of Educational Psychology, 86,* 439–456.

Marsh, H. W., Chessor, D., Craven, R., & Roche, L. (1995). The effects of gifted and talented programs on academic self-concept: The big fish strikes again. *American Educational Research Journal, 32,* 285–321.

Marsh, H. W., & Holmes, I. W. M. (1990). Multidimensional self-concepts: Construct validation of responses by children. *American Educational Research Journal, 27,* 89–118.

Marsh, H. W., & Shavelson, R. (1985). Self-concept: Its multifaceted, hierarchical structure. *Educational Psychologist, 20,* 107–123.

Marsh, H. W., & Yeung, A. S. (1997). Coursework selection: Relation to academic self-concept and achievement. *American Educational Research Journal, 34,* 691–720.

Marsh, H. W., Walker, R., & Debus, R. (1991). Subject-specific components of academic self-concept and self-efficacy. *Contemporary Educational Psychology, 16,* 331–345.

Marshall, H. (1996). Implications of differentiating and understanding constructivist approaches. *Journal of Educational Psychology, 31,* 235–240.

Marshall, H. H. (1987). Motivational strategies of three fifth-grade teachers. *Elementary School Journal, 88,* 135–150.

Marshall, H. H. (1989). The development of self-concept. *Young Children, 44*(5), 44–51.

Marshall, H. H. (Ed.). (1992). *Redefining student learning: Roots of educational change.* Norwood, NJ: Ablex.

Martin, C. L. (1989). Children's use of gender-related information in making social judgments. *Developmental Psychology, 25,* 80–88.

Martin, C. L., & Little, J. K. (1990). The relation of gender understanding to children's sex-typed preferences and gender stereotypes. *Child Development, 61,* 1427–1439.

Martin, G., & Pear, J. (1992). *Behavior modification: What it is and how to do it* (4th ed.). Englewood Cliffs, NJ: Prentice-Hall.

Martindale, C. (1991). *Cognitive psychology: A neural-network approach.* Pacific Grove, CA: Brooks/Cole.

Maslow, A. H. (1968). *Toward a psychology of being* (2nd ed.). New York: Van Nostrand.

Maslow, A. H. (1970). *Motivation and personality* (2nd ed.). New York: Harper and Row.

Mason, D. A., & Good, T. L. (1993). Effects of two-group and whole-class teaching on regrouped elementary students' mathematics achievement. *American Educational Research Journal, 30,* 328–360.

Matlin, M. W., & Foley, H. J. (1997). *Sensation and perception* (4th ed.). Boston: Allyn & Bacon.

Mayer, J. D., & Salovey, P. (1993). The intelligence of emotional intelligence. *Intelligence, 17,* 433–442.

Mayer, J. D., & Salovey, P. (1997). What is emotional intelligence? In P. Salovey & D. Sluyter (Eds.), *Emotional development, emotional literacy, and emotional intelligence.* New York: Basic Books.

Mayer, R. E. (1982). Memory for algebra story problems. *Journal of Educational Psychology, 74,* 199–216.

Mayer, R. E. (1983a). Can you repeat that? Qualitative and quantitative effects of repetition and advance organizers on learning from science prose. *Journal of Educational Psychology, 75,* 40–49.

Mayer, R. E. (1983b). *Thinking, problem solving, cognition.* San Francisco: Freeman.

Mayer, R. E. (1984). Twenty-five years of research on advance organizers. *Instructional Science, 8,* 133–169.

Mayer, R. E. (1992). Cognition and instruction: Their historic meeting within educational psychology. *Journal of Educational Psychology, 84,* 405–412.

Mayer, R. E. (1992). *Thinking, problem solving, cognition* (2nd ed.). New York: Freeman.

Mayer, R. E. (1996). Learners as information processors: Legacies and limitations of educational psychology's second metaphor. *Journal of Educational Psychology, 31,* 151–161.

Mayer, R. E., & Sims, V. K. (1994). For whom is a picture worth a thousand words? Extensions of a dual-coding theory of multimedia learning. *Journal of Educational Psychology, 86,* 389–401.

Mayer, R. E., & Wittrock, M. C. (1996). Problem-solving transfer. In D. Berliner & R. Calfee (Eds.), *Handbook of educational psychology* (pp. 47–62). New York: Macmillan.

McCaslin, M., & Good, T. (1996). The informal curriculum. In D. Berliner & R. Calfee (Eds.), *Handbook of educational psychology* (pp. 622–670). New York: Macmillan.

McClelland, D. (1985). *Human motivation.* Glenview, IL: Scott, Foresman.

McClelland, D. C. (1993). Intelligence is not the best predictor of job performance. *Current Directions in Psychological Science, 2,* 5–6.

McCombs, B. L., & Marzano, R. J. (1990). Putting the self in self-regulated learning: The self as agent in integrating skill and will. *Educational Psychologist, 25,* 51–70.

McCormack, S. (1989). Response to Render, Padilla, and Krank: But practitioners say it works! *Educational Leadership, 46*(6), 77–79.

McCormick, C. B., & Levin, J. R. (1987). Mnemonic prose-learning strategies. In M. Pressley & M. McDaniel (Eds.), *Imaginary and related mnemonic processes* (pp. 407–427). New York: Springer-Verlag.

McDonald, J. P. (1993). Three pictures of an exhibition: Warm, cool, and hard. *Phi Delta Kappan, 6,* 480–485.

McGee, L. M., & Richgels, D. J. (1990). *Literacy's beginnings.* Boston: Allyn & Bacon.

McGuire, J. (1988). Gender stereotypes of parents with two-year-olds and beliefs about gender differences in behavior. *Sex Roles, 19,* 233–240.

McKenzie, T. L., & Rushall, B. S. (1974). Effects of self-recording on attendance and performance in a competitive swimming training environment. *Journal of Applied Behavior Analysis, 7,* 199–206.

McLaughlin, J. (1991). Reconciling care and control: Authority in classroom relationships. *Journal of Teacher Education, 40*(3), 182–195.

McLaughlin, T. F., & Gnagey, W. J. (1981, April). *Self-management and pupil self-control.* Paper presented at the annual meeting of the American Educational Research Association, Los Angeles.

McLoyd, V. C. (1998). Economic disadvantage and child development. *American Psychologist, 53,* 185–204.

McNemar, Q. (1964). Lost: Our intelligence? Why? *American Psychologist, 19,* 871–882.

Means, B., & Knapp, M. S. (1991). Cognitive approaches to teaching advanced skills to educationally disadvantaged students. *Phi Delta Kappan, 73,* 282–289.

Mediascope. (1996). *National television violence study: Executive summary 1994–1995.* Studio City, CA: Author.

Medley, D. M. (1979). The effectiveness of teachers. In P. Peterson & H. Walberg (Eds.), *Research on teaching: Concepts, findings, and implications* (pp. 11–27). Berkeley, CA: McCutchan.

Meece, J. L. (1997). *Child and adolescent development for educators.* New York: McGraw-Hill.

Meek, A. (1991). On thinking about teaching: A conversation with Eleanor Duckworth. *Educational Leadership, 48*(6), 30–34.

Meichenbaum, D. (1977). *Cognitive behavior modification: An integrative approach.* New York: Plenum.

Meichenbaum, D. (1986). Cognitive behavior modification. In F. Kanfer & A. Goldstein (Eds.), *Helping people change: A textbook of methods* (3rd ed.) (pp. 346–380). New York: Pergamon.

Meichenbaum, D., Burland, S., Gruson, L., & Cameron, R. (1985). Metacognitive assessment. In S. Yussen (Ed.), *The growth of reflection in children* (pp. 1–30). Orlando, FL: Academic Press.

Meisels, S. J. (1989). High-stakes testing in kindergarten. *Educational Leadership, 46*(7), 16–22.

Mendell, P. R. (1971). Retrieval and representation in long-term memory. *Psychonomic Science, 23,* 295–296.

Messick, S. (1975). The standard problem: Meaning and values in measurement and evaluation. *American Psychologist, 35,* 1012–1027.

Messick, S. (1994). The matter of style: Manifestations of personality in cognition, learning, and teaching. *Educational Psychologist, 29,* 121–136.

Metcalfe, B. (1981). Self-concept and attitude toward school. *British Journal of Educational Psychology, 51,* 66–76.

Metcalfe, J., & Shimamura, A. P. (Eds.). (1994). *Metacognition: Knowledge about knowing.* Cambridge, MA: MIT Press.

Meyer, D. R., & Garasky, S. (1993). Custodial fathers: Myths, realities, and child support. *Journal of Marriage and the Family, 55,* 73–79.

Meyer, M., Delgardelle, M., & Middleton, J. (1996). Addressing parents' concerns over curriculum reform. *Educational Leadership, 53*(7), 54–57.

Michael, R. T., Gagnon, J. H., Laumann, E. O., & Kolata, G. (1994). *Sex in America.* Boston: Little Brown.

Miller, E. (1994). Peer mediation catches on, but some adults don't. *Harvard Education Letter, 10*(3), 8.

Miller, G. A. (1956). The magical number seven, plus or minus two: Some limits on our capacity for processing information. *Psychological Review, 63,* 81–97.

Miller, G. A., Galanter, E., & Pribram, K. H. (1960). *Plans and the structure of behavior.* New York: Holt, Rinehart & Winston.

Miller, K., & Gelman, R. (1983). The child's representation of number: A multidimensional scaling analysis. *Child Development, 54,* 1470–1479.

Miller, P. H. (1993). *Theories of developmental psychology* (3rd ed.). New York: Freeman.

Miller, R. B. (1962). Analysis and specification of behavior for training. In R. Glaser (Ed.), *Training research and education: Science edition.* New York: Wiley.

Mills, C. J., Ablard, K. E., & Stumpf, H. (1993). Gender differences in academically talented young students' mathematical reasoning: Patterns across age and subskills. *Journal of Educational Psychology, 85,* 340–346.

Mills, J. R., & Jackson, N. E. (1990). Predictive significance of early giftedness: The case of precocious reading. *Journal of Educational Psychology, 82,* 410–419.

Mitchell, B. M. (1984). An update on gifted and talented education in the U.S. *Roeper Review, 6,* 161–163.

Moely, B. E., Hart, S. S., Santulli, K., Leal, L., Johnson, T., Rao, N., & Burney, L. (1986). How do teachers teach memory skills? In J. Levin & M. Pressley (Eds.), *Educational Psychologist, 21* (Special issue on learning strategies), 55–72.

Moll, L. C., & Whitmore, K. F. (1993). Vygotsky in classroom practice: Moving from individual transmission to social transaction. In E. Forman, N. Minick, & C. A. Stone (Eds.), *Contexts for learning: Sociocultural dynamics in children's development* (pp. 19–42). New York: Oxford University Press.

Moll, L. C., Amanti, C., Neff, D., & Gonzalez, N. (1992). Funds of knowledge: Using a qualitative approach to connect homes and classrooms. *Theory Into Practice, 31,* 132–141.

Moos, R. H., & Moos, B. S. (1978). Classroom social climate and student absences and grades. *Journal of Educational Psychology, 70,* 263–269.

Morine Dershimer, G. (1993). Tracing conceptual change in preservice teachers. *Teaching and Teacher Education, 9,* 15–26.

Morris, C. G. (1991). *Psychology: An introduction* (7th ed.). Englewood Cliffs, NJ: Prentice-Hall.

Morris, P. F. (1990). Metacognition. In M. W. Eysenck, (Ed.), *The Blackwell dictionary of cognitive psychology* (pp. 225–229). Oxford, UK: Basil Blackwell.

Morrow, L. M. (1983). Home and school correlates of early interest in literature. *Journal of Educational Research, 76,* 221–230.

Morrow, L. M. (1992). The impact of a literature-based program on literacy achievement, use of literature, and attitudes of children from minority backgrounds. *Reading Research Quarterly, 27,* 251–275.

Morrow, L. M. (1997). *Literacy development in the early years: Helping children to read and write* (3rd ed.). Boston: Allyn & Bacon.

Morrow, L. M., & Weinstein, C. (1986). Encouraging voluntary reading: The impact of a literature program on children's use of library centers. *Reading Research Quarterly, 21,* 330–346.

Moshman, D. (1982). Exogenous, endogenous, and dialectical constructivism. *Developmental Review, 2,* 371–384.

Moshman, D. (1997). Pluralist rational constructivism. *Issues in Education: Contributions from Educational Psychology, 3,* 229–234.

Moshman, D., Glover, J. A., & Bruning, R. H. (1987). *Developmental psychology.* Boston: Little, Brown.

Moskowitz, G., & Hayman, M. L. (1976). Successful strategies of inner-city teachers: A year-long study. *Journal of Educational Research, 69,* 283–289.

Moss, P. A. (1992). Shifting conceptions of validity in educational measurement: Implications for performance assessment. *Review of Educational Research, 62,* 229–258.

Mueller, C. M., & Dweck, C. S. (1998). Praise for intelligence can undermine children's motivation and performance. *Journal of Personality and Social Psychology, 75,* 33–52.

Mumford, M. D., Costanza, D. P., Baughman, W. A., Threlfall, V., & Fleishman, E. A. (1994). Influence of abilities on performance during practice: Effects of massed and distributed practice. *Journal of Educational Psychology, 86,* 134–144.

Murphy, P. K., & Alexander, P. A. (2000). A motivated exploration of motivation terminology. *Contemporary Educational Psychology, 25,* 3–53.

Murray, H. G. (1983). Low inference classroom teaching behavior and student ratings of college teaching effectiveness. *Journal of Educational Psychology, 75,* 138–149.

Mussen, P., Conger, J. J., & Kagan, J. (1984). *Child development and personality* (6th ed.). New York: Harper & Row.

Muth, K. D., & Alverman, D. E. (1999). *Teaching and learning in the middle grades.* Boston: Allyn & Bacon.

National Center for Research on Cultural Diversity and Second Language Learning, Center for Applied Linguistics (1992). *Instructional conversations.* Washington, DC: ERIC Document #EDO-FL-92-01.

National Council of Teachers of Mathematics (NCTM). (1989). *Curriculum and evaluation standards for school mathematics.* Reston, VA: Author.

National Council of Teachers of Mathematics (NCTM). (1991). *Professional standards for teaching mathematics.* Reston, VA: Author.

National Governors Association (NGA). (1989). *Results in education: 1989.* Washington, DC: Author.

National Joint Committee on Learning Disabilities (NJCLD). (1989). *Letter from NJCLD to member organizations. Topic: Modifications to the NJCLD definition of learning disabilities.* Washington, DC: Author.

National Science Foundation (NSF). (1988). *Women and minorities in science and engineering* (NSF 88-301). Washington, DC: Author.

Naveh-Benjamin, M. (1991). A comparison of training programs intended for different types of test-anxious students: Further support for an information-processing model. *Journal of Educational Psychology, 83,* 134–139.

Naveh-Benjamin, M., McKeachie, W. J., & Lin, Y. (1987). Two types of test-anxious students: Support for an information processing model. *Journal of Educational Psychology, 79,* 131–136.

Needles, M., & Knapp, M. (1994). Teaching writing to children who are undeserved. *Journal of Educational Psychology, 86*, 339–349.

Neimark, E. (1975). Intellectual development during adolescence. In F. D. Horowitz (Ed.), *Review of child development research* (Vol. 4). Chicago: University of Chicago Press.

Neisser, U., Boodoo, G., Bouchard, A., Boykin, W., Brody, N., Ceci, S. J., Halpern, D. F., Loehlin, J. C., Perloff, R., Sternberg, R. J., & Urbina, S. (1996). Intelligence: Knowns and unknowns. *American Psychologist, 51*, 77–101.

Nelson, G. (1993). Risk, resistance, and self-esteem: A longitudinal study of elementary school-aged children from mother-custody and two-parent families. *Journal of Divorce and Remarriage, 19*, 99–119.

Nelson, K. (1986). *Event knowledge.* Hillsdale, NJ: Erlbaum.

Nelson, T. O. (1996). Consciousness and metacognition. *American Psychologist, 51*, 102–116.

Nestor-Baker, N. S. (1999). *Tacit knowledge in the superintendency: An exploratory analysis.* Unpublished doctoral dissertation, The Ohio State University, Columbus, OH.

Neuman, R. S., & Schwager, M. T. (1995). Students' help seeking during problem solving: Effects of grade, goal, and prior achievement. *American Educational Research Journal, 32*, 352–376.

Neuman, S. B., & Roskos, K. (1992). Literacy objects as cultural tools: Effects on children's literacy behaviors in play. *Reading Research Quarterly, 27*, 255–275.

Newby, T. J. (1991). Classroom motivation: Strategies of first-year teachers. *Journal of Educational Psychology, 83*, 195–200.

Newcombe, N., & Baenninger, M. (1990). The role of expectations in spatial test performance: A meta-analysis. *Sex Roles, 16*, 25–37.

Newmann, F. M., & Wehlage, G. G. (1993). Five standards of authentic instruction. *Educational Leadership, 50*(7), 8–12.

Newstead, S. E., Franklyn-Stokes, A., & Armstead, P. (1996). Individual differences in student cheating. *Journal of Educational Psychology, 88*, 229–241.

Nicholls, J. G., & Miller, A. (1984). Conceptions of ability and achievement motivation. In R. Ames & C. Ames (Eds.), *Research on motivation in education. Vol. 1: Student Motivation* (pp. 39–73). New York: Academic Press.

Nicholls, J. G., Nelson, J. R., Gleaves, K. (1995). Learning facts versus learning that most questions have many answers: Students' evaluations of contrasting curricula. *Journal of Educational Psychology, 87*, 253–260.

Nielsen, L. (1993). Students from divorced and blended families. *Educational Psychology Review, 5*, 177–199.

Nissani, M., & Hoefler-Nissani, D. M. (1992). Experimental studies of belief dependence of observations and of resistance to conceptual change. *Cognition and Instruction, 9*, 97–111.

Noddings, N. (1990). Constructivism in mathematics education. In R. Davis, C. Maher, & N. Noddings (Eds.), *Constructivist views on the teaching and learning of mathematics* (pp. 7–18). Monograph 4 of the National Council of Teachers of Mathematics, Reston, VA.

Noddings, N. (1992). *The challenge to care in schools: An alternative approach to education.* New York: Teachers College Press.

Noddings, N. (1995). Teaching themes of care. *Phi Delta Kappan, 76*, 675–679.

Norman, D. P. (1982). *Learning and memory.* San Francisco: Freeman.

Novak, J. D., & Musonda, D. (1991). A twelve-year longitudinal study of science concept learning. *American Educational Research Journal, 28*, 117–154.

Nucci, L. (1987). Synthesis of research on moral development. *Educational Leadership, 44*(5), 86–92.

Nungester, R. J., & Duchastel, P. C. (1982). Testing versus review: Effects on retention. *Journal of Educational Psychology, 74*, 18–22.

Nuthall, G., & Alton-Lee, A. (1990). Research on teaching and learning: Thirty years of change. *Elementary School Journal, 90*, 546–570.

Nuthall, G., & Alton-Lee, A. (1992). Understanding how students learn in classrooms. In M. Pressley, K. Harris, & J. Guthrie (Eds.), *Promoting academic competence and literacy in school* (pp. 57–87). San Diego: Academic Press.

Nuthall, G., & Alton-Lee, A. (1993). Predicting learning from student experience of teaching: A theory of student knowledge in classrooms. *American Educational Research Journal, 30*, 799–840.

Nuthall, G., & Alton-Lee, A. (1995). Assessing classroom knowledge: How students use their knowledge and experience to answer classroom achievement test questions in science and social studies. *American Educational Research Journal, 32*, 185–197.

O'Boyle, M. W., & Gill, H. S. (1998). On the relevance of research findings in cognitive neuroscience to educational practice. *Educational Psychology Review, 10*, 397–410.

O'Connor, C. (1997). Dispositions toward (collective) struggle and educational resilience in the inner city: A case analysis of six African American high school students. *American Educational Research Journal, 34*, 593–629.

O'Donnell, A. M., & O'Kelly, J. (1994). Learning from peers: Beyond the rhetoric of positive results. *Educational Psychology Review, 6*, 321–350.

O'Leary, K. D. (1980). Pills or skills for hyperactive children? *Journal of Applied Behavior Analysis, 13*, 191–204.

O'Leary, K. D., & O'Leary, S. (Eds.). (1977). *Classroom management: The successful use of behavior modification* (2nd ed.). Elmsford, NY: Pergamon.

O'Leary, K. D., & Wilson, G. T. (1987). *Behavior therapy: Application and outcome.* Englewood Cliffs, NJ: Prentice-Hall.

O'Leary, K. D., Kaufman, K. F., Kass, R. E., & Drabman, R. S. (1970). The effects of loud and soft reprimands on the behavior of disruptive students. *Exceptional Children, 37*, 145–155.

O'Leary, S. (1995). Parental discipline mistakes. *Current Directions in Psychological Science, 4*, 11–13.

O'Leary, S. G., & O'Leary, K. D. (1976). Behavior modification in the schools. In H. Leitenberg (Ed.), *Handbook of behavior modification and behavior therapy.* Englewood Cliffs, NJ: Prentice-Hall.

O'Neil, J. (1990a). Link between style, culture proves divisive. *Educational Leadership, 48*(2), 8.

O'Neil, J. (1990b). Piecing together the restructuring puzzle. *Educational Leadership, 47*(7), 4–10.

O'Neil, J. (1991). Drive for national standards picking up steam. *Educational Leadership, 48*(5), 4–8.

O'Neil, J. (1993). Can national standards make a difference? *Educational Leadership, 50*(5), 4–8.

Oakes, J. (1985). *Keeping track.* New Haven: Yale University Press.

Oakes, J. (1990a). Opportunities, achievement, and choice: Women and minority students in science and math. *Review of Research in Education, 16*, 153–222.

Oakes, J. (1990b). *Multiplying inequities: The effects of race, social class, and tracking on opportunities to learn mathematics and science.* Santa Monica, CA: Rand.

Oakes, J. (1999). Promotion or retention: Which one is social? *Harvard Education Letter, 15*(1), 8.

Ogbu, J. U. (1987). Variability in minority school performance: A problem in search of an explanation. *Anthropology and Education Quarterly, 18*, 312–334.

Ogbu, J. U. (1997). Understanding the school performance of urban blacks: Some essential background knowledge. In H. Walberg, O. Reyes, & R. P. Weissberg (Eds.), *Children and youth: Interdisciplinary perspectives* (pp. 190–140). Norwood, NJ: Ablex.

Ogbu, J. U. (1999). Beyond language: Ebonics, Proper English, and identity in a Black-American speech community. *American Educational Research Journal, 36*, 147–184.

Ogden, J. E., Brophy, J. E., & Evertson, C. M. (1977, April). *An experimental investigation of organization and management techniques in first-grade reading groups.* Paper presented at the annual meeting of the American Educational Research Association, New York.

Ollendick, T. H., Dailey, D., & Shapiro, E. S. (1983). Vicarious reinforcement: Expected and unexpected effects. *Journal of Applied Behavior Analysis, 16,* 485–491.

Olsen, L. (1988). *Crossing the schoolhouse border: Immigrant students and the California public schools.* San Francisco: California Tomorrow.

Onslow, M. (1992). Choosing a treatment program for early stuttering: Issues and future directions. *Journal of Speech and Hearing Research, 35,* 983–993.

Orlando L., & Machado, A. (1996). In defense of Piaget's theory: A reply to 10 common criticisms. *Psychological Review, 103,* 143–164.

Ormrod, J. E. (1999). *Human learning* (3rd ed.). Upper Saddle River: NJ: Merrill/Prentice-Hall.

Ortony, A., Clore, G. L., & Collins, A. (1988). *The cognitive structure of emotions.* Cambridge: Cambridge University Press.

Osborn, A. F. (1963). *Applied imagination* (3rd ed.). New York: Scribner's.

Ovando, C. J. (1989). Language diversity and education. In J. Banks & C. McGee Banks (Eds.), *Multicultural education: Issues and perspectives* (pp. 208–228). Boston: Allyn & Bacon.

Owen, L. (1985). *None of the above: Behind the myth of scholastic aptitude.* Boston: Houghton Mifflin.

Owens, R. E. (1995). *Language disorders* (2nd ed.) Boston: Allyn & Bacon.

Padilla, F. M. (1992). *The gang as an American enterprise.* New Brunswick, NJ: Rutgers University Press.

Paivio, A. (1971). *Imagery and verbal processes.* New York: Holt, Rinehart & Winston.

Paivio, A. (1986). *Mental representations: A dual-coding approach.* New York: Oxford University Press.

Pajares, F. (1997). Current directions in self-efficacy research. In M. L. Maehr & P. R. Pintrich (Eds.), *Advances in motivation and achievement* (Vol. 10, pp. 1–49). Greenwich, CT: JAI Press.

Palincsar, A. S. (1986). The role of dialogue in providing scaffolded instruction. In J. Levin & M. Pressley (Eds.), *Educational Psychologist, 21* (Special issue on learning strategies), 73–98.

Palincsar, A. S. (1998). Social constructivist perspectives on teaching and learning. In J. T. Spence, J. M. Darley, & D. J. Foss (Eds.), *Annual Review of Psychology* (pp. 345–375). Palo Alto, CA: Annual Reviews.

Palincsar, A. S., & Brown, A. L. (1984). Reciprocal teaching of comprehension-fostering and monitoring activities. *Cognition and Instruction, 1,* 117–175.

Palincsar, A. S., & Brown, A. L. (1989). Classroom dialogues to promote self-regulated comprehension. In J. Brophy (Ed.), *Advances in research on teaching* (Vol. 1, pp. 35–67). Greenwich, CT: JAI Press.

Palincsar, A. S., Magnuson, S. J., Marano, N., Ford, D., & Brown, N. (1998). Designing a community of practice: Principles and practices of the GIsML community. *Teaching and Teacher Education, 14,* 5–19.

Pallas, A. M., & Alexander, K. (1983). Sex differences in quantitative SAT performance: New evidence on the differential coursework hypothesis. *American Educational Research Journal, 20,* 165–182.

Panksepp, J. (1998). Attention deficit hyperactivity disorders, psychostimulants, and intolerance of playfulness: A tragedy in the making? *Current Directions in Psychological Science, 7,* 91–98

Papert, S. (1993). *The children's machine: Rethinking school in the age of the computer.* New York: Basic Books.

Paris, S. (1988, April). *Fusing skill and will: The integration of cognitive and motivational psychology.* Paper presented at the annual meeting of the American Educational Research Association, New Orleans.

Paris, S. G., & Cunningham, A. E. (1996). Children becoming students. In D. Berliner & R. Calfee, (Eds.), *Handbook of Educational Psychology* (pp. 117–146). New York: Macmillan.

Paris, S. G., Lipson, M. Y., & Wixson, K. K. (1983). Becoming a strategic reader. *Contemporary Educational Psychology, 8,* 293–316.

Parks, C. P. (1995). Gang behavior in the schools: Myth or reality? *Educational Psychology Review, 7,* 41–68.

Pasch, M., Sparks-Langer, G., Gardner, T. G., Starko, A. J., & Moody, C. D. (1991). *Teaching as decision making: Instructional practices for the successful teacher.* New York: Longman.

Pate, P. E., McGinnis, K., & Homestead, E. (1995). Creating coherence through curriculum integration. In M. Harmin (1994). *Inspiring active learning: A handbook for teachers* (pp. 62–70). Alexandria, VA: Association for Supervision and Curriculum Development.

Paulman, R. G., & Kennelly, K. J. (1984). Test anxiety and ineffective test taking: Different names, same construct? *Journal of Educational Psychology, 76,* 279–288.

Paulson, F. L., Paulson, P. R., & Meyer, C. A. (1991). What makes a portfolio a portfolio? *Educational Leadership, 48*(5), 60–63.

Payne, K. J., & Biddle, B. J. (1999). Poor school funding, child poverty, and mathematics achievement. *Educational Researcher, 28*(6), 4–12.

Pearson, P. D. (1989). Commentary: Reading the whole language movement. *Elementary School Journal, 90,* 231–241.

Pelham, W. E. (1981). Attention deficits in hyperactive and learning-disabled children. *Exceptional Education Quarterly, 2,* 13–23.

Pelham, W. E., & Murphy, H. A. (1986). Attention deficit and conduct disorders. In M. Hersen (Ed.), *Pharmacological and behavioral treatment: An integrative approach* (pp. 108–148). New York: Wiley.

Pellegrini, A. D., Bartini, M., & Brooks, F. (1999). School bullies, victims, and aggressive victims: Factors relating to group affiliation and victimization in early adolescence. *Journal of Educational Psychology, 91,* 216–224.

Peneul, W. R., & Wertsch, J. V. (1995). Vygotsky and identity formation: A sociocultural approach. *Educational Psychologist, 30,* 83–92.

Peng, S., & Lee, R. (1992, April). *Home variables, parent-child activities, and academic achievement: A study of 1988 eighth graders.* Paper presented at the annual meeting of the American Educational Research Association, San Francisco.

Perkins, D. N. (1986). Thinking frames. *Educational Leadership, 43,* 4–11.

Perkins, D. N. (1987). Thinking frames: An integrative perspective on teaching cognitive skills. In J. B. Baron & R. J. Sternberg (Eds.), *Teaching thinking skills: Theory and practice* (pp. 41–85). New York: Freeman.

Perkins, D. N., & Blythe, T. (1994). Putting understanding up front. *Educational Leadership, 51*(5), 4–7.

Perkins, D. N., Jay, E., & Tishman, S. (1993). New conceptions of thinking: From ontology to education. *Educational Psychologist, 28,* 67–85.

Perkins, D. N., & Salomon, G. (1989). Are cognitive skills context-bound? *Educational Researcher, 18,* 16–25.

Perrone, V. (1994). How to engage students in learning. *Educational Leadership, 51*(5), 11–13.

Perry, N. E., VandeKamp, K., & Mercer, L. (2000, April). *Investigating teacher-student interactions that foster self-regulated learning.* In N. E. Perry (Chair), Symposium conducted at the meeting of the American Educational Research Association, New Orleans.

Peterson, C., & Barrett, L. C. (1987). Explanatory style and academic performance among university freshmen. *Journal of Personality and Social Psychology, 53,* 603–607.

Peterson, M. P. (1993). Physical and sexual abuse among school children: Prevalence and prevention. *Educational Psychology Review, 5,* 63–86.

Peterson, P. L. (1992). Revising their thinking: Keisha Coleman and her third-grade mathematics class. In H. Marshall (Ed.), *Redefining student learning: Roots of educational change* (pp. 151–176). Norwood, NJ: Ablex.

Peterson, P. L., & Comeaux, M. A. (1989). Assessing the teacher as a reflective professional: New perspectives on teacher evaluation. In A. Woolfolk (Ed.), *Research perspectives on the graduate preparation of teachers* (pp. 132–152). Englewood Cliffs, NJ: Prentice-Hall.

Peterson, P. L., Fennema, E., & Carpenter, T. (1989). Using knowledge of how students think about mathematics. *Educational Leadership, 46*(4), 42–46.

Peterson, S. E., DeGracie, J. S., & Ayabe, C. R. (1987). A longitudinal study of the effects of retention/promotion on academic achievement. *American Educational Research Journal, 24,* 107–118.

Pettigrew, T. (1998). Intergroup contact theory. In J. T. Spence, J. M. Darley, & D. J. Foss (Eds.), *Annual Review of Psychology* (pp. 65–85). Palo Alto, CA: Annual Reviews.

Pfeffer, C. R. (1981). Developmental issues among children of separation and divorce. In I. Stuart & L. Abt (Eds.), *Children of separation and divorce.* New York: Van Nostrand Reinhold.

Pfiffner, L. J., Rosen, L. A., & O'Leary, S. G. (1985). The efficacy of an all-positive approach to classroom management. *Journal of Applied Behavior Analysis, 18,* 257–261.

Phillips, D. (1995). The good, the bad, and the ugly: The many faces of constructivism. *Educational Researcher, 24*(7), 5–12.

Phillips, D. (1997). How, why, what, when, and where: Perspectives on constructivism and education. *Issues in Education: Contributions from Educational Psychology, 3,* 151–194.

Phillips, D., & Zimmerman, M. (1990). The developmental course of perceived competence and incompetence among competent children. In R. Sternberg & J. Kolligian (Eds.), *Competence considered* (pp. 41–66). New Haven, CT: Yale University Press.

Phinney, J., & Alipiria, L. (1990). Ethnic identity in college students from four ethnic groups. *Journal of Adolescence, 13,* 171–183.

Phinney, J. S. (1993). Multiple group identities: Differentiation, conflict, and integration. In J. Kroger (Ed.), *Discussions on ego identity* (pp. 47–73). Hillsdale, NJ: Lawrence Erlbaum.

Phye, G. D. (1992). Strategic transfer: A tool for academic problem solving. *Educational Psychology Review, 4,* 393–421.

Phye, G. D., & Sanders, C. E. (1994). Advice and feedback: Elements of practice for problem solving. *Contemporary Educational Psychology, 17,* 211–223.

Phye, G. D., & Sanders, C. E. (1994). Advice and feedback: Elements of practice for problem solving. *Contemporary Educational Psychology, 19,* 286–301.

Piaget, J. (1954). *The construction of reality in the child* (M. Cook, Trans.). New York: Basic Books.

Piaget, J. (1962). *Comments on Vygotsky's critical remarks concerning "The language and thought of the child" and "Judgment and reasoning in the child."* Cambridge, MA: MIT Press.

Piaget, J. (1963). *Origins of intelligence in children.* New York: Norton.

Piaget, J. (1965). *The moral judgment of the child.* New York: Free Press.

Piaget, J. (1970a). Piaget's theory. In P. Mussen (Ed.), *Handbook of child psychology* (3rd ed.) (Vol. 1, pp. 703–732). New York: Wiley.

Piaget, J. (1970b). *The science of education and the psychology of the child.* New York: Orion Press.

Piaget, J. (1973). *To understand is to invent: The future of education* (G.-A. Roberts, Trans.). New York : Grossman.

Piaget, J. (1974). *Understanding causality* (D. Miles and M. Miles, Trans.). New York: Norton.

Piaget, J. (1985). *The equilibrium of cognitive structures: The central problem of intellectual development* (T. Brown & K. L. Thampy, Trans.). Chicago: University of Chicago Press.

Pierson, L. H., & Connell, J. P. (1992). Effect of grade retention on self-system processes, school engagement, and academic performance. *Journal of Educational Psychology, 84,* 300–307.

Pine, G. J., & Hilliard, A. G., III (1990). Rx for racism: Imperatives for America's schools. *Phi Delta Kappan, 71,* 593–600.

Pintrich, P. R. (1994). Continuities and discontinuities: Future directions for research in educational psychology. *Educational Psychologist, 29,* 137–148.

Pintrich, P. R., Marx, R. W., & Boyle, R. A. (1993). Beyond cold conceptual change: The role of motivational beliefs and classroom contextual factors in the process of conceptual change. *Review of Educational Research, 63,* 167–199.

Pintrich, P. R., & Schrauben, B. (1992). Students' motivational beliefs and their cognitive engagement in academic tasks. In D. Schunk & J. Meece (Eds.), *Students' perceptions in the classroom: Causes and consequences* (pp. 149–183). Hillsdale, NJ: Erlbaum.

Pintrich, P. R., & Schunk, D. H. (1996). *Motivation in education: Theory, research, and applications.* Columbus, OH: Merrill.

Pitts, J. M. (1992). Constructivism: Learning rethought. In J. B. Smith & J. C. Coleman, Jr. (Eds.), *School Library Media Annual* (Vol. 10, pp. 14–25). Englewood, CO: Libraries Unlimited.

Polson, P. G., & Jeffries, R. (1985). Instruction in general problem-solving skills: An analysis of four approaches. In J. Segal, S. Chipman, & R. Glaser (Eds.), *Thinking and learning skills* (Vol. 1, pp. 417–455). Mahwah, NJ: Erlbaum.

Popham, W. J. (1993). *Educational evaluation* (3rd ed.). Boston: Allyn & Bacon.

Popham, W. J. (1999). *Classroom assessment: What teachers need to know.* Boston: Allyn & Bacon.

Posner, M. I. (1973). *Cognition: An introduction.* Glenview, IL: Scott, Foresman.

Powell, R. R., Garcia, J., & Denton, J. J. (1985, March). *The portrayal of minorities and women in selected elementary science series.* Paper presented at the annual meeting of the American Educational Research Association, Chicago.

Powers, S. I., Hauser, S. T., & Kilner, L. A. (1989). Adolescent mental health. *American Psychologist, 44,* 200–208.

Prawat, R. S. (1991). The value of ideas: The immersion approach to the development of thinking. *Educational Researcher, 20,* 3–10.

Prawat, R. S. (1992). Teachers beliefs about teaching and learning: A constructivist perspective. *American Journal of Education, 100,* 354–395.

Prawat, R. S. (1996). Constructivism, modern and postmodern. *Issues in Education: Contributions from Educational Psychology, 3,* 215–226.

Prawat, R. S., & Floden, R. E. (1994). Philosophical perspectives on constructivist view of learning. *Educational Psychologist, 29,* 37–48.

Premack, D. (1965). Reinforcement theory. In D. Levine (Ed.), *Nebraska symposium on motivation* (Vol. 13). Lincoln, NE: University of Nebraska Press.

Pressley, M. (1986). The relevance of the good strategy user model to the teaching of mathematics. In J. Levin & M. Pressley (Eds.), *Educational Psychologist, 21* (Special issue on learning strategies), 139–161.

Pressley, M. (1991). Comparing Hall (1988) with related research on elaborative mnemonics. *Journal of Educational Psychology, 83,* 165–170.

Pressley, M. (1995). More about the development of self-regulation: complex, long-term, and thoroughly social. *Educational Psychologist, 30,* 207–212.

Pressley, M. (1996, August). *Getting beyond whole language: Elementary reading instruction that makes sense in light of recent psychological research.* Paper presented at the Annual meeting of the American Psychological Association, Toronto.

Pressley, M. (1998). *Reading instruction that works: The case for balanced teaching.* New York: The Guilford Press.

Pressley, M., Barkowski, J. G., & Schneider, W. (1987). Cognitive strategies: Good strategy users coordinate metacognition and knowledge. In R. Vasta & G. Whitehurst (Eds.), *Annals of Child Development,* Vol. 5 (pp. 89–129). Greenwich, CT: JAI Press.

Pressley, M., Levin, J., & Delaney, H. D. (1982). The mnemonic keyword method. *Review of Research in Education, 52,* 61–91.

Price, G., & O'Leary, K. D. (1974). *Teaching children to develop high performance standards.* Unpublished manuscript. State University of New York at Stony Brook.

Pring, R. (1971). Bloom's taxonomy: A philosophical critique. *Cambridge Journal of Education, 1,* 83–91.

Public Agenda Foundation. (1994). *First things first: What Americans expect from public schools.* New York: Author.

Purcell, P., & Stewart, L. (1990). Dick and Jane in 1989. *Sex Roles, 22,* 177–185.

Putnam, R. T., & Borko, H. (in press). Teacher learning: Implications of new views of cognition. In B. J. Biddle, T. L. Good, & I. F. Goodson (Eds.), *The international handbook of teachers and teaching.* Dordrecht, the Netherlands: Kluwer.

Quay, H. C., & Peterson, D. R. (1987). *Manual for the revised behavior problem checklist.* Coral Cables, FL: Author.

Rachlin, H. (1991). *Introduction to modern behaviorism* (3rd ed.), New York: W. H. Freeman.

Raffini, J. P. (1996). *150 ways to increase intrinsic motivation in the classroom.* Boston: Allyn & Bacon.

Ramirez, J., Yuen, S., & Ramey, D. (1991). *Executive summary: Longitudinal study of structured English immersion strategy, early-exit, late-exit transitional bilingual education programs for language minority children.* San Mateo, CA: Aguirre International.

Range, L. M. (1993). Suicide prevention: Guidelines for schools. *Educational Psychology Review, 5,* 135–154.

Rathus, S. A. (1988). *Understanding child development.* New York: Holt, Rinehart & Winston.

Raudenbush, S. (1984). Magnitude of teacher expectancy effects on pupil IQ as a function of the credibility of expectancy induction: A synthesis of findings from 18 experiments. *Journal of Educational Psychology, 76,* 85–97.

Raudsepp, E., & Haugh, G. P. (1977). *Creative growth games.* New York: Harcourt Brace Jovanovich.

Ravitch, D. (1995). *National standards in American education: A citizens's guide.* Washington, DC: Brookings Institution.

Recht, D. R., & Leslie, L. (1988). Effect of prior knowledge on good and poor readers' memory of text. *Journal of Educational Psychology, 80,* 16–20.

Reder, L. M. (1996). Different research programs on metacognition: Are the boundaries imaginary? *Learning and Individual Differences, 8,* 383–390.

Redfield, D. L., & Rousseau, E. W. (1981). A meta-analysis of experimental research on teacher questioning behavior. *Review of Educational Research, 51,* 181–193.

Reed, S., & Sautter, R. C. (1990). Children of poverty: The status of 12 million Americans. *Phi Delta Kappan, 71*(10), K1–K12.

Reeve, J. (1996). *Motivating others: Nurturing inner motivational resources.* Boston: Allyn & Bacon.

Reeve, J., Bolt, E., & Cai, Y. (1999). Autonomy-supportive teachers: How they teach and motivate students. *Journal of Educational Psychology, 91,* 537–548.

Reich, P. A. (1986). *Language development.* Englewood Cliffs, NJ: Prentice-Hall.

Reid, D. K., Hresko, W. P., & Swanson, H. L. (1991). *A cognitive approach to learning disabilities* (2nd ed.). Austin, TX: Pro-Ed.

Reid, M. K., & Borkowski, J. G. (1987). Causal attributions of hyperactive children: Implications for teaching strategies and self control. *Journal of Educational Psychology, 79,* 296–307.

Reisberg, D., & Heuer, F. (1992). Remembering the details of emotional events. In E. Winograd & U. Neisser (Eds.), *Affect and accuracy in recall: Studies of "flashbulb" memories.* Cambridge, England: Cambridge University Press.

Rembolt, C. (1998). Making violence unacceptable. *Educational Leadership, 56* (1), 32–38.

Render, G. F., Padilla, J. N. M., & Krank, H. M. (1989). What research really shows about assertive discipline. *Educational Leadership, 46*(6), 72–75.

Rennie, L. J., & Parker, L. H. (1987). Detecting and accounting for gender differences in mixed-sex and single-sex groupings in science lessons. *Educational Review, 39*(1), 65–73.

Renninger, K. A., Hidi, S., & Krapp, A. (Eds.). (1992). *The role of interest in learning and development.* Hillsdale, NJ: Lawrence Erlbaum.

Rentel, V. (1994). Preparing clinical faculty members: Research on teachers' reasoning. In K. Howey & N. Zimpher (Eds.), *The professional development of teacher educators.* Norwood, NJ: Ablex.

Renzulli, J. S., & Reis, S. M. (1991). The schoolwide enrichment model: A comprehensive plan for the development of creative productivity. In N. Colangelo & G. Davis (Eds.), *Handbook of gifted education* (pp. 111–141). Boston: Allyn & Bacon.

Renzulli, J. S., & Smith, L. H. (1978). *The Learning Styles Inventory: A measure of student preferences for instructional techniques.* Mansfield Center, CT: Creative Learning Press.

Resnick, L. B. (1981). Instructional psychology. *Annual Review of Psychology, 32,* 659–704.

Resnick, L. B. (1987). Learning in school and out. *Educational Researcher, 16*(9), 13–20.

Resnick, L. B., & Klopfer, L. E. (1989). Toward the thinking curriculum: An overview. In *Toward the thinking curriculum: Current cognitive research* (pp. 1–18). Alexandria, VA: Association for Supervision and Curriculum Development.

Resnick, L. B., & Nolan, K. (1995). Where in the world are world-class standards? *Educational Leadership, 52*(6), 6–11.

Reynolds, A. (1992). Grade retention and school adjustment: An explanatory analysis. *Educational Evaluation and Policy Analysis, 14*(2), 101–121.

Reynolds, M. C., & Birch, J. W. (1988). *Adaptive mainstreaming: A primer for teachers and principals* (3rd ed.). New York: Longman.

Reynolds, W. M. (1980). Self-esteem and classroom behavior in elementary school children. *Psychology in the Schools, 17,* 273–277.

Rhode, G., Morgan, D. P., & Young, K. R. (1983). Generalization and maintenance of treatment gains of behaviorally handicapped students from resource rooms to regular classrooms using self-evaluation procedures. *Journal of Applied Behavior Analysis, 16,* 171–188.

Ricciardelli, L. A. (1992). Bilingualism and cognitive development: Relation to threshold theory. *Journal of Psycholinguistic Research, 21,* 301–316.

Rice, F. P. (1999). *The adolescent: Development, relationships, and culture* (9th ed.). Boston: Allyn & Bacon.

Rice, M. L. (1989). Children's language acquisition. *American Psychologist, 44,* 149–156.

Richardson, T. M., & Benbow, C. P. (1990). Long-term effects of acceleration on the social-emotional adjustment of mathematically precocious youths. *Journal of Educational Psychology, 82,* 464–470.

Riley, M. S., & Greeno, J. G. (1991). Developmental analysis of understanding language about quantities and of solving problems. *Cognition and Instruction, 5,* 49–101.

Robbins, P. A. (1990). Implementing whole language: Bridging children and books. *Educational Leadership, 47*(6), 50–55.

Robert Wood Johnson Foundation (1988). *Serving handicapped children: A special report.* Princeton, NJ: Author.

Robinsin, A., & Clinkenbeard, P. R. (1998). Giftedness: An exceptionality examined. In J. T. Spence, J. M. Darley, & D. J. Foss (Eds.), *Annual Review of Psychology* (pp. 117–139). Palo Alto, CA: Annual Reviews.

Robinson, C. S., & Hayes, J. R. (1978). Making inferences about relevance in understanding problems. In R. Revlin & R. E. Mayer (Eds.), *Human reasoning.* Washington, DC: Winston.

Robinson, D. H. (1998). Graphic organizers as aids to test learning. *Reading Research and Instruction, 37,* 85–105.

Robinson, D. H., & Kiewra, K. A. (1995). Visual argument: Graphic outlines are superior to outlines in improving learning from text. *Journal of Educational Psychology, 87,* 455–467.

Roderick, M. (1994). Grade retention and school dropout: Investigating an association, *American Educational Research Journal, 31,* 729–760.

Rodriguez, R. (1987, September 9). What is an American education? *Education Week, 7*(1).

Rogers, C. R. (1969). *Freedom to learn.* Columbus, OH: Charles E. Merrill.

Rogers, C. R., & Freiberg, H. J. (1994). *Freedom to learn* (3rd ed.). Columbus, OH: Charles E. Merrill.

Rogoff, B. (1990). *Apprenticeship in thinking: Cognitive development in social context.* New York: Oxford University Press.

Rogoff, B., & Chavajay, P. (1995). What's become of the research on the cultural basis of cognitive development? *American Psychologist, 50,* 859–877.

Rogoff, B., & Morelii, G. (1989). Perspectives on children's development from cultural psychology. *American Psychologist, 44,* 343–348.

Rogoff, B., & Wertsch, J. V. (Eds.). (1984). *Children's learning in the "zone of proximal development."* San Francisco: Jossey-Bass.

Rohwer, W. D., Jr., & Sloane, K. (1994). Psychological perspectives. In L. Anderson & L. Sosniak (Eds.), *Bloom's taxonomy: A forty-year retrospective.* Ninety-third yearbook for the National Society for the Study of Education: Part II (pp. 41–63). Chicago: University of Chicago Press.

Rokos, K., & Neuman, S. B. (1998). Play as an opportunity for literacy. In O. N. Saracho & B. Spodek (Eds.), *Multiple perspectives on play in early childhood education* (pp. 100–115). Albany: State University of New York Press.

Rop, C. (1997/1998). Breaking the gender barrier in the physical sciences. *Educational Leadership, 55*(4), 58–60.

Rosch, E. H. (1973). On the internal structure of perceptual and semantic categories. In T. Moore (Ed.), *Cognitive development and the acquisition of language* (pp. 111–144). New York: Academic Press.

Rosch, E. H. (1975). Cognitive representations of semantic categories. *Journal of Experimental Psychology: General, 104,* 192–233.

Roschelle, J., & Clancey, W. J. (1992). Learning as social and neural. *Educational Psychologist, 27,* 435–454.

Rose, A. (1962). The causes of prejudice. In I. M. Barron (Ed.), *American cultural minorities: A textbook in intergroup relations.* New York: Alfred A. Knopf.

Rose, L. C., & Gallup, A. M. (1996). The 28th annual Phi Delta Kappa/Gallup Poll of the public's attitude toward the public schools. *Phi Delta Kappan, 78*(1), 41–59.

Rose, L. C. & Gallup, A. M. (1999). The 31st annual Phi Delta Kappa/Gallup Poll of the public's attitude toward the public schools. *Phi Delta Kappan, 81*(1), 41–58.

Rosen, L. A., O'Leary, S. G., Joyce, S. A., Conway, G., & Pfiffner, L. J. (1984). The importance of prudent negative consequences for maintaining the appropriate behavior of hyperactive students. *Journal of Abnormal Child Psychology, 12,* 581–604.

Rosenman, A. A. (1987, November 11). The value of multicultural curricula. *Education Week, 7*(10).

Rosenshine, B. (1977, April). *Primary grades instruction and student achievement.* Paper presented at the annual meeting of the American Educational Research Association, New York.

Rosenshine, B. (1979). Content, time, and direct instruction. In P. Peterson & H. Walberg (Eds.), *Research on teaching: Concepts, findings, and implications* (pp. 28–56). Berkeley, CA: McCutchan.

Rosenshine, B. (1986). Synthesis of research on explicit teaching. *Educational Leadership, 43*(7), 60–69.

Rosenshine, B. (1988). Explicit teaching. In D. Berliner & B. Rosenshine (Eds.), *Talks to teachers* (pp. 75–92). New York: Random House.

Rosenshine, B., & Furst, N. (1973). The use of direct observation to study teaching. In R. Travers (Ed.), *Second handbook of research on teaching.* Chicago: Rand McNally.

Rosenshine, B., & Meister, C. (1992, April). *The uses of scaffolds for teaching less structured academic tasks.* Paper presented at the annual meeting of the American Educational Research Association, San Francisco.

Rosenshine, B., & Meister, C. (1994). Reciprocal teaching: A review of the research. *Review of Educational Research, 64,* 479–530.

Rosenshine, B., & Stevens, R. (1986). Teaching functions. In M. Wittrock (Ed.), *Handbook of research on teaching* (3rd ed.) (pp. 376–391). New York: Macmillan.

Rosenthal, R. (1973). The Pygmalion effect lives. *Psychology Today,* 56–63.

Rosenthal, R. (1987). Pygmalion effects: Existence, magnitude and social importance. A reply to Wineburg. *Educational Researcher, 16,* 37–41.

Rosenthal, R. (1995). Critiquing Pygmalion: A 25-year perspective. *Current Directions in Psychological Science, 4,* 171–172.

Rosenthal, R., & Jacobson, L. (1968). *Pygmalion in the classroom.* New York: Holt, Rinehart, Winston.

Roskos, K., & Neuman, S. B. (1993). Descriptive observation of adults' facilitation of literacy in young children's play. *Early Childhood Research Quarterly, 8,* 77–98.

Roskos, K., & Neuman, S. B. (1995). Two beginning kindergarten teachers' planning for integrated literacy instruction. *Elementary School Journal, 96,* 195–215.

Rosser, R. (1994). *Cognitive development: Psychological and biological perspectives.* Boston: Allyn & Bacon.

Roth, W-M., & Bowen, G. M. (1995). Knowing and interacting: A study of culture, practices, and resources in a grade 8 open-inquiry science guided by an apprenticeship metaphor. *Cognition and Instruction, 13,* 73–128.

Rothenberg, J. (1989). The open classroom reconsidered. *Elementary School Journal, 90,* 68–86.

Rotherham-Borus, M. J. (1994). Bicultural reference group orientations and adjustment. In M. Bernal & G. Knight (Eds.), *Ethnic identity.* Albany, NY: State University of New York Press.

Rowe, M. B. (1974). Wait-time and rewards as instructional variables: Their influence on language, logic, and fate control. Part 1: Wait-time. *Journal of Research in Science Teaching, 11,* 81–94.

Rumelhart, D., & Ortony, A. (1977). The representation of knowledge in memory. In R. Anderson, R. Spiro, & W. Montague (Eds.), *Schooling and the acquisition of knowledge* (pp. 99–135). Hillsdale, NJ: Erlbaum.

Ruopp, F., & Driscoll, M. (1990, January/February). Access to algebra. *Harvard Education Letter, 6*(A), 4–5.

Ryan, R. M. (1991). The nature of the self in autonomy and relatedness. In G. R. Goethals & J. Strauss (Eds.), *Multidisciplinary perspectives on the self.* New York: Springer-Verlag.

Ryan, R. M., & Deci, E. L. (1996). When paradigms clash: Comments on Cameron and Pierce's claim that rewards do not undermine intrinsic motivation. *Review of Educational Research, 66,* 33–38.

Ryan, R. M., & Grolnick, W. S. (1986). Origins and pawns in the classroom: Self-report and projective assessments of individual differences in the children's perceptions. *Journal of Personality and Social Psychology, 50,* 550–558.

Ryans, D. G. (1960). *Characteristics of effective teachers, their descriptions, comparisons and appraisal: A research study.* Washington, DC: American Council on Education.

Sabers, D. S., Cushing, K. S., & Berliner, D. C. (1991). Differences among teachers in a task characterized by simultaneity, multidimensionality, and immediacy. *American Educational Research Journal, 28,* 68–87.

Sadker, M., & Sadker, D. (1986a). Questioning skills. In J. Cooper (Ed.), *Classroom teaching skills* (3rd ed.) (pp. 143–180). Lexington, MA: D. C. Heath.

Sadker, M., & Sadker, D. (1986b). Sexism in the classroom: From grade school to graduate school. *Phi Delta Kappan, 68,* 512.

Sadker, M., & Sadker, D. (1994). *Failing at fairness: How America's schools cheat girls.* New York; Scribner.

Sadker, M., Sadker, D., & Klein, S. (1991). The issue of gender in elementary and secondary education. *Review of Research in Education, 17,* 269–334.

Salomon, G., & Perkins, D. N. (1989). Rocky roads to transfer: Rethinking mechanisms of a neglected phenomenon. *Educational Psychologist, 24,* 113–142.

Salovey, P. & Mayer, J. D. (1990). Emotional intelligence. *Imagination, Cognition, and Personality, 9,* 185–211.

Sanchez, F., & Anderson, M. L. (1990, May). Gang mediation: A process that works. *Principal,* 54–56.

Sanchez, R. (1995, April 6). Educators reexamine the way teachers are taught. *The Washington Post,* pp. A1.

Sandrock, J. W. (1996). *Adolescence.* Dubuque, IA: Brown & Benchmark.

Sattler, J. (1992). *Assessment of children* (3rd ed. rev.). San Diego: Jerome M. Sattler.

Savage, T. V. (1999). *Teaching self-control through management and discipline.* Boston: Allyn & Bacon.

Sawyer, R. J., Graham, S., & Harris, K. R. (1992). Direct teaching, strategy instruction, and strategy instruction with explicit self-regulation: Effects on the composition skills and self-efficacy of learning disabled students. *Journal of Educational Psychology, 84,* 340–352.

Saxe, G. B. (1988). Candy selling and math learning. *Educational Researcher, 17*(6), 14–21.

Scardamalia, M., & Bereiter, C. (1996). Adaptation and understanding: A case for new cultures of schooling. In S. Vosniado, E. De Corte, R. Glasse, & H. Mandl (Eds.), *International perspectives on the design of technology-supported learning environments* (pp. 149–163). Hillsdale, NJ: Lawrence Erlbaum.

Scarr, S., & Carter-Saltzman, L. (1982). Genetics and intelligence. In R. Sternberg (Ed.), *Handbook of human intelligence* (pp. 792–896). New York: Cambridge University Press.

Scarr, S., Weinberg, R. A., & Levine, A. (1986). *Understanding development.* New York: Harcourt Brace Jovanovich.

Scherer, M. (1993). On savage inequalities: A conversation with Jonathan Kozol. *Educational Leadership, 50*(4), 4–9.

Scherer, M. (1999). The discipline of hope: A conversation with Herb Kohl. *Educational Leadership, 56*(1), 8–13.

Schiefele, U. (1991). Interest, learning, and motivation. *Educational Psychologist, 26,* 299–324.

Schneider, W., & Bjorklund, D. F. (1992). Expertise, aptitude, and strategic remembering. *Child Development, 63,* 416–473.

Schoenfeld, A. H. (1979). Explicit heuristic training as a variable in problem solving performance. *Journal for Research in Mathematics Education, 10,* 173–187.

Schofield, J. W. (1991). School desegregation and intergroup relations. *Review of Research in Education, 17,* 235–412.

Schofield, J. W. (1995). Review of research on school desegregation's impact on elementary and secondary school students. In J. A. Banks & C. Banks (Eds.), *Handbook of research on multicultural education.* New York: Macmillan.

Schofield, J. W., Eurch-Fulcer, R., & Britt, C. L. (1994). Teachers, computer tutors, and teaching: The artificially intelligent tutor as an agent for classroom change. *American Educational Research Journal, 31,* 579–607.

Schon, D. (1983). *The reflective practitioner.* New York: Basic Books.

Schraw, G., & Moshman, D. (1995). Metacognitive theories. *Educational Psychology Review, 7,* 351–371.

Schuder, T. (1994). The genesis of transactional strategies for at-risk students. *Elementary School Journal, 94,* 235–254.

Schunk, D. H. (1987). Peer models and children's behavioral change. *Review of Educational Research, 57,* 149–174.

Schunk, D. H. (1991). Self-efficacy and academic motivation. *Educational Psychologist, 26,* 207–232.

Schunk, D. H. (1996). Goal and self-evaluative influences during childrens' cognitive skill learning. *American Educational Research Journal, 33,* 359–382.

Schunk, D. H. (1996). *Learning theories: An educational perspective* (2nd ed.). Columbus, OH: Merrill.

Schunk, D. H. (2000). *Learning theories: An educational perspective* (3rd ed.). Columbus, OH: Merrill/Prentice-Hall.

Schunk, D. H., & Hanson, A. R. (1985). Peer models: Influence on children's self-efficacy and achievement. *Journal of Educational Psychology, 77,* 313–322.

Schwartz, B., & Reisberg, D. (1991). *Learning and memory.* New York: Norton.

Schwartz, B., & Robbins, S. J. (1995). *Psychology of learning and behavior* (4th ed.). New York, Norton.

Seddon, G. M. (1978). The properties of Bloom's taxonomy of educational objectives for the cognitive domain. *Review of Educational Research, 48,* 303–323.

Seifert, K. L., & Hoffnung, R. J. (1991). *Child and adolescent development.* Boston: Houghton Mifflin.

Seligman, M. E. P. (1975). *Helplessness: On depression, development, and death.* San Francisco: Freeman.

Selman, R. L. (1980). *The growth of interpersonal understanding.* New York: Academic Press.

Selman, R. L., & Byrne, D. F. (1974). A structural-developmental analysis of levels of role taking in middle childhood. *Child Development, 45,* 803–806.

Semb, G. B., & Ellis, J. A. (1994). Knowledge taught in school: What is remembered? *Review of Educational Research, 64,* 253–286.

Serbin, L., & O'Leary, D. (1975, January). How nursery schools teach girls to shut up. *Psychology Today,* 56–58.

Serpell, R. (1993). Interface between sociocultural and psychological aspects of cognition. In E. Forman, N. Minick, & C. A. Stone (Eds.), *Contexts for learning: Sociocultural dynamics in children's development* (pp. 357–368). New York: Oxford University Press.

Shapiro, B. C. (1995). The NBPTS sets standards for accomplished teaching. *Educational Leadership, 52*(6), 55–57.

Shapiro, E. S., & Ager, C. (1992). Assessment of special education students in regular education programs: Linking assessment to instruction. *The Elementary School Journal, 92,* 283–296.

Shavelson, R. J. (1987). Planning. In M. Dunkin (Ed.), *The international encyclopedia of teaching and teacher education* (pp. 483–486). New York: Pergamon Press.

Shavelson, R. J., & Bolus, R. (1982). Self-concept: The interplay of theory and methods. *Psychology, 74,* 3–17.

Shavelson, R. J., Gao, X., & Baxter, G. (1993). *Sampling variability of performance assessments.* CSE Technical Report 361. Los Angeles: UCLA Center for the Study of Evaluation.

Shepard, L. A., & Smith, M. L. (1989). Academic and emotional effects of kindergarten retention. In L. Shepard & M. Smith (Eds.), *Flunking grades: Research and policies on retention* (pp. 79–107). Philadelphia: Falmer Press.

Sherman, A. (1994). *Wasting America's future: The Children's Defense Fund report on the costs of child poverty.* Boston: Beacon Press.

Sherman, J. G., Ruskin, R. S., & Semb, G. B. (Eds.) (1982). *The Personalized System of Instruction: 48 seminal papers.* Lawrence, KS: TRI Publications.

Sherman, J. W., & Bessenoff, G. R. (1999). Stereotypes as source-monitoring cues: On the interaction between episodic and semantic memory. *Psychological Science, 10,* 106–110.

Sherry, M. (1990). Implementing an integrated instructional system: Critical issues. *Phi Delta Kappan, 72,* 118–120.

Shields, P., Gordon, J., & Dupree, D. (1983). Influence of parent practices upon the reading achievement of good and poor readers. *Journal of Negro Education, 52,* 436–445.

Shimahara, N. K., & Sakai, A. (1995). *Learning to teach in two cultures.* New York: Garland.

Shoda, Y., Mischel, W., & Peake, P. K. (1990). Predicting adolescent cognitive and self-regulatory competencies from preschool delay of gratification. *Developmental Psychology, 26,* 978–986.

Shuell, T. J. (1981, April). *Toward a model of learning from instruction.* Paper presented at a meeting of the American Educational Research Association, Los Angeles.

Shuell, T. J. (1986). Cognitive conceptions of learning. *Review of Educational Research, 56,* 411–436.

Shuell, T. J. (1990). Phases of meaningful learning. *Review of Educational Psychology, 60,* 531–548.

Shuell, T. J. (1996). Teaching and learning in a classroom context. In D. Berliner & R. Calfee (Eds.), *Handbook of educational psychology* (pp. 726–764). New York: Macmillan.

Shulman, L. S. (1987). Knowledge and teaching: Foundations of the new reform. *Harvard Educational Review, 19*(2), 4–14.

Shulman, L. S. (1992). Toward a pedagogy of cases. In J. Shulman (Ed.), *Case method in teacher education* (pp. 1–30). New York: Teachers College Press.

Shultz, J., & Florio, S. (1979). Stop and freeze: The negotiation of social and physical space in a kindergarten/first grade classroom. *Anthropology and Education Quarterly, 10,* 166–181.

Siegel, J., & Shaughnessy, M. F. (1994). Educating for understanding: An interview with Howard Gardner. *Phi Delta Kappan, 75,* 536–566.

Siegler, R. S. (1991). *Children's thinking* (2nd ed.). Englewood Cliffs, NJ: Prentice-Hall.

Siegler, R. S. (1993). Adaptive and non-adaptive characteristics of low-income children's mathematical strategy use. In B. Penner (Ed.), *The challenge in mathematics and science education: Psychology's response* (pp. 341–366). Washington, DC: American Psychological Association.

Simmons, R. G., & Blyth, D. A. (1987). *Moving into adolescence.* New York: Aldine De Gruyter.

Simon, D. P., & Chase, W. G. (1973). Skill in chess. *American Scientist, 61,* 394–403.

Simon, H. A. (1995). The information-processing view of mind. *American Psychologist, 50,* 507–508.

Simon, P. (1980). *The tongue-tied American: Confronting the foreign language crisis.* New York: Continuum.

Simpson, E. J. (1972). The classification of educational objectives in the psychomotor domain. *The Psychomotor Domain. Vol. 3.* Washington: Gryphon House.

Singley, K., & Anderson, J. R. (1989). *The transfer of cognitive skill.* Cambridge, MA: Harvard University Press.

Sisk, D. A. (1988). Children at risk: The identification of the gifted among the minority. *Gifted Education International, 5,* 138–141.

Sizer, T. (1984). *Horace's compromise: The dilemma of the American high school* (updated ed.). Princeton, NJ: Houghton Mifflin.

Skinner, B. F. (1950). Are theories of learning necessary? *Psychological Review, 57,* 193–216.

Skinner, B. F. (1953). *Science and human behavior.* New York: Macmillan.

Skinner, B. F. (1989). The origins of cognitive thought. *American Psychologist, 44,* 13–18.

Skoe, E. E., Pratt, M. W., Matthews, M., & Curror, S. E. (1996). The ethic of care: Stability over time, gender differences, and correlates in mid-to late adulthood. *Psychology and Aging, 11,* 280–292.

Slaby, R. G., Roedell, W. C., Arezzo, D., & Hendrix, K. (1995). *Early violence prevention.* Washington, DC: National Association for the Education of Young Children.

Slavin, R. E. (1984). Students motivating students to excel: Cooperative incentives, cooperative tasks, and student achievement. *Elementary School Journal, 85,* 53–64.

Slavin, R. E. (1987). Ability grouping and student achievement in elementary schools: A best-evidence synthesis. *Review of Educational Research, 57,* 293–336.

Slavin, R. E. (1990). Achievement effects of ability grouping in secondary schools: A best-evidence synthesis. *Review of Educational Research, 60,* 471–500.

Slavin, R. E. (1995). *Cooperative learning* (2nd ed.). Boston: Allyn & Bacon.

Slavin, R. E., & Karweit, N. (1985). Effects of whole class, ability grouped, and individualized instruction on mathematics achievement. *American Educational Research Journal, 22,* 351–368.

Slavin, R. E., Karweit, N. L., & Madden, N. A. (1989). *Effective programs for students at risk.* Boston: Allyn & Bacon.

Sleeter, C. E. (1995). Curriculum controversies in multicultural education. In E. Flaxman & H. Passow (Eds.), *94th Yearbook of the National Society for the Study of Education: Part II: Changing populations, changing schools* (pp. 162–185). Chicago: University of Chicago Press.

Smetana, J. G., & Braeges, J. L. (1990). The development of toddlers' moral and conventional judgments. *Merrill-Palmer Quarterly, 36,* 329–346.

Smith, C. B. (Moderator) (1994). *Whole language: The debate.* Bloomington, IN: EDINFO Press.

Smith, D. D. (1998). *Introduction to special education: Teaching in an age of challenge* (3rd ed.). Boston: Allyn & Bacon.

Smith, F. (1975). *Comprehension and learning: A conceptual framework for teachers.* New York: Holt, Rinehart & Winston.

Smith, F. (1992). Learning to read: The never-ending debate. *Phi Delta Kappan, 73,* 432–442.

Smith, J. D., & Caplan, J. (1988). Cultural differences in cognitive style development. *Developmental Psychology, 24,* 46–52.

Smith, M. (1993). Some school-based violence prevention strategies. *NASSP Bulletin, 77*(557), 70–75.

Smith, M. L. (1991). Put to the test: The effects of external testing on teachers. *Educational Researcher, 20*(5), 8–11.

Smith, S. M., Glenberg, A., & Bjork, R. A. (1978). Environmental context and human memory. *Memory and Cognition, 6,* 342–353.

Snider, V. E. (1990). What we know about learning styles from research in special education. *Educational Leadership, 48*(2), 53.

Snow, C. E. (1987). Beyond conversation: Second language learners' acquisition of description and explanation. In J. P. Lantolf & A. Labarca (Eds.), *Research in second language learning: Focus on the classroom* (pp. 3–16). Norwood, NJ: Ablex.

Snow, C. E. (1993). Families as social contexts for literacy development. In C. Daiute (Ed.), *New directions for child development* (No. 61, pp. 11–24). San Francisco: Jossey-Bass.

Snow, M. A. (1986). *Innovative second language education: Bilingual immersion programs* (Education Report 1). Los Angeles: Center of Language Education and Research, University of California.

Snow, R. E. (1995). Pygmalion and intelligence. *Current Directions in Psychological Science, 4,* 169–171.

Snow, R. E., Corno, L., & Jackson, D. (1996). Individual differences in affective and cognitive functions. In D. Berliner & R. Calfee (Eds.), *Handbook of educational psychology* (pp. 243–310). New York: Macmillan.

Snowman, J. (1984). Learning tactics and strategies. In G. Phye & T. Andre (Eds.), *Cognitive instructional psychology* (pp. 243–275). Orlando, FL: Academic Press.

Soar, R. S., & Soar, R. M. (1979). Emotional climate and management. In P. Peterson & H. Walberg (Eds.), *Research on teaching: Concepts, findings, and implications* (pp. 97–119). Berkeley, CA: McCutchan.

Sobesky, W. E. (1983). The effects of situational factors on moral judgment. *Child Development, 54,* 575–584.

Sokolove, S., Garrett, J., Sadker, D., & Sadker, M. (1986). Interpersonal communications skills. In J. Cooper (Ed.), *Classroom teaching skills: A handbook* (pp. 233–278). Lexington, MA: D. C. Heath.

Spearman, C. (1927). *The abilities of man: Their nature and measurement.* New York: Macmillan.

Spector, J. E. (1992). Predicting progress in beginning reading: Dynamic assessment of phonemic awareness. *Journal of Educational Psychology, 84,* 353–363.

Spencer, M. B., & Markstrom-Adams, C. (1990). Identity processes among racial and ethnic-minority children in America. *Child Development, 61,* 290–310.

Spiro, R. J., Feltovich, P. J., Jacobson, M. L., & Coulson, R. L. (1991). Cognitive flexibility, constructivism, and hypertext: Random access instruction for advanced knowledge acquisition in ill-structured domains. *Educational Technology, 31*(5), 24–33.

Stahl, S. A., & Miller, P. D. (1989). Whole language and language experience approaches for beginning reading: A quantitative research synthesis. *Review of Educational Research, 59,* 87–116.

Stainback, S., & Stainback, W. (1992). Schools as inclusive communities. In W. Stainback & S. Stainback (Eds.), *Controversial issues confronting special education: Divergent perspectives* (pp. 29–43). Boston: Allyn & Bacon.

Stanovich, K. E. (1991). Reading disability: Assessment issues. In H. Swanson (Ed.), *Handbook of assessment of learning disabilities: Theory, research, and practice* (pp. 147–175). Austin, TX: Pro-Ed.

Stanovich, K. E. (1992). *How to think straight about psychology* (3rd ed.). Glenview, IL: Scott, Foresman.

Stanovich, K. E. (1998). Cognitive neuroscience and educational psychology: What season is it? *Educational Psychology Review, 10,* 419–426.

Starch, D., & Elliot, E. C. (1912). Reliability of grading high school work in English. *Scholastic Review, 20,* 442–457.

Starch, D., & Elliot, E. C. (1913a). Reliability of grading work in history. *Scholastic Review, 21,* 676–681.

Starch, D., & Elliot, E. C. (1913b). Reliability of grading work in mathematics. *Scholastic Review, 21,* 254–259.

Starr, R. H., Jr. (1979). Child abuse. *American Psychologist, 34,* 872–878.

Steele, C. M., & Aronson, J. Stereotype threat and the intellectual test performance of African Americans. *Journal of Personality and Social Psychology, 69,* 797–811.

Stein, B. S., Littlefield, J., Bransford, J. D., & Persampieri, M. (1984). Elaboration and knowledge acquisition. *Memory and Cognition, 12,* 522–529.

Stephen, J., Fraser, E., & Marcia, J. E. (1992). Moratorium achievement (Mama) cycles in life span identity development: Vale orientations and reasoning system correlates. *Journal of Adolescence, 15,* 283–300.

Stepien, W., & Gallagher, S. (1993). Problem-based learning: As authentic as it gets. *Educational Leadership, 50*(7), 25–28.

Sternberg, R. J. (1985). *Beyond IQ: A triarchic theory of human intelligence.* New York: Cambridge University Press.

Sternberg, R. J. (1986). *Intelligence applied: Understanding and increasing your own intellectual skills.* New York: Harcourt Brace Jovanovich.

Sternberg, R. J. (1990). *Metaphors of mind: Conceptions of the nature of intelligence.* New York: Cambridge University Press.

Sternberg, R. J. (1998). Myths, countermyths, and truths about intelligence. In A. Woolfolk (Ed.), *Readings in educational psychology* (2nd ed.) (pp. 53–60). Boston: Allyn & Bacon.

Sternberg, R. J. (1999). *Cognitive psychology* (2nd ed.). Ft. Worth, TX: Harcourt Brace.

Sternberg, R. J., & Davidson, J. (1982, June). The mind of the puzzler. *Psychology Today,* 37–44.

Sternberg, R. J., & Detterman, D. L. (Eds.). (1986). *What is intelligence? Contemporary viewpoints on its nature and definition.* Norwood, NJ: Ablex.

Sternberg, R. J., & Kaufman, J. C. (1998). Human abilities. In J. T. Spence, J. M. Darley, & D. J. Foss (Eds.), *Annual Review of Psychology* (pp. 479–502). Palo Alto, CA: Annual Reviews.

Sternberg, R. J., & Wagner, R. K. (1993). The g-ocentric view of intelligence and job performance is wrong. *Current Directions in Psychological Science, 2,* 1–5.

Sternberg, R. J., Wagner, R. K., Williams, W. M., & Horvath, J. A. (1995). Testing common sense. *American Psychologist, 50,* 912–927.

Stevenson, H. W, & Stigler, J. (1992). *The learning gap.* New York: Summit Books.

Stigler, J. W., Lee, S., & Stevenson, H. W. (1987). Mathematics classrooms in Japan, Taiwan, and the United States. *Child Development, 58,* 1272–1285.

Stipek, D. J. (1993). *Motivation to learn* (2nd ed.). Boston: Allyn & Bacon.

Stipek, D. J. (1996). Motivation and instruction. In D. Berliner & R. Calfee (Eds.), *Handbook of educational psychology* (pp. 85–109). New York: Macmillan.

Stipek, D. J. (1998). *Motivation to learn* (3rd ed.). Boston: Allyn & Bacon.

Stodolsky, S. S. (1988). *The subject matters: Classroom activity in math and social studies.* Chicago: University of Chicago Press.

Straus, M. A., Gelles, R. J., & Steinmetz, S. K. (1980). *Behind closed doors: Violence in the American family.* New York: Doubleday.

Strauss, S. (1993). Teachers' pedagogical content knowledge about children's minds and learning: Implications for teacher education. *Educational Psychologist, 28,* 279–290.

Strike, K. (1975). The logic of discovery. *Review of Educational Research, 45,* 461–483.

Stumpf, H. (1995). Gender differences on test of cognitive abilities: Experimental design issues and empirical results. *Learning and Individual Differences, 7,* 275–288.

Sulzby, E., & Teale, W. (1991). Emergent literacy. In R. Barr, M. L. Kamil, P. B. Mosenthal, & P. D. Pearson (Eds.), *Handbook of reading research, Vol. II* (pp. 727–758). New York: Longman.

Sulzer-Azaroff, B., & Mayer, G. R. (1986). *Achieving educational excellence using behavioral strategies.* New York: Holt, Rinehart & Winston.

Suzuki, B. H. (1983). The education of Asian and Pacific Americans: An introductory overview. In D. Nakanishi & M. Hirano-Nakanishi (Eds.), *The education of Asian and Pacific Americans: Historical perspectives and prescriptions for the future* (pp. 1–14). Phoenix, AZ: Oryx Press.

Swanson, H. L. (1990). The influence of metacognitive knowledge and aptitude on problem solving. *Journal of Educational Psychology, 82,* 306–314.

Swanson, H. L., O'Conner, J. E., & Cooney, J. B. (1990). An information processing analysis of expert and novice teachers' problem solving. *American Educational Research Journal, 27,* 533–556.

Sweller, J., van Merrienboer, J. J. G., & Paas, F. G. W. C. (1998). Cognitive architecture and instructional design. *Educational Psychology Review, 10,* 251–296.

Symons, S., Woloshyn, V., & Pressley, M. (1994). The scientific evaluation of the whole language approach to literacy development [Special issue]. *Educational Psychologist, 29*(4).

Tait, H., & Enwistle, N. J. (in press). Identifying students at risk through ineffective study strategies. *Higher Education.*

Tal, Z., & Babad, E. (1990). The teachers' pet phenomenon: Rate of occurrence, correlates, and psychological costs. *Journal of Educational Psychology, 82,* 637–645.

Tanner, J. M. (1990). *Foetus to man* (2nd ed.). Cambridge: Harvard University Press.

Task Force on Pediatric AIDS: American Psychological Association. (1989). Pediatric AIDS and human immunodeficiency virus infection: Psychological issues. *American Psychologist, 44,* 258–264.

Tavris, C. (1998, September 13). Peer pressure. [Review of the book *The nurture assumption: Why children turn out the way they do; parents matter less than you think and peers matter more*]. *New York Review of Books,* 14–15.

Taylor, J. B. (1983). Influence of speech variety on teachers' evaluation of reading comprehension. *Journal of Educational Psychology, 75,* 662–667.

Tennyson, R. D. (1981, April). *Concept learning effectiveness using prototype and skill development presentation forms.* Paper presented at the annual meeting of the American Educational Research Association, Los Angeles.

Tennyson, R. D., & Cocchiarella, M. J. (1986). An empirically based instructional design theory for teaching concepts. *Review of Educational Research, 56,* 40–71.

Terman, L. M., & Oden, M. H. (1947). The gifted child grows up. In L. M. Terman (Ed.), *Genetic studies of genius* (Vol. 4). Stanford, CA: Stanford University Press.

Terman, L. M., & Oden, M. H. (1959). The gifted group in mid-life. In L. M. Terman (Ed.), *Genetic studies of genius* (Vol. 5). Stanford, CA: Stanford University Press.

Terman, L. M., Baldwin, B. T., & Bronson, E. (1925). Mental and physical traits of a thousand gifted children. In L. M. Terman (Ed.), *Genetic studies of genius* (Vol. 1). Stanford, CA: Stanford University Press.

Tharp, R. G. (1989). Psychocultural variables and constants: Effects on teaching and learning in schools. *American Psychologist, 44*, 349–359.

Tharp, R. G., & Gallimore, R. (1988). *Rousing minds to life: Teaching, learning, and schooling in social context.* New York: Cambridge University Press.

Tharp, R. G., & Gallimore, R. (1991). *The instructional conversation: Teaching and learning in social activity.* Washington, DC: National Center for Research on Cultural Diversity and Second Language Learning.

Thoma, S. J. (1986). Estimating gender differences in the comprehension and preference of moral issues. *Developmental Review, 6*, 165–180.

Thomas, E. L., & Robinson, H. A. (1972). *Improving reading in every class: A sourcebook for teachers.* Boston: Allyn & Bacon.

Thompson, R. A., & Wyatt, J. M. (1999). Current research on child maltreatment: Implications for educators. *Educational Psychology Review, 11*, 173–202.

Thompson, G. (1991). *Teaching through themes.* New York: Scholastic.

Thorkildsen, T. A., Nolen, S. B., & Fournier, J. (1994). What is fair? Children's critiques of practices that influence motivation. *Journal of Educational Psychology, 86*, 475–486.

Thorndike, E. L. (1913). *Educational psychology: Vol. 2. The psychology of learning.* New York: Teachers College, Columbia University.

Thorndike, R., Hagen, E., & Sattler, J. (1986). *The Stanford-Binet Intelligence Scale* (4th ed.). Chicago: Riverside.

Thurstone, L. L. (1938). Primary mental abilities. *Psychometric Monographs*, No. 1.

Tiedt, P. L., & Tiedt, I. M. (1990). *Multicultural education: A handbook of activities, information, and resources.* Boston: Allyn & Bacon.

Tierney, R. J., Readence, J. E., & Dishner, E. K. (1990). *Reading strategies and practices: A compendium* (3rd ed.). Boston: Allyn & Bacon.

Timmer, S. G., Eccles, J., & O'Brien, K. (1988). How children use time. In F. Juster & F. Stafford (Eds.), *Time, goods, and well-being.* Ann Arbor, MI: Institute for Social Research, University of Michigan.

Tishman, S., Perkins, D., & Jay, E., (1995). *The thinking classroom: Creating a culture of thinking.* Boston: Allyn & Bacon.

Tobias, S. (1982). When do instructional methods make a difference? *Educational Researcher, 11*(4), 4–10.

Tobias, S. (1985). Text anxiety: Interference, defective skills, and cognitive capacity. *Educational Psychologist, 20*, 135–142.

Tobias, S., & Duchastel, P. (1974). Behavioral objectives, sequence, and anxiety in CAI. *Instructional Science, 3*, 232–242.

Tobin, K. (1987). The role of wait time in higher cognitive learning. *Review of Educational Research, 56*, 69–95.

Tobin, K. (1990, April). *Metaphors in the construction of teacher knowledge.* Paper presented at the Annual Meeting of the American Educational Research Association, Boston.

Tobin, K., & Dawson, G. (1992). Constraints to curriculum reform: Teachers and the myths of schooling. *Educational Technology Research and Development, 40*(1), 81–92.

Tochon, F., & Munby, H. (1993). Novice and expert teachers' time epistemology: A wave function from didactics to pedagogy. *Teaching and Teacher Education, 9*, 205–218.

Tomasello, M., Kruger, A. C., & Ratner, H. H. (1993). Cultural learning. *Behavioral and Brain Sciences, 16*, 495–552.

Tomlinson-Keasey, C. (1990). Developing our intellectual resources for the 21st century: Educating the gifted. *Journal of Educational Psychology, 82*, 399–403.

Tomlinson-Keasey, C., & Little, T. D. (1990). Predicting educational attainment, occupational achievement intellectual skill, and personal adjustment among gifted men and women. *Journal of Educational Psychology, 82*, 442–455.

Torrance, E. P. (1972). Predictive validity of the Torrance tests of creative thinking. *Journal of Creative Behavior, 6*, 236–262.

Torrance, E. P. (1986). Teaching creative and gifted learners. In M. Wittrock (Ed.), *Handbook of research on teaching* (3rd ed.) (pp. 630–647). New York: Macmillan.

Torrance, E. P., & Hall, L. K. (1980). Assessing the future reaches of creative potential. *Journal of Creative Behavior, 14*, 1–19.

Tschannen-Moran, M., Woolfolk Hoy, A. & Hoy, W. K. (1998). Teacher efficacy: Its meaning and measure. *Review of Educational Research, 68*, 202–248.

Turiel E. (1983). *The development of social knowledge: Morality and convention.* New York: Cambridge University Press.

U. S. Bureau of the Census. (1997). *Statistical abstract of the United States.* Washington DC: US Government Printing Office.

U. S. Department of Health and Human Services. (1997). *Youth risk behavior surveillance—U.S., 1995.* MMWR, 45 (No. SS-4).

Urdan, T. C., & Maehr, M. L. (1995). Beyond a two-goal theory of motivation and achievement: A case for social goals. *Review of Educational Research, 65*, 213–243.

Vacc, N. N. (1989). Writing evaluation: Examining four teachers' holistic and analytic scores. *Elementary School Journal, 90*, 88–95.

Van Houten, R., & Doleys, D. M. (1983). Are social reprimands effective? In S. Axelrod & J. Apsche (Eds.), *The effects of punishment on human behavior.* San Diego: Academic Press.

Van Meter, P., Yokoi, L., & Pressley, M. (1994). College students' theory of note-taking derived from their perceptions of note-taking. *Journal of Educational Psychology, 86*, 323–338.

Vasquez, J. A. (1990). Teaching to the distinctive traits of minority students. *The Clearing House, 63*, 299–304.

Vaughn, S., Bos, C. S., & Schumm, J. S. (1996). *Teaching mainstreamed, diverse, and at-risk students in the general education classroom.* Boston: Allyn & Bacon.

Veenman, S. (1984). Perceived problems of beginning teachers. *Review of Educational Research, 54*, 143–178.

Vellutino, F. R. (1991). Introduction to three studies on reading acquisition: Convergent findings on theoretical foundations of code-oriented versus whole-language approaches to reading instruction. *Journal of Educational Psychology, 83*, 437–443.

Vera, A. H., & Simon, H. A. (1993). Situated action: A symbolic interpretation. *Cognitive Science, 17*, 7–48.

Viadero, D. (1990). Battle over multicultural education rises in intensity. *Education Week, 10*(13), 1, 11, 13, 14.

Vispoel, W. P. (1995). Self-concept inartistic domains: An extension of the Shavelson, Hubmner, and Stanton (1976) model. *Journal of Educational Psychology, 87*, 134–153.

Vispoel, W. P., & Austin, J. R. (1995). Success and failure in junior high school: A critical incident approach to understanding students' attributional beliefs. *American Educational Research Journal, 32*, 377–412.

von Glaserfeld, E. (1990). An exposition of constructivism: Why some like it radical. In R. Davis, C. Maher, & N. Noddings (Eds.), *Constructivist views on the teaching and learning of mathematics* (pp. 19–30). Monograph 4 of the National Council of Teachers of Mathematics, Reston, VA.

von Glaserfeld, E. (1995). A constructivist approach to teaching. In L. Steffe & J. Gale (Eds.), *Constructivism in education* (p. 5). Hillsdale, NJ: Lawrence Erlbaum.

von Glaserfeld, E. (1997). Amplification of a constructivist perspective. *Issues in Education: Contributions from Educational Psychology, 3*, 203–210.

Vroom, V. (1964). *Work and motivation.* New York: Wiley.

Vygotsky, L. S. (1978). *Mind in society: The development of higher mental process.* Cambridge, MA: Harvard University Press.

Vygotsky, L. S. (1986). *Thought and language.* Cambridge, MA: MIT Press.

Vygotsky, L. S. (1987). *Problems of general psychology.* New York: Plenum.

Vygotsky, L. S. (1993). *The collected works of L. S. Vygotsky: Vol. 2* (J. Knox & C. Stevens, Trans.). New York: Plenum.

Wadsworth, B. J. (1978). *Piaget for the classroom teacher.* New York: Longman.

Wadsworth, B. J. (1989). *Piaget's theory of cognitive development: An introduction for students of psychology and education* (4th ed.). New York: Longman.

Wadsworth, B. J. (1996). *Piaget's theory of cognitive and affective development* (5th ed.). New York: Addison, Wesley, Longman.

Walberg, H. J. (1990). Productive teaching and instruction: Assessing the knowledge base. *Phi Delta Kappan, 72,* 470–478.

Walberg, H. J., Pascal, R. A., & Weinstein, T. (1985). Homework's powerful effects on learning. *Educational Leadership, 42*(7), 76–79.

Walker, L. J. (1991). Sex differences in moral reasoning. In W. M. Kurtines & J. L. Gewirtz (Eds.), *Handbook of moral behavior and development* (Vol. 2) (pp. 333–362). Hillsdale, NJ: Erlbaum.

Walker, L. J., & Pitts, R. C. (1998). Naturalistic conceptions of moral maturity. *Developmental Psychology, 34,* 403–419.

Walker, L. J., Pitts, R. C., Hennig, K. H., & Matsuba, M. K. (1995). Reasoning about morality and real-life moral problems. In M. Killen & D. Hart (Eds.), *Morality in everyday life: Developmental perspectives* (pp. 371–407). Cambridge, England: Cambridge University Press

Wallerstein, J. S. (1991). The long-term effects of divorce on children: A review. *Journal of the American Academy of Child and Adolescent Psychiatry, 30,* 349–360.

Walton, G. *Identification of the intellectually gifted children in the public school kindergarten.* Unpublished doctoral dissertation, University of California, Los Angeles, 1961.

Wang, A. Y., & Thomas, M. H. (1995). Effects of keywords on long-term retention: Help or hindrance? *Journal of Educational Psychology, 87,* 468–475.

Wang, A. Y., Thomas, M. H., & Ouellette, J. A. (1992). Keyword mnemonic and retention of second-language vocabulary words. *Journal of Educational Psychology, 84,* 520–528.

Wang, M. C., & Palincsar, A. S. (1989). Teaching students to assume an active role in their learning. In M. Reynolds (Ed.), *Knowledge base for the beginning teacher* (pp. 71–84). New York: Pergamon.

Ward, M., & Sweller, J. (1990). Structuring effective worked examples. *Cognition and Instruction, 7,* 1–40.

Wasserman, E. A., & Miller, R. R. (1997). What's elementary about associative learning. In J. T. Spence, J. M. Darley, & D. J. Foss (Eds.), *Annual Review of Psychology* (pp. 573–607). Palo Alto, CA: Annual Reviews.

Wasserman, S. (1993). *Getting down to cases.* New York: Teachers College Press.

Waterman, A. S. (1992). Identity as an affect of optimal psychological functioning. In G. Adams, T. Gullota, & R. Montemayoor (Eds.), *Adolescent identity formation.* Newbury Park, CA: Sage.

Waters, H. F. (1993, July 12). Networks under the gun. *Newsweek,* 64–66.

Webb, N. (1985). Verbal interaction and learning in peer-directed groups. *Theory Into Practice, 24,* 32–39.

Webb, N., & Palincsar, A. (1996). Group processes in the classroom. In D. C. Berliner & R. C. Calfee (Eds.), *Handbook of educational psychology* (pp. 841–876). New York: Macmillan.

Weiland, A., & Coughlin, R. (1979). Self-identification and preferences: A comparison of White and Mexican-American first- and third-graders. *Journal of Cross-Cultural Psychology, 10,* 356–365.

Weinberg, R. A. (1989). Intelligence and IQ. *American Psychologist, 44,* 98–104.

Weiner, B. (1979). A theory of motivation for some classroom experiences. *Journal of Educational Psychology, 71,* 3–25.

Weiner, B. (1980). The role of affect in rational (attributional) approaches to human motivation. *Educational Researcher, 9,* 4–11.

Weiner, B. (1986). *An attributional theory of motivation and emotion.* New York: Springer.

Weiner, B. (1990). History of motivational research in education. *Journal of Educational Psychology, 82,* 616–622.

Weiner, B. (1992). *Human motivation: Metaphors, theories, and research.* Newbury Park, CA: Sage.

Weiner, B. (1994). Ability versus effort revisited: The moral determinants of achievement evaluation an achievement as a moral system. *Educational Psychologist, 29,* 163–172.

Weiner, B. (1994). Integrating social and persons theories of achievement striving. *Review of Educational Research, 64,* 557–575.

Weiner, B., & Graham, S. (1989). Understanding the motivational role of affect: Lifespan research from an attributional perspective. *Cognition and Emotion, 4,* 401–419.

Weiner, B., Russell, D., & Lerman, D. (1978). Affective consequences of causal ascriptions. In J. H. Harvey, W. J. Ickes, & R. F. Kidd (Eds.), *New directions in attribution research* (Vol. 2). Hillsdale, NJ: Erlbaum.

Weinert, F. E., & Helmke, A. (1995). Learning from wise mother nature or big brother instructor: The wrong choice as seen from an educational perspective. *Educational Psychologist, 30,* 135–143.

Weinstein, C., Woolfolk, A., Dittmeier, L. & Shanker, U. (1994). Protector or prison guard: Using metaphors and media to explore student teachers' thinking about classroom management. *Action in Teacher Education, 16*(1), 41–54.

Weinstein, C. E. (1994). Learning strategies and learning to learn. *Encyclopedia of Education.*

Weinstein, C. E., & Mayer, R. E. (1985). The teaching of learning strategies. In M. C. Wittrock (Ed.), *Handbook of research on teaching* (3rd ed.) (pp. 315–327). New York: Macmillan.

Weinstein, C. E., & McCombs, B. (in press). A model of strategic learning. In C. Weinstein & B. McCombs (Eds.), *Strategic learning: Skill, will, and self-regulation.* Hillsdale, NJ: Erlbaum.

Weinstein, C. S. (1977). Modifying student behavior in an open classroom through changes in the physical design. *American Educational Research Journal, 14,* 249–262.

Weinstein, C. S. (1996). *Secondary classroom management: Lessons from research and practice.* New York: McGraw-Hill.

Weinstein, C. S. (1999). Reflections on best practices and promising programs: Beyond assertive classroom discipline. In H. J. Freiberg (Ed.), *Beyond behaviorism: Changing the classroom management paradigm* (pp. 147–163). Boston: Allyn & Bacon.

Weinstein, C. S., & Mignano, A. J., Jr. (1997). *Elementary classroom management: Lessons from research and practice* (2nd ed.) New York: McGraw-Hill.

Weinstein, R. S., Madison, S. M., & Kuklinski, M. R. (1995). Raising expectations in schools: Obstacles and opportunities for change. *American Educational Research Journal, 32,* 121–159.

Weisberg, R. W. (1993). *Creativity: Beyond the myth of genius.* New York: W. H. Freemen.

Weiss, G., & Hechtman, L. T. (1993). *Hyperactive children grow up: ADHD in children, adolescents, and adults* (2nd ed.). New York: Guilford Press.

Wells, A. S., & Crain, R. L. (1994). Perpetuation theory and the long-term effects of school desegregation. *Review of Educational Research, 64,* 531–55.

Wentzel, K. R. (1999). Social-motivational processes and interpersonal relations: Implications for understanding motivation in school. *Journal of Educational Psychology, 91,* 76–97.

Wertsch, J. V. (1985). *Vygotsky and the social formation of the mind.* Cambridge, MA: Harvard University Press.

Wertsch, J. V. (1991). *Voices of the mind: A sociocultural approach to mediated action.* Cambridge, MA: Harvard University Press.

Wertsch, J., & Tulviste, P. (1992). L. S. Vygotsky and contemporary developmental psychology. *Developmental Psychology, 28,* 548–557.

Wessells, M. G. (1982). *Cognitive psychology.* New York: Harper & Row.

Wessman, A. (1972). Scholastic and psychological effects of a compensatory education program for disadvantaged high school students: Project A B C. *American Educational Research Journal, 9,* 361–372.

Wharton-McDonald, R. Pressley, M., & Mistretta, J. (1996). *Outstanding literacy instruction in first grade: Teacher practices and student achievement.* Albany, NY: National Reading Research Center.

Wheelock, A. (1992). *Crossing the tracks: How untracking can save America's schools.* New York: the New Press.

When the student becomes the teacher. (1986, March). *Harvard Education Letter, 2*(3), 5–6.

White, B. Y. (1993). TinkerTools: Causal models, conceptual change, and science education. *Cognition and Instruction, 10,* 1–100.

White, E. M. (1984). Holisticism. *College Composition and Communication, 35,* 400–409.

White, H. (1986). Damsels in distress: Dependency themes in fiction for children and adolescents. *Adolescence, 21,* 251–256.

White, K. R. (1982). The relation between socioeconomic status and academic achievement. *Psychological Bulletin, 91*(3), 461–481.

White, S., & Tharp, R. G. (1988, April). *Questioning and wait-time: A cross cultural analysis.* Paper presented at the annual meeting of the American Educational Research Association, New Orleans.

Whitehead, A. N. (1929). *The aims of education.* New York: Macmillan.

Whitehurst, G. J., Epstein, J. N., Angell, A. L., Payne, A. C., Crone, D. A., & Fischel, J. E. (1994). Outcomes of an emergent literacy program in headstart. *Journal of Educational Psychology, 86,* 542–555.

Wigfield, A., & Eccles, J. (1989). Test anxiety in elementary and secondary school students. *Educational Psychologist, 24,* 159–183.

Wigfield, A., Eccles, J., MacIver, D., Rueman, D., & Midgley, C. (1991). Transitions at early adolescence: Changes in children's domain-specific self-perceptions and general self-esteem across the transition to junior high school. *Developmental Psychology, 27,* 552–565.

Wigfield, A., Eccles, J. S., & Pintrich, P. R. (1996). Development between the ages of 11 and 25. In D. Berliner & R. Calfee, (Eds.), *Handbook of Educational Psychology* (pp. 148–185). New York: Macmillan.

Wiggins, G. (1989). Teaching to the authentic test. *Educational Leadership, 46*(7), 41–47.

Wiggins, G. (1991). Assessment, authenticity, context, and validity. *Phi Delta Kappan, 75,* 200–214.

Wiggins, G. (1991). Standards, not standardization: Evoking quality student work. *Educational Leadership, 48*(5), 18–25.

Wiggins, G. (1993). Assessment, authenticity, context, and validity. *Phi Delta Kappan, 75,* 200–214.

Wiig, E. H. (1982). Communication disorders. In H. Haring (Ed.), *Exceptional children and youth* (pp. 81–110). Columbus, OH: Charles E. Merrill.

Wilen, W. (1990). Forms and phases of discussion. In W. Wilen (Ed.), *Teaching and learning through discussion* (pp. 3–24). Springfield, IL: Charles C. Thomas.

Wilkins, W. E., & Glock, M. D. (1973). *Teacher expectations and student achievement: A replication and extension.* Ithaca, NY: Cornell University Press.

Willerman, L. (1979). *The psychology of individual and group differences.* San Francisco: Freeman.

Williams, C., & Bybee J. (1994). What do children feel guilty about? Developmental and gender differences. *Developmental Psychology, 30,* 617–623.

Williams, G. C., Wiener, M. W., Markakis, K. M., Reeve, J., & Deci, E. L. (1993). Medical student motivation for internal medicine. *Annals of Internal Medicine.*

Williams, W., Blythe, T., White, N., Li, J., Sternberg, R., & Gardner, H. (1996). *Practical Intelligence in school.* New York: HarperCollins.

Willingham, W. W., & Cole, N. S. (1997). *Gender and fair assessment.* Mahwah, NJ: Lawrence Erlbaum Associates.

Willis, P. (1977). *Learning to labor.* Lexington, MA: D. C. Heath.

Wilson, C. W., & Hopkins, B. L. (1973). The effects of contingent music on the intensity of noise in junior high home economics classes. *Journal of Applied Behavior Analysis, 6,* 269–275.

Winett, R. A., & Winkler, R. C. (1972). Current behavior modification in the classroom: Be still, be quiet, be docile. *Journal of Applied Behavior Analysis, 15,* 499–504.

Wingate, N. (1986). Sexism in the classroom. *Equity and Excellence, 22,* 105–110.

Winne, P. H. (1995). Inherent details in self-regulated learning. *Educational Psychologist, 30,* 173–188.

Winograd, P., & Johnston, P. (1982). Comprehension monitoring and the error-detection paradigm. *Journal of Reading Behavior, 14,* 61–76.

Witkin, H. A., Moore, C. A., Goodenough, D. R., & Cox, R. W. (1977). Field-dependent and field-independent cognitive styles and their educational implications. *Review of Educational Research, 47,* 1–64.

Wittrock, M. C. (1982, March). *Educational implications of recent research on learning and memory.* Paper presented at the annual meeting of the American Educational Research Association, New York.

Wittrock, M. C. (1992). An empowering conception of educational psychology. *Educational Psychologist, 27,* 129–142.

Wolf, D., Bixby, J., Glenn, J., III, & Gardner, H. (1991). To use their minds well: New forms of student assessment. *Review of Research in Education, 17,* 31–74.

Wolters, C. A., Yu, S. L., & Pintrich, P. R. (1996). The relation between goal orientation and students' motivational beliefs and self-regulated learning. *Learning and Individual Differences, 8,* 211–238.

Women on Words and Images. (1975). *Dick and Jane as victims: Sex stereotyping in children's readers.* Available from author, P. O. Box 2163, Princeton, NJ.

Wong, L. (1987). Reaction to research findings: Is the feeling of obviousness warranted? *Dissertation Abstracts International, 48/12,* 3709B (University Microfilms #DA 8801059).

Wood, D., Bruner, J., & Ross, S. (1976). The role of tutoring in problem solving. *British Journal of Psychology, 66,* 181–191.

Wood, S. E., & Wood, E. G. (1999). *The world of psychology* (3rd ed.). Boston: Allyn & Bacon.

Woolfolk, A. E., & Brooks, D. (1983). Nonverbal communication in teaching. In E. Gordon (Ed.), *Review of research in education* (Vol. 10, pp. 103–150). Washington, DC: American Educational Research Association.

Woolfolk, A. E., & Brooks, D. (1985). The influence of teachers' nonverbal behaviors on students' perceptions and performance. *Elementary School Journal, 85,* 514–528.

Woolfolk, A. E., & Hoy, W. K. (1990). Prospective teachers' sense of efficacy and beliefs about control. *Journal of Educational Psychology, 82,* 81–91.

Woolfolk, A. E., Rosoff, B., & Hoy, W. K. (1990). Teachers' sense of efficacy and their beliefs about managing students. *Teaching and Teacher Education, 6,* 137–148.

Woolfolk, A. E., & Woolfolk, R. L. (1974). A contingency management technique for increasing student attention in a small group. *Journal of School Psychology, 12,* 204–212.

Woolfolk Hoy, A., & Tschannen-Moran. M. (1999). Implications of cognitive approaches to peer learning for teacher education. In A.

O'Donnell & A. King (Eds.), *Cognitive perspectives on peer learning* (pp. 257–284). Mahwah, NJ: Lawrence Erlbaum.

Worthen, B. R. (1993). Critical issues that will determine the future of alternative assessment. *Phi Delta Kappan, 74,* 444–457.

Worthen, B. R., & Spandel, V. (1991). Putting the standardized text debate in perspective. *Educational Leadership, 48*(5), 65–70.

Wright, S. C., & Taylor, D. M. (1995). Identity and the language of the classroom: Investigating the impact of heritage versus second language instruction on personal and collective self-esteem. *Journal of Educational Psychology, 87,* 241–252.

Wyler, R. S. (1988). Social memory and social judgment. In P. Solomon, G. Goethals, C. Kelly, & B. Stephans (Eds.), *Perspectives on memory research.* New York: Springer-Verlag.

Yee, A. H. (1992). Asians as stereotypes and students: Misperceptions that persist. *Educational Psychology Review, 4,* 95–132.

Yell, M. L. (1990). The use of corporal punishment, suspension, expulsion, and timeout with behaviorally disordered students in public schools: Legal considerations. *Behavioral Disorders, 15,* 100–109.

Yerkes, R. M., & Dodson, J. D. (1908). The relation of strength of stimulus to rapidity of habit formation. *Journal of Comparative Neurology, 18,* 459–482.

Yetman, N. R. (1999). *Majority and minority: The dynamics of race and ethnicity in American life.* (6th ed.). Boston: Allyn & Bacon.

Yinger, R. (1999). The role of standards in teaching and teacher education. In G. Griffin (Ed.), *The education of teachers: Ninety-eighth yearbook of the National Society for the Study of Education (Part 1)* (pp. 85–113). Chicago: University of Chicago Press.

You and the system. (1991, April). *Teacher Magazine,* 32H.

Young, A. J. (1997). I think, therefore I'm motivated: The relations among cognitive strategy use, motivational orientation, and classroom perceptions over time. *Learning and Individual Differences, 9,* 249–283.

Zeichner, K., & Gore, J. (1990). Teacher socialization. In W. R. Houston (Ed.), *Handbook of research on teacher education* (pp. 329–348). New York: Macmillan.

Zeidner, M. (1995). Adaptive coping with test situations. *Educational Psychologist, 30,* 123–134.

Zelli, A, Dodge, K. A., Lochman, J. E., & Laird, R. D. (1999). The distinction between beliefs legitimizing aggression and deviant processing of social cues: Testing measurement validity and the hypothesis that biased processing mediates the effects of beliefs on aggression. *Journal of Personality and Social Psychology, 77,* 150–166.

Zigmond, N., Jenkins, J., Fuchs, D., Deno, S., & Fuchs, L. S. (1995). When students fail to achieve satisfactorily: A reply to Leskey and Waldron. *Phi Delta Kappan, 77,* 303–306.

Zimmerman, B. J. (1990). Self-regulated learning and academic achievement: An overview. *Educational Psychologist, 21,* 3–18.

Zimmerman. B. J. (1995). Self-efficacy and educational development. In A. Bandura (Ed.), *Self-efficacy in changing societies* (pp. 202–231). New York: Cambridge University Press.

Zimmerman, B. J., Bandura, A., & Martinez-Pons, M. (1992). Self-motivation for academic attainment: The role of self-efficacy beliefs and goal-setting. *American Educational Research Journal, 29,* 663–676.

Zimmerman, B. J., & Schunk, D. H. (Eds.). (1989). *Self-regulated learning and academic achievement: Theory, research, and practice.* New York: Springer-Verlag.

Zimmerman, D. W. (1981). On the perennial argument about grading "on the curve" in college courses. *Educational Psychologist, 16,* 175–178.

Ziomek, R. L., & Maxey, J. M. (1993). To nationally test or not to nationally test: That is the question! *Measurement and Evaluation in Counseling and Development, 26,* 64–68.

Name Index

Klausmeier, H. J., 280, 281
Klavas, A., 129
Klein, R., 83
Kling, K. C., 75
Klinzing, H. G., 6
Knapp, M. S., 160, 191, 334, 501
Kneedler, P., 355
Kneedler, R., 139
Koestner, R., 230, 369
Kogan, N., 127
Kohlberg, L., 47, 78, 80
Kohn, A., 230, 231, 232, 578
Kolata, G. B., 95, 179
Kolb, G., 27
Kolbe, L., 462–463
Korenman, S., 165
Korn, Z., 226
Koser, L., 13
Kotrez, D., 549
Kounin, J. S., 327, 451
Kozulin, A., 45, 51, 545, 547
Krank, H. M., 461
Krapp, A., 381
Krathwohl, D. R., 278, 479, 480
Kreitzer, A. E., 479
Kroger, J., 68
Kronsberg, S., 176
Kruger, A. C., 49
Krumboltz, H. B., 216, 218
Krumboltz, J. D., 216, 218
Kucan, L., 492
Kuklinski, M. R., 419
Kulik, C. C., 118, 126, 544, 573
Kulik, C. L., 221
Kulik, J. A., 118, 126, 221, 544, 573
Kulikowich, J. M., 263

Ladson-Billings, G., 189, 190, 191
Laird, R. D., 83
Lake, K., 577
Lambert, 171
Land, M. L., 495
Larrivee, B., 502
Latham, G. P., 372, 377
Latta, R. M., 221
Lau, S., 374
Laumann, E. O., 95
Lave, J., 311, 334, 349, 376
Leary, M. R., 379
Leavy, J., 138
Lee, A. Y., 293, 296
Lee, R., 165
Lee, S., 487
Lefton, L. A., 65
Leinbach, M. D., 176
Leinhardt, G., 6, 301

LeMahieu, P., 571
Leming, J. S., 372
LePore, P. C., 118
Lepper, M. R., 225, 232, 381, 390, 406, 419
Lerman, D., 374
Lerner, R. M., 97
Leslie, L., 241
Levin, J. R., 264, 265, 266, 454, 455
Levine, A., 95
Lewinsohn, P. M., 98
Lewis, A. C., 542
Liben, L. S., 175
Lin, Y., 385
Lindsay, P. H., 245
Linn, M. C., 177, 178
Linn, R. L., 523, 532, 539, 540
Lipscomb, T. J., 82
Lipsky, D. K., 134
Lipson, M. Y., 242
Little, J. K., 175
Little, T. D., 124
Littlefield, J., 255
Livingston, C., 5, 14, 301
Lloyd, J. W., 134
Lochman, J. E., 83
Locke, E. A., 372, 377
Lockhart, R. S., 249, 256
Loftus, E., 258
Lohman, D. L., 108
Lomask, M. S., 543
Loomis, L. S., 87
Lopez, S. R., 158, 165
Lord, S., 94
Lortie, D., 9
Loveless, T., 164
Lowe, R., 170
Lowenstein, G., 383, 407
Lowry, R., 462–463
Luiten, J., 289
Lustina, M. J., 172, 173
Luyben, P. D., 216
Lyman, H. B., 525
Lytton, H., 175
Ma, X., 73
Mabry, L., 570, 571
MacAllister, H. A., 82
McCarthy, K., 94
McCaslin, M., 342
McClelland, D. C., 117, 393
McClelland, P., 161
Maccoby, E. E., 85, 175
McCombs, B. L., 10, 129
McCormack, S., 461
McCormick, C. B., 264, 266
McDevitt, T., 164, 167

McDill, E. L., 161
McDonald, J. P., 568, 572
McGee, L. M., 55
McGinnis, K., 483
McGregor, L. N., 82
Machado, A., 30, 41
Macionis, J. J., 160, 165, 170, 171
MacIver, D. J., 94, 164
McKeachie, W. J., 385
McKenzie, T. L., 227
McKeown, M. G., 492
McLaughlin, T. F., 226
McLoyd, V. C., 156, 160, 161, 162
MacMillan, D. L., 107, 123, 126
McNemar, Q., 108
Macrae, C. N., 172
Madaus, G. F., 479, 539
Madison, S. M., 419
Madsen, C. H., 13, 213
Maehr, M. L., 378, 381, 387, 404, 405
Mager, R., 476, 477
Magnuson, D., 462, 464
Magusson, S. J., 337, 338
Maher, C. A., 335, 499
Mahn, H., 44, 46
Maier, N. R. F., 297
Major, B., 174
Maker, C. J., 125
Mandlebaum, L. H., 460
Mangione, P. L., 93
Manning, B. H., 225, 228, 229
Manning, M. L., 187
Mantzicopolos, P., 573
Marano, N., 337
Maratsos, M. P., 53
Marcia, J. E., 68
Mare, 164
Markakis, K. M., 390
Markman, E. M., 53, 261
Marks, C., 309
Markstrom-Adams, C., 75
Marsh, H. W., 71, 72, 73, 75, 93, 388
Marshall, H. H., 74, 329, 330, 334, 358, 413
Marshall, S., 118
Martin, C. L., 80, 175, 176
Martin, G., 223
Martin, J., 454
Martin, J. A., 85
Martin, J. M., 74
Martin, W. R., 486, 487
Martindale, C., 244
Marx, R. W., 302, 366, 381
Maryland, S. P., 123
Marzano, R. J., 10
Masia, B. B., 480

Subject Index

Page numbers in boldface type indicate pages on which key terms and concepts are defined.

Persuasion, social, **388**
Phonics, 507–508
Physical development, **24**, 89–92
Piaget's theory of cognitive development, 27–43
  basic tendencies in thinking and, 28–30
  implications for teachers, 39–43
  influences on development and, 28
  limitations of, 40–43
  stages of development and, 30–39
  Vygotsky's theory compared with, 46–47
Planning
  of learning environments, 444–447
  for testing, 557–559
Planning for teaching, 474–485
  from constructivist perspective, 481–485
  objectives and, 476–478
  taxonomies for, 478–481
PLAN program, 423–424
Play, creativity and, 122
Point system, for grading, 579–580
Portfolios, **566**, 567, 568–572
  evaluating, 568–572
Positive correlations, **14**
Positive practice, **216**
Positive reinforcement, **207**, 217
Poverty, 160–161
PQ4R, 306, 309
Practical/contextual intelligence, 114
Practice
  distributed, **264**
  massed, **264**
  positive, **216**
Praise, appropriate use of, 214
Praise-and-ignore approach, 213
Praxis Series, 542
Preferences, learning, **128**, 128–129
Pregnancy, during adolescence, 95
Prejudice, 170–172, **171**
  continuing, 170–171
  development of, 171–172
Premack principle, **214**, 214–215
Preoperational stage, **31**, 31–33
Preschool children
  gender-role stereotyping in, 175–176
  physical development of, 89–90
  psychosocial development of, 65–66, 67
Presentation punishment, **208**
Pretests, **556**, 557
Principles, **16**

Private speech, cognitive development and, 46–48
Problem(s), **290**
Problem-based learning, **338**, 338–339, **407**, 407–408
Problem solving, **290**, 290–301, 353
  anticipating, acting, and looking back and, 296–297
  defining goals and representing problems and, 291–294
  effective, 298–301
  exploring possible solution strategies and, 294–296
  factors hindering, 297–298
  general versus domain-specific, 290–291
  problem finding and, 291
Procedural knowledge, **242**
Procedural memory, **255**
Procedures, **440**
  for classrooms, 440, 441
Production(s), **255**
  observational learning and, 324
Prompts, **210**, 211
Pronunciation
  dialects and, 180
  in language development, 53
Propositional networks, **252**
Prototypes, **279**
PSI (Personalized System of Instruction), 219
Psychological/individual constructivism, 330
Psychomotor domain, 481
Psychosocial development, **64**. *See also* Erikson's theory of psychosocial development; Moral development
Psychotic behavior, 14
Puberty, **91**
Punishment, **207**, 207–209, 220
  presentation, **208**
  removal, **208**, 208–209
Pygmalion effect, 416, **417**

Question(s)
  convergent, **490**
  divergent, **490**
  multiple-choice, 559–560
Questioning, 490–492
  reciprocal, **345**

Race, **165**. *See also* Ethnicity and race
Radical constructivism, **332**, 332–333
Random procedures, **15**
Range, **527**

Ratio reinforcement schedules, **209**
Readiness testing, **540**, 540–541
Reading strategies, 306–309
Reading/writing instruction, 507–510
  sensible approach to, 508–510
  skills and phonics and, 507–510
  whole language and, 507
READS, 306, 309
Reasoning
  deductive, **286**, 287
  inductive, **285**
  moral, 78, **79**
Reciprocal determinism, **328**, 328–329
Reciprocal questioning, **345**
Reciprocal teaching, **349**, 349–351
Recitation, **489**, 489–492
Recognizing accomplishment, 409–410
Reconstruction, **257**, 257–258
Referrals, for special services, 147
Reflectiveness, 7
Reflectivity, **127**, 127–128
Regular education initiative, **128**, 129
Rehearsal, long-term memory and, 249
Reinforcement, 206–207, **207**
  negative, 217–218
  observational learning and, 324–325
  positive, 217
  selecting reinforcers and, 214–215
  of self, 226–227
  teacher attention as, 213–214
  vicarious, **325**
Reinforcement schedules, 209–210
Reinforcers, 206, **207**
Relatedness, need for, 379
Reliability, **531**
  of performance and exhibition assessment, 571
  of tests, 531, 534
Removal punishment, **208**, 208–209
Report cards, 578–579
Reprimands, **218**, 219
Research, 14–16
  on bilingual education, 184–185
  common sense versus, 12–13
  correlational, 14
  descriptive, 14
  experimental, 14–15
  on learning environments, 439
  on learning styles, 187–188
  teaching theories and, 15–16
Resistance cultures, 163

Credits

Text Credits

p. 4 From "Teachers Who Make a Difference," by Robert Coles, 1990, *Instructor*, September 1990, pp. 58–59. Copyright © 1990 by Scholastic, Inc. Reprinted with permission.

p. 6 From R. Roupp and M. Driscoll, *Harvard Education Letter*, 6 (1) January – February 1990, p. 5. Copyright President and Fellows of Harvard College. Reprinted with permission. All rights reserved.

p. 7 L. S. Schulman, "Knowledge & Teaching: Foundations of the New Reform." *Harvard Educational Review* 19(2), 4–14.

p. 134, National Joint Committee on Learning Disabilities 1989, p. 1.

p. 140 American Association on Mental Deficiency AAMD Ad Hoc Committee on Terminology and Classification, 1992, p. 5.

p. 177 From "Sex Differences in Choice of College Student Majors," by N. C. Ware and V. E. Lee, *American Educational Research Journal*, 25, 59–614. Copyright © 1988.

p. 222 From "Students' Perceptions of Teachers' Instructional and Management Adaptations for Students with Learning or Behavior Problems," by C. L. Fulk and P. J. Smith, 1995, *The Elementary School Journal*, 95, 409–419.

p. 225 From, *Applied Behavior Analysis in Education: A Structured Teaching Approach* (p. 272) by W. R. Jensen, H. N. Sloane, and K. R. Young. Copyright © 1988 Prentice-Hall, Inc.

p. 261 From "Thinking About Thinking," by E. Bondy, 1989, *Annual Editions: Educational Psychology*, pp. 83–86.

p. 280 Abstract from "An Empirically Based Instructional Design Theory for Teaching Concepts," by R. D. Tennyson and M. M. Cocchiarella, 1986, *Review of Educational Research*, 56, pp. 40–71.

p. 298 From "Explicit Heuristic Training as a Variable in Problem Solving Performance," by A. H. Schoenfeld, 1979, *Journal for Research in Mathematics Education*, 10, pp. 173–187.

p. 301 From "Taking into Account Student Conceptions in Instructional Strategy: An Example of Physics," by S. Joshua and J. J. Dupin, 1988, *Cognition and Instruction*, 5, pp. 193–222.

p. 338 From "Whole Language—What a Bargain," by C. Espe, C. Worner, and M. Hotkevich, *Educational Leadership*, 47(6) p. 45. Reprinted by permission of the Association for Supervision and Curriculum Development. Copyright © 1990 by ASCD. All rights reserved.

p. 350 From "When the Student Becomes the Teacher," *Harvard Education Letter*, 2(3), March 1986, pp. 5–6. Copyright President and Fellows of Harvard College. Reprinted with permission. All rights reserved.

p. 374 "Why Can't Susie and Johnny Do Math?" *Harvard Education Letter*, 3(4), 1987, pp. 6–7. Copyright President and Fellows of Harvard College. Reprinted with permission. All rights reserved.

p. 406 "Reasons for Studying: Motivational Orientatons and Study Strategies," by S. B. Nolen, *Cognition and Instruction*, 5, pp. 269-288. Copyright © 1988.

p. 415 "The 'Teacher's Pet' Phenomenon, Students' Perceptions of Differential Behavior, and Students' Morale," by E. Babad, *Journal of Educational Psychology*, 87, pp. 361–374. Copyright © 1995.

Chapter Opener Art Credits

Chapter 1: © Cathlyn Melloan/Stone.

Chapter 2: Charles Sharp Collection/© Robert Frerck/Odyssey/Chicago.

Chapter 3: Peter W. Michel, *Fathers & Sons*, © 1999. Painted wood, 24" x 23.5" in diameter.

Chapter 4: Joseph Cornel, *Untitled*, c. mid 1950s. Box construction, 18" x 11-1/2" x 2-3/4". Photograph courtesy of Pace Wildenstein. © The Joseph and Robert Cornell Memorial Foundation/Licensed by VAGA, New York, NY.

Chapter 5: Unknown Artist, *Mbulu Ngulu*, Franceville. Christie's Images.

Chapter 6: Rafael Ferrer, *Yo-Yo-Yo-Yo-Yo*, 1975. Mixed media, 105" x 106" x 9-1/2". Nancy Hoffman Gallery.

Chapter 7: John Okulick, *Crown*, 1989–90. Painted wood and metal, 26" x 42" x 7". Nancy Hoffman Gallery.

Chapter 8: Charles Pratt, *Kachina Doll Chess Set*, Christof Gallery, Santa Fe, NM. © Dewitt Jones/Corbis.

Chapter 9: Alexander Calder, *Boomerang and Sickle Moon*, 1971. Metal. Pucker Safrai Gallery, Boston, MA. © 2001 Alexander Calder/Artists Rights Society (ARS), New York. Burstein Collection/Corbis.

Chapter 10: © Carol Grigg, *Big Black Boot Dance*. Authorized by Joan Cawley Licensing, Ltd.

Chapter 11: Frank Stella, *Valletta (Malta Series #6)*, 1983. Honeycombed aluminum with etched magnesium surface, wood with fiberglass, ink and paint, 107" x 101" x 52". Collection of Mr. and Mrs. Graham Gund. © 2001 Frank Stella/Artists Rights Society (ARS), New York.

Chapter 12: Arman, *Pure Epic*, 1988. Oil and paintbrushes on canvas and panel, 111 cm. x 87 cm. Private Collection/ The Bridgeman Art Library.

Chapter 13: Peter W. Michel, *Mind Folk*, © 1995. Painted wood, 18" x 9-1/4" x 5-3/4".

Chapter 14: Orlando A.B., *Cubiculo*. Engman International Fine Art.

Chapter 15: John Scott, *Take the A-Frame*, 1984. Painted brass and wood, flagstone base, 26-1/2" x 34-1/2" x 7-3/4". Collection of Elizabeth Harris and Edward Dugger III.

Photo Credits

p. 7, Will Hart; p. 8, Kelly Hoy, Arlington Writers; p. 11, Courtesy of Lynn Corno; p. 12, Michael Newman/Photo-Edit; p. 28, Anderson/Monkmeyer; p. 32, Brian Smith; p. 34, Michael Newman/PhotoEdit; p. 44, James V. Wertsch/Washington University; p. 45, Owen Franken/ Stock Boston; p. 48, Will Hart; p. 64, Ted Streshinsky/ Corbis; p. 66 and 73, Will Hart; p. 76, Brian Smith; p. 80, Courtesy of Carol Gilligan; p. 82, Will Hart; p. 87, Michael Newman/PhotoEdit; p. 93, Myrleen Ferguson Cate/Photo-Edit; p. 106, Brian Smith; p. 109, Tom Herde/Boston Globe; p. 113, AP/Wide World Photos; p. 115, Bob Daemmrich/The Image Works; p. 121, David Young-Wolff/PhotoEdit; p. 125, Will Hart; p. 130, Courtesy National Easter Seals Society; p. 139, Will Faller; p. 165, Bruce Ayres/Stone; p. 167, Spencer Grant/PhotoEdit; p. 170, Carl Iwasaki/Life Magazine © Time Inc.; p. 175, Lori Adamski Peek/Stone; p. 183 and 186, Brian Smith; p. 202, Will Hart; p. 206, Falk/Monkmeyer; p. 210, Charles Pefley/Stock Boston; p. 213 and 222, Will Hart; p. 241, Lawrence Migdale/Stone; p. 246, Will Hart; p. 248, Aaron Haupt/Stock Boston; p. 260, Michael Newman/ PhotoEdit; p. 265, Stephen Frisch/Stock Boston; p. 283, Will Faller; p. 286, Will Hart; p. 296, Walter Hodges/ Stone; p. 304, Stephen Marks; p. 312, Syracuse Newspapers/The Image Works; p. 323, Stanford University News Service; p. 324, Tony Freeman/PhotoEdit; p. 326 and 330, Will Hart; p. 334, Brian Smith; p. 342, Will Hart/Photo-Edit; p. 345, Mary Kate Denny/Stone; p. 349, Courtesy of Annmarie Palinscar; p. 368, Kelly Hoy, Arlington Writers; p. 370, Steve Woit/Index Stock Imagery; p. 379, Andy Sacks/Stone; p. 381, Ian Shaw/Stone; p. 389, Will Hart; p. 405, Bob Daemmrich/Stock Boston; p. 411, Kelly Hoy, Arlington Writers; p. 418, Mary Kate Denny/PhotoEdit; p. 423, 435, and 440, Will Hart; p. 452, Kelly Hoy, Arlington Writers; p. 457, Frank Siteman/PhotoEdit; p. 475, Bruce Forster/Stone; p. 486, David Lissy/Index Stock Imagery; p. 494, Chip Henderson/Stone; p. 503, Capece/ Monkmeyer; p. 507, Ernest Braun/Stone; p. 523, Richard Clintsman/Stone; p. 525, Bob Daemmrich/The Image Works; p. 540, Tony Freeman/PhotoEdit; p. 548, Ed Lallo/ Liaison Agency; p. 557, Will Hart; p. 563, Bob Daemmrich/Stock Boston; p. 567 and 574, Will Hart; p. 583, Robert E. Daemmrich/Stone.

You should carefully read the following terms and conditions before opening this disk package.
Opening this disk package indicates your acceptance of these terms and conditions.
If you do not agree with them, you should promptly return the package unopened.

Allyn and Bacon provides this Program and License for its use. You assume responsibility for the selection of the Program to achieve your intended results, and for the installation, use, and results obtained from the Program. This License extends only to use of the Program in the United States or countries in which the Program is marketed by duly authorized distributors.

License Grant

You hereby accept a nonexclusive, nontransferable, permanent License to install and use the Program on a single computer at any given time. You may copy the Program solely for backup or archival purposes in support of your use of the Program on the single computer. You may **not** modify, translate, disassemble, decompile, or reverse engineer the Program, in whole or in part.

Term

This License is effective until terminated. Allyn and Bacon reserves the right to terminate this License automatically if any provision of the License is violated. You may terminate the License at any time. To terminate this License, you must return the Program, including documentation, along with a written warranty stating that all copies of the Program in your possession have been returned or destroyed.

Limited Warranty

The Program is provided "As Is" without warranty of any kind, either express or implied, including, but **not** limited to, the implied warranties or merchantability and fitness for a particular purpose. The entire risk as to the quality and performance of the Program is with you. Should the Program prove defective, you (and **not** Allyn and Bacon or any authorized distributor) assume the entire cost of all necessary servicing, repair, or correction. No oral or written information or advice given by Allyn and Bacon, its dealers, distributors, or agents shall create a warranty or increase the scope of its warranty.

Some states do **not** allow the exclusion of implied warranty, so the above exclusion may **not** apply to you. This warranty gives you specific legal rights and you may also have other rights that vary from state to state.

Allyn and Bacon does **not** warrant that the functions contained in the Program will meet your requirements or that the operation of the Program will be uninterrupted or error-free.

However, Allyn and Bacon warrants the disk(s) on which the Program is furnished to be free from defects in material and workmanship under normal use for a period of ninety (90) days from the date of delivery to you as evidenced by a copy of your receipt.

The Program should **not** be relied on as the sole basis to solve a problem whose incorrect solution could result in injury to a person or property. If the Program is employed in such a manner, it is at the user's own risk and Allyn and Bacon explicitly disclaims all liability for such misuse.

Limitation of Remedies

Allyn and Bacon's entire liability and your exclusive remedy shall be:

1. The replacement of any disk **not** meeting Allyn and Bacon's "Limited Warranty" and that is returned to Allyn and Bacon or

2. If Allyn and Bacon is unable to deliver a replacement disk or cassette that is free of defects in materials or workmanship, you may terminate this Agreement by returning the Program.

In no event will Allyn and Bacon be liable to you for any damages, including any lost profits, lost savings, or other incidental or consequential damages arising out of the use or inability to use such Program even if Allyn and Bacon or an authorized distributor has been advised of the possibility or such damages or for any claim by any other party.

Some states do **not** allow the limitation or exclusion of liability for incidental or consequential damages, so the above limitation or exclusion may **not** apply to you.

General

You may **not** sublicense, assign, or transfer the License of the Program. Any attempt to sublicense, assign, or transfer any of the rights, duties, or obligations hereunder is void.

This Agreement will be governed by the laws of the State of Massachusetts.

Should you have any questions concerning this Agreement, or any questions concerning technical support, you may contact Allyn and Bacon by writing to:

Allyn and Bacon
Pearson Education
160 Gould Street
Needham Heights, MA 02494

You acknowledge that you have read this Agreement, understand it, and agree to be bound by its terms and conditions. You further agree that it is the complete and exclusive statement of the Agreement between us that supersedes any proposal or prior Agreement, oral or written, and any other communications between us relating to the subject matter of this Agreement.

Notice To Government End Users

The Program is provided with restricted rights. Use, duplication, or disclosure by the Government is subject to restrictions set forth in subdivison (b)(3)(iii) of The Rights in Technical Data and Computer Software Clause 252.227-7013.